ETHICAL THEORY

BLACKWELL PHILOSOPHY ANTHOLOGIES

Each volume in this outstanding series provides an authoritative and comprehensive collection of the essential primary readings from philosophy's main fields of study. Designed to complement the *Blackwell Companions to Philosophy* series, each volume represents an unparalleled resource in its own right, and will provide the ideal platform for course use.

ETHICAL THEORY: AN ANTHOLOGY

Edited by Russ Shafer-Landau

Blackwell
Publishing

Editorial material and organization © 2007 by Blackwell Publishing Ltd

BLACKWELL PUBLISHING
350 Main Street, Malden, MA 02148-5020, USA
9600 Garsington Road, Oxford OX4 2DQ, UK
550 Swanston Street, Carlton, Victoria 3053, Australia

The right of Russ Shafer-Landau to be identified as the Author of the Editorial Material in this Work has been asserted in accordance with the UK Copyright, Designs, and Patents Act 1988.

First published 2007 by Blackwell Publishing Ltd

7   2011

Library of Congress Cataloging-in-Publication Data

Ethical theory : an anthology / edited by Russ Shafer-Landau.
    p. cm. — (Blackwell philosophy anthologies)
  Includes bibliographical references.
  ISBN: 978-1-4051-3319-7 (hardcover : alk. paper)
  ISBN: 978-1-4051-3320-3 (pbk. : alk. paper) 1. Ethics. I. Shafer-Landau, Russ.
  BJ1012.E88346   2007
  170—dc22

                                    2006102119

A catalogue record for this title is available from the British Library.

Set in 9.5/11.5pt Minion
by SPi Publisher Services, Pondicherry, India
Printed and bound in Singapore
by COS Printers Pte Ltd

The publisher's policy is to use permanent paper from mills that operate a sustainable forestry policy, and which has been manufactured from pulp processed using acid-free and elementary chlorine-free practices. Furthermore, the publisher ensures that the text paper and cover board used have met acceptable environmental accreditation standards.

For further information on
Blackwell Publishing, visit our website:
www.blackwellpublishing.com

Contents

Preface

As a cursory scan through the table of contents will show, the realm of ethical theory is an expansive one. If I had my way, this book would have been half again as long, to reflect this breadth, but then my editor rightly drew my attention to certain practicalities of the publishing world. I am hopeful, nonetheless, that most of the centrally important questions in ethical theory receive attention within these covers.

At the heart of ethics are two questions: (i) What should I do?, and (ii) What sort of person should I be? Though philosophers sometimes proceed as if these questions were really quite distinct from one another, it is artificial to suppose that we can plausibly answer the one without making important commitments that go some ways towards answering the other. We can also, of course, ask about the status of our answers to these questions, by asking, for instance, whether such answers are in some way reflective only of personal opinion, or whether they might be best measured against some more objective standard. And again, we might be puzzled at how we can gain ethical knowledge in the first place (if we can), and wonder at the rational authority of morality (if there is any). All of these questions, and many others, are addressed, if not conclusively answered, in the readings that follow.

Any contemporary ethics anthology worth its salt will be sure to include coverage of consequentialism, deontology, contractarianism, and virtue ethics. This book does that, but I have been intent on ensuring that other areas, less often surveyed in such books, receive attention as well. This explains the separate sections on moral standing, moral responsibility, moral knowledge, and a concluding sampling of work that asks about the very possibility of systematic ethical theory. These are matters about which students tend to be quite interested, though for various reasons these issues are usually omitted, or given only scant representation, in anthologies such as this one.

I have also made the difficult decision, in the last several sections devoted to normative ethics, to forgo the usual point-counterpoint sampling of contrasting views, in favor of devoting each such section entirely to proponents of the theory being represented. Thus, in the section on consequentialism, for instance, I omit the usual critics of the doctrine, and restrict myself to allowing only its defenders a voice therein. This makes the reader's work a bit more difficult, but also, I think, much more interesting. What this approach allows is a richer and subtler representation of the normative theory under scrutiny. Readers will not have criticisms of the theories presented and ready to hand. As a compensation, however, they will have a more nuanced target to aim at when seeking to identify for themselves the vulnerabilities (and the strengths) of the views they are exploring.

The task of comprehending, within the pages of even this large work, the entire compass of ethical theory is not one that any sane philosopher would think possible. (Not that it hasn't been fun trying.) I'm sure that those with experience of this area will doubtless be disappointed to find that a favorite paper has gone missing here or there. But I hope to have provided enough in the way of pleasant surprises and compensating rewards to make up for that sort of thing. My own goal is to have included here articles that are exemplary in their accessibility, their being centrally representative of an important view within ethical theory, and their being first-rate works of philosophy. In a very small number of cases I have included pieces that I know to have failed in one of these aspects, because they have been so successful in the others.

I've greatly enjoyed acquainting and reacquainting myself with these terrific pieces of philosophy. A further source of genuine pleasure comes from acknowledging the very kind, expert advice I have received from so many talented and generous philosophers. My sincere thanks to Jim Anderson, Steven Arkonovich, Paul Bloomfield, Ben Bradley, Claudia Card, Tom Carson, Terence Cuneo, Jonathan Dancy, Ben Eggleston, Dan Hausman, Dan Haybron, Chris Heathwood, Thomas Hill, Jr., Dan Jacobson, Robert Johnson, Thaddeus Metz, Carolina Sartorio, Sam Scheffler, Rob Streiffer, and Pekka Väyrynen. Don Hubin, Simon Keller, and James S. Taylor reviewed all of my introductory essays and offered excellent suggestions for improvement. Bekka Williams and David Killoren significantly aided in the research, and Brad Majors was a superb assistant in every way.

Jeff Dean prompted me to put this book together, and I'd like to express my appreciation to him not only for encouraging me along these lines, but also for being such a thoughtful and reasonable editor. His assistant, Danielle Descoteaux, served as my regular correspondent at Blackwell, and was the very model of cheery, intelligent efficiency. I couldn't have asked for a better editorial team.

RSL
Madison, August 2006

Acknowledgments

The editor and publisher gratefully acknowledge the permission granted to reproduce the copyright material in this book:

1: David Hume, "Of the Influencing Motives of the Will" and "Moral Distinctions Not Derived from Reason," from *Treatise of Human Nature*, Book III, 1737.

2: A. J. Ayer, "A Critique of Ethics," pp. 102–13 from *Language, Truth and Logic*. New York: Dover, 1952. Reprinted by permission of Dover Publications Inc.

3: J. L. Mackie, "The Subjectivity of Values," pp. 15–18, 27–46 from *Ethics: Inventing Right and Wrong*. New York: Penguin, 1977. Copyright © J. L. Mackie, 1977. Reproduced by permission of Penguin Books Ltd.

4: Gilbert Harman, "Ethics and Observation," pp. 3–10 from *The Nature of Morality*. Oxford: Oxford University Press, 1977. By permission of Oxford University Press.

5: Gilbert Harman, "Moral Relativism Defended." Reprinted by permission of Duke University Press.

6: G. E. Moore, "The Subject-Matter of Ethics," from *Principia Ethica*, 1903.

7: Mary Midgley, "Trying Out One's New Sword," from *Heart and Mind: The Varieties of Moral Experience*. New York: St Martin's Press, 1981. Reproduced with permission of Palgrave Macmillan.

8: Russ Shafer-Landau, "Ethics as Philosophy: A Defense of Ethical Nonnaturalism," from Mark Timmons and Terence Horgan (eds.), *Metaethics After Moore*. Oxford: Oxford University Press, 2005. By permission of Oxford University Press.

9: Michael Smith, "Realism," pp. 399–410 from Peter Singer (ed.), *A Companion to Ethics*. Oxford: Blackwell, 1993. Reprinted by permission of the publishers, Blackwell Publishing.

10: Shelly Kagan, "Thinking About Cases," pp. 44–63 from Ellen Frankel Paul, Fred D. Miller, Jr, and Jeffrey Paul (eds.), *Moral Knowledge*. Cambridge: Cambridge University Press, 2001. © Social Philosophy and Policy Foundation, reproduced with permission. Reprinted by permission of the author Shelly Kagan.

11: George Sher, "But I Could Be Wrong," pp. 64–78 from *Social Philosophy & Policy*, 18(2), 2001. © Social Philosophy and Policy Foundation, reproduced with permission. Reprinted by permission of the author George Sher.

12: Renford Brambrough, "Proof," pp. 11–13, 15–27 from *Moral Skepticism and Moral Knowledge*. London: Routledge, 1979.

13: Robert Audi, "Moral Knowledge and Ethical Pluralism," pp. 275–6, 278–85, 288–95 from John Greco and Ernest

Sosa (eds.), *The Blackwell Guide to Epistemology*. Oxford: Blackwell, 1999. Reprinted by permission of the publishers, Blackwell Publishing.

14: Geoffrey Sayre-McCord, "Coherentism and the Justification of Moral Beliefs," from Mark Timmons and Walter Sinnott-Armstrong (eds.), *Moral Knowledge?* Oxford: Oxford University Press, 1996. By permission of Oxford University Press, Inc.

15: Plato, "The Immoralist's Challenge," pp. 496–502 from *The Republic*, Book II, 357A–367E, trans. G. M. A. Grube; revised by C. D. C. Reeve. Indianapolis: Hackett, 1992. Reprinted by permission of Hackett Publishing Company, Inc. All rights reserved.

16: Philippa Foot, "Morality as a System of Hypothetical Imperatives," pp. 305–15 from *Philosophical Review*, 81, 1972. Reprinted by permission of Duke University Press.

17: Gregory S. Kavka, "The Reconciliation Project," pp. 279–319 from David Zimmerman and David Copp (eds.), *Morality, Reason and Truth*. Totowa, NJ: Rowman and Allanheld, 1985. Reprinted by permission of Rowman & Littlefield Publishers Inc.

18: Russ Shafer-Landau, "Moral Rationalism," excerpted from chapters 7 and 8 of *Moral Realism: A Defence*. Oxford: Oxford University Press, 2003. By permission of Oxford University Press.

19: Joel Feinberg, "Psychological Egoism," pp. 476–88 from Russ Shafer-Landau and Joel Feinberg (eds.), *Reason and Responsibility*. Belmont: Wadsworth, 2004. Reprinted with permission of Wadsworth, a division of Thomson Learning. Reprinted with permission of Mrs Betty Feinberg.

20: Lester Hunt, "Flourishing Egoism," pp. 72–95 from *Social Philosophy and Policy*, Cambridge University Press, 1999. © Social Philosophy and Policy Foundation, reproduced with permission. Reprinted by permission of the author Lester Hunt.

21: James Rachels, "Ethical Egoism," from *The Elements of Moral Philosophy*, Fourth Edition. New York: Random House, 1986. Reproduced with permission of The McGraw-Hill Companies.

22: Susan Wolf, "Moral Saints," pp. 419–39 from *The Journal of Philosophy*, 79(8), 1982. Reprinted by permission of *The Journal of Philosophy*. Reprinted by permission of Susan Wolf.

23: Plato, "Euthyphro," trans. Benjamin Jowett, Oxford, 1892.

24: Robert Merrihew Adams, "A New Divine Command Theory," pp. 66–79 from *Journal of Religious Ethics*, 7, 1979. Reprinted by permission of the publishers, Blackwell Publishing.

25: William Lane Craig and Walter Sinnott-Armstrong, "God and Objective Morality: A Debate," pp. 17–21, 33–6 from *God? A Debate Between a Christian and an Athiest*. Oxford: Oxford University Press, 2004. By permission of Oxford University Press.

26: Immanuel Kant, "God and Immortality as Postulates of Pure Practical Reason," from *Critique of Practical Reason*, trans. T. K. Abbott. London: Longmans, Green and Company, 1873.

27: C. Stephen Layman, "God and the Moral Order," pp. 304–16 from *Faith and Philosophy*, 19(3), 2002. Reprinted by permission of the Editor and *Faith and Philosophy*.

28: Erik Wielenberg, "God and Morality," pp. 39–42, 48–65 from *Value and Virtue in a Godless Universe*. Cambridge: Cambridge University Press, 2005. © Cambridge University Press, reproduced with permission. Reprinted by permission of the author Erik Wielenberg.

29: John Stuart Mill, "Hedonism," from *Utilitarianism*, 1859.

30: Robert Nozick, "The Experience Machine," pp. 42–5 from *Anarchy, State and Utopia*. New York: Basic Books, 1974. © 1974 by Basic Books. Reprinted by permission of Basic Books, a member of Perseus Books, LLC.

31: Fred Feldman, "The Good Life: A Defense of Attitudinal Hedonism," pp. 605–623 from *Philosophy and Phenomenological Research* 65(3), 2002. Reprinted by permission of the author Fred Feldman.

32: James Griffin, "The Informed Desire Account," pp. 12–17, 21–31 from *Well-Being*. Oxford: Oxford University Press, 1986. By permission of Oxford University Press.

33: Richard Kraut, "Desire and the Human Good," pp. 39–49 from *Proceedings and Addresses of the American Philosophical Association*, 68(2), 1995. Reprinted by permission of The American Philosophical Association.

34: W. D. Ross, "What Things are Good?" pp. 134–41 from *The Right and the Good*. Oxford: Oxford University Press, 1930. By permission of Oxford University Press.

35: Derek Parfit, "What Makes Someone's Life Go Best", pp. 493–502 from *Reasons and Persons*. Oxford: Oxford University Press, 1984. By permission of Oxford University Press.

36: Richard Taylor, "Determinism and the Theory of Agency," pp. 224–30 from Sidney Hook (ed.), *Determinism and Freedom*. New York: Macmillan, 1979.

37: Galen Strawson, "The Impossibility of Moral Responsibility," pp. 5, 7–10, 13–15, 25 from *Philosophical Studies*, 75, 1994. With kind permission from Springer Science and Business Media. Reprinted by permission of the author Galen Strawson.

38: A. J. Ayer, "Freedom and Necessity," pp. 271–84 from *Philosophical Essays*. New York: Bedford/St. Martin's Press, 1969. Reproduced with permission of Palgrave Macmillan.

39: Thomas Nagel, "Moral Luck," pp. 137–55 from *Proceedings of the Aristotelian Society*, 50, 1976. Reprinted by permission of the publishers, Blackwell Publishing.

40: Susan Wolf, "Sanity and the Metaphysics of Responsibility," pp. 46–62 from Ferdinand David Schoeman (ed.), *Responsibility, Character and the Emotions: New Essays in Moral Psychology*. New York: Cambridge University Press, 1988. Reprinted by permission of Cambridge University Press. Reprinted by permission of the author Susan Wolf.

41: Peter Strawson, "Freedom and Resentment," pp. 1–25 from *Proceedings of the British Academy*, 48, 1962. Reproduced by permission *Proceedings of the British Academy*.

42: Immanuel Kant, "We Have No Duties to Animals," pp. 239–41 from *Lectures on Ethics*, trans. Louis Infield. London: Methuen Press, 1930. Reproduced by permission of Taylor & Francis Books UK.

43: Peter Singer, "All Animals Are Equal," pp. 1–21 from *Animal Liberation*, Second Edition. New York: Ecco Press, 1990.

44: Joel Feinberg, "The Rights of Animals and Unborn Generations," pp. 43–6, 49–50, 55, 57–63 from William Blackstone (ed.), *Philosophy and Environmental Crisis*. Athens: University of Georgia Press, 1974. Reprinted by permission of Jean T. Blackstone.

45: Kenneth Goodpaster, "On Being Morally Considerable," pp. 308, 310–25 from *Journal of Philosophy*, 75, 1978. Reprinted by permission of *The Journal of Philosophy*. Reprinted by permission of the author Kenneth Goodpaster.

46: Michael Tooley, "Abortion and Infanticide," pp. 44–55, 58–64 from *Philosophy of Public Affairs*, 1, 1972. Reprinted by permission of the publishers, Blackwell Publishing.

47: Don Marquis, "An Argument that Abortion is Wrong," pp. 91–102 from Hugh LaFollette (ed.), *Ethics in Practice*. Oxford: Blackwell, 1997. Reprinted by permission of the publishers, Blackwell Publishing.

48: John Stuart Mill, "Utilitarianism," from *Utilitarianism*, 1859.

49: William Shaw, "The Consequentialist Perspective," pp. 5–20 from James Dreier, *Contemporary Debates in Moral Theory*. Oxford: Blackwell, 2005. Reprinted by permission of the publishers, Blackwell Publishing.

50: J. J. C. Smart, "Extreme and Restricted Utilitarianism," pp. 344–54 from *Philosophical Quarterly*, 6, 1956. Reprinted by permission of the publishers, Blackwell Publishing.

51: Brad Hooker, "Rule-Consequentialism," pp. 183–204 from Hugh LaFollette (ed.), *The Blackwell Guide to Ethical Theory*. Oxford: Blackwell, 1999. Reprinted by permission of the publishers, Blackwell Publishing.

52: R. M. Hare, "What is Wrong with Slavery," pp. 103–21 from *Philosophy and Public Affairs*, 8(2), 1979. Reprinted by permission of the publishers, Blackwell Publishing.

53: Peter Singer, "Famine, Affluence and Morality," pp. 229–43 from *Philosophy and Public Affairs*, 1(3), 1972. Reprinted by permission of the publishers, Blackwell Publishing.

54: John Harris, "The Survival Lottery," pp. 81–7 from *Philosophy*, 50, 1975. © by The Royal Institute of Philosophy, published by Cambridge University Press, reproduced with permission. Reprinted with permission of Professor John Harris.

55: Immanuel Kant, pp. 7–16, 25–39 from *Groundwork of the Metaphysics of Morals*, trans. Mary J. Gregor. Cambridge: Cambridge University Press, 1998. © by Cambridge University Press, reprinted with permission. Reprinted by permission of Betty Kiehl, The Estate of Professor M. J. Gregor.

56: Christine Korsgaard, "Kant's Formula of Universal Law," pp. 24–47 from *Pacific Philosophical Quarterly*, 66, 1985. Reprinted by permission of the publishers, Blackwell Publishing.

57: Onora O'Neill, "Kantian Approaches to Some Famine Problems," pp. 258–70 from Tom Regan (ed.), *Matters of Life and Death: New Introductory Essays in Moral Philosophy*, Third Edition. New York: McGraw-Hill, 1980.

58: Robert Nozick, "The Rationality of Side Constraints," pp. 27–33 from *Anarchy, State and Utopia*. New York: Basic Books. © 1974 by Basic Books. Reprinted by permission of Basic Books, a member of Perseus Books, LLC.

59: Alan Gewirth, "The Golden Rule Rationalized," pp. 133–47 from *Midwest Studies in Philosophy*, 3, 1978. Reprinted by permission of the publishers, Blackwell Publishing.

60: Philippa Foot, "The Problem of Abortion and the Doctrine of the Double Effect," pp. 5–15 from *Oxford Review*, 5, 1967.

61: Judith Jarvis Thomson, "Killing, Letting Die, and the Trolley Problem," *The Monist*, 52(2), April 1976. © 1976, *The Monist: An International Quarterly Journal of General Philosophical Inquiry*, Peru, IL, USA 61354. Reprinted by permission.

62: Thomas Hobbes, from *Leviathan*, 1651.

63: David Gauthier, "Why Contractarianism?," pp. 15–30 from Peter Vallentyne (ed.), *Contractarianism and Rational Choice*. New York: Cambridge University Press, 1991. Reprinted by permission of Cambridge University Press.

64: John Rawls, "A Theory of Justice," pp. 11–21, 60–3, 136–40, 153–6 from *A Theory of Justice*. Cambridge, MA: Harvard University Press, 1971. Reprinted by permission of the publisher, Harvard University Press.

65: T. M. Scanlon, "Contractualism and Utilitarianism," pp. 103–29 from Amartya Sen and Bernard Williams (eds.), *Utilitarianism and Beyond*. Cambridge: Cambridge University Press, 1982. © 1982 by Maison des Sciences de l'Homme and Cambridge University Press, reproduced with permission. Reprinted by permission of Professor T. Scanlon.

66: Aristotle, "The Nature of Virtue," pp. 1–5, 7–12, 15–29, 163–9 from *Nichomachean Ethics*, Second Edition, trans. Terence Irwin. Indianapolis: Hackett, 1999. Reprinted by permission of Hackett Publishing Company, Inc. All rights reserved.

67: Martha Nussbaum, "Non-Relative Virtues: An Aristotelian Approach," pp. 32–50 from Peter A. French, Theodore E. Uehling, Jr. and Howard K. Wettstein (eds.), *Ethical Theory: Character and Virtue, Midwest Studies in Philosophy* 13. Notre Dame, IN: University of Notre Dame Press, 1988. Reprinted by permission of the publishers, Blackwell Publishing.

68: Rosalind Hursthouse, "Normative Virtue Ethics," pp. 19–33 from Roger Crisp (ed.), *How Should One Live?* Oxford: Oxford

University Press, 1996. By permission of Oxford University Press.

69: Michael Slote, "Agent-Based Virtue Ethics," pp. 83–101 from *Midwest Studies in Philosophy*, 20, 1995. Reprinted by permission of the publishers, Blackwell Publishing.

70: Christine Swanton, "A Virtue Ethical Account of Right Action," pp. 32–52 from *Ethics*, 112, 2001. Reprinted by permission of the publisher, The University of Chicago Press.

71: Julia Annas, "Being Virtuous and Doing the Right Thing," pp. 61–74 from *Proceedings and Addresses of the American Philosophical Association*, 78, 2004. Reprinted by permission of The American Philosophical Association.

72: W. D. Ross, "What Makes Right Acts Right?," pp. 18–22, 29–32, 39–41 from *The Right and the Good*. Oxford: Oxford

University Press, 1930. By permission of Oxford University Press.

73: David McNaughton, "An Unconnected Heap of Duties?," pp. 433–47 from *Philosophical Quarterly*, 46, 1996. Reprinted by permission of the publishers, Blackwell Publishing.

74: Jonathan Dancy, "An Unprincipled Morality." Reprinted by permission of Professor Jonathan Dancy.

75: Margaret Olivia Little, "On Knowing the 'Why': Particularism and Moral Theory," pp. 32-40 from *Hastings Center Report*, 31(4), 2001. Reprinted by permission of The Hastings Center.

76: Gerald Dworkin, "Unprincipled Ethics," pp. 224–38 from *Midwest Studies in Philosophy*, 20, 1995. Reprinted by permission of the publishers, Blackwell Publishing.

PART I
The Status of Morality

Introduction to Part I

Suppose that we are puzzled about whether we ought to lend our support to a war that our government has initiated. We mull things over, we talk to our friends, we listen to what politicians and opinion writers have to say about the matter, and then, finally, we do manage to make up our minds. Can our moral view of the matter be true? If so, what could make it true?

Suppose that we have thought things out quite a bit, and have arrived, not at a particular assessment of this war or that war, but of all wars – we have developed a theory of just war. This theory tells us the conditions under which the activities of war are just and right. Can this theory be true? If so, what makes it true?

Suppose, finally, that our thinking has become so sophisticated that we are able, after a great deal of effort, to develop an entire ethic. We have, to our satisfaction, identified the conditions that determine whether actions are moral or immoral. Can *this* sort of theory be true? If so, what makes it true?

The questions I have posed are not questions about the content of morality. I am not asking about what should go on the laundry list of moral dos and don'ts. The questions I posed above are about the status of our moral opinions, and our moral theories. What are we doing when we arrive at moral verdicts and theories? So long as we are speaking sincerely, we are surely voicing our personal opinion

about such matters. But is that all there is to it? Do our opinions answer to any independent authority? Are actions right just because someone approves of them? Because a society approves of them? Because God approves of them? Or might it be that actions are right independently of all such sources of approval? Or, more pessimistically, might it be the case that morality is a fraud, a system of merely conventional rules that have no real authority at all? On this last view, all of our moral talk is fraught with error: we think that genocide is immoral, and think it our duty to tend to the weak, but these views, like all moral views, are (on this line) simply mistaken.

The possibilities just canvassed represent the wide variety of views in *metaethics*. Metaethics is that branch of ethical theory that asks, not about the content of morality, but about its status. Is morality a human invention? A divine creation? Something else? Can we have moral knowledge, and, if so, how? Are moral requirements rationally compelling – do we always have excellent reason to do as morality says? For present purposes, the central metaethical question is whether moral views can be true, and, if so, whether they can be objectively true. A claim is objectively true just in case it is true independently of what any human being actually thinks of it. There are lots of objective truths: that two and two are four; that oxygen is denser than helium, that the planet Mars is smaller than the planet Jupiter. The big question here is whether there are any moral claims that share this status.

Many of our writers do not think so. David Hume, our lead-off author, wrote his magnificent *Treatise of Human Nature* when he was still in his twenties. Contained therein is a series of very powerful arguments against the objectivity of ethics. Many of these arguments are, either on their own or with an updating, taken today as cogent reasons for rejecting ethical objectivity. One of the more famous arguments is this:

1 All claims that can be known by reason are either empirical matters of fact, or conceptual truths (such as "all bachelors are unmarried," or "all cubes have six sides").
2 Moral claims do not represent empirical matters of fact.
3 Moral claims do not represent conceptual truths.
4 Therefore reason cannot give us moral knowledge.

Hume was also notable for emphasizing the impossibility of deducing an *ought* from an *is*, i.e., deducing a moral claim, or a prescription about what should be done, from a factual claim that describes what is the case. One is making no logical error in accepting this description: "that action is a premeditated killing of a defenseless child," but failing to infer that "therefore that action is immoral." If the person who knows of the killing fails to deem it immoral, she is not making a logical error. But what other sort of error could she be making? It is no error of reason, says Hume, for it is an implication of his argument, above, that errors of reason are limited to two kinds: mistaking empirical matters of fact, or misunderstanding the concepts one is employing. But such a callous individual may know all of the nonmoral facts surrounding the killing, and may be as conceptually sophisticated as the rest of us. If there is any error made by such a person, it cannot be that she has failed to get at the truth. For reason is the faculty that gets at truth, and if, according to Hume, there is no error of reason, then there is no failure to light

on the truth. Perhaps, as many commentators read him, that is because Hume didn't believe that there was such a thing as ethical truth.

Here is another argument taken from Hume's classic work:

1 Moral judgments are intrinsically motivating.
2 Beliefs are not intrinsically motivating – they need desires to generate motivation.
3 Therefore moral judgments are not beliefs.

If moral judgments are not beliefs, then what are they? A.J. Ayer, whose views on ethics clearly bear a Humean influence, claims that our moral judgments are just expressions of our emotions. If I judge that eating meat is immoral, for instance, I am not reporting a putative fact about meat eating. Rather, I am expressing my aversion to it. It's as if I were saying: "meating-eating – yechhh!" Such an expression, pretty clearly, cannot be true. But neither can it be false. It is not the sort of thing discernible by reason, since it doesn't seek to represent the way things really are. Moral judgments are not reports or descriptions of the world. They are our emotional responses to a world that contains no values at all.

J.L. Mackie holds a view that is pretty close to Ayer's. Mackie agrees with Ayer that the world contains no values. Nothing is morally right or wrong. Of course, almost all of us resort to moral vocabulary to register our approvals or disapprovals of things. But our moral judgments are never true.

There is a subtle but important disagreement between these two thinkers. Ayer denies that moral judgments are truth-apt, i.e., capable of being true or false. He thinks this because of his attachment to the verifiability criterion of meaning, according to which a sentence is meaningful only if it is either a conceptual truth or empirically verifiable. Ayer basically takes Hume's criterion for what could be discovered by reason, and applies it to the theory of meaning. Ayer denies that moral claims are conceptual truths, and he also thinks it impossible to verify them through the evidence of the senses. So Ayer judges them meaningless. And a meaningless sentence is not truth-apt – it is neither true nor false.

Mackie, by contrast, thinks that moral claims are meaningful, but always fail to state the truth. That's because, for Mackie, there is no moral truth. Morality is entirely made-up, though we all suppose that it answers to some objective criteria of right and wrong. Since there are no such criteria, all of our moral claims rest on a massive failure of presupposition. We assume the existence of objective values in our moral judgments. We try to accurately report on the details of an objective morality. But we invariably fail, and lapse into error, because the very thing required to make our moral judgments true (i.e., an objective moral reality) does not exist.

Mackie's arguments for this view are numerous. One of the most important ones is this:

1 The degree of disagreement in ethics is much greater than that found in science.
2 The best explanation of this is that science explores a realm of objective facts, while ethics comprises a set of judgments that reflect non-objective, parochial opinion.
3 The view likeliest to be true is the one that best explains the available evidence.
4 Therefore, the view likeliest to be true is that ethics comprises a set of judgments that reflect non-objective, parochial opinion.

The comparative breadth and depth of ethical disagreement has long been a source of suspicion about the objectivity of ethics. So, too, has this concern, again well-expressed by Mackie in another of his arguments:

1 If there are any genuine moral requirements, then they must be intrinsically motivating and intrinsically reason-giving.
2 Nothing is either intrinsically motivating or intrinsically reason-giving.
3 Therefore, there are no genuine moral requirements.

Mackie argues that anything that is either intrinsically motivating or reason-giving would be "queer" – quite unlike anything else we know of in the universe. Following Hume, he thinks that motivation is entirely contingent on what one happens to believe and desire. No fact

or putative requirement can motivate all by itself. Mackie also thinks that the very concept of a moral requirement entails that it supply an excellent or overriding reason for all to whom it applies. But again, he thinks that reasons depend on contingent facts about people's desires or interests. No consideration can supply a reason for action all by itself; whether it does so or not depends on whether it is conducive to one's ends. Since, by Mackie's lights, something counts as a moral requirement only if it supplies, by itself, a reason for compliance, and since, as he sees it, there can be no such intrinsically reason-giving entities, it follows that there are no genuine moral requirements.

Gilbert Harman is the last representative in our readings of those who are deeply suspicious of the objectivity of ethics. Updating an argument that can be found in our selection from Hume's *Treatise*, Harman argues that we have good reason to deny the existence of objective moral facts. The argument is this: all objective facts are indispensable in explaining what we observe; no putative moral facts are thus indispensable; therefore there are no objective moral facts. We can explain all that needs explaining without introducing any moral features. If we want to discover why people are born or die, why banks operate as they do, why crops flourish or fail, we needn't invoke moral facts in the explanations. Indeed, everything we observe about the world can be explained, at least in principle, without the use of any moral notions or categories at all. This seems straightforward when we are seeking to explain scientific phenomena, such as the workings of enzymes, or the motions of planets. But it is also true when we are trying to explain why we think, for instance, that (in Harman's example) lighting a cat on fire is immoral. We have the moral thoughts we do because of our upbringing. We are not attuned to some odd realm of objective moral fact; rather, we express our socially inculcated views of right and wrong when we issue our moral judgments. This last view, very like one of Mackie's, says that the simpler hypothesis by far is that our moral judgments are nothing more than expressions of parochial attitudes formed during our maturation. Why complicate things by introducing a realm of objective moral facts, when all that needs explaining – including our propensity to have confident moral views – can be explained without them?

Though sharing a good deal of Mackie's suspicion about moral objectivity, Harman does not think that our moral views are all erroneous. Rather, Harman endorses a thesis known as *ethical relativism*. When we judge actions right or wrong, we are doing so only relative to a conventional moral standard – the one that we have agreed (with others) to accept. Though Harman offers a number of considerations on behalf of his favored view, perhaps the most powerful is given by the following line of argument: Moral requirements provide reasons for action. Further, people have reasons to act in certain ways only if such actions serve their ends. Since people's ends (i.e., their desires and commitments) differ from person to person, people's reasons for action differ in this way as well. It follows that people's moral requirements differ in this way as well. What counts as the correct moral requirements are thus contingent on what we happen to care about. Harman thus parts company with Ayer and Mackie in thinking that there are, in fact, real moral requirements. But he accepts their claim that moral demands have no objective authority.

Ethical relativism is here critically examined by Mary Midgley. Midgley introduces us to the samurai practice of assessing one's new sword by using it to kill innocent onlookers, and asks whether we are really prepared to regard such conventional practices as morally equivalent to ones that forbid such "sport." She thinks that when we consider the implications of ethical relativism, we will see that it deeply conflicts with what we really believe about the nature of morality.

The readings of this part also include an excerpt from G.E. Moore's influential work, *Principia Ethica*, written just over a century ago. Moore thinks that there are three major options for ethics: (1) ethical naturalism, according to which moral features of the world are nothing more than scientific features, and so as real as scientific features; (2) ethical nonnaturalism, according to which moral features, while real, are non-scientific; or (3) a view, that he leaves nameless, according to

which moral talk is meaningless, because there aren't any real moral features of the world. Moore thinks that the last option is preposterous, and dismisses it nearly out of hand. This is the view that came later to be endorsed by Ayer and others. Moore famously argues against option (1), ethical naturalism, by means of his open-question argument: if it is an open question whether some natural feature of the world is identical to some moral feature, then they can't really be identical. For any natural feature and any moral feature, there will be an open question as to whether they are really just one feature, or two. Therefore moral features are not natural, scientific features of the world.

Moore's preferred view, ethical nonnaturalism, has been out of favor for the past several decades. This is partly explained by the great increase in philosophical naturalism, the world view that claims that all of the world's contents are explicable scientifically. It is also attributable to a suspicion that if ethical nonnaturalism were true, we would have no access to moral facts except through intuition. Since different people have different intuitions, and intuitionism seems to have no method for adjudicating conflicts among intuitions, this moral epistemology has struck many as lacking credibility. Philosophers also worry about how unscientific moral facts could either motivate or provide moral agents with reasons for action, something that, as we saw above, many think is part of the job description of a moral requirement.

I think that some form of ethical nonnaturalism is correct, and offer a partial defense of it here. The article doesn't answer all of the objections that have been leveled against this view. Discussion of some of these criticisms is pursued in subsequent Parts: see especially Part II, where moral intuitionism is defended (by Brambrough and Audi) and criticized (by Geoffrey Sayre-McCord), and Part III, where there is much discussion about whether moral requirements are intrinsically reason-giving (see especially the papers by Philippa Foot, who denies this, and my contribution there, which affirms it). In addition to trying to reply to objections, I do offer a positive argument on behalf of nonnaturalism, which highlights the parallels between philosophy generally, and ethics in particular. Philosophical questions admit of objectively correct answers, and philosophy is not a natural science. Since ethics is a branch of philosophy, we should expect that the same things are true of ethics, namely, that moral questions have objectively correct answers, which are no part of natural science to discover.

Michael Smith's selection on *moral realism* – the technical term for the view that there is objective ethical truth – both describes and defends this metaethical position. He seeks to answer perennial worries about how we could know what is right and wrong, and how moral requirements could intrinsically motivate and provide reasons for action. He does this by developing an ideal advisor view of ethics. He thinks that what you are required to do is whatever you would want yourself to do, were you purged of false beliefs and possessed of a fully coherent set of desires. Because this ideal advisor is basically you, only new and improved, you already have built-in a motivation to adhere to his or her recommendations. You have reason to take the advice seriously, since it is given by a highly informed counterpart who shares your basic outlook on life. And you can know what the advice is, provided that you can approximate the position of someone who has gathered relevant nonmoral information, and has managed to eliminate conflicts among relevant desires. In this way, if Smith is correct, we can address the most pressing objections to the possibility of ethical objectivity.

CHAPTER 1

"Of the Influencing Motives of the Will" & "Moral Distinctions Not Derived from Reason"

DAVID HUME

Of the Influencing Motives of the Will

Nothing is more usual in philosophy, and even in common life, than to talk of the combat of passion and reason, to give the preference to reason, and assert that men are only so far virtuous as they conform themselves to its dictates. Every rational creature, it is said, is obliged to regulate his actions by reason; and if any other motive or principle challenge the direction of his conduct, he ought to oppose it, till it be entirely subdued, or at least brought to a conformity with that superior principle. On this method of thinking the greatest part of moral philosophy, ancient and modern, seems to be founded; nor is there an ampler field, as well for metaphysical arguments, as popular declamations, than this supposed preëminence of reason above passion. The eternity, invariableness, and divine origin of the former, have been displayed to the best advantage: the blindness, inconstancy, and deceitfulness of the latter, have been as strongly insisted on. In

David Hume, "Of the Influencing Motives of the Will" and "Moral Distinctions Not Derived from Reason," from *Treatise of Human Nature*, Book III, 1737.

order to show the fallacy of all this philosophy, I shall endeavour to prove *first*, that reason alone can never be a motive to any action of the will; and *secondly*, that it can never oppose passion in the direction of the will.

The understanding exerts itself after two different ways, as it judges from demonstration or probability; as it regards the abstract relations of our ideas, or those relations of objects of which experience only gives us information. I believe it scarce will be asserted, that the first species of reasoning alone is ever the cause of any action. As its proper province is the world of ideas, and as the will always places us in that of realities, demonstration and volition seem upon that account to be totally removed from each other. Mathematics, indeed, are useful in all mechanical operations, and arithmetic in almost every art and profession: but it is not of themselves they have any influence. Mechanics are the art of regulating the motions of bodies *to some designed end or purpose;* and the reason why we employ arithmetic in fixing the proportions of numbers, is only that we may discover the proportions of their influence and operation. A merchant is desirous of knowing the sum total of his accounts with any person: why? but that he may learn what sum will have the same *effects* in paying his debt, and going to market, as all the particular articles taken together. Abstract or demonstrative reasoning, therefore, never influences any of our actions, but only as it directs our judgment concerning causes and effects; which leads us to the second operation of the understanding.

It is obvious, that when we have the prospect of pain or pleasure from any object, we feel a consequent emotion of aversion or propensity, and are carried to avoid or embrace what will give us this uneasiness or satisfaction. It is also obvious, that this emotion rests not here, but, making us cast our view on every side, comprehends whatever objects are connected with its original one by the relation of cause and effect. Here then reasoning takes place to discover this relation; and according as our reasoning varies, our actions receive a subsequent variation. But it is evident, in this case, that the impulse arises not from reason, but is only directed by it. It is from the prospect of pain or pleasure that the aversion or propensity arises towards any object: and these emotions extend themselves to the causes and effects of that object, as they are pointed out to us by reason and experience. It can never in the least concern us to know, that such objects are causes, and such others effects, if both the causes and effects be indifferent to us. Where the objects themselves do not affect us, their connection can never give them any influence; and it is plain that, as reason is nothing but the discovery of this connection, it cannot be by its means that the objects are able to affect us.

Since reason alone can never produce any action, or give rise to volition, I infer, that the same faculty is as incapable of preventing volition, or of disputing the preference with any passion or emotion. This consequence is necessary. It is impossible reason could have the latter effect of preventing volition, but by giving an impulse in a contrary direction to our passions; and that impulse, had it operated alone, would have been ample to produce volition. Nothing can oppose or retard the impulse of passion, but a contrary impulse; and if this contrary impulse ever arises from reason, that latter faculty must have an original influence on the will, and must be able to

cause, as well as hinder, any act of volition. But if reason has no original influence, it is impossible it can withstand any principle which has such an efficacy, or ever keep the mind in suspense a moment. Thus, it appears, that the principle which opposes our passion cannot be the same with reason, and is only called so in an improper sense. We speak not strictly and philosophically, when we talk of the combat of passion and of reason. Reason is, and ought only to be, the slave of the passions, and can never pretend to any other office than to serve and obey them. As this opinion may appear somewhat extraordinary, it may not be improper to confirm it by some other considerations.

A passion is an original existence, or, if you will, modification of existence, and contains not any representative quality, which renders it a copy of any other existence or modification. When I am angry, I am actually possessed with the passion, and in that emotion have no more a reference to any other object, than when I am thirsty, or sick, or more than five feet high. It is impossible, therefore, that this passion can be opposed by, or be contradictory to truth and reason; since this contradiction consists in the disagreement of ideas, considered as copies, with those objects which they represent.

What may at first occur on this head is, that as nothing can be contrary to truth or reason, except what has a reference to it, and as the judgments of our understanding only have this reference, it must follow that passions can be contrary to reason only, so far as they are *accompanied* with some judgment or opinion. According to this principle, which is so obvious and natural, it is only in two senses that any affection can be called unreasonable. First, when a passion, such as hope or fear, grief or joy, despair or security, is founded on the supposition of the existence of objects, which really do not exist. Secondly, When in exerting any passion in action, we choose means sufficient for the designed end, and deceive ourselves in our judgment of causes and effects. Where a passion is neither founded on false suppositions, nor chooses means insufficient for the end, the understanding can neither justify nor condemn it. It is not contrary to reason to prefer the destruction of the whole world to the scratching of my finger. It is not contrary to reason for me to choose my total ruin, to prevent the least uneasiness of an Indian, or person wholly unknown to me. It is as little contrary to reason to prefer even my own acknowledged lesser good to my greater, and have a more ardent affection for the former than the latter. A trivial good may, from certain circumstances, produce a desire superior to what arises from the greatest and most valuable enjoyment; nor is there anything more extraordinary in this, than in mechanics to see one pound weight raise up a hundred by the advantage of its situation. In short, a passion must be accompanied with some false judgment, in order to its being unreasonable; and even then it is not the passion, properly speaking, which is unreasonable, but the judgment.

The consequences are evident. Since a passion can never, in any sense, be called unreasonable, but when founded on a false supposition, or when it chooses means insufficient for the designed end, it is impossible that reason and passion can ever oppose each other, or dispute for the government of the will and actions. The moment we perceive the falsehood of any supposition, or the insufficiency of any means, our passions yield to our reason without any opposition. I may desire any fruit as of an excellent relish; but whenever you convince me of my mistake, my longing ceases. I may will the performance of certain actions as means of obtaining any desired good; but as my willing of these actions is only secondary, and founded on the supposition that they are causes of the proposed effect; as soon as I discover the falsehood of that supposition, they must become indifferent to me.

It is natural for one, that does not examine objects with a strict philosophic eye, to imagine, that those actions of the mind are entirely the same, which produce not a different sensation, and are not immediately distinguishable to the feeling and perception. Reason, for instance, exerts itself without producing any sensible emotions; and except in the more sublime disquisitions of philosophy, or in the frivolous subtilties of the schools, scarce ever conveys any pleasure or uneasiness. Hence it proceeds, that every action of the mind which operates with the same calmness and tranquillity, is confounded with reason by all those who judge of things from the first view and appearance. Now it is certain there are certain calm desires and tendencies, which, though they be real passions, produce little emotion in the mind, and are more known by their effects than by the immediate feeling or sensation. These desires are of two kinds; either certain instincts originally implanted in our natures, such as benevolence and resentment, the love of life, and kindness to children; or the general appetite to good, and aversion to evil, considered merely as such. When any of these passions are calm, and cause no disorder in the soul, they are very readily taken for the determinations of reason, and are supposed to proceed from the same faculty with that which judges of truth and falsehood. Their nature and principles have been supposed the same, because their sensations are not evidently different.

Beside these calm passions, which often determine the will, there are certain violent emotions of the same kind, which have likewise a great influence on that faculty. When I receive any injury from another, I often feel a violent passion of resentment, which makes me desire his evil and punishment, independent of all considerations of pleasure and advantage to myself. When I am immediately threatened with any grievous ill, my fears, apprehensions, and aversions rise to a great height, and produce a sensible emotion.

The common error of metaphysicians has lain in ascribing the direction of the will entirely to one of these principles, and supposing the other to have no influence. Men often act knowingly against their interest; for which reason, the view of the greatest possible good does not always influence them. Men often counteract a violent passion in prosecution of their interests and designs; it is not, therefore, the present uneasiness alone which determines them. In general we may observe that both these principles operate on the will; and where they are contrary, that either of them prevails, according to the *general* character or *present* disposition of the person. What we call strength of mind, implies the prevalence of the calm passions above the violent; though we may easily observe, there is no man so constantly possessed of this virtue as never on any occasion to yield to the solicitations of passion and desire. From these variations of temper proceeds the great difficulty of deciding concerning the actions and resolutions of men, where there is any contrariety of motives and passions.

Moral Distinctions Not Derived from Reason

There is an inconvenience which attends all abstruse reasoning, that it may silence, without convincing an antagonist, and requires the same intense study to make us sensible of its force, that was at first requisite for its invention. When we leave our closet, and engage in the common affairs of life, its conclusions seem to vanish like the phantoms of the night on the appearance of the morning; and it is difficult for us to retain even that conviction which we had attained with difficulty. This is still more conspicuous in a long chain of reasoning, where we must preserve to the end the evidence of the first propositions, and where we often lose sight of all the most received maxims, either of philosophy or common life. I am not, however, without hopes, that the present system of philosophy will acquire new force as it advances; and that our reasonings concerning *morals* will corroborate whatever has been said concerning the *understanding* and the *passions*. Morality is a subject that interests us above all others; we fancy the peace of society to be at stake in every decision concerning it; and it is evident that this concern must make our speculations appear more real and solid, than where the subject is in a great measure indifferent to us. What affects us, we conclude, can never be a chimera; and, as our passion is engaged on the one side or the other, we naturally think that the question lies within human comprehension; which, in other cases of this nature, we are apt to entertain some doubt of. Without this advantage, I never should have ventured upon a third volume of such abstruse philosophy, in an age wherein the greatest part of men seem agreed to convert reading into an amusement, and to reject

everything that requires any considerable degree of attention to be comprehended.

It has been observed, that nothing is ever present to the mind but its perceptions; and that all the actions of seeing, hearing, judging, loving, hating, and thinking, fall under this denomination. The mind can never exert itself in any action which we may not comprehend under the term of *perception;* and consequently that term is no less applicable to those judgments by which we distinguish moral good and evil, than to every other operation of the mind. To approve of one character, to condemn another, are only so many different perceptions.

Now, as perceptions resolve themselves into two kinds, viz. *impressions* and *ideas*, this distinction gives rise to a question, with which we shall open up our present inquiry concerning morals, *whether it is by means of our* ideas *or* impressions *we distinguish betwixt vice and virtue, and pronounce an action blamable or praiseworthy?* This will immediately cut off all loose discourses and declamations, and reduce us to something precise and exact on the present subject.

Those who affirm that virtue is nothing but a conformity to reason; that there are eternal fitnesses and unfitnesses of things, which are the same to every rational being that considers them; that the immutable measure of right and wrong impose an obligation, not only on human creatures, but also on the Deity himself: all these systems concur in the opinion, that morality, like truth, is discerned merely by ideas, and by their juxtaposition and comparison. In order, therefore, to judge of these systems, we need only consider whether it be possible from reason alone, to distinguish betwixt moral good and evil, or whether there must concur some other principles to enable us to make that distinction.

If morality had naturally no influence on human passions and actions, it were in vain to take such pains to inculcate it; and nothing would be more fruitless than that multitude of rules and precepts with which all moralists abound. Philosophy is commonly divided into *speculative* and *practical;* and as morality is always comprehended under the latter division, it is supposed to influence our passions and actions, and to go beyond the calm and indolent judgments of the understanding. And this is confirmed by common experience, which informs us that men are often governed by their duties, and are deterred from some actions by the opinion of injustice, and impelled to others by that of obligation.

Since morals, therefore, have an influence on the actions and affections, it follows that they cannot be derived from reason; and that because reason alone, as we have already proved, can never have any such influence. Morals excite passions, and produce or prevent actions. Reason of itself is utterly impotent in this particular. The rules of morality, therefore, are not conclusions of our reason.

No one, I believe, will deny the justness of this inference; nor is there any other means of evading it, than by denying that principle on which it is founded. As long as it is allowed, that reason has no influence on our passions and actions, it is in vain to pretend that morality is discovered only by a deduction of reason. An active principle can never be founded on an inactive; and if reason be inactive in itself, it must remain so in all its shapes and appearances, whether it exerts itself in natural or moral subjects, whether it considers the powers of external bodies, or the actions of rational beings.

It would be tedious to repeat all the arguments by which I have proved[1] that reason is perfectly inert, and can never either prevent or produce any action or affection. It will be easy to recollect what has been said upon that subject. I shall only recall on this occasion one of these arguments, which I shall endeavour to render still more conclusive, and more applicable to the present subject.

Reason is the discovery of truth or falsehood. Truth or falsehood consists in an agreement or disagreement either to the *real* relations of ideas, or to *real* existence and matter of fact. Whatever therefore is not susceptible of this agreement or disagreement, is incapable of being true or false, and can never be an object of our reason. Now, it is evident our passions, volitions, and actions, are not susceptible of any such agreement or disagreement; being original facts and realities, complete in themselves, and implying no reference to other passions, volitions, and actions. It is impossible,

therefore, they can be pronounced either true or false, and be either contrary or conformable to reason.

This argument is of double advantage to our present purpose. For it proves *directly*, that actions do not derive their merit from a conformity to reason, nor their blame from a contrariety to it; and it proves the same truth more *indirectly*, by showing us, that as reason can never immediately prevent or produce any action by contradicting or approving of it, it cannot be the source of moral good and evil, which are found to have that influence. Actions may be laudable or blamable; but they cannot be reasonable or unreasonable: laudable or blamable, therefore, are not the same with reasonable or unreasonable. The merit and demerit of actions frequently contradict, and sometimes control our natural propensities. But reason has no such influence. Moral distinctions, therefore, are not the offspring of reason. Reason is wholly inactive, and can never be the source of so active a principle as conscience, or a sense of morals.

But perhaps it may be said, that though no will or action can be immediately contradictory to reason, yet we may find such a contradiction in some of the attendants of the actions, that is, in its causes or effects. The action may cause a judgment, or may be *obliquely* caused by one, when the judgment concurs with a passion; and by an abusive way of speaking, which philosophy will scarce allow of, the same contrariety may, upon that account, be ascribed to the action. How far this truth or falsehood may be the source of morals, it will now be proper to consider.

It has been observed that reason, in a strict and philosophical sense, can have an influence on our conduct only after two ways: either when it excites a passion, by informing us of the existence of something which is a proper object of it; or when it discovers the connection of causes and effects, so as to afford us means of exerting any passion. These are the only kinds of judgment which can accompany our actions, or can be said to produce them in any manner; and it must be allowed, that these judgments may often be false and erroneous. A person may be affected with passion, by supposing a pain or pleasure to lie in an object which has no tendency to produce either of these sensations, or which produces the contrary to what is imagined. A person may also take false measures for the attaining of his end, and may retard, by his foolish conduct, instead of forwarding the execution of any object. These false judgments may be thought to affect the passions and actions, which are connected with them, and may be said to render them unreasonable, in a figurative and improper way of speaking. But though this be acknowledged, it is easy to observe, that these errors are so far from being the source of all immorality, that they are commonly very innocent, and draw no manner of guilt upon the person who is so unfortunate as to fall into them. They extend not beyond a mistake of *fact*, which moralists have not generally supposed criminal, as being perfectly involuntary. I am more to be lamented than blamed, if I am mistaken with regard to the influence of objects in producing pain or pleasure, or if I know not the proper means of satisfying my desires. No one can ever regard such errors as a defect in my moral character. A fruit, for instance, that is really disagreeable, appears to me at a distance, and, through mistake, I fancy it to be pleasant and delicious. Here is one error. I choose certain means of reaching this fruit, which are not proper for my end. Here is a second error; nor is there any third one, which can ever possibly enter into our reasonings concerning actions. I ask, therefore, if a man in this situation, and guilty of these two errors, is to be regarded as vicious and criminal, however unavoidable they might have been? Or if it be possible to imagine that such errors are the sources of all immorality?

And here it may be proper to observe, that if moral distinctions be derived from the truth or falsehood of those judgments, they must take place wherever we form the judgments; nor will there be any difference, whether the question be concerning an apple or a kingdom, or whether the error be avoidable or unavoidable.

For as the very essence of morality is supposed to consist in an agreement or disagreement to reason, the other circumstances are entirely arbitrary, and can never either bestow on any action the character of virtuous or vicious, or deprive it of that character. To which we may add, that this agreement or disagreement, not admitting of degrees, all virtues and vices would of course be equal.

Should it be pretended, that though a mistake of *fact* be not criminal, yet a mistake of *right* often is; and that this may be the source of immorality: I would answer, that it is impossible such a mistake can ever be the original source of immorality, since it supposes a real right and wrong; that is, a real distinction in morals, independent of these judgments. A mistake, therefore, of right, may become a species of immorality; but it is only a secondary one, and is founded on some other antecedent to it.

As to those judgments which are the *effects* of our actions, and which, when false, give occasion to pronounce the actions contrary to truth and reason; we may observe, that our actions never cause any judgment, either true or false, in ourselves, and that it is only on others they have such an influence. It is certain that an action, on many occasions, may give rise to false conclusions in others; and that a person, who, through a window, sees any lewd behaviour of mine with my neighbour's wife, may be so simple as to imagine she is certainly my own. In this respect my action resembles somewhat a lie or falsehood; only with this difference, which is material, that I perform not the action with any intention of giving rise to a false judgment in another, but merely to satisfy my lust and passion. It causes, however, a mistake and false judgment by accident; and the falsehood of its effects may be ascribed, by some odd figurative way of speaking, to the action itself. But still I can see no pretext of reason for asserting, that the tendency to cause such an error is the first spring or original source of all immorality.

Thus, upon the whole, it is impossible that the distinction betwixt moral good and evil can be made by reason; since that distinction has an influence upon our actions, of which reason alone is incapable. Reason and judgment may, indeed, be the mediate cause of an action, by prompting or by directing a passion; but it is not pretended that a judgment of this kind, either in its truth or falsehood, is attended with virtue or vice. And as to the judgments, which are caused by our judgments, they can still less bestow those moral qualities on the actions which are their causes.

But, to be more particular, and to show that those eternal immutable fitnesses and unfitnesses of things cannot be defended by sound philosophy, we may weigh the following considerations.

If the thought and understanding were alone capable of fixing the boundaries of right and wrong, the character of virtuous and vicious either must lie in some relations of objects, or must be a matter of fact which is discovered by our reasoning. This consequence is evident. As the operations of human understanding divide themselves into two kinds, the comparing of ideas, and the inferring of matter of fact, were virtue discovered by the understanding, it must be an object of one of these operations; nor is there any third operation of the understanding which can discover it. There has been an opinion very industriously propagated by certain philosophers, that morality is susceptible of demonstration; and though no one has ever been able to advance a single step in those demonstrations, yet it is taken for granted that this science may be brought to an equal certainty with geometry or algebra. Upon this supposition, vice and virtue must consist in some relations; since it is allowed on all hands, that no matter of fact is capable of being demonstrated. Let us therefore begin with examining this hypothesis, and endeavour, if possible, to fix those moral qualities which have been so long the objects of our fruitless researches; point out distinctly the relations which constitute morality or obligation, that we may know wherein they consist, and after what manner we must judge of them.

If you assert that vice and virtue consist in relations susceptible of certainty and demonstration, you must confine yourself to those *four* relations which alone admit of that degree of evidence; and in that case you run into absurdities from which you will never be able to extricate yourself. For as you make the very essence of morality to lie in the relations, and as there is no one of these relations but what is applicable, not only to an irrational but also to an inanimate object, it follows that even such objects must be susceptible of merit or demerit. *Resemblance, contrariety, degrees in quality,* and *proportions in quantity and number*; all these relations belong as properly to matter as to our actions, passions, and volitions. It is unquestionable, therefore, that morality lies not in any of these relations, nor the sense of it in their discovery.[2]

Should it be asserted, that the sense of morality consists in the discovery of some relation distinct from these, and that our enumeration was not complete when we comprehended all demonstrable relations under four general heads; to this I know not what to reply, till some one be so good as to point out to me this new relation. It is impossible to refute a system which has never yet been explained. In such a manner of fighting in the dark, a man loses his blows in the air, and often places them where the enemy is not present.

I must therefore, on this occasion, rest contented with requiring the two following conditions of any one that would undertake to clear up this system. *First,* as moral good and evil belong only to the actions of the mind, and are derived from our situation with regard to external objects, the relations from which these moral distinctions arise must lie only betwixt internal actions and external objects, and must not be applicable either to internal actions, compared among themselves, or to external objects, when placed in opposition to other external objects. For as morality is supposed to attend certain relations, if these relations could belong to internal actions considered singly, it would follow, that we might be guilty of crimes in ourselves, and independent of our situation with respect to the universe; and in like manner, if these moral relations could be applied to external objects, it would follow that even inanimate beings would be susceptible of moral beauty and deformity. Now, it seems difficult to imagine that any relation can be discovered betwixt our passions, volitions, and actions, compared to external objects, which relation might not belong either to these passions and volitions, or to these external objects, compared among *themselves.*

But it will be still more difficult to fulfil the *second* condition, requisite to justify this system. According to the principles of those who maintain an abstract rational difference betwixt moral good and evil, and a natural fitness and unfitness of things, it is not only supposed, that these relations, being eternal and immutable, are the same, when considered by every rational creature, but their *effects* are also supposed to be necessarily the same; and it is concluded they have no less, or rather a greater, influence in directing the will of the Deity, than in governing the rational and virtuous of our own species. These two particulars are evidently distinct. It is one thing to know virtue, and another to conform the will to it. In order, therefore, to prove that the measures of right and wrong are eternal laws, *obligatory* on every rational mind, it is not sufficient to show the relations upon which they are founded: we must also point out the connection betwixt the relation and the will; and must prove that this connection is so necessary, that in every well-disposed mind, it must take place and have its influence; though the difference betwixt these minds be in other respects immense and infinite. Now, besides what I have already proved, that even in human nature no relation can ever alone produce any action; besides this, I say, it has been shown, in treating of the understanding, that there is no connection of cause and effect, such as this is supposed to be, which is discoverable otherwise than by experience, and of which we can pretend to have any security by the simple consideration of the objects. All beings in the universe, considered in themselves, appear entirely loose and independent of each other. It is only by experience we learn their influence and connection; and this influence we ought never to extend beyond experience.

Thus it will be impossible to fulfil the *first* condition required to the system of eternal rational measures of right and wrong; because it is impossible to show those relations, upon which such a distinction may be founded: and it is as impossible to fulfil the *second* condition: because we cannot prove *a priori*, that these relations, if they really existed and were perceived, would be universally forcible and obligatory.

But to make these general reflections more clear and convincing, we may illustrate them by some particular instances, wherein this character of moral good or evil is the most universally acknowledged. Of all crimes that human creatures are capable of committing, the most horrid and unnatural is ingratitude, especially when it is committed against parents, and appears in the more flagrant instances of wounds and death. This is acknowledged by all mankind, philosophers as well as the people: the question only arises among philosophers, whether the guilt or moral deformity of this action be discovered by demonstrative reasoning, or be felt by an internal sense, and by means of some sentiment, which the reflecting on such an action naturally occasions. This question will soon be decided against the former opinion, if we can show the same relations in other objects, without the notion of any guilt or iniquity attending them. Reason or science is nothing but the comparing of ideas, and the discovery of their relations; and if the same relations have different characters, it must evidently follow, that those characters are not discovered merely by reason. To put the affair, therefore, to this trial, let us choose any inanimate object, such as an oak or elm; and let us suppose, that, by the dropping of its seed, it produces a sapling below it, which, springing up by degrees, at last overtops and destroys the parent tree: I ask, if, in this instance, there be wanting any relation which is discoverable in parricide or ingratitude? Is not the one tree the cause of the other's existence; and the latter the cause of the destruction of the former, in the same manner as when a child murders his parent? It is not sufficient to reply, that a choice or will is wanting. For in the case of parricide, a will does not give rise to any *different* relations, but is only the cause from which the action is derived; and consequently produces the *same* relations, that in the oak or elm arise from some other principles. It is a will or choice that determines a man to kill his parent: and they are the laws of matter and motion that determine a sapling to destroy the oak from which it sprung. Here then the same relations have different causes; but still the relations are the same: and as their discovery is not in both cases attended with a notion of immorality, it follows, that that notion does not arise from such a discovery.

But to choose an instance still more resembling; I would fain ask any one, why incest in the human species is criminal, and why the very same action, and the same relations in animals, have not the smallest moral turpitude and deformity? If it be answered, that this action is innocent in animals, because they have not reason sufficient to discover its turpitude; but that man, being endowed with that faculty, which *ought* to restrain him to his duty, the same action instantly becomes criminal to him. Should this be said, I would reply, that this is evidently arguing in a circle. For, before reason can perceive this turpitude, the turpitude must exist; and consequently is independent of the decisions of our reason, and is their object more properly than their effect. According to this system, then, every animal that has sense and appetite and will, that is, every animal must be susceptible of all the same virtues and vices, for which we ascribe praise and blame to human creatures. All the difference is, that our superior reason may serve to discover the vice or virtue, and by that means may augment the blame or praise: but still this discovery supposes a separate being in these moral distinctions, and a being which depends only on the will and appetite, and which, both in thought and reality, may be distinguished from reason. Animals are susceptible of the same relations with respect to each other as the human species, and therefore would also be susceptible of the same morality, if the essence of morality consisted in these relations. Their want of a sufficient degree of reason may hinder them from perceiving the duties and obligations of morality, but can never hinder these duties from existing; since they must antecedently exist, in order to their being perceived. Reason must find them, and can never produce them. This argument deserves to be weighed, as being, in my opinion, entirely decisive.

Nor does this reasoning only prove, that morality consists not in any relations that are the objects of science; but if examined, will prove with equal certainty, that it consists not in any *matter of fact*, which can be discovered by the understanding. This is the *second* part of our argument; and if it can be made evident, we may conclude that morality is not an object of reason. But can there be any difficulty in proving that vice and virtue are not matters of fact, whose existence we can infer by reason? Take any action allowed to be vicious; wilful

murder, for instance. Examine it in all lights, and see if you can find that matter of fact, or real existence, which you call *vice*. In whichever way you take it, you find only certain passions, motives, volitions, and thoughts. There is no other matter of fact in the case. The vice entirely escapes you, as long as you consider the object. You never can find it, till you turn your reflection into your own breast, and find a sentiment of disapprobation, which arises in you, towards this action. Here is a matter of fact; but it is the object of feeling, not of reason. It lies in yourself, not in the object. So that when you pronounce any action or character to be vicious, you mean nothing, but that from the constitution of your nature you have a feeling or sentiment of blame from the contemplation of it. Vice and virtue, therefore, may be compared to sounds, colours, heat, and cold, which, according to modern philosophy, are not qualities in objects, but perceptions in the mind: and this discovery in morals, like that other in physics, is to be regarded as a considerable advancement of the speculative sciences; though, like that too, it has little or no influence on practice. Nothing can be more real, or concern us more, than our own sentiments of pleasure and uneasiness; and if these be favourable to virtue, and unfavourable to vice, no more can be requisite to the regulation of our conduct and behaviour.

I cannot forbear adding to these reasonings an observation, which may, perhaps, be found of some importance. In every system of morality which I have hitherto met with, I have always remarked, that the author proceeds for some time in the ordinary way of reasoning, and establishes the being of a God, or makes observations concerning human affairs; when of a sudden I am surprised to find, that instead of the usual copulations of propositions, *is*, and *is not*, I meet with no proposition that is not connected with an *ought*, or an *ought not*. This change is imperceptible; but is, however, of the last consequence. For as this *ought*, or *ought not*, expresses some new relation or affirmation, it is necessary that it should be observed and explained; and at the same time that a reason should be given, for what seems altogether inconceivable, how this new relation can be a deduction from others, which are entirely different from it. But as authors do not commonly use this precaution, I shall presume to recommend it to the readers; and am persuaded, that this small attention would subvert all the vulgar systems of morality, and let us see that the distinction of vice and virtue is not founded merely on the relations of objects, nor is perceived by reason.

Notes

1. Book II. Part III. Sect. 3
2. As a proof how confused our way of thinking on this subject commonly is, we may observe, that those who assert that morality is demonstrable, do not say that morality lies in the relations, and that the relations are distinguishable by reason. They only say, that reason can discover such an action, in such relations, to be virtuous, and such another vicious. It seems they thought it sufficient if they could bring the word Relation into the proposition, without troubling themselves whether it was to the purpose or not. But here, I think, is plain argument. Demonstrative reason discovers only relations. But that reason, according to this hypothesis, discovers also vice and virtue. These moral qualities, therefore, must be relations. When we blame any action, in any situation, the whole complicated object of action and situation must form certain relations, wherein the essence of vice consists. This hypothesis is not otherwise intelligible. For what does reason discover, when it pronounces any action vicious? Does it discover a relation or a matter of fact? These questions are decisive, and must not be eluded.

CHAPTER 2
A Critique of Ethics

A. J. AYER

There is still one objection to be met before we can claim to have justified our view that all synthetic propositions are empirical hypotheses. This objection is based on the common supposition that our speculative knowledge is of two distinct kinds – that which relates to questions of empirical fact, and that which relates to questions of value. It will be said that "statements of value" are genuine synthetic propositions, but that they cannot with any show of justice be represented as hypotheses, which are used to predict the course of our sensations; and, accordingly, that the existence of ethics and æsthetics as branches of speculative knowledge presents an insuperable objection to our radical empiricist thesis.

In face of this objection, it is our business to give an account of "judgments of value" which is both satisfactory in itself and consistent with our general empiricist principles. We shall set ourselves to show that in so far as statements of value are significant, they are ordinary "scientific" statements; and that in so far as they are not scientific, they are not in the literal sense significant, but are simply expressions of emotion which can be neither true nor false. In maintaining this view, we may confine ourselves for the present to the case of ethical

A. J. Ayer, "A Critique of Ethics," pp. 102–13 from *Language, Truth and Logic*. New York: Dover, 1952. Reprinted by permission of Dover Publications Inc.

statements. What is said about them will be found to apply, *mutatis mutandis*, to the case of æsthetic statements also.

The ordinary system of ethics, as elaborated in the works of ethical philosophers, is very far from being a homogeneous whole. Not only is it apt to contain pieces of metaphysics, and analyses of non-ethical concepts: its actual ethical contents are themselves of very different kinds. We may divide them, indeed, into four main classes. There are, first of all, propositions which express definitions of ethical terms, or judgments about the legitimacy or possibility of certain definitions. Secondly, there are propositions describing the phenomena of moral experience, and their causes. Thirdly, there are exhortations to moral virtue. And, lastly, there are actual ethical judgments. It is unfortunately the case that the distinction between these four classes, plain as it is, is commonly ignored by ethical philosophers; with the result that it is often very difficult to tell from their works what it is that they are seeking to discover or prove.

In fact, it is easy to see that only the first of our four classes, namely that which comprises the propositions relating to the definitions of ethical terms, can be said to constitute ethical philosophy. The propositions which describe the phenomena of moral experience, and their causes, must be assigned to the science of psychology, or sociology. The exhortations to moral virtue are not propositions at all, but ejaculations or commands which are designed to provoke the reader to action of a certain sort. Accordingly, they do not belong to any branch of philosophy or science. As for the expressions of ethical judgments, we have not yet determined how they should be classified. But inasmuch as they are certainly neither definitions nor comments upon definitions, nor quotations, we may say decisively that they do not belong to ethical philosophy. A strictly philosophical treatise on ethics should therefore make no ethical pronouncements. But it should, by giving an analysis of ethical terms, show what is the category to which all such pronouncements belong. And this is what we are now about to do.

A question which is often discussed by ethical philosophers is whether it is possible to find definitions which would reduce all ethical terms to one or two fundamental terms. But this question, though it undeniably belongs to ethical philosophy, is not relevant to our present enquiry. We are not now concerned to discover which term, within the sphere of ethical terms, is to be taken as fundamental; whether, for example, "good" can be defined in terms of "right" or "right" in terms of "good," or both in terms of "value." What we are interested in is the possibility of reducing the whole sphere of ethical terms to non-ethical terms. We are enquiring whether statements of ethical value can be translated into statements of empirical fact.

That they can be so translated is the contention of those ethical philosophers who are commonly called subjectivists, and of those who are known as utilitarians. For the utilitarian defines the rightness of actions, and the goodness of ends, in terms of the pleasure, or happiness, or satisfaction, to which they give rise; the subjectivist, in terms of the feelings of approval which a certain person, or group of people, has towards them. Each of these types of definition makes moral judgments into a sub-class of psychological or sociological judgments; and for this reason they are very attractive to us. For, if either was correct, it would follow that ethical assertions were not generically different from the factual assertions which are ordinarily contrasted with them; and the

account which we have already given of empirical hypotheses would apply to them also.

Nevertheless we shall not adopt either a subjectivist or a utilitarian analysis of ethical terms. We reject the subjectivist view that to call an action right, or a thing good, is to say that it is generally approved of, because it is not self-contradictory to assert that some actions which are generally approved of are not right, or that some things which are generally approved of are not good. And we reject the alternative subjectivist view that a man who asserts that a certain action is right, or that a certain thing is good, is saying that he himself approves of it, on the ground that a man who confessed that he sometimes approved of what was bad or wrong would not be contradicting himself. And a similar argument is fatal to utilitarianism. We cannot agree that to call an action right is to say that of all the actions possible in the circumstances it would cause, or be likely to cause, the greatest happiness, or the greatest balance of pleasure over pain, or the greatest balance of satisfied over unsatisfied desire, because we find that it is not self-contradictory to say that it is sometimes wrong to perform the action which would actually or probably cause the greatest happiness, or the greatest balance of pleasure over pain, or of satisfied over unsatisfied desire. And since it is not self-contradictory to say that some pleasant things are not good, or that some bad things are desired, it cannot be the case that the sentence "x is good" is equivalent to "x is pleasant," or to "x is desired." And to every other variant of utilitarianism with which I am acquainted the same objection can be made. And therefore we should, I think, conclude that the validity of ethical judgments is not determined by the felicific tendencies of actions, any more than by the nature of people's feelings; but that it must be regarded as "absolute" or "intrinsic," and not empirically calculable.

If we say this, we are not, of course, denying that it is possible to invent a language in which all ethical symbols are definable in non-ethical terms, or even that it is desirable to invent such a language and adopt it in place of our own; what we are denying is that the suggested reduction of ethical to non-ethical statements is consistent with the conventions of our actual language. That is, we reject utilitarianism and subjectivism, not as proposals to replace our existing ethical notions by new ones, but as analyses of our existing ethical notions. Our contention is simply that, in our language, sentences which contain normative ethical symbols are not equivalent to sentences which express psychological propositions, or indeed empirical propositions of any kind.

It is advisable here to make it plain that it is only normative ethical symbols, and not descriptive ethical symbols, that are held by us to be indefinable in factual terms. There is a danger of confusing these two types of symbols, because they are commonly constituted by signs of the same sensible form. Thus a complex sign of the form "x is wrong" may constitute a sentence which expresses a moral judgment concerning a certain type of conduct, or it may constitute a sentence which states that a certain type of conduct is repugnant to the moral sense of a particular society. In the latter case, the symbol "wrong" is a descriptive ethical symbol, and the sentence in which it occurs expresses an ordinary sociological proposition; in the former case, the symbol "wrong" is a normative ethical symbol, and the sentence in which it occurs does not, we maintain, express an empirical proposition at all. It is only with normative ethics that we are at present concerned; so that whenever ethical symbols are used in the course of this argument without qualification, they are always to be interpreted as symbols of the normative type.

In admitting that normative ethical concepts are irreducible to empirical concepts, we seem to be leaving the way clear for the "absolutist" view of ethics – that is, the view that statements of value are not controlled by observation, as ordinary empirical propositions are, but only by a mysterious "intellectual intuition." A feature of this theory, which is seldom recognized by its advocates, is that it makes statements of value unverifiable. For it is notorious that what seems intuitively certain to one person may seem doubtful, or even false, to another. So that unless it is possible to provide some criterion by which one may decide between conflicting intuitions, a mere appeal to intuition is worthless as a test of a proposition's

validity. But in the case of moral judgments, no such criterion can be given. Some moralists claim to settle the matter by saying that they "know" that their own moral judgments are correct. But such an assertion is of purely psychological interest, and has not the slightest tendency to prove the validity of any moral judgment. For dissentient moralists may equally well "know" that their ethical views are correct. And, as far as subjective certainty goes, there will be nothing to choose between them. When such differences of opinion arise in connection with an ordinary empirical proposition, one may attempt to resolve them by referring to, or actually carrying out, some relevant empirical test. But with regard to ethical statements, there is, on the "absolutist" or "intuitionist" theory, no relevant empirical test. We are therefore justified in saying that on this theory ethical statements are held to be unverifiable. They are, of course, also held to be genuine synthetic propositions.

Considering the use which we have made of the principle that a synthetic proposition is significant only if it is empirically verifiable, it is clear that the acceptance of an "absolutist" theory of ethics would undermine the whole of our main argument. And as we have already rejected the "naturalistic" theories which are commonly supposed to provide the only alternative to "absolutism" in ethics, we seem to have reached a difficult position. We shall meet the difficulty by showing that the correct treatment of ethical statements is afforded by a third theory, which is wholly compatible with our radical empiricism.

We begin by admitting that the fundamental ethical concepts are unanalyzable, inasmuch as there is no criterion by which one can test the validity of the judgments in which they occur. So far we are in agreement with the absolutists. But, unlike the absolutists, we are able to give an explanation of this fact about ethical concepts. We say that the reason why they are unanalyzable is that they are mere pseudo-concepts. The presence of an ethical symbol in a proposition adds nothing to its factual content. Thus if I say to someone, "You acted wrongly in stealing that money," I am not stating anything more than if I had simply said, "You stole that money." In adding that this action is wrong I am not making any further statement about it. I am simply evincing my moral disapproval of it. It is as if I had said, "You stole that money," in a peculiar tone of horror, or written it with the addition of some special exclamation marks. The tone, or the exclamation marks, adds nothing to the literal meaning of the sentence. It merely serves to show that the expression of it is attended by certain feelings in the speaker.

If now I generalize my previous statement and say, "Stealing money is wrong," I produce a sentence which has no factual meaning – that is, expresses no proposition which can be either true or false. It is as if I had written "Stealing money!!" – where the shape and thickness of the exclamation marks show, by a suitable convention, that a special sort of moral disapproval is the feeling which is being expressed. It is clear that there is nothing said here which can be true or false. Another man may disagree with me about the wrongness of stealing, in the sense that he may not have the same feelings about stealing as I have, and he may quarrel with me on account of my moral sentiments. But he cannot, strictly speaking, contradict me. For in saying that a certain type of action is right or wrong, I am not making any factual statement, not even a statement about my own state of mind. I am merely expressing certain moral sentiments. And the man who is ostensibly contradicting me is merely expressing his moral sentiments. So that there is plainly no sense in asking which of us is in the right. For neither of us is asserting a genuine proposition.

What we have just been saying about the symbol "wrong" applies to all normative ethical symbols. Sometimes they occur in sentences which record ordinary empirical facts besides expressing ethical feeling about those facts: sometimes they occur in sentences which simply express ethical feeling about a certain type of action, or situation, without making any statement of fact. But in every case in which one would commonly be said to be making an ethical judgment, the function of the relevant ethical word is purely "emotive." It is used to express feeling about certain objects, but not to make any assertion about them.

It is worth mentioning that ethical terms do not serve only to express feeling. They are calculated also to arouse feeling, and so to stimulate action. Indeed some of them are used in such a way as to give the sentences in which they occur the effect of commands. Thus the sentence "It is your duty to tell the truth" may be regarded both as the expression of a certain sort of ethical feeling about truthfulness and as the expression of the command "Tell the truth." The sentence "You ought to tell the truth" also involves the command "Tell the truth," but here the tone of the command is less emphatic. In the sentence "It is good to tell the truth" the command has become little more than a suggestion. And thus the "meaning" of the word "good," in its ethical usage, is differentiated from that of the word "duty" or the word "ought." In fact we may define the meaning of the various ethical words in terms both of the different feelings they are ordinarily taken to express, and also the different responses which they are calculated to provoke.

We can now see why it is impossible to find a criterion for determining the validity of ethical judgments. It is not because they have an "absolute" validity which is mysteriously independent of ordinary sense-experience, but because they have no objective validity whatsoever. If a sentence makes no statement at all, there is obviously no sense in asking whether what it says is true or false. And we have seen that sentences which simply express moral judgments do not say anything. They are pure expressions of feeling and as such do not come under the category of truth and falsehood. They are unverifiable for the same reason as a cry of pain or a word of command is unverifiable – because they do not express genuine propositions.

Thus, although our theory of ethics might fairly be said to be radically subjectivist, it differs in a very important respect from the orthodox subjectivist theory. For the orthodox subjectivist does not deny, as we do, that the sentences of a moralizer express genuine propositions. All he denies is that they express propositions of a unique non-empirical character. His own view is that they express propositions about the speaker's feelings. If this were so, ethical judgments clearly would be capable of being true or false. They would be true if the speaker had the relevant feelings, and false if he had not. And this is a matter which is, in principle, empirically verifiable. Furthermore they could be significantly contradicted. For if I say, "Tolerance is a virtue," and someone answers, "You don't approve of it," he would, on the ordinary subjectivist theory, be contradicting me. On our theory, he would not be contradicting me, because, in saying that tolerance was a virtue, I should not be making any statement about my own feelings or about anything else. I should simply be evincing my feelings, which is not at all the same thing as saying that I have them.

The distinction between the expression of feeling and the assertion of feeling is complicated by the fact that the assertion that one has a certain feeling often accompanies the expression of that feeling, and is then, indeed, a factor in the expression of that feeling. Thus I may simultaneously express boredom and say that I am bored, and in that case my utterance of the words, "I am bored," is one of the circumstances which make it true to say that I am expressing or evincing boredom. But I can express boredom without actually saying that I am bored. I can express it by my tone and gestures, while making a statement about something wholly unconnected with it, or by an ejaculation, or without uttering any words at all. So that even if the assertion that one has a certain feeling always involves the expression of that feeling, the expression of a feeling assuredly does not always involve the assertion that one has it. And this is the important point to grasp in considering the distinction between our theory and the ordinary subjectivist theory. For whereas the subjectivist holds that ethical statements actually assert the existence of certain feelings, we hold that ethical statements are expressions and excitants of feeling which do not necessarily involve any assertions.

We have already remarked that the main objection to the ordinary subjectivist theory is that the validity of ethical judgments is not determined by the nature of their author's feelings. And this is an objection which our theory escapes. For it does not imply that the existence of any feelings is a necessary and sufficient condition of the validity of an ethical judgment. It implies, on the contrary, that ethical judgments have no validity.

There is, however, a celebrated argument against subjectivist theories which our theory does not escape. It has been pointed out by Moore that if ethical statements were simply statements about the speaker's feelings, it would be impossible to argue about questions of value.[1] To take a typical example: if a man said that thrift was a virtue, and another replied that it was a vice, they would not, on this theory, be disputing with one another. One would be saying that he approved of thrift, and the other that *he* didn't; and there is no reason why both these statements should not be true. Now Moore held it to be obvious that we do dispute about questions of value, and accordingly concluded that the particular form of subjectivism which he was discussing was false.

It is plain that the conclusion that it is impossible to dispute about questions of value follows from our theory also. For as we hold that such sentences as "Thrift is a virtue" and "Thrift is a vice" do not express propositions at all, we clearly cannot hold that they express incompatible propositions. We must therefore admit that if Moore's argument really refutes the ordinary subjectivist theory, it also refutes ours. But, in fact, we deny that it does refute even the ordinary subjectivist theory. For we hold that one really never does dispute about questions of value.

This may seem, at first sight, to be a very paradoxical assertion. For we certainly do engage in disputes which are ordinarily regarded as disputes about questions of value. But, in all such cases, we find, if we consider the matter closely, that the dispute is not really about a question of value, but about a question of fact. When someone disagrees with us about the moral value of a certain action or type of action, we do admittedly resort to argument in order to win him over to our way of thinking. But we do not attempt to show by our arguments that he has the "wrong" ethical feeling towards a situation whose nature he has correctly apprehended. What we attempt to show is that he is mistaken about the facts of the case. We argue that he has misconceived the agent's motive: or that he has misjudged the effects of the action, or its probable effects in view of the agent's knowledge; or that he has failed to take into account the special circumstances in which the agent was placed. Or else we employ more general arguments about the effects which actions of a certain type tend to produce, or the qualities which are usually manifested in their performance. We do this in the hope that we have only to get our opponent to agree with us about the nature of the empirical facts for him to adopt the same moral attitude towards them as we do. And as the people with whom we argue have generally received the same moral education as ourselves, and live in the same social order, our expectation is usually justified. But if our opponent happens to have undergone a different process of moral "conditioning" from ourselves, so that, even when he acknowledges all the facts, he still disagrees with us about the moral value of the actions under discussion, then we abandon the attempt to convince him by argument. We say that it is impossible to argue with him because he has a distorted or undeveloped moral sense; which signifies merely that he employs a different set of values from our own. We feel that our own system of values is superior, and therefore speak in such derogatory terms of his. But we cannot bring forward any arguments to show that our system is superior. For our judgment that it is so is itself a judgment of value, and accordingly outside the scope of argument. It is because argument fails us when we come to deal with pure questions of value, as distinct from questions of fact, that we finally resort to mere abuse.

In short, we find that argument is possible on moral questions only if some system of values is presupposed. If our opponent concurs with us in expressing moral disapproval of all actions of a given type *t*, then we may get him to condemn a particular action A, by bringing forward arguments to show that A is of type *t*. For the question whether A does or does not belong to that type is a plain question of fact. Given that a man has certain moral principles, we argue that he must, in order to be consistent, react morally to certain things in a certain way. What we do not and cannot argue about is the validity of these moral principles. We merely praise or condemn them in the light of our own feelings.

If anyone doubts the accuracy of this account of moral disputes, let him try to construct even an imaginary argument on a question of value which does not reduce itself to an argument about a question of logic or about an empirical matter of fact. I am confident that he will not succeed in producing a single example. And if that is the case, he must allow that its involving the impossibility of purely ethical arguments is not, as Moore thought, a ground of objection to our theory, but rather a point in favor of it.

Having upheld our theory against the only criticism which appeared to threaten it, we may now use it to define the nature of all ethical enquiries. We find that ethical philosophy consists simply in saying that ethical concepts are pseudo-concepts and therefore unanalyzable. The further task of describing the different feelings that the different ethical terms are used to express, and the different reactions that they customarily provoke, is a task for the psychologist. There cannot be such a thing as ethical science, if by ethical science one means the elaboration of a "true" system of morals. For we have seen that, as ethical judgments are mere expressions of feeling, there can be no way of determining the validity of any ethical system, and, indeed, no sense in asking whether any such system is true. All that one may legitimately enquire in this connection is, What are the moral habits of a given person or group of people, and what causes them to have precisely those habits and feelings? And this enquiry falls wholly within the scope of the existing social sciences.

It appears, then, that ethics, as a branch of knowledge, is nothing more than a department of psychology and sociology. And in case anyone thinks that we are overlooking the existence of casuistry, we may remark that casuistry is not a science, but is a purely analytical investigation of the structure of a given moral system. In other words, it is an exercise in formal logic.

When one comes to pursue the psychological enquiries which constitute ethical science, one is immediately enabled to account for the Kantian and hedonistic theories of morals. For one finds that one of the chief causes of moral behavior is fear, both conscious and unconscious, of a god's displeasure, and fear of the enmity of society. And this, indeed, is the reason why moral precepts present themselves to some people as "categorical" commands. And one finds, also, that the moral code of a society is partly determined by the beliefs of that society concerning the conditions of its own happiness – or, in other words, that a society tends to encourage or discourage a given type of conduct by the use of moral sanctions according as it appears to promote or detract from the contentment of the society as a whole. And this is the reason why altruism is recommended in most moral codes and egotism condemned. It is from the observation of this connection between morality and happiness that hedonistic or eudæmonistic theories of morals ultimately spring, just as the moral theory of Kant is based on the fact, previously explained, that moral precepts have for some people the force of inexorable commands. As each of these theories ignores the fact which lies at the root of the other, both may be criticized as being one-sided; but this is not the main objection to either of them. Their essential defect is that they treat propositions which refer to the causes and attributes of our ethical feelings as if they were definitions of ethical concepts. And thus they fail to recognize that ethical concepts are pseudo-concepts and consequently indefinable.

Note

1. cf. *Philosophical Studies*, "The Nature of Moral Philosophy."

CHAPTER 3
The Subjectivity of Values

J. L. MACKIE

Moral Scepticism

There are no objective values. This is a bald statement of the thesis of this chapter, but before arguing for it I shall try to clarify and restrict it in ways that may meet some objections and prevent some misunderstanding.

The statement of this thesis is liable to provoke one of three very different reactions. Some will think it not merely false but pernicious; they will see it as a threat to morality and to everything else that is worthwhile, and they will find the presenting of such a thesis in what purports to be a book on ethics paradoxical or even outrageous. Others will regard it as a trivial truth, almost too obvious to be worth mentioning, and certainly too plain to be worth much argument. Others again will say that it is meaningless or empty, that no real issue is raised by the question whether values are or are not part of the fabric of the world. But, precisely because there can be these three different reactions, much more needs to be said.

The claim that values are not objective, are not part of the fabric of the world, is meant to include not only moral goodness, which might

J. L. Mackie, "The Subjectivity of Values," pp. 15–18, 27–46 from *Ethics: Inventing Right and Wrong*. New York: Penguin, 1977. Copyright © J. L. Mackie, 1977. Reproduced by permission of Penguin Books Ltd.

be most naturally equated with moral value, but also other things that could be more loosely called moral values or disvalues – rightness and wrongness, duty, obligation, an action's being rotten and contemptible, and so on. It also includes non-moral values, notably aesthetic ones, beauty and various kinds of artistic merit. I shall not discuss these explicitly, but clearly much the same considerations apply to aesthetic and to moral values, and there would be at least some initial implausibility in a view that gave the one a different status from the other.

Since it is with moral values that I am primarily concerned, the view I am adopting may be called moral scepticism. But this name is likely to be misunderstood: 'moral scepticism' might also be used as a name for either of two first order views, or perhaps for an incoherent mixture of the two. A moral sceptic might be the sort of person who says 'All this talk of morality is tripe,' who rejects morality and will take no notice of it. Such a person may be literally rejecting all moral judgements; he is more likely to be making moral judgements of his own, expressing a positive moral condemnation of all that conventionally passes for morality; or he may be confusing these two logically incompatible views, and saying that he rejects all morality, while he is in fact rejecting only a particular morality that is current in the society in which he has grown up. But I am

Moral Relativism

not at present concerned with the merits or faults of such a position. These are first order moral views, positive or negative: the person who adopts either of them is taking a certain practical, normative, stand. By contrast, what I am discussing is a second order view, a view about the status of moral values and the nature of moral valuing, about where and how they fit into the world. These first and second order views are not merely distinct but completely independent: one could be a second order moral sceptic without being a first order one, or again the other way round. A man could hold strong moral views, and indeed ones whose content was thoroughly conventional, while believing that they were simply attitudes and policies with regard to conduct that he and other people held. Conversely, a man could reject all established morality while believing it to be an objective truth that it was evil or corrupt.

With another sort of misunderstanding moral scepticism would seem not so much pernicious as absurd. How could anyone deny that there is a difference between a kind action and a cruel one, or that a coward and a brave man behave differently in the face of danger? Of course, this is undeniable; but it is not to the point. The kinds of behaviour to which moral values and disvalues are ascribed are indeed part of the furniture of the world, and so are the natural, descriptive, differences between them; but not, perhaps, their differences in value. It is a hard fact that cruel actions differ from kind ones, and hence that we can learn, as in fact we all do, to distinguish them fairly well in practice, and to use the words 'cruel' and 'kind' with fairly clear descriptive meanings; but is it an equally hard fact that actions which are cruel in such a descriptive sense are to be condemned? The present issue is with regard to the objectivity specifically of value, not with regard to the objectivity of those natural, factual, differences on the basis of which differing values are assigned.

Subjectivism

Another name often used, as an alternative to 'moral scepticism', for the view I am discussing is 'subjectivism'. But this too has more than one meaning. Moral subjectivism too could be a first order, normative, view, namely that everyone really ought to do whatever he thinks he should. This plainly is a (systematic) first order view; on examination it soon ceases to be plausible, but that is beside the point, for it is quite independent of the second order thesis at present under consideration. What is more confusing is that different second order views compete for the name 'subjectivism'. Several of these are doctrines about the meaning of moral terms and moral statements. What is often called moral subjectivism is the doctrine that, for example, 'This action is right' *means* 'I approve of this action', or more generally that moral judgements are equivalent to reports of the speaker's own feelings or attitudes. But the view I am now discussing is to be distinguished in two vital respects from any such doctrine as this. First, what I have called moral scepticism is a negative doctrine, not a positive one: it says what there isn't, not what there is. It says that there do not exist entities or relations of a certain kind, objective values or requirements, which many people have believed to exist. Of course, the moral sceptic cannot leave it at that. If his position is to be at all plausible, he must give some account of how other people have fallen into what he regards as an error, and this account will have to include some positive suggestions about how values fail to be objective, about what has been mistaken for, or has led to false beliefs about, objective values. But this will be a development of his theory, not its core: its core is the negation. Secondly, what I have called moral scepticism is an ontological thesis, not a linguistic or conceptual one. It is not, like the other doctrine often called moral subjectivism, a view about the meanings of moral statements. Again, no doubt, if it is to be at all plausible, it will have to give some account of their meanings, and I shall say something about this [in a later section of the original work.] But this too will be a development of the theory, not its core.

It is true that those who have accepted the moral subjectivism which is the doctrine that moral judgements are equivalent to reports of the speaker's own feelings or attitudes have usually presupposed what I am calling moral scepticism. It is because they have assumed that there are no objective values that they have looked elsewhere for an analysis of what moral statements might mean, and have settled upon subjective reports. Indeed, if all our moral statements were such subjective reports, it would follow that, at least so far as we are aware, there are no objective moral values. If we were aware of them, we would say something about them. In this sense this sort of subjectivism entails moral scepticism. But the converse entailment does not hold. The denial that there are objective values does not commit one to any particular view about what moral statements mean, and certainly not to the view that they are equivalent to subjective reports. No doubt if moral values are not objective they are in some very broad sense subjective, and for this reason I would accept 'moral subjectivism' as an alternative name to 'moral scepticism'. But subjectivism in this broad sense must be distinguished from the specific doctrine about meaning referred to above. Neither name is altogether satisfactory: we simply have to guard against the (different) misinterpretations which each may suggest.

[. . .]

Hypothetical and Categorical Imperatives

We may make this issue clearer by referring to Kant's distinction between hypothetical and categorical imperatives, though what he called imperatives are more naturally expressed as 'ought'-statements than in the imperative mood. 'If you want X, do Y' (or 'You ought to do Y') will be a hypothetical imperative if it is based on the supposed fact that Y is, in the circumstances, the only (or the best) available means to X, that is, on a causal relation between Y and X. The reason for doing Y lies in its causal connection with the desired end, X; the oughtness is contingent upon the desire. But 'You ought to do Y' will be a categorical imperative if you ought to do Y irrespective of any such desire for any end to which Y would contribute, if the oughtness is not thus contingent upon any desire.

[. . .]

A categorical imperative, then, would express a reason for acting which was unconditional in the sense of not being contingent upon any present desire of the agent to whose satisfaction the recommended action would contribute as a means – or more directly: 'You ought to dance', if the implied reason is just that you want to dance or like dancing, is still a hypothetical imperative. Now Kant himself held that moral judgements are categorical imperatives, or perhaps are all applications of one categorical imperative, and it can plausibly be maintained at least that many moral judgements contain a categorically imperative element. So far as ethics is concerned, my thesis that there are no objective values is specifically the denial that any such categorically imperative element is objectively valid. The objective values which I am denying would be action-directing absolutely, not contingently (in the way indicated) upon the agent's desires and inclinations.

[. . .]

The Claim to Objectivity

If I have succeeded in specifying precisely enough the moral values whose objectivity I am denying, my thesis may now seem to be trivially true. Of course, some will say, valuing, preferring, choosing, recommending, rejecting, condemning, and so on, are human activities, and there is no need to look for values that are prior to and logically independent of all such activities. There may be widespread agreement in valuing, and particular value-judgements are not in general arbitrary or isolated: they typically cohere with others, or can be criticized if they do not, reasons can be given for them, and so on: but if all that the subjectivist is maintaining is that desires, ends, purposes, and the like figure somewhere in the system of reasons, and that no ends or purposes are objective as opposed to being merely inter-subjective, then this may be conceded without much fuss.

But I do not think that this should be conceded so easily. As I have said, the main tradition of European moral philosophy includes the contrary claim, that there are objective values of just the sort I have denied. I have referred already [in the original work] to Plato, Kant, and Sidgwick. Kant in particular holds that the categorical imperative is not only categorical and imperative but objectively so: though a rational being gives the moral law to himself, the law that he thus makes is determinate and necessary. Aristotle begins the *Nicomachean Ethics* by saying that the good is that at which all things aim, and that ethics is part of a science which he calls 'politics', whose goal is not knowledge but practice; yet he does not doubt that there can be *knowledge* of what is the good for man, nor, once he has identified this as well-being or happiness, *eudaimonia*, that it can be known, rationally determined, in what happiness consists; and it is plain that he thinks that this happiness is intrinsically desirable, not good simply because it is desired. The rationalist Samuel Clarke holds that

> these eternal and necessary differences of things make it *fit and reasonable* for creatures so to act . . . even separate from the consideration of these rules being the *positive will* or *command of God*; and also antecedent to any respect or regard, expectation or apprehension, of any *particular private and personal advantage or disadvantage, reward or punishment*, either present or future . . .

Even the sentimentalist Hutcheson defines moral goodness as 'some quality apprehended in actions, which procures approbation . . .', while saying that the moral sense by which we perceive virtue and vice has been given to us (by the Author of nature) to direct our actions. Hume indeed was on the other side, but he is still a witness to the dominance of the objectivist tradition, since he claims that when we 'see that the distinction of vice and virtue is not founded merely on the relations of objects, nor is perceiv'd by reason', this 'wou'd subvert all the vulgar systems of morality'. And Richard Price insists that right and wrong are 'real characters of actions', not 'qualities of our minds', and are perceived by the understanding; he criticizes the notion of moral sense on the ground that it would make virtue an affair of taste, and moral right and wrong "nothing in the objects themselves"; he rejects

Hutcheson's view because (perhaps mistakenly) he sees it as collapsing into Hume's.

But this objectivism about values is not only a feature of the philosophical tradition. It has also a firm basis in ordinary thought, and even in the meanings of moral terms. No doubt it was an extravagance for Moore to say that 'good' is the name of a non-natural quality, but it would not be so far wrong to say that in moral contexts it is used as if it were the name of a supposed non-natural quality, where the description "non-natural" leaves room for the peculiar evaluative, prescriptive, intrinsically action-guiding aspects of this supposed quality. This point can be illustrated by reflection on the conflicts and swings of opinion in recent years between non-cognitivist and naturalist views about the central, basic, meanings of ethical terms. If we reject the view that it is the function of such terms to introduce objective values into discourse about conduct and choices of action, there seem to be two main alternative types of account. One (which has importantly different subdivisions) is that they conventionally express either attitudes which the speaker purports to adopt towards whatever it is that he characterizes morally, or prescriptions or recommendations, subject perhaps to the logical constraint of universalizability. Different views of this type share the central thesis that ethical terms have, at least partly and primarily, some sort of non-cognitive, non-descriptive, meaning. Views of the other type hold that they are descriptive in meaning, but descriptive of natural features, partly of such features as everyone, even the non-cognitivist, would recognize as distinguishing kind actions from cruel ones, courage from cowardice, politeness from rudeness, and so on, and partly (though these two overlap) of relations between the actions and some human wants, satisfactions, and the like. I believe that views of both these types capture part of the truth. Each approach can account for the fact that moral judgements are action-guiding or practical. Yet each gains much of its plausibility from the felt inadequacy of the other. It is a very natural reaction to any non-cognitive analysis of ethical terms to protest that there is more to ethics than this, something more external to the maker of moral judgements, more authoritative over both him and those of or to whom he speaks, and this reaction is likely to persist even when full allowance has been made for the logical, formal, constraints of full-blooded prescriptivity and universalizability. Ethics, we are inclined to believe, is more a matter of knowledge and less a matter of decision than any non-cognitive analysis allows. And of course naturalism satisfies this demand. It will not be a matter of choice or decision whether an action is cruel or unjust or imprudent or whether it is likely to produce more distress than pleasure. But in satisfying this demand, it introduces a converse deficiency. On a naturalist analysis, moral judgements can be practical, but their practicality is wholly relative to desires or possible satisfactions of the person or persons whose actions are to be guided; but moral judgements seem to say more than this. This view leaves out the categorical quality of moral requirements. In fact both naturalist and non-cognitive analyses leave out the apparent authority of ethics, the one by excluding the categorically imperative aspect, the other the claim to objective validity or truth. The ordinary user of moral language means to say something about whatever it is that he characterizes morally, for example a possible action, as it is in itself, or would be if it were realized, and not about, or even simply expressive of, his, or anyone else's, attitude or relation to it. But the something he wants to say is not purely descriptive, certainly not inert, but something that involves a call for action or for the refraining from action, and one that is absolute, not contingent upon any desire or preference or policy or choice, his own or anyone else's. Someone in a state of moral perplexity, wondering whether it would be wrong for him to engage, say, in research related to bacteriological warfare, wants to arrive at some judgement about this concrete case, his doing this work at this time in these actual circumstances; his relevant characteristics will be part of the subject of the judgement, but no relation between him and the proposed action will be part of the predicate. The question is not, for example, whether he really wants to do this work, whether it will satisfy or dissatisfy him, whether he will in the long run have a pro-attitude towards it, or even whether this is an

action of a sort that he can happily and sincerely recommend in all relevantly similar cases. Nor is he even wondering just whether to recommend such action in all relevantly similar cases. He wants to know whether this course of action would be wrong in itself. Something like this is the everyday objectivist concept of which talk about non-natural qualities is a philosopher's reconstruction.

The prevalence of this tendency to objectify values – and not only moral ones – is confirmed by a pattern of thinking that we find in existentialists and those influenced by them. The denial of objective values can carry with it an extreme emotional reaction, a feeling that nothing matters at all, that life has lost its purpose. Of course this does not follow; the lack of objective values is not a good reason for abandoning subjective concern or for ceasing to want anything. But the abandonment of a belief in objective values can cause, at least temporarily, a decay of subjective concern and sense of purpose. That it does so is evidence that the people in whom this reaction occurs have been tending to objectify their concerns and purposes, have been giving them a fictitious external authority. A claim to objectivity has been so strongly associated with their subjective concerns and purposes that the collapse of the former seems to undermine the latter as well.

This view, that conceptual analysis would reveal a claim to objectivity, is sometimes dramatically confirmed by philosophers who are officially on the other side. Bertrand Russell, for example, says that 'ethical propositions should be expressed in the optative mood, not in the indicative'; he defends himself effectively against the charge of inconsistency in both holding ultimate ethical valuations to be subjective and expressing emphatic opinions on ethical questions. Yet at the end he admits:

> Certainly there *seems* to be something more. Suppose, for example, that some one were to advocate the introduction of bull-fighting in this country. In opposing the proposal, I should *feel*, not only that I was expressing my desires, but that my desires in the matter are *right*, whatever that may mean. As a matter of argument, I can, I think, show that I am not

guilty of any logical inconsistency in holding to the above interpretation of ethics and at the same time expressing strong ethical preferences. But in feeling I am not satisfied.

But he concludes, reasonably enough, with the remark: 'I can only say that, while my own opinions as to ethics do not satisfy me, other people's satisfy me still less.'

I conclude, then, that ordinary moral judgements include a claim to objectivity, an assumption that there are objective values in just the sense in which I am concerned to deny this. And I do not think it is going too far to say that this assumption has been incorporated in the basic, conventional, meanings of moral terms. Any analysis of the meanings of moral terms which omits this claim to objective, intrinsic, prescriptivity is to that extent incomplete; and this is true of any non-cognitive analysis, any naturalist one, and any combination of the two.

If second order ethics were confined, then, to linguistic and conceptual analysis, it ought to conclude that moral values at least are objective: that they are so is part of what our ordinary moral statements mean: the traditional moral concepts of the ordinary man as well as of the main line of western philosophers are concepts of objective value. But it is precisely for this reason that linguistic and conceptual analysis is not enough. The claim to objectivity, however ingrained in our language and thought, is not self-validating. It can and should be questioned. But the denial of objective values will have to be put forward not as the result of an analytic approach, but as an 'error theory', a theory that although most people in making moral judgements implicitly claim, among other things, to be pointing to something objectively prescriptive, these claims are all false. It is this that makes the name 'moral scepticism' appropriate.

But since this is an error theory, since it goes against assumptions ingrained in our thought and built into some of the ways in which language is used, since it conflicts with what is sometimes called common sense, it needs very solid support. It is not something we can accept lightly or casually and then quietly pass on. If we are to adopt this view, we must argue

explicitly for it. Traditionally it has been supported by arguments of two main kinds, which I shall call the argument from relativity and the argument from queerness, but these can, as I shall show, be supplemented in several ways.

The Argument from Relativity

The argument from relativity has as its premiss the well-known variation in moral codes from one society to another and from one period to another, and also the differences in moral beliefs between different groups and classes within a complex community. Such variation is in itself merely a truth of descriptive morality, a fact of anthropology which entails neither first order nor second order ethical views. Yet it may indirectly support second order subjectivism: radical differences between first order moral judgements make it difficult to treat those judgements as apprehensions of objective truths. But it is not the mere occurrence of disagreements that tells against the objectivity of values. Disagreement on questions in history or biology or cosmology does not show that there are no objective issues in these fields for investigators to disagree about. But such scientific disagreement results from speculative inferences or explanatory hypotheses based on inadequate evidence, and it is hardly plausible to interpret moral disagreement in the same way. Disagreement about moral codes seems to reflect people's adherence to and participation in different ways of life. The causal connection seems to be mainly that way round: it is that people approve of monogamy because they participate in a monogamous way of life rather than that they participate in a monogamous way of life because they approve of monogamy. Of course, the standards may be an idealization of the way of life from which they arise: the monogamy in which people participate may be less complete, less rigid, than that of which it leads them to approve. This is not to say that moral judgements are purely conventional. Of course there have been and are moral heretics and moral reformers, people who have turned against the established rules and practices of their own communities for moral reasons, and often for moral reasons that we would endorse. But this can usually be understood as the extension, in ways which, though new and unconventional, seemed to them to be required for consistency, of rules to which they already adhered as arising out of an existing way of life. In short, the argument from relativity has some force simply because the actual variations in the moral codes are more readily explained by the hypothesis that they reflect ways of life than by the hypothesis that they express perceptions, most of them seriously inadequate and badly distorted, of objective values.

But there is a well-known counter to this argument from relativity, namely to say that the items for which objective validity is in the first place to be claimed are not specific moral rules or codes but very general basic principles which are recognized at least implicitly to some extent in all society – such principles as provide the foundations of what Sidgwick has called different methods of ethics: the principle of universalizability, perhaps, or the rule that one ought to conform to the specific rules of any way of life in which one takes part, from which one profits, and on which one relies, or some utilitarian principle of doing what tends, or seems likely, to promote the general happiness. It is easy to show that such general principles, married with differing concrete circumstances, different existing social patterns or different preferences, will beget different specific moral rules; and there is some plausibility in the claim that the specific rules thus generated will vary from community to community or from group to group in close agreement with the actual variations in accepted codes.

The argument from relativity can be only partly countered in this way. To take this line the moral objectivist has to stay that it is only in these principles that the objective moral character attaches immediately to its descriptively specified ground or subject: other moral judgements are objectively valid or true, but only derivatively and contingently – if things had been otherwise, quite different sorts of actions would have been right. And despite the prominence in recent philosophical ethics of universalization, utilitarian principles, and the like, these are very far from constituting the whole of what is actually affirmed as basic in ordinary moral thought. Much of this is concerned rather with what Hare calls "ideals" or, less kindly, 'fanaticism'. That is, people judge that some things are good or right, and others are bad or wrong, not because – or at any rate not only because – they exemplify some general principle for which widespread implicit acceptance could be claimed, but because something about those things arouses certain responses immediately in them, though they would arouse radically and irresolvably different responses in others. 'Moral sense' or 'intuition' is an initially more plausible description of what supplies many of our basic moral judgements than 'reason'. With regard to all these starting points of moral thinking the argument from relativity remains in full force.

The Argument from Queerness

Even more important, however, and certainly more generally applicable, is the argument from queerness. This has two parts, one metaphysical, the other epistemological. If there were objective values, then they would be entities or qualities or relations of a very strange sort, utterly different from anything else in the universe. Correspondingly, if we were aware of them, it would have to be by some special faculty of moral perception or intuition, utterly different from our ordinary ways of knowing everything else. These points were recognized by Moore when he spoke of non-natural qualities, and by the intuitionists in their talk about a 'faculty of moral intuition'. Intuitionism has long been out of favour, and it is indeed easy to point out its implausibilities. What is not so often stressed, but is more important, is that the central thesis of intuitionism is one to which any objectivist view of values is in the end committed: intuitionism merely makes unpalatably plain what other forms of objectivism wrap up. Of course the suggestion that moral judgements are made or moral problems solved by just sitting down and having an ethical intuition is a travesty of actual moral thinking. But, however complex the real process, it will require (if it is to yield authoritatively prescriptive conclusions) some input of this distinctive sort, either premisses or forms of argument or both. When we ask the awkward question, how we can be aware of this authoritative prescriptivity, of the truth of these distinctively ethical premisses or of the cogency of this distinctively ethical pattern of reasoning, none of our ordinary accounts of sensory perception or introspection or the framing and confirming of explanatory hypotheses or inference or logical construction or conceptual analysis, or any combination of these, will provide a satisfactory answer; 'a special sort of intuition' is a lame answer, but it is the one to which the clear-headed objectivist is compelled to resort.

Indeed, the best move for the moral objectivist is not to evade this issue, but to look for companions in guilt. For example, Richard Price argues that it is not moral knowledge alone that such an empiricism as those of Locke and Hume is unable to account for, but also our knowledge and even our ideas of essence, number, identity, diversity, solidity, inertia, substance, the necessary existence and infinite extension of time and space, necessity and possibility in general, power, and causation. If the understanding, which Price defines as the faculty within us that discerns truth, is also a source of new simple ideas of so many other sorts, may it not also be a power of immediately perceiving right and wrong, which yet are real characters of actions?

This is an important counter to the argument from queerness. The only adequate reply to it would be to show how, on empiricist foundations, we can construct an account of the ideas and beliefs and knowledge that we have of all these matters. I cannot even begin to do that here, though I have undertaken some parts of the task elsewhere. I can only state my belief that satisfactory accounts of most of these can be given in empirical terms. If some supposed metaphysical necessities or essences resist such treatment, then they too should be included, along with objective values, among the targets of the argument from queerness.

This queerness does not consist simply in the fact that ethical statements are 'unverifiable'. Although logical positivism with its verifiability theory of descriptive meaning gave an impetus to non-cognitive accounts of ethics, it is not only logical positivists but also empiricists of a much more liberal sort who should find objective values hard to accommodate. Indeed, I would not only reject the verifiability principle but also deny the conclusion commonly drawn from it, that moral judgements lack descriptive meaning. The assertion that there are objective values or intrinsically prescriptive entities or features of some kind, which ordinary moral judgements presuppose, is, I hold, not meaningless but false.

Plato's Forms give a dramatic picture of what objective values would have to be. The Form of the Good is such that knowledge of it provides the knower with both a direction and an overriding motive; something's being good both tells the person who knows this to pursue it and makes him pursue it. An objective good would be sought by anyone who was acquainted with it, not because of any contingent fact that this person, or every person, is so constituted that he desires this end, but just because the end has to-be-pursuedness somehow built into it. Similarly, if there were objective principles of right and wrong, any wrong (possible) course of action would have not-to-be-doneness somehow built into it. Or we should have something like Clarke's necessary relations of fitness between situations and actions, so that a situation would have a demand for such-and-such an action somehow built into it.

The need for an argument of this sort can be brought out by reflection on Hume's argument that 'reason' – in which at this stage he includes all sorts of knowing as well as reasoning – can never be an 'influencing motive of the will'. Someone might object that Hume has argued unfairly from the lack of influencing power (not contingent upon desires) in ordinary objects of knowledge and ordinary reasoning, and might maintain that values differ from natural objects precisely in their power, when known, automatically to influence the will. To this Hume could, and would need to, reply that this objection involves the postulating of value-entities or value-features of quite a different order from anything else with which we are acquainted, and of a corresponding faculty with which to detect them. That is, he would have to supplement his explicit argument with what I have called the argument from queerness.

Another way of bringing out this queerness is to ask, about anything that is supposed to have some objective moral quality, how this is linked with its natural features. What is the connection between the natural fact that an action is a piece of deliberate cruelty – say, causing pain just for fun – and the moral fact that it is wrong? It cannot be an entailment, a logical or semantic necessity. Yet it is not merely that the two features occur together. The wrongness must somehow be 'consequential' or 'supervenient'; it is wrong because it is a piece of deliberate cruelty. But just what *in the world* is signified by this 'because'? And how do we know the relation that it signifies, if this is something more than such actions being socially condemned, and condemned by us too, perhaps through our having absorbed attitudes from our social environment? It is not even sufficient to postulate a faculty which 'sees' the wrongness: something must be postulated which can see at once the natural features that constitute the cruelty, and the wrongness, and the mysterious consequential link between the two. Alternatively, the intuition required might be the perception that wrongness is a higher order property belonging to certain natural properties; but what is this belonging of properties to other properties, and how can we discern it? How much simpler and more comprehensible the situation would be if we could replace the moral quality with some sort of subjective response which could be causally related to the detection of the natural features on which the supposed quality is said to be consequential.

It may be thought that the argument from queerness is given an unfair start if we thus relate it to what are admittedly among the wilder products of philosophical fancy – Platonic Forms, non-natural qualities, self-evident relations of fitness, faculties of intuition, and the like. Is it equally forceful if applied to the terms in which everyday moral judgements are more likely to be expressed – though still, as has been argued [in the original work], with a claim to objectivity – 'you must do this', 'you can't do that', 'obligation', 'unjust', 'rotten', 'disgraceful', 'mean', or talk about good

reasons for or against possible actions? Admittedly not; but that is because the objective prescriptivity, the element a claim for whose authoritativeness is embedded in ordinary moral thought and language, is not yet isolated in these forms of speech, but is presented along with relations to desires and feelings, reasoning about the means to desired ends, inter-personal demands, the injustice which consists in the violation of what are in the context the accepted standards of merit, the psychological constituents of meanness, and so on. There is nothing queer about any of these, and under cover of them the claim for moral authority may pass unnoticed. But if I am right in arguing that it is ordinarily there, and is therefore very likely to be incorporated almost automatically in philosophical accounts of ethics which systematize our ordinary thought even in such apparently innocent terms as these, it needs to be examined, and for this purpose it needs to be isolated and exposed as it is by the less cautious philosophical reconstructions.

Patterns of Objectification

Considerations of these kinds suggest that it is in the end less paradoxical to reject than to retain the common-sense belief in the objectivity of moral values, provided that we can explain how this belief, if it is false, has become established and is so resistant to criticisms. This proviso is not difficult to satisfy.

On a subjectivist view, the supposedly objective values will be based in fact upon attitudes which the person has who takes himself to be recognizing and responding to those values. If we admit what Hume calls the mind's 'propensity to spread itself on external objects', we can understand the supposed objectivity of moral qualities as arising from what we can call the projection or objectification of moral attitudes. This would be analogous to what is called the 'pathetic fallacy', the tendency to read our feelings into their objects. If a fungus, say, fills us with disgust, we may be inclined to ascribe to the fungus itself a non-natural quality of foulness. But in moral contexts there is more than this propensity at work. Moral attitudes themselves are at least partly social in origin: socially established – and socially necessary – patterns of behaviour put pressure on individuals, and each individual tends to internalize these pressures and to join in requiring these patterns of behaviour of himself and of others. The attitudes that are objectified into moral values have indeed an external source, though not the one assigned to them by the belief in their absolute authority. Moreover, there are motives that would support objectification. We need morality to regulate interpersonal relations, to control some of the ways in which people behave towards one another, often in opposition to contrary inclinations. We therefore want our moral judgements to be authoritative for other agents as well as for ourselves: objective validity would give them the authority required. Aesthetic values are logically in the same position as moral ones; much the same metaphysical and epistemological considerations apply to them. But aesthetic values are less strongly objectified than moral ones; their subjective status, and an 'error theory' with regard to such claims to objectivity as are incorporated in aesthetic judgements, will be more readily accepted, just because the motives for their objectification are less compelling.

But it would be misleading to think of the objectification of moral values as primarily the projection of feelings, as in the pathetic fallacy. More important are wants and demands. As Hobbes says, 'whatsoever is the object of any man's Appetite or Desire, that is it, which he for his part calleth *Good*'; and certainly both the adjective 'good' and the noun 'goods' are used in non-moral contexts of things because they are such as to satisfy desires. We get the notion of something's being objectively good, or having intrinsic value, by reversing the direction of dependence here, by making the desire depend upon the goodness, instead of the goodness on the desire. And this is aided by the fact that the desired thing will indeed have features that make it desired, that enable it to arouse a desire or that make it such as to satisfy some desire that is already there. It is fairly easy to confuse the way in which a thing's desirability is indeed objective with its having in our sense objective value. The fact that the word 'good' serves as one of our main

moral terms is a trace of this pattern of objectification.

[. . .]

Another way of explaining the objectification of moral values is to say that ethics is a system of law from which the legislator has been removed. This might have been derived either from the positive law of a state or from a supposed system of divine law. There can be no doubt that some features of modern European moral concepts are traceable to the theological ethics of Christianity. The stress on quasi-imperative notions, on what ought to be done or on what is wrong in a sense that is close to that of 'forbidden', are surely relics of divine commands. Admittedly, the central ethical concepts for Plato and Aristotle also are in a broad sense prescriptive or intrinsically action-guiding, but in concentrating rather on 'good' than on 'ought' they show that their moral thought is an objectification of the desired and the satisfying rather than of the commanded. Elizabeth Anscombe has argued that modern, non-Aristotelian, concepts of *moral* obligation, *moral* duty, of what is *morally* right and wrong, and of the *moral* sense of 'ought' are survivals outside the framework of thought that made them really intelligible, namely the belief in divine law. She infers that 'ought' has 'become a word of mere mesmeric force', with only a 'delusive appearance of content', and that we would do better to discard such terms and concepts altogether, and go back to Aristotelian ones.

There is much to be said for this view. But while we can explain some distinctive features of modern moral philosophy in this way, it would be a mistake to see the whole problem of the claim to objective prescriptivity as merely local and unnecessary, as a post-operative complication of a society from which a dominant system of theistic belief has recently been rather hastily excised. As Cudworth and Clarke and Price, for example, show, even those who still admit divine commands, or the positive law of God, may believe moral values to have an independent objective but still action-guiding authority. Responding to Plato's *Euthyphro* dilemma, they believe that God commands what he commands because it is in itself good or right, not that it is good or right merely because and in that he commands it. Otherwise God himself could not be called good. Price asks, 'What can be more preposterous, than to make the Deity nothing but will; and to exalt this on the ruins of all his attributes?' The apparent objectivity of moral value is a widespread phenomenon which has more than one source: the persistence of a belief in something like divine law when the belief in the divine legislator has faded out is only one factor among others. There are several different patterns of objectification, all of which have left characteristic traces in our actual moral concepts and moral language.

CHAPTER 4

Ethics and Observation

GILBERT HARMAN

The Basic Issue

Can moral principles be tested and confirmed in the way scientific principles can? Consider the principle that, if you are given a choice between five people alive and one dead or five people dead and one alive, you should always choose to have five people alive and one dead rather than the other way round. We can easily imagine examples that appear to confirm this principle. Here is one:

> You are a doctor in a hospital's emergency room when six accident victims are brought in. All six are in danger of dying but one is much worse off than the others. You can just barely save that person if you devote all of your resources to him and let the others die. Alternatively, you can save the other five if you are willing to ignore the most seriously injured person.

It would seem that in this case you, the doctor, would be right to save the five and let the other person die. So this example, taken by itself, confirms the principle under consideration. Next, consider the following case.

Gilbert Harman, "Ethics and Observation," pp. 3–10 from *The Nature of Morality*. Oxford: Oxford University Press, 1977.

You have five patients in the hospital who are dying, each in need of a separate organ. One needs a kidney, another a lung, a third a heart, and so forth. You can save all five if you take a single healthy person and remove his heart, lungs, kidneys, and so forth, to distribute to these five patients. Just such a healthy person is in room 306. He is in the hospital for routine tests. Having seen his test results, you know that he is perfectly healthy and of the right tissue compatibility. If you do nothing, he will survive without incident; the other patients will die, however. The other five patients can be saved only if the person in Room 306 is cut up and his organs distributed. In that case, there would be one dead but five saved.

The principle in question tells us that you should cut up the patient in Room 306. But in this case, surely you must not sacrifice this innocent bystander, even to save the five other patients. Here a moral principle has been tested and disconfirmed in what may seem to be a surprising way.

This, of course, was a "thought experiment." We did not really compare a hypothesis with the world. We compared an explicit principle with our feelings about certain imagined examples. In the same way, a physicist performs thought experiments in order to compare explicit hypotheses with his "sense" of what should happen in certain situations, a "sense" that he has acquired as a result of his long working familiarity with current theory. But scientific hypotheses can also be tested in real experiments, out in the world.

Can moral principles be tested in the same way, out in the world? You can observe someone do something, but can you ever perceive the rightness or wrongness of what he does? If you round a corner and see a group of young hoodlums pour gasoline on a cat and ignite it, you do not need to *conclude* that what they are doing is wrong; you do not need to figure anything out; you can *see* that it is wrong. But is your reaction due to the actual wrongness of what you see or is it simply a reflection of your moral "sense," a "sense" that you have acquired perhaps as a result of your moral upbringing?

Observation

The issue is complicated. There are no pure observations. Observations are always "theory laden." What you perceive depends to some extent on the theory you hold, consciously or unconsciously. You see some children pour gasoline on a cat and ignite it. To really see that, you have to possess a great deal of knowledge, know about a considerable number of objects, know about people: that people pass through the life stages infant, baby, child, adolescent, adult. You must know what flesh and blood animals are, and in particular, cats. You must have some idea of life. You must know what gasoline is, what burning is, and much more. In one sense, what you "see" is a pattern of light on your retina, a shifting array of splotches, although, even that is theory, and you could never adequately describe what you see in that sense. In another sense, you see what you do because of the theories you hold. Change those theories and you would see something else, given the same pattern of light.

Similarly, if you hold a moral view, whether it is held consciously or unconsciously, you will be able to perceive rightness or wrongness, goodness or badness, justice or injustice. There is no difference in this respect between moral propositions and other theoretical propositions. If there is a difference, it must be found elsewhere.

Observation depends on theory because perception involves forming a belief as a fairly direct result of observing something; you can form a belief only if you understand the relevant concepts and a concept is what it is by virtue of its role in some theory or system of beliefs. To recognize a child as a child is to employ, consciously or unconsciously, a concept that is defined by its place in a framework of the stages of human life. Similarly, burning is an empty concept apart from its theoretical connections to the concepts of heat, destruction, smoke, and fire.

Moral concepts – Right and Wrong, Good and Bad, Justice and Injustice – also have a place in your theory or system of beliefs and are the concepts they are because of their context. If we say that observation has occurred whenever an opinion is a direct result of perception, we must allow that there is moral observation, because such an opinion can be a moral opinion as easily as any other sort. In this sense, observation may be used to confirm or disconfirm moral theories. The observational opinions that, in this sense, you find yourself with can be in either agreement or conflict with your consciously explicit moral principles. When they are in conflict, you must choose between your explicit theory and observation. In ethics, as in science, you sometimes opt for theory, and say that you made an error in observation or were biased or whatever, or you sometimes opt for observation, and modify your theory.

In other words, in both science and ethics, general principles are invoked to explain particular cases and, therefore, in both science and ethics, the general principles you accept can be tested by appealing to particular judgments that certain things are right or wrong, just or unjust, and so forth; and these judgments are analogous to direct perceptual judgments about facts.

Observational Evidence

Nevertheless, observation plays a role in science that it does not seem to play in ethics. The difference is that you need to make assumptions about certain physical facts to explain the occurrence of the observations that support a scientific theory, but you do not seem to need to make assumptions about any moral facts to explain the occurrence of the so-called moral observations I have been talking about. In the moral case, it would seem that you need only make assumptions about the psychology or moral sensibility of the person making the moral observation. In the scientific case, theory is tested against the world.

The point is subtle but important. Consider a physicist making an observation to test a scientific theory. Seeing a vapor trail in a cloud chamber, he thinks, "There goes a proton." Let us suppose that this is an observation in the relevant sense, namely, an immediate judgment made in response to the situation without any conscious reasoning having taken place. Let us also suppose that his observation confirms his theory, a theory that helps give meaning to the very term "proton" as it occurs in his observational judgment. Such a confirmation rests on inferring an explanation. He can count his making the observation as confirming evidence for his theory only to the extent that it is reasonable to explain his making the observation by assuming that, not only is he in a certain psychological "set," given the theory he accepts and his beliefs about the experimental apparatus, but furthermore, there really was a proton going through the cloud chamber, causing the vapor trail, which he saw as a proton. (This is evidence for the theory to the extent that the theory can explain the proton's being there better than competing theories can.) But, if his having made that observation could have been equally well explained by his psychological set alone, without the need for any assumption about a proton, then the observation would not have been evidence for the existence of that proton and therefore would not have been evidence for the theory. His making the observation supports the theory only because, in order to explain his making the observation, it is reasonable to assume something about the world over and above the assumptions made about the observer's psychology. In particular, it is reasonable to assume that there was a proton going through the cloud chamber, causing the vapor trail.

Compare this case with one in which you make a moral judgment immediately and with-out conscious reasoning, say, that the children are wrong to set the cat on fire, or that the doctor would be wrong to cut up one healthy patient to save five dying patients. In order to explain your making the first of these judgments, it would be reasonable to assume, perhaps, that the children really are pouring gasoline on a cat and you are seeing them do it. But, in neither case is there any obvious reason to assume anything about "moral facts," such as that it really is wrong to set the cat on fire or to cut up the patient in Room 306. Indeed, an assumption about moral facts would seem to be totally irrelevant to the explanation of your making the judgment you make. It would seem that all we need assume is that you have certain more or less well articulated moral principles that are reflected in the judgments you make, based on your moral sensibility. It seems to be completely irrelevant to our explanation whether your intuitive immediate judgment is true or false.

The observation of an event can provide observational evidence for or against a scientific theory in the sense that the truth of that observation can be relevant to a reasonable explanation of why that observation was made. A moral observation does not seem, in the same sense, to be observational evidence for or against any moral theory, since the truth or falsity of the moral observation seems to be completely irrelevant to any reasonable explanation of why that observation was made. The fact that an observation of an event was made at the time it was made is evidence not only about the observer but also about the physical facts. The fact that you made a particular moral observation when you did does not seem to be evidence about moral facts, only evidence about you and your moral sensibility. Facts about protons can affect what you observe, since a proton passing through the cloud chamber can cause a vapor trail that reflects light to your eye in a way that, given your scientific training and psychological set, leads you to judge that what you see is a proton. But there does not seem to be any way in which the actual rightness or wrongness of a given situation can have any effect on your perceptual apparatus. In this respect, ethics seems to differ from science.

In considering whether moral principles can help explain observations, it is therefore important to note an ambiguity in the word "observation." You see the children set the cat on fire and immediately think, "That's wrong." In one sense, your observation is that what the children are doing is wrong. In another sense, your observation is your thinking that thought. Moral observations might explain observations in the first sense but not in the second sense. Certain moral principles might help to explain why it was *wrong* of the children to set the cat on fire, but moral principles seem to be of no help in explaining *your thinking* that that is wrong. In the first sense of "observation," moral principles can be tested by observation – "That this act is wrong is evidence that causing unnecessary suffering is wrong." But in the second sense of "observation," moral principles cannot clearly be tested by observation, since they do not appear to help explain observations in this second sense of "observation." Moral principles do not seem to help explain your observing what you observe.

Of course, if you are already given the moral principle that it is wrong to cause unnecessary suffering, you can take your seeing the children setting the cat on fire as observational evidence that they are doing something wrong. Similarly, you can suppose that your seeing the vapor trail is observational evidence that a proton is going through the cloud chamber, if you are given the relevant physical theory. But there is an important apparent difference between the two cases. In the scientific case, your making that observation is itself evidence for the physical theory because the physical theory explains the proton, which explains the trail, which explains your observation. In the moral case, your making your observation does not seem to be evidence for the relevant moral principle because that principle does not seem to help explain your observation. The explanatory chain from principle to observation seems to be broken in morality. The moral principle may "explain" why it is wrong for the children to set the cat on fire. But the wrongness of that act does not appear to help explain the act, which you observe, itself. The explanatory chain appears to be broken in such a way that neither the moral principle nor the wrongness

of the act can help explain why you observe what you observe.

A qualification may seem to be needed here. Perhaps the children perversely set the cat on fire simply "because it is wrong." Here it may seem at first that the actual wrongness of the act does help explain why they do it and therefore indirectly helps explain why you observe what you observe just as a physical theory, by explaining why the proton is producing a vapor trail, indirectly helps explain why the observer observes what he observes. But on reflection we must agree that this is probably an illusion. What explains the children's act is not clearly the actual wrongness of the act but, rather, their belief that the act is wrong. The actual rightness or wrongness of their act seems to have nothing to do with why they do it.

Observational evidence plays a part in science it does not appear to play in ethics, because scientific principles can be justified ultimately by their role in explaining observations, in the second sense of observation – by their explanatory role. Apparently, moral principles cannot be justified in the same way. It appears to be true that there can be no explanatory chain between moral principles and particular observings in the way that there can be such a chain between scientific principles and particular observings. Conceived as an explanatory theory, morality, unlike science, seems to be cut off from observation.

Not that every legitimate scientific hypothesis susceptible to direct observational testing. Certain hypotheses about "black holes" in space cannot be directly tested, for example, because no signal is emitted from within a black hole. The connection with observation in such a case is indirect. And there are many similar examples. Nevertheless, seen in the large, there is the apparent difference between science and ethics we have noted. The scientific realm is accessible to observation in a way the moral realm is not.

Ethics and Mathematics

Perhaps ethics is to be compared, not with physics, but with mathematics. Perhaps such a moral principle as "You ought to keep your promises" is confirmed or disconfirmed in the way (whatever it is) in which such a mathematical principle as "5 + 7 = 12" is. Observation does not seem to play the role in mathematics it plays in physics. We do not and cannot perceive numbers, for example, since we cannot be in causal contact with them. We do not even understand what it would be like to be in causal contact with the number 12, say. Relations among numbers cannot have any more of an effect on our perceptual apparatus than moral facts can.

Observation, however, *is* relevant to mathematics. In explaining the observations that support a physical theory, scientists typically appeal to mathematical principles. On the other hand, one never seems to need to appeal in this way to moral principles. Since an observation is evidence for what best explains it, and since mathematics often figures in the explanations of scientific observations, there is indirect observational evidence for mathematics. There does not seem to be observational evidence, even indirectly, for basic moral principles. In explaining why certain observations have been made, we never seem to use purely moral assumptions. In this respect, then, ethics appears to differ not only from physics but also from mathematics.

CHAPTER 5

Moral Relativism Defended

GILBERT HARMAN

My thesis is that morality arises when a group of people reach an implicit agreement or come to a tacit understanding about their relations with one another. Part of what I mean by this is that moral judgments – or, rather, an important class of them – make sense only in relation to and with reference to one or another such agreement or understanding. This is vague, and I shall try to make it more precise in what follows. But it should be clear that I intend to argue for a version of what has been called moral relativism.

In doing so, I am taking sides in an ancient controversy. Many people have supposed that the sort of view which I am going to defend is obviously correct – indeed, that it is the only sort of account that could make sense of the phenomenon of morality. At the same time there have also been many who have supposed that moral relativism is confused, incoherent, and even immoral, at the very least obviously wrong.

Most arguments against relativism make use of a strategy of dissuasive definition; they define moral relativism as an inconsistent thesis. For example, they define it as the assertion that (a) there are no universal moral principles and (b) one ought to act in accordance with the principles of one's own group, where

Gilbert Harman, "Moral Relativism Defended," Reprinted by permission of Duke University Press.

this latter principle, (b), *is* supposed to be a universal moral principle.[1] It is easy enough to show that this version of moral relativism will not do, but that is no reason to think that a defender of moral relativism cannot find a better definition.

My moral relativism is a soberly logical thesis – a thesis about logical form, if you like. Just as the judgment that something is large makes sense only in relation to one or another comparison class, so too, I will argue, the judgment that it is wrong of someone to do something makes sense only in relation to an agreement or understanding. A dog may be large in relation to chihuahuas but not large in relation to dogs in general. Similarly, I will argue, an action may be wrong in relation to one agreement but not in relation to another. Just as it makes no sense to ask whether a dog is large, period, apart from any relation to a comparison class, so too, I will argue, it makes no sense to ask whether an action is wrong, period, apart from any relation to an agreement.

There is an agreement, in the relevant sense, if each of a number of people intends to adhere to some schedule, plan, or set of principles, intending to do this on the understanding that the others similarly intend. The agreement or understanding need not be conscious or explicit; and I will not here try to say what distinguishes moral agreements from, for example, conventions of the road or conventions of etiquette, since these distinctions will not be important as regards the purely logical thesis that I will be defending.

Although I want to say that certain moral judgments are made in relation to an agreement, I do not want to say this about all moral judgments. Perhaps it is true that all moral judgments are made in relation to an agreement; nevertheless, that is not what I will be arguing. For I want to say that there is a way in which certain moral judgments are relative to an agreement but other moral judgments are not. My relativism is a thesis only about what I will call "inner judgments," such as the judgment that someone ought or ought not to have acted in a certain way or the judgment that it was right or wrong of him to have done so. My relativism is not meant to apply, for example, to the judgment that someone is evil or the judgment that a given institution is unjust.

In particular, I am not denying (nor am I asserting) that some moralities are "objectively" better than others or that there are objective standards for assessing moralities. My thesis is a soberly logical thesis about logical form.

1.   Inner Judgments

We make inner judgments about a person only if we suppose that he is capable of being motivated by the relevant moral considerations. We make other sorts of judgment about those who we suppose are not susceptible of such motivation. Inner judgments include judgments in which we say that someone should or ought to have done something or that someone was right or wrong to have done something. Inner judgments do not include judgments in which we call someone (literally) a savage or say that someone is (literally) inhuman, evil, a betrayer, a traitor, or an enemy.

Consider this example. Intelligent beings from outer space land on Earth, beings without the slightest concern for human life and happiness. That a certain course of action on their part might injure one of us means nothing to them; that fact by itself gives them no reason to avoid the action. In such a case it would be odd to say that nevertheless the beings ought to avoid injuring us or that it would be wrong for them to attack us. Of course we will want to resist them if they do such things and we will make negative judgments about them; but we will judge that they are dreadful enemies to be repelled and even destroyed, not that they should not act as they do.

Similarly, if we learn that a band of cannibals has captured and eaten the sole survivor of a ship-wreck, we will speak of the primitive morality of the cannibals and may call them savages, but we will not say that they ought not to have eaten their captive.

Again, suppose that a contented employee of Murder, Incorporated was raised as a child to honor and respect members of the "family" but to have nothing but contempt for the rest of society. His current assignment, let us suppose, is to kill a certain bank manager, Bernard J. Ortcutt. Since Ortcutt is not a member of the "family," the employee in question has no compunction about carrying out his assignment. In particular, if we were to try to convince him that he should not kill Ortcutt, our argument would merely amuse him. We would not provide him with the slightest reason to desist unless we were to point to practical difficulties, such as the likelihood of his getting caught. Now, in this case it would be a misuse of language to say of him that he ought not to kill Ortcutt or that it would be wrong of him to do so, since that would imply that our own moral considerations carry some weight with him, which they do not. Instead we can only judge that he is a criminal, someone to be hunted down by the police, an enemy of peace-loving citizens, and so forth.

It is true that we can make certain judgments about him using the word "ought." For example, investigators who have been tipped off by an informer and who are waiting for the assassin to appear at the bank can use the "ought" of expectation to say, "He ought to arrive soon," meaning that on the basis of their information one would expect him to arrive soon. And, in thinking over how the assassin might carry out his assignment, we can use the "ought" of rationality to say that he ought to go in by the rear door, meaning that it would be more rational for him to do that than to go in by the front door. In neither of these cases is the moral "ought" in question.

There is another use of "ought" which is normative and in a sense moral but which is distinct from what I am calling the moral "ought." This is the use which occurs when we say that something ought or ought not to be the case. It ought not to be the case that members of Murder, Incorporated go around killing people; in other words, it is a terrible thing that they do so. The same thought can perhaps be expressed as "They ought not to go around killing people," meaning that it ought not to be the case that they do, not that they are wrong to do what they do. The normative "ought to be" is used to assess a situation; the moral "ought to do" is used to describe a relation between an agent and a type of act that he might perform or has performed.

The sentence "They ought not to go around killing people" is therefore multiply ambiguous. It can mean that one would not expect them to do so (the "ought" of expectation), that it is not in their interest to do so (the "ought" of rationality), that it is a bad thing that they do so (the normative "ought to be"), or that they are wrong to do so (the moral "ought to do"). For the most part I am here concerned only with the last of these interpretations.

The word "should" behaves very much like "ought to." There is a "should" of expectation ("They should be here soon"), a "should" of rationality ("He should go in by the back door"), a normative "should be" ("They shouldn't go around killing people like that"), and the moral "should do" ("You should keep that promise"). I am of course concerned mainly with the last sense of "should."

"Right" and "wrong" also have multiple uses; I will not try to say what all of them are. But I do want to distinguish using the word "wrong" to say that a particular situation or action is wrong from using the word to say that it is wrong *of someone* to do something. In the former case, the word "wrong" is used to assess an act or situation. In the latter case it is used to describe a relation between an agent and an act. Only the latter sort of judgment is an inner judgment. Although we would not say concerning the contented employee of Murder,

Incorporated mentioned earlier that it was wrong *of him* to kill Ortcutt, we could say that *his action* was wrong and we could say that it is wrong that there is so much killing.

To take another example, it sounds odd to say that Hitler should not have ordered the extermination of the Jews, that it was wrong of him to have done so. That sounds somehow "too weak" a thing to say. Instead we want to say that Hitler was an evil man. Yet we can properly say, "Hitler ought not to have ordered the extermination of the Jews," if what we mean is that it ought never to have happened; and we can say without oddity that what Hitler did was wrong. Oddity attends only the inner judgment that Hitler was wrong to have acted in that way. That is what sounds "too weak."

It is worth noting that the inner judgments sound too weak not because of the enormity of what Hitler did but because we suppose that in acting as he did he shows that he could not have been susceptible to the moral considerations on the basis of which we make our judgment. He is in the relevant sense beyond the pale and we therefore cannot make inner judgments about him. To see that this is so, consider, say, Stalin, another massmurderer. We can perhaps imagine someone taking a sympathetic view of Stalin. In such a view, Stalin realized that the course he was going to pursue would mean the murder of millions of people and he dreaded such a prospect; however, the alternative seemed to offer an even greater disaster – so, reluctantly and with great anguish, he went ahead. In relation to such a view of Stalin, inner judgments about Stalin are not as odd as similar judgments about Hitler. For we might easily continue the story by saying that, despite what he hoped to gain, Stalin should not have undertaken the course he did, that it was wrong of him to have done so. What makes inner judgments about Hitler odd, "too weak," is not that the acts judged seem too terrible for the words used but rather that the agent judged seems beyond the pale – in other words beyond the motivational reach of the relevant moral considerations.

Of course, I do not want to deny that for various reasons a speaker might pretend that an agent is or is not susceptible to certain moral considerations. For example, a speaker may for rhetorical or political reasons wish to suggest that someone is beyond the pale, that he should not be listened to, that he can be treated as an enemy. On the other hand, a speaker may pretend that someone is susceptible to certain moral considerations in an effort to make that person or others susceptible to those considerations. Inner judgments about one's children sometimes have this function. So do inner judgments made in political speeches that aim at restoring a lapsed sense of morality in government.

II.   The Logical Form of Inner Judgments

Inner judgments have two important characteristics. First, they imply that the agent has reasons to do something. Second, the speaker in some sense endorses these reasons and supposes that the audience also endorses them. Other moral judgments about an agent, on the other hand, do not have such implications; they do not imply that the agent has reasons for acting that are endorsed by the speaker.

If someone S says that A (morally) ought to do D, S implies that A has reasons to do D and S endorses those reasons – whereas if S says that B was evil in what B did, S does not imply that the reasons S would endorse for not doing what B did were reasons for B not to do that thing; in fact, S implies that they were not reasons for B.

Let us examine this more closely. If S says that (morally) A ought to do D, S implies that A has reasons to do D which S endorses. I shall assume that such reasons would have to have their source in goals, desires, or intentions that S takes A to have and that S approves of A's having because S shares those goals, desires, or intentions. So, if S says that (morally) A ought to do D, there are certain motivational attitudes M which S assumes are shared by S, A, and S's audience.

Now, in supposing that reasons for action must have their source in goals, desires, or intentions, I am assuming something like an Aristotelian or Humean account of these matters, as opposed, for example, to a Kantian approach which sees a possible source of motivation in reason itself. I must defer a full-scale discussion of the issue to another occasion. Here I simply assume that the Kantian approach is wrong. In particular, I assume that there might be no reasons at all for a being from outer space to avoid harm to us; that, for Hitler, there might have been no reason at all not to order the extermination of the Jews; that the contented employee of Murder, Incorporated might have no reason at all not to kill Ortcutt; that the cannibals might have no reason not to eat their captive. In other words, I assume that the possession of rationality is not sufficient to provide a source for relevant reasons, that certain desires, goals, or intentions are also necessary. Those who accept this assumption will, I think, find that they distinguish inner moral judgments from other moral judgments in the way that I have indicated.

Ultimately, I want to argue that the shared motivational attitudes M are intentions to keep an agreement (supposing that others similarly intend). For I want to argue that inner moral judgments are made relative to such an agreement. That is, I want to argue that, when S makes the inner judgment that A ought to do D, S assumes that A intends to act in accordance with an agreement which S and S's audience also intend to observe. In other words, I want to argue that the source of the reasons for doing D which S ascribes to A is A's sincere intention to observe a certain agreement. I have not yet argued for the stronger thesis, however. I have argued only that S makes his judgment relative to some motivational attitudes M which S assumes are shared by S, A, and S's audience.

Formulating this as a logical thesis, I want to treat the moral "ought" as a four-place predicate (or "operator"), "Ought (A, D, C, M)," which relates an agent A, a type of act D, considerations C, and motivating attitudes M. The relativity to considerations C can be brought out by considering what are sometimes called statements of prima-facie obligation, "Considering that you promised, you ought to go to the board meeting, but considering that you are the sole surviving relative, you ought to go to the funeral; all things considered, it is not clear what you ought to do." The claim that there is this relativity, to considerations, is not, of course, what makes my thesis a version of moral relativism, since any theory must acknowledge relativity to considerations. The relativity to considerations does, however, provide a model for a coherent interpretation of moral relativism as a similar kind of relativity.

It is not as easy to exhibit the relativity to motivating attitudes as it is to exhibit the relativity to considerations, since normally a speaker who makes a moral "ought" judgment intends the relevant motivating attitudes to be ones that the speaker shares with the agent and the audience, and normally it will be obvious what attitudes these are. But sometimes a speaker does invoke different attitudes by invoking a morality the speaker does not share. Someone may say, for example, "As a Christian, you ought to turn the other cheek; I, however, propose to strike back." A spy who has been found out by a friend might say, "As a citizen, you ought to turn me in, but I hope that you will not." In these and similar cases a speaker makes a moral "ought" judgment that is explicitly relative to motivating attitudes that the speaker does not share.

In order to be somewhat more precise, then, my thesis is this. "Ought (A, D, C, M)" means roughly that, given that A has motivating attitudes M and given C, D is the course of action for A that is supported by the best reasons. In judgements using this sense of "ought," C and M are often not explicit mentioned by are indicated by the context of utterance. Normally, when that happens, C will be "all things considered" and M will be attitudes that are shared by the speaker and audience.

I mentioned that inner judgements have two characteristics. First, they imply that the agent has reasons to do something that are capable of motivating the agent. Second, the speaker endorses those reasons and supposes that the audience does too. Now, any "Ought (A, D, C, M)" judgment has the first of these characteristics, but as we have just seen a judgment of this sort will not necessarily have the second characteristic if made with explicit reference to motivating attitudes not shared by the speaker. If reference is made either implicitly or explicitly (for example, through the use of the adverb "morally") to attitudes that are shared by the speaker and audience, the resulting judgement has both characteristics and is an inner judgment. If reference is made to attitudes that are not shared by the speaker, the resulting judgment is not an inner judgment and does not represent a full-fledged moral judgment on the part of the speaker. In such a case we have an example of what has been called an inverted-commas use of "ought."[2]

III.   Moral Bargaining

I have argued that moral "ought" judgments are relational, "Ought (A, D, C, M)," where M represents certain motivating attitudes. I now want to argue that the attitudes M derive from an agreement. That is, they are intentions to adhere to a particular agreement on the understanding that others also intend to do so. Really, it might be better for me to say that I put this forward as a hypothesis, since I cannot pretend to be able to prove that it is true. I will argue, however, that this hypothesis accounts for an otherwise puzzling aspect of our moral views that, as far as I know, there is not other way to account for.

I will use the word "intention" in a somewhat extended sense to cover certain dispositions or habits. Someone may habitually act in accordance with the relevant understanding and therefore may be disposed to act in that way without having any more or less conscious intention. In such a case it may sound odd to say that he *intends* to act in accordance with the moral understanding. Nevertheless, for present purposes I will count that as his having the relevant intention in a dispositional sense.

I now want to consider the following puzzle about our moral views, a puzzle that has figured in recent philosophical discussion of issues such as abortion. It has been observed that most of us assign greater weight to the duty not to harm others than to the duty to help others. For example, most of us believe that a doctor ought not to save five of his patients who would otherwise die by cutting up a sixth patient and distributing his healthy organs where needed to the others, even though we do think that the doctor has a duty to try to help as many of his patients as he can. For we also think that he has a stronger duty to try not to harm any of his patients (or anyone else) even if by so doing he could help five others.

This aspect of our moral views can seem very puzzling, especially if one supposes that moral feelings derive from sympathy and concern for others. But the hypothesis that morality derives from an agreement among people of varying powers and resources provides a plausible explanation. The rich, the poor, the strong, and the weak would all benefit if all were to try to avoid harming one another. So everyone could agree to that arrangement. But the rich and the strong would not benefit from an arrangement whereby everyone would try to do as much as possible to help those in need. The poor and weak would get all of the benefit of this latter arrangement. Since the rich and the strong could foresee that they would be required to do most of the helping and that they would receive little in return, they would be reluctant to agree to a strong principle of mutual aid. A compromise would be likely and a weaker principle would probably be accepted. In other words, although everyone could agree to a strong principle concerning the avoidance of harm, it would not be true that everyone would favor an equally strong principle of mutual aid. It is likely that only a weaker principle of the latter sort would gain general acceptance. So the hypothesis that morality derives from an understanding among people of different powers and resources can explain (and, according to me, does explain) why in our morality avoiding harm to others is taken to be more important than helping those who need help.

By the way, I am here only trying to *explain* an aspect of our moral views. I am not therefore *endorsing* that aspect. And I defer until later a relativistic account of the way in which aspects of our moral view can be criticized "from within."

Now we need not suppose that the agreement or understanding in question is explicit. It is enough if various members of society knowingly reach an agreement in intentions – each intending to act in certain ways on the understanding that the others have similar intentions. Such an implicit agreement is reached through a process of mutual adjustment and implicit bargaining.

Indeed, it is essential to the proposed explanation of this aspect of our moral views to suppose that the relevant moral understanding is thus the result of *bargaining*. It is necessary to suppose that, in order to further our interests, we form certain conditional intentions, hoping that others will do the same. The others, who have different interests, will form somewhat different conditional intentions. After implicit bargaining, some sort of compromise is reached.

Seeing morality in this way as a compromise based on implicit bargaining helps to explain why our morality takes it to be worse to harm someone than to refuse to help someone. The explanation requires that we view our morality as an implicit agreement about what to do. This sort of explanation could not be given if we were to suppose, say, that our morality represented an agreement only about the facts (naturalism). Nor is it enough simply to suppose that our morality represents an agreement in attitude, if we forget that such agreement can be reached, not only by way of such principles as are mentioned, for example, in Hare's "logic of imperatives,"[3] but also through bargaining. According to Hare, to accept a general moral principle is to intend to do something.[4] If we add to his theory that the relevant intentions can be reached through implicit bargaining, the resulting theory begins to look like the one that I am defending.

Many aspects of our moral views can be given a utilitarian explanation. We could account for these aspects, using the logical analysis I presented in the previous section of this paper, by supposing that the relevant "ought" judgments presuppose shared attitudes of sympathy and benevolence. We can equally well explain them by supposing that considerations of utility have influenced our implicit agreements, so that the appeal is to a shared intention to adhere to those agreements. Any aspect of morality that is susceptible of a utilitarian explanation can also be explained by an implicit agreement, but not conversely. There are aspects of our moral views that seem to be explicable only in the second way, on the assumption that morality derives from an agreement. One example, already cited, is the distinction we make between harming and not helping. Another is our feeling that each person has an inalienable right of self-defense and self-preservation. Philosophers have not been able to come up with a really satisfactory utilitarian justification of such a right, but it is easily intelligible on our present hypothesis, as Hobbes observed many years ago. You cannot, except in very special circumstances, rationally form the intention not to try to preserve your life if it should ever be threatened, say, by society or the state, since you know that you cannot now control what you would do in such a situation. No matter what you now decided to do, when the time came, you would ignore your prior decision and try to save your life. Since you cannot now intend to do something later which you now know that you would not do, you cannot now intend to keep an agreement not to preserve your life if it is threatened by others in your society.[5]

This concludes the positive side of my argument that what I have called inner moral judgments are made in relation to an implicit agreement. I now want to argue that this theory avoids difficulties traditionally associated with implicit agreement theories of morality.

IV. Objections and Replies

One traditional difficulty for implicit agreement theories concerns what motivates us to do what we have agreed to do. It will, obviously, not be enough to say that we have implicitly agreed to keep agreements, since the issue would then be why we keep *that* agreement. And this suggests an objection to implicit agreement theories. But the apparent force of the objection derives entirely from taking an agreement to be a kind of ritual. To agree in the relevant sense is not just to say something; it is to intend to do something – namely, to intend to carry out one's part of the agreement on the condition that others do their parts. If we agree in this sense to do something, we intend to do it and intending to do it is already to be motivated to do it. So there is no problem as to why we are motivated to keep our agreements in this sense.

We do believe that in general you ought not to pretend to agree in this sense in order to

trick someone else into agreeing. But that suggests no objection to the present view. All that it indicates is that *our* moral understanding contains or implies an agreement to be open and honest with others. If it is supposed that this leaves a problem about someone who has not accepted our agreement – "What reason does *he* have not to pretend to accept our agreement so that he can then trick others into agreeing to various things?" – the answer is that such a person may or may not have such a reason. If someone does not already accept something of our morality it may or may not be possible to find reasons why he should.

A second traditional objection to implicit agreement theories is that there is not a perfect correlation between what is generally believed to be morally right and what actually is morally right. Not everything generally agreed on is right and sometimes courses of action are right that would not be generally agreed to be right. But this is no objection to my thesis. My thesis is not that the implicit agreement from which a morality derives is an agreement in moral judgment; the thesis is rather that moral judgments make reference to and are made in relation to an agreement in intentions. Given that a group of people have agreed in this sense, there can still be disputes as to what the agreement implies for various situations. In my view, many moral disputes are of this sort. They presuppose a basic agreement and they concern what implications that agreement has for particular cases.

There can also be various things wrong with the agreement that a group of people reach, even from the point of view of that agreement, just as there can be defects in an individual's plan of action even from the point of view of that plan. Given what is known about the situation, a plan or agreement can in various ways be inconsistent, incoherent, or self-defeating. In my view, certain moral disputes are concerned with internal defects of the basic moral understanding of a group, and what changes should be made from the perspective of that understanding itself. This is another way in which moral disputes make sense with reference to and in relation to an underlying agreement.

Another objection to implicit agreement theories is that not all agreements are morally

binding – for example, those made under com-
plusion or from a position of unfair disadvantage, which may seem to indicate that there are
moral principles prior to those that derive from
an implicit agreement. But, again, the force of
the objection derives from an equivocation
concerning what an agreement is. The principle
that compelled agreements do not obligate
concerns agreement in the sense of a certain
sort of ritual indicating that one agrees. My
thesis concerns a kind of agreement in intentions. The principle about compelled agreements is part of, or is implied by, our
agreement in intentions. According to me it is
only with reference to some such agreement in
intentions that a principle of this sort makes
sense.

Now it may be true our moral agreement in
intentions also implies that it is wrong to compel people who are in a greatly inferior position
to accept an agreement in intentions that they
would not otherwise accept, and it may even be
true that there is in our society at least one class
of people in an inferior position who have been
compelled thus to settle for accepting a basic
moral understanding, aspects of which they
would not have accepted had they not been in
such an inferior position. In that case there
would be an incoherence in our basic moral
understanding and various suggestions might
be made concerning the ways in which this
understanding should be modified. But this
moral critique of the understanding can proceed from that understanding itself rather than
from "prior" moral principles.

In order to fix ideas, let us consider a society
in which there is a well-established and long-
standing tradition of hereditary slavery. Let us
suppose that everyone accepts this institution,
including the slaves. Everyone treats it as in the
nature of things that there should be such
slavery. Furthermore, let us suppose that there
are also aspects of the basic moral agreement
which speak against slavery. That is, these
aspects together with certain facts about the
situation imply that people should not own
slaves and that slaves have no obligation to
acquiesce in their condition. In such a case,
the moral understanding would be defective,
although its defectiveness would presumably
be hidden in one or another manner, perhaps

by means of a myth that slaves are physically
and mentally subhuman in a way that makes
appropriate the sort of treatment elsewhere
reserved for beasts of burden. If this myth
were to be exposed, the members of the society
would then be faced with an obvious incoherence in their basic moral agreement and might
come eventually to modify their agreement so
as to eliminate its acceptance of slavery.

In such a case, even relative to the old agreement it might be true that slave owners ought
to free their slaves, that slaves need not obey
their masters, and that people ought to work to
eliminate slavery. For the course supported by
the best reasons, given that one starts out with
the intention of adhering to a particular agreement, may be that one should stop intending
to adhere to certain aspects of that agreement
and should try to get others to do the same.

We can also (perhaps – but see below) envision a second society with hereditary slavery
whose agreement has no aspects that speak
against slavery. In that case, even if the facts
of the situation were fully appreciated, no
incoherence would appear in the basic moral
understanding of the society and it would not
be true in relation to that understanding that
slave owners ought to free their slaves, that
slaves need not obey their masters, and so
forth. There might nevertheless come a time
when there were reasons of a different sort to
modify the basic understanding, either because
of an external threat from societies opposed
to slavery or because of an internal threat of
rebellion by the slaves.

Now it is easier for us to make what I have
called inner moral judgments about slave
owners in the first society than in the second.
For we can with reference to members of the
first society invoke principles that they share
with us and, with reference to those principles,
we can say of them that they ought not to have
kept slaves and that they were immoral to
have done so. This sort of inner judgment
becomes increasingly inappropriate, however,
the more distant they are from us and the less
easy it is for us to think of our moral understanding as continuous with and perhaps a
later development of theirs. Furthermore, it
seems appropriate to make only non-inner
judgments of the slave owners in the second

society. We can say that the second society is unfair and unjust, that the slavery that exists is wrong, that it ought not to exist. But it would be inappropriate in this case to say that it was morally wrong of the slave owners to own slaves. The relevant aspects of our moral understanding, which we would invoke in moral judgments about them, are not aspects of the moral understanding that exists in the second society.

[. . .]

Let me turn now to another objection to implicit agreement theories, an objection which challenges the idea that there is an agreement of the relevant sort. For, if we have agreed, when did we do it? Does anyone really remember having agreed? How did we indicate our agreement? What about those who do not want to agree? How do they indicate that they do not agree and what are the consequences of their not agreeing? Reflection on these and similar questions can make the hypothesis of implicit agreement seem too weak a basis on which to found morality.

But once again there is equivocation about agreements. The objection treats the thesis as the claim that morality is based on some sort of ritual rather than an agreement in intentions. But, as I have said, there is an agreement in the relevant sense when each of a number of people has an intention on the assumption that others have the same intention. In this sense of "agreement," there is no given moment at which one agrees, since one continues to agree in this sense as long as one continues to have the relevant intentions. Someone refuses to agree to the extent that he or she does not share these intentions. Those who do not agree are outside the agreement; in extreme cases they are outlaws or enemies. It does not follow, however, that there are no constraints on how those who agree may act toward those who do not, since for various reasons the agreement itself may contain provisions for dealing with outlaws and enemies.

This brings me to one last objection, which derives from the difficulty people have in trying to give an explicit and systematic account of their moral views. If one actually agrees to something, why is it so hard to say what one has agreed? In response I can say only that many understandings appear to be of this sort. It is often possible to recognize what is in accordance with the understanding and what would violate it without being able to specify the understanding in any general way. Consider, for example, the understanding that exists among the members of a team of acrobats or a symphony orchestra.

Another reason why it is so difficult to give a precise and systematic specification of any actual moral understanding is that such an understanding will not in general be constituted by absolute rules but will take a vaguer form, specifying goals and areas of responsibility. For example, the agreement may indicate that one is to show respect for others by trying where possible to avoid actions that will harm them or interfere with what they are doing; it may indicate the duties and responsibilities of various members of the family, who is to be responsible for bringing up the children, and so forth. Often what will be important will be not so much exactly what actions are done as how willing participants are to do their parts and what attitudes they have – for example, whether they give sufficient weight to the interests of others.

The vague nature of moral understandings is to some extent alleviated in practice. One learns what can and cannot be done in various situations. Expectations are adjusted to other expectations. But moral disputes arise nonetheless. Such disputes may concern what the basic moral agreement implies for particular situations; and, if so, that can happen either because of disputes over the facts or because of a difference in basic understanding. Moral disputes may also arise concerning whether or not changes should be made in the basic agreement. Racial and sexual issues seem often to be of this second sort; but there is no clear line between the two kinds of dispute. When the implications of an agreement for a particular situation are considered, one possible outcome is that it becomes clear that the agreement should be modified.

[. . .]

Finally, I would like to say a few brief words about the limiting case of group morality, when the group has only one member; then, as it were, a person comes to an understanding with himself. In my view, a person can make inner judgments in relation to such an individual morality only about himself. A familiar form of pacifism is of this sort. Certain pacifists judge that it would be wrong of them to participate in killing, although they are not willing to make a similar judgment about others. Observe that such a pacifist is unwilling only to make *inner* moral judgments about others. Although he is unwilling to judge that those who do participate are wrong to do so, he is perfectly willing to say that it is a bad thing that they participate. There are of course many other examples of individual morality in this sense, when a person imposes standards on himself that he does not apply to others. The existence of such examples is further con-

firmation of the relativist thesis that I have presented.

My conclusion is that relativism can be formulated as an intelligible thesis, the thesis that morality derives from an implicit agreement and that moral judgments are in a logical sense made in relation to such an agreement. Such a theory helps to explain otherwise puzzling aspects of our own moral views, in particular why we think that it is more important to avoid harm to others than to help others. The theory is also partially confirmed by what is, as far as I can tell, a previously unnoticed distinction between inner and non-inner moral judgments. Furthermore, traditional objections to implicit agreement theories can be met.

Notes

1. Bernard Williams, *Morality: An Introduction to Ethics* (New York, 1972), pp. 20–1; Marcus Singer, *Generalization in Ethics* (New York, 1961), p. 332.
2. R. M. Hare, *The Language of Morals* (Oxford, 1952), pp. 164–8.
3. R. M. Hare, *op. cit.* and *Freedom and Reason* (Oxford, 1963).
4. *The Language of Morals*, pp. 18–20, 168–9.
5. Cf. Thomas Hobbes, *Leviathan* (Oxford, 1957, *inter alia*), pt. I, ch. 14, "Of the First and Second Natural Laws, And of Contracts."

CHAPTER 6
The Subject-Matter of Ethics

G. E. MOORE

[...]

What, then, is good? How is good to be defined? Now, it may be thought that this is a verbal question. A definition does indeed often mean the expressing of one word's meaning in other words. But this is not the sort of definition I am asking for. Such a definition can never be of ultimate importance in any study except lexicography. If I wanted that kind of definition I should have to consider in the first place how people generally used the word "good"; but my business is not with its proper usage, as established by custom. I should, indeed, be foolish, if I tried to use it for something which it did not usually denote: if, for instance, I were to announce that, whenever I used the word "good," I must be understood to be thinking of that object which is usually denoted by the word "table." I shall, therefore, use the word in the sense in which I think it is ordinarily used; but at the same time I am not anxious to discuss whether I am right in thinking that it is so used. My business is solely with that object or idea, which I hold, rightly or wrongly, that the word is generally used to stand for. What I want to discover is the nature of that object or idea, and about this I am extremely anxious to arrive at an agreement.

But, if we understand the question in this sense, my answer to it may seem a very disappointing one. If I am asked "What is good?" my answer is that good is good, and that is the end of the matter. Or if I am asked "How is good to be defined?" my answer is that it cannot be defined, and that is all I have to say about it. But disappointing as these answers may appear, they are of the very last importance. To readers who are familiar with philosophic terminology, I can express their importance by saying that they amount to this: That propositions about the good are all of them synthetic and never analytic; and that is plainly no trivial matter. And the same thing may be expressed more popularly, by saying that, if I am right, then nobody can foist upon us such an axiom as that "Pleasure is the only good" or that "The good is the desired" on the pretence that this is "the very meaning of the word."

Let us, then, consider this position. My point is that "good" is a simple notion, just as "yellow" is a simple notion; that, just as you cannot, by any manner of means, explain to any one who does not already know it, what yellow is, so you cannot explain what good is. Definitions of the kind that I was asking for, definitions which describe the real nature of the object or notion denoted by a word, and which do not merely tell us what the word is used to mean, are only possible when the object or notion in question is something complex.

G. E. Moore, "The Subject-Matter of Ethics," from *Principia Ethica*, 1903.

You can give a definition of a horse, because a horse has many different properties and qualities, all of which you can enumerate. But when you have enumerated them all, when you have reduced a horse to his simplest terms, then you can no longer define those terms. They are simply something which you think of or perceive, and to any one who cannot think of or perceive them, you can never, by any definition, make their nature known. It may perhaps be objected to this that we are able to describe to others, objects which they have never seen or thought of. We can, for instance, make a man understand what a chimaera is, although he has never heard of one or seen one. You can tell him that it is an animal with a lioness's head and body, with a goat's head growing from the middle of its back, and with a snake in place of a tail. But here the object which you are describing is a complex object; it is entirely composed of parts, with which we are all perfectly familiar—a snake, a goat, a lioness; and we know, too, the manner in which those parts are to be put together, because we know what is meant by the middle of a lioness's back, and where her tail is wont to grow. And so it is with all objects, not previously known, which we are able to define: they are all complex; all composed of parts, which may themselves, in the first instance, be capable of similar definition, but which must in the end be reducible to simplest parts, which can no longer be defined. But yellow and good, we say, are not complex: they are notions of that simple kind, out of which definitions are composed and with which the power of further defining ceases.

When we say, as Webster says, "The definition of horse is 'A hoofed quadruped of the genus Equus,' " we may, in fact, mean three different things. (1) We may mean merely: "When I say 'horse,' you are to understand that I am talking about a hoofed quadruped of the genus Equus." This might be called the arbitrary verbal definition: and I do not mean that good is indefinable in that sense. (2) We may mean, as Webster ought to mean: "When most English people say 'horse,' they mean a hoofed quadruped of the genus Equus." This may be called the verbal definition proper, and I do not say that good is indefinable in this sense either; for it is certainly possible to

discover how people use a word: otherwise, we could never have known that "good" may be translated by "gut" in German and by "bon" in French. But (3) we may, when we define horse, mean something much more important. We may mean that a certain object, which we all of us know, is composed in a certain manner: that it has four legs, a head, a heart, a liver, etc., etc., all of them arranged in definite relations to one another. It is in this sense that I deny good to be definable. I say that it is not composed of any parts, which we can substitute for it in our minds when we are thinking of it. We might think just as clearly and correctly about a horse, if we thought of all its parts and their arrangement instead of thinking of the whole: we could, I say, think how a horse differed from a donkey just as well, just as truly, in this way, as now we do, only not so easily; but there is nothing whatsoever which we could so substitute for good; and that is what I mean, when I say that good is indefinable.

But I am afraid I have still not removed the chief difficulty which may prevent acceptance of the proposition that good is indefinable. I do not mean to say that *the* good, that which is good, is thus indefinable; if I did think so, I should not be writing on Ethics, for my main object is to help towards discovering that definition. It is just because I think there will be less risk of error in our search for a definition of "the good," that I am now insisting that *good* is indefinable. I must try to explain the difference between these two. I suppose it may be granted that "good" is an adjective. Well "the good," "that which is good," must therefore be the substantive to which the adjective "good" will apply: it must be the whole of that to which the adjective will apply, and the adjective must *always* truly apply to it. But if it is that to which the adjective will apply, it must be something different from that adjective itself; and the whole of that something different, whatever it is, will be our definition of *the* good. Now it may be that this something will have other adjectives, beside "good," that will apply to it. It may be full of pleasure, for example; it may be intelligent: and if these two adjectives are really part of its definition, then it will certainly be true, that pleasure and intelligence are good. And many people appear to think that, if we say "Pleasure and intelligence are good," or if we say "Only pleasure and intelligence are good," we are defining "good." Well, I cannot deny that propositions of this nature may sometimes be called definitions; I do not know well enough how the word is generally used to decide upon this point. I only wish it to be understood that is not what I mean when I say there is no possible definition of good, and that I shall not mean this if I use the word again. I do most fully believe that some true proposition of the form "Intelligence is good and intelligence alone is good" can be found; if none could be found, our definition of *the* good would be impossible. As it is, I believe *the* good to be definable; and yet I still say that good itself is indefinable.

"Good," then, if we mean by it that quality which we assert to belong to a thing, when we say that the thing is good, is incapable of any definition, in the most important sense of that word. The most important sense of "definition" is that in which a definition states what are the parts which invariably compose a certain whole; and in this sense "good" has no definition because it is simple and has no parts. It is one of those innumerable objects of thought which are themselves incapable of definition, because they are the ultimate terms by reference to which whatever *is* capable of definition must be defined. That there must be an indefinite number of such terms is obvious, on reflection; since we cannot define anything except by analysis, which, when carried as far as it will go, refers us to something, which is simply different from anything else, and which by that ultimate difference explains the peculiarity of the whole which we are defining: for every whole contains some parts which are common to other wholes also. There is, therefore, no intrinsic difficulty in the contention that "good" denotes a simple and indefinable quality. There are many other instances of such qualities.

Consider yellow, for example. We may try to define it, by describing its physical equivalent; we may state what kind of light-vibrations must stimulate the normal eye, in order that we may perceive it. But a moment's reflection is sufficient to show that those light-vibrations are not themselves what we mean by yellow.

They are not what we perceive. Indeed we should never have been able to discover their existence, unless we had first been struck by the patent difference of quality between the different colors. The most we can be entitled to say of those vibrations is that they are what corresponds in space to the yellow which we actually perceive.

Yet a mistake of this simple kind has commonly been made about "good." It may be true that all things which are good are *also* something else, just as it is true that all things which are yellow produce a certain kind of vibration in the light. And it is a fact, that Ethics aims at discovering what are those other properties belonging to all things which are good. But far too many philosophers have thought that when they named those other properties they were actually defining good; that these properties, in fact, were simply not "other," but absolutely and entirely the same with goodness. This view I propose to call the "naturalistic fallacy" and of it I shall now endeavor to dispose.

Let us consider what it is such philosophers say. And first it is to be noticed that they do not agree among themselves. They not only say that they are right as to what good is, but they endeavor to prove that other people who say that it is something else, are wrong. One, for instance, will affirm that good is pleasure, another, perhaps, that good is that which is desired; and each of these will argue eagerly to prove that the other is wrong. But how is that possible? One of them says that good is nothing but the object of desire, and at the same time tries to prove that it is not pleasure. But from his first assertion, that good just means the object of desire, one of two things must follow as regards his proof:

(1) He may be trying to prove that the object of desire is not pleasure. But, if this be all, where is his Ethics? The position he is maintaining is merely a psychological one. Desire is something which occurs in our minds, and pleasure is something else which so occurs; and our would-be ethical philosopher is merely holding that the latter is not the object of the former. But what has that to do with the question

in dispute? His opponent held the ethical position that pleasure was the good, and although he should prove a million times over the psychological proposition that pleasure is not the object of desire, he is no nearer proving his opponent to be wrong. The position is like this. One man says a triangle is a circle: another replies "A triangle is a straight line, and I will prove to you that I am right: *for*" (this is the only argument) "a straight line is not a circle." "That is quite true," the other may reply; "but nevertheless a triangle is a circle, and you have said nothing whatever to prove the contrary. What is proved is that one of us is wrong, for we agree that a triangle cannot be both a straight line and a circle: but which is wrong, there can be no earthly means of proving, since you define triangle as straight line and I define it as circle." – Well, that is one alternative which any naturalistic Ethics has to face; if good is *defined* as something else, it is then impossible either to prove that any other definition is wrong or even to deny such definition.

(2) The other alternative will scarcely be more welcome. It is that the discussion is after all a verbal one. When A says "Good means pleasant" and B says "Good means desired," they may merely wish to assert that most people have used the word for what is pleasant and for what is desired respectively. And this is quite an interesting subject for discussion: only it is not a whit more an ethical discussion than the last was. Nor do I think that any exponent of naturalistic Ethics would be willing to allow that this was all he meant. They are all so anxious to persuade us that what they call the good is what we really ought to do. "Do, pray, act so, because the word 'good' is generally used to denote actions of this nature": such, on this view, would be the substance of their teaching. And in so far as they tell us how we ought to act, their teaching is truly ethical, as they mean it to be. But how perfectly absurd is the reason they would give for it! "You

are to do this, because most people use a certain word to denote conduct such as this." "You are to say the thing which is not, because most people call it lying." That is an argument just as good! – My dear sirs, what we want to know from you as ethical teachers, is not how people use a word; it is not even, what kind of actions they approve, which the use of this word "good" may certainly imply: what we want to know is simply what *is* good. We may indeed agree that what most people do think good, is actually so; we shall at all events be glad to know their opinions: but when we say their opinions about what *is* good, we do mean what we say; we do not care whether they call that thing which they mean "horse" or "table" or "chair," "gut" or "bon" or "ἀγαθός"; we want to know what it is that they so call. When they say "Pleasure is good," we cannot believe that they merely mean "Pleasure is pleasure" and nothing more than that.

Suppose a man says "I am pleased"; and suppose that is not a lie or a mistake but the truth. Well, if it is true, what does that mean? It means that his mind, a certain definite mind, distinguished by certain definite marks from all others, has at this moment a certain definite feeling called pleasure. "Pleased" *means* nothing but having pleasure, and though we may be more pleased or less pleased, and even, we may admit for the present, have one or another kind of pleasure; yet in so far as it is pleasure we have, whether there be more or less of it, and whether it be of one kind of another, what we have is one definite thing, absolutely indefinable, some one thing that is the same in all the various degrees and in all the various kinds of it that there may be. We may be able to say how it is related to other things: that, for example, it is in the mind, that it causes desire, that we are conscious of it, etc., etc. We can, I say, describe its relations to other things, but define it we can *not*. And if anybody tried to define pleasure for us as being any other natural object; if anybody were to say, for instance, that pleasure *means* the sensation of red, and were to proceed to deduce from that pleasure is a color, we should be entitled to laugh at him and to distrust his future statements about pleasure. Well, that would be the same fallacy which I have called the naturalistic fallacy. That "pleased" does not mean "having the sensation of red," or anything else whatever, does not prevent us from understanding what it does mean. It is enough for us to know that "pleased" does mean "having the sensation of pleasure," and though pleasure is absolutely indefinable, though pleasure is pleasure and nothing else whatever, yet we feel no difficulty in saying that we are pleased. The reason is, of course, that when I say "I am pleased," I do *not* mean that "I" am the same thing as "having pleasure." And similarly no difficulty need be found in my saying that "pleasure is good" and yet not meaning that "pleasure" is the same thing as "good," that pleasure *means* good, and that good *means* pleasure. If I were to imagine that when I said "I am pleased," I meant that I was exactly the same thing as "pleased," I should not indeed call that a naturalistic fallacy, although it would be the same fallacy as I have called naturalistic with reference to Ethics. The reason of this is obvious enough. When a man confuses two natural objects with one another, defining the one by the other, if for instance, he confuses himself, who is one natural object, with "pleased" or with "pleasure" which are others, then there is no reason to call the fallacy naturalistic. But if he confuses "good," which is not in the same sense a natural object, with any natural object whatever, then there is a reason for calling that a naturalistic fallacy; its being made with regard to "good" marks it as something quite specific, and this specific mistake deserves a name because it is so common. As for the reasons why good is not to be considered a natural object, they may be reserved for discussion in another place. But, for the present, it is sufficient to notice this: Even if it were a natural object, that would not alter the nature of the fallacy nor diminish its importance one whit. All that I have said about it would remain quite equally true: only the name which I have called it would not be so appropriate as I think it is. And I do not care about the name: what I do care about is the fallacy. It does not matter what we call it, provided we recognize it when we meet with it. It is to be met with in almost every book on Ethics; and yet it is not recognized: and that is why it is necessary to multiply illustrations of it, and convenient to give it a name. It is a very simple fallacy indeed. When we say that an orange is yellow, we do not think our statement binds us to hold that "orange" means nothing else than "yellow," or that nothing can be yellow but an orange. Supposing the orange is also sweet! Does that bind us to say that "sweet" is exactly the same thing as "yellow," that "sweet" must be defined as "yellow"? And supposing it be recognized that "yellow" just means "yellow" and nothing else whatever, does that make it any more difficult to hold that oranges are yellow? Most certainly it does not: on the contrary, it would be absolutely meaningless to say that oranges were yellow, unless yellow did in the end mean just "yellow" and nothing else whatever – unless it was absolutely indefinable. We should not get any very clear notion about things which are yellow – we should not get very far with our science, if we were bound to hold that everything which was yellow, *meant* exactly the same thing as yellow. We should find we had to hold that an orange was exactly the same thing as a stool, a piece of paper, a lemon, anything you like. We could prove any number of absurdities; but should we be the nearer to the truth? Why, then, should it be different with "good"? Why, if good is good and indefinable, should I be held to deny that pleasure is good? Is there any difficulty in holding both to be true at once? On the contrary, there is no meaning in saying that pleasure is good, unless good is something different from pleasure. It is absolutely useless, so far as Ethics is concerned, to prove, as Mr. Spencer tries to do, that increase of pleasure coincides with increase of life, unless good *means* something different from either life or pleasure. He might just as well try to prove that an orange is yellow by showing that it always is wrapped up in paper.

In fact, if it is not the case that "good" denotes something simple and indefinable, only two alternatives are possible: either it is a complex, a given whole, about the correct analysis of which there may be disagreement; or else it means nothing at all, and there is no such subject as Ethics. In general, however, ethical philosophers have attempted to define good, without recognizing what such an attempt must mean. They actually use arguments which involve one or both of the absurdities considered [earlier]. We are, therefore, justified in concluding that the attempt to define good is chiefly due to want of clearness as to the possible nature of definition. There are, in fact, only two serious alternatives to be considered, in order to establish the conclusion that "good" does denote a simple and indefinable notion. It might possibly denote a complex, as "horse" does; or it might have no meaning at all. Neither of these possibilities has, however, been clearly conceived and seriously maintained, as such, by those who presume to define good; and both may be dismissed by a simple appeal to facts.

(1)   The hypothesis that disagreement about the meaning of good is disagreement with regard to the correct analysis of a given whole, may be most plainly seen to be incorrect by consideration of the fact that, whatever definition be offered, it may be always asked, with significance, of the complex so defined, whether it is itself good. To take, for instance, one of the more plausible, because one of the more complicated, of such proposed definitions, it may easily be thought, at first sight, that to be good may mean to be that which we desire to desire. Thus if we apply this definition to a particular instance and say "When we think that A is good, we are thinking that A is one of the things which we desire to desire," our proposition may seem quite plausible. But, if we carry the investigation further, and ask ourselves "Is it good to desire to desire A?" it is apparent, on a little reflection, that this question is itself as intelligible, as the original question "Is A good?" – that we are, in fact, now asking for exactly the same information about the desire to desire A, for which we formerly asked with regard to A itself. But it is also apparent that the meaning of this second question cannot be correctly analyzed into "Is the desire to desire A one of the things which we desire to desire?": we

have not before our minds anything so complicated as the question "Do we desire to desire to desire to desire A?" Moreover any one can easily convince himself by inspection that the predicate of this proposition – "good" – is positively different from the notion of "desiring to desire" which enters into its subject: "That we should desire to desire A is good" is *not* merely equivalent to "That A should be good is good." It may indeed be true that what we desire to desire is always also good; perhaps, even the converse may be true: but it is very doubtful whether this is the case, and the mere fact that we understand very well what is meant by doubting it, shows clearly that we have two different notions before our minds.

(2)   And the same consideration is sufficient to dismiss the hypothesis that "good" has no meaning whatsoever. It is very natural to make the mistake of supposing that what is universally true is of such a nature that its negation would be self-contradictory: the importance which has been assigned to analytic propositions in the history of philosophy shows how easy such a mistake is. And thus it is very easy to conclude that what seems to be a universal ethical principle is in fact an identical proposition; that, if, for example, whatever is called "good" seems to be pleasant, the proposition "Pleasure is the good" does not assert a connection between two different notions, but involves only one, that of pleasure, which is easily recognized as a distinct entity. But whoever will attentively consider with himself what is actually before his mind when he asks the question "Is pleasure (or whatever it may be) after all good?" can easily satisfy himself that he is not merely wondering whether pleasure is pleasant. And if he will try this experiment with each suggested definition in succession, he may become expert enough to recognize that in every case he has before his mind a unique object, with regard to the connection of which with any other object, a distinct question

may be asked. Every one does in fact understand the question "Is this good?" When he thinks of it, his state of mind is different from what it would be, were he asked "Is this pleasant, or desired, or approved?" It has a distinct meaning for him, even though he may not recognize in what respect it is distinct. Whenever he thinks of "intrinsic value," or "intrinsic worth," or says that a thing "ought to exist," he has before his mind the unique object – the unique property of things – which I mean by "good." Everybody is constantly aware of this notion, although he may never become aware at all that it is different from other notions of which he is also aware. But, for correct ethical reasoning, it is extremely important that he should become aware of this fact; and, as soon as the nature of the problem is clearly understood, there should be little difficulty in advancing so far in analysis.

CHAPTER 7
Trying Out One's New Sword

MARY MIDGLEY

All of us are, more or less, in trouble today about trying to understand cultures strange to us. We hear constantly of alien customs. We see changes in our lifetime which would have astonished our parents. I want to discuss here one very short way of dealing with this difficulty, a drastic way which many people now theoretically favour. It consists in simply denying that we can ever understand any culture except our own well enough to make judgements about it. Those who recommend this hold that the world is sharply divided into separate societies, sealed units, each with its own system of thought. They feel that the respect and tolerance due from one system to another forbids us ever to take up a critical position to any other culture. Moral judgement, they suggest, is a kind of coinage valid only in its country of origin.

I shall call this position "moral isolationism". I shall suggest that it is certainly not forced upon us, and indeed that it makes no sense at all. People usually take it up because they think it is a respectful attitude to other cultures. In fact, however, it is not respectful. Nobody can respect what is entirely unintelligible to them. To respect someone, we have to know enough

about him to make a *favourable* judgement, however general and tentative. And we do understand people in other cultures to this extent. Otherwise a great mass of our most valuable thinking would be paralysed.

To show this, I shall take a remote example, because we shall probably find it easier to think calmly about it than we should with a contemporary one, such as female circumcision in Africa or the Chinese Cultural Revolution. The principles involved will still be the same. My example is this. There is, it seems, a verb in classical Japanese which means "to try out one's new sword on a chance wayfarer". (The word is *tsujigiri*, literally "crossroads-cut".) A samurai sword had to be tried out because, if it was to work properly, it had to slice through someone at a single blow, from the shoulder to the opposite flank. Otherwise, the warrior bungled his stroke. This could injure his honour, offend his ancestors, and even let down his emperor. So tests were needed, and wayfarers had to be expended. Any wayfarer would do – provided, of course, that he was not another Samurai. Scientists will recognize a familiar problem about the rights of experimental subjects.

Now when we hear of a custom like this, we may well reflect that we simply do not understand it; and therefore are not qualified to criticize it at all, because we are not members of that culture. But we are not members of any

Mary Midgley, "Trying Out One's New Sword," from *Heart and Mind: The Varieties of Moral Experience*. New York: St Martin's Press, 1981. Reproduced with permission of Palgrave Macmillan.

other culture either, except our own. So we extend the principle to cover all extraneous cultures, and we seem therefore to be moral isolationists. But this is, as we shall see, an impossible position. Let us ask what it would involve.

We must ask first: Does the isolating barrier work both ways? Are people in other cultures equally unable to criticize *us*? This question struck me sharply when I read a remark in *The Guardian* by an anthropologist about a South American Indian who had been taken into a Brazilian town for an operation, which saved his life. When he came back to his village, he made several highly critical remarks about the white Brazilians' way of life. They may very well have been justified. But the interesting point was that the anthropologist called these remarks "a damning indictment of Western civilization". Now the Indian had been in that town about two weeks. Was he in a position to deliver a damning indictment? Would we ourselves be qualified to deliver such an indictment on the Samurai, provided we could spend two weeks in ancient Japan? What do we really think about this?

My own impression is that we believe that outsiders can, in principle, deliver perfectly good indictments – only, it usually takes more than two weeks to make them damning. Understanding has degrees. It is not a slapdash yes-or-no matter. Intelligent outsiders can progress in it, and in some ways will be at an advantage over the locals. But if this is so, it must clearly apply to ourselves as much as anybody else.

Our next question is this: Does the isolating barrier between cultures block praise as well as blame? If I want to say that the Samurai culture has many virtues, or to praise the South American Indians, am I prevented from doing *that* by my outside status? Now, we certainly do need to praise other societies in this way. But it is hardly possible that we could praise them effectively if we could not, in principle, criticize them. Our praise would be worthless if it rested on no definite grounds, if it did not flow from some understanding. Certainly we may need to praise things which we do not *fully* understand. We say "there's something very good here, but I can't quite

make out what it is yet". This happens when we want to learn from strangers. And we can learn from strangers. But to do this we have to distinguish between those strangers who are worth learning from and those who are not. Can we then judge which is which?

This brings us to our third question: What is involved in judging? Now plainly there is no question here of sitting on a bench in a red robe and sentencing people. Judging simply means forming an opinion, and expressing it if it is called for. Is there anything wrong about this? Naturally, we ought to avoid forming – and expressing – *crude* opinions, like that of a simple-minded missionary, who might dismiss the whole Samurai culture as entirely bad, because non-Christian. But this is a different objection. The trouble with crude opinions is that they are crude, whoever forms them, not that they are formed by the wrong people. Anthropologists, after all, are outsiders quite as much as missionaries. Moral isolationism forbids us to form *any* opinions on these matters. Its ground for doing so is that we don't understand them. But there is much that we don't understand in our own culture too. This brings us to our last question: If we can't judge other cultures, can we really judge our own? Our efforts to do so will be much damaged if we are really deprived of our opinions about other societies, because these provide the range of comparison, the spectrum of alternatives against which we set what we want to understand. We would have to stop using the mirror which anthropology so helpfully holds up to us.

In short, moral isolationism would lay down a general ban on moral reasoning. Essentially, this is the programme of immoralism, and it carries a distressing logical difficulty. Immoralists like Nietzsche are actually just a rather specialized sect of moralists. They can no more afford to put moralizing out of business than smugglers can afford to abolish customs regulations. The power of moral judgement is, in fact, not a luxury, not a perverse indulgence of the self-righteous. It is a necessity. When we judge something to be bad or good, better or worse than something else, we are taking it as an example to aim at or avoid. Without opinions of this sort, we would have no framework of comparison for our own policy, no chance of profiting by other people's insights or mistakes. In this vacuum, we could form no judgements on our own actions.

Now it would be odd if Homo sapiens had really got himself into a position as bad as this – a position where his main evolutionary asset, his brain, was so little use to him. None of us is going to accept this sceptical diagnosis. We cannot do so, because our involvement in moral isolationism does not flow from apathy, but from a rather acute concern about human hypocrisy and other forms of wickedness. But we polarize that concern around a few selected moral truths. We are rightly angry with those who despise, oppress or steamroll other cultures. We think that doing these things is actually *wrong*. But this is itself a moral judgement. We could not condemn oppression and insolence if we thought that all our condemnation were just a trivial local quirk of our own culture. We could still less do it if we tried to stop judging altogether.

Real moral scepticism, in fact, could lead only to inaction, to our losing all interest in moral questions, most of all in those which concern other societies. When we discus these things, it becomes instantly clear how far we are from doing this. Suppose, for instance, that I criticize the bisecting Samurai, that I say his behaviour is brutal. What will usually happen next is that someone will protest, will say that I have no right to make criticisms like that of another culture. But it is most unlikely that he will use this move to end the discussion of the subject. Instead, he will justify the Samurai. He will try to fill in the background, to make me understand the custom, by explaining the exalted ideals of discipline and devotion which produced it. He will probably talk of the lower value which the ancient Japanese placed on individual life generally. He may well suggest that this is a healthier attitude than our own obsession with security. He may add, too, that the wayfarers did not seriously mind being bisected, that in principle they accepted the whole arrangement.

Now an objector who talks like this is implying that it *is* possible to understand alien customs. That is just what he is trying to make me do. And he implies, too, that if I do

succeed in understanding them, I shall do something better than giving up judging them. He expects me to change my present judgement to a truer one – namely, one that is favourable. And the standards I must use to do this cannot just be Samurai standards. They have to be ones current in my own culture. Ideals like discipline and devotion will not move anybody unless he himself accepts them. As it happens, neither discipline nor devotion is very popular in the West at present. Anyone who appeals to them may well have to do some more arguing to make *them* acceptable, before he can use them to explain the Samurai. But if he does succeed here, he will have persuaded us, not just that there was something to be said for them in ancient Japan, but that there would be here as well.

Isolating barriers simply cannot arise here. If we accept something as a serious moral truth about one culture, we can't refuse to apply it – in however different an outward form – to other cultures as well, wherever circumstances admit it. If we refuse to do this, we just are not taking the other culture seriously. This becomes clear if we look at the last argument used by my objector – that of justification by consent of the victim. It is suggested that sudden bisection is quite in order, *provided* that it takes place between consenting adults. I cannot now discuss how conclusive this justification is. What I am pointing out is simply that it can only work if we believe that *consent* can make such a transaction respectable – and this is a thoroughly modern and Western idea. It would probably never occur to a Samurai; if it did, it would surprise him very much. It is *our* standard. In applying it, too, we are likely to make another typically Western demand. We shall ask for good factual evidence that the wayfarers actually do have this rather surprising taste – that they are really willing to be bisected. In applying Western standards in this way, we are not being confused or irrelevant. We are asking the questions which arise *from where we stand*, questions which we can see the sense of. We do this because asking questions which you can't see the sense of is humbug. Certainly we can extend our questioning by imaginative effort. We can come to understand other societies better. By doing so, we may make their questions our own, or we may see that they are really forms of the questions which we are asking already. This is not impossible. It is just very hard work. The obstacles which often prevent it are simply those of ordinary ignorance, laziness and prejudice.

If there were really an isolating barrier, of course, our own culture could never have been formed. It is no sealed box, but a fertile jungle of different influences – Greek, Jewish, Roman, Norse, Celtic and so forth, into which further influences are still pouring – American, Indian, Japanese, Jamaican, you name it. The moral isolationist's picture of separate unmixable cultures is quite unreal. People who talk about British history usually stress the value of this fertilizing mix, no doubt rightly. But this is not just an odd fact about Britain. Except for the very smallest and most remote, all cultures are formed out of many streams. All have the problem of digesting and assimilating things which, at the start, they do not understand. All have the choice of learning something from this challenge, or, alternatively, of refusing to learn, and fighting it mindlessly instead.

This universal predicament has been obscured by the fact that anthropologists used to concentrate largely on very small and remote cultures, which did not seem to have this problem. These tiny societies, which had often forgotten their own history, made neat, self-contained subjects for study. No doubt it was valuable to emphasize their remoteness, their extreme strangeness, their independence of our cultural tradition. This emphasis was, I think, the root of moral isolationism. But, as the tribal studies themselves showed, even there the anthropologists were able to interpret what they saw and make judgements – often favourable – about the tribesmen. And the tribesmen, too, were quite equal to making judgements about the anthropologists – and about the tourists and Coca-Cola salesmen who followed them. Both sets of judgements, no doubt, were somewhat hasty, both have been refined in the light of further experience. A similar transaction between us and the Samurai might take even longer. But that is no reason at all for deeming it impossible. Morally as well as physically, there is only one world, and we all have to live in it.

CHAPTER 8

Ethics as Philosophy: A Defense of Ethical Nonnaturalism

RUSS SHAFER-LANDAU

I. Introduction

Moral realism is the view that (i) moral judgments are beliefs that are meant to describe the
way things really are; (ii) some of these beliefs
are true, and (iii) moral judgments are made
true in some way other than by virtue of the
attitudes taken towards their content by any
actual or idealized human agent. If torturing a
child is wrong, it is not because of anyone's
disapproval of such an action. It is not because
the action falls afoul of standards that I
endorse, or rules that any society accepts.
Even the disapproval of an ideal observer –
say, someone who knows all nonmoral facts,
and is fully rational – is not what makes an
action wrong. For moral realists, the ultimate
standard(s) of morality are as much a part of
reality as the ultimate laws of logic, or the basic
principles of physics. Perhaps God (if there
is a God) made them up, but human beings
certainly didn't. We humans have created for
ourselves a number of different sets of conventional moral standards, but these are never the
final word in the moral arena. The flaws and
attractions of any conventional morality are
rightly measured against those of a moral system that human beings did not create.

II. Ethics as Philosophy

Ethics is a branch of philosophy. Few would
dispute that. Yet this fact has significant, wide-
ranging implications, many of which have gone
little noticed in debates about the status of
ethical judgments. My central claim is that
there are very close parallels between ethical
investigation and that pursued in philosophy
quite generally. These parallels provide excellent reason for rejecting some of the perennial
criticisms that moral realism has faced.

I locate the central claim within a central
argument. Here it is:

1. Ethics is a species of inquiry; philosophy is
    its genus.
2. A species inherits the essential traits of its
    genus.
3. One essential trait of philosophy is the
    realistic status of its truths.
4. Therefore moral realism is true.

Both premise (1) and (2) strike me as
extremely plausible – so plausible, in fact, that
I will proceed here by assuming, rather than
arguing for, their truth. If one is willing to

Russ Shafer-Landau, "Ethics as Philosophy: A Defense of
Ethical Nonnaturalism," from Mark Timmons and Terence
Horgan (eds.), *Metaethics After Moore*. Oxford: Oxford
University Press, 2005.

make these concessions, then all the attention must focus on premise (3).

To see ethics as philosophy is to appreciate a certain kind and degree of methodological similarity. Philosophy is not primarily an empirical discipline, but an *a priori* one. Its truths are ordinarily discoverable, when they are, not exclusively by appeal to what our senses can tell us. We don't bump into such things as universals, free will, or modalities; we can't see them, or hear or touch them. We may have reason to deny the existence of such things, but not because we aren't sure what they taste like. Dismissing such things from our ontology, or ratifying their inclusion in it, is something that no scientist is able to do. Such things are dealt with in an *a priori* way.

Substantiating the claim that fundamental philosophical truths are *a priori* is work for a chapter unto itself (at the least). This isn't that chapter. Yet this claim about philosophy, while contentious, isn't on the face of it that implausible. Of course there are those who deny the very possibility or existence of *a priori* knowledge. But for all others, basic philosophical principles should be quite attractive candidates. Philosophy must run a close second to mathematics as an exemplar of an *a priori* discipline (if indeed there are any such exemplars). Part of this is explicable by reference to the metaphysically or conceptually necessary status of the principles that are the object of philosophical investigation. And part of this is explicable by reflection on cases. Consider for a moment Leibniz's law of the indiscernibility of identicals, or the modal principle that anything that is necessary is possibly necessary. These certainly don't seem to be inductive generalizations, or conclusions of inferences to the best explanation. The role of sensory evidence in establishing such claims is peripheral, at best. I might be mistaken about this, and nothing to come will absolutely protect against this possibility. But the view that makes the justification of such principles a matter of empirical confirmation is (much) more contentious than the one I am prepared to rely on.

As ethics is a branch of philosophy, we have excellent reason to think that fundamental ethical principles share the same status as fundamental philosophical principles. When we want to know whether something is right or wrong, admirable or vicious, we will certainly want to know what's going on in the world. The evidence of our senses may tell us that happiness has been maximized, or that the words of a promise have been uttered, but that's only the beginning, not the end, of our ethical investigations. When trying to verify the basic standards that govern the application of moral predicates, we will only secondarily (if at all) advert to what the physicists and botanists and hydrologists say. The conditions under which actions are right, and motives and characters good, aren't confirmed by the folks with lab coats. They are confirmed, if at all, by those who think philosophically. And much of that thinking, especially when focused on nonderivative, core principles, is undertaken without clear reliance on what we can see, or hear, or touch.

Since doing ethics is doing a kind of philosophy, we shouldn't be surprised at the similarities just mentioned. In what follows, I will rely on the parallels between the species (ethics) and its genus (philosophy) in a way that aids moral realists in answering three of the most pressing objections against their views.

The first objection says that the intractability of ethical disagreement sustains an antirealist diagnosis of ethical thought and talk. The second criticism claims that this disagreement in any event undermines any justified belief we may have for our moral views, provided that they are meant to tell us about how the world really is. The third asserts that the causal inefficacy of moral facts provides excellent reason to deny their existence. These aren't the only criticisms that moral realists have faced,[1] but they are among the most important. I think that they can be met. That is work enough for a day, if it can be accomplished.

III.   Moral Disagreement as a Metaphysical Objection

If there is an objective truth about what is morally right and wrong, why is there so much disagreement about such matters? Many believe that objective truths of any kind must be such as to garner consensus about them, at least among people who are well situated to appreciate such things. But it doesn't take an expert to realize that such consensus is extremely elusive in ethics. So persistent moral disagreement presents us with a choice. Perhaps there are no moral facts at all. Or there are, but ones that are not objective. Either way, the moral realist loses.

There are really two ways to run this skeptical argument, though they usually remain entangled in the literature. One is as an argument that seeks to best explain the scope of actual ethical disagreement we see in our world. The second is as an *a priori* argument, that has us anticipating persistent disagreement even among hypothetical, idealized moral deliberators. In both cases, the presence of intractable disagreement is said to be sufficient to draw an antirealist conclusion: there are no real, objective moral standards that could serve as guideposts to our moral investigations. In ethics, we make it all up.

The first version of the argument, as an inference to the best explanation, is inconclusive at best. Certainly there is intractable moral disagreement – plenty of it. But just as surely, such disagreement might be well explained as a product of insufficient nonmoral information, or adequate information insufficiently "processed." Such processing failures cover a wide range of cases, from errors of instrumental reasoning, to a failure of nerve, sympathy, empathy, or imagination. One explanation (not the only one) of these errors is that there's typically much more personally at stake in ethical matters than in scientific ones, and these stakes tend to introduce biasing factors that skew correct perception. It may be that for any given real-world ethical disagreement, we could cite at least one of these failings as an explanation for its continued existence.

I think that one's expectations of (lack of) consensus is largely an expression of one's antecedent metaethical commitments, rather than anything that could serve as an independent argument in this context. Imagine away all of the failings mentioned in the previous paragraph: will there or won't there be any disagreement left to threaten moral realism? I'm not sure. If not, then the realist can rest easy. But suppose disagreement persists, even in the imagined situation in which we rid our agents of the flaws that impede correct moral reasoning. Even here, however, realists can sustain their view with a minimum of damage. They will have to say that impeccable reasoning may nevertheless fail to land on the truth. There can be a gap between epistemic accessibility and truth. If we are to posit an absence of consensus even among perfected inquirers, then the idealized picture of moral inquirers will fail to guard against their fallibility.

At this point we can introduce the ethics–philosophy parallel and use it to defend moral realism from the argument from disagreement. The breadth and depth of philosophical disagreement is just as great as that found within ethics (perhaps greater). There's still no consensus on whether we have free will, on the analysis of knowledge, or on the relation of the mental and the physical. Nor is there broad agreement about which methods are best suited to confirm the right answers for us.

If the intractability of disagreement in an area is best explained by antirealist assumptions about its status, then we must be global philosophical antirealists. The judgments we render, and the arguments we offer on their behalf, must all be seen either as incapable of truth, as expressions of conative commitments only, or as claims whose truth is contingent on personal or interpersonal endorsement. But that's not a very plausible take on the status of our philosophical views. There is a truth – a real, objective truth – about whether the mental is identical to the physical, or about whether certain kinds of freedom are compatible with determinism. Once we are sure of our terms and concepts, the judgments that affirm or deny the existence of such things are literally either true or false, in as robust a sense as we can imagine. We don't have the final say about the truth of such judgments, and the content of these judgments is indeed something other than whatever practical commitments contingently accompany them.

I invite you to reflect on the status of the philosophical judgments you hold most dear, and have worked most carefully to defend. Do you imagine that your views, and their supporting arguments, are either untrue, or possessed of only the sort of minimal truth that is attainable by having been sincerely endorsed from within a parochial perspective? No matter how skeptical you might be about some alleged philosophical entities (universals, free will, or moral facts), you presumably take your confident opinions about such matters as having registered a real truth, one that is a function neither of your attitudes towards it, nor of the language you have used to comprehend it. That truth, you believe, is independent of the circle you inhabit, the agreements you've entered, the conventions you are part of, and the era in which you find yourself.

And yet one's philosophical views are bound to be as controversial as one's ethical views. Disagreements in core (and peripheral) philosophical areas are apparently intractable. Empirical evidence hasn't yet been able to solve any major philosophical problem, and any prediction that it someday might is as likely to divide philosophers as any other philosophical question. If intractable disagreement about verdicts and methods is enough to warrant an antirealist diagnosis of an area, then the whole of philosophy must be demoted. That simply is implausible: there really is (or isn't) such a thing as an omnipotent God, numbers without spatio-temporal location, actions that are both free and determined, etc. My say-so doesn't make it so. Neither does anyone else's.

The philosophical stance that denies the existence of objective moral properties is itself the subject of intractable disagreement. If such disagreement is sufficient to undermine the realistic status of the controversial judgments, then the views of the moral antirealist cannot be objectively correct. They are either untrue, or are true reports of the attitudes they themselves take toward moral realism, or are noncognitive expressions that reflect their own practical commitments. If they are *any* of those things, then they cannot rationally command the allegiance of their detractors. Moral realists needn't be making any error when rejecting such views.

The alternative is to see our beliefs about such matters as aspiring to, and possibly succeeding in, representing a philosophical reality not of our own making. This reality is constituted by a set of claims whose truth is independent of our endorsement of their content. And this despite the presence of intractable philosophical disagreement.

Of course, one might say that were we free of the shortcomings that beset all of us actual inquirers, we would converge on a set of philosophical claims about free will, the mind, the existence of God, etc. The disputes that seem to us so intractable would vanish with more information, more efficient and comprehensive application of that information, etc. That may be so. But then we have every reason to render the same verdict in the ethical case. Since ethics is a branch of philosophy, it would be very surprising to come to any other conclusion.

IV.   Moral Disagreement as an Epistemic Defeater

For any nontrivial moral view one holds, there are bound to be others who disagree with it. This very fact is probably not enough to undermine any epistemic justification one may have for the belief. One might, after all, be unaware of the disagreement, and this ignorance might be non-culpable. Yet what of the ordinary situation, where we realize that our own moral views fail to command universal allegiance? Suppose not only that you know of such disagreement, but that you also rightly believe that your opponents, reasoning correctly from their own incompatible but justified beliefs, will never come over to your side. What does that do to the status of your own beliefs?

As I see it, such awareness does not, by itself, constitute a defeater of one's views. It does not entail that one ought to suspend judgment about what one believes. For one may well think – and this is the usual case – that one has justifying reasons that the other is failing to appreciate. That she is reasoning impeccably from her own starting points does not mean that her beliefs must be true, since her starting points may be way off-base. And, as you will see things, they almost certainly are.

Surely it is possible that any defense you offer of your contested views will invoke other beliefs that are as controversial as the ones you are intending to support. In fact, this happens all the time in moral discussions. Perhaps, for many such cases, there is nothing one can do but beg the question. And question-begging arguments never confer justification.

There are two things to say here. First, one's belief might continue to be justified, even if defending it to others has one begging questions. A belief's justification is distinct from an agent's ability to justify it to others. So long as the belief was initially justified, it is possible that its justification survives, despite an agent's inability to advance considerations that an audience finds compelling. (Someone rightly convinced that tomatoes are fruits might be justified in her belief, even if she's unable to bring others around to the idea.) Second, there is excellent reason to believe that the presence of another's incompatible, justified belief doesn't always undermine justification; indeed, there might even be a case for thinking that question-begging arguments can supply positive justification for one's contested beliefs.

We can see this with the help of series of examples. Suppose that you are engaged in conversation with a principled fanatic. He thinks that the fundamental ethical imperative is to gain power over others; everything else is subsidiary to this primary goal. Any argument you offer for beneficence is bound to be treated as the product of an effective brainwashing. Nothing you can say will convince him. Moreover, suppose that he's not contradicting himself, and isn't making any false empirical claims to support his ultimate principle. In the context of your conversation, you are bound to beg the question.

But you might be justified in your beliefs anyway. For the presence of an intelligent, consistent and indefatigable opponent does not necessarily undermine a belief that one is otherwise justified in holding. This is a general point. It holds for one's ethical views, but also for perceptual, memorial, and philosophical ones, as well.

To simplify, consider a case in which one's perceptual beliefs later form the basis of a memorial belief. I saw and remember talking to my hated nemesis Smith the moment before he made that fatal misstep that no one else witnessed. I try to convince others of what I have seen, and am met with disbelief. They know of our rivalry, and they think I killed

him. (Suppose I've done just that in other, similar cases.) That others have excellent reason to doubt my word is compatible with my original belief, and its memorial descendant, both being highly justified. In this case, not only do the incompatible, well-justified beliefs of others fail to undermine my justification, but my own question-begging attitudes (e.g., regarding my own innocence in this case) do appear to be enough to constitute positive justification for the beliefs I hold.

We can broaden the picture in an obvious way. Informed, rational and attentive skeptics, possessed of internally consistent and coherent attitudes, might remain unconvinced by any of our empirical claims. According to this version of the argument from disagreement, that resistance defeats any justification we might have for our empirical beliefs. Though we can't absolutely discount that possibility, the conclusion is so drastic as to call into question the soundness of the argument that generated it. If we assume, as everyone reading this chapter will, that we do have some positively justified empirical beliefs, then, so far as I can tell, it follows that question-begging grounds can confer positive justification. For anything one might cite as evidence on behalf of one's empirical beliefs will surely be regarded as question-begging by the skeptic.

A similar story can be told regarding all of our philosophical beliefs. The most brilliant philosophers, rational, open-minded, and well-informed, have failed to agree among themselves on just about every key philosophical issue. If pervasive and intractable disagreement signaled an absence of justification, this would mean that none of those philosophers (much less the rest of us) would be at all justified in holding the philosophical views that they (we) do. But this seems false; it's certainly belied by anyone who sincerely undertakes to argue philosophically. One who has developed a theoretically sophisticated take on some philosophical issue, coming to grips with deep criticisms and developing novel and integrated positive proposals, is surely justified to some extent in thinking her views correct. Of course such a person will see that some others will fail to be convinced – even some others who are as smart, ingenious and imaginative as she is. She will recognize her fallibility and appreciate a salient feature of philosophical history – namely, the failure of greater minds to attract even near-unanimity on most of the major points that they had advanced. Still, awareness of this history, and the skepticism of some of her contemporaries, is not enough to force her to suspend judgment on the views that she has so skillfully defended.

I see no reason to register a different verdict for ethics. Deep disagreement there, as elsewhere, should give one pause. It can sap one's confidence, and if it does, then that (but not the disagreement *per se*) may be sufficient to undercut one's justification. But this is no different from the general case. Provided that one brings to a dispute a moral belief that is justified, then exposure to conflicting belief needn't defeat one's justification, even if one is unable to convince an intelligent other of the error of his ways.

The present argument against the epistemic justification of moral belief relies on the following principle (or something very like it):

> (E) If (i) S believes that p, and R believes that not-p, and (ii) S and R know of this disagreement, and (iii) S and R have formed their beliefs in rational and informed ways, then S is not justified in a belief that p, and R is not justified in a belief that not-p.

(E) may be true. But no one could be justified in believing it. (E) itself is the subject of intractable disagreement – there are informed and rational people who endorse it, and equally qualified people who reject it. By its own lights, then, we must suspend judgment about (E). Having done that, however, we are no longer epistemically forbidden from positively embracing a contested belief, even if our opponents are as smart we as are.

We can reveal another kind of skeptical self-defeat if we renew our emphasis on establishing a parity between ethical investigation and philosophical investigations generally. A familiar skeptical line is that there isn't, really, any adequate evidence that can be called upon to support our ethical opinions. Unlike empirical investigations, we haven't anything tangible that can, at the end of the day, finally settle a

disputed moral question. All the sensory evidence at our disposal will underdetermine an ethical verdict. And what's left? Only our emotional responses and our moral convictions, both of which are traceable to accidents of birth and upbringing. Their genesis marks them as unreliable indicators of any truth there might be. But there's nothing else to rely on in ethics. And, therefore, our moral views lack justification, one and all.

The problem with such an argument should by now be apparent. There is a striking equivalence between the nature and source of our evidence in philosophy, and in ethics. We have no choice but to rely on our intuitions and considered judgments in both. What tells us, for example, that many proposed analyses of knowledge are no good is not some empirical finding that scientists have unearthed. It is instead our conceptual intuitions about counter-examples. If we want to know whether determinism is compatible with free will, we will consult arguments that invariably appeal to our intuitive responses to hypothetical cases. If such convictions and responses have no evidential credibility, then we should have to regard all philosophical beliefs as unjustified. Perhaps they are. But then those of the moral antirealist are similarly undone.

V. The Causal Inefficacy of Moral Facts

Gilbert Harman (see his reading earlier in this Part) has famously charged that moral facts are causally inert, and are, therefore, best construed antirealistically. If I am right, his basic line of attack is misdirected.

Harman doesn't put things in quite this way, but I think his position, and that of many who take his lead, can be accurately captured in the following argument:

1. If something exists, and its existence is best construed realistically, then it must possess independent causal powers.
2. Moral facts possess no independent causal powers.
3. Therefore, either moral facts don't exist, or their existence isn't best construed realistically.

Harman himself believes in moral facts, though he regards them as artifacts of social agreements. He is an ethical relativist, not a moral realist.

Since the argument is valid, any realist must choose either or both of the premises to come in for criticism. I opt for (1), because I suspect that (2) is true. A fact has independent causal powers only if its causal powers obtain regardless of the causal powers of any other facts it depends upon or is realized by. I'm not confident that moral facts possess such powers.

I won't try to vindicate my lack of confidence here. If it is misplaced, then so much the better for moral realism. Moral facts would possess independent causal power, and thereby pass the most stringent test for ontological inclusion. But let's instead imagine that my suspicion is correct, and that we are thus placed in what many have considered a worst-case scenario: trying to defend the existence of moral facts, realistically construed, while acknowledging that they are fundamentally different in kind from those whose existence is ratified by the natural sciences. If I am right, then such things as a benefactor's generosity, a regime's injustice, a friend's thoughtfulness, are causes (if they are) only by virtue of inheriting the causal powers of the facts that realize them at a time. Any causal power they have is exhausted by that of the subvening facts that fix a situation's moral status. Nothing follows from this admission unless we are also prepared to insist on a causal test of ontological credibility, of the sort espoused in Harman's first premise.

Such a test is powerfully motivated, but is ultimately resistible. This test is an application of Occam's razor, and is responsible for our having pared down our ontology in many sensible ways. We're quite finished with explanations that invoke Osiris or golems or centaurs, and Occam's razor is responsible for that. All that these entities were once invoked to explain can be more parsimoniously explained by relying on facts or properties whose existence is vindicated through scientific confirmation. And such confirmation makes essential reference to a putative entity's causal powers.

So out with the trolls, the ancient pantheon, and the vampires. That's not so bad, is it? Such things aren't required to explain the goings-on in our world. But then, by my admission, neither are moral facts. So, by parity of reasoning, either we keep moral facts, but at the expense of a bloated ontology that implausibly lets these minor supernatural agents sneak back in, or we abolish the lot of them. Why should morality get special treatment here, when, as we all agree, the causal test has done its good work in so many other areas? Very conveniently for me, I don't have the time in this context to provide the full answer to this question.[2] But in lieu of that long story, let me offer a brief reply, and then a longer one that invokes the ethics–philosophy parallel that I have already relied on.

The brief reply: application of the causal test has highly counter-intuitive implications. This is so on two assumptions: first, that only physical facts and properties possess independent causal powers, and second, that at least most of the properties of the special sciences are not identical to, but only supervenient upon, those of physics. From these assumptions, allied with the causal test, it follows that nothing exists but (roughly) atoms and the void. There certainly won't be any such things as atmospheres, rock strata, newts, and dandelions, if we grant that such things are not identical to anything referred to in a physics journal. It seems to me that such things do exist, but are composed of, and not identical to, particular physical facts and properties. Thus the causal test eliminates too much from our ontology.

Suppose that doesn't faze you – you can live with such a parsimonious ontology, or you don't endorse one of the two assumptions that got us there.[3] Still, we can invoke the ethics–philosophy parallel in the service of a further argument that should worry proponents of the causal test. By way of introduction, we can note that moral facts are a species of *normative fact*. Normative facts are those that tell us what we *ought* to do; they rely on norms, or standards, for conduct within a given realm. Normative facts cause nothing of their own accord.

We can be helped to see this by comparing ethics, not to philosophy as a whole, but to one of its close philosophical cousins. In my opinion, moral facts are *sui generis*, but they are most similar to another kind of normative fact – epistemic facts. Epistemic facts concern what we ought to believe, provided that our beliefs are aimed at the truth. Once one understands the concept of logical validity, then if confronted with a modus ponens argument, one *ought to* believe that it is logically valid. This is a true epistemic principle.

It's also the case that you oughtn't believe things that you have no evidence for, and much evidence against. What does this epistemic truth cause? Nothing. Nor are particular, concrete epistemic duties – duties had by agents at a time – at all independently causally efficacious. Epistemic facts have as their primary function the specification of standards that should or must be met. Unlike scientific principles and facts, such normative standards may be perfectly correct even if they are honored only in the breach. The epistemic requirement that we proportion our beliefs to the evidence can be true even in a world populated wholly by spell-casters and astrologers. The normative facts that specify the conditions under which we ought to believe the truth, or behave morally, lack the ability to explain the workings of the natural order. Our epistemic and moral duties cannot explain why apples fall from trees, why smallpox takes its victims, why leopards have their spots. But they may exist for all that.

Nor is this failure something specific to the moral or epistemological realms. Consider prudential or instrumental duties – those that require us to enhance self-interest or efficiently satisfy our desires. Such normative demands do not explain what goes on in the world. Alternatively, if they are thought, for instance, to be powerful enough to explain why agents act as they do, then surely moral and epistemic requirements are capable of doing so as well. I see no basis for distinguishing the causal powers of any of these normative types from one another.

I don't mean to suggest for a moment that the causal test is useless. Rather, I think we should recognize its limits. The causal test fails as a general ontological test: it doesn't work when applied to the normative realm.

Scientific principles are vindicated, when they are, because they are able to do two closely related things: cite the causes of past events, and accurately predict the nature and occurrence of future events. Their claim to be genuinely explanatory depends almost entirely on their ability to discharge these two tasks.

But moral rules are not like that. Moral principles aren't viewed in the first instance as hypotheses that predict the actions of agents, but rather as requirements that everyone knows will encounter predictive failures. True, moral principles will reliably predict the doings of good and bad agents. But that presupposes the reality of moral goodness and badness, and there's no reason to make such a concession at this stage, especially given the seriousness of antirealist charges, and the aim (given a naturalistic vantage point) of beginning from a neutral perspective and relying on the causal test as a way to determine the nature of reality.[4] Yes, we can enshrine moral predicates within true counterfactuals, even (in some cases) counterfactuals of greater generality than those describable at the physical level. But that is no proof of moral realism, as we can do the same for the predicates of etiquette and the civil law, which obviously cannot be construed realistically. Moral principles and facts aren't meant to explain behavior, or anticipate our actions, but rather to *prescribe* how we ought to behave, or *evaluate* states or events. They don't cite the causes of outcomes, but rather indicate what sort of conduct would merit approval, or justify our gratitude, or legitimate some result. Science can't tell us such things.

If I am right, then an allegiance to the causal test entirely eliminates the normative realm. But this is highly implausible. There *are* reasons to believe things, reasons to satisfy one's desires, reasons to look out for oneself. There are also moral duties to aid others and refrain from harming them, even if doing so isn't going to improve one's lot in life. The standards that supply such reasons are not capable of causing anything. Nor, it seems, are the reasons or obligations themselves. (Again, if they are, all the better for moral realists.) If there is any such thing as a genuine reason, the test must fail. Alternatively, if the test is retained, then such reasons must be capable of passing it. And then the causal argument against moral facts evaporates.

Maybe we can have our cake and it eat, too? Why not retain the causal test, allow that normative facts exist, but view them, as Harman does moral facts, as by-products of human choice and election? The causal test is a realist's test. Failure to pass it doesn't mean that a putative fact doesn't exist. It just means that the fact cannot be construed realistically. Normative facts may be like this. If so, we could retain the test, and also retain a global normative antirealism. Perfectly in keeping with the physicalist leanings of so many of our contemporaries.

The animating spirit behind the causal test is the ontological principle that the real is limited to what is scientifically confirmable, and the epistemic principle that we have good reason to believe in something only if it impinges on our experience, or is required in the best explanation of that which does. The causal test obviously supports, and derives support from, both the ontological and the epistemic principle. Yet both principles are dubious. The case for the causal test is considerably diminished once we see why.

The epistemic principle is problematic because it invokes an entity – a good reason – whose existence is not itself scientifically confirmable. It's like saying that God sustains a universe that contains no supernatural beings. There's a kind of internal incoherence here: the claim discounts the existence of the kind of thing that is presupposed by the claim itself.

Further, a belief's being justified is not the sort of thing that we can empirically detect. Nor, seemingly, is reference to its epistemic status required to explain anything that we have ever observed. But then, by the epistemic principle under scrutiny, we have no good reason to think that there is any such thing as the property of being epistemically justified. But if there is no such property, then the principle that implies such a thing cannot itself be justified. And so we can be rid of it.

Here's another way to get to the same result. We needn't make essential reference to this epistemic principle to explain why we see or hear or feel the things we do. Nor, so far as I can see, is any epistemic principle required in the best account of why various observable events have occurred in the world. So if the

principle is true, then we lack a good reason for thinking it so. This principle, like normative standards quite generally, seeks to regulate and appraise conduct, rather than to describe its causal antecedents or powers. If that's sufficient to render it unreal, or sufficient to remove any justification we might have for believing it, then it can't rightly be used to constrain our epistemic findings or practices.

And the ontological view? The relevant ontological principle tells us that the only existential truths there are (i.e., truths about what exists) are those that are scientifically confirmed. This is certainly false if we are concerned with science as it stands, as some such truths have yet to be discovered. Yet the view is no more plausible if we are envisioning the edicts of a perfected natural science.

Here's why. Consider this existential claim:

(O) There are no existential truths other than those ratified by perfected natural sciences.

Either (O) is true or false. If false, let's drop it: our ontology wouldn't then be entirely fixed by the natural sciences. But if it's true, then it must be false: it's self-referentially incoherent. For (O) cannot itself be scientifically confirmed. If it were true, it would be an instance of a non-scientifically confirmable existential truth. Thus either way we go, (O) must be false.

(O) is a thesis from metaphysics, not physics. Philosophers, not natural scientists, are the ones who will end up pronouncing on its merits. This is another application of the general idea that there are specifically philosophical truths that escape the ambit of scientific confirmation. There might be abstract entities, or such a thing as conceptual necessity, justified belief, or goodness. Bring your beakers, your electron microscopes, your calculators and calipers – you'll never find them. You can't abolish such things just because they lack independent causal power, and so escape empirical detection. After all, the principle calling for such abolition isn't itself scientifically confirmable.

In the end, the absence of independent causal power is not a good reason to deny the existence of moral facts, realistically construed. Of course, nothing I've said in this section supplies any argument for thinking that there are such things. I doubt that causal considerations could do that. But undermining their role in antirealist arguments can go some way towards removing a familiar barrier to justified belief in the sort of moral realism that I find appealing.

VI.   Conclusion

Once we attend to the fact that ethics is a branch of philosophy, the plausibility of moral realism is greatly enhanced. Basic, fundamental philosophical principles are realistic in nature. And central ethical principles are philosophical ones. This combination of claims gives us excellent reason to suppose that fundamental ethical truths are best construed realistically.

This seems to me to be a very powerful argument that can aid the moral realist in replying to a number of perennial criticisms. One such criticism – that persistent, intractable moral disagreement is best explained as antirealists would do – can be met once we avail ourselves of the ethics–philosophy parallel. Moral disagreement shares all structural features with philosophical disagreement generally, and yet a global philosophical anti

realism is very implausible. Moral disagreement also fails to provide a strong epistemic defeater for one's own already-justified moral beliefs. Controversial philosophical beliefs might be justifiedly held; things are no different in the specifically moral domain. And the causal inefficacy of moral facts can be admitted without threatening moral realism, since the causal test is too restrictive a standard for ontological credibility. Alternatively, if (contrary to my suspicions) moral facts do manage to pass that test, then retaining the test will entitle moral facts to admission into our ontology.

Once we attend to the fact that ethics is a branch of philosophy, a defense of moral realism becomes a bit easier than it otherwise might be. That's not to say that the project is easy, and there are other criticisms of realism that I have not been able to discuss here. Still, reliance on the ethics–philosophy parallel enables us to plausibly respond to *some* of the critical obstacles to the development of a plausible moral realism. We can hardly hope to vindicate a complex metaethical theory in one fell swoop. We can, if the preceding arguments are any good, manage to show that some of the sources of its unpopularity have been overrated. I hope to have done that here.

Notes

1. Perhaps the most important additional objection – one leveled by Hume and Mackie in their readings in this Part – is that if moral realism is true, then moral duties must supply all people with an excellent reason to do as they command. But moral duties cannot do this. Therefore, either there are no moral duties (Mackie), or those moral duties that do exist are best construed anti-realistically (Hume). I try to answer this objection, by trying to show that moral duties *do* entail excellent reasons for action, in my article on moral rationalism in Part III.

2. I try my hand in *Moral Realism: A Defence* (Oxford University Press, 2003), pp. 98–114.

3. Beware: arguments for rejecting either assumption may well allow moral facts to pass the causal test.

4. So in this respect I think that Harman was wrong to concede to his opponents the existence of moral facts. The proper starting point for an antirealist is one in which we suspend judgment on the existence of such facts, and demand of the realist some positive arguments for believing in them. Harman instead was willing to grant the existence of moral facts, but claimed that even so they possessed no independent causal powers, and so could not be construed realistically.

CHAPTER 9

Realism

MICHAEL SMITH

Most of us take moral appraisal pretty much for granted. To the extent that we worry, we simply worry about *getting it right*. Philosophers too worry about getting the answers to moral questions right. However, traditionally, they have also been worried about the whole business of moral appraisal itself. The problem they have grappled with emerges when we focus on two distinctive features of moral practice; for, surprisingly, these features pull against each other, threatening to make the very idea of morality look altogether incoherent.

The first feature is implicit in our concern to get the answers to moral questions *right*, for this concern presupposes that there are correct answers to moral questions to be had, and thus that there exists a domain of distinctively *moral* facts. Moreover, we seem to think that these facts have a particular character, for the only relevant determinant of the rightness of an act would seem to be the circumstances in which that action takes place. Agents whose circumstances are identical face the same moral choice: if they perform the same act then either they both act rightly or they both act wrongly.

Something like this conception of moral facts seems to explain our pre-occupation

with moral argument. Since we are all in the same boat, so, it seems, we think that a conversation in which agents carefully muster and assess each other's reasons for and against their moral opinions is the best way to discover what the moral facts are. If the participants are open-minded and thinking clearly then we seem to think that such an argument should result in a *convergence* in moral opinion – a convergence upon the truth.

We may summarise this first feature of moral practice as follows: we seem to think that moral questions have correct answers, that these answers are made correct by objective moral facts, that these facts are determined by circumstances, and that, by arguing, we can discover what these facts are. The term "objective" here simply signifies the possibility of a convergence in moral views of the kind just mentioned.

Consider now the second feature. Suppose we reflect and decide that we did the wrong thing in (say) refusing to give to famine relief. It seems we come to think we failed to do something for which there was a good reason. And this has motivational implications. For now imagine the situation if we refuse again when next the opportunity arises. We will have refused to do what we think we have good reason to do, and this will occasion serious puzzlement. An explanation of some sort will need to be forthcoming (perhaps weakness of will or irrationality of some other kind). Why?

Michael Smith, "Realism," pp. 399–410 from Peter Singer (ed.), *A Companion to Ethics*. Oxford: Blackwell, 1993. Reprinted by permission of the publishers, Blackwell Publishing.

Because, other things being equal, having a moral opinion seems to require having a corresponding reason, and therefore motivation, to act accordingly.

These two distinctive features of moral practice – the *objectivity* and the *practicality* of moral judgement – are widely thought to have both metaphysical and psychological implications. However, and unfortunately, these implications are the exact opposite of each other. In order to see why, we need to pause for a moment to reflect on the nature of human psychology.

According to the standard picture of human psychology – a picture we owe to David Hume – there are two main kinds of psychological state. On the one hand there are beliefs, states that purport to represent the way the world is. Since our beliefs purport to represent the world, they are subject to rational criticism: specifically, they are assessable in terms of truth and falsehood. And on the other hand there are also desires, states that represent how the world is to be. Desires are unlike beliefs in that they do not even purport to represent the way the world is. They are therefore not assessable in terms of truth and falsehood. Indeed, according to the standard picture, our desires are not subject to any sort of rational criticism at all. The fact that we have a certain desire is, with a proviso to be mentioned presently, simply a fact about ourselves to be acknowledged. In themselves, desires are all on a par, rationally neutral.

This is important, for it suggests that though facts about the world may rightly affect our beliefs, such facts should, again with a proviso to be mentioned presently, have no rational impact upon our desires. They may of course, have some *non*-rational impact. Seeing a spider, I may be overcome with a morbid fear and desire never to be near one. However this is not a change in my desires mandated by reason. It is a *non*-rational change in my desires.

Now for the proviso. Suppose, contrary to the example just given, I acquire an aversion to spiders because I come to believe, falsely, that they have an unpleasant odour. This is certainly an irrational aversion. However, this is not contrary to the spirit of the standard picture. For my aversion is *based on* a further desire and

belief: my desire not to smell that unpleasant odour and my belief that that odour is given off by spiders. Since I can be rationally criticised for having the belief, as it is false, so I can be rationally criticised for having the aversion it helps to produce. The proviso is thus fairly minor: desires are subject to rational criticism, but only insofar as they are based on irrational beliefs. Desires that do not have this feature are not subject to rational criticism at all.

According to the standard picture, then, there are two kinds of psychological state – beliefs and desires – utterly distinct and different from each other. This picture is important because it provides us with a model for understanding human action. A human action is the product of these two forces: a desire representing the way the world is to be and a belief telling us how the world is, and thus how it has to be changed, so as to make it that way.

We said earlier that the objectivity and the practicality of moral judgement have both metaphysical and psychological implications. We can now say what they are. Consider first the objectivity of moral judgement: the idea that there are moral facts, determined by circumstances, and that, by arguing, we can discover what these objective moral facts are. This implies, metaphysically, that amongst the various facts there are in the world there aren't just facts about (say) the consequences of our actions on the well-being of sentient creatures, there are also distinctively *moral* facts: facts about the rightness and wrongness of our actions having these consequences. And, psychologically, the implication is thus that when we make a moral judgement we express our *beliefs* about the way these moral facts are. Our moral beliefs are representations of the way the world is *morally*.

Given the standard picture of human psychology, there is a further psychological implication. For whether or not people who have a certain moral belief desire to act accordingly must now be seen as a further and entirely separate question. They may happen to have a corresponding desire, they may not. However, either way, they cannot be rationally criticised.

But now consider the second feature, the practicality of moral judgement, the idea that to have a moral opinion simply *is*, contrary to

what has just been said, to have a corresponding reason, and thus motivation, to act accordingly. Psychologically, since making a moral
judgement entails having a certain desire, and
no recognition of a fact about the world could
rationally compel us to have one desire rather
than another, this seems to imply that our
judgement must really simply *be* an expression
of that desire. And this psychological implication has a metaphysical counterpart. For, contrary to initial appearance, it seems that when
we judge it right to give to famine relief (say),
we *are not* responding to any moral fact. In
judging it right to give to famine relief, we are
really simply expressing our desire that people
give to famine relief. It is as if we were yelling
"Hooray for giving to famine relief!" – no
mention of a moral fact there, in fact, no
factual claim at all.

We are now in a position to see why philosophers have been worried about the whole
business of moral appraisal. The problem is
that the *objectivity* and the *practicality* of
moral judgement pull in quite opposite directions from each other. The objectivity of moral
judgement suggests that there are moral facts,
determined by circumstances, and that our
moral judgements express our beliefs about
what these facts are. But though this is presupposed by moral argument, it leaves it entirely
mysterious how or why having a moral view
has special links with what we are motivated to
do. And the practicality of moral judgement
suggests just the opposite, that our moral
judgements express our desires. While this
seems presupposed in the link between moral
judgement and motivation, it leaves it entirely
mysterious how or why moral judgements can
be the subject of moral argument.

The very idea of morality may therefore be
incoherent, for what is required to make sense
of a moral judgement is a queer sort of fact
about the universe: a fact whose recognition
necessarily impacts upon our desires. But the
standard picture of human psychology tells us
that there are no such facts. Nothing could be
everything a moral judgement purports to be –
or so the standard picture tells us.

At long last we are in a position to see what
this essay is about. For *moral realism* is simply
the metaphysical view that there exist moral

facts. The psychological counterpart to realism
is cognitivism, the view that moral judgements
express our beliefs about what these moral facts
are. Moral realism thus contrasts with two
alternative metaphysical views: *irrealism* and
moral nihilism. According to the irrealists,
there are no moral facts, but neither are
moral facts required to make sense of moral
practice. We can happily acknowledge that our
moral judgements simply express our desires
about how people behave. This is non-
cognitivism, the psychological counterpart to
irrealism. By contrast, according to the moral
nihilists, the irrealists are right that there are
no moral facts, but wrong about what is
required to make sense of moral practice.
Without moral facts moral practice is all a
sham, much like religious practice without
belief in God.

Which, then, should we believe: realism,
irrealism or nihilism? I favour realism. Let me
say why. We have assumed from the outset that
judgements of right and wrong are judgements
about our reasons for action. But though these
judgements seem to concern a realm of facts
about our reasons, what casts doubt on this is
the standard picture of human psychology. For
it tells us that, since judgements about our
reasons have motivational implications, so
they must really simply be expressions of our
desires. It seems to me that here we see the real
devil of the piece: the standard picture of
human psychology's tacit conflation of *reasons*
with *motives.* Seeing why this is so enables us to
see why we may legitimately talk about our
beliefs about the reasons we have, and why
having such beliefs makes it rational to have
corresponding desires; why such beliefs have
motivational implications.

Imagine giving the baby a bath. As you do, it
begins to scream uncontrollably. Nothing you
do seems to help. As you watch, you are overcome with a desire to drown it in the bath-
water. You are *motivated* to drown the baby.
Does this entail that you have a *reason* to
drown the baby? Commonsense tells us that,
since this desire is not *worth* satisfying, it does
not provide you with such a reason; that, in
this case, you are motivated to do something
you have *no* reason to do. But can the standard
picture agree with commonsense on this score?

No, it cannot. For your desire to drown the baby need be based on no false belief, and, as such, the standard picture tells us it is beyond rational criticism. There is no sense in which it is not worth satisfying – or so the standard picture tells us. But this is surely wrong.

The problem is that the standard picture gives no special privilege to what we would want if we were 'cool, calm and collected'. Yet commonsense tells us that not being cool, calm and collected may lead to·all sorts of irrational emotional outbursts. Having those desires that we would have if we were cool, calm and collected thus seems to be an *independent* rational ideal. When cool, calm and collected, you would want that the baby isn't drowned, no matter how much it screams, and no matter how overcome you may be, in your uncool, uncalm and uncollected state, with a desire to drown it. This is why you have no reason to drown the baby. It seems to me that this insight is the key to reconciling the objectivity with the practicality of moral judgement.

Judgements of right and wrong express our beliefs about our reasons. But what sort of fact is a fact about our reasons? The preceding discussion suggests that they are not facts about what we *actually* desire, as the standard picture would have it, but are rather facts about what we *would* desire if we were in certain idealised conditions of reflection: if, say, we were well informed, cool, calm and collected.

According to this account, then, I have a reason to give to famine relief in my particular circumstances just in case, if I were in such idealised conditions of reflection, I would desire that, even when in my particular circumstances, I give to famine relief. Now this sort of fact may certainly be the object of a belief. And moreover having such a belief – a belief about our reasons – certainly seems to rationally require of us that we have corresponding desires.

In order to see this, suppose I believe I would desire to give to famine relief if I were cool, calm and collected but, being uncool, uncalm and uncollected, I don't desire to give to famine relief. Am I rationally criticizable for not having the desire? I surely am. After all, from my own point of view my beliefs and desires form a more coherent, and thus a rationally

preferable, package if I do in fact desire what I believe I would desire if I were cool, calm and collected. This is because, since it is an independent rational ideal to have the desires I would have if I were cool, calm and collected so, from my own point of view, if I believe that I would have a certain desire under such conditions and yet fail to have it, my beliefs and desires fail to meet this ideal. To believe that I would desire to give to famine relief if I were cool, calm and collected and yet fail to desire to give to famine relief is thus to manifest a commonly recognizable species of rational failure.

If this is right then, contrary to the standard picture, a broader class of desires may be rationally criticized. The desires of those who fail to desire to do what they believe they have reason to do can be rationally criticized even though they may not be based on any false belief. And, if this is right, then the standard picture is wrong to suggest that a judgement with motivational implications must really be the expression of a desire. For a judgement about an agent's reasons has motivational implications – the rational agent is motivated accordingly – and yet it is the expression of a belief.

Have we said enough to solve the problem facing the moral realist? Not yet. Moral judgements aren't *just* judgements about the reasons we have. They are judgements about the reasons we have *where those reasons are determined entirely by our circumstances*. People in the same circumstances face the same moral choice: if they do the same then either they both act rightly (they both do what they have reason to do) or they both act wrongly (they both do what they have reason not to do). Does the account of reasons we have given support this?

Suppose our circumstances are identical. Is it right for each of us to give to famine relief? According to the story just told, it is right that I give to famine relief just in case I have a reason to do so, and I have such a reason just in case, if I were in idealised conditions of reflection – well informed, cool, calm and collected – I would desire to give to famine relief. And the same is true of you. If our circumstances are the same then, supposedly, we should both have such a reason or both lack such a reason. But do we?

The question is whether, if we were well informed, cool, calm and collected, we would all *converge* in the desires we have. Would we converge or would there always be the possibility of some non-rationally-explicable difference in our desires *even under such conditions?* The standard picture of human psychology now returns to center-stage. For it tells us that there is always the possibility of some non-rationally-explicable difference in our desires *even under such idealised conditions of reflection.* This is the residue of the standard picture's conception of desire as a psychological state that is beyond rational criticism.

If there is such a possibility then the realist's attempt to reconcile the objectivity and the practicality of moral judgement simply fails. For we are forced to accept that there is a *fundamental relativity* in the reasons we have. What we have reason to do is relative to what we would desire under idealised conditions of reflection, and this may differ from person to person. It is not wholly determined by our circumstances, as moral facts are supposed to be.

Many philosophers believe that there is always such a possibility; that our reasons are fundamentally relative. But this seems unwarranted to me. For it seems to me that moral practice is itself the forum in which we will *discover* whether there is a fundamental relativity in our reasons.

After all, in moral practice we attempt to change people's moral beliefs by engaging them in rational argument: i.e. by getting their beliefs to approximate those they would have under more idealised conditions of reflection. And sometimes we succeed. When we succeed, other things being equal, we succeed in changing their desires. How, then, can we say in advance that this procedure will never result in a massive *convergence* in moral beliefs? And, if it did result in a massive convergence in our moral beliefs – and thus in our desires – then why not say that this convergence would itself be best explained by the fact that the beliefs and desires that emerge have some *privileged* rational status? Something like such a convergence on certain mathematical judgements in mathematical practice lies behind our conviction that those claims enjoy a privileged rational status. So why not think that a like convergence in moral practice would show that those moral judgements and concerns enjoy the same privileged rational status? At this point, the standard picture's insistence that there is a fundamental relativity in our reasons begins to sound all too much like a hollow dogma.

The kind of moral realism described here endorses a conception of moral facts that is a far cry from the picture noted at the outset: moral facts as queer facts about the universe whose recognition necessarily impacts upon our desires. The realist has eschewed queer facts about the universe in favour of a more 'subjectivist' conception of moral facts. The realist's point, however, is that such a conception of moral facts may make them subjective only in the innocuous sense that they are facts about our reasons: i.e. facts about what we would *want* under certain idealised conditions of reflection. For wants are, admittedly, states enjoyed by subjects. But moral facts remain objective insofar as they are facts about what *we*, not just *you* or *I*, would want under such conditions. The existence of a moral fact – say, the rightness of giving to famine relief in certain circumstances – requires that, under idealised conditions of reflection, rational creatures would *converge* upon a desire to give to famine relief in such circumstances.

Of course, it must be said that moral argument has not yet produced the sort of convergence in our desires that would make the idea of a moral fact – a fact about the reasons we have entirely determined by our circumstances – look plausible. But neither has moral argument had much of a history in times in which we can engage in free reflection unhampered by a false biology (the Aristotelian tradition) or a false belief in God (the Judeo-Christian tradition). It remains to be seen whether sustained moral argument can elicit the requisite convergence in our moral beliefs, and corresponding desires, to make the idea of a moral fact look plausible. The kind of moral realism described here holds out the hope that it will. Only time will tell.

PART II
Moral Knowledge

Introduction to Part II

How can we gain moral knowledge? In some cases, philosophers treat this question as a specific instance of the more general question: how we can gain knowledge of anything? This more general question is usually framed by reference to a variety of skeptical challenges. The deepest of these, and the ones hardest to answer, are those that cast doubt on our ability to know anything at all.

Consider, for instance, the relevant alternatives argument: in order to know that some claim is true, one must first be able to decisively exclude all views that are incompatible with the original claim. But one can never do that. So one can never know anything.

Or consider the vicious circle argument: in order to know that some claim is true, one must first know that one's methods for sorting true from false beliefs are reliable. But in order to know that one's methods are reliable, one must first know some particular facts, whose existence is vindicated by those methods. Since knowing the facts requires knowing the methods, and knowing the methods requires knowing the facts, we can't escape from this vicious circle, and consequently, we know nothing.

There are plenty of other general skeptical arguments, i.e., arguments designed to impugn our knowledge of anything at all. If knowledge requires a decisive refutation of such skepticism, then knowledge may well be an impossibility, since it is notoriously difficult to refute the skeptical position that refuses to credit anyone with knowledge.

Discussions in moral epistemology rarely start by considering these most radical forms of skepticism. Instead, such discussions usually begin with the assumption that we can know at least some things – that two and two are four, that there are rivers and mountains and volcanoes on earth, that other people are alive, can think, and can feel roughly as we do. Importantly, the knowledge that gets taken for granted in such discussions is straightforward, nonmoral knowledge. The challenge in ethics typically originates by noting important differences between the nonmoral claims that are usually accepted as knowledge, and moral claims, which often are not.

One perennial source of skepticism about moral knowledge is the comparatively greater degree of disagreement about moral claims than about mathematical or empirical claims. As we saw in Part I, some philosophers use this fact about the scope of moral disagreement to argue that ethics is not objective. But other philosophers cite this fact as the basis for a more modest claim. Even if widespread moral disagreement is compatible with ethical objectivity, such extensive disagreement undermines the chance of ever knowing right from wrong. For (it is claimed) if a belief remains controversial among intelligent and rational people, then we should suspend judgment on its merits. All moral beliefs are controversial in this way. And so we should suspend belief about all moral matters.

Renford Brambrough, in his selection here, tries to rebut this traditional criticism. (I also try my hand at rebutting this argument in my article in Part I.) Brambrough argues that we must ensure that comparisons between moral and nonmoral knowledge are fair, and that when we do, we will see that moral knowledge fares no worse than nonmoral knowledge. It wouldn't do to impugn the possibility of scientific knowledge just because there are a number of unsolved scientific questions that engender controversy. After all, there are a great many scientific claims that garner near-universal consensus. But things are no different when it comes to morality. Discussions of moral knowledge often highlight the disputed cases, but there is also a great deal of near-unanimity on many moral matters – for instance, that it is wrong to deliberately withhold available anesthesia from a patient when performing a very painful surgery.

In his very interesting selection here, George Sher argues that it isn't the presence of widespread disagreement alone that generates problems for moral knowledge. Rather, it is this disagreement combined with what he calls *Contingency* – namely, the claim that we hold most of the moral beliefs we do largely as a result of accidents of birth and upbringing. Were we born in very different circumstances, or exposed to very different influences, we'd have very different moral beliefs from the ones we presently hold. This fact, combined with the existence of such broad ethical disagreement, casts doubt on the reliability of our moral beliefs.

Bambrough's article considers this objection, too, as well as a number of other traditional arguments for moral skepticism. His reply is, as before, to try to establish the parity between moral and nonmoral beliefs. It is true, says Bambrough, that we would have very different *nonmoral* beliefs from the ones we presently hold, were we to have been born or raised in very different circumstances from our actual ones. But just as that fact does not undermine our claims to ordinary nonmoral knowledge,

neither should it undermine our otherwise warranted claims to moral knowledge.

Still, we might ask why most of us are so confident of having at least some moral knowledge – that surgeons ought to use easily available anesthetics, that genocide and slavery are immoral, that offering nourishment and love to a starving child is a morally good thing. Shelly Kagan has an answer – namely, that we rely on our case-specific intuitions to serve as a basis, and a criterion, for establishing our network of justified moral beliefs. We have very strong convictions about cases, and though we needn't regard them as self-certifying, we do regard them as warranted starting points for ethical investigation. He is no doubt correct about the way in which we actually proceed in our moral justifications. Indeed, he doesn't see any other plausible way to proceed in trying to decide what is right and wrong. As Kagan argues, however, our reliance on such convictions may well fail to yield justified moral beliefs.

Kagan's doubts are rooted in a set of disanalogies drawn between the way in which we acquire justified empirical belief and the manner in which we come to hold the moral beliefs we do. The problem isn't that there is more disagreement in ethics than in science. Rather, the problem is that while we have some account of the reliability of empirical belief, we lack such an account in ethics. Certain of our empirical beliefs strike us immediately as being correct, and, further, we have a roughly coherent picture of the way the natural world works that explains how our senses are reliable indicators of its contents. Granted, certain of our moral beliefs, too, strike us immediately as being clearly correct. But here, claims Kagan, we lack a coherent overall theory of morality that underwrites our moral intuitions. Until we have a better-developed account of the moral world, and of the moral sense that would intuit its contours, it is doubtful that we are justified in relying on intuitions in the crucial ways we do when thinking about ethics.

Robert Audi's contribution to this section offers a detailed account and defense of ethical intuitionism, which seeks precisely to justify our reliance on our moral intuitions – our strongly held, non-inferentially formed moral beliefs. Intuitionism has a long history, and Audi traces some of it, while updating its formulation in several important ways. Intuitionism has frequently been relied on to solve the regress problem, an especially difficult skeptical worry about moral belief. The regress problem states that every justified moral belief requires supporting reasons that confer its justification. These reasons have to come from other beliefs. But these other beliefs will be either nonmoral or moral. They can't be nonmoral, since, following Hume, no moral belief is entailed by a nonmoral one. But the supporting beliefs cannot be moral, either, since any such supporting belief must itself be supported by yet other moral beliefs, and so on, and so on (this is the regress that gives the argument its name). Since moral beliefs require support, and no support can be offered, no moral beliefs are justified. Hence we cannot have any moral knowledge.

The ethical intuitionist solves this problem by denying that all justified moral beliefs must receive support from other beliefs. Rather, we are justified in believing some moral claims just because we understand them. Such beliefs are known as *self-evident* moral beliefs. Suppose you believe – as you very likely do – that it is immoral to torture children for the sole purpose of generating sadistic pleasure. Do you really need to introduce evidence in support of such a claim? All argument must stop somewhere. Intuitionists claim that some highly credible moral beliefs are satisfactory stopping points. That these beliefs may not garner universal consensus is neither here nor there. There are many truths, and some justified beliefs, that will not attract the endorsement of everyone. If some moral outliers fail to see the truth of certain moral claims, that reveals a defect in their understanding. It does not show that the self-evident beliefs require outside support. Nor does it undermine the status of such beliefs as self-evident.

The moral coherentist will have none of this. Coherentists, here represented by Geoffrey Sayre-McCord, claim that beliefs are justified if, and to the extent that, they cohere with one's other beliefs. No beliefs are self-evident. Sayre-McCord here provides a powerful argument against self-evidence. In a nutshell: we are justified in holding a belief only if we have reasons that support it; these reasons must come from other beliefs, and not the belief itself; therefore all epistemic justification must be inferential; therefore there are no self-evident beliefs. If a line of moral questioning cannot stop, though, with a self-evident belief, then how can we avoid an infinite regress? The coherentist argues that we need to abandon the idea of a wholly linear chain of justification, and instead consider that a belief can receive support, and in turn lend support to, a variety of other beliefs. So long as there is this mutual support, a belief is justified.

This of course looks like an endorsement of circular reasoning, since a belief's supporting evidence will consist of other beliefs whose justification is ultimately a matter of having received support from the initial belief under scrutiny. Coherentists reply that fans of self-evidence are no better off. Indeed, say coherentists, they are worse off, since self-evidence is the epitome of circular reasoning. To claim that a belief can provide evidence for itself is to use the very belief in question as its own support – a very small circle indeed.

The debate between fans of self-evidence and fans of coherentism represents a series of ongoing controversies in moral epistemology. Readers are well-advised to consider these arguments, and whether those of either side can adequately address the worries raised by Kagan and Sher.

CHAPTER 10
Thinking About Cases

SHELLY KAGAN

1. The Priority of Case Specific Intuitions

Anyone who reflects on the way we go about arguing for or against moral claims is likely to be struck by the central importance we give to thinking about cases. Intuitive reactions to cases – real or imagined – are carefully noted, and then appealed to as providing reason to accept (or reject) various claims. When trying on a general moral theory for size, for example, we typically get a feel for its overall plausibility by considering its implications in a range of cases. Similarly, when we try to refine the statement of a principle meant to cover a fairly specific part of morality, we guide ourselves by testing the various possible revisions against a carefully constructed set of cases (often differing only in rather subtle ways). And when arguing against a claim, we take ourselves to have shown something significant if we can find an intuitively compelling counterexample, and such counterexamples almost always take the form of a description of one or another case

Shelly Kagan, "Thinking About Cases," pp. 44–63 from Ellen Frankel Paul, Fred. D. Miller, Jr, and Jeffrey Paul (eds.), *Moral Knowledge*. Cambridge: Cambridge University Press, 2001. © Social Philosophy and Policy Foundation, reproduced with permission. Reprinted by permission of the author Shelly Kagan.

where the implications of the claim in question seem implausible. Even when we find ourselves faced with a case where we have no immediate and clear reaction, or where we have such a reaction, but others don't share it and we need to persuade them, in what is probably the most common way of trying to make progress we consider various analogies and disanalogies; that is to say, we appeal to still other cases, and by seeing what we want to say there, we discover (or confirm) what it is plausible to say in the original case. In these and other ways, then, the appeal to cases plays a central and ubiquitous role in our moral thinking.
[. . .]

Absent compelling reason to dismiss some particular intuition, most of us are inclined to give our intuitions about cases considerable weight. We trust them to a remarkable extent, using them, as I have already indicated, as the touchstones against which our various moral claims are to be judged. We take our intuitions about cases to constitute not only evidence, but compelling evidence indeed. I think it fair to say that almost all of us trust intuitions about particular cases over general theories, so that given a conflict between a theory – even one that seems otherwise attractive – and an intuitive judgment about a particular case that conflicts with that theory, we will almost always give priority to the intuition.
[. . .]

It is not at all clear to me what to make of this fact. Perhaps our pervasive and deep-seated reliance on intuitions about particular cases – what we might call "case specific intuitions" – is misguided. It is puzzling, at any rate, for it seems to me that although the extent to which we rely upon intuitions about cases is widely recognized, we don't yet have anything like an adequate account of our practice – that is, a careful description of the various ways in which we appeal to, and give priority to, our case specific intuitions. Nor, I think, do we have anything like an adequate justification of our practice. While it is obvious that we constantly appeal to our intuitions about cases, it is far from clear what, if anything, makes it legitimate for us to give these intuitions the kind of priority we typically give them.

One ("deflationary") possibility, of course, is that our reliance upon intuitions about particular cases is simply a reflection of a more general epistemic policy of relying on *all* of our various beliefs – and inclinations to believe – to the extent that we are confident about them. On such an account, all we could say is that we just happen to be especially confident about our various case specific intuitions; and while this might be a fact that would call for some sort of explanation (perhaps along evolutionary grounds), it would need no further *justification.* But the more ambitious epistemological alternative is to think that there is indeed some special justification for our reliance on case specific moral intuitions, something that warrants our particular confidence in them and our giving them the kind of priority that we do. I take it that most of us are actually drawn to this second view, and so the question remains whether there is in fact a plausible way to defend this idea, a way to justify our particular confidence in and reliance upon case specific intuitions.

II.   The Analogy to Empirical Observation

The closest we typically come, I think, to justifying this reliance on moral intuition is to appeal to a certain analogy. It is often suggested (and it is, at any rate, a natural suggestion to make) that we should think of case specific intuitions as playing a role in moral theory similar to that of *observation* in empirical theory. The suggestion, I presume, is sufficiently familiar that a bare sketch of the analogy should suffice.

Let's start with the role of observation. When arguing for or against empirical theories, we give unique weight to accommodating our observations of the world. We can simply see – immediately, and typically without further ado – that the liquid in the test tube has turned red or that the needle on the meter is pointing to 3, and an adequate empirical theory must take account of these facts. We appeal to such observations to provide support for a given theory, and we are very strongly inclined to reject any theory that runs afoul of them. Even a theory that seems otherwise attractive, and that strikes us as intuitively plausible in its own right, will be rejected if it contradicts the evidence provided by our empirical observations. To be sure, any given observation can itself be rejected (we might discover, for example, that we had unwittingly observed the test tube in red light), but for all that, no one seriously proposes that we should give no weight to our observations at all; and typically we give far greater priority to preserving the judgments of our observations than we do to maintaining our allegiance to any particular general empirical theory.

Similarly, then, when arguing for or against a moral theory we should think of our case specific intuitions as akin to observations. When thinking about particular cases we can simply see – immediately, and typically without further ado – whether, say, a given act would be right or wrong, or that it is morally relevant whether or not you have made a promise. An adequate moral theory must take account of these facts, it must accommodate these intuitions. To be sure, any given intuition can be challenged or rejected (we might, for example, realize that we made some judgment while inappropriately angry or embarrassed), but it would be quite implausible to suggest that we should give no weight to our moral intuitions at all. Indeed, even an otherwise plausible moral theory should be rejected if it contradicts the evidence provided by these intuitions; and so typically we appropriately give far greater priority to endorsing the judgments of intuition than we do to maintaining our allegiance to any particular general moral principle.

The analogy is indeed an appealing one, and it would be silly to dismiss it out of hand. But if we try to take it seriously certain points of disanalogy immediately suggest themselves. The most obvious worry – also familiar, and a natural one to think about – is this: in the case of empirical observation we have a tolerably good idea of how it is that the observations are produced. Visual observations depend upon the eyes, auditory observations depend upon the ears, and so forth. More generally, empirical observations depend upon the presence of well-functioning sense organs. In contrast, in the moral case, it is not at all obvious how it is that the corresponding "observations" – the moral intuitions – are produced. Is there a corresponding organ, a "moral sense," that is at work here? If so, it must be admitted that we know precious little about it.

Now this complaint must not be misunderstood. The main complaint about an appeal to a moral sense had better not be that we don't know how it *works*. For if that were the complaint it might not be especially worrisome. I take it, after all, that for most of human history we knew next to nothing about how the various sense organs worked either. But despite our ignorance, what was never in question was the existence of the various sense organs themselves (or that they were, indeed, sense organs). It was always fairly obvious, for example, that eyes were tied to visual observation, ears to auditory observation, and so on. In contrast, talk of a "moral sense" is nothing more than a place holder, a name for a supposed organ of moral intuition, something whose existence we may be led to infer (so as to have an account of the generation of moral intuitions), but concerning which we know virtually nothing else. And it is this, I take it, that gives us ground for skepticism, leaving us worried that there may be no such organ at all. Yet without a moral sense to correspond to the sense organs, the analogy to empirical observation is threatened.

Just how serious is the threat? Actually, this isn't at all obvious. Even if there were no moral sense, no organ generating moral intuitions, the rest of the analogy might still go through. We could still regard moral intuitions as "input" for our moral theories, in roughly the way that we let empirical observations function as input for empirical theories. Perhaps there is no single moral organ (or set of organs) corresponding to the sense organs; still, the fact of the matter is that we have the various intuitions and we can treat them as input, accommodating them and giving them priority in the way that empirical observations are accommodated and given priority.

In any event, given the undeniable fact that we do have our various moral intuitions, it is not clear what harm there is in simply going ahead and positing a moral sense in the first place. Presumably, *something* generates the intuitions – they do not arise out of thin air – and if we want to talk of the mechanism (or mechanisms) responsible for generating them as a "moral sense" or a "moral faculty" it is not clear what objection there can be to doing so, so long as we don't thereby presuppose anything further about the structure or inner workings of that faculty.

The important question, rather, is whether we have special reason to *trust* our moral intuitions. Whether or not we posit a moral sense, the question remains whether there is good reason to take our intuitive judgments as *evidence* in anything like the way we do. Even if there is a moral sense, an organ capable of generating moral intuitions, we still need to know whether it is more or less reliable.

It is precisely at this point, of course, that the analogy to empirical observation seems to beg the crucial question. After all, we all come to the discussion already convinced of the general reliability of the sense organs. (That is, we come to *this* discussion convinced of it; skepticism about the senses is not a worry we normally embrace when doing moral philosophy) Roughly speaking, then, we take the sense organs to be generally reliable, which is to say that empirical observations are generally reliable as well: *that* is why empirical theories must accommodate them. Similarly, then, once we make the assumption that our moral intuitions are generally reliable – that our moral sense, whatever it is, is generally reliable – then of course it will follow that our moral theories must accommodate our intuitions as well. But what justifies our assumption that our moral intuitions are reliable? Insofar as the analogy to empirical observation *presupposes* the reliability of our moral intuitions, it is not obvious how it can provide us with any reason to accept the claim that they are indeed reliable.

It is possible, however, that the analogy to empirical observation might still be found helpful, even here. For it might be suggested that our reasons for trusting our moral intuitions are analogous to our reasons for trusting the evidence of our senses.

Very well, then, what exactly *is* it that justifies us in thinking our empirical observations generally reliable in the first place? This is, of course, a complicated and much contested question, but at least one attractive answer begins by emphasizing the fact that we find ourselves strongly inclined to believe these observations – immediately, and without further ado – and so in the absence of a good reason to reject them, it is reasonable to (continue to) accept them. What's more, we are able to incorporate these observations into an overall attractive theory of the empirical world, one which admittedly rejects some of the observations as erroneous, but which for the most part endorses the claims of observation as correct. These two facts – the lack of reason for wholesale skepticism concerning our senses, and our ability to construct an overall theory that in the main endorses our observations – together go a considerable way toward justifying us in taking our senses to be reliable.

Of course, to say that our senses are reliable is to say more than that they *happen* to be accurate, that empirical observations happen to be true. It is to claim that this level of accuracy is nonaccidental, that there is a connection between the truth of the relevant claims and the fact that they are given by empirical observation. (Very roughly, the presumed connection is this: it is because of the fact that P is true that we make the empirical observation that P; and were it not the case that P, we would not "observe" that P.) As we normally put it, our sense organs *respond* to the underlying empirical realities (and do so accurately, of course).

[. . .]

But what justifies us in taking our sense organs to be not just (accidentally) accurate, but reliably responsive in this way? I suspect it is primarily the very two facts already noted: we are strongly and immediately inclined to believe our empirical observations, and we can offer an (admittedly incomplete) overall theory of the empirical world that largely endorses the claims of observation as correct.

Given these two facts, we are justified in believing that ultimately – even if not initially – an account will be forthcoming which will display the inner mechanics of the sense organs in such a way as to explain just how this responsiveness is accomplished (that is, how it is that the non-accidental connection between observation and fact is maintained). Of course, to believe that such an account can be produced is not yet to produce it. And eventually, no doubt, that promissory note must be made good: the account must indeed be produced. But I take it that our belief in the possibility of such an account can justifiably remain a mere promissory note for a good long time, since, as I have already noted, for much of human history we couldn't actually produce even the basic outlines of the relevant accounts. Still, given that we *were* able to produce an attractive overall theory of the empirical world that largely accommodated our empirical observations, it was nonetheless reasonable to conclude (albeit provisionally) that empirical observations are, indeed, not only accurate, but reliably so.

Analogously, then, it might be argued that we are also justified in taking our moral intuitions to be reliable. We certainly find ourselves strongly inclined to believe our moral intuitions – immediately, and without further ado – and so, in the absence of good reason to reject them, it is reasonable to (continue to) accept them. And if, going beyond this, we are also able to incorporate our intuitions into an overall attractive theory of morality, one which for the most part endorses these intuitions as correct, then even if the theory rejects some of the intuitions as erroneous, we will still be justified in taking our moral intuitions to be generally reliable.

Here too, of course, we will still find ourselves with a further explanatory obligation. If we are to justify our *reliance* on moral intuition it won't suffice if moral intuitions merely happen to be accurate: there must be, instead, a non-accidental connection between moral intuition and the underlying moral realities. Thus, we must believe that ultimately an account will be forthcoming that will display the inner mechanics of the moral sense in such a way as to reveal how it succeeds in being responsive to the moral "facts." Eventually, no doubt, we will need to make good on this promissory note, and produce the requisite account. But just as we were justified in taking sense organs to be reliably responsive, even though we lacked (for most of human history) an account of how it is that this responsiveness was accomplished, we may still be justified (for the time being) in taking our moral sense to be reliably responsive as well, even if we still lack an account of how *that* responsiveness is accomplished. In short, given the compelling nature of our immediate moral intuitions, and given the existence of an overall moral theory that largely accommodates those intuitions, we are justified in believing that the requisite account of the moral sense may yet be forthcoming. Which is to say: we are justified in taking intuition to be reliable.

If an answer along these lines is to be accepted, however, it is important to give due weight to the claim that our various moral intuitions can indeed be incorporated into an overall attractive theory of morality. For it is only if we are truly able to construct such a theory that we are entitled to take our moral intuitions to be reliable.

To see this, consider the case of empirical observation again, and imagine that we were unable to construct a theory of the empirical world which largely endorsed our empirical observations. We would then dismiss the evidence of our senses as unreliable – illusory, not to be trusted. After all, our sense organs can hardly be reliable if empirical observations are not generally accurate, but we are only justified in taking empirical observation to be accurate given our ability to construct a plausible theory of the empirical world that largely endorses the observations. Thus, if we were unable to construct such a theory, we would be forced to dismiss the evidence of our senses as inaccurate and unreliable.

The point can perhaps be put this way: the fact that we find ourselves immediately and unreflectively inclined to accept our empirical "observations" only gives us reason to accept these observations as reliable *given* that we have no reason to be skeptical of their accuracy. It provides only a presumptive argument for accepting them. But if we find that we cannot construct an overall theory of the empirical world that (in the main) endorses the observations, then this very failure provides us with good reason to be skeptical. The presumptive argument provided by the intuitive force of the observations is overcome. Similarly, then, in and of itself the mere fact that we find ourselves immediately and unreflectively inclined to accept our case specific moral intuitions provides us with only a presumptive argument for accepting them. If we were to discover that we could not actually construct an attractive overall moral theory that (in the main) endorses these intuitions, then this presumptive argument would be overcome, and we would have reason to be skeptical about our moral intuitions. So the question we must ask ourselves is this: can we indeed produce a moral theory that appropriately accommodates our moral intuitions, incorporating them into an overall theory of morality that is itself plausible and attractive?

I don't think the answer to this question is obvious, especially once we bear in mind that the requisite theory presumably must go beyond merely *organizing* the various "appearances," but must itself be sufficiently explanatory so as to provide at least the beginnings of an account of the relevant phenomena. Consider the empirical case, yet again: we are satisfied that the requisite theory of the empirical world can indeed be produced, but we would not be satisfied if all we could do was organize our various empirical observations into systematic patterns. Instead, what we want, and what we take ourselves to be able to produce, is a theory that goes below the surface and provides something of an explanation of the empirical phenomena that are the subject matter of our empirical observations. We offer, that is, a theory of objects in space and time, interacting with one another and with ourselves, a theory that begins to explain how it is that the empirical world can have the particular features reported in our observations.

Similarly, then, in looking for a moral theory that will accommodate our case specific moral intuitions, it won't suffice if all we can do is organize these intuitions into systematic patterns. Instead, what we need to find is a moral theory that goes below the surface and provides at least the beginnings of an explanation of the moral phenomena that are the subject matter of our moral intuitions. That is to say: we need a theory that offers at least the outlines of an explanation of how the moral domain can indeed have the particular features ascribed by our various intuitions. What I take to be far from obvious is whether we can in fact produce an overall moral theory that is sufficiently explanatory in this way, while still accommodating the bulk of our moral intuitions.

Of course, the difficulty of this task will depend on at least two further issues: first, the precise content of the moral intuitions we are trying to accommodate, and second, the standards we impose concerning what will constitute an explanatorily adequate moral theory. Unfortunately, pursuing either of these issues here would take us too far afield. But let me register the following skeptical note. I have argued elsewhere[1] that, in point of fact, certain widely accepted views – views central to commonsense morality and supported by the case specific intuitions of a great many individuals – cannot be provided with the kind of theoretical underpinnings we are here calling for. If I am right about this, then despite the immediate appeal of the relevant intuitions, they cannot be incorporated into an adequate overall moral theory, and in this regard, at least, our moral intuitions are unreliable.

I realize, of course, that many people would reject the particular arguments I've previously offered concerning the impossibility of providing an appealing and coherent moral theory that endorses these common moral intuitions. It is important to note, however, that in at least some cases the rejection of these arguments would simply take the form of pointing out how counterintuitive the implications of these arguments are, and in the present context, at least, such an appeal to intuition would

constitute begging the question. For insofar as we are trying to establish whether our case specific moral intuitions are to be trusted or not, a simple appeal to the *force* of these intuitions shows nothing. We are only justified in trusting our intuitions if we can indeed construct a moral theory that adequately explains and incorporates them, and this, of course, is precisely what I am saying we cannot do. Thus, the mere fact that the conclusions for which I have argued are incompatible with many forceful and widely held intuitions does nothing to show that the requisite moral theory *can* be constructed. Indeed, as I have already noted, I think there are good reasons to conclude that we cannot, in fact, produce the requisite moral theory.

III. Error Theories

Let's recap. We have been taking seriously the analogy between moral intuitions and empirical observations, so as to see what might justify our practice of giving our case specific intuitions the kind of priority that we do. I have been suggesting, of course, that if we are to be justified in trusting our intuitions in this way, there must be an explanatorlly adequate moral theory that endorses (not all, but most of) our case specific intuitions, just as we take ourselves to be justified in trusting our empirical observations by virtue of having an explanatorily adequate empirical theory that endorses (most of) our empirical observations. And as I have already noted, my own opinion is that once we take seriously the need to construct a general moral theory that would endorse our case specific intuitions as being for the most part accurate, we will find it difficult, indeed impossible, to produce the requisite theory. Theories that attempt to accommodate the bulk of our various case specific intuitions fall, I believe, at one or another explanatory task, and fall short in overall plausibility. What we are led to, instead, is a general moral theory according to which many of our specific moral intuitions are simply mistaken.

If I am right about this, then at a minimum we will have reason to be skeptical about these particular common moral intuitions. More generally, however, and for our current purposes more importantly, we will have reason to conclude as well that moral intuition is not, on the whole, reliable. Instead, the appropriate stance to take toward our moral intuitions will involve accepting an *error theory*, according to which at least many of our case specific moral intuitions are mistaken.

Of course, there are various kinds of error theories – some more radical than others – and we've not yet addressed the question of whether our moral intuitions need to be discounted altogether. At one extreme lies just such wholesale skepticism concerning our case specific moral intuitions. But more modest versions of error theories are possible as well, and it might be that our best overall moral theory still endorses some specified range of moral intuitions, while nonetheless writing off other classes of intuitions as mistaken.

However, even such moderate error theories will seem unattractive to many. They will hold, correctly, that to accept an error theory – even a modest one – is to retreat significantly from our current practice, where appeals to intuition are generally taken across the board to be a particularly important source of evidence concerning the moral domain.

And so, despite my own skepticism, many will insist on remaining optimistic about the prospects for constructing a moral theory that actually succeeds quite generally in accommodating our case specific intuitions. They will want to reject any error theoretic approach to moral intuition at all. They will claim that our moral intuitions are, in point of fact, typically accurate, and that we are justified in thinking that it is nonaccidental that this is so. Thus, they will insist that we are justified in taking moral intuition to be reliable.

There are, however, still further grounds for skepticism about the overall reliability of our moral intuitions that we have not yet considered. What I have in mind is the surprising – and typically overlooked – extent to which people's intuitions actually differ with regard to specific cases. The extent of the disagreement is overlooked for the simple reason that we normally don't *look* for such disagreement. We barely entertain the possibility that others may not agree with us, and so we typically don't look around very carefully to see just how widely shared our particular intuitions actually are. And when we do stumble upon such cases of intuitive disagreement, it surprises us. Our own intuitions are sufficiently compelling and powerful that the relevant judgments strike us as virtually self-evident, and we are, accordingly, shocked if other, apparently reasonable individuals don't share them.

I do not mean to suggest, of course, that intuitive disagreements arise with regard to every case, though it does seem to me – based on years of discussing such cases with students and others – that even the most compelling examples typically fall short of garnering complete agreement. And in many cases, I think, once one probes a bit one finds that there is actually a considerable amount of disagreement. Consider, for example, "trolley problems" of the kind frequently used to determine the precise nature of the prohibition against harming others.[2] In my own classes I generally find that only about three fourths of the students share the majority intuition (say, that it is permissible to turn the trolley), while up to a fourth disagree; and even the apparent agreement of the three fourths majority dissolves when one asks further questions (for example, whether one is required, or only permitted, to turn the trolley).

To be sure, it is difficult to be confident that the opinions being reported in such informal polls truly state the immediate moral intuitions of the students in my classes. As we have already noted, we need to distinguish between the immediate pronouncements of our case specific intuitions and the various beliefs about a case one might have instead (for example, as a result of conscious reflection). In short, when students vote in such polls, are they reporting moral intuitions, or simply stating their own tentative beliefs about the cases? It might well be that despite the existence of widespread disagreement in opinions about the relevant cases, there is actually far greater agreement with regard to the immediate intuitions themselves.

This is certainly a possibility, and I don't mean to suggest that I conduct my polls with sufficient care to rule it out. (It would be useful to have some careful empirical studies of these matters.) Still, it seems to me likely that intuitive disagreement is indeed a fairly widespread phenomenon.

What's more, I suspect that such disagreement is far from a random affair. It is not that any given individual almost always agrees with the majority, but sporadically finds himself faced with an idiosyncratic intuition, one as much at odds with the rest of his own intuitions (at other times, or in other cases) as it is at odds with the majority. If this were the nature of intuitive disagreement, we might well feel free to write off the occasional, quirky intuition as a mere aberration – a random misfiring in an otherwise reliable moral sense. In fact, however, it seems to me that moral disagreement is systematic and patterned. A given individual is likely to be regularly responsive to certain features that cases might display, while other individuals are routinely indifferent to the presence (or absence) of those features, or react to them in quite different ways. In short, intuitive disagreement doesn't take the form of norm and aberration, Rather, it is as though moral senses fall into distinct types, each with its own regular pattern of intuitive responses.

If I am right about this, obviously enough, it greatly complicates the position of anyone who hopes to endorse moral intuitions as largely correct. For if people actually differ considerably as to the content of those intuitions, even when thinking about the very same cases, then clearly not everyone's intuitions can be largely reliable. So what should we say?

One possibility, I suppose, would be to hold that everyone's intuition is indeed reliable, but only in those areas where there is complete agreement (assuming that such an area of complete agreement is to be found at all). But if we do say this, then we face the difficult task of explaining why intuition is indeed reliable in exactly those areas. What is it about the areas of agreement that makes intuition there function properly, and what is it about the other areas that causes intuition to break down and malfunction? Apparently, even those who hope to endorse moral intuition to this limited extent require an error theory, and an error theory of a fairly subtle sort, for they need to explain why intuition malfunctions in certain areas while

working reliably in others. Absent a story about the mechanics of moral intuitions – the workings of the moral sense – any confidence that intuition is indeed to be trusted at all, even where there is agreement, may seem strained or premature.

More ambitiously still, some might hold out the hope of justifying reliance upon moral intuition even in those cases (considerable, as I believe) where there is intuitive disagreement. Clearly, however, this requires dismissing as flawed the moral senses of all those who stand in intuitive disagreement with the intuitions being endorsed. At best, the moral intuitions of only certain individuals can be held to be generally reliable. For the rest, then, we will inevitably need to embrace an error theory of a different sort: we will require an account which explains how most (or at least many) people end up with unreliable moral intuitions, while the moral sense of others nonetheless ends up functioning properly and reliably. And we will need an epistemological account as well, so as to justify us in our position concerning just whose intuition is to be trusted as reliable. (Obviously, it won't do to simply assume without further ado that it is *mine* that functions properly.)

This is not to say that these various explanatory burdens could not possibly be met. Once again, empirical observation provides a helpful analogy, for we do find ourselves, in the case of color blindness, arguing for something at least roughly comparable. Certain individuals are said to have damaged or flawed visual senses – leading to inaccurate visual observations, in at least a specifiable range of cases – while the rest of us are held to have properly functioning and reliable visual senses nonetheless. If something like this can be plausibly held to occur in the case of empirical observation, why not in the case of moral intuition as well? Is it so implausible to think that certain individuals are "morally blind" – cursed with inaccurate moral intuitions, in at least a specifiable range of cases?

The analogy to color blindness certainly suggests that something similar might arise in the case of moral intuition as well. But it is one thing to admit the mere possibility of something like this, it is quite another to make good on the claim that "moral blindness" actually occurs, and still another thing to warrant applying this label to some particular individual. In the case of color blindness, after all, we are able to demonstrate, even to the satisfaction of the color blind themselves, that their visual apparatus is indeed impaired, and that they fail to respond accurately to genuine features of the empirical world, features that the rest of us are able to detect through our own unimpaired visual senses. It is far from clear whether anything analogous can be done in the case of disagreement of moral intuitions, or even how one would go about trying to make out a comparable case. Instead, the charge of moral blindness more typically seems little more than name calling, where we blithely dismiss the intuitions of those who disagree with us, assuming without any further evidence than the mere fact of the disagreement itself that it is they who are blind, rather than us.[3]

I have been arguing that given the nature of intuitive moral disagreement, no one, not even those who hope to endorse moral intuition as generally reliable, can escape the need to accept some kind of error theory with regard to at least many moral intuitions. And I have suggested as well that until we produce at least the beginnings of a story about the mechanics of moral intuition it is difficult to be confident that the requisite error theory can be produced. Attempts to limit the error theory – so that it impugns only a certain range of intuitions, or a certain group of moral senses – may easily fail, so that we are left with no good reason to believe our moral intuitions to be especially reliable at all.

But I do not mean to suggest that matters are particularly easier for those who hope to embrace far more radical error theories, dismissing most, or all, of our moral intuitions as suspect. For the fact is, producing a plausible error theory even of this radical sort is extremely difficult as well.

Consider, for example, the suggestion that is sometimes made that our case specific intuitions can be dismissed out of hand, as the mere historical by product of outdated religious views or neuroses about sex, or that they are merely the results of internalizing

dubious moral teachings received in childhood. Were this the case, there might well be little reason to give any weight at all to our case specific moral intuitions, and the wiser course of action would be to attempt to elaborate moral theories simply without appeal to them, however difficult that might prove to be.

But although accounts along these lines may well rightly cast doubt upon certain case specific intuitions (say, about sex), they seem rather inadequate as general explanations of the origins of our moral intuitions. Consider again the appeal to trolley problems as a means of determining the precise content of the prohibition against harming. Such cases are highly stylized, and unlike anything most of us have ever faced in real life, read about, or even imagined before being introduced to them for the first time as adults. Yet once the given case is described, we typically find ourselves with a moral intuition about it. I think it highly implausible, accordingly, to suggest that what happens here is that some vestige of a (perhaps forgotten) religious teaching now comes into play. No one is taught about trolley problems in childhood – nor even anything remotely similar to them – and yet we still find ourselves with intuitive reactions to the cases once they are described. Thus, whatever the actual origins of these case specific intuitions, we cannot dismiss them as artifacts of outmoded or unjustified teachings and accidental historical influences. For the simple fact of the matter is that most of our case specific intuitions cannot be plausibly explained in this way.

We may do somewhat better if we appeal, instead, to some of the primitive beliefs about physics or the nature of agency that we may well inherit as a result of our evolutionary history, as well as to certain innate psychological biases in terms of how to group people and events. An error theory that dismisses (many of) our case specific intuitions on the ground that they are implicitly based on inherited but dubious physical theories may well have an easier time of it explaining how we can have immediate and intuitive reactions to trolley cases, say, despite never having considered such cases previously. We may, for example, react to a given case as we do because we are innately disposed to view it in terms of mistaken concepts of causation and agency.

Here, too, such an account may rightly cast doubt upon certain of our case specific moral intuitions. But even an account of this sort seems inadequate, in large part because of the very universality of the inherited biases and beliefs that it presupposes. If our case specific intuitions are to be explained in terms of innate (though false) views about physics, say, then we would expect that people's intuitions would be fairly uniform – all reflecting the same set of inherited, though dubious, physical beliefs or psychological dispositions. In fact, however, as I have already suggested, it seems to me that we differ from one another in terms of our moral intuitions, in ways that this sort of account cannot easily accommodate. Intuitive disagreement is widespread and systematic, and it is implausible to dismiss our case specific intuitions on the ground that they are based on shared, inherited – and false! – views about the world, if in point of fact many of the relevant intuitions are not universally shared at all.

An error theory adequate to the facts about our moral intuitions would apparently have to be a rather subtle affair. It would need to accommodate the simple fact that we readily have intuitive reactions to cases quite unlike anything that we have faced or been taught about previously, and yet at the same time it would need to accommodate the fact that when we think about such cases our intuitive reactions are not all the same: people's intuitions differ, in systematic and patterned ways. It is not at all obvious what such an error theory would look like.[4]

I don't mean to suggest, however, that it will be impossible to produce an error theory adequate to the facts. Indeed, if I am right that everyone needs an error theory of some sort – both those on the whole trusting of moral intuition, and those on the whole skeptical of it – then it seems inevitable that *some* sort of error theory must be right, and I see no particular reason to assume that we cannot eventually articulate and defend this theory, whatever it is. But for the time being, at any rate, it seems to me that we are rather far from having an adequate account of what this theory looks like, and so, lacking it, we are rather far

from knowing to what extent our moral intuitions can be trusted.

IV. Particular Cases and General Claims

Let me close by noting one further complication. Recall the fact, previously noted, that our moral intuition is capable of responding not only to particular cases but also to general moral principles and moral theories. Consider how different this is from the case of empirical observation, where all we can directly observe are the features of particular cases. I can simply see that the meter is pointing to 3, but I cannot simply see the truth of Ohm's law or other principles of physics at all. General empirical claims must be inferred from the evidence; one cannot simply observe their truth. Apparently, our sense organs are incapable of responding directly to general empirical truths in this way.

In itself, this may be no more than a striking disanalogy between the case of moral intuition and the case of empirical observation. But it points to a deeper problem. For we have also already noted the fact that we do not give the same kind of priority to our intuitions about general moral claims. What we particularly trust, rather, are our case specific intuitions, so that given a conflict between an intuition about a particular case and an intuition about a general moral claim, we are almost always inclined to endorse the intuition about the particular case (at least, insofar as what we are attending to is the evidential force of the intuitions themselves). We give priority not to intuition in general, but, more particularly, to our case specific intuitions.

Yet how is this fact to be explained? If the situation were like that of empirical observation – with the relevant sense only capable of responding directly to particular cases rather than to general principles as well – there would, of course, be nothing further *to* explain (although, no doubt, we would ultimately want to explain just why it is that the given sense can respond only to particulars). But given that moral intuition is capable of reacting both to particular cases and to general principles, we do need a further explanation: we need to understand just why it should be the case that intuition is particularly reliable only with regard to specific cases. What makes our intuition more reliable for the one sort of object rather than the other?

Once we put the question this way, however, it may seem that the answer won't be particularly hard to come by. Even if moral intuition (unlike empirical observation) is capable of reacting both to particular cases and to general claims, there is no particular reason to assume that it will be equally adept at handling both *kinds* of objects. Although, no doubt, the details of the explanation will need to await a theory of the inner mechanics of moral sense, there is nothing particularly perplexing in the claim that intuition reacts more reliably when directed to one particular kind of object.

But this reassuring answer is itself threatened by the realization that this very distinction between two *kinds* of objects for intuition may well be misguided. For the fact of the matter, I believe, is that when we react to particular cases we are actually reacting to things of the very same type as when we react to general moral claims. It is easy to lose sight of this, given our common practice – one that I have followed in this paper as well – of saying that we are reacting to *particular* cases. But what we are actually reacting to, I think, are *types* of cases.

This is easiest to see in the situation where the kind of case we are thinking about is purely imaginary. What we are presented with, then, is only a description – and typically, all things considered, a fairly thin description at that. There is no actual, particular, concrete case that we are confronted with. So when our intuition tells us, say, that some particular act would be the right thing to do in that particular case, what we are actually intuiting, it seems, is that a certain *kind* of act would be the right thing to do in a certain *kind* of case. And this, of course, is a general moral claim.

The same thing is true, I think, even when the particular case being judged is an actual one. Again, this is easiest to see if the case, despite being real, is not one that we actually observe. We might only be *told* about the case, which means, of course, that we are again presented with a mere description. But this means, I take it, that we are not actually reacting to a particular, concrete case, but rather to a *type* of case. So here, too, when we react to the case what we are actually intuitively responding to is, it seems, something general: we are intuitively seeing that, say, this kind of act would be the right thing to do in this kind of case.

Although the point is controversial, I think the same is probably true even in those situations where we are literally faced with an actual, concrete case. Even in cases like this, I suspect that what we are actually responding to is its being a case with various salient features. By virtue of being literally faced with the case – able to observe it for ourselves – we better come to see that it has certain features, and we then intuit that the right thing to do, given a case with *these* features, is such and such. But if that is right, then here, too, we are reacting to something general: we are seeing that such and such an act is the right thing to do in this *kind* of case.

This is not to deny that being actually presented with a concrete case may elicit a different intuitive reaction than merely being presented with a description of the case. (When we literally *see* the needs of others we may intuitively see the importance of helping them, in a way that no mere description of their needs would elicit.) But even if it is true that in such cases there can be something special about intuition in the face of genuinely concrete particulars, the fact would remain that typically when we think about cases, we are only thinking about *kinds* of cases. Which is to say, typically when we think about cases we are intuitively reacting to something general.

This makes it harder to explain the priority we want to give to our intuitive reactions to "particular" cases. If all, or at least most, case specific intuitions are not actually reactions to something concrete and particular at all, then we cannot readily claim that what makes intuition more reliable here is that it is directed at a different kind of object than when we intuitively respond to a general moral claim. In both cases, it seems, what we see is something general.

Of course, there will still be differences in degrees of generality, and it might be that what we should give priority to are our intuitive reactions to the less general rather than to the more general. But this, too, calls out for explanation, and it is not clear what could be said in its defense.

For when we face the fact that typically (at least) when we think about a case, we are indeed only *thinking* about it, we are reminded of the fact that intuitive reactions are, in some suitably broad sense of the term, *a priori*. Typically, at least, we don't need to actually see the case; we only need to think about it. But it is not, as far as I can see, a general feature of the *a priori* that such thoughts are more reliable when they are directed to the less general rather than the more general. So it remains unclear why moral intuition should be thought particularly reliable in just such cases.

V. Conclusion

I have been arguing that our reliance upon case specific moral intuitions is problematic, and in need of a justification that we do not yet posses. Most importantly, of course, anyone who is going to rely on intuition at all – and that, I think, means all of us – needs to explain exactly why we are justified in taking intuition to be particularly reliable in the first place. This is a justificatory burden that has not, I think, been satisfactorily discharged. In particular, despite the obvious appeal of an analogy to the case of empirical observation, there are, it seems, sufficient disanalogies here, so that at a minimum considerably more needs to be said. Furthermore, if, as I think, we must all accept some sort of error theory (whether modest or radical) with regard to moral intuition, then we must face the further fact that providing an adequate error theory is itself a surprisingly difficult task. Apparently, our reliance upon intuition must be tempered; but how, or in what ways, is not yet clear.

In sum, the extent to which intuition is to be trusted – if at all – remains unsettled. Our reliance upon moral intuition remains troubling.

Still, the fact remains as we I that despite these questions we are all inclined to attend to our case specific intuitions. We worry when our moral beliefs run afoul of them and we take comfort in the extent to which our moral beliefs accord with them. It may well be, as I believe, that our moral intuition deserves considerably less respect than it is normally accorded. But it is difficult to believe that we could ever make do without it altogether. No moral argument – no claim, no theory – will ever seem compelling if it has not been subjected to the testing we provide when we think about cases.

Notes

1. See, especially, Shelly Kagan, *The Limits of Morality* (Oxford: Oxford University Press, 1989).

2. In the basic case, a runaway trolley will hit and kill five children, unless you throw a switch which will divert the trolley onto a side track, saving the five, but killing a sixth child trapped on that side track (who would otherwise be safe). A large number of variants of this basic case have been discussed. See, e.g., Judith Jarvis Thomson, "Killing, Letting Die, and the Trolley Problem," in Thomson, *Rights, Restitution, and Risk*, 78–93; and Frances Kamm, "Harming some to Save Others," *Philosophical Studies* 57, no. 3 (1989); 227–60.

3. The situation is further complicated by the fact that *each* side may fall to respond to features that the other side's intuitions mark out as morally significant. Thus, unlike the normal case of color blindness, moral disagreement may actually be closer to a situation in which many groups claim to see one or more colors that some other groups do not, and yet each group still fails to see some of the colors that other groups claim to see.

4. It might seem that an emotivist or expressivist account of moral claims would have an easy time accommodating these facts, since there is nothing especially surprising in the suggestion that people's emotional (and other) attitudes vary, and that they can be readily generated in response to never before considered cases. But even accounts of this kind, it seems to me, should be troubled by the ease and force with which intuitions can be generated in response to trolley problems (and the like) since it is not at all obvious why these should so readily engage our emotions or other pro-attitudes, nor why minor changes in the cases should elicit such drastically altered reactions.

CHAPTER 11

But I Could Be Wrong

GEORGE SHER

I. Introduction

My aim in this essay is to explore the implications of the fact that even our most deeply held
moral beliefs have been profoundly affected by
our upbringing and experience – that if any of
us had a sufficiently different upbringing and
set of experiences, he almost certainly would
now have a very different set of moral beliefs
and very different habits of moral judgment.
This fact, together with the associated proliferation of incompatible moral doctrines, is
sometimes invoked in support of liberal policies of toleration and restraint, but the relevance of these considerations to individual
moral deliberation has received less attention.
In Sections II through V, I shall argue that this
combination of contingency and controversy
poses a serious challenge to the authority of
our moral judgments. In Section VI, I shall
explore a promising way of responding to this
challenge.

George Sher, "But I Could Be Wrong," pp. 64–78 from
Social Philosophy & Policy, 18(2), 2001. © Social Philosophy
and Policy Foundation, reproduced with permission. Reprinted by permission of the author George Sher.

II. The Challenge to My Moral Judgments

In Chapter II of *On Liberty*, John Stuart Mill
observes that the person who uncritically
accepts the opinion of "the world"

> devolves upon his own world the responsibil-
> ity of being in the right against the dissentient
> worlds of other people; and it never troubles
> him that mere accident has decided which of
> these numerous worlds is the object of his
> reliance, and that the same causes which
> made him a churchman in London would
> have made him a Buddhist or a Confucian in
> Peking.[1]

Along similar lines, John Rawls observes in
Political Liberalism that the "burdens of judgment" that make moral disagreement inevitable include the fact that

> to some extent (how great we cannot tell) the
> way we assess evidence and weight moral and
> political values is shaped by our total experi-
> ence, our whole course of life up to now; and
> our total experiences must always differ.[2]

Despite their sketchiness, both passages appear
to contain much truth. Moreover, the two passages are complementary in that Mill emphasizes the influence of contingent factors on the

content of a person's most basic religious (and, by extension, moral and philosophical) convictions, while Rawls focuses more on the influence that contingent factors have on the inferences and judgments that a person makes *within* his basic framework. Thus, taken together, the two passages suggest that the influence of contingent factors on moral judgment is certainly extensive and may well be pervasive.

The principles that Mill and Rawls are defending in these passages are not the same: the passage from Mill appears in his famous defense of freedom of speech, while Rawls's point is that in a pluralistic society, a conception of justice must be defensible in terms accessible to all. However, each of these principles purports to provide a reason not to act in all the ways that initially appear to be called for by one's moral beliefs. This is why Mill and Rawls are both comfortable invoking a consideration – the influence of contingent factors on our moral beliefs – which, if taken seriously, is bound to undermine our confidence in the truth or rational defensibility of these moral beliefs.

But the same consideration that is so congenial to liberal principles that require us to distance ourselves from our moral beliefs in political contexts is decidedly uncongenial to our efforts to marshal these moral beliefs when we deliberate as individuals. My awareness that I would now have different moral convictions if I had a different upbringing or different experiences may make it easier for me to put my moral beliefs out of play in the interest of allowing competing beliefs a fair hearing, or for the sake of arriving at terms of social cooperation acceptable to all. This same awareness, however, makes it correspondingly *harder* for me to act on my moral convictions when these conflict with the moral convictions of others. There is an obvious tension between my belief that my moral assessment of a situation is right while yours is wrong and my further belief that it is only an accident of fate that I assess the situation in my way rather than yours.

This tension raises questions about what I have reason to do in various practical interpersonal contexts. Perhaps most obviously, it raises such questions when I take myself to be morally justified in treating you in a way that

you find morally objectionable – when, for example, I think I am not obligated to finance your dubious business venture despite our long friendship, or when you demand attention that I feel I do not owe. The tension also muddies the waters when you and I disagree about something we must do together – when, for example, I want to give our failing student a retest but you worry about fairness to other students, or when we disagree about how much of our joint income we should donate to charity. It even raises doubts when I am contemplating taking some action that will not affect you at all, but of which you morally disapprove – when, for example, I am considering joining the Marines, contributing to a pro-choice candidate, or taking spectacular revenge on a hated rival, but you offer dissenting counsel. In all of the aforementioned contexts, my awareness that I might well have taken a position like yours if my history had been sufficiently different will not sit well with my belief that I have more reason to act on my moral beliefs than I have to act on yours.

Why, exactly, do these beliefs not sit well together? The answer, I think, is that my belief that I have more reason to act on my own moral beliefs than on yours appears to rest on a further belief that my own moral beliefs are somehow *better* – that they are truer, more defensible, more reasonable, or something similar. However, if I believe that it is only an accident of history that I hold my own moral beliefs rather than yours, then I must also believe that which of us has the better moral beliefs is also an accident of history. This of course does not mean that my belief that my own moral beliefs are better is wrong or baseless, but it does mean that I would have that same belief even if it *were* wrong or baseless. However, once I realize that I would have this belief whether or not it were true, I no longer seem entitled to use it in my practical deliberations.

III. The Challenge Not a Form of Skepticism

As just presented, the problems raised by the contingent origins of our moral beliefs bear a striking similarity to certain familiar skeptical worries. There is, in particular, an obvious affinity between the claim advanced at the end of the preceding section – that we are not in a position to tell whether we hold our moral beliefs because they are defensible or true or merely because of our upbringing – and the standard skeptical claim that we are not in a position to tell whether we hold our empirical beliefs because they represent reality accurately or merely because they have been instilled in us by an evil demon or a mad scientist stimulating a brain in a vat. Thus, isn't the current problem merely a special case of a far more general skeptical challenge – a challenge whose force we all acknowledge, but with which we long ago learned to coexist?

There is both something right and something wrong about this suggestion. What is right is its premise that the current problem has the same abstract structure as a very common form of skepticism; what is wrong is its conclusion that we can therefore live with the current problem as easily as we can live with skepticism. In fact, for three reasons, the current problem is far more vexing and urgent.

First, unlike the standard skeptical hypotheses, the claim that each person's moral beliefs were shaped by his upbringing and life experiences has an obvious basis in fact. We have no evidence at all that any of our empirical beliefs were caused by an evil demon or a mad scientist; and even the hypothesis that I am now dreaming, though somewhat more realistic, is improbable in light of the low frequency with which experiences with all the marks of wakefulness – vividness, continuity, coherence, self-consciousness, and the rest – have in the past turned out to be dreams. Thus, the most that any skeptical hypothesis can show is that all of our beliefs about the world *might* have had causes that operate independently of the truth of what we believe. In stark contrast, however, the fact that people's moral beliefs vary systematically with their backgrounds and life experiences shows considerably more, for in becoming aware of this, I acquire a positive reason to suspect that when you and I disagree about what morality demands, my taking the position I do has less to do with the superiority of my moral insight than with the nature of the causes that have operated on me.

The second reason that the current problem is harder to live with than is general skepticism is that we have significant second-order reason to be confident in our shared empirical beliefs, but no corresponding second-order reason to be confident in our controversial moral beliefs. In the case of our shared empirical beliefs, the second-order reason for confidence is provided by the various background theories that imply the reliability, within broad limits, of the processes through which these beliefs were formed – physiological theories about the mechanisms through which our sensory receptors put us in contact with the world, biological theories that imply that reliable belief-forming mechanisms have survival value, and so on. Even if appealing to these theories begs the question against global skepticism, our acceptance of them still makes such skepticism easier to ignore by reinforcing the confidence that we feel in our empirical beliefs when we are not contemplating the skeptical challenge. By contrast, my acceptance of the same background theories does not similarly reinforce my confidence that my own moral beliefs are better than yours, for because the theories imply the reliability of belief-forming mechanisms that are common to all members of our species, they provide no basis for any distinctions *among* individuals. Indeed, if anything, my awareness that a different upbringing and set of experiences would have caused me to acquire a different set of moral beliefs provides evidence that the processes through which I acquired my actual moral beliefs are probably *not* reliable.

Even by themselves, these two reasons would suggest that the current problem is much harder to live with than is general skepticism. However, a third reason makes the case even more strongly. Simply put, the most serious obstacle to our bracketing the current problem in the same way we routinely bracket skepticism is that unlike the fabrications of the skeptic, the current challenge to our moral beliefs is directly relevant to action.

For, as is often remarked, the hypotheses that all of my beliefs are being orchestrated by an evil demon or a master neuromanipulator, or that I am now dreaming, have no obvious impact either on what I *ought* to do or on what I am *inclined* to do. Even if I were able to suspend my commonsense beliefs, my awareness that various types of experience have been regularly connected in the past might well justify my "acting" as if the world were exactly as it seemed; and, in any case, suspending my commonsense beliefs in practical contexts is not a live option. As Hume famously observed, even if I find skepticism convincing in the isolation of my study, I will, as soon as I emerge, "find myself absolutely and necessarily determined to live, and talk, and act like other people in the common affairs of life."[3] When it comes time to act, our robust animal realism will always dominate.

But not so our corresponding tendency to *moral* realism, for although we standardly do proceed as though our moral convictions are in some sense true, our confidence in their truth is neither anchored in our animal nature (since nonhuman animals evidently do not share it) nor invulnerable to reflective challenge. Because this confidence is relatively superficial, we cannot assume that it would survive a compelling demonstration that it cannot be defended. There is, to be sure, a real question about what it would be rational for me to do if I did lose confidence in my own moral beliefs – I would, after all, have exactly the same grounds for doubt about your moral beliefs as I would about mine – but at a minimum, this loss of confidence would reopen many questions that my own moral beliefs were previously thought to settle. Because of this, the challenge to the authority of my moral judgments seems capable of destabilizing my practical deliberation in a way that general skepticism cannot.

IV.   The Interplay of Controversy and Contingency

As just presented, the challenge to the authority of my moral judgments has a dual focus, for it appears to rest both on a premise about moral disagreement and on a premise about the contingent origins of my moral beliefs and ways of assessing evidence and weighting competing values. (For brevity, I shall henceforth refer to the combination of a person's moral beliefs and

his ways of assessing evidence and weighting values as his *moral outlook*.) Respectively, these premises are as follows:

(1)   I often disagree with others about what I morally ought to do.

(2)   The moral outlook that supports my current judgment about what I ought to do has been shaped by my upbringing and experiences; for (just about) any alternative judgment, there is some different upbringing and set of experiences that would have caused me to acquire a moral outlook that would in turn have supported this alternative judgment.

These premises are logically distinct – it could be true that you and I disagree about what one of us ought to do but false that our backgrounds have shaped our moral outlooks, or true that our backgrounds have shaped our moral outlooks but false that we disagree. [. . .] having the moral outlook that informs my specific moral judgments is unlikely to have much to do with that outlook's justifiability or truth. [. . .]

To give the challenge to the authority of my moral judgments the strongest possible run for its money, we cannot represent it as resting exclusively on either (1) or (2). Just as the version of the challenge that begins by appealing to (1) is unlikely to succeed without supplementation by (2), the version that begins by appealing to (2) is unlikely to succeed without supplementation by (1). Hence, no matter where we start, we will end by concluding that (1) and (2) work best when they work together.[4]

V.   The Role of Reflection

How well, though, *does* the combined appeal to (1) and (2) work? Must I really accept its corrosive implication that I often have no better reason to rely on my own moral judgments than on the judgments of those with whom I strongly disagree? Are (1) and (2) both firmly enough grounded to support this disturbing conclusion?

There is, I think, little point in contesting (1), for its claim that I often disagree with others about what I morally ought to do is all too obviously true. However, when we turn to (2)'s claim that I would now view my moral obligations differently if my upbringing and experiences had been sufficiently different, the issue becomes more complicated. Briefly put, the complication is that although a person's upbringing and experiences clearly do cause him to acquire various moral beliefs and habits of judgment, these cannot be assumed to persist unaltered over time. No less than any other beliefs and habits, our moral beliefs and habits of moral judgment can be expected to evolve in response to various intellectual pressures.

We may not fully register this if we focus too exclusively on Mill's claim that "the same causes that made [someone] a churchman in London would have made him a Buddhist or a Confucian in Peking," for this claim draws attention to a single aspect of what a person believes – the particular religion he accepts – that often *is* a direct result of his background. It is obviously impossible for someone who has only been exposed to one religion to become devout in another. However, the more pertinent question is whether a person who has only been exposed to a single religion may nevertheless come to reject some or all of its teachings; and to this further question, the answer is clearly "Yes."

For because any set of claims about religion (or, by extension, morality) can be subjected to rational scrutiny, people can and often do reject even the religious and moral doctrines to which they have been most relentlessly exposed. Even when someone has at first been nonrationally caused to acquire a certain religious or moral belief, it is open to him rationally to evaluate that belief at any later point. Of course, in so doing, he will rely on various ways of assessing evidence and weighting values, and it is likely that the ways he uses will themselves have been shaped by his experiences (and, we may add, by his culture). Still, no matter how far these influences extend – and, as Rawls notes about the influence of experience, this is something we cannot know – their introduction does not alter the basic point because any resulting ways of assessing evidence and weighting values can be rationally scrutinized in turn. Thus, properly understood, the moral outlook that we have been nonrationally caused to acquire is best viewed not as a permanent fixture of our thought, but rather as a starting point that we may hope successively to improve through ongoing critical reflection.

There is, of course, no guarantee that this hope will be realized. Despite my best efforts, it remains possible that my moral outlook has from the start been hopelessly compromised by some massive error, and that my lack of access to the source of error has systematically subverted all my ameliorative endeavors. However, this hypothesis, if backed by no positive argument, is no less speculative than is the hypothesis that all my experiences are caused by a scientist stimulating a brain in a vat. Thus, as long as I have no concrete reason to believe otherwise, it may well be reasonable for me to assume that my efforts to think through the arguments for and against my fundamental moral convictions, and to correct for the distortions, biases, and false beliefs that my upbringing and earlier experiences have inevitably introduced, have on the whole made things better rather than worse.

How, exactly, would the truth of this meliorist assumption bear on (2)'s claim that if I had a sufficiently different upbringing and set of experiences, I would now judge my moral obligations differently? The answer, I think, is complicated. The truth of the meliorist assumption would not show that (2)'s claim is false, but would indeed lessen (2)'s sting. However, it would also leave intact the challenge to the authority of my moral judgments that (2) poses in conjunction with (1). Let me argue briefly for each of these three points in turn.

At first glance, the assumption that reflecting on one's moral outlook tends to improve it may indeed seem to tell against (2), for if this assumption is correct, then even two radically different moral outlooks can be expected eventually to converge if subjected to enough reflection. However, for at least two reasons, this way of arguing against (2) does not seem promising. First, even if we grant both that I would have reflected seriously on the alternative moral outlook that a given alternative history would have caused me to acquire and that

I did reflect seriously on the moral outlook that my actual history caused me to acquire, there is no guarantee that the two starting points are close enough to allow anything approaching full convergence within my lifetime (or, *a fortiori*, now). In addition, at least some of the alternative histories that would have caused me to acquire a different moral outlook would also have caused me to be disinclined to engage in the kind of reflection that would be necessary to secure *any* degree of convergence. For both reasons, the assumption that reflecting on one's moral outlook generally improves it does not seem capable of supporting a refutation of (2).

Even if this is so, however, the assumption does make (2) more palatable, for as long as I can even partially overcome the nonrational origins of my moral outlook by critically reflecting on it, the fact that my moral outlook would now be different if my history had been different will not entirely undermine its credibility. Given the validating effects of critical reflection, I will, by virtue of engaging in it, at least partly transcend my moral outlook's merely contingent origins.

Yet even if *this* is so, it will hardly follow that I have any more reason to rely on my own moral judgments than on the judgments of others with whom I strongly disagree; for because these disagreements take place within a society that prizes reflection (and because, as an academic, I tend to interact with the more reflective segment of my society), I cannot assume that those with whom I disagree have been any less reflective than I. Given that they, too, may well have sought to transcend the merely historical origins of their moral outlooks, an appeal to the validating effects of my reflections will not resolve my problem, but will only reraise it at a higher level. When you and I disagree about what I ought to do – when, for example, my own conscientious reflection leaves me convinced that the revenge I am planning falls well within tolerable moral limits, while yours leaves you no less convinced that I really ought to resist my ugly, vengeful urges – I cannot reasonably assume that it is I rather than you who has successfully thought his way out of his causally induced errors.

And if I am tempted to think otherwise, I need only remind myself of how often such situations arise. If I am entitled to assume that you have been less successful than me in purging your thinking of causally induced error, then I must be entitled to make the same assumption about the great majority of others with whom I disagree – about vast numbers of intelligent and sophisticated vegetarians, pacifists, postmodernists, deconstructionists, gender feminists, pro-lifers, proponents of partial-birth abortion, neutralists, advocates of hate-speech codes, fundamentalists, libertines, rigorists, and egoists, to name just a few. But although it is certainly possible that I have been more successful in avoiding error than some of these others – this is likely on statistical grounds alone – it strains credulity to suppose that I have been more successful than all, or even most, of them. It would be something of a miracle if, out of all the disputants, it was just me who got it all right.

VI.   Practical Solution to These Doubts?

So what should I do? More precisely, how should I respond to the challenge to my ability to decide on rational grounds what I should do? I can see three main possibilities: first, to renew my quest for a convincing reason to believe that my own moral judgments are more likely to be true or justified than are those of the innumerable others with whom I disagree; second, to concede both that no such reason is likely to be forthcoming and that I therefore cannot rationally base my actions on my own moral judgments; and third, to acknowledge that no such reason is forthcoming but *deny* that this makes it irrational to base my actions on my own moral judgments. Unfortunately, of these three strategies, the first is pretty clearly doomed, while the second would commit me to a wholesale rejection of the moral point of view. Thus, if I am to avoid the twin pitfalls of futility and moral skepticism, I will probably have to implement some variant of the third strategy.

To do this, I will have to block the inference from "I have no good reason to believe that my own moral judgments are more likely to be justified or true than those of innumerable others who disagree with me" to "I cannot rationally base my actions on my own moral judgments." This in turn requires a demonstration that what makes it rational for me to base my actions on my own moral judgments is not simply the strength of my reasons for believing that these judgments are justified or true. More specifically, what I must show is that even when I realize that my own moral judgments are no more likely to be true or justified than are yours, it nevertheless remains rational for me to act on my own judgments simply because they *are* my own.

Can anything like this be shown? If so, it seems the argument would likely have to turn on certain features of practical reason itself. In particular, its pivotal premise seems likely to be that because no one can act rationally without basing his decisions on his *own* assessment of the reasons for and against the actions available to him, practical reason itself *requires* that I give pride of place to my own judgments. Although I can of course rationally discount any particular judgment that I take to be false or unjustified, the reason I can do this is that to discount a particular judgment is not to abdicate the task of judging; rather, it is only to allow one of my own judgments to trump another. Because acting rationally necessarily involves basing my decisions on the way *I* see things, I cannot entirely transcend my own outlook without moving decisively beyond the bounds of practical reason.

This much, I think, is clear enough. However, because not all reasons for acting are moral reasons – because, for example, I can also have reasons that are prudential, hedonistic, or aesthetic – the mere fact that practical reason requires that I base my actions on my own judgments about what I have reason to do is not sufficient to vindicate the rationality of acting on my own best *moral* judgments. To show that practical reason requires this, I must take the further step of arguing that even an attempt to transcend my own *moral* outlook would take me beyond the bounds of practical reason; and unlike the previous step, this one may seem problematic indeed.

For because my moral outlook encompasses only a small fraction of what I believe, want, and aim at, simply disregarding it would hardly leave me with nothing, or too little, upon which to base my practical decisions. Even if I

were to set aside every one of my moral beliefs, I could still choose one action over another on any number of further grounds – for example, because the chosen action would be fun, because it would advance the aims of some person I care about, or because it is required for the completion of some project I have undertaken. Thus, given my awareness that my own moral judgments are no more likely to be true or justified than are the moral judgments of any number of others, isn't it indeed rational for me to set moral considerations aside and make my decisions exclusively on other grounds?

The answer, I think, is that this is *not* rational, for if I were to do it, I would merely be discounting one set of practical judgments in favor of another whose members are no less compromised by the now-familiar combination of controversy and contingency. Although a full defense of this final claim is beyond my scope, I shall end this section with a brief sketch of the argument for it.

The first thing that needs to be said is that just as the great majority of my *moral* judgments would be contested by various persons who are no less reflective than I, so too would the great majority of my *nonmoral practical* judgments. Indeed, the latter disagreements seem if anything to be even more wide-ranging, since they encompass both disagreements about which *sorts* of nonmoral considerations are relevant to the decision at hand – for example, disagreements about whether I should make the decision mainly on hedonistic, prudential, aesthetic, or affectional grounds – and disagreements about what each type of consideration gives me reason to do. Although some such disagreements obviously turn on different understandings of the facts of a given situation, many others do not. Also, while many endorse the metaprinciple that what I ought to do depends on my *own* weighting of the competing nonmoral considerations, there are also many who reject this metaprinciple. Thus, all in all, my nonmoral practical judgments are sure to be every bit as controversial as my moral judgments.

Moreover, second, my having the beliefs and habits of thought that combine to support the relevant practical judgments seems equally contingent in both the moral and nonmoral cases. Just as it is true that if I had had a sufficiently different upbringing and set of experiences, I would now hold your view rather than mine about what I *morally* ought to do, so too is it true that if I had had a sufficiently different upbringing and set of experiences, I would now hold your view rather than mine about what I have *nonmoral* reason to do. Our attitudes about the value of culture, work, friendship, planning, and much else are no less accidents of our upbringing and experiences, and are no less influential in shaping our judgments about how to live, than are our beliefs about virtue and vice and what we owe to each other.

Thus, in the end, my moral and nonmoral judgments about what I ought to do – or, better, the moral and nonmoral components of my integrated judgments about what, all things considered, I ought to do – seem likely to stand or fall together. Either it is rational for me to set both components of my own practical judgments aside or it is not rational for me to set either of them aside. If I were to set both components aside, I would indeed lack any basis upon which to make reasoned decisions about what to do. Hence, given the inescapability of my commitment to acting for reasons, my tentative conclusion is that practical rationality precludes my setting either of the components aside.

VII. Conclusion

My main contention in this essay has been that given the degree to which merely contingent factors appear to have shaped our moral outlooks, there is a serious question about whether I ever have good grounds for believing that I am right and you are wrong when you and I disagree about what I ought to do. However, I have also suggested that even if I never *do* have good grounds for believing this, it may nevertheless often remain rational for me to base my actions on my own moral judgments rather than yours. When they are combined, these claims have the paradoxical implication that it is often rational for me to act on the basis of moral judgments the objective likelihood of whose truth or justifiability I have good reason to regard as quite low. This implication casts (fresh) doubt on our ability to integrate our reasons for believing and for acting – that is, on our ability to square the demands of theoretical and practical reason. It also suggests that the price we pay for being clear-eyed moral agents may be a disconcerting awareness of a certain inescapable form of bad faith. Whether these are the only conclusions that the paradoxical implication warrants, or whether, in addition, it provides a platform for some further thrust by the moral skeptic, is a question I will not attempt to answer here.

Notes

1. John Stuart Mill, *On Liberty* (Indianapolis, IN: Hackett, 1978), 17.
2. John Rawls, *Political Liberalism* (New York: Columbia University Press, 1993), 56–57.
3. David Hume, *A Treatise of Human Nature*, ed. L. A. Selby-Bigge (Oxford: Clarendon Press, 1960), bk. I, sec. 7, p. 269.
4. The authority of my empirical beliefs faces a challenge analogous to that faced by my moral judgments. As is the case with moral judgments, I disagree with others about various empirical matters, and for (just about) any empirical belief that I reject but someone else accepts, there is some different upbringing and set of experiences that would have caused me to accept that empirical belief.

Because I have taken the fact that a different background would have caused me to weigh the evidence in a way that supports your moral judgment rather than mine to undermine the authority of my own moral judgment, I can hardly deny that the fact that a different background would have caused me to weigh the evidence in a way that supports your empirical belief rather than mine is similarly subversive of the authority of my own empirical belief. However, there are several things worth noting here. First, very few of my actual empirical beliefs *are* disputed by thoughtful, conscientious people who have simply weighed the evidence differently. Second, when an empirical disagreement *is* of this nature – when, for example, you and I disagree about what to make of the evidence about the causes of a phenomenon such as intergenerational poverty – considerable diffidence on both sides is indeed in order. It is worth noting, too, that if those with whom I disagree have not merely assessed the shared evidence differently but either lack or are unresponsive to evidence I have – if, for example, they are members of a prescientific society that attributes diseases to spirits rather than micro-organisms, or are creationists – then the fact that I would have their beliefs if I had their background does *not* undermine the authority of my own beliefs. Here I can see that, and why, my own background is the more favored. Taken together, these considerations suggest that the combination of controversy and contingency poses far less of a threat to the authority of my empirical beliefs than it does to the authority of my moral judgments.

CHAPTER 12

Proof

RENFORD BRAMBROUGH

[. . .]

When a philosopher reasons with us about knowledge of good and evil, we may lose our grip on this knowledge and understanding. A lack of realism besets us in this as in other philosophical disputes, so that moral knowledge, like any other kind of knowledge, becomes prey to philosophical scepticism. Moral scepticism has often tempted philosophers whose understanding of the sources and grounds and functions of sceptical doctrines generally might have been expected to protect them against the bewitchment of a scepticism so extravagant that Hume declines to discuss it (*Enquiries*, § 133):

> Those who have denied the reality of moral distinctions, may be ranked among the disingenuous disputants; nor is it conceivable, that any human creature could ever seriously believe, that all characters and actions were alike entitled to the affection and regard of everyone. The difference, which nature has placed between one man and another, is so wide, and this difference is still so much farther widened, by education, example, and habit, that, where the opposite extremes come at

> once under our apprehension, there is no scepticism so scrupulous, and scarce any assurance so determined, as absolutely to deny all distinction between them. Let a man's insensibility be ever so great, he must often be touched with the images of Right and Wrong; and let his prejudices be ever so obstinate, he must observe, that others are susceptible of like impressions. The only way, therefore, of converting an antagonist of this kind, is to leave him to himself. For, finding that nobody keeps up the controversy with him, it is probable he will, at last, of himself, from mere weariness, come over to the side of common sense and reason.

It is well known that recent [. . .] philosophy, under the leadership of Moore and Wittgenstein, has defended common sense and common language against what seem to many contemporary philosophers to be the paradoxes, the obscurities and the mystifications of earlier metaphysical philosophers. The spirit of this work is shown by the titles of two of the most famous of Moore's papers: 'A Defence of Common Sense' and 'Proof of an External World'. It can be more fully but still briefly described by saying something about Moore's defence of the commonsense belief that there are external material objects. His proof of an external world consists essentially in holding up his hands and saying, 'Here are two hands; therefore there are at least two material

Renford Brambrough, "Proof," pp. 11–13, 15–27 from *Moral Skepticism and Moral Knowledge*. London: Routledge, 1979.

objects.' He argues that no proposition that could plausibly be alleged as a reason in favour of doubting the truth of the proposition that I have two hands can possibly be more certainly true than that proposition itself. If a philosopher produces an argument against my claim to *know* that I have two hands, I can therefore be sure in advance that *either* at least one of the premises of argument is false, *or* there is a mistake in the reasoning by which he purports to derive from his premises the conclusion that I do not know that I have two hands.

Moore himself speaks largely in terms of knowledge and belief and truth and falsehood rather than of the language in which we make our commonsense claims and the language in which the sceptic or metaphysician attacks them, but his procedures and conclusions are similar to those of other and later philosophers who have treated the same topic in terms of adherence to or departure from common language. A so-called linguistic philosopher would say of the sceptic that he was using words in unusual senses, and that when he said that we do not know anything about the external world he was using the word 'know' so differently from the way in which we ordinarily use it that his claim was not in conflict with the claim that we make when we say that we *do* know something about the external world. Moore takes the words of the sceptic literally, and shows that what he says is literally false. The linguistic philosopher recognises that what the sceptic says is literally false, and goes on to conclude that the sceptic, who must be as well aware as we are that what he says is literally false, is not speaking literally. Both Moore and the linguistic philosopher maintain with emphasis (Moore is famous for his *emphasis*) that we literally *do* know of some propositions about the external world that they are true; they both hold fast to common sense and common language.

[...]

What is apparently not very well known is that there is a conflict between the fashionable allegiance to common sense and common language and the fashionable rejection of objectivism in moral philosophy.

[...]

Many contemporary [...] philosophers accept Moore's proof of an external world.

Many contemporary [...] philosophers reject the claim that we have moral knowledge. There are some contemporary [...] philosophers who both accept Moore's proof of an external world and reject the claim that we have moral knowledge. The position of these philosophers is self-contradictory. If we can show by Moore's argument that there is an external world, then we can show *by parity of reasoning*, by an exactly analogous argument, that we have moral knowledge, that there are some propositions of morals which are *certainly* true, and which we *know* to be true.

My proof that we have moral knowledge consists essentially in saying, 'We know that this child, who is about to undergo what would otherwise be painful surgery, should be given an anaesthetic before the operation. Therefore we know at least one moral proposition to be true.' I argue that no proposition that could plausibly be alleged as a reason in favour of doubting the truth of the proposition that the child should be given an anaesthetic can possibly be more certainly true than that proposition itself. If a philosopher produces an argument against my claim to *know* that the child should be given an anaesthetic, I can therefore be sure in advance that *either* at least one of the premises of his argument is false, *or* there is a mistake in the reasoning by which he purports to derive from his premises the conclusion that I do not know that the child should be given an anaesthetic.

When Moore proves that there is an external world he is defending a commonsense belief. When I prove that we have moral knowledge I am defending a commonsense belief. The contemporary philosophers who both accept Moore's proof of an external world and reject the claim that we have moral knowledge defend common sense in one field and attack common sense in another field. They hold fast to common sense when they speak of our knowledge of the external world, and depart from common sense when they speak of morality.

When they speak of our knowledge of the external world they not only do not give reasons for confining their respect for common sense to their treatment of that single topic but assume and imply that their respect for common sense is *in general* justified. When they go on to speak of morality they not only do not give reasons for abandoning the respect for common sense that they showed when they spoke of our knowledge of the external world, but assume and imply that they are still showing the same respect for common sense. But this is just what they are *not* doing.

The commonsense view is that we *know* that stealing is wrong, that promise-keeping is right, that unselfishness is good, that cruelty is bad. Common language uses in moral contexts the whole range of expressions that it also uses in non-moral contexts when it is concerned with knowledge and ignorance, truth and falsehood, reason and unreason, questions and answers. We speak as naturally of a child's not knowing the difference between right and wrong as we do of his not knowing the difference between right and left. We say that we do not know what to do as naturally as we say that we do not know what is the case. We say that a man's moral views are unreasonable as naturally as we say that his views on a matter of fact are unreasonable. In moral contexts, just as naturally as in non-moral contexts, we speak of thinking, wondering, asking; of beliefs, opinions, convictions, arguments, conclusions; of dilemmas, problems, solutions; of perplexity, confusion, consistency and inconsistency, of errors and mistakes, of teaching, learning, training, showing, proving, finding out, understanding, realising, recognising and coming to see.

I am not now saying that we are right to speak of all these things as naturally in one type of context as in another, though that is what I do in fact believe. Still less am I saying that the fact that we speak in a particular way is itself a sufficient justification for speaking in that particular way. What I am saying now is that a philosopher who defends common sense when he is talking about our knowledge of the external world must *either* defend common sense when he talks about morality (that is to say, he must admit that we have moral knowledge) *or* give us reasons why in the one case common sense is to be defended, while in the other case it is *not* to be defended. If he does neither of these things we shall be entitled to accuse him of inconsistency. I do accuse such philosophers of inconsistency.

Moore did not expect the sceptic of the senses to be satisfied with his proof of an external world, and I do not expect the moral sceptic to be satisfied with my proof of the objectivity of morals. Even somebody who is not a sceptic of the senses may be dissatisfied with Moore's proof, and even somebody who is not a moral sceptic may be dissatisfied with my proof. Even somebody who regards either proof as a conclusive argument for its conclusion may nevertheless be dissatisfied. He may reasonably wish to be given not only a conclusive demonstration of the truth of the conclusion, but also a detailed answer to the most popular or plausible arguments against the conclusion.

Those who reject the commonsense account of moral knowledge, like those who reject the commonsense account of our knowledge of the external world, do of course offer arguments in favour of their rejection. In both cases those who reject the commonsense account offer very much the same arguments whether or not they recognise that the account they are rejecting is in fact the commonsense account. If we now look at the arguments that can be offered against the commonsense account of moral knowledge we shall be able to see whether they are sufficiently similar to the arguments that can be offered against the commonsense account of our knowledge of the external world to enable us to sustain our charge of inconsistency against a philosopher who attacks common sense in one field and defends it in the other. (We may note in passing that many philosophers in the past have committed the converse form of the same *prima facie* inconsistency: they have rejected the commonsense account of our knowledge of the external world but have accepted the commonsense account of moral knowledge.)

'*Moral disagreement is more widespread, more radical and more persistent than disagreement about matters of fact.*'

I have two main comments to make on this suggestion: the first is that it is almost certainly untrue, and the second is that it is quite certainly irrelevant.

The objection loses much of its plausibility as soon as we insist on comparing the comparable. We are usually invited to contrast our admirably close agreement that there is a glass of water on the table with the depth, vigour and tenacity of our disagreements about capital punishment, abortion, birth control and nuclear disarmament. But this game may be played by two or more players. A sufficient reply in kind is to contrast our general agreement that this child should have an anaesthetic with the strength and warmth of the disagreements between cosmologists and radio astronomers about the interpretation of certain radioastronomical observations. If the moral sceptic then reminds us of Christian Science we can offer him in exchange the Flat Earth Society.

But this is a side issue. Even if it is true that moral disagreement is more acute and more persistent than other forms of disagreement, it does not follow that moral knowledge is impossible. However long and violent a dispute may be, and however few or many heads may be counted on this side or on that, it remains possible that one party to the dispute is right and the others wrong. Galileo was right when he contradicted the cardinals; and so was Wilberforce when he rebuked the slave-owners.

There is a more direct and decisive way of showing the irrelevance of the argument from persistent disagreement. The question of whether a given type of enquiry is objective is the question whether it is *logically capable* of reaching knowledge, and is therefore an *a priori*, logical question. The question of how much agreement or disagreement there is between those who actually engage in that enquiry is a question of psychological or sociological fact. It follows that the question about the actual extent of agreement or disagreement has no bearing on the question of the objectivity of the enquiry. If this were not so, the objectivity of every enquiry might wax and wane through the centuries as men become more or less disputatious or more or less proficient in the arts of persuasion.

'*Our moral opinions are conditioned by our environment and upbringing.*'

It is under this heading that we are reminded of the variegated customs and beliefs of Hottentots, Eskimos, Polynesians and American Indians, which do indeed differ widely from each other and from our own. But this objection is really a special case of the general argument from disagreement, and it can be answered on the same lines. The beliefs of the Hottentots and the Polynesians about straightforwardly factual matters differ widely from our own, but that does not tempt us to say that science is subjective. It is true that most of those who are born and bred in the stately homes of England have a different outlook on life from that of the Welsh miner or the Highland crofter, but it is also true that all these classes of people differ widely in their factual beliefs, and not least in their factual beliefs about themselves and each other.

The moral sceptic's favourite examples are often presented as though they settled the issue beyond further argument.

(1)   Herodotus reports that within the Persian Empire there were some tribes that buried their dead and some that burned them. Each group thought that the other's practice was barbarous. But (a) they agreed that respect must be shown to the dead; (b) they lived under very different climatic conditions; (c) we can now see that they were guilty of moral myopia in setting such store by what happened, for good or bad reasons, to be their own particular practice. Moral progress in this field has consisted in coming to recognise that burying-versus-burning is not an issue on which it is necessary for the whole of mankind to have a single, fixed, universal standpoint, regardless of variations of conditions in time and place.

(2)   Some societies practice polygamous marriage. Others favour monogamy. Here again there need be no absolute and unvarying rule. In societies where women heavily outnumber men, institutions may be appropriate which would be out of place in societies where the numbers of men and women are roughly equal. The moralist who insists that monogamy is

right, regardless of circumstances, is like the inhabitant of the Northern Hemisphere who insists that it is always and everywhere cold at Christmas, or the inhabitant of the Southern Hemisphere who cannot believe that it is ever or anywhere cold at Christmas.

(3) Some societies do not disapprove of what we condemn as 'stealing'. In such societies, anybody may take from anybody else's house anything he may need or want. This case serves further to illustrate that circumstances objectively alter cases, that relativity is not only compatible with, but actually required by, the objective and rational determination of questions of right and wrong. I can maintain that Bill Sykes is a rogue, and that prudence requires me to lock all my doors and windows against him, without being committed to holding that if an Eskimo takes whalemeat from the unlocked igloo of another Eskimo, then one of them is a knave and the other a fool. It is not that we disapprove of stealing and that the Eskimos do not, but that their circumstances differ so much from ours as to call for new consideration and a different judgement, which may be that in their situation stealing is innocent, or that in their situation there is no private property and therefore no possibility of *stealing* at all.

(4) Some tribes leave their elderly and useless members to die in the forest. Others, including our own, provide old-age pensions and geriatric hospitals. But we should have to reconsider our arrangements if we found that the care of the aged involved for us the consequences that it might involve for a nomadic and pastoral people: general starvation because the old could not keep pace with the necessary movement to new pastures; children and domestic animals a prey to wild beasts; a life burdensome to all and destined to end with the early extinction of the tribe.

'*When I say that something is good or bad or right or wrong I commit myself, and reveal something of my attitudes and feelings.*'

This is quite true, but it is equally and analogously true that when I say that something is true or false, or even that something is red or round, I also commit myself and reveal something of my *beliefs*. Emotivist and imperativist philosophers have sometimes failed to draw a clear enough distinction between what is said or meant by a particular form of expression and what is implied or suggested by it, and even those who have distinguished clearly and correctly between meaning and implication in the case of moral propositions have often failed to see that exactly the same distinction can be drawn in the case of non-moral propositions. If I say 'this is good' and then add 'but I do not approve of it', I certainly behave oddly enough to owe you an explanation; but I behave equally oddly and owe you a comparable explanation if I say 'that is true, but I don't believe it.' If it is held that I contradict myself in the first case, it must be allowed that I contradict myself in the second case. If it is claimed that I do not contradict myself in the second case, then it must be allowed that I do not contradict myself in the first case. If this point can be used as an argument against the objectivity of morals, then it can also be used as an argument against the objectivity of science, logic, and of every other branch of enquiry.

The parallel between *approve* and *believe* and between *good* and *true* is so close that it provides a useful test of the paradoxes of subjectivism and emotivism. The emotivist puts the cart before the horse in trying to explain goodness in terms of approval, just as he would if he tried to explain truth in terms of belief. Belief cannot be explained without introducing the notion of truth, and approval cannot be explained without introducing the notion of goodness. To believe is (roughly) to hold to be true, and to approve is (equally roughly) to hold to be good. Hence it is as unsatisfactory to try to reduce goodness to approval, or to approval plus some other component, as it would be to try to reduce truth to belief, or to belief plus some other component.

If we are to give a correct account of the logical character of morality we must preserve the distinction between appearance and reality, between seeming and really being, that we clearly and admittedly have to preserve if we are to give a correct account of truth and belief. Just as we do and must hope that what we believe (what seems to us to be true) is in fact true, so we must hope that what we approve (what seems to us to be good) is in fact good.

I can say of another, 'He thinks it is raining, but it is not,' and of myself, 'I thought it was raining, but it was not.' I can also say of another, 'He thinks it is good, but it is not,' and of myself, 'I thought it was good, but it was not.'

> 'After every circumstance, every relation is known, the understanding has no further room to operate, nor any object on which it could employ itself.'

This sentence from the first Appendix to Hume's *Enquiry Concerning the Principles of Morals* is the moral sceptic's favourite quotation, and he uses it for several purposes, including some that are alien to Hume's intentions. Sometimes it is no more than a flourish added to the argument from disagreement. Sometimes it is used in support of the claim that there comes a point in every moral dispute when further reasoning is not so much ineffective as impossible in principle. In either case the answer is once again a firm *tu quoque*. In any sense in which it is true that there may or must come a point in moral enquiry beyond which no further reasoning is possible, it is in that same sense equally true that there may or must be a point in *any* enquiry at which the reasoning has to stop. Nothing can be proved to a man who will accept nothing that has not been proved. Moore recognises that his proof of an external world uses premises which have not themselves been proved. Not even in pure mathematics, that paradigm of strict security of reasoning, can we *force* a man to accept our premises or our modes of inference; and therefore we cannot force him to accept our conclusions. Once again the moral sceptic counts as a reason for doubting the objectivity of morals a feature of moral enquiry which is exactly paralleled in other departments of enquiry where he does not count it as a reason for scepticism. If he is to be consistent, he must either withdraw his argument against the objectivity of morals or subscribe also to an analogous

argument against the objectivity of mathematics, physics, history, and every other branch of enquiry.

But of course such an argument gives no support to a sceptical conclusion about any of these enquiries. However conclusive a mode of reasoning may be, and however accurately we may use it, it always remains possible that we shall fail to convince a man who disagrees with us. There may come a point in a moral dispute when it is wiser to agree to differ than to persist with fruitless efforts to convince an opponent. But this by itself is no more a reason for doubting the truth of our premises and the validity of our arguments than the teacher's failure to convince a pupil of the validity of a proof of Pythagoras's theorem is a reason for doubting the validity of the proof and the truth of the theorem. It is notorious that even an expert physicist may fail to convince a member of the Flat Earth Society that the earth is not flat, but we nevertheless *know* that the earth is not flat. Lewis Carroll's tortoise ingeniously resisted the best efforts of Achilles to convince him of the validity of a simple deductive argument, but of course the argument *is* valid.

> 'A dispute which is purely *moral* is inconclusive in principle. The specifically *moral* element in moral disputes is one which cannot be resolved by investigation and reflection.'

This objection brings into the open an assumption that is made at least implicitly by most of those who use Hume's remark as a subjectivist weapon: the assumption that whatever is a logical or factual dispute, or a mixture of logical and factual disputes, is necessarily *not* a moral dispute; that nothing is a moral dispute unless it is *purely* moral in the sense that it is a dispute between parties who agree on *all* the relevant factual and logical questions. But the *purely moral* dispute envisaged by this assumption is a pure fiction. The search for the 'specifically moral element' in moral disputes is a wild-goose chase, and is the result of the initial confusion of supposing that no feature of moral reasoning is *really* a feature of moral reasoning, or is *characteristic* of moral reasoning, unless it is peculiar to moral reasoning. It is as if one insisted that a ginger cake could be fully characterised, and could only be characterised, by saying that there is ginger in it. It is true that ginger is the peculiar ingredient of a ginger cake as contrasted with other cakes, but no cake can be made entirely of ginger, and the ingredients that are combined with ginger to make ginger cakes are the same as those that are combined with chocolate, lemon, orange or vanilla to make other kinds of cakes; and ginger itself, when combined with other ingredients and treated in other ways, goes into the making of ginger puddings, ginger biscuits and ginger beer.

To the question 'What is the place of reason in ethics?' why should we not answer: 'The place of reason in ethics is exactly what it is in other enquiries, to enable us to find out the relevant facts and to make our judgements mutually consistent, to expose factual errors and detect logical inconsistencies'? This might seem to imply that there are some moral judgements which will serve as starting points for any moral enquiry, and will not themselves be proved, as others may be proved by being derived from them or disproved by being shown to be incompatible with them, and also to imply that we cannot engage in moral argument with a man with whom we agree on *no* moral question. In so far as these implications are correct they apply to all enquiry, and not only to moral enquiry; and they do not, when correctly construed, constitute any objection to the rationality and objectivity of morality or of any other mode of enquiry. They seem to make difficulties for moral objectivity only when they are associated with a picture of rationality which, though it has always been powerful in the minds of philosophers, can be shown to be an unacceptable caricature.

Here again the moral sceptic is partial and selective in his use of an argument of indefinitely wide scope: if it were true that a man must accept unprovable moral premises before I could prove to him that there is such a thing as moral knowledge it would equally be true that a man must accept an unprovable material object proposition before Moore could prove to him that there is an external world. Similarly, if a moral conclusion can be proved only to a man who accepts unprovable moral premises then a physical conclusion can be proved only to a man who accepts unprovable physical premises.

'*There are recognised methods for settling factual and logical disputes, but there are no recognised methods for settling moral disputes.*'

This is either false, or true but irrelevant, according to how it is understood. Too often those who make this complaint are arguing in a circle, since they will count nothing as a recognised method of argument unless it is a recognised method of logical or scientific argument. If we adopt this interpretation, then it is true that there are no recognised methods of moral argument, but the lack of such methods does not affect the claim that morality is objective. One department of enquiry has not been shown to be no true department of enquiry when all that has been shown is that it cannot be carried on by exactly the methods that are appropriate to some other department of enquiry. We know without the help of the sceptic that morality is not identical with logic or science.

But in its most straightforward sense the claim is simply false. There *are* recognised methods of moral argument. Whenever we say 'How would you like it if somebody did this to you?' or 'How would it be if we all acted like this?' we are arguing according to recognised and established methods, and are in fact appealing to the consistency requirement to which I have already referred. It is true that such appeals are often ineffective, but it is also true that well-founded logical or scientific arguments often fail to convince those to whom they are addressed. If the present objection is pursued beyond this point it turns into the argument from radical disagreement.

The moral sceptic is even more inclined to exaggerate the amount of disagreement that there is about methods of moral argument than he is inclined to exaggerate the amount of disagreement in moral belief as such. One reason for this is that he concentrates his attention on the admittedly striking and important fact that there is an enormous amount of immoral *conduct*. But most of those who *behave* immorally appeal to the very same methods of moral argument as those who condemn their immoral conduct. Hitler broke many promises, but he did not explicitly hold that promise-breaking as such and in general was permissible. When others broke their promises to him he complained with the same force and in the same terms as those with whom he himself had failed to keep faith. And whenever he broke a promise he tried to *justify* his breach by claiming that other obligations overrode the duty to keep the promise. He did not simply deny that it was his duty to keep promises. He thus entered into the very process of argument by which it is possible to condemn so many of his own actions. He was *inconsistent* in requiring of other nations and their leaders standards of conduct to which he himself did not conform, and in failing to produce *convincing reasons* for his own departures from the agreed standards.

CHAPTER 13

Moral Knowledge and Ethical Pluralism

ROBERT AUDI

Intuitionism

[. . .] To see the main epistemological thrust of intuitionism, consider how one might explain the justification of an ordinary moral principle such as the proposition that we should (*prima facie*) keep our promises. Why believe this? I could explain why I do; but explaining need not justify, and perhaps I cannot justify the principle by appeal to any more fundamental proposition. According to intuitionism, this would not show that I do not know or justifiedly believe it. At some point or other in defending a factual (say, perceptual) judgment, I may be equally incapable of giving a further justification. It would not follow that the judgment I am defending does not express knowledge or justified belief.

The issue should be explicitly considered in the light of a general commitment of most (and arguably the most plausible) intuitionist ethical theories: epistemological foundationalism. This view (in a generic form) says above all that if there is any knowledge or justification, it traces to some non-inferential knowledge or justification. A foundationalist may say that

Robert Audi, "Moral Knowledge and Ethical Pluralism," pp. 275–6, 278–85, 288–95 from John Greco and Ernest Sosa (eds.), *The Blackwell Guide to Epistemology*. Oxford: Blackwell, 1999. Reprinted by permission of the publishers, Blackwell Publishing.

(with some special exceptions) the principle that one should keep one's promises, or at least some more general principle, such as that people should be treated with respect, is self-evident, hence intuitively knowable, and needs no defense by derivation from prior principles. Intuitionism so viewed does not claim that *everyone* who considers the relevant principle will find it obvious (especially immediately); but that will hold for certain theorems in logic, the kind that are initially hard to understand but, when they are finally understood, are comfortably accepted as self-evident, or at least as logically true.[1] The appeal to self-evident propositions, then, should not be assimilated to the appeal to obviousness nor expected to be made with a view to cutting off discussion.

Foundationalists will tend to argue that an appeal to what is self-evident can be warranted when we get to certain stages in a process of justification. For they take some beliefs (including many that lack self-evident propositions as objects) as foundational in a way that warrants holding them without having prior premises. Self-evident propositions are paradigms of appropriate objects of foundational beliefs. For foundationalism, if there were no non-inferentially justified beliefs, then we would not be justified in holding anything. A coherentist seeking to justify the promising principle may be willing to go on arguing, perhaps pointing out that if we do not keep promises life will be unbearable, and then, for each thesis attacked, defending it with respect to one or more others that can support it. A skeptic may not be pacified by either approach. But neither can simply be rejected out of hand.

[. . .]

The Epistemological Resources of Moderate Intuitionism

This section will set out a moderate version of intuitionism, a version intended to improve on the one proposed by W. D. Ross in *the Right and the Good* (1930), which remains the statement of intuitionism most often illustratively referred to by writers in ethical theory.

Rossian intuitionism

As Ross portrayed it, intuitionism as a kind of ethical theory has three main characteristics. (1) It affirms an irreducible plurality of basic moral principles. (2) Each principle centers on a different kind of ground, in the sense of a factor, such as an injury occurring in one's presence, implying a *prima facie* moral duty, say a duty to aid someone just injured. (3) Each principle is in some sense intuitively (hence non-inferentially) known by those who appropriately understand it. All three points seem appropriate to any full-blooded version of intuitionism. On the normative side, Ross proposed, as fundamental both in guiding daily life and in articulating a sound ethical theory, a list (which he did not claim to be complete) of *prima facie* duties: duties of fidelity (promise-keeping, including honesty conceived as fidelity to one's word); reparation; justice (particularly rectification of injustice, such as exploitation of the poor); gratitude; beneficence; self-improvement; and non-injury.[2]

Epistemologically, Ross emphasized the self-evidence of the propositions expressing our *prima facie* duties:

> That an act, *qua* fulfilling a promise, or *qua* effecting a just distribution of good . . . is *prima facie* right, is self-evident; not in the

sense that it is evident from the beginning of our lives, or as soon as we attend to the proposition for the first time, but in the sense that when we have reached sufficient mental maturity and have given sufficient attention to the proposition it is evident without any need of proof, or of evidence beyond itself. It is evident just as a mathematical axiom, or the validity of a form of inference, is evident . . . In our confidence that these propositions are true there is involved the same confidence in our reason that is involved in our confidence in mathematics . . . In both cases we are dealing with propositions that cannot be proved, but that just as certainly need no proof.[3]

In explaining how we apprehend the self-evident, unprovable moral truths in question, Ross appealed to something like what we commonly call intuitions (his term here is "conviction" and apparently designates a cognition held at least partly on the basis of understanding its propositional object). He said, e.g., that if someone challenges

> our view that there is a special obligatoriness attaching to the keeping of promises because [according to the challenger] it is self-evident that the only duty is to produce as much good as possible, we have to ask ourselves whether we really, when we reflect, *are* convinced that [as he takes G. E. Moore to hold] this is self-evident . . . it seems self-evident that a promise simply as such, is something that *prima facie* ought to be kept . . . the moral convictions of thoughtful and well-educated people are the data of ethics, just as sense-perceptions are the data of a natural science. Just as some of the latter have to be rejected as illusory, so have some of the former; but as the latter are rejected only when they conflict with other more accurate sense-perceptions, the former are rejected only when they conflict with convictions which stand better the test of refection.[4]

I want to stress that Ross speaks here not only of our grasping (or apprehending) the truth of the relevant moral and mathematical propositions, but also of what I think he conceives as our apprehending their self-evidence. One indication of this latter focus is his taking us to be aware that we are dealing with proposi- tions which are not in need of proof – *proof- exempt*, we might say. He is influenced, I believe, by the dialectic of argument with other philosophers about what is self-evident, and he is here not concentrating on the more basic question of how we can know the truth of first-order moral propositions. Such a shift of focus is particularly easy if one thinks that the relevant *kind* of proposition, if true, is self- evident. For then one does not expect to find cogent premises for such a proposition – or, like Moore and Ross, thinks there can be none – and, as a philosopher, one will want to explain *why* one has none by maintaining that the proposition is self-evident.

Whatever the reason for it, Ross does not always distinguish (or does not explicitly dis- tinguish) apprehending the truth of a propos- ition that *is* self-evident from apprehending *its self-evidence*. This is a point whose significance is easily missed. The truth of at least some self-evident propositions is easy to appre- hend. Self-evident propositions have even been thought to be so luminous that one can- not grasp them *without* believing them. But the epistemic *status* of propositions, for instance their justification or self-evidence, is a para- digm source of disagreement. Two people attending to the same proposition can agree that it is true but differ concerning its status, one of them thinking it self-evident and the other taking it to be merely empirical. Intu- itionism as most plausibly developed does not require positing non-inferential knowledge of the self-evidence, as opposed to the truth, of its basic principles. If I am correct, then one apparently common view of intuitionism is a mistake. Let me clarify the crucial distinction.

We might know that a moral principle, say that promise-keeping is a *prima facie* duty, is self-evident only on the basis of sophisticated considerations, say from knowing the concep- tual as opposed to empirical (e.g., observa- tional) character of the grounds on which we know that principle to be true. We would know its truth *on* these grounds; we would know its self-evidence through knowledge *about* the grounds. It is, however, that first-order prop- osition, the principle that promise-keeping is a duty, not the second-order thesis that this

principle is self-evident, which is the funda- mental thing we must be able to know intui- tively if intuitionism (whether in Ross's version or any other plausible one) is to succeed.

One might indeed consider the concept of self-evidence, by contrast with that of truth, to be an epistemically explanatory notion more appropriate to the metaethics of intuitionism than to its basic formulation as a normative theory. Its application to a proposition explains both how it can be known (roughly, through understanding it in its own terms) and why knowing it requires no premises. Ross naturally wanted to indicated why his principles are true and how they are known, not just *that* they are true; but one might surely know their truth, intuitively or otherwise, without knowing either why they are true or how they are known.

Granted, then, that intuitionists hold that moral agents need and have intuitive know- ledge of their duties, neither intuitionists as moral theorists nor we as moral agents need intuitive knowledge of the status of the prin- ciples of duty. Nor need an intuitionist hold that conscientious moral agents must in gen- eral even know that they know the moral principles that guide them. The first-order knowledge does the crucial day-to-day norma- tive work.

These reflections bring us to another major element in the most common conception of intuitionism: the idea that, for cognition grounded in genuine intuition, intuitionism implies *indefeasible justification* – roughly, jus- tification that cannot be undermined or over- ridden. Intuitionism (even in Ross) is not committed to this general idea, though he may have accepted it for certain cases. For ethical intuitionism as a normative theory, the primary role of intuition is to give us direct, i.e., non-inferential, knowledge or justified belief of the *truth* of certain moral proposi- tions. It is not, as one might think from reading Ross and some other intuitionists, to provide either knowledge of the self-evidence of basic moral propositions (especially certain moral principles) or what one might naturally take to follow from the existence of such knowledge – indefeasible justification for believing those propositions. Intuition can yield a kind of insight into, and non-inferential knowledge of, first-order propositions without yielding such knowledge of or any insight into second-order propositions about their status.

What reason remains, then, to think that intuitively grounded beliefs of moral principles are indefeasibly justified? To be sure, self-evidence apparently entails necessity; but even the necessary truth of a principle would not imply that one's *justification* for believing it is indefeasible. Clearly, we can cease to be justified in believing even a genuine theorem that is necessary and even a priori, because our "proof" of it is shown to be defective.

Conclusions of inference versus conclusions of reflection

If I have eliminated one significant element from Ross's view and thereby provided a more moderate intuitionism, on a related matter I want to claim some-what more than he did. In a sense, an intuition (or intuitive judgment) *can* be a conclusion formed though rational inquiry or searching reflection, and when this is understood it will be apparent that there is room for a still wider intuitionism than so far described. Consider reading a poem to decide whether the language is artificial. After two readings, one silent and the other aloud, one might judge that the language is indeed artificial. This judgment could be a response to evidential propositions, say that the author has manipulated words to make the lines scan. But the judgment need not so arise: if the artificiality is subtler, there may just be a stilted quality that one can hardly pin down. In this second case, one judges from a global, intuitive sense of the integration of vocabulary, movement, and content. Call the first judgment of artificiality a *conclusion of inference*: it is premised on propositions one has noted as evidence. Call the second judgment a *conclusion of reflection*: it emerges from thinking about the poem, but not from one or more evidential premises. It is more like a response to viewing a painting than like an inference from propositionally represented information. You respond to a pattern: you notice a stiff movement in the otherwise flowing meter; you are irritated by an inapt simile; and so on. The conclusion of reflection is a

kind of wrapping up of the question, akin to concluding a practical matter with a *decision*. One has not added up the evidences and inferred their implication; one has obtained a view of the whole and broadly characterized it. Far from starting with a checklist of artificialities, one could not even compose the relevant list until after studying the poem.

By no means all moral intuitions are conclusions of reflection (and the point apparently holds for intuitions in general); and in this respect, as in other aspects of intuitive reactivity, people differ and may themselves change over time, even in relation to the same proposition. Moreover, there is no need to deny that in principle, where one arrives at such a conclusion, one *could* figure out why and *then* formulate, in explicit premises, one's basis for the conclusion. But that a ground of judgment can be so formulated does not entail that it must do its work in that inferential way. An intuitive judgment or belief may not emerge until reflection proceeds for some time, even when inference is not a factor in the formation of that judgment or belief. This delay is particularly likely when the object of judgment is complicated. Such an intuition can be a conclusion of reflection, temporally as well as epistemically; and in content it may be either empirical or a priori.

On the conception of intuition I am developing, then, it is, in the "faculty" sense, chiefly a non-inferential cognitive capacity, not a non-reflective one. The cognitions in question – intuitions – instantiate intuition in what we might call the experiential sense: they are cognitive responses to the relevant object, such as a moral assessment. Understanding of that object is required for these cognitions to possess intuitive justification or constitute intuitive knowledge, and, often, understanding comes only with time.[5] Achieving understanding may be so labored that even a self-evident truth it finally reveals, even non-inferentially, *seems* not to be self-evident and is either not believed or not believed with much conviction. Let me develop this idea.

Self-evidence and understanding

The contrast between conclusions of inference and conclusions of reflection is related to a distinction that is highly pertinent to understanding intuitionism. It is between two kinds of self-evidence. Let me first sketch a general conception of self-evident propositions; we can then distinguish two kinds. Taking off from the idea that a self-evident proposition is one whose truth is in some way evident "in itself," I propose the following sketch of the basic notion of self-evidence. A self-evident proposition is (roughly) a truth such that an adequate understanding of it meets two conditions: (a) in virtue of that understanding, one is justified in believing the proposition (i.e., has justification for believing it, whether one in fact believes it or not) – this is why such a truth is evident *in itself*; and (b) if one believes the proposition on the *basis* of that understanding of it, then one knows it. Thus (abbreviating and slightly altering the characterization), a proposition is self-evident provided an adequate understanding of it is sufficient for being justified in believing it and for knowing it if one believes it on the basis of that understanding. Three clarifications are needed immediately.

First, as (a) indicates, it does not follow from the self-evidence of a proposition that if one understands (and considers) the proposition, then one believes it. Self-evident propositions may be *withholdable* and indeed *disbelievable*: there are some that one might fail to believe or even believe false. This non-belief-entailing conception of self-evidence is plausible because one can fail initially to "see" a self-evident truth and later grasp it in just the way one grasps the truth of a paradigmatically self-evident proposition: one that is obvious in itself the moment one considers it. Take, e.g., a self-evident proposition that is perhaps not immediately obvious: the existence of great-grandchildren is impossible apart from that of at least four generations of people. A delay in seeing a truth (such as this) need not change the character of what one sees. What is self-evident can be justifiedly believed on its "intrinsic" merits, but they need not leap out immediately. Granted, rational persons tend to believe self-evident propositions they adequately understand when they comprehendingly consider them. In some cases, however, one can see *what* a self-evident

proposition says – and thus understand it – before seeing *that*, or how, it is true.

Second, though I offer no full analysis of adequate understanding, I have several clarifying points. It is to be contrasted with mistaken or partial or clouded understanding. Adequate understanding of a proposition is more than simply getting the general sense of a sentence expressing it, as where one can parse the sentence grammatically, indicate something of what it means through examples, and perhaps translate it into another language one knows well. Adequacy here implies not only seeing what the proposition says, but also being able to apply it to (and withhold its application from) an appropriately wide range of cases, and being able to see some of its logical implications, to distinguish it from a certain range of close relatives, and to comprehend its elements and some of their relations. An inadequate understanding of a self-evident proposition is not sufficient for knowledge or justified belief of it.

Third, there is both an occurrent and a dispositional use of "understanding." The former is illustrated by one's comprehension of a proposition one is considering, the latter by such comprehension as is retained after one's attention turns elsewhere. A weaker dispositional use is illustrated by "She understands such ideas," uttered where one has in mind something like this: she has never entertained them, but would (occurrently) understand them upon considering them.

Leaving further subtleties aside, the crucial point is that in the above characterization of self-evidence, "understanding", in clause (a), may bear any of the suggested senses so long as justification is construed accordingly. If you have occurrent understanding of a self-evident proposition, you have occurrent justification for it; if you have strong dispositional understanding of it, you have dispositional justification; and if you have weak dispositional understanding, you have only *structural justification* for it: roughly, there is an appropriate path leading from justificatory materials accessible to you to an occurrent justification for the proposition but you lack dispositional justification. (I shall assume that when knowledge of a self-evident proposition is based on understanding it, the understanding must be occurrent or strongly dispositional, but even here one could devise a conception of knowledge with a looser connection to understanding.)

Two kinds of self-evidence

Given the points about self-evidence expressed in (a) and (b), we may distinguish those self-evident propositions that are readily understood by normal adults (or by people of some relevant description, e.g. mature moral agents) and those they understand only through reflection on them. Call the first *immediately self-evident* and the second *mediately self-evident*, since their truth can be grasped only through the mediation of reflection (as opposed to inference from one or more premises. This is not a logical or epistemological distinction, but a psychological and pragmatic one concerning comprehensibility to a certain kind of mind. It will soon be clear why the distinction is nonetheless important for understanding intuitionism.

The reflection in question may involve drawing inferences, say about what it means, for both perpetrator and victim, to flog an infant for pleasure. But the role of inferences is limited largely to clarifying what the proposition in question says: as self-evidence is normally understood, a self-evident proposition is knowable without relying on inferential *grounds* for it. One may require time to get it in clear focus, but need not reach it by an inferential path from one or more premises. To see one kind of role inference *can* have, however, consider the proposition that if *p* entails *q* and *q* entails *r* and yet *r* is false, then *p* is false. One may instantly just see the truth of this; but even if one must first infer that *p* entails *r*, this is not a ground for believing the whole conditional proposition. It is an implicate of a part of it (of the if-clause) that helps one to see how it is that the whole conditional is true. Even if such *internal inference* is required to know the truth of a proposition, it may still be mediately self-evident.

Internal inferences may also be purely clarificatory, say semantically, as where, from the proposition that there is a great-grandchild,

one infers that there are parental, grandparental, and great-grandparental generations. We might say, then, that knowledge of a self-evident proposition (and justification for believing it) may depend *internally* on inference, above all where inference is needed for understanding the proposition, but may not depend *externally* on inference, where this is a matter of epistemic dependence on one or more premises (the kind of dependence entailing independent evidential support for the proposition in question).

In the light of the distinction between the mediately and the immediately self-evident, the characteristic intuitionist claim that basic moral principles are self-evident can be seen to require only that a kind of reflection will yield adequate justification for them – the kind of justification that yields knowledge when belief of a true proposition is based on such reflection. Given how much time and thought this reflection may require, the intuitionist view may be seen as closer to Kant's moral epistemology than one might think, at least assuming that for Kant it is the apriority of the categorical imperative itself that is epistemologically most important, as opposed to the inferential character of our knowledge of it.

Even supposing that it is crucial for Kant that knowledge of the categorical imperative be inferential (as one might think from his arguing for it from considerations about the nature of practical reason), it should be stressed that the Rossian principles of duty, as first-order moral principles, need not be in the same epistemic boat. If they are even mediately self-evident, they may be taken to be non-inferentially knowable. Still, surely any (or virtually any) proposition that can be known non-inferentially can also be known inferentially. Ross, apparently following Moore and Prichard, implicitly denied this,[6] but there is no need for a intuitionism, either as a moral epistemology positing intuitive knowledge of moral principles or as an ethical pluralism, to deny it.

As long as basic moral principles *can* be known (or at least justifiedly accepted) independently of relying on grounding premises, morality can be understood and practiced as intuitionists understand it. Life would be very different if we could not move our legs except by doing something else, such as activating a machine that moves them; but we *can* do such things and at times may find it desirable. The possibility of moving our legs in a secondary way does not change the nature of our primary leg movements. So it can be with knowledge of basic moral principles. It is only ethical theory (of a certain kind) that must provide for the possibility of overdetermined justification or knowledge of moral principles by virtue of their being supported independently by both intuitive and inferential grounds. Providing for this possibility is in no way hostile to any major intuitionist purpose.

[. . .]

Rationalist intuitionism

[I]ntuitionism in moral epistemology [. . .] is best conceived, given the overall views of Ross and its other major proponents, as a rationalist position, and in answering some objections to it I will stress the rationalism of the reconstructed Rossian intuitionism developed above – in outline, the view that we have intuitive justification for both some of our particular moral judgments and a plurality of mediately self-evident moral principles.

A common objection to intuitionism centers on the claim that the basic principles of ethics are self-evident. If so, why is there so much disagreement on them? I suggest three points in reply.

First, if mediate self-evidence is the only kind that need be claimed for basic moral principles, such as Ross's principles of *prima facie* duty, there is no presumption that there should be consensus on them, even after some discussion or reflection. Indeed, given the complexities of the notion of the *prima facie* justified (and even of the notion of justification itself), some people may be expected to have difficulty understanding Ross's principles in the first place.

Second, some of the apparent hesitation in accepting the truth of the principles may come from *thinking* of their truth as a kind requiring endorsement of their self-evidence – the status intuitionists have prominently claimed for them – or of their necessity, a property that, at least since Kant, has commonly been taken

to be grasped *in* seeing the truth of an a priori proposition. But I have stressed that the second-order claim that they are self-evident need not also be self-evident in order for them to have this status themselves, and, unlike Ross, I argue that it should not be expected to be self-evident. Seeing its truth requires some theoretical premises.

Third, even if there should be persisting disagreement on the truth or status of the Rossian principles, there need not be disagreement about the basic moral force of the considerations they cite. For instance, whether or not we accept Ross's principles concerning promising and non-injury, we might, both in our abstract thinking and in regulating our conduct, take our having promised to do something as a basic moral reason to do it, or the fact that leaving now would strand a friend about to be attacked by a mad dog, as a basic reason not to do that. Such agreement *in* reasons for action – *operative agreement*, we might call it – does not require agreement *on* them, for instance on some principle expressing them, or on their force. We can agree that a factor, such as avoidance of abandoning a friend, is a good reason for action even if we cannot formulate, or cannot both accept, a principle subsuming the case.

More commonly, we agree on the positive or negative relevance of a reason yet differ on its force; this may occur even where we can agree on a principle subsuming the case, and it can lead to at least temporary disagreement on the final resolution of a moral issue. If there is the kind of wide agreement in moral practice that I think there is among civilized people, then the most important kind of consensus needed for the success of intuitionism as a moral theory is in place. It can at least be argued that the truth and non-inferential justifiability of the relevant principles best explains the high degree of consensus among civilized people in wide segments of their everyday moral practice.

Incommensurability as a problem for intuitionism

Supposing this threefold reply to the first objection succeeds, we must acknowledge a further problem for intuitionism – though it besets virtually any pluralistic ethical view. Non-inferential knowledge or justified belief that a consideration morally favors an action is one thing; such knowledge or justification for taking it as an overriding reason for action is quite another. One might speak of an *incommensurability problem*, since intuitionism grants that there are irreducibly different kinds of moral grounds. Intuitionists deny that there are, say, just hedonic grounds that can be aggregatively assessed to determine what our obligations are. There are at least three crucial points here.

First, intuitionism does not imply that we typically have non-inferential knowledge of *final* duty. We may, for instance, have to compare the case at hand with earlier ones or hypothetical cases and then reason from relevant information to a conclusion. Thus, we might note that if we submit a certain appraisal we may be accused of bias, and we may begin to see the question in relation to conflict of interest. Our final judgment may arise from formulating a sufficient condition for a conflict of interest and judging that the prospective action satisfies it and is thereby impermissible.

Second, it is essential to distinguish higher-order knowledge (or justification) regarding the overridingness of a duty (or other kind of reason) from the first-order knowledge that a given action, say keeping one's promise in spite of a good excuse for non-performance, is obligatory (or otherwise reasonable in some overall way). One can know what one is obligated to do, even in a situation of conflicting duties, yet lack the kind of comparative knowledge one might get from, say, a utilitarian calculation or a Kantian deduction. Perhaps if I know that I should wait for a distressed friend, in a case where I realize this means missing an appointment, I am in a *position* to figure out that one of the two duties is overriding, or even to reach the second-order knowledge that I know this comparative proposition. But I do not in such cases automatically know either of these propositions; and if I am not skilled in moral reasoning, it may be hard for me to do any more than sketch an account of why one duty is overriding. That we easily make mistakes in such sketches is one

reason why knowledge of overridingness, and particularly of just *why* it obtains, is often hard to come by.

Third, the difficulty of achieving knowledge or justification in the fact of conflicting grounds is not peculiar to ethics. Consider divided evidence for a scientific hypothesis. Sometimes we must suspend judgment on a hypothesis or cannot reasonably choose between two alternative ones. This does not imply that we never have grounds good enough for knowledge; and the conditions for a degree of justification sufficient to warrant acceptance of a hypothesis are less stringent than the conditions for knowledge. So it is in ethics, sometimes with lesser justification than is common in rational scientific acceptance, but in many cases with greater: even when lying would spare someone pain, it can sometimes be utterly and immediately clear that we should not do it. If there is incommensurability, in the sense of the absence of a common measure for all moral considerations, there is nonetheless *comparability* in the sense implying the possibility of a rational weighting in the context of the relevant facts.

Intuitionism can also maintain (though it may leave open) that final duty is like *prima facie* duty in supervening on natural facts. This plausible view implies that, even where there is no single quantitative or otherwise arguably straightforward basis for comparing conflicting duties, it is possible to describe the various grounds of duty in each case, to compare the cases in that respect with similar cases resolved in the past, bring to bear hypothetical examples, and the like. This is the sort of stuff on which practical wisdom is made.

The charge of dogmatism

Because the controversy between empiricism and rationalism as epistemological perspectives is apparently very much with us in ethical theory, despite how few ethical theorists avowedly maintain either perspective, I want to examine some plausible objections to the intuitionism developed here that are either motivated by empiricism or best seen as objections, not to appeal to intuitions, but to the underlying rationalism of the prominent intuitionist views: roughly, to their taking reason, as opposed to observation, to be capable of grounding justification for substantive truths, such as (arguably) Ross's moral principles of *prima facie* duty.

Is intuitionism dogmatic, as some have held? It might well be dogmatic to claim both that we have intuitive, certain knowledge of what our *prima facie* duties are *and* cannot ground that knowledge on any kind of evidence or in some way support it by examples. But I have argued that a plausible intuitionism, including Ross's, is not committed to our having "certain knowledge" here – where such certainty implies indefeasible justification. Moreover, dogmatism – as distinct from mere stubbornness – is a second-order attitude, such as believing, on a controversial matter, that one is obviously right. Even holding that basic moral principles are self-evident does not entail taking a dogmatic attitude toward them or one's critics. The self-evident may not even be readily understood, much less obvious. A related point is that intuitionism also does not invite moral agents to be dogmatic. Moral principles can *be* basic in our ethical life and non-inferentially justified for us, even if we do not take them to be self-evident (or perhaps even true).

Despite Ross's in some ways unfortunate analogy between moral principles and elementary logical and mathematical ones, he provides a place for reflective equilibrium, which is roughly a kind of fairly stable balance among one's principles and one's judgments about particular cases, to enhance – or for its unobtainability to undermine – our justification for an "intuitive" moral judgment. Nor does anything he must hold, *qua* intuitionist, preclude his allowing a systematization of his moral principles in terms of something more general. Indeed, in at least one place he speaks as if one of the *prima facie* duties might be derivable from another.[7] If such systematization is achieved, then contrary to what the dogmatism charge suggests, that systematization might provide both reasons for the principles and a source of correctives for certain false intuitions or for merely apparent intuitions. An intuition can be mistaken, and a mere prejudice can masquerade as an intuition.

Suppose, e.g., that one uses the categorical imperative to systematize first-order moral principles like Ross's. This would enable one to justify them with whatever force that higher-order principle transmits. Suppose that principle is itself either non-inferentially knowable – in which case intuitionism might claim to encompass among self-evident principles a higher-order moral standard as well as its typical workaday ones – or well justified by arguments from premises, say general truths about practical reason. In either case, it is a good premise for first-order principles of duty. And might it not follow from the categorical imperative that there is (e.g.) *prima facie* moral reason to keep promises? After all, breaking them is *prima facie* something the intrinsic end formulation explicitly forbids: treating people merely as means – giving them an expectation and then, for one's own ends, letting them down. Quite apart from how successful such a unifying enterprise is, if it is even possible as a critical and clarificatory perspective on first-order intuitive principles, this reduces the plausibility of claiming that positing such principles invites dogmatism.

Moreover, given how intuitions are understood – as deriving from the exercise of reason and as having evidential weight – it is incumbent on conscientious intuitionists to factor into their moral thinking, particularly on controversial issues, the apparent intuitions of *others*. If mine have evidential weight, should not others' too? Ross appealed repeatedly to "what we really think" and drew attention to the analogy between intuitions in ethics and perceptions in science. Intuitions, then, are not properly conceived as arbitrary. Many have a basis in reflection and are shared by people of very different experience. Moreover, any rule of conduct arbitrarily posited or grounded in the special interests of its proponents would be hard-pressed to survive the kind of reflection to which conscientious intuitionists will subject their basic moral standards. Thus, even if an apparent intuition might sometimes arise as an arbitrary cognition, it would not necessarily have even *prima facie* justification; and, where a genuine intuition, which presumably does have some degree of *prime facie* justification, is misleading, it can at least normally be defeated by other intuitions that reflection might generate or by those together with further elements in the reflective equilibrium a reasonable intuitionist would seek.

Some philosophical commitments of intuitionism

[. . .]

I turn now to the matter of epistemic principles, roughly principles indicating the grounds or nature of knowledge and justification, say that if, on the basis of a clear visual impression of print on paper, I believe there is printed paper before me, then I am justified in so believing. Is moderate intuitionism (Rossian or other) committed to implausible epistemic principles? I have already suggested that intuitionists as such need not take a self-evident proposition to be incapable of being evidenced by anything else. I now want to suggest that, quite apart from whether they can be evidenced by something else, Ross's basic principles of duty are at least candidates for a priori justification in the way they should be if they are mediately self-evident.

Keeping in mind what constitutes a *prima facie* duty, consider how we would regard some native speaker of English who denied that there is (say) a *prima facie* duty not to injure other people and meant by this something which implies that doing it would not in general be even *prima facie* wrong. This is not amoralism, in the most common sense – the point is not that the person would not be *moved*. Rather, such a person apparently exhibits a kind of *moral deafness*. As with any denial of a clearly true a priori proposition, our first thought might be that there is misunderstanding of some key term, such as "prima facie". Apart from misunderstanding, I doubt that anyone not in the grip of a competing theory would deny the proposition, and I believe that any plausible competing theory would tend to support the same moral judgment, perhaps disguised in different clothing. To be sure, it may be that some skeptical consideration could lead someone who adequately understands a properly formulated Rossian principle to deny it. But some skeptical considerations can be brought against nonmoral a priori propositions and in any event are not necessarily good reasons to doubt either the truth or the a priori status of the challenged proposition.

What is perhaps less controversial is that if we do not ascribe to reason the minimal power required in order for a moderate intuitionism of the kind I have described to be epistemologically plausible, then we face serious problems that must be solved before any instrumentalist or empiricist ethical theory is plausible. For one thing, instrumentalists must account for their fundamental principle that if, on our beliefs, an action serves a basic (roughly, non-instrumental) desire of ours, then there is a reason for us to perform the action. This proposition seems a better candidate for mediate self-evidence than for empirical confirmation. None of this entails that a moderate intuitionism is true; the point is that unless reason has sufficient power to make principles like Ross's plausible candidates for truth, then it is not clear that instrumentalist principles are plausible candidates either.

The Gap between Intuitive Moral Judgment and Rational Action

It may easily seem that to show that moral knowledge is possible is to vanquish moral skepticism. But if moral skepticism includes the full range of skeptical positions in ethics, this is not so. Granted that general moral knowledge, say of principles expressing basic *prima facie* duties, is significant, it can exist quite apart from knowledge of singular moral judgments – even the self-addressed, action-guiding kind that moral life depends on. I have argued that despite the problem raised by the plurality of values, such singular judgments can express knowledge, and certainly justified belief. But is either moral knowledge or justified moral belief extensive enough to give us moral guidance in daily life?
[. . .]

Some challenges of moral skepticism

On the first question, concerning the possibility of knowledge or justified belief regarding the moral status of individual actions, I maintain that although singular moral judgments should not be considered self-evident, they may still be noninferentially knowable (or justified). This point may be obscured because it may seem that intuitionism requires self-evidence for justified belief of singular as well as certain general moral propositions. But it does not and in fact cannot plausibly require this if I am right in taking self-evident propositions to be knowable on conceptual grounds. Nor does intuitionism imply that only self-evident propositions are intuitively knowable. A singular moral judgment about a particular person can be intuitively knowable, especially when it is an application of a principle of *prima facie* as opposed to final duty.

One may also be tempted to think that if, in making singular moral judgments, we are guided by moral principles, and if, afterwards, we can frame a principle to cover the action in question, then we should be able to see the relevant judgments as derivable from principles in a way that as it were certifies them as knowledge. This idea neglects a point essential to a particularist intuitionism such as Ross's: at least some intuitions regarding concrete cases are epistemically more basic than, or in any event indispensable to, intuitive knowledge of the corresponding generalizations. It may be only when we think of a deed concretely and realize it is wrong that we see (or are justified in believing) that all deeds of that kind are wrong.

The idea that singular moral judgments are knowable only as applications of generalizations may also arise from the correct point that in many cases one must be able to see two or more conflicting (*prima facie*) generalizations to apply to one's options before one can tell what, overall, one should do. Still, the applicability of several generalizations to a case does not imply that one's final obligation therein is determined by applying a further, reconciling generalization. That point holds even if such a generalization is in principle formulable after the fact.

To be sure, supposing that (all) moral properties supervene on a finite set of natural ones and that the relevant natural ones and their grounding relations to the moral ones are discernible by ordinary kinds of inquiry, then in principle one can, given a good grasp of a sound moral judgment in a case of conflicting obligations, formulate a generalization that nontrivially applies to similar cases. For the overall obligatoriness one discerns will be based on natural properties that one can in principle discriminate and appeal to in framing a generalization. But this generalization possibility is not a necessary condition for one's forming a justified judgment (or one expressing knowledge), say a judgment that one must rectify an injustice. One can achieve a sound result whether or not one generalizes on it or is even able to do so. It could be, for instance, that overall obligation is *organic*, and that given the sense in which it is, we can have no guarantee of being able to specify just what properties are the basis of it. Even if *prima facie* obligation is entailed by certain natural properties (a view that intuitionists commonly hold), overall obligation apparently requires a more complicated account.

A further point concerning the epistemic resources of the intuitionism I am developing is that in many cases of a singular judgment settling a conflict of duties, there is the possibility of reaching a reflective equilibrium between this judgment and various moral principles and other singular judgments. This equilibrium may contribute to the justification of that judgment; the former or elements in it may even produce the latter. Here, then, is one way a judgment that begins as a hypothesis can graduate to the status of justified belief or even knowledge.

[. . .]

If the (ideally moderate) foundationalism that I suggest is crucial for a plausible intuitionism is sound, we can make at least two significant points here. First, if we distinguish between rebutting a skeptical view – showing that the case for it is unsound – and refuting it, which is showing it false by establishing that there *is* the relevant kind of knowledge or justification, then there is reason to think rebuttal is possible. What we can do, I contend, is consider the various epistemic standards the skeptic says moral judgment cannot meet and argue that either the standard is too high or the judgment can meet it. Second, although refuting skepticism is harder than rebutting it, it may yet be possible given epistemic standards that are not unrealistically high. For one thing, there is a chance that some paradigms will simply be more intuitive than any competing intuitions that serve skepticism. Surely it is more intuitive that we are justified in judging that flogging infants for pleasure is wrong than that no one is justified in holding moral judgments. Perhaps we can exhibit or argue for our justification here in a compelling way that counts as showing that we have moral justification.

[. . .]

Notes

1. This is the kind of thing W. D. Ross and other intuitionists have said about basic moral principles: they are intuitively knowable and self-evident, though seeing their truth may take a good deal of reflection. See e.g. Ross's *The Right and the Good* (Oxford: Oxford University Press, 1930), esp. ch. 2. The point is developed below.
2. See Ross, p. 21.
3. Ibid., pp. 29–30.
4. Ibid., pp. 39–41.
5. I speak here only of intuitions *that*, as opposed to property intuitions, intuitions *of* or regarding something; the latter do not admit of justification or knowledge in the same way.
6. Ross said (e.g., in the quotation given from pp. 29–30) that his principles do not admit of proof, and Moore went so far as to say that in calling propositions intuitions he means "*merely* to assert that they are incapable of proof; I imply nothing whatever as to the manner or origin of our cognition of them." *Principia Ethica* (London: Cambridge University Press, 1903), p. x. See also p. 145.
7. He says that "[E]ven before the implicit undertaking to tell the truth was established [by a contract] I had a duty not to tell lies, since to tell lies is *prima facie* to do a positive injury to a person," *The Right and the Good*, p. 55. This seems to countenance a derivation of a duty of fidelity (Ross conceived honesty as fidelity to one's implicit agreement in speaking) from one of non-injury.

CHAPTER 14

Coherentism and the Justification of Moral Beliefs

GEOFFREY SAYRE-McCORD

What I hope to offer here is an account of epistemic justification that can do justice to the epistemic challenges our moral beliefs face, while leaving room for some of those beliefs, sometimes, to count as justified in precisely the same way our more mundane non-moral beliefs, sometimes, do. I don't mean to suggest, and I certainly won't argue, that our moral beliefs are actually as justified as many of our other beliefs are. I think many of them are not; the challenges they face properly induce epistemic humility. But I do think that some of our moral beliefs are justified and justified in the same sense (if not always to the same degree) as are many of our other beliefs.

As a result, what I'll be doing is primarily defending in general – and without special regard for morality – a theory of the epistemic justification of belief that applies across the board to all our beliefs.

Foundationalism and Coherentism

What does it take for a person to be *epistemically* (as opposed to morally or pragmatically)

Geoffrey Sayre-McCord, "Coherentism and the Justification of Moral Beliefs," from Mark Timmons and Walter Sinnott-Armstrong (eds.), *Moral Knowledge?* Oxford: Oxford University Press, 1996. By permission of Oxford University Press, Inc.

justified in holding the belief she does? Under what conditions, for instance, would she be justified in accepting utilitarianism or in rejecting Naziism, or in thinking courage virtuous, or pleasure good?

When concerned with belief in general, with no special focus on moral beliefs, answers have traditionally divided into two camps, one foundationalist, the other coherentist. The foundationalist's account involves appealing to some class of *epistemically privileged* beliefs (that enjoy their privilege independently of their inferential/evidential connections) and then holding that a belief, any belief, moral or otherwise, is justified if and only if either: (i) it is member of that privileged class; or (ii) it bears an appropriate evidential/inferential relation to a belief that is a member of the class.

Different versions of foundationalism emerge as different classes of belief are singled out as foundational and as different evidential/inferential relations are countenanced as appropriate. Just to mention a few of the familiar suggestions, beliefs might count as foundational in virtue of being certain, or incorrigible, or formed under the appropriate circumstances, while an inferential relation might count as appropriate if it is deductive, or inductive, or abductive, or explanatory. Precisely how the details are filled in will make a huge difference to both the stringency of the requirements imposed and the plausibility of the theory that results. What all the versions share, though, is the view that there is an epistemically privileged class of beliefs that are justified independently of the evidential/inferential relations they might bear to other beliefs and that all other beliefs are justified, when they are, in virtue of the support they receive from foundational beliefs[1] [. . .]

Suppose, then, that some of our moral views are justified. How would our justified moral beliefs (assuming there are some) fit into the foundationalist's picture of justification? Foundationalists who hold that some moral beliefs *are* justified must hold either that some moral beliefs are epistemically privileged or that, although none are, some moral beliefs are nonetheless justified inferentially by appeal ultimately to some nonmoral beliefs that are.

The vast majority of foundationalists working in moral theory have gone the first route and embraced a *moral foundation*, holding that some of our moral beliefs qualify as epistemically privileged. Influenced by Hume's observation that one cannot legitimately infer an "ought" from and "is," they've held that our nonmoral beliefs, taken alone, can provide no evidence whatsoever for our moral convictions.[2] There is, they think, an inferentially unbridgeable gap between nonmoral and moral beliefs (or at least between nonevaluative and evaluative beliefs) [. . .]

If this is right, it means that, on a foundationalist's view of justification, the only way any of our moral beliefs could be justified is if some of them are epistemically privileged – otherwise they all are ultimately unjustifiable. The central problem facing such a position is to make plausible the suggestion that at least some moral beliefs are properly viewed as epistemically privileged. And this is no small problem since all the concerns that raise general epistemic worries about our moral views devolve onto any particular proposal one might make to the effect that some subset of those views is epistemically privileged.

Coherentists, in contrast, reject precisely this view, maintaining that whatever justification our moral beliefs enjoy is due entirely to the relations they bear to other things we believe. Those who think the gap between nonmoral and moral beliefs (or at least between nonevaluative and evaluative beliefs) is forever unbridgeable, maintain that all our moral beliefs receive what justification they have only from other moral (or at least evaluative) beliefs. Others, though, hold that, whatever the nature of the "is"/"ought" gap, it does not work to insulate completely our moral judgments from nonmoral (and nonevaluative) considerations. On their view, metaphysical, epistemological, social, and psychological considerations might all be relevant to the justification of our moral views. Significantly, defenders of this version of moral coherentism needn't hold that nonmoral beliefs *alone* either entail or in some other way inferentially support moral conclusions; they may well hold that our moral views themselves establish the epistemic relevance of nonmoral considerations. This means that a coherentist can accept all the standard arguments for the "is"/"ought" gap without being committed to holding that all the evidence we have for our moral views come from moral considerations. In fact, given just how implausible it is to see any of our moral views as epistemically privileged, a great attraction of coherentism is its ability to make sense of our moral views being (to a greater or lesser extent) justified even in the face of the "is"/"ought" gap.

The heart of the difference between foundationalism and coherentism, as the distinction applies generally, is found in coherentism's rejection of the view that there is an epistemically privileged subset of beliefs (moral or not), and its rejection of the view that all other beliefs are justified only in virtue of the relations they bear to such privileged beliefs. This difference turns on what foundationalism asserts and coherentism denies.[3] Yet coherentism goes beyond the denial and offers a positive account of what it takes for a person's belief to be epistemically justified.[4]

The coherentist's positive account involves articulating a conception of what it is for one belief to cohere with others, and then arguing that a person's belief is epistemically justified only if, and then to the extent that, the belief in question coheres well with her other beliefs. There is, on the coherentist's view, no subset of beliefs that counts as epistemically privileged (at least none whose privilege is independent of the inferential connections its members bear to other beliefs). Instead, beliefs, moral and otherwise, enjoy whatever epistemic credentials they have thanks to the evidential/inferential relations they bear to other beliefs. The more and better the relations, the greater the degree of coherence enjoyed by the set and the stronger the justification. Predictably, different versions of coherentism emerge as different evidential/inferential relations are countenanced as appropriate. Also predictably, precisely how the details are filled in will make a huge difference to both the stringency of the requirements imposed and the plausibility of the theory that results. What all the versions share, though, is the view that the extent to which a belief is justified turns simply on the evidential/inferential relations it bears to other beliefs [. . .]

I am going to put off, for a time, offering a positive account of coherence and its relation to justification, turning first to one argument, *the regress argument*, that is commonly thought to show that no version of coherentism has a chance of being right regardless of the specific account of coherence it offers. I will, in the next two sections, argue that a coherentist can consistently recognize the force of the regress argument and yet satisfyingly stop the regress without having her position collapse into a version of foundationalism. With that argument made, I will then offer a positive account of coherence as a backdrop for replying to several other objections to coherentism many have found persuasive.

The Regress Argument

The regress argument is by far the most influential argument against both coherentism in general and coherentism as applied to our moral beliefs. As this argument would have it, if any beliefs are justified at all, some must be justified independently of the relations they bear to other beliefs. In other words, coherentism has got to be false.

The argument begins with the assumption that one belief provides justification for another only if it is, itself, justified. For any given belief, then, the question arises: what sort of justification does it enjoy? If it is justified by other beliefs from which it is inferable, then the beliefs on which its justification depends must themselves be justified and we can raise the same question about them, and then again about whatever beliefs justify those. If we are to avoid an infinite regress, there are only two possibilities (compatible with holding that the initial belief is justified). Either:

(i)   The path of justification from one belief to those from which it is inferable, to those from which they are inferable, leads back to the initial belief, in which case the justification comes objectionably full circle; or

(ii) There are some justified beliefs that are justified independently of the support they might receive from others (say, because they are self-justifying or because they are justified by something other than a belief, perhaps an experience), in which case the regress can be satisfyingly stopped.

Foundationalists have taken comfort from this argument thinking, first, that coherentism is saddled with defending some version of the apparently indefensible (i) and, second, that the kind of beliefs their theories identify as epistemically privileged would play just the role that (ii) makes clear needs to be filled.

Coherentists hold (at least) one of three things: that the way in which one's justification for a belief might come full circle is not, after all, objectionable; or that a coherentist might, despite appearances, acknowledge that there are some justified beliefs that are justified independently of the support they might receive from others; or that there's some third option. Although I am tempted by the first option, in the course of what follows, I shall defend the second as available to a coherentist [. . .]

Whether the regress can actually be stopped [. . .] depends on how the assumption that starts the regress is interpreted. As originally put, that assumption was: one belief provides justification for another only if it is, itself, justified. We can distinguish two relevant readings of this assumption. On one reading, the assumption is: One belief provides *positive* justification for another only if it is, itself, *positively* justified. On the other, it is: One belief provides *positive* justification for another only if it is, itself, *permissively* justified [where a belief is *positively* justified only if the available evidence counts in its favor, while a belief is *permissively* justified as long as the balance of available evidence does not count against it].[5] [. . .] [T]he second reading of the assumption is both strong enough to get the regress going and weak enough to allow the regress to come to an end in beliefs that require no others for their justification [. . .]

This distinction between permissive and positive justification, and the resulting appeal to permissively justified beliefs, has at least three advantages. First, it can explain how the regress might be stopped; it comes to an end if and when we arrive at beliefs that are permissively justified. Second, it leaves room for regress-stoppers that, despite their "regress-stopping" role, might be both over-ridable and underminable; permissively justified beliefs will lose their status when, for instance, new evidence is acquired that tells against them. Third, it avoids saying that among a person's reasons for believing as she does are reasons constituted by considerations that are unavailable to her; whether a belief counts as permissively justified turns only on whether the other things she believes provide, on balance, evidence against the belief.[6] [. . .]

Strikingly, though, coherentists can admit permissively justified beliefs, and rely on them to stop the regress in just the way the foundationalist is proposing, *without abandoning coherentism*. Such a coherentist will still deny that there is an *epistemically privileged set of* beliefs that enjoy their privilege independently of their inferential connections – since which beliefs count as permissively justified depends upon the evidential/inferential relations they bear to others. Moreover, such a coherentist can continue to hold that what positive reason we have for any belief will still always depend solely on what other beliefs a person has. This sort of coherentism, then, grants the regress argument's initial assumption: that a belief can provide (positive) justification for another belief only if it is, itself (permissively) justified. It grants as well that, to the extent an unacceptable regress threatens, it can be brought to a stop with the recognition that beliefs can be justified in either of two senses. What it denies is foundationalism's characteristic – and defining – claim that some beliefs (the regress stoppers) are epistemically privileged independently of the inferential/evidential relations they bear to other beliefs. It insists instead that whether a belief can serve to stop the regress, whether it counts as permissively justified or not, is fully determined by the evidential relations it bears to other beliefs, and that when it does so count it itself enjoys no positive justification, even as it is available to provide positive support for other beliefs.

The coherentist won't hold that the permissively justified beliefs that bring the regress to a stop have anything else to recommend them independently of how they relate to other beliefs; their primary role is to provide the epistemic input – the initial bits of evidence – one justifiably relies upon in seeking out views that are positively justified.

Nor will the coherentist say that every belief spontaneously formed will count as permissively justified. Even if one forms a belief non-inferentially, say as a direct result of some experience, whether it counts as permissively justified will depend on what else one believes. If I turn my head and come to think there's a dog at my feet, the proven past reliability of beliefs of this kind gives me reason to trust this belief as well, and it will count as one I am positively (and not just permissively) justified in believing, even though it is cognitively spontaneous. Whereas, if I find myself yet again confident that this time, finally, I will win the lottery, I have ample reason to distrust the belief, and if I believe it any way, it will count as unjustified (and not permissively justified at all). In the great majority of cases, we might expect, people will have various background beliefs that serve either to support or to undermine the new beliefs they just happen to find themselves with.

And, standardly, any belief's status as merely permissively justified will be comparatively unstable, in that it is likely either to emerge as positively justified as it becomes intertwined with, and in various ways supported by, other beliefs or to become unjustified as one discovers reasons not to trust it. Looked at over time, one's initially merely permissively justified beliefs will regularly get swept up by others so as to become positively justified (as we find reason to think them true) or get sifted out as unjustified (as we find reason to think them suspect).

Permissively Justified Beliefs and Positive Support

As long as beliefs that are merely permissively justified can provide positive justification for other beliefs, foundationalists and coherentists alike can successfully stop the regress, and the regress argument will tell not at all against coherentism. However, if permissively justified beliefs cannot provide positive justification, an appeal to permissively justified beliefs won't help either the coherentist or the foundationalist, when it comes to stopping the regress.

So we need to ask: Can beliefs we have no reason to accept really provide positive support? The temptation is to think not. Even if some permissively justified beliefs (say, the visually prompted belief that there's something red in front of me) can serve to justify others (say, that there's something colored in front of me), it looks as if not all permissively justified beliefs can play this role. In fact, people often seem to hold beliefs that are apparently permissively justified (since they seem to have on balance no reason to reject them) that pretty clearly couldn't serve to justify any other belief. Wild hunches, weird forebodings, and spurious superstitions are, after all, commonplace; and permissively justified though they may be, such beliefs seem not at all able to justify those beliefs that are based on them.

Now a foundationalist might step in at this point hoping to re-establish a role for epistemically privileged beliefs. Unlike coherentists, she is able to distinguish those permissively justified beliefs that can justify others from those that can't, by treating some as epistemically privileged and others not. She might hold that the difference is found in whether the person is being epistemically responsible in holding the belief or in whether the belief is properly caused by experience, or in whether it is suitably concerned with one's private

experience. It is open to the foundationalist to hold that epistemic responsibility, or proper etiology, or appropriate content, might mark the difference between those permissively justified beliefs that can, and those that can't, provide positive justification for other beliefs. A coherentist, in contrast, has to say that all permissively justified beliefs can serve to justify other beliefs, if she is to avoid a surreptitious appeal to privileged beliefs.

Problems arise for the foundationalist, however, as soon as one turns to the question: Why do the specific features identified (whatever they are) make a difference to one's justification? Any attempt to distinguish between permissively justified beliefs that will and those that won't provide positive evidence seems inevitably to face a dilemma.

In every case, the proposed grounds for drawing the distinction will either involve considerations that are potentially unavailable to the person in question or not. If they do, then the account will involve, I'll argue, an implausible kind of [what has come to be called] externalism; if they don't, then by adducing considerations that are available to that person, the view will in the end not be able to mark a difference among permissively justified beliefs in a way that counts only some as capable of providing positive support for other beliefs.

Suppose the foundationalist embraces externalism and (for instance) takes the etiology of the particular belief to be crucial to its ability to justify other beliefs. In a particular case, a person might then hold a belief that lacks the proper history and yet be unaware of that fact. And so far as her evidence is concerned, the belief will be no different from other beliefs of hers that enjoy the proper history. When it comes to the evidence she has, her merely permissively justified beliefs are indistinguishable. That the difference would nonetheless make a difference to her being able justifiably to rely on her belief to justify others seems quite implausible.

It's easy to imagine situations in which two people have the very same beliefs, rely on them identically in reaching various other beliefs, and so are *apparently* equally justified in what they believe, even though they differ (unbeknownst to them) in what originally caused their permissively justified beliefs. One of the two might be in the hands of an evil demon or entranced by a virtual reality machine while the other is not, or one might be experiencing a drug-induced hallucination while the other is really living the life the first imagines, or one might be undergoing an optical illusion indistinguishable ("from the inside") from the accurate visual experiences the other is having.[7] In each of these cases, if we were to assume that only those beliefs with the proper etiology will serve to justify other beliefs, we would be committed to holding that those who have no reason whatsoever to think they are victims of deception, manipulation, drugs, or illusion, though they are, differ substantially, in the justification they have for believing as they do, from those others who are not victims but who have exactly the same grounds available to them for believing as they do. No doubt they are not equally well-placed epistemically. No doubt too we have reason to distinguish between them. Yet when it comes to the justification each has for her own view, they appear to be identically situated. Similar concerns plague any other externalist proposal a foundationalist might offer as grounds for distinguishing among permissively justified beliefs when it comes to their ability to contribute positively to the justification of other beliefs.

Alternatively, and for good reason, the foundationalist might avoid externalism and suggest marking the distinction between permissively justified beliefs that can, and those that can't, provide positive support, by appealing to considerations the person in question has available. But then the considerations adduced will either tell against certain putatively permissively justified beliefs, and so establish the beliefs as not permissively justified at all, or tell in favor of certain beliefs, and so establish them as positively justified. If the first, if the person herself has reason not to hold the belief in question, then coherentist and foundationalist alike will rightly resist seeing the beliefs that are at issue as capable of establishing positive justification, since the beliefs are not even permissively justified. If the second, if the person has reason to rely on the belief, then the belief is positively justified and we simply shift the issue back to the status of the

considerations the foundationalist identifies and ask of them whether they can provide positive support. At some point, if an infinite regress is to be avoided, we will inevitably appeal to some permissively justified belief as providing positive support for others, but at this point with no grounds for saying that only some such permissively justified beliefs can play this role [. . .]

[R]esistance to the idea that permissively justified beliefs might provide positive support for other beliefs is bolstered substantially by the cases of wild hunches, weird forebodings, spurious superstitions, etc., that I have already mentioned. These seem to be cases where a person's permissively justified beliefs pretty clearly couldn't serve to justify others. Yet the appearance is misleading, not usually because the beliefs can serve to justify others but because (when the cases are compelling) the beliefs are not actually permissively justified. A great many of the supposedly permissively justified beliefs we reject as unable to support others are beliefs we think the person herself has reason to suspect (even if she doesn't in fact suspect them). In fact, cases of wild hunches, weird forebodings, and spurious superstitions, count as *wild*, *weird*, or *spurious*, precisely because we think of the beliefs in question as ones the person has reason to reject [. . .]

Still, one might be inclined to think that any belief one has, on balance, no reason to hold can't possibly serve to justify anything else. This will seem reasonable, even unavoidable, as long as we think of evidential relations roughly on the model of logical relations as simply justification preserving in the way logical relations are truth preserving. If evidential relations among beliefs serve merely as conduits of justification, one belief will receive positive support from others only to the extent those others themselves have some positive support to convey. On this view, some belief may, thanks to the support it receives from several other beliefs, itself enjoy more positive justification than any of the others, yet the total positive justification it can enjoy is limited nonetheless by the positive justification those other beliefs collectively have to offer. Underwriting this view of evidential relations is the intuition that one belief can be seen as epistemically valuable in light of the relation it bears to others only if the others are themselves epistemically valuable. Just as one action will count as good because of its consequences only if its consequences are good, so too some belief will count as positively justified by other beliefs only if those others are positively justified. Clearly, if this view is right, then beliefs that are merely permissively justified will be useless when it comes to providing positive support for others and an appeal to them won't serve to stop the regress on behalf of either foundationalists or coherentists.

What the coherentist must say (and the foundationalist will have reason to say as well) is that the intuition, and the view of justification it underwrites, are mistaken. Fortunately, in ethics and in epistemology, there's an alternative view that has its own appeal: that the value of an action or a belief depends upon both what it is related to and, more importantly for our purposes, how it is related to them. The intuition here is that the value of the whole may not be a function of the value of its parts considered independently of how they are related.[8] Just as things that are valueless considered in isolation may come to be related in such a way as to constitute something of significant value, so too beliefs that enjoy no positive justification considered in isolation may come to be evidentially related in such a way as to constitute a set of positively justified beliefs.

The appeal of this alternative view depends upon our ability to see the evidential relations themselves as making a difference to the justificatory status of the beliefs they relate. They might be seen as making a difference in either of two ways: The relations themselves might work to enhance and not merely preserve justificatory value; or they might serve as a condition for the justificatory value of the beliefs they relate. The first suggestion, which is the more straightforward (but I think in the end less attractive) one, would enable us to appeal to the justificatory value of the evidential relations when it comes to explaining how it is that a belief supported by another that is merely permissively justified may in light of the relation they bear to one another count as positively justified.[9] The second suggestion would pick up on the fact that the common distinc-

tion between things that are good in themselves and things that are good for their consequences, can be supplemented with a distinction between things that are only conditionally good and those that are unconditionally good. The idea, then, would be that our beliefs, to the extent they are justified, are only conditionally justified – the condition being set by their being appropriately related to other beliefs the person has. Significantly, this latter view needn't be accompanied by any commitment to there being beliefs (or evidential relations) that are unconditionally justified; it would be enough if some beliefs might be conditionally justified. In any case, either account would serve to explain how it is that a belief's being properly related to another that is only permissively justified might render it positively justified.[10]

A full story following up either suggestion would involve explaining the distinctive epistemic contribution the evidential relations are supposed to play. However the details go, the epistemic role of such relations – their status as *evidential* relations – will presumably be bound up with their having a systematic if indirect connection to truth. Of course, evidential relations won't be such that, when they hold among beliefs, the beliefs are thereby sure to be, or even likely to be, true. Rather, I suspect, the relations that are in fact evidential will be those determined by cannons of reasoning that are truth conducive (and not just truth preserving) in that systematically respecting them would have the tendency of shifting views towards the truth in the long haul, given accurate information. Obviously, a person might respect the relevant cannons of reasoning over time and so hold beliefs that are evidentially related (on this view) and yet, because of lack of evidence, or misleading evidence, actually consistently have evidence for false views. But in these cases, as well as happier ones, if the beliefs are in fact supported by the weight of the evidence available to the person, they count as justified, at least according to the coherentist. In any case, while coherentism is committed to there being a fact of the matter as to whether, and to what extent, two beliefs are evidentially related, it is not wedded to any particular account of those evidential relations [. . .]

The Nature and Role of Coherence

To address several of the concerns one might have about the coherence theory of justification, I need now to say something more specific about the connection between the relative coherence of a set of beliefs and the evidential/inferential relations that hold among the beliefs. According to coherentism, I've said, a belief is justified only if, and then to the extent that, it coheres well with the other things the person believes.[11] Along the way, though, I've also attributed to the coherentist the view that a belief is: (i) permissively justified if and only if the weight of the evidence available to the person does not, on balance, tell against the belief; and (ii) positively justified if and only if the weight of the evidence, again on balance, tells in favor of the belief (just how positively justified it is will be a matter of how strong the evidence, on balance, is). Seeing how these characterizations of justification relate to one another is crucial to seeing the sort of coherence theory I am advancing.

How then does the relative coherence of a set of beliefs reflect the evidential relations that hold among those beliefs? And how does the relative coherence of one's beliefs relate to their being justified? I will take these questions in order.

The relative coherence of a set of beliefs is a matter of whether, and to what degree, the set exhibits (what I will call) *evidential consistency, connectedness,* and *comprehensiveness.*[12] The first, evidential consistency, sets a necessary and sufficient condition for (minimal) coherence, while the second and third, connectedness and comprehensiveness, serve, when present, to increase the relative coherence of a set that is minimally coherent. Each, though, is a property of a set of beliefs, if it is at all, only in virtue of the evidential relations that hold among the contents of the beliefs in the set.

Thus, a set of beliefs counts as (minimally) coherent if and only if the set is evidentially consistent – that is, if and only if the weight of the evidence provided by the various beliefs in the set don't tell, on balance, against any of the others.[13] Given an evidentially consistent, and so at least minimally coherent, set, just how coherent the set is will be a matter of the connectedness and comprehensiveness it exhibits.

Clearly, a set of beliefs can count as minimally coherent even if none of the beliefs in the set are evidentially supported by any of the others. However, an evidentially consistent (and so coherent) set might contain some beliefs that are, to a greater or lesser extent, evidentially related to others in the set in a way that means they, on balance, receive support from the others, or provide support for them, or both. In these cases, the evidential relations among the beliefs induce in the set some degree of what I've called connectedness. The stronger and more extensive the support, the more connected, and more coherent, the set. Thus, a set will be more or less coherent, assuming it is evidentially consistent, to the extent the beliefs in it enjoy positive support from others in the set. At the same time, for any given set that is at least minimally coherent, its relative coherence, because of comprehensiveness, will increase when other beliefs are added to the set, assuming it remains evidentially consistent. The more comprehensive the set, other things equal, the more coherent it will be.[14]

It goes without saying that virtually no one's total set of beliefs will count as even minimally coherent, although subsets of those beliefs will presumably count as more than minimally coherent. Similarly, virtually no one holds beliefs all of which are justified, although subsets of most peoples' beliefs will presumably count as positively and not just permissively justified.

When it comes to relating the relative coherence of a person's beliefs to their status as justified beliefs, the coherentist's suggestion is, first, that those beliefs of her's that are justified are all and only those that belong to the subset of her beliefs that is maximally coherent and, second, that a belief will belong or not to that subset in virtue of the evidential relations it bears to everything else she believes. A subset of a person's beliefs will count as maximally coherent only if it is evidentially consistent and then if, when compared to all the subsets of her total belief set that are evidentially consistent, it exhibits a greater degree of coherence over-all (thanks to its connectedness and comprehensiveness) than do the others. [. . .]

How well a particular belief coheres with the other things the person believes, we can now say, is determined by whether it is a member of the maximally coherent subset of what she believes (it doesn't count as cohering at all if it is not), and if it is, whether, and to what extent, it is evidentially supported by other beliefs in that set (the more support it receives the better it coheres). Any belief in the set will at least be permissively justified, and will be more or less positively justified as it receives more or less evidential support from other beliefs in the set. Thus, to say that a belief is justified only if, and then to the extent that, it coheres well with the other things the person believes, is to register the way in which one's justification turns on how one's belief relates evidentially to whatever else one believes.

A full articulation of the coherence theory I've been describing would of course involve developing a theory of what relations count as evidential. And clearly this is not the place to begin that project. But I should emphasize that any plausible theory of justification will require supplementation by an account of evidential relations, since all such theories recognize and rely in some way or other on there being evidential relations that our beliefs might bear to one another [. . .]

Against this background, we can also characterize what it would be for a potential belief to cohere well with what a person actually believes. Whether such a belief would cohere at all with the other beliefs a person holds depends on whether, were the person to believe it, it would then be a member of the (perhaps, in light of the new belief, dramatically different) maximally coherent subset of everything she believes. And how well such a belief would cohere with the others depends on the degree to which the resulting maximally coherent set would be more coherent than its predecessor. If such a belief would cohere with whatever else she believes, then should she believe it, the belief would be justified.[15] [. . .]

Some Objections

I can't here do full justice to the range of objections that have been raised to coherentism.

However, I would like to indicate the extent to which some of the more common objections miss their mark, at least when it comes to the version of coherentism I am advancing. The objections I have in mind are that coherentism has got to be false because the mere fact that a set of beliefs is coherent is no reason to think they are true; that coherentism is objectionably conservative and inappropriately privileges one's actual beliefs; and that coherentism fails to recognize sufficiently the importance of experience. I will take these objections in order and suggest that each either misunderstands coherentism or underestimates the resources available to it.

Aside from the regress argument, the most common objection to coherentism turns on noticing that for any coherent set of beliefs a person might actually hold, there's another possible set of beliefs that is equally or more coherent. This observation raises two concerns: First, isn't coherentism committed to the obviously false view that the mere coherence of a set of beliefs is reason to think them true; and second, isn't the coherentist consequently unable to account for the fact that we can justifiably reject views we recognize to be more coherent than our own? These concerns are all the more pressing because it looks as if we have exceedingly strong inductive grounds for thinking that any coherent set of beliefs, our own included, is likely to be false.[16]

To respond to these worries we need to distinguish two questions: What is it for a belief to be justified? and What is it that justifies a belief? Coherentism, of the sort I am defending, is addressed to the first question but not the second – a belief is justified if and then to the extent that it coheres well with a person's other beliefs, but it is not *justified by* the fact that it is a member of a coherent set of beliefs. What a person's beliefs are justified by are her other beliefs – or, more accurately, by the facts, as she takes them to be, so far as they provide evidence for her view.

A useful analogy can be found in the expected utility theory of rational choice. According to that theory, a person's choice is rational if and only if, given the available options, the choice maximizes her expected utility. But the fact that the option maximizes her expected utility is not an extra reason for the person to choose it – rather it's status as the option that maximizes expected utility is a reflection of (what the theory supposes to be) the reasons the person has for choosing it.[17] Now of course one might have all sorts of objections to this theory, and I don't rest my case for the coherence theory on the acceptability of rational choice theory. Far from it. Still, I do want to suggest that the relation between expected utility and the reasons an agent has for making one choice over another (according to this theory) provides a nice analogue to the relation between relative coherence and the reasons a person has for holding one belief rather than another. As the analogy would have it, the fact that a belief coheres better than do the available alternatives with a person's other beliefs is not an extra reason for the person to hold it – rather it's status as the belief that maximizes coherence is a reflection of the reasons the person has for holding it. So thought of, the coherence theory is not committed to saying that the coherence of our beliefs is a reason to think they are true. Instead, what evidence we have for the truth of our beliefs is found in, and only in, what else we believe [about experience as a course of information about the world]. This means a coherentist can and should admit that the mere fact that a set of beliefs is coherent provides one with no reason to think they are true, even though, if the beliefs in question are one's own, their relative coherence will reflect the extent to which one's evidence gives one reason to think they are true.

Just as the maximizing theory of rationality doesn't offer substantive reasons for a person to act, so too the coherence theory doesn't offer substantive reasons for a person to believe or not. In both cases, the theories are offered as accurate and informative characterizations of the link between what we value or believe and the rationality or justification of what we do or believe. In each case, the plausibility of the theory depends, of course, on whether it actually captures the conditions under which someone counts as having chosen rationally or believed with justification. While I have my doubts about the theory of rationality on that front, I think the coherence theory of justification does a surprisingly good job.

What, then, does the coherentist say about those situations in which one recognizes that someone else holds a view that is more coherent than is one's own? If justification is a matter of coherence shouldn't I abandon my beliefs if I discover there is an alternative set of beliefs that are more coherent? The coherentist does have to hold that, if the person's beliefs really are more coherent, then that person has more justification for believing as she does, given her evidence, than one has for one's own view. However, acknowledging this is not yet to say that one has any reason to reject one's views in favor of hers, not least of all because the mere fact that her view is more coherent is no reason to think it true, but also because her evidence, such as it is, might justifiably be rejected by you as misleading, ill informed, or otherwise unacceptable (even if the other person is justified in relying on it).

Often, of course, the alternative coherent views [. . .] will be ones that we ourselves see some reason to accept, even if we think on balance the evidence tells against them. To take a moral example: Suppose that concerning various matters I am inclined to think consequentialist considerations are relevant and often decisive. I think, for instance, that when it comes to public policy the fact that one policy would produce more happiness for all than some other policy is a reason to choose it, or I think the fact that some present would ease someone's sorrow is a reason to give it, or whatever. Suppose too, though, that I resist the utilitarian view that some action is right if and only if it produces the greatest happiness for the greatest number, on the grounds that there are some things one cannot legitimately do to another person no matter how much happiness would be produced. In this situation I might well recognize that the utilitarian's position, given her other beliefs, is more coherent than mine. And I may have no single overarching moral principle to propose in place of the utilitarian's. Am I then required to accept utilitarianism? Is a coherentist committed to saying I am? The utilitarian and I share a good number of beliefs concerning the sort of considerations that might be relevant to moral evaluation, and to this extent we both have some grounds for thinking utilitarianism is true. Yet we differ on crucial points; in particular, I think (say) that willful murder is always wrong, no matter what, and that a sadist's pleasures are utterly worthless, and I think the rightness of an act depends as much on why it was performed as on the effects it happens to produce. She believes that I am wrong about these things (and others). I may, of course, be brought around to the utilitarian's view if she offers compelling grounds for seeing my own beliefs as explicable but false. And part of her argument in defense of utilitarianism will reasonably be that the utilitarian view does an good job of accounting for a number of things we both believe, which itself provides some evidence for the principle. Still, and even as I give due weight to the fact that the utilitarian principle captures well a number of considerations, I will justifiably reject it if (but only if) the weight of the evidence provided by what else I believe (some of which she denies) tells on balance against her view.

In the end, whether one is justified in retaining one's original view in light of another depends on whether one's own evidence tells in favor of the other view or not. In the face of (even) coherent alternatives, one justifiably rejects the others, when one does, on the basis of what one justifiably believes.[18] Often, the weight of one's evidence will tell against views one recognizes would be more coherent, and one justifiably rejects them on the grounds that one has reason for thinking them false. Given what else one believes, the alternative views do not after all count as coherent alternatives for you despite their being recognizably coherent when held by others. This means, of course, that had one's initial beliefs been different, had one believed one thing rather than another, one would have justifiably rejected the views that one actually (and with justification) accepts. But this doesn't mean that the fact that one believes as one does is one's reason for rejecting the alternative; rather one's reason is that the alternative clashes with the facts (as you take them to be).

Recognizing the crucial role played by one's actual beliefs naturally raises two more worries about the coherence theory: that it will have objectionably conservative implications and that it inappropriately privileges the beliefs one merely happens to have. The conservativism of the view, however, goes just as far as, but no farther than, the conservativism that comes with allowing that one must base one's beliefs on the available evidence. This inevitable limitation requires acknowledging that throughout our epistemic endeavors we will be appealing to what we believe, because what evidence one has is limited to that provided by one's beliefs (and other relevantly similar cognitive states). We are never able to stand fully apart from those beliefs without then loosing all grounds for believing anything at all. Yet this reliance on what we happen to believe has no seriously conservative implications, since those beliefs themselves, especially in light of the new evidence experience and reflection regularly provide, won't stand as fixed points but will instead shift in response to the new evidence (if they are to continue to count as justified).

When it comes to privileging actual beliefs, it is no part of this coherence theory that the mere fact that one believes something, considered alone, provides any reason whatsoever for thinking the belief true; that evidence must come from other things one believes, if it is to come at all. Absent such a background, a person will take the content of her belief to be true, but that is a reflection of what it is for an attitude to count as a belief. And the content of that belief does serve as evidence for other things she might believe, but in relying on that evidence, she is not taking the fact that she believes it to be evidence for something else, rather she is taking what she believes (say, that the coffee is hot, or that willful cruelty is wrong) as her evidence.[19] [. . .]

Still, because the coherence theory treats as evidence only what we already believe, it might seem to ignore a crucial impetus for change: experience. On the one hand, the theory may seem unable even to accommodate experiential input and observation. On the other hand, although it might be able to accommodate such input, it may seem not properly to recognize its importance. And surely any adequate theory must acknowledge the role and importance of experience and observation when it comes to the justification of belief.

The first concern, I think, is undercut by the role cognitively spontaneous beliefs are able to play within coherentism. It's true, coherentism doesn't allow experience as relevant to justification unless and until the experience comes into the person's cognitive economy. Yet, especially in its recognition of cognitively spontaneous beliefs, coherentism leaves room for experiences to enter that cognitive economy unbidden, either thanks to the experiences themselves having a cognitive content (in which case it is the content of the experience that serves as evidence) or by their being the content of an appropriate cognitive attitude (in which case it is the fact that such an experience occurred that serves as evidence). [. . .] [C]oherentists, no less than foundationalists, are able to recognize these beliefs, and other noninferred beliefs, as a regular source of new evidence that plays a crucial role in determining what we are justified in believing. What is distinctive about coherentism is its claim that the epistemic credentials these beliefs, and all others, enjoy is dependent on the evidential/inferential relations they bear to others. And a belief can bear the appropriate sort of relation to others even if, as it happens, it was caused directly by experience or is concerned directly with experience.

The second concern is encouraged by the thought that the coherence theory is committed to treating a set of beliefs as justified as long as it is coherent, regardless of whether those beliefs have been properly informed by experience. Even if the coherence theory can allow experiential input, the concern is that it treats such input as incidentally important rather than crucial.

The worry can be brought out with an example. Imagine that someone holds an exceedingly coherent set of beliefs, as coherent as any coherentist could demand. But imagine too that because of some neural accident, or a Mad Scientist's mucking about, or God's intervention, her beliefs become insensitive to experience. Her beliefs remain in a coherent stasis, although now they are uninfluenced one way or the other by her accumulating experience. Surely, one is inclined to say, she is no longer justified in holding her beliefs despite their continued coherence and this shows that, as the foundationalist can hold, the status of our beliefs as

justified depends on their being properly responsive to experience and not on their being coherent.[20]

So far, the case is crucially underdescribed. We need to distinguish between: (i) the person who's experiences continue to provide her with evidence that she unfortunately fails to take into account; and (ii) the person who may in a sense continue to have experiences although the link between her experience and her cognitive states is severed in a way that keeps her from acquiring new evidence from those experiences. In the first case, she is clearly unjustified in holding her beliefs precisely for the reasons a coherentist can acknowledge: She violates the basing requirement. Whatever explains her continuing to hold the beliefs she does, it is not the evidence available to her. What she believes may or may not be justified; whether it is depends on whether the evidence provided by her experiences (to which she is unresponsive) tells against them, on balance. But because she doesn't believe as she does because her beliefs cohere well with her evidence, she is not justified in holding those beliefs even on the coherentist's view. In the second case, though, the coherentist will say that the person may in fact be justified in holding her beliefs, though she is in an epistemically sad situation. For in this case she is, by hypothesis, not receiving new evidence from her senses and so her failure to respond to those experiences by changing her beliefs is no reflection on the justification she has for them. To think otherwise is to fall back on the sort of externalism that holds people strictly liable for what they believe even in cases where they have no reason to believe otherwise.[21] Either way, I think the example doesn't support the idea that coherentism ignores the importance of one's being properly responsive to one's experiences.

Nonetheless, coherentism requires experience only to the extent experience (broadly construed) is the source of new evidence. It imposes no specific requirement on the nature of that experience (on either its source or content) nor on how a person must see her views as being related to experience. And it's liberalness on these matters may be problematic. There are two plausible claims that together suggest that peoples' beliefs are justified only if they see those beliefs as grounded in their experience. The first is that a person's beliefs are justified only if the supposition that they are true figures as part of the best explanation that person has of her holding the belief. The second is that such an explanation will inevitably, at some point, appeal to that person's experiences. The first claim gets its plausibility from the conviction that we would have reason to rely on our beliefs only if we thought they were responsive to the facts they concern, just as we would have reason to rely on someone else's beliefs only if we thought their beliefs responsive to the facts they concern. The second gets its plausibility from the general conviction that only experience establishes an appropriate link between our beliefs and what they are about [. . .]

The important thing to notice about both the explanatory requirement and the empiricist assumption, is that they represent at most substantive restrictions on what *we* can justifiably believe, given what else we believe. And coherentism can perfectly well acknowledge these restrictions as ones we justifiably believe appropriate; they are more or less justified, according to the coherentist, to the extent to which they are actually supported by the evidence available to those who hold them. All that coherentism denies is that satisfying them represents a necessary condition on justification. On the coherentist's view, even if, on balance, we have reason to reject any belief not properly grounded in experience, other people may, depending on what else they believe, be justified in holding their beliefs even when they have no explanation of them or no explanation of them that links them to experience.

Incidentally, I do think that the truth of our moral beliefs often plays a role in explaining both why we hold them and why we have the experiences we take as evidence for them. Thus we might appeal to the injustice of certain institutions to explain the social unrest we observe; to the value of an activity to explain why it regularly gives rise to satisfaction; to the evilness of a character to explain a person's willingness to act as we learn someone has. Yet these explanations rely on our justifiably

believing institutions of that type unjust, or activities of that sort good, or characters of that kind evil; they go through only if, in giving them, we can legitimately invoke other background moral views in accounting for the relation between morality and the experiences we hope to explain. If instead we had to build up, piecemeal, and without recourse to background views, an explanation of moral beliefs relying initially only on certain privileged beliefs (say concerning our sensory experiences) we would, I suspect, never find ourselves having to appeal to the truth of our moral views to explain our holding them. At the same time, though, I suspect as well that were we similarly obliged to explain our nonmoral views in this piecemeal fashion the truth of few of them would figure in an explanation of our holding them.

An important advantage of the coherence theory is that it can make good sense of our legitimately relying in this way on background assumptions, whether moral or not: If these assumptions cohere well with the other things we believe, then when it comes time to show that our particular beliefs, say, some of our moral beliefs, are properly responsive to our experiences, the background assumptions are among the beliefs we may legitimately take into account. If everything comes together appropriately, and the explanations actually go through, we can justifiably believe that our moral beliefs play a role in explaining our experiences. Of course, everything might not come together appropriately; even as we find ourselves initially justified in relying on moral assumptions in trying to explain our experiences, we may discover the explanations are not good. In that case, we need to weigh the justification we have for those beliefs against the recognition that they might be explanatorily impotent. While I think the bulk of the justification we have for our moral beliefs really has nothing to do with their playing an important role in explaining our experiences, I am inclined to think that we would not be justified in believing of some moral principles, that they were true, unless we also thought their being true made some difference to, and so contribute to an explanation of, our believing them.[22]

Conclusion

Most of this chapter has been given over to articulating and defending a version of the coherence theory of justification. As that theory would have it, a belief is justified if, and then to the extent that, it coheres well with the other things a person believes. And a person is justified in holding some belief if and only if the belief itself is justified and she holds it because it is justified. In various crucial ways the theory differs from most versions of the coherence theory. First of all, rather than dodging the regress argument by embracing a holistic theory of justification, this version meets the argument head on and, with the foundationalist, acknowledges that certain beliefs may serve as suitable regress-stoppers. Unlike foundationalism, however, it insists that these regress-stoppers – the beliefs that count as permissively, but not positively, justified – enjoy no special epistemic privilege and are themselves characterizable only in terms of the evidential connections they bear to other beliefs. When beliefs are permissively justified it is only in light of the relations they bear to other beliefs. Second of all, while it treats the coherence of one's beliefs as a criterion of justification, it treats coherence itself not as a justifying property of those beliefs but rather as a measure of the evidential support the beliefs enjoy. In every case, what evidence a person has for her beliefs is found not in their relative coherence, but in the contents of her other beliefs.

Thus there is in coherentism a built-in commitment to relativism about justification. What a person in fact believes, and so what evidence she happens to have available, is crucial to whether her views are justified, and a belief one person is justified in accepting may be such that others would be justified in rejecting it. The relativism doesn't collapse, of course, into the view that anything one takes to be justified is. The coherentist says a person's belief is justified only if it coheres well with her other beliefs; whether it does is independent of whether she thinks it does (except as such a belief might be countenanced as evidentially related to other things she believes). In any given case, according to coherentism, there is a fact of the matter about whether someone is justified and they, as well as anyone else, might get that fact wrong.

There is as well a deep seated recognition of fallibilism. Not only does a coherentist treat each belief as open to revision in light of others, she recognizes also that even a fully coherent, and so wonderfully justified, set of beliefs might turn out to be false. Justification's link to truth, such as it is, is not provided by coherence itself, but instead by the evidential relations that bind beliefs together into coherent sets. Thus the theory makes good sense of how we can look back on our own earlier beliefs as having been justified and yet now justifiably thought wrong; and it makes good sense out of how we can distinguish among others as between those who are justified in holding their differing (and as we see it false) views and those that aren't.

At the same time, the theory finds a good place for the thought that, while we recognize that any of our beliefs might be wrong, that fact about us and our beliefs doesn't in and of itself count as strong reason to reject our view – certainly not nearly as strong as would be our coming to think we actually had made a mistake (in which case we've got reasons precisely as strong as the support that view has, for changing the view in question). Thus the coherentist responds to the sceptic neither decisively nor simply by deciding not to worry about her challenge, but by advancing a positive view about what sort of evidence the mere possibility of error constitutes. Each suggestion that a person might have made a mistake is appropriately countered, when it can be, by appeal to the evidence available that supports the view. A person might of course be wrong in the positive view she advances – a possibility the sceptic will push – but that fact too tells only so far against the weight of the evidence the person might be able to marshal in defense of her own view. Whether, concerning any particular issue, a person is justified in accepting scepticism will turn (as does the justification for all beliefs) on the weight of the evidence available.

Notes

1. See William Alston's "Two Types of Foundationalism," in the *Journal of Philosophy* 73 (1976), pp. 165–85.

2. See David Hume's *A Treatise of Human Nature*, 2nd edition (Oxford: Oxford University Press, 1978), p. 469.

3. Compatible with this crucial difference, coherentism may have a great deal in common with foundationalism. It might, for instance, recognize different classes of belief (even as it rejects the suggestion that any class is epistemically privileged), or embrace the same inferential principles, or even allow that justified beliefs take on, for instance, a pyramid structure.

4. Although foundationalism and coherentism, as I have characterized them, are mutually exclusive, they clearly don't exhaust the possibilities. Someone might well reject foundationalism's commitment to an epistemically privileged class of beliefs and yet resist coherentism's positive account of justification in terms of coherence. One might hold, for instance, that one's beliefs are justified if they are reliable indicators of the facts they concern, or, alternatively, if they are the product of a reliable belief-forming mechanism. In neither case would their justification turn on their cohering with one's other beliefs, except to the extent the relevant sort of reliability is related to coherence.

5. Clearly there are two other possible readings: (i) one belief provides (permissive) justification for another only if it is, itself, (permissively) justified; and (ii) one belief provides (permissive) justification for another only if it is, itself, (positively) justified. The first of these is weaker even than the weak reading defended in what follows, and would in any case be irrelevant to establishing that we ever have positive reason to believe as we do; and the second would, like the strong reading rejected in what follows, make an appeal to permissive justification useless when it comes to stopping the regress.

6. Although permissively justified beliefs can serve to stop the regress, presumably only positively justified beliefs enjoy the sort of support that knowledge is usually thought to presuppose. In any case, a belief that is *merely* permissively justified will be a belief one has, on balance, no reason to believe – it enjoys no positive justification.

7. Whether these cases are ultimately intelligible is open to question. It's arguable (but I think not true) that the beliefs we are able to attribute to two people so differently situated must always be different. If so, then the supposition that they share beliefs can't be sustained. What matters, though, is not so much whether these represent real possibilities; what matters is that, were they possible, we would normally count the people involved as being equally justified, though not equally well-situated epistemically.

8. G. E. Moore articulates this idea as he spells out what it would be for something to exhibit *organic unity*. See *Principia Ethica*.

9. If this suggestion is to be worked out in a way that is compatible with the version of internalism I've defended, the justification enhancing role of evidential relations cannot be that of giving a person more reason to believe as she does (since the presence of the relation may be something about which she has no beliefs even when it holds).

10. Incidentally, even if the relations themselves are seen as being valuable, the value they have might itself be conditional on their relating real evidence. Thus while the relations will presumably be characterized in terms that allow them to stand among propositions (whether believed or not), the evidential value of these relations might depend upon the status of those propositions as evidence – which status they will have, I've argued, only as they become the content of the relevant person's beliefs.

11. How well, and whether, a belief coheres with the others a person holds will depend, in part, on what alternatives are available to her. Before Newton came on the scene, people were justified in believing things about the workings of the world that later they would have been unjustified in accepting in light of the evidence and options available. So we might say, a bit more precisely, that a belief is justified only if, and then to the extent that, it coheres *better than does any competitor belief* with the other things the person believes (where two beliefs will compete with one another if either might, but both can't, be held by the person in question).

12. Although here I will be characterizing the coherence of a set of beliefs, the same considerations of evidential consistency, connectedness, and comprehensiveness, will serve to characterize the relative coherence of sets of propositions directly. So, for instance, a set of propositions that constitute a theory will

count as minimally coherent if appropriately
consistent, and then as more than minimally
coherent as the theory is connected and comprehensive.

13. The evidential consistency requirement insists
on both more and less than would a requirement that demanded logical consistency from
the contents of the beliefs in the set. It demands
more because a set that contained only logically
consistent beliefs would nonetheless fall short of
evidential consistency if the evidence provided
by some of the beliefs, on balance, told against
one of the beliefs. It demands less because a set
that contained logically inconsistent beliefs that
were equally well supported by the evidence
provided by the other beliefs would count as
evidentially consistent (and so minimally coherent). For arguments against requiring logical
consistency, see Richard Foley's "Justified
Inconsistent Beliefs," in *American Philosophical
Quarterly* (1979), pp. 247–57.

14. I don't suppose that there is any algorithm for
determining the relative contributions connectedness and comprehensiveness make to the
over-all coherence of a set. It would be a mistake, though, to think that connectedness and
comprehensiveness will never compete. While
any belief that increases the connectedness of
an evidentially consistent set will likewise
increase comprehensiveness, and any belief
that increases comprehensiveness in such a set
will at worst make no difference to connectedness, when it comes to comparing one coherent
set with another, we may be faced with one
that's more connected but less comprehensive
than another and sometimes, at least, comprehensiveness may win out over connectedness or
vice versa.

15. Nice complications emerge when we consider
situations in which the person herself is considering various things she might believe, each
of which would cohere well with the other
things she believes. In that case, which belief
would be justified will depend on which of the
options would cohere *better* with the other
things she believes (including her beliefs concerning which of the options is more justified),
and, having considered the options, believing
one that coheres less well, but still well, with
her beliefs, would presumably be unjustified.

16. In "Coherence and Models for Moral Theorizing," in Mark Timmons and Walter Sinnott-
Armstrong (eds.) *Moral Knowledge?* (Oxford:
Oxford University Press), I raise this objection
to the all too common practice, in moral theory,

of treating the fact that one theory is more
coherent than another as an independent reason to think the theory true.

17. A person may, of course, be wrong in the probabilities she associates with various outcomes,
or the value she attributes to those outcomes.
Expected utility often differs from actual utility.
Yet, according to this theory, so far as the
rationality of her choice is concerned, it is
rational if given those views the choice she
makes maximizes expected utility.

18. Here the analogy with decision theory may be
helpful again. We might well recognize another
person as making a choice, from among the
same options we face, that maximizes her
expected utility, and (if only we could make
good sense of interpersonal utility comparisons) we might recognize too that given her
expectations and values, the option she takes
has a greater expected utility for her than our
best option has for us. Nonetheless, that provides us with no reason whatsoever to embrace
the option she rationally chooses. We might of
course take the fact that she has the expectations or values she does as evidence that ours
are misguided, and if so, we will have reason to
change ours, but often enough we have good
reason to think what she expects or values is
irrelevant.

19. Just as the theory of rational choice is not
committed to saying that the fact that something advances one's own interests need be a
reason a person has for acting, since people's
preferences may all be other-directed, so too
the coherence theory is not committed to saying that the fact that one believes something
need be a reason a person has for believing,
since people's beliefs may all have as their content things other than their own beliefs. Now in
fact we can expect people to be interested in
their own interests and to have beliefs concerning their beliefs, but these interests and beliefs
constitute only a fraction of the interests and
beliefs a person usually has and neither the
maximizing theory of rationality nor the
coherence theory of justification gives them
any special weight or importance.

20. See Alvin Plantinga's *Warrant: The Current
Debate* (Oxford: Oxford University Press,
1993).

21. We may need yet a third case: It may be that the
person has actually had her beliefs "frozen" so
that she is not simply insensitive to the beliefs
she forms on the basis of experience, nor simply cognitively cut off from her experiences.

In this case, I think the most reasonable thing to say is that she is no longer believing anything. But if we still count her as believing, she will still fail the basing requirement because, once her beliefs are "frozen," what explains her holding of them is no longer her evidence but the fact that they are now unchangeable.

22. For discussion of these issues, see Gilbert Harman's *The Nature of Morality* (New York: Oxford University Press, 1977); and Nicholas Sturgeon's "Moral Explanations," in *Morality, Reason and Truth* (Totowa, NJ: Rowman and Allanheld, 1985), ed. by David Copp and David Zimmerman, pp. 49–78; as well as my "Moral Theory and Explanatory Impotence," *Midwest Studies* XII, ed. by Peter French *et al.*, (University of Minnesota Press, 1988), pp. 433–57, and "Normative Explanations" *Philosophical Perspectives* VII, ed. by James Tomberlin (1992), pp. 55–72.

PART III
Why Be Moral?

Introduction to Part III

If we make the value of moral behavior dependent on its serving self-interest or getting us what we want, then the value of being moral is precarious. Sometimes fulfilling our duty comes at the expense of our interests and desires. When it does, why should we be moral?

Plato has his brother Glaucon put this question to Socrates, in the early pages of his masterpiece, *Republic*. Glaucon asks Socrates to show that justice is a good in and of itself, quite apart from any benefits it may bring. To hone the challenge, he imagines a person wholly just, though with a reputation for grave injustice. This is meant to ensure that any benefits wrought by justice alone will be distinguished from the merely instrumental benefits achieved by the (possibly misleading) appearance of being just. What is so good about being just, especially if others mistreat you because of their (false) belief in your corrupted, dishonest nature?

The remainder of the *Republic*, not included here, provides a long, complicated answer to this question. Plato believes that providing this answer requires showing how being just will be a genuine benefit for the person himself – even if his true character remains hidden, and he is persecuted, even tortured, as a result. In other words, Plato thinks that we should be moral because being so will serve our self-interest.

Of course, if self-interest is measured in terms of popularity, wealth, or political power, then being moral is no guarantee of enhancing self-interest. There is no denying that such things are what many people really, truly want. But Plato denies that our true interests are determined by what we want. We are often out of touch with what really matters. Those who have had experience with being truly just, know that its value far surpasses the ephemeral enjoyments afforded by wealth and fame. Not only are such goals inherently worthless, says Plato; their pursuit is far more likely to bring distraction and internal conflict than the pursuits involved in the moral life. As the French say: the softest pillow is a clean conscience.

So Plato can address our primary question with confidence, because he thinks that he can establish a necessary link between morality and self-interest. Since almost everyone agrees that we have excellent reason to see to our own interests, it would follow that we have excellent reason to be moral.

Philippa Foot takes issue with this view. She claims that our reasons stem from one of two sources: either what we desire, or what is in our self-interest. Not all of our desires, if satisfied, will in fact serve our interests. Sometimes we want things that, when achieved or possessed, only turn out to have been bad for us. If we label our wants and interests our *ends*, we can characterize Foot's argument like so: we have reason to do something only if it serves our ends; being moral won't always serve our ends; therefore we don't always have reason to be moral. Specifically, we lack reason to be moral whenever being moral fails to get us what we want, or to promote our self-interest.

Foot thinks, in effect, that there is not always a good answer to the question: *why be moral?* Sometimes we lack good reason to adhere to morality's requirements. These requirements are relevantly like those of the law, or etiquette. They apply to us regardless of whether adhering to them serves our ends. But there is good reason to obey them only if doing so furthers our ends. If respecting a requirement of etiquette really gained me nothing, and didn't fulfill a desire of mine, then what possible reason could I have for obeying it? Foot can think of none. The situation, she claims, is just the same when it comes to our moral duty.

Gregory Kavka shares this basic outlook, though he believes that when we really think things through, we will see that for almost all of us, almost all the time, we have excellent reason to be moral. He registers an important distinction, glossed over thus far in this introduction, between acting morally on specific occasions, and cultivating a moral character. He admits that it is far harder to show that doing one's moral duty will invariably serve one's ends. But he thinks that it is ordinarily possible to show that we have excellent reason to develop and reinforce dispositions to give priority to morality over self-interest. We have such reason because, strange as it may at first sound, we are likeliest to enhance our self-interest if we develop traits that motivate us to behave morally, even when doing so likely comes at the expense of self-interest. Kavka here endorses Thomas Hobbes' view of rationality (developed in Hobbes's *Leviathan*), which tells us that conduct is rational provided that it is reasonably likely to enhance self-interest. It is rational to be a moral person, because being such a person is reasonably likely to make us better off in the end.

Of course, there are some circumstances where this just isn't so. If one has the very bad luck to have been born in a highly corrupt and violent society, then cultivating one's moral character may be a recipe for a short and painful life. When there is a genuine conflict between the demands of morality and self-interest, what should we do? Before answering that, we should follow Kavka's lead and determine whether we can't, after all, effect some reconciliation between these demands. For many of us, living in stable societies and possessed of at least moderate comforts, we can do just that. But in other cases, the question presses.

It is common for philosophers, and others, to approach this question as Foot and Kavka have done. They have assumed that our reasons must stem from our desires or our self-interest, or both. In my paper here on this subject, I reject this assumption, and argue that there are conceptual reasons to think that moral demands entail excellent reasons for action. I also try to counter the most powerful arguments, including Foot's argument by analogy (to law and etiquette), that have tried to limit the power of moral demands to generate reasons for obedience.

When we ask ourselves about whether we ought to cultivate moral traits of character in ourselves, we naturally assume that such a thing is possible. But what if it weren't? What if, instead, the only motives we could have were self-interested ones? *Psychological egoism* claims that it is impossible for us to be motivated by anything other than self-interest. Psychological egoism is not an ethical view. It is a descriptive view about the way that human motivation operates. Still, it earns a place in the present text because, if it were true, and if (as many philosophers believe) it were also true that the impossibility of doing something entails the absence of a moral obligation to do it, then we could never be obligated to be altruistically motivated. Motivations of kindness, generosity, compassion – all paradigmatically moral motivations – would be morally optional (at best).

Thus our picture of the moral life would have to be drastically altered were psychological egoism to turn out to be true. Joel Feinberg here comes to the aid of our conventional view of the requirements of the moral life, with an exposition and critique of psychological egoism. His article introduces us to the most popular arguments for psychological egoism, and a diagnosis of their error.

Another form of egoism has long been thought a threat to morality. This is *ethical egoism*, the doctrine that imposes just a single, ultimate ethical requirement: to maximize the chances of enhancing self-interest. This form of egoism has rarely been explicitly defended, since it has seemed to so many to license the sort of behavior that is paradigmatically immoral. If killing or torturing were likely to enhance self-interest, as they sometimes seem to do, then ethical egoism would generate a moral requirement to undertake such actions. But few people have been willing to sign on to the existence of such requirements, at least for the reason given. Even if it is sometimes permissible to kill or torture – say, to many save innocent lives – promotion of self-interest isn't what justifies our doing so.

Lester Hunt seeks to rehabilitate ethical egoism by showing how moral demands and those of self-interest will invariably coincide. He does this by taking a leaf from Plato's book. Ethical egoism demands that we give paramount attention to our own interests. And this will indeed license the actions of the politically power-hungry, the manipulative con-man, the hired gun, but only if their self-interest lies in gaining what they want. Hunt follows Plato in denying this. Self-interest consists in living a flourishing life, and one may fail to live such a life, even if one's desires are well satisfied. For one might want the wrong things, things that fail, in fact, to give importance and meaning to a life. Hunt thinks that the elements of a flourishing life will require one to act in ways that respect our moral views about what is paradigmatically right and wrong. If he is right, we have a neat way of reconciling morality and self-interest after all.

James Rachels next summarizes the major arguments for and against ethical egoism. He ultimately comes down against it, charging that it is a form of unjustified discrimination. He believes that any form of preferential treatment must be justified, and that ethical egoism, requiring as it does that one give absolute priority to self-interest over the interests of others, is a form of preferential treatment. It thus requires justification for the assignment of this absolute priority. But none is forthcoming – or so Rachels argues. If he is right, then we must abandon the age-old dream of justifying the rationality of moral conduct with the claim that morality always serves self-interest. And if this noble dream is only that, never destined to be fulfilled, then our original question presses even more forcefully. If acting morally sometimes requires a sacrifice of self-interest – perhaps even the ultimate sacrifice – then why be moral?

Susan Wolf encourages us not to be. It's not that she counsels a life of debauchery and cruelty. Nor does she advise against morality because of the vulnerability to unhappiness that it creates. Rather, the morally exemplary life is not as valuable as it's cracked up to be. She invites us to contemplate the moral saint, one who lives wholly by and entirely for the demands of morality. Whether these demands are set by the standards of common sense, or those of contemporary moral theories, the life of a moral saint, says Wolf, is not an attractive ideal. Even where it might be possible for the demands of morality and self-interest to coincide, as in the case of one whose heartfelt commitments are exhausted by the requirements of morality, the model of such a life is one that we would hesitate to commend either for ourselves or for our loved ones. There is more to life than morality – indeed, what morality leaves out can be more important, can contain more that is truly good, than the life of one who is wholly committed to morality. This is not, of course, to say that it is never good to exemplify moral virtues, or to perform actions that are morally required. Still, if you are considering what sort of person to be (as opposed to what particular action to undertake at a given moment), you should take a pass on being a moral saint, in favor of setting your sights elsewhere. If Wolf is right, then the best lives are led by those whose moral imperfections allow them to pursue even greater goods than those available to the moral saint.

CHAPTER 15
The Immoralist's Challenge

PLATO

When I said this, I thought I had done with the discussion, but it turned out to have been only a prelude. Glaucon showed his characteristic courage on this occasion too and refused to accept Thrasymachus' abandonment of the argument. Socrates, he said, do you want to seem to have persuaded us that it is better in every way to be just than unjust, or do you want truly to convince us of this?

I want truly to convince you, I said, if I can.

Well, then, you certainly aren't doing what you want. Tell me, do you think there is a kind of good we welcome, not because we desire what comes from it, but because we welcome it for its own sake – joy, for example, and all the harmless pleasures that have no results beyond the joy of having them?

Certainly, I think there are such things.

And is there a kind of good we like for its own sake and also for the sake of what comes from it – knowing, for example, and seeing and being healthy? We welcome such things, I suppose, on both counts.

Yes.

And do you also see a third kind of good, such as physical training,[1] medical treatment when sick, medicine itself, and the other ways of making money? We'd say that these are onerous but beneficial to us, and we wouldn't choose them for their own sakes, but for the sake of the rewards and other things that come from them.

There is also this third kind. But what of it?

Where do you put justice?

I myself put it among the finest goods, as something to be valued by anyone who is going to be blessed with happiness, both because of itself and because of what comes from it.

That isn't most people's opinion. They'd say that justice belongs to the onerous kind, and is to be practiced for the sake of the rewards and popularity that come from a reputation for justice, but is to be avoided because of itself as something burdensome.

I know that's the general opinion. Thrasymachus faulted justice on these grounds a moment ago and praised injustice, but it seems that I'm a slow learner.

Come, then, and listen to me as well, and see whether you still have that problem, for I think that Thrasymachus gave up before he had to, charmed by you as if he were a snake. But I'm not yet satisfied by the argument on either side. I want to know what justice and injustice are and what power each itself has when it's by itself in the soul. I want to leave out of account their rewards and what comes from each of them. So, if you agree, I'll renew the argument

Plato, "The Immoralist's Challenge," pp. 496–502 from *The Republic*, Book II, 357A–367E, trans. G. M. A. Grube; revised by C. D. C. Reeve. Indianapolis: Hackett, 1992. Reprinted by permission of Hackett Publishing Company, Inc. All rights reserved.

of Thrasymachus. First, I'll state what kind of thing people consider justice to be and what its origins are. Second, I'll argue that all who practice it do so unwillingly, as something necessary, not as something good. Third, I'll argue that they have good reason to act as they do, for the life of an unjust person is, they say, much better than that of a just one.

It isn't, Socrates, that I believe any of that myself. I'm perplexed, indeed, and my ears are deafened listening to Thrasymachus and countless others. But I've yet to hear anyone defend justice in the way I want, proving that it is better than injustice. I want to hear it praised *by itself*, and I think that I'm most likely to hear this from you. Therefore, I'm going to speak at length in praise of the unjust life, and in doing so I'll show you the way I want to hear you praising justice and denouncing injustice. But see whether you want me to do that or not.

I want that most of all. Indeed, what subject could someone with any understanding enjoy discussing more often?

Excellent. Then let's discuss the first subject I mentioned – what justice is and what its origins are.

They say that to do injustice is naturally good and to suffer injustice bad, but that the badness of suffering it so far exceeds the goodness of doing it that those who have done and suffered injustice and tasted both, but who lack the power to do it and avoid suffering it, decide that it is profitable to come to an agreement with each other neither to do injustice nor to suffer it. As a result, they begin to make laws and covenants, and what the law commands they call lawful and just. This, they say, is the origin and essence of justice. It is intermediate between the best and the worst. The best is to do injustice without paying the penalty; the worst is to suffer it without being able to take revenge. Justice is a mean between these two extremes. People value it not as a good but because they are too weak to do injustice with impunity. Someone who has the power to do this, however, and is a true man wouldn't make an agreement with anyone not to do injustice in order not to suffer it. For him that would be madness. This is the nature of justice, according to the argument, Socrates, and these are its natural origins.

We can see most clearly that those who practice justice do it unwillingly and because they lack the power to do injustice, if in our thoughts we grant to a just and an unjust person the freedom to do whatever they like. We can then follow both of them and see where their desires would lead. And we'll catch the just person red-handed travelling the same road as the unjust. The reason for this is the desire to outdo others and get more and more.[2] This is what anyone's nature naturally pursues as good, but nature is forced by law into the perversion of treating fairness with respect.

The freedom I mentioned would be most easily realized if both people had the power they say the ancestor of Gyges of Lydia possessed. The story goes that he was a shepherd in the service of the ruler of Lydia. There was a violent thunderstorm, and an earthquake broke open the ground and created a chasm at the place where he was tending his sheep. Seeing this, he was filled with amazement and went down into it. And there, in addition to many other wonders of which we're told, he saw a hollow bronze horse. There were windowlike openings in it, and, peeping in, he saw a corpse, which seemed to be of more than human size, wearing nothing but a gold ring on its finger. He took the ring and came out of the chasm. He wore the ring at the usual monthly meeting that reported to the king on the state of the flocks. And as he was sitting among the others, he happened to turn the setting of the ring towards himself to the inside of his hand. When he did this, he became invisible to those sitting near him, and they went on talking as if he had gone. He wondered at this, and, fingering the ring, he turned the setting outwards again and became visible. So he experimented with the ring to test whether it indeed had this power – and it did. If he turned the setting inward, he became invisible; if he turned it outward, he became visible again. When he realized this, he at once arranged to become one of the messengers sent to report to the king. And when he arrived there, he seduced the king's wife, attacked the king with her help, killed him, and took over the kingdom.

Let's suppose, then, that there were two such rings, one worn by a just and the other by an unjust person. Now, no one, it seems, would be so incorruptible that he would stay on the path of justice or stay away from other people's property, when he could take whatever he wanted from the market-place with impunity, go into people's houses and have sex with anyone he wished, kill or release from prison anyone he wished, and do all the other things that would make him like a god among humans. Rather his actions would be in no way different from those of an unjust person, and both would follow the same path. This, some would say, is a great proof that one is never just willingly but only when compelled to be. No one believes justice to be a good when it is kept private, since, wherever either person thinks he can do injustice with impunity, he does it. Indeed, every man believes that injustice is far more profitable to himself than justice. And any exponent of this argument will say he's right, for someone who didn't want to do injustice, given this sort of opportunity, and who didn't touch other people's property would be thought wretched and stupid by everyone aware of the situation, though, of course, they'd praise him in public, deceiving each other for fear of suffering injustice. So much for my second topic.

As for the choice between the lives we're discussing, we'll be able to make a correct judgment about that only if we separate the most just and the most unjust. Otherwise we won't be able to do it. Here's the separation I have in mind. We'll subtract nothing from the injustice of an unjust person and nothing from the justice of a just one, but we'll take each to be complete in his own way of life. First, therefore, we must suppose that an unjust person will act as clever craftsmen do: A first-rate captain or doctor, for example, knows the difference between what his craft can and can't do. He attempts the first but lets the second go by, and if he happens to slip, he can put things right. In the same way, an unjust person's successful attempts at injustice must remain undetected, if he is to be fully unjust. Anyone who is caught should be thought inept, for the extreme of injustice is to be believed to be just without being just. And our completely unjust person must be given complete injustice; nothing may be subtracted from it. We must allow

that, while doing the greatest injustice, he has nonetheless provided himself with the greatest reputation for justice. If he happens to make a slip, he must be able to put it right. If any of his unjust activities should be discovered, he must be able to speak persuasively or to use force. And if force is needed, he must have the help of courage and strength and of the substantial wealth and friends with which he has provided himself.

Having hypothesized such a person, let's now in our argument put beside him a just man, who is simple and noble and who, as Aeschylus says, doesn't want to be believed to be good but to be so.[3] We must take away his reputation, for a reputation for justice would bring him honor and rewards, so that it wouldn't be clear whether he is just for the sake of justice itself or for the sake of those honors and rewards. We must strip him of everything except justice and make his situation the opposite of an unjust person's. Though he does no injustice, he must have the greatest reputation for it, so that his justice may be tested fullstrength and not diluted by wrong-doing and what comes from it. Let him stay like that unchanged until he dies – just, but all his life believed to be unjust. In this way, both will reach the extremes, the one of justice and the other of injustice, and we'll be able to judge which of them is happier.

Whew! Glaucon, I said, how vigorously you've scoured each of the men for our competition, just as you would a pair of statues for an art competition.

I do the best I can, he replied. Since the two are as I've described, in any case, it shouldn't be difficult to complete the account of the kind of life that awaits each of them, but it must be done. And if what I say sounds crude, Socrates, remember that it isn't I who speak but those who praise injustice at the expense of justice. They'll say that a just person in such circumstances will be whipped, stretched on a rack, chained, blinded with fire, and, at the end, when he has suffered every kind of evil, he'll be impaled, and will realize then that one shouldn't want to be just but to be believed to be just. Indeed, Aeschylus' words are far more correctly applied to unjust people than to just ones, for the supporters of injustice will say that a really unjust person, having a way of life based on the truth about things and not living in accordance with opinion, doesn't want simply to be believed to be unjust but actually to be so –

Harvesting a deep furrow in his mind,
Where wise counsels propagate.

He rules his city because of his reputation for justice; he marries into any family he wishes; he gives his children in marriage to anyone he wishes; he has contracts and partnerships with anyone he wants; and besides benefiting himself in all these ways, he profits because he has no scruples about doing injustice. In any contest, public or private, he's the winner and outdoes[4] his enemies. And by outdoing them, he becomes wealthy, benefiting his friends and harming his enemies. He makes adequate sacrifices to the gods and sets up magnificent offerings to them. He takes better care of the gods, therefore, (and, indeed, of the human beings he's fond of) than a just person does. Hence it's likely that the gods, in turn, will take better care of him than of a just person. That's what they say, Socrates, that gods and humans provide a better life for unjust people than for just ones.

When Glaucon had said this, I had it in mind to respond, but his brother Adeimantus intervened: You surely don't think that the position has been adequately stated?

Why not? I said.

The most important thing to say hasn't been said yet.

Well, then, I replied, a man's brother must stand by him, as the saying goes.[5] If Glaucon has omitted something, you must help him. Yet what he has said is enough to throw me to the canvas and make me unable to come to the aid of justice.

Nonsense, he said. Hear what more I have to say, for we should also fully explore the arguments that are opposed to the ones Glaucon gave, the ones that praise justice and find fault with injustice, so that what I take to be his intention may be clearer.

When fathers speak to their sons, they say that one must be just, as do all the others who have charge of anyone. But they don't praise justice itself, only the high reputations it leads to and the consequences of being thought to be just, such as the public offices, marriages, and other things Glaucon listed. But they elaborate even further on the consequences of reputation. By bringing in the esteem of the gods, they are able to talk about the abundant good things that they themselves and the noble Hesiod and Homer say that the gods give to the pious,[6] for Hesiod says that the gods make the oak trees

Bear acorns at the top and bees in the middle
And make fleecy sheep heavy laden with wool

for the just, and tells of many other good things akin to these. And Homer is similar:

When a good king, in his piety,
Upholds justice, the black earth bears
Wheat and barley for him, and his trees are
heavy with fruit.
His sheep bear lambs unfailingly, and the sea
yields up its fish.

Musaeus and his son make the gods give the just more headstrong goods than these.[7] In their stories, they lead the just to Hades, seat them on couches, provide them with a symposium of pious people, crown them with wreaths, and make them spend all their time drinking – as if they thought drunkenness was the finest wage of virtue. Others stretch even further the wages that virtue receives from the gods, for they say that someone who is pious and keeps his promises leaves his children's children and a whole race behind him. In these and other similar ways, they praise justice. They bury the impious and unjust in mud in Hades; force them to carry water in a sieve; bring them into bad repute while they're still alive, and all those penalties that Glaucon gave to the just person they give to the unjust. But they have nothing else to say. This, then, is the way people praise justice and find fault with injustice.

Besides this, Socrates, consider another form of argument about justice and injustice employed both by private individuals and by poets. All go on repeating with one voice that justice and moderation are fine things, but hard and onerous, while licentiousness and injustice are sweet and easy to acquire and are shameful only in opinion and law. They add that unjust deeds are for the most part more profitable than just ones, and, whether in public or private, they willingly honor vicious people who have wealth and other types of power and declare them to be happy. But they dishonor and disregard the weak and the poor, even though they agree that they are better than the others.

But the most wonderful of all these arguments concerns what they have to say about the gods and virtue. They say that the gods, too, assign misfortune and a bad life to many good people, and the opposite fate to their opposites. Begging priests and prophets frequent the doors of the rich and persuade them that they possess a god-given power founded on sacrifices and incantations. If the rich person or any of his ancestors has committed an injustice, they can fix it with pleasant rituals. Moreover, if he wishes to injure some enemy, then, at little expense, he'll be able to harm just and unjust alike, for by means of spells and enchantments they can persuade the gods to serve them. And the poets are brought forward as witnesses to all these accounts. Some harp on the ease of vice, as follows:

> Vice in abundance is easy to get;
> The road is smooth and begins beside you,
> But the gods have put sweat between us and
> virtue,

and a road that is long, rough, and steep.[8] Others quote Homer to bear witness that the gods can be influenced by humans, since he said:

> The gods themselves can be swayed by prayer,
> And with sacrifices and soothing promises,
> Incense and libations, human beings turn
> them from their purpose
> When someone has transgressed and sinned.[9]

And they present a noisy throng of books by Musaeus and Orpheus, offspring as they say of Selene and the Muses, in accordance with which they perform their rituals.[10] And they persuade not only individuals but whole cities

that the unjust deeds of the living or the dead can be absolved or purified through sacrifices and pleasant games. These initiations, as they call them, free people from punishment hereafter, while a terrible fate awaits the uninitiated.

When all such sayings about the attitudes of gods and humans to virtue and vice are so often repeated, Socrates, what effect do you suppose they have on the souls of young people? I mean those who are clever and are able to flit from one of these sayings to another, so to speak, and gather from them an impression of what sort of person he should be and of how best to travel the road of life. He would surely ask himself Pindar's question, "Should I by justice or by crooked deceit scale this high wall and live my life guarded and secure?" And he'll answer: "The various sayings suggest that there is no advantage in my being just if I'm not also thought just, while the troubles and penalties of being just are apparent. But they tell me that an unjust person, who has secured for himself a reputation for justice, lives the life of a god. Since, then, 'opinion forcibly overcomes truth' and 'controls happiness,' as the wise men say, I must surely turn entirely to it.[11] I should create a façade of illusory virtue around me to deceive those who come near, but keep behind it the greedy and crafty fox of the wise Archilochus."[12]

"But surely," someone will object, "it isn't easy for vice to remain always hidden." We'll reply that nothing great is easy. And, in any case, if we're to be happy, we must follow the path indicated in these accounts. To remain undiscovered we'll form secret societies and political clubs. And there are teachers of persuasion to make us clever in dealing with assemblies and law courts. Therefore, using persuasion in one place and force in another, we'll outdo others[13] without paying a penalty.

"What about the gods? Surely, we can't hide from them or use violent force against them!" Well, if the gods don't exist or don't concern themselves with human affairs, why should we worry at all about hiding from them? If they do exist and do concern themselves with us, we've learned all we know about them from the laws and the poets who give their genealogies – nowhere else. But these are the very people who tell us that the gods can be persuaded and influenced by sacrifices, gentle prayers, and offerings. Hence, we should believe them on both matters or neither. If we believe them, we should be unjust and offer sacrifices from the fruits of our injustice. If we are just, our only gain is not to be punished by the gods, since we lose the profits of injustice. But if we are unjust, we get the profits of our crimes and transgressions and afterwards persuade the gods by prayer and escape without punishment.

"But in Hades won't we pay the penalty for crimes committed here, either ourselves or our children's children?" "My friend," the young man will say as he does his calculation, "mystery rites have great power and the gods have great power of absolution. The greatest cities tell us this, as do those children of the gods who have become poets and prophets."

Why, then, should we still choose justice over the greatest injustice? Many eminent authorities agree that, if we practice such injustice with a false façade, we'll do well at the hands of gods and humans, living and dying as we've a mind to. So, given all that has been said, Socrates, how is it possible for anyone of any power – whether of mind, wealth, body, or birth – to be willing to honor justice and not laugh aloud when he hears it praised? Indeed, if anyone can show that what we've said is false and has adequate knowledge that justice is best, he'll surely be full not of anger but of forgiveness for the unjust. He knows that, apart from someone of godlike character who is disgusted by injustice or one who has gained knowledge and avoids injustice for that reason, no one is just willingly. Through cowardice or old age or some other weakness, people do indeed object to injustice. But it's obvious that they do so only because they lack the power to do injustice, for the first of them to acquire it is the first to do as much injustice as he can.

And all of this has no other cause than the one that led Glaucon and me to say to you: "Socrates, of all of you who claim to praise justice, from the original heroes of old whose words survive, to the men of the present day, not one has ever blamed injustice or praised justice except by mentioning the reputations, honors, and rewards that are their consequences. No one has ever adequately described

what each itself does of its own power by its presence in the soul of the person who possesses it, even if it remains hidden from gods and humans. No one, whether in poetry or in private conversations, has adequately argued that injustice is the worst thing a soul can have in it and that justice is the greatest good. If you had treated the subject in this way and persuaded us from youth, we wouldn't now be guarding against one another's injustices, but each would be his own best guardian, afraid that by doing injustice he'd be living with the worst thing possible."

Thrasymachus or anyone else might say what we've said, Socrates, or maybe even more, in discussing justice and injustice – crudely inverting their powers, in my opinion. And, frankly, it's because I want to hear the opposite from you that I speak with all the force I can muster. So don't merely give us a theoretical argument that justice is stronger than injustice, but tell us what each itself does, because of its own powers, to someone who possesses it, that makes injustice bad and justice good. Follow Glaucon's advice, and don't take reputations into account, for if you don't deprive justice and injustice of their true reputations and attach false ones to them, we'll say that you are not praising them but their reputations and that you're encouraging us to be unjust in secret. In that case, we'll say that you agree with Thrasymachus that justice is the good of another, the advantage of the stronger, while injustice is one's own advantage and profit, though not the advantage of the weaker.

You agree that justice is one of the greatest goods, the ones that are worth getting for the sake of what comes from them, but much more so for their own sake, such as seeing, hearing, knowing, being healthy, and all other goods that are fruitful by their own nature and not simply because of reputation. Therefore, praise justice as a good of that kind, explaining how – because of its very self – it benefits its possessors and how injustice harms them. Leave wages and reputations for others to praise.

Others would satisfy me if they praised justice and blamed injustice in that way, extolling the wages of one and denigrating those of the other. But you, unless you order me to be satisfied, wouldn't, for you've spent your whole life investigating this and nothing else. Don't, then, give us only a theoretical argument that justice is stronger than injustice, but show what effect each has because of itself on the person who has it – the one for good and the other for bad – whether it remains hidden from gods and human beings or not.

Notes

1. "Music" or "music and poetry" and "physical training" are more transliterations than translations of *mousikē* and *gymnastikē*, which have no English equivalents. It is clear from Plato's discussion, for example, that *mousikē* includes poetry and stories, as well as music proper, and that *gymnastikē* includes dance and training in warfare, as well as what we call physical training. The aims of *mousikē* and *gymnastikē* are characterized at 522a. For further discussion see F.A.G. Beck, *Greek Education 430–350* B.C. (London: Methuen, 1964).

2. *Pleonexian.* See 343e n. 18.

3. In *Seven Against Thebes*, 592–94, it is said of Amphiaraus that "he did not wish to be believed to be the best but to be it." The passage continues with the words Glaucon quotes below at 362a–b.

4. *pleonektein.* See 343e n. 18.

5. See Homer, *Odyssey* 16.97–98.

6. The two quotations which follow are from Hesiod, *Works and Days* 332–33, and Homer, *Odyssey* 19.109.

7. Musaeus was a legendary poet closely associated with the mystery religion of Orphism.

8. *Works and Days* 287–89, with minor alterations.

9. *Iliad* 9.497–501, with minor alterations.

10. It is not clear whether Orpheus was a real person or a mythical figure. His fame in Greek myth rests on the poems in which the doctrines of the Orphic religion are set forth. These are discussed in W. Burkert, *Greek Religion* (Cambridge: Harvard University Press, 1985). Musaeus was a mythical singer closely related to Orpheus. Selene is the Moon.

11. The quotation is attributed to Simonides, whom Polemarchus cites in Book I.

12. Archilochus of Paros (c. 756–16 B.C.), was an iambic and elegiac poet who composed a famous fable about the fox and the hedgehog.

13. *Pleonektountes.* See 343e n. 18.

CHAPTER 16

Morality as a System of Hypothetical Imperatives

PHILIPPA FOOT

There are many difficulties and obscurities in Kant's moral philosophy, and few contemporary moralists will try to defend it all. Many, for instance, agree in rejecting Kant's derivation of duties from the mere form of the law expressed in terms of a universally legislative will. Nevertheless, it is generally supposed, even by those who would not dream of calling themselves his followers, that Kant established one thing beyond doubt – namely, the necessity of distinguishing moral judgements from hypothetical imperatives. That moral judgements cannot be hypothetical imperatives has come to seem an unquestionable truth. It will be argued here that it is not.

In discussing so thoroughly Kantian a notion as that of the hypothetical imperative, one naturally begins by asking what Kant himself meant by a hypothetical imperative, and it may be useful to say a little about the idea of an imperative as this appears in Kant's works. In writing about imperatives Kant seems to be thinking at least as much of statements about what ought to be or should be done, as of injunctions expressed in the imperative mood. He even describes as an imperative the assertion that it would be 'good to do or refrain from doing something'[1] and explains that for a will that 'does not always do something simply because it is presented to it as a good thing to do' this has the force of a command of reason. We may therefore think of Kant's imperatives as statements to the effect that something ought to be done or that it would be good to do it.

The distinction between hypothetical imperatives and categorical imperatives, which plays so important a part in Kant's ethics, appears in characteristic form in the following passages from the *Foundations of the Metaphysics of Morals*:

> All imperatives command either hypothetically or categorically. The former present the practical necessity of a possible action as a means to achieving something else which one desires (or which one may possibly desire). The categorical imperative would be one which presented an action as of itself objectively necessary, without regard to any other end.[2]

> If the action is good only as a means to something else, the imperative is hypothetical; but if it is thought of as good in itself, and hence as necessary in a will which of itself conforms to reason as the principle of this will, the imperative is categorical.[3]

The hypothetical imperative, as Kant defines it, 'says only that the action is good to some purpose' and the purpose, he explains, may

Philippa Foot, "Morality as a System of Hypothetical Imperatives," pp. 305–15 from *Philosophical Review*, 81, 1972. Reprinted by permission of Duke University Press.

be possible or actual. Among imperatives related to actual purposes Kant mentions rules of prudence, since he believes that all men necessarily desire their own happiness. Without committing ourselves to this view it will be useful to follow Kant in classing together as 'hypothetical imperatives' those telling a man what he ought to do because (or if) he wants something and those telling him what he ought to do on grounds of self-interest. Common opinion agrees with Kant in insisting that a moral man must accept a rule of duty whatever his interests or desires.[4]

Having given a rough description of the class of Kantian hypothetical imperatives it may be useful to point to the heterogeneity within it. Sometimes what a man should do depends on his passing inclination, as when he wants his coffee hot and should warm the jug. Sometimes it depends on some long-term project, when the feelings and inclinations of the moment are irrelevant. If one wants to be a respectable philosopher one should get up in the mornings and do some work, though just at that moment when one should do it the thought of being a respectable philosopher leaves one cold. It is true nevertheless to say of one, at that moment, that one wants to be a respectable philosopher,[5] and this can be the foundation of a desire-dependent hypothetical imperative. The term 'desire' as used in the original account of the hypothetical imperative was meant as a grammatically convenient substitute for 'want', and was not meant to carry any implication of inclination rather than long-term aim or project. Even the word 'project', taken strictly, introduces undesirable restrictions. If someone is devoted to his family or his country or to any cause, there are certain things he wants, which may then be the basis of hypothetical imperatives, without either inclinations or projects being quite what is in question. Hypothetical imperatives should already be appearing as extremely diverse; a further important distinction is between those that concern an individual and those that concern a group. The desires on which a hypothetical imperative is dependent may be those of one man, or may be taken for granted as belonging to a number of people engaged in some common project or sharing common aims.

Is Kant right to say that moral judgements are categorical, not hypothetical, imperatives? It may seem that he is, for we find in our language two different uses of words such as 'should' and 'ought', apparently corresponding to Kant's hypothetical and categorical imperatives, and we find moral judgements on the 'categorical' side. Suppose, for instance, we have advised a traveller that he should take a certain train, believing him to be journeying to his home. If we find that he has decided to go elsewhere, we will most likely have to take back what we said: the 'should' will now be unsupported and in need of support. Similarly, we must be prepared to withdraw our statement about what he should do if we find that the right relation does not hold between the action and the end – that it is either no way of getting what he wants (or doing what he wants to do) or not the most eligible among possible means. The use of 'should' and 'ought' in moral contexts is, however, quite different. When we say that a man should do something and intend a moral judgement we do not have to back up what we say by considerations about his interests or his desires; if no such connexion can be found the 'should' need not be withdrawn. It follows that the agent cannot rebut an assertion about what, morally speaking, he should do by showing that the action is not ancillary to his interests or desires. Without such a connexion the 'should' does not stand unsupported and in need of support the support that *it* requires is of another kind.

There is, then, one clear difference between moral judgements and the class of 'hypothetical imperatives' so far discussed. In the latter 'should' is 'used hypothetically', in the sense defined, and if Kant were merely drawing attention to this piece of linguistic usage his point would easily be proved. But obviously Kant meant more than this; in describing moral judgements as non-hypothetical – that is, categorical imperatives – he is ascribing to them a special dignity and necessity which this usage cannot give. Modern philosophers follow Kant in talking, for example, about the 'unconditional requirement' expressed in moral judgements. These, they say, tell us what we have to do whatever our interests or desires, and by their inescapability they are distinguished from hypothetical imperatives.

The problem is to find proof for this further feature of moral judgements. If anyone fails to see the gap that has to be filled it will be useful to point out to him that we find 'should' used non-hypothetically in some non-moral statements to which no one attributes the special dignity and necessity conveyed by the description 'categorical imperative'. For instance, we find this non-hypothetical use of 'should' in sentences enunciating rules of etiquette, as, for example, that an invitation in the third person should be answered in the third person, where the rule does not *fail to apply* to someone who has his own good reasons for ignoring this piece of nonsense, or who simply does not care about what, from the point of view of etiquette, he should do. Similarly, there is a non-hypothetical use of 'should' in contexts where something like a club rule is in question. The club secretary who has told a member that he should not bring ladies into the smoking-room does not say, 'Sorry, I was mistaken' when informed that this member is resigning tomorrow and cares nothing about his reputation in the club. Lacking a connexion with the agent's desires or interests, this 'should' does not stand 'unsupported and in need of support'; it requires only the backing of the rule. The use of 'should' is therefore 'non-hypothetical' in the sense defined.

It follows that if a hypothetical use of 'should' gave a hypothetical imperative, and a non-hypothetical use of 'should' a categorical imperative, then 'should' statements based on rules of etiquette, or rules of a club would be categorical imperatives. Since this would not be accepted by defenders of the categorical imperative in ethics, who would insist that these other 'should' statements give hypothetical imperatives, they must be using this expression in some other sense. We must therefore ask what they mean when they say that 'You should answer . . . in the third person' is a hypothetical imperative. Very roughly the idea seems to be that one may reasonably ask why anyone should bother about what should (from the point of view of etiquette) be done, and that such considerations deserve no notice unless reason is shown. So although

people give as their reason for doing something the fact that it is required by etiquette, we do not take this consideration as *in itself giving us reason to act*. Considerations of etiquette do not have any automatic reason-giving force, and a man might be right if he denied that he had reason to do 'what's done'.

This seems to take us to the heart of the matter, for, by contrast, it is supposed that moral considerations necessarily give reasons for acting to any man. The difficulty is, of course, to defend this proposition which is more often repeated than explained. Unless it is said, implausibly, that all 'should' or 'ought' statements give reasons for acting, which leaves the old problem of assigning a special categorical status to moral judgement, we must be told what it is that makes the moral 'should' relevantly different from the 'shoulds' appearing in normative statements of other kinds.[6] Attempts have sometimes been made to show that some kind of irrationality is involved in ignoring the 'should' of morality: in saying 'Immoral – so what?' as one says 'Not *comme il faut* – so what?' But as far as I can see these have all rested on some illegitimate assumption, as, for instance, of thinking that the amoral man, who agrees that some piece of conduct is immoral but takes no notice of that, is inconsistently disregarding a rule of conduct that he has accepted; or again of thinking it inconsistent to desire that others will not do to one what one proposes to do to them. The fact is that the man who rejects morality because he sees no reason to obey its rules can be convicted of villainy but not of inconsistency. Nor will his action necessarily be irrational. Irrational actions are those in which a man in some way defeats his own purposes, doing what is calculated to be disadvantageous or to frustrate his ends. Immorality does not *necessarily* involve any such thing.

It is obvious that the normative character of moral judgement does not guarantee its reason-giving force. Moral judgements are normative, but so are judgements of manners, statements of club rules, and many others. Why should the first provide reasons for acting as the others do not? In every case it is because there is a background of teaching that the non-hypothetical 'should' can be used. The behaviour is required, not simply recommended, but the question remains as to why we should do what we are required to do. It is true that moral rules are often enforced much more strictly than the rules of etiquette, and our reluctance to press the non-hypothetical 'should' of etiquette may be one reason why we think of the rules of etiquette as hypothetical imperatives. But are we then to say that there is nothing behind the idea that moral judgements are categorical imperatives but the relative stringency of our moral teaching? I believe that this may have more to do with the matter than the defenders of the categorical imperative would like to admit. For if we look at the kind of thing that is said in its defence we may find ourselves puzzled about what the words can even mean unless we connect them with the feelings that this stringent teaching implants. People talk, for instance, about the 'binding force' of morality, but it is not clear what this means if not that we *feel* ourselves unable to escape. Indeed the 'inescapability' of moral requirements is often cited when they are being contrasted with hypothetical imperatives. No one, it is said, escapes the requirements of ethics by having or not having particular interests or desires. Taken in one way this only reiterates the contrast between the 'should' of morality and the hypothetical 'should', and once more places morality alongside of etiquette. Both are inescapable in that behaviour does not cease to offend against either morality or etiquette because the agent is indifferent to their purposes and to the disapproval he will incur by flouting them. But morality is supposed to be inescapable in some special way and this may turn out to be merely the reflection of the way morality is taught. Of course, we must try other ways of expressing the fugitive thought. It may be said, for instance, that moral judgements have a kind of necessity since they tell us what we "must do" or "have to do" whatever our interests and desires. The sense of this is, again, obscure. Sometimes when we use such expressions we are referring to physical or mental compulsion. (A man has to go along if he is pulled by strong men and he has to give in if tortured beyond endurance.) But it is only in the absence of such conditions that moral judgements apply. Another and more common sense of the words is found in sentences such as 'I caught a bad cold and had to stay in bed' where a penalty for acting otherwise is in the offing. The necessity of acting morally is not, however, supposed to depend on such penalties. Another range of examples, not necessarily having to do with penalties, is found where there is an unquestioned acceptance of some project or rôle, as when a nurse tells us that she has to make her rounds at a certain time, or we say that we have to run for a certain train[7] But these too are irrelevant in the present context, since the acceptance condition can always be revoked.

No doubt it will be suggested that it is in some other sense of the words 'have to' or 'must' that one has to or must do what morality demands. But why should one insist that there must be such a sense when it proves so difficult to say what it is? Suppose that what we take for a puzzling thought were really no thought at all but only the reflection of our *feelings* about morality? Perhaps it makes no sense to say that we 'have to' submit to the moral law, or that morality is 'inescapable' in some special way. For just as one may feel as if one is falling without believing that one is moving downward, so one may feel as if one has to do what is morally required without believing oneself to be under physical or psychological compulsion, or about to incur a penalty if one does not comply. No one thinks that if the word 'falling' is used in a statement reporting one's sensations it must be used in a special sense. But this kind of mistake may be involved in looking for the special sense in which one 'has to' do what morality demands. There is no difficulty about the idea that we feel we *have to* behave morally, and given the psychological conditions of the learning of moral behaviour it is natural that we should have such feelings. What we cannot do is quote them in support of the doctrine of the categorical imperative. It seems, then, that in so far as it is backed up by statements to the effect that the moral law *is* inescapable, or that we *do* have to do what is morally required of us, it is uncertain whether the doctrine of the categorical imperative even makes sense.

The conclusion we should draw is that moral judgements have no better claim to be categorical imperatives than do statements about matters of etiquette. People may indeed follow either morality or etiquette without asking why they should do so, but equally well they may not. They may ask for reasons and may reasonably refuse to follow either if reasons are not to be found.

It will be said that this way of viewing moral considerations must be totally destructive of morality, because no one could ever act morally unless he accepted such considerations as in themselves sufficient reason for action. Actions that are truly moral must be done 'for their own sake', 'because they are right', and not for some ulterior purpose. This argument we must examine with care, for the doctrine of the categorical imperative has owed much to its persuasion.

Is there anything to be said for the thesis that a truly moral man acts 'out of respect for the moral law' or that he does what is morally right because it is morally right? That such propositions are not prima facie absurd depends on the fact that moral judgement concerns itself with a man's reasons for acting as well as with what he does. Law and etiquette require only that certain things are done or left undone, but no one is counted as charitable if he gives alms 'for the praise of men', and one who is honest only because it pays him to be honest does not have the virtue of honesty. This kind of consideration was crucial in shaping Kant's moral philosophy. He many times contrasts acting out of respect for the moral law with acting from an ulterior motive, and what is more from one that is self-interested. In the early *Lectures on Ethics* he gave the principle of truth-telling under a system of hypothetical imperatives as that of not lying *if it harms one* to lie. In the *Metaphysics of Morals* he says that ethics cannot start from the ends which a man may propose to himself, since these are all 'selfish'.[8] In the *Critique of Practical Reason* he argues explicitly that when acting not out of respect for moral law but 'on a material maxim' men do what they do for the sake of pleasure or happiness.

All material practical principles are, as such, of one and the same kind and belong under the general principle of self love or one's own happiness.[9]

Kant, in fact, was a psychological hedonist in respect of all actions except those done for the sake of the moral law, and this faulty theory of human nature was one of the things preventing him from seeing that moral virtue might be compatible with the rejection of the categorical imperative.

If we put this theory of human action aside, and allow as ends the things that seem to be ends, the picture changes. It will surely be allowed that quite apart from thoughts of duty a man may care about the suffering of others, having a sense of identification with them, and wanting to help if he can. Of course he must want not the reputation of charity, nor even a gratifying rôle helping others, but, quite simply, their good. If this is what he does care about, then he will be attached to the end proper to the virtue of charity and a comparison with someone acting from an ulterior motive (even a respectable ulterior motive) is out of place. Nor will the conformity of his action to the rule of charity be merely contingent. Honest action may happen to further a man's career; charitable actions do not *happen* to further the good of others.[10]

Can a man accepting only hypothetical imperatives possess other virtues besides that of charity? Could he be just or honest? This problem is more complex because there is no end related to such virtues as the good of others is related to charity. But what reason could there be for refusing to call a man a just man if he acted justly because he loved truth and liberty, and wanted every man to be treated with a certain respect? And why should the truly honest man not follow honesty for the sake of the good that honest dealing brings to men? Of course, the usual difficulties can be raised about the rare case in which no good is foreseen from an individual act of honesty. But it is not evident that a man's desires could not give him reason to act honestly even here. He wants to live openly and in good faith with his neighbours; it is not all the same to him to lie and conceal.

If one wants to know whether there could be a truly moral man who accepted moral principles as hypothetical rules of conduct, as many people accept rules of etiquette as hypothetical rules of conduct, one must consider the right kind of example. A man who demanded that morality should be brought under the heading of self-interest would not be a good candidate, nor would anyone who was ready to be charitable or honest only so long as he felt inclined. A cause such as justice makes strenuous demands, but this is not peculiar to morality, and men are prepared to toil to achieve many ends not endorsed by morality. That they are prepared to fight so hard for moral ends – for example, for liberty and justice – depends on the fact that these are the kinds of ends that arouse devotion. To sacrifice a great deal for the sake of etiquette one would need to be under the spell of the emphatic 'ought'. One could hardly be devoted to behaving *comme il faut*.

In spite of all that has been urged in favour of the hypothetical imperative in ethics, I am sure that many people will be unconvinced and will argue that one element essential to moral virtue is still missing. This missing feature is the recognition of a *duty* to adopt those ends which we have attributed to the moral man. We have said that he *does* care about others, and about causes such as liberty and justice; that it is on this account that he will accept a system of morality. But what if he never cared about such things, or what if he ceased to care? Is it not the case that he *ought* to care? This is exactly what Kant would say, for though at times he sounds as if he thought that morality is not concerned with ends, at others he insists that the adoption of ends such as the happiness of others is itself dictated by morality.[11] How is this proposition to be regarded by one who rejects all talk about the binding force of the moral law? He will agree that a moral man has moral ends and cannot be indifferent to matters such as suffering and injustice. Further, he will recognise in the statement that one *ought*

to care about these things a correct application of the non-hypothetical moral 'ought' by which society is apt to voice its demands. He will not, however, take the fact that he ought to have certain ends as in itself reason to adopt them. If he himself is a moral man then he cares about such things, but not 'because he ought'. If he is an amoral man he may deny that he has any reason to trouble his head over this or any other moral demand. Of course he may be mistaken, and his life as well as others' lives may be most sadly spoiled by his selfishness. But this is not what is urged by those who think they can close the matter by an emphatic use of 'ought'. My argument is that they are relying on an illusion, as if trying to give the moral 'ought' a magic force.[12]

This conclusion may, as I said, appear dangerous and subversive of morality. We are apt to panic at the thought that we ourselves, or other people, might stop caring about the things we do care about, and we feel that the categorical imperative gives us some control over the situation. But it is interesting that the people of Leningrad were not struck by the thought that only the *contingent* fact that other citizens shared their loyalty and devotion to the city stood between them and the Germans during the terrible years of the siege. Perhaps we should be less troubled than we are by fear of defection from the moral cause; perhaps we should even have less reason to fear it if people thought of themselves as volunteers banded together to fight for liberty and justice and against inhumanity and oppression. It is often felt, even if obscurely, that there is an element of deception in the official line about morality. And while some have been persuaded by talk about the authority of the moral law, others have turned away with a sense of distrust.

Notes

1. *Foundations of the Metaphysics of Morals*, Sec. II, trans. by L. W. Beck.
2. Ibid.
3. Ibid.
4. According to the position sketched here we have three forms of hypothetical imperative: 'If you want x you should do y', 'Because you want x

you should do y', and 'Because x is in your interest you should do y'. For Kant the third would automatically be covered by the second.

5. To say that at that moment one wants to be a respectable philosopher would be another matter. Such a statement requires a special connexion between the desire and the moment.

6. To say that moral considerations are *called* reasons is blatantly to ignore the problem.

In the case of etiquette or club rules it is obvious that the non-hypothetical use of 'should' has resulted in the loss of the usual connexion between what one should do and what one has reason to do. Someone who objects that in the moral case a man cannot be justified in restricting his practical reasoning in this way, since every moral 'should' gives reasons for acting, must face the following dilemma. Either it is possible to create reasons for acting simply by putting together any silly rules and introducing a non-hypothetical 'should', or else the non-hypothetical 'should' does not necessarily imply reasons for acting. If it does not necessarily imply reasons for acting we may ask why it is supposed to do so in the case of morality. Why cannot the indifferent amoral man say that for him 'should$_m$' gives no reason for acting, treating 'should$_m$' as most of us treat 'should$_e$'? Those who insist that 'should$_m$' is categorical in this second 'reason-giving' sense do not seem to realise that they never prove this to be so. They sometimes say that moral considerations 'just do' give reasons for acting, without explaining why some devotee of etiquette could not say the same about the rules of etiquette.

7. I am grateful to Rogers Albritton for drawing my attention to this interesting use of expressions such as 'have to' or 'must'.

8. Pt. II, Introduction, sec. II.

9. Immanuel Kant, *Critique of Practical Reason*, trans. L. W. Beck, p. 133.

10. It is not, of course, necessary that charitable actions should *succeed* in helping others; but when they do so they do not *happen* to do so, since that is necessarily their aim. (Footnote added, 1977.)

11. See, e.g., *The Metaphysics of Morals*, pt. II, sec. 30.

12. See G. E. M. Anscombe, 'Modern Moral Philosophy', *Philosophy* (1958). My view is different from Miss Anscombe's, but I have learned from her.

CHAPTER 17
The Reconciliation Project

GREGORY S. KAVKA

Clarifying the nature of the relationship between ethical and self-interested conduct is one of the oldest problems of moral philosophy. As far back as Plato's *Republic*, philosophers have approached it with the aim of reconciling morality and self-interest by showing that moral behavior is required by, or at least is consistent with, rational prudence. Let us call this undertaking the Reconciliation Project. In modern times this project is generally viewed as doomed to failure. It is believed that unless we make an outdated and implausible appeal to divine sanctions, we cannot expect to find agreement between moral and prudential requirements.

Can this negative verdict on the Reconciliation Project be avoided? Before we can deal with this question, we must distinguish among versions of the project along four dimensions. The *audience* dimension concerns to whom our arguments about coincidence of duty and interest are addressed. Sometimes it is supposed that a successful version of the Reconciliation Project must be capable of converting to virtue a hardened cynic or immoralist. . . . This is too much to ask. Immoralists are not

likely to understand or appreciate the benefits of living morally, nor are they usually the sort of people who will listen to, or be swayed by, abstract rational arguments. A more modest aim is to speak convincingly to the puzzled ordinary person, such as Glaucon, who fears that in following the path of morality he is being irrational and is harming himself, but who is willing to listen to and ponder arguments to the contrary. We shall here be concerned with versions of the Reconciliation Project having this more modest aim.

A second dimension concerns the sort of *agent* for whom morality and self-interest are supposed to coincide. Versions of the Reconciliation Project that are ambitious along this dimension might attempt to demonstrate such coincidence in the case of all actual human beings, or even all possible human beings. More restrained versions would concentrate on more limited classes, such as persons without severe emotional disturbances or persons capable of self-assessment and love for others. The audience and agent dimensions of the Reconciliation Project are related. If one's aim in pursuing the project is to create or strengthen moral motivation, one would normally choose an agent class that just encompasses one's audience, so as to convince one's listeners that it pays *them* (promotes their own interests) to be moral, while at the same time exposing one's argument to the fewest possible objections. But

Gregory S. Kavka, "The Reconciliation Project," pp. 279–319 from David Zimmerman and David Copp (eds.), *Morality, Reason and Truth*. Totowa, NJ: Rowman and Allanheld, 1985. Reprinted by permission of Rowman & Littlefield Publishers Inc.

if one aims at promoting theoretical understanding, one's agent class may be broader or narrower than one's audience. One may, for example, seek to convince reflective persons of goodwill that it pays everyone to be moral. Agent and audience classes need not even overlap; one might argue to sophisticated theorists that morality pays for the unsophisticated, who could not be expected successfully to disguise their immoralities.

The third dimension of the Reconciliation Project is the *social* one. Whether morality pays is partly a function of others' responses to one's immoralities. Are morality and prudence supposed to coincide, then, in all imaginable social environments, all feasible ones, all (or most) actual ones, some feasible ones, or some imaginable ones? Different answers to this question yield importantly different versions of the Reconciliation Project.

Fourth and finally, if we say that morality and prudence coincide, does this mean that (i) each individual ethical act is prudent or (ii) that there are sufficient prudential reasons for adopting a moral way of life and acting in accordance with moral rules? This question concerns the nature of the objects or entities to be reconciled and calls attention to the *object* dimension of the Reconciliation Project. Reconciling all particular acts of duty with prudence is so unpromising a task as to have been largely shunned by the major philosophical exponents of the project. (Although, as we shall see below, much depends on whether prudential evaluations of acts are undertaken prospectively or retrospectively.) Thus Plato argues the prudential advantages of moral dispositions or ways of life, while Hobbes focuses on providing a prudential grounding for moral rules.

Taking note of the object dimension allows us to clarify the Reconciliation Project by answering a preliminary objection to it. According to this objection, the project must fail because supposedly moral actions are not really moral if they are motivated by prudential concerns. We may, however, accept this observation about motivation and moral action without damaging the Reconciliation Project properly construed. For that project is not committed to morality and prudence being identical, or to moral and prudential motives

or reasons for action being the same. Rather, prudence and morality are supposed to be reconcilable in two senses. They recommend the same courses of conduct (where conduct is described in some motive-neutral way). Further, it is consistent with the requirements of prudence to adopt and live a moral way of life, even though this involves developing a pattern of motivation in which nonprudential considerations play an important role. Thus the Reconciliation Project survives the preliminary objection because it concerns, along its object dimension, acts or rules of action or ways of life, rather than motives or reasons for action.

Still, the Reconciliation Project is hopeless if we adopt very stringent interpretations of it along most or all of its four dimensions. We cannot expect to convince a clever immoralist that it pays everyone to act morally on every specific occasion in any sort of society. But why should we consider only such extreme versions of the project? Taking account of the dimensions of variation of the Reconciliation Project, I propose instead to discuss some less extreme versions (and modifications) of it to see to what extent they can be carried out and why they fail when they do. In the course of this investigation, I hope partly to vindicate the rationality of being moral and to clarify further the relationship between morality, prudence, and rationality.

I begin by sketching a Hobbesian version of the Reconciliation Project that presupposes psychological egoism and relies exclusively on external sanctions (social rewards and punishments) to reconcile obligation and interest. This Hobbesian approach provides considerable illumination, but it suffers from serious defects. To correct some of these, I consider the significance of internal (self-imposed psychological) sanctions. Next, I take up the two most intractable objections to all forms of the project. These concern the obligation to die for others, and those duties owed by members of strong groups to members of weak groups who are apparently not in a position to reciprocate benefits bestowed on them. Finally, I note how the recognition of nonegoistic motives transforms the Reconciliation Project. Throughout, my remarks are largely programmatic. I sketch alternatives, problems, and general strategies for solving problems and leave much detail to be filled in later. I hope nonetheless to say enough to show that the Reconciliation Project is still philosophically interesting and important.

I.   The Hobbesian Strategy

As a starting point, let us consider Hobbes's version of the Reconciliation Project. In seeking to reconcile duty and interest, Hobbes is limited by two self-imposed restrictions: He rules out appeal to religious sanctions, and he leaves no place for internal sanctions (such as guilt feelings) in his account of human psychology. Hence, Hobbes is reduced to arguing his case solely in terms of external sanctions; that is, social rewards and punishments. He does, however, marshall these relatively meager resources to good advantage.

The core of Hobbes's view is that the general rules of conduct that a farsighted prudent man concerned with his own survival, security, and well-being would follow are essentially the rules of traditional morality. The function of these rules is to promote peace, cooperation, and mutual restraint for the benefit of all parties. The rules therefore forbid killing, assault, and robbery, and they require keeping one's agreements, settling disputes by arbitration, providing aid to others when the cost to one is small and the benefit to them is large, and so on. The self-interested individual, if sufficiently rational and farsighted, will follow these rules because doing so is the best (and only reliable) way to ensure peaceful and cooperative relations with others. The person, for example, who wastes on luxuries what others need to survive is not likely to be helped by others if he later falls into want; nor will his person and property ever be safe from the desperate acts of the needy. The dangers of hostile reactions by others that confront the habitual assailant, thief, or contract-breaker are even more obvious. And while people may try to conceal their violations of moral rules, the long-run dangers of exposure and retaliation by others are great. Thus, argues Hobbes, morality is superior to immorality as a general policy, from the viewpoint of rational prudence.

One may agree that normally morality is a more prudent general policy than immorality but raise doubts about its prudential rationality in two special circumstances: when one is confident that a violation would go undiscovered and unpunished, and when others are not willing to reciprocate restraint. In the first case, it appears that one would benefit by *offensively* violating moral rules; that is, by not complying with them when others are complying. In the second case, prudence seems to call for a *defensive* violation – for noncompliance motivated by the belief that others are not complying and the desire not to put oneself at a disadvantage. Hobbes recognizes and attempts to deal with both cases.

Hobbes's argument against offensive violations of moral rules is presented in his famous reply to the Fool (1651, 1958, pp. 120–122). He acknowledges that such violations will in some cases turn out, *in retrospect*, to best serve the agent's interests. But because they risk serious external sanctions (such as the withdrawal of all future cooperation by others), they are never *prospectively* rational. Since the consequences of failure are horrible and the chances of failure are not precisely calculable, it is not a rational gamble to offensively violate moral rules. Underlying this Hobbesian argument is an intuition about rational prudence that is reflected in the usual connotation of the word *prudence*. To be prudent is to play it safe and not take large, uncontrollable risks. It is not implausible to suppose that rational pursuit of one's own interests requires being prudent in this sense when one's vital interests are at stake.

To develop this point, let us follow decision theorists in drawing a distinction between choices under *risk* and under *uncertainty*. In the former cases, one has reliable knowledge of the probabilities that the various possible outcomes would follow the different available courses of action. In choices under uncertainty, one lacks such knowledge. Rawls contends that rationality requires that, when making vitally important choices under uncertainty, one follow a Maximin Strategy – choose the act with the best worst outcome (1971, pp. 152–158). I have argued elsewhere for using a Disaster Avoidance Strategy in such circumstances – choosing the alternative that maximizes one's chances of avoiding all unacceptable outcomes.[1] Both strategies favor playing it safe in the sense of aiming at avoidance (or minimization) of the risk of unacceptable outcomes.

Now suppose we view choices among actions in the real world as made under uncertainty. (This is plausible for the most part, given our limited understanding of the complex factors that determine the consequences of our actions.) If, as Hobbes suggests, offensive violators risk the application of serious external sanctions, offensive violations would be irrational according to both the Maximin and Disaster Avoidance viewpoints. For the offensive violator accepts, under uncertainty, an unnecessary (or greater than necessary) risk of suffering disastrous consequences. So if either Rawls's analysis of rational prudential choice under uncertainty or my own is correct, Hobbes's argument against offensive violations under uncertainty is largely vindicated.

The considerations just presented attempt in effect to reconcile the requirements of morality and prudence as applied to (a certain class of) particular actions. They may serve, that is, as part of a Reconciliation Project focusing along the object dimension on *acts*. They function ever more effectively as part of an argument for the coincidence of *rules* of morality and prudence. We can imagine someone claiming that living by some rule such as the following would better serve one's interests than following moral rules: "Follow the moral rules except when you believe (or confidently believe) you can get away with violating them." But if one lives by this sort of rule, one is likely to undergo the risks inherent in offensive violations on a good number of occasions. And even if one is cautious in selecting the occasions, the risk of getting caught and suffering serious sanctions on one or more occasions will be substantial and much greater than the chance of getting caught on one particular occasion. Hence, insofar as rational prudence requires avoiding or minimizing risks of suffering serious sanctions, it would not recommend a policy of clever "compromise" between moral and immoral conduct as exemplified in this rule.

We have seen that Hobbes tries to reconcile duty and prudence in the case of offensive violations by denying that such violations are prudential. The opposite tack is adopted for defensive violations. These, Hobbes claims, are not contrary to moral duty. Agents are not obligated to follow the constraints of traditional morality unless others are reciprocating their restraint. To comply with moral rules unilaterally is to render oneself prey to others, and this, Hobbes urges, one is not required to do (1651, 1958, pp. 110, 130).

The governing principle of Hobbesian morality, then, is what I call the Copper Rule: "Do unto others as they *do* unto you." This principle enunciates a less glittering moral ideal than the familiar Golden Rule, which requires us to treat others well regardless of whether they treat us well in return. In thus opting for a reciprocal rather than unilateral interpretation of moral requirements, is Hobbes abandoning traditional morality?

To answer this question, we must distinguish between two aspects of morality – practice morality and ideal morality. Practice morality encompasses the standards of conduct actually expected of, and generally practiced by, persons living within a given moral tradition. It is roughly the part of morality concerned with *requirements*, those standards for which people are blamed, criticized, or punished for failing to live up to. Ideal morality refers to standards of moral excellence that a tradition sets up as models to aspire to and admire. Praise, honor, and respect are the rewards of those who live by its higher, more demanding standards. But, in general, people are not blamed for falling short of such ideals, or even for not aiming at them.

Now there surely are important strands of unilateralism in the ideal morality of the Western tradition. The Golden Rule, the admonition to love thine enemy, and the principle of turning the other cheek, all concern treating well even those who do not reciprocate. But if we turn to practice, and the standards of conduct that are actually treated as moral requirements, we find Copper Rule reciprocity to be a reasonable summary of much of what we observe. For practice morality allows us considerable leeway to engage in otherwise forbidden conduct toward those who violate moral constraints, especially when this is necessary for protection. Thus individuals may kill in self-defense, society may deprive criminals of their liberty, contracts may be broken when reciprocal fulfillment cannot be expected, and so forth.

We may then, without committing Hobbes to absurdity, attribute to him the claim that, in practice, traditional moral rules contain exception clauses allowing for defensive "violations" of the main clauses of the rule, if these are aimed at other violators. In adopting this pruned-down conception of moral requirements, Hobbes has abandoned the ambitious dream of achieving a reconciliation between ideal morality and prudence. But he has avoided one telling objection to the Reconciliation Project: that morality requires us (as prudence does not) to sacrifice our interests to the immoral, who will be all too ready to take advantage of such a sacrifice. Note, however, that the companion objection that morality sometimes requires us to sacrifice our interests for others who are moral is not dealt with by the Copper Rule interpretation of morality. Forms of this objection will be considered later.

As we have seen, Hobbes treats offensive and defensive violations of moral rules quite differently. In the former case, he reconciles prudence to morality by altering cynical interpretations of what prudence demands, while in the latter case he reconciles morality to prudence by offering a nonstandard interpretation of morality. Yet in each case he draws our attention to the oft-neglected social dimension of the Reconciliation Project. His discussion of defensive violations suggests that under certain conditions – anarchy or general noncompliance with traditional moral rules – moral and prudential requirements coincide, but only as a result of the effective loosening or disappearance of the former. Hence, *how* duty and interest are reconciled is a function of the social environment. In arguing for the imprudence of offensive violations of moral rules, Hobbes presupposes threats of external sanctions that are serious enough to make such violations a bad gamble. Therefore, his argument does not apply to imaginary situations in which society rewards immoral actions, or even certain real ones in which it ignores serious immoralities when they are committed by members of some privileged groups.

Suppose, then, that our aim is to reconcile prudence with traditional moral requirements (without the exception clauses); that is, do not kill or steal, aid the needy when the costs are small, and so on. Hobbes suggests that this reconciliation is possible only in a certain sort of social environment – one we may call *punitive*. In a punitive environment, serious violators of moral norms are sought out, apprehended, and given stiff punishments frequently enough to make immorality a bad prudential risk. As a result, there is general compliance with moral rules and little need for one to undertake defensive violations. In a punitive social environment, offensive violations of moral rules are irrational and defensive ones are unnecessary. If an actual social environment is punitive, the Reconciliation Project seems to have succeeded with respect to it. And if such an environment is feasible but nonactual, those who wish people to act morally but fear the distracting influence of self-interest will have some reason to create it.

Let us now briefly summarize the Hobbesian approach to the Reconciliation Project, which is based on external sanctions. It consists first of proposing specific interpretations of that project along two of the four dimensions. With respect to the object dimension, it focuses on rules or policies rather than on individual acts. (Although the reply to the Fool fits within an act version of the project as well.) And it presupposes a punitive social environment, avoiding the dubious claim that duty and interest coincide in any social context. Further, it provides a novel interpretation of moral requirements – the Copper Rule or reciprocal interpretation – and it rests on a "playing it safe" theory of rational prudential choice under uncertainty. All of these aspects of the Hobbesian strategy make contributions to the interpretation and development of the Reconciliation Project. None is without plausibility. However, there are two fatal objections that the Hobbesian Strategy cannot adequately answer.

The first concerns punitive social environments. These are beneficial in discouraging immoral conduct, but they have costs. To render immorality a bad risk solely via threats of punishments, such punishments must be made very heavy and/or very probable. In a society of significant size, doing the latter would normally require a massive policing establishment with large monetary costs (borne by the citizens), interferences with personal liberty and privacy (searches, eavesdropping, surveillance), and dangers of police power and influence over the political and economic institutions of society. Heavy penalties also have social costs – monetary costs of supporting prisons, lessened chances of reconciliation between offenders and society, dangers of gross injustice if the innocent might sometimes be punished, and so on. In short, we must accept trade-offs between various things that we value and the deterence of serious immorality. And it may not always be possible for society, by use of external sanctions alone, to ensure that "crime does not pay" without sacrificing too much in the way of individual liberty, privacy, and protection from excessive state and police power.

Our second objection concedes that immorality generally does not pay, and even allows, that immorality is prudentially irrational under genuine uncertainty. However, *some* opportunities for immoral gain may present themselves under risk; that is, the probabilities of detection and punishment may be reliably known. In these situations, maximizing expected personal utility is arguably the most rational course, and this may imply engaging in an offensive violation. A slumlord, for example, may have relatively precise statistical data that allow him to estimate reliably the odds of his getting caught and punished if he hires a professional arsonist to burn one of his buildings so that he can collect the insurance. If the chances of arrest and conviction are low and the return is high, the crime may have positive expected value for him, and it will be prudentially rational for him to undertake it. The rules of a system of rational self-interest will be formulated to allow agents to take advantage of such situations.

These two objections reveal that while external sanctions alone can take us, via the Hobbesian Strategy, some considerable way toward reconciling duty and interest, they cannot take us far enough. We at least need some device other than a punitive social environment that can alter the calculations or dispositions of the slumlord and other potential criminals. The obvious candidates here are internal sanctions,

psychic structures that punish immorality and reward virtue. Unlike external sanctions, these are relatively free of problems concerning evasion and detection, since one's conscience follows one everywhere, and they do not threaten privacy and democracy as do secret police forces. In the next section, I will explore how their inclusion may extend and strengthen the Hobbesian arguments for the coincidence for morality and prudence.

II. Internal Sanctions

Internal sanctions come in two varieties, negative and positive. The negative sanctions are guilt feelings and related forms of psychic distress that most of us are subject to feel when we believe we have done wrong. We develop the tendency to experience such feelings under such circumstances as part of the socialization process we undergo in growing up. It is no mystery why society nurtures and encourages the development of this tendency; it benefits others to the extent that it inhibits or deters misconduct by the individual. And once one possesses the tendency, it imposes extra – and relatively certain – costs on immorality, costs which may tip the prudential balance in favor of restraint. Arson may not be the most rational option for our slumlord, for example, if in addition to prison he risks, with high probability, significant guilt feelings over endangering the lives of tenants or over cheating his insurance company. With internal sanctions operating along with external sanctions in this way, the social environment need not be so punitive as to keep serious immorality within tolerable limits.

There is no entirely satisfactory label for the positive internal sanctions, the agreeable feelings that typically accompany moral action and the realization that one has acted rightly, justly, or benevolently. So let us opt for the vague term "the satisfactions of morality." Moral people have long testified as to the strength and value of such satisfactions, often claiming that they are the most agreeable satisfactions we can attain. This last claim goes beyond what is necessary for our purposes. All we need to assert is that there are special significant pleasures or satisfactions that accompany regular moral action and the practice of a moral way of life that are not available to (unreformed) immoralists and others of their ilk. For if this is so, then the forgoing of these potential satisfactions must be charged as a significant opportunity cost of choosing an immoral way of life.

Can an individual have it both ways, enjoying the psychic benefits of morality while living an immoral life? He could, perhaps, if he lived immorally while sincerely believing he was not. Certain fanatics who selflessly devote themselves to false moral ideals, such as purifying the human race by eugenics or pleasing God by destroying nonbelievers, might fall in this category. Of more concern in the present context, however, is the individual who adopts morality as a provisional way of life or policy while planning to abandon it if a chance to gain much by immorality should arise later. This person, we would say, is not truly moral, and it is hard to believe that he would perceive himself to be, so long as his motives are purely prudential and his commitment to morality is only conditional. In any case, we would not expect him to experience the satisfactions of morality in the same way, or to the same degree, as the genuinely moral individual who is aware of the (relative) purity of his motives and the nature and depth of his commitment.

Note that if this is so we have arrived at a paradox of self-interest: *being* purely self-interested will not always best serve one's interests. For there may be certain substantial personal advantages that accrue only to those who are not purely self-interested, such as moral people. Thus it may be rational for you, as a purely self-interested person, to cease being one if you can, to transform yourself into a genuinely moral person. And once you are such a person, you will not be disposed to act immorally, under risk, whenever so doing promises to maximize personal expected utility.

The lesson of this paradox, and the opportunity cost of being immoral, does not apply, though, to those (if any) who are no longer capable of learning to enjoy the satisfactions of living a moral life. Further, some people may still be capable of developing an appreciation of

these satisfactions, but the transition costs of moving to this state from their present immoral condition may outweigh the advantages gained. For people such as these, especially those who are immune from guilt feelings, the prudential argument for being moral must essentially rest on external sanctions. And with respect to some individuals, such as hardened but cautious immoralists or clever psychopaths, the argument may fail.

Thus we must acknowledge a restriction of the Reconciliation Project along its agent dimension. It is too much to claim that it pays one to be moral, irrespective of one's psychological characteristics. Rather, the argument from internal sanctions supports the prudential rationality of living a moral life for the two classes of people constituting the vast majority of humankind: First, those who are already endowed with conscience and moral motivations, so that they experience the satisfactions of living morally and are liable to suffering guilt feelings when they do wrong. Second, those who are capable of developing into moral persons without excessive cost – immoralists who are not fully committed to that way of life, and children.

Should we be dismayed that the Reconciliation Project may not encompass, along its agent dimension, those incapable of enjoying the satisfactions of morality? This depends upon our aims in pursuing the project and the audience to whom its arguments are addressed. Insofar as our aim is to reassure the ordinary good man that he is not harming himself by being moral, or to encourage parents who want to do the best for their children to give them moral education, we need not worry. And if we seek theoretical illumination, we achieve more by recognizing the variation along the agent dimension than by denying it. Only if our aim were the hopeless one of convincing dedicated immoralists to be moral, by using rational arguments, would we be in difficulty. Am I confessing, then, that we are helpless in the face of the immoralist? No, we are not helpless in the practical sense, for we can use external sanctions to restrain immoralists. Nor should we perceive an immoralist's gloating that it does not pay him to be moral (because the satisfactions of morality are not for him) as a victory over us. It is more like the pathetic boast of a deaf person that he saves money because it does not pay him to buy opera records.

III.   The Ultimate Sacrifice

We have seen how the recognition of internal sanctions allows us to deal with two objections that undermine the Hobbesian external-sanctions approach to the Reconciliation Project. Two difficult objections remain, however, even when internal sanctions are taken into account. The first is that morality sometimes requires the sacrifice of one's life, and this cannot be in one's interests. The second is that morality requires powerful groups to treat weak groups fairly and decently, while it better serves the interests of the powerful group's members not to do so.

The objection concerning death runs as follows. In certain circumstances, morality requires of us that we give up our lives to protect others. We are bound by obligations of fair play, gratitude, and perhaps consent to fight in just wars of national defense. Fulfilling these obligations costs many people their lives. Extreme situations can also arise in civilian life in which morality requires one to accept one's own death. If gangsters credibly threaten to kill me unless I kill an innocent person, I must refrain. If I am a loser in a fair and necessary lifeboat lottery, I am morally bound to abide by the outcome. If half of the expedition's necessary food supply is lost as a result of my recklessness, I must be the first to agree to go without food on the long return trip so that others may survive. And so on. In each of these cases, however, self-interest seems to counsel taking the opposite course. Where there is life there is hope, and even if the likely cost of saving my life is to suffer severe internal and external sanctions (such as imprisonment, depression, and guilt for the military deserter), that cost must be less than the premature loss of my life, since such loss would deprive me of all future enjoyments and frustrate all of my main plans and desires.

In response to this objection, let us first note that there are fates worse than death. And for some people, living with the knowledge that one has preserved one's life at the cost of the lives of others, the sacrifice of one's principles, or the desertion of a cause one loves may be such a fate. In addition, society is aware of the heavy value that people place on the continuation of their own lives and typically responds by using heavy external sanctions to encourage appropriate life-risking behavior in defense of society. Thus infantry officers may stand behind their own lines and shoot those who retreat, thereby rendering advance a safer course than retreat. (Even if advance is virtually suicidal, death with honor at the hands of the enemy may be a lesser evil than death with dishonor at the hands of one's own officers.) On the positive side, those who risk or lose their lives in battle are often offered significant rewards by their fellow citizens – medals, honors, praise, and material compensation for themselves or their families.

The upshot of this is that in a substantial number of cases the sacrifice of one's life for moral ends may be consistent with the requirements of prudence because it constitutes the lesser of two extreme personal evils. It would, however, be disingenuous to suggest that this is so in most, much less all, cases. Officers cannot shoot all deserters or retreaters, nor are courts likely to sentence to death those who cheat in lifeboat lotteries. And relatively few are so committed to morality that they could not eventually recover, at least partially, from the negative psychic effects of abandoning principle to preserve their lives. So we must concede that self-interest and morality will frequently, or usually, recommend divergent courses of action when there is a stark choice between immoral action and certain death.

Does this concession destroy the Reconciliation Project? Only if we have in mind a version of the project that focuses, along the object dimension, on acts. If instead we consider, as we have been, whether adopting the moral *way of life* is consistent with prudence, the answer may well be different. In adopting or pursuing a moral way of life, we are, it is true, running a *risk* of sacrificing our lives imprudently. For the requirements of morality may sometimes call for us to give up (or risk) our lives. And if we do develop the habits and dispositions appropriate to the moral life, we are likely (or at least more likely than otherwise) to live up to these requirements at the cost of our lives, if we find ourselves in appropriate circumstances. Notice, however, that in assessing this risk and weighing it against the advantages of the moral life, we must consider how likely we are to find ourselves in such circumstances.

Now this depends, in turn, on our view of what the substantive rules of morality require of us. If they demand that one right all wrongs and fight all injustices anywhere at any time with all the means one possesses and regardless of the personal cost, the likelihood that one would be morally obligated to lay down (or seriously risk) one's life at some time or another is obviously large. But surely on any reasonable conception they require much less than this. Perhaps you are obligated to give up your life (i) to protect your country in a just war; (ii) to protect those to whom you owe special duties of protection (your children, your passengers if you are a ship's captain); (iii) to protect those you owe immense debts of gratitude (your parents); (iv) to avoid seriously violating the rights of innocent others (as in the gangster threat situation); (v) to save others from dangers that your misconduct, recklessness, or negligence has created; (vi) to keep important agreements you have made (such as accepting employment as a bodyguard); or (vii) to save the lives of large numbers of innocent people when you are the only one who can do so. And perhaps there are other specific duties of sacrifice that I have left off this list. But as a whole, the duties are limited to special and quite unlikely circumstances. (Military service is the only seriously life-endangering-required activity that is at all likely to confront a significant segment of the population. Presumably such service is morally obligatory only if the war is just, which frequently is not the case. Further, in most wars the percentage of those serving who are killed is rather low.)

Now if the chances are small that you will ever confront a situation in which you are morally obligated to surrender your life, it may well pay you to adopt a moral way of life, even if doing so increases the likelihood

that you would sacrifice your life in such a situation. For the relatively certain external and internal benefits of the moral life should far out-weigh the very unlikely loss of one's life. Further, it is worth noting that many immoral lifestyles – crime, debauchery, deception of all those around you – may have much higher premature death rates than the moral life. Insofar as adoption of a moral way of life ensures that you will not lapse into one of these alternatives, it may even on balance increase your life expectancy.

The argument, then, is that adopting a moral way of life carries at most a very small net risk to one's life. Since it provides significant benefits with high probability, it is a reasonable prudential choice. It is useful in understanding this argument to compare adopting a moral way of life with two other activities that are not generally thought to be imprudent: joining the military and entering into a long-term love relationship, such as by marrying or having children. These undertakings are like becoming moral in the main respect relevant to our argument. They are likely to involve or produce changes in one's motivational structure that would render one more likely to risk or sacrifice one's life in certain circumstances, such as when your loved ones or comrades in arms are in danger. (In addition, military service carries a nonnegligible risk of finding yourself in precisely these circumstances.) But this feature of these undertakings is not usually thought to render them in-eligible choices from a prudential perspective. Why, then, should the same feature render becoming moral a generally imprudent course of conduct? This activity, like entering a long-term love relationship, promises very large external and internal rewards while involving a relatively tiny risk of loss of life. The gamble is hardly more foolish in the case of virtue than in the case of love.

IV.   Group Immorality

Human beings, as has often been remarked, are social creatures. We need one another for a variety of practical and emotional reasons – for help in securing satisfaction of our material needs, for physical protection, for companionship, for love, and so on. The above arguments that duty and interest coincide all rest on this fact. Individuals need the help rather than the hostility of society to prosper, and in the process of social learning they internalize norms of conscience that further fuse their interests with those of the social group. However, one does not require the aid or cooperation of *all* others, only of a sufficient number of those with whom one is likely to come in contact. This fact generates the most telling objection to the Reconciliation Project: That it is not in the interests of powerful *groups* and their members to treat decently and to help, as morality demands, the members of weak groups, who are apparently not in a position to return good for good and evil for evil.

It is clear that when we consider relations among groups, our earlier tools for reconciling interest and obligation cannot be used in the same way. External sanctions operate effectively, to the extent they do, because it is in the general interest of society and its members to restrain individuals from harming others. But if there is a split between groups in society, there may be no effective sanction against members of a dominant group harming members of a powerless group. For the others in the dominant group may condone, or even approve, such conduct, while the members of the powerless group are too weak to punish the offenders. And if the norms of the dominant group allow, or even encourage, mistreatment of the powerless group – as throughout history they often have – even well-socialized members of the dominant group may carry out such mistreatment without suffering substantial guilt feelings.

This objection shows that there cannot be a satisfactory solution to the Reconciliation Project if the project is strictly interpreted along the social and degree dimensions. That is, we cannot hope to show that in all historically actual (much less all conceivable) social circumstances it has been (or would be) in the interests of all groups and their members to act morally toward members of other groups. Instead, particular cases of supposed divergence of group duty and interest must be considered on an ad hoc basis, and the most we

can reasonably aspire to is the presentation of arguments that make it plausible that obligation and interest coincide in *actual* present circumstances. This will not ease the anxiety of moralists who seek a noncontingent guarantee that interest and duty will never diverge. But it could suffice to convince the attentive moral individual, or group leader, that he or she is not being foolish in acting morally, or in leading his or her group in a moral direction.

Before discussing the three most important specific instances of the objection before us, it should be pointed out that whether there is hope of reconciling group interest and duty depends on what we take the demands of duty to be. In the case of individuals, we saw that a unilateralist-idealistic interpretation of moral requirements might render the Reconciliation Project impossible. Similarly, if we interpret morality as requiring rich and powerful groups to share so much with the poor and weak as to create absolute equality, there is very little prospect that duty and interest can be reconciled. But it is far from obvious that morality demands this much. What morality does clearly require is that the rich and powerful refrain from actively harming the poor and weak, and that the former aid the latter when the costs of giving are small and the benefits of receiving are large. We shall see that with this modest interpretation of the obligations of the powerful, reconciling their obligations with their interests may be possible.

Let us turn to our examples, the first concerning justice within a society. Why should rich and powerful groups in a nation allow the poor opportunities for education, employment, and advancement and provide social-welfare programs that benefit the poor as morality requires? Why shouldn't they simply oppress and exploit the poor? There are several reasons why, in modern times, it is most probably in the long-term interest of the rich and powerful to treat the domestic poor well. First, some rich individuals, and more likely some of their children, may be poor at some time in the future and thus benefit from programs to help the poor. Second, offering opportunities to members of all groups widens the pool of talent available to fill socially useful jobs, which should provide long-run economic benefits to members of all groups. Third, and most important, there is the reason that has impressed social theorists from Hobbes to Rawls: Decent treatment of all promotes social stability and cohesion and discourages revolution. This reason is especially important in contemporary times, when ideals of human dignity, equality, and justice are known and espoused virtually everywhere, and when revolution is frequently proposed as a legitimate means of attaining such ideals.

Taken together, these reasons constitute a strong case, on prudential grounds, for decent treatment of the domestic poor by a nation's dominant groups. In fact, if we apply Disaster Avoidance reasoning, it turns out that the third reason alone shows that good treatment of the poor is prudentially rational. For if the poor find the status quo unacceptable and apply such reasoning, they will revolt. Thus Hobbes writes, "Needy men and hardy, not contented with their present condition, . . . are inclined to . . . stir up trouble and sedition; for there is no . . . such hope to mend an ill game as by causing a new shuffle" (1651, 1958, p. 87). The rich, being aware of this, will (if they follow a Disaster Avoidance strategy) seek to prevent the poor from falling into such unacceptable circumstances. For the rich thereby maximize their chances of obtaining an outcome acceptable to them: preservation of something resembling the status quo.

What about a wealthy and powerful nation aiding poor, weak nations? Is this in the long-run interest of the former as well as the latter? In a world of advanced technology, international markets, ideological conflicts among powerful nations, and nuclear weapons, it most probably is. In competition with other powerful nations, allies – even poor nations – are useful for political, economic, and military reasons. And economic development of poor nations should, in the long run, produce economic benefits for richer nations, such as by providing markets and reliable supplies of various raw and finished goods. Most important, continued poverty in the Third World is likely to produce continued political turmoil, civil wars, and regional wars between nations. In a world armed to the teeth with nuclear weapons, and with more and more

nations acquiring such weapons, the long-run danger of rich developed countries being drawn into a devastating military conflict started by a desperate poor nation, or some desperate group within such a nation, is far from negligible.

The above arguments about domestic and international justice suggest there is, after all, a form of reciprocity between powerful and weak groups because of interdependencies between the two in economic and security matters. The poor cannot return the aid of the rich in kind, but they can offer their talents, their purchasing power, and so on. If not treated well, they cannot directly punish the rich and powerful, but they can stir up serious trouble for them if they are willing to experience such trouble themselves. Thus they are able, and likely, to return good for good and evil for evil to the rich in the long run, and it will be rational for the rich to act accordingly.

Even this form of reciprocity is not available, however, to deal with our third and most puzzling example – the treatment of future generations. Future generations (beyond the next few) are powerless to act upon us, since they will not exist until after we are dead. Yet we have substantial power to determine the quality of their lives by influencing their numbers and the nature of the social and natural environment into which they will be born. Given this absolute asymmetry in power to affect one another, how can it be in our interest to act morally toward future generations? Morality requires us, at a minimum, to leave our descendants with enough resources to allow future people to live decent lives. But this would necessitate having a lower material standard of living than we could obtain by depleting resources and contaminating the environment whenever it is convenient to do so. If future generations cannot punish us for ruthlessly exploiting the earth in this way, doesn't rational prudence require it of us?

The supporter of the Reconciliation Project can come some considerable way toward answering even this objection. He might point out first that misuse of resources and damage to the environment will often produce substantial negative effects within our own lifetimes. So, for the most part, it is in our own interests to follow conservation policies that will turn out to benefit future generations. This reply will take us only so far, however. For there are policies whose benefits are experienced now and most of whose costs will be borne generations later (such as building nuclear power plants without having solved the long-term waste storage problem). Also, optimal *rates* of use of scarce nonrenewable resources will vary greatly depending upon how long we care about the resource lasting. Hence, there is a far from perfect overlap between the resource and environmental policies likely to most benefit present people and those likely to ensure a decent life for future generations.

A more promising argument begins from the fact that most people care very deeply about the happiness of their own children and grandchildren, and hence their own happiness would be diminished by contemplating the prospect of these descendants having to live in a resource-depleted world. Further, they realize that their children's and grandchildren's happiness will in turn be affected by the prospects for happiness of *their* children and grandchildren, and so forth. Hence, the happiness of present people is linked, generation by generation, to the prospects for happiness of some likely members of distant future generations. This "chain-connection" argument has considerable force, but it falls short of constituting a full solution to the problem before us. This is because the perceived happiness of one's children and grandchildren is only one component of the well-being or happiness of the typical parent. And the perceived happiness of *their* children and grandchildren is, in turn, only one component of the happiness of one's children and grandchildren. So there is a multiplier effect over generations that quickly diminishes the influence on a present person's happiness of the prospects for happiness of his later descendants. And we must seek some other device to link living peoples' interests firmly with those of distant future generations.

The most promising such device is an appeal to our need to give meaning to our lives and endeavors. I have suggested elsewhere that one strong reason we have for providing future people with the means to survive and

prosper is that this is our best hope for the successful continuation of certain human enterprises that we value (and may have contributed to) – science, the arts and humanities, morality, religion, democratic government.[2] Similarly, Ernest Partridge has argued that human beings have a psychological need for "self-transcendence"; that is, a need to contribute to projects that are outside themselves and that will continue after their deaths (1981). Those without such goals are unlikely to find meaning in their lives, especially during the middle and later stages of life, when people typically reflect on their own mortality. Thus Partridge says, "We need the future, *now*" (1981, p. 217).

There is a great deal of truth in this argument, but there are some limits to what it can show. It cannot reconcile the interests and obligations to posterity of the narcissist who has no self-transcending goals and is incapable of developing them. However, this need not worry us anymore than did the corresponding remark made earlier about the person no longer capable of becoming moral. The self-transcending life may be the happier life for the vast majority who still can live it, and these people have good prudential reasons for doing so. The more important problem is that not all self-transcending concerns need be directed toward the distant future. They may involve goals that do not extend much beyond one's lifetime (such as the prosperity of one's children, or the eventual rise to power of one's favorite political movement). Such goals may give meaning to one's life without supplying reasons to provide for the welfare of distant generations. Perhaps, though, it is a psychological fact that enterprises that promise to continue into the indefinite future are better able to provide meaning in our lives, or to provide consolation for our mortality. If so, there would be powerful prudential reasons for one's adopting self-transcending concerns of unlimited temporal scope, and for protecting the social and natural environments for future generations.

These are the best arguments I can think of for a coincidence of self-interest and our obligations to posterity. Many (including myself at times) will find them only partly convincing.

Does this lack of complete conviction indicate that we should abandon the Reconciliation Project? No. Instead, we may broaden our interpretation of that project.

V. The Wider Project

The general strategy I have followed in outlining a defense of the Reconciliation Project has been to restrain the project's ambitions where necessary. Thus the scope of the project has been narrowed in several ways. It applies to ways of life rather than particular actions and to practice morality rather than ideal morality. It succeeds with respect to most people and groups in actual social circumstances, but not with respect to all people and groups in all actual or possible circumstances. It may not convince the skeptical immoralist to change his ways, but it provides good reasons for moral people not to regret (or abandon) their way of life and for loving parents to raise their children to be moral.

However, to understand better the relationship between morality, rationality, and self-interest, we must briefly consider an important *widening* of the Reconciliation Project. For that project may be viewed as but a specific instance of a more general project: reconciling morality with the requirements of practical rationality. Given two special assumptions – the truth of Psychological Egoism and the interpretation of practical rationality as the efficient pursuit of the agent's ends (whatever they may be) – this Wider Reconciliation Project would collapse into our original version concerning morality and self-interest. But the first of these assumptions is surely false; on any construal that does not render all motives self-interested by definition, people sometimes do have unselfish aims and possess and act upon non-self-interested motives. As a result, the question of whether moral requirements are consistent with the rational pursuit of the actual ends that people have is both distinct from and more important than the question of whether these requirements cohere with the demands of prudence.

Would shifting our focus to the Wider Reconciliation Project render irrelevant all we have said about the original project? If self-interested concerns played only an insignificant role in human motivation, it would. But clearly this is not the case. In fact, while Psychological Egoism is false, I would venture to propose that a milder doctrine, which I call Predominant Egoism, is probably true. Predominant Egoism says that human beings are, as a matter of fact, predominantly self-interested in the following sense. At least until they have achieved a satisfactory level of security and well-being, people's self-interested concerns tend to override their other regarding, idealistic, and altruistic motives in determining their actions. Further, those nonselfish concerns that are sufficiently powerful to move people to acts that seriously conflict with self-interest tend to be limited in scope, such as to the well-being of family and friends and the advancement of specific favored projects or institutions.

Now if it is true that people are predominantly self-interested, in this sense, many or most of their strongest motives and dearest ends are self-interested ones. And the above arguments about reconciling duty and interest will be highly relevant to the task of reconciling duty and the rational pursuit of people's actual ends. But in carrying out this Wider Reconciliation Project, there would be a new resource to appeal to – the altruistic and nonselfish ends that most everyone actually has to some degree. The presence of these ends may extend the range of cases in which the requirements of reason and morality coincide beyond those in which prudence and morality coincide.

Consider again our relationship to future generations. Most of us do have significant nonselfish concerns about the well-being of our children and grandchildren and the survival and prospering of the human species. So we have reason to provide for these things *over and above* the contribution that our awareness of such provision makes to our own psychic well-being. This further strengthens both the chain-connection and self-transcendence arguments for reconciling practical rationality with our duties to posterity. For it shows that in carrying out such duties we are fulfilling ends of ours not previously considered (that is, nonselfish ends) in addition to contributing to our own happiness.

The recognition of nonselfish ends also provides a fresh perspective on the sustenance of moral motivation over generations. We suggested earlier that parents seeking to promote their children's interests would have good reasons to raise their children to be moral. This suggestion would have little significance if we were operating upon an assumption of the truth of Psychological Egoism. (For then the only relevant question would be whether it is in a *parent's* interest to raise his or her children to be moral.) Since, however, concern for the well-being of one's children is among the strongest and most universal of non-self-interested human concerns, the suggestion is crucial to our understanding of how morality is rationally passed on from generation to generation. Typical parents who care strongly for the well-being of their children and care somewhat for the well-being of others have three significant reasons for raising those children to be moral: This will likely benefit the children (in accordance with our earlier arguments that being moral usually pays), it will likely benefit others who are affected by the children, and it will likely benefit the parents

themselves (because their children will treat them better). And when children grow up as moral beings possessing consciences and the potential to experience the satisfactions of morality, it is, we have argued, most always in their interest to continue to live a moral life. Further, they, as parents, will have the same reasons for raising their children to be moral as their parents had for raising them in this manner. Thus morality can be seen to be potentially self-sustaining from generation to generation, without even taking into account socializing influences on the child from outside the family.

In raising children to be moral, and in providing for future generations, some of the ends that we seek to achieve are non-self-interested ones. Given the content of moral rules and their connection with protecting the interests of others, many morally required actions will satisfy ends of this kind. As a result, the Wider Reconciliation Project should be successful in more cases than the original project. We may restate this crucial point: While it is normally prudent to be moral, it is sometimes rational to be moral even if it is not prudent.

Notes

1. "Deterrence, Utility, and Rational Choice" (1980). A similar view is hinted at in Fishkin (1979), pp. 34 and 149 (fn. 17). To employ the Disaster Avoidance Strategy, ordinal knowledge of the relevant probabilities is required.

2. See section IV of my "The Futurity Problem" (1978). I there discuss reasons for wanting the continuation of the species, but some of the same points apply to assuring future people decent lives.

CHAPTER 18
Moral Rationalism

RUSS SHAFER-LANDAU

Moral rationalism is the view that moral obligations entail reasons for action: necessarily, if one has a moral obligation to do something, then one has a reason to do it. I think that rationalism is more plausible than most people have thought. After briefly sketching some positive considerations on its behalf, I want to focus on trying to disarm what I think are the four most serious criticisms of it. I'll conclude by trying to draw some general lessons about how difficult it is to justify claims about the ultimate sources of normativity.

Suppose someone does an act because she thinks it right – she acts from the motive of duty, and, let us suppose, in this case she is on target about what duty requires. What justifies her in performing such an act? If someone correctly cites an action's rightness as her reason for performing it, we don't ordinarily question the legitimacy or conceptual coherence of her doing so. But if the rightness of an act itself was no reason at all for performing it, then we would have to do just that. It could never be the case that the rightness of an act was what justified or legitimated its performance, made its performance appropriate under the circumstances. For legitimacy, appropriateness, and justification are all normative notions, and

their proper application depends crucially on the existence of reasons. If the rightness of an act was itself no reason to perform it, then even the *prima facie* justification of virtuous conduct would always be contingent on a showing that it (say) serves self-interest or satisfies the agent's desires. Almost no one believes this. This implies that an action's rightness constitutes a good justifying reason for performing it.

We can support this view by considering immoral acts as well. When we deem someone's behavior morally unjustified, we imply that he has violated a standard of appropriate conduct. Suppose such standards did not by themselves supply reasons for action. Then we'd be forced to allow that though some actions are unjustified, immoral, improper, illegitimate, or inappropriate, there nevertheless may be no reason at all to avoid them. But this seems wrong – not only conceptually confused, but also gravely unfair. It seems a conceptual error to cite a standard as a guide to conduct and a basis for evaluation – to say, for instance, that S ought to have kept her promise, and was wrong for having failed to keep her promise – and yet claim that there was no reason at all for S to have kept her promise. And it seems unfair to criticize violations of such standards while admitting that an agent responsible for offensive conduct may have had no reason to do otherwise. The fairness and appropriateness of moral evaluation rest on an agent's

Russ Shafer-Landau, "Moral Rationalism," excerpted from chapters 7 and 8 of *Moral Realism: A Defence*. Oxford: Oxford University Press, 2003.

attentiveness to reasons. An agent who correctly claims to have ignored no reasons for action cannot be held to have violated any moral standard. This plausible thought is true only if moral rationalism is true.

We are left, therefore, with the choice of either endorsing moral rationalism, or endorsing the idea that proper moral evaluation of an agent has nothing to do with the agent's attentiveness to reasons. Those who take the latter option must shoulder the burden of explaining just what (other than reasons) could serve as the basis for moral assessment, and just how this basis will manage to avoid the apparent unfairness of criticizing agents for conduct they had no reason to avoid.

I think that the considerations just offered provide some presumptive argument for the truth of moral rationalism. We can strengthen the case if we are able defuse the strongest arguments against it. Let me proceed directly to this task.

The first of the critical arguments is what I shall call *The Reasons Internalist Argument*:

1. Reasons Internalism is true: reasons must be capable of motivating those for whom they are reasons.
2. Desires are required for motivation.
3. Moral obligations apply to agents independently of their desires.
4. Therefore moral rationalism is false.

According to this argument, what reasons we have depends on our motivational capacity, which in turn depends on our desires. What moral obligations we have does not depend on our desires. Therefore we may entirely lack reason to fulfill our moral obligations. Therefore moral rationalism is false.

Here I want to consider only the merits of the first premise of this argument. According to those who favor reasons internalism, a reason must be capable of motivating in the sense that there is some rational relation that obtains between the putative reason and one's existing motivations; there must be, as Bernard Williams (1981: 104–5) puts it, a "sound deliberative route" from one's "subjective motivational set" to the belief or action for which there is a putative reason. So if internalism is true, then

one's reasons are restricted to those results attainable from rationally deliberating from one's existing motivations. I believe that this restriction is spurious, and that internalism is, therefore, false.

Consider a person so misanthropic, so heedless of others' regard, so bent on cruelty, that nothing in his present set of motives would prevent him from committing the worst kind of horrors. He cannot, in the relevant sense, be moved to forbear from such behavior. But why should this unfortunate fact force us to revise our standards for appropriate conduct? Nothing we say to him will convince him to modify his behavior. But is this intransigence a basis for holding him to different standards, or isn't it rather a justification for convicting him of a kind of blindness? It is natural to say that people have reason to refrain from behavior that is fiendish, callous, brutal, arrogant or craven. We don't withdraw such evaluations just because their targets fail (or would, after deliberation, fail) to find them compelling.

Internalists are in a difficult position here. If internalism is true, then the absence of a sound deliberative link from one's motivations to Φ-ing means that there is no reason to Φ. Now if blame requires failure to adhere to good reasons, and the absence of this motivational link entails an absence of reasons, then agents are morally blameless if avoidance of evil bears no such link to their motivations. The worst of the lot – hatemongers and misanthropes, the Streichers or the Himmlers of the world – would thereby be immune from blame. And hence, presumably, from punishment, since proper punishment is predicated on blameworthiness.

The argument can be put more straightforwardly as follows:

1. If internalism is true, then one has no reason to Φ if Φ-ing is rationally unrelated to one's existing motivations.
2. If one has no reason to Φ, then one can't be justly blamed or punished for not Φ-ing.
3. Therefore if internalism is true, then one can't be justly blamed or punished for not Φ-ing, if Φ-ing is rationally unrelated to one's existing motivations.

4. Some agents *are* justly blamed or punished for their evil deeds, even though avoidance of such conduct was rationally unrelated to their motivations.
5. Therefore internalism is false.

Those who dislike the conclusion have just two premises to choose from, since the first premise is a conceptual truth. The second premise is strong. It ties blameworthiness (and suitability for punishment) to the existence of reasons. To reject the second premise is to insist that agents may be blameworthy despite lacking any reason to refrain from their unseemly conduct. Such a stand commits one to the view that one could be properly blameworthy for Φ-ing even though one had no reason not to Φ; blameable for Φ-ing, though no consideration at all inclined against Φ-ing. I think that is a very strange view. For we rightly suppose that whenever someone is blameworthy, there is in principle some explanation of this fact, some feature in virtue of which an agent is blameworthy. That feature must embody a failing. And this failure is best understood as a failure to appreciate or adhere to considerations that favor or oppose some attitude, choice, or action. But such considerations are just what reasons are. So rejecting the second premise leaves one with an unrecognizable view of the conditions under which agents are properly subject to blame.

The last option is to reject the fourth premise. In this context, it helps if we focus again on various malefactors, say, on the disciplined immoralist, or the single-minded, principled fanatic. Those who reject the fourth premise must say of such agents that they ought to be immune from blame and punishment. Yet if anyone merits such assessments, surely those committed to evil do. As far as I can tell, the only way to justify withholding censure from such wrongdoers is to withhold it from everyone, and argue against the existence of any moral responsibility. Perhaps, in the final analysis, no one is properly liable to blame or punishment. There are well-known arguments to this conclusion, which almost no one believes. Nevertheless, this is an option for the internalist.

So internalists are faced with the choice of withholding blame from the very worst that humanity has to offer, or embracing an unpalatable view of blameworthiness that severs its connection with sensitivity and adherence to reasons. Externalism easily avoids this dilemma, and that is good reason to prefer it to internalism. Since that is so, we are justified in rejecting the first premise of the reasons internalist argument, and so the argument itself.

Call a second antirationalist argument *The Rational Egoist Argument*:

1. Rational Egoism is true.
2. Ethical Egoism is false.
3. Therefore Moral Rationalism is false.

Both premises have broad appeal. Rational egoism is the thesis that one has a reason to Φ if and only if Φ-ing will promote one's interests. Ethical egoism is the view that one is morally obligated to Φ if and only if Φ-ing will promote one's self-interest. The denial of ethical egoism entails that adherence to moral requirements may sometimes fail to promote one's self-interest. The endorsement of rational egoism entails that one lacks reason to perform actions that fail in this way. Therefore, the combination of these views entails that one may be morally obligated to Φ even though one lacks a reason to Φ. Therefore this combination entails that moral rationalism is false.

Here I just want to assume that ethical egoism is false; in other words, that premise (2) is true. Since I reject the conclusion, and the argument is valid, I will take issue with the first premise – the endorsement of rational egoism.

It may be that promotion of self-interest always supplies a good reason for action. But why believe that this is the only kind of good reason there is? Most of us firmly hold judgments that imply the falsity of this thesis. If I see someone distractedly crossing the street, about to be run over, I have reason to yell out and warn her. If I see a gang of youths corner a young woman, taunt her and begin to drag her into a dark alley, I have reason to notify the police, immediately intervene, and call for the assistance of others to help. If I spot a seriously dehydrated hiker while in the backwoods, I have reason to offer up my canteen. Of course we can imagine situations where, all things considered, I have most reason not to perform these actions. Nevertheless, such cases certainly appear to provide at least defeasible reason for action, even though our interests are not served, and may only be hindered, by rendering such aid.

The appeal to our deeply-held beliefs about what reasons we have can be supplemented by two arguments designed to undermine rational egoism. The first relies on the importance of autonomy. Autonomous choices for desired or valued ends at least sometimes supply reasons for action, even when such choices are known by the agent not to enhance (or perhaps only to damage) his self-interest. If a soldier decides to sacrifice himself for his comrades, then he has some reason to take the means necessary to saving their lives, even though such actions are condemned from the rational egoist standpoint. If, less dramatically, a person autonomously decides to bestow an anonymous charitable donation sufficiently large to do herself some harm, she nevertheless has some reason to carry through with her resolution. Reasons here, as in the soldier case, may also stem from the needs of those the agent is trying to help. But that isn't necessary to make the relevant point. All that is needed is a recognition that autonomous choices do sometimes supply reasons for action, even though such choices fail to promote the agent's own interests.

There are only two ways to dispute this anti-egoist conclusion. The first is simply to deny the independent value of autonomy, and claim that one's welfare alone is all that should matter to an agent. Autonomous choice may in some cases supply reasons, but only derivatively – only because and to the extent that acting on such a choice promotes one's own welfare. As far as I am aware, however, there is no good argument for this conclusion – no sound argument that shows that autonomy is only derivatively valuable in this way.

The alternative is to allow for the independent importance of autonomy, but to claim that autonomous choice and self-interest can never conflict, because autonomous choice invariably promotes self-interest: one has reason to Φ if and only if Φ-ing promotes one's self interest, and, necessarily, Φ-ing promotes one's self-interest if one autonomously chooses to Φ.

But why think this? Why think it impossible for an agent to know that an action will damage his interests but to autonomously choose to do it anyway? It certainly seems possible that agents may, with relevantly full information and a minimum of external pressure, choose to perform actions that they believe will damage their interests. Surely the burden is on one who claims that in every such case the agent must either mistake his interests, be ignorant of relevant facts, or somehow be subject to far greater external pressure than was initially imagined.

A second argument against rational egoism takes its inspiration from an argument against a strong form of ethical egoism, which claims that acts are right if and only if, *and because*, they promote one's self-interest. The strongest criticism of ethical egoism is its inability to justify its policy of preferential treatment. In effect, ethical egoism sanctions a policy in which each person gets to elevate his or her interests over all others. Such a policy is a departure from the default ethical position in which equals should receive equal treatment. In response to the charge that ethical egoism licenses discriminatory treatment (because it sanctions treating the welfare of others as less important than one's own, without justifying this preference), egoists have two replies. The first is to accept that their theory *is* a policy of unequal treatment, but to deny that this is damaging, by citing a relevant feature that justifies such unequal treatment. The second is to argue that ethical egoism is not a policy of preferential treatment, but is perfectly egalitarian.

The second reply doesn't work. It says that egoism is egalitarian because it confers on every person the same privileges. *Everyone* gets to treat her interests as more important than anyone else's. But this is not enough to insulate the egoist from charges of undue preference. That everyone gets to treat others abominably does not justify such treatment. Ethical egoism is egalitarian in one sense – everyone gets the same moral privileges. But it is inegalitarian in another – it allows one person to give herself complete priority over another for no reason other than the fact that she is the author of the action.

The other reply admits that ethical egoism is a policy of unequal treatment, but seeks to justify this policy by citing a relevant difference that justifies the inequality. Not all discrimination is bad – some students, for instance, deservedly get As, others Bs, and so on. So long as one can cite a relevant difference that justifies the differential treatment, such treatment is completely above-board. Now suppose that you've worked very hard to earn what you have. Suppose also that I correctly judge that I would benefit by taking your goods by force. In that case, I am not only allowed to do so, but morally must do so. I am treating myself and you differently. What licenses such treatment? I'd be better off if I took your things. But you'd be better off if I didn't. Why am I allowed to give the nod to my own interests? That I would benefit does not explain why I am allowed (or required) to give my own interests priority over yours, since you would benefit (or at least avoid harm) were I to refrain from the forcible taking.

There is a stronger and a weaker criticism of ethical egoism at work here. The stronger criticism, leveled by utilitarians, says that the fact that an act will promote one's own interests supplies no basis whatever for priority. The weaker criticism claims that this fact does give some reason for priority in some contexts, but that this priority is defeasible and is in fact often defeated by such things as other persons' deserts, needs and interests. We need only the weaker claim to establish the anti-egoist point. We could go so far as to concede that it is just a brute fact that one is morally allowed to give some priority to oneself, while still demanding justification for the egoist's claim that such priority is the only morally relevant consideration there is.

It strikes me that the rational egoist faces precisely the same objections. We might allow that it is simply a brute fact that there is always reason to promote one's self-interest. But we need an argument for thinking that this is the only reason there could possibly be. Such a claim isn't self-evident, and it conflicts with some of our other very deeply held beliefs. The rational egoist claims that the only consideration that can support or justify an action is its conduciveness to self-interest. But why don't the like interests, needs, wants and autono-

mous choices of others also constitute a basis for rationalizing action that serves them? They are different from one's own interests, etc., in only one respect: that they are not one's own. Even if we concede (as many do not) that this difference makes some difference, why does it make *all* the difference? It seems instead simply to be an assertion of an unjustified policy of preferential treatment. What is it about oneself that gives one license in every situation to give one's own concerns priority over others? That everyone has such license does not justify it. It isn't clear what could.

Rational egoism conflicts with many firm convictions we have about cases. It cannot accommodate a suitable role for autonomy in supplying reasons for action. And rational egoism forces us away from a default position of equality, in ways that are structurally similar to those of ethical egoism, and yet fails to justify the policy of preferential treatment that it is committed to.

If in the end rational egoism is unsupported, then the Rational Egoist Argument fails to supply good grounds for rejecting moral rationalism. Consider, then, the The Analogical Argument, clearly inspired by an important article by Philippa Foot (1972). Requirements of law and etiquette apply to individuals regardless of their desires to comply. Yet these requirements do not entail reasons for action – one might be perfectly rational or reasonable to reject their strictures. Foot's claim is that the same goes for morality. Just because its edicts apply to agents regardless of their desires or interests – they are categorical in this regard – doesn't mean that moral obligations necessarily supply agents with reasons to behave morally. As an argument from analogy, this can't be absolutely watertight, but it can shift the burden of proof to the rationalist, who, in the face of this argument, must take either of two options.

The first is to argue that the demands of law and etiquette are in fact intrinsically reason-giving. The alternative is allow that they are not, but to point up a relevant disanalogy between moral requirements and those of law and etiquette.

The first path seems problematic. While it is true, as anyone who reads Miss Manners will know, that most rules of etiquette have a moral basis, no one would deny that certain of these rules, such as that dictating where to lay the fish knife on a table setting, are morally arbitrary. Such rules apply even to those who haven't any desire or interest in obeying them. But such rules don't generate reasons for conformity all by themselves – they generate reasons, when they do, only because the rules are coextensive with moral requirements, or because adhering to the rules will advance some other interest one may have. If in a given context properly laying the fish knife serves no moral ends, and serves no personal ones, either, then it is difficult to see what reason one could have for concern about its placement.

So there are requirements that are categorical in one sense without being categorical in another: such requirements apply to individuals regardless of their desires, but do not necessarily supply such individuals with any reason for action. It is incumbent on the moral rationalist to explain this.

The explanation, I believe, invokes the idea of jurisdiction. A jurisdiction comprises a set of standards that dictate behavior for a defined set of members. (The set may be defined territorially, as in the law, or may be defined by voluntary allegiance, as with a charitable association or bridge club, etc. Discussion of the different sources of membership is important for other contexts, especially political philosophy, but don't much matter here.) The rules of etiquette, or those of a board game, do not necessarily supply reasons for action, because they are not necessarily applicable; they are inapplicable to all who find themselves outside the relevant jurisdictions. A variety of factors can explain one's extra-jurisdictional status. An accident of birth explains why I am not subject to the civil statutes of Ethiopia. An autonomous choice explains why the code of the Benevolent Protective Order of Elks does not apply to me. The choices of others explain why I am not bound to uphold the duties of a Prime Minister or President. For these reasons, and others, the strictures of the relevant domain (law, etiquette, fraternal societies, etc.) may fail to apply in a given case. And if such standards fail to apply to one's actions, then *a fortiori*

they will fail to supply one with reasons for action.

In this sense, the scope of the relevant rules is limited. The limit is explained by the conventional origin of such rules. For any given convention, whether it be focused on law, etiquette or play, one may lack reason to adhere to its rules because one is not a party to the convention. The requirements of law, etiquette, and games are all circumscribed. For any requirements of conventional origin, it is always in principle possible find oneself outside of the jurisdiction. The reasons generated by conventional rules are therefore reasons that exist only contingently.

Morality is different. Its scope is pervasive. Every action is morally evaluable – even if the pronouncement is simply one of permissibility. There is no exiting the "morality game." One may renounce morality, may act without regard to the moral status of one's conduct, may in fact act with the intention of behaving immorally, but all such dissociative strategies do not free one from susceptibility to moral assessment. This distinguishes moral requirements from those in the law, etiquette or games.

What explains this special character of moral assessment? I think it must be the claim that morality is objective, in the sense of being correct independently of whether anyone thinks so. We don't create the principles that generate moral requirements. The principles are not constituted by and do not apply to us in virtue of conventional agreements. Moral requirements are inescapable because they are not of our own making.

This does not explain why moral rationalism is true. The pervasive scope of moral evaluation does not explain why moral facts are necessarily reason-giving. But it does serve as the basis for resisting the Analogical Argument, because a relevant disanalogy among kinds of desire-independent requirements has been identified. Not every categorical requirement is necessarily reason-giving, because some such requirements are conventional in origin, and so supply reasons only contingently. Morality's content is not conventionally fixed, and so we lack this basis for thinking that it supplies reasons only contingently.

This reply assumes that moral requirements are not conventional. If morality is conventional, then the Analogical Argument, so far as I can see, is sound, and we should reject moral rationalism. But to assume that morality is conventional at this stage is just to beg the question against the moral rationalist, by supposing that his favored reply to the Analogical Argument cannot work. By contrast, there is nothing question-begging *at this stage* about assuming the truth of moral objectivism, since objectivism by itself is neutral with respect to the merits of rationalism – indeed, many moral objectivists reject moral rationalism. There are independent grounds for doubting moral objectivism, of course – all of which, in the end, I think can be answered – but I cannot do that here. (I make an effort in Shafer-Landau, 2003)

Consider then a final argument that I will call *The Argument from Extrinsic Reasons:*

1. If moral rationalism is true, then moral facts are intrinsically reason-giving.
2. There are no intrinsically reason-giving facts.
3. Therefore moral rationalism is false.

I think that premise (2) is false, and will spend my time here trying to show it so. I also think, perhaps surprisingly, that the first premise may be false. But I won't go into that here. Antirationalists will say that all reasons derive from an agent's perspective. For consider the alternative: if reasons exist regardless of one's desires or interests, then where do they come from? (And how can we know them?) What, other than an agent's own perspective, could serve as a source of normative authority? To insist that a set of facts could contain within themselves normative authority for agents, regardless of their outlooks on life, seems obscurantist, and appears to have the effect of prematurely cutting off any helpful explanation of normativity.

If this is obscurantist, I think we have no choice but to embrace the mysteries. I think there must be some intrinsically normative entities. To see this, consider the parallels between conditions of epistemic and moral assessment. We say that agents have reasons to believe the truth, and to conform their reasoning to truth-preserving schemas, even if believing the truth is not conducive to the goals they set themselves. Suppose someone accepts the truth of a conditional and its antecedent, but denies that she has any reason to accept the consequent. It's not just that she may have (possibly overriding) reasons which oppose making such an inference. Someone might correctly believe that all passengers aboard a downed airliner have been killed, while knowing that her brother was among them, and yet resist drawing the terrible conclusion. Practical considerations, such as sustaining emotional stability, may militate against believing the truth, and may, for anything said thus far, be so strong as to outweigh it in given instances. But the sister who holds out hope against all evidence, and contrary to the logical implications of her own beliefs, is in some real sense acting against reason. Indeed, she is, in one sense, behaving irrationally, though also in a way that is fully understandable. She is acting contrary to sufficiently good reasons – reasons that are there to tell her, and anyone in her epistemic situation, that she ought to believe something that she cannot bring herself to believe.

To say such a thing commits one to the existence of what I shall call *nonperspectival* or *intrinsic* reasons. I believe that there is intrinsic reason to think that two and two are four – the fact itself provides one with reason to believe it. One needn't show that such belief is somehow related to one's adopted goals in order to justify believing such a thing. If, unusually, success at basic mathematics was entirely unrelated to one's preferred activities, one would still have good reason to think that two and two were four, not five or three.

The basic idea here is that certain things can be intrinsically normative – reason-giving independently of the instrumental, final or unconditional value actually attached to things by agents. The opposing view insists that all reasons stem entirely from an agent's own contingent commitments. Antirationalists might allow for the existence of objective values, but would insist that whatever reason-giving force such values have is entirely dependent on the agent's own investment. There are no reasons at all apart from a particular agent's perspective.

The rationalist insists that the reasons generated from within these perspectives can be assessed and can in cases collude with, or compete against, reasons that are nonperspectival. The epistemic rationalist claims that certain (kinds of) reasons for belief are like this. We behave in an epistemically appropriate fashion when our practices track these reasons, which are not all of our own making. There is reason to believe that the earth is roughly round, that two and two are four, and that the consequent follows from a conditional and its antecedent. We don't make these reasons up; most perspectives recognize such reasons, but their existence does not depend on the perspective one takes to the world. Those perspectives that fail to recognize these reasons are missing something.

There are clear parallels with moral rationalism. The moral rationalist says that certain kinds of facts – moral facts – necessarily supply us with reasons for action, as well as reasons for belief. Everyone has a reason to regard genocide as evil, because it is true that genocide is evil. And everyone has reason not to participate in genocide, because it is a fact that we are obligated to refrain from such participation. Or, to take the usual example, no worse for being usual: we have reason to alleviate another person's excruciating pain, if we can do so effectively at very little cost to ourselves. There are considerations in such cases that *justify* alleviating such pain, even if doing so is neither desired for its own sake, nor instrumental to one's desires. Those who overcome their indifference and manage to offer assistance in such cases are acting appropriately, or more than appropriately. Their actions are proper, legitimate and justified. They wouldn't be, were there no reason at all to undertake them. Such reasons may be defeasible, but they apply to us even in the absence of any instrumental relation to one's goals.

Here is the crucial failure of antirationalism. In its effort to cast doubt on the possibility of intrinsic reasons, it must commit itself to the view that what reasons we have – for belief and for action – depend entirely on one's outlook. If they weren't dependent in this way, then they would be nonperspectival – there would be intrinsic reasons after all. Yet once we meet the conditions of an antirationalist theory, we see that any such theory is hoist by its own petard. For by its own lights such a view has

nothing in itself to recommend it to anyone not already convinced of its merits. If antirationalism is true, then all reasons are contingent on one's perspective. Importantly, no perspective is superior to another (except as judged so from within a given perspective, which perspective is itself in no way rationally or epistemically superior to another). For if any perspective were nonperspectivally superior, this would mean that agents would have, regardless of their perspective, more reason to endorse the superior outlook. And this is just what is disallowed by antirationalism. So antirationalism succumbs to the kind of argument that undermines a global relativism.

All of this still leaves us short of an account of why moral facts *are* intrinsically reason-giving – thus far we've attempted to display the attractions of rationalism, and have tried to undermine the anti-rationalist arguments, but haven't offered any concrete explanation of *why* moral facts supply reasons (for action or evaluation). One possibility is to explain the normativity of moral facts by positing a necessary connection between them and other kinds of intrinsically reason-giving considerations. For instance, one might claim that all moral obligations entailed a reason for action, because, necessarily, fulfilling a moral obligation made one better off, and one always has reason to make oneself better off. I am not optimistic about any such strategy. But if this explanatory route is barred, what other route is available?

The worry here is the same as that which besets accounts of candidate intrinsic values. We ordinarily explain the value of something by showing its relation to something else acknowledged to be intrinsically valuable. But when one's candidate intrinsic values are themselves questioned, this strategy must fail. Suppose one claims that any situation in which an innocent child is maimed solely to produce pleasure for his tormentor is bad, in itself. Isn't this true? But there's very little one can say to someone who doesn't believe this. The intrinsic moral rationalist is in much the same boat when defending the normativity of moral facts. According to her, there is no more fundamental kind of normative consideration from which moral facts can derive their reason-giving force. But just as the inability to cite a more fundamental consideration doesn't necessarily undermine the claim about intrinsic value, so too it needn't undermine the claim about normativity. One must recognize the limits of normative explanation.

That said, rationalists must concede that their favored theory does not enjoy the same degree of endorsement as the verdict we reach in the example in which a child is maimed. But this shouldn't be seen as a stumbling block to acceptance of rationalism. Moral rationalism is a much more complicated, less obvious and less immediately appealing view than the one expressed in the example. Further, the parallel with defending claims of intrinsic value should alert us to the difficulty of justification in these contexts. Justification here is a matter of defusing arguments designed to undermine the relevant view, and adducing some non-conclusive considerations that favor it. In case such a strategy is thought by its nature to be too weak to establish the requisite degree of justification, we need to remind ourselves that this is all that can be hoped for even for those theories of practical reasons whose allegiance is much broader than moral rationalism. The brute inexplicability of the normativity of moral facts is not different in kind from that which besets other, familiar theories of practical reasons.

Consider both rational egoism and instrumentalism. Proponents of these theories claim, respectively, that self-interest or desire satisfaction are the sole kind of intrinsically reason-giving consideration. When they defend their favored claims, they do so by trying to reply to criticisms and offer probative evidence far short of demonstrable proof as positive support for their views. Indeed, on the assumption that self-interest is not identical with or best measured exclusively by desire-satisfaction, at least one of these popular theories must be false. The relevant point here is that strategies for defending

any such view – any candidate for intrinsically normative consideration – are similar across the board. The rational egoist will not be able to point to a kind of normative consideration more fundamental than self-interest, to which the reason-giving force of self-interest is of necessity related. The instrumentalist is likewise handicapped when trying to establish the intrinsic normativity of desire-satisfaction. This kind of explanatory failure is not itself an argument against any one of these theories. In response to the charge that intrinsic moral rationalists are unable to explain the normativity of moral facts, rationalists should be prepared to point to partners in crime. They needn't look very far.

If I am right, one always has reason to do as morality says. Whether this is the best possible reason – whether moral considerations are invariably overriding – is another matter. One can't settle that issue without having in hand a theory of normative ethics, an inventory of kinds of non-moral reasons, and a method for measuring their relative strength. We don't need to undertake such extensive investigations to establish the more circumscribed claim of moral rationalism's plausibility.

I have tried to show that moral rationalism can survive the strongest arguments designed to undermine it. The Reasons Internalist Argument, the Rational Egoist Argument, the Analogical Argument and the Argument from Extrinsic Reasons do not, in the end, point up insuperable difficulties for the rationalist. There are strong considerations to do with the conceptual coherence and the fairness of moral evaluation that support moral rationalism. And rationalism's insistence on the irreducibly normative character of moral facts should not be an impediment to its acceptance. Any problem that may arise in this context is one shared by any competing theory which aims to identify an intrinsically normative kind of consideration.

References

Foot, Philippa. 1972. "Morality as a System of Hypothetical Imperatives," *Philosophical Review* (82), pp. 306–315.

Shafer-Landau, Russ. 2003. *Moral Realism: A Defence*. Oxford University Press.

Williams, Bernard. 1981. "Internal and External Reasons," as reprinted in his *Moral Luck*, Cambridge University Press 1985.

CHAPTER 19
Psychological Egoism

JOEL FEINBERG

A. The Theory

1. "Psychological egoism" is the name given to a theory widely held by ordinary people, and at one time almost universally accepted by political economists, philosophers, and psychologists, according to which all human actions when properly understood can be seen to be motivated by selfish desires. More precisely, psychological egoism is the doctrine that the only thing anyone is capable of desiring or pursuing ultimately (as an end in itself) is his *own* self-interest. No psychological egoist denies that people sometimes do desire things other than their own welfare – the happiness of other people, for example; but all psychological egoists insist that people are capable of desiring the happiness of others only when they take it to be a *means* to their own happiness. In short, purely altruistic and benevolent actions and desires do not exist; but people sometimes appear to be acting unselfishly and disinterestedly when they take the interests of others to be means to the promotion of their own self-interest.

2. This theory is called *psychological* egoism to indicate that it is not a theory about what

 ought to be the case, but rather about what, as a matter of fact, *is* the case. That is, the theory claims to be a description of psychological facts, not a prescription of ethical ideals. It asserts, however, not merely that all men do as a contingent matter of fact "put their own interests first," but also that they are capable of nothing else, human nature being what it is. Universal selfishness is not just an accident or a coincidence on this view; rather, it is an unavoidable consequence of psychological laws.

The theory is to be distinguished from another doctrine, so-called "ethical egoism," according to which all people *ought* to pursue their own wellbeing. This doctrine, being a prescription of what *ought* to be the case, makes no claim to be a psychological theory of human motives; hence the word "ethical" appears in its name to distinguish it from *psychological* egoism.

3. There are a number of types of motives and desires which might reasonably be called "egoistic" or "selfish," and corresponding to each of them is a possible version of psychological egoism. Perhaps the most common version of the theory is that apparently held by Jeremy Bentham.[1] According to this version, all persons have only one ultimate motive in all their voluntary behavior and that motive is a selfish one; more specifically, it is one particular kind of selfish motive – namely, a desire for one's own *pleasure*. According to this version of

Joel Feinberg, "Psychological Egoism," pp. 476–88 from Russ Shafer-Landau and Joel Feinberg (eds.), *Reason and Responsibility*. Belmont: Wadsworth, 2004. Reprinted with permission of Wadsworth, a division of Thomson Learning.

the theory, "the only kind of ultimate desire is the desire to get or to prolong pleasant experiences, and to avoid or to cut short unpleasant experiences for oneself."[2] This form of psychological egoism is often given the cumbersome name – *psychological egoistic hedonism.*

B.   Prima Facie Reasons in Support of the Theory

4. Psychological egoism has seemed plausible to many people for a variety of reasons, of which the following are typical:

a.   "Every action of mine is prompted by motives or desires or impulses which are *my* motives and not somebody else's. This fact might be expressed by saying that whenever I act I am always pursuing my own ends or trying to satisfy my own desires. And from this we might pass on to – 'I am always pursuing something for myself or seeking my own satisfaction.' Here is what seems like a proper description of a man acting selfishly, and if the description applies to all actions of all men, then it follows that all men in all their actions are selfish."[3]

b.   It is a truism that when a person gets what he wants he characteristically feels pleasure. This has suggested to many people that what we really want in every case is our own pleasure, and that we pursue other things only as a means.

c.   *Self-Deception.* Often we deceive ourselves into thinking that we desire something fine or noble when what we really want is to be thought well of by others or to be able to congratulate ourselves, or to be able to enjoy the pleasures of a good conscience. It is a well-known fact that people tend to conceal their true motives from themselves by camouflaging them with words like "virtue," "duty," etc. Since we are so often misled concerning both our own real motives and the real motives of others, is it not reasonable to suspect that we might *always* be deceived when we think motives disinterested and altruistic? Indeed, it is a simple matter to explain away all allegedly unselfish motives: "Once the conviction

that selfishness is universal finds root in a person's mind, it is very likely to burgeon out in a thousand corroborating generalizations. It will be discovered that a friendly smile is really only an attempt to win an approving nod from a more or less gullible recording angel; that a charitable deed is, for its performer, only an opportunity to congratulate himself on the good fortune or the cleverness that enables him to be charitable; that a public benefaction is just plain good business advertising. It will emerge that gods are worshipped only because they indulge men's selfish fears, or tastes, or hopes; that the 'golden rule' is no more than an eminently sound success formula; that social and political codes are created and subscribed to only because they serve to restrain other men's egoism as much as one's own, morality being only a special sort of 'racket' or intrigue using weapons of persuasion in place of bombs and machine guns. Under this interpretation of human nature, the categories of commercialism replace those of disinterested service and the spirit of the horse trader broods over the face of the earth."[4]

d.   *Moral Education.* Morality, good manners, decency, and other virtues must be teachable. Psychological egoists often notice that moral education and the inculcation of manners usually utilize what Bentham calls the "sanctions of pleasure and pain."[5] Children are made to acquire the civilizing virtues only by the method of enticing rewards and painful punishments. Much the same is true of the history of the race. People in general have been inclined to behave well only when it is made plain to them that there is "something in it for them." It is not then highly probable that just such a mechanism of human motivation as Bentham describes must be presupposed by our methods of moral education?

C.   Critique of Psychological Egoism: Confusions in the Arguments

5. *Non-Empirical Character of the Arguments.* If the arguments of the psychological egoist

consisted for the most part of carefully acquired empirical evidence (well-documented reports of controlled experiments, surveys, interviews, laboratory data, and so on), then the critical philosopher would have no business carping at them. After all, since psychological egoism purports to be a scientific theory of human motives, it is the concern of the experimental psychologist, not the philosopher, to accept or reject it. But as a matter of fact, empirical evidence of the required sort is seldom presented in support of psychological egoism. Psychologists, on the whole, shy away from generalizations about human motives which are so sweeping and so vaguely formulated that they are virtually incapable of scientific testing. It is usually the "armchair scientist" who holds the theory of universal selfishness, and his usual arguments are either based simply on his "impressions" or else are largely of a non-empirical sort. The latter are often shot full of a very subtle kind of logical confusion, and this makes their criticism a matter of special interest to the analytic philosopher.

6. The psychological egoist's first argument (4a, above) is a good example of logical confusion. It begins with a truism – namely, that all of my motives and desires are *my* motives and desires and not someone else's. (Who would deny this?) But from this simple tautology nothing whatever concerning the nature of my motives or the objective of my desires can possibly follow. The fallacy of this argument consists in its violation of the general logical rule that analytic statements (tautologies) cannot entail synthetic (factual) ones.[6] That every voluntary act is prompted by the agent's own motives is a tautology; hence, it cannot be equivalent to "A person is always seeking something for himself" or "All of a person's motives are selfish," which are synthetic. What the egoist must prove is not merely:

(i) Every voluntary action is prompted by a motive of the agent's own.

but rather:

(ii) Every voluntary action is prompted by a motive of a quite particular kind, viz. a selfish one.

Statement (i) is obviously true, but it cannot all by itself give any logical support to statement (ii).

The source of the confusion in this argument is readily apparent. It is not the genesis of an action or the *origin* of its motives which makes it a "selfish" one, but rather the "purpose" of the act or the *objective* of its motives; *not where the motive comes from* (in voluntary actions it always comes from the agent) but *what it aims at* determines whether or not it is selfish. There is surely a valid distinction between voluntary behavior, in which the agent's action is motivated by purposes of his own, and *selfish* behavior in which the agent's motives are of one exclusive sort. The egoist's argument assimilates all voluntary action into the class of selfish action, by requiring, in effect, that an unselfish action be one which is not really motivated at all. In the words of Lucius Garvin, "to say that an act proceeds from our own . . . desire is only to say that the act is our own. To demand that we should act on motives that are not our own is to ask us to make ourselves living contradictions in terms."[7]

7. But if argument 4a fails to prove its point, argument 4b does no better. From the fact that all our successful actions (those in which we get what we were after) are accompanied or followed by pleasure it does not follow, as the egoist claims, that the *objective* of every action is to get pleasure for oneself. To begin with, the premise of the argument is not, strictly speaking, even true. Fulfillment of desire (simply getting what one was after) is no guarantee of satisfaction (pleasant feelings of gratification in the mind of the agent). Sometimes when we get what we want we *also* get, as a kind of extra dividend, a warm, glowing feeling of contentment; but often, far too often, we get no dividend at all, or, even worse, the bitter taste of ashes. Indeed, it has been said that the characteristic psychological problem of our time is the *dissatisfaction* that attends the fulfillment of our very most powerful desires.

Even if we grant, however, for the sake of argument, that getting what one wants *usually* yields satisfaction, the egoist's conclusion does not follow. We can concede that we normally get pleasure (in the sense of satisfaction) when our desires are satisfied, *no matter what our desires are for;* but it does not follow from this roughly accurate generalization that the only thing we ever desire is our own satisfaction. Pleasure may well be the usual accompaniment of all actions in which the agent gets what he wants; but to infer from this that what the agent always wants is his own pleasure is like arguing, in William James's example,[8] that because an ocean liner constantly consumes coal on its trans-Atlantic passage that therefore the *purpose* of its voyage is to consume coal. The immediate inference from even constant accompaniment to purpose (or motive) is always a *non sequitur.*

Perhaps there is a sense of "satisfaction" (desire fulfillment) such that it is certainly and universally true that we get satisfaction whenever we get what we want. But satisfaction in this sense is simply the "coming into existence of that which is desired." Hence, to say that desire fulfillment always yields "satisfaction" in this sense is to say no more than that we always get what we want when we get what we want, which is to utter a tautology like "a rose is a rose." It can no more entail a synthetic truth in psychology (like the egoistic thesis) than "a rose is a rose" can entail significant information in botany.

8. *Disinterested Benevolence.* The fallacy in argument 4b then consists, as Garvin puts it, "in the supposition that the apparently unselfish desire to benefit others is transformed into a selfish one by the fact that we derive pleasure from carrying it out."[9] Not only is this argument fallacious; it also provides us with a suggestion of a counterargument to show that its conclusion (psychological egoistic hedonism) is false. Not only is the presence of pleasure (satisfaction) as a by-product of an action no proof that the action was selfish; in some special cases it provides rather conclusive proof that the action was *unselfish.* For in those special cases the fact that we get pleasure from a particular action *presupposes that we desired something else* – something other than our own pleasure – as an end in itself and not merely as a means to our own pleasant state of mind.

This way of turning the egoistic hedonist's argument back on him can be illustrated by taking a typical egoist argument, one attributed

(perhaps apocryphally) to Abraham Lincoln, and then examining it closely:

> Mr. Lincoln once remarked to a fellow-passenger on an old-time mud-coach that all men were prompted by selfishness in doing good. His fellow-passenger was antagonizing this position when they were passing over a corduroy bridge that spanned a slough. As they crossed this bridge they espied an old razor-backed sow on the bank making a terrible noise because her pigs had got into the slough and were in danger of drowning. As the old coach began to climb the hill, Mr. Lincoln called out, "Driver, can't you stop just a moment?" Then Mr. Lincoln jumped out, ran back and lifted the little pigs out of the mud and water and placed them on the bank. When he returned, his companion remarked: "Now Abe, where does selfishness come in on this little episode?" "Why, bless your soul Ed, that was the very essence of selfishness. I should have had no peace of mind all day had I gone on and left that suffering old sow worrying over those pigs. I did it to get peace of mind, don't you see?"[10]

If Lincoln had cared not a whit for the welfare of the little pigs and their "suffering" mother, but only for his own "peace of mind," it would be difficult to explain how he could have derived pleasure from helping them. The very fact that he did feel satisfaction as a result of helping the pigs presupposes that he had a pre-existing desire for something other than his own happiness. Then when *that* desire was satisfied, Lincoln of course derived pleasure. The *object* of Lincoln's desire was not pleasure; rather pleasure was the *consequence* of his pre-existing desire for something else. If Lincoln had been wholly indifferent to the plight of the little pigs as he claimed, how could he possibly have derived any pleasure from helping them? He could not have achieved peace of mind from rescuing the pigs, had he not a prior concern – on which his peace of mind depended – for the welfare of the pigs for its own sake.

In general, the psychological hedonist analyzes apparent benevolence into a desire for "benevolent pleasure." No doubt the benevolent person does get pleasure from his benevolence, but in most cases, this is only because he has previously desired the good of some person, or animal, or mankind at large. Where there is no such desire, benevolent conduct is not generally found to give pleasure to the agent.

9. *Malevolence.* Difficult cases for the psychological egoist include not only instances of disinterested benevolence, but also cases of "disinterested malevolence." Indeed, malice and hatred are generally no more "selfish" than benevolence. Both are motives likely to cause an agent to sacrifice his own interests – in the case of benevolence, in order to help someone else, in the case of malevolence in order to harm someone else. The selfish person is concerned ultimately only with his own pleasure, happiness, or power; the benevolent person is often equally concerned with the happiness of others; to the malevolent person, the *injury* of another is often an end in itself – an end to be pursued sometimes with no thought for his own interests. There is reason to think that people have as often sacrificed themselves to injure or kill others as to help or to save others, and with as much "heroism" in the one case as in the other. The unselfish nature of malevolence was first noticed by the Anglican Bishop and moral philosopher Joseph Butler (1692–1752), who regretted that people are no more selfish than they are.[11]

10. *Lack of Evidence for Universal Self-Deception.* The more cynical sort of psychological egoist who is impressed by the widespread phenomenon of self-deception (see 4c above) cannot be so quickly disposed of, for he has committed no *logical* mistakes. We can only argue that the acknowledged frequency of self-deception is insufficient evidence for his universal generalization. His argument is not fallacious, but inconclusive.

No one but the agent himself can ever be certain what conscious motives really prompted his action, and where motives are disreputable, even the agent may not admit to himself the true nature of his desires. Thus, for every apparent case of altruistic behavior, the psychological egoist can argue, with some plausibility, that the true motivation *might* be selfish, appearance to the contrary. Philanthropic acts are really motivated by the desire to receive gratitude; acts of self-sacrifice, when truly understood, are seen to be motivated by the desire to feel self-esteem; and so on. We must concede to the egoist that all apparent altruism might be deceptive in this way; but such a sweeping generalization requires considerable empirical evidence, and such evidence is not presently available.

11. *The "Paradox of Hedonism" and Its Consequences for Education.* The psychological egoistic Hedonist (e.g., Jeremy Bentham) has the simplest possible theory of human motivation. According to this variety of egoistic theory, all human motives without exception can be reduced to one – namely, the desire for one's own pleasure. But this theory, despite its attractive simplicity, or perhaps because of it, involves one immediately in a paradox. Astute observers of human affairs from the time of the ancient Greeks have often noticed that pleasure, happiness, and satisfaction are states of mind which stand in a very peculiar relation to desire. An exclusive desire for happiness is the surest way to prevent happiness from coming into being. Happiness has a way of "sneaking up" on persons when they are preoccupied with other things; but when persons deliberately and single-mindedly set off in pursuit of happiness, it vanishes utterly from sight and cannot be captured. This is the famous "paradox of hedonism": the single-minded pursuit of happiness is necessarily self-defeating, for *the way to get happiness is to forget it*; then perhaps it will come to you. If you aim exclusively at pleasure itself, with no concern for the things that bring pleasure, then pleasure will never come. To derive satisfaction, one must ordinarily first desire something other than satisfaction, and then find the means to get what one desires.

To feel the full force of the paradox of hedonism the reader should conduct an experiment in his imagination. Imagine a person (let's call him "Jones") who is, first of all, devoid of intellectual curiosity. He has no desire to acquire any kind of knowledge for its own sake, and thus is utterly indifferent to questions of science, mathematics, and philosophy. Imagine further that the beauties of nature leave Jones cold: he is unimpressed by the autumn foliage, the snow-capped mountains, and the rolling oceans. Long walks in the country on spring mornings and skiing forays in the winter are to him equally a bore. Moreover, let us suppose that Jones can find no appeal in art. Novels are dull, poetry a pain, paintings nonsense and music just noise. Suppose further that Jones has neither the participant's nor the spectator's passion for baseball, football, tennis, or any other sport. Swimming to him is a cruel aquatic form of calisthenics, the sun only a cause of sunburn. Dancing is coeducational idiocy, conversation a waste of time, the other sex an unappealing mystery. Politics is a fraud, religion mere superstition; and the misery of millions of underprivileged human beings is nothing to be concerned with or excited about. Suppose finally that Jones has no talent for any kind of handicraft, industry, or commerce, and that he does not regret that fact.

What then is Jones interested in? He must desire something. To be sure, he does. Jones has an overwhelming passion for, a complete preoccupation with, his own happiness. The one exclusive desire of his life is *to be happy*. It takes little imagination at this point to see that Jones's one desire is bound to be frustrated. People who – like Jones – most hotly pursue their own happiness are the least likely to find it. Happy people are those who successfully pursue such things as aesthetic or religious experience, self-expression, service to others, victory in competitions, knowledge, power, and so on. If none of these things in themselves and for their own sakes mean anything to a person, if they are valued at all then only as a means to one's own pleasant states of mind – then that pleasure can never come. The way to achieve happiness is to pursue something else.

Almost all people at one time or another in their lives feel pleasure. Some people (though perhaps not many) really do live lives which are on the whole happy. But if pleasure and happiness presuppose desires for something other than pleasure and happiness, then the existence of pleasure and happiness in the experience of some people proves that those people have strong desires for something other than their own happiness – egoistic hedonism to the contrary.

The implications of the "paradox of hedonism" for educational theory should be obvious. The parents least likely to raise a happy child are those who, even with the best intentions, train their child to seek happiness directly. How often have we heard parents say:

> I don't care if my child does not become an intellectual, or a sports star, or a great artist. I just want her to be a plain average sort of person. Happiness does not require great ambitions and great frustrations; it's not worth it to suffer and become neurotic for the sake of science, art, or do-goodism. I just want my child to be happy.

This can be a dangerous mistake, for it is the child (and the adult for that matter) without "outerdirected" interests who is the most likely to be unhappy. The pure egoist would be the most wretched of persons.

The educator might well beware of "life adjustment" as the conscious goal of the educational process for similar reasons. "Life adjustment" can be achieved only as a by-product of other pursuits. A whole curriculum of "life adjustment courses" unsupplemented by courses designed to incite an interest in things other than life adjustment would be tragically self-defeating.

As for moral education, it is probably true that punishment and reward are indispensable means of inculcation. But if the child comes to believe that the *sole* reasons for being moral are that he will escape the pain of punishment thereby and/or that he will gain the pleasure of a good reputation, then what is to prevent him from doing the immoral thing whenever he is sure that he will not be found out? While punishment and reward then are important tools for the moral educator, they obviously have their limitations. Beware of the man who does the moral thing only out of fear of pain or love of pleasure. He is not likely to be wholly trustworthy. Moral education is truly successful when it produces persons who are willing to do the right thing *simply because it is right*, and not merely because it is popular or safe.

12. *Pleasure as Sensation.* One final argument against psychological hedonism should suffice to put that form of the egoistic psychology to

rest once and for all. The egoistic hedonist claims that all desires can be reduced to the single desire for one's own *pleasure*. Now the word "pleasure" is ambiguous. On the one hand, it can stand for a certain indefinable, but very familiar and specific kind of sensation, or more accurately, a property of sensations; and it is generally, if not exclusively, associated with the senses. For example, certain taste sensations such as sweetness, thermal sensations of the sort derived from a hot bath or the feel of the August sun while one lies on a sandy beach, erotic sensations, olfactory sensations (say) of the fragrance of flowers or perfume, and tactual and kinesthetic sensations from a good massage, are all pleasant in this sense. Let us call this sense of "pleasure," which is the converse of "physical pain," pleasure$_1$.

On the other hand, the word "pleasure" is often used simply as a synonym for "satisfaction" (in the sense of gratification, not mere desire fulfillment.) In this sense, the existence of pleasure presupposes the prior existence of desire. Knowledge, religious experience, aesthetic expression, and other so-called "spiritual activities" often give pleasure in this sense. In fact, as we have seen, we tend to get pleasure in this sense whenever we get what we desire, no matter what we desire. The masochist even derives pleasure (in the sense of "satisfaction") from his own physically painful sensations. Let us call the sense of "pleasure" which means "satisfaction" – pleasure$_2$.

Now we can evaluate the psychological hedonist's claim that the sole human motive is a desire for one's own pleasure, bearing in mind (as he often does not) the ambiguity of the word "pleasure." First, let us take the hedonist to be saying that it is the desire for pleasure$_1$ (pleasant sensation) which is the sole ultimate desire of all people and the sole desire capable of providing a motive for action. Now I have little doubt that all (or most) people desire their own pleasure, *sometimes*. But even this familiar kind of desire occurs, I think, rather rarely. When I am very hungry, I often desire to eat, or, more specifically, to eat this piece of steak and these potatoes. Much less often do I desire to eat certain morsels simply for the sake of the pleasant gustatory sensations they might cause. I have, on the other hand, been motivated in the latter way when I have gone to especially exotic (and expensive) French or Chinese restaurants; but normally, pleasant gastronomic sensations are simply a happy consequence or by-product of my eating, not the antecedently desired objective of my eating. There are, of course, others who take gustatory sensations far more seriously: the *gourmet* who eats only to savor the textures and flavors of fine foods, and the wine fancier who "collects" the exquisitely subtle and very pleasant tastes of rare old wines. Such people are truly absorbed in their taste sensations when they eat and drink, and there may even be some (rich) persons whose desire for such sensations is the sole motive for eating and drinking. It should take little argument, however, to convince the reader that such persons are extremely rare.

Similarly, I usually derive pleasure from taking a hot bath, and on occasion (though not very often) I even decide to bathe simply for the sake of such sensations. Even if this is equally true of everyone, however, it hardly provides grounds for inferring that *no one ever* bathes from *any* other motive. It should be empirically obvious that we sometimes bathe simply in order to get clean, or to please others, or simply from habit.

The view then that we are never after anything in our actions but our own pleasure – that all people are complete "gourmets" of one sort or another – is not only morally cynical; it is also contrary to common sense and everyday experience. In fact, the view that pleasant sensations play such an enormous role in human affairs is so patently false, on the available evidence, that we must conclude that the psychological hedonist has the other sense of "pleasure" – satisfaction – in mind when he states his thesis. If, on the other hand, he really does try to reduce the apparent multitude of human motives to the one desire for pleasant sensations, then the abundance of historical counter examples justifies our rejection out of hand of his thesis. It surely seems incredible that the Christian martyrs were ardently pursuing their own pleasure when they marched off to face the lions, or that what the Russian soldiers at Stalingrad "really" wanted when they doused themselves with gasoline, ignited themselves, and then threw the flaming torches of their own bodies on German tanks, was simply the experience of pleasant physical sensations.

13. *Pleasure as Satisfaction.* Let us consider now the other interpretation of the hedonist's thesis, that according to which it is one's own pleasure$_2$ (satisfaction) and not merely pleasure$_1$ (pleasant sensation) which is the sole ultimate objective of all voluntary behavior. In one respect, the "satisfaction thesis" is even less plausible than the "physical sensation thesis"; for the latter at least is a genuine empirical hypothesis, testable in experience, though contrary to the facts which experience discloses. The former, however, is so confused that it cannot even be completely stated without paradox. It is, so to speak, defeated in its own formulation. Any attempted explication of the theory that all men at all times desire only their own satisfaction leads to an *infinite regress* in the following way:

"All men desire only satisfaction."
"Satisfaction of what?"
"Satisfaction of their desires."
"Their desires for what?"
"Their desires for satisfaction."
"Satisfaction of what?"
"Their desires."
"For what?"
"For satisfaction" – etc., *ad infinitum.*

In short, psychological hedonism interpreted in this way attributes to all people as their sole motive a wholly vacuous and infinitely self-defeating desire. The source of this absurdity is in the notion that satisfaction can, so to speak, feed on itself, and perform the miracle of perpetual self-regeneration in the absence of desires for anything other than itself.

To summarize the argument of sections 12 and 13: The word "pleasure" is ambiguous. Pleasure$_1$ means a certain indefinable characteristic of physical sensation. Pleasure$_2$ refers to the feeling of satisfaction that often comes when one gets what one desires whatever be the nature of that which one desires. Now, if the hedonist means pleasure$_1$ when he says that one's own pleasure is the ultimate objective of all of one's own pleasure is the ultimate objective of all of one's behavior, then his view is not supported by the facts. On the other hand, if he

means pleasure$_2$, then his theory cannot even be clearly formulated, since it leads to the following infinite regress: "I desire only satisfaction of my desire for satisfaction of my desire for satisfaction . . . etc., *ad infinitum.*" I conclude then that psychological hedonism (the most common form of psychological egoism), however interpreted, is untenable.

D.   Critique of Psychological Egoism: Unclear Logical Status of the Theory

14. There remain, however, other possible forms of the egoistic psychology. The egoist might admit that not all human motives can be reduced to the one ultimate desire for one's own pleasure, or happiness, and yet still maintain that our ultimate motives, whether they be desire for happiness (J. S. Mill), self-fulfillment (Aristotle), power (Hobbes), or whatever, are always *self-regarding* motives. He might still maintain that, given our common human nature, wholly disinterested action impelled by exclusively other-regarding motives is psychologically impossible, and that therefore there is a profoundly important sense in which it is true that, whether they be hedonists or not, *all people are selfish.*

Now it seems to me that this highly paradoxical claim cannot be finally evaluated until it is properly understood, and that it cannot be properly understood until one knows what the psychological egoist is willing to accept as evidence either for or against it. In short, there are two things that must be decided: (a) whether the theory is true or false and (b) whether its truth or falsity (its truth value) depends entirely on the *meanings* of the words in which it is expressed or whether it is made true or false by certain *facts*, in this case the facts of psychology.

15. *Analytic Statements.* Statements whose truth is determined solely by the meanings of the words in which they are expressed, and thus can be held immune from empirical evidence, are often called analytic statements or tautologies. The following are examples of tautologies:

(1)   All bachelors are unmarried.
(2)   All effects have causes.
(3)   Either Providence is the capital of Rhode Island or it is not.

The truth of (1) is derived solely from the meaning of the word "bachelor," which is defined (in part) as "unmarried man." To find out whether (1) is true or false we need not conduct interviews, compile statistics, or perform experiments. All empirical evidence is superfluous and irrelevant; for if we know the meanings of "bachelor" and "unmarried," then we know not only that (1) is true, but that it is *necessarily* true – i.e., that it cannot possibly be false, that no future experiences or observations could possibly upset it, that to deny it would be to assert a logical contradiction. But notice that what a tautology gains in certainty ("necessary truth") it loses in descriptive content. Statement (1) imparts no information whatever about any matter of fact; it simply records our determination to use certain words in a certain way. As we say, "It is true by definition."

Similarly, (2) is (necessarily) true solely in virtue of the meanings of the words "cause" and "effect" and thus requires no further observations to confirm it. And of course, no possible observations could falsify it, since it asserts no matter of fact. And finally, statement (3) is (necessarily) true solely in virtue of the meaning of the English expression "either . . . or." Such terms as "either . . . or," "If . . . then," "and," and "not" are called by logicians "logical constants." The *definitions* of logical constants are made explicit in the so-called "laws of thought" – the law of contradiction, the law of the excluded middle, and the law of identity. These "laws" are not laws in the same sense as are (say) the laws of physics. Rather, they are merely consequences of the *definitions* of logical constants, and as such, though they are necessarily true, they impart no information about the world. "Either Providence is the capital of Rhode Island or it is not" tells us nothing about geography; and "Either it is now raining or else it is not" tells us nothing about the weather. You don't have to look at a map or look out the window to know that they are true. Rather, they are known to be true *a priori* (independently of experience); and, like all (or many)[12] *a priori* statements, they are *vacuous*, i.e., devoid of informative content.

The denial of an analytic statement is called a contradiction. The following are typical examples of contradictions: "Some bachelors are married," "Some causes have no effects," "Providence both is and is not the capital of Rhode Island." As in the case of tautologies, the truth value of contradictions (their falsehood) is logically necessary, not contingent on any facts of experience, and uninformative. Their falsity is derived from the meanings (definitions) of the words in which they are expressed.

16. *Synthetic Statements.* On the other hand, statements whose truth or falsity is derived not from the meanings of words but rather from the facts of experience (observations) are called *synthetic.*[13] Prior to experience, there can be no good reason to think either that they are true or that they are false. That is to say, their truth value is *contingent*; and they can be confirmed or disconfirmed only by *empirical* evidence,[14] i.e., controlled observations of the world. Unlike analytic statements, they do impart information about matters of fact. Obviously, "It is raining in Newport now," if true, is more informative than "Either it is raining in Newport now or it is not," even though the former *could* be false, while the latter is necessarily true. I take the following to be examples of synthetic (contingent) statements:

(1′)   All bachelors are neurotic.
(2′)   All events have causes.
(3′)   Providence is the capital of Rhode Island.
(3″)   Newport is the capital of Rhode Island.

Statement (3′) is true; (3″) is false; and (1′) is a matter for a psychologist (not for a philosopher) to decide; and the psychologist himself can only decide *empirically*, i.e., by making many observations. The status of (2′) is very difficult and its truth value is a matter of great controversy. That is because its truth or falsity depends on *all* the facts ("all events"); and, needless to say, not all of the evidence is in.

17. *Empirical Hypotheses.* Perhaps the most interesting subclass of synthetic statements are those generalizations of experience of the sort characteristically made by scientists; e.g., "All released objects heavier than air fall," "All swans are white," "All men have Oedipus complexes." I shall call such statements "empirical hypotheses" to indicate that their function is

to sum up past experience and enable us successfully to predict or anticipate future experience.[15] They are never logically certain, since it is always at least conceivable that future experience will disconfirm them. For example, zoologists once believed that all swans are white, until black swans were discovered in Australia. The most important characteristic of empirical hypotheses for our present purposes is their relation to evidence. A person can be said to understand an empirical hypothesis only if he knows how to recognize evidence against it. *If a person asserts or believes a general statement in such a way that he cannot conceive of any possible experience which he would count as evidence against it, then he cannot be said to be asserting or believing an empirical hypothesis.* We can refer to this important characteristic of empirical hypotheses as *falsifiability in principle.*

Some statements only appear to be empirical hypotheses but are in fact disguised tautologies reflecting the speaker's determination to use words in certain (often eccentric) ways. For example, a zoologist might refuse to allow the existence of "Australian swans" to count as evidence against the generalization that all swans are white, on the grounds that the black Australian swans are not "really" swans at all. This would indicate that he is holding *whiteness* to be part of the definition of "swan," and that therefore, the statement "All swans are white" is, for him, "true by definition" — and thus just as immune from counterevidence as the statement "All spinsters are unmarried." Similarly, most of us would refuse to allow any possible experience to count as evidence against "2 + 2 = 4" or "Either unicorns exist or they do not," indicating that the propositions of arithmetic and logic are not empirical hypotheses.

18. *Ordinary Language and Equivocation.* Philosophers, even more than ordinary people, are prone to make startling and paradoxical claims that take the form of universal generalizations and hence resemble empirical hypotheses. For example, "All things are mental (there are no physical objects)," "All things are good (there is no evil)," "All voluntary behavior is selfish," etc. Let us confine our attention for the moment to the latter which is a rough statement of psychological egoism. At first sight, the statement "All voluntary behavior is selfish" seems obviously false. One might reply to the psychological egoist in some such manner as this:

> I *know* some behavior, at least, is unselfish, because I saw my Aunt Emma yesterday give her last cent to a beggar. Now she will have to go a whole week with nothing to eat. Surely, *that* was not selfish of her.

Nevertheless, the psychological egoist is likely not to be convinced, and insist that, in this case, if we knew enough about Aunt Emma, we would learn that her primary motive in helping the beggar was to promote her own happiness or assuage her own conscience, or increase her own selfesteem, etc. We might then present the egoist with even more difficult cases for his theory – saints, martyrs, military heroes, patriots, and others who have sacrificed themselves for a cause. If psychological egoists nevertheless refuse to accept any of these as examples of unselfish behavior, then we have a right to be puzzled about what they are saying. Until we know what they would count as *unselfish* behavior, we can't very well know what they mean when they say that all voluntary behavior is *selfish.* And at this point we may suspect that they are holding their theory in a "privileged position" – that of immunity to evidence, that they would allow no *conceivable* behavior to count as evidence against it. What they say then, if true, must be true in virtue of the way they define – or redefine – the word "selfish." And in that case, it cannot be an empirical hypothesis.

If what the psychological egoist says is "true by redefinition," then I can "agree" with him and say "It is true that in *your* sense of the word 'selfish' my Aunt Emma's behavior was selfish; but in the ordinary sense of 'selfish,' which implies blameworthiness, she surely was not selfish." There is no point of course in arguing about a mere word. The important thing is not what particular words a person uses, but rather whether what he wishes to say in those words is true. Departures from ordinary language can often be justified by their utility for certain purposes; but they are dangerous when they invite equivocation. The psychological egoist may be saying something which is true when he says that Emma is selfish in *his* sense, but if he doesn't realize that his sense of "selfish" differs from the ordinary one, he may be tempted to infer that Emma is selfish in the ordinary sense which implies blameworthiness; and this of course would be unfair and illegitimate. It is indeed an extraordinary extension of the meaning of the word "self-indulgent" (as C. G. Chesterton remarks somewhere) which allows a philosopher to say that a man is self-indulgent when he wants to be burned at the stake.

19. *The Fallacy of the Suppressed Correlative.* Certain words in the English language operate in pairs – e.g., "selfish-unselfish," "good-bad," "large-small," "mental-physical." To assert that a thing has one of the above characteristics is to *contrast* it with the opposite in the pair. To know the meaning of one term in the pair, we must know the meaning of the correlative term with which it is contrasted. If we could not conceive of what it would be like for a thing to be bad, for example, then we could not possibly understand what is being said of a thing when it is called "good." Similarly, unless we had a notion of what it would be like for action to be *unselfish*, we could hardly understand the sentence "So-and-so acted selfishly"; for we would have nothing to contrast "selfishly" with. The so-called "fallacy of the suppressed correlative"[16] is committed by a person who consciously or unconsciously redefines one of the terms in a contrasting pair in such a way that its new meaning incorporates the sense of its correlative.

Webster's Collegiate Dictionary defines "selfish" (in part) as "regarding one's own comfort, advantage, etc. in disregard of, or at the expense of that of others." In this ordinary and proper sense of "selfish," Aunt Emma's action in giving her last cent to the beggar certainly was *not* selfish. Emma *disregarded* her *own* comfort (it is not "comfortable" to go a week without eating) and advantage (there is no "advantage" in malnutrition) *for the sake of* (not "at the expense of") another. Similarly, the martyr marching off to the stake is foregoing (not indulging) his "comfort" and indeed his very life for the sake of (not at the

expense of) a cause. If Emma and the martyr then are "selfish," they must be so in a strange new sense of the word.

A careful examination of the egoist's arguments (see especially 4b above) reveals what new sense he gives to the word "selfish." He redefines the word so that it means (roughly) "motivated," or perhaps "intentional." "After all," says the egoist, "Aunt Emma had some *purpose* in giving the beggar all her money, and this purpose (desire, intention, motive, aim) was *her* purpose and no one else's. She was out to further some aim of her own, wasn't she? Therefore, she was pursuing her own ends (acting from her own motives); she was after something *for herself* in so acting, and that's what I mean by calling her action selfish. Moreover, all intentional action – action done 'on purpose,' deliberately from the agent's own motives – is selfish in the same sense." We can see now, from this reply, that since the egoist apparently means by "selfish" simply "motivated," when he says that all motivated action is selfish *he is not asserting a synthetic empirical hypothesis about human motives; rather, his statement is a tautology roughly equivalent to "all motivated actions are motivated."* And if that is the case, then what he says is true enough; but, like all tautologies, it is empty, uninteresting, and trivial.

Moreover, in redefining "selfish" in this way, the psychological egoist has committed the fallacy of the suppressed correlative. For what can we now contrast "selfish voluntary action" with? Not only are there no *actual* cases of unselfish voluntary actions on the new definition; there are not even any *theoretically possible* or *conceivable* cases of unselfish voluntary actions. And if we cannot even conceive of what an unselfish voluntary action would be like, how can we give any sense to the expression "selfish voluntary action"? The egoist, so to speak, has so blown up the sense of "selfish" that, like in-flated currency, it will no longer buy anything.

20. *Psychological Egoism as a Linguistic Proposal.* There is still one way out for the egoist. He might admit that his theory is not really a psychological hypothesis about human nature designed to account for the facts and enable us to predict or anticipate future events. He may

even willingly concede that his theory is really a disguised redefinition of a word. Still, he might argue, he has made no claim to be giving an accurate description of actual linguistic usage. Rather, he is making a proposal to *revise* our usage in the interest of economy and convenience, just as the biologists once proposed that we change the ordinary meaning of "insect" in such a way that spiders are no longer called insects, and the ordinary meaning of "fish" so that whales and seals are no longer called fish.

What are we to say to this suggestion? First of all, stipulative definitions (proposals to revise usage) are never true or false. They are simply useful or not useful. Would it be useful to redefine "selfish" in the way the egoist recommends? It is difficult to see what would be gained thereby. The egoist has noticed some respects in which actions normally called "selfish" and actions normally called "unselfish" are alike, namely they are both motivated and they both can give satisfaction – either in prospect or in retrospect – to the agent. Because of these likenesses, the egoist feels justified in attaching the label "selfish" to *all* actions. Thus one word – "selfish" – must for him do the work of two words ("selfish" and "unselfish" in their old meanings); and, as a result, a very real distinction, that between actions for the sake of others and actions at the expense of others,

can no longer be expressed in the language. Because the egoist has noticed some respects in which two types of actions are alike, he wishes to make it impossible to describe the respects in which they differ. It is difficult to see any utility in this state of affairs.

But suppose we adopt the egoist's "proposal" nevertheless. Now we would have to say that all actions are selfish, but, in addition, we would want to say that there are two different kinds of selfish actions, those which regard the interests of others and those which disregard the interests of others, and, furthermore, that only the latter are blameworthy. After a time our ear would adjust to the new uses of the word "selfish," and we would find nothing at all strange in such statements as "Some selfish actions are morally praise-worthy." After a while, we might even invent two new words, perhaps "selfitic" and "unselfitic," to distinguish the two important classes of "selfish" actions. Then we would be right back where we started, with new linguistic tools ("selfish" for "motivated," "selfitic" for "selfish," and "unselfitic" for "unselfish") to do the same old necessary jobs. That is, until some new egoistic philosopher arose to announce with an air of discovery that "All selfish behavior is really selfitic – there are no truly unselfitic selfish actions." Then, God help us!

Notes

1. See his *Introduction to the Principles of Morals and Legislation* (1789), Chap. I, first paragraph: "Nature has placed mankind under the governance of two sovereign masters, *pain* and *pleasure*. It is for them alone to point out what we ought to do, as well as to determine what we shall do. . . . They govern us in all we do, in all we say, in all we think: every effort we can make to throw off our subjection will serve but to demonstrate and confirm it."

2. C. D. Broad, *Ethics and the History of Philosophy* (New York: The Humanities Press, 1952), Essay 10 – "Egoism as a Theory of Human Motives," p. 218. This essay is highly recommended.

3. Austin Duncan-Jones, *Butler's Moral Philosophy* (London; Penguin Books, 1952), p. 96. Duncan-Jones goes on to reject this argument. See p. 512f.

4. Lucius Garvin, *A Modern Introduction to Ethics* (Boston: Houghton Mifflin, 1953), p. 37. Quoted here by permission of the author and publisher.

5. *Op. cit.*, Chap. III.

6. See Part D, 15 and 16, below.

7. *Op. cit.*, p. 39.

8. *The Principles of Psychology* (New York: Henry Holt, 1890), Vol. II, p. 558.

9. *Op. cit.*, p. 39.

10. Quoted from the *Springfield* (Illinois) *Monitor*, by F. C. Sharp in his *Ethics* (New York: Appleton-Century, 1928), p. 75.

11. See his *Fifteen Sermons on Human Nature Preached at the Rolls Chapel* (1726), especially the first and eleventh.

12. Whether or not there are some *a priori* statements that are not merely analytic, and hence

not vacuous, is still a highly controversial question among philosophers.

13. Some philosophers (those called "rationalists") believe that there are some synthetic statements whose truth can be known *a priori* (see note 12). If they are right, then the statement above is not entirely accurate.

14. Again, subject to the qualification in notes 12 and 13.

15. The three examples given above all have the generic character there indicated, but they also differ from one another in various other ways, some of which are quite important. For our present purposes however, we can ignore the ways in which they differ from one another and concentrate on their common character as generalizations of experience ("inductive generalizations"). As such they are sharply contrasted with such a generalization as "All puppies are young dogs," which is analytic.

16. The phrase was coined by J. Lowenberg. See his article "What Is Empirical?" in the *Journal of Philosophy*, May 1940.

CHAPTER 20
Flourishing Egoism

LESTER HUNT

I. Virtue and Self-Interest

Early in Peter Abelard's *Dialogue between a Philosopher, a Jew, and a Christian*, the philosopher (that is, the ancient Greek) and the Christian easily come to agreement about what the point of ethics is: "[T]he culmination of true ethics . . . is gathered together in this: that it reveal where the ultimate good is and by what road we are to arrive there." They also agree that, since the enjoyment of this ultimate good "comprises true blessedness," ethics "far surpasses other teachings in both usefulness and worthiness."[1] As Abelard understood them, both fundamental elements of his twelfth-century ethical culture – Greek philosophy and Christian religion – held a common view of the nature of ethical inquiry, one that was so obvious to them that his characters do not even state it in a fully explicit way. They take for granted, as we take the ground we stand on, the premise that the most important function of ethical theory is to tell you what sort of life is most desirable, or most worth living. That is, the point of ethics is that it is good for you, that it serves your self-interest.

Lester Hunt, "Flourishing Egoism," pp. 72–95 from *Social Philosophy and Policy*, 16(1), 1999. © Social Philosophy and Policy Foundation, reproduced with permission. Reprinted by permission of the author Lester Hunt.

This idea sounds very strange to modern ears, and is scarcely made less so when it is stated, as it is by Abelard, in terms of the concept of happiness or, to use the somewhat broader term that is now widely used, of "flourishing." It still sounds as if things are being combined that cannot be put together. Nonetheless, Abelard's depiction of his intellectual heritage suggests – at least to me – a historical generalization which I think is at least close to being right: the idea of self-interest, as expressed through the notions of happiness or flourishing, dominates the ethical thinking of both ancient Greek and medieval Christian philosophy in more or less the way I have just described. It is also fair to say that there is at least one other idea that very characteristically dominates thought during the same periods: namely, the idea of virtue. It was generally assumed at that time that ethics tells you what sort of person you should be: it discovers which traits, if you should have them, would make you a good person.

This close historical association between virtue and self-interest suggests (again, to me at any rate) a further hypothesis: that there is some close connection between the concept of virtue and that of self-interest. This impression is reinforced by the fact that, as the concept of self-interest and related notions receded from the focal point of Western ethics, the idea of virtue did so as well. Both ideas were already sharply demoted in the work of Hobbes, beginning a trend that resulted (sometime in the middle of the twentieth century) in an ethical orthodoxy within which virtue was never mentioned and the agent's own well-being was regarded as at best irrelevant to his or her ethical merit, and at worst in conflict with it.

In what follows, I would like to present one piece of evidence that these two ideas do indeed belong together, related in something like the way they are in the classical, pre-Hobbesian tradition. More precisely, I will argue that the notion of happiness or (the term I will use hereafter) "flourishing" enables us to entertain a much closer connection between virtue and self-interest than modern prejudices will generally allow.

To make this point, I will focus on an ethical doctrine in which this connection is alleged in its most extreme form, namely, ethical egoism. It is perhaps obvious that the notion of flourishing can be relevant to the development of egoistic theories. Though there are various forms of egoism, it must be definition hold, in one way or another, that a distinguishing mark of the right or the good in human conduct is the fact that it conduces to the self-interest of the agent. The concept of flourishing can readily serve as a first approach toward understanding what self-interest is, as an outline sketch that can be filled in later in various ways. One way to explain what self-interest is – among other ways, some crucially different – would be to specify that what is in a person's self-interest is to live the sort of life that is most desirable, most worth living. In a word, self-interest is flourishing. One can then inquire about what sort of life this is, and what it is that makes it the best life.

If flourishing can be used to explain, or begin to explain, what self-interest is, then it can also be used to specify the content of a doctrine of ethical egoism. I will argue in what follows that it makes a great deal of difference whether an egoistic theory begins in this way or in a certain alternative way. It makes a difference to the plausibility of ethical theories and, more fundamentally, to the relevance of self-interest to ethics and to central ethical concepts, most particularly including virtue.

I will begin by setting out some familiar difficulties confronting egoistic theories, together with solutions to these difficulties which can be drawn from the work of one proponent of flourishing-based egoism, one who is often mentioned in discussions of egoism but seldom read closely or discussed with care by professional philosophers. I am referring, as some readers may already have surmised, to Ayn Rand.

II. Difficulties for Egoism

The first difficulty I want to focus on is a very simple but also, I think, very influential objection to ethical egoism. It is based on the fundamental fact that ethical egoism is, as one might put it, a theory of reasons: it does not, as such, pass judgment on people, their traits, their ways of life, or the acts that they do, but, rather, tells us what constitutes a good reason for such judgments. Egoism says that in some ultimate way, actions, traits, and ways of life have value because they are beneficial to the agent who has or does them. This is what gives us a reason to do actions, to have traits, to live a given way of life, or to admire them in others. The objection I have in mind alleges that egoism, regarded as a theory of reasons, and in particular as a theory of reasons for action, clearly clashes with common sense.[2] Most of us think that the good of others is, to take a phrase used by Michael Slote in a similar context, a "ground floor" reason for action – that the fact that an action produces some good for some other person is sometimes, simply in itself, a reason for doing it.[3] Yet this seems to be just the sort of thing that egoism denies.

To the extent that a theory does clash with common sense, it must present people with arguments to change their minds, at least if its proponents mean to convince people who do not already agree with them. Here the clash with common sense seems very deep, and the burden of proof correspondingly large. In the absence of compelling arguments to the contrary, Slote says, "a properly conservative approach seems to dictate . . . that we prefer a common-sense account . . . to the egoistic view."[4]

The second objection I want to consider is one to which Derek Parfit drew attention a few years ago. Like the first one, it arises, more or less naturally, when we regard egoism as a theory of reasons for action. It goes like this: Egoism, interpreted as a theory of reasons for action, distinguishes between good reasons and bad ones by using a certain aim, or outcome, as the standard: namely, the agent's own good. The problem, according to this objection, is that this outcome will probably not be achieved most effectively by people who are trying to achieve it, and who have no other ultimate aim. We can readily imagine reasons why this might well be the case. If people were to realize that I act as if I value their well-being simply in order to get something out of them, all sorts of results that are bad for me will tend follow: to one extent or another, other people will object to being "used" in this way and will refuse to cooperate with me. They will also dislike me, and they will think I am a bad person. However, it is good for me that others cooperate with me, like me, and think I am a good person; thus, to the extent that these results can be expected to follow from it, ego-istic behavior undermines the aim of egoism.

As Parfit has pointed out in his own response to this sort of objection, the problem it raises is not a logical contradiction: it does not mean that egoism logically entails its own falsity.[5] We could take it to mean, rather, that egoism advises us to conceal our ultimate aim from others and perhaps from ourselves. It may actually be easier to get others to respond in a favorable way to us if we actually come to value their well-being as an end in itself. This, in turn, may mean that egoism would require us to believe theories that are inconsistent with itself, that it would require us to think (for instance) that things are actually good that, according to egoism, are really worthless. It would not follow from this, however, that according to egoism, egoism is false. Strictly speaking, it would only entail that, according to egoism, we really should have these attitudes and believe these theories. Egoism would (according to itself) give the true account of why we ought to do and believe these things.

Parfit has apparently taken the position that, if this objection does not convict egoism of self-contradiction, it is no objection at all.[6] It seems to me, though, that it *is* an objection, and one that should be taken seriously. Ethical egoism, like any other ethical doctrine, is meant to guide the conduct of life. If it should turn out to be true that it can only be followed by using secrecy, lying, self-deception, and holding contradictory beliefs, this would raise several problems for anyone who wants to believe the doctrine. To mention only the most obvious one, it would seem to mean that this guide to life is an extremely difficult one to follow. To the extent that one guide is difficult to follow and another is not, that other is, all other things being equal (for instance, if the reasons for thinking they *are* true are about evenly balanced), clearly preferable as a guide. Later, I will say more to reinforce the idea that this constitutes a problem. For the time being, I hope it has enough intuitive appeal to at least motivate the reader to continue to follow what I am saying.

III.   One Version of Egoism

Neither of these two objections, as I have described them, is a knockdown refutation of ethical egoism. Both have the character, rather, of considerations that weigh against it and must somehow be balanced by considerations that weigh on the other side, creating a burden of proof that apparently must be shouldered by anyone who wishes to defend ethical egoism to people not already convinced of its truth. Despite this appearance, I will argue in what follows that there is at least one sort of egoism that can afford to lay down this burden. I am referring to egoistic doctrines that make suit-able use of the idea of flourishing. Such theor-ies can be formulated in such a way that the above objections simply do not apply to them. This, in fact, is one of the principal advantages these theories enjoy over other varieties of eth-ical egoism, for there are varieties to which these objections do apply. To make a case for these claims, I will, as already indicated, focus on one particular example of flourishing-based egoism: the one formulated and defended by Ayn Rand. In the present section of this essay, I will describe this version in what I hope is enough detail to provide a basis for discussion. In the next section, I will briefly show how the possibilities opened by the flourishing-based approach enable it to side-step these two otherwise persuasive objections.

One of the most direct and revealing statements of Rand's ethical egoism is a statement in her philosophical novel *Atlas Shrugged*, one that she deemed important enough to quote some years later in her essay "The Objectivist Ethics":

> Man has to be man – by choice; he has to hold his life as a value – by choice; he has to learn to sustain it – by choice; he has to discover the values it requires and practice his virtues – by choice. A code of values accepted by choice is a code of morality.[7]

There is much in this statement that invites comment of one sort or another, but for the present I will only call attention to one aspect of it, one that I will later argue is important. She does not describe the moral task as, fundamentally, one of selecting acts nor, by the same token, as one of selecting acts that optimally achieve some goal. In place of a goal, she presents something that cannot in any straightforward sense be maximized, something we would not ordinarily think of as a goal at all: namely, one's own life. It is the value that must be achieved – or, as she says, "sustained." Further, she presents this task as one that apparently can *only* be carried out by one means or method: by identifying the requisite values and – what is evidently a closely related matter – practicing the appropriate virtues.

When she gives an even more explicit statement of her ethical egoism, a few pages after quoting the passage from *Atlas Shrugged*, she says:

> The Objectivist ethics proudly advocates and upholds *rational selfishness* – which means: the values required for man's survival *qua* man.[8]

Here, again, though the reference to virtue is dropped, there is still no direct reference to action at all. This pattern, as far as I know, is sustained throughout her work: in her direct statements of her doctrine, she does not

present it as a thesis that is *directly* about what we should do.

Naturally, as with any ethical theory, action must come into it at some point. In a rough sort of way, it is relatively easy to say how action enters into this one. Among the many values that can become helpful in sustaining the ultimate value, three are of such importance that they can be singled out as *the* means to its achievement:

> The three cardinal values of the Objectivist ethics – the three values which, taken together, are the means to and the realization of one's ultimate values, one's own life – are Reason, Purpose, Self-Esteem.[9]

In turn, "these three values," as she has her character John Galt say, "imply and require all of man's virtues."[10] In "The Objectivist Ethics" she selects three virtues for special consideration as "corresponding" to the three cardinal values: rationality, productiveness, and pride.

Finally, though Rand does not directly connect self-interest with action, she does establish such a connection between action and virtue: "*Value*," she says, "is that which one acts to gain and/or keep – *virtue* is the act by which one gains and/or keeps it."[11] Self-interest as an ethical standard is connected with action, but the connection is made indirectly, through the intermediary concepts of value and virtue. One's interests are sustained only by achieving that which is of value, while that which is of value is achieved by means of virtue. The acts of which such virtue consists, whatever they might be, are the ones that her ethical standard singles out for praise and commendation.

To see just what these connections between standard and action amount to, it is probably most helpful to understand what self-interest means for Rand. To that end, consider the following story, which I draw from the life of the great architect Louis Sullivan. In 1917, Sullivan's career was in desperate condition. His innovative aesthetic was out of fashion, and he had completed no projects of any importance for three years. If he did not receive a commission soon, he was facing the degrading possibility of real poverty. Then the directors of a small banking firm in Sidney, Ohio approached him about designing a building for them. He traveled to Sidney and, after inspecting the site and reflecting on their specifications, had a meeting with the directors which an early biographer describes in this way:

> He announced to the directors that the design was made – in his head – proceeded to draw a rapid sketch before them, and announced an estimate of the cost. One of the directors was somewhat disturbed by the unfamiliarity of the style, and suggested that he had rather fancied some classic columns and pilasters for the façade. Sullivan very brusquely rolled up his sketch and started to depart, saying that the directors could get a thousand architects to design a classic bank but only one to design them this kind of bank, and that as far as he was concerned, it was either the one thing or the other. After some conference, the directors accepted the sketch design and the bank was forthwith built with not a single essential change in the design.[12]

This incident presents us with a definite narrative sequence, concluding with a happy ending: Sullivan is in serious danger, yet faces it with unflinching courage and, perhaps because of this, things turn out very well for him. He is able to pay his rent a while longer, and he avoids violating his architectural ideals. But wherein does this "turning out well" consist?

Rand created a memorable fictional incident, probably inspired by this historical one, which poses a striking answer to this question. There is an episode in her novel *The Fountainhead* in which the architect-hero, Howard Roark, confronts a professional crisis virtually identical to the one we have just seen Sullivan facing: if he does not get an architectural commission almost immediately, he will have to go to work as a laborer, possibly giving up his career forever. He is asked to design a commercial building, and there is a request for classical ornaments that are inconsistent with the rest of the design. But Roark is not as lucky as Sullivan was. The board makes it clear that this represents their final offer. As he prepares to leave, a representative of the company begs him to reconsider, if only for the sake of his own well-being:

> "We want your building. You need the commission. Do you have to be quite so fanatical and selfless about it?"
> "What?" Roark asked, incredulously.
> "Fanatical and selfless."
> Roark smiled. He looked down at his drawings. His elbow moved a little, pressing them to his body. He said:
> "That was the most selfish thing you've ever seen a man do."[13]

By making things turn out worse for Roark than they did for Sullivan, Rand compels us to consider what self-interest really is. Sullivan manages to secure for himself two sorts of goods: those involved in designing the sort of building he believes in, and those involved in being able to pay his rent. Because he achieves both, we have no need to think about the relative roles of these two sorts of values – which we might roughly capture by calling them "ideals" and "money" – in constituting the interests of the individual involved. In Roark's case these two sorts of goods conflict, and he must choose between them. In evaluating the effect of this episode on the hero's fortunes, we must consider which choice better supports his well-being.

Rand and her character make it very clear that their solution to this problem is not the one that many people would give, including many philosophers who have discussed ethical egoism. Typically, one's ideals are thought to be for the most part antithetical to one's interests, while money is treated as if it were infallibly conducive to them, and this is clearly not what Rand and Roark think. Obviously, there is a heterodox theory about the nature of self-interest involved here.

Whatever this theory might be, it certainly cannot simply amount to the claim that acting on one's ideals is necessarily in one's interest. It is too evident that some people's ideals really are bad for them. What, then, *is* self-interest? Rand never says, quite directly and explicitly, what "interest" or "self-interest" mean when she uses them, but she does make some relevant and highly illuminating comments on the thing that she takes as representing the opposite of these things: namely, sacrifice. " 'Sacrifice," she tells us, "is the surrender of a greater value for the sake of a lesser one or of a non-value."[14] She goes on to give an example:

> If a man who is passionately in love with his wife spends a fortune to cure her of a dangerous illness, it would be absurd to claim that he does it as a "sacrifice" for *her* sake, not his own, and that it makes no difference to *him*, personally and selfishly, whether she lives or dies. . . . But suppose he let her die in order to spend his money on saving the lives of ten other women, none of whom meant anything to him. . . . *That* would be a sacrifice.[15]

Now I am in a position to say more about how it is, in Rand's theory, that value and virtue connect action with self-interest. An account of the connection that is both suggested by and consistent with the passages I have quoted in the last several paragraphs would go like this. One's interests consist in achieving what is of value. Since things that are of value are unequally valuable and conflict with one another, this would have to mean achieving what is of *greatest* value. But this cannot be accomplished without knowing what is, in a given situation, of greater value and what is of less. Since acting on the basis of this understanding is what virtue is, this also means that achieving one's own interest would be impossible without virtue.

IV.   Difficulties Avoided

How does this version of ethical egoism fare in the face of the objections against egoism that I raised earlier? In the case of the first one, I think the answer is fairly straightforward. This objection rested on the claim that egoism clashes with the idea that the good of others is a "ground floor" reason for action, and that, consequently, egoism is incompatible with common sense. As I have presented it, this claim could mean two different things.

First, it could mean that common sense holds that the fact that a given act advances the good of others is a reason for doing that act and, further, that there is no reason why *this* is so. There is no reason why it is a reason. This, of course, does not seem to be a tenet of common sense at all. Indeed, it seems consistent with common sense to say that the good of people you know is a reason for action because other people are of great value to you, that promoting the good of others, at least of certain others, is an indispensable part of the sort of life that it is best to live, the sort of life that is the most desirable. In fact, parents – most of whom can be taken to represent common sense to some extent – often try to convince their children that this is true. Of course, it is debatable whether such common-sense ways of explaining the value of the good of others are egoistic; but it is worth noting that, if they are, they are instances of flourishing-based egoism. We show that something is in one's self-interest by showing that it is part of a certain sort of life. This sort of life, it is assumed, is what self-interest is.

However, it seems likely that few people would be influenced by this objection to ethical egoism if this is what it meant. An alternative and more persuasive way of understanding the objection would be to view it as the claim that common sense denies a *certain* conception of the reason why the good of others is a reason for action. According to this conception, the *only* reason for which we should seek to bring about the good of others is that their well-being in turn brings about a certain further result – namely, of course, our own self-interest.

It is certainly very plausible to say that this conception clashes with common sense. However, it is not so obvious that it is implied by ethical egoism. In particular, Rand's theory seems to have no such implication. It does not recommend that we seek the well-being of others on the grounds that their well-being causes one's own interests to be realized. Rather, one's own interest is (consists in) the attainment of value, and one of the most valuable things is the good of other – that is, certain other – people. One's own self-interest is not some further result, in addition to the attainment of one's values; and one's values include, as a part of them, the good of certain other people.

What this means is that, as I have already hinted, Rand's egoism is of the flourishing-based sort. The notion of attaining value functions here as part of her account of which sort of life is best. We show that things are in one's interest by showing that they are part of this sort of life. The reason why something does fit into such a life – why it is a value – may be a matter of what further effects it has on the agent, but that is another matter. Saying that the good of others fits into such a life is not the same thing as saying that it has such effects. This is why Rand can claim that she is an ethical egoist and yet embrace the common-sense view that the good of others *is* a ground-floor reason for action in that it is worth pursuing in itself.

So much for the first objection to ethical egoism. As for the second one, which alleges that egoism requires one to adopt a certain self-defeating attitude toward other people, a closely related reply is also available. The reply I just gave to the second, and more likely, interpretation of the first objection rested on the idea that it assumed an arbitrarily narrow notion of egoism as a theory of reasons. The existence of flourishing-based explanations of self-interest opens up the possibility of an egoism that is more inclusive in the reasons for action that it treats as legitimate. The same sort of thing can be said in connection with the second objection. In both cases, it is assumed that, according to egoism, a consideration becomes a good reason for action simply and solely because, if one acts on it, it brings about a certain result: the agent's own self-interest. In the second objection this assumption implies that, if we act as egoism recommends, we are viewing the interests of others in a certain way: as mere instruments to be manipulated to produce a certain result. As we have already seen, this assumption is not necessarily true, and, in particular, it is not true of Rand's egoism. In her view, the achievement of one's values is related to self-interest, not by causality, but by identity. That is what self-interest is. Given that the good of (at least certain) others properly is among one's values, it is in one's self-interest to pursue it, even apart from further, future results it might bring. To put the same idea in more abstract and theory-neutral language: it is in one's self-interest, not because it causes flourishing, but because it is partly constitutive of it.

Of course, whether an ethical egoism that is formulated in this way is true, or even fully coherent, is another matter; but at least we can say that this form of egoism is not logically committed to a repulsively manipulative attitude toward other people, an attitude which, according to the second objection, must be concealed from them and, possibly, from oneself.

V. Consequentialist Egoism

My responses to the two objections, as I have presented them so far, are very brief. Obviously, much more remains to be said about them; in particular, I must deal with the inevitable replies, and that is what I will do for most of the remainder of this essay. I have claimed that these objections do not necessarily apply to a certain sort of egoism: namely, the sort that, at least implicitly, uses the flourishing-based approach to explaining what self-interest is. In addition, some of my comments have suggested rather strongly that such objections *do* apply to a certain other sort of egoism, and may even cause it some serious damage. Accordingly, I have exposed myself to two sorts of attack: one from people who find fault with the type of egoism I have defended, and the other from people who find fault with the way I have implicitly rejected the other type. Some people would likely wish to claim that the notion of flourishing cannot help egoism in the way I have suggested it can, while others will say that non-flourishing-based egoism has no need of such help.

I will take the latter sort of attack first, using as my principal focus a version of the attack presented by Peter Railton.[16] Following some suggestions by Parfit to which I have already referred, Railton contends that, contrary to what I have supposed, the second objection, properly understood, really presents no problem at all for the theories at which it is aimed: the self-defeatingness with which it charges them is actually not a bad thing. What prevents it from being a bad thing, in part, is the concept of virtue. Railton states his argument in terms of egoistic hedonism, but it is easy to see how it can be generalized to apply to egoism in general.

Egoistic hedonism ("hedonism" for short) is the theory that says that all actions that an agent might do are good only if they cause a certain state of consciousness in the agent: namely, happiness or pleasure (which, for brevity, I will call "pleasure" from now on). Stated as a problem about hedonism, the second objection rests on the familiar truism that people who make pleasure their sole ultimate aim often achieve this end less well than people who have ultimate ends – goods sought as good in themselves – other than (perhaps in addition to) pleasure. Doing something because it results in a certain state of consciousness in oneself is quite a different thing from doing it for love of the activity itself. They are different, in spite of the fact that the latter way of acting will also produce pleasure. In fact, for a number of reasons, a life filled with these sorts of activities will probably contain more pleasure than a life in which everything is calculated to achieve this result.

As Railton treats it, this problem is simply an instance of a more general psychological one, which is created by the fact that the temptation to indulge in excessive reflection about one's ends tends to interfere with the achievement of those ends. A problem that seems to function as a paradigm for him is one that he calls "a famous old conundrum for consequentialism": If all actions are to be judged by their outcomes, then it would seem that we must deliberate not only about actions but about how much time to spend on any deliberation, including these deliberations about our deliberations, and so on to infinity.

One can avoid this problem, he says, simply by refraining from deliberating about time allocation. The "sophisticated consequentialist" can "develop standing dispositions to give more or less time to decisions depending upon their perceived importance, the amount of information available, the predictability of his choice, and so on."[17] Similar things, he points out, can be said of a wide range of problems involving self-defeatingly goal-based thinking. There is the tennis enthusiast who is so obsessed with winning that he would actually win more if he forgot the score and became absorbed in the details of the game,[18] the timid employee who will never have the nerve to ask for a needed raise if he deliberates about whether to do it, the self-conscious man who,

if he thinks about how he should act at a party he is attending, will fail to achieve the goal of such thinking, which is to act naturally and, ultimately, to enjoy the party. Finally, there is the tightrope walker who will not be able to concentrate if he consciously focuses on the fact that his life depends on his keeping his concentration. In each of these cases, Railton tells us, the individuals involved can improve the consequences of their action by avoiding "consequentialist deliberation." This can be done by developing personal traits, "habits of thought," which tend to forestall such deliberation.[19] Because of their manifest importance in enabling us to live as we should, such traits would naturally be regarded as virtues.

This argument brings to the surface two important threads in the tangle of issues I am treating here, threads I want to comment on very briefly before going on to the question of the cogency of Railton's argument. First, one moral that can be drawn from examples like the case of the tightrope walker and the others just cited is that deliberation and conscious reflection are not the same thing as rationality, even when they contain only factually accurate thoughts and are carried out without violating the formal constraints of logic. There are times when conscious reflection, just because it is conscious reflection, would be profoundly irrational.[20]

The other thread that deserves some immediate comment has to do with the nature of Railton's ultimate concerns. He is not defending egoistic hedonism against attack because he believes it is true. His interest is based on the fact that his own doctrine, what is usually called consequentialism, has been subjected to the same attack, and he believes both can be given the same defense. Fundamentally, the defense he offers for egoistic hedonism is the one he also offers for consequentialism. The fact that an intelligent person could find such a strategy plausible rather obviously suggests a further fact, which I believe is both true and important: namely, that consequentialism is indeed closely related to egoism. This, however, is only true of a certain sort of egoism.

Consequentialism decides the rightness or wrongness of actions based on their total causal outcome, their effects on *everyone* who is affected by them. The relevant sort of egoism decides the rightness or wrongness of acts based on their effects on the agent alone. Obviously, these two ideas have something in common: both are ethical theories which decide the rightness of acts, and both do so based entirely on the results that these acts produce. Since both of these views appeal only to consequences, they probably should both be treated as varieties of "consequentialism": one might be called "collective consequentialism," and the other could be called "individual consequentialism." It is worth bearing in mind the possibility that the problem Railton poses and tries to solve for egoistic hedonism is indeed a problem for consequentialism in general, including all consequentialist varieties of egoism, as well as his favored collective variety of the doctrine. If his solution is not a satisfactory one, then this doctrine may be flawed in all its varieties.

I say this is worth bearing in mind because I think that, in fact, the proposed solution is not a satisfactory one. The reason for this has to do with the nature of the traits that are to solve the problem faced by the tennis player, the tightrope walker, and the others who experience the temptation to become irrationally reflective and deliberative.

Those traits are, as Railton says, "habits of thought." It is important to ask exactly what this means. Habits are traits on the basis of which individuals act. The fact that an act is done from habit has no necessary connection with the thoughts, beliefs, or values of the person who does it. It is in this sense that habits might be said to be mindless. Suppose that I develop a habit of abstaining from fatty foods because I value health. Later, I change my way of thinking and no longer value health, but from habit I still refrain (for a while) from eating those foods. In both cases the actions involved (which happen to be abstentions) are habitual and are done from the *same* habit. The relation between habit and thought is loose. This does not mean that there is tension or incompatibility between habit and thought, any more than there is any tension between an inert hammer and the skillful deliberation of the carpenter. It means that, to the extent that it is habitual, the act does not necessarily proceed from any thought or any valuation.

It is partly for this reason that such habits are not traits of character. If I develop a habit of not thinking about my score while playing a game, this might be a result of wisdom. It might also be a cowardly evasion, in which I conceal from myself the fact that my real goals and interests are of a sort that I despise. Wisdom and cowardice are traits of character, while the habit of thinking or not thinking of something is not. This is, in part, because conduct that is wise or cowardly necessarily arises from what one thinks or values, while habitual behaviors, including habitual thoughts, do not.[21]

In spite of their mindlessness, or perhaps because if it, these habits of thought serve to advance the purposes set by our thoughts and evaluations. This can be so, for instance, when conscious thinking would take more time than we should spend on it, or when its results would be so inaccurate that a very rough but readily available approximation to the right answer would actually serve better. Things that do not have the nature of thought can serve as a substitute for thought. These particular substitutes can mimic, approximately, the results that conscious thought could be expected to produce if it could only work in some ideally rapid, logical, and well-informed manner.

There are times when such thought-substitutes are desirable, and the particular way in which they are desirable can help to explain why they are feasible as well. To see why such an explanation is necessary, consider the state of mind of the tightrope walker who finds that he must develop a habit of avoiding certain states of consciousness: he must not look down; he must not think about what it would feel like to lose his balance; he must not visualize the ugly results of landing on the ground beneath him. Usually, avoiding thought in a situation where there are important problems to solve is not only undesirable but, for the sort of person who is good at solving problems, difficult to do. Why, then, is the performer able to do so in this case?

Part of the answer, no doubt, lies in the fact that here one is not avoiding thought in general, but only certain particular thoughts. These particular thoughts, moreover, are, from the agent's point of view, eminently worthy of being avoided. Admittedly, the information that the tightrope walker can represent to himself by imagining his mangled body lying far beneath him might be accurate, but this is not a situation in which the collection of accurate data is per se valuable. His only concern at the moment is what he should do, and only the data that can inform him on that point have any legitimate interest. The data that he fails to collect by not looking down have no implications that go beyond what he already knows – indeed, beyond what he is already doing. The fact that he would become a bloody mess if he were to fall is all the more reason why he should focus his consciousness on the rope and on his destination at the other end. If he refrains from thinking about this fact, the only thing he misses that is connected with his present concerns is the emotional power the fact has to confuse and disorient him.

It would be easy, though tedious, to show that similar things can be said about the tennis enthusiast, the self-conscious man, and the timid employee. The general idea that applies to all of them is this: When we deliberate, we think about which particular act is the right one to do. There are various thoughts which, if we experience them, can interfere with identifying and doing the right thing. Under such circumstances, developing a certain habit of thought, in which such thoughts are avoided, can help to achieve the end of deliberation. Developing such a habit is possible, in part, because the individual literally *has no reason* to think these thoughts. In such situations, though habit does not have the nature of a mental process, it serves, so to speak, as a mind-mimic.

Railton's argument fails because the problem faced by the hedonist, and by consequentialists in general, whether individual or collective, is fundamentally different from situations of this kind. In particular, the problem lacks the characteristic that, as we have just seen, allows habits of thought to be a feasible solution. To see why, we must look a little closer at what this problem actually amounts to.

First, it has to be admitted that the problem involved in this sort of case is in one way the same as that faced by the tightrope walker and the others: in both cases, the problem is how to avoid having certain thoughts. Consider, however, concrete instances of the thought to be avoided in the case of the hedonist. A plausible example of the sort of thought that would give me trouble if I were an egoistic hedonist would be the realization that, by stealing the contents of my friend's wallet, I can expect to be better off on balance than I am now. Insofar as the consequences of individual acts can be calculated, this seems to be the sort of thought that can be supported by the preponderance of evidence. Further, it seems to be a plausible thought, not only from the point of view of an egoistic hedonist, but from that of any sort of consequentialist egoism.

It is easy to find examples of thoughts that would have the same sort of plausibility for the collective consequentialist and would create the same sort of trouble. Consider, for instance, the following facts. I spend some of my income on making my son's diet nutritious, varied, and interesting to him. This is not needed to keep him alive; it only serves to improve the quality of his life. If I were to give this money to the right charities, I could probably save the life of some child in the Third World. Resources at my disposal that merely bring goods like improved health to my son might very likely mean the difference between life and death to a stranger on the other side of the earth.

There is one good reason for avoiding the thoughts involved in these two cases that applies equally to both of them. At the moment when I see increasing my property as a good enough reason to take my friend's wallet, I view my friend as having a definite and very limited sort of value. Similarly, at the moment when I decide to divert resources away from my son simply because it would benefit the larger group of which he is a mere part, I am viewing his value as limited in exactly the same way. In both cases, the other person is seen as an entity whose interests can conflict with that of some other entity, and that conflict is seen as, in itself, a good enough reason to sacrifice the interests of the person.

Obviously, it would be very bad if one's attitude toward other people amounted simply to this. In particular, it would be regarded as bad within the points of view of both individual and collective consequentialism. As far as the individual standard is concerned, this willingness instantly to sacrifice everyone for the sake of some advantage to oneself is the source of the problems I cited earlier, involving loss of trust and respect from others and resulting in damage to one's own well-being. It also harms one's interest in a more immediate and possibly more devastating way. Anyone who, supposing it is possible, has this attitude toward others is obviously incapable of forming close personal attachments to other people, the sorts of attachments that are involved in love and friendship. Such attachments seem to be absolutely essential components of human well-being.

From the point of view of individual consequentialism, this fact is very important. It is also important, and equally so, from the point of view of collective consequentialism. If everyone used consequentialist ideas in the daily course of deliberation, everyone would be incapable of close personal attachments to others. But this would mean that no one would be living a good life, which runs directly against the standard that defines this point of view.

From the point of view of consequentialism, whether individual or collective, it is crucial that this same point of view be kept out of the perspective of deliberation, in which human beings actually choose their conduct. One problem faced by the consequentialist, the one we are now considering, is how to do this. We can now see why habits of thought are not a feasible solution to it: we have reason to think that a genuine consequentialist – someone who consistently believes consequentialism – will likely not be able to develop effective habits of suppressing the relevant thoughts.

The problem of the consequentialist differs from the sort of problem for which habits of thought are clearly a workable solution in at least two relevant ways. First, the troublesome thoughts in the case of the tightrope walker (and related cases) are simply a miscellaneous collection of facts united only by an emotional connection with the issue faced by the deliberator. In the consequentialist cases, the thoughts really are about the issue at hand: the problem of which course of action is the right one to follow. This, of course, is exactly what deliberation is about. This immediately creates a problem, for people whose habits of mind are those of a rational human being, of how to motivate oneself to screen these thoughts out of one's consciousness. Such people would view the possibility of developing such a habit with deep suspicion, partly because they would need assurance that such habits would not also suppress thoughts that they really should be having.

Naturally, if we know that these habits only suppress certain thoughts, and if we know that if they have any bearing on the issue at all, they have the same implications that the preponderance of one's unsuppressed thoughts have, then we have the assurance we need. As I have pointed out, in cases like that of the tightrope walker, this is just what we do have. In the consequentialist cases, however, this assurance is starkly absent, and this is the second way in which such cases differ from the others. In fact, the thoughts to be avoided would imply that the action supported by one's unsuppressed thoughts would be *wrong*. According to individual consequentialism, failure to steal my friend's wallet, under the circumstances we have imagined, would be the wrong thing to do. The same thing is true, according to collective consequentialism, of failure to deprive one's child of resources that could bring greater benefits to the children of strangers in other countries.

It is crucial, from the point of view of consequentialism, to keep such thoughts out of one's deliberative thinking. One thing that makes this particularly difficult to do is the fact that, to put it bluntly, such thoughts *should not* be systematically suppressed. After all, according to any conceivable ethical standard, there really are times when we ought to prefer our interests to those of our friends, and there really are times when we ought to prefer the interests of stricken and desperate strangers over the desires of our children. However, for consequentialists, thinking about the consequences of one's conduct in such contexts is not a safe enterprise. For non-consequentialists, such considerations are a normal and inevitable part of deliberation. For consequentialists, ironically, they are not: such thoughts threaten to engulf their deliberative thoughts and poison their relations with others and with themselves.

The problem is a particularly nasty one because of the nature of the obstacles that consequentialists, whether individual or collective, must try to overcome. Among the things they would have working against them are their desire to consider everything that is relevant to issues about which they are thinking, and their eagerness to identify the things that, by their standards, are the right things to do. I think this means that their adversaries would include both their rationality and their moral integrity. These are not the sort of obstacles we ought to be contending with.

VI.   The Possibility of Flourishing-Based Egoism

I think it is clear from what I have already said that flourishing-based egoism is not doomed to face these problems. The flourishing-based explanation of self-interest makes it possible for me to say that my friend's good is partly constitutive of my own good. If I do take this position, there is no prima facie reason to think that I will advance my interests by stealing his wallet, even if he never suspects me and, in purely consequentialist terms, I "get away with it." If my relationship with my friend is, to use Rand's terminology, "one of my highest values," then by betraying his trust and victimizing him I would be damaging my own life just as I am damaging his.

This said, however, I must deal with the remaining one of the potential attacks on my line of reasoning as set out at the beginning of Section V: the one that I can expect to be launched by people who find the notion of flourishing-based egoism, in one way or another, implausible. Here I face a somewhat awkward problem. The particular aspect of this sort of egoism that I have chosen to focus on and defend, the aspect that is relevant to the point I wish to make, is its potential for being developed in non-consequentialist ways. The problem is that, as far as I know, this aspect of this sort of theory has never been clearly and unambiguously identified and attacked. I will have to guess what sorts of criticisms might be made against it.

The apparent fact that this sort of view has not been criticized suggests that the most likely doubts that people might have about it would concern whether there really is such a thing as nonconsequentialist egoism. That is, one might doubt that the doctrine can be fully formulated without collapsing either into consequentialist egoism or into some nonegoist doctrine. The following would be one way of setting out these doubts: One's interests, one might say, consist in achieving what is of value or, in more antique language, possessing the good. But not just any value or good will do. It is not in my interest to have what is good for, or of value to, someone else but is not good for or of value to me. It must be good for me, of value to me. If something is good for me, it must have some effect that falls on me rather than someone else, an effect that is in some way favorable to me. Now, if self-interest is the standard of ethical merit, that would have to mean, in one way or another, that actions are evaluated on the basis of how much good they produce for the agent, and this would mean that actions are evaluated on the basis of the effects that they have on the agent. But this, of course, is consequentialist egoism. The only way egoism can avoid being consequentialist is by avoiding egoism, probably by opting for an impersonal, non-agent-relative notion of the good.

What should immediately arouse suspicion against this argument is the fact that the conception of self-interest that it uses carries the implication – in fact, this is virtually the point of it as employed here – that actions can never have value in themselves for the agent who performs them. Presumably, insofar as an act has value in itself, it is not good for any one person as distinguished from everyone else. This is not plausible on the face of it. People treat many of the things that they do with friends and lovers as good in themselves and, precisely as such, as good for them. There is no obvious reason why they should not do so. Further, most people live their lives as ends in themselves, and not as processes that only have value because they serve some end other than themselves. Since a life is made up of actions – one's life is simply everything one does – this would seem to mean that many actions, and probably many kinds of actions, are being treated as good for the individuals who do them, *and* as good in themselves. The people who would raise the objection I am considering here would have to say what is wrong with this – and it is not obvious what their explanation could be.

No doubt such people would also claim that nonconsequentialist egoists also have something *they* need to explain. One might well ask precisely how the good of others can become good for oneself in a nonconsequentialist way. This seems a very reasonable question. Consider the image that is most naturally formed when we try to imagine how it is that human beings are actually related to each other. I am here and my friend is over there. Between us, there is empty space through which a slight draft is blowing. Nonetheless, there are many sorts of relations that hold between us. Inclusion is obviously not one of them, however; I am not included in him, and he is not part of me. How then can his good be included in mine, as a part of it?

There is no way I can present a full answer to this interesting question here, but I think it will suffice if I suggest a way in which it *can* be answered.[22] What I would like to suggest is this. My friend's good is not a characteristic of my friend as an inert object, but as a living being. More precisely, it is characteristic of his life, of the way he lives and functions. This, of course, is simply a way of putting the matter in flourishing-based terms. But events in my friend's life can also be, and often are, events in my life as well. This is partly because many of our actions are actually shared projects, or things that we both do. The dinner we shared the other day in a Vietnamese restaurant, the book we are writing together, the long conversation we had with his former classmates from Germany – these are all things we *both* did. Thus, although my friend's body does not overlap my body, his life does overlap my life. Beyond that, many of the other events in my friend's life, the ones in which I do not share as fellow-agent, are things of which I am conscious, and my well-being is raised or lowered by this consciousness. For these reasons, good things in my friend's life will be goods in my life as well.[23]

There is at least one more thing, however, that critics of nonconsequentialist egoism

would probably say its proponents would need to explain. Whatever the faults of consequentialism might be, these critics might point out, at least it has an explanation of how a course of action can be good for or of value to me and not to someone else. Supposing that this explanation is not adequate, what is it that *does* make the things we do good for, of value to, or in the interests of one person rather than another?

This, of course, is a reasonable question and must be answered by any theory that claims to be egoistic. All I am prepared to do here is to make a few comments about how one sort of answer can begin. We can find an interesting clue to an answer in a comment that Rand makes immediately after she presents the definition of sacrifice I quoted in Section III above:

> The rational principle of conduct is the exact opposite [of sacrifice]: always act in accordance with the hierarchy of your values, and never sacrifice a greater value to a lesser one. This . . . requires that one possess a defined hierarchy of *rational* values (values chosen and validated by a rational standard). Without such a hierarchy, neither rational conduct nor considered value judgments nor moral choices are possible.[24]

Presumably, the exact opposite of sacrifice would be doing what is in one's own interest. The argument involved here seems to be this. The reason it would be a sacrifice on my part to save the lives of ten women I do not know while letting my own wife die is that it would involve preferring a lesser value to a greater one. In that case, the reason a particular act is an instance of acting in my own interest must be that it would involve preferring a greater value to a lesser one. Of course, it is possible for people to have perverse or foolish values or to rank their values in perverse or foolish ways, so not just any values will count. There must be a way to limit which ones count. The way that Rand uses is the same as the one employed by the Stoics: the values and their ranking must be rational.[25] Given that assumption, a course of action will be in your interest – and thus of value to you or good for you – if it meets two conditions: first, that it is in accordance with your values, and, second, that your values and their hierarchical order are rational.

Of course, this way of answering our question is no doubt apt to be controversial, in no small part because some people would disagree with the conception of reason it employs. Given my rather limited objectives, I will confine my comments to two other aspects of this answer, ones that should be considerably less controversial.

First, the explanation of self-interest Rand has given is plainly a flourishing-based one. Describing a settled hierarchy of values is equivalent to describing a way of life: the sort of life that is lived on the basis of that hierarchy. She has explained what self-interest is, not by tracing the consequences of the actions involved, but by asserting that self-interest must fit into a way of life, one that is good or the best, and by offering an account of what it is that makes this life good or the best.[26]

Second, this way of explaining self-interest leads very naturally to an explanation of virtue or, more precisely, of why certain traits have the status of virtues. Many traits that are traditionally viewed as vices could be seen as errors which involve valuing something too much or too little. Cowardice is valuing safety too highly, for instance, and gluttony is valuing certain pleasures too highly. The contrary virtues, then, would seem to consist in placing the right value on the same goods, neither valuing them too much nor too little. This is precisely what having a rational hierarchy of values would mean. This, on the flourishing-based notion of self-interest we are now considering, can explain why they *are* virtues. They are essential to human well-being, not because they lead to it, in a consequentialist sense, but because they are constitutive of it. The order that these traits bring to our values is what well-being is, or an essential part of it.[27]

VII. Virtue and Self-Interest, Again

If we adopt the flourishing-based explanation of self-interest, ethical egoism loses some of the wildly counterintuitive appearance it is apt to present on first hearing. It is, in that case, not liable to the two rather obvious objections I have discussed, which might otherwise provoke reasonable people to reject it. Of course, one might still reject it on other grounds, and nothing I have said here is meant to affect that possibility.

Nonetheless, I hope that what we have seen here might prove to be useful even to people who have no interest in this particular ethical doctrine. After all, the features of the consequentialist notion of self-interest that give the egoistic doctrines that make use of it their strange and repugnant appearance are problematic for nonegoists as well. The consequences that we have seen following from the idea that self-interest is simply a matter of the causal outcome of one's acts make the notion unattractive for any sort of ethical use at all. If this is what self-interest is, then pursuing it would seem to require a state of mind dominated by a calculating sort of attitude toward the future, and toward other people. In particular, the attitude toward other people that would seem to be required is manipulative and possibly dishonest. To try to explain the value of a virtue by connecting it with self-interest in this sense is to degrade it somewhat, to make it seem less lofty than other virtues. It is very natural to try to segregate an idea like self-interest from all issues having to do with ethical merit. That, of course, is just what the post-Hobbesian tradition did.

On the other hand, if we accept an appropriate flourishing-based explanation of self-interest, it becomes equally natural to see self-interest and considerations of merit as far more closely related.[28] This is true even if one balks at making the relation as close as the ethical egoist does. In particular, the ancient, flourishing-based conceptions of self-interest have an especially close connection with the ancient and long-ignored notion of virtue. At the very least, such notions of self-interest can explain why certain traits are virtues: they are traits that maintain a properly hierarchical relationship among the values that the agent holds. This is surely an important fact even if one holds that self-interest is not the *full* explanation of why these traits are virtues, and even if one thinks that there are other virtues to which this explanation does not apply.[29]

Egoists are distinguished by the fact that they hold that self-interest in some sense is *the* explanation for one feature or another of the ethical realm, and perhaps of the entire realm itself. In a way, they are monists. Those who resist monistic views can at least be open to the possibility that self-interest is *an* explanation.

To the extent that one accepts the flourishing-based explanation of self-interest, this possibility ought to be an attractive one. Then another possibility will arise, as eminently worthy of exploration: that at least *part* of the point of ethics is that, as Abelard was trying to tell us, it is good for us.

Notes

1. Peter Abelard, "Dialogue 2: Between the Philosopher and the Christian," in Abelard, *Ethical Writings*, trans. Paul Vincent Spade (Indianapolis: Hackett, 1995), pp. 93–94.
2. "Common sense," in this context, means: the views that people in a given culture hold before theoretical considerations convince them to change those views.
3. Michael Slote, *From Morality to Virtue* (New York: Oxford University Press, 1992), p. 91.
4. *Ibid.*, p. 92. The objection to egoism that Slote raises in this passage is actually about egoism regarded as a theory of what makes actions admirable, and not (at least not explicitly) about egoism as a theory of reasons for performing actions. His claim is that egoism clashes with "the ground floor admiration for acts and traits that help others" which "most of us are disposed – and happy to be disposed – to feel." The objection I have just presented is stated as an objection to egoism as a theory of reasons for acting and thus constitutes a different, though related, problem. It seems likely that a satisfactory response to the objection I am considering would contain clues pointing to a response to the problem Slote raises, but an adequate discussion of the latter problem would require more attention than I will be able to devote to it in this essay.
5. This theme runs throughout much of Derek Parfit's *Reasons and Persons* (New York: Oxford University Press, 1984), ch. 1, esp. sections 1–8.
6. See the preceding footnote.
7. Ayn Rand, "The Objectivist Ethics," in Rand, *The Virtue of Selfishness* (New York: Signet, 1964), p. 23.
8. *Ibid.*, p. 31.
9. *Ibid.*, p. 27.
10. Ayn Rand, *Atlas Shrugged* (New York: Random House, 1957), p. 1018.
11. Rand, "The Objectivist Ethics," p. 25.
12. Hugh Morrison, *Louis Sullivan: Prophet of Modern Architecture* (New York: Norton, 1935), pp. 180–81.
13. Ayn Rand, *The Fountainhead* (New York: Bobbs-Merrill, 1943), p. 206.
14. Rand, "The Ethics of Emergencies," in *The Virtue of Selfishness* (*supra* note 7), p. 44.
15. *Ibid.*, pp. 44–5. Rand has John Galt put the same idea this way: "If you exchange a penny for a dollar, it is *not* a sacrifice; if you exchange a dollar for a penny, it is. If you achieve the career you wanted, after years of struggle, it is *not* a sacrifice; if you then renounce it for the sake of a rival, it *is*. If you own a bottle of milk and give it to your starving child, it is *not* a sacrifice; if you give it to your neighbor's child and let your own die, it *is*" (Rand, *Atlas Shrugged*, p. 1028).
16. My main source is Peter Railton, "Alienation, Consequentialism, and the Demands of Morality," *Philosophy and Public Affairs*, vol. 13, no. 2 (Spring 1984), pp. 134–71. See also his "How Thinking about Character and Utilitarianism Might Lead to Rethinking the Character of Utilitarianism," *Midwest Studies in Philosophy*, vol. 13 (1988), pp. 398–416.
17. Railton, "Alienation, Consequentialism, and the Demands of Morality," pp. 153–4.
18. *Ibid.*, p. 144.
19. *Ibid.*, p. 154.
20. For discussions of the ways in which human reason is able to avoid pointless or counterproductive thinking, see Michael Polanyi, *The Tacit Dimension* (New York: Double-day, 1966), ch. 1; and Polanyi, *Knowing and Being* (Chicago: University of Chicago Press, 1969), Part III.
21. For further discussion of the difference between habits and traits of character, see my *Character and Culture* (Lanham, MD: Rowman and Littlefield, 1997), ch. 1.
22. I can also refer the reader to Aristotle's account of the value of character friendship, which is both egoistic and nonconsequentialist; see Aristotle, *Nicomachean Ethics*, Book IX, chs. 4 and 9. Another example would be Rand's account of love relationships, which is actually

rather similar to Aristotle's account of character friendship, and which can be found dramatized and discussed in various passages in *Atlas Shrugged*, but especially in the character Francisco d'Anconia's speech about the meaning of sex (Rand, *Atlas Shrugged*, pp. 489–95).

23. The fundamental idea that underlies what I have just said is a point made in a number of ways by Aristotle: my friend and the good of my friend can be valuable in themselves and for me, if only because my being conscious of them is valuable in the same ways. An episode from Ayn Rand's life illustrates this idea vividly. In a letter to John Hospers, she explained why a favorable letter from him about a book she had just published was more important to her than a blisteringly unfavorable review in *Newsweek*: "It is not an issue of how many people will see your letter vs. how many people will see the review. Your letter proves the existence of a man of intelligence and integrity; the review proves the existence of a fool and a knave. The first is important, the second is not. (Or, to use *your* terms: the existence of the former is an 'intrinsic' good – while the existence of the latter is not even an instrumental evil.)" Michael S. Berliner, ed., *The Letters of Ayn Rand* (New York: Dutton, 1995), p. 562. It would not be so plausible to say that, if Hospers had written the same letter to someone else and Rand had never learned of it, the letter and its author would still be "intrinsic" goods (i.e., good in themselves) for her. But she does know about them, and that in itself seems to suffice to give them that status. This suggests a solution to a problem that I have so far not touched on directly: What about the good of strangers? To avoid wildly counterintuitive results, it seems that the nonconsequentialist egoist would need to show how the good of strangers, and not just the good of my friends, can to some degree be included in my own good as a part. The solution I have in mind would be based on the notion that strangers I do not know about pose no ethical problems, but once I become aware of them, to some extent my consciousness of their weal or woe adds to mine.

24. Rand, "The Ethics of Emergencies," p. 44.

25. See Epictetus, *The Discourses*, 1.2 and 1.4.

26. This may be the place to briefly raise an exegetical issue. Tara Smith and Irfan Khawaja have pointed out to me that Rand, in one of her later writings, uses strongly consequentialist language which appears to conflict with the nonconsequentialist interpretation of her position that I am presenting here. See Rand, "Causality versus Duty," in her *Philosophy: Who Needs It?* (New York: Signet, 1982). In the main, this essay is a critique of Kantian deontology on the grounds that thinking in terms of consequences and, more generally, causal thinking, is absolutely essential to rationality. I think the first thing to say about this is that this argument is, so far, perfectly consistent with the view I am attributing to Rand. Nonconsequentialist egoism does not claim (as deontology does) that thinking in terms of consequences does not belong in the ethical realm; it only denies the consequentialist claim that nothing else *does* belong there. It can also claim (what seems clearly true) that thinking in terms of consequences (e.g., Will this food nourish me or poison me?) is an absolutely indispensable part of discerning what one's interests are. It only denies that the relationship between them is identity. There is, however, one passage in which Rand seems to go beyond this and claim that thinking in terms of consequences *is* identical to rationality in ethics ("Causality versus Duty," p. 99, third full paragraph). I would argue that here she is falling into the understandable temptation of overstating the difference between herself and Kant, and that the argument she is giving in that passage can be stated in overtly nonconsequentialist terms.

27. If we introduce the assumption that the function of virtue is precisely to maintain this rational hierarchy of values, then virtue and self-interest would appear to be very nearly the same thing. The idea that something like this is indeed the case is typical of philosophers in the tradition of flourishing-based egoism, including Plato, Aristotle, and the Stoics. For an insightful discussion of the views of the Stoics on this issue, see Michael Slote's comments on Stoicism and Epicureanism as opposed forms of ethical egoism in *From Morality to Virtue*, pp. 201–10. The Epicureans, of course, were proponents of consequentialist egoism.

28. I cannot resist making the following comment, which will have to wait for fuller development. One could say that what flourishing traditionally did for the concept of self-interest is precisely analogous to what virtue traditionally did for the concept of ethical merit. In both cases, there is a certain shift from the act to the agent and from the episodic to the settled and the structural. When we evaluate what a person does from a virtue-based point of view, we do

so on the basis of what an act indicates about the person who performed it, and the things that it indicates are relatively enduring aspects of the person. In that case, the value of the act is explained by the sort of life of which it is a part. This is exactly what happens when we understand self-interest by way of the notion of flourishing.

29. I should mention that, according to my own view of these matters, there are a number of radically different sorts of virtues, and only one of them has the hierarchy-preserving function that is essential to the argument I have just given. See my *Character and Culture*, chs. 1–4. The virtues that do have this function are the subject of ch. 2. It would take us too far afield to discuss how self-interest and egoism are related to the other sorts of virtues and, to tell the truth, my views on this subject are presently amorphous and changing.

CHAPTER 21

Ethical Egoism

JAMES RACHELS

Is There a Duty to Contribute for Famine Relief ?

Each year millions of people die of malnutrition and related health problems. A common pattern among children in poor countries is death from dehydration caused by diarrhea brought on by malnutrition. James Grant, executive director of the United Nations Children's Fund (UNICEF), estimates that about 15,000 children die in this way *every day*. That comes to 5,475,000 children annually. Even if his estimate is too high, the number that die is staggering.

For those of us in the affluent countries, this poses an acute moral problem. We spend money on ourselves, not only for the necessities of life but for innumerable luxuries – for fine automobiles, fancy clothes, stereos, sports, movies, and so on. In our country, even people with modest incomes enjoy such things. The problem is that we *could* forgo our luxuries and give the money for famine relief instead. The fact that we don't suggests that we regard our luxuries as more important than feeding the hungry.

James Rachels, "Ethical Egoism," from *The Elements of Moral Philosophy*, Fourth Edition. New York: Random House, 1986. Reproduced with permission of The McGraw-Hill Companies.

Why do we allow people to starve to death when we could save them? Very few of us actually believe our luxuries are that important. Most of us, if asked the question directly, would probably be a bit embarrassed, and we would say that we probably should do more for famine relief. The explanation of why we do not is, at least in part, that we hardly ever think of the problem. Living our own comfortable lives, we are effectively insulated from it. The starving people are dying at some distance from us; we do not see them, and we can avoid even thinking of them. When we do think of them, it is only abstractly, as bloodless statistics. Unfortunately for the starving, statistics do not have much power to motivate action.

But leaving aside the question of *why* we behave as we do, what is our *duty*? What *should* we do? We might think of this as the "common-sense" view of the matter: morality requires that we balance our own interests against the interests of others. It is understandable, of course, that we look out for our own interests, and no one can be faulted for attending to his own basic needs. But at the same time the needs of others are also important, and when we can help others – especially at little cost to ourselves – we should do so. Suppose you are thinking of spending ten dollars on a trip to the movies, when you are reminded that ten dollars could buy food for a starving child. Thus you could do a great service for the child at little cost to yourself. Common-sense morality would say, then, that you should give the money for famine relief rather than spending it on the movies.

This way of thinking involves a general assumption about our moral duties: it is assumed that we have moral duties *to other people* – and not merely duties that we create, such as by making a promise or incurring a debt. We have "natural" duties to others *simply because they are people who could be helped or harmed by our actions*. If a certain action would benefit (or harm) other people, then that is a reason why we should (or should not) do that action. The common-sense assumption is that other people's interests *count*, for their own sakes, from a moral point of view.

But one person's common sense is another person's naive platitude. Some thinkers have maintained that, in fact, we have no "natural" duties to other people. *Ethical Egoism* is the idea that each person ought to pursue his or her own self-interest exclusively. It is different from Psychological Egoism, which is a theory of human nature concerned with how people *do* behave – Psychological Egoism says that people do in fact always pursue their own interests. Ethical Egoism, by contrast, is a normative theory – that is, a theory about how we *ought* to behave. Regardless of how we do behave, Ethical Egoism says we have no moral duty except to do what is best for ourselves.

It is a challenging theory. It contradicts some of our deepest moral beliefs – beliefs held by most of us, at any rate – but it is not easy to refute. We will examine the most important arguments for and against it. If it turns out to be true, then of course that is immensely important. But even if it turns out to be false, there is still much to be learned from examining it – we may, for example, gain some insight into the reasons why we *do* have obligations to other people.

But before looking at the arguments, we should be a little clearer about exactly what this theory says and what it does not say. In the first place, Ethical Egoism does not say that one should promote one's own interests *as well as* the interests of others. That would be an ordinary, unexceptional view. Ethical Egoism

is the radical view that one's *only* duty is to promote one's own interests. According to Ethical Egoism, there is only one ultimate principle of conduct, the principle of self-interest, and this principle sums up *all* of one's natural duties and obligations.

However, Ethical Egoism does not say that you should *avoid* actions that help others, either. It may very well be that in many instances your interests coincide with the interests of others, so that in helping yourself you will be aiding others willynilly. Or it may happen that aiding others is an effective *means* for creating some benefit for yourself. Ethical Egoism does not forbid such actions; in fact, it may demand them. The theory insists only that in such cases the benefit to others is not what makes the act right. What makes the act right is, rather, the fact that it is to one's own advantage.

Finally, Ethical Egoism does not imply that in pursuing one's interests one ought always to do what one wants to do, or what gives one the most pleasure in the short run. Someone may want to do something that is not good for himself or that will eventually cause himself more grief than pleasure – he may want to drink a lot or smoke cigarettes or take drugs or waste his best years at the race track. Ethical Egoism would frown on all this, regardless of the momentary pleasure it affords. It says that a person ought to do what *really is* to his or her own best advantage, *over the long run*. It endorses selfishness, but it doesn't endorses foolishness.

Three Arguments in Favor of Ethical Egoism

What reasons can be advanced to support this doctrine? Why should anyone think it is true? Unfortunately, the theory is asserted more often than it is argued for. Many of its supporters apparently think its truth is self-evident, so that arguments are not needed. When it *is* argued for, three lines of reasoning are most commonly used.

1. The first argument has several variations, each suggesting the same general point:

a.   Each of us is intimately familiar with our own individual wants and needs.

Moreover, each of us is uniquely placed to pursue those wants and needs effectively. At the same time, we know the desires and needs of other people only imperfectly, and we are not well situated to pursue them. Therefore, it is reasonable to believe that if we set out to be "our brother's keeper," we would often bungle the job and end up doing more mischief than good.

b. At the same time, the policy of "looking out for others" is an offensive intrusion into other people's privacy; it is essentially a policy of minding other people's business.

c. Making other people the object of one's "charity" is degrading to them; it robs them of their individual dignity and self-respect. The offer of charity says, in effect, that they are not competent to care for themselves; and the statement is self-fulfilling – they cease to be self-reliant and become passively dependent on others. That is why the recipients of "charity" are so often resentful rather than appreciative.

What this adds up to is that the policy of "looking out for others" is self-defeating. If we want to promote the best interests of everyone alike, we should *not* adopt so-called altruistic policies of behavior. On the contrary, if each person looks after his or her *own* interests, it is more likely that everyone will be better off, in terms of both physical and emotional well-being. Thus Robert G. Olson says in his book *The Morality of Self-Interest* (1965), "The individual is most likely to contribute to social betterment by rationally pursuing his own best long-range interests." Or as Alexander Pope said more poetically,

Thus God and nature formed the general frame
And bade self-love and social be the same.

It is possible to quarrel with this argument on a number of grounds. Of course no one favors bungling, butting in, or depriving people of their self-respect. But is this really what we are doing when we feed hungry children? Is the starving child in Ethiopia really harmed when we "intrude" into "her business" by supplying food? It hardly seems likely. Yet we can set this point aside, for considered as an argument for

Ethical Egoism, this way of thinking has an even more serious defect.

The trouble is that it isn't really an argument *for Ethical Egoism* at all. The argument concludes that we should adopt certain policies of action; and on the surface they appear to be egoistic policies. However, the *reason* it is said we should adopt those policies is decidedly *un*egoistic. The reason is one that to an egoist shouldn't matter. It is said that we should adopt those policies because doing so will promote the "betterment of society" – but according to Ethical Egoism, that is something we should not be concerned about. Spelled out fully, with everything laid on the table, the argument says:

(1) We ought to do whatever will promote the best interests of everyone alike.
(2) The interests of everyone will best be promoted if each of us adopts the policy of pursuing our own interests exclusively.
(3) Therefore, each of us should adopt the policy of pursuing our own interests exclusively.

If we accept this reasoning, then we are not ethical egoists at all. Even though we might end up *behaving* like egoists, our ultimate principle is one of beneficence – we are doing what we think will help everyone, not merely what we think will benefit ourselves. Rather than being egoists, we turn out to be altruists with a peculiar view of what in fact promotes the general welfare.

2. The second argument was put forward with some force by Ayn Rand, a writer little heeded by professional philosophers but who nevertheless was enormously popular on college campuses during the 1960s and 1970s. Ethical Egoism, in her view, is the only ethical philosophy that respects the integrity of the individual human life. She regarded the ethics of "altruism" as a totally destructive idea, both in society as a whole and in the lives of individuals taken in by it. Altruism, to her way of thinking, leads to a denial of the value of the individual. It says to a person: *your* life is merely something that may be sacrificed. "If a man accepts the ethics of altruism," she writes, "his first concern is not how to live his life, but

how to sacrifice it." Moreover, those who would *promote* this idea are beneath contempt – they are parasites who, rather than working to build and sustain their own lives, leech off those who do. Again, she writes:

> Parasites, moochers, looters, brutes and thugs can be of no value to a human being – nor can he gain any benefit from living in a society geared to *their* needs, demands and protections, a society that treats him as a sacrificial animal and penalizes him for his virtues in order to reward *them* for their vices, which means: a society based on the ethics of altruism.

By "sacrificing one's life" Rand does not necessarily mean anything so dramatic as dying. A person's life consists (in part) of projects undertaken and goods earned and created. To demand that a person abandon his projects or give up his goods is also a clear effort to "sacrifice his life." Furthermore, throughout her writings Rand also suggests that there is a *metaphysical* basis for egoistic ethics. Somehow, it is the only ethics that takes seriously the *reality* of the individual person. She bemoans "the enormity of the extent to which altruism erodes men's capacity to grasp . . . the value of an individual life; it reveals a mind from which the reality of a human being has been wiped out."

What, then, of the starving people? It might be argued, in response, that Ethical Egoism "reveals a mind from which the reality of a human being has been wiped out" – namely, the human being who is starving. Rand quotes with approval the evasive answer given by one of her followers: "Once, when Barbara Brandon was asked by a student: 'What will happen to the poor . . . ?' – she answered: 'If *you* want to help them, you will not be stopped.' " All these remarks are, I think, part of one continuous argument that can be summarized like this:

(1) A person has only one life to live. If we place any value on the individual – that is, if the individual has any moral worth – then we must agree that this life is of supreme importance. After all, it is all one has, and all one is.

(2) The ethics of altruism regards the life of the individual as something one must be ready to sacrifice for the good of others.

(3) Therefore, the ethics of altruism does not take seriously the value of the human individual.

(4) Ethical Egoism, which allows each person to view his or her own life as being of ultimate value, *does* take the human individual seriously – in fact, it is the only philosophy that does so.

(5) Thus, Ethical Egoism is the philosophy that ought to be accepted.

The problem with this argument, as you may already have noticed, is that it relies on picturing the alternatives in such an extreme way. "The ethics of altruism" is taken to be such an extreme philosophy that *nobody*, with the possible exception of certain monks, would find it congenial. As Ayn Rand presents it, altruism implies that one's own interests have *no* value, and that *any* demand by others calls for sacrificing them. If that is the alternative, then any other view, including Ethical Egoism, will look good by comparison. But this is hardly a fair picture of the choices. What we called the common-sense view stands somewhere between the two extremes. It says that one's own interests and the interests of others are both important and must be balanced against one another. Sometimes, when the balancing is done, it will turn out that one should act in the interests of others; other times, it will turn out that one should take care of oneself. So even if the Randian argument refutes the extreme "ethics of altruism," it does not follow that one must accept the other extreme of Ethical Egoism.

3. The third line of reasoning takes a somewhat different approach. Ethical Egoism is usually presented as a *revisionist* moral philosophy, that is, as a philosophy that says our common-sense moral views are mistaken and need to be changed. It is possible, however, to interpret Ethical Egoism in a much less radical way, as a theory that *accepts* common-sense morality and offers a surprising account of its basis.

The less radical interpretation goes as follows. In everyday life, we assume that we are obliged to obey certain rules. We must avoid doing harm to others, speak the truth, keep our promises, and so on. At first glance, these duties appear to be very different from one another. They appear to have little in common. Yet from a theoretical point of view, we may wonder whether there is not some hidden *unity* underlying the hodgepodge of separate duties. Perhaps there is some small number of fundamental principles that explain all the rest, just as in physics there are basic principles that bring together and explain diverse phenomena. From a theoretical point of view, the smaller the number of basic principles, the better. Best of all would be *one* fundamental principle, from which all the rest could be derived. Ethical Egoism, then, would be the theory that all our duties are ultimately derived from the one fundamental principle of self-interest.

Taken in this way, Ethical Egoism is not such a radical doctrine. It does not challenge commonsense morality; it only tries to explain and systematize it. And it does a surprisingly successful job. It can provide plausible explanations of the duties mentioned above, and more:

a. If we make a habit of doing things that are harmful to other people, people will not be reluctant to do things that will harm *us*. We will be shunned and despised; others will not have us as friends and will not do us favors when we need them. If our offenses against others are serious enough, we may even end up in jail. Thus it is to our own advantage to avoid harming others.

b. If we lie to other people, we will suffer all the ill effects of a bad reputation. People will distrust us and avoid doing business with us. We will often need for people to be honest with us, but we can hardly expect them to feel much of an obligation to be honest with us if they know we have not been honest with them. Thus it is to our own advantage to be truthful.

c. It is to our own advantage to be able to enter into mutually beneficial arrangements with other people. To benefit from those arrangements, we need to be able to rely on others to keep their parts of the bargains we make with them – we need to be able to rely on them to keep their promises to us. But we can hardly expect others to keep their promises to us if we are not willing to keep our promises to them. Therefore, from the point of view of self-interest, we should keep our promises.

Pursuing this line of reasoning, Thomas Hobbes suggested that the principle of Ethical Egoism leads to nothing less than the Golden Rule: we should "do unto others" *because* if we do, others will be more likely to "do unto us."

Does this argument succeed in establishing Ethical Egoism as a viable theory of morality? It is, in my opinion at least, the best try. But there are two serious objections to it. In the first place, the argument does not prove quite as much as it needs to prove. At best, it shows only that *as a general rule* it is to one's own advantage to avoid harming others. It does not show that this is *always* so. And it could not show that, for even though it may usually be to one's advantage to avoid harming others, sometimes it is not. Sometimes one might even *gain* from treating another person badly. In that case, the obligation not to harm the other person could *not* be derived from the principle of Ethical Egoism. Thus it appears that not all our moral obligations can be explained as derivable from self-interest.

But set that point aside. There is still a more fundamental question to be asked about the proposed theory. Suppose it is true that, say, contributing money for famine relief is somehow to one's own advantage. It does not follow that this is the only reason, or even the most basic reason, why doing so is a morally good thing. (For example, the most basic reason might be *in order to help the starving people*. The fact that doing so is also to one's own advantage might be only a secondary, less important, consideration.) A demonstration that one could *derive* this duty from self-interest does not prove that self-interest is the *only reason* one has this duty. Only if you accept an additional proposition – namely, the proposition that there is no reason for giving *other than* self-interest – will you find Ethical Egoism a plausible theory.

Three Arguments Against Ethical Egoism

Ethical Egoism has haunted twentieth-century moral philosophy. It has not been a popular doctrine; the most important philosophers have rejected it outright. But it has never been very far from their minds. Although no thinker of consequence has defended it, almost everyone has felt it necessary to explain why he was rejecting it – as though the very possibility that it might be correct was hanging in the air, threatening to smother their other ideas. As the merits of the various "refutations" have been debated, philosophers have returned to it again and again.

The following three arguments are typical of the refutations proposed by contemporary philosophers.

1. In his book *The Moral Point of View* (1958), Kurt Baier argues that Ethical Egoism cannot be correct because it cannot provide solutions for conflicts of interest. We need moral rules, he says, only because our interests sometimes come into conflict. (If they never conflicted, then there would be no problems to solve and hence no need for the kind of guidance that morality provides.) But Ethical Egoism does not help to resolve conflicts of interest; it only exacerbates them. Baier argues for this by introducing a fanciful example:

> Let B and K be candidates for the presidency of a certain country and let it be granted that it is in the interest of either to be elected, but that only one can succeed. It would then be in the interest of B but against the interest of K if B were elected, and vice versa, and therefore in the interest of B but against the interest of K if K were liquidated, and vice versa. But from this it would follow that B ought to liquidate K, that it is wrong for B not to do so, that B has not "done his duty" until he has liquidated K; and vice versa. Similarly K, knowing that his own liquidation is in the interest of B and therefore, anticipating B's attempts to secure it, ought to take steps to foil B's endeavors. It would be wrong for him not to do so. He would "not have done his duty" until he had made sure of stopping B. . . .
>
> This is obviously absurd. For morality is designed to apply in just such cases, namely,

those where interests conflict. But if the point of view of morality were that of self-interest, then there could never be moral solutions of conflicts of interest.

Does this argument prove that Ethical Egoism is unacceptable? It does, *if* the conception of morality to which it appeals is accepted. The argument assumes that an adequate morality must provide solutions for conflicts of interest in such a way that everyone concerned can live together harmoniously. The conflict between B and K, for example, should be resolved so that they would no longer be at odds with one another. (One would not then have a duty to do something that the other has a duty to prevent.) Ethical Egoism does not do that, and if you think an ethical theory should, then you will not find Ethical Egoism acceptable.

But a defender of Ethical Egoism might reply that *he* does not accept this conception of morality. For him, life is essentially a long series of conflicts in which each person is struggling to come out on top: and the principle he accepts – the principle of Ethical Egoism – simply urges each one to do his or her best to win. On his view, the moralist is not like a courtroom judge, who resolves disputes. Instead, he is like the Commissioner of Boxing, who urges each fighter to do his best. So the conflict between B and K will be "resolved" not by the application of an ethical theory but by one or the other of them winning the struggle. The egoist will not be embarrassed by this – on the contrary, he will think it no more than a realistic view of the nature of things.

2. Some philosophers, including Baier, have leveled an even more serious charge against Ethical Egoism. They have argued that it is a *logically inconsistent* doctrine – that is, they say it leads to logical contradictions. If this is true, then Ethical Egoism is indeed a mistaken theory, for no theory can be true if it is self-contradictory.

Consider B and K again. As Baier explains their predicament, it is in B's interest to kill K, and obviously it is in K's interest to prevent it. But, Baier says,

> if K prevents B from liquidating him, his act must be said to be both wrong and not

wrong – wrong because it is the prevention of what B ought to do, his duty, and wrong for B not to do it; not wrong because it is what K ought to do, his duty, and wrong for K not to do it. But one and the same act (logically) cannot be both morally wrong and not morally wrong.

Now, does *this* argument prove that Ethical Egoism is unacceptable? At first glance it seems persuasive. However, it is a complicated argument, so we need to set it out with each step individually identified. Then we will be in a better position to evaluate it. Spelled out fully, it looks like this:

(1)   Suppose it is each person's duty to do what is in his own best interests.
(2)   It is in B's best interest to liquidate K.
(3)   It is in K's best interest to prevent B from liquidating him.
(4)   Therefore B's duty is to liquidate K, and K's duty is to prevent B from doing it.
(5)   But it is wrong to prevent someone from doing his duty.
(6)   Therefore it is wrong for K to prevent B from liquidating him.
(7)   Therefore it is both wrong and not wrong for K to prevent B from liquidating him.
(8)   But no act can be both wrong and not wrong – that is a self-contradiction.
(9)   Therefore the assumption with which we started – that it is each person's duty to do what is in his own best interests – cannot be true.

When the argument is set out in this way, we can see its hidden flaw. The logical contradiction – that it is both wrong and not wrong for K to prevent B from liquidating him – does *not* follow simply from the principle of Ethical Egoism. It follows from that principle *and* the additional premise expressed in step (5) – namely, that "it is wrong to prevent someone from doing his duty." Thus we are not compelled by the logic of the argument to reject Ethical Egoism. Instead, we could simply reject this additional premise, and the contradiction would be avoided. That is surely what the ethical egoist would want to do, for the ethical egoist would never say, without qualification, that it is

always wrong to prevent someone from doing his duty. He would say, instead, that *whether one ought to prevent someone from doing his duty depends entirely on whether it would be to one's own advantage to do so.* Regardless of whether we think this is a correct view, it is, at the very least, a *consistent* view, and so this attempt to convict the egoist of self-contradiction fails.

3. Finally, we come to the argument that I think comes closest to an outright refutation of Ethical Egoism. It is also the most interesting of the arguments, because at the same time it provides the most insight into why the interests of other people *should* matter to a moral agent.

Before this argument is presented, we need to look briefly at a general point about moral values. So let us set Ethical Egoism aside for a moment and consider this related matter.

There is a whole family of moral views that have this in common: they all involve dividing people into groups and saying that the interests of some groups count for more than the interests of other groups. Racism is the most conspicuous example; it involves dividing people into groups according to race and assigning greater importance to the interests of one race than to others. The practical result is that members of the preferred race are to be *treated better* than the others. Anti-Semitism works the same way, and so can nationalism. People in the grip of such views will think, in effect: "*My* race counts for more," or "Those who believe in *my* religion count for more," or "*My* country counts for more," and so on.

Can such views be defended? Those who accept them are usually not much interested in argument – racists, for example, rarely try to offer rational grounds for their position. But suppose they did. What could they say?

There is a general principle that stands in the way of any such defense, namely: *We can justify treating people differently only if we can show that there is some factual difference between them that is relevant to justifying the difference in treatment.* For example, if one person is admitted to law school while another is rejected, this can be justified by pointing out that the first graduated from college with honors and scored well on the admissions test, while the second dropped out of college and never took the test. However, if *both* graduated with honors and did well on the entrance examination – in other words, if they are in all relevant respects equally well qualified – then it is merely arbitrary to admit one but not the other.

Can a racist point to any differences between, say, white people and black people that would justify treating them differently? In the past, racists have sometimes attempted to do this by picturing blacks as stupid, lacking in ambition, and the like. *If* this were true, then it might justify treating them differently, in at least some circumstances. (This is the deep purpose of racist stereotypes – to provide the "relevant differences" needed to justify differences in treatment.) But of course it is not true, and in fact there are no such general differences between the races. Thus racism is an *arbitrary* doctrine, in that it advocates treating some people differently even though there are no differences between them to justify it.

Ethical Egoism is a moral theory of the same type. It advocates that each of us divide the world into two categories of people – ourselves and all the rest – and that we regard the interests of those in the first group as more important than the interests of those in the second group. But each of us can ask, what is the difference between myself and others that justifies placing myself in this special category? Am I more intelligent? Do I enjoy my life more? Are my accomplishments greater? Do I have needs or abilities that are so different from the needs or abilities of others? *What is it that makes me so special?* Failing an answer, it turns out that Ethical Egoism is an arbitrary doctrine, in the same way that racism is arbitrary.

The argument, then, is this:

(1) Any moral doctrine that assigns greater importance to the interests of one group than to those of another is unacceptably arbitrary unless there is some difference between the members of the groups that justifies treating them differently.

(2) Ethical Egoism would have each person assign greater importance to his or her own interests than to the interests of others. *But there is no general difference between oneself and others, to which each person can appeal, that justifies this difference in treatment.*

(3) Therefore, Ethical Egoism is unacceptably arbitrary.

And this, in addition to arguing against Ethical Egoism, also sheds some light on the question of why we should care about others.

We should care about the interests of other people *for the very same reason we care about our own interests;* for their needs and desires are comparable to our own. Consider, one last time, the starving people we could feed by giving up some of our luxuries. Why should we care about them? We care about ourselves, of course – if *we* were starving, we would go to almost any lengths to get food. But what is the difference between us and them? Does hunger affect them any less? Are they somehow less deserving than we? If we can find no relevant difference between us and them, then we must admit that if *our* needs should be met, so should *theirs.* It is this realization, that we are on a par with one another, that is the deepest reason why our morality must include some recognition of the needs of others, and why, then, Ethical Egoism fails as a moral theory.

CHAPTER 22
Moral Saints

SUSAN WOLF

I don't know whether there are any moral saints. But if there are, I am glad that neither I nor those about whom I care most are among them. By *moral saint* I mean a person whose every action is as morally good as possible, a person, that is, who is as morally worthy as can be. Though I shall in a moment acknowledge the variety of types of person that might be thought to satisfy this description, it seems to me that none of these types serve as unequivocally compelling personal ideals. In other words, I believe that moral perfection, in the sense of moral saintliness, does not constitute a model of personal well-being toward which it would be particularly rational or good or desirable for a human being to strive.

Outside the context of moral discussion, this will strike many as an obvious point. But, within that context, the point, if it be granted, will be granted with some discomfort. For within that context it is generally assumed that one ought to be as morally good as possible and that what limits there are to morality's hold on us are set by features of human nature of which we ought not to be proud. If, as I believe, the ideals that are derivable from common sense and philosophically popular moral theories do not support these assumptions, then something has

Susan Wolf, "Moral Saints," pp. 419–39 from *The Journal of Philosophy*, 79(8), 1982. Reprinted by permission of *The Journal of Philosophy*.

to change. Either we must change our moral theories in ways that will make them yield more palatable ideals, or, as I shall argue, we must change our conception of what is involved in affirming a moral theory.

In this paper, I wish to examine the notion of a moral saint, first, to understand what a moral saint would be like and why such a being would be unattractive, and, second, to raise some questions about the significance of this paradoxical figure for moral philosophy. I shall look first at the model(s) of moral sainthood that might be extrapolated from the morality or moralities of common sense. Then I shall consider what relations these have to conclusions that can be drawn from utilitarian and Kantian moral theories. Finally, I shall speculate on the implications of these considerations for moral philosophy.

Moral Saints and Common Sense

Consider first what, pretheoretically, would count for us – contemporary members of Western culture – as a moral saint. A necessary condition of moral sainthood would be that one's life be dominated by a commitment to improving the welfare of others or of society as a whole. As to what role this commitment must play in the individual's motivational system, two contrasting accounts suggest themselves to me which might equally be thought to qualify a person for moral sainthood.

First, a moral saint might be someone whose concern for others plays the role that is played in most of our lives by more selfish, or, at any rate, less morally worthy concerns. For the moral saint, the promotion of the welfare of others might play the role that is played for most of us by the enjoyment of material comforts, the opportunity to engage in the intellectual and physical activities of our choice, and the love, respect, and companionship of people whom we love, respect, and enjoy. The happiness of the moral saint, then, would truly lie in the happiness of others, and so he would devote himself to others gladly, and with a whole and open heart.

On the other hand, a moral saint might be someone for whom the basic ingredients of happiness are not unlike those of most of the rest of us. What makes him a moral saint is rather that he pays little or no attention to his own happiness in light of the overriding importance he gives to the wider concerns of morality. In other words, this person sacrifices his own interests to the interests of others, and feels the sacrifice as such.

Roughly, these two models may be distinguished according to whether one thinks of the moral saint as being a saint out of love or one thinks of the moral saint as being a saint out of duty (or some other intellectual appreciation and recognition of moral principles). We may refer to the first model of the Loving Saint; to the second, as the model of the Rational Saint.

The two models differ considerably with respect to the qualities of the motives of the individuals who conform to them. But this difference would have limited effect on the saints' respective public personalities. The shared content of what these individuals are motivated to be – namely, as morally good as possible – would play the dominant role in the determination of their characters. Of course, just as a variety of large-scale projects, from tending the sick to political campaigning, may be equally and maximally morally worthy, so a variety of characters are compatible with the ideal of moral sainthood. One moral saint may be more or less jovial, more or less garrulous, more or less athletic than another. But, above

all, a moral saint must have and cultivate those qualities which are apt to allow him to treat others as justly and kindly as possible. He will have the standard moral virtues to a nonstandard degree. He will be patient, considerate, even-tempered, hospitable, charitable in thought as well as in deed. He will be very reluctant to make negative judgments of other people. He will be careful not to favor some people over others on the basis of properties they could not help but have.

Perhaps what I have already said is enough to make some people begin to regard the absence of moral saints in their lives as a blessing. For there comes a point in the listing of virtues that a moral saint is likely to have where one might naturally begin to wonder whether the moral saint isn't, after all, too good – if not too good for his own good, at least too good for his own well-being. For the moral virtues, given that they are, by hypothesis, *all* present in the same individual, and to an extreme degree, are apt to crowd out the nonmoral virtues, as well as many of the interests and personal characteristics that we generally think contribute to a healthy, well-rounded, richly developed character.

In other words, if the moral saint is devoting all his time to feeding the hungry or healing the sick or raising money for Oxfam, then necessarily he is not reading Victorian novels, playing the oboe, or improving his backhand. Although no one of the interests or tastes in the category containing these latter activities could be claimed to be a necessary element in a life well lived, a life in which *none* of these possible aspects of character are developed may seem to be a life strangely barren.

The reasons why a moral saint cannot, in general, encourage the discovery and development of significant nonmoral interests and skills are not logical but practical reasons. There are, in addition, a class of nonmoral characteristics that a moral saint cannot encourage in himself for reasons that are not just practical. There is a more substantial tension between having any of these qualities unashamedly and being a moral saint. These qualities might be described as going against the moral grain. For example, a cynical or sarcastic wit, or a sense of humor that appreciates this kind of wit in others, requires that one take an attitude of resignation and pessimism toward the flaws and vices to be found in the world. A moral saint, on the other hand, has reason to take an attitude in opposition to this – he should try to look for the best in people, give them the benefit of the doubt as long as possible, try to improve regrettable situations as long as there is any hope of success. This suggests that, although a moral saint might well enjoy a good episode of *Father Knows Best*, he may not in good conscience be able to laugh at a Marx Brothers movie or enjoy a play by George Bernard Shaw.

An interest in something like gourmet cooking will be, for different reasons, difficult for a moral saint to rest easy with. For it seems to me that no plausible argument can justify the use of human resources involved in producing a *paté de canard en croute* against possible alternative beneficent ends to which these resources might be put. If there is a justification for the institution of haute cuisine, it is one which rests on the decision *not* to justify every activity against morally beneficial alternatives, and this is a decision a moral saint will never make. Presumably, an interest in high fashion or interior design will fare much the same, as will, very possibly, a cultivation of the finer arts as well.

A moral saint will have to be very, very nice. It is important that he not be offensive. The worry is that, as a result, he will have to be dull-witted or humorless or bland.

This worry is confirmed when we consider what sorts of characters, taken and refined both from life and from fiction, typically form our ideals. One would hope they would be figures who are morally good – and by this I mean more than just not morally bad – but one would hope, too, that they are not *just* morally good, but talented or accomplished or attractive in nonmoral ways as well. We may make ideals out of athletes, scholars, artists – more frivolously, out of cowboys, private eyes, and rock stars. We may strive for Katharine Hepburn's grace, Paul Newman's "cool"; we are attracted to the high-spirited passionate nature of Natasha Rostov; we admire the keen perceptiveness of Lambert Strether. Though there is certainly nothing immoral about the ideal

characters or traits I have in mind, they cannot be superimposed upon the ideal of a moral saint. For although it is a part of many of these ideals that the characters set high, and not merely acceptable, moral standards for themselves, it is also essential to their power and attractiveness that the moral strengths go, so to speak, along-side of specific, independently admirable, nonmoral ground projects and dominant personal traits.

When one does finally turn one's eyes toward lives that are dominated by explicitly moral commitments, moreover, one finds oneself relieved at the discovery of idiosyncrasies or eccentricities not quite in line with the picture of moral perfection. One prefers the blunt, tactless, and opinionated Betsy Trotwood to the unfailingly kind and patient Agnes Copperfield; one prefers the mischievousness and the sense of irony in Chesterton's Father Brown to the innocence and undiscriminating love of St. Francis.

It seems that, as we look in our ideals for people who achieve nonmoral varieties of personal excellence in conjunction with or colored by some version of high moral tone, we look in our paragons of moral excellence for people whose moral achievements occur in conjunction with or colored by some interests or traits that have low moral tone. In other words, there seems to be a limit to how much morality we can stand.

One might suspect that the essence of the problem is simply that there is a limit to how much of *any* single value, or any single type of value, we can stand. Our objection then would not be specific to a life in which one's dominant concern is morality, but would apply to any life that can be so completely characterized by an extraordinarily dominant concern. The objection in that case would reduce to the recognition that such a life is incompatible with well-roundedness. If that were the objection, one could fairly reply that well-roundedness is no more supreme a virtue than the totality of moral virtues embodied by the ideal it is being used to criticize. But I think this misidentifies the objection. For the way in which a concern for morality may dominate a life, or, more to the point, the way in which it may dominate an ideal of life, is not easily imagined by analogy to the dominance an aspiration to become an Olympic swimmer or a concern pianist might have.

A person who is passionately committed to one of these latter concerns might decide that her attachment to it is strong enough to be worth the sacrifice of her ability to maintain and pursue a significant portion of what else life might offer which a proper devotion to her dominant passion would require. But a desire to be as morally good as possible is not likely to take the form of one desire among others which, because of its peculiar psychological strength, requires one to forego the pursuit of other weaker and separately less demanding desires. Rather, the desire to be as morally good as possible is apt to have the character not just of a stronger, but of a higher desire, which does not merely successfully compete with one's other desires but which rather subsumes or demotes them. The sacrifice of other interests for the interest in morality, then, will have the character, not of a choice, but of an imperative.

Moreover, there is something odd about the idea of morality itself, or moral goodness, serving as the object of a dominant passion in the way that a more concrete and specific vision of a goal (even a concrete *moral* goal) might be imagined to serve. Morality itself does not seem to be a suitable object of passion. Thus, when one reflects, for example, on the Loving Saint easily and gladly giving up his fishing trip or his stereo or his hot fudge sundae at the drop of the moral hat, one is apt to wonder not at how much he loves morality, but at how little he loves these other things. One thinks that, if he can give these up so easily, he does not know what it *is* to truly love them. There seems, in other words, to be a kind of joy which the Loving Saint, either by nature or by practice, is incapable of experiencing. The Rational Saint, on the other hand, might retain strong nonmoral and concrete desires – he simply denies himself the opportunity to act on them. But this is no less troubling. The Loving Saint one might suspect of missing a piece of perceptual machinery, of being blind to some of what the world has to offer. The Rational Saint, who sees it but foregoes it, one suspects of having a different problem – a pathological

fear of damnation, perhaps, or an extreme form of self-hatred that interferes with his ability to enjoy the enjoyable in life.

In other words, the ideal of a life of moral sainthood disturbs not simply because it is an ideal of a life in which morality unduly dominates. The normal person's direct and specific desires for objects, activities, and events that conflict with the attainment of moral perfection are not simply sacrificed but removed, suppressed, or subsumed. The way in which morality, unlike other possible goals, is apt to dominate is particularly disturbing, for it seems to require either the lack or the denial of the existence of an identifiable, personal self.

This distinctively troubling feature is not, I think, absolutely unique to the ideal of the moral saint, as I have been using that phrase. It is shared by the conception of the pure aesthete, by a certain kind of religious ideal, and, somewhat paradoxically, by the model of the thorough-going, self-conscious egoist. It is not a coincidence that the ways of comprehending the world of which these ideals are the extreme embodiments are sometimes described as 'moralities' themselves. At any rate, they compete with what we ordinarily mean by "morality". Nor is it a coincidence that these ideals are naturally described as fanatical. But it is easy to see that these other types of perfection cannot serve as satisfactory personal ideals; for the realization of these ideals would be straightforwardly immoral. It may come as a surprise to some that there may in addition be such a thing as a *moral* fanatic.

Some will object that I am being unfair to "common-sense morality" – that it does not really require a moral saint to be either a disgusting goody-goody or an obsessive ascetic. Admittedly, there is no logical inconsistency between having any of the personal characteristics I have mentioned and being a moral saint. It is not morally wrong to notice the faults and shortcomings of others or to recognize and appreciate nonmoral talents and skills. Nor is it immoral to be an avid Celtics fan or to have a passion for caviar or to be an excellent cellist. With enough imagination, we can always contrive a suitable history and set of circumstances that will embrace such characteristics in one or another specific fictional story of a perfect moral saint.

If one turned onto the path of moral sainthood relatively late in life, one may have already developed interests that can be turned to moral purposes. It may be that a good golf game is just what is needed to secure that big donation to Oxfam. Perhaps the cultivation of one's exceptional artistic talent will turn out to be the way one can make one's greatest contribution to society. Furthermore, one might stumble upon joys and skills in the very service of morality. If, because the children are short a ninth player for the team, one's generous offer to serve reveals a natural fielding arm or if one's part in the campaign against nuclear power requires accepting a lobbyist's invitation to lunch at Le Lion d'Or, there is no moral gain in denying the satisfaction one gets from these activities. The moral saint, then, may, by happy accident, find himself with nonmoral virtues on which he can capitalize morally or which make psychological demands to which he has no choice but to attend. The point is that, for a moral saint, the existence of these interests and skills can be given at best the status of happy accidents – they cannot be encouraged for their own sakes as distinct, independent aspects of the realization of human good.

It must be remembered that from the fact that there is a tension between having any of these qualities and being a moral saint it does not follow that having any of these qualities is immoral. For it is not part of common-sense morality that one ought to be a moral saint. Still, if someone just happened to want to be a moral saint, he or she would not have or encourage these qualities, and, on the basis of our common-sense values, this counts as a reason *not* to want to be a moral saint.

One might still wonder what kind of reason this is, and what kind of conclusion this properly allows us to draw. For the fact that the models of moral saints are unattractive does not necessarily mean that they are unsuitable ideals. Perhaps they are unattractive because they make us feel uncomfortable – they highlight our own weaknesses, vices, and flaws. If so, the fault lies not in the haracters of the saints, but in those of our unsaintly selves.

To be sure, some of the reasons behind the disaffection we feel for the model of moral sainthood have to do with a reluctance to criticize ourselves and a reluctance to committing ourselves to trying to give up activities and interests that we heartily enjoy. These considerations might provide an *excuse* for the fact that we are not moral saints, but they do not provide a basis for criticizing sainthood as a possible ideal. Since these considerations rely on an appeal to the egoistic, hedonistic side of our natures, to use them as a basis for criticizing the ideal of the moral saint would be at best to beg the question and at worst to glorify features of ourselves that ought to be condemned.

The fact that the moral saint would be without qualities which we have and which, indeed, we like to have, does not in itself provide reason to condemn the ideal of the moral saint. The fact that some of these qualities are good qualities, however, and that they are qualities we *ought* to like, does provide reason to discourage this ideal and to offer other ideals in its place. In other words, some of the qualities the moral saint necessarily lacks are virtues, albeit nonmoral virtues, in the unsaintly characters who have them. The feats of Groucho Marx, Reggie Jackson, and the head chef at Lutèce are impressive accomplishments that it is not only permissible but positively appropriate to recognize as such. In general, the admiration of and striving toward achieving any of a great variety of forms of personal excellence are character traits it is valuable and desirable for people to have. In advocating the development of these varieties of excellence, we advocate nonmoral reasons for acting, and in thinking that it is good for a person to strive for an ideal that gives a substantial role to the interests and values that correspond to these virtues, we implicitly acknowledge the goodness of ideals incompatible with that of the moral saint. Finally, if we think that it is *as* good, or even better for a person to strive for one of these ideals than it is for him or her to strive for and realize the ideal of the moral saint, we express a conviction that it is good not to be a moral saint.

Moral Saints and Moral Theories

I have tried so far to paint a picture – or, rather, two pictures – of what a moral saint might be like, drawing on what I take to be the attitudes and beliefs about morality prevalent in contemporary, common-sense thought. To my suggestion that common-sense morality generates conceptions of moral saints that are unattractive or otherwise unacceptable, it is open to someone to reply, "so much the worse for common-sense morality." After all, it is often claimed that the goal of moral philosophy is to correct and improve upon common-sense morality, and I have as yet given no attention to the question of what conceptions of moral sainthood, if any, are generated from the leading moral theories of our time.

A quick, breezy reading of utilitarian and Kantian writings will suggest the images, respectively, of the Loving Saint and the Rational Saint. A utilitarian, with his emphasis on happiness, will certainly prefer the Loving Saint to the Rational one, since the Loving Saint will himself be a happier person than the Rational Saint. A Kantian, with his emphasis on reason, on the other hand, will find at least as much to praise in the latter as in the former. Still, both models, drawn as they are from common sense, appeal to an impure mixture of utilitarian and Kantian intuitions. A more careful examination of these moral theories raises questions about whether either model of moral sainthood would really be advocated by a believer in the explicit doctrines associated with either of these views.

Certainly, the utilitarian in no way denies the value of self-realization. He in no way disparages the development of interests, talents, and other personally attractive traits that I have claimed the moral saint would be without. Indeed, since just these features enhance the happiness both of the individuals who possess them and of those with whom they associate, the ability to promote these features both in oneself and in others will have considerable positive weight in utilitarian calculations.

This implies that the utilitarian would not support moral sainthood as a universal ideal. A world in which everyone, or even a large number of people, achieved moral sainthood – even a world in which they *strove* to achieve it – would probably contain less happiness than a world in which people realized a diversity of ideals involving a variety of personal and perfectionist values. More pragmatic considerations also suggest that, if the utilitarian wants to influence more people to achieve more good, then he would do better to encourage them to pursue happiness-producing goals that are more attractive and more within a normal person's reach.

These considerations still leave open, however, the question of what kind of an ideal the committed utilitarian should privately aspire to himself. Utilitarianism requires him to want to achieve the greatest general happiness, and this would seem to commit him to the ideal of the moral saint.

One might try to use the claims I made earlier as a basis for an argument that a utilitarian should choose to give up utilitarianism. If, as I have said, a moral saint would be a less happy person both to be and to be around than many other possible ideals, perhaps one could create more total happiness by not trying too hard to promote the total happiness. But this argument is simply unconvincing in light of the empirical circumstances of our world. The gain in happiness that would accrue to oneself and one's neighbors by a more well-rounded, richer life than that of the moral saint would be pathetically small in comparison to the amount by which one could increase the general happiness if one devoted oneself explicitly to the care of the sick, the downtrodden, the starving, and the homeless. Of course, there may be psychological limits to the extent to which a person can devote himself to such things without going crazy. But the utilitarian's individual limitations would not thereby become a positive feature of his personal ideals.

The unattractiveness of the moral saint, then, ought not rationally convince the utilitarian to abandon his utilitarianism. It may, however, convince him to take efforts not to wear his saintly moral aspirations on his sleeve. If it is not too difficult, the utilitarian will try not to make those around him uncomfortable. He will not want to appear "holier than thou"; he will not want to inhibit others' ability to enjoy themselves. In practice, this might make the perfect utilitarian a less nauseating companion than the moral saint I earlier portrayed. But insofar as this kind of reasoning produces a more bearable public personality, it is at the cost of giving him a personality that must be evaluated as hypocritical and condescending when his private thoughts and attitudes are taken into account.

Still, the criticisms I have raised against the saint of common-sense morality should make some difference to the utilitarian's conception of an ideal which neither requires him to abandon his utilitarian principles nor forces him to fake an interest he does not have or a judgment he does not make. For it may be that a limited and carefully monitored allotment of time and energy to be devoted to the pursuit of some nonmoral interests or to the development of some nonmoral talents would make a person a better contributor to the general welfare than he would be if he allowed himself no indulgences of this sort. The enjoyment of such activities in no way compromises a commitment to utilitarian principles as long as the involvement with these activities is conditioned by a willingness to give them up whenever it is recognized that they cease to be in the general interest.

This will go some way in mitigating the picture of the loving saint that an understanding of utilitarianism will on first impression suggest. But I think it will not go very far. For the limitations on time and energy will have to be rather severe, and the need to monitor will restrict not only the extent but also the quality of one's attachment to these interests and traits. They are only weak and somewhat peculiar sorts of passions to which one can consciously remain so conditionally committed. Moreover, the way in which the utilitarian can enjoy these "extra-curricular" aspects of his life is simply not the way in which these aspects are to be enjoyed insofar as they figure into our less saintly ideals.

The problem is not exactly that the utilitarian values these aspects of his life only as a means to an end, for the enjoyment he and others get from these aspects are not a means to, but a part of, the general happiness. Nonetheless, he values these things only because of and insofar as they *are* a part of the general happiness. He values them, as it were, under the description 'a contribution to the general happiness'. This is to be contrasted with the various ways in which these aspects of life may be valued by nonutilitarians. A person might love literature because of the insights into human nature literature affords. Another might love the cultivation of roses because roses are things of great beauty and delicacy. It may be true that these features of the respective activities also explain why these activities are happiness-producing. But, to the nonutilitarian, this may not be to the point. For if one values these activities in these more direct ways, one may not be willing to exchange them for others that produce an equal, or even a greater amount of happiness. From that point of view, it is not because they produce happiness that these activities are valuable; it is because these activities are valuable in more direct and specific ways that they produce happiness.

To adopt a phrase of Bernard Williams', the utilitarian's manner of valuing the not explicitly moral aspects of his life "provides (him) with one thought too many".[1] The requirement that the utilitarian have this thought – periodically, at least – is indicative of not only a weakness but a shallowness in his appreciation of the aspects in question. Thus, the ideals toward which a utilitarian could acceptably strive would remain too close to the model of the common-sense moral saint to escape the criticisms of that model which I earlier suggested. Whether a Kantian would be similarly committed to so restrictive and unattractive a range of possible ideals is a somewhat more difficult question.

The Kantian believes that being morally worthy consists in always acting from maxims that one could will to be universal law, and doing this not out of any pathological desire but out of reverence for the moral law as such. Or, to take a different formulation of the categorical imperative, the Kantian believes that moral action consists in treating other persons always as ends and never as means only. Presumably, and according to Kant himself, the Kantian thereby commits himself to some degree of benevolence as well as to the rules of fair play. But we surely would not will that *every* person become a moral saint, and treating others as ends hardly requires bending over backwards to protect and promote their interests. On one interpretation of Kantian doctrine, then, moral perfection would be achieved simply by unerring obedience to a limited set of side-constraints. On this interpretation, Kantian theory simply does not yield an ideal conception of a person of any fullness comparable to that of the moral saints I have so far been portraying.

On the other hand, Kant does say explicitly that we have a duty of benevolence, a duty not only to allow others to pursue their ends, but to take up their ends as our own. In addition, we have positive duties to ourselves, duties to increase our natural as well as our moral perfection. These duties are unlimited in the degree to which they *may* dominate a life. If action in accordance with and motivated by the thought of these duties is considered virtuous, it is natural to assume that the more one performs such actions, the more virtuous one is. Moreover, of virtue in general Kant says, "it is an ideal which is unattainable while yet our duty is constantly to approximate to it".[2] On this interpretation, then, the Kantian moral saint, like the other moral saints I have been considering, is dominated by the motivation to be moral.

Which of these interpretations of Kant one prefers will depend on the interpretation and the importance one gives to the role of the imperfect duties in Kant's over-all system. Rather than choose between them here, I shall consider each briefly in turn.

On the second interpretation of Kant, the Kantian moral saint is, not surprisingly, subject to many of the same objections I have been raising against other versions of moral sainthood. Though the Kantian saint may differ from the utilitarian saint as to *which* actions he is bound to perform and which he is bound to refrain from performing, I suspect that the range of activities acceptable to the Kantian saint will remain objectionably restrictive. Moreover, the manner in which the Kantian saint must think about and justify the activities he pursues and the character traits he develops will strike us, as it did with the utilitarian saint, as containing "one thought too many." As the

utilitarian could value his activities and character traits only insofar as they fell under the description of 'contributions to the general happiness', the Kantian would have to value his activities and character traits insofar as they were manifestations of respect for the moral law. If the development of our powers to achieve physical, intellectual, or artistic excellence, or the activities directed toward making others happy are to have any moral worth, they must arise from a reverence for the dignity that members of our species have as a result of being endowed with pure practical reason. This is a good and noble motivation, to be sure. But it is hardly what one expects to be dominantly behind a person's aspirations to dance as well as Fred Astaire, to paint as well as Picasso, or to solve some outstanding problem in abstract algebra, and it is hardly what one hopes to find lying dominantly behind a father's action on behalf of his son or a lover's on behalf of her beloved.

Since the basic problem with any of the models of moral sainthood we have been considering is that they are dominated by a single, all-important value under which all other possible values must be subsumed, it may seem that the alternative interpretation of Kant, as providing a stringent but finite set of obligations and constraints, might provide a more acceptable morality. According to this interpretation of Kant, one is as morally good as can be so long as one devotes some limited portion of one's energies toward altruism and the maintenance of one's physical and spiritual health, and otherwise pursues one's independently motivated interests and values in such a way as to avoid overstepping certain bounds. Certainly, if it be a requirement of an acceptable moral theory that perfect obedience to its laws and maximal devotion to its interests and concerns be something we can wholeheartedly strive for in ourselves and wish for in those around us, it will count in favor of this brand of Kantianism that its commands can be fulfilled without swallowing up the perfect moral agent's entire personality.

Even this more limited understanding of morality, if its connection to Kant's views is to be taken at all seriously, is not likely to give an unqualified seal of approval to the nonmorally directed ideals I have been advocating. For Kant is explicit about what he calls "duties of apathy and self-mastery" (69/70) – duties to ensure that our passions are never so strong as to interfere with calm, practical deliberation, or so deep as to wrest control from the more disinterested, rational part of ourselves. The tight and self-conscious rein we are thus obliged to keep on our commitments to specific individuals and causes will doubtless restrict our value in these things, assigning them a necessarily attenuated place.

A more interesting objection to this brand of Kantianism, however, comes when we consider the implications of placing the kind of upper bound on moral worthiness which seemed to count in favor of this conception of morality. For to put such a limit on one's capacity to be moral is effectively to deny, not just the moral necessity, but the moral goodness of a devotion to benevolence and the maintenance of justice that passes beyond a certain, required point. It is to deny the possibility of going morally above and beyond the call of a restricted set of duties. Despite my claim that all-consuming moral saintliness is not a particularly healthy and desirable ideal, it seems perverse to insist that, were moral saints to exist, they would not, in their way, be remarkably noble and admirable figures. Despite my conviction that it is as rational and as good for a person to take Katharine Hepburn or Jane Austen as her role model instead of Mother Theresa, it would be absurd to deny that Mother Theresa is a morally better person.

I can think of two ways of viewing morality as having an upper bound. First, we can think that altruism and impartiality are indeed positive moral interests, but that they are moral only if the degree to which these interests are actively pursued remains within certain fixed limits. Second, we can think that these positive interests are only incidentally related to morality and that the essence of morality lies elsewhere, in, say, an implicit social contract or in the recognition of our own dignified rationality. According to the first conception of morality, there is a cut-off line to the amount of altruism or to the extent of devotion to justice and fairness that is worthy of moral praise. But to draw this line earlier than the line that brings the altruist in question into a worse-off position than all those to whom he devotes himself seems unacceptably artificial and gratuitous. According to the second conception, these positive interests are not essentially related to morality at all. But then we are unable to regard a more affectionate and generous expression of good will toward others as a natural and reasonable extension of morality, and we encourage a cold and unduly self-centered approach to the development and evaluation of our motivations and concerns.

A moral theory that does not contain the seeds of an all-consuming ideal of moral sainthood thus seems to place false and unnatural limits on our opportunity to do moral good and our potential to deserve moral praise. Yet the main thrust of the arguments of this paper has been leading to the conclusion that, when such ideals are present, they are not ideals to which it is particularly reasonable or healthy or desirable for human beings to aspire. These claims, taken together, have the appearance of a dilemma from which there is no obvious escape. In a moment, I shall argue that, despite appearances, these claims should not be understood as constituting a dilemma. But, before I do, let me briefly describe another path which those who are convinced by my above remarks may feel inclined to take.

If the above remarks are understood to be implicitly critical of the views on the content of morality which seem most popular today, an alternative that naturally suggests itself is that we revise our views about the content of morality. More specifically, my remarks may be taken to support a more Aristotelian, or even a more Nietzschean, approach to moral philosophy. Such a change in approach involves substantially broadening or replacing our contemporary intuitions about which character traits constitute moral virtues and vices and which interests constitute moral interests. If, for example, we include personal bearing, or creativity, or sense of style, as features that contribute to one's *moral* personality, then we can create moral ideals which are incompatible with and probably more attractive than the Kantian and utilitarian ideals I have discussed. Given such an alteration of our conception of morality, the figures with which I have been concerned above might, far from being considered to be moral saints, be seen as morally inferior to other more appealing or more interesting models of individuals.

This approach seems unlikely to succeed, if for no other reason, because it is doubtful that any single, or even any reasonably small number of substantial personal ideals could capture the full range of possible ways of realizing human potential or achieving human good which deserve encouragement and praise. Even if we could provide a sufficiently broad characterization of the range of positive ways for human beings to live, however, I think there are strong reasons not to want to incorporate such a characterization more centrally into the framework of morality itself. For, in claiming that a character trait or activity is morally good, one claims that there is a certain kind of reason for developing that trait or engaging in that activity. Yet, lying behind our criticism of more conventional conceptions of moral sainthood, there seems to be a recognition that among the immensely valuable traits and activities that a human life might positively embrace are some of which we hope that, if a person does embrace them, he does so *not* for moral reasons. In other words, no matter how flexible we make the guide to conduct which we choose to label "morality," no matter how rich we make the life in which perfect obedience to this guide would result, we will have reason to hope that a person does not wholly rule and direct his life by the abstract and impersonal consideration that such a life would be morally good.

Once it is recognized that morality itself should not serve as a comprehensive guide to conduct, moreover, we can see reasons to retain the admittedly vague contemporary intuitions about what the classification of moral and non-moral virtues, interests, and the like should be. That is, there seem to be important differences between the aspects of a person's life which are currently considered appropriate objects of moral evaluation and the aspects that might be included under the altered conception of morality we are now considering, which the latter approach would tend wrongly to blur or to neglect. Moral evaluation now is focused primarily on features of a person's life over

which that person has control; it is largely restricted to aspects of his life which are likely to have considerable effect on other people. These restrictions seem as they should be. Even if responsible people could reach agreement as to what constituted good taste or a healthy degree of well-roundedness, for example, it seems wrong to insist that everyone try to achieve these things or to blame someone who fails or refuses to conform.

If we are not to respond to the unattractiveness of the moral ideals that contemporary theories yield either by offering alternative theories with more palatable ideals or by understanding these theories in such a way as to prevent them from yielding ideals at all, how, then, are we to respond? Simply, I think, by admitting that moral ideals do not, and need not, make the best personal ideals. Earlier, I mentioned one of the consequences of regarding as a test of an adequate moral theory that perfect obedience to its laws and maximal devotion to its interests be something we can whole-heartedly strive for in ourselves and wish for in those around us. Drawing out the consequences somewhat further should, I think, make us more doubtful of the proposed test than of the theories which, on this test, would fail. Given the empirical circumstances of our world, it seems to be an ethical fact that we have unlimited potential to be morally good, and endless opportunity to promote moral interests. But this is not incompatible with the not-so-ethical fact that we have sound, compelling, and not particularly selfish reasons to choose not to devote ourselves univocally to realizing this potential or to taking up this opportunity.

Thus, in one sense at least, I am not really criticizing either Kantianism or utilitarianism. Insofar as the point of view I am offering bears directly on recent work in moral philosophy, in fact, it bears on critics of these theories who, in a spirit not unlike the spirit of most of this paper, point out that the perfect utilitarian would be flawed in this way or the perfect Kantian flawed in that.[3] The assumption lying behind these claims, implicitly or explicitly, has been that the recognition of these flaws shows us something wrong with utilitarianism as opposed to Kantianism, or something wrong with Kantianism as opposed to utilitarianism, or something wrong with both of these theories as opposed to some nameless third alternative. The claims of this paper suggest, however, that this assumption is unwarranted. The flaws of a perfect master of a moral theory need not reflect flaws in the intramoral content of the theory itself.

Moral Saints and Moral Philosophy

In pointing out the regrettable features and the necessary absence of some desirable features in a moral saint, I have not meant to condemn the moral saint or the person who aspires to become one. Rather, I have meant to insist that the ideal of moral sainthood should not be held as a standard against which any other ideal must be judged or justified, and that the posture we take in response to the recognition that our lives are not as morally good as they might be need not be defensive.[4] It is misleading to insist that one is *permitted* to live a life in which the goals, relationships, activities, and interests that one pursues are not maximally morally good. For our lives are not so comprehensively subject to the requirement that we apply for permission, and our nonmoral reasons for the goals we set ourselves are not excuses, but may rather be positive, good reasons which do not exist *despite* any reasons that might threaten to outweigh them. In other words, a person may be *perfectly wonderful* without being *perfectly moral.*

Recognizing this requires a perspective which contemporary moral philosophy has generally ignored. This perspective yields judgments of a type that is neither moral nor egoistic. Like moral judgments, judgments about what it would be good for a person to be are made from a point of view outside the limits set by the values, interests, and desires that the person might actually have. And, like moral judgments, these judgments claim for themselves a kind of objectivity or a grounding in a perspective which any rational and perceptive being can take up. Unlike moral judgments, however, the good with which these judgments are concerned is not the good of anyone or any group other than the individual himself.

Nonetheless, it would be equally misleading to say that these judgments are made for the sake of the individual himself. For these judgments are not concerned with what kind of life it is in a person's interest to lead, but with what kind of interests it would be good for a person to have, and it need not be in a person's interest that he acquire or maintain objectively good interests. Indeed, the model of the Loving Saint, whose interests are identified with the interests of morality, is a model of a person for whom the dictates of rational self-interest and the dictates of morality coincide. Yet, I have urged that we have reason not to aspire to this ideal and that some of us would have reason to be sorry if our children aspired to and achieved it.

The moral point of view, we might say, is the point of view one takes up insofar as one takes the recognition of the fact that one is just one person among others equally real and deserving of the good things in life as a fact with practical consequences, a fact the recognition of which demands expression in one's actions and in the form of one's practical deliberations. Competing moral theories offer alternative answers to the question of what the most correct or the best way to express this fact is. In doing so, they offer alternative ways to evaluate and to compare the variety of actions, states of affairs, and so on that appear good and bad to agents from other, nonmoral points of view. But it seems that alternative interpretations of the moral point of view do not exhaust the ways in which our actions, characters, and their consequences can be comprehensively and objectively evaluated. Let us call the point of view from which we consider what kinds of lives are good lives, and what kinds of persons it would be good for ourselves and others to be, the *point of view of individual perfection.*

Since either point of view provides a way of comprehensively evaluating a person's life, each point of view takes account of, and, in a sense, subsumes the other. From the moral point of view, the perfection of an individual life will have some, but limited, value – for each individual remains, after all, just one person among others. From the perfectionist point of view, the moral worth of an individual's relation to his world will likewise have some, but limited, value – for, as I have argued, the (perfectionist) goodness of an individual's life does not vary proportionally with the degree to which it exemplifies moral goodness.

It may not be the case that the perfectionist point of view is like the moral point of view in being a point of view we are ever *obliged* to take up and express in our actions. Nonetheless, it provides us with reasons that are independent of moral reasons for wanting ourselves and others to develop our characters and live our lives in certain ways. When we take up this point of view and ask how much it would be good for an individual to act from the moral point of view, we do not find an obvious answer.[5]

The considerations of this paper suggest, at any rate, that the answer is not "as much as possible." This has implications both for the continued development of moral theories and for the development of metamoral views and for our conception of moral philosophy more generally. From the moral point of view, we have reasons to want people to live lives that seem good from outside that point of view. If, as I have argued, this means that we have reason to want people to live lives that are not morally perfect, then any plausible moral theory must make use of some conception of supererogation.[6]

If moral philosophers are to address themselves at the most basic level to the question of how people should live, however, they must do more than adjust the content of their moral theories in ways that leave room for the affirmation of nonmoral values. They must examine explicitly the range and nature of these nonmoral values, and, in light of this examination, they must ask how the acceptance of a moral theory is to be understood and acted upon. For the claims of this paper do not so much conflict with the content of any particular currently popular moral theory as they call into question a metamoral assumption that implicitly surrounds discussions of moral theory more generally. Specifically, they call into question the assumption that it is always better to be morally better.

The role morality plays in the development of our characters and the shape of our practical deliberations need be neither that of a universal medium into which all other values must be translated nor that of an ever-present filter through which all other values must pass. This is not to say that moral value should not be an important, even the most important, kind of value we attend to in evaluating and improving ourselves and our world. It is to say that our values cannot be fully comprehended on the model of a hierarchical system with morality at the top.

The philosophical temperament will naturally incline, at this point, toward asking, "What, then, *is* at the top – or, if there is no top, how *are* we to decide when and how much to be moral?" In other words, there is a temptation to seek a metamoral – though not, in the standard sense, metaethical – theory that will give us principles, or, at least, informal directives on the basis of which we can develop and evaluate more comprehensive personal ideals. Perhaps a theory that distinguishes among the various roles a person is expected to play within a life – as professional, as citizen, as friend, and so on – might give us some rules that would offer us, if nothing else, a better framework in which to think about and discuss these questions. I am pessimistic, however, about the chances of such a theory to yield substantial and satisfying results. For I do not see how a metamoral theory could be constructed which would not be subject to considerations parallel to those which seem inherently to limit the appropriateness of regarding moral theories as ultimate comprehensive guides for action.

This suggests that, at some point, both in our philosophizing and in our lives, we must be willing to raise normative questions from a perspective that is unattached to a commitment to any particular well-ordered system of values. It must be admitted that, in doing so, we run the risk of finding normative answers that diverge from the answers given by whatever moral theory one accepts. This, I take it, is the grain of truth in G. E. Moore's "open question" argument. In the background of this paper, then, there lurks a commitment to what seems to me to be a healthy form of intuitionism. It is a form of intuitionism which is not intended to take the place of more rigorous, systematically developed, moral theories – rather, it is intended to put these more rigorous and systematic moral theories in their place.

Notes

1. "Persons, Character and Morality" in Amelie Rorty, ed., *The Identities of Persons* (Berkeley: Univ. of California Press, 1976), p. 214.
2. Immanuel Kant, *The Doctrine of Virtue*, Mary J. Gregor, trans. (New York: Harper & Row, 1964), p. 71.
3. See, e.g., Williams, *op. cit.* and J. J. C. Smart and Bernard Williams, *Utilitarianism: For and Against* (New York: Cambridge, 1973). Also, Michael Stocker, "The Schizophrenia of Modern Ethical Theories," *The Journal of Philosophy*, LXIII, 14 (Aug. 12, 1976): 453–66.
4. George Orwell makes a similar point in "Reflections on Gandhi," in *A Collection of Essays by George Orwell* (New York: Harcourt Brace Jovanovich, 1945), p. 176: "sainthood is . . . a thing that human beings must avoid . . . It is too readily assumed that . . . the ordinary man only rejects it because it is too difficult; in other words, that the average human being is a failed saint. It is doubtful whether this is true. Many people genuinely do not wish to be saints, and it is probable that some who achieve or aspire to sainthood have never felt much temptation to be human beings."
5. A similar view, which has strongly influenced mine, is expressed by Thomas Nagel in "The Fragmentation of Value," in *Mortal Questions* (New York: Cambridge, 1979), pp. 128–41. Nagel focuses on the difficulties such apparently incommensurable points of view create for specific, isolable practical decisions that must be made both by individuals and by societies. In focusing on the way in which these points of view figure into the development of individual personal ideals, the questions with which I am concerned are more likely to lurk in the background of any individual's life.
6. The variety of forms that a conception of supererogation might take, however, has not generally been noticed. Moral theories that make use of this notion typically do so by identifying some specific set of principles as universal moral requirements and supplement this list with a further set of directives which it is morally praise-worthy but not required for an agent to follow. [See, e.g., Charles Fried, *Right and Wrong* (Cambridge, Mass.: Harvard, 1979).] But it is possible that the ability to live a morally blameless life cannot be so easily or definitely secured as this type of theory would suggest. The fact that there are some situations in which an agent is morally required to do something and other situations in which it would be good but not required for an agent to do something does not imply that there are specific principles such that, in any situation, an agent is required to act in accordance with these principles and other specific principles such that, in any situation, it would be good but not required for an agent to act in accordance with those principles.

PART IV
Ethics and Religion

Introduction to Part IV

For as long as there have been theists (those who believe in the existence of a god), there have been debates about the relation between God (or the gods) and morality. In Western philosophy, this debate first crystallized in an early Platonic dialogue, *Euthyphro*. It was in this short work that Socrates asks Euthyphro whether the gods love an action because it is pious, or whether actions are pious because the gods love them. Socrates tries to show that preference for the latter option leaves us with a picture of the gods that renders their choices and affections arbitrary.

We can cast the discussion in monotheistic terms, at no cost to the underlying philosophical stakes. And let us can shift the focus from piety, to moral rightness. The question, then, is whether acts are morally right in virtue of their having been divinely commanded. If Socrates is correct, then the answer must be No, for an affirmative answer would leave us with a picture of God as one whose commands are arbitrary, which clashes with the traditional picture of God as wholly perfect. A perfect God does not issue arbitrary commands, or make arbitrary choices.

Imagine God's deliberations in determining the content of morality. Either there are, or there are not, excellent reasons that support God's prohibitions on (say) torture and rape. If there are no such reasons, then God's choice is arbitrary, i.e., insufficiently well-supported by reason and argument. This clashes with the traditional view of God as all-perfect. We mere mortals sometimes act arbitrarily. But if we were perfectly informed about things, and were also perfectly motivated to comply with the balance of reasons, then we would never choose or act arbitrarily. Though arbitrary gods are common features of many polytheistic cultures, Western monotheism has long been at pains to depict its divinity as one possessed of perfect knowledge, perfect motivation, and perfect power to translate motivation into action. This is not a picture that allows arbitrariness to infect divine choices or actions.

Moreover, if no reasons adequately supported God's forbidding such behavior, then torture and rape are not inherently immoral. Without a divine prohibition, such actions, on the present view, would be morally neutral, not morally wrong. What makes an action wrong, on such a view, is God's having forbidden it. Absent divine disapproval, nothing is immoral. And yet if we want to see God's moral proclamations as backed by excellent reasons (rather than as arbitrary choices), we are compelled to think that it is the immoral nature of certain actions that provide God with the best possible reasons for their prohibition, and the morally salutary nature of other actions that provide God with excellent reasons for approving of them.

Most theologians and philosophers who have thought about the matter have come to the conclusion that if God is to avoid arbitrariness, we must envision God as issuing commands based on excellent reasons. And God must avoid arbitrariness, since arbitrariness is incompatible with divine perfection. (The alternative, of course, is to allow for divine imperfection, as many religions do – but as traditional Western monotheism does not.) If God is in fact issuing commands based on excellent reasons – indeed, the very best reasons there could be – then it is those excellent reasons, and not the fact of God's having commanded various actions, that makes those actions right. The excellent reasons that support the requirements of charity and kindness are what make it right be charitable and kind. God's commands don't make such things right; rather, God loves such things because they are right. Seeing that they are right, God commands them.

Though it strikes many as blasphemous to say such things, this picture preserves the perfection of God. On this view, God, being omniscient, knows everything (including all moral facts). And God, being wholly good and so caring for his creation, imparts the most important of these moral truths to us, in the form of personal communication or biblical scripture. This picture of God sees the divine creator as an infallible purveyor of moral messages, rather than as the author of the moral law.

Most philosophers have found this line of reasoning persuasive. But the philosopher Robert Adams has sought to vindicate something like the old-fashioned divine command theory (i.e., the theory according to which acts are right just because God commands them, and wrong just because God forbids them). Adams recognizes the problems for the traditional view, but thinks that a small alteration can provide the needed repair. If we think of morality as based on the commands, not just of any God, but rather of a *loving* God, then all of the traditional concerns about divine command theory disappear. Or so he thinks. Read the piece for yourself to see whether he has provided the needed fix.

The debates surrounding the divine command theory take place, of course, within the confines of a religious world view. And that world view may be fundamentally in error. God may not exist. If there is no God, then the question of God's relation to morality is moot.

The view that nothing does, in fact, answer to the traditional Western conception of God (the wholly perfect creator of the universe), is nowadays shared by many philosophers. But there are some who seek to vindicate God's existence, by arguing that many of our deepest ethical convictions actually presuppose such a belief. For instance, William Lane Craig argues that the objectivity of ethics, and the meaning of life, hinge on the existence of a supremely authoritative being. Whether atheists realize it or not, a godless universe deprives life of meaning and leaves us without any firm moral foundations. This popular form of argument is rebutted by Walter Sinnott-Armstrong, Craig's debate partner in the selection excerpted here. Sinnott-Armstrong does not seek to establish the truth of atheism (the view that God does not exist) in this selection, but instead restricts himself to criticizing Craig's familiar line of thinking.

Immanuel Kant, whose *Critique of Pure Reason* includes devastating criticisms of traditional argument for God's existence, argues here that ethical thinking presupposes the existence of God and immortality. This is not a direct argument for either, but rather a Kantian transcendental argument, which seeks to establish the existence of something by showing how it is presupposed in a kind of thinking that human beings find inescapable. Ethical thinking is one such form of thought. According to Kant, morality enjoins us to be morally flawless. But since, as Kant believes, a moral requirement entails the possibility of fulfilling it, and since, as Kant also believes, we are incapable of moral perfection here on earth, the demand that we be morally flawless entails immortality, for an afterlife is the only context in which we might reach such a state.

Kant also believes that God is a "necessary postulate" of morality because morality requires that justice be done. Justice requires that the virtuous be rewarded, and the wicked be punished. Since justice isn't always done here on earth, morality again requires immortality, so as to provide a context in which people will receive their just deserts. But this distribution of benefit and burden will not come of its own accord, even if we are all immortal. It must come from someone with enough wisdom and power to allocate the necessary rewards and punishments. And that person is God.

Kant recognizes that this does not constitute a proof of God's existence. Rather, Kant is arguing that if we persist in our moral thinking, then we must accept the truth of these presuppositions (God and immortality). There are two standard replies to this sort of argument. The first is to deny that morality rests on the presuppositions that Kant has identified. On this line, we can vindicate ordinary moral thought without committing ourselves to these allegedly necessary postulates. The second reply allows that morality does indeed presuppose the existence of God and immortality, but rejects the truth of the presuppositions, and so rejects the coherence or truth of morality.

Another familiar line of thinking in this area is one that is well formulated by the philosopher Stephen Layman, who provides a modern updating of the Kantian argument. Layman argues that if there is no God, and no afterlife, then there will be cases in which people do not have most reason to do their moral duty. But, he argues, people always have most reason to do their moral duty. Part of the concept of genuine moral duty, as it applies to us here on earth, is that something is our duty only if it supplies us with a reason for compliance that is more powerful than any competing considerations. It follows that there is either a God, or an afterlife, or both.

Those who want to resist Layman's conclusion will need to challenge his initial claim (that the absence of God or the afterlife allows for cases in which morality fails to supply overriding reasons), or deny his second claim (that moral reasons always trump competing considerations). Readers are encouraged to consider Layman's arguments in tandem with those offered in Part III, where the issues surrounding the reasons to be moral are at center stage.

Erik Wielenberg's contribution represents a thorough critique of many of the most prominent theistic arguments that have sought to establish a link between religion and ethics. Like his fellow atheist Sinnott-Armstrong, Wielenberg is not arguing here against God's existence. Rather, he is trying to undermine theistic attempts to establish a necessary link between morality and God. Wielenberg focuses especially on variations of the divine command theory (including that developed by Robert Adams), and argues that there is no coherent and plausible picture according to which God's commands lie at the heart of morality.

CHAPTER 23
Euthyphro

PLATO

SOCRATES: But shall we . . . say that whatever all the gods hate is unholy, and whatever they all love is holy: while whatever some of them love, and others hate, is either both or neither? Do you wish us now to define holiness and unholiness in this manner?

EUTHYPHRO: Why not, Socrates?

SOCRATES: There is no reason why I should not, Euthyphro. It is for you to consider whether that definition will help you to instruct me as you promised.

EUTHYPHRO: Well, I should say that holiness is what all the gods love, and that unholiness is what they all hate.

SOCRATES: Are we to examine this definition, Euthyphro, and see if it is a good one? Or are we to be content to accept the bare assertions of other men, or of ourselves, without asking any questions? Or must we examine the assertions?

EUTHYPHRO: We must examine them. But for my part I think that the definition is right this time.

SOCRATES: We shall know that better in a little while, my good friend. Now consider this

Plato, "Euthyphro," trans. Benjamin Jowett, Oxford, 1892.

question. Do the gods love holiness because it is holy, or is it holy because they love it?

EUTHYPHRO: I do not understand you, Socrates.

SOCRATES: I will try to explain myself: we speak of a thing being carried and carrying, and being led and leading, and being seen and seeing; and you understand that all such expressions mean different things, and what the difference is.

EUTHYPHRO: Yes, I think I understand.

SOCRATES: And we talk of a thing being loved, and, which is different, of a thing loving?

EUTHYPHRO: Of course.

SOCRATES: Now tell me: is a thing which is being carried in a state of being carried, because it is carried, or for some other reason?

EUTHYPHRO: No, because it is carried.

SOCRATES: And a thing is in a state of being led, because it is led, and of being seen, because it is seen?

EUTHYPHRO: Certainly.

SOCRATES: Then a thing is not seen because it is in a state of being seen; it is in a state of being seen because it is seen: and a thing is not led because it is in a state of being led; it is in a state of being led because it is led: and a thing is not carried because it is in a state of being carried; it is in a state of being carried because it is carried. Is my meaning clear now, Euthyphro? I mean this: if anything becomes or is affected, it does not become because it is in a state of becoming; it is in a state of becoming because it becomes; and it is not affected because it is in a state of being affected: it is in a state of being affected because it is affected. Do you not agree?

EUTHYPHRO: I do.

SOCRATES: Is not that which is being loved in a state, either of becoming, or of being affected in some way by something?

EUTHYPHRO: Certainly.

SOCRATES: Then the same is true here as in the former cases. A thing is not loved by those who love it because it is in a state of being loved. It is in a state of being loved because they love it.

EUTHYPHRO: Necessarily.

SOCRATES: Well, then, Euthyphro, what do we say about holiness? Is it not loved by all the gods, according to your definition?

EUTHYPHRO: Yes.

SOCRATES: Because it is holy, or for some other reason?

EUTHYPHRO: No, because it is holy.

SOCRATES: Then it is loved by the gods because it is holy: it is not holy because it is loved by them?

EUTHYPHRO: It seems so.

SOCRATES: But then what is pleasing to the gods is pleasing to them, and is in a state of being loved by them, because they love it?

EUTHYPHRO: Of course.

SOCRATES: Then holiness is not what is pleasing to the gods, and what is pleasing to the gods is not holy, as you say, Euthyphro. They are different things.

EUTHYPHRO: And why, Socrates?

SOCRATES: Because we are agreed that the gods love holiness because it is holy: and that it is not holy because they love it. Is not this so?

EUTHYPHRO: Yes.

SOCRATES: And that what is pleasing to the gods because they love it, is pleasing to them by reason of this same love: and that they do not love it because it is pleasing to them.

EUTHYPHRO: True.

SOCRATES: Then, my dear Euthyphro, holiness, and what is pleasing to the gods, are different things. If the gods had loved holiness because it is holy, they would also have loved what is pleasing to them because it is pleasing to them; but if what is pleasing to them had been pleasing to them because they loved it, then holiness too would have been holiness, because they loved it. But now you see that they are opposite things, and wholly different from each other. For the one is of a sort to be loved because it is loved: while the other is loved, because it is of a sort to be loved. My question, Euthyphro, was, What is holiness? But it turns out that you have not explained to me the essence of holiness; you have been content to mention an attribute which belongs to it, namely, that all the gods love it. You have not yet told me what is its essence. Do not, if you please, keep from me what holiness is; begin again and tell me that. Never mind whether the gods love it, or whether it has other attributes: we shall not differ on that point. Do your best to make it clear to me what is holiness and what is unholiness.

CHAPTER 24

A New Divine Command Theory

ROBERT MERRIHEW ADAMS

In a recent issue of *The Journal of Religious Ethics*, Jeffrey Stout (1978) has written about an earlier paper of mine (Adams, 1973) urging development and modification of the very point on which, as it happens, my own metaethical views have changed most. My thoughts have been moving in a rather different direction from his, however.[1] For that reason, and because of his paper's interesting and perceptive linkage of metaethical issues with the most fundamental questions in the theory of meaning I would like to respond to him.

My Old Position

My modified divine command theory was proposed as a partial analysis of the *meaning* of "(ethically) wrong." Recognizing that it would be most implausible as an analysis of the sense in which the expression is used by many speakers (for instance, by atheists), I proposed the theory only as an analysis of the meaning of "wrong" in the discourse of some Jewish and Christian believers. In the theory that I now prefer, as we shall see, the identification of wrongness with contrariety to God's commands is neither pre-

Robert Merrihew Adams, "A New Divine Command Theory," pp. 66–79 from *Journal of Religious Ethics*, 7, 1979. Reprinted by permission of the publishers, Blackwell Publishing.

sented as a meaning analysis nor relativized to a group of believers. According to the old theory, however, it is part of the meaning of "(ethically) wrong" for at least some believers that

(1) (for any action X) X is ethically wrong if and only if X is contrary to God's commands,

but also that

(2) "X is wrong" normally expresses opposition or certain other negative attitudes toward X.

The meaning of "wrong" seems to be overdetermined by (1) and (2). Conflicts could arise. Suppose God commanded me to practice cruelty for its own sake. (More precisely, suppose he commanded me to make it my chief end in life to inflict suffering on other human beings, for no other reason than that he commanded it.) I cannot summon up the relevant sort of opposition or negative attitude toward disobedience to such a command, and I will not say that it would be wrong to disobey it.

Such conflicts within the religious ethical belief system are prevented by various background beliefs, which are *presupposed* by (1). Particularly important is the belief that

(3) God is loving, and therefore does not and will not command such things as (e.g.) the practice of cruelty for its own sake.

But (3) is contingent. It is allowed by the theory to be logically possible for God to command cruelty for its own sake, although the believer is confident he will not do such a thing. Were the believer to come to think (3) false, however, I suggested that his concept of ethical wrongness would "break down." It would not function as it now does, because he would not be prepared to use it to say that any action is wrong (Adams, 1973:322–4). Because of the interplay and tension of the various considerations involved in it, this picture of the meaning of "(ethically) wrong" is (as I acknowledged) somewhat "untidy." But its untidiness should not obscure the fact that I meant it quite definitely to follow from the theory that the following are necessary truths:

(4) If X is wrong, then X is contrary to the commands of God.
(5) If X is obligatory, then X is required by the commands of God.
(6) If X is ethically permitted, then X is permitted by the commands of God.
(7) If there is not a *loving* God, then nothing is ethically wrong or obligatory or permitted.

These four theses are still taken to be necessary truths in my present divine command theory. [. . .]

The Nature of Wrongness and the Meaning of "Wrong"

I do not think that every competent user of "wrong" in its ethical sense must know what the nature of wrongness is. The word is used – with the same meaning, I would now say – by people who have different views, or none at all, about the nature of wrongness. As I remarked in my earlier paper, "There is probably much less agreement about the most basic issues in moral theory than there is about many ethical issues of less generality" (Adams, 1973:343). That people can use an expression to signify an ethical property, knowing it is a property they seek (or shun, as the case may be), but not knowing what its nature is, was realized by Plato when he characterized the good as

That which every soul pursues, doing everything for the sake of it, divining that it is something, but perplexed and unable to grasp adequately what it is or to have such a stable belief as about other things (*Republic* 505D–E).

What every competent user of "wrong" must know about wrongness is first of all, that wrongness is a property of actions (perhaps also of intentions and of various attitudes, but certainly of actions); and second that people are generally opposed to actions they regard as wrong, and count wrongness as a reason (often a conclusive reason) for opposing an action. In addition I think the competent user must have some opinion about what actions have this property, and some fairly settled disposition as to what he will count as reasons for and against regarding an action as wrong. There is an important measure of agreement among competent users in these opinions and dispositions – not complete agreement, nor universal agreement on some points and disagreement on others, but overlapping agreements of one person with another on some points and with still others on other points. "To call an action 'wrong' is, among other things, to classify it with certain other actions," as having a common property, "and there is considerable agreement . . . as to what actions those are" (Adams, 1973:344). Torturing children for fun is one of them in virtually everyone's opinion.

Analysis of the concept or understanding with which the word "wrong" is used is not sufficient to determine what wrongness is. What it can tell us about the nature of wrongness, I think, is that wrongness will be the property of actions (if there is one) that best fills the role assigned to wrongness by the concept. My theory is that contrariety to the command of a loving God is that property; but we will come to that in [the next] section. Meanwhile I will try to say something about what is involved in being the property that *best* fills the relevant role, though I do not claim to be giving an adequate set of individually necessary and jointly sufficient conditions.

(i) We normally speak of actions being right and wrong as of facts that obtain objectively, independently of whether we think they do. "Wrong" has the syntax of an ordinary predicate, and we worry that we may be mistaken in our ethical judgments. This feature of ethical concepts gives emotivism and prescriptivism in metaethics much of their initial implausibility. If possible, therefore, the property to be identified with ethical wrongness should be one that actions have or lack objectively.

(ii) The property that is wrongness should belong to those types of action that are thought to be wrong – or at least it should belong to an important central group of them. It would be unreasonable to expect a theory of the nature of wrongness to yield results that agree perfectly with pre-theoretical opinion. One of the purposes a metaethical theory may serve is to give guidance in revising one's particular ethical opinions. But there is a limit to how far those opinions may be revised without changing the subject entirely; and we are bound to take it as a major test of the acceptability of a theory of the nature of wrongness that it should in some sense account for the wrongness of a major portion of the types of action we have believed to be wrong.

(iii) Wrongness should be a property that not only belongs to the most important types of action that are thought to be wrong, but also plays a causal role (or a role as object of perception) in their coming to be regarded as wrong. It should not be connected in a merely fortuitous way with our classification of actions as wrong and not wrong.

(iv) Understanding the nature of wrongness should give one more rather than less reason to oppose wrong actions as such. Even if it were discovered (as it surely will not be) that there is a certain sensory pleasure produced by all and only wrong actions, it would be absurd to say that wrongness *is* the property of producing that pleasure. For the property of producing such a pleasure, in itself, gives us no reason whatever to oppose an action that has the property.

(v) The best theory about the nature of wrongness should satisfy other intuitions about wrongness as far as possible. One intuition that is rather widely held and is relevant to theological metaethics is that rightness and wrongness are determined by a law or standard that has a sanctity that is greater than that of any merely human will or institution.

We are left, on this view, with a concept of wrongness that has both objective and subjective aspects. The best theory of the nature of wrongness, I think, will be one that identifies wrongness with some property that actions have or lack objectively. But we do not have a fully objective procedure for determining which theory of the nature of wrongness is the best, and therefore which property is wrongness.

For example, the property that is wrongness should belong to the most important types of action that are believed to be wrong. But the concept possessed by every competent user of "wrong" does not dictate exactly which types of action those are. A sufficiently eccentric classification of types of action as right or wrong would not fit the concept. But there is still room for much difference of opinion. In testing theories of the nature of wrongness by their implications about what types of action are wrong, I will be guided by my own classification of types of action as right and wrong, and by my own sense of which parts of the classification are most important.

Similarly, in considering whether identifying wrongness with a given property, *P*, makes wrongness more or less of a reason for opposing an action, I will decide partly on the basis of how *P* weighs with me. And in general I think that this much is right about prescriptivist intuitions in metaethics: to identify a property with ethical wrongness is in part to assign it a certain complex role in my life (and, for my part, in the life of society); in deciding to do that I will (quite reasonably) be influenced by what attracts and repels me personally. But it does not follow that the theory I should choose is not one that identifies wrongness with a property that actions would have or lack regardless of how I felt about them.

A New Divine Command Theory

The account I have given of the concept of wrongness that every competent user of "wrong" must have is consistent with many different theories about the nature of wrongness – for example, with the view that wrongness is the property of failing to maximize human happiness, and with a Marxist theory that wrongness is the property of being contrary to the objective interests of the progressive class or classes. But given typical Christian beliefs about God, it seems to me most plausible to identify wrongness with the property of being contrary to the commands of [a] loving God. (i) This is a property that actions have or lack objectively, regardless of whether we think they do. (I assume the theory can be filled out with a satisfactory account of what love consists in here.) (ii) The property of being contrary to the commands of a loving God is certainly believed by Christians to belong to all and only wrong actions. (iii) It also plays a causal role in our classification of actions as wrong, in so far as God has created our moral faculties to reflect his commands. (iv) Because of what is believed about God's actions, purposes, character, and power, he inspires such devotion and/or fear that contrariness to his commands is seen as a supremely weighty reason for opposing an action. Indeed, (v) God's commands constitute a law or standard that seems to believers to have sanctity that is not possessed by any merely human will or institution.

My new divine command theory of the nature of ethical wrongness, then, is that ethical wrongness *is* (i.e., is identical with) the property of being contrary to the commands of a loving God. I regard this as a metaphysically necessary, but not an analytic or *a priori* truth. Because it is not conceptual analysis, this claim is not relative to a religious sub-community of the larger linguistic community. It purports to be the correct theory of the nature of the ethical wrongness that *everybody* (or almost everybody) is talking about.

Further explanation is in order, first about the notion of a divine *command*, and second about the *necessity* that is claimed here. On the first point I can only indicate here the character of the explanation that is needed; for it amounts to nothing less than a theory of revelation. Theists sometimes speak of wrong action as action contrary to the "will" of God, but that way of speaking ignores some important distinctions. One is the distinction between the absolute will of God (his "good pleasure") and his revealed will. Any Christian theology will grant that God in his godly pleasure sometimes decides, for reasons that may be mysterious to us, not to do everything he could to prevent a wrong action. According to some theologies nothing at all can happen contrary to God's good pleasure. It is difficult, therefore, to suppose that all wrong actions are unqualified, contrary to God's will in the sense of his good pleasure. It is God's *revealed* will – not what he wants or plans to have happen, but what he has told us to do – that is thought to determine the rightness and wrongness of human actions. Roman Catholic theology has made a further distinction, within God's revealed will, between his commands, which it would be wrong not to follow, and "counsels (of perfection)," which it would be better to follow but not wrong not to follow. It is best, therefore, in our metaethical theory, to say that wrongness is contrariety to God's *commands*; and commands must have been issued, promulgated, or somehow revealed.

The notion of the issuance of a divine command requires a theory of revelation for its adequate development. The first such theory that comes to mind may be a Biblical literalism that takes divine commands to be just what is written in the Bible as commanded by God. But there will also be Roman Catholic theories involving the *magisterium* of the Church, a Quaker theory about "the inner light," theories about "general revelation" through the moral feelings and intuitions of unbelievers as well as believers – and other theories as well. To develop these theories and choose among them is far too large a task for the present essay.

The thesis that wrongness is (identical with) contrariety to a loving God's commands must be *metaphysically necessary* if it is true. That is, it cannot be false in any possible world if it is true in the actual world. For if it were false in some possible world, then wrongness would be non-identical with contrariety to God's commands in the actual world as well, by the transitivity of identity, just as Matthew and Levi must be non-identical in all worlds if they are non-identical in any.

This argument establishes the metaphysical necessity of property identities in general; and that leads me to identify wrongness with contrariety to the commands of a *loving* God, rather than simply with contrariety to the commands of God. Most theists believe that both of those properties are in fact possessed by all and only wrong actions. But if wrongness is simply contrariety to the commands of God, it is necessarily so, which implies that it would be wrong to disobey God even if he were so unloving as to command the practice of cruelty for its own sake. That consequence is unacceptable. I am not prepared to adopt the negative attitude toward possible disobedience in that situation that would be involved in identifying wrongness simply with contrariety to God's commands. The loving character of the God who issues them seems to me therefore to be a metaethically relevant feature of divine commands. (I assume that in deciding what property is wrongness, and therefore would be wrongness in all possible worlds, we are to rely on our own actual moral feelings and convictions, rather than on those that we or others would have in other possible worlds.)

If it is necessary that ethical wrongness is contrariety to a loving God's commands, it follows that no actions would be ethically wrong if there were not a loving God. This consequence will seem (at least initially) implausible to many, but I will try to dispel as much as I can of the air of paradox. It should be emphasized, first of all, that my theory does not imply what would ordinarily be meant by saying that no actions *are* ethically wrong if there *is* no loving God. If there is no loving God, then the theological part of my theory is false; but the more general part presented in [the previous] section, implies that in that case ethical wrongness is the property with which it is identified by the best remaining alternative theory.

Similarly, if there is in fact a loving God, and if ethical wrongness is the property of being contrary to the commands of a loving God, there is still, I suppose, a possible world, w_1; in which there would not be a loving God but there would be people to whom w_1 would seem much as the actual world seems to us, and who would use the world "wrong" much as we use it. We may say that they would associate it with the same *concept* as we do although the property it would signify in their mouths is not wrongness. The actions they call "wrong" would not be wrong – that is, they would not have the property that actually is wrongness (the property of being contrary to the commands of a loving God). But that is not to say that they would be mistaken whenever they predicated "is wrong" of an action. For "wrong" in their speech would signify the property (if any) that is assigned to it by the metaethical theory that would be the best in relation to an accurate knowledge of their situation in w_1. We can even say that they would believe, as we do, that cruelty is wrong, if by that we mean, not that the property they would ascribe to cruelty by calling it "wrong" is the same as the property that we so ascribe, but that the subjective psychological state that they would express by the ascription is that same that we express.

Readers who think that I have not sufficiently dispelled the air of paradox may wish to consider a slightly different divine command theory, according to which it is a contingent truth that contrariety to God's commands constitutes the nature of wrongness. Instead of saying that wrongness is the property that in the actual world best fills a certain role, we could say that wrongness is the property of having whatever property best fills that role in whatever possible world is in question. On the latter view it would be reasonable to say that the property that best fills the role constitutes the nature of wrongness, but that the nature of wrongness may differ in different possible worlds. The theist could still hold that the nature of wrongness in the actual world is constituted by contrariety to the commands of God (or of a loving God – it does not make as much difference which we say, on this view, since the theist believes God is loving in the actual world anyway). But it might be constituted by other properties in some other possible worlds. This theory does not imply that no action would be wrong if there were no loving God; and that may still seem to be an advantage. On the other hand I think there is also an air of paradox about the idea that wrongness may have different natures in different possible worlds; and if a loving God does issue commands, actual wrongness has a very different character from anything that could occur in a world without a loving God.

The difference between this alternative theory and the one I have endorsed should not be exaggerated. On both theories the nature of wrongness is actually constituted by contrariety to the commands of (a loving) God. And on both theories there may be other possible worlds in which other properties best fill the role by which contrariety to a loving God's commands is linked in the actual world to our concept of wrongness.

Note

1. The metaethical position to be presented here was briefly indicated in Adams (1979). Though not all the arguments given there in favor of the theory are repeated here, the position is much more fully expounded in the present essay.

References

Adams, Robert Merrihew 1973 "A modified divine command theory of ethical wrongness." pp. 318–47 in Gene Outka and John P. Reeder, Jr. (eds), *Religion and Morality*. Garden City: Anchor.

Adams, Robert Merrihew 1979 "Moral arguments for theistic belief." In C. F. Delaney (ed.), *Rationality and Religious Belief*. Notre Dame, In: University of Notre Dame Press.

Stout, Jeffrey L. 1978 "Metaethics and the death of meaning: Adams' tantalizing closing." *The Journal of Religious Ethics* (Spring) 6:1–18.

CHAPTER 25

God and Objective Morality: A Debate

WILLIAM LANE CRAIG AND WALTER SINNOTT-ARMSTRONG

God Makes Sense of Objective Values in the World

If God does not exist, then objective moral values do not exist. When I speak of *objective* moral values, I mean moral values that are valid and binding whether anybody believes in them or not. Thus, to say, for example, that the Holocaust was objectively wrong is to say that it was wrong even though the Nazis who carried it out thought that it was right and that it would still have been wrong even if the Nazis had won World War II and succeeded in exterminating or brain-washing everyone who disagreed with them. Now if God does not exist, then moral values are not objective in this way.

Many theists and atheists alike concur on this point. For example, Bertrand Russell observed,

> . . . ethics arises from the pressures of the community on the individual. Man . . . does not always instinctively feel the desires which are useful to his herd. The herd, being anxious

that the individual should act in its interests, has invented various devices for causing the individual's interest to be in harmony with that of the herd. One of these . . . is morality.[1]

Michael Ruse, a philosopher of science at the University of Guelph, agrees. He explains,

> Morality is a biological adaptation no less than are hands and feet and teeth. Considered as a rationally justifiable set of claims about an objective something, ethics is illusory. I appreciate that when somebody says "Love thy neighbor as thyself," they think they are referring above and beyond themselves. Nevertheless, such reference is truly without foundation. Morality is just an aid to survival and reproduction . . . and any deeper meaning is illusory.[2]

Friedrich Nietzsche, the great nineteenth century atheist who proclaimed the death of God, understood that the death of God meant the destruction of all meaning and value in life. I think that Friedrich Nietzsche was right.

But we must be very careful here. The question here is *not*: "Must we believe in God in

William Lane Craig and Walter Sinnott-Armstrong, "God and Objective Morality: A Debate," pp. 17–21, 33–6 from *God? A Debate Between a Christian and an Athiest*. Oxford: Oxford University Press, 2004.

order to live moral lives?" I'm not claiming that we must. Nor is the question: "Can we *recognize* objective moral values without believing in God?" I think that we can. Nor is the question: "Can we formulate an adequate system of ethics without reference to God?" So long as we assume that human beings have objective moral value, the atheist could probably draft a moral code that the theist would largely agree with.

Rather the question is: "If God does not exist, do objective moral values exist?" Like Russell and Ruse, I don't see any reason to think that in the absence of God, the herd morality evolved by *homo sapiens* is objective. After all, if there is no God, then what's so special about human beings? They're just accidental by-products of nature that have evolved relatively recently on an infinitesimal speck of dust lost somewhere in a hostile and mindless universe and that are doomed to perish individually and collectively in a relatively short time. On the atheistic view, some action, say, rape, may not be socially advantageous, and so in the course of human development has become taboo; but that does absolutely nothing to prove that rape is really wrong. On the atheistic view, there's nothing really *wrong* with your raping someone. Thus, without God there is no absolute right and wrong that imposes itself on our conscience.

But the problem is that objective values *do* exist, and deep down we all know it. There's no more reason to deny the objective reality of moral values than the objective reality of the physical world. As John Healey, the Executive Director of Amnesty International, wrote in a fund-raising letter, "I am writing you today because I think you share my profound belief that *there are indeed some moral absolutes.* When it comes to torture, to government-sanctioned murder, to 'disappearances' – there are no lesser evils. These are outrages against all of us."[3] Actions like rape, cruelty, and child abuse aren't just socially unacceptable behavior – they're moral abominations. Some things are really wrong. Similarly love, equality, and self-sacrifice are really good. But if moral values cannot exist without God and moral values do exist, then it follows logically and inescapably that God exists.

We can summarize this argument as follows:

1. If God does not exist, objective moral values do not exist.
2. Objective moral values do exist.
3. Therefore, God exists.

Again, let's consider possible objections that might be raised against this argument.

Some atheist philosophers, unwilling to bite the bullet and affirm that acts like rape or torturing a child are morally neutral actions, have tried to affirm objective moral values in the absence of God, thus in effect denying premise (1). Let's call this alternative Atheistic Moral Realism. Atheistic moral realists affirm that moral values and duties do exist in reality and are not dependent upon evolution or human opinion, but they insist that they are not grounded in God. Indeed, moral values have no further foundation. They just exist.

I must confess that this alternative strikes me as incomprehensible, an example of trying to have your cake and eat it, too. What does it mean to say, for example, that the moral value *Justice* simply exists? I don't know what this means. I understand what it is for a person to be just; but I draw a complete blank when it is said that, in the absence of any people, *Justice* itself exists. Moral values seem to exist as properties of persons, not as abstractions – or at any rate, I don't know what it is for a moral value to exist as an abstraction. Atheistic moral realists seem to lack any adequate foundation in reality for moral values, but just leave them floating in an unintelligible way.

Further, the nature of moral duty or obligation seems incompatible with Atheistic Moral Realism. Let's suppose for the sake of argument that moral values do exist independently of God. Suppose that values like *Mercy, Justice, Love, Forbearance,* and the like just exist. How does that result in any moral obligations for me? Why would I have a moral duty, say, to be merciful? Who or what lays such an obligation on me? As the ethicist Richard Taylor points out, "A duty is something that is owed. . . . But something can be owed only to some person or persons. There can be no such thing as duty in isolation. . . ."[4] God makes sense of moral obligation because His commands constitute for us our moral duties. Taylor writes, "Our moral obligations can . . . be understood as those that are imposed by God. . . . But what if this higher-than-human lawgiver is no longer taken into account? Does the concept of a moral obligation . . . still make sense? . . . the concept of moral obligation [is] unintelligible apart from the idea of God. The words remain but their meaning is gone."[5] As a non-theist, Taylor therefore thinks that we literally have no moral obligations, that there is no right or wrong. The Atheistic Moral Realist rightly finds this abhorrent, but, as Taylor clearly sees, on an atheistic view there simply is no ground for duty, even if moral values somehow exist.

Finally, it is fantastically improbable that just that sort of creature would emerge from the blind evolutionary process who corresponds to the abstractly existing realm of moral values.[6] This seems to be an utterly incredible coincidence, when you think about it. It is almost as though the moral realm *knew* that we were coming. It is far more plausible to regard both the natural realm and the moral realm as under the hegemony or authority of a divine Designer and Law-giver than to think that these two entirely independent orders of reality just happened to mesh.

Thus it seems to me that Atheistic Moral Realism is not a plausible view, but is basically a halfway house for philosophers who don't have the stomach for the moral nihilism or meaninglessness that their own atheism implies.

What, then, about premise (2) **Objective moral values do exist?** Some people, as we have seen, deny that objective moral values exist. I agree with them that IF there is no God, then moral values are just the products of socio-biological evolution or expressions of personal taste. But I see no reason to think that that is in fact all that moral values are. Those who think so seem to commit the genetic fallacy, which is trying to invalidate something by showing how it *originated*. For example, a socialist who tried to refute your belief in democratic government by saying, "The only reason you believe in democracy is that you were raised in a democratic society!" would be guilty of the genetic fallacy. For even if it

were true that your belief is totally the result of cultural conditioning, that does absolutely nothing to show that your belief is false (think of people who have been culturally conditioned to believe that the Earth is round!). The truth of an idea is not dependent upon how that idea originated. It's the same with moral values. If moral values are *discovered* rather than *invented*, then our gradual and fallible apprehension of the moral realm no more undermines the objective reality of that realm than our gradual, fallible apprehension of the physical world undermines the objective reality of the physical realm. We know objective moral values exist because we clearly apprehend some of them. The best way to show this is simply to describe moral situations in which we clearly see right and wrong: torturing a child, incest, rape, ethnic cleansing, racism, witch burning, the Inquisition, and so forth. If someone really fails to see the objective moral truth about such matters, then he is simply morally handicapped, like a color-blind person who cannot tell the difference between red and green, and there's no reason to think that his impairment should make us call into question what we see clearly.

From the truth of the two premises the conclusion follows logically that (3) **Therefore, God exists.** Thus, God makes sense of ethics in a way that atheism really cannot. So in addition to the metaphysical and scientific arguments for God, we have a powerful moral argument for God.

[. . .]

Morality

One example of a questionable appeal to authority occurs in Craig's argument from objective morality. Craig quotes Russell, Ruse, and Nietzsche, saying that there could not be objective values without God. Then he claims that there are objective values. He concludes that God exists.

It is important to get this argument out of the way right at the start, because it leads many religious believers to think that all atheists are immoral and dangerous. This is false. Many atheists are nice (including me, I hope). Craig admits this, but then he writes, "On the atheistic view, there's nothing really *wrong* with your raping someone." Such misleading and inaccurate allegations inhibit mutual understanding.

In fact, many atheists are happy to embrace objective moral values. I agree with them. Rape is morally wrong. So is discrimination against gays and lesbians. Even if somebody or some group *thinks* that these acts are not morally wrong, they still *are* morally wrong, so their immorality is objective by Craig's own definition. Craig and I might not always agree about what is objectively morally wrong, but we do agree that some acts are objectively morally wrong.

This admission implies nothing about God, unless objective values depend on God. Why should we believe that they do? Because Russell, Ruse, and Nietzsche say so? But their claims are denied by many philosophers, atheists as well as theists. Even Russell and Ruse themselves denied these claims at other times in their careers. So Craig needs a reason to believe some authorities rather than others.

Craig does give some reasons to back up his authorities. One is that atheists see morality as a biological adaptation, but moral values are not objective if they depend on our biology. This argument commits a fallacy of *equivocation*. When anthropologists talk about a culture's morality, they describe a group of beliefs about what is right and wrong or good and bad. In contrast, when philosophers present a moral system, they seek a set of rules or principles that prescribes what really *is* morally right and wrong or good and bad. Morality in the philosophical sense can be objective, even if people's beliefs about it are subjective. After all, scientific beliefs have biological and cultural origins as well. Just as it is objectively true that the earth moves around the sun, although biology and culture lead some people to believe otherwise, so rape is objectively morally wrong, although biology and culture lead some people to believe otherwise. At least this position is not excluded by the biological and cultural origins of moral beliefs, so atheists can recognize those origins and still consistently believe in objective values.

Craig next asks, "If God did not forbid rape, what makes rape immoral objectively?" This question is supposed to be hard for atheists to answer, because Craig seems to assume that on "the atheistic view" (which one?) what makes rape wrong is some cost to the rapist or to society. These views are inadequate because rape would still be immoral even if the rapist got away with it and even if society was not harmed. But atheists can give a better answer: What makes rape immoral is that rape harms *the victim* in terrible ways. The victim feels pain, loses freedom, is subordinated, and so on. These harms are not justified by any benefits to anyone. Craig still might ask, "What's immoral about causing serious harms to other people without justification?" But now it seems natural to answer, "It simply is. Objectively. Don't you agree?"

This simple answer implies nothing like "in the absence of any people, *Justice* itself exists," so atheists can agree with Craig that they "don't know what this means." Atheists can also agree with Craig and Taylor that "A duty is something that is owed. . . . But something can be owed only to some person or persons." The duty not to rape is owed to the victim. Thus, Craig's criticisms of "Atheistic Moral Realism" attack a *straw man*.

Craig suggests a deeper problem when he asks, "what's so special about human beings?" If harm to the victim is what makes rape immoral, why isn't it also immoral when a lion causes harm by having forced sex with another lion? Atheists can answer that lower animals, such as lions, are not moral agents. They do not make free choices. Their actions are not determined by any conception of what is moral or not. That explains why moral rules and principles do not apply to lower animals any more than they apply to avalanches that kill people. You don't need to add that humans were made in God's image or that we are His favorite species or anything religious.

Philosophers still might long for deeper explanations of why it is immoral for moral agents to cause unjustified harm. Many atheists offer various explanations, but I do not want to commit myself to any particular account here. And I don't need to. Even if atheists were stuck with saying, "It *just is* immoral," that would be a problem for atheism only if theists could give a better answer. They cannot.

In the end, Craig himself says, "If someone really fails to see the objective moral truth about [rape], then he is simply morally handicapped." This is no better (or worse) than saying, "Rape just is morally wrong."

Theists might give deeper accounts of morality, but atheists can adopt or adapt the same accounts – with only one exception. The only theory of morality that atheists cannot accept is one that refers to God, such as when theists claim that what makes rape immoral is that God commands us not to rape. This view faces a difficult question: Why should we obey God's commands? The answer cannot be that God will punish us if we disobey, since might does not make right. Even if a government commands you to turn in runaway slaves and will punish you if you don't, that does not make it morally wrong to hide runaway slaves. Some theists answer that we should obey God's commands because God gave us life. But our parents also gave us life, and yet, at least in modern societies, we do not have to marry whomever our parents tell us to. Theists might answer that it is simply immoral to disobey God, but that claim is no more illuminating than when atheists say that it is simply immoral to cause unjustified harm. A better answer is that God has good reasons for his commands. God commands us not to rape because rape harms the victim. But then that harm (not the command) is what makes rape immoral. Rape would be just as harmful without God, so rape would be morally wrong without God. To think otherwise is like a boy imagining that, once his parents leave, he may beat up his little sister, because the only thing that makes it wrong for him to beat up his sister is that his parents told him not to.

This basic point was presented long ago as a dilemma in Plato's dialogue, *The Euthyphro*: Is rape immoral because God commanded us not to rape or did God command us not to rape because rape is immoral? If God forbids rape because it is immoral, rape must be immoral prior to His command, so His command is not necessary to make it immoral. On the other hand, if God forbids rape but not because it is already immoral, God could have failed to forbid rape, and then there would be nothing immoral about raping whenever we want. That implication is unacceptable. Theists often respond that God cannot fail to command us not to rape, because He is good, and rape is bad. That response brings us right back to the first horn of the dilemma. If God's nature ensures that He will forbid rape because of how bad rape is, then God's command is not needed to make rape wrong. Rape is immoral anyway, and God is superfluous, except maybe for punishment or as a conduit of information.

This dilemma arises not only for rape but for all kinds of immorality. God's commands are arbitrary if He has no reason to command one act rather than another; but, if He does have reasons for His commands, then His *reasons* rather than His *commands* are what make acts immoral. Divine command theorists think that they can solve this dilemma, but all of their solutions fail, in my opinion. Anyway, I don't need to claim that much here. My current task is only to refute Craig's argument, so all I need to show is that atheists can coherently believe in an objective morality. They can, and I do.

Notes

1. Bertrand Russell, *Human Society in Ethics and Politics* (New York: Simon and Schuster, 1955), 124.
2. Michael Ruse, "Evolutionary Theory and Christian Ethics," in *The Darwinian Paradigm* (London: Routledge, 1989), 262–269.
3. John Healey, Amnesty International fund-raising letter, 1991.
4. Richard Taylor, *Ethics, Faith, and Reason* (Englewood Cliffs, N.J.: Prentice-Hall, 1985), 83.
5. Ibid., pp. 83–84.
6. See Gregory E. Ganssle, "Necessary Moral Truths and the Need for Explanation," *Philosophia Christi* 2 (2000): 105–112.

CHAPTER 26

God and Immortality as Postulates of Pure Practical Reason

IMMANUEL KANT

The Immortality of the Soul as a Postulate of Pure Practical Reason

The realization of the *summum bonum* in the world is the necessary object of a will determinable by the moral. But in this will the *perfect accordance* of the mind with the moral law is the supreme condition of the *summum bonum*. This then must be possible, as well as its object, since it is contained in the command to promote the latter. Now, the perfect accordance of the will with the moral law is *holiness*, a perfection of which no rational being of the sensible world is capable at any moment of his existence. Since, nevertheless, it is required as practically necessary, it can only be found in a *progress in infinitum* toward that perfect accordance, and on the principles of pure practical reason it is necessary to assume such a practical progress as the real object of our will.

Now, this endless progress is only possible on the supposition of an *endless* duration of the *existence* and personality of the same rational being (which is called the immortality of the soul). The *summum bonum*, then, practically is only possible on the supposition of the immortality of the soul; consequently this

Immanuel Kant, "God and Immortality as Postulates of Pure Practical Reason," from *Critique of Practical Reason*, trans. T. K. Abbott. London: Longmans, Green and Company, 1873.

immortality, being inseparably connected with the moral law, is a postulate of pure practical reason (by which I mean a *theoretical* proposition, not demonstrable as such, but which is an inseparable result of an unconditional *a priori practical* law).

This principle of the moral destination of our nature, namely, that it is only in an endless progress that we can attain perfect accordance with the moral law, is of the greatest use, not merely for the present purpose of supplementing the impotence of speculative reason, but also with respect to religion. In default of it, either the moral law is quite degraded from its *holiness*, being made out to be *indulgent*, and conformable to our convenience, or else men strain their notions of their vocation and their expectation to an unattainable goal, hoping to acquire complete holiness of will, and so they lose themselves in fantastical *theosophic* dreams, which wholly contradict self-knowledge. In both cases the unceasing *effort* to obey punctually and thoroughly a strict and inflexible command of reason, which yet is not ideal but real, is only hindered. For a rational but finite being, the only thing possible is an endless progress from the lower to higher degrees of moral perfection. The *Infinite* Being, to whom the condition of time is nothing, sees in this series, which is to us endless succession a whole of accordance with the moral law; and the holiness which His command inexorably requires, in order to be true to His justice in the share which He assigns to each in the *summum bonum*, is to be found in a single intellectual intuition of the whole existence of rational beings. All that can be expected of the creature in respect of the hope of this participation would be the consciousness of his tried character, by which, from the progress he has hitherto made from the worse to the morally better, and the immutability of purpose which has thus become known to him, he may hope for a further unbroken continuance of the same, however long his existence may last, even beyond this life, and thus he may hope, not indeed here, nor in any imaginable point of his future existence, but only in the endlessness of his duration (which God alone can survey) to be perfectly adequate to his will (without indulgence or excuse, which do not harmonize with justice).

The Existence of God as Postulate of Pure Practical Reason

In the foregoing analysis the moral law led to a practical problem which is prescribed by pure reason alone, without the aid of any sensible motives, namely, that of the necessary completeness of the first and principal element of the *summum bonum*, viz. Morality; and as this can be perfectly solved only in eternity, to the postulate of *immortality*. The same law must also lead us to affirm the possibility of the second element of the *summum bonum*, viz. Happiness proportioned to that morality, and this on grounds as disinterested as before, and solely from impartial reason; that is, it must lead to the supposition of the existence of a cause adequate to this effect; in other words, it must postulate the *existence of God*, as the necessary condition of the possibility of the *summum bonum* (an object of the will which is necessarily connected with the moral legislation of pure reason). We proceed to exhibit this connexion in a convincing manner.

Happiness is the condition of a rational being in the world with whom *everything goes according to his wish and will*; it rests, therefore, on the harmony of physical nature with his whole end, and likewise with the essential determining principle of his will. Now the moral law as a law of freedom commands by determining principles, which ought to be quite independent on nature and on its harmony with our faculty of desire (as springs). But the acting rational being in the world is not the cause of the world and of nature itself. There is not the least ground, therefore, in the moral law for a necessary connexion between morality and proportionate happiness in a being that belongs to the world as part of it, and therefore dependent on it, and which for that reason cannot by his will be a cause of his nature, nor by his own power make it thoroughly harmonize, as far as his happiness is concerned, with his practical principles. Nevertheless, in the practical problem of pure reason, i.e. the necessary pursuit of the *summum bonum*, such a connexion is postulated as necessary: we ought to endeavour to promote the *summum bonum*, which, therefore, must be possible. Accordingly, the existence of a cause of all nature, distinct from nature itself, and containing the principle of this connexion, namely, of the exact harmony of happiness with morality, is also *postulated*. Now, this supreme cause must contain the principle of the harmony of nature, not merely with a law of the will of rational beings, but with the conception of this *law*, in so far as they make it the *supreme determining principle of the will*, and consequently not merely with the form of morals, but with their morality as their motive, that is, with their moral character. Therefore, the *summum bonum* is possible in the world only on the supposition of a Supreme Being having a causality corresponding to moral character. Now a being that is capable of acting on the conception of laws is an *intelligence* (a rational being), and the causality of such a being according to this conception of laws is his *will*; therefore the supreme cause of nature, which must be presupposed as a condition of the *summum bonum*, is a being which is the cause of nature by *intelligence* and *will*, consequently its author, that is God. It follows that the postulate of the possibility of the *highest derived good* (the best world) is likewise the postulate of the reality of a *highest original good*, that is to say, of the existence of God. Now it was seen to be a duty for us to promote the *summum bonum*; consequently it is not merely allowable, but it is a necessity connected with duty as a requisite, that we should pre-suppose the possibility of this *summum bonum*; and as this is possible only on condition of the existence of God, it inseparably connects the supposition of this with duty; that is, it is morally necessary to assume the existence of God.

It must be remarked here that this moral necessity is *subjective*, that is, it is a want, and to *objective*, that is, itself a duty, for there cannot be a duty to suppose the existence of anything (since this concerns only the theoretical employment of reason). Moreover, it is not meant by this that it is necessary to suppose the existence of God *as a basis of all obligation in general* (for this rests, as has been sufficiently proved, simply on the autonomy of reason itself). What belongs to duty here is only the endeavour to realize and promote the *summum bonum* in the world, the possibility of which can therefore be postulated; and as our reason finds it not conceivable except on the supposition of a supreme intelligence, the admission of this existence is therefore connected with the consciousness of our duty, although the admission itself belongs to the domain of speculative reason. Considered in respect of this alone, as a principle of explanation, it may be called a *hypothesis*, but in reference to the intelligibility of an object given us by the moral law (the *summum bonum*), and consequently of a requirement for practical purposes, it may be called *faith*, that is to say a pure *rational faith*, since pure reason (both in its theoretical and its practical use) is the sole source from which it springs. . . .

The doctrine of Christianity, even if we do not yet consider it as a religious doctrine, gives, touching this point, a conception of the *summum bonum* (the kingdom of God), which alone satisfies the strictest demand of practical reason. The moral law is holy (unyielding) and demands holiness of morals, although all the moral perfection to which man can attain is still only virtue, that is, a rightful disposition arising from *respect* for the law, implying consciousness of a constant propensity to transgression, or at least a want of purity, that is, a mixture of many spurious (not moral) motives

of obedience to the law, consequently a self-esteem combined with humility. In respect, then, of the holiness which the Christian law requires, this leaves the creature nothing but a progress *in infinitum*, but for that very reason it justifies him in hoping for an endless duration of his existence. The *worth* of a character *perfectly* accordant with the moral law is infinite, since the only restriction on all possible happiness in the judgment of a wise and all-powerful distributor of it is the absence of conformity of rational beings to their duty. But the moral law of itself does not *promise* any happiness, for according to our conceptions of an order of nature in general, this is not necessarily connected with obedience to the law. Now Christian morality supplies this defect (of the second indispensable element of the *summum bonum*) by representing the world, in which rational beings devote themselves with all their soul to the moral law, as a *kingdom of God*, in which nature and morality are brought into a harmony foreign to each of itself, by a holy Author who makes the derived *summum bonum* possible. *Holiness* of life is prescribed to them as a rule even in this life, while the welfare proportioned to it, namely, *bliss*, is represented, as attainable only in an eternity; because the *former* must always be the pattern of their conduct in every state, and progress toward it is already possible and necessary in this life; while the *latter*, under the name of happiness, cannot be attained at all in this world (so far as our own power is concerned), and therefore is made simply an object of hope. Nevertheless, the Christian principle of *morality* itself is not theological (so as to be heteronomy), but is autonomy of pure practical reason, since it does not make the knowledge of God and His will the foundation of these laws, but only of the attainment of the *summum bonum*, on condition of following these laws, and it does not even place the proper *spring* of this obedience in the desired results, but solely in the conception of duty, as that of which the faithful observance alone constitutes the worthiness to obtain those happy consequences.

In this manner the moral laws lead through the conception of the *summum bonum* as the object and final end of pure practical reason to *religion*, that is, to the *recognition of all duties as divine commands, not as sanctions, that is to say, arbitrary ordinances of a foreign will and contingent in themselves,* but as essential *laws* of every free will in itself, which, nevertheless, must be regarded as commands of the Supreme Being, because it is only from a morally perfect (holy and good) and at the same time all-powerful will, and consequently only through harmony with this will, that we can hope to attain the *summum bonum* which the moral law makes it our duty to take as the object of our endeavours. Here again, then, all remains disinterested and founded merely on duty; neither fear nor hope being made the fundamental springs, which if taken as principles would destroy the whole moral worth of actions. The moral law commands me to make the highest possible good in a world the ultimate object of all my conduct. But I cannot hope to effect this otherwise than by the harmony of my will with that of a holy and good Author of the world; and although the conception of the *summum bonum* is a whole, in which the greatest happiness is conceived as combined in the most exact proportion with the highest degree of moral perfection (possible in creatures), includes *my own happiness,* yet it is not this that is the determining principle of the will which is enjoined to promote the *summum bonum,* but the moral law, which, on the contrary, limits by strict conditions my unbounded desire of happiness.

Hence also morality is not properly the doctrine how we should *make* ourselves happy, but how we should become *worthy* of happiness. It is only when religion is added that there also comes in the hope of participating some day in happiness in proportion as we have endeavoured to be not unworthy of it.

A man is *worthy* to possess a thing or a state when his possession of it is in harmony with the *summum bonum.* We can now easily see that all worthiness depends on moral conduct, since in the conception of the *summum bonum* this constitutes the condition of the rest (which belongs to one's state), namely, the participation of happiness. Now it follows from this that *morality* should never be treated as a *doctrine of happiness,* that is, an instruction how to become happy; for it has to do simply with the rational condition (*conditio sine qua non*)

of happiness, not with the means of attaining it. But when morality has been completely expounded (which merely imposes duties instead of providing rules for selfish desires), then first, after the moral desire to promote the *summum bonum* (to bring the kingdom of God to us) has been awakened, a desire founded on a law, and which could not previously arise in any selfish mind, and when for the behoof of this desire the step to religion has been taken, then this ethical doctrine may be also called a doctrine of happiness because the *hope* of happiness first begins with religion only.

We can also see from this that, when we ask what is *God's ultimate end* in creating the world, we must not name the *happiness* of the rational beings in it, but the *summum bonum,* which adds a further condition to that wish of such beings, namely, the condition of being worthy of happiness, that is, the *morality* of these same rational beings, a condition which alone contains the rule by which only they can hope to share in the former at the hand of a *wise* Author. For as *wisdom* theoretically considered signifies *the knowledge of the summum bonum,* and practically *the accordance of the will with the summum bonum,* we cannot attribute to a supreme independent wisdom an end based merely on *goodness.* For we cannot conceive the action of this goodness (in respect of the happiness of rational beings) as suitable to the highest original good, except under the restrictive conditions of harmony with the holiness[1] of His will. Therefore those who placed the end of creation in the glory of God (provided that this is not conceived anthropomorphically as a desire to be praised) have perhaps hit upon the best expression. For nothing glorifies God more than that which is the most estimable thing in the world, respect for His command, the observance of the holy duty that His law imposes on us, when there is added thereto His glorious plan of crowning such a beautiful order of things with corresponding happiness. If the latter (to speak humanly) make Him worthy of love, by the *former* He is an object of adoration. Even men can never acquire respect by benevolence alone, though they may gain love, so that the greatest beneficence only procures them honour when it is regulated by worthiness.

That in the order of ends, man (and with him every rational being) is *an end in himself*, that is, that he can never be used merely as a means by any (not even by God) without being at the same time an end also himself, that therefore *humanity* in our person must be *holy* to ourselves, this follows now of itself because he is the *subject of the moral law*, in other words, of that which is holy in itself, and on account of which and in agreement with which alone can anything be termed holy. For this moral law is founded on the autonomy of his will, as a free will which by its universal laws must necessarily be able to agree with that to which it is to submit itself.

Note

1. In order to make these characteristics of these conceptions clear, I add the remark that whilst we ascribe to God various attributes, the quality of which we also find applicable to creatures, only that in Him they are raised to the highest degree, e.g. power, knowledge, presence, goodness, &c., under the designations of omnipotence, omniscience, omnipresence, &c., there are three that are ascribed to God exclusively, and yet without the addition of greatness, and which are all moral. He is the *only holy*, the *only blessed*, the *only wise*, because these conceptions already imply the absence of limitation. In the order of these attributes He is also the *holy lawgiver* (and creator), the *good governor* (and preserver), and the *just judge*, three attributes which include everything by which God is the object of religion, and in conformity with which the metaphysical perfections are added of themselves in the reason.

CHAPTER 27

God and the Moral Order

C. STEPHEN LAYMAN

I argue that three theses about the moral order are defensible, that they do not, beg the question of God's existence, and that they support theism over naturalism. The three theses are:

1. In every actual case, one has most reason to do what is morally required. (One has most reason to do act x if and only if the strongest relevant reasons favor doing x.)
2. If there is no God and no life after death, then there are cases in which morality requires that one make a great sacrifice that confers relatively modest benefits (or prevents relatively modest harms).
3. If in a given situation one must make a great sacrifice in order to do what is morally required, but the sacrifice confers relatively modest benefits (or prevents relatively modest harms), then one does not have most reason to do what is morally required.

("Sacrifice" is here used in a technical way to indicate a permanent and uncompensated loss of something that is in the agent's long-term best interests.) After arguing for theses three theses, I claim that since theism can accommo-

date them and naturalism cannot, theism has a theoretical advantage over naturalism.

Skepticism about the value of moral arguments for theism is widespread among philosophers. But I maintain that there is a conjunction of theses about the moral order that increases the probability of theism. None of these theses begs the question of God's existence and each is, I believe, plausible upon reflection.

Prior to stating my argument, a number of preliminaries are in order. First, in this paper "God" means "an almighty and wholly good being." By "theism" I mean simply the view that God exists. I assume that a wholly good being is perfectly loving. I also assume that God would not order reality in such a way that being moral would disadvantage agents in the long run. And I assume that "the long term" likely involves life after death, given theism.[1]

Second, I do not think the moral argument I am advancing can stand alone. Hence, in putting it forward, I assume either that other theistic arguments provide some significant support for the existence of God or that belief in God is properly basic.[2] Thus, I claim merely that my moral argument makes a positive contribution to a larger, rational case for (or defense of) theism.

Third, the argument I wish to advance is primarily an attempt to show that a certain

C. Stephen Layman, "God and the Moral Order," pp. 304–16 from *Faith and Philosophy*, 19(3), 2002. Reprinted by permission of the Editor and *Faith and Philosophy*.

body of evidence supports theism over *naturalism*. By "naturalism" I mean roughly the view that (a) whatever exists is material or dependent (causally or by supervenience) on material things and (b) material things are entirely governed by natural laws. There is no God according to the naturalist and no life after death. When we die, our bodies decay, and we cease to exist.

Fourth, my argument is designed to appeal to those who believe that there are irreducibly moral facts. I assume, for example, that it is a moral fact that *it is wrong to torture people for fun.* Some individuals or groups may deny or ignore this fact, but it remains a fact. (Analogously, it is fact that the earth is round, and this remains a fact even though it is denied by the Flat Earth Society.) In saying that there are *irreducibly* moral facts, I mean that the facts in question cannot correctly be identified with non-evaluative or non-normative facts, such as merely psychological or sociological facts. To illustrate, the fact that *murder is wrong* cannot be identified with the fact that *most humans disapprove of murder.*

Fifth, my argument is meant to appeal to those who accept a fairly traditional understanding of what is morally right and wrong. I shall simply assume, for example, that lying, stealing, and killing are generally wrong, though I shall not beg any questions about cases commonly regarded as allowable exceptions. For instance, I shall assume that it is generally wrong to intentionally kill a human being, but I shall not beg any questions about the usual range of possible exceptions, e.g., killing in self-defense. Of course, some moral theorists reject what I here call a "fairly traditional understanding of what is right and wrong." To illustrate, some act-utilitarians find killing, stealing, and lying permissible in many situations in which these acts are traditionally considered wrong. In my opinion, ethical theories that justify killing, stealing, and lying in a much wider range of cases than is traditionally allowed are, for that very reason, highly problematic; but I shall not argue that case here. I can only say that those who reject a fairly traditional view about the wrongness of killing, stealing, and lying need read no further, for this paper is unlikely to be of any interest to them.

Sixth, in this paper, locutions such as "This is a moral duty" or "This is a moral requirement" express not merely *prima facie* moral duties but *ultima facie* moral duties. That is, when I say that an act is a moral duty (or that it is morally required), I mean that, in the situation in question, the act is what one morally ought to do *all things considered.* For example, if I say that one is morally required *not to steal* in a certain situation, I do not mean simply that there are some moral considerations against stealing that may be outweighed by other moral considerations in favor of stealing; rather I mean that, taking all morally relevant factors into account, one ought not to steal in that situation.

Seventh, I shall frequently use the locution "x has most reason to do y." A person has "most reason" to do something, in my sense, when the weightiest or strongest reasons favor doing that thing. So, if an agent has most reason to do act A, then taking all relevant reasons into account (e.g., prudential, moral, and aesthetic reasons), they on balance favor performing A. And I assume that "the balance of reasons" is not a merely subjective notion; agents can make mistakes in weighing up reasons for and against an action. For example, in my view, a person who thinks that moral requirements are typically outweighed by personal whims would be making a grave mistake.

Finally, I shall use the word "sacrifice" in a somewhat technical way to indicate *a permanent, net loss of something that is in the long-term best interests of the agent.* So, for present purposes, the word "sacrifice" indicates a permanent loss to the agent, not a temporary one; moreover, it indicates a loss that is not "made up for" in the long run. Of course, as the term is ordinarily used, sacrifices are often temporary and/or compensated, so let me provide some examples of a sacrifice in my sense. Suppose, for the sake of illustration, that there is no life after death, and hence that this earthly life is the only one we've got. On this supposition, if one gave up one's eyesight permanently and this loss was not compensated in any way, then one would have made a sacrifice in my sense of the term, indeed a great sacrifice. Similarly, if a person who is not poor were to give up all of her material goods, and this loss was not compensated in any way, she would have made a sacrifice in my sense of the term, presumably a great one.

I. The Argument Briefly Stated

In this section I will state my argument. My intent is to summarize the basic intuitions that give the argument its plausibility. In the next section I will consider some important objections to the argument and amplify some key points.

My argument has three main premises. Premise (1) is this: *In every actual case one has most reason to do what is morally required.* In other words, in every actual case, if a person is morally required to do some act, then (taking all relevant reasons into account) the balance of reasons favors performing that act. Why think (1) is true? Consider an actual case in which someone has performed an action that you initially find quite puzzling or odd. Then imagine that you become convinced that in performing the action the person was doing his or her moral duty. The act was morally required. Would you not assume that the action was fully justified on this basis? Most of us would and most moral theorists (theist or non-theist) would agree. If an act is my moral duty, then I have overriding reason to perform it. In short, premise (1) is part of our pre-theoretical conception of morality. [. . .]

We can, however, say a bit more in favor of (1): If one does not always have most reason to do what is morally required, then why should one be moral? In a given case, considerations of prudence, aesthetics, and/or etiquette may conflict with moral considerations and one faces the question, "How should one act?", where the "should" is not moral but may be interpreted along the following lines: "Which alternative course of action is backed by the strongest or weightiest reasons?" And if we grant that a certain course of action X is backed by the strongest or weightiest reasons, then from a rational point of view X should be done. Moreover, if we agree that the best reasons sometimes favor immoral actions, and yet we give our full allegiance to morality, then our allegiance to morality is irrational in the sense that

it involves acting on inferior reasons. But I presume that most of my readers give morality their full allegiance and do not regard this allegiance as involving such irrationality. So, I assume that my readers will find themselves strongly inclined to accept (1).

Before going on, however, I should point out that premise (1) is *not* the claim that one has most reason to do what is morally required in every *logically possible* case. In other words, I have not claimed that (1) is a necessary truth, I have merely claimed that it is true. And I shall soon describe some *logically possible* cases or situations in which it seems to me that the agent would not have most reason to do what is morally required. I regard these cases as *merely* logically possible – I myself do not think that cases combining all of the relevant features occur in the actual world. However, those who are convinced that there is no God and no life after death may be inclined to regard cases of the relevant type as actual, and this may raise questions about premise (1). I shall return to this matter in section II, but for now I will simply make three assertions: (a) since we are discussing an argument for God's existence, I take it that the non-existence of God is not properly assumed in evaluating the truth of my premises, (b) I hope to show that each of my three main premises is either embedded in our pre-theoretical conception of morality or defensible via argument (or both), and (c) my overall strategy is to argue that theism has a theoretical advantage over naturalism because theism can accommodate my three main premises while naturalism cannot.

Premise (2) is as follows: *If there is no God and no life after death, then there are cases in which morality requires that one make a great sacrifice that confers relatively modest benefits (or prevents relatively modest harms).* The following case – let us call it the "Ms. Poore case" – is offered in support of premise (2). Suppose Ms. Poore has lived many years in grinding poverty. She is not starving, but has only the bare necessities. She has tried very hard to get ahead by hard work, but nothing has come of her efforts. An opportunity to steal a large sum of money arises. If Ms. Poore steals the money and invests it wisely, she can obtain many desirable things her poverty has denied her: cure for a painful (but nonfatal) medical condition, a well-balanced diet, decent housing, adequate heat in the winter, health insurance, new career opportunities through education, etc. Moreover, if she steals the money, her chances of being caught are very low and she knows this. She is also aware that the person who owns the money is very wealthy and will not be greatly harmed by the theft. Let us add that Ms. Poore rationally believes that if she fails to steal the money, she will likely live in poverty for the remainder of her life. In short, Ms. Poore faces the choice of stealing the money or living in grinding poverty the rest of her life. In such a case, I think it would be *morally* wrong for Ms. Poore to steal the money; and yet, assuming there is no God and no life after death, failing to steal the money will likely deny her a large measure of personal fulfillment, i.e., a large measure of *what is in her long-term best interests.*

I believe that the Ms. Poore case offers intuitive support for premise (2). However, some may reject (2) on the grounds that *virtue is its own reward,* and hence we are *necessarily* compensated for our *morally required* losses because moral virtue is a great enough benefit to those who possess it to compensate fully for any losses it entails. Now, I do not doubt that virtue is a benefit to those who possess it. But the suggestion that *perfect* virtue is *necessarily* a great enough benefit to its possessor to compensate fully for any loss it entails strikes me as highly implausible. Consider the following thought experiment.[3] Imagine two people, Mr. Gladwin and Ms. Goodwin. Mr. Gladwin is a morally lukewarm person who happens to be regarded as a paragon of virtue. He is admired by most people, prosperous, loved by his family and friends, and enjoys his life very much. Ms. Goodwin on the other hand is genuinely virtuous – honest, just, and pure in heart. Unfortunately, because of some clever enemies, Ms. Goodwin is widely regarded as wicked. She is in prison for life on false charges. Her family and friends, convinced that she is guilty, have turned against her. She subsists on a bread and water diet. Leaving God out of the picture for the moment, which of these two people is better off? Which is more fulfilled assuming there is no God? Surely it is Gladwin,

not Goodwin. And note that even if virtue is of value for its own sake, it isn't the *only* thing of value. In particular, freedom is valuable too. Suppose the warden agrees to release Ms. Goodwin if and only if she commits one morally wrong act. Perhaps her accounting skills enable her to help steal some money for the warden. Now, it seems to me that if there is no God and no life after death, it could easily be in Ms. Goodwin's long-term best interest to act immorally in this sort of case. The choice is roughly between life-long misery and an action that is immoral but produces relatively modest harms. So, it does not seem *necessarily* true that the rewards of *perfect* virtue compensate for the rewards of wrongdoing; nor does it seem *necessarily* true that being *perfectly* virtuous is in the agent's long-term best interest. I conclude that the cases of Ms. Poore and Ms. Goodwin provide strong intuitive support for (2).

The above cases also help to support premise (3): *If in a given case one must make a great sacrifice in order to do what is morally required, but the sacrifice confers relatively modest benefits (or prevents relatively modest harms), then one does not have most reason to do what is morally required.* Further support for this third premise comes from the following principle: *It is always and necessarily prudent to act so as to promote one's long-term best interests.* And therefore, making a great sacrifice (where a sacrifice is an *uncompensated* giving-up of something that is in one's long-term best interests) is not prudent. Premise (3) makes explicit what the cases of Ms. Poore and Ms. Goodwin strongly suggest, namely, that *when considerations of prudence and morality clash, if the prudential considerations are truly momentous while the results of behaving immorally are relatively minor, then morality does not override prudence.*

There are, I recognize, multiple barriers to the acceptance of (3). I shall make two brief comments here and leave more technical issues for the next section. First, it may be helpful to note that if God exists, there will be no genuine conflicts between prudence and morality. The reason is this: to act immorally is to sin; to sin is to alienate oneself from God; and it is never in one's long-term best interests to alienate oneself from God. Accordingly, the situation envisioned in the antecedent of premise (3) could not be actual if God exists, for in doing one's moral duty one prevents a very great harm to oneself, namely, alienation from God.

Second, it might be claimed that (a) acting immorally even just once will ruin one's character and (b) to ruin one's character is to incur a great loss; hence, one always has most reason to act morally. The problem with this objection to premise (3) is that (a) is manifestly false. For one's character can be summed up in terms of traits (e.g., being fair, being responsible, being wise, being loving, etc.), each trait being a tendency to act in a certain way. But many or even most people can do something wrong *in what they regard as a rare special case* without thereby altering significantly the basic behavioral tendencies associated with their traits of character.

We have, then, three premises, each of which is plausible on reflection and none of which begs the question of God's existence. Let us now examine the logic of the situation:

> Premise 1. In every actual case, one has most reason to do what is morally required.
> Premise 2. If there is no God and no life after death, then there are cases in which morality requires that one make a great sacrifice that confers relatively modest benefits (or prevents relatively modest harms).
> Premise 3. If in a given case one must make a great sacrifice in order to do what is morally required, but the sacrifice confers relatively modest benefits (or prevents relatively modest harms), then one does not have most reason to do what is morally required.

Premises (2) and (3) imply the following subconclusion:

> 4. If there is no God and no life after death, then in some cases one does not have most reason to do what is morally required.

But (4) and (1) combine to yield:

> 5. "There is no God and no life after death" is false, i.e., either God exists or there is life after death (or both).

Given (5), one can still avoid the conclusion that God exists by arguing that there would be (or at least might well be) a life after death *in which the best interests of morally virtuous persons are realized* even if God does not exist. This move is not, however, open to the naturalist. So, let us consider some objections that, if correct, would prevent us from arriving at step (5).

II.   Objections and Replies

Objection 1. Your argument presupposes that, on pain of irrationality, one needs some nonmoral or prudential reason to do what is morally required; but this presupposition is false. In fact, to be genuinely morally virtuous, one must do the morally right thing simply because it is right. Those who do the right thing for an ulterior, prudential reason are, from a moral point of view, substandard.

Reply. My argument does not involve this presupposition. Granted, from the moral standpoint, one should do the right thing for moral reasons. But what if there are possible situations in which the weightiest reasons favor doing something *besides* what's morally required? On the assumption that agents can find themselves in such situations, it would seem that agents are rationally justified in doing something other than what's morally required. So, I'm not suggesting people should behave morally for ulterior motives, I'm raising the question whether they "should" behave morally at all in certain hypothetical situations. (The "should" in scare quotes does not express the dictates of morality, but the dictates of rationality, i.e., what one *should* do is what one has the weightiest reasons to do). Let me elaborate briefly.

Assuming that conflicts between morality and prudence occur, I agree that moral reasons *can* outweigh prudential ones. For example, suppose ten children will die a very painful death if I don't help them, but helping them will produce a very slight *net* decrease in the satisfaction of my longterm best interests. Such cases are not actual, in my view, but if they do occur, then it seems clear to me that the moral reasons would outweigh the conflicting prudential ones. And so, in such cases, I would have most reason to act morally even though prudence runs contrary to morality.

What I question is the rationality of doing what's morally required if the gains (for all affected) are relatively minor and the long-term disadvantages to the agent are momentous. In such hypothetical cases it seems to me that the strongest reasons do not back morality. Thus, my argument draws attention to the fact that certain metaphysical views are demoralizing, in the sense that they make acting on weaker reasons the price of moral virtue in some instances. It may be useful to illustrate this point with a rather farfetched metaphysical view: Suppose a very powerful Deity is in control of the universe but the Deity particularly delights in ensuring that those who do their duty for duty's sake fare very poorly as compared to the self-serving phonies, the morally lukewarm, and the wicked. And suppose the free agents are well aware of these grim metaphysical facts. In such a situation it seems to me that the free agents would often lack overriding reason to do their moral duty. Again, my point is not that people should do the right things to get a reward; rather, my point is not that in certain hypothetical situations people lack overriding reason to do the right thing.

Objection 2. The cases you describe in support of premises (2) and (3) are bound to be taken by the naturalist as evidence against premise (1). Also, by attacking or qualifying the thesis that *virtue is its own reward*, you have undermined the only ground a naturalist has for accepting (1). Thus, although your premises may be logically consistent, your argument is dialectically flawed; in effect you give the naturalist good reason to reject premise (1).

Reply. First of all, my moral cases (i.e., Ms. Poore, Ms. Goodwin) provide evidence against premise (1) *only* on the assumption that there is no God and no life after death. But one can hardly make this assumption and give the argument an open-minded run for its money; it is after all an argument for God's existence! So, if the naturalist regards my moral cases as evidence against (1), the naturalist is begging the question, and the dialectical error is on the naturalist's side.

Second, I doubt that many people accept (1) on the grounds that *virtue is its own reward*. I doubt that (1) is typically accepted on the basis of an argument at all. Rather, when certain questions are posed, we simply find that we are presupposing (1). To illustrate, consider an (admittedly contrived) moral theory: *one is always morally required to do what is best for others.*[5] On this theory, the agent's interests are irrelevant to morality – the agent must do what is best for others regardless of the cost to himself. But suppose a significant sacrifice on my part would only marginally improve someone else's lot, e.g., Sue's minor headache can somehow be relieved if I give up my annual two-week vacation. This moral theory seems to demand that I give up my vacation. Well, why not accept this theory of morality? One good reason seems to be this: it fails to give self-interest its due, and thus yields a situation in which *alleged* moral requirements are overridden by self-interest. The point, of course, is not that self-interest does override morality, but rather that the overridingness of moral reasons is presupposed in our moral theorizing. And of course, we bring this presupposition to our moral theorizing because it is deeply embedded in our pre-theoretical conception of morality.[6]

Third, the appeal to *virtue is its own reward* is not the only possible defense of premise (1). As noted previously, if (1) is false, then immoral actions are sometimes backed by reasons as strong as (or stronger than) those backing the moral alternative. But if immoral actions are sometimes backed by reasons as strong as (or stronger than) those backing the moral alternative, then the institution of morality lacks rational authority. That is, the system of morality does not a have blanket endorsement from the rational point of view – only parts of it do. And even if those parts are very large, this consequence is not something most of us can readily accept.

Objection 3. Some moral theorists, in company with Kant and R.M. Hare, claim that moral reasons necessarily or by definition override all others. If such views are correct, then premise (3) must be false. For if moral reasons necessarily override all other kinds of reasons, then there can be no situation in which one lacks most reason to act morally; but (3) presupposes that such situations are possible.

Reply. No dictionary defines "morality" in terms of overridingness. So, those who *define* moral reasons as overriding ones are offering a *theory* and we need evidence for the theory. Similarly, the claim that moral reasons *necessarily* override all others is not obvious, and it won't do to argue for it in an inductive fashion by citing cases. The problem with such an inductive approach is that it runs afoul of the very sorts of cases that serve as the focus of this paper. The hypothetical cases described in section I cast doubt on the claim that "It is *necessarily* true that moral reasons are overriding." So, the situation seems to be that most of us find ourselves believing that, in every actual case, moral reasons are overriding; but – unless we take for granted certain highly controversial metaphysical theses [. . .] – we lack good reason to think that "Moral reasons are overriding" is a *necessary truth.*

Objection 4. Kantians argue that *whenever an agent acts immorally, she acts on a maxim that she cannot consistently will to be universal law.* But it is irrational to act on a maxim one cannot consistently will to be universal law; hence, one always has most reason to act morally; therefore, premise (3) is false.

Reply. My reply is twofold. First, the Kantian thesis is in fact highly dubious. Consider the case of Ms. Poore. How should we describe the maxim she is acting on? Presumably along the following lines: *Whenever I find myself in a circumstance in which (a) I am very poor but not destitute, (b) I can easily steal a large sum of money with impunity from a very rich person, (c) I will doom myself to enduring and wretched poverty by not stealing, and (d) I will inflict little harm by stealing, I shall steal.* Why can't Ms. Poore consistently will this maxim to be universal law? The clauses of the maxim ensure that it can be applied only rarely. And I see no conceptual difficulties regarding theft (or the institution of private property) if we contemplate a world (similar to the actual world but) in which all relevantly situated persons act in accord with the maxim. And although Ms. Poore might not *like* to have money stolen from her if she were rich, she might nevertheless be *willing* to have anyone in her current

circumstances act in accord with the stated maxim, and willing to take a chance on being stolen from in the event that she herself should become rich. Perhaps a few Kantians (certainly not Kant himself) will agree with all this and adopt a revisionist morality that allows stealing (lying, etc.) in the cases I've described. But since such revisionism runs contrary to my settled judgment of the cases, I do not think it provides the naturalist with a cost-free response to my argument.

Second, suppose we grant that *if one acts immorally, one acts on a maxim one cannot consistently will to be universal law.* Does it follow logically that one has most reason to be moral? Not clearly. For one may have very strong reasons to make a special exception in one's own case. And even if making a special exception in one's own case is always immoral, it may sometimes be rational. One can imagine Ms. Poore saying, "Even if I cannot consistently will that all possible agents in my situation commit theft, the fact is relatively few people will ever be in my situation and in this case there's just too much at stake for me personally in doing the moral thing."
[. . .]

III.   Completing the Argument

If my argument up to this point is any good, then it has given some support to step (5), i.e., the thesis that either God exists or there is life after death (or both). However, (5) could be true even if God does not exist; for it may be that there is no God but there is a life after death in which the best interests of the morally virtuous are realized. So, in this section I wish to complete my moral argument for theism by defending the following premise:

> 6. It is likely that if there is a life after death in which the long-term best interests of the morally virtuous are realized, then God exists.

If premise (6) is defensible, then if it is conjoined with premises (1) through (3), we have an argument that lends positive support to theism. In defending (6), I shall rely on two assumptions. First, I shall assume that there is no life after death given naturalism. Second, I shall assume that the two best theories of the afterlife centrally involve either theism or reincarnation.

Given that reincarnation occurs, each person's soul is transferred to another body at some time after death. So, given reincarnation, there is life after death. And given the doctrine of karma, one's degree of moral virtue determines one's circumstances in the next life. Indeed, if the law of karma governs the universe, the more nearly one lives up to the demands of morality, the better one's circumstances in the next life.[7] Thus, the traditional Hindu doctrines of reincarnation and karma combine to yield a cosmic moral order.

Of course, a doctrine of reincarnation could be combined with theism, but we are here concerned with versions of reincarnation that are in logical competition with theism, i.e., views that deny the existence of any sort of personal Deity. And it seems to me that such views are self-undermining, for the complexity of the moral order they postulate provides good evidence of an Intelligent and Moral Designer. Consider: given that reincarnation and karma hold in the absence of any Deity, the universe is governed not only by physical laws but by impersonal moral laws. These moral laws must be very complicated, for they have to regulate the connection between each soul's moral record in one life and that soul's total circumstances in its next life, including which body it has and the degree of happiness (and/or misery) it experiences. Accordingly, these laws must some-how take into account every act, every intention, and every choice of every moral agent and ensure that the agent receives nothing less than his or her just deserts in the next life. Now, the degree of complexity involved here is not only extraordinarily high, it is also complexity that serves a moral end, namely, justice. Such complexity can hardly be accepted as a brute fact. *Highly complex order serving a moral end* is a phenomenon that legitimates appeal to an intelligent cause. And if the order is on a scale far surpassing what can reasonably be attributed to human intelligence, the appeal to divine intelligence is surely justified. Thus, the moral order postulated by non-theistic reincarnation provides evidence for theism.[8]

To sum up, even if reincarnation occurs in accordance with the principle of karma, the nature of the postulated moral order lends support to theism. Therefore, it seems likely that if there is a life after death in which the ultimate fulfillment of the morally virtuous is realized, then God exists. And this thesis, together with the argument of section I, provides at least some positive support for the proposition that God exists.

Seattle Pacific University

Notes

1. Here is a sketch of an argument linking theism and life after death: A wholly loving God would care deeply about the fulfillment of human creatures and would not leave human creatures frustrated and unfulfilled if he is able to provide the means of fulfillment. Yet, as virtually everyone will admit, in this earthly life, the deepest yearnings of human beings are not fulfilled, and many human beings have led lives characterized by frustration. An almighty God is surely able to provide the means of fulfillment by providing human creatures with a form of existence after death in which their deepest yearnings can be satisfied. So, if God exists, life after death seems likely.

2. A belief is *properly basic* if it does not need to be based on other beliefs in order to be rational or warranted.

3. This thought experiment is borrowed in its essentials from Richard Taylor, "Value and the Origin of Right and Wrong," in Louis Pojman, ed., *Ethical Theory: Classical and Contemporary Readings* (Belmont, California: Wadsworth, 1989), 115–21. For some interesting, brief reflections on the difficulty of showing that it is in everyone's best interest to be virtuous, see Bernard Williams, *Ethics and the Limits of Philosophy* (Cambridge, Massachusetts: Harvard University Press, 1985), 43–5. Also see, Peter Singer, *Practical Ethics* (London: Cambridge University Press, 1979), 201–20.

4. I am indebted to Eleonore Stump for helping me to phrase this objection in a clear fashion.

5. The example is borrowed from Sarah Stroud, "Moral Overridingness and Moral Theory," *Pacific Philosophical Quarterly 79* (1998), 170–89.

6. Here perhaps is the place to note that some ethicists have rejected the thesis that moral requirements always override all other considerations. See, for example, Philippa Foot, "Are Moral Considerations Overriding?" in *Virtues and Vices* (Berkeley and Los Angeles: University of California Press, 1978), pp. 181–8. The argumentation in Foot's essay seems to me unconvincing, however. For example, Foot points out that people who care about morality will sometimes say things of this sort, "It was morally wrong to do X but I *had to* do X to avoid disaster for myself, my family, or my country." But it seems to me that this sort of statement does not prove even that the speaker believes that the moral reasons are overridden by other reasons. After all, a smoker may say, "I know that the best and strongest reasons favor not smoking, but I *had to* light up anyway." Notoriously, we humans often feel we "have to" do things that are backed by inferior reasons.

7. According to traditional Hindu thought, if one is *perfectly* moral, one deserves *moksha* (salvation), i.e., deliverance from *samsara* (the cycle of birth and death). This deliverance is generally equated with a kind of oneness with ultimate reality.

8. The main point of this paragraph is borrowed from Robin Collins, "Eastern Religions," in Michael J. Murray, ed., *Reason for the Hope Within* (Grand Rapids, MI: Eerdmans, 1999), 206.

CHAPTER 28

God and Morality

ERIK WIELENBERG

God as the Omnipotent Creator of Ethics

[. . .]

Theists typically maintain that God is the omnipotent creator of the universe. This thesis usually is understood as implying at least that God is the ultimate source of all contingently existing things and of all contingent truths. Some theists hold that God's creative powers extend not just to the way the universe is and the things that it contains, but also to the way the universe ought to be and the values it contains. Philip Quinn (1998) explains this approach nicely:

> Theists customarily wish to insist on a sharp distinction between God and the world, between the creator and the created realm. According to traditional accounts of creation and conservation, each contingent thing depends on God's power for its existence whenever it exists. God, by contrast, depends on nothing external to himself for his existence. So God has complete sovereignty over contingent existence. . . . Considerations of theoretical unity of a familiar sort then make

it attractive to extend the scope of divine sovereignty . . . from the realm of fact into the realm of value.[1]

Theists who hold the sort of view described by Quinn maintain that just as it is God's creative activity that brought it about that atoms exist and that light has the speed it does, it is also God's creative activity that determines which things are good and evil, which actions are morally right, wrong, and obligatory, which traits of character are virtues and vices, which human lives are worth living, and so on. According to a particularly strong version of this view, God has the power to arrange morality as He sees fit; He is the author of the laws of morality in the same sense that He is the author of the laws of nature. Moreover, because He is omnipotent, the only constraint on which laws of morality God creates is the limit of possibility. If we understand *ethical claims* as claims about which things are good, evil, morally right, wrong, obligatory, virtuous, or vicious, then we can capture the essence of this view with the following pair of theses:[2]

> Control Thesis: Every *logically consistent* ethical claim, E, is such that God could make E true.
> Dependency Thesis: Every *true* ethical claim is true in virtue of some act of will on the part of God.

Erik Wielenberg, "God and Morality," pp. 39–42, 48–65 from *Value and Virtue in a Godless Universe*. Cambridge: Cambridge University Press, 2005. © Cambridge University Press, reproduced with permission. Reprinted by permission of the author Erik Wielenberg.

The Dependency Thesis may be held as a contingent truth or as a necessary truth. If it is a necessary truth, then the presence of ethical truths in the universe entails that God exists. If the thesis is necessarily true then without God, nothing can be good, bad, right, wrong, virtuous, or vicious. As Craig puts it, "In a universe without God, good and evil do not exist. There is only the bare, valueless, fact of existence."[3] This sort of argument – from the premise that the Dependency Thesis is necessarily true to the conclusion that there are no ethical truths if God does not exist – is the *God as the source of ethics* argument.[4]

Some theists who accept the conclusion of the God as the source of ethics argument fail to appreciate its consequences fully. Craig is an example. One of his central themes is how *awful* it would be if God did not exist. Consider, for instance, Craig's account of the realization of his own mortality:

> I can remember very vividly the first time my father told me, as a child, that someday, I was going to die. Somehow as a child the thought had just never occurred to me, and when he told me, I was just over-whelmed with an unbearable fear and sadness, and I cried and cried and cried, and although my father tried to reassure me repeatedly that this event was a long way off, to me that just didn't matter. The fact was that I was going to die and would be no more. And that thought just overwhelmed me.[5]

Later, Craig refers to the "horror of modern man" – facing life in (what "modern man" takes to be) a Godless universe. But if there can be no good or evil if God does not exist, then there can be no *evil* if God does not exist. So if God doesn't exist, nothing *bad* can ever happen to anyone. The conclusion of the God as the source of ethics argument implies that there is nothing good about a Godless universe – but it equally implies that there is nothing *bad* about it either. If this argument is sound there can be nothing awful or horrible about a Godless universe. The short version of Craig's self-contradictory message is "Without God there would be no value in the universe – and think how horrible that would be!"

Still, this confusion by itself does not constitute an objection to the God as the source of ethics argument. To criticize that argument, I will consider two positions. The stronger position consists of both the Control Thesis and the Dependency Thesis. The weaker position denies the Control Thesis but accepts the Dependency Thesis. Ultimately I will conclude that both theses are false. If this is right, then the God as the source of ethics argument fails.

Since the God as the source of ethics argument relies only on the Dependency Thesis, some might wonder why I bother to discuss the Control Thesis at all. One reason is my suspicion that some theists may find the Dependency Thesis attractive because they accept the Control Thesis. Although the latter does not entail the former, acceptance of the latter naturally suggests acceptance of the former. Another reason is that the fact that the Control Thesis is false is an important piece of information that will help us understand properly the relationship between God and ethical truth. After criticizing both the strong and the weak positions, I will sketch an alternative account of God's relationship to ethical truth. The earlier rejection of both the strong and weak positions will help to motivate this account.

Criticism of the Strong Position

One difficulty with the Control Thesis can be illustrated by a simple example. Imagine a contest in which the prize is omnipotence. There are two competitors in this contest. The first competitor hopes to win the prize and use his omnipotence for the good of humanity. He intends to bring peace, justice, and happiness to the entire world. The second competitor hopes to win the prize and use his omnipotence for his own selfish, nefarious purposes. He plans to slaughter most of humanity and force the rest to live in excrement pits where they will work themselves to death as his slaves and be subject to torture at his hand for his amusement. As it happens, the second competitor wins the contest and becomes omnipotent. It seems clear that the worst has happened – a thoroughly vicious being has become all-powerful and the world is on the verge of being plunged into evil. Fortunately, this does not happen. This is because the first use to which the winner puts his newly acquired omnipotence is to change certain ethical facts. He makes it the case that the slaughter of innocents is fantastically good, that undeserved suffering is just, and that a human life devoted to serving him has the greatest possible amount of internal meaning. He also makes it the case that he himself is a morally perfect being. He does this not by changing the nature of his character (his desires, motives, goals, and so on are just the same as before), but rather by *changing the nature of moral perfection*. He then implements his now fantastically good and just plan. He slaughters most of the humans, throws the rest into the pits, and so on. But, because he changed the ethical facts first, the story has a happy ending. All is for the best. The film version of this scenario would leave you grinning like a fool as you left the theater.

There is just one problem with all of this: The story in question is crazy. What is crazy about the story is precisely the idea that a being could be powerful enough to make it the case that, for instance, the slaughter of innocents is fantastically good. There simply is no amount of power that would enable a being to make that true. Power – even omnipotence – may be used in the service of good or evil, but its use is to be evaluated within a moral framework that is itself not subject to the power in question. This story seems to get things backward by making morality subject to power. We might put the point this way: A (putatively) moral framework that could be completely rearranged by a sufficiently powerful being is not a *moral* framework at all. The moral of this story is that omnipotence does not include power over all ethical claims. But presumably if the Control Thesis is true at all, it is true in virtue of the fact that omnipotence does include this sort of power. Hence, the Control Thesis is false.
[...]

Criticism of the Weak Position

There are, then, good reasons for theist and naturalist alike to reject the Control Thesis. However, even if this is right, it doesn't refute the God as the source of ethics argument because that argument is based on the Dependency Thesis. Moreover, some theists have proposed a way of rejecting the Control Thesis while continuing to hold the Dependency Thesis. We may broach this proposal by way of an objection to the Strong Position proposed by Ralph Cudworth (1976):

> [D]iverse modern theologers do not only seriously, but zealously contend . . . that there is nothing absolutely, intrinsically, and naturally good and evil, just and unjust, antecedently to any positive command or prohibition of God; but that the arbitrary will and pleasure of God . . . by its commands and prohibitions, is the first and only rule and measure thereof. Whence it follows unavoidably, that nothing can be imagined so grossly wicked, or so foully unjust or dishonest, but if it were supposed to be commanded by this omnipotent Deity, must needs upon that hypothesis forthwith become holy, just, and righteous.[6]

Cudworth's point seems to be that if the Control Thesis were true, then anything could be "holy, just, and righteous" – which seems absurd. The problematic implication of the Control Thesis, as Cudworth sees it, is the *contingency* of certain ethical truths. The Control Thesis allegedly implies, for instance, that it could be morally permissible for one person gratuitously to pummel another.

A popular strategy for responding to this kind of objection is to maintain that because it is part of God's essential nature to have a certain type of character (say, to be loving), there are some things such that making them good or right is incompatible with God's essential nature. For example, Edward Wierenga (1983) suggests that because God is all-loving, "He would not command an action which, were it to be performed, would be a gratuitous pummeling of another human being."[7] In this way, it is denied that God could make just any logically consistent ethical claim true. There are some logically consistent ethical claims – for instance that it would be obligatory for someone to inflict a gratuitous pummeling on another human being – that God cannot make true because doing so is inconsistent with His essential nature. Nevertheless, all true ethical claims are true in virtue of some act of will on the part of God. It is still divine *willing* that determines which ethical claims are true, but the scope of divine willing is limited by the divine character. According to this proposal, the Control Thesis is false because it is incompatible with the claim that God essentially has a character of a certain sort, but the Dependency Thesis is nevertheless true.

I think the revised proposal is unacceptable for two reasons. First, implicit in the proposal is the notion that God has the *power* to make any logically consistent ethical claim true; it is only His character that prevents Him from being able to exercise this power. This implies that if, *per impossible*, God were not loving, He could make it the case that it is obligatory for someone to inflict a gratuitous pummeling on another human being. But I think that the story about the good competitor – evil competitor contest . . . shows that even this more modest claim is false. [. . .]

Second, notice that the Dependency Thesis implies that nothing distinct from God is intrinsically good or evil. The claim that the Dependency Thesis is necessarily true implies that it is *impossible* for anything distinct from God to be intrinsically good or evil. This is because intrinsic value is the value a thing has in virtue of its intrinsic nature. If an act of will on the part of God bestows value on something distinct from God, that value cannot be intrinsic. It will be value that the thing has in virtue of something distinct from itself. I think this implication is problematic for the simple reason that some things distinct from God actually are intrinsically good and some things actually are intrinsically evil. Pain, for example, seems to be an intrinsic evil. It is evil in and of itself; its badness is part of its intrinsic nature and is not bestowed upon it from some external source. Yet the theist who accepts the Dependency Thesis must reject this, and maintain instead that pain is bad only because God made it so.

It may be replied that in making this claim I am begging the question against someone who holds the Dependency Thesis. Do I have an *argument* for my claim that some things are

intrinsically good or evil? In response to this charge I appeal to some remarks Roderick Chisholm (1973) makes in *The Problem of the Criterion*. Chisholm's topic in that book is epistemology, and he suggests that if we must choose whether to accept some philosophical principle about knowledge or to accept some obvious truth such as that I know I have hands, we should accept the obvious truth.[8] Similarly, it seems to me that if we must choose between the Dependency Thesis and the claim that pain is intrinsically evil or that falling in love is intrinsically good, it is the Dependency Thesis that should go. An epistemology that leads to the conclusion that individuals cannot know they have hands should be rejected; similarly, a metaphysics that leads to the conclusion that falling in love is not intrinsically good, or that pain is not intrinsically evil, should be rejected. In this vein Nielsen writes:

> God or no God, the torturing of innocents is vile. More generally, even if we can make nothing of the concept of God, we can readily come to appreciate . . . that, if anything is evil, inflicting or tolerating unnecessary and pointless suffering is evil, especially when something can be done about it. . . . Can't we be more confident about this than we can about any abstract or general philosophical point we might make in ethical theory?[9]

I conclude, therefore, that the Dependency Thesis should be rejected along with the Control Thesis. If this is correct, then the God as the source of ethics argument, because it is based on the claim that the Dependency Thesis is necessarily true, fails.

An Alternative Account

Rejecting these two theses raises some questions. If the Dependency Thesis is false, then there are some true ethical claims whose truth is not due to some act of will on the part of God. What, then, makes these ethical claims true? If the Control Thesis is false, then there are some logically consistent ethical claims that not even God could make true. Why is

God unable to make such claims true? Is this inability consistent with God's omnipotence?

One view that provides answers to these questions is the view that *some ethical truths are necessary truths*. Consider, for instance, the claim that suffering is intrinsically evil. I suggest that this ethical claim is true, and, furthermore, that it is a necessary truth. This claim is true not just in the actual world but in every possible world. Just as there is no possible universe in which $2 + 2 = 5$, there is no possible universe in which suffering is not intrinsically evil. Suffering is bad in virtue of its intrinsic nature – and this is true in every possible universe.

This is a view that can be accepted by atheist and theist alike. With respect to the question, what makes these ethical claims true? my answer is that it is the same sort of thing that makes other necessary truths true – namely, the essential nature of the entities that those claims are about. It is the essential character of the numbers 2 and 5, and of the relations addition and identity, that make it the case that necessarily, $2 + 2$ is not equal to 5. It is the essential nature of pain that makes it the case that it is intrinsically evil. This view also explains why God is unable to render such claims false and how this is compatible with His omnipotence. He is unable to render them false because they simply cannot be rendered false; as necessary truths, they have but one possible truth value – true. It is widely held that omnipotence does not include the ability to do what is impossible. Making necessary falsehoods true is impossible. Thus the fact that God cannot make baby-torture for the sake of entertainment morally permissible does not imply that He is not omnipotent.

I do not mean to suggest that all ethical truths are necessarily true. Indeed, it is clear that many ethical truths are contingent truths. For instance, suppose that I promise to meet you for lunch on a certain occasion. Also suppose that on the occasion in question I have no sufficiently weighty reason not to keep my promise. It follows that I am obligated to meet you for lunch. This is an ethical truth, yet it is a contingent truth. I might not have promised to meet you in the first place; indeed, I might not have been born at all. In either case,

the ethical claim in question would have been false. But it seems to me that contingent ethical truths like these are always partly grounded in some necessary ethical truth (or truths). In this case, the relevant truth is something like, "It is morally wrong to fail to keep a promise unless you have some sufficiently weighty reason for doing so."[10]

These necessary ethical truths, I believe, are part of the furniture of the universe. If God exists, they are not rendered true by Him nor are they dependent upon His will for their truth. Moreover, at least some of them are such that He lacks the power to render them false. These necessary ethical truths constitute the ethical background of every possible universe. It is within this framework that all beings and their actions, divine and human alike, are to be evaluated.

Still, it is consistent with this view that God, if He exists, has some role in shaping the moral system to which human beings are subject. That this is so may be seen by considering a familiar kind of case involving humans. Suppose a friend of yours does a huge favor for you. He is happy to do you the favor, but notes (correctly) that "you owe me one." A few weeks later, we may suppose, your friend calls you and informs you that he really needs to borrow your car for the day. You have no pressing need for the car yourself and your friend gently reminds you of the favor he did for you. It is plausible to suppose that, under these circumstances, you have a moral obligation to loan your friend your car for the day.[11] In this case, your friend's request to borrow the car has imposed an obligation on you that you would not otherwise have had. Moreover, there are a variety of obligations your friend could have imposed on you other than the obligation to loan him your car, as there are plenty of other reasonable requests he might have made instead. But of course your friend is not an all-powerful arbiter of morality. It is precisely the framework of necessary ethical truth that enables your friend to impose the obligation in question upon you. The system of morality itself licenses this sort of thing under certain circumstances. This case suggests another possible relationship between God and ethics. This type of relationship is the topic of the next section.

God as Divine Commander

We often find ourselves faced with certain obligations because of how we are related to others. When someone is my friend or spouse, I have obligations to that other person that I would not otherwise have. For example, if I am married to X, then I am morally obligated to be faithful toward X in a way that I would not be if I were not married to X. Some of these relationships seem to be essential to the human condition. For instance, every human being has two genetic parents. This feature of the human condition imposes obligations on humans that they would not otherwise have; arguably, we have obligations toward our parents that we do not have toward any other human being. Imagine for a moment that a theory of spontaneous generation of humans is correct – that is, that rather than being born, human beings have no parents and instead simply grow spontaneously out of the ground from time to time. In a world like that, no human being would be genetically related to any other human being, and the obligations of humans in such a world would be quite different from the obligations of humans in our world. This suggests that whether or not human beings have a *divine creator* may affect the moral obligations that human beings have. If God did exist, then perhaps we would have moral obligations that we in fact do not have (supposing that naturalism is true). It is important to distinguish two claims here. The first is the modest claim that the existence of God brings with it *some* moral obligations that we would not have if God did not exist. The other claim is the so-called "Karamazov's Thesis."[12] This is the thesis that if God does not exist, then all human actions are morally permissible and human beings have no moral obligations at all. Without God, anything goes.

Why might someone accept Karamazov's Thesis? One answer to this question has its roots in the Platonic (1977) dialogue *Phaedo*. In that dialogue, Socrates says that "the gods are our guardians and that men are one of their possessions."[13] Some Biblical passages indicate the presence of this strand of thought in the Judeo-Christian tradition as well. In the Old Testament, God sometimes refers to the Israelites as His "treasured possession."[14] Picking up on this idea, Baruch Brody (1974) makes the following tentative suggestion:

> [I]f we are the property of God, then perhaps we just have an obligation to do whatever he says, and then perhaps we can . . . consider the possible claim that . . . actions are right (wrong) for us to do just in case and only because God, who has created and owns us and whom we therefore have an obligation to follow, wants us to do (refrain from doing) them.[15]

[. . .]

According to Brody's principle, if God does not exist then nothing is morally wrong – but nothing is morally right either. Still, Brody's principle implies that without God, human beings have no moral obligations – and that is the claim in which we are most interested.

Brody considers the objection that owning a human being is "an unjust act, one that cannot meaningfully be ascribed to an all just being."[16] As Brody sees it, the crucial question is, "is it unjust for God, who is vastly superior to us and is our creator, to possess human beings?"[17] But let us suppose that it is just for God to possess human beings, and that if God exists all human are His property. It seems to me that it does not follow from this that without God, human beings have no moral obligations. This is because the claim that (1) Being X owns Being Y does not imply (2) the *only* moral obligations Y has are the ones imposed by X. Such an inference is open to a variety of counter examples; I will present just one. Suppose that X and Y are married to each other and both are the property of Z. Under these circumstances, X and Y will have a variety of obligations. Some of these obligations may derive from Z's ownership of X and Y – but others will derive from the marriage relation that obtains between X and Y themselves. If X and Y were not owned by Z, they might have fewer obligations than they do have – but they would still have some obligations. Specifically, they would still have the various obligations that arise from the fact that they are married to each other. So the claim that human beings are God's property does not establish Karamazov's Thesis.

There are grounds for maintaining that God has the authority to impose moral obligations on us other than the claim that we are God's property. Brody considers the idea that "we have an obligation to follow God's wishes because he is our creator."[18] Brody's suggestion is that even if we are not God's property, the fact that He is our creator may put Him in a position to impose various moral obligations upon us. Recall the example of your friend who was in a position to impose certain moral obligations upon you because you "owed him one." If God did exist, perhaps we, too, would "owe Him one" for creating us, and consequently He would be in a position to impose obligations upon us.

Adams examines the idea that the gratitude we owe to God might license Him to impose obligations upon us. Among the reasons humans might have to obey God, Adams includes "reasons of gratitude," such as the facts that "God is our creator . . . God loves us . . . God gives us all the goods we enjoy . . . [the] covenants God has made with us for our good . . . or other things God has done to save us or bring us to the greatest good."[19] Similarly, in his book *The God Who Commands*, Richard Mouw (1996) writes:

The God who issues the "Thou shalts" of Exodus 20 is the one who prefaces those directives with the reminder that we have been delivered from the house of bondage. And the one who, in the New Testament, tells us to keep his commandments, does so on the basis of the fact that when we were yet sinners he died for us. The God who commands in the Scriptures is the one who offers the broken chariots of the Egpytians and the nail-scarred hands of the divine Son as a vindication of the right to tell us what to do.[20]

A second possible basis for God's status as our rightful commander has to do not with the gratitude we owe God but rather with God's intrinsic nature:

God is supremely knowledgeable and wise. . . . God is the Good itself, supremely beautiful and rich in nonmoral as well as moral perfection. . . . One important

excellence is justice. It clearly matters to the persuasive power of God's character, as a source of moral obligation, that the divine will is just.[21]

Adams also points to the goodness of God's commands themselves, declaring that, "[I]t is crucial . . . that the behavior that God commands is not bad, but good, either intrinsically or by serving a pattern of life that is very good."[22] Still another ground is suggested by Swinburne:

God is the creator of the inanimate world and, not being known to have ceded ownership of it, is properly judged its owner. . . . The owner of property has the right to tell those to whom he has loaned it what they are allowed to do with it. Consequently God has a right to lay down how that property, the inanimate world, shall be used and by whom. If God has made the Earth, he can say which of his children can use which part.[23]

There are, then, a wide range of plausible reasons for the idea that if God did exist, He would be authorized to impose certain moral obligations on human beings.[24] It is important to notice that the sort of view suggested by Adams and the others is quite different from the view that in virtue of His omnipotence, God has the power of constructing ethics through the force of His will. The view under consideration now is that in virtue of some *ethical* feature or features of God (such as His goodness) or some ethically significant relationship between humans and God (He is our creator, or our savior), God is authorized to impose moral obligations upon us. According to this sort of view, God is our duly authorized commander. Though both kinds of view reasonably may be labeled 'divine command theories,' they differ from each other in significant ways. I have already argued that the first sort of view is false. Now I will argue not that the second sort of view is false, but rather that it is inconsistent with Karamazov's Thesis and hence hardly can be used to establish that thesis. The second type of divine command theory can be used legitimately to establish that if God exists, then *some* of our moral obligations are imposed on us by God. But it cannot be used to establish the stronger conclusion that if God exists, then *all* of our moral obligations are imposed on us by God.

My argument turns on the following question: *How* exactly could God impose obligations on human beings? That is, suppose that God is our duly authorized commander. Through what *process* could God impose obligations on us? This question does not seem to arise on the previously discussed view that God is the omnipotent creator of ethical truth. On that view, God renders certain ethical claims true in much the same way that He renders certain physical claims true – by simply willing that they be true. But a duly authorized commander cannot impose moral obligations *merely* by willing them into existence. So if we are thinking of God according to this model, we must inquire into the nature of the process by which God imposes obligations upon us. In his paper "Divine Command, Divine Will, and Moral Obligation" Mark Murphy (1998) usefully outlines the three main options, which are that God can impose on person S the moral obligation to do A: (1) by *commanding* S to do A; (2) by *willing that S be morally obligated to* do A; or (3) by *willing* that S do A.[25]

Let us consider the three possibilities in reverse order. One of the main problems facing a proponent of option (3) is that of specifying the appropriate sense of 'willing' as it appears in (3):

> The difficulty that lurks in specifying such a sense is this. If one specifies a sense of willing that is too strong, it would follow that no one could possibly violate a moral requirement; if one specifies a sense of willing that is too weak, it does not seem appropriate to connect that sense to moral obligation; and it is not easy to specify a sense of willing that falls between these unacceptable extremes.[26]

[. . .]

Adams suggests that this type of view fails because of the possibility of cases in which "God wants us to do something but does not command us to do it."[27] Adams elaborates on this point as follows:

> For many reasons, we often do not want people to be *obliged* to do what we want them to *do*. So far as I can see, God can have such reasons too, so that we should not expect God to want God's wanting someone to do something to impose, automatically, an obligation to do it.[28]

The point here is that option (3) implies that it is impossible for God merely to want a person to perform a certain action without that person being morally obligated to perform the action. According to (3), the willing itself imposes the obligation. A possible case of the sort Adams has in mind occurs in Milton's *Paradise Lost*. After the creation of Adam but prior to the creation of Eve, Adam asks God to create an equal companion for him. Initially God resists, first suggesting that Adam's complaint that he is lonely is unwarranted, declaring "What call'st thou solitude? Is not the earth / With various living creatures and the air / Replenish'd, and all these at thy command / To come and play before thee?"[29] Adam persists, and God next points out that He, despite lacking an equal companion, is perfectly happy; why, then, should Adam's lack of such a companion prevent him from being happy?[30] Adam replies that God is perfect whereas man is not; hence man's need for an equal companion. Finally, God relents.

[. . .]

It turns out that God wanted Adam to have an equal companion all along – and He wanted Adam to recognize his need for such a companion on his own and to ask God to create a companion for him. But it seems implausible to suppose that in wanting this, God thereby imposed on Adam the moral obligation to ask God for a companion. It is surely possible that God wanted Adam to ask for a companion without Adam being obligated to make the request. One problem with option (3), then, is that it actually seems to impose unacceptable restrictions on what God can do.

Another difficulty with (3) may be seen by recalling the case of the friend to whom you owe the favor. It seems absurd to suppose that your friend could impose on you the obligation to loan him your car merely by *willing* that you do so! If he fails to communicate his will to you in some fashion, no obligation is imposed upon you. But the same thing would seem to be true with respect to God. From the fact that God has the authority to impose obligations on human beings it does not follow that He can impose obligations merely by willing that people perform certain actions. As Adams puts it: "Games in which one party incurs guilt for failing to guess the unexpressed wishes of the other party are not nice games. They are no nicer if God is thought of as a party to them."[31]

This latter point tells against option (2) as well. Option (2) implies that God, our duly authorized commander, can impose moral obligations on us merely by willing that we have certain moral obligations but without communicating to us what these obligations might be. Again, this seems implausible; your friend may want you to be obligated to loan him your car, but no such obligation exists until he actually makes the request.

These considerations suggest that option (1) is the most plausible option of the three. I will argue, however, that if the only way God can impose moral obligations on human beings is by commanding them to perform certain actions, there will be limits to the obligations God can impose – and the nature of these limits will provide a reason for rejecting the view that God could be the source of *all* of our moral obligations.

Adams favors option (1), and he points out that to evaluate it, something must be said about what it is for God to issue a command to a human being. Adams specifies three conditions that must be met:

(1) A divine command will always involve a *sign*, as we may call it, that is intentionally caused by God. (2) In causing the sign God must intend to issue a command, and *what* is commanded is what God intends to command thereby. (3) The sign must be such that the intended audience could understand it as conveying the intended command.[32]

It is not clear if Adams intends these three conditions to be jointly sufficient for God to impose a moral obligation on human beings by

way of a divine command. If he does, though, then I think Adams has left out an important condition. Recall the example of the friend to whom you owe a favor. Suppose your friend (call him "Dave") sends you an anonymous note. The note reads: "Loan Dave your car." In this case, your friend has given you a sign that he intentionally caused and, in so doing, intends to issue to you the command to loan him your car. Moreover, you are clearly capable of understanding the note as conveying the command to you to loan Dave your car. Are you now morally obligated to loan Dave your car? The answer clearly enough is no, and it is not hard to see why: You have no idea who issued this command. More specifically, you don't know that the command was issued by Dave. Moreover, Dave (we may reasonably suppose) knew that you would not be able to tell who issued the command. In these circumstances, it seems clear that Dave, despite being capable of imposing on you the obligation to loan him your car, has failed to do so in the case at hand. He has failed to do so because he has failed to get you to recognize that the command is coming from a legitimate source.

[. . .]

If God is to impose moral obligations on humans by way of His divine commands, He must get his intended audience to recognize that the commands are coming from Him. The case of Dave illustrates that it is not enough merely for God to have the right credentials; those whom He would command must *recognize* that the commands in question are coming from an appropriately credentialed God. But it seems clear that there are plenty of people who do not believe that God has issued any commands to anyone – naturalists, for example. A naturalist denies the existence of supernatural beings of any sort. Furthermore, a naturalist does not believe that there is someone who created us, or made the relevant covenants with us, or died for our sins, or is omniscient and perfectly good.

We may distinguish two kinds of naturalist. The first is a *reasonable naturalist*. A reasonable naturalist holds an epistemic position such that it is reasonable to withhold belief in God. The second is an *unreasonable naturalist*, whose epistemic position makes it *not* reasonable to withhold belief in God.

It seems clear that God has not imposed any obligations on reasonable naturalists by way of divine commands. A reasonable naturalist does not believe that any command has God as its source. Moreover, it is logical for a reasonable naturalist to withhold belief that a given command is a divine command. It might be thought that any divine command would *obviously* have God as its source. But if this were true, and if divine commands had been issued to everyone, then the existence of God would be *obvious* to everyone – which it plainly is not. Moreover, some of the things that Adams counts as divine commands do not obviously have God as their source:

> Principles of moral obligation constituted by divine commands are not timeless truths, because the commands are given by signs that occur in time. People who are not in the region of space–time in which a sign can be known are not subject to a command given by it. Of course, if the signs by which some divine commands are given are moral impulses and sensibilities common to practically all adult human beings since some (not too recent) point in the evolution of our species, all of us can fairly be counted as subject to those commands.[33]

Here Adams suggests that "moral impulses and sensibilities" can be the signs by which God issues divine commands. But these are hardly signs whose divine origin is obvious; they seem fairly akin to anonymous notes.

If God does not impose moral obligations on reasonable naturalists by way of divine commands, it follows either that (1) reasonable naturalists have no moral obligations, or (2) some humans have moral obligations that are not derived from divine commands. Option (1) is implausible and something no theist would want to accept. Surely the theist will not allow that the naturalist, in virtue of his naturalism, is allowed to do whatever he wants! It seems, therefore, that we must conclude that there are some moral obligations that are not derived from divine commands. God as the divine commander is not the source of all of our moral obligations; even the theist ought to admit that at least some obligations have some other basis.

It might be objected that all naturalists are unreasonable naturalists. Even if this dubious claim is true, it still follows that there are moral obligations that are not derived from divine commands. Consider once more the example of you and Dave. Suppose that Dave knows that you are unreasonable in the following way: You refuse to believe of anyone who calls you on the telephone that he is who he says he is. Knowing this, Dave cannot impose a moral obligation on you by way of a command issued over the phone, because he knows that you will (unreasonably) fail to recognize that the command is coming from him. Similarly, God cannot impose moral obligations on unreasonable naturalists by way of divine commands because they will (unreasonably, we may suppose) fail to recognize that such commands are coming from God. There are two points worth making here. First, this case is to be carefully distinguished from the case of a person who does recognize that a given command is coming from God but who refuses to admit this. This is not the case of the unreasonable naturalist, who genuinely fails to recognize a divine source for any command. Second, the claim here is not that an unreasonable naturalist is entirely above criticism. Suppose that God issues a command to a certain unreasonable naturalist to perform action A. The unreasonable naturalist, failing to recognize God as the source of this command, fails to perform action A. The unreasonable naturalist may be open to criticism: Failure to recognize that the command has a divine source may be *irrational*. Nevertheless, God has failed to impose on the unreasonable naturalist the moral obligation *to perform action A*, and so we cannot say that something morally wrong was done in failing to perform action A (unless of course there was already an obligation to perform A for some other reason). Returning to the case of Dave, you can be criticized for unreasonably failing to believe that it is Dave on the other end of the line, but it cannot be said that you have violated a moral obligation in failing to loan Dave your car. Dave failed to impose that moral obligation on you because you failed to recognize his command to loan him your car as coming from him.

We can conclude, therefore, that the presence of naturalists in the world – whether they are reasonable or unreasonable – teaches us that there are some moral obligations that are not derived from divine commands. God may impose *some* moral obligations on human beings by way of His divine commands, but not all of our moral obligations are so imposed. [. . .]

These points allow us to respond to some rhetorical questions posed by Craig (1996): "If God does not exist, then it is difficult to see any reason to think that human beings are special or that their morality is objectively true. Moreover, why think that we have any moral obligations to do anything? Who or what imposes any moral duties upon us?"[34]

The proper response to Craig's first rhetorical question is that we have some moral obligations that derive from our relationships with other human beings and we have other moral obligations that derive from intrinsic values. The proper response to Craig's second question is that many of our moral duties are such that no being *imposes* them upon us. Craig's mistake is in thinking that the set of moral obligations we have is coextensive with the set of moral obligations that are imposed on us by some being. The truth is that even if God exists, the latter is a proper subset of the former.

It appears, then, that the idea that if God does not exist everything is permissible is an overreaction. Consider the case of a man who, having extricated himself from an increasingly unhappy romantic relationship, thinks, "I'm free! I can do whatever I want!" Of course if taken literally this claim is false, but most likely what he means is that it is morally permissible for him to do all sorts of things that it was not permissible for him to do while he was in the relationship. Breaking up with his girlfriend has not made it permissible for him to torture babies for fun. Similarly, if modern man has discovered that God does not exist, he has not thereby also discovered that it is permissible for him to do anything he wants. Instead, he has merely discovered that it is permissible from him to do some things that he previously believed were not permissible for him to do. He has discovered, for instance, that he has much more latitude, morally speaking, in how he spends his Sundays. He has not discovered, though, that it is permissible for him to devote his Sunday afternoons to the torture of helpless infants.

There is, of course, much more to be said about the basis of the moral obligations we have that are not imposed on us by God. My goal here, however, is not to develop a complete atheistic metaethical theory. My goal instead has been to show that the idea that God is the complete source of all ethical truths, or even of all our moral obligations, leads to problematic consequences and hence should be rejected.

Notes

1. Philip Quinn, "The Primacy of God's Will in Christian Ethics," in *Christian Theism and Moral Philosophy* (Macon, GA: Mercer Univ. Press, 1998), 263.
2. The view captured by these two theses is different from the view Quinn later proposes; specifically, Quinn does not endorse the Control Thesis, 263–4.
3. William Lane Craig, "The Absurdity of Life Without God." Craig often argues from the existence of "objective moral values" to the existence of God. For transcripts of some of Craig's debates, see www.leaderu.com/offices/billcraig/menus/debates.html (accessed March 26, 2004).

4. One who holds the Dependency Thesis merely as a contingent truth can consistently maintain that while God is in fact the author of all ethical truth, there are possible worlds with ethical truths in which God does not exist. In such worlds the ethical truths have some source other than God.
5. Craig, "Absurdity of Life."
6. Ralph Cudworth, *A Treatise Concerning Eternal and Immutable Morality* (New York: Garland, 1976), 9–10.
7. Edward Wierenga, "A Defensible Divine Command Theory," *Nous* 17 (September 1983), 394.

8. Roderick Chisholm, *The Problem of the Criterion* (Milwaukee, WI: Marquette Univ. Press, 1973), 21.

9. Kai Nielsen, *Ethics Without God*, 10.

10. The ideas developed in the three previous paragraphs are similar to some suggestions made by Richard Swinburne in "Duty and the Will of God," in *Divine Commands and Morality*, ed. P. Helm (Oxford: Oxford Univ. Press, 1981), 125–6.

11. Unless of course your friend is an alcoholic whose driver's license was revoked for driving under the influence; or he is narcoleptic; or. . . . But let us suppose none of the infinitely many circumstances of this sort that may be true are not.

12. Wierenga calls it this in "Divine Command," 389.

13. Plato, *Phaedo*, trans. G. M. A. Grube (Indianapolis: Hackett, 1977), 10, 62b.

14. See, for example, Exodus 19:5 and Deuteronomy 7:6.

15. Baruch Brody, "Morality and Religion Reconsidered," in *Readings in the Philosophy of Religion*, ed. B. Brody (Englewood Cliffs, NJ: Prentice Hall, 1974), 601.

16. Brody, "Morality and Religion," 601.

17. Ibid.

18. Ibid., 595.

19. Robert Adams, *Finite and Infinite Goods* (Oxford: Oxford University Press, 1999), 252.

20. Richard Mouw, *The God Who Commands* (Notre Dame: Univ. of Notre Dame Press, 1996), 19–20.

21. Adams, *Finite and Infinite*, 253–4.

22. Ibid., 255.

23. John Hick, *Evil and the God of Love* (New York: Macmillan, 1966), 132–3.

24. For an account of a somewhat more complicated ground, see Chapter 3 of John Hare's *God's Call* (Grand Rapids MI: Wm. B. Eerdmans, 2001), particularly 110–11.

25. Mark Murphy, "Divine Command, Divine Will, and Moral Obligation," *Faith and Philosophy* 15:1 (January 1998), 4; I have revised Murphy's formulations slightly.

26. Ibid., 16.

27. Adams, *Finite and Infinite*, 260.

28. Ibid., 261.

29. Milton, *Paradise Lost*, 192, Book VIII, lines 369–72.

30. Ibid., 193–4, Book VIII, lines 399–411.

31. Adams, *Finite and Infinite*, 261.

32. Ibid., 265.

33. Ibid., 270.

34. William Lane Craig, "The Indispensability of Theological Meta-ethical Foundations for Morality," 1996, home.apu.edu/~CTRF/papers/1996_papers/craig.html (accessed March 26, 2004).

PART V
Value

Introduction to Part V

What sorts of things have value, and why? Naturally, philosophers have returned different answers to this question. And, naturally (being philosophers), they have usually begun their replies with a distinction – that between intrinsic and extrinsic value. An activity or a thing or a state of affairs possesses intrinsic value just in case its value derives from its own nature, rather than its place within a larger whole, or its ability to generate good results. When searching for what is intrinsically valuable, we are trying to fix on what is good in itself, in its own right, apart from any extrinsic considerations.

Intrinsic value is often contrasted with instrumental value – the value associated with an ability to generate intrinsically good results. A vaccination, for instance, possesses only instrumental value. Were the vaccination entirely ineffective at inoculating a patient against harm, then there would be nothing good about it at all. Its goodness derives entirely from the results it causes. Instrumental goods are good only contingently. If the circumstances change, so that such things (e.g., vaccinations, tedious work, dieting) fail to cause the good results that they often do, then such things lose what value they might have had.

There is another form of extrinsic value, what philosophers nowadays label *constitutive value*. This is the value possessed by certain elements of a valuable whole, in virtue of their contribution to the larger whole. Constitutive values are not themselves intrinsically valuable. Nor are they necessarily instrumentally valuable. Consider a particular brushstroke in a Van Gogh painting. The brushstroke is not, in itself, of any particular value. Nor is it causing something good to come about. Rather, its value derives from the role it plays in constituting something that is itself worthy of our desire and interest.

When it comes to philosophical value theory, questions of intrinsic value have always stood front and center. The current sampling of work reflects this tradition. Many philosophers agree that we can discern what is intrinsically valuable by discovering what is worth desiring for its own sake. The list of popular candidates is not as long as one might think: pleasure, knowledge, beauty, inner harmony, loving relations, health, and virtue. Unquestionably, the view that has attracted the greatest single number of adherents (and detractors) is hedonism: the claim that pleasure is the sole intrinsic value. The historical importance of hedonism is reflected in the heavy sampling here of work devoted to its defense and criticism.

Hedonism is an essential element of classical utilitarianism, here represented in excerpts from John Stuart Mill's *Utilitarianism*. Mill's discussion is famous for many things. He argues that ultimate ends are not susceptible of hard proof, that the value of virtue is really assimilable to that of pleasure, and that there are higher and lower pleasures, not all of which are equally valuable. In this last, he parts company with the views of his godfather, Jeremy Bentham, who had famously said that "pushpin [a tavern game] is as good as poetry." Bentham thought that all pleasures, understood as intrinsically enjoyable states of mind, were equally valuable. Today, Benthamites would say that a life on the couch, in front of the TV or video screen, is as good (if as pleasant) as a life of service, or a life of scholarship. Mill would have none of that. He sought to defend hedonism against the view that it was a doctrine worthy only of the swine, and claimed that it was better to be Socrates dissatisfied, than a pig satisfied. As to the question of how we might rank some pleasures as superior to others, Mill argued that we must defer to the preference of those who had experienced all kinds of pleasures – base as well as elevated ones. Such people invariably preferred the subtler, harder to gain, longer-lasting pleasures of the mind to those of the flesh. Or so he claimed.

Mill's discussion in also famous for his consideration of a classic anti-hedonist criticism: that virtue, not pleasure, is what is truly valuable. Here Mill claims that virtue, like all else, is valuable only as a means to pleasure. His discussion, however, has been variously interpreted, and readers might ask whether Mill is pointing here to virtue's constitutive value in a life of pleasure, rather than to its instrumental value in bringing about a state (pleasure) discrete from virtue.

The philosopher Robert Nozick next offers us a pithy thought experiment designed to undermine hedonism, and, more generally, any view according to which the sole intrinsic value is some kind of positive experience. He invites us to contemplate an activity-less life inside an *experience machine*. This machine creates for its inhabitants an experience that is so lifelike that those inside cannot tell that their experiences are illusory. They think that they are in the world, engaging in all of the activities that the rest of us are engaged in. But all the while they are lying still, inside the machine. Suppose that we could program the machine to create a set of experiences, designed to last a

natural lifetime, that were immensely pleasurable – far more pleasurable than the lives of those of us who actually have to do a bit of slogging and trudging each day. Given that, by hypothesis, the life of a machine inhabitant would be more pleasurable than any of our lives, it should follow from hedonism that (i) the inhabitants' lives are more valuable than any of our own, and (ii) there are no values that are available to us that are unavailable to those within the machine. After all, if pleasure is the only thing of intrinsic value, and if pleasure is a state of mind, then every instance of intrinsic value should be available, in principle, to inhabitants of the experience machine. Nozick thinks that this is preposterous, and asks us to reflect on the sorts of valuable things that cannot be had by those within the machine. These are additional sources of intrinsic value, no one of which is identical to pleasure. Therefore hedonism is false.

In a sophisticated rejoinder to traditional and more recent critiques of hedonism (including Nozick's), Fred Feldman develops a view that he calls *attitudinal hedonism*. This brand of hedonism claims that pleasure is indeed the sole intrinsic value, but that pleasure is not a feeling; rather, it is an attitude of enjoyment. When we take enjoyment in what merits enjoyment, then this enjoyment is genuinely, intrinsically valuable. This sort of pleasure is what makes a life go well for the one who lives it; pain is what makes a life go poorly. Feldman is careful to explain that he is concentrating not on what is morally good, or on what makes the world as a whole valuable, but rather, on what makes a person's life valuable. It may be, for all he says, that a world of beauty is (other things equal) a better world, containing more that is intrinsically valuable, than a world that is wholly without it. But if we restrict our focus, as most of us do, to asking about what will make a life truly valuable, and worth living, then we should answer: a life short on pain, and filled with instances of taking pleasure in what merits our affection.

Feldman considers a number of objections to hedonism, and indeed, a great many have been leveled over the past many centuries. One that he does not consider, but that seems to have played a large role in generating suspicions about hedonism, is the common thought that there is simply much more that is valuable in its own right than pleasure. Trying to narrow the whole realm of intrinsic value to just one thing – pleasure – has struck many as yielding an unduly cramped view of value.

This allegiance to value pluralism has generated two quite distinct views. The first is, in a way, *very* pluralistic, but is also, in its way, a different form of monism (the view that there is ultimately only a single relevant rule or value). This first theory is the desire-satisfaction view. Its adherents are impressed by the wide variety of things that people actually do value for their own sake. Desire satisfaction theorists decline to identify just a subset of these valued items as possessed of intrinsic value. Indeed, such theorists reject the idea that *any* of the familiar candidates – pleasure, health, beauty, etc. – possesses intrinsic value. Nothing is valuable in its own right except having one's desires satisfied. And these desires can be for anything – for winning the lottery, becoming a celebrity, being a good friend, or avoiding sidewalk cracks, cutting one's hair short, or having peanut butter on Tuesdays. What matters is not what the desires are for, but rather that they are satisfied. To the extent that they are, one is living a life of value. And to the extent that one's desires are frustrated – no matter, again, the object of these desires – one's life is going poorly.

There appear to be clear counter-examples to the claim that the satisfaction of a desire is, in itself, a thing of value, making the desirer's life better to that extent than it would otherwise be. If my desire is based on false information, then its satisfaction may contribute nothing (except hardship) to my life. If my desire stems from setting unduly self-effacing goals, because I have been cast down so long that I have come to identify with the interests of my oppressors, then again, getting me what I want may gain me nothing truly valuable.

Some philosophers have thought that the desire-satisfaction account can be made to work, provided a crucial modification is made. What makes one's life go well is the satisfaction of one's *informed* desires – those that do, or would, result from a fully considered and informed assessment of one's options.

James Griffin advances a view of this kind. In the selection here, he outlines the classic worries for desire-based accounts of goodness, and shows how best to motivate the modified position he favors. The view comes in for criticism by Richard Kraut, who articulates worries for even the improved desire-based view. Like Griffin, and other desire-based theorists, Kraut too endorses value pluralism. But he denies that any version of a desire-based account can accommodate all that is plausible about such pluralism. Rather, he endorses (but does not argue in any detail for) an objective, pluralistic account, according to which a variety of things are objectively intrinsically good. Such things are good not because they are desired for their own sakes, but rather because of their objective nature as such. There is something about them that makes them intrinsically worthy of being desired or admired. Further, according to Kraut, there is no single overarching value in virtue of which all valuable things are good.

Derek Parfit endorses this very view, and reveals its attractions partly by pointing to the difficulties that beset hedonism and the desire-based views. For Parfit, as well as for Kraut, the absence of a unifying super-value does not render the realm of intrinsic value incoherent. There is no single thing whose possession, in varying degrees, determines the value of a life.

Note that we are here on Feldman's playing field. We are asking about what makes life worth living, rather than what makes the world contain intrinsic goodness. W.D. Ross, the last of our contributors in this section, has his sights set on this last matter. He develops a famous thought experiment that has us consider two worlds identical in all respects, but for some candidate intrinsic value. He then asks whether the presence of this candidate (e.g., pleasure, knowledge, justice) makes the world more valuable than it would be in its absence. Ross would agree with Mill, our first author, that there is no strict proof of ultimate values. Still, Ross believes that his test shows us that Mill is mistaken in thinking that pleasure is, in itself, of value (much less that it is the only thing of such value). For if it is enjoyed by those who deserve pain instead, it is positively bad. Ross's rejection of hedonism, and his defense of value pluralism, have themselves attracted a lot of attention. One thing is sure – the debate in this area of ethical theory is still very much alive, and certainly very much worth pursuing, focusing as it does on our efforts to identify what is most valuable – in human life, and in the world around us.

CHAPTER 29

Hedonism

JOHN STUART MILL

The creed which accepts, as the foundation of morals, Utility, or the Greatest-happiness Principle, holds that actions are right in proportion as they tend to promote happiness, wrong as they tend to produce the reverse of happiness. By happiness is intended pleasure and the absence of pain; by unhappiness, pain and the privation of pleasure. To give a clear view of the moral standard set up by the theory, much more requires to be said; in particular, what things it includes in the ideas of pain and pleasure, and to what extent this is left an open question. But these supplementary explanations do not affect the theory of life on which this theory of morality is grounded – namely, that pleasure, and freedom from pain, are the only things desirable as ends; and that all desirable things (which are as numerous in the utilitarian as in any other scheme) are desirable either for the pleasure inherent in themselves, or as means to the promotion of pleasure and the prevention of pain.

Now, such a theory of life excites in many minds, and among them in some of the most estimable in feeling and purpose, inveterate dislike. To suppose that life has (as they express it) no higher end than pleasure – no better and nobler object of desire and pursuit – they designate as utterly mean and groveling; as a

John Stuart Mill, "Hedonism," from *Utiliarianism*, 1859.

doctrine worthy only of swine, to whom the followers of Epicurus were, at a very early period, contemptuously likened: and modern holders of the doctrine are occasionally made the subject of equally polite comparisons by its German, French, and English assailants.

When thus attacked, the Epicureans have always answered, that it is not they, but their accusers, who represent human nature in a degrading light, since the accusation supposes human beings to be capable of no pleasures except those of which swine are capable. If this supposition were true, the charge could not gainsaid, but would then be no longer an imputation; for, if the sources of pleasure were precisely the same to human beings and to swine, the rule of life which is good enough for the one would be good enough for the other. The comparison of the Epicurean life to that of beasts is felt as degrading, precisely because a beast's pleasures do not satisfy a human being's conceptions of happiness. Human beings have faculties more elevated than the animal appetites; and, when once made conscious of them, do not regard any thing as happiness which does not include their gratification. I do not, indeed, consider the Epicureans to have been by any means faultless in drawing out their scheme of consequences from the utilitarian principle. To do this in any sufficient manner, many Stoic as well as Christian elements require to be included. But there is no known Epicurean theory of life which does not assign to the pleasures of the intellect, of the feeling and imagination, and of the moral sentiments, a much higher value as pleasures than to those of mere sensation. It must be admitted, however, that utilitarian writers in general have placed the superiority of mental over bodily pleasures chiefly in the greater permanency, safety, uncostliness, &c., of the former – that is, in their circumstantial advantages rather than in their intrinsic nature. And, on all these points, utilitarians have fully proved their case; but they might have taken the other, and, as it may be called, higher ground, with entire consistency. It is quite compatible with the principle of utility to recognize the fact, that some *kinds* of pleasure are more desirable and more valuable than others. It would be absurd, that while, in estimating all other things, quality is considered as well as quantity, the estimation of pleasures should be supposed to depend on quantity alone.

If I am asked what I mean by difference of quality in pleasures, or what makes one pleasure more valuable than another, merely as a pleasure, except its being greater in amount, there is but one possible answer. Of two pleasures, if there be one to which all or almost all who have experience of both give a decided preference, irrespective of any feeling of moral obligation to prefer it, that is the more desirable pleasure. If one of the two is, by those who are competently acquainted with both, placed so far above the other that they prefer it, even though knowing it to be attended with a greater amount of discontent, and would not resign it for any quantity of the other pleasure which their nature is capable of, we are justified in ascribing to the preferred enjoyment a superiority in quality, so far outweighing quantity, as to render it, in comparison, of small account.

Now, it is an unquestionable fact, that those who are equally acquainted with and equally capable of appreciating and enjoying both do give a most marked preference to the manner of existence which employs their higher faculties. Few human creatures would consent to be changed into any of the lower animals, for a promise of the fullest allowance of a beast's pleasures: no intelligent human being would consent to be a fool, no instructed person would be an ignoramus, no person of feeling and conscience would be selfish and base, even though they should be persuaded that the fool, the dunce, or the rascal is better satisfied with his lot than they are with theirs. They would not resign what they possess more than he for the most complete satisfaction of all the desires which they have in common with him. If they ever fancy they would, it is only in cases of unhappiness so extreme, that, to escape from it, they would exchange their lot for almost any other, however undesirable in their own eyes. A being of higher faculties requires more to make him happy, is capable probably of more acute suffering, and certainly accessible to it at more points, than one of an inferior type; but, in spite of these liabilities, he can never really wish to sink into what he feels to be a lower grade of existence. We may give what explanation we please of this unwillingness; we may attribute it to pride, a name which is given indiscriminately to some of the most and to some of the least estimable feelings of which mankind are capable; we may refer it to the love of liberty and personal independence – an appeal to which was with the Stoics one of the most effective means for the inculcation of it; to the love of power, or to the love of excitement, both of which do really enter into and contribute to it: but its most appropriate appellation is a sense of dignity, which all human beings possess in one form or other, and in some, though by no means in exact, proportion to their higher faculties, and which is so essential a part of the happiness of those in whom it is strong, that nothing which conflicts with it could be, otherwise than momentarily, an object of desire to them. Whoever supposes that this preference takes place at a sacrifice of happiness; that the superior being, in any thing like equal circumstances, is not happier than the inferior – confounds the two very different ideas of happiness and content. It is indisputable, that the being whose capacities of enjoyment are low has the greatest chance of having them fully satisfied; and a highly endowed being will always feel that any happiness which he can look for, as the world is constituted, is imperfect. But he can learn to bear its imperfections, if they are at all bearable; and they will not make him envy the being who is indeed unconscious of the imperfections, but only because he feels not at all the good which those imperfections qualify. It is better to be a human being dissatisfied, than a pig satisfied; better to be Socrates dissatisfied, than a fool satisfied. And if the fool or the pig are of a different opinion, it is because they only know their own side of the question. The other party to the comparison knows both sides.

It may be objected, that many who are capable of the higher pleasures, occasionally, under the influence of temptation, postpone them to the lower. But this is quite compatible with a full appreciation of the intrinsic superiority of the higher. Men often, from infirmity of character, make their election for the nearer good, though they know it to be the less valuable, and this no less when the choice is between two bodily pleasures than when it is between bodily and mental. They pursue sensual indulgences to the injury of health, though perfectly aware that health is the greater good. It may be further objected, that many who begin with youthful enthusiasm for everything noble, as they advance in years sink into indolence and selfishness. But I do not believe that those who undergo this very common change voluntarily choose the lower description of pleasures in preference to the higher. I believe, that, before they devote themselves exclusively to the one, they have already become incapable of the other. Capacity for the nobler feelings is in most natures a very tender plant, easily killed, not only by hostile influences, but by mere want of sustenance; and, in the majority of young persons, it speedily dies away if the occupations to which their position in life has devoted them, and the society into which it has thrown them, are not favorable to keeping that higher capacity in exercise. Men lose their high aspirations as they lose their intellectual tastes, because they have not time or opportunity for indulging them; and they addict themselves to inferior pleasures, not because they deliberately prefer them, but because they are either the only ones to which they have access, or the only ones which they are any longer capable of enjoying. It may be questioned whether any

one, who has remained equally susceptible to both classes of pleasures, ever knowingly and calmly preferred the lower; though many in all ages have broken down in an ineffectual attempt to combine both.

From this verdict of the only competent judges, I apprehend there can be no appeal. On a question, which is the best worth having of two pleasures, or which of two modes of existence is the most grateful to the feelings, apart from its moral attributes and from its consequences, the judgment of those who are qualified by knowledge of both, or, if they differ, that of the majority among them, must be admitted as final. And there needs be the less hesitation to accept this judgment respecting the quality of pleasures, since there is no other tribunal to be referred to even on the question of quantity. What means are there of determining which is the acutest of two pains, or the intensest of two pleasurable sensations, except the general suffrage of those who are familiar with both? Neither pains nor pleasures are homogeneous, and pain is always heterogeneous with pleasure. What is there to decide whether a particular pleasure is worth purchasing at the cost of particular pain, except the feelings and judgment of the experienced? When, therefore, those feelings and judgment declare the pleasures derived from the higher faculties to be preferable *in kind*, apart from the question of intensity, to those of which the animal nature, disjoined from the higher faculties, is susceptible, they are entitled on this subject to the same regard.

Of What Sort of Proof the Principle of Utility is Susceptible

It has already been remarked, that questions of ultimate ends do not admit of proof, in the ordinary acceptation of the term. To be incapable of proof by reasoning is common to all first principles; to the first premises of our knowledge, as well as to those of our conduct. But the former, being matters of fact, may be the subject of a direct appeal to the faculties which judge of fact – namely, our senses, and our internal consciousness. Can an appeal be made to the same faculties on questions of practical ends? Or by what other faculty is cognizance taken of them?

Questions about ends are, in other words, questions what things are desirable. The utilitarian doctrine is, that happiness is desirable, and the only thing desirable, as an end; all other things being only desirable as means to that end. What ought to be required of this doctrine – what conditions is it requisite that the doctrine should fulfil – to make good its claim to be believed?

The only proof capable of being given that an object is visible, is that people actually see it. The only proof that a sound is audible, is that people hear it: and so of the other sources of our experience. In like manner, I apprehend, the sole evidence it is possible to produce that anything is desirable, is that people do actually desire it. If the end which the utilitarian doctrine proposes to itself were not, in theory and in practice, acknowledged to be an end, nothing could ever convince any person that it was so. No reason can be given why the general happiness is desirable, except that each person, so far as he believes it to be attainable, desires his own happiness. This, however, being a fact, we have not only all the proof which the case admits of, but all which it is possible to require, that happiness is a good: that each person's happiness is a good to that person, and the general happiness, therefore, a good to the aggregate of all persons. Happiness has made out its title as *one* of the ends of conduct, and consequently one of the criteria of morality.

But it has not, by this alone, proved itself to be the sole criterion. To do that, it would seem, by the same rule, necessary to show, not only that people desire happiness, but that they never desire anything else. Now it is palpable that they do desire things which, in common language, are decidedly distinguished from happiness. They desire, for example, virtue and the absence of vice, no less really than pleasure and the absence of pain. The desire of virtue is not as universal, but it is as authentic a fact, as the desire of happiness. And hence the opponents of the utilitarian standard deem that they have a right to infer that there are other ends of human action besides happiness, and that happiness is not the standard of approbation and disapprobation.

But does the utilitarian doctrine deny that people desire virtue, or maintain that virtue is not a thing to be desired? The very reverse. It maintains not only that virtue is to be desired, but that it is to be desired disinterestedly, for itself. Whatever may be the opinion of utilitarian moralists as to the original conditions by which virtue is made virtue; however they may believe (as they do) that actions and dispositions are only virtuous because they promote another end than virtue; yet this being granted, and it having been decided, from considerations of this description, what *is* virtuous, they not only place virtue at the very head of the things which are good as means to the ultimate end, but they also recognise as a psychological fact the possibility of its being, to the individual, a good in itself, without looking to any end beyond it; and hold, that the mind is not in a right state, not in a state conformable to Utility, not in the state most conducive to the general happiness, unless it does love virtue in this manner – as a thing desirable in itself, even although, in the individual instance, it should not produce those other desirable consequences which it tends to produce, and on account of which it is held to be virtue. This opinion is not, in the smallest degree, a departure from the Happiness principle. The ingredients of happiness are very various, and each of them is desirable in itself, and not merely when considered as swelling an aggregate. The principle of utility does not mean that any given pleasure, as music, for instance, or any given exemption from pain, as for example health, are to be looked upon as means to a collective something termed happiness, and to be desired on that account. They are desired and desirable in and for themselves; besides being means, they are a part of the end. Virtue, according to the utilitarian doctrine, is not naturally and originally part of the end, but it is capable of becoming so; and is desired and cherished, not as a means to happiness, but as a part of their happiness.

To illustrate this farther, we may remember that virtue is not the only thing, originally a means, and which if it were not a means to anything else, would be and remain indifferent, but which by association with what it is a means to, comes to be desired for itself, and that too with the utmost intensity. What, for example, shall we say of the love of money? There is nothing originally more desirable about money than about any heap of glittering pebbles. Its worth is solely that of the things which it will buy; the desires for other things than itself, which it is a means of gratifying. Yet the love of money is not only one of the strongest moving forces of human life, but money is, in many cases, desired in and for itself; the desire to possess it is often stronger than the desire to use it, and goes on increasing when all the desires which point to ends beyond it, to be compassed by it, are falling off. It may be then said truly, that money is desired not for the sake of an end, but as part of the end. From being a means to happiness, it has come to be itself a principal ingredient of the individual's conception of happiness. The same may be said of the majority of the great objects of human life – power, for example, or fame; except that to each of these there is a certain amount of immediate pleasure annexed, which has at least the semblance of being naturally inherent in them; a thing which cannot be said of money. Still, however, the strongest natural attraction, both of power and of fame, is the immense aid they give to the attainment of our other wishes; and it is the strong association thus generated between them and all our objects of desire, which gives to the direct desire of them the intensity it often assumes, so as in some characters to surpass in strength all other desires. In these cases the means have become a part of the end, and a more important part of it than any of the things which they are means to. What was once desired as an instrument for the attainment of happiness, has come to be desired for its own sake. In being desired for its own sake it is, however, desired as *part* of happiness. The person is made, or thinks he would be made, happy by its mere possession; and is made unhappy by failure to obtain it. The desire of it is not a different thing from the desire of happiness, any more than the love of music, or the desire of health. They are included in happiness. They are some of the elements of which the desire of happiness is made up. Happiness is not an abstract idea, but a concrete whole; and these are some of its parts. And the utilitarian standard sanctions

and approves their being so. Life would be a poor thing, very ill provided with sources of happiness, if there were not this provision of nature, by which things originally indifferent, but conducive to, or otherwise associated with, the satisfaction of our primitive desires, become in themselves sources of pleasure more valuable than the primitive pleasures, both in permanency, in the space of human existence that they are capable of covering, and even in intensity.

Virtue, according to the utilitarian conception, is a good of this description. There was no original desire of it, or motive to it, save its conduciveness to pleasure, and especially to protection from pain. But through the association thus formed, it may be felt a good in itself, and desired as such with as great intensity as any other good; and with this difference between it and the love of money, of power, or of fame, that all of these may, and often do, render the individual noxious to the other members of the society to which he belongs, whereas there is nothing which makes him so much a blessing to them as the cultivation of the disinterested love of virtue. And consequently, the utilitarian standard, while it tolerates and approves those other acquired desires, up to the point beyond which they would be more injurious to the general happiness than promotive of it, enjoins and requires the cultivation of the love of virtue up to the greatest strength possible, as being above all things important to the general happiness.

It results from the preceding considerations, that there is in reality nothing desired except happiness. Whatever is desired otherwise than as a means to some end beyond itself, and ultimately to happiness, is desired as itself a part of happiness, and is not desired for itself until it has become so. Those who desire virtue for its own sake, desire it either because the consciousness of it is a pleasure, or because the consciousness of being without it is a pain, or for both reasons united; as in truth the pleasure and pain seldom exist separately, but almost always together, the same person feeling pleasure in the degree of virtue attained, and pain in not having attained more. If one of these gave him no pleasure, and the other no pain, he would not love or desire virtue, or would desire it only for the other benefits which it might produce to himself or to persons whom he cared for.

We have now, then, an answer to the question, of what sort of proof the principle of utility is susceptible. If the opinion which I have now stated is psychologically true – if human nature is so constituted as to desire nothing which is not either a part of happiness or a means of happiness, we can have no other proof, and we require no other, that these are the only things desirable. If so, happiness is the sole end of human action, and the promotion of it the test by which to judge of all human conduct; from whence it necessarily follows that it must be the criterion of morality, since a part is included in the whole.

And now to decide whether this is really so; whether mankind do desire nothing for itself but that which is a pleasure to them, or of which the absence is a pain; we have evidently arrived at a question of fact and experience, dependent, like all similar questions, upon evidence. It can only be determined by practised self-consciousness and self-observation, assisted by observation of others. I believe that these sources of evidence, impartially consulted, will declare that desiring a thing and finding it pleasant, aversion to it and thinking of it as painful, are phenomena entirely inseparable, or rather two parts of the same phenomenon; in strictness of language, two different modes of naming the same psychological fact: that to think of an object as desirable (unless for the sake of its consequences), and to think of it as pleasant, are one and the same thing; and that to desire anything, except in proportion as the idea of it is pleasant, is a physical and metaphysical impossibility.

So obvious does this appear to me, that I expect it will hardly be disputed: and the objection made will be, not that desire can possibly be directed to anything ultimately except pleasure and exemption from pain, but that the will is a different thing from desire; that a person of confirmed virtue, or any other person whose purposes are fixed, carries out his purposes without any thought of the pleasure he has in contemplating them, or expects to derive from their fulfilment; and persists in acting on them, even though these pleasures are much diminished, by changes in his character or decay of his passive sensibilities, or are outweighed by the pains which the pursuit of the purposes may bring upon him. All this I fully admit, and have stated it elsewhere, as positively and emphatically as any one. Will, the active phenomenon, is a different thing from desire, the state of passive sensibility, and though originally an offshoot from it, may in time take root and detach itself from the parent stock; so much so, that in the case of an habitual purpose, instead of willing the thing because we desire it, we often desire it only because we will it. This, however, is but an instance of that familiar fact, the power of habit, and is nowise confined to the case of virtuous actions. Many indifferent things, which men originally did from a motive of some sort, they continue to do from habit. Sometimes this is done unconsciously, the consciousness coming only after the action: at other times with conscious volition, but volition which has became habitual, and is put into operation by the force of habit, in opposition perhaps to the deliberate preference, as often happens with those who have contracted habits of vicious or hurtful indulgence. Third and last comes the case in which the habitual act of will in the individual instance is not in contradiction to the general intention prevailing at other times, but in fulfilment of it; as in the case of the person of confirmed virtue, and of all who pursue deliberately and consistently any determinate end. The distinction between will and desire thus understood, is an authentic and highly important psychological fact; but the fact consists solely in this – that will, like all other parts of our constitution, is amenable to habit, and that we may will from habit what we no longer desire for itself, or desire only because we will it. It is not the less true that will, in the beginning, is entirely produced by desire; including in that term the repelling influence of pain as well as the attractive one of pleasure. Let us take into consideration, no longer the person who has a confirmed will to do right, but him in whom that virtuous will is still feeble, conquerable by temptation, and not to be fully relied on; by what means can it be strengthened? How can the will to be virtuous, where it does not exist in sufficient force, be implanted or awakened? Only by making the person *desire* virtue – by making him think of it in a pleasurable light, or of its absence in a painful one. It is by associating the doing right with pleasure, or the doing wrong with pain, or by eliciting and impressing and bringing home to the person's experience the pleasure naturally involved in the one or the pain in the other, that it is possible to call forth that will to be virtuous, which, when confirmed, acts without any thought of either pleasure or pain. Will is the child of desire, and passes out of the dominion of its parent only to come under that of habit. That which is the result of habit affords no presumption of being intrinsically good; and there would be no reason for wishing that the purpose of virtue should become independent of pleasure and pain, were it not that the influence of the pleasurable and painful associations which prompt to virtue is not sufficiently to be depended on for unerring constancy of action until it has acquired the support of habit. Both in feeling and in conduct, habit is the only thing which imparts certainty; and it is because of the importance to others of being able to rely absolutely on one's feelings and conduct, and to oneself of being able to rely on one's own, that the will to do right ought to be cultivated into this habitual independence. In other words, this state of the will is a means to good, not intrinsically a good; and does not contradict the doctrine that nothing is a good to human beings but in so far as it is either itself pleasurable, or a means of attaining pleasure or averting pain.

But if this doctrine be true, the principle of utility is proved. Whether it is so or not, must now be left to the consideration of the thoughtful reader.

CHAPTER 30

The Experience Machine

ROBERT NOZICK

. . . Suppose there were an experience machine that would give you any experience you desired. Superduper neuropsychologists could stimulate your brain so that you would think and feel you were writing a great novel, or making a friend, or reading an interesting book. All the time you would be floating in a tank, with electrodes attached to your brain. Should you plug into this machine for life, preprogramming your life's experiences? If you are worried about missing out on desirable experiences, we can suppose that business enterprises have researched thoroughly the lives of many others. You can pick and choose from their large library or smorgasbord of such experiences, selecting your life's experiences for, say, the next two years. After two years have passed, you will have ten minutes or ten hours out of the tank, to select the experiences of your *next* two years. Of course, while in the tank you won't know that you're there; you'll think it's all actually happening. Others can also plug in to have the experiences they want, so there's no need to stay unplugged to serve them. (Ignore problems such as who will service the machines if everybody plugs in.) Would you plug in? *What else*

Robert Nozick, "The Experience Machine," pp. 42–5 from *Anarchy, State and Utopia*. New York: Basic Books, 1974. © 1974 by Basic Books. Reprinted by permission of Basic Books, a member of Perseus Books, LLC.

can matter to us, other than how our lives feel from the inside? Nor should you refrain because of the few moments of distress between the moment you've decided and the moment you're plugged. What's a few moments of distress compared to a lifetime of bliss (if that's what you choose), and why feel any distress at all if your decision *is* the best one?

What does matter to us in addition to our experiences? First, we want to *do* certain things, and not just have the experience of doing them. In the case of certain experiences, it is only because first we want to do the actions that we want the experiences of doing them or thinking we've done them. (But *why* do we want to do the activities rather than merely to experience them?) A second reason for not plugging in is that we want to *be* a certain way, to be a certain sort of person. Someone floating in a tank is an indeterminate blob. There is no answer to the question of what a person is like who has long been in the tank. Is he courageous, kind, intelligent, witty, loving? It's not merely that it's difficult to tell; there's no way he is. Plugging into the machine is a kind of suicide. It will seem to some, trapped by a picture, that nothing about what we are like can matter except as it gets reflected in our experiences. But should it be surprising that what *we are* is important to us? Why should we be concerned only with how our time is filled, but not with what we are?

Thirdly, plugging into an experience machine limits us to a man-made reality, to a world no deeper or more important than that which people can construct. There is no *actual* contact with any deeper reality, though the experience of it can be simulated. Many persons desire to leave themselves open to such contact and to a plumbing of deeper significance.[1] This clarifies the intensity of the conflict over psychoactive drugs, which some view as mere local experience machines, and others view as avenues to a deeper reality; what some view as equivalent to surrender to the experience machine, others view as following one of the reasons *not* to surrender!

We learn that something matters to us in addition to experience by imagining an experience machine and then realizing that we would not use it. We can continue to imagine a sequence of machines each designed to fill lacks suggested for the earlier machines. For example, since the experience machine doesn't meet our desire to *be* a certain way, imagine a transformation machine which transforms us into whatever sort of person we'd like to be (compatible with our staying us). Surely one would not use the transformation machine to become as one would wish, and thereupon plug into the experience machine![2] So

something matters in addition to one's experiences *and* what one is like. Nor is the reason merely that one's experiences are unconnected with what one is like. For the experience machine might be limited to provide only experiences possible to the sort of person plugged in. Is it that we want to make a difference in the world? Consider then the result machine, which produces in the world any result you would produce and injects your vector input into any joint activity. We shall not pursue here the fascinating details of these or other machines. What is most disturbing about them is their living of our lives for us. Is it misguided to search for *particular* additional functions beyond the competence of machines to do for us? Perhaps what we desire is to live (an active verb) ourselves, in contact with reality. (And this, machines cannot do *for* us.) Without elaborating on the implications of this, which I believe connect surprisingly with issues about free will and causal accounts of knowledge, we need merely note the intricacy of the question of what matters *for people* other than their experiences. Until one finds a satisfactory answer, and determines that this answer does not *also* apply to animals, one cannot reasonably claim that only the felt experiences of animals limit what we may do to them.

Notes

1. Traditional religious views differ on the *point* of contact with a transcendent reality. Some say that contact yields eternal bliss or Nirvana, but they have not distinguished this sufficiently from merely a *very* long run on the experience machine. Others think it is intrinsically desirable to do the will of a higher being which created us all, though presumably no one would think this if we discovered we had been created as an object of amusement by some superpowerful child from another galaxy or dimension. Still others imagine an eventual merging with a higher reality, leaving unclear its desirability, or where that merging leaves us.
2. Some wouldn't use the transformation machine at all; it seems like *cheating*. But the one-time use

of the transformation machine would not remove all challenges; there would still be obstacles for the new us to overcome, a new plateau from which to strive even higher. And is this plateau any the less earned or deserved than that provided by genetic endowment and early childhood environment? But if the transformation machine could be used indefinitely often, so that we could accomplish anything by pushing a button to transform ourselves into someone who could do it easily, there would remain no limits we *need* to strain against or try to transcend. Would there be anything left *to do*? Do some theological views place God outside of time because an omniscient omnipotent being couldn't fill up his days?

CHAPTER 31

The Good Life: A Defense of Attitudinal Hedonism

FRED FELDMAN

1. The Good Life

[...]

Let us say that any view is a form of "hedonism" if, according to that view, what makes a life go well for the one who lives it is fundamentally a matter of enjoyment. The one who lives the life enjoys, or "takes pleasure in", the things that befall him in that life. That's the sort of view I will be discussing here.

I have several goals. One is to distinguish among several forms of hedonism. Another is to consider some of the classic objections to hedonism. I want to show that while some of these objections might be effective against some naive forms of hedonism, they are irrelevant to other forms. I will be suggesting that one particular form of hedonism survives all the main objections. For those who do not share my axiological intuitions, I will describe other forms of hedonism that they may find more attractive. I will close by discussing some unfinished business. I will mention some problems that remain even if one of my preferred forms of hedonism can overcome the classic objections here considered.

Before turning to the theories and arguments, however, I need to say a few words

Fred Feldman, "The Good Life: A Defense of Attitudinal Hedonism," pp. 605–27 from *Philosophy and Phenomenological Research*, 65(3), 2002.

about some of the concepts that figure centrally in what follows.

2. Pleasure as a "Feeling" vs. Pleasure as an Attitude

2a. *Pleasure as a "feeling"*. Discussions of hedonism often proceed on the assumption that pleasure is some sort of "feeling", or sensation. Perhaps it is thought that pleasure is distinctive sort of sensation – one that we invariably enjoy, or seek, or try to prolong. Perhaps (on the other hand) it is thought that there is no such *distinctive* feeling of pleasure. On this view, the word "pleasure" properly applies to feelings of various sorts. All that is required is that the one who experiences the feeling enjoys it, or takes pleasure in it. For present purposes I can be neutral on this question about the nature of pleasure as a feeling. Nevertheless, I will need to say a few more things about it.

It seems to me that if we use the word "feeling" strictly and literally, we use it in such a way that something counts as a feeling only if it is something we can really *feel*, or sense. Consider, for example, a feeling of pressure on your back when getting a massage. In such a case there is an immediate sensory quality – the feeling of pressure on the back. That's a paradigm case of a feeling. Consider, for another example, the feeling of heat in your foot when you first step into a hot bath. That feeling of heat is another paradigm example of a feeling. If pleasure were strictly and literally a feeling, it would be relevantly like these feelings of heat and cold and pressure.

[. . .]

While of course I acknowledge that there are things properly called "feelings of pleasure", they are not central to my project here. I discuss them primarily to get them out of the way. The sorts of hedonism that fascinate me are not based on the idea that it is the presence of any such sensory feeling of pleasure that helps to enhance the quality of a person's life. My sorts of hedonism are based on the different idea that it is the presence of "enjoyment" – not a feeling – that makes a life better. Let's consider what enjoyment is.

2b. Enjoyment. Enjoyment is not a feeling. It is an attitude. Like so many other attitudes, it takes propositional entities (or states of affairs) as its objects. Thus, suppose I am reading an insightful and amusing philosophy paper. Suppose I find the paper to be enlightening and entertaining. In such a case, it makes sense to say that I am enjoying various facts about the paper. More ponderously, we might say that as I read the paper, I take attitudinal pleasure in the fact that the paper is so well written, or in the fact that it is filled with such interesting arguments and insights. Perhaps I take pleasure in the fact that the examples are so apt. To enjoy some state of affairs is to take attitudinal pleasure in this way in it.

Attitudinal pleasure is a mode of consciousness. It is a way of being aware of a state of affairs. It takes its place among such attitudes as hope and fear, belief and doubt, and recollection and anticipation. In order to take up any of these attitudes toward some state of affairs, one must be able to conceive that state of affairs. This is not to suggest that one must be able to express the state in words – even an inarticulate person can hope for a drink of water, or fear that there might be something under the bed. As I see it, it does not take tremendous intellectual sophistication to have such attitudes. By the wagging of her little tail, my dog Pippin indicates that she takes pleasure in the fact that we are about to take a ride in the truck.

Some features of enjoyment will play a role in the theories to be discussed. One of these is that enjoyments happen at times. Thus, it makes sense to say that I was enjoying the paper for a while, but eventually I came to some parts that were too complicated. Then I didn't enjoy it so much. Another feature of enjoyment is that it is a matter of degree: I might enjoy reading several of the term papers, but I might enjoy some of them more than others. For simplicity in exposition, we can assume that these intensities can be represented with numbers. Thus, we can say that at about 8:00 pm I was enjoying to intensity $+12$ the reading of this paper, but that at about 10:30 pm I was enjoying to intensity $+2$ the reading of this other paper. Papers read after midnight were not enjoyed at all.[1]

Can we enjoy, or take pleasure in, a state of affairs that does not occur? Our ordinary ways of talking about enjoyment might suggest that this is impossible, but further reflection suggests that things are more complicated. [Roderick] Chisholm has provided a good example.[2] Suppose a candidate for office mistakenly thinks he won the election. Chisholm suggests that this candidate could be pleased about winning the election even though in fact he didn't win it. Here's another case that might seem even more convincing: suppose I mistakenly think that I will be meeting G. E. Moore soon. Suppose I am delighted about this. Clearly, I am pleased about *something*. It seems wrong to say that what I am pleased about is the fact that *I think I will meet Moore*. It seems better to say that I am pleased that *I am going to meet him* (even though I am not going to meet him). In what follows I will not assume that attitudinal pleasure is always directed toward truths. Perhaps the most we can say is that if you take pleasure in some state of affairs, then you must at least think that it's true.

Another aspect of the epistemology of enjoyment is puzzling, too. In an earlier era, philosophers sometimes said that such states as enjoyment are "transparent" or "self-revealing". Some of them may have meant to suggest that if you are enjoying something, then you must know immediately that you are enjoying it. I have my doubts. I think we can deceive ourselves about our enjoyments. A person might think he is enjoying the taste and aroma of the wine when in fact he is really enjoying being seen in possession of a bottle with an impressive label.

Enjoyment has its opposite number. We might call this "disenjoyment" but it is easier to call it attitudinal pain. Just as we say that someone takes pleasure in some things, we can say that he "takes pain" in others. To take pain in something is to disenjoy it. If we represent amounts of enjoyment with numbers, then we can introduce a simplifying assumption: to disenjoy something to some extent, n, is to enjoy it to some negative extent, −n.

Some people are convinced that there is a deep conceptual link between the attitude of enjoyment and the feeling of sensory pleasure. For example, they may tell us that to enjoy something is to feel pleasure as a result of it (or as a result of thinking of it). I am convinced that this view is false[3] but I will not debate it here. For present purposes it is sufficient that the distinction between attitudinal pleasure and sensory pleasure is clear. After a brief discussion of sensory hedonism, I will not be talking much about sensory pleasure. Most of the views to be discussed here concern attitudinal pleasure.

3. The Evaluation of Lives

[. . .]

My questions here concern neither extrinsic goodness nor moral goodness. I am interested in the value of a life *for the one who lives it*. Some like to say that this scale measures "welfare". Others would say it measures "quality of life". Aristotle seems to have this scale in mind when he wonders what makes a person "happy", and seriously considers the question whether things that happen after death might affect this score.[4] Parfit sometimes talks of "a life well worth living".[5] I think he is alluding to this same scale of measurement. This is the sort of evaluation with which we will be concerned here.

When students and colleagues think back with affection on Chisholm and hope that his life went well for him, we are hoping that

his life ranked high on this third scale. We are hoping that he led a life that was good for him. (Of course, some of us might also be concerned to know whether his life was good for others, and some might be curious about whether his life was morally good. However interesting such inquiries might be, they are not my topic here.)

From now on when I speak of "the value of a person's life", I will be referring to that person's score on this third scale. Thus, I mean to be discussing the question whether the value of a person's life is determined by the extent to which he enjoys the things that happen to him in that life.

4. A Simple Form of Hedonism; Why it Fails

Some people (especially critics) insist on understanding hedonism as a view about sensory pleasure and sensory pain. They insist that the hedonist must mean that the value of a life is determined by the total amount of sensory pleasure it contains, minus the total amount of sensory pain it contains. Views of this sort may be said to be forms of 'Sensory Hedonism'.

I am not interested in defending Sensory Hedonism. It is not my view. I reject it for a variety of reasons. For one thing, I reject it because it gives what I take to be the wrong evaluation of a life such as the life of Stoicus. According to the story, Stoicus just wants peace and quiet. He wants to live an unruffled life. We must be clear about Stoicus's desires: it's not that he wants peace and quiet because he thinks these will give him sensory pleasure. He wants peace and quiet as ends in themselves. In fact, he prefers not to have sensory pleasure. He prefers not to have sensory pleasure in part because he fears that if he had some sensory pleasure, it would ruffle his life. He feels the same way about sensory pain: he does not want it.

Suppose Stoicus gets exactly what he wants – peace, quiet, no sensory pleasure, and no sensory pain. Suppose that as he receives his daily dose of peace and quiet, Stoicus is pleased. That is, suppose he enjoys the peace and quiet. Suppose he takes attitudinal pleasure in various facts about his life, including the fact that he is not experiencing any sensory pleasure. Suppose Stoicus eventually dies a happy man. He lived 90 years of somewhat boring but on the whole quite enjoyable peace and quiet. Stoicus thinks (right before he dies) that his has been an outstandingly good life.

Sensory Hedonism implies that Stoicus did not have a good life. This follows from the fact that the life of Stoicus did not contain any episodes of sensory pleasure. But if Stoicus was happy with his life, and enjoyed the experiences that came his way, and got precisely what he wanted at every moment, it seems strange to say that there was nothing good about his life. Although it is not the sort of life I would like to lead, I must confess that it seems quite a nice life for someone with Stoicus's tastes. Dull perhaps, but at the same time pleasant enough (in its non-sensory way).

I mention the example of Stoicus for several reasons. For one, it is supposed to show that Sensory Hedonism is false. It does this by showing that it is possible for a person to have quite a good life (as measured on the third scale) even though he experiences no sensory pleasure. Another reason to mention the life of Stoicus is that it is supposed to drive home the difference between sensory pleasure and attitudinal pleasure. Stoicus had none of the former, but plenty of the latter. And the third reason to mention Stoicus is that reflection on his case may highlight the plausibility of attitudinal hedonism.[6]

Attitudinal hedonism is the view that what makes a life good for the one who lives it is that it contains a lot of enjoyment, or attitudinal pleasure, and relatively little disenjoyment, or attitudinal pain. I now turn to a discussion of this sort of view.

5.   Attitudinal Hedonism

One form of attitudinal hedonism can be constructed as follows: first we assume that whenever a person takes attitudinal pleasure in any state of affairs, he does so for some period of time and at some average intensity. Of course, in real-life cases it may be difficult or even impossible to determine the intensity

of a person's pleasure, and there may be some difficulty in determining precisely when the pleasure begins and when it ends. But I will assume that such problems are not deeply conceptual – they are merely practical difficulties. Thus, I assume that whenever a person is pleased about something, there is some amount of attitudinal pleasure he takes in this something. Let's assume at the outset that this amount is determined by the intensity and duration of his pleasure.

I make similar assumptions about attitudinal pain.

Let us imagine a numerical scale on which these attitudinal pleasures can be measured. Assume that the scale assigns positive numbers to pleasures, with higher number representing more intense and longer lasting pleasures. Assume that it assigns negative numbers, with lower (absolutely greater) negative numbers representing more intense and longer lasting pains.

We might suppose that the value of a person's life according to attitudinal hedonism would be the sum, for all the attitudinal pleasures and pains that person ever experiences in that life, of these numbers. Alas, things are not quite so simple.

We must recognize *basic attitudinal pleasures and pains*. Otherwise, we will run into some nagging problems about double-counting. To see this in a concrete case, imagine that Stoicus is pleased to degree +10 that there is fresh water in the pitcher. Imagine further that he is pleased that there is fresh water because he realizes that he will be able to drink it, and he is pleased to degree +10 that he will be able to drink it. Still further, imagine that he is pleased that he will be able to drink it because he realizes that if he drinks it, he will not be thirsty, and he will be pleased to degree +10 to avoid thirst. Finally, imagine that he is pleased that he will avoid thirst because he believes that thirst would be unpleasant.

I think it would be wrong to give Stoicus a score of +40 in such a case. To do so would be to give extra credit merely for having longer chains of belief. I cannot see that having such extra-long chains makes a person's life any better. I propose instead to count only the pleasures at the ends of the chains. Thus, in the present case, Stoicus should get only 10 points for his water-in-the pitcher/drinking-it/avoiding thirst pleasure.

Thus, I propose that we say that *S is intrinsically attitudinally pleased to degree n about p at t* if S is attitudinally pleased to degree n about p at t, but not in virtue of the fact that he is attitudinally pleased about something else at t. Intrinsic pleasure is pleasure taken in a thing "for its own sake". I assume that there is also intrinsic attitudinal displeasure.

Another sort of double-counting must be avoided, too. Consider the case in which Stoicus is intrinsically pleased about three things at once: that he feels no thirst, that he feels no sensory pain, and that he feels no sensory pleasure. Suppose he takes exactly 10 units of attitudinal pleasure in each of these states. But he also takes pleasure in the various conjunctions and disjunctions of these states. For example, he takes pleasure (perhaps 20 units of it) in the fact that he feels neither sensory pleasure nor sensory pain. Surely we would be guilty of an overcount if we added all these 20s and 30s to the score already assigned to Stoicus.

Let us assume that whenever a person takes pleasure in some complex state of affairs such as the conjunctions just illustrated, that he takes this pleasure in virtue of the fact that he takes pleasure in the simpler components of which these are composed. Thus, there is a non-causal way in which you can take pleasure in p *in virtue of the fact that* you take pleasure in q. Let us understand "in virtue of" in this broader way, so that the proposed account of intrinsic attitudinal pleasure is sensitive to both ways of being intrinsic.

For purposes of discussion, then, let us understand Intrinsic Attitudinal Hedonism (IAH) to be the view that the value of a person's life is determined by the total amount of intrinsic attitudinal pleasure the person enjoys during that life (counting intrinsic attitudinal pain as "negative pleasure"). This theory implies that someone like Stoicus leads a pretty good life. That's because Stoicus was described as enjoying his peace and quiet and his lack of sensory pain and pleasure, and as not disenjoying anything. I assume that these enjoyments are either themselves intrinsic, or depend upon some other intrinsic enjoyments lying deeper

in the psyche of Stoicus. So Stoicus gets quite a few positive points, and no negative points. His life is good, just as he declared it to be.

It's interesting to see what IAH implies about the life of a garden-variety sensory hedonist. Suppose Hugh enjoys sex, drugs, and rock 'n' roll. Suppose he has many delightful sensory experiences. He takes great intrinsic attitudinal pleasure in the various states of affairs consisting of his feeling this sensory pleasure, or his feeling that sensory pleasure. As a result of the sheerest good fortune, Hugh never suffers much pain beyond the occasional hangover, or mild bout of indigestion. IAH implies that Hugh's life was excellent.[7] This seems reasonable to me. Furthermore, it is the sort of thing some sensory hedonists would want to say. And IAH yields precisely this result.

It's interesting to note that IAH does not imply that the goodness of Hugh's life is ultimately determined by the fact that he experienced a lot of sensory pleasures. (That would be the basis on which typical forms of Sensory Hedonism would evaluate his life.) Rather, IAH bases its judgment upon the fact that Hugh took intrinsic attitudinal pleasure in the fact that he was having these experiences. If another person (Stoicus perhaps) were forced to endure precisely these experiences, but didn't enjoy them, IAH would declare (correctly in my view) that his life was worthless. And IAH would reach this conclusion in spite of the fact that the sensory experiences were, sense-datum for sense-datum, indiscernible from those enjoyed by Hugh.

6.   Some Classic Objections to Hedonism

I hope at this point that the general outlines of attitudinal hedonism are clear enough to permit critical discussion. I now turn to consideration of some classic objections to hedonism. It is not clear that the philosophers who presented these objections intended to be attacking a view precisely like IAH. But I will take the liberty of interpreting these objections as objections to the view I have sketched. Perhaps this will serve to make attitudinal hedonism clearer. It will also eventually lead me to introduce some alternatives to the theory.

6a. Shelly Kagan discusses one of the most common and forceful objections to hedonism in his "Me and My Life".[8] According to Kagan, hedonism implies that what determines the quality of a person's life is something completely internal to the person – in this case a certain mental state. Kagan thus says that hedonism is a form of "mental statism". Hedonism, like all forms of mental statism, implies that if two lives are alike with respect to mental states, they must also be alike with respect to value. In particular, hedonism implies that if two lives are alike with respect to pleasures and pains, then those lives are of equal value. This remains true even if one of the individuals takes his pleasures from correctly perceived interactions with real human beings, and the other individual is a mere brain in a vat, utterly unconnected with other people but taking himself to be living a life like the first person's. Kagan thinks that this is a source of trouble for hedonism.

Rather than letting the issue turn on far-fetched cases involving brains in vats, Kagan, following Tom Nagel, considers the fairly realistic case of a happy businessman. The businessman is happy because, as he thinks, his career is going well, he is respected in his community, and he has a loving family. In the example, all of his assumptions are false. The businessman is in fact held in utter contempt by his colleagues, deeply deceived by his adulterous wife, and hated by his children. Each has his or her reasons for engaging in the deception, but the result is the same: the businessman's happiness is completely dependent upon his widespread misapprehension of his circumstances. If he knew the truth about his colleagues, his wife, and his children, he would be miserable. Kagan concludes the discussion of this example by saying, "In thinking about this man's life, it is difficult to believe that it is all a life could be, that this life has gone about as well as a life could go. Yet this seems to be the very conclusion mental state theories must reach. . . . So mental state theories must be wrong."[9]

Since we are considering a form of attitudinal hedonism, let us be sure to understand the case appropriately for present purposes. Let us stipulate that the businessman takes immediate attitudinal pleasure in many states of affairs, taking them all to be true. But they are all false. So, for example, this businessman is intrinsically pleased that he is respected by his colleagues, but in fact he is not respected by his colleagues. He is intrinsically pleased that he his loved by children, but in fact he is not loved by his children, and so on.

The objection should be clear. Attitudinal hedonism implies that the businessman's life is a good one, yet none of us would want such a life; none of us would wish such a life for our loved ones; such a life is not easily thought to be ideal.

Variants of this objection have been presented by a number of anti-hedonists and some of them may seem pretty persuasive.[10] Nevertheless, the attitudinal hedonist need not be utterly crushed. Some such hedonists might reply by saying that the life of the deceived businessman is not so bad after all. Perhaps we can explain away our sense that something is amiss in the businessman's life by pointing out that we would not like to be deceived, and we would be pained to learn that our colleagues and family have been holding us in contempt for all these years. This helps to explain the fact that none of us would voluntarily choose the life of the deceived businessman. We know things about his life that he does not know. Since we know these things, we would not enjoy the experiences he enjoys. Hence, his life seems unattractive to us.

Furthermore, if any of his deceivers should slip up, the businessman might discover his real situation. Then he would be miserable. We would not like to have a life constantly on the brink of misery. However, in the case as described, it is stipulated that he does not discover his real situation, and is not miserable. If we were to ask him how his life is going, he would surely insist that he is living a fine life. Some would say that since the businessman does not know about the deception, it does not hurt him. Hence, it is not entirely clear that hedonism's implications are indefensible. Perhaps considerations such as these help to explain away our intuitive sense that his life is not all a life could be.

But the defender of Attitudinal Hedonism does not have to take this "bite the bullet" line. He can move to higher ground. He can slightly revise the axiology. As before, he can say that the fundamental goods are takings of intrinsic pleasure in various states of affairs, but he can modify this by saying that such takings of pleasures enhance the value of a life more when they are takings of pleasures in *true* states of affairs. This single modification yields a view according to which the life of the deceived businessman is not very good, even if internally indiscernible from the life of his cousin the undeceived businessman whose mental life is just the same, but whose family and colleagues are in reality as they appear to him to be.

It's not clear that the revised axiology is a form of mental statism, since it implies that it's possible for there to be two lives exactly alike ("from the inside") with respect to mental states, but unlike in value. But on the other hand, it's interesting to note that even the revised theory makes the value of a life depend on mental states – enjoyments after all are mental states – it's just that the question how much a certain state counts depends in part upon whether the object of that state is true. So I don't know whether Kagan would categorize this as a form of mental statism or not. Since the view itself is fairly clear, I see no reason to worry about whether it is a form of mental statism. In any case, it is clearly a form of hedonism. Let us call the revised theory "Veridical Intrinsic Attitudinal Hedonism", or "VIAH".

My point here is to show that attitudinal hedonism has the resources to deal with the example of the deceived businessman. If you think that the deceived businessman's life is less valuable than the life of his undeceived internal duplicate, then I offer VIAH for you. If you think that the twin businessmen lead lives of equal value – that where pleasure is concerned, truth does not matter – then I offer IAH for you. Either way, there should be some form of hedonism that will yield results consistent with your axiological intuitions about these cases.

6b. *The Argument from Worthless Pleasures.* A number of philosophers have claimed that certain kinds of pleasure are not good, and do not serve to enhance the value of any life.

They have appealed to such pleasures in their attacks on hedonism.

Aristotle hints at this in the *Nicomachean Ethics* (X.3) where he speaks of "disgraceful" and "base" pleasures. Broad makes the case quite persuasively in *Five Types of Ethical Theory*. He more or less defines malice in such a way that a person enjoys malicious pleasure iff s/he takes pleasure in some other person's suffering.[11] Brandt makes a similar point in his argument against hedonism in *Ethical Theory*. He describes some women who attended beheadings in evening dress in Germany.[12] He suggests that if they enjoyed the occasion, their enjoyment was not intrinsically desirable. Moore does not (so far as I know) make explicit use of precisely this argument, but he apparently accepts the main premise. He speaks of cruelty, and he says that one essential component of it is the enjoyment of pain in other people.[13] He says that cruelty is a great mixed evil, containing a good part (enjoyment, which is a sort of pleasure) and a bad part (the pain of the other person). The whole thus formed is judged to be intrinsically bad. Brentano makes a similar claim, although his discussion is open to various interpretations.

In "Two Unique Cases of Preferability", Brentano says:

> What of pleasure in the bad? Is it itself something that is good? Aristotle says that it is not. . . . The hedonists expressed the contrary view, . . . But their view is to be rejected. . . . Pleasure in the bad is, as pleasure, something that is good, but at the same time, as an incorrect emotion, it is something that is bad.[14]

I will attempt to formulate the argument clearly, so that useful discussion may ensue. And as I formulate, I will try to construe the argument in such a way as to make it directly relevant to the forms of intrinsic attitudinal hedonism I have introduced. Thus, I will not be speaking of "feelings of pleasure". I will be speaking of attitudinal pleasures whose objects are bad, or unworthy of pleasurable contemplation.

Suppose some terrorist really hates children. Suppose he sets off a bomb at a playground, and then watches the news on TV. When he sees the suffering children choking and gasping and bleeding, and learns of the many injuries and deaths, this terrorist is delighted. He takes pleasure in the misery of his victims. More precisely, he takes veridical intrinsic attitudinal pleasure of a high degree in the fact that the innocent children are suffering.

Suppose the terrorist does this many times over, and each time thoroughly enjoys the fruits of his labor. Suppose at the same time that his life is not filled with counterbalancing pains. If VIAH were true, the life of this terrorist would be a good one. We would have to agree that things turned out well for him, and the quality of his life was high. Many of us, I suspect, would be inclined to reject this evaluation, and with it attitudinal hedonism. The problem here is that while the life of the terrorist was filled with large doses of veridical intrinsic attitudinal pleasure, these pleasures were the pleasures of cruelty. Pleasures such as these might seem to make a life worse, rather than better.[15]

Other philosophers have reminded us of other worthless pleasures. In a memorable passage, Moore says: "It is commonly held that certain of what would be called the lowest forms of sexual enjoyment" might be "the most pleasant states we ever experience."[16] And in this context he speaks of "a perpetual indulgence in bestiality". He says (roughly) that if hedonism were true, then this perpetual indulgence in bestiality would be "heaven indeed, and all human endeavors should be devoted to its realisation. I venture to think [says Moore] that this view is as false as it is paradoxical".

Let us try to visualize the life to which Moore here alludes, adjusted so as to be directly relevant to VIAH. Imagine a person – we can call him "Porky" – who spends all his time in the pigsty, engaging in the most obscene sexual activities imaginable. I stipulate that Porky takes great intrinsic attitudinal pleasure in these activities and the feelings they stimulate. In the example, he really does engage in the activities and feel the feelings. Thus, his pleasures are veridical, too. Let's imagine that Porky happily carries on like this for many years. Imagine also that Porky has no human

friends; has no other sources of pleasure; has no interesting knowledge.

Moore's point (as modified to apply here) is that VIAH implies that Porky's life is one of the best we can imagine – "heaven indeed". Yet, as Moore indicates, that implication is a bit hard to swallow.

Objectors claim that Porky's life is not very good in spite of the stipulated fact that it contains a lot of veridical intrinsic attitudinal pleasure. This example is thought to illustrate a second way in which pleasure can be worthless. As Aristotle said, base pleasures do not enhance the value of a life.

7.   A More Complex Form of Hedonism

I think it is possible to modify our attitudinal hedonism so as to make it generate the desired results in these cases, too. Moore, Brentano, and Chisholm have pointed the way. Roughly, the idea is to say that the intrinsic value of an attitudinal pleasure is determined not simply by the intensity and duration and truthfulness of that pleasure, but by these in combination with the appropriateness of the object of that pleasure. (Similarly for attitudinal pains.) More exactly, the value of a pleasure is enhanced when it is pleasure taken in a worthy object, such as something good, or beautiful. The value of a pleasure is mitigated when it is pleasure taken in an unworthy object, such as something evil, or ugly. The disvalue of a pain is mitigated (made less bad) when it is pain taken in an object worthy of pain, such as something evil, or ugly. The value of a pain is enhanced (made yet worse) when it is pain taken in an object unworthy of this attitude, such as something good or beautiful.[17]

I think it's reasonable to describe certain objects by saying that they "deserve to be objects of pleasure". In the case of such objects it is fitting, or appropriate, that someone take pleasure in them. Thus, for example, if an object is genuinely beautiful, then it deserves to be appreciated. If an object is good, then it deserves to be admired. So we can identify the objects worthy of pleasure as those that deserve to have pleasure taken in them. (And similarly for pain and its objects.) In this way we make essential use of the concept of *desert* in the formulation of our hedonistic axiology.

While we are making this adjustment for pleasure-worthiness, we might as well incorporate the adjustment for truth. That is, we can view the veridicalness of the object of a pleasure as yet another factor that enhances its worthiness of pleasure. We therefore can say that when someone takes pleasure in a true state of affairs, his pleasure is more valuable, other things being equal, than it would have been if the object of his pleasure had been false.

One version of the resulting theory may be called "Desert Adjusted Intrinsic Attitudinal Hedonism" (or DAIAH). It is structurally similar to views discussed by Moore, Brentano, Chisholm, [. . .] and others.[18] It is intended to generate the desired results in the cases involving malicious and base pleasures. Since the objects of those pleasures are respectively evil and disgusting, DAIAH declares the pleasures to be much less valuable. If the life of the terrorist is filled with pleasures of this first worthless sort, and the life of Porky is filled with pleasures of the second worthless sort, then DAIAH declares those lives to be of little value. I claim – though I cannot take the time to show it in detail here – that the view also deals adequately with what we may dub "worthwhile pains", such as intrinsic attitudinal pain taken in evil or ugly objects.

8.   Yet Another Objection

I like DAIAH. I think I know some of its implications, and I am happy to accept them. I think I am in a state approaching reflective equilibrium while believing it. However, my point here is not to show that DAIAH is the one true form of hedonism. Rather, my point is merely to show that it is possible to formulate a kind of hedonism that is immune to the objections presented by Aristotle, Broad, Moore and the others based on the possibility of misdirected pleasure. We can be hedonists without saying that base and malicious pleasures improve a life as much as pleasures taken in worthier objects.

Yet a further classic objection to hedonism remains. A number of anti-hedonists have

made use of this argument, and I make no claims about priority. I cite the version to be found in Ross mainly because I think it is a neat and persuasive formulation of the argument.

Ross says:

> If we compare two imaginary states of the universe, alike in the total amounts of virtue and vice and of pleasure and pain present in the two, but in one of which the virtuous were all happy and the vicious miserable, while in the other the virtuous were miserable and the vicious happy, very few people would hesitate to say that the first was a much better state of the universe than the second. It would seem then that, besides virtue and pleasure, we must recognize, as a third independent good, the apportionment of pleasure and pain to the virtuous and the vicious respectively.[19]

Although Ross says it quite well himself, I'd like to say it again in my own words to ensure that the objection bears directly on the forms of attitudinal hedonism under consideration here. I think Ross wants us to imagine two possible worlds. The worlds are supposed to be exactly alike with respect to several important features – virtue and vice, pleasure and pain. So let us stipulate that each world contains a million virtuous people and a million vicious people, and let us stipulate that each world contains a million people who enjoy lives filled with object-appropriate intrinsic attitudinal pleasure, and each world also contains a million people who live lives filled with object-inappropriate intrinsic attitudinal pain. So the worlds are very similar. The central difference concerns who gets what. In W1, the virtuous people get to live the lives filled with object appropriate pleasure and the vicious people get to live the lives filled with pain. It's the reverse in W2. There "bad things happen to good people" and "good things happen to bad people".

I want to be clear about what goes on in W2. Imagine a life filled with pleasures taken in appropriate objects. Here the pleasure-seeker is no Porky or perverted terrorist. This is an educated, tasteful aesthete. He takes deep pleasure in such things as genuinely beautiful works of art, and the innocent frolicking of healthy, happy children. The only problem is that this aesthete is also a thief who has stolen the art from those to whom it rightly belongs, and a kidnapper who has kidnapped the frolicking children. So while the *objects* deserve to be enjoyed, *this thief and kidnapper* does not deserve to be enjoying them.

The crucial thing to note about these worlds is that they are exactly alike with respect to veridical intrinsic attitudinal pleasures and pains. Ross's point (modified to apply to the theory currently under consideration) is that DAIAH implies that these worlds are equally valuable. Yet Ross thinks (and I think too) that the just world, W1, is much better than the equally pleasant but unjust world, W2. This might seem to refute DAIAH.

Ross's example is interesting and insightful. It draws our attention to an important consideration. Nevertheless, I think it does not refute DAIAH. Note that DAIAH as so far stated says nothing about values of worlds. It speaks only about the values of *lives*. Yet Ross's argument is not based on any alleged misevaluation of *lives*. He did not say that the lives of the happy vicious people were misevaluated by hedonism. Indeed, it seems to me that DAIAH might get this right. Rather, Ross's claim concerns the evaluation of *worlds*. Since DAIAH gives no evaluation of worlds, it cannot be guilty of giving the wrong evaluation of the worlds described by Ross.

If we add a certain assumption to DAIAH, we will get the conclusion Ross attacks. The assumption is that the value of a world is equal to the sum of the values of the lives lived there. Since DAIAH gives equivalent evaluations of the lives in W1 and W2, it would then yield the conclusion that W1 is equal in value to W2. Ross could then launch his attack. But perhaps the defender of DAIAH would not endorse this aggregative principle. Perhaps he would acknowledge that a world could be filled with good lives, and yet be a bad world because the wrong people get to live those good lives. Then Ross's argument would lose its target.

It seems to me that an axiological theory should give an account of what makes a life worth living. DAIAH does this. It tells us that the value of a life is determined by the net extent to which the liver of that life experiences object appropriate veridical intrinsic attitudinal pleasures. Ross's example does not raise any serious trouble for DAIAH on these grounds. But an axiological theory should also give an account of what makes a world worth creating, or aiming for. If we jettison the idea that the value of a world is the sum of the values of the lives lived there, then DAIAH says nothing about this question. We should address this issue.

9. Double Desert Adjusted Hedonism

We have adjusted the value of a pleasure to reflect the extent to which the object of that pleasure deserves to be enjoyed. This (I claim) solves the problem of worthless pleasures (and worthwhile pains) and gives the proper basis for the evaluation of lives. I propose that we adjust this value again, this time to reflect the extent to which the *subject* – the one who experiences the pleasure – deserves to be experiencing it. This "double desert adjustment" will give the proper basis for the evaluation of worlds and will solve the problem set by Ross.

Suppose a person takes intrinsic attitudinal pleasure in some object. To find the double desert adjusted value of his pleasure, we need to take several steps. First, we need to determine the intensity and duration and truthfulness of the pleasure. Other things being equal, longer and stronger and true pleasures are more valuable. Next we need to determine the extent to which the object of the pleasure deserves to be enjoyed. We ask if the object is a worthy object of pleasure. Other things being equal, pleasure taken in more worthy objects is more valuable. (This is the first adjustment in value for desert, taken to ensure that the *object* of the pleasure deserves to be enjoyed.) Then finally we need to determine the extent to which the *subject* of the pleasure deserves to be taking that particular pleasure. Other things being equal, pleasures enjoyed by more deserving subjects are more valuable than otherwise similar pleasures enjoyed by less deserving subjects. This is the second adjustment in value for desert, taken to ensure that the *subject* of the pleasure deserves to be enjoying it.

Similar adjustments in value would be made to episodes of intrinsic attitudinal pain. Roughly, the idea here would be that when a person who fully deserves to be taking pain in a certain object does take pain in that object, then the badness of his pain is mitigated. Other things being equal, such pains are less bad for the world than similar pains suffered by people who do not deserve to be undergoing them. Pains suffered by people who deserve not to be suffering them are worse, other things being equal, than similar pains suffered by people who do deserve to be suffering them. As a result of all this, we can see that the worst pains (on this double-adjusted scale) are intense, long-lasting pains taken in objects that deserve not to be objects of pain, suffered by people who deserve not to be suffering them.

Considerations of space and time do not permit me to give a full account of the nature, sources, and structure of desert. (I have discussed these issues elsewhere, and hope to say more in the future.) Such things as excessive or deficient prior receipt, legal or moral "rights" to pleasure, hard work, virtue and vice, etc. probably influence the extent to which someone deserves some pleasure. I recognize that more needs to be said, but this is not the place to say it.

The resulting value may be called the Double Desert Adjusted Value of the pleasure. Similar procedures would yield the DDAV of any intrinsic attitudinal pains. Double Desert Adjusted Intrinsic Attitudinal Hedonism (DDAIAH) is the view that the value of a world (or outcome, or other complex state of affairs) is the sum of the Double Desert Adjusted Values of the intrinsic attitudinal pleasures enjoyed and pains suffered in that world (or outcome, or whatever). My answer to Ross is this: "Yes, Ross, you have presented a problem for an extension of DAIAH. You have shown that we would go wrong if we evaluated worlds strictly in terms of *single* desert-adjusted intrinsic attitudinal pleasures and pains. But we are not forced to endorse that extension. Instead, we can endorse DDAIAH."

My view as a whole is roughly this:

1. The fundamental bearers of value are complex states of affairs of this form: *S takes intrinsic attitudinal pleasure (pain) of intensity n and duration m in object P at time t, when S deserves to degree r to be taking that pleasure (pain) and P deserves to degree s to be the object of that pleasure (pain).*

2. The desert adjusted value of such a state is a function of intensity, duration, truth, and pleasure (pain) worthiness of its object.

3. The double desert adjusted value of such a state is a function of intensity, duration, truth, pleasure (pain) worthiness of its object, and the pleasure (pain) worthiness of its subject.

4. The value (on the third scale) of a life is the sum of the desert adjusted values of the fundamental intrinsic attitudinal pleasure (pain) states in that life.

5. The value (on the third scale) of a world is the sum of the double desert adjusted values of the fundamental intrinsic attitudinal pleasure (pain) states in that world.

Notes

1. The intensity of enjoyment must not be confused with the "strength" or "intensity" of any feeling. One can take great pleasure in some state of affairs even though one does not experience any intense sensations while thinking about that state of affairs. Indeed, Stoicus (whose case is discussed below) might be *very* pleased that he is not feeling any intense feelings at all.

2. In *Brentano and Intrinsic Value*, pp. 28–9.

3. And I presented a variety of arguments against it in "Two Questions about Pleasure".

4. *Nicomachean Ethics*, Book I, Chapters 10–11.

5. *Reasons and Persons*, passim. For an especially insightful discussion of various views on these topics, see Parfit's Appendix I, "What Makes Someone's Life Go Best". pp. 493–502.

6. It might appear that the real moral of the story of Stoicus is that we should consider some form

of satisfactionism – the idea that what makes a life worth living is that it is filled with satisfied desires. I am convinced that this sort of view is indefensible. This is not the place to present arguments. For an impressive critical discussion, see Section 1 of Chapter 3 of Adams' *Finite and Infinite Goods*.

7. Excellent on the *third scale*. This sort of hedonism makes no evaluation of Hugh's life on any other scale. So it is consistent with what I have said to say in addition that Hugh's life ranks low in terms of value to others as well as in terms of moral value.

8. *Proceedings of the Aristotelian Society* (1984): 309–24.

9. *Normative Ethics*, 35.

10. Robert Nozick's example of the 'experience machine' comes to mind here. See his *Anarchy, State, and Utopia*, pp. 42–5.

11. Broad, *Five Types of Ethical Theory*, pp. 53–4 in the excerpt included in Brandt's *Value and Obligation*.

12. Brandt, *Ethical Theory*, p. 316.

13. Moore, *Principia Ethica* Chapter VI, Section 125.

14. *The Origin of Our Knowledge of Right and Wrong*, p. 90.

15. It is important, in considering a case such as this, to be sure to keep in mind the fact that we are talking about evaluation *on the third scale*. We are not asking whether the terrorist led a morally good life, or whether he led a life that

was good for others. Nor are we asking whether his pleasures were 'admirable'. We are asking whether he led a life that was "good for him". Though his pleasures were directed toward wholly inappropriate objects, one could still insist that if he enjoyed these things, his life was good for him. Many antihedonists prefer not to say this.

16. Moore, *Principia Ethica* Chapter III, Section 56.

17. I speak loosely here. I do not mean to suggest that pleasures have variable intrinsic values – values that can be increased or decreased depending upon changes in the nature of their objects. Rather, what I mean is that the fundamental bearers of intrinsic value should be taken to be complex states of affairs involving not only the intensity and duration and truthfulness of a pleasure, but something also about the worthiness of its object – the extent to which that object deserves to be enjoyed. Thus, a basic value state, on this axiology, would be something of this form: *S takes intrinsic attitudinal pleasure of intensity n1 and duration m1 in state of affairs P, while P is worthy of pleasure of intensity n2 and duration m2.*

18. Moore endorses something like this in Chapter VI of *Principia Ethica*. Brentano did it in *The Origin of Our Knowledge of Right and Wrong*. Chisholm does it in Chapter 5 of *Brentano and Intrinsic Value*.

19. From *The Right and the Good*, p. 138.

References

Adams, Robert, *Finite and Infinite Goods: A Framework for Ethics* (New York and Oxford: Oxford University Press, 1999).

Brandt, Richard, *Ethical Theory: The Problems of Normative and Critical Ethics* (Englewood Cliffs: Prentice-Hall, Inc., 1959).

——, *Value and Obligation: Systematic Readings in Ethics* (New York: Harcourt, Brace & World, Inc., 1961).

Brentano, Franz, *The Origin of Our Knowledge of Right and Wrong*, ed. by Oskar Kraus, English edition edited by Roderick M. Chisholm, translated by Roderick M. Chisholm and Elizabeth Schneewind (London: Routledge & Kegan Paul, 1969).

Broad, C. D., *Five Types of Ethical Theory* (London: Kegan, Paul, 1930).

Chisholm, Roderick M., *Brentano and Intrinsic Value* (Cambridge: Cambridge University Press, 1986).

Feldman, Fred, "Two Questions about Pleasure", in David Austin, (ed.) *Philosophical Analysis* (Dordrecht: Kluwer Academic Publishers, 1988), pp. 59–81. Reprinted in *Utilitarianism, Hedonism and Desert*.

Kagan, Shelly, 'Me and My Life' *Proceedings of the Aristotelian Society* 94 (1994), pp. 309–24.

——, *Normative Ethics* (Boulder, Colorado: Westview Press, 1998).

Moore, G. E., *Principia Ethica* (Cambridge: Cambridge University Press, 1962; first published 1903).

Nozick, Robert, *Anarchy, State and Utopia* (New York: Basic Books, 1974).

Parfit, Derek, *Reasons and Persons* (Oxford: Oxford University Press, 1984).

Ross, Sir William David, *The Right and the Good* (Oxford: Oxford University Press, 1930).

CHAPTER 32
The Informed Desire Account

JAMES GRIFFIN

The Informed Desire Account

[. . .]

The informed-desire account starts with the recognition that actual desires can be faulty. What sorts of fault matter? Obviously, for one, lack of information. Some of our strongest desires rest on mistakes of fact. I make my fortune, say, only to discover I am no better off because I was after people's respect all along and mistakenly thought that making a fortune would command respect. Or I want an operation to restore me to health, not realizing that some pill will do just as well. What matters is the ultimate, not the immediate, object of my desire, and factual mistakes creep into matching the one to the other. Or I develop one set of material desires not realizing that they are the sort that, once satisfied, are replaced by another set that are just as clamorous and I am no better off. The consumer-desires at the centre of the economists' stage can be like that. Then another relevant fault is logical mistake. A lot of practical reasoning is about adapting means to ends and, like any reasoning, it can be confused, irrelevant, or question-begging. Then there are subtler faults. Sometimes desires are defective because we have not got enough, or

James Griffin, "The Informed Desire Account," pp. 12–17, 21–31 from *Well-Being*. Oxford: Oxford University Press, 1986.

the right, concepts. Theories need building which will supply new or better concepts, including value concepts. For instance, it is easy to concentrate on desires to possess this or that object, at the cost of the more elusive, difficult-to-formulate, desires to live a certain sort of life. And it is almost impossible to strike the right balance between the two main components of happiness – on the one hand, the discontent that leads to better and, on the other, contentment with one's lot. One needs more than facts and logic to sort those problems out: one needs insight and subtle, perspicuous concepts. And with information, more is not always better. It might cripple me to know what someone thinks of me, and I might sensibly prefer to remain in ignorance. What seems most important to the informed-desire account is that desires have a structure; they are not all on one level. We have local desires (say, for a drink) but also higher order desires (say, to distance oneself from consumers' material desires) and global desires (say, to live one's life autonomously). The structure of desires provides the criterion for "informed" desire: *information* is what advances plans of life; information is *full* when more, even when there is more, will not advance them further. So there is only one way to avoid all the faults that matter to 'utility': namely, by understanding completely what makes life go well.

This brings out another break with classical utilitarian tradition. Bentham, Mill, and Sidgwick all saw utility as having to enter our experience. But we desire things other than states of mind; I might sometimes prefer, say, bitter truth to comforting delusion. The informed-desire account has the advantage of being able to accommodate such desires. But the desire account does this by severing the link between 'fulfilment of desire' and the requirement that the person in some way experience its fulfilment, dropping what we might call the Experience Requirement. If the delusion is complete, one believes that one has the truth; the mental states involved in believing something that really is true and believing a successful deception are the same. Or if a father wants his children to be happy, what he wants, what is valuable to him, is a state of the world, not a state of his mind; merely to delude him into thinking that his children flourish, therefore, does not give him what he values. That is the important point; the informed-desire account does not require that fulfilment of desire translates itself in every case into the experience of the person who has the desire, and that is what gives the account its breadth and attraction as a theory of what makes life valuable. This seems to me the way that the informed-desire account has to develop. The definition itself is short: 'utility' is the fulfilment of informed desires, the stronger the desires, the greater the utility. The way that the account develops, however, shows that all of those key terms are to a fairly large degree technical.

(a) '*Desire*'. In the present technical sense, desires clearly do not have to have felt intensities; they need not be linked exclusively with appetitive states (some are, but others are aims we adopt as a result of understanding and judgement); they need not have existed before fulfilment. Rather, desiring something is, in the right circumstances, going for it, or not avoiding or being indifferent to getting it.

(b) '*Informed*'. In its technical sense, 'informed' is the absence of all the faults that I listed just a moment ago. There is a historically important account of practical reason that goes roughly like this: reason alone can never determine action. The end of action must be something fixed on, in its own reasonless way,

by desire; we reason, but deliberation is only of means. It is hard to see what is at issue between those who say, with Hume, that reason alone cannot supply a motive and those who say, with Kant, that it can. But those of the latter pursuasion are right to this extent: in deciding how to act, we must try to understand what properties things and states of affairs have, and we must put our desires through a lot of criticism and refinement to reach this understanding. In this sense, deliberation may be of ends, and important deliberation often is. So an 'informed' desire is one formed by appreciation of the nature of its object, and it includes anything necessary to achieve it.

(c) '*Fulfilment*'. Being 'fulfilled' cannot be understood in a psychological way, or we should be back with mental state accounts. A desire is 'fulfilled' in the sense in which a clause in a contract is fulfilled: namely, what was agreed (desired) comes about.

(d) '*Strength*'. 'Strength of desire' has several senses, appropriate to different theoretical settings. The 'strongest' desire can be the winner, or it can be the most intensely felt. But strength of desire, in its technical sense here, has to be understood in connection with the structure that informed desires have. One does not most satisfy someone's desires simply by satisfying as many as possible, or as large a proportion. One must assess their strength, not in the sense of felt intensity, but in a sense supplied by the natural structure of desire. The desires I feel most intensely could be satisfied by your constantly imperilling my life and saving me only at the last moment, whereas I should clearly prefer peace to peril; anyway, felt intensity is too often a mark of such relatively superficial matters as convention or training to be a reliable sign of anything as deep as well-being. That I prefer peace to peril suggests that global desires provide, in large part, the relevant notion of strength of desire: I desire the one form of life more than the other. True, sometimes we form global desires only on the basis of having summed local desires (for example, the global desire for a way of life based on a reckoning that day-to-day pleasures will be maximized that way). But even then we must rank that way of life against others that it excludes, and our preference between them will, it seems, be basic – that is, a global judgment not based on any other quantitative judgments. This means that the relevant notion of aggregation cannot be simply that of summing up small utilities from local satisfactions; the structure of desires already incorporates, constitutes, aggregation. It means also that the relevant sense of 'strength' is not simply the desire that wins out in motivation. If my doctor tells me that I shall die if I do not lay off drink, I shall want to lay off it. But I may later crack and go on a binge, and at that point my desire to drink will, in a perfectly clear sense, be strongest. If strength were interpreted as motivational force, then 'utility' would lose its links with well-being; what would be good for me would then be fulfilment not of my informed desires but of what I 'ought to desire' or 'have reason to desire'. So to retain the links with well-being, the relevant sense of 'strength' has to be, not motivational force, but rank in a cool preference ordering, an ordering that reflects appreciation of the nature of the objects of desire.

Troubles with the Informed-Desire Account

There are strong objections to such an account. Is it even intelligible? If our desires never changed with time, then each of us would have a single preference order, by reference to which what most fulfilled his desires over the course of his life could be calculated. However, life is not so simple; preferences change, and not always in a way that allows us totally to discount earlier ones. Suppose that for much of his life a person wanted his friends to keep him from vegetating when he retired but, now that he is retired, wants to be left to vegetate. Is there any intelligible programme for weighing desires that change with time and hence for maximizing fulfilment? If not, we may be driven back to a happiness or mental state account.

Yet all the problems that we have just seen with mental state accounts remain; defects in one account do not obligingly disappear with the appearance of defects in another. How do we determine how happy a person is? Is happiness a single mental state? If many, how are they linked? Mental state accounts are hardly a refuge from troubles. Moreover, there may be an acceptable programme for handling cases where preferences change with time. The notion of an informed desire needs still further development and may eventually be able to supply the weighting of desires that we need in these troublesome cases. Has our retired friend simply forgotten the satisfactions of a busy life? If so, his later desire has much less weight. Is it just a change in taste, on the model of no longer liking ice cream? If so, his earlier desire has much less weight. We shall have to come back to these problems when we discuss measurement, but for now I have to be content with suggesting that the prospects of making the informed-desire account work are certainly not less rosy than those of making a mental state account work.

The other troubles are much more worrying. The breadth of the account, which is its attraction, is also its great flaw. The account drops the Experience Requirement, as we called it. It allows my utility to be determined not only by things that I am not aware of (that seems right: if you cheat me out of an inheritance that I never expected, I might not know but still be worse off for it), but also by things that do not affect my life in any way at all. The trouble is that one's desires spread themselves so widely over the world that their objects extend far outside the bound of what, with any plausibility, one could take as touching one's own well-being. The restriction to *informed* desire is no help here. I might meet a stranger on a train and, listening to his ambitions, form a strong, informed desire that he succeed, but never hear of him again. And any moderately decent person wants people living in the twenty-second century to be happy and prosperous. And we know that Leonardo had an informed desire that humans fly, which the Wright brothers fulfilled centuries later. Indeed, without the Experience Requirement, why would utility not include the desires of the dead? And would that not mean the account had gone badly awry? And if we exclude these desires that extend beyond the bounds of what affects well-being, would we not, in order to avoid arbitrariness, have to reintroduce the Experience Requirement, thereby losing the breadth that makes the informed-desire account attractive? The difficulty goes deep in the theory. In fact, it goes deep, one way or other, in any account of well-being.

Another attraction of the account is that desires have to be shaped by appreciation of the nature of their objects. Without that restriction, the account is not even a starter. But with it, do desires even matter any longer? It may be somewhat too simple to say that things are desired because valuable, not valuable because desired. Yet the informed-desire account concedes much of the case for saying so. What makes us desire the things we desire, when informed, is something about them – *their* features or properties. But why bother then with informed desire, when we can go directly to what it is about objects that shape informed desires in the first place? If what really matter are certain sorts of reason for action, to be found outside desires in qualities of their objects, why not explain well-being directly in terms of them? It does not seem that it is fulfilled desire that is the basis of well-being, but certain of its objects. And that points us, depending on what we decide those objects are, either back towards mental states or beyond utility altogether.

[. . .]

How may we restrict the desire account?

THE informed-desire account will have to be abandoned unless we can find a way to restrict the desires that count. But we cannot do it with the Experience Requirement. [. . .]

The trouble, you will recall, comes from examples like these: I want the sympathetic stranger I meet on the train to succeed; I want people in the twenty-second century to prosper; Leonardo wanted humans to fly. All of them informed desires, but (the trouble is) their fulfilment not part of well-being.

The notion we are after is not the notion of value in general, but the narrower notion of a life's being valuable solely to the person who lives it. And this must itself impose restrictions on which desires count. As these examples show, the desires that count have to enter our lives in a way beyond just being our desires. So what we need to do is to make clear the sense in which only certain informed desires enter our lives in this further way. Think of the difference between my desire that the stranger succeed and my desire that my children prosper. I want both, but they enter my life in different ways. The first desire does not become one of my aims. The second desire, on the other hand, is one of my central ends, on the achievement of which the success of my life will turn. It is not that, deep down, what I really want is my own achievement, and that I want my children's prosperity only as a means to it. What I want is *their* prosperity, and it distorts the value I attach to it to make it only a means to such a purely personal end as my own achievement. It is just that their prosperity also becomes part of my life's being successful in a way that the prosperity of the stranger on the train does not.

But that can be only part of the story. It is not that informed desires count only if they become the sort of aims or goals or aspirations on which the success of a life turns. Good things can just happen; manna from heaven counts too. So we should try saying, to introduce more breadth, that what count are what we aim at and what we would not avoid or be indifferent to getting. What counts for me, therefore, is what enters my life with no doing from me, what I bring into my life, and what I do with my life. The range of that list is not so great as to include things that I cannot (e.g. the prosperity of our twenty-second-century successors) or do not (e.g. the sympathetic stranger's success) take into my life as an aim or goal. And Leonardo's wanting humans to fly would not count either; to the extent it became an aim of his life it was unsuccessful, and to the extent it was merely a wish it does not count.

In a way the account is now circular. I appeal to our rough notion of well-being in deciding which informed desires to exclude from this account of well-being. But that, I think, does not matter. If what we were doing were taking a totally empty term, 'well-being', and stipulating a sense for it, then we could not, in the middle of the job, appeal to 'well-being'. But our job is not that. The notion of 'well-being' we want to account for is not empty to start with; utilitarians use our everyday notion, and our job is to make it clearer. So we are free to move back and forth between our judgments about which cases fall inside the boundary and our descriptions of the boundary. Every account of this type will do the same. There is the same sort of undamaging circularity in mental state and enjoyment accounts, because they need to get beyond the ordinary senses of 'pleasure' and 'enjoyment', and they would have to go about fixing a new boundary in just the same way.

This narrowing of the desire account still does not get rid of the great embarrassment of the desires of the dead. Of course, a lot of the desires of the dead do count morally, but that is because they affect the living. There is a good case for honouring wishes expressed in wills. Inheritance satisfies the desires of the living to provide for their offspring and encourages saving that benefits society generally. There is a good case, too, for granting rights to the dead – say, to determine whether their bodies are used for medical purposes. But that, again, does not require appeal beyond the well-being of the living. And, anyway, that a desire of a dead person counts *morally* does not show that it counts towards his well-being.

The real trouble is our counting the fulfilment of aims even if (as it seems we must) we do not require that the fulfilment enter experience. Some of our aims are not fulfilled until we are dead; some, indeed, being desires for then, could not be. But is this so embarrassing, after all? You might have a desire – it could be an informed one, I think – to have your achievements recognized and acknowledged. An enemy of yours might go around slandering you behind your back, successfully persuading everyone that you stole all your ideas, and they, to avoid unpleasantness, pretend in your presence to believe you. If that could make your life less good, then why could it not be made less good by his slandering you with the extra distance behind your back that death brings? You might well be willing to exert yourself, at risk of your life, to prevent these slanders being disseminated after your death. You might, with eyes full open, prefer that course to longer life with a ruined reputation after it. There seems nothing irrational in attaching this value to posthumous reputation. And the value being attached to it does not seem to be moral or aesthetic or any kind other than the value to be attached to the life as a life to be lived. Here is another example. It would not have been at all absurd for Bertrand Russell to have thought that if his work for nuclear disarmament had, after his death, actually reduced the risk of nuclear war, his last years would have been more worthwhile, and his life altogether more valuable, than if it all proved futile. True, if Russell had indeed succeeded, his life clearly would have been more valuable to others. But Russell could also have considered it more valuable from the point of view of his own self-interest. For instance, it would not have been absurd for Russell to think the same about devoting his last years to some purely intellectual project without effects on others' well-being, such as patching up the holes in the Theory of Descriptions. A lot of desires of the dead would be ruled out on the grounds we have already mentioned, but it seems right for some still to count.

Why We Should Resist Restricting it More

Excluding some desires raises the general question of whether the best account of 'utility' will not exclude desires of several further sorts. Should not other-regarding desires be excluded? Those who not only want their own welfare but also, luckily for them, have others wanting it too count more heavily than those who do not; for instance, orphans count less than children with loving parents. But that yields Bentham out of Orwell: each to count for at least one but some for more than one. Should not irrational desires be excluded? The principle of utility is a normative principle and ought perhaps, therefore, to grant weight only to what are, by its own standards, good reasons, such as benefit and freedom from harm, and to grant weight only to desires justifiable in terms of these reasons. Should not, for obvious reasons, immoral desires be excluded? Indeed, should not desires of any sort of moral character be excluded? If the concern of the principle of utility is with what ought to be done, then the desire for something because it is what ought to be done appears when the principle delivers its result and seems improper as a ground for the result.

[. . .]

First of all, it is impossible to separate self-regarding and other-regarding desires. Each of us wants certain pure states of himself (e.g. to be free from pain); but we also want our lives to have some point, and this desired state can be hard to separate from states of others. Also, if we accepted the restriction to self-regarding desires, we should sever the connection between utility and happiness (and happiness is a large part of utility even on the informed-desire account). A father's happiness can be at stake in his child's happiness – two persons' welfare riding on one person's fate. Allowing that is no violation of everybody's counting for one; it merely allows the father, like everyone else, also to count for one. We have to swallow a little harder when we shift from involvements such as love to involvements such as hate, envy, spite, prejudice, and intolerance. If these sorts of desires are going to count too, what awful distortions will creep into political decision? But if a lover's happiness counts, so does a hater's *schadenfreude*. It is an ugly sort of pleasure, and as pleasures go slight and trouble-somely mixed, but still a pleasure. If it ought not to have weight in moral or political calculation, then we had better find a way to keep it out. But out of moral and political calculation, where it probably does not belong, not out of 'utility', where in some small way it probably does. Also letting other-regarding desires enter moral calculation seems to distort the notion of a moral reason. If one of my aims is to convince Britain that it ought to go over to comprehensive schools, why should you think that my desire constitutes yet another moral reason for going over to comprehensive schools? It would be absurd to introduce comprehensive education because it satisfied the desires of its advocates. What has overwhelming weight here, of course, is the good of the children and of society at large. But all that one really has to swallow is that the happiness of the advocates of comprehensives may in some small way turn on what happens, and that, at least, seems right.

Simply to rule out irrational desires would also go too far. A compulsive hand-washer's desire is irrational, but its fulfilment affects his utility. So since irrational desires cannot be excluded wholesale, why not let them in, and if their fulfilment is sometimes morally intolerable, look to other moral matters besides utility to block it. True, the fulfilment of other sorts of irrational desires is more worrying. A misogynist might be put off his food by a woman's sitting next to him in the Senior Common Room. Consistency would seem to require that his desire not to have women around counts too. Well, why not? The suggestion earlier was that desires that are irrational on utilitarian grounds should not be given weight, because no utilitarian value is at stake. But if someone is upset or distressed, then there is a utilitarian value at stake. The theoretical oddity would come, not in giving weight to such desires, but in giving them none.

What if desires are not only irrational but downright immoral? Should we count, for instance, sadistic desires? This has seemed more of a challenge than it really is, simply because people still tend to think of "utility" in rather narrow hedonistic terms. Anyone with much understanding would regard his own sadistic desires – even purely from the point of view of how good his life is for him to lead – as making virtually no claim upon being fulfilled. He would have formed second-order desires not to encourage or indulge them; he would know that, in his case at least, their gratification is mixed and brings no lasting or deep enjoyment; he would know that their opportunity cost is enormous. In fact, it is hard to think of any fairly normal sort who would not be better off, from his own point of view, frustrating his sadistic desires and trying for something better. Still, it would be a mistake simply to rule out sadistic desires. Not everyone is fairly normal. Perhaps there is someone for whom sadistic kicks are all he has, who is incapable of better. It might even be right, if he were also an inept sadist who aims to shock and upset but succeeds only in boring, to play along with him. The same holds for a desire to do something because it would be morally right. There are people for whom living morally is so much at the centre of their lives that their success there is a large part of their lives' being successful. The ideal development of human nature is for 'ethical push' (self-interest) and 'ethical pull' (obligation) to get progressively closer to each other. That too complicates the notion of 'well-being', but desirably so.

All these cases for further restrictions focus not on 'well-being' itself but on how it fits into moral theory. So this is another time when we have to remind ourselves that the question, "What is the best account of "utility"?', is quite distinct from the question, 'What is the best account, as *ad hoc* as you like, that yields the most adequate one principle, utility maximizing, moral theory?'

How Value and Desire are Related

The danger is that desire accounts get plausible only by, in effect, ceasing to be desire accounts. We had to qualify *desire* with *informed*, and that gave prominence to the features or qualities of the objects of desire, and not to the mere existence of desire. Then, to prevent informed desires from spreading too widely, we had to give prominence to only a certain range of features or qualities. Does this not confirm the suspicion that desire is no longer playing any real part, and remains only as a token of piety to a utilitarian tradition that has now effectively been abandoned? The issue widens. Could desire be a *ground* of value, or is it at best only a *mark* of it? Are things valuable because desired, or desired because valuable? And widest of all, what place do reason (cognition, perception, judgment) and desire (will, appetite, conation) have in explaining value?

In a way the order of explanation must be from *value* to *desire*. We see that an object has certain features, such as that it is pleasant or healthy or that it gives security, or that it would be an accomplishment. And therefore we desire it. We have always to be able to cite some feature that makes the desirability of the object intelligible; otherwise the notion of 'value' loses hold. And that feature has to be generally intelligible as one that makes things desirable. No one can just make something valuable by adopting it as his own personal aim. Of course,

people can disagree in their values. I might find mountain-climbing exciting and value it highly; you may find it simply terrifying and not value it at all. But we do not disagree here in our values in any deep or interesting way. Virtually everyone values excitement and does not value pure terror, though people differ in what they find exciting and terrifying. We all have to be able to connect what we value to some generally intelligible desirability feature. What is more, we sometimes discover values. You may be happy-go-lucky and not even think about accomplishing anything with your life, but then come upon someone whose accomplishment makes his life seem to you exhilarating and fulfilled. And with time you may come to discover more and more what this desirable accomplishment really is; you see how to separate it from mere achievement and its value from merely gaining praise. When you see what accomplishment is, you form a desire. And there need not be any pre-existent background desire (except those of vacuous generality) of which your new desire is merely another instance.

But what is interesting is how little any of this shows. It still leaves a strong case for saying that the order of explanation is quite the reverse: from *desire* to *value*. True, objects are valuable because of *their* features. But how do we explain these various desirability features? How do we separate *desirability* features from the rest? Here we have to guard against taking one or two examples as paradigms, and missing the variety of cases. So consider the following ones.

Case I: I have tasted both apples and pears. I like both but prefer pears. How do we explain my attaching more value to having a pear? The only relevant desirability feature is that they taste good. However, it is not a plausible explanation of *tasting better* that I perceive that pears possess this desirability feature to a greater degree than apples. We need to explain my liking pears more in terms of my wanting them more. That is true whether different persons' tastes coincide or not. But another important feature of tastes is that often they do not. We have no reason to expect, with many tastes, that differences in valuing shows that there is any lack of perception or

THE INFORMED DESIRE ACCOUNT

understanding. My preference for pears is not open to criticism (though others of my tastes are – for lack of discrimination, experience, attention). There is a tradition, especially strong in the social sciences, that sees all preference on the model of the simplest tastes: a pre-existent motivation, not subject to criticism, unaffected by understanding; the explanation running from *desire* to *value*. But this is only one kind of case.

Case 2: A recluse may see what he is missing and come to prefer good company. Here perception plays a large part; it may even be a case of discovering a value. But why is good company itself seen as desirable? The explanation cannot be just in terms of perception; there is an important pre-existent motivation. The motivation is not a taste, which typically can vary from person to person; it is more a feature of human nature. We are social creatures; we want and, other things being equal, go for company.

Case 3: Freud, in his last days, preferred thinking clearly to drugged comfort. Here there is a large element of perception but no obvious, at least simple, pre-existent motivation. We get no plausible explanation of this case unless we bring in both understanding what it is to think clearly and wanting it more. Explaining the state of *thinking clearly* as a desirability feature needs both perception and desire, without priority to either. To see this feature as desirable and to desire it on seeing it are the same. There is no plausible explanation of the one in terms of the other.

Case 4: A person who in the past has frittered his life away comes to value accomplishing something with it. Here understanding plays an enormous role, and desire may seem to disappear altogether. Accomplishment, in the general sense I have in mind (making one's life valuable and not just frittering it away), is valuable for everyone; anyone who fails to recognize it as valuable lacks understanding. It is true that there will be odd types for whom, all things considered, it will be better not to try for it. Perhaps someone for whom any ambition sets up intense anxieties had better not. But that is a case of conflict of values, in which accomplishment is still a value. Does the priority now run the other way? Do we see a life of

accomplishment as valuable and then, on the basis of that, form a desire for it? Clearly, this is not a case of first perceiving facts neutrally and then desire's entering and blindly fixing on one object and not another. The way in which we talk about the objects we value is far from neutral; we call it 'accomplishment' and explain it in terms of giving life weight and substance or not wasting life. The language we use in reporting our perceptions already organizes our experience and selects what we see as important; it is designed to show how we view certain things in a favourable light. Desire here does not blindly fix on an object; it is obviously pointed in certain directions by what we perceive favourably. But all of this, though true, explains too little. We also have to explain what goes on in our perceiving things favourably. And here desire comes back at a deeper level, as part of this explanation. Hume was wrong to see desire and understanding (appetite and cognition) as distinct existences. He was wrong to make desire blind. But it is a variety of the same mistake to think that one can explain our fixing on desirability features purely in terms of understanding. It is a mistake not only to keep understanding out of all desire but also to keep desire out of all understanding. Some understanding – the sort that involves fixing on certain features and seeing them in a favourable light – is also a kind of movement. It requires a will to go for what has those features. There is no adequate explanation of their being *desirability* features without appeal to this kind of movement. So we cannot, even in the case of a desirability feature such as *accomplishment*, separate understanding and desire. Once we see something as 'accomplishment', as 'giving weight and substance to our lives', as 'avoiding wasting our lives', there is no space left for desire to follow along in a secondary, subordinate position. Desire is not blind. Understanding is not bloodless. Neither is the slave of the other. There is no priority.

It may still seem that a value such as accomplishment has to have some priority to desire. It may seem that such a value cannot even depend upon what, if informed, persons would desire. One thing that would show this is our deciding that accomplishment is of absolute value. But few of us believe that; it is much more plausible to think there could be the very rare case in which trying to accomplish something was so painful that it was not worth doing. Another thing that would show it is our deciding that the value of accomplishment, while not absolute, is not given by its place in informed desires either, in other words that reflectively wanting accomplishment and recognizing its value to one can differ. But what would the difference be? Where, for instance, would trade-offs sanctioned by these different conceptions of the value of accomplishment diverge?

So desire is more than merely a mark of value. It is a ground, in the following sense: it is part of the full explanation of prudential value. But this does not give desire priority. Nor does the appearance of *desiring* in *valuing* mean that we are free to make an existential choice of values. The desires that count are not brute and unconstrained; they are informed.

It is the strength of the notion of 'informed desire' that it straddles – that is, does not accept any sharp form of – the divide between reason and desire.

The advantages of the informed desire account, therefore, seem to me to be these. It provides the materials needed to encompass the complexity of prudential value. It has the advantages of scope and flexibility over explanations of 'well-being' in terms of desirability features. It has scope, because all prudential values, from objects of simple varying tastes to objects of universal informed agreement, register somewhere in informed preferences. It has flexibility, because not everyone's well-being is affected in the same way by a certain desirability feature, and we want a notion sensitive to these individual differences. We want to know not only that something is valuable, but how valuable it is, and how valuable to different persons.

[. . .]

CHAPTER 33

Desire and the Human Good

RICHARD KRAUT

I

When we compare contemporary moral philosophy with the well-known moral systems of earlier centuries, we should be struck by the fact that a certain assumption about human well being that is now widely taken for granted was universally rejected in the past. The contemporary moral climate predisposes us to be pluralistic about the human good, whereas earlier systems of ethics embraced a conception of well being that we would now call narrow and restrictive. One way to convey the sort of contrast I have in mind is to note that according to Plato and Aristotle, there is one kind of life, that of the philosopher, that represents the summit of human flourishing, and all other lives are worth leading to the extent that they approximate this ideal. Certain other ethical theories of the past were in a way more narrow than this, for whereas Plato and Aristotle maintained that many things are in themselves worthwhile, others argued that there is only one intrinsic good – pleasure according to the Epicureans, virtue according to the Stoics. By contrast, it is now widely assumed that all such approaches are too exclusive, that not only are there many types of intrinsic goods but there is no one specific kind of life – whether it is that of a philosopher or a poet or anyone else – that is the single human ideal. Even hedonism, a conception of the good that had a powerful influence in the modern period, has few contemporary proponents. A consensus has arisen in our time that there is no single ultimate end that provides the measure by which the worth of all other goods must be assessed.

But if we want not merely to take note of our departure from the past, but also to show why we are justified in being pluralists about the good, then we must have something to say about what human well being is. We should not simply assert that there are many goods and many kinds of good lives, but must offer some general account of what well being is that explains why it is so multiform. In response to this demand, many philosophers would, as a first approximation, equate the human good with the satisfaction of desire, and would explain the multiplicity of the good by pointing out that because of the enormous variety of our interests and tastes, our desires exhibit a similar heterogeneity. Roughly speaking, what makes a state of affairs good for someone is its satisfaction of one of that person's desires; accordingly our lives go well to the extent that our desires, or the ones to which we give the greatest weight, are satisfied.

Richard Kraut, "Desire and the Human Good," pp. 39–49 from *Proceedings and Addresses of the American Philosophical Association*, 68(2), 1995. Reprinted by permission of the American Philosophical Association.

A complication is created by the fact that sometimes we have desires – those created by addictions, for example – that we wish we were without. But this can easily be handled in familiar ways by giving special weight to second-order desires. The general idea is that so long as one wants something wholeheartedly and with open eyes, then it is good for one's desire to be satisfied, regardless of the content of the desire. The objects we now want or will want are made good for us by our wanting them; they are not already good for us, apart from our having a present or future desire for them. There are no facts about what is ultimately good for me that are independent of my aims, facts that I need to discover in order to know what to aim at. No wonder, then, that well being is multiform. Our good is invented and constructed rather than discovered; and because of the great variation in our personalities and abilities, we invent different plans of life and our desires are directed at many different kinds of objects.

Although the "desire theory," as it might be called, is widely accepted, in part because it gives some backing to the assumption that the good is multiform, I will argue that it nonetheless has weaknesses serious enough to justify its rejection. At bottom, its main deficiency is that it is too accepting of desires as they stand, and cannot account for some of the ways in which they are subject to evaluation. What we need is a theory that is more objective and in this respect closer to the eudaimonistic theories of ancient and medieval philosophy. I would like to show now we can abandon the desire theory and still hold onto our sense that many different kinds of life are worth living – more than earlier systems realized, but not so many as the desire theory endorses.

II

I begin with a point that, despite its familiarity, cannot easily be accommodated by the desire theory. It is conceptually and psychologically possible for people to decide, voluntarily and with due deliberation, to renounce their good in favor of an alternative goal. They can clear-headedly design a long-range plan and fulfill it,

thereby satisfying their deepest desires, in spite of the fact that they realize all the while that what they are doing is bad for them. In fact, they can carry out certain plans precisely *because* they think that it is bad for them to do so. For example, suppose a man has committed a serious crime at an earlier point in his life, and although he now regrets having done so, he realizes that no one will believe him if he confesses. So he decides to inflict a punishment upon himself for a period of several years. He abandons his current line of work, which he loves, and takes a job that he considers boring, arduous, and insignificant. He does not regard this as a way of serving others, because he realizes that what he will be doing is useless. His aim is simply to balance the evil he has done to others with a comparable evil for himself. Taking a pill to relieve his pangs of guilt would be of no use, since his aim is to do himself harm, not to make himself feel good. He punishes himself because he regards this as a moral necessity, and when he carries out his punishment, he does so from a sense of duty rather than a joyful love of justice and certainly with no relish for the particular job he is doing. In an ordinary sense of "want," he doesn't want to punish himself, but the desire theory cannot take refuge in this point, since it uses a much broader notion of desire, according to which what we voluntarily seek is what we desire. And in this sense, our self-punisher does want above all to punish himself.

Spending one's days performing a task that one rightly regards as boring, arduous and useless is not something we would ordinarily consider advantageous, and so we can plausibly assume that when the self-punisher carries out his plan, he is not only trying to act against his good, but he succeeds in harming himself, despite the fact that he gets precisely what he wants. It would be dogmatic and counter-intuitive to insist that he must benefit from his punishment simply because he desires it. The more reasonable response is to concede that sometimes carrying out one's plans and getting what one above all wants conflicts with one's good.

Furthermore, I see no plausible way for the desire theory to make adjustments that convincingly accommodate this sort of counter-example. Bringing in the notions of rationality and full information will not help. The self-punisher is not violating any obvious principle of rationality and he has all the empirical information he needs. The moral that is most naturally drawn from this case is that there are circumstances in which people voluntarily renounce their good. When they do so, they are still getting what they want, and so we cannot equate well being with the satisfaction of desires, even when these desires are rational and exposed to full information. Other sorts of cases in which this happens, which are more common than self-punishment, are those in which we willingly make sacrifices in our well-being in order to promote the good of others. But rather than pursue this idea, I will turn to another type of objection to the desire theory. The weakness of the theory is best appreciated when we see the variety of difficulties it encounters.

III

Imagine a boy who, while walking through the park, sees a duck, and at the same time spots a rock on the ground. Impulsively, he picks up the rock and throws it at the duck. Is it good for him, to some extent, if his desire to hit the duck is satisfied? I find that implausible. Surely he would be no worse off if he had never felt an impulse to hit the duck; and once this impulse does arise, he would be no worse off if it evaporated before he acted on it. We might even say, with some plausibility, that it is *bad* for him to satisfy this desire, that for his own good he should be free of such destructive impulses. Someone who wants to defend the desire theory may suggest that we should salvage it by making a slight modification. The boy's desire to hit the duck is a mere passing whim, and so what we should say is that satisfying desires is good for us only when they are more enduring than fleeting urges. The desires that are good to satisfy are those that organize our lives and lead to projects that absorb considerable time and energy. The problem with this idea is that we can easily imagine desires that are unobjectionable as whims but become perverse when given more significance than that. Consider for example the impulse one might feel on a

winter walk to reach out and knock an icicle to the ground. And imagine someone who has more than a fleeting urge to do this. Rather, he has the project of knocking down as many icicles as he can before they melt. He hires a crew of workers and a fleet of trucks, so that he can reach icicles hanging from tall buildings; and this is how he spends his winters. It is implausible to suppose that now that this desire is no mere whim but a grand project, its satisfaction has become good. Rather, our reaction to the example is that the subject has become the victim of a senseless passion. The amount of time and effort he devotes to his plan does not make us confident that this is where his good lies; on the contrary, this feature of the example is precisely what inclines us to think that he is wasting his time.

Some philosophers will react to this case by saying that if the icicle fanatic really has carefully considered all of the alternatives available to him, and decides after due deliberation that this is the plan he wishes to pursue, then, peculiar as it may seem, the satisfaction of this desire *is* where his good lies. Who are we, it might be asked rhetorically, to stand in judgment of his conception of the good? To this it can be replied that we cannot responsibly avoid considering the specific content of people's projects when we make decisions about whether we should assist them. If the icicle fanatic appealed to us for financial support, we would not and should not set aside doubts about whether he is doing himself any good, and these doubts arise precisely because we focus on the object of his desire and fail to see why it is worth his while to undertake this project.

IV

There is one other aspect of the desire theory that should be considered, before I propose an alternative approach. The theory holds that it is the satisfaction of *my* desires that constitutes my good. We can gain a better perspective on the theory if we construe it as one among a family of closely related views. For example, what we might call the parental desire theory would hold that what makes something good for a person is the fact that it is something *his parents* want for him. The sibling desire theory and the grandparent desire theory would have the same structure: each could identify the good of X with the satisfaction of the desires some Y has regarding X, alternative versions of the theory picking out a different Y. The desire theory is the special case in which Y is identical to X. This leads us to ask why we should take the desire theory to be more plausible than the parental desire theory or any other member of this family of theories. We cannot reply: because each person knows where his best interest lies. For we recognize that as a hazardous generalization. If the parental desire theory must be rejected because there are times when parents fail to have the necessary love and knowledge to guide the lives of their children, then we will be faced with the question why these failures cannot also occur in the relation one has to oneself.

Perhaps the parental desire theory (and all other variations in which X is not identical to Y) should be rejected because its general acceptance would lead to passivity and submissiveness. Children would continually make their most important decisions by looking to the blueprint for their lives drawn up by others, and they would fail to develop such qualities as self-reliance, creativity, autonomy and the like. But why should we think that these are qualities that children should develop? An appealing answer is that it is part of a person's good to be a designer of one's life and a molder of one's desires. But that is not a suggestion the desire theorist can accept because, according to that theory, if my good consists partly in exercising initiative and expressing autonomy, then that is true only on condition that these are qualities I want to have. If I don't want them because I haven't been educated to value them, then, according to the desire theory, my lacking them is in itself no loss.

Although no one thinks that the parental desire theory is correct, there is nonetheless a modest and obvious truth that lies in its vicinity, namely that in the first stages of human life, it is best for children to be looked after by adults who take responsibility for their present and future good. And one reason why this is so is because there are many things that are or will be good for children that they are in no position to know about and cannot be said to want. A baby wants food, warmth, stimulation, and contact; but we cannot attribute to it a desire to develop its capacities or to be nurtured in the customs of its society. Education about these matters is beneficial for children, but the desire-theory cannot easily explain why, because children are for a time too young to have any desire for such learning. The desire-theory says that one's well-being is constituted by the satisfaction of one's desires, but the example of small children forces us to recognize a gap in the theory: it cannot be one's present desires alone that constitute one's well-being.

The gap could be filled if we say that the satisfaction of one's future desires is also a component of well-being. Even though a child may not now want an education she will want this at some future time, and so it is in her interests if we prepare her for the satisfaction of this future desire. But this way of expanding the desire theory does not fully capture our reasons for educating children: the child isn't going to have a desire to be educated independently of the way we bring her up; rather we train her so that she develops this desire and can satisfy it, and we do so because we think that having and satisfying this desire will be good for her. We encourage the interest children show in music, or their curiosity about the natural world, because we think it is and will be good for them to have a love of music or of nature. But there is nothing inevitable about their developing these desires. When we promote the future good of young children, we do not merely aim at desire satisfaction in general, but we try to instill certain desires rather than others on the grounds that some things are worth developing a desire for, and others are not.

V

I conclude from what I have said so far that wanting something does not by itself confer desirability on what we want or getting it. It is intelligible and at times appropriate to act on the thought, "I want to do this, even though

I don't think that it's good for me or will make my life better." That expresses the attitude many of us normally have towards our whims and impulses. Although we act on them, and need not be subject to criticism for doing so, we don't puff up the importance of these desires by supposing that it will be good even to the slightest degree if they are satisfied.

But if wanting something does not make it good for the want to be satisfied, then we have to ask what does. My response is that what makes a desire good to satisfy is its being a desire for something that has features that make it worth wanting. Notice the difference between this approach and the one that lies behind the desire theory. It says that we confer goodness on objects by wanting them; by contrast, my idea is that the objects we desire must prove themselves worthy of being wanted by having certain characteristics. If they lack features that make them worth wanting, then the fact that we want them does not make up for that deficiency.

The sort of view I have in mind can also be expressed if I switch for the moment from talking about what people want to talking about what they love. It is widely accepted that someone who is living a good life should love something or someone. If one has no interests or attachments at all, how can one's life be going well? Or if one is only slightly interested in things, if one has no strong emotional attachments, then that too is a deficiency, because there are objects to which a more enthusiastic response is appropriate. But, according to the conception of the good that I am presenting, some things are worthy of our interest and love, whereas others are not. So what makes one's life a good one is one's caring about something worth caring about. But of course that cannot be the whole story, because we can care a great deal about what is worthy of love and yet be cut off from it in some way. Imagine someone who loves painting but is imprisoned and unable to carry out her work; or someone who loves his children but is prevented from having any relationship with them. These people may love what is worth loving, but they don't have a satisfactory relationship with what they love, and as a result their lives are not going well. So, there are at least three conditions that make a life a good one: one must love something, what one loves must be worth loving, and one must be related in the right way to what one loves. Perhaps other conditions must be specified, but I will not explore that possibility here.

It might be objected that the thesis I am proposing is empty unless it is backed by a systematic theory that enables us to decide which among alternative ways of life is most worth living and which objects are most worth loving. It would of course be nice to have such a theory, but it is possible to do without one and still make defensible judgments about what is worth wanting and what is not. Recall the examples used earlier: we can judge, without having a systematic conception of the good, that the self-punisher is harming himself by doing boring, arduous, and insignificant work; or that the icicle fanatic is wasting his time. To take other cases: We believe that in normal circumstances only a certain amount of attention deserves to be paid to such things as neatness, appearance, or health, and we consider an interest that goes beyond this to be obsessive, because it undermine's a person's good. We think that certain intellectual or artistic projects would be a waste of time because they would produce uninteresting results or none at all. To take another sort of case: if someone devotes considerable time to friendships with people who are contemptible and undeserving of affection, then we think that his life is to some degree misspent.

What these examples suggest is that when we choose the objects of our interests successfully we can justify our choice of a way of life by pointing to the qualities of those objects. We have more to say in these cases than "this is what I want to do;" we can explain why we want to do these things by describing the admirable qualities of the objects we love. And by educating others to recognize and care about those qualities, we can rationally persuade them that it was worth their while for them to develop an interest in objects to which they were initially indifferent.

If this approach is correct, then certain widespread and powerful human desires may be such that their satisfaction does us no good. Consider, for example, the desire to have positions of power over other people, simply for its own sake. Those who love power in this way are not making any obvious error of fact or reasoning. Yet, if one asks what it is about power that makes it worth loving, it is hard to know how to answer or even to see that the question admits of an answer. Someone who develops a desire for power does not do so by being trained to focus on its properties; we don't become sensitized or educated so that we can respond to or articulate the admirable qualities that power has. So it's no wonder that we draw a blank when we ask what it is about power that makes it desirable.

Notice how different the situation is when it comes to certain other things we care about. If we are experienced and articulate, we can say a great deal about why we love our favorite novel or piece of music or friend. This is because we become attached to these objects through a process of training that makes us adept at recognizing and articulating certain properties that we respond to. Power, by contrast, is typically sought for no reason at all. And if we reject the desire theory, then we have no reason to think that satisfying the desire for power is in itself good for people. The same holds true of other deep-seated worldly motives, such as the desires for fame, recognition, and wealth.

It is here that we find one of the greatest contrasts between certain traditional conceptions of the good and the desire theory. The older conceptions took the desires for power, reputation, wealth, and the like to be, at best, of limited value; in fact, despite many disagreements among Platonists, Aristotelians, Stoics, Epicureans, and Christians about what the good is, there was until recent times a striking consensus among philosophers in these traditions that strong desires for power, status, material goods, and the like are contrary to self-interest properly understood. By contrast, the desire theory must hold that, so long as we pursue these goals without psychological division and with open eyes, making no mistake of fact or logic, then they are no less worth pursuing as ends than any other possible goals. That is why I said earlier that the chief weakness of the desire theory is that it is too accepting of desires as they stand and that it underestimates the ways in which we can

subject desires to criticism. The desire theory does not demand that the objects in which we take an interest have in themselves desirable features, since its basic idea is that we invest those objects with desirability by being attracted to them. Traditional conceptions are more able to criticize desires as they stand because they insist that the objects we love prove themselves worthy of our interest by their possession of desirable characteristics.

VI

The controversial nature of the proposal I am making can be brought out still further if we notice what it says about pain. It is often taken to be obvious that physical pain is in itself bad; but my doubts about the intrinsic goodness of power lead me also to question the intrinsic badness of pain. When I said that power is not good in itself, my reason was that I saw no feature of it that makes it worth wanting. Similarly, even though we all want to avoid pain, I see no feature of it that makes it worthy of avoidance. We don't notice any characteristic of pain that grounds our aversion to it; we just hate the way it feels. But according to my proposal that is not enough to show that it really is bad in itself. Just as our going for something does not show it to be good, so our avoiding it does not show it to be bad. And the fact that we *all* avoid it, and instinctively so, does not show it to be bad either. Our instincts are subject to evaluation, and so something more must be said about our aversion to pain besides its instinctual character, if we are to conclude that it is bad in itself.

To avoid misunderstanding, let me add that of course I think that pain is almost always bad to some extent. But my reason for thinking this has to do with the things that physical pain normally accompanies, namely some injury or the interruption of healthy processes. Almost every pain distracts us from devoting full attention to the things we care about, and over time pain depresses the level of energy we have. Pain is an animal's generally reliable mechanism for keeping it out of harm's way, and this applies no less to human animals than others. When we take into account the other events that accompany pain, we can see why it is generally bad for us to some degree. What I am questioning is whether, when we leave aside these other features of pain and just concentrate on the way it feels, we have any reason to think it is bad, and not merely something we dislike.

Perhaps I can create some doubt about whether pain is intrinsically bad by calling attention to a number of other sensations that are disliked even though they are not physically painful: for example, foul odors and grating noises. Should we say that these are in themselves bad to experience, apart from the harm they typically bring about by distracting or annoying us? Suppose I am the only person who is repelled by a certain sound, and everyone else is indifferent to it: if we say that it is intrinsically bad for me but not for others to hear the sound, then we are presupposing that it is a person's likes and dislikes that create what is good and bad for him. And we will then have to say that satisfying our whims and urges is good, and in particular that it is good for the boy in our earlier example to hit the duck. On the other hand, if we say that a grating sound is bad for me to hear only if everyone else has the same response then we have to explain why the reaction of others should be so important to my good. The most plausible way of disposing of this whole problem is to say that we should not infer from our aversion to something that it is contrary to our good, just as we should not infer from the presence of an urge that it does one good to satisfy it. If we accept this proposal, then we should become doubtful abut the intrinsic badness of pain.

VII

There is one further matter that should be addressed before we return to the theme of pluralism with which we began. I have been focusing exclusively on the *human* good and have said nothing about the good of other sorts of animals. But it might be objected that this is the wrong way to go about things, because we need to locate the human good within a framework that has broader application. And it should be obvious that much of what I have said about the human good does not apply to other animals. I claim that for a human life to go well one must love something worth loving. But it would be absurd to hold that the life of a non-human animal goes well only on this condition. What in the life of a salmon or a snake or a mole is worth loving? Can these animals be said to love anything at all?

The inapplicability of these conditions of human well being to non-human life might suggest that we have been on the wrong track all along. Perhaps we should have begun by looking for an account of well being that covers all cases, not just the human condition. Such a thought may partially account for the attraction of hedonism to earlier thinkers. Pleasure and pain guide the behavior of all animals; and hedonists, ancient and modern, have always appealed to the universality of these forces to support their doctrine. Hedonism has an apparent advantage in that it determines the good of all animals with one fell swoop. But we should not be impressed, for the implausibility of hedonism as applied to human life still stands. What we must do therefore is find some substitute for it. We need a general account of the well being of all animals, and then we must ask how the more specific conception of human well being is related to this broader framework.

The general formula that we should apply across the board is one that we find in Aristotle and the Stoics, namely that the good for each animal consists in leading the kind of life that is appropriate to its nature. And since each animal species has a different nature, we must consider the peculiar physical characteristics of each species to determine more specifically where its good lies. The nature of non-human animals is fixed by their bodies and physical capacities, and so for them living well consists in the maintenance of physical health and the full use of the capacities of their bodies. That is why the confinement of a bird to a small space would be contrary to its good, even if it were attached during its confinement to a machine that constantly stimulated the pleasure center of its brain.

But what should we say about the peculiar nature of human beings? Because of our possession of the kind of brain we have, the lives we can lead are far less restricted than are those of other animals. Our intellectual capacity allows far greater plasticity in our development, and it makes the kind of life we lead far more a matter of choice than it is for other animals. The good of a non-human animal is, as it were, built into its body, whereas for human beings the good is an object of rational choice and its achievement requires the training of desires and emotions so that they take appropriate objects as determined by reason. This is not to deny that we have a nature. Rather, it is to say that it is our nature to be choosers, to be capable of using reason to make choices and to mold our desires and emotions. And so the nature of human beings is reflected in our theory of the good when we say that in order for our lives to go well our desires and emotions must be directed at objects whose features make them appropriate choices for us. It is implicit in the notion of choiceworthiness that the objects of our desires are open to evaluation by means of reflection. By insisting that desire satisfaction is not in itself good, that the object of the desire must be worth wanting, we bring in the need for evaluation and reflection, and we thus ground our good in our capacity for rational choice. We explain the human good not as hedonism does, by means of a single comprehensive theory applicable to all animals, but by a two-stage process in which a broad account that applies universally is then made more specific by being tied to the peculiarities of the human situation.

Since I have accepted the traditional view that our nature as human beings consists in the exercise of our capacity for rational choice, it might be asked why I do not go further and accept a more determinate conception of the good, one that holds that human lives are worthwhile to the extent that they are devoted to reasoning. My reply is that the extent to which it is intrinsically worthwhile to engage in reasoning, or good reasoning, is itself a matter that is subject to rational evaluation; there is no self-contradiction in the idea that one might *reason* to the conclusion that there are activities that are better than *reasoning*, or that one's life goes best if reason plays a secondary or minor role. So the fact that reasoning is distinctive of human beings does not itself determine the proper place of reasoning in a human life. The best way of establishing the importance of reason in a good life is to take note of the various kinds of worthwhile activities there are, and recognize how many of them we would be incapable of undertaking, if our capacity for reasoning were seriously impaired.

VIII

We can now return to the ideas with which we started: that the good for human beings is highly varied, that there is no single master good that measures the worth of all others; that there is no specific kind of life that is best for everyone. Pluralism, so construed, is a newcomer to the philosophical scene, and it is worth asking whether any arguments can be found for it. One of the apparent attractions of the desire theory is that it offers an explanation for this variety, but in light of that theory's deficiencies we have reason to seek an alternative account of why pluralism about the good might be true.

A better way to defend pluralistic intuitions, I suggest, is to accept the general thesis that some objects of human pursuit have qualities that make them objectively worth wanting and that others are without merit, but to reject any of the more specific theses that have been proposed in the past about how to achieve a more determinate ranking of human lives. The modern philosopher's sense that many different kinds of lives are worth living, but that we cannot arrange them in a hierarchy ranging from best to worst, is best supported by concrete illustration rather than a highly general argument: the favored strategy should be to take note of all of the different objects that are worth pursuing and the diversity of worthwhile lives devoted to these pursuits, and then to show that none of the objective conceptions of the good with which we are familiar from the history of philosophy does justice to this rich variety. But this pluralistic project cannot succeed simply by pointing to the great variety of lives people in fact lead; what must be shown is considerably more difficult, namely that these different kinds of lives are worth living, and none more so than any others.

If this is correct, then the hierarchical conceptions of the good that are now out of favor cannot be undermined with a single blow; if there is no supremely desirable object or life, in comparison with which all other objects or lives must be evaluated, then this must be established on a case-by-case basis by showing why each proposed candidate fails to provide a plausible standard. The defender of the multiplicity of the human good must support this thesis by persuading us that many different types of thing are worth wanting and by showing why we should reject attempts to assign each of them a discrete place on a single hierarchical scale. Although I am sympathetic to such a project, I have not undertaken it here. My main point has been that the multiplicity of the good cannot be directly inferred from the variability of human desire. So my conclusion is a conditional one: if we wish to be pluralists, then we should accept the point, once widely taken for granted, that in deciding which sorts of lives it is good to live, we cannot bypass the task of evaluating our desires by asking whether their objects possess the qualities that make them worth wanting.

CHAPTER 34

What Things are Good?

W. D. ROSS

Our next step is to inquire what kinds of thing are intrinsically good. (1) The first thing for which I would claim that it is intrinsically good is virtuous disposition and action, i.e. action, or disposition to act, from any one of certain motives, of which at all events the most notable are the desire to do one's duty, the desire to bring into being something that is good, and the desire to give pleasure or save pain to others. It seems clear that we regard all such actions and dispositions as having value in themselves apart from any consequence. And if any one is inclined to doubt this and to think that, say, pleasure alone is intrinsically good, it seems to me enough to ask the question whether, of two states of the universe holding equal amounts of pleasure, we should really think no better of one in which the actions and dispositions of all the persons in it were thoroughly virtuous than of one in which they were highly vicious. To this there can be only one answer. Most hedonists would shrink from giving the plainly false answer which their theory requires, and would take refuge in saying that the question rests on a false abstraction. Since virtue, as they conceive it, is a disposition to do just the acts which will produce most pleasure, a universe full of virtuous persons

W. D. Ross, "What Things are Good?" pp. 134–41 from *The Right and the Good*. Oxford: Oxford University Press, 1930.

would be bound, they might say, to contain more pleasure than a universe full of vicious persons. To this two answers may be made. (*a*) Much pleasure, and much pain, do not spring from virtuous or vicious actions at all but from the operation of natural laws. Thus even if a universe filled with virtuous persons were bound to contain more of the pleasure and less of the pain that springs from human action than a universe filled with vicious persons would, that inequality of pleasantness might easily be supposed to be precisely counteracted by, for instance, a much greater incidence of disease. The two states of affairs would then, on balance, be equally pleasant; would they be equally good? And (*b*) even if we could not imagine any circumstances in which two states of the universe equal in pleasantness but unequal in virtue could exist, the supposition is a legitimate one, since it is only intended to bring before us in a vivid way what is really self-evident, that virtue is good apart from its consequences.

(2) It seems at first sight equally clear that pleasure is good in itself. Some will perhaps be helped to realize this if they make the corresponding supposition to that we have just made; if they suppose two states of the universe including equal amounts of virtue but the one including also widespread and intense pleasure and the other widespread and intense pain. Here too it might be objected that

the supposition is an impossible one, since virtue always tends to promote general pleasure, and vice to promote general misery. But this objection may be answered just as we have answered the corresponding objection above.

Apart from this, however, there are two ways in which even the most austere moralists and the most anti-hedonistic philosophers are apt to betray the conviction that pleasure is good in itself. (*a*) One is the attitude which they, like all other normal human beings, take towards kindness and towards cruelty. If the desire to give pleasure to others is approved, and the desire to inflict pain on others condemned, this seems to imply the conviction that pleasure is good and pain bad. Some may think, no doubt, that the mere thought that a certain state of affairs would be *painful* for another person is enough to account for our conviction that the desire to produce it is bad. But I am inclined to think that there is involved the further thought that a state of affairs in virtue of being painful is *prima facie* (i.e. where other considerations do not enter into the case) one that a rational spectator would not approve, i.e. is *bad*; and that similarly our attitude towards kindness involves the thought that pleasure is good. (*b*) The other is the insistence, which we find in the most austere moralists as in other people, on the conception of merit. If virtue deserves to be rewarded by happiness (whether or not vice also deserves to be rewarded by unhappiness), this seems at first sight to imply that happiness and unhappiness are not in themselves things indifferent, but are good and bad respectively.

Kant's view on this question is not as clear as might be wished. He points out that the Latin *bonum* covers two notions, distinguished in German as *das Gute* (the good) and *das Wohl* (well-being, i.e. pleasure or happiness); and he speaks of 'good' as being properly applied only to actions,[1] i.e. he treats 'good' as equivalent to 'morally good', and by implication denies that pleasure (even deserved pleasure) is good. It might seem then that when he speaks of the union of virtue with the happiness it deserves as the *bonum consummatum* he is not thinking of deserved happiness as good but only as *das Wohl*, a source of satisfaction to the person who

has it. But if this exhausted his meaning, he would have no right to speak of virtue, as he repeatedly does, as *das oberste Gut*; he should call it simply *das Gute*, and happiness *das Wohl*. Further, he describes the union of virtue with happiness not merely as 'the object of the desires of rational finite beings,' but adds that it approves itself 'even in the judgement of an impartial reason' as 'the whole and perfect good', rather than virtue alone. And he adds that 'happiness, while it is pleasant to the possessor of it, is not of itself absolutely and in all respects good, but always presupposes morally right behaviour as its condition'; which implies that *when* that condition is fulfilled, happiness *is* good.[2] All this seems to point to the conclusion that in the end he had to recognize that while virtue alone is morally good, deserved happiness also is not merely a source of satisfaction to its possessor, but objectively good.

But reflection on the conception of merit does not support the view that pleasure is always good in itself and pain always bad in itself. For while this conception implies the conviction that pleasure when deserved is good, and pain when undeserved bad, it also suggests strongly that pleasure when undeserved is bad and pain when deserved good.

There is also another set of facts which casts doubt on the view that pleasure is always good and pain always bad. We have a decided conviction that there are bad pleasures and (though this is less obvious) that there are good pains. We think that the pleasure taken either by the agent or by a spectator in, for instance, a lustful or cruel action is bad; and we think it a good thing that people should be pained rather than pleased by contemplating vice or misery.

Thus the view that pleasure is always good and pain always bad, while it seems to be strongly supported by some of our convictions, seems to be equally strongly opposed by others. The difficulty can, I think, be removed by ceasing to speak simply of pleasure and pain as good or bad, and by asking more carefully what it is that we mean. Consideration of the question is aided if we adopt the view (tentatively adopted already)[3] that what is good or bad is always something properly expressed by a that-clause, i.e. an objective, or as I should prefer to call it, a *fact*. If we look at the matter thus, I think we can agree that the fact that a sentient being is in a state of pleasure is always in itself good, and the fact that a sentient being is in a state of pain always in itself bad, when this fact is not an element in a more complex fact having some other characteristic relevant to goodness or badness. And where considerations of desert or of moral good or evil do not enter, i.e. in the case of animals, the fact that a sentient being is feeling pleasure or pain is the whole fact (or the fact sufficiently described to enable us to judge of its goodness or badness), and we need not hesitate to say that the pleasure of animals is always good, and the pain of animals always bad, in itself and apart from its consequences. But when a moral being is feeling a pleasure or pain that is deserved or undeserved, or a pleasure or pain that implies a good or a bad disposition, the total fact is quite inadequately described if we say "a sentient being is feeling pleasure, or pain". The total fact may be that 'a sentient and moral being is feeling a pleasure that is undeserved, or that is the realization of a vicious disposition', and though the fact included in this, that 'a sentient being is feeling pleasure' would be good if it stood alone, that creates only a presumption that the total fact is good, and a presumption that is outweighed by the other element in the total fact.

Pleasure seems, indeed, to have a property analogous to that which we have previously recognized under the name of conditional or *prima facie* rightness. An act of promise-keeping has the property, not necessarily of being right but of being something that is right if the act has no other morally significant characteristic (such as that of causing much pain to another person). And similarly a state of pleasure has the property, not necessarily of being good, but of being something that is good if the state has no other characteristics that prevents it from being good. The two characteristics that may interfere with its being good are (*a*) that of being contrary to desert, and (*b*) that of being a state which is the

realization of a bad disposition. Thus the pleasures of which we can say without doubt that they are good are (i) the pleasures of non-moral beings (animals), (ii) the pleasures of moral beings that are deserved and are either realizations of good moral dispositions or realizations of neutral capacities (such as the pleasures of the senses).

In so far as the goodness or badness of a particular pleasure depends on its being the realization of a virtuous or vicious disposition, this has been allowed for by our recognition of virtue as a thing good in itself. But the mere recognition of virtue as a thing good in itself, and of pleasure as a thing *prima facie* good in itself, does not do justice to the conception of merit. If we compare two imaginary states of the universe, alike in the total amounts of virtue and vice and of pleasure and pain present in the two, but in one of which the virtuous were all happy and the vicious miserable, while in the other the virtuous were miserable and the vicious happy, very few people would hesitate to say that the first was a much better state of the universe than the second. It would seem then that, besides virtue and pleasure, we must recognize (3), as a third independent good, the apportionment of pleasure and pain to the virtuous and the vicious respectively. And it is on the recognition of this as a separate good that the recognition of the duty of justice, in distinction from fidelity to promises on the one hand and from beneficence on the other, rests.

(4) It seems clear that knowledge, and in a less degree what we may for the present call 'right opinion', are states of mind good in themselves. Here too we may, if we please, help ourselves to realize the fact by supposing two states of the universe equal in respect of virtue and of pleasure and of the allocation of pleasure to the virtuous, but such that the persons in the one had a far greater understanding of the nature and laws of the universe than those in the other. Can any one doubt that the first would be a better state of the universe?

From one point of view it seems doubtful whether knowledge and right opinion, no matter what it is of or about, should be considered good. Knowledge of mere matters of fact (say of the number of stories in a building), without knowledge of their relation to other facts, might seem to be worthless; it certainly seems to be worth much less than the knowledge of general principles, or of facts as depending on general principles – what we might call insight or understanding as opposed to mere knowledge. But on reflection it seems clear that even about matters of fact right opinion is in itself a better state of mind to be in than wrong, and knowledge than right opinion.

There is another objection which may naturally be made to the view that knowledge is as such good. There are many pieces of knowledge which we in fact think it well for people *not* to have; e.g. we may think it a bad thing for a sick man to know how ill he is, or for a vicious man to know how he may most conveniently indulge his vicious tendencies. But it seems that in such cases it is not the knowledge but the consequences in the way of pain or of vicious action that we think bad.

It might perhaps be objected that knowledge is not a better state than right opinion, but merely a source of greater satisfaction to its possessor. It no doubt is a source of greater satisfaction. Curiosity is the desire to *know*, and is never really satisfied by mere opinion. Yet there are two facts which seem to show that this is not the whole truth. (*a*) While opinion recognized to be such is never thoroughly satisfactory to its possessor, there is another state of mind which is not knowledge – which may even be mistaken – yet which through lack of reflection is not distinguished from knowledge by its possessor, the state of mind which Professor Cook Wilson has called 'that of being under the impression that so-and-so is the case'.[4] Such a state of mind may be as great a source of satisfaction to its possessor as knowledge, yet we should all think it to be an inferior state of mind to knowledge. This surely points to a recognition by us that knowledge has a worth other than that of being a source of satisfaction to its possessor. (*b*) Wrong opinion, so long as its wrongness is not discovered, may be as great a source of satisfaction as right. Yet we should agree that it is an inferior state of mind, because it is to a less extent founded on knowledge and is itself a less close approximation to knowledge; which again seems to point to our recognizing knowledge as something good in itself.

Four things, then, seem to be intrinsically good – virtue, pleasure, the allocation of pleasure to the virtuous, and knowledge (and in a less degree right opinion). And I am unable to discover anything that is intrinsically good, which is not either one of these or a combination of two or more of them. And while this list of goods has been arrived at on its own merits, by reflection on what we really think to be good, it perhaps derives some support from the fact that it harmonizes with a widely accepted classification of the elements in the life of the soul. It is usual to enumerate these as cognition, feeling, and conation. Now knowledge is the ideal state of the mind, and right opinion an approximation to the ideal, on the cognitive or intellectual side; pleasure is its ideal state on the side of feeling; and virtue is its ideal state on the side of conation; while the allocation of happiness to virtue is a good which we recognize when we reflect on the ideal relation between the conative side and the side of feeling. It might of course be objected that there are or may be intrinsic goods that are not states of mind or relations between states of mind at all, but in this suggestion I can find no plausibility. Contemplate any imaginary universe from which you suppose mind entirely absent, and you will fail to find anything in it that you can call good in itself. That is not to say, of course, that the existence of a material universe may not be a necessary condition for the existence of many things that are good in themselves. Our knowledge and our true opinions are to a large extent about the material world, and to that extent could not exist unless it existed. Our pleasures are to a large extent derived from material objects. Virtue owes many of its opportunities to the existence of material conditions of good and material hindrances to good. But the value of material things appears to be purely instrumental, not intrinsic.

Of the three elements virtue, knowledge, and pleasure are compounded all the complex states of mind that we think good in themselves. Aesthetic enjoyment, for example, seems to be a blend of pleasure with insight into the nature of the object that inspires it.

Mutual love seems to be a blend of virtuous disposition of two minds towards each other, with the knowledge which each has of the character and disposition of the other, and with the pleasure which arises from such disposition and knowledge. And a similar analysis may probably be applied to all other complex goods.

Notes

1. *Kritik der pr. Vernunft*, 59–60 (Akad. Ausgabe, vol. v), 150–1 (Abbott's Trans., ed. 6).
2. Ib. 110–11 (Akad. Ausgabe), 206–7 (Abbott).
3. [In the original text], pp. 111–13.
4. *Statement and Inference*, i. 113.

CHAPTER 35

What Makes Someone's Life Go Best

DEREK PARFIT

What would be best for someone, or would be most in this person's interests, or would make this person's life go, for him, as well as possible? Answers to this question I call *theories about self-interest*. There are three kinds of theory. On *Hedonistic Theories*, what would be best for someone is what would make his life happiest. On *Desire-Fulfilment Theories*, what would be best for someone is what, throughout his life, would best fulfil his desires. On *Objective List Theories*, certain things are good or bad for us, whether or not we want to have the good things, or to avoid the bad things.

Narrow Hedonists assume, falsely, that pleasure and pain are two distinctive kinds of experience. Compare the pleasures of satisfying an intense thirst or lust, listening to music, solving an intellectual problem, reading a tragedy, and knowing that one's child is happy. These various experiences do not contain any distinctive common quality.

What pains and pleasures have in common are their relations to our desires. On the use of 'pain' which has rational and moral significance, all pains are when experienced unwanted, and a pain is worse or greater the more it is unwanted. Similarly, all pleasures are when experienced wanted, and they are better

or greater the more they are wanted. These are the claims of *Preference-Hedonism*. On this view, one of two experiences is more pleasant if it is preferred.

This theory need not follow the ordinary uses of the words 'pain' and 'pleasure'. Suppose that I could go to a party to enjoy the various pleasures of eating, drinking, laughing, dancing, and talking to my friends. I could instead stay at home and read *King Lear*. Knowing what both alternatives would be like, I prefer to read *King Lear*. It extends the ordinary use to say that this would give me more pleasure. But on Preference-Hedonism, if we add some further assumptions given below, reading *King Lear* would give me a better evening. Griffin cites a more extreme case. Near the end of his life Freud refused pain-killing drugs, preferring to think in torment than to be confusedly euphoric. Of these two mental states, euphoria is more pleasant. But on Preference-Hedonism thinking in torment was, for Freud, a better mental state. It is clearer here not to stretch the meaning of the word 'pleasant'. A Preference-Hedonist should merely claim that, since Freud preferred to think clearly though in torment, his life went better if it went as he preferred.[1]

Consider next Desire-Fulfilment Theories. The simplest is the *Unrestricted* Theory. This claims that what is best for someone is what would best fulfil *all* of his desires, throughout

Derek Parfit, "What Makes Someone's Life Go Best", pp. 493–502 from *Reasons and Persons*. Oxford: Oxford University Press, 1984.

his life. Suppose that I meet a stranger who has what is believed to be a fatal disease. My sympathy is aroused, and I strongly want this stranger to be cured. Much later, when I have forgotten our meeting, the stranger is cured. On the Unrestricted Desire-Fulfilment Theory, this event is good for me, and makes my life go better. This is not plausible. We should reject this theory.

Another theory appeals only to someone's desires about his own life. I call this the *Success Theory*. This theory differs from Preference-Hedonism in only one way. The Success Theory appeals to all of our preferences about our own lives. A Preference-Hedonist appeals only to preferences about those present features of our lives that are introspectively discernible. Suppose that I strongly want not to be deceived by other people. On Preference-Hedonism it would be better for me if I believe that I am not being deceived. It would be irrelevant if my belief is false, since this makes no difference to my state of mind. On the Success Theory, it would be worse for me if my belief is false. I have a strong desire about my own life – that I should not be deceived in this way. It is bad for me if this desire is not fulfilled, even if I falsely believe that it is.

When this theory appeals only to desires that are about our own lives, it may be unclear what this excludes. Suppose that I want my life to be such that all of my desires, whatever their objects, are fulfilled. This may seem to make the Success Theory, when applied to me, coincide with the Unrestricted Desire-Fulfilment Theory. But a Success Theorist should claim that this desire is not really about my own life. This is like the distinction between a real change in some object, and a so-called *Cambridge-change*. An object undergoes a Cambridge-change if there is any change in the true statements that can be made about this object. Suppose that I cut my cheek while shaving. This causes a real change in me. It also causes a change in Confucius. It becomes true, of Confucius, that he lived on a planet in which later one more cheek was cut. This is merely a Cambridge-change.

Suppose that I am an exile, and cannot communicate with my children. I want their lives to go well. I might claim that I want to live the life

of someone whose children's lives go well. A Success Theorist should again claim that this is not really a desire about my own life. If unknown to me one of my children is killed by an avalanche, this is not bad for me, and does not make my life go worse.

A Success Theorist *would* count some similar desires. Suppose that I try to give my children a good start in life. I try to give them the right education, good habits, and psychological strength. Once again, I am now an exile, and will never be able to learn what happens to my children. Suppose that, unknown to me, my children's lives go badly. One finds that the education that I gave him makes him unemployable, another has a mental breakdown, another becomes a petty thief. If my children's lives fail in these ways, and these failures are in part the result of mistakes I made as their parent, these failures in my children's lives would be judged to be bad for me on the Success Theory. One of my strongest desires was to be a successful parent. What is now happening to my children, though it is unknown to me, shows that this desire is not fulfilled. My life failed in one of the ways in which I most wanted it to succeed. Though I do not know this fact, it is bad for me, and makes it true that I have had a worse life. This is like the case where I strongly want not to be deceived. Even if I never know, it is bad for me both if I am deceived and if I turn out to be an unsuccessful parent. These are not introspectively discernible differences in my conscious life. On Preference-Hedonism, these events are not bad for me. On the Success Theory, they are.

Because they are thought by some to need special treatment, I mention next the desires that people have about what happens after they are dead. For a Preference-Hedonist, once I am dead, nothing bad can happen to me. A Success Theorist should deny this. Return to the case where all my children have wretched lives, because of the mistakes I made as their parent. Suppose that my children's lives all go badly only after I am dead. My life turns out to have been a failure, in one of the ways I cared about most. A Success Theorist should claim that, here too, this makes it true that I had a worse life.

Some Success Theorists would reject this claim. Their theory ignores the desires of the dead. I believe this theory to be indefensible. Suppose that I was asked, 'Do you want it to be true that you were a successful parent even after you are dead?' I would answer 'Yes'. It is irrelevant to my desire whether it is fulfilled before or after I am dead. These Success Theorists count it as bad for me if my desire is not fulfilled, even if, because I am an exile, I never know this. How then can it matter whether, when my desire is not fulfilled, I am dead? All that my death does is to *ensure* that I will never know this. If we think it irrelevant that I never know about the non-fulfilment of my desire, we cannot defensibly claim that my death makes a difference.

I turn now to questions and objections which arise for both Preference-Hedonism and the Success Theory.

Should we appeal only to the desires and preferences that someone actually has? Return to my choice between going to a party or staying at home to read *King Lear*. Suppose that, knowing what both alternatives would be like, I choose to stay at home. And suppose that I never later regret this choice. On one theory, this shows that staying at home to read *King Lear* gave me a better evening. This is a mistake. It might be true that, if I had chosen to go to the party, I would never have regretted that choice. According to this theory, this would have shown that going to the party gave me a better evening. This theory thus implies that each alternative would have been better than the other. Since this theory implies such contradictions, it must be revised. The obvious revision is to appeal not only to my actual preferences, in the alternative I choose, but also to the preferences that I would have had if I had chosen otherwise.[2]

In this example, whichever alternative I choose, I would never regret this choice. If this is true, can we still claim that one of the alternatives would give me a better evening? On some theories, when in two alternatives I would have such contrary preferences, neither alternative is better or worse for me. This is not plausible when one of my contrary preferences would have been much stronger. Suppose that, if I choose to go to the party, I shall be only mildly glad that I made this choice, but that, if I choose to stay and read *King Lear*, I shall be extremely glad. If this is true, reading *King Lear* gives me a better evening.

Whether we appeal to Preference-Hedonism or the Success Theory, we should not appeal only to the desires or preferences that I actually have. We should also appeal to the desires and preferences that I would have had, in the various alternatives that were, at different times, open to me. One of these alternatives would be best for me if it is the one in which I would have the strongest desires and preferences fulfilled. This allows us to claim that some alternative life would have been better for me, even if throughout my actual life I am glad that I chose this life rather than this alternative. [. . .]

Turn now to the third kind of Theory that I mentioned: the Objective List Theory. According to this theory, certain things are good or bad for people, whether or not these people would want to have the good things, or to avoid the bad things. The good things might include moral goodness, rational activity, the development of one's abilities, having children and being a good parent, knowledge, and the awareness of true beauty. The bad things might include being betrayed, manipulated, slandered, deceived, being deprived of liberty or dignity, and enjoying either sadistic pleasure, or aesthetic pleasure in what is in fact ugly.[3]

An Objective List Theorist might claim that his theory coincides with the Global version of the Success Theory. On this theory, what would make my life go best depends on what I would prefer, now and in the various alternatives, if I knew all of the relevant facts about these alternatives. An Objective List Theorist might say that the most relevant facts are what his theory claims – what would in fact be good or bad for me. And he might claim that anyone who knew these facts would want what is truly good for him, and want to avoid what would be bad for him.

If this was true, though the Objective List Theory would coincide with the Success Theory, the two theories would remain distinct. A Success Theorist would reject this description of the coincidence. On his theory, nothing is good or bad for people, whatever their preferences are. Something is bad for someone only if, knowing the facts, he wants to avoid it. And the relevant facts do not include the alleged facts cited by the Objective List Theorist. On the Success Theory it is, for instance, bad for someone to be deceived if and because this is not what he wants. The Objective List Theorist makes the reverse claim. People want not to be deceived because this is bad for them.

As these remarks imply, there is one important difference between on the one hand Preference-Hedonism and the Success Theory, and on the other hand the Objective List Theory. The first two kinds of theory give an account of self-interest which is entirely factual, or which does not appeal to facts about value. The account appeals to what a person does and would prefer, given full knowledge of the purely non-evaluative facts about the alternatives. In contrast, the Objective List Theory appeals directly to facts about value.

In choosing between these theories, we must decide how much weight to give to imagined cases in which someone's fully informed preferences would be bizarre. If we can appeal to these cases, they cast doubt on both Preference-Hedonism and the Success Theory. Consider the man that Rawls imagined who wants to spend his life counting the numbers of blades of grass in different lawns. Suppose that this man knows that he could achieve great progress if instead he worked in some especially useful part of Applied Mathematics. Though he could achieve such significant results, he prefers to go on counting blades of grass. On the Success Theory, if we allow this theory to cover all imaginable cases, it could be better for this person if he counts his blades of grass rather than achieves great and beneficial results in Mathematics.

The counter-example might be more offensive. Suppose that what someone would most prefer, knowing the alternatives, is a life in which, without being detected, he causes as much pain as he can to other people. On the Success Theory, such a life would be what is best for this person.

We may be unable to accept these conclusions. Ought we therefore to abandon this theory? [. . .] Suppose we agree that, in some imagined cases, what someone would most want both now and later, fully knowing about the alternatives, would *not* be what would be best for him. If we accept this conclusion, it may seem that we must reject both Preference-Hedonism and the Success Theory. [. . .]

It might be claimed instead that we can dismiss the appeal to such imagined cases. It might be claimed that what people would in fact prefer, if they knew the relevant facts, would always be something that we could accept as what is really good for them. Is this a good reply? If we agree that in the imagined cases what someone would prefer might be something that is bad for him, in these cases we have abandoned our theory. If this is so, can we defend our theory by saying that, in the actual cases, it would not go astray? I believe that this is not an adequate defence. But I shall not pursue this question here.

This objection may apply with less force to Preference-Hedonism. On this theory, what can be good or bad for someone can only be discernible features of his conscious life. These are the features that, at the time, he either wants or does not want. I asked above whether it is bad for people to be deceived because they prefer not to be, or whether they prefer not to be deceived because this is bad for them. Consider the comparable question with respect to pain. Some have claimed that pain is intrinsically bad, and that this is why we dislike it. As I have suggested, I doubt this claim. After taking certain kinds of drug, people claim that the quality of their sensations has not altered, but they no longer dislike these sensations. We would regard such drugs as effective analgesics. This suggests that the badness of a pain consists in its being disliked, and that it is not disliked because it is bad. The disagreement between these views would need much more discussion. But, if the second view is better, it is more plausible to claim that whatever someone wants or does not want to experience – however bizarre we find his desires – should be counted as being for this person truly pleasant or painful, and as being for that reason good or bad for him. There may still be cases where it is plausible to claim that it would be bad for someone if he enjoys certain kinds of pleasure. This might be claimed, for instance, about sadistic pleasure. But there may be few such cases.

If instead we appeal to the Success Theory, we are not concerned only with the experienced quality of our conscious life. We are concerned with such things as whether we are achieving what we are trying to achieve, whether we are being deceived, and the like. When considering this theory, we can more often plausibly claim that, even if someone knew the facts, his preferences might go astray, and fail to correspond to what would be good or bad for him.

Which of these different theories should we accept? I shall not attempt an answer here. But I shall end by mentioning another theory, which might be claimed to combine what is most plausible in these conflicting theories. It is a striking fact that those who have addressed this question have disagreed so fundamentally. Many philosophers have been convinced Hedonists; many others have been as much convinced that Hedonism is a gross mistake.

Some Hedonists have reached their view as follows. They consider an opposing view, such as that which claims that what is good for someone is to have knowledge, to engage in rational activity, and to be aware of true beauty. These Hedonists ask, 'Would these states of mind be good, if they brought no enjoyment, and if the person in these states of mind had not the slightest desire that they continue?' Since they answer No, they conclude that the value of these states of mind must lie in their being liked, and in their arousing a desire that they continue.

This reasoning assumes that the value of a whole is just the sum of the value of its parts. If we remove the part to which the Hedonist appeals, what is left seems to have no value, hence Hedonism is the truth.

Suppose instead that we claim that the value of a whole may not be a mere sum of the value of its parts. We might then claim that what is best for people is a composite. It is not just their being in the conscious states that they want to be in. Nor is it just their having knowledge, engaging in rational activity, being aware of true beauty, and the like. What is good for someone is neither just what Hedonists claim, nor just what is claimed by Objective List Theorists. We might believe that if we had *either* of these, *without the other*, what we had would have little or no value. We might claim, for example, that what is good or bad for someone is to have knowledge, to be engaged in rational activity, to experience mutual love, and to be aware of beauty, while strongly wanting just these things. On this view, each side in this disagreement saw only half of the truth. Each put forward as sufficient something that was only necessary. Pleasure with many other kinds of object has no value. And, if they are entirely devoid of pleasure, there is no value in knowledge, rational activity, love, or the awareness of beauty. What is of value, or is good for someone, is to have both; to be engaged in these activities, and to be strongly wanting to be so engaged.

Notes

1. J. P. Griffin, 'Are There Incommensurable Values?', *Philosophy and Public Affairs*, 7/1 (Autumn, 1977).

2. See P. Bricker, 'Prudence', *The Journal of Philosophy*, 83/7 (July, 1980).

3. H. Sidgwick, *The Methods of Ethics*, (Macmillan: London, 1907), 111–12.

PART VI
Moral Responsibility

Introduction to Part VI

Our susceptibility to moral praise and blame seems to be at the very heart of what it is to be a person. So much of what distinguishes us from everything else on earth has to do with the capacities we possess that make us liable to such praise and blame. And yet understanding this special set of capacities has proven to be an extremely difficult philosophical task.

The classic worry is that the conditions under which people are morally responsible are impossible to fulfill. This worry is developed in the first two readings of this section, by Richard Taylor, and Galen Strawson.

Taylor is considering an ages-old difficulty. We can call it "the problem of determinism," though to speak as if there were only one such problem is no doubt misleading. Determinism is the view that everything that occurs does so as a result of a set of causes that, taken together, necessitate the outcome. If determinism is true, then events in our world are never random, but rather necessitated to occur just as they do by the way the world is, and the laws of nature that regulate it. In principle, everything that happens can be explained by a set of causes that (in tandem with natural laws) have made that outcome unavoidable.

Taylor believes that determinism and moral responsibility are incompatible. Though it is difficult, as he argues, to show that we can indeed be morally responsible, it is impossible to show it if determinism is true. For if we

cannot but choose and act as we do, then we cannot be rightly blamed or praised for our choices and conduct. If determinism is true, it seems that we lack control over our decisions, since control seems to require a kind of freedom that determinism makes impossible. And if we lack control over our decisions, then how could we be held morally responsible for them, and the actions they cause?

Taylor argues that what is required for moral responsibility is the falsity of determinism. But even if Taylor is right, the falsity of determinism would be only necessary, but not sufficient, for our having moral responsibility. Galen Strawson's article makes this plain. Strawson agrees with Taylor that moral responsibility and determinism are incompatible. But if determinism is false, that leaves us no better off. For, as Strawson argues, if events are not necessitated to occur just as they do, then we are *still* unable to exert control over our choices and actions. If events are not necessitated, then they are random, and random choices and actions are not ones for which we are responsible.

Taylor points to what is needed – a conception of an entity that is unique in the universe: an agent. An agent is one who can make choices without being necessitated to do so, while still avoiding randomness and exerting control over the content of her choices. She somehow slips between the horns of Strawson's dilemma, which can be simply stated: either our choices and actions are determined by prior causes, in which case we cannot be morally responsible; or our choices and actions are not determined, in which case they are random, and so again we cannot be morally responsible. Taylor does not argue for the existence of agents, and does not try to show how people can exhibit the relevant sort of control compatibly with indeterminism. He is just trying to show what must be the case if we are to be genuinely morally responsible. Whether those conditions are satisfied is the subject of much continuing philosophical debate.

A. J. Ayer rejects the terms of this debate. He believes that determinism and moral responsibility are perfectly compatible. Those who think otherwise are, he argues, failing to properly distinguish between an action's being caused, and an action's being constrained. Ayer believes that actions can be causally determined without also being constrained. Constraint undermines freedom, and with it, moral responsibility. But causation need not.

Ayer agrees that a person's action is free, and one for which he is morally responsible, only if he could have done something other than he in fact did. But Ayer thinks that we usually do have such power, since he analyses the power in this way: a person has the ability to do otherwise just in case he would have done something else had he chosen to do something else. Had my choices been different, my actions would have been different (since, when I act freely, my choices determine my actions). But this is compatible with my actions and choices being causally necessitated. And so we have a reconciliation between determinism and moral responsibility.

This sort of view is known as *compatibilism*. Though Ayer's version of it is nowadays little loved (see Taylor's article for an explanation), the compatibilist project is today the predominant one in this area of philosophy. The articles here by Susan Wolf and Peter Strawson develop alternative versions of it. Before considering their views, however, we should take note of Thomas Nagel's contribution to this literature. Nagel's focus is the Kantian claim that moral responsibility requires that an

agent be in control of the circumstances for which she is being morally assessed. Neither good nor bad luck should affect an agent's liability to praise or blame. And yet, as Nagel points out, many of our commonsense moral judgments do allow luck to play a role in determining culpability. We judge a reckless driver and his action to be morally worse if he runs over a bystander than if he doesn't. And yet the presence of the bystander on his route is not something over which he has any control. We judge a ruthless person and his actions to be morally worse if he manages to live in a place and time in which he has the opportunity to exercise his ruthlessness over others. But that a person is living in (say) Nazi Germany, rather than in a society under an enlightened rule of law, is something that is not within that person's control. Actions that, when performed, would be judged folly (at best), and traitorous (at worst), are sometimes judged in a more kindly light if their results turn out for the best. The extreme actions of a revolutionary will earn praise if successful, and condemnation if not. And yet such results are rarely wholly within the power of the revolutionary to effect.

Nagel isn't afraid to push his analysis to its logical extreme: our decisions to act as we do are also a product of circumstances that we do not control. We make the choices we do because of our beliefs, desires, and dispositions. And yet the elements of our character have been shaped by factors outside of our control. We don't control our genetic endowment. Nor are we able to determine who our parents are, what culture we grow up in, what social pressures we are subject to in our formative years. These are the major influences on the choices that we eventually make. If Kant is correct, then these choices are ones for which we are morally responsible only if such choices are uninfluenced by luck. That doesn't seem a possibility. So either, says Nagel, we must abandon Kant's criterion of responsibility, or we must abandon the many commonsensical moral appraisals of persons and their actions. It isn't a very happy choice.

Susan Wolf is clear about which alternative to choose. She does not believe that we can eliminate all aspects of luck in the formation of our character. Like other compatibilists, she is intent on showing how a relevant sense of control is compatible with causal necessitation, such that we can be relevantly in control of our decisions, and so be morally responsible for them, even though our decisions are themselves a product of factors that, ultimately, lie beyond our control. According to Wolf, we are responsible for our actions and their results only if the actions are within the control of our will, and our will is within control of our "deeper self." This last notion is a complicated one, but we can get an intuitive sense of it by contrasting it with one's drunken, or temporarily ill-informed self. One's deeper self includes those attitudes about the sort of person one really is, and really aims to be. These two conditions must be supplemented by a third, namely, that one's deeper self is sane. Wolf tries to unpack this concept by considering what it is to be insane, which, on her understanding, involves having unavoidably mistaken moral beliefs and values. According to Wolf, a person is morally responsible for her choices provided that all three of these conditions have been met.

Peter Strawson thinks that the focus on determinism is largely out of place in discussions of moral responsibility. When we consider our practices of moral appraisal, we find ourselves enmeshed in a complicated network of *reactive attitudes* (such as forgiveness, goodwill and affection, thoughtfulness and indifference) that reflect a person's susceptibility to warranted praise or blame. This intricate pattern of interpersonal responses is largely untouched by any concern for determinism. We give praise to those who exemplify certain attitudes, and condemn others for their different attitudes. We do wholly excuse some (e.g., infants and the insane) who are incapable of having reactive attitudes at all. But the entire practice of assigning moral responsibility is a self-standing form of life with its own rules, and one that is not aptly scrutinized from without. For Strawson, there is no reason to suspect the integrity of our moral practices, which require that we maintain the network of reactive attitudes towards others (and ourselves). To think that we must abandon our moral practices were we to accept determinism is to accept the possibility of an external critique of these practices. Strawson thinks that such a thing is impossible. Taking up the stance that determinism is true, and then using that assumption to scrutinize our practices, is thus an illicit form of criticism.

Strawson's article has been extremely influential. It isn't easy going, to be sure, and its influence has cut both ways. Some philosophers reject the idea that our moral practices are wholly self-standing and are immune from rational "external" assessment. They deny that the threat of determinism can be dispelled as readily as Strawson insists. Readers more sympathetic to its central claims, however, have found in it the basis of a new research program for compatibilism, and for vindicating our practices of praise and blame even if it turns out that determinism is true.

CHAPTER 36

Determinism and the Theory of Agency

RICHARD TAYLOR

I shall neither prove nor disprove determinism. Instead, I shall (1) give a precise statement of it, as I think Edwards and Hospers understand it, (2) show that it does, as they maintain, entail that men have no moral responsibilities, (3) elicit the defects of the usual answers to this claim, (4) indicate how a simple indeterminism supplies no better basis for responsibility, and (5) sketch a theory of agency that I think anyone insisting on moral responsibility must be driven to.

Determinism

Determinism is the thesis that whatever occurs occurs under conditions given which nothing else could occur. Indeterminism is simply the minimum denial of this, viz., that at least some things occur under conditions given which something else could occur instead. But these statements need to be made precise.
[. . .]
Determinism, then, is the thesis that in the case of any true statement of the form "*e* occurs" the event whose name or description replaces "*e*" is causally necessitated, never contingent. Indeterminism is the thesis that in the case of some true statement of that form, the event named or described is contingent.

Responsibility

Edwards and Hospers believe that determinism is incompatible with responsibility and obligation on the basis, I believe, of the following argument. It is assumed (*a*) that responsibility and obligation, in their strictly ethical sense, if they have any application at all, figure only in the context of human conduct, not in that of the behavior of animals, and (*b*) that a necessary (not sufficient) condition for ascribing this responsibility to a man for what he has done, or obligation for what he has yet to do, is that he could have done, or could do, something else; that is, that the occurrence for which he is responsible or obligated is contingent. But (*c*) this condition is never fulfilled. Hence (*d*) no man has ever been morally responsible for anything he has ever done, or will ever be morally obligated to do anything else. A corollary of this is that the notions of "ought" and "ought not" have no application to human conduct in any sense in which they do not equally apply to the behavior of animals.

Richard Taylor, "Determinism and the Theory of Agency," pp. 224–30 from Sidney Hook (ed.), *Determinism and Freedom*. New York: Macmillan, 1979.

"Soft determinism"

Determinists unwilling to accept this conclusion have tried several rejoinders, of which I shall cite, and reject, the four most common.

1. It is said that, even assuming determinism, the necessary condition for responsibility is often fulfilled, for to say that an agent could have done otherwise means only that he would have done otherwise had he chosen to.

But this neglects the fact that, if determinism is true, he could not have chosen otherwise. Indeed, by this kind of argument, one could say that, though a man has died of decapitation, he did not *have* to die, that he *could* have lived on – meaning only that he *would* have lived had he somehow kept his head on! And this is hardly the sort of contingency we want.

2. Again, it is said that a *sufficient* condition for ascribing moral responsibility is that an agent act from deliberation with knowledge of the consequences, and that this condition is often fulfilled.

But this presupposes the necessary condition for such responsibility that according to determinism is never fulfilled, for, as Hart reminded us (citing Aristotle), it makes sense to deliberate only about things that are, or are believed to be, contingent. This point becomes clear if we remind ourselves that, according to determinism, not only is a man's behavior causally necessitated (among other things, by the course of his deliberations), but so also is every step and detail of his deliberations, and so *also* are his beliefs (true or false) about the future, and *hence* his beliefs concerning the effects of his actions. Under these conditions one can no more ascribe moral responsibility to a man than to a robot who "deliberates," and then "acts," in response to our pushing various buttons (labeled "deliberate" etc.), every step of the chain then following by causal necessity.

3. Determinists sometimes say that we are, after all, responsible only for our *acts,* not our intentions, choices, or decisions. A man is not punished or rewarded for deciding to do something unless he then goes ahead and does it, and since even advocates of "free will" concede that our acts are causally determined (by our choices or "wills," for instance), there is

evidently no absurdity in being held responsible for what is determined.

But an indeterminist is not likely to concede that all our acts are causally determined. Moreover, this view conceives of responsibility only in terms of reward and punishment, confusing moral responsibility with corrigibility. What I am referring to as *moral* responsibility comes out more clearly if we consider cases in which no questions of law, no questions of benefiting or harming others, and no questions of reward, punishment, or retribution are at all involved. If, for instance, an intelligent man studies what is in fact a valid philosophical argument, understands it, accepts the premises as true and the reasoning as valid, and yet refuses to accept the conclusion, there is no philosopher, save those who deny obligation altogether, who would not say that he *ought* to accept the conclusion. But here no overt act is involved, but only a decision, and no question of reward, punishment, or retribution comes into the picture, much less one of legality. It cannot be true, therefore, that men have no responsibilities or obligations with respect to their decisions, unless it should turn out that they have no responsibilities or obligations whatever.

4. Finally, many determinists have said that moral responsibility consists only in amenability to a change of behavior through the force of real or anticipated rewards or punishments; in other words, that responsibility simply consists in corrigibility – a view that not only is compatible with determinism but presupposes it.

This definition of responsibility, however, violates what was assumed at the outset – namely, that lower animals have neither moral obligations nor responsibilities. The behavior of almost any sentient thing – rodents and fish, for instance – is alterable by the stimulus of reward or punishment. Moreover, this queer conception of moral responsibility and obligation, in addition to applying to situations to which moral concepts do not apply, fails to cover cases of the sort we just considered. For when one says that a man *ought* to accept a conclusion, in the light of probative evidence known to him, he does *not* mean merely that he can be *induced* to do so by threat or reward; indeed, the obligation might hold when this condition does not.

I regard it as reasonable, then, that if determinism is true no man has ever been morally responsible for anything he has ever done, and no man ever will be under any obligation to do anything. This is a painful conclusion to accept, particularly in view of the fact that, if one does accept it, one can try to persuade others to do so only by threats, blows, or arguments, but can never say that they *ought* to accept it, even if it is proved. But the conclusion may well be true nonetheless, for it seems to be entailed by what most philosophers regard as obviously true, viz., determinism.

Indeterminism

The denial of determinism, however, seems no more compatible with moral judgment than determinism, for it would seem to rob human actions, in Liebnitz's phrase, of any "rhyme or reason." Since this thought is fairly familiar I shall not elaborate it but only illustrate it.

Suppose an agent so constituted that his actions are determined by the numbers that turn up on a roulette wheel, and suppose, further, that the wheel obeys no causal laws whatever, so that its behavior is unpredictable in principle. Now, it would be plainly irrational to consider an agent so constituted morally responsible for those acts or obligated to perform others, since they are obviously utterly beyond his control; yet this situation corresponds exactly, so far as moral judgment is concerned, to that of an agent whose acts are quite undetermined.

Agency

To salvage moral responsibility one must resort to certain odd metaphysical notions that have long since been out of fashion and that are admittedly most difficult to comprehend clearly. What is needed, that is, is a view according to which (*a*) there is a reason for everything that happens, but (*b*) some such happenings – viz., some human acts – are contingent. The only way of satisfying these seemingly incompatible requirements is to suppose that an act for which an agent is responsible is performed by him, but that he, in turn, is not causally necessitated to do it. Now, this does, I think, accord with what men take themselves to be – namely, *agents* (cf. Latin *agere*) or beings that *act* rather than things all aspects of whose behavior are the causal consequences of the way they are acted upon. It now remains to elicit just what this theory involves, and see whether it is compatible with responsibility.

First, then, it involves the conception of a self or person (i.e., an agent) that is not merely a congeries or series of states or events, for on this view it is an agent who performs certain acts (i.e., who acts) rather than states or events in his history that causally determine them – these states or events being, presumably, if not things done by himself, then simply the causal consequences of other states or events, whether of his own history or that of other things.

Second, it involves an extraordinary conception of causation, according to which something that is not an event can nevertheless bring about an event – a conception, that is, according to which a "cause" can be something other than a sufficient condition; for if we say that a person is the "cause" of his act, we are not saying that *he* is a sufficient condition for its occurrence, since he plainly is not. We must accordingly not speak of an agent as *causing* an act, since "being a cause" ordinarily just means "being a sufficient condition," but rather of his originating it or, simply, of his *performing* it – in a manner in which things in the physical world, so far as we know, are never done or brought about. And this is evidently the conception of Aristotle, who spoke of living things as "self-moved." It is also what later philosophers, like Thomas Reid, meant by "active power," viz., the power to act without being acted upon, and it may be what Kant meant when he obscurely spoke of a "noumenal" self that is free.

Now, both of these conceptions – that of an *agent* as distinct from the states or events of his history, and that of *performing* as distinct from being a sufficient condition – are certainly odd and hard to conceive of clearly. Indeed, a philosopher could not be accused of stubbornness if he preferred to give up moral responsibility to embracing these two notions. But I am sure that only by accepting them can one *also* accept the notions of moral responsibility, obligation, and what Professor Hook referred to as "dignity."

It still remains to see, however, whether this conception of agency is compatible with responsibility. To show that it is, it needs to be shown that *on this view* (*a*) some human acts are contingent, in the sense defined; (*b*) animals are not rendered morally responsible; and (*c*) acts do not arise "without rhyme or reason," i.e., are not capricious.

With regard to the first point: some acts *are* contingent on this view, for they are not simply the causal consequences of antecedent conditions. Now, it will be tempting to say that there *must* be sufficient conditions for an agent's doing just what he does, but this simply begs the question, being just what the theory denies. There are certainly always conditions under which any event occurs, but such conditions do not in all cases necessitate just that event to the exclusion of any other; otherwise there would be no such thing as an *act*, nor would anything ever be *done*. We may further assume that for any act that is performed, there are reasons why it is performed; but such reasons need not be causal conditions. Rather, they may be, for example, motives or purposes, which are not sufficient conditions. To say, for instance, that an agent acted in a certain way in order to achieve a certain purpose is to give an explanation, but not a causal one, for his conduct. And if it is now insisted that there must, in any case, be conditions sufficient for an agent's having just such purposes and motives as he has, this may or may not be true (I think it is not); it is in any case irrelevant, for it would mean that only his purposes and motives – but not thereby his acts – are causally determined.

Secondly, as to the question whether this theory would render animals morally responsible: it evidently would not. If animals are "self-moving," as Aristotle thought, they do indeed satisfy a necessary condition for responsibility; but it does not follow that they satisfy any sufficient condition for it, and, in fact, they evidently do not.

Finally, as to the question whether this theory avoids capriciousness in human acts: it plainly does not, *if* by "capricious" *nothing more* is meant than "contingent." That is, it does deny that there are conditions sufficient for the occurrence of all events that occur. But it does not deny that there is an explanation or reason for every event, as we have just seen, for there are ways of explaining a man's conduct otherwise than by a recitation of causal conditions. The concept of agency, then, is quite unlike that of a thing whose behavior is arranged to coincide with the random selections of a roulette; for, assuming the wheel to be causally undetermined, there is *no* ultimate explanation for the roulette's behavior, whereas there is for the agent's. Moreover, saying of an agent that *he* acts makes sense; but we cannot conceive of a wheel – no agent at all – as "deciding" what is to be "done."

Conclusion

I do not claim to have proved a theory of agency, but I believe I have shown that, if it is intelligible, it renders moral responsibility possible. The conditions of moral responsibility can thus be elicited, in terms of agency, as follows.

Consider a situation in which some object *O* grasps a knife and cuts off a man's hand. Now assume: (1) there were no conditions sufficient for this event – i.e., it was contingent; (2) *O* is an agent, e.g., a man; (3) the event described is an act of *O*'s and not, for example, a reflex; (4) *O* realized, while contemplating the act, what it consisted in, and (5) he knew what its consequences would be, and that they would be evil.

A. Each of these assumptions can be true, and they can all be true together; that is, there is no proposition known to be true with which the conjunction of these five is causally or logically incompatible.
B. If (1) were false, *O* would not be morally responsible for the event described.
C. *Hence* neither (2), nor (3), (4), nor (5) is a sufficient condition for responsibility; nor are these four together sufficient, except as they may presuppose (1).
D. But (1), (2), (3), (4), and (5) are each a necessary condition for moral responsibility for this event, and
E. Together they are sufficient.

If one denies *E* one must, I believe, either deny *B*, as Edwards and Hospers do not, or else deny *A*, which would seem arbitrary and implausible.

CHAPTER 37

The Impossibility of Moral Responsibility

GALEN STRAWSON

I

There is an argument, which I will call the Basic Argument, which appears to prove that we cannot be truly or ultimately morally responsible for our actions. According to the Basic Argument, it makes no difference whether determinism is true or false. We cannot be truly or ultimately morally responsible for our actions in either case.

The Basic Argument has various expressions in the literature of free will, and its central idea can be quickly conveyed. (1) Nothing can be *causa sui* – nothing can be the cause of itself. (2) In order to be truly morally responsible for one's actions one would have to be *causa sui*, at least in certain crucial mental respects. (3) Therefore nothing can be truly morally responsible.

In this paper I want to reconsider the Basic Argument, in the hope that anyone who thinks that we can be truly or ultimately morally responsible for our actions will be prepared to say exactly what is wrong with it. I think that the point that it has to make is obvious, and that it has been underrated in recent discussion of free will – perhaps because it admits of no

Galen Strawson, "The Impossibility of Moral Responsibility," pp. 5, 7–10, 13–15, 25 from *Philosophical Studies*, 75, 1994.

answer. I suspect that it is obvious in such a way that insisting on it too much is likely to make it seem less obvious than it is, given the innate contrasuggestibility of human beings in general and philosophers in particular. But I am not worried about making it seem less obvious than it is so long as it gets adequate attention. As far as its validity is concerned, it can look after itself.

[. . .]

[E]ssentially the same argument can be given in a more natural form. (1) It is undeniable that one is the way one is, initially, as a result of heredity and early experience, and it is undeniable that these are things for which one cannot be held to be in any way responsible (morally or otherwise). (2) One cannot at any later stage of life hope to accede to true moral responsibility for the way one is by trying to change the way one already is as a result of heredity and previous experience. For (3) both the particular way in which one is moved to try to change oneself, and the degree of one's success in one's attempt at change, will be determined by how one already is as a result of heredity and previous experience. And (4) any further changes that one can bring about only after one has brought about certain initial changes will in turn be determined, via the initial changes, by heredity and previous experience. (5) This may not be the whole story, for it may be that some changes in the way one is are traceable not to heredity and experience but to the influence of indeterministic or random factors. But it is absurd to suppose that indeterministic or random factors, for which one is ex hypothesi in no way responsible, can in themselves contribute in any way to one's being truly morally responsible for how one is.

The claim, then, is not that people cannot change the way they are. They can, in certain respects (which tend to be exaggerated by North Americans and underestimated, perhaps, by Europeans). The claim is only that people cannot be supposed to change themselves in such a way as to be or become truly or ultimately morally responsible for the way they are, and hence for their actions.

II

I have encountered two main reactions to the Basic Argument. On the one hand it convinces almost all the students with whom I have discussed the topic of free will and moral responsibility. On the other hand it often tends to be dismissed, in contemporary discussion of free will and moral responsibility, as wrong, or irrelevant, or fatuous, or too rapid, or an expression of metaphysical megalomania.

I think that the Basic Argument is certainly valid in showing that we cannot be morally responsible in the way that many suppose. And I think that it is the natural light, not fear, that has convinced the students I have taught that this is so. That is why it seems worthwhile to restate the argument in a slightly different – simpler and looser – version, and to ask again what is wrong with it.

Some may say that there is nothing wrong with it, but that it is not very interesting, and not very central to the free will debate. I doubt whether any non-philosopher or beginner in philosophy would agree with this view. If one wants to think about free will and moral responsibility, consideration of some version of the Basic Argument is an over-whelmingly natural place to start. It certainly has to be considered at some point in a full discussion of free will and moral responsibility, even if the point it has to make is obvious. Belief in the kind of absolute moral responsibility that it shows to be impossible has for a long time been central to the Western religious, moral, and cultural tradition, even if it is now slightly on the wane (a disputable view). It is a matter of historical fact that concern about moral responsibility has been the main motor . . . of discussion of the issue of free will. The only way in which one might hope to show (1) that the Basic Argument was not central to the free will debate would be to show (2) that the issue of moral responsibility was not central to the free will debate. There are, obviously, ways of taking the word 'free' in which (2) can be maintained. But (2) is clearly false none the less.

In saying that the notion of moral responsibility criticized by the Basic Argument is central to the Western tradition, I am not suggesting that it is some artificial and local Judaeo-Christian-Kantian construct that is found nowhere else in the history of the peoples of the world, although even if it were that would hardly diminish its interest and importance for us. It is natural to suppose that Aristotle also subscribed to it, and it is significant that anthropologists have suggested that most human societies can be classified either as 'guilt cultures' or as 'shame cultures'. It is true that neither of these two fundamental moral emotions necessarily presupposes a conception of oneself as truly morally responsible for what one has done. But the fact that both are widespread does at least suggest that a conception of moral responsibility similar to our own is a natural part of the human moral-conceptual repertoire.

In fact the notion of moral responsibility connects more tightly with the notion of guilt than with the notion of shame. In many cultures shame can attach to one because of what some member of one's family – or government – has done, and not because of anything one has done oneself; and in such cases the feeling of shame need not (although it may) involve some obscure, irrational feeling that one is somehow responsible for the behaviour of one's family or government. The case of guilt is less clear. There is no doubt that people can feel guilty (or can believe that they feel guilty) about things for which they are not responsible, let alone morally responsible. But it is much less obvious that they can do this without any sense or belief that they are in fact responsible.

III

Such complications are typical of moral psychology, and they show that it is important to try to be precise about what sort of responsibility is under discussion. What sort of 'true' moral responsibility is being said to be both impossible and widely believed in?

An old story is very helpful in clarifying this question. This is the story of heaven and hell. As I understand it, true moral responsibility is responsibility of such a kind that, if we have it, then it *makes sense*, at least, to suppose that it could be just to punish some of us with (eternal) torment in hell and reward others with (eternal) bliss in heaven. The stress on the words 'makes sense' is important, for one certainly does not have to believe in any version of the story of heaven and hell in order to understand the notion of true moral responsibility that it is being used to illustrate. Nor does one have to believe in any version of the story of heaven and hell in order to believe in the existence of true moral responsibility. On the contrary: many atheists have believed in the existence of true moral responsibility. The story of heaven and hell is useful simply because it illustrates, in a peculiarly vivid way, the *kind* of absolute or ultimate accountability or responsibility that many have supposed themselves to have, and that many do still suppose themselves to have. It very clearly expresses its scope and force.

But one does not have to refer to religious faith in order to describe the sorts of everyday situation that are perhaps primarily influential in giving rise to our belief in true responsibility. Suppose you set off for a shop on the evening of a national holiday, intending to buy a cake with your last ten pound note. On the steps of the shop someone is shaking an Oxfam tin. You stop, and it seems completely clear to you that it is entirely up to you what you do next. That is, it seems to you that you are truly, radically free to choose, in such a way that you will be ultimately morally responsible for whatever you do choose. Even if you believe that determinism is true, and that you will in five minutes time be able to look back and say that what you did was determined, this does not seem to undermine your sense of the absoluteness and inescapability of your freedom, and of your moral responsibility for your choice. The same seems to be true even if you accept the validity of the Basic Argument stated in section I, which concludes that one cannot be in any way ultimately responsible for the way one is and decides. In both cases, it remains true that as one stands there, one's freedom and true moral responsibility seem obvious and absolute to one.

Large and small, morally significant or morally neutral, such situations of choice occur regularly in human life. I think they lie at the heart of the experience of freedom and moral responsibility. They are the fundamental source of our inability to give up belief in true or ultimate moral responsibility. There are further questions to be asked about why human beings experience these situations of choice as they do. It is an interesting question whether any cognitively sophisticated, rational, self-conscious agent must experience situations of choice in this way. But they are the experiential rock on which the belief in true moral responsibility is founded.

[. . .]

IV

Let me now restate the Basic Argument in very loose – as it were conversational – terms. New forms of words allow for new forms of objection, but they may be helpful none the less.

(1) You do what you do, in any situation in which you find yourself, because of the way you are.

So

(2) To be truly morally responsible for what you do you must be truly responsible for the way you are – at least in certain crucial mental respects.

Or:

(1) What you intentionally do, given the circumstances in which you (believe you) find yourself, flows necessarily from how you are.

Hence

(2) you have to get to have some responsibility for how you are in order to get to have some responsibility for what you intentionally do, given the circumstances in which you (believe you) find yourself.

Comment: Once again the qualification about 'certain mental respects' is one I will take for granted. Obviously one is not responsible for one's sex, one's basic body pattern, one's height, and so on. But if one were not responsible for anything about oneself, how one could be responsible for what one did, given the truth of (1)? This is the fundamental question, and it seems clear that if one is going to be responsible for any aspect of oneself, it had better be some aspect of one's mental nature.

I take it that (1) is incontrovertible, and that it is (2) that must be resisted. For if (1) and (2) are conceded the case seems lost, because the full argument runs as follows.

(1) You do what you do because of the way you are.

So

(2) To be truly morally responsible for what you do you must be truly responsible for the way you are – at least in certain crucial mental respects.

But

(3) You cannot be truly responsible for the way you are, so you cannot be truly responsible for what you do.

Why can't you be truly responsible for the way you are? Because

(4) To be truly responsible for the way you are, you must have intentionally brought it about that you are the way you are, and this is impossible.

Why is it impossible? Well, suppose it is not. Suppose that

(5) You have somehow intentionally brought it about that you are the way

you now are, and that you have brought this about in such a way that you can now be said to be truly responsible for being the way you are now.

For this to be true

(6) You must already have had a certain nature N in the light of which you intentionally brought it about that you are as you now are.

But then

(7) For it to be true that you and you alone are truly responsible for how you now are, you must be truly responsible for having had the nature N in the light of which you intentionally brought it about that you are the way you now are.

So

(8) You must have intentionally brought it about that you had that nature N, in which case you must have existed already with a prior nature in the light of which you intentionally brought it about that you had the nature N in the light of which you intentionally brought it about that you are the way you now are . . .

Here one is setting off on the regress. Nothing can be *causa sui* in the required way. Even if such causal 'aseity' is allowed to belong unintelligibly to God, it cannot be plausibly be supposed to be possessed by ordinary finite human beings. 'The *causa sui* is the best self-contradiction that has been conceived so far', as Nietzsche remarked in 1886:

it is a sort of rape and perversion of logic. But the extravagant pride of man has managed to entangle itself profoundly and frightfully with just this nonsense. The desire for 'freedom of the will' in the superlative metaphysical sense, which still holds sway, unfortunately, in the minds of the half-educated; the desire to bear the entire and ultimate responsibility for one's actions oneself, and to absolve God, the world, ancestors, chance, and society involves nothing less than to be precisely this *causa sui* and, with more than Baron Münchhausen's audacity, to pull oneself up into existence by the hair, out of the swamps of nothingness . . . (*Beyond Good and Evil*, § 21).

The rephrased argument is essentially exactly the same as before, although the first two steps are now more simply stated. It may seem pointless to repeat it, but the questions remain. Can the Basic Argument simply be dismissed? It is really of no importance in the discussion of free will and moral responsibility? (No and No) Shouldn't any serious defense of free will and moral responsibility thoroughly acknowledge the respect in which the Basic Argument is valid before going on to try to give its own positive account of the nature of free will and moral responsibility? Doesn't the argument go to the heart of things if the heart of the free will debate is a concern about whether we can be truly morally responsible in the absolute way that we ordinarily suppose? (Yes and Yes)

We are what we are, and we cannot be thought to have made ourselves *in such a way* that we can be held to be free in our actions *in such a way* that we can be held to be morally responsible for our actions *in such a way* that any punishment or reward for our actions is ultimately just or fair. Punishments and rewards may seem deeply appropriate or intrinsically 'fitting' to us in spite of this argument, and many of the various institutions of punishment and reward in human society appear to be practically indispensable in both their legal and non-legal forms. But if one takes the notion of justice that is central to our intellectual and cultural tradition seriously, then the evident consequence of the Basic Argument is that there is a fundamental sense in which no punishment or reward is ever ultimately just. It is exactly as just to punish or reward people for their actions as it is to punish or reward them for the (natural) colour of their hair or the (natural) shape of their faces.

[. . .]

V

There is nothing new in the somewhat incantatory argument of this paper. It restates certain points that may be in need of restatement. 'Everything has been said before', said André Gide, echoing La Bruyère, 'but since nobody listens we have to keep going back and beginning all over again.' This is an exaggeration, but it may not be a gross exaggeration, so far as general observations about the human condition are concerned.

The present claim, in any case, is simply this: time would be saved, and a great deal of readily available clarity would be introduced into the discussion of the nature of moral responsibility, if the simple point that is established by the Basic Argument were more generally acknowledged and clearly stated. Nietzsche thought that thorough-going acknowledgement of the point was long overdue, and his belief that there might be moral advantages in such an acknowledgement may deserve further consideration.

CHAPTER 38
Freedom and Necessity

A. J. AYER

When I am said to have done something of my own free will it is implied that I could have acted otherwise; and it is only when it is believed that I could have acted otherwise that I am held to be morally responsible for what I have done. For a man is not thought to be morally responsible for an action that it was not in his power to avoid. But if human behaviour is entirely governed by causal laws, it is not clear how any action that is done could ever have been avoided. It may be said of the agent that he would have acted otherwise if the causes of his action had been different, but they being what they were, it seems to follow that he was bound to act as he did. Now it is commonly assumed both that men are capable of acting freely, in the sense that is required to make them morally responsible, and that human behaviour is entirely governed by causal laws: and it is the apparent conflict between these two assumptions that gives rise to the philosophical problem of the freedom of the will.

Confronted with this problem, many people will be inclined to agree with Dr. Johnson: 'Sir, we *know* our will is free, and *there's* an end on't.' But, while this does very well for those

A. J. Ayer, "Freedom and Necessity," pp. 271–84 from *Philosophical Essays*. New York: Bedford/St. Martin's Press, 1969. Reproduced with permission of Palgrave Macmillan.

who accept Dr. Johnson's premiss, it would hardly convince anyone who denied the freedom of the will. Certainly, if we do know that our wills are free, it follows that they are so. But the logical reply to this might be that since our wills are not free, it follows that no one can know that they are: so that if anyone claims, like Dr. Johnson, to know that they are, he must be mistaken. What is evident, indeed, is that people often believe themselves to be acting freely; and it is to this 'feeling' of freedom that some philosophers appeal when they wish, in the supposed interests of morality, to prove that not all human action is causally determined. But if these philosophers are right in their assumption that a man cannot be acting freely if his action is causally determined, then the fact that someone feels free to do, or not to do, a certain action does not prove that he really is so. It may prove that the agent does not himself know what it is that makes him act in one way rather than another: but from the fact that a man is unaware of the causes of his action, it does not follow that no such causes exist.

So much may be allowed to the determinist; but his belief that all human actions are subservient to causal laws still remains to be justified. If, indeed, it is necessary that every event should have a cause, then the rule must apply to human behaviour as much as to anything else. But why should it be supposed that every event must have a cause? The contrary is not unthinkable. Nor is the law of universal causation a necessary presupposition of scientific thought. The scientist may try to discover causal laws, and in many cases he succeeds; but sometimes he has to be content with statistical laws, and sometimes he comes upon events which, in the present state of his knowledge, he is not able to subsume under any law at all. In the case of these events he assumes that if he knew more he would be able to discover some law, whether causal or statistical, which would enable him to account for them. And this assumption cannot be disproved. For however far he may have carried his investigation, it is always open to him to carry it further; and it is always conceivable that if he carried it further he would discover the connection which had hitherto escaped him. Nevertheless, it is also conceivable that the events with which he is concerned are not systematically connected with any others: so that the reason why he does not discover the sort of laws that he requires is simply that they do not obtain.

Now in the case of human conduct the search for explanations has not in fact been altogether fruitless. Certain scientific laws have been established; and with the help of these laws we do make a number of successful predictions about the ways in which different people will behave. But these predictions do not always cover every detail. We may be able to predict that in certain circumstances a particular man will be angry, without being able to prescribe the precise form that the expression of his anger will take. We may be reasonably sure that he will shout, but not sure how loud his shout will be, or exactly what words he will use. And it is only a small proportion of human actions that we are able to forecast even so precisely as this. But that, it may be said, is because we have not carried our investigations very far. The science of psychology is still in its infancy and, as it is developed, not only will more human actions be explained, but the explanations will go into greater detail. The ideal of complete explanation may never in fact be attained: but it is theoretically attainable. Well, this may be so: and certainly it is impossible to show *a priori* that it is not so: but equally it cannot be shown that it is. This will

not, however, discourage the scientist who, in the field of human behaviour, as elsewhere, will continue to formulate theories and test them by the facts. And in this he is justified. For since he has no reason *a priori* to admit that there is a limit to what he can discover, the fact that he also cannot be sure that there is no limit does not make it unreasonable for him to devise theories, nor, having devised them, to try constantly to improve them.

But now suppose it to be claimed that, so far as men's actions are concerned, there is a limit: and that this limit is set by the fact of human freedom. An obvious objection is that in many cases in which a person feels himself to be free to do, or not to do, a certain action, we are even now able to explain, in causal terms, why it is that he acts as he does. But it might be argued that even if men are sometimes mistaken in believing that they act freely, it does not follow that they are always so mistaken. For it is not always the case that when a man believes that he has acted freely we are in fact able to account for his action in causal terms. A determinist would say that we should be able to account for it if we had more knowledge of the circumstances, and had been able to discover the appropriate natural laws. But until those discoveries have been made, this remains only a pious hope. And may it not be true that, in some cases at least, the reason why we can give no causal explanation is that no causal explanation is available; and that this is because the agent's choice was literally free, as he himself felt it to be?

The answer is that this may indeed be true, inasmuch as it is open to anyone to hold that no explanation is possible until some explanation is actually found. But even so it does not give the moralist what he wants. For he is anxious to show that men are capable of acting freely in order to infer that they can be morally responsible for what they do. But if it is a matter of pure chance that a man should act in one way rather than another, he may be free but can hardly be responsible. And indeed when a man's actions seem to us quite unpredictable, when, as we say, there is no knowing what he will do, we do not look upon him as a moral agent. We look upon him as a lunatic.

To this it may be objected that we are not dealing fairly with the moralist. For when he makes it a condition of my being morally responsible that I should act freely, he does not wish to imply that it is purely a matter of chance that I act as I do. What he wishes to imply is that my actions are the result of my own free choice: and it is because they are the result of my own free choice that I am held to be morally responsible for them.

But now we must ask how it is that I come to make my choice. Either it is an accident that I choose to act as I do or it is not. If it is an accident, then it is merely a matter of chance that I did not choose otherwise; and if it is merely a matter of chance that I did not choose otherwise, it is surely irrational to hold me morally responsible for choosing as I did. But if it is not an accident that I choose to do one thing rather than another, then presumably there is some causal explanation of my choice: and in that case we are led back to determinism.

Again, the objection may be raised that we are not doing justice to the moralist's case. His view is not that it is a matter of chance that I choose to act as I do, but rather that my choice depends upon my character. Nevertheless he holds that I can still be free in the sense that he requires; for it is I who am responsible for my character. But in what way am I responsible for my character? Only, surely, in the sense that there is a causal connection between what I do now and what I have done in the past. It is only this that justifies the statement that I have made myself what I am: and even so this is an over-simplification, since it takes no account of the external influences to which I have been subjected. But, ignoring the external influences, let us assume that it is in fact the case that I have made myself what I am. Then it is still legitimate to ask how it is that I have come to make myself one sort of person rather than another. And if it be answered that it is a matter of my strength of will, we can put the same question in another form by asking how it is that my will has the strength that it has and not some other degree of strength. Once more, either it is an accident or it is not. If it is an accident, then by the same argument as before, I am not morally responsible, and if it is not an accident we are led back to determinism.

Furthermore, to say that my actions proceed from my character or, more colloquially, that I

act in character, is to say that my behaviour is consistent and to that extent predictable: and since it is, above all, for the actions that I perform in character that I am held to be morally responsible, it looks as if the admission of moral responsibility, so far from being incompatible with determinism, tends rather to pre-suppose it. But how can this be so if it is a necessary condition of moral responsibility that the person who is held responsible should have acted freely? It seems that if we are to retain this idea of moral responsibility, we must either show that men can be held responsible for actions which they do not do freely, or else find some way of reconciling determinism with the freedom of the will.

It is no doubt with the object of effecting this reconciliation that some philosophers have defined freedom as the consciousness of necessity. And by so doing they are able to say not only that a man can be acting freely when his action is causally determined, but even that his action must be causally determined for it to be possible for him to be acting freely. Nevertheless this definition has the serious disadvantage that it gives to the word 'freedom' a meaning quite different from any that it ordinarily bears. It is indeed obvious that if we are allowed to give the word 'freedom' any meaning that we please, we can find a meaning that will reconcile it with determinism: but this is no more a solution of our present problem than the fact that the word 'horse' could be arbitrarily used to mean what is ordinarily meant by "sparrow" is a proof that horses have wings. For suppose that I am compelled by another person to do something 'against my will.' In that case, as the word 'freedom' is ordinarily used, I should not be said to be acting freely: and the fact that I am fully aware of the constraint to which I am subjected makes no difference to the matter. I do not become free by becoming conscious that I am not. It may, indeed, be possible to show that my being aware that my action is causally determined is not incompatible with my acting freely: but it by no means follows that it is in this that my freedom consists. Moreover, I suspect that one of the reasons why people are inclined to define freedom as the consciousness of necessity is that they think that if one is conscious of necessity one may somehow be able to master it. But this is a fallacy. It is like someone's saying that he wishes he could see into the future, because if he did he would know what calamities lay in wait for him and so would be able to avoid them. But if he avoids the calamities then they don't lie in the future and it is not true that he foresees them. And similarly if I am able to master necessity, in the sense of escaping the operation of a necessary law, then the law in question is not necessary. And if the law is not necessary, then neither my freedom nor anything else can consist in my knowing that it is.

Let it be granted, then, when we speak of reconciling freedom with determination we are using the word 'freedom' in an ordinary sense. It still remains for us to make this usage clear: and perhaps the best way to make it clear is to show what it is that freedom, in this sense, is contrasted with. Now we began with the assumption that freedom is contrasted with causality: so that a man cannot be said to be acting freely if his action is causally determined. But this assumption has led us into difficulties and I now wish to suggest that it is mistaken. For it is not, I think, causality that freedom is to be contrasted with, but constraint. And while it is true that being constrained to do an action entails being caused to do it, I shall try to show that the converse does not hold. I shall try to show that from the fact that my action is causally determined it does not necessarily follow that I am constrained to do it: and this is equivalent to saying that it does not necessarily follow that I am not free.

If I am constrained, I do not act freely. But in what circumstances can I legitimately be said to be constrained? An obvious instance is the case in which I am compelled by another person to do what he wants. In a case of this sort the compulsion need not be such as to deprive one of the power of choice. It is not required that the other person should have hypnotized me, or that he should make it physically impossible for me to go against his will. It is enough that he should induce me to do what he wants by making it clear to me that, if I do not, he will bring about some situation that I regard as even more undesirable than the consequences of the action that he wishes me to do. Thus, if the man points a pistol at my head I may still choose to disobey him: but this does not prevent its being true that if I do fall in with his wishes he can legitimately be said to have compelled me. And if the circumstances are such that no reasonable person would be expected to choose the other alternative, then the action that I am made to do is not one for which I am held to be morally responsible.

A similar, but still somewhat different, case is that in which another person has obtained an habitual ascendancy over me. Where this is so, there may be no question of my being induced to act as the other person wishes by being confronted with a still more disagreeable alternative: for if I am sufficiently under his influence this special stimulus will not be necessary. Nevertheless I do not act freely, for the reason that I have been deprived of the power of choice. And this means that I have acquired so strong a habit of obedience that I no longer go through any process of deciding whether or not to do what the other person wants. About other matters I may still deliberate: but as regards the fulfilment of this other person's wishes, my own deliberations have ceased to be a causal factor in my behaviour. And it is in this sense that I may be said to be constrained. It is not, however, necessary that such constraint should take the form of subservience to another person. A kleptomaniac is not a free agent, in respect of his stealing, because he does not go through any process of deciding whether or not to steal. Or rather, if he does go through such a process, it is irrelevant to his behaviour. Whatever he resolved to do, he would steal all the same. And it is this that distinguishes him from the ordinary thief.

But now it may be asked whether there is any essential difference between these cases and those in which the agent is commonly thought to be free. No doubt the ordinary thief does go through a process of deciding whether or not to steal, and no doubt it does affect his behaviour. If he resolved to refrain from stealing, he could carry his resolution out. But if it be allowed that his making or not making this resolution is causally determined, then how can he be any more free than the kleptomaniac? It may be true that unlike the kleptomaniac he could refrain from stealing if he chose: but if there is a cause, or set of causes, which necessitate his choosing as he does, how can he be said to have the power of choice? Again, it may be true that no one now compels me to get up and walk across the room: but if my doing so can be causally explained in terms of my history or my environment, or whatever it may be, then how am I any more free than if some other person had compelled me? I do not have the feeling of constraint that I have when a pistol is manifestly pointed at my head: but the chains of causation by which I am bound are no less effective for being invisible.

The answer to this is that the cases I have mentioned as examples of constraint do differ from the others: and they differ just in the ways that I have tried to bring out. If I suffered from a compulsion neurosis, so that I got up and walked across the room, whether I wanted to or not, or if I did so because somebody else compelled me, then I should not be acting freely. But if I do it now, I shall be acting freely, just because these conditions do not obtain; and the fact that my action may nevertheless have a cause is, from this point of view, irrelevant. For it is not when my action has any cause at all, but only when it has a special sort of cause, that it is reckoned not to be free.

But here it may be objected that, even if this distinction corresponds to ordinary usage, it is still very irrational. For why should we distinguish, with regard to a person's freedom, between the operations of one sort of cause and those of another? Do not all causes equally necessitate? And is it not therefore arbitrary to say that a person is free when he is necessitated in one fashion but not when he is necessitated in another?

That all causes equally necessitate is indeed a tautology, if the word 'necessitate' is taken merely as equivalent to 'cause': but if, as the objection requires, it is taken as equivalent to 'constrain' or 'compel,' then I do not think that this proposition is true. For all that is needed for one event to be the cause of another is that, in the given circumstances, the event which is said to be the effect would not have occurred if it had not been for the occurrence of the event which is said to be the cause, or vice versa, according as causes are interpreted as necessary, or sufficient, conditions: and this fact is usually deducible from some causal law which states that whenever an event of the one kind occurs then, given suitable conditions, an event of the other kind will occur in a certain temporal or spatio-temporal relationship to it. In short, there is an invariable concomitance between the two classes of events; but there is no compulsion, in any but a metaphorical sense. Suppose, for example, that a psycho-analyst is able to account for some aspect of my behaviour by referring it to some lesion that I suffered in my childhood. In that case, it may be said that my childhood experience, together with certain other events, necessitates my behaving as I do. But all that this involves is that it is found to be true in general that when people have had certain experiences as children, they subsequently behave in certain specifiable ways; and my case is just another instance of this general law. It is in this way indeed that my behaviour is explained. But from the fact that my behaviour is capable of being explained, in the sense that it can be subsumed under some natural law, it does not follow that I am acting under constraint.

If this is correct, to say that I could have acted otherwise is to say, first, that I should have acted otherwise if I had so chosen; secondly, that my action was voluntary in the sense in which the actions, say, of the kleptomaniac are not; and thirdly, that nobody compelled me to choose as I did: and these three conditions may very well be fulfilled. When they are fulfilled, I may be said to have acted freely. But this is not to say that it was a matter of chance that I acted as I did, or, in other words, that my action could not be explained. And that my actions should be capable of being explained is all that is required by the postulate of determinism.

If more than this seems to be required it is, I think, because the use of the very word 'determinism' is in some degree misleading. For it tends to suggest that one event is somehow in the power of another, whereas the truth is merely that they are factually correlated. And the same applies to the use, in this context, of the word 'necessity' and even of the word 'cause' itself. Moreover, there are various reasons for this. One is the tendency to confuse causal with logical necessitation, and so to infer mistakenly that the effect is contained in the cause. Another is the uncritical use of a concept of force which is derived from primitive experiences of pushing and striking. A third is the survival of an animistic conception of causality, in which all causal relationships are modelled on the example of one person's exercising authority over another. As a result we tend to form an imaginative picture of an unhappy effect trying vainly to escape from the clutches of an over-mastering cause. But, I repeat, the fact is simply that when an event of one type occurs, an event of another type occurs also, in a certain temporal or spatio-temporal relation to the first. The rest is only metaphor. And it is because of the metaphor, and not because of the fact, that we come to think that there is an antithesis between causality and freedom.

Nevertheless, it may be said, if the postulate of determinism is valid, then the future can be explained in terms of the past: and this means that if one knew enough about the past one would be able to predict the future. But in that case what will happen in the future is already decided. And how then can I be said to be free? What is going to happen is going to happen and nothing that I do can prevent it. If the determinist is right, I am the helpless prisoner of fate.

But what is meant by saying that the future course of events is already decided? If the implication is that some person has arranged it, then the proposition is false. But if all that is meant is that it is possible, in principle, to deduce it from a set of particular facts about the past, together with the appropriate general laws, then, even if this is true, it does not in the least entail that I am the helpless prisoner of fate. It does not even entail that my actions make no difference to the future: for they are causes as well as effects; so that if they were different their consequences would be different also. What it does entail is that my behaviour can be predicted: but to say that my behaviour can be predicted is not to say that I am acting under constraint. It is indeed true that I cannot escape my destiny if this is taken to mean no more than that I shall do what I shall do. But this is a tautology, just as it is a tautology that what is going to happen is going to happen. And such tautologies as these prove nothing whatsoever about the freedom of the will.

CHAPTER 39
Moral Luck

THOMAS NAGEL

Kant believed that good or bad luck should influence neither our moral judgment of a person and his actions, nor his moral assessment of himself.

> The good will is not good because of what it effects or accomplishes or because of its adequacy to achieve some proposed end; it is good only because of its willing, i.e., it is good of itself. And, regarded for itself, it is to be esteemed incomparably higher than anything which could be brought about by it in favor of any inclination or even of the sum total of all inclinations. Even if it should happen that, by a particularly unfortunate fate or by the niggardly provision of a stepmotherly nature, this will should be wholly lacking in power to accomplish its purpose, and if even the greatest effort should not avail it to achieve anything of its end, and if there remained only the good will (not as a mere wish but as the summoning of all the means in our power), it would sparkle like a jewel in its own right, as something that had its full worth in itself. Usefulness or fruitlessness can neither diminish nor augment this worth.[1]

He would presumably have said the same about a bad will: whether it accomplishes its evil

purposes is morally irrelevant. And a course of action that would be condemned if it had a bad outcome cannot be vindicated if by luck it turns out well. There cannot be moral risk. This view seems to be wrong, but it arises in response to a fundamental problem about moral responsibility to which we possess no satisfactory solution.

The problem develops out of the ordinary conditions of moral judgment. Prior to reflection it is intuitively plausible that people cannot be morally assessed for what is not their fault, or for what is due to factors beyond their control. Such judgment is different from the evaluation of something as a good or bad thing, or state of affairs. The latter may be present in addition to moral judgment, but when we blame someone for his actions we are not merely saying it is bad that they happened, or bad that he exists: we are judging *him*, saying he is bad, which is different from his being a bad thing. This kind of judgment takes only a certain kind of object. Without being able to explain exactly why, we feel that the appropriateness of moral assessment is easily undermined by the discovery that the act or attribute, no matter how good or bad, is not under the person's control. While other evaluations remain, this one seems to lose its footing. So a clear absence of control, produced by involuntary movement, physical force, or ignorance of the circumstances, excuses what

Thomas Nagel, "Moral Luck," pp. 137–55 from *Proceedings of the Aristotelian Society*, 50, 1976. Reprinted by permission of the publishers, Blackwell Publishing.

is done from moral judgment. But what we do depends in many more ways than these on what is not under our control – what is not produced by a good or a bad will, in Kant's phrase. And external influences in this broader range are not usually thought to excuse what is done from moral judgment, positive or negative.

Let me give a few examples, beginning with the type of case Kant has in mind. Whether we succeed or fail in what we try to do nearly always depends to some extent on factors beyond our control. This is true of murder, altruism, revolution, the sacrifice of certain interests for the sake of others – almost any morally important act. What has been done, and what is morally judged, is partly determined by external factors. However jewel-like the goodwill may be in its own right, there is a morally significant difference between rescuing someone from a burning building and dropping him from a twelfth-story window while trying to rescue him. Similarly, there is a morally significant difference between reckless driving and manslaughter. But whether a reckless driver hits a pedestrian depends on the presence of the pedestrian at the point where he recklessly passes a red light. What we do is also limited by the opportunities and choices with which we are faced, and these are largely determined by factors beyond our control. Someone who was an officer in a concentration camp might have led a quiet and harmless life if the Nazis had never come to power in Germany. And someone who led a quiet and harmless life in Argentina might have become an officer in a concentration camp if he had not left Germany for business reasons in 1930.

I shall say more later about these and other examples. I introduce them here to illustrate a general point. Where a significant aspect of what someone does depends on factors beyond his control, yet we continue to treat him in that respect as an object of moral judgment, it can be called moral luck. Such luck can be good or bad. And the problem posed by this phenomenon, which led Kant to deny its possibility, is that the broad range of external influences here identified seems on close examination to undermine moral assessment as surely as does the narrower range of familiar excusing condi-

tions. If the condition of control is consistently applied, it threatens to erode most of the moral assessments we find it natural to make. The things for which people are morally judged are determined in more ways than we at first realize by what is beyond their control. And when the seemingly natural requirement of fault or responsibility is applied in light of these facts, it leaves few pre-reflective moral judgments intact. Ultimately, nothing or almost nothing about what a person does seems to be under his control.

Why not conclude, then, that the condition of control is false – that it is an initially plausible hypothesis refuted by clear counterexamples? One could in that case look instead for a more refined condition which picked out the *kinds* of lack of control that really undermine certain moral judgments, without yielding the unacceptable conclusion derived from the broader condition, that most or all ordinary moral judgments are illegitimate.

What rules out this escape is that we are dealing not with a theoretical conjecture but with a philosophical problem. The condition of control does not suggest itself merely as a generalization from certain clear cases. It seems *correct* in the further cases to which it is extended beyond the original set. When we undermine moral assessment by considering new ways in which control is absent, we are not just discovering what *would* follow given the general hypothesis, but are actually being persuaded that in itself the absence of control is relevant in these cases too. The erosion of moral judgment emerges not as the absurd consequence of an over-simple theory, but as a natural consequence of the ordinary idea of moral assessment, when it is applied in view of a more complete and precise account of the facts. It would therefore be a mistake to argue from the unacceptability of the conclusions to the need for a different account of the conditions of moral responsibility. The view that moral luck is paradoxical is not a *mistake*, ethical or logical, but a perception of one of the ways in which the intuitively acceptable conditions of moral judgment threaten to undermine it all.

It resembles the situation in another area of philosophy, the theory of knowledge. There too conditions which seem perfectly natural, and which grow out of the ordinary procedures for challenging and defending claims to knowledge, threaten to undermine all such claims if consistently applied. Most skeptical arguments have this quality: they do not depend on the imposition of arbitrarily stringent standards of knowledge, arrived at by misunderstanding, but appear to grow inevitably from the consistent application of ordinary standards. There is a substantive parallel as well, for epistemological skepticism arises from consideration of the respects in which our beliefs and their relation to reality depend on factors beyond our control. External and internal causes produce our beliefs. We may subject these processes to scrutiny in an effort to avoid error, but our conclusions at this next level also result, in part, from influences which we do not control directly. The same will be true no matter how far we carry the investigation. Our beliefs are always, ultimately, due to factors outside our control, and the impossibility of encompassing those factors without being at the mercy of others leads us to doubt whether we know anything. It looks as though, if any of our beliefs are true, it is pure biological luck rather than knowledge.

Moral luck is like this because while there are various respects in which the natural objects of moral assessment are out of our control or influenced by what is out of our control, we cannot reflect on these facts without losing our grip on the judgments.

There are roughly four ways in which the natural objects of moral assessment are disturbingly subject to luck. One is the phenomenon of constitutive luck – the kind of person you are, where this is not just a question of what you deliberately do, but of your inclinations, capacities, and temperament. Another category is luck in one's circumstances – the kind of problems and situations one faces. The other two have to do with the causes and effects of action: luck in how one is determined by antecedent circumstances, and luck in the way one's actions and projects turn out. All of them present a common problem. They are all opposed by the idea that one cannot be more culpable or estimable for anything than one is for that fraction of it which is under

one's control. It seems irrational to take or dispense credit or blame for matters over which a person has no control, or for their influence on results over which he has partial control. Such things may create the conditions for action, but action can be judged only to the extent that it goes beyond these conditions and does not just result from them.

Let us first consider luck, good and bad, in the way things turn out. Kant, in the above-quoted passage, has one example of this in mind, but the category covers a wide range. It includes the truck driver who accidentally runs over a child, the artist who abandons his wife and five children to devote himself to painting,[2] and other cases in which the possibilities of success and failure are even greater. The driver, if he is entirely without fault, will feel terrible about his role in the event, but will not have to reproach himself. Therefore this example of agent-regret[3] is not yet a case of *moral* bad luck. However, if the driver was guilty of even a minor degree of negligence – failing to have his brakes checked recently, for example – then if that negligence contributes to the death of the child, he will not merely feel terrible. He will blame himself for the death. And what makes this an example of moral luck is that he would have to blame himself only slightly for the negligence itself if no situation arose which required him to brake suddenly and violently to avoid hitting a child. Yet the *negligence* is the same in both cases, and the driver has no control over whether a child will run into his path.

The same is true at higher levels of negligence. If someone has had too much to drink and his car swerves onto the sidewalk, he can count himself morally lucky if there are no pedestrians in its path. If there were, he would be to blame for their deaths, and would probably be prosecuted for manslaughter. But if he hurts no one, although his recklessness is exactly the same, he is guilty of a far less serious legal offense and will certainly reproach himself and be reproached by others much less severely. To take another legal example, the penalty for attempted murder is less than that for successful murder – however similar the intentions and motives of the assailant may be in the two cases. His degree of culpability can depend, it would seem, on whether the victim happened to be wearing a bullet-proof vest, or whether a bird flew into the path of the bullet – matters beyond his control.

Finally, there are cases of decision under uncertainty – common in public and in private life. Anna Karenina goes off with Vronsky, Gauguin leaves his family, Chamberlain signs the Munich agreement, the Decembrists persuade the troops under their command to revolt against the czar, the American colonies declare their independence from Britain, you introduce two people in an attempt at matchmaking. It is tempting in all such cases to feel that some decision must be possible, in the light of what is known at the time, which will make reproach unsuitable no matter how things turn out. But this is not true; when someone acts in such ways he takes his life, or his moral position, into his hands, because how things turn out determines what he has done. It is possible *also* to assess the decision from the point of view of what could be known at the time, but this is not the end of the story. If the Decembrists had succeeded in overthrowing Nicholas I in 1825 and establishing a constitutional regime, they would be heroes. As it is, not only did they fail and pay for it, but they bore some responsibility for the terrible punishments meted out to the troops who had been persuaded to follow them. If the American Revolution had been a bloody failure resulting in greater repression, then Jefferson, Franklin and Washington would still have made a noble attempt, and might not even have regretted it on their way to the scaffold, but they would also have had to blame themselves for what they had helped to bring on their compatriots. (Perhaps peaceful efforts at reform would eventually have succeeded.) If Hitler had not overrun Europe and exterminated millions, but instead had died of a heart attack after occupying the Sudetenland, Chamberlain's action at Munich would still have utterly betrayed the Czechs, but it would not be the great moral disaster that has made his name a household word.

In many cases of difficult choice the outcome cannot be foreseen with certainty. One kind of assessment of the choice is possible in advance, but another kind must await the outcome, because the outcome determines what has been done. The same degree of culpability or estimability in intention, motive, or concern is compatible with a wide range of judgments, positive or negative, depending on what happened beyond the point of decision. The *mens rea* which could have existed in the absence of any consequences does not exhaust the grounds of moral judgment. Actual results influence culpability or esteem in a large class of unquestionably ethical cases ranging from negligence through political choice.

That these are genuine moral judgments rather than expressions of temporary attitude is evident from the fact that one can say *in advance* how the moral verdict will depend on the results. If one negligently leaves the bath running with the baby in it, one will realize, as one bounds up the stairs toward the bathroom, that if the baby has drowned one has done something awful, whereas if it has not one has merely been careless. Someone who launches a violent revolution against an authoritarian regime knows that if he fails he will be responsible for much suffering that is in vain, but if he succeeds he will be justified by the outcome. I do not mean that *any* action can be retroactively justified by history. Certain things are so bad in themselves, or so risky, that no results can make them all right. Nevertheless, when moral judgment does depend on the outcome, it is objective and timeless and not dependent on a change of standpoint produced by success or failure. The judgment after the fact follows from an hypothetical judgment that can be made beforehand, and it can be made as easily by someone else as by the agent.

From the point of view which makes responsibility dependent on control, all this seems absurd. How is it possible to be more or less culpable depending on whether a child gets into the path of one's car, or a bird into the path of one's bullet? Perhaps it is true that what is done depends on more than the agent's state of mind or intention. The problem then is, why is it not irrational to base moral assessment on what people do, in this broad sense? It amounts to holding them responsible for the contributions of fate as well as for their own – provided they have made some contribution to begin with. If we look at cases of negligence or attempt, the pattern seems to be that overall culpability corresponds to the product of mental or intentional fault and the seriousness of the outcome. Cases of decision under uncertainty are less easily explained in this way, for it seems that the overall judgment can even shift from positive to negative depending on the outcome. But here too it seems rational to subtract the effects of occurrences subsequent to the choice, that were merely possible at the time, and concentrate moral assessment on the actual decision in light of the probabilities. If the object of moral judgment is the *person*, then to hold him accountable for what he has done in the broader sense is akin to strict liability, which may have its legal uses but seems irrational as a moral position.

The result of such a line of thought is to pare down each act to its morally essential core, an inner act of pure will assessed by motive and intention. Adam Smith advocates such a position in *The Theory of Moral Sentiments*, but notes that it runs contrary to our actual judgments.

> But how well soever we may seem to be persuaded of the truth of this equitable maxim, when we consider it after this manner, in abstract, yet when we come to particular cases, the actual consequences which happen to proceed from any action, have a very great effect upon our sentiments concerning its merit or demerit, and almost always either enhance or diminish our sense of both. Scarce, in any one instance, perhaps, will our sentiments be found, after examination, to be entirely regulated by this rule, which we all acknowledge ought entirely to regulate them.[4]

Joel Feinberg points out further that restricting the domain of moral responsibility to the inner world will not immunize it to luck. Factors beyond the agent's control, like a coughing fit, can interfere with his decisions as surely as they can with the path of a bullet from his gun.[5] Nevertheless the tendency to cut down the scope of moral assessment is pervasive, and does not limit itself to the influence of effects. It attempts to isolate the will from the other direction, so to speak, by separating out constitutive luck. Let us consider that next.

Kant was particularly insistent on the moral irrelevance of qualities of temperament and personality that are not under the control of the will. Such qualities as sympathy or coldness might provide the background against which obedience to moral requirements is more or less difficult, but they could not be objects of moral assessment themselves, and might well interfere with confident assessment of its proper object – the determination of the will by the motive of duty. This rules out moral judgment of many of the virtues and vices, which are states of character that influence choice but are certainly not exhausted by dispositions to act deliberately in certain ways. A person may be greedy, envious, cowardly, cold, ungenerous, unkind, vain, or conceited, but *behave* perfectly by a monumental effort of will. To possess these vices is to be unable to help having certain feelings under certain circumstances, and to have strong spontaneous impulses to act badly. Even if one controls the impulses, one still has the vice. An envious person hates the greater success of others. He can be morally condemned as envious even if he congratulates them cordially and does nothing to denigrate or spoil their success. Conceit, likewise, need not be displayed. It is fully present in someone who cannot help dwelling with secret satisfaction on the superiority of his own achievements, talents, beauty, intelligence, or virtue. To some extent such a quality may be the product of earlier choices; to some extent it may be amenable to change by current actions. But it is largely a matter of constitutive bad fortune. Yet people are morally condemned for such qualities, and esteemed for others equally beyond control of the will: they are assessed for what they are *like*.

To Kant this seems incoherent because virtue is enjoined on everyone and therefore must in principle be possible for everyone. It may be easier for some than for others, but it must be possible to achieve it by making the right choices, against whatever temperamental background.[6] One may want to have a generous spirit, or regret not having one, but it makes no sense to condemn oneself or anyone else for a quality which is not within the control of the will. Condemnation implies that you should not be like that, not that it is unfortunate that you are.

Nevertheless, Kant's conclusion remains intuitively unacceptable. We may be persuaded that these moral judgments are irrational, but they reappear involuntarily as soon as the argument is over. This is the pattern throughout the subject.

The third category to consider is luck in one's circumstances, and I shall mention it briefly. The things we are called upon to do, the moral tests we face, are importantly determined by factors beyond our control. It may be true of someone that in a dangerous situation he would behave in a cowardly or heroic fashion, but if the situation never arises, he will never have the chance to distinguish or disgrace himself in this way, and his moral record will be different.

A conspicuous example of this is political. Ordinary citizens of Nazi Germany had an opportunity to behave heroically by opposing the regime. They also had an opportunity to behave badly, and most of them are culpable for having failed this test. But it is a test to which the citizens of other countries were not subjected, with the result that even if they, or some of them, would have behaved as badly as the Germans in like circumstances, they simply did not and therefore are not similarly culpable. Here again one is morally at the mercy of fate, and it may seem irrational upon reflection, but our ordinary moral attitudes would be unrecognizable without it. We judge people for what they actually do or fail to do, not just for what they would have done if circumstances had been different.[7]

This form of moral determination by the actual is also paradoxical, but we can begin to see how deep in the concept of responsibility the paradox is embedded. A person can be morally responsible only for what he does; but what he does results from a great deal that he does not do; therefore he is not morally responsible for what he is and is not responsible for. (This is not a contradiction, but it is a paradox.)

It should be obvious that there is a connection between these problems about responsibility and control and an even more familiar problem, that of freedom of the will. That is the last type of moral luck I want to take up, though I can do no more within the scope of this essay than indicate its connection with the other types.

If one cannot be responsible for consequences of one's acts due to factors beyond one's control, or for antecedents of one's acts that are properties of temperament not subject to one's will, or for the circumstances that pose one's moral choices, then how can one be responsible even for the stripped-down acts of the will itself, if *they* are the product of antecedent circumstances outside of the will's control?

The area of genuine agency, and therefore of legitimate moral judgment, seems to shrink under this scrutiny to an extensionless point. Everything seems to result from the combined influence of factors, antecedent and posterior to action, that are not within the agent's control. Since he cannot be responsible for them, he cannot be responsible for their results – though it may remain possible to take up the aesthetic or other evaluative analogues of the moral attitudes that are thus displaced.

It is also possible, of course, to brazen it out and refuse to accept the results, which indeed seem unacceptable as soon as we stop thinking about the arguments. Admittedly, if certain surrounding circumstances had been different, then no unfortunate consequences would have followed from a wicked intention, and no seriously culpable act would have been performed; but since the circumstances were *not* different, and the agent *in fact* succeeded in perpetrating a particularly cruel murder, *that* is what he did, and that is what he is responsible for. Similarly, we may admit that if certain antecedent circumstances had been different, the agent would never have developed into the sort of person who would do such a thing; but since he *did* develop (as the inevitable result of those antecedent circumstances) into the sort of swine he is, and into the person who committed such a murder, *that* is what he is blameable for. In both cases one is responsible for what one actually does – even if what one actually does depends in important ways on what is not within one's control. This compatibilist account of our moral judgments would leave room for the ordinary conditions of responsibility – the absence of coercion, ignorance, or involuntary movement – as part of the determination of what someone has done – but it is understood not to exclude the influence of a great deal that he has not done.

The only thing wrong with this solution is its failure to explain how skeptical problems arise. For they arise not from the imposition of an arbitrary external requirement, but from the nature of moral judgment itself. Something in the ordinary idea of what someone does must explain how it can seem necessary to subtract from it anything that merely happens – even though the ultimate consequence of such subtraction is that nothing remains. And something in the ordinary idea of knowledge must explain why it seems to be undermined by any influences on belief not within the control of the subject – so that knowledge seems impossible without an impossible foundation in autonomous reason. But let us leave epistemology aside and concentrate on action, character, and moral assessment.

The problem arises, I believe, because the self which acts and is the object of moral judgment is threatened with dissolution by the absorption of its acts and impulses into the class of events. Moral judgment of a person is judgment not of what happens to him, but of him. It does not say merely that a certain event or state of affairs is fortunate or unfortunate or even terrible. It is not an evaluation of a state of the world, or of an individual as part of the world. We are not thinking just that it would be better if he were different, or did not exist, or had not done some of the things he has done. We are judging *him*, rather than his existence or characteristics. The effect of concentrating on the influence of what is not under his control is to make this responsible self seem to disappear, swallowed up by the order of mere events.

What, however, do we have in mind that a person must *be* to be the object of these moral attitudes? While the concept of agency is easily undermined, it is very difficult to give it a positive characterization. That is familiar from the literature on Free Will.

I believe that in a sense the problem has no solution, because something in the idea of agency is incompatible with actions being events, or people being things. But as the external determinants of what someone has done are gradually exposed, in their effect on consequences, character, and choice itself, it becomes gradually clear that actions are events and people things. Eventually nothing remains which can be ascribed to the responsible self, and we are left with nothing but a portion of the larger sequence of events, which can be deplored or celebrated, but not blamed or praised.

Though I cannot define the idea of the active self that is thus undermined, it is possible to say something about its sources. There is a close connection between our feelings about ourselves and our feelings about others. Guilt and indignation, shame and contempt, pride and admiration are internal and external sides of the same moral attitudes. We are unable to view ourselves simply as portions of the world, and from inside we have a rough idea of the boundary between what is us and what is not, what we do and what happens to us, what is our personality and what is an accidental handicap. We apply the same essentially internal conception of the self to others. About ourselves we feel pride, shame, guilt, remorse – and agent-regret. We do not regard our actions and our characters merely as fortunate or unfortunate episodes – though they may also be that. We cannot *simply* take an external evaluative view of ourselves – of what we most essentially are and what we do. And this remains true even when we have seen that we are not responsible for our own existence, or our nature, or the choices we have to make, or the circumstances that give our acts the consequences they have. Those acts remain ours and we remain ourselves, despite the persuasiveness of the reasons that seem to argue us out of existence.

It is this internal view that we extend to others in moral judgment – when we judge *them* rather than their desirability or utility. We extend to others the refusal to limit ourselves to external evaluation, and we accord to them selves like our own. But in both cases this comes up against the brutal inclusion of humans and everything about them in a world from which they cannot be separated and of which they are nothing but contents. The external view forces itself on us at the same time that we resist it. One way this occurs is through the gradual erosion of what we do by the subtraction of what happens.

The inclusion of consequences in the conception of what we have done is an acknowledgment that we are parts of the world, but the paradoxical character of moral luck which emerges from this acknowledgment shows that we are unable to operate with such a view, for it leaves us with no one to be. The same thing is revealed in the appearance that determinism obliterates responsibility. Once we see an aspect of what we or someone else does as something that happens, we lose our grip on the idea that it has been done and that we can judge the doer and not just the happening. This explains why the absence of determinism is no more hospitable to the concept of agency than is its presence – a point that has been noticed often. Either way the act is viewed externally, as part of the course of events.

The problem of moral luck cannot be understood without an account of the internal conception of agency and its special connection with the moral attitudes as opposed to other types of value. I do not have such an account. The degree to which the problem has a solution can be determined only by seeing whether in some degree the incompatibility between this conception and the various ways in which we do not control what we do is only apparent. I have nothing to offer on that topic either. But it is not enough to say merely that our basic moral attitudes toward ourselves and others are determined by what is actual; for they are also threatened by the sources of that actuality, and by the external view of action which forces itself on us when we see how everything we do belongs to a world that we have not created.

Notes

1. *Foundations of the Metaphysics of Morals*, first section, third paragraph.
2. Such a case, modelled on the life of Gauguin, is discussed by Bernard Williams in "Moral Luck" *Proceedings of the Aristotelian Society*, supplementary vol. L (1976), 115–35 (to which the original version of this essay was a reply). He points out that though success or failure cannot be predicted in advance, Gauguin's most basic retrospective feelings about the decision will be determined by the development of his talent. My disagreement with Williams is that his account fails to explain why such retrospective attitudes can be called moral. If success does not permit Gauguin to justify himself to others, but still determines his most basic feelings, that shows only that his most basic feelings need not be moral. It does not show that morality is subject to luck. If the retrospective judgment were moral, it would imply the truth of a hypothetical judgment made in advance, of the form "If I leave my family and become a great painter, I will be justified by success; if I don't become a great painter, the act will be unforgivable."
3. Williams' term (*ibid.*).
4. Pt II, sect. 3, Introduction, para. 5.
5. "Problematic Responsibility in Law and Morals," in Joel Feinberg, *Doing and Deserving* (Princeton: Princeton University Press, 1970).
6. "If nature has put little sympathy in the heart of a man, and if he, though an honest man, is by temperament cold and indifferent to the sufferings of others, perhaps because he is provided with special gifts of patience and fortitude and expects or even requires that others should have the same – and such a man would certainly not be the meanest product of nature – would not he find in himself a source from which to give himself a far higher worth than he could have got by having a good-natured temperament?" (*Foundations of the Metaphysics of Morals*, first section, eleventh paragraph).
7. Circumstantial luck can extend to aspects of the situation other than individual behavior. For example, during the Vietnam War even U.S. citizens who had opposed their country's actions vigorously from the start often felt compromised by its crimes. Here they were not even responsible; there was probably nothing they could do to stop what was happening, so the feeling of being implicated may seem unintelligible. But it is nearly impossible to view the crimes of one's own country in the same way that one views the crimes of another country, no matter how equal one's lack of power to stop them in the two cases. One *is* a citizen of one of them, and has a connection with its actions (even if only through taxes that cannot be withheld) – that one does not have with the other's. This makes it possible to be ashamed of one's country, and to feel a victim of moral bad luck that one was an American in the 1960s.

CHAPTER 40

Sanity and the Metaphysics of Responsibility

SUSAN WOLF

Philosophers who study the problems of free will and responsibility have an easier time than most in meeting challenges about the relevance of their work to ordinary, practical concerns. Indeed, philosophers who study these problems are rarely faced with such challenges at all, since questions concerning the conditions of responsibility come up so obviously and so frequently in everyday life. Under scrutiny, however, one might question whether the connections between philosophical and nonphilosophical concerns in this area are real.

In everyday contexts, when lawyers, judges, parents, and others are concerned with issues of responsibility, they know, or think they know, what in general the conditions of responsibility are. Their questions are questions of application: Does this or that particular person meet this or that particular condition? Is this person mature enough, or informed enough, or sane enough to be responsible? Was he or she acting under posthypnotic suggestion or under the influence of a mind-impairing drug? It is assumed, in these contexts, that normal, fully developed adult human beings are

responsible beings. The questions have to do with whether a given individual falls within the normal range.

By contrast, philosophers tend to be uncertain about the general conditions of responsibility, and they care less about dividing the responsible from the nonresponsible agents than about determining whether, and if so why, any of us are ever responsible for anything at all.

In the classroom, we might argue that the philosophical concerns grow out of the nonphilosophical ones, that they take off where the nonphilosophical questions stop. In this way, we might convince our students that even if they are not plagued by the philosophical worries, they ought to be. If they worry about whether a person is mature enough, informed enough, and sane enough to be responsible, then they should worry about whether that person is metaphysically free enough, too.

The argument I make here, however, goes in the opposite direction. My aim is not to convince people who are interested in the apparently nonphilosophical conditions of responsibility that they should go on to worry about the philosophical conditions as well, but rather to urge those who already worry about the philosophical problems not to leave the more mundane, prephilosophical problems behind. In particular, I suggest that the mundane recognition that *sanity* is a condition of

Susan Wolf, "Sanity and the Metaphysics of Responsibility," pp. 46–62 from Ferdinand David Schoeman (ed.), *Responsibility, Character and the Emotions: New Essays in Moral Psychology*. New York: Cambridge University Press, 1988. Reprinted by permission of Cambridge University Press. Reprinted by permission of the author Susan Wolf.

responsibility has more to do with the murky and apparently metaphysical problems which surround the issue of responsibility than at first meets the eye. Once the significance of the condition of sanity is fully appreciated, at least some of the apparently insuperable metaphysical aspects of the problem of responsibility will dissolve.

My strategy is to examine a recent trend in philosophical discussions of responsibility, a trend that tries, but I think ultimately fails, to give an acceptable analysis of the conditions of responsibility. It fails due to what at first appear to be deep and irresolvable metaphysical problems. It is here that I suggest that the condition of sanity comes to the rescue. What at first appears to be an impossible requirement for responsibility – the requirement that the responsible agent have created her- or himself – turns out to be the vastly more mundane and non controversial requirement that the responsible agent must, in a fairly standard sense, be sane.

Frankfurt, Watson, and Taylor

The trend I have in mind is exemplified by the writings of Harry Frankfurt, Gary Watson, and Charles Taylor. I will briefly discuss each of their separate proposals, and then offer a composite view that, while lacking the subtlety of any of the separate accounts, will highlight some important insights and some important blind spots they share.

In his seminal article "Freedom of the Will and the Concept of a Person,"[1] Harry Frankfurt notes a distinction between freedom of action and freedom of the will. A person has freedom of action, he points out, if she (or he) has the freedom to do whatever she wills to do – the freedom to walk or sit, to vote liberal or conservative, to publish a book or open a store, in accordance with her strongest desires. Even a person who has freedom of action may fail to be responsible for her actions, however, if the wants or desires she has the freedom to convert into action are themselves not subject to her control. Thus, the person who acts under post-hypnotic suggestion, the victim of brainwashing, and the kleptomaniac might all possess

freedom of action. In the standard contexts in which these examples are raised, it is assumed that none of the individuals is locked up or bound. Rather, these individuals are understood to act on what, at one level at least, must be called *their own desires*. Their exemption from responsibility stems from the fact that their own desires (or at least the ones governing their actions) are not up to them. These cases may be described in Frankfurt's terms as cases of people who possess freedom of action, but who fail to be responsible agents because they lack freedom of the will.

Philosophical problems about the conditions of responsibility naturally focus on an analysis of this latter kind of freedom: What *is* freedom of the will, and under what conditions can we reasonably be thought to possess it? Frankfurt's proposal is to understand freedom of the will by analogy to freedom of action. As freedom of action is the freedom to do whatever one wills to do, freedom of the will is the freedom to will whatever one wants to will. To make this point clearer, Frankfurt introduces a distinction between first-order and second-order desires. First-order desires are desires to do or to have various things; second-order desires are desires about what desires to have or what desires to make effective in action. In order for an agent to have both freedom of action and freedom of the will, that agent must be capable of governing his or her actions by first-order desires *and* capable of governing his or her first-order desires by second-order desires.

Gary Watson's view of free agency[2] – free and responsible agency, that is – is similar to Frankfurt's in holding that an agent is responsible for an action only if the desires expressed by that action are of a particular kind. While Frankfurt identifies the right kind of desires as desires that are supported by second-order desires, however, Watson draws a distinction between "mere" desires, so to speak, and desires that are *values*. According to Watson, the difference between free action and unfree action cannot be analyzed by reference to the logical form of the desires from which these various actions arise, but rather must relate to a difference in the quality of their source. Whereas some of my desires are just appetites or conditioned responses I find myself "stuck with," others are expressions of judgments on my part that the objects I desire are good. Insofar as my actions can be governed by the latter type of desire – governed, that is, by my values or valuational system – they are actions that I perform freely and for which I am responsible.

Frankfurt's and Watson's accounts may be under stood as alternate developments of the intuition that in order to be responsible for one's actions, one must be responsible for the self that performs these actions. Charles Taylor, in an article entitled "Responsibility for Self,"[3] is concerned with the same intuition. Although Taylor does not describe his view in terms of different levels or types of desire, his view is related, for he claims that our freedom and responsibility depend on our ability to reflect on, criticize, and revise our selves. Like Frankfurt and Watson, Taylor seems to believe that if the characters from which our actions flowed were simply and permanently *given* to us, implanted by heredity, environment, or God, then we would be mere vehicles through which the causal forces of the world traveled, no more responsible than dumb animals or young children or machines. But like the others, he points out that, for most of us, our characters and desires are not so brutely implanted – or, at any rate, if they are, they are subject to revision by our own reflecting, valuing, or second-order desiring selves. We human beings – and as far as we know, only we human beings – have the ability to step back from ourselves and decide whether we are the selves we want to be. Because of this, these philosophers think, we are responsible for our selves and for the actions that we produce.

Although there are subtle and interesting differences among the accounts of Frankfurt, Watson, and Taylor, my concern is with features of their views that are common to them all. All share the idea that responsible agency involves something more than intentional agency. All agree that if we are responsible agents, it is not just because our actions are within the control of our wills, but because, in addition, our wills are not just psychological states *in* us, but expressions of characters that come *from* us, or that at any rate are acknowledged and affirmed *by* us. For Frankfurt, this means that our wills must be ruled by our

second-order desires; for Watson, that our wills must be governable by our system of values: for Taylor, that our wills must issue from selves that are subject to self-assessment and redefinition in terms of a vocabulary of worth. In one way or another, all these philosophers seem to be saying that the key to responsibility lies in the fact that responsible agents are those for whom it is not just the case that their actions are within the control of their wills, but also the case that their wills are within the control of their *selves* in some deeper sense. Because, at one level, the differences among Frankfurt, Watson, and Taylor may be understood as differences in the analysis or interpretation of what it is for an action to be under the control of this deeper self, we may speak of their separate positions as variations of one basic view about responsibility: the *deep-self view.*

The Deep-Self View

Much more must be said about the notion of a deep self before a fully satisfactory account of this view can be given. Providing a careful, detailed analysis of that notion poses an interesting, important, and difficult task in its own right. The degree of understanding achieved by abstraction from the views of Frankfurt, Watson, and Taylor, however, should be sufficient to allow us to recognize some important virtues as well as some important drawbacks of the deep-self view.

One virtue is that this view explains a good portion of our pretheoretical intuitions about responsibility. It explains why kleptomaniacs, victims of brainwashing, and people acting under posthypnotic suggestion may not be responsible for their actions, although most of us typically are. In the cases of people in these special categories, the connection between the agents' deep selves and their wills is dramatically severed – their wills are governed not by their deep selves, but by forces external to and independent from them. A different intuition is that we adult human beings can be responsible for our actions in a way that dumb animals, infants, and machines cannot. Here the explanation is not in terms of a split between these beings' deep selves and their wills; rather, the point is that these beings *lack* deep selves altogether. Kleptomaniacs and victims of hypnosis exemplify individuals whose selves are *alienated* from their actions; lower animals and machines, on the other hand, do not have the sorts of selves from which actions *can* be alienated, and so they do not have the sort of selves from which, in the happier cases, actions can responsibly flow.

At a more theoretical level, the deep-self view has another virtue: It responds to at least one way in which the fear of determinism presents itself.

A naive reaction to the idea that everything we do is completely determined by a causal chain that extends backward beyond the times of our births involves thinking that in that case we would have no control over our behavior whatsoever. If everything is determined, it is thought, then what happens happens, whether we want it to or not. A common, and proper, response to this concern points out that determinism does not deny the causal efficacy an agent's desires might have on his or her behavior. On the contrary, determinism in its more plausible forms tends to affirm this connection, merely adding that as one's behavior is determined by one's desires, so one's desires are determined by something else.[4]

Those who were initially worried that determinism implied fatalism, however, are apt to find their fears merely transformed rather than erased. If our desires are governed by something else, they might say, they are not *really* ours after all – or, at any rate, they are ours in only a superficial sense.

The deep-self view offers an answer to this transformed fear of determinism, for it allows us to distinguish cases in which desires are determined by forces foreign to oneself from desires which are determined *by* one's self – by one's "real," or second-order desiring, or valuing, or deep self, that is. Admittedly, there are cases, like that of the kleptomaniac or the victim of hypnosis, in which the agent acts on desires that "belong to" him or her in only a superficial sense. But the proponent of the deep-self view will point out that even if determinism is true, ordinary adult human action can be distinguished from this. Determinism implies that the desires which govern our actions are in turn governed by something else, but that something else will, in the fortunate cases, be our own deeper selves.

This account of responsibility thus offers a response to our fear of determinism; but it is a response with which many will remain unsatisfied. Even if my actions are governed by my desires and my desires are governed by my own deeper self, there remains the question: Who, or what, is responsible for this deeper self? The response above seems only to have pushed the problem further back.

Admittedly, some versions of the deep-self view, including Frankfurt's and Taylor's seem to anticipate this question by providing a place for the ideal that an agent's deep self may be governed by a still deeper self. Thus, for Frankfurt, second-order desires may themselves be governed by third-order desires, third-order desires by fourth-order desires, and so on. Also, Taylor points out that, as we can reflect on and evaluate our prereflective selves, so we can reflect on and evaluate the selves who are doing the first reflecting and evaluating, and so on. However, this capacity to recursively create endless levels of depth ultimately misses the criticism's point.

First of all, even if there is no *logical* limit to the number of levels of reflection or depth a person may have, there is certainly a psychological limit – it is virtually impossible imaginatively to conceive a fourth-, much less an eighth-order, desire. More important, no matter how many levels of self we posit, there will still, in any individual case, be a last level – a deepest self about whom the question "What governs it?" will arise, as problematic as ever. If determinism is true, it implies that even if my actions are governed by my desires, and my desires are governed by my deepest self, my deepest self will still be governed by something that must, logically, be external to myself altogether. Though I can step back from the values my parents and teachers have given me and ask whether these are the values I really want, the "I" that steps back will itself be a product of the parents and teachers I am questioning.

The problem seems even worse when one sees that one fares no better if determinism is false. For if my deepest self is not determined by something external to myself, it will still not be determined by *me*. Whether I am a product of carefully controlled forces or a result of random mutations, whether there is a complete explanation of my origin or no explanation at all, *I* am not, in any case, responsible for my existence; I am not in control of my deepest self.

Thus, though the claim that an agent is responsible for only those actions that are within the control of his or her deep self correctly identifies a necessary condition for responsibility – a condition that separates the hypnotized and the brainwashed, the immature and the lower animals from ourselves, for example – it fails to provide a sufficient condition of responsibility that puts all fears of determinism to rest. For one of the fears invoked by the thought of determinism seems to be connected to its implication that we are but intermediate links in a causal chain, rather than ultimate, self-initiating sources of movement and change. From the point of view of one who has this fear, the deep-self view seems merely to add loops to the chain, complicating the picture but not really improving it. From the point of view of one who has this fear, responsibility seems to require being a prime mover unmoved, whose deepest self is itself neither random *nor* externally determined, but is rather determined *by* itself – who is, in other words, self-created.

At this point, however, proponents of the deep-self view may wonder whether this fear is legitimate. For although people evidently can be brought to the point where they feel that responsible agency requires them to be ultimate sources of power, to the point where it seems that nothing short of self-creation will do, a return to the internal standpoint of the agent whose responsibility is in question makes it hard to see what good this metaphysical status is supposed to provide or what evil its absence is supposed to impose.

From the external standpoint, which discussions of determinism and indeterminism encourage us to take up, it may appear that a special metaphysical status is required to distinguish us significantly from other members of the natural world. But proponents of the deep-self view will suggest this is an illusion that a return to the internal standpoint should dispel. The possession of a deep self that is effective in governing one's actions is a sufficient distinction, they will say. For while other members of the natural world are not in control of the selves that they are, we, possessors of effective deep selves, are in control. We can reflect on what sorts of beings we are, and on what sorts of marks we make on the world. We can change what we don't like about ourselves, and keep what we do. Admittedly, we do not create ourselves from nothing. But as long as we can revise ourselves, they will suggest, it is hard to find reason to complain. Harry Frankfurt writes that a person who is free to do what he wants to do and also free to want what he wants to want has "all the freedom it is possible to desire or to conceive."[5] This suggests a rhetorical question: If you are free to control your actions by your desires, and free to control your desires by your deeper desires, and free to control those desires by still deeper desires, what further kind of freedom can you want?

The Condition of Sanity

Unfortunately, there is a further kind of freedom we can want, which it is reasonable to think necessary for responsible agency. The deep-self view fails to be convincing when it is offered as a complete account of the conditions of responsibility. To see why, it will be helpful to consider another example of an agent whose responsibility is in question.

JoJo is the favorite son of Jo the First, an evil and sadistic dictator of a small, undeveloped country. Because of his father's special feelings for the boy, JoJo is given a special education and is allowed to accompany his father and observe his daily routine. In light of this treatment, it is not surprising that little JoJo takes his father as a role model and develops values very much like Dad's. As an adult, he does many of the same sorts of things his father did, including sending people to prison or to death or to torture chambers on the basis of whim. He is not *coerced* to do these things, he acts according to his own desires. Moreover, these are desires he wholly *wants* to have.

When he steps back and asks, "Do I really want to be this sort of person?" his answer is resoundingly "Yes," for this way of life expresses a crazy sort of power that forms part of his deepest ideal.

In light of JoJo's heritage and upbringing – both of which he was powerless to control – it is dubious at best that he should be regarded as responsible for what he does. It is unclear whether anyone with a childhood such as his could have developed into anything but the twisted and perverse sort of person that he has become. However, note that JoJo is someone whose actions are controlled by his desires and whose desires are the desires he wants to have: That is, his actions are governed by desires that are governed by and expressive of his deepest self.

The Frankfurt – Watson – Taylor strategy that allowed us to differentiate our normal selves from the victims of hypnosis and brainwashing will not allow us to differentiate ourselves from the son of Jo the First. In the case of these earlier victims, we were able to say that although the actions of these individuals were, at one level, in control of the individuals themselves, these individuals themselves, qua agents, were not the selves they more deeply wanted to be. In this respect, these people were unlike our happily more integrated selves. However, we cannot say of JoJo that his self, qua agent, is not the self he wants it to be. It *is* the self he wants it to be. From the inside, he feels as integrated, free, and responsible as we do.

Our judgment that JoJo is not a responsible agent is one that we can make only from the outside – from reflecting on the fact, it seems, that his deepest self is not up to him. Looked at from the outside, however, our situation seems no different from his – for in the last analysis, it is not up to any of us to have the deepest selves we do. Once more, the problem seems metaphysical – and not just metaphysical, but insuperable. For, as I mentioned before, the problem is independent of the truth of determinism. Whether we are determined or undetermined, we cannot have created our deepest selves. Literal self-creation is not just empirically, but logically impossible.

If JoJo is not responsible because his deepest self is not up to him, then we are not responsible either. Indeed, in that case responsibility would be impossible for anyone to achieve. But I believe the appearance that literal self-creation is required for freedom and responsibility is itself mistaken.

The deep-self view was right in pointing out that freedom and responsibility require us to have certain distinctive types of control over our behavior and our selves. Specifically, our actions need to be under the control of our selves, and our (superficial) selves need to be under the control of our deep selves. Having seen that these types of control are not enough to guarantee us the status of responsible agents, we are tempted to go on to suppose that we must have yet another kind of control to assure us that even our deepest selves are somehow up to us. But not all the things necessary for freedom and responsibility must be types of power and control. We may need simply to *be* a certain way, even though it is not within our power to determine whether we are that way or not.

Indeed, it becomes obvious that at least one condition of responsibility is of this form as soon as we remember what, in everyday contexts, we have known all along – namely, that in order to be responsible, an agent must be *sane*. It is not ordinarily in our power to determine whether we are or are not sane. Most of us, it would seem, are lucky, but some of us are not. Moreover, being sane does not necessarily mean that one has any type of power or control an insane person lacks. Some insane people, like JoJo and some actual political leaders who resemble him, may have complete control of their actions, and even complete control of their acting selves. The desire to be sane is thus not a desire for another form of control; it is rather a desire that one's self be connected to the world in a certain way – we could even say it is a desire that one's self be *controlled by* the world in certain ways and not in others.

This becomes clear if we attend to the criteria for sanity that have historically been dominant in legal questions about responsibility. According to the M'Naughten Rule, a person is sane if (1) he knows what he is doing and (2) he knows that what he is doing is, as the case may be, right or wrong. Insofar as one's desire to be sane involves a desire to know what one is doing – or more generally, a desire to live in the real world – it is a desire to be a controlled (to have, in this case, one's *beliefs* controlled) by perceptions and sound reasoning that produce an accurate conception of the world, rather than by blind or distorted forms of response. The same goes for the second constituent of sanity – only, in this case, one's hope is that one's *values* be controlled by processes that afford an accurate conception of the world.[6] Putting these two conditions together, we may understand sanity, then, as the minimally sufficient ability cognitively and normatively to recognize and appreciate the world for what it is.

There are problems with this definition of sanity, at least some of which will become obvious in what follows, that make it ultimately unacceptable either as a gloss on or an improvement of the meaning of the term in many of the contexts in which it is used. The definition offered does seem to bring out the interest sanity has for us in connection with issues of responsibility, however, and some pedagogical as well as stylistic purposes will be served if we use sanity hereafter in this admittedly specialized sense.

The Sane Deep-Self View

So far I have argued that the conditions of responsible agency offered by the deep-self view are necessary but not sufficient. Moreover, the gap left open by the deep-self view seems to be one that can be filled only by a metaphysical, and, as it happens, metaphysically impossible addition. I now wish to argue, however, that the condition of sanity, as characterized above, is sufficient to fill the gap. In other words, the deep-self view, supplemented by the condition of sanity, provides a satisfying conception of responsibility. The conception of responsibility I am proposing, then, agrees with the deep-self view in requiring that a responsible agent be able to govern her (or his) actions by her desires and to govern her desires by her deep self. In addition, my conception insists that the agent's deep self be sane, and claims that this is *all* that is needed for responsible agency. By contrast to the plain deep-self view, let us call this new proposal the *sane deep-self view*.

It is worth noting, to begin with, that this new proposal deals with the case of JoJo and related cases of deprived childhood victims in ways that better match our pretheoretical intuitions. Unlike the plain deep-self view, the sane deep-self view offers a way of explaining why JoJo is not responsible for his actions without throwing our own responsibility into doubt. For, although like us, JoJo's actions flow from desires that flow from his deep self, unlike us, JoJo's deep self is itself insane. Sanity, remember, involves the ability to know the difference between right and wrong, and a person who, even on reflection, cannot see that having someone tortured because he failed to salute you is wrong plainly lacks the requisite ability.

Less obviously, but quite analogously, this new proposal explains why we give less than full responsibility to persons who, though acting badly, act in ways that are strongly encouraged by their societies – the slaveowners of the 1850s, the Nazis of the 1930s, and many male chauvinists of our fathers' generation, for example. These are people, we imagine, who falsely believe that the ways in which they are acting are morally acceptable, and so, we may assume, their behavior is expressive of or at least in accordance with these agents' deep selves. But their false beliefs in the moral permissibility of their actions and the false values from which these beliefs derived may have been inevitable, given the social circumstances in which they developed. If we think that the agents could not help but be mistaken about their values, we do not blame them for the actions those values inspired?[7]

It would unduly distort ordinary linguistic practice to call the slaveowner, the Nazi, or the male chauvinist even partially or locally insane. Nonetheless, the reason for withholding blame from them is at bottom the same as the reason for withholding it from JoJo. Like JoJo, they are, at the deepest level, unable cognitively and normatively to recognize and appreciate the world for what it is. In our sense of the term, their deepest selves are not fully *sane*.

The sane deep-self view thus offers an account of why victims of deprived childhoods as well as victims of misguided societies may not be responsible for their actions, without implying that we are not responsible for ours.

The actions of these others are governed by mistaken conceptions of value that the agents in question cannot help but have. Since, as far as we know, our values are not, like theirs, unavoidably mistaken, the fact that these others are not responsible for their actions need not force us to conclude that we are not responsible for ours.

But it may not yet be clear why sanity, in this special sense, should make such a difference – why, in particular, the question of whether someone's values are unavoidably *mistaken* should have any bearing on their status as responsible agents. The fact that the sane deep-self view implies judgments that match our intuitions about the difference in status between characters like JoJo and ourselves provides little support for it if it cannot also defend these intuitions. So we must consider an objection that comes from the point of view we considered earlier which rejects the intuition that a relevant difference can be found.

Earlier, it seemed that the reason JoJo was not responsible for his actions was that although his actions were governed by his deep self, his deep self was not up to him. But this had nothing to do with his deep self's being mistaken or not mistaken, evil or good, insane or sane. If JoJo's values are unavoidably mistaken, our values, even if not mistaken, appear to be just as unavoidable. When it comes to freedom and responsibility, isn't it the unavoidability, rather than the mistakenness, that matters?

Before answering this question, it is useful to point out a way in which it is ambiguous: The concepts of avoidability and mistakenness are not unequivocally distinct. One may, to be sure, construe the notion of avoidability in a purely meta-physical way. Whether an event or state of affairs is unavoidable under this construal depends, as it were, on the tightness of the causal connections that bear on the event's or state of affairs' coming about. In this sense, our deep selves do seem as unavoidable for us as JoJo's and the others' are for them. For presumably we are just as influenced by our parents, our cultures, and our schooling as they are influenced by theirs. In another sense, however, our characters are not similarly unavoidable.

In particular, in the cases of JoJo and the others, there are certain features of their characters that they cannot avoid *even though these features are seriously mistaken, misguided, or bad.* This is so because, in our special sense of the term, these characters are less than fully sane. Since these characters lack the ability to know right from wrong, they are unable to revise their characters on the basis of right and wrong, and so their deep selves lack the resources and the reasons that might have served as a basis for self-correction. Since the deep selves *we* unavoidably have, however, are sane deep selves – deep selves, that is, that unavoidably *contain* the ability to know right from wrong – we unavoidably do have the resources and reasons on which to base self-correction. What this means is that though in one sense we are no more in control of our deepest selves than JoJo et al., it does not follow in our case, as it does in theirs, that we would be the way we are, even if it is a bad or wrong way to be. However, if this does not follow, it seems to me, our absence of control at the deepest level should not upset us.

Consider what the absence of control at the deepest level amounts to for us: Whereas JoJo is unable to control the fact that, at the deepest level, he is not fully sane, we are not responsible for the fact that, at the deepest level, we are. It is not up to us to *have* minimally sufficient abilities cognitively and normatively to recognize and appreciate the world for what it is. Also, presumably, it is not up to us to have lots of other properties, at least to begin with – a fondness for purple, perhaps, or an antipathy for beets. As the proponents of the plain deep-self view have been at pains to point out, however, we do, if we are lucky, have the ability to revise our selves in terms of the values that are held by or constitutive of our deep selves. If we are lucky enough both to have this ability and to have our deep selves be sane, it follows that although there is much in our characters that we did not choose to have, there is nothing irrational or objectionable in our characters that we are compelled to keep.

Being sane, we are able to understand and evaluate our characters in a reasonable way, to notice what there is reason to hold on to, what there is reason to eliminate, and what, from a rational and reasonable standpoint, we may retain or get rid of as we please. Being able as well to govern our superficial selves by our deep selves, then, we are able to change the things we find there is reason to change. This being so, it seems that although we may not be *metaphysically* responsible for ourselves – for, after all, we did not create ourselves from nothing – we are *morally* responsible for ourselves, for we are able to understand and appreciate right and wrong, and to change our characters and our actions accordingly.

Self-Creation, Self-Revision, and Self-Correction

At the beginning of this chapter, I claimed that recalling that sanity was a condition of responsibility would dissolve at least some of the appearance that responsibility was metaphysically impossible. To see how this is so, and to get a fuller sense of the sane deep-self view, it may be helpful to put that view into perspective by comparing it to the other views we have discussed along the way.

As Frankfurt, Watson, and Taylor showed us, in order to be free and responsible we need not only to be able to control our actions in accordance with our desires, we need to be able to control our desires in accordance with our deepest selves. We need, in other words, to be able to *revise* ourselves – to get rid of some desires and traits, and perhaps replace them with others on the basis of our deeper desires or values or reflections. However, consideration of the fact that the selves who are doing the revising might themselves be either brute products of external forces or arbitrary outputs of random generation made us wonder whether the capacity for self-revision was enough to assure us of responsibility – and the example of JoJo added force to the suspicion that it was not. Still, if the ability to revise ourselves is not enough, the ability to create ourselves does not seem necessary either. Indeed, when you think of it, it is unclear why anyone should want self-creation. Why should anyone be disappointed at having to accept the idea that one has to get one's start somewhere? It is an idea that most of us have lived with

quite contentedly all along. What we do have reason to want, then, is something more than the ability to revise ourselves, but less than the ability to create ourselves. Implicit in the sane deep-self view is the idea that what is needed is the ability to *correct* (or improve) ourselves.

Recognizing that in order to be responsible for our actions, we have to be responsible for our selves, the sane deep-self view analyzes what is necessary in order to be responsible for our selves as (1) the ability to evaluate ourselves sensibly and accurately, and (2) the ability to transform ourselves insofar as our evaluation tells us to do so. We may understand the exercise of these abilities as a process whereby we *take* responsibility for the selves that we are but did not ultimately create. The condition of sanity is intrinsically connected to the first ability; the condition that we able to control our superficial selves by our deep selves is intrinsically connected to the second.

The difference between the plain deep-self view and the sane deep-self view, then, is the difference between the requirement of the capacity for self-revision and the requirement of the capacity for self-correction. Anyone with the first capacity can *try* to take responsibility for himself or herself. However, only someone with a sane deep self – a deep self that can see and appreciate the world for what it is – can self-evaluate sensibly and accurately. Therefore, although insane selves can try to take responsibility for themselves, only sane selves will properly be accorded responsibility.

Two Objections Considered

At least two problems with the sane deep-self view are so glaring as to have certainly struck many readers. In closing, I shall briefly address them. First, some will be wondering how, in light of my specialized use of the term "sanity," I can be so sure that "we" are any saner than the nonresponsible individuals I have discussed. What justifies my confidence that, unlike the slaveowners, Nazis, and male chauvinists, not to mention JoJo himself, we are able to understand and appreciate the world for what it is? The answer to this is that nothing justifies this except widespread intersubjective agreement and the considerable success we have in getting around in the world and satisfying our needs. These are not sufficient grounds for the smug assumption that we are in a position to see the truth about *all* aspects of ethical and social life. Indeed, it seems more reasonable to expect that time will reveal blind spots in our cognitive and normative outlook, just as it has revealed errors in the outlooks of those who have lived before. But our judgments of responsibility can only be made from here, on the basis of the understandings and values that we can develop by exercising the abilities we do possess as well and as fully as possible.

If some have been worried that my view implicitly expresses an overconfidence in the assumption that we are sane and therefore right about the world, others will be worried that my view too closely connects sanity with being right about the world, and fear that my view implies that anyone who acts wrongly or has false beliefs about the world is therefore insane and so not responsible for his or her actions. This seems to me to be a more serious worry, which I am sure I cannot answer to everyone's satisfaction.

First, it must be admitted that the sane deep-self view embraces a conception of sanity that is explicitly normative. But this seems to me a strength of that view, rather than a defect. Sanity *is* a normative concept, in its ordinary as well as in its specialized sense, and severely deviant behavior, such as that of a serial murderer of a sadistic dictator, does constitute evidence of a psychological defect in the agent. The suggestion that the most horrendous, stomach-turning crimes could be committed only by an insane person – an inverse of Catch-22, as it were – must be regarded as a serious possibility, despite the practical problems that would accompany general acceptance of that conclusion.

But, it will be objected, there is no justification, in the sane deep-self view, for regarding only horrendous and stomach-turning crimes as evidence of insanity in its specialized sense. If sanity is the ability cognitively and normatively to understand and appreciate the world for what it is, then *any* wrong action or false

belief will count as evidence of the absence of that ability. This point may also be granted, but we must be careful about what conclusion to draw. To be sure, when someone acts in a way that is not in accordance with acceptable standards of rationality and reasonableness, it is always appropriate to look for an explanation of why he or she acted that way. The hypothesis that the person was unable to understand and appreciate that an action fell outside acceptable bound will always be a possible explanation. Bad performance on a math test always suggests the possibility that the testee is stupid. Typically, however, other explanations will be possible, too – for example, that the agent was too lazy to consider whether his or her action was acceptable, or too greedy to care, or, in the case of the math testee, that he or she was too occupied with other interests to attend class or study. Other facts about the agent's history will help us decide among these hypotheses.

This brings out the need to emphasize that sanity, in the specialized sense, is defined as the *ability* cognitively and normatively to understand and appreciate the world for what it is. According to our commonsense understandings, having this ability is one thing and exercising it is another – at least some wrong-acting, responsible agents presumably fall within the gap. The notion of "ability" is notoriously problematic, however, and there is a long history of controversy about whether the truth of determinism would show our ordinary ways of thinking to be simply confused on this matter. At this point, then, metaphysical concerns may voice themselves again – but at least they will have been pushed into a narrower, and perhaps a more manageable, corner.

The sane deep-self view does not, then, solve all the philosophical problems connected to the topics of free will and responsibility. If anything, it highlights some of the practical and empirical problems, rather than solves them. It may, however, resolve some of the philosophical, and particularly, some of the metaphysical problems, and reveal how intimate are the connections between the remaining philosophical problems and the practical ones.

Notes

1. Harry Frankfurt, "Freedom of the Will and the Concept of a Person," *Journal of Philosophy* LXVIII (1971), 5–20.

2. Gary Watson, "Free Agency," *Journal of Philosophy* LXXII (1975), 205–20.

3. Charles Taylor, "Responsibility for Self," in A. E. Rorty, ed., *The Identities of Persons* (Berkeley: University of California Press, 1976), pp. 381–99.

4. See, e.g., David Hume. *A Treatise of Human Nature* (Oxford: Oxford University Press, 1967), pp. 399–406, and R. E. Hobart, "Free Will as Involving Determination and Inconceivable Without It," *Mind* 43 (1934).

5. Frankfurt, p. 16.

6. Strictly speaking, perception and sound reasoning may not be enough to ensure the ability to achieve an accurate conception of what one is doing and especially to achieve a reasonable normative assessment of one's situation. Sensitivity and exposure to certain realms of experience may also be necessary for these goals. For the purpose of this essay, I understand "sanity" to include whatever it takes to enable one to develop an adequate conception of one's world. In other contexts, however, this would be an implausibly broad construction of the term.

7. Admittedly, it is open to question whether these individuals were in fact unable to help having mistaken values, and indeed, whether recognizing the errors of their society would even have required exceptional independence or strength of mind. This is presumably an empirical question, the answer to which is extraordinarily hard to determine. My point here is simply that *if* we believe they are unable to recognize that their values are mistaken, we do not hold them responsible for the actions that flow from these values, and *if* we believe their ability to recognize their normative errors is impaired, we hold them less than fully responsible for relevant actions.

CHAPTER 41

Freedom and Resentment

PETER STRAWSON

I

Some philosophers say they do not know what the thesis of determinism is. Others say, or imply, that they do know what it is. Of these, some – the pessimists perhaps – hold that if the thesis is true, then the concepts of moral obligation and responsibility really have no application, and the practices of punishing and blaming, of expressing moral condemnation and approval, are really unjustified. Others – the optimists perhaps – hold that these concepts and practices in no way lose their *raison d'être* if the thesis of determinism is true. Some hold even that the justification of these concepts and practices requires the truth of the thesis. There is another opinion which is less frequently voiced: the opinion, it might be said, of the genuine moral sceptic. This is that the notions of moral guilt, of blame, of moral responsibility are inherently confused and that we can see this to be so if we consider the consequences either of the truth of determinism or of its falsity. The holders of this opinion agree with the pessimists that these notions lack application if determinism is true, and add simply that they also lack it if determinism is false. If I am asked which of

these parties I belong to, I must say it is the first of all, the party of those who do not know what the thesis of determinism is. But this does not stop me from having some sympathy with the others, and a wish to reconcile them. Should not ignorance, rationally, inhibit such sympathies? Well, of course, though darkling, one has some inkling – some notion of what sort of thing is being talked about. This lecture is intended as a move towards reconciliation; so is likely to seem wrongheaded to everyone.

But can there be any possibility of reconciliation between such clearly opposed positions as those of pessimists and optimists about determinism? Well, there might be a formal withdrawal on one side in return for a substantial concession on the other. Thus, suppose the optimist's position were put like this: (1) the facts as we know them do not show determinism to be false; (2) the facts as we know them supply an adequate basis for the concepts and practices which the pessimist feels to be imperilled by the possibility of determinism's truth. Now it might be that the optimist is right in this, but is apt to give an inadequate account of the facts as we know them, and of how they constitute an adequate basis for the problematic concepts and practices; that the reasons he gives for the adequacy of the basis are themselves inadequate and leave out something vital. It might be that the pessimist is rightly anxious to get this vital thing back

Peter Strawson, "Freedom and Resentment," pp. 1–25 from *Proceedings of the British Academy*, 48, 1962.

and, in the grip of his anxiety, feels he has to go beyond the facts as we know them; feels that the vital thing can be secure only if, beyond the facts as we know them, there is the further fact that determinism is false. Might *he* not be brought to make a formal withdrawal in return for a vital concession?

II

Let me enlarge very briefly on this, by way of preliminary only. Some optimists about determinism point to the efficacy of the practices of punishment, and of moral condemnation and approval, in regulating behaviour in socially desirable ways.[1] In the fact of their efficacy, they suggest, is an adequate basis for these practices; and this fact certainly does not show determinism to be false. To this the pessimists reply, all in a rush, that *just* punishment and *moral* condemnation imply moral guilt and guilt implies moral responsibility and moral responsibility implies freedom and freedom implies the falsity of determinism. And to this the optimists are wont to reply in turn that it is true that these practices require freedom in a sense, and the existence of freedom in this sense is one of the facts as we know them. But what "freedom" means here is nothing but the absence of certain conditions the presence of which would make moral condemnation or punishment inappropriate. They have in mind conditions like compulsion by another, or innate incapacity, or insanity, or other less extreme forms of psychological disorder, or the existence of circumstances in which the making of any other choice would be morally inadmissible or would be too much to expect of any man. To this list they are constrained to add other factors which, without exactly being limitations of freedom, may also make moral condemnation or punishment inappropriate or mitigate their force: as some forms of ignorance, mistake, or accident. And the general reason why moral condemnation or punishment are inappropriate when these factors or conditions are present is held to be that the practices in question will be generally efficacious means of regulating behaviour in desirable ways only in cases where these factors are

not present. Now the pessimist admits that the facts as we know them include the existence of freedom, the occurrence of cases of free action, in the negative sense which the optimist concedes; and admits, or rather insists, that the existence of freedom in this sense is compatible with the truth of determinism. Then what does the pessimist find missing? When he tries to answer this question, his language is apt to alternate between the very familiar and the very unfamiliar.[2] Thus he may say, familiarly enough, that the man who is the subject of justified punishment, blame or moral condemnation must really *deserve* it; and then add, perhaps, that, in the case at least where he is blamed for a positive act rather than an omission, the condition of his really deserving blame is something that goes beyond the negative freedoms that the optimist concedes. It is, say, a genuinely free identification of the will with the act. And this is the condition that is incompatible with the truth of determinism.

The conventional, but conciliatory, optimist need not give up yet. He may say: Well, people often decide to do things, really intend to do what they do, know just what they're doing in doing it; the reasons they think they have for doing what they do, often really are their reasons and not their rationalizations. These facts, too, are included in the facts as we know them. If this is what you mean by freedom – by the identification of the will with the act – then freedom may again be conceded. But again the concession is compatible with the truth of the determinist thesis. For it would not follow from that thesis that nobody decides to do anything; that nobody ever does anything intentionally; that it is false that people sometimes know perfectly well what they are doing. I tried to define freedom negatively. You want to give it a more positive look. But it comes to the same thing. Nobody denies freedom in this sense, or these senses, and nobody claims that the existence of freedom in these senses shows determinism to be false.

But it is here that the lacuna in the optimistic story can be made to show. For the pessimist may be supposed to ask: But *why* does freedom in this sense justify blame, etc.? You turn towards me first the negative, and then the positive, faces of a freedom which nobody challenges. But the only reason you have given for the practices of moral condemnation and punishment in cases where this freedom is present is the efficacy of these practices in regulating behaviour in socially desirable ways. But this is not a sufficient basis, it is not even the right *sort* of basis, for these practices as we understand them.

Now my optimist, being the sort of man he is, is not likely to invoke an intuition of fittingness at this point. So he really has no more to say. And my pessimist, being the sort of man he is, has only one more thing to say; and that is that the admissibility of these practices, as we understand them, demands another kind of freedom, the kind that in turn demands the falsity of the thesis of determinism. But might we not induce the pessimist to give up saying this by giving the optimist something more to say?

III

I have mentioned punishing and moral condemnation and approval; and it is in connection with these practices or attitudes that the issue between optimists and pessimists – or, if one is a pessimist, the issue between determinists and libertarians – is felt to be particularly important. But it is not of these practices and attitudes that I propose, at first, to speak. These practices or attitudes permit, where they do not imply, a certain detachment from the actions or agents which are their objects. I want to speak, at least at first, of something else: of the non-detached attitudes and reactions of people directly involved in transactions with each other; of the attitudes and reactions of offended parties and beneficiaries; of such things as gratitude, resentment, forgiveness, love, and hurt feelings. Perhaps something like the issue between optimists and pessimists arises in this neighbouring field too; and since this field is less crowded with disputants, the issue might here be easier to settle; and if it is settled here, then it might become easier to settle it in the disputant-crowded field.

What I have to say consists largely of commonplaces. So my language, like that of commonplace generally, will be quite unscientific and imprecise. The central commonplace that I want to insist on is the very great importance that we attach to the attitudes and intentions towards us of other human beings, and the great extent to which our personal feelings and reactions depend upon, or involve, our beliefs about these attitudes and intentions. I can give no simple description of the field of phenomena at the centre of which stands this commonplace truth; for the field is too complex. Much imaginative literature is devoted to exploring its complexities; and we have a large vocabulary for the purpose. There are simplifying styles of handling it in a general way. Thus we may, like La Rochefoucauld, put self-love or self-esteem or vanity at the centre of the picture and point out how it may be caressed by the esteem, or wounded by the indifference or contempt, of others. We might speak, in another jargon, of the need for love, and the loss of security which results from its withdrawal; or, in another, of human self-respect and its connection with the recognition of the individual's dignity. These simplifications are of use to me only if they help to emphasize how much we actually mind, how much it matters to us, whether the actions of other people – and particularly of *some* other people – reflect attitudes towards us of goodwill, affection, or esteem on the one hand or contempt, indifference, or malevolence on the other. If someone treads on my hand accidentally, while trying to help me, the pain may be no less acute than if he treads on it in contemptuous disregard of my existence or with a malevolent wish to injure me. But I shall generally feel in the second case a kind and degree of resentment that I shall not feel in the first. If someone's actions help me to some benefit I desire, than I am benefited in any case; but if he intended them so to benefit me because of his general goodwill towards me, I shall reasonably feel a gratitude which I should not feel at all if the benefit was an incidental consequence, unintended or even regretted by him, of some plan of action with a different aim.

These examples are of actions which confer benefits or inflict injuries over and above any conferred or inflicted by the mere manifestation of attitude and intention themselves. We should consider also in how much of our behaviour the benefit or injury resides mainly or entirely in the manifestation of attitude itself. So it is with good manners, and much of what we call kindness, on the one hand; with deliberate rudeness, studied indifference, or insult on the other.

Besides resentment and gratitude, I mentioned just now forgiveness. This is a rather unfashionable subject in moral philosophy at present; but to be forgiven is something we sometimes ask, and forgiving is something we sometimes say we do. To ask to be forgiven is in part to acknowledge that the attitude displayed in our actions was such as might properly be resented and in part to repudiate that attitude for the future (or at least for the immediate future); and to forgive is to accept the repudiation and to forswear the resentment.

We should think of the many different kinds of relationship which we can have with other people – as sharers of a common interest; as members of the same family; as colleagues; as friends; as lovers; as chance parties to an enormous range of transactions and encounters. Then we should think, in each of these connections in turn, and in others, of the kind of importance we attach to the attitudes and intentions towards us of those who stand in these relationships to us, and of the kinds of *reactive* attitudes and feelings to which we ourselves are prone. In general, we demand some degree of goodwill or regard on the part of those who stand in these relationships to us, though the forms we require it to take vary widely in different connections. The range and intensity of our *reactive* attitudes towards goodwill, its absence or its opposite vary no less widely. I have mentioned, specifically, resentment and gratitude; and they are a usefully opposed pair. But, of course, there is a whole continuum of reactive attitude and feeling stretching on both sides of these and – the most comfortable area – in between them.

The object of these commonplaces is to try to keep before our minds something it is easy to forget when we are engaged in philosophy, especially in our cool, contemporary style, viz. what it is actually like to be involved in ordinary inter-personal relationships, ranging from the most intimate to the most casual.

IV

It is one thing to ask about the general causes of these reactive attitudes I have alluded to; it is another to ask about the variations to which they are subject, the particular conditions in which they do or do not seem natural or reasonable or appropriate; and it is a third thing to ask what it would be like, what it *is* like, not to suffer them. I am not much concerned with the first question; but I am with the second; and perhaps even more with the third.

Let us consider, then, occasions for resentment: situations in which one person is offended or injured by the action of another and in which – in the absence of special considerations – the offended person might naturally or normally be expected to feel resentment. Then let us consider what sorts of special considerations might be expected to modify or mollify this feeling or remove it altogether. It needs no saying now how multifarious these considerations are. But, for my purpose, I think they can be roughly divided into two kinds. To the first group belong all those which might give occasion for the employment of such expressions as 'He didn't mean to', 'He hadn't realized', 'He didn't know'; and also all those which might give occasion for the use of the phrase 'He couldn't help it', when this is supported by such phrases as 'He was pushed', 'He had to do it', 'It was the only way', 'They left him no alternative', etc. Obviously these various pleas, and the kinds of situations in which they would be appropriate, differ from each other in striking and important ways. But for my present purpose they have something still more important in common. None of them invites us to suspend towards the agent, either at the time of his action or in general, our ordinary reactive attitudes. They do not invite us to view the *agent* as one in respect of whom these attitudes are in any way inappropriate. They invite us to view the *injury* as one in respect of whom a particular one of these attitudes is inappropriate. They do not invite us to see the *agent* as other than a fully responsible agent. They invite us to see the *injury* as one for which he was not fully, or at all, responsible. They do not suggest that the agent is in any way an inappropriate object of that kind of demand for goodwill or regard which is reflected in our ordinary reactive attitudes. They suggest instead that the fact of injury was not in this case incompatible with that demand's being fulfilled, that the fact of injury was quite consistent with the agent's attitude and intentions being just what we demand they should be.[3] The agent was just ignorant of the injury he was causing, or had lost his balance through being pushed or had reluctantly to cause the injury for reasons which acceptably override his reluctance. The offering of such pleas by the agent and their acceptance by the sufferer is something in no way opposed to, or outside the context of, ordinary interpersonal relationships and the manifestation of ordinary reactive attitudes. Since things go wrong and situations are complicated, it is an essential and integral element in the transactions which are the life of these relationships.

The second group of considerations is very different. I shall take them in two sub-groups of which the first is far less important than the second. In connection with the first sub-group we may think of such statements as 'He wasn't himself', 'He has been under very great strain recently', 'He was acting under post-hypnotic suggestion'; in connection with the second, we may think of 'He's only a child', 'He's a hopeless schizophrenic', 'His mind has been systematically perverted', 'That's purely compulsive behaviour on his part'. Such pleas as these do, as pleas of my first general group do not, invite us to suspend our ordinary reactive attitudes towards the agent, either at the time of his action or all the time. They do not invite us to see the agent's action in a way consistent with the full retention of ordinary inter-personal attitudes and merely inconsistent with one particular attitude. They invite us to view the agent himself in a different light from the light in which we should normally view one who has acted as he has acted. I shall not linger over the first subgroup of cases. Though they perhaps raise, in the short term, questions akin to those raised, in the long term, by the second subgroup, we may dismiss them without considering those questions by taking that admirably suggestive phrase, 'He wasn't himself', with the seriousness that – for all its being

logically comic – it deserves. We shall not feel resentment against the man he is for the action done by the man he is not; or at least we shall feel less. We normally have to deal with him under normal stresses; so we shall not feel towards him, when he acts as he does under abnormal stresses, as we should have felt towards him had he acted as he did under normal stresses.

The second and more important subgroup of cases allows that the circumstances were normal, but presents the agent as psychologically abnormal – or as morally undeveloped. The agent was himself; but he is warped or deranged, neurotic or just a child. When we see someone in such a light as this, all our reactive attitudes tend to be profoundly modified. I must deal here in crude dichotomies and ignore the ever-interesting and everilluminating varieties of case. What I want to contrast is the attitude (or range of attitudes) of involvement or participation in a human relationship, on the one hand, and what might be called the objective attitude (or range of attitudes) to another human being, on the other. Even in the same situation, I must add, they are not altogether *exclusive* of each other; but they are, profoundly, *opposed* to each other. To adopt the objective attitude to another human being is to see him, perhaps, as an object of social policy; as a subject for what, in a wide range of sense, might be called treatment; as something certainly to be taken account, perhaps precautionary account, of; to be managed or handled or cured or trained; perhaps simply to be avoided, though *this* gerundive is not peculiar to cases of objectivity of attitude. The objective attitude may be emotionally toned in many ways, but not in all ways: it may include repulsion or fear, it may include pity or even love, though not all kinds of love. But it cannot include the range of reactive feelings and attitudes which belong to involvement or participation with others in inter-personal human relationships; it cannot include resentment, gratitude, forgiveness, anger, or the sort of love which two adults can sometimes be said to feel reciprocally, for each other. If your attitude towards someone is wholly objective, then though you may fight him, you cannot quarrel with him, and though you may talk to him, even negotiate with him, you cannot reason with him. You can at most pretend to quarrel, or to reason, with him.

Seeing someone, then, as warped or deranged or compulsive in behaviour or peculiarly unfortunate in his formative circumstances – seeing someone so tends, at least to some extent, to set him apart from normal participant reactive attitudes on the part of one who sees him, tends to promote, at least in the civilized, objective attitudes. But there is something curious to add to this. The objective attitude is not only something we naturally tend to fall into in cases like these, where participant attitudes are partially or wholly inhibited by abnormalities or by immaturity. It is also something which is available as a resource in other cases too. We look with an objective eye on the compulsive behaviour of the neurotic or the tiresome behaviour of a very young child, thinking in terms of treatment or training. But we *can* sometimes look with something like the same eye on the behaviour of the normal and the mature. We *have* this resource and can sometimes use it: as a refuge, say, from the strains of involvement; or as an aid to policy; or simply out of intellectual curiosity. Being human, we cannot, in the normal case, do this for long, or altogether. If the strains of involvement, say, continue to be too great, then we have to do something else – like severing a relationship. But what is above all interesting is the tension there is, in us, between the participant attitude and the objective attitude. One is tempted to say: between our humanity and our intelligence. But to say this would be to distort both notions.

What I have called the participant reactive attitudes are essentially natural human reactions to the good or ill will or indifference of others towards us, as displayed in *their* attitudes and actions. The question we have to ask is: What effect would, or should, the acceptance of the truth of a general thesis of determinism have upon these reactive attitudes? More specifically, would, or should, the acceptance of the truth of the thesis lead to the decay or the repudiation of all such attitudes? Would, or should, it mean the end of gratitude, resentment, and forgiveness; of all reciprocated adult loves; of all the essentially *personal* antagonisms?

But how can I answer, or even pose, this question without knowing *exactly* what the thesis of determinism is? Well, there is one thing we do know: that if there is a coherent thesis of determinism, then there must be a sense of 'determined' such that, if that thesis is true, then all behaviour whatever is determined in that sense. Remembering this, we can consider at least what possibilities lie formally open; and then perhaps we shall see that the question can be answered *without* knowing exactly what the thesis of determinism is. We can consider what possibilities lie open because we have already before us an account of the ways in which particular reactive attitudes, or reactive attitudes in general, may be, and, sometimes, we judge, should be, inhibited. Thus I considered earlier a group of considerations which tend to inhibit, and, we judge, should inhibit, resentment, in particular cases of an agent causing an injury, without inhibiting reactive attitudes in general towards that agent. Obviously this group of considerations cannot strictly bear upon our question; for that question concerns reactive attitudes in general. But resentment has a particular interest; so it is worth adding that it has never been claimed as a consequence of the truth of determinism that one or another of *these* considerations was operative in every case of an injury being caused by an agent; that it would follow from the truth of determinism that anyone who caused an injury *either* was quite simply ignorant of causing it *or* had acceptably overriding reasons for acquiescing reluctantly in causing it *or . . .* , etc. The prevalence of this happy state of affairs would not be a consequence of the reign of universal determinism, but of the reign of universal goodwill. We cannot, then, find here the possibility of an affirmative answer to our question, even for the particular case of resentment.

Next, I remarked that the participant attitude, and the personal reactive attitudes in general, tend to give place, and, it is judged by the civilized, should give place, to objective attitudes, just in so far as the agent is seen as excluded from ordinary adult human relationships by deep-rooted psychological abnormality – or simply by being a child. But it cannot be a consequence of any thesis which is not itself self-contradictory that abnormality is the universal condition.

Now this dismissal might seem altogether too facile; and so, in a sense, it is. But whatever is too quickly dismissed in this dismissal is allowed for in the only possible form of affirmative answer that remains. We can sometimes, and in part, I have remarked, look on the normal (those we rate as 'normal') in the objective way in which we have learned to look on certain classified cases of abnormality. And our question reduces to this: could, or should, the acceptance of the determinist thesis lead us always to look on everyone exclusively in this way? For this is the only condition worth considering under which the acceptance of determinism could lead to the decay or repudiation of participant reactive attitudes.

It does not seem to be self-contradictory to suppose that this might happen. So I suppose we must say that it is not absolutely inconceivable that it should happen. But I am strongly inclined to think that it is, for us as we are, practically inconceivable. The human commitment to participation in ordinary inter-personal relationships is, I think, too thoroughgoing and deeply rooted for us to take seriously the thought that a general theoretical conviction might so change our world that, in it, there were no longer any such things as inter-personal relationships as we normally understand them; and being involved in inter-personal relationships as we normally understand them precisely is being exposed to the range of reactive attitudes and feelings that is in question.

This, then, is a part of the reply to our question. A sustained objectivity of inter-personal attitude, and the human isolation which that would entail, does not seem to be something of which human beings would be capable, even if some general truth were a theoretical ground for it. But this is not all. There is a further point, implicit in the foregoing, which must be made explicit. Exceptionally, I have said, we can have direct dealings with human beings without any degree of personal involvement, treating them simply as creatures to be handled in our own interests, or our side's, or society's – or even theirs. In the extreme case of the mentally deranged, it is easy

to see the connection between the possibility of a wholly objective attitude and the impossibility of what we understand by ordinary inter-personal relationships. Given this latter impossibility, no other civilized attitude is available than that of viewing the deranged person simply as something to be understood and controlled in the most desirable fashion. To view him as outside the reach of personal relationships is already, for the civilized, to view him in this way. For reasons of policy or self-protection we may have occasion, perhaps temporary, to adopt a fundamentally similar attitude to a 'normal' human being; to concentrate, that is, on understanding 'how he works', with a view to determining our policy accordingly or to finding in that very understanding a relief from the strains of involvement. Now it is certainly true that in the case of the abnormal, though not in the case of the normal, our adoption of the objective attitude is a consequence of our viewing the agent as *incapacitated* in some or all respects for ordinary interpersonal relationships. He is thus incapacitated, perhaps, by the fact that his picture of reality is pure fantasy, that he does not, in a sense, live in the real world at all; or by the fact that his behaviour is, in part, an unrealistic acting out of unconscious purposes; or by the fact that he is an idiot, or a moral idiot. But there is something else which, *because* this is true, is equally certainly *not* true. And that is that there is a sense of 'determined' such that (1) if determinism is true, all behaviour is determined in this sense, and (2) determinism might be true, i.e. it is not inconsistent with the facts as we know them to suppose that all behaviour might be determined in this sense, and (3) our adoption of the objective attitude towards the abnormal is the result of prior embracing of the belief that the behaviour, or the relevant stretch of behaviour, of the human being in question *is* determined in this sense. Neither in the case of the normal, then, nor in the case of the abnormal is it true that, when we adopt an objective attitude, we do so *because* we hold such a belief. So my answer has two parts. The first is that we cannot, as we are, seriously envisage ourselves adopting a thoroughgoing objectivity of attitude to others as a result of theoretical conviction of the truth of determinism; and the second is that when we do in fact adopt such an attitude in a particular case, our doing so is not the consequence of a theoretical conviction which might be expressed as 'Determinism in this case', but is a consequence of our abandoning, for different reasons in different cases, the ordinary inter-personal attitudes.

It might be said that all this leaves the real question unanswered, and that we cannot hope to answer it without knowing exactly what the thesis of determinism is. For the real question is not a question about what we actually do, or why we do it. It is not even a question about what we would *in fact* do if a certain theoretical conviction gained general acceptance. It is a question about what it would be *rational* to do if determinism were true, a question about the rational justification of ordinary inter-personal attitudes in general. To this I shall reply, first, that such a question could seem real only to one who had utterly failed to grasp the purport of the preceding answer, the fact of our natural human commitment to ordinary interpersonal attitudes. This commitment is part of the general framework of human life, not something that can come up for review as particular cases can come up for review within this general framework. And I shall reply, second, that if we could imagine what we cannot have, viz. a choice in this matter, then we could choose rationally only in the light of an assessment of the gains and losses to human life, its enrichment or impoverishment; and the truth or falsity of a general thesis of determinism would not bear on the rationality of *this* choice.[4]

V

The point of this discussion of the reactive attitudes in their relation – or lack of it – to the thesis of determinism was to bring us, if possible, nearer to a position of compromise in a more usual area of debate. We are not now to discuss reactive attitudes which are essentially those of offended parties or beneficiaries. We are to discuss reactive attitudes which are essentially not those, or only incidentally are those, of offended parties or beneficiaries, but are nevertheless, I shall claim, kindred attitudes to those I have discussed. I put resentment in the centre of the previous discussion. I shall put moral indignation – or, more weakly, moral disapprobation – in the centre of this one.

The reactive attitudes I have so far discussed are essentially reactions to the quality of others' wills towards us, as manifested in their behaviour: to their good or ill will or indifference or lack of concern. Thus resentment, or what I have called resentment, is a reaction to injury or indifference. The reactive attitudes I have now to discuss might be described as the sympathetic or vicarious or impersonal or disinterested or generalized analogues of the reactive attitudes I have already discussed. They are reactions to the qualities of others' wills, not towards ourselves, but towards others. Because of this impersonal or vicarious character, we give them different names. Thus one who experiences the vicarious analogue of resentment is said to be indignant or disapproving, or morally indignant or disapproving. What we have here is, as it were, resentment on behalf of another, where one's own interest and dignity are not involved; and it is this impersonal or vicarious character of the attitude, added to its others, which entitle it to the qualification "moral". Both my description of, and my name for, these attitudes are, in one important respect, a little misleading. It is not that these attitudes are essentially vicarious – one can feel indignation on one's own account – but that they are essentially capable of being vicarious. But I shall retain the name for the sake of its suggestiveness; and I hope that what is misleading about it will be corrected in what follows.

The personal reactive attitudes rest on, and reflect, an expectation of, and demand for, the manifestation of a certain degree of goodwill or regard on the part of other human beings towards ourselves; or at least on the expectation of, and demand for, an absence of the manifestation of active ill will or indifferent disregard. (What will, in particular cases, *count* as manifestations of good or ill will or disregard will vary in accordance with the particular relationship in which we stand to another human being.) The generalized or vicarious analogues of the personal reactive attitudes rest on, and reflect, exactly the same expectation or demand in a generalized form; they rest on, or reflect, that is, the demand for the manifestation of a reasonable degree of goodwill or regard, on the part of others, not simply towards oneself, but towards all those on whose behalf moral indignation may be felt, i.e. as we now think, towards all men. The generalized and non-generalized forms of demand, and the vicarious and personal reactive attitudes which rest upon, and reflect, them are connected not merely logically. They are connected humanly; and not merely with each other. They are connected also with yet another set of attitudes which I must mention now in order to complete the picture. I have considered from two points of view the demands we make on others and our reactions to their possibly injurious actions. These were the points of view of one whose interest was directly involved (who suffers, say, the injury) and of others whose interest was not directly involved (who do not themselves suffer the injury). Thus I have spoken of personal reactive attitudes in the first connection and of their vicarious analogues in the second. But the picture is not complete unless we consider also the correlates of these attitudes on the part of those on whom the demands are made, on the part of the agents. Just as there are personal and vicarious reactive attitudes associated with demands on others for oneself and demands on others for others, so there are self-reactive attitudes associated with demands on oneself for others. And here we have to mention such phenomena as feeling bound or obliged (the "sense of obligation"); feeling compunction; feeling guilty or remorseful or at least responsible; and the more complicated phenomenon of shame.

All these three types of attitude are humanly connected. One who manifested the personal reactive attitudes in a high degree but showed no inclination at all to their vicarious analogues would appear as an abnormal case of moral egocentricity, as a kind of moral solipsist. Let him be supposed fully to acknowledge the claims to regard that others had on him, to be susceptible of the whole range of self-reactive attitudes. He would then see himself as unique both as one (*the* one) who had a general claim on human regard and as one (*the* one) on whom

human beings in general had such a claim. This would be a kind of moral solipsism. But it is barely more than a conceptual possibility; if it is that. In general, though within varying limits, we demand of others for others, as well as of ourselves for others, something of the regard which we demand of others for ourselves. Can we imagine, besides that of the moral solipsist, any other case of one or two of these three types of attitude being fully developed, but quite unaccompanied by any trace, however slight, of the remaining two or one? If we can, then we imagine something far below or far above the level of our common humanity – a moral idiot or a saint. For all these types of attitude alike have common roots in our human nature and our membership of human communities.

[. . .]

What concerns us now is to inquire, as previously in connection with the personal reactive attitudes, what relevance any general thesis of determinism might have to their vicarious analogues. The answers once more are parallel; though I shall take them in a slightly different order. First, we must note, as before, that when the suspension of such an attitude or such attitudes occurs in a particular case, it is *never* the consequence of the belief that the piece of behaviour in question was determined in a sense such that all behaviour *might be*, and, if determinism is true, all behaviour *is*, determined in that sense. For it is not a consequence of any general thesis of determinism which might be true that nobody knows what he's doing or that everybody's behaviour is unintelligible in terms of conscious purposes or that everybody lives in a world of delusion or that nobody has a moral sense, i.e. is susceptible of self-reactive attitudes, etc. In fact no such sense of 'determined' as would be required for a general thesis of determinism is ever relevant to our actual suspensions of moral reactive attitudes. Second, suppose it granted, as I have already argued, that we cannot take seriously the thought that theoretical conviction of such a general thesis would lead to the total decay of the personal reactive attitudes. Can we then take seriously the thought that such a conviction – a conviction, after all, that many have held or said they held – would nevertheless lead to the total decay or repudiation of the vicarious analogues of these attitudes? I think that the change in our social world which would leave us exposed to the personal reactive attitudes but not all to their vicarious analogues, the generalization of abnormal ego-centricity which this would entail, is perhaps even harder for us to envisage as a real possibility than the decay of both kinds of attitude together. Though there are some necessary and some contingent differences between the ways and cases in which these two kinds of attitudes operate or are inhibited in their operation, yet, as general human capacities or pronenesses, they stand or lapse together. Finally, to the further question whether it would not be *rational*, given a general theoretical conviction of the truth of determinism, so to change our world that in it all these attitudes were wholly suspended, I must answer, as before, that one who presses this question has wholly failed to grasp the import of the preceding answer, the nature of the human commitment that is here involved: it is *useless* to ask whether it would not be rational for us to do what it is not in our nature to (be able to) do. To this I must add, as before, that if there were, say, for a moment open to us the possibility of such a godlike choice, the rationality of making or refusing it would be determined by quite other consider-ations than the truth or falsity of the general theoretical doctrine in question. The latter would be simply irrelevant; and this becomes ironically clear when we remember that for those convinced that the truth of determinism nevertheless really would make the one choice rational, there has always been the insuperable difficulty of explaining in intelligible terms how its falsity would make the opposite choice rational.

I am aware that in presenting the argument as I have done, neglecting the ever-interesting varieties of case, I have presented nothing more than a schema, using sometimes a crude opposition of phrase where we have a great intricacy of phenomena. In particular the sim-ple opposition of objective attitudes on the one hand and the various contrasted attitudes which I have opposed to them must seem as grossly crude as it is central. Let me pause to mitigate this crudity a little, and also to strengthen one of my central contentions, by

mentioning some things which straddle these contrasted kinds of attitude. Thus parents and others concerned with the care and upbringing of young children cannot have to their charges either kind of attitude in a pure or unqualified form. They are dealing with creatures who are potentially and increasingly capable both of holding, and being objects of, the full range of human and moral attitudes, but are not yet truly capable of either. The treatment of such creatures must therefore represent a kind of compromise, constantly shifting in one direc-tion, between objectivity of attitude and devel-oped human attitudes. Rehearsals insensibly modulate towards true performances. The punishment of a child is both like and unlike the punishment of an adult. Suppose we try to relate this progressive emergence of the child as a responsible being, as an object of non-objective attitudes, to that sense of 'determined' in which, if determinism is a possibly true thesis, all behaviour *may* be determined, and in which, if it is a true thesis, all behaviour *is* determined. What bearing *could* such a sense of "determined" have upon the progressive modification of attitudes towards the child? Would it not be grotesque to think of the development of the child as a progressive or patchy emergence from an area in which its behaviour is in this sense determined into an area in which it isn't? Whatever sense of 'determined' is required for stating the thesis of determinism, it can scarcely be such as to allow of compromise, borderline-style answers to the question, 'Is this bit of behaviour deter-mined or isn't it?' But in this matter of young children, it is essentially a borderline, penum-bral area that we move in. Again, consider – a very different matter – the strain in the attitude of a psychoanalyst to his patient. *His* objectiv-ity of attitude, *his* suspension of ordinary moral reactive attitudes, is profoundly modi-fied by the fact that the aim of the enterprise is to make such suspension unnecessary or less necessary. Here we may and do naturally speak of restoring the agent's freedom. But here the restoring of freedom means bringing it about that the agent's behaviour shall be intelligible in terms of conscious purposes rather than in terms only of unconscious purposes. *This* is the object of the enterprise; and it is in so far as *this* object is attained that the suspension, or half-suspension, of ordinary moral attitudes is deemed no longer necessary or appropriate. And in this we see once again the *irrelevance* of that concept of 'being determined' which must be the central concept of determinism. For we cannot both agree that this object is attainable and that its attainment has this consequence and yet hold (1) that neurotic behaviour is determined in a sense in which, it may be, all behaviour is determined, and (2) that it is because neurotic behaviour is determined in this sense that objective attitudes are deemed appropriate to neurotic behaviour. Not, at least, without accusing ourselves of incoherence in our attitude to psychoanalytic treatment.

VI

And now we can try to fill in the lacuna which the pessimist finds in the optimist's account of the concept of moral responsibility, and of the bases of moral condemnation and punishment; and to fill it in from the facts as we know them. For, as I have already remarked, when the pessimist himself seeks to fill it in, he rushes beyond the facts as we know them and proclaims that it cannot be filled in at all unless determinism is false.

Yet a partial sense of the facts as we know them is certainly present to the pessimist's mind. When his opponent, the optimist, undertakes to show that the truth of determinism would not shake the foundations of the concept of moral responsibility and of the practices of moral condemnation and punishment, he typically refers, in a more or less elaborated way, to the efficacy of these practices in regulating behaviour in socially desirable ways. These practices are represented solely as instruments of policy, as methods of individual treatment and social control. The pessimist recoils from this picture; and in his recoil there is, typically, an element of emotional shock. He is apt to say, among much else, that the humanity of the offender himself is offended by *this* picture of his condemnation and punishment.

The reasons for this recoil – the explanation of the sense of an emotional, as well as a conceptual, shock – we have already before us. The picture painted by the optimists is painted in a style appropriate to a situation envisaged as wholly dominated by objectivity of attitude. The only operative notions invoked in this picture are such as those of policy, treatment, control. But a thoroughgoing objectivity of attitude, excluding as it does the moral reactive attitudes, excludes at the same time essential elements in the concepts of *moral* condemnation and *moral* responsibility. This is the reason for the conceptual shock. The deeper emotional shock is a reaction, not simply to an inadequate conceptual analysis, but to the suggestion of a change in our world. I have remarked that it is possible to cultivate an exclusive objectivity of attitude in some cases, and for some reasons, where the object of the attitude is not set aside from developed interpersonal and moral attitudes by immaturity or abnormality. And the suggestion which seems to be contained in the optimist's account is that such an attitude should be universally adopted to all offenders. This is shocking enough in the pessimist's eyes. But, sharpened by shock, his eyes see further. It would be hard to make *this* division in our natures. If to all offenders, then to all mankind. Moreover, to whom could this recommendation be, in any real sense, addressed? Only to the powerful, the authorities. So abysses seem to open.[5]

But we will confine our attention to the case of the offenders. The concepts we are concerned with are those of responsibility and guilt, qualified as 'moral', on the one hand – together with that of membership of a moral community; of demand, indignation, disapprobation and condemnation, qualified as 'moral', on the other hand – together with that of punishment. Indignation, disapprobation, like resentment, tend to inhibit or at least to limit our goodwill towards the object of these attitudes, tend to promote an at least partial and temporary withdrawal of goodwill; they do so in proportion as they are strong; and their strength is in general proportioned to what is felt to be the magnitude of the injury and to the degree to which the agent's will is identified with, or indifferent to, it. (These, of course, are not contingent connections.) But these attitudes of disapprobation and indignation are precisely the correlates of the moral demand in the case where the demand is felt to be disregarded. The making of the demand *is* the proneness to such attitudes. The holding of them does not, as the holding of objective attitudes does, involve as a part of itself viewing their object other than as a member of the moral community. The partial withdrawal of goodwill which *these* attitudes entail, the modification *they* entail of the general demand that another should, if possible, be spared suffering, is, rather, the consequence of *continuing* to view him as a member of the moral community; only as one who has offended against its demands. So the preparedness to acquiesce in that infliction of suffering on the offender which is an essential part of punishment is all of a piece with this whole range of attitudes of which I have been speaking. It is not only moral reactive attitudes towards the offender which are in question here. We must mention also the self-reactive attitudes of offenders themselves. Just as the other-reactive attitudes are associated with a readiness to acquiesce in the infliction of suffering on an offender, within the 'institution' of punishment, so the self-reactive attitudes are associated with a readiness on the part of the offender to acquiesce in such infliction *without* developing the reactions (e.g. of resentment) which he would normally develop to the infliction of injury upon him; i.e. with a readiness, as we say, to accept punishment[6] as 'his due' or as 'just'.

I am not in the least suggesting that these readinesses to acquiesce, either on the part of the offender himself or on the part of others, are always or commonly accompanied or preceded by indignant boilings or remorseful pangs; only that we have here a continuum of attitudes and feelings to which these readinesses to acquiesce themselves belong. Nor am I in the least suggesting that it belongs to this continuum of attitudes that we should be ready to acquiesce in the infliction of injury on offenders in a fashion which we saw to be quite indiscriminate or in accordance with procedures which we knew to be wholly useless. On the contrary, savage or civilized, we have some belief in the utility of practices of condemnation and punishment. But the social utility of these practices, on which the optimist lays such exclusive stress, is not what is now in question. What is in question is the pessimist's justified sense that to speak in terms of social utility alone is to leave out something vital in our conception of these practices. The vital thing can be restored by attending to that complicated web of attitudes and feelings which form an essential part of the moral life as we know it, and which are quite opposed to objectivity of attitude. Only by attending to this range of attitudes can we recover from the facts as we know them a sense of what we mean, i.e. of *all* we mean, when, speaking the language of morals, we speak of desert, responsibility, guilt, condemnation, and justice. But we *do* recover it from the facts as we know them. We do not have to go beyond them. Because the optimist neglects or misconstrues these attitudes, the pessimist rightly claims to find a lacuna in his account. We can fill the lacuna for him. But in return we must demand of the pessimist a surrender of his metaphysics.

Optimist and pessimist misconstrue the facts in very different styles. But in a profound sense there is something in common to their misunderstandings. Both seek, in different ways, to overintellectualize the facts. Inside the general structure or web of human attitudes and feelings of which I have been speaking, there is endless room for modification, redirection, criticism, and justification. But questions of justification are internal to the structure or relate to modifications internal to it. The existence of the general framework of attitudes itself is something we are given with the fact of human society. As a whole, it neither calls for, nor permits, an external 'rational' justification. Pessimist and optimist alike show themselves, in different ways, unable to accept this.[7] The optimist's style of over-intellectualizing the facts is that of a characteristically incomplete empiricism, a one-eyed utilitarianism. He seeks to find an adequate basis for certain social practices in calculated consequences, and loses sight (perhaps wishes to lose sight) of the human attitudes of which these practices are, in part, the expression. The pessimist does not lose sight of these attitudes, but is unable to accept the fact that it is just these attitudes themselves which fill the gap in the optimist's account. Because of this, he thinks the gap can be filled only if some general metaphysical proposition is repeatedly verified, verified in all cases where it is appropriate to attribute moral responsibility. This proposition he finds it as difficult to state coherently and with intelligible relevance as its determinist contradictory. Even when a formula has been found ('contra-causal freedom' or something of the kind) there still seems to remain a gap between its applicability in particular cases and its supposed moral consequences. Sometimes he plugs this gap with an intuition of fittingness – a pitiful intellectualist trinket for a philosopher to wear as a charm against the recognition of his own humanity.

Even the moral sceptic is not immune from his own form of the wish to over-intellectualize such notions as those of moral responsibility, guilt, and blame. He sees that the optimist's account is inadequate and the pessimist's libertarian alternative inane; and finds no resource except to declare that the notions in question are inherently confused, that 'blame is metaphysical'. But the metaphysics was in the eye of the metaphysician. It is a pity that talk of the moral sentiments has fallen out of favour. The phrase would be quite a good name for that network of human attitudes in acknowledging the character and place of which we find, I suggest, the only possibility of reconciling these disputants to each other and the facts.

There are, at present, factors which add, in a slightly paradoxical way, to the difficulty of making this acknowledgement. These human attitudes themselves, in their development and in the variety of their manifestations, have to an increasing extent become objects of study in the social and psychological sciences; and this growth of human self-consciousness, which we might expect to reduce the difficulty of acceptance, in fact increases it in several ways. One factor of comparatively minor importance is an increased historical and anthropological awareness of the great variety of forms which these human attitudes may take at different times and in different cultures. This makes one rightly chary of claiming as essential features of the concept of morality in general, forms of these attitudes which may have a local and temporary prominence. No doubt to some extent my own descriptions of human attitudes have reflected local and temporary features of our own culture. But an awareness of variety of forms should not prevent us from acknowledging also that in the absence of *any* forms of these attitudes it is doubtful whether we should have anything that *we* could find intelligible as a system of human relationships, as human society. A quite different factor of greater importance is that psychological studies have made us rightly mistrustful of many particular manifestations of the attitudes I have spoken of. They are a prime realm of self-deception, of the ambiguous and the shady, of guilt-transference, unconscious sadism and the rest. But it is an exaggerated horror, itself suspect, which would make us unable to acknowledge the facts because of the seamy side of the facts. Finally, perhaps the most important factor of all is the prestige of these theoretical studies themselves. That prestige is great, and is apt to make us forget that in philosophy, though it also is a theoretical study, we have to take account of the facts in *all* their bearings; we are not to suppose that we are required, or permitted, as philosophers, to regard ourselves, as human beings, as detached from the attitudes which, as scientists, we study with detachment. This is in no way to deny the possibility and desirability of redirection and modification of our human attitudes in the light of these studies. But we may reasonably think it unlikely that our progressively greater understanding of certain aspects of ourselves will lead to the total disappearance of those aspects. Perhaps it is not inconceivable that it should; and perhaps, then, the dreams of some philosophers will be realized.

If we sufficiently, that is *radically*, modify the view of the optimist, his view is the right one. It is far from wrong to emphasize the efficacy of all those practices which express or manifest our moral attitudes, in regulating behaviour in ways considered desirable; or to add that when certain of our beliefs about the efficacy of some of these practices turns out to be false, then we may have good reason for dropping or modifying those practices. What *is* wrong is to forget that these practices, and their reception, the reactions to them, really *are* expressions of our moral attitudes and not merely devices we calculatingly employ for regulative purposes. Our practices do not merely exploit our natures, they express them. Indeed the very understanding of the kind of efficacy these expressions of our attitudes have turns on our remembering this. When we do remember this, and modify the optimist's position accordingly, we simultaneously correct its conceptual deficiencies and ward off the dangers it seems to entail, without recourse to the obscure and panicky metaphysics of libertarianism.

Notes

1. Cf. P. H. Nowell-Smith, 'Freewill and Moral Responsibility', *Mind*, 1948.
2. As Nowell-Smith pointed out in a later article: 'Determinists and Libertarians', *Mind*, 1954.
3. Perhaps not in every case *just* what we demand they should be, but in any case *not* just what we demand they should not be. For my present purpose these differences do not matter.
4. The question, then, of the connection between rationality and the adoption of the objective attitude to others is misposed when it is made to seem dependent on the issue of determinism. But there is another question which should be raised, if only to distinguish it from the misposed question. Quite apart from the issue of determinism might it not be said that we should be nearer to being purely rational creatures in proportion as our relation to others was in fact dominated by the objective attitude? I think this might be said; only it would have to be added, once more, that if such a choice were possible, it would not necessarily be rational to choose to be more purely rational than we are.
5. See J. D. Mabbott's 'Freewill and Punishment', in *Contemporary British Philosophy*, 3rd ser. (London: Allen & Unwin, 1956).
6. Of course not *any* punishment for *anything* deemed an offence.
7. Compare the question of the justification of induction. The human commitment to inductive belief-formation is original, natural, non-rational (not *ir*rational), in no way something we choose or could give up. Yet rational criticism and reflection can refine standards and their application, supply 'rules for judging of cause and effect'. Ever since the facts were made clear by Hume, people have been resisting acceptance of them.

PART VII
Moral Standing

Introduction to Part VII

Factory farming practices in North America and Europe are often extremely cruel. Farm animals are frequently confined in terribly cramped quarters, are separated from their mothers well before they would otherwise become independent, and are often killed in a process that is both painful and filled with terror for the animals that must undergo it. Is there anything immoral about such practices?

Answering this question forces us to consider the moral standing of nonhuman animals. Something's moral standing is its intrinsic moral importance – its ability to impose moral demands on others just by virtue of its own nature. A person, or animal, or ecosystem, has moral standing provided that we must respect it even when doing so might only thwart our purposes and interests.

Immanuel Kant had a way of demarcating the scope of the moral community, i.e., distinguishing those who do, from those who don't, possess moral standing. Kant thought that the line was formed by reference to a being's autonomy and rationality. If someone possesses both features – both the ability to form goals free of external influence, and the ability to reason appropriately about the implications of one's goals – then, and only then, is the person a member of the moral community. Such people have moral rights, and these rights explain why others have duties *to* them – duties to respect their property, for instance, and duties not to interfere with their harmless projects.

Contrast the status of us persons with that of a nonhuman animal. For Kant, such animals lack moral standing. They have no rights, for they lack both autonomy and rationality. Still, Kant does not believe that we are permitted to treat animals in just any way we like. Even though my watch has no moral standing, you are not permitted to just pick it up and smash it to pieces. You have a duty *to* me (since I possess rights), *regarding* my watch (which doesn't). So even though pets, for instance, have no rights, one isn't allowed to steal and kill them, for in doing so, the perpetrator is wronging a human being.

But what of animals who roam the wild – is it permissible to treat them in just any way we please? Kant says no, since such behavior will make us more likely to treat our fellow human beings, who do possess rights, in the same way. But this is a weak argument. By prohibiting such action on the basis of its likely bad results, this rationale is unavailable to the Kantian. (Much more on this in Part IX). And it in any event assumes that we are unable to draw relevant distinctions between our treatment of those who (on Kantian grounds) are within the moral community, and those without. People who mistreat animals are often respectful of their fellow human beings. If we took Kant's view to heart, we'd see nothing intrinsically wrong with torturing animals, but plenty that is intrinsically wrong with treating our fellow human beings that way. On the assumption that we could carry this distinction over to our actions, and conform our behavior to Kantian principles, then those who hurt animals would not be likelier to mistreat humans. In that case, Kant has no argument against such behavior. That is because, for him, animals have no moral standing.

Peter Singer will have none of this. Singer follows Jeremy Bentham, the first philosopher to offer a highly developed account of Utilitarianism, in thinking that the essential feature that determines moral standing is *sentience*. Strictly speaking, sentience is the capacity to have sense experience – experience that is derived from taste, sight, hearing, etc. But in the context of the present debates, sentience refers to the capacity to experience pleasure and pain. According to Singer, a being has moral importance in its own right if, and only if, it is sentient. Rationality and autonomy do not determine the scope of the moral community. Neither does anything else. Throughout the history of civilization many criteria have been put forward to decide matters of moral standing. In addition to rationality and autonomy, thinkers have proposed such criteria as linguistic ability, having a range of emotions, intelligence, communicative ability, having a soul, and being a member of the human species. None of these criteria is acceptable, according to Singer. Indeed, he focuses especially on this last standard, and argues that species membership is in itself irrelevant to moral standing. Those who think otherwise are, to his mind, guilty of a prejudice – *speciesism* – that is, in all essentials, morally equivalent to racism and sexism.

Singer offers a master argument for forcing us to reconsider our views about the moral standing of nonhuman animals:

1. If it is wrong to prematurely kill, eat and experiment upon severely brain damaged human orphans, then it is wrong to prematurely kill, eat and experiment upon nonhuman animals.
2. It is almost always wrong to prematurely kill, eat and experiment upon severely brain damaged human orphans.

3. Therefore it is almost always wrong to prematurely kill, eat and experiment upon nonhuman animals.

The first premise is the contentious one. Singer claims that both animals and brain damaged human infants are equally sentient, and possessed of identical interests. In that case, argues Singer, there is no plausible basis for assigning greater moral importance to one over the other. If one denies this, and thinks that the human is morally more important than the nonhuman animal, then one must defend a criterion of moral standing that will generate that result. Singer does not believe that this can be successfully done. He thinks that any candidates other than sentience are bound to exclude from the moral community those we would like to see within it. If we consider the short but influential list, above, we can see that human infants, or the severely mentally retarded, either lack the relevant features (linguistic ability, intelligence, etc.), or possess them in no greater degree than animals do. If that is so, then it seems that we must regard the human and the nonhuman as morally on a par with one another. Giving moral priority to the one over the other would be an unjustified form of discrimination.

Singer's emphasis on sentience allows him to draw a principled line that has humans and other animals on one side, and plants and inanimate objects on the other. We can act immorally *towards* plants – say, by stealing them, or destroying them if they belong to others – but we cannot wrong a plant. Plants lack moral standing – they possess no intrinsic moral importance. And so we have no duties to them.

Joel Feinberg agrees with Singer's conclusion here, but offers a different basis for it. According to Feinberg, beings are eligible to possess rights only if they have interests. Without interests, a thing can have no good of its own, no well-being. And, says Feinberg, interests require conative ability – the ability to want, desire, and hope for things. Since humans and animals possess such abilities, they also possess interests. There is a way that their lives can go better or worse for them. These interests are capable of being protected, which is what rights do. Those things that lack interests – individual plants, species of plants, ecosystems, and first trimester fetuses – lack moral standing, as they have no conative life. Such things have no interests, and hence no rights, since there is nothing for such rights to protect.

Feinberg thinks that interests play this crucial role in the determination of moral standing for two reasons. First, a right holder must be capable of being represented, and it is impossible to represent a being that has no interests. Second, a right holder must be capable of being benefited, and only beings with interests can be benefited.

Kenneth Goodpaster finds something attractive in Feinberg's claim that moral standing presupposes the possession of interests. Yet Goodpaster denies that interests require conation. There is a legitimate sense in which plants, for instance, have interests. Their lives can go better or worse – they can flourish, or do poorly and decline. To insist that interests require the possession of a mental life is to beg the question against those, such as Goodpaster, who would seek to expand the scope of the moral community. Goodpaster's vision of this scope is the broadest of all of our authors. He ultimately endorses what he calls a *life principle*, which assigns intrinsic moral importance to all living things. This would allow us to exclude paradigmatic instances of things that lack moral standing (e.g., chairs, rocks, and hammers), while enfranchising even such things as shellfish, insects, and plants.

Are fetuses within the scope of the moral community? Do they count for nearly nothing, as the philosopher Mary Anne Warren has written – likening their moral status to that of newborn guppies?[1] Michael Tooley, in his selection here, takes this line, basing it on what he calls the *self-consciousness requirement*. This is the view that a being has a serious right to life only if it has a self-conception, regarding itself as an entity that persists through time. Since fetuses lack such a self-conception, they lack a serious right to life.

We can employ an oft-used distinction from this literature – that between persons, who are rights-holders, and humans, who are defined by species membership. It follows, on Tooley's view, that not all humans are persons. Most are. But fetuses aren't – they are humans, but not persons. Conversely, some nonhuman animals may possess the requisite self-conception, and so, according to Tooley, may qualify as persons. If they do, then many of our current animal husbandry and experimentation practices amount to murder.

True, infants, the temporarily comatose, and some severely retarded adult human beings also lack such a self-conception. It follows that these groups of human beings are also non-persons – they also lack a serious right to life. Yet their lacking a right to life does not automatically license our mistreatment of them. There might be good reason to treat a non-person with respect, though the reason cannot stem from a moral requirement to honor its right to life (since non-persons do not, by Tooley's lights, possess any such right). By denying personhood to infants and the severely mentally retarded, as well as to fetuses, we make the preservation of their lives contingent on their bearing some special relation to persons.

At the other end of the spectrum, some philosophers have argued that a fetus, from conception, possesses the same moral standing as you or I. On this view, fetuses at any stage of gestation are full-fledged persons. Most writers who favor such a view do so because of religious commitments. But Don Marquis, who here defends this position, crafts his argument in a way that is entirely free of religious claims.

Marquis thinks that we can sidestep the exceedingly difficult question of the proper criteria for personhood, and ask instead about the ultimate reason for thinking that killing an acknowledged person is immoral. The answer, he thinks, is that in perpetrating such an act, one is depriving the victim of a future of value – a future in which the victim would come to value the activities, experiences and relations available to him were he still alive. Not everyone has a future of value – some people, for instance, are terminally ill and face the prospect of only a miserable remaining amount of time before their death. But most human beings do possess a future of value, and so, in almost all cases, it would be immoral to kill our fellow human beings. And that tallies nicely with what we already believe.

However, most fetuses also possess a future of value. Some do not – some, for instance, are born without brains, or are born with incredibly debilitating illnesses that promise a life of only misery. But these are the exceptions, not the rule. If Marquis has correctly identified the wrong-making feature of ordinary killing, then it follows that, in most cases, it is as immoral to perform or submit to an abortion as it is to perform or abet the murder of an adult human being.

The questions of moral standing are highly complex and remain quite controversial. Though a number of philosophers, including many represented in this section, have tried to provide solutions to these questions by offering fairly self-standing views, others have sought to answer such questions within the context of a developed, coherent normative ethical theory. A developed normative ethic will, among many other things, identify the crucial features needed for moral standing. To give just one example:

Hobbesian contractarians (whose views receive much fuller treatment in Part X) have a principled account of why the moral community should be limited to those who can credibly threaten to withhold benefits from others, unless these others renounce violence and offer cooperation. Since we can gain any benefit we'd like from fetuses, infants, and nonhuman animals, without having to offer any promise of nonviolence or cooperation on our part, it follows on this account that such vulnerable beings lack intrinsic moral importance, and are excluded from the moral community.

This of course is only one of many possible views about moral standing. Its plausibility depends on that of the larger normative ethic that frames it. The remainder of this book is devoted to these more comprehensive ethical views, and readers are encouraged to pursue our current questions within the context of the more detailed normative ethical offerings that follow.

Note

1. "On the Moral and Legal Status of Abortion," *The Monist*, 57 (1973).

CHAPTER 42
We Have No Duties to Animals

IMMANUEL KANT

Baumgarten speaks of duties towards beings which are beneath us and beings which are above us. But so far as animals are concerned, we have no direct duties. Animals are not self-conscious and are there merely as a means to an end. That end is man. We can ask, "Why do animals exist?" But to ask, "Why does man exist?" is a meaningless question. Our duties towards animals are merely indirect duties towards humanity. Animal nature has analogies to human nature, and by doing our duties to animals in respect of manifestations which correspond to manifestations of human nature, we indirectly do our duty towards humanity. Thus, if a dog has served his master long and faithfully, his service, on the analogy of human service, deserves reward, and when the dog has grown too old to serve, his master ought to keep him until he dies. Such action helps to support us in our duties towards human beings, where they are bounden duties. If then any acts of animals are analogous to human acts and spring from the same principles, we have duties towards the animals because thus we cultivate the corresponding duties towards human beings. If a man shoots his dog because the animal is no longer capable of service, he does not fail in his duty to the dog, for the dog cannot judge, but his act is inhuman and damages in himself that humanity which it is his duty to show towards mankind. If he is not to stifle his human feelings, he must practice kindness towards animals, for he who is cruel to animals becomes hard also in his dealings with men. We can judge the heart of a man by his treatment of animals. Hogarth depicts this in his engravings. He shows how cruelty grows and develops. He shows the child's cruelty to animals, pinching the tail of a dog or a cat; he then depicts the grown man in his cart running over a child; and lastly, the culmination of cruelty in murder. He thus brings home to us in a terrible fashion the rewards of cruelty, and this should be an impressive lesson to children. The more we come in contact with animals and observe their behaviour, the more we love them, for we see how great is their care for their young. It is then difficult for us to be cruel in thought even to a wolf. Leibnitz used a tiny worm for purposes of observation, and then carefully replaced it with its leaf on the tree so that it should not come to harm through any act of his. He would have been sorry – a natural feeling for a humane man – to destroy such a creature for no reason. Tender feelings towards dumb animals develop humane feelings toward mankind. In England butchers and doctors do not sit on a jury

Immanuel Kant, "We Have No Duties to Animals," pp. 239–41 from *Lectures on Ethics*, trans. Louis Infield. London: Methuen Press, 1930.

because they are accustomed to the sight of death and hardened. Vivisectionists, who use living animals for their experiments, certainly act cruelly, although their aim is praiseworthy, and they can justify their cruelty, since animals must be regarded as man's instruments; but any such cruelty for sport cannot be justified. A master who turns out his ass or his dog because the animal can no longer earn its keep manifests a small mind. The Greeks' ideas in this respect were high-minded, as can be seen from the fable of the ass and the bell of ingratitude. Our duties towards animals, then, are indirect duties towards mankind.

CHAPTER 43

All Animals are Equal

PETER SINGER

"Animal liberation" may sound more like a parody of other liberation movements than a serious objective. The idea of "The Rights of Animals" actually was once used to parody the case for women's rights. When Mary Wollstonecraft, a forerunner of today's feminists, published her *Vindication of the Rights of Woman* in 1792, her views were widely regarded as absurd, and before long an anonymous publication appeared entitled *A Vindication of the Rights of Brutes*. The author of this satirical work (now known to have been Thomas Taylor, a distinguished Cambridge philosopher) tried to refute Mary Wollstonecraft's arguments by showing that they could be carried one stage further. If the argument for equality was sound when applied to women, why should it not be applied to dogs, cats, and horses? The reasoning seemed to hold for these "brutes" too; yet to hold that brutes had rights was manifestly absurd. Therefore the reasoning by which this conclusion had been reached must be unsound, and if unsound when applied to brutes, it must also be unsound when applied to women, since the very same arguments had been used in each case.

In order to explain the basis of the case for the equality of animals, it will be helpful to start with an examination of the case for the equality of women. Let us assume that we wish to defend the case for women's rights against the attack by Thomas Taylor. How should we reply?

One way in which we might reply is by saying that the case for equality between men and women cannot validly be extended to nonhuman animals. Women have a right to vote, for instance, because they are just as capable of making rational decisions about the future as men are; dogs, on the other hand, are incapable of understanding the significance of voting, so they cannot have the right to vote. There are many other obvious ways in which men and women resemble each other closely, while humans and animals differ greatly. So, it might be said, men and women are similar beings and should have similar rights, while humans and nonhumans are different and should not have equal rights.

The reasoning behind this reply to Taylor's analogy is correct up to a point, but it does not go far enough. There are obviously important differences between humans and other animals, and these differences must give rise to some differences in the rights that each have. Recognizing this evident fact, however, is no barrier to the case for extending the basic principle of equality to nonhuman animals. The differences

Peter Singer, "All Animals Are Equal," pp. 1–21 from *Animal Liberation*, Second Edition. New York: Ecco Press, 1990.

that exist between men and women are equally undeniable, and the supporters of Women's Liberation are aware that these differences may give rise to different rights. Many feminists hold that women have the right to an abortion on request. It does not follow that since these same feminists are campaigning for equality between men and women they must support the right of men to have abortions too. Since a man cannot have an abortion, it is meaningless to talk of his right to have one. Since dogs can't vote, it is meaningless to talk of their right to vote. There is no reason why either Women's Liberation or Animal Liberation should get involved in such nonsense. The extension of the basic principle of equality from one group to another does not imply that we must treat both groups in exactly the same way, or grant exactly the same rights to both groups. Whether we should do so will depend on the nature of the members of the two groups. The basic principle of equality does not require equal or identical *treatment*; it requires equal consideration. Equal consideration for different beings may lead to different treatment and different rights.

So there is a different way of replying to Taylor's attempt to parody the case for women's rights, a way that does not deny the obvious differences between human beings and nonhumans but goes more deeply into the question of equality and concludes by finding nothing absurd in the idea that the basic principle of equality applies to so-called brutes. At this point such a conclusion may appear odd; but if we examine more deeply the basis on which our opposition to discrimination on grounds of race or sex ultimately rests, we will see that we would be on shaky ground if we were to demand equality for blacks, women, and other groups of oppressed humans while denying equal consideration to non-humans. To make this clear we need to see, first, exactly why racism and sexism are wrong. When we say that all human beings, whatever their race, creed, or sex, are equal, what is it that we are asserting? Those who wish to defend hierarchical, inegalitarian societies have often pointed out that by whatever test we choose it simply is not true that all humans are equal. Like it or not we must face the fact that humans come in

different shapes and sizes; they come with different moral capacities, different intellectual abilities, different amounts of benevolent feeling and sensitivity to the needs of others, different abilities to communicate effectively, and different capacities to experience pleasure and pain. In short, if the demand for equality were based on the actual equality of all human beings, we would have to stop demanding equality.

Still, one might cling to the view that the demand for equality among human beings is based on the actual equality of the different races and sexes. Although, it may be said, humans differ as individuals, there are no differences between the races and sexes as such. From the mere fact that a person is black or a woman we cannot infer anything about that person's intellectual or moral capacities. This, it may be said, is why racism and sexism are wrong. The white racist claims that whites are superior to blacks, but this is false; although there are differences among individuals, some blacks are superior to some whites in all of the capacities and abilities that could conceivably be relevant. The opponent of sexism would say the same: a person's sex is no guide to his or her abilities, and this is why it is unjustifiable to discriminate on the basis of sex.

The existence of individual variations that cut across the lines of race or sex, however, provides us with no defense at all against a more sophisticated opponent of equality, one who proposes that, say, the interests of all those with IQ scores below 100 be given less consideration than the interests of those with ratings over 100. Perhaps those scoring below the mark would, in this society, be made the slaves of those scoring higher. Would a hierarchical society of this sort really be so much better than one based on race or sex? I think not. But if we tie the moral principle of equality to the factual equality of the different races or sexes, taken as a whole, our opposition to racism and sexism does not provide us with any basis for objecting to this kind of inegalitarianism.

There is a second important reason why we ought not to base our opposition to racism and sexism on any kind of factual equality, even the limited kind that asserts that variations in capacities and abilities are spread evenly among the different races and between the sexes: we can have no absolute guarantee that these capacities and abilities really are distributed evenly, without regard to race or sex, among human beings. So far as actual abilities are concerned there do seem to be certain measurable differences both among races and between sexes. These differences do not, of course, appear in every case, but only when averages are taken. More important still, we do not yet know how many of these differences are really due to the different genetic endowments of the different races and sexes, and how many are due to poor schools, poor housing, and other factors that are the result of past and continuing discrimination. Perhaps all of the important differences will eventually prove to be environmental rather than genetic. Anyone opposed to racism and sexism will certainly hope that this will be so, for it will make the task of ending discrimination a lot easier; nevertheless, it would be dangerous to rest the case against racism and sexism on the belief that all significant differences are environmental in origin. The opponent of, say, racism who takes this line will be unable to avoid conceding that if differences in ability did after all prove to have some genetic connection with race, racism would in some way be defensible.

Fortunately there is no need to pin the case for equality to one particular outcome of a scientific investigation. The appropriate response to those who claim to have found evidence of genetically based differences in ability among the races or between the sexes is not to stick to the belief that the genetic explanation must be wrong, whatever evidence to the contrary may turn up; instead we should make it quite clear that the claim to equality does not depend on intelligence, moral capacity, physical strength, or similar matters of fact. Equality is a moral idea, not an assertion of fact. There is no logically compelling reason for assuming that a factual difference in ability between two people justifies any difference in the amount of consideration we give to their needs and interests. *The principle of the equality of human beings is not a description of an alleged actual equality among humans: it is a prescription of how we should treat human beings.*

Jeremy Bentham, the founder of the reforming utilitarian school of moral philosophy, incorporated the essential basis of moral equality into his system of ethics by means of the formula: "Each to count for one and none for more than one." In other words, the interests of every being affected by an action are to be taken into account and given the same weight as the like interests of any other being. A later utilitarian, Henry Sidgwick, put the point in this way: "The good of any one individual is of no more importance, from the point of view (if I may say so) of the Universe, than the good of any other." More recently the leading figures in contemporary moral philosophy have shown a great deal of agreement in specifying as a fundamental presupposition of their moral theories some similar requirement that works to give everyone's interests equal consideration – although these writers generally cannot agree on how this requirement is best formulated.

It is an implication of this principle of equality that our concern for others and our readiness to consider their interests ought not to depend on what they are like or on what abilities they may possess. Precisely what our concern or consideration requires us to do may vary according to the characteristics of those affected by what we do: concern for the well-being of children growing up in America would require that we teach them to read; concern for the well-being of pigs may require no more than that we leave them with other pigs in a place where there is adequate food and room to run freely. But the basic element – the taking into account of the interests of the being, whatever those interests may be – must, according to the principle of equality, be extended to all beings, black or white, masculine or feminine, human or nonhuman.

Thomas Jefferson, who was responsible for writing the principle of the equality of men into the American Declaration of Independence, saw this point. It led him to oppose slavery even though he was unable to free himself fully from his slaveholding background. He wrote in a letter to the author of a book that emphasized the notable intellectual achievements of Negroes in order to refute the then common view that they had limited intellectual capacities:

Be assured that no person living wishes more sincerely than I do, to see a complete refutation of the doubts I myself have entertained and expressed on the grade of understanding allotted to them by nature, and to find that they are on a par with ourselves . . . but whatever be their degree of talent it is no measure of their rights. Because Sir Isaac Newton was superior to others in understanding, he was not therefore lord of the property or persons of others.[1]

Similarly, when in the 1850s the call for women's rights was raised in the United States, a remarkable black feminist named Sojourner Truth made the same point in more robust terms at a feminist convention:

They talk about this thing in the head; what do they call it? ["Intellect," whispered someone nearby.] That's it. What's that got to do with women's rights or Negroes' rights? If my cup won't hold but a pint and yours holds a quart, wouldn't you be mean not to let me have my little half-measure full?[2]

It is on this basis that the case against racism and the case against sexism must both ultimately rest; and it is in accordance with this principle that the attitude that we may call "speciesism," by analogy with racism, must also be condemned. Speciesism – the word is not an attractive one, but I can think of no better term – is a prejudice or attitude of bias in favor of the interests of members of one's own species and against those of members of other species. It should be obvious that the fundamental objections to racism and sexism made by Thomas Jefferson and Sojourner Truth apply equally to speciesism. If possessing a higher degree of intelligence does not entitle one human to use another for his or her own ends, how can it entitle humans to exploit nonhumans for the same purpose?

Many philosophers and other writers have proposed the principle of equal consideration of interests, in some form or other, as a basic moral principle; but not many of them have recognized that this principle applies to members of other species as well as to our own. Jeremy Bentham was one of the few who did

realize this. In a forward-looking passage written at a time when black slaves had been freed by the French but in the British dominions were still being treated in the way we now treat animals, Bentham wrote:

The day *may* come when the rest of the animal creation may acquire those rights which never could have been withholden from them but by the hand of tyranny. The French have already discovered that the blackness of the skin is no reason why a human being should be abandoned without redress to the caprice of a tormentor. It may one day come to be recognized that the number of the legs, the villosity of the skin, or the termination of the *os sacrum* are reasons equally insufficient for abandoning a sensitive being to the same fate. What else is it that should trace the insuperable line? Is it the faculty of reason, or perhaps the faculty of discourse? But a full-grown horse or dog is beyond comparison a more rational, as well as a more conversable animal, than an infant of a day or a week or even a month, old. But suppose they were otherwise, what would it avail? The question is not, Can they *reason*? nor Can they *talk*? but, Can they *suffer*?[3]

In this passage Bentham points to the capacity for suffering as the vital characteristic that gives a being the right to equal consideration. The capacity for suffering – or more strictly, for suffering and/or enjoyment or happiness – is not just another characteristic like the capacity for language or higher mathematics. Bentham is not saying that those who try to mark "the insuperable line" that determines whether the interests of a being should be considered happen to have chosen the wrong characteristic. By saying that we must consider the interests of all beings with the capacity for suffering or enjoyment Bentham does not arbitrarily exclude from consideration any interests at all – as those who draw the line with reference to the possession of reason or language do. The capacity for suffering and enjoyment is a *prerequisite for having interests at all*, a condition that must be satisfied before we can speak of interests in a meaningful way. It would be nonsense to say that it was not in the interests of a stone to be kicked along the road by a schoolboy. A stone does not have interests because it cannot suffer. Nothing that we can do to it could possibly make any difference to its welfare. The capacity for suffering and enjoyment is, however, not only necessary, but also sufficient for us to say that a being has interests – at an absolute minimum, an interest in not suffering. A mouse, for example, does have an interest in not being kicked along the road, because it will suffer if it is.

Although Bentham speaks of "rights" in the passage I have quoted, the argument is really about equality rather than about rights. Indeed, in a different passage, Bentham famously described "natural rights" as "nonsense" and "natural and imprescriptible rights" as "nonsense upon stilts." He talked of moral rights as a shorthand way of referring to protections that people and animals morally ought to have; but the real weight of the moral argument does not rest on the assertion of the existence of the right, for this in turn has to be justified on the basis of the possibilities for suffering and happiness. In this way we can argue for equality for animals without getting embroiled in philosophical controversies about the ultimate nature of rights.

In misguided attempts to refute the arguments of this book, some philosophers have gone to much trouble developing arguments to show that animals do not have rights. They have claimed that to have rights a being must be autonomous, or must be a member of a community, or must have the ability to respect the rights of others, or must possess a sense of justice. These claims are irrelevant to the case for Animal Liberation. The language of rights is a convenient political shorthand. It is even more valuable in the era of thirty-second TV news clips than it was in Bentham's day; but in the argument for a radical change in our attitude to animals, it is in no way necessary.

If a being suffers there can be no moral justification for refusing to take that suffering into consideration. No matter what the nature of the being, the principle of equality requires that its suffering be counted equally with the like suffering – insofar as rough comparisons can be made – of any other being. If a being is not capable of suffering, or of experiencing enjoyment or happiness, there is nothing to

be taken into account. So the limit of sentience (using the term as a convenient if not strictly accurate shorthand for the capacity to suffer and/or experience enjoyment) is the only defensible boundary of concern for the interests of others. To mark this boundary by some other characteristic like intelligence or rationality would be to mark it in an arbitrary manner. Why not choose some other characteristic, like skin color?

Racists violate the principle of equality by giving greater weight to the interests of members of their own race when there is a clash between their interests and the interests of those of another race. Sexists violate the principle of equality by favoring the interests of their own sex. Similarly, speciesists allow the interests of their own species to override the greater interests of members of other species. The pattern is identical in each case.

Most human beings are speciesists. The following chapters in the original show that ordinary human beings – not a few exceptionally cruel or heartless humans, but the overwhelming majority of humans – take an active part in, acquiesce in, and allow their taxes to pay for practices that require the sacrifice of the most important interests of members of other species in order to promote the most trivial interests of our own species.

There is, however, one general defense of the practices to be described in the next two chapters that needs to be disposed of before we discuss the practices themselves. It is a defense which, if true, would allow us to do anything at all to nonhumans for the slightest reason, or for no reason at all, without incurring any justifiable reproach. This defense claims that we are never guilty of neglecting the interests of other animals for one breathtakingly simple reason: they have no interests. Nonhuman animals have no interests, according to this view, because they are not capable of suffering. By this is not meant merely that they are not capable of suffering in all the ways that human beings are – for instance, that a calf is not capable of suffering from the knowledge that it will be killed in six months time. That modest claim is, no doubt, true; but it does not clear humans of the charge of speciesism, since it allows that animals may suffer in other ways – for instance, by being given electric shocks, or being kept in small, cramped cages. The defense I am about to discuss is the much more sweeping, although correspondingly less plausible, claim that animals are incapable of suffering in any way at all; that they are, in fact, unconscious automata, possessing neither thoughts nor feelings nor a mental life of any kind.

Although, as we shall see in a later chapter in the original, the view that animals are automata was proposed by the seventeenth-century French philosopher René Descartes, to most people, then and now, it is obvious that if, for example, we stick a sharp knife into the stomach of an unanesthetized dog, the dog will feel pain. That this is so is assumed by the laws in most civilized countries that prohibit wanton cruelty to animals. Readers whose common sense tells them that animals do suffer may prefer to skip the remainder of this section, moving straight on to the next section, since the pages in between do nothing but refute a position that they do not hold. Implausible as it is, though, for the sake of completeness this skeptical position must be discussed.

Do animals other than humans feel pain? How do we know? Well, how do we know if anyone, human or nonhuman, feels pain? We know that we ourselves can feel pain. We know this from the direct experience of pain that we have when, for instance, somebody presses a lighted cigarette against the back of our hand. But how do we know that anyone else feels pain? We cannot directly experience anyone else's pain, whether that "anyone" is our best friend or a stray dog. Pain is a state of con-sciousness, a "mental event," and as such it can never be observed. Behavior like writhing, screaming, or drawing one's hand away from the lighted cigarette is not pain itself; nor are the recordings a neurologist might make of activity within the brain observations of pain itself. Pain is something that we feel, and we can only infer that others are feeling it from various external indications.

In theory, we *could* always be mistaken when we assume that other human beings feel pain. It is conceivable that one of our close friends is really a cleverly constructed robot, controlled by a brilliant scientist so as to give all the signs of feeling pain, but really no more sensitive than any other machine. We can never know, with absolute certainty, that this is not the case. But while this might present a puzzle for philosophers, none of us has the slightest real doubt that our close friends feel pain just as we do. This is an inference, but a perfectly reasonable one, based on observations of their behavior in situations in which we would feel pain, and on the fact that we have every reason to assume that our friends are beings like us, with nervous systems like ours that can be assumed to function as ours do and to produce similar feelings in similar circumstances.

If it is justifiable to assume that other human beings feel pain as we do, is there any reason why a similar inference should be unjustifiable in the case of other animals?

Nearly all the external signs that lead us to infer pain in other humans can be seen in other species, especially the species most closely re-lated to us – the species of mammals and birds. The behavioral signs include writhing, facial contortions, moaning, yelping or other forms of calling, attempts to avoid the source of pain, appearance of fear at the prospect of its rep-etition, and so on. In addition, we know that these animals have nervous systems very like ours, which respond physiologically as ours do when the animal is in circumstances in which we would feel pain: an initial rise of blood pressure, dilated pupils, perspiration, an increased pulse rate, and, if the stimulus continues, a fall in blood pressure. Although human beings have a more developed cerebral cortex than other animals, this part of the brain is concerned with thinking functions rather than with basic impulses, emotions, and feel-ings. These impulses, emotions, and feelings are located in the diencephalon, which is well developed in many other species of animals, especially mammals and birds.[4]

We also know that the nervous systems of other animals were not artificially constructed – as a robot might be artificially constructed – to mimic the pain behavior of humans. The nervous systems of animals evolved as our own did, and in fact the evolutionary history of human beings and other animals, especially mammals, did not diverge until the central features of our nervous systems were already in existence. A capacity to feel pain obviously enhances a species' prospects of survival, since it causes members of the species to avoid sources of injury. It is surely unreasonable to suppose that nervous systems that are virtually identical physiologically, have a common origin and a common evolutionary function, and result in similar forms of behavior in similar circumstances should actually operate in an entirely different manner on the level of subjective feelings.

It has long been accepted as sound policy in science to search for the simplest possible explanation of whatever it is we are trying to explain. Occasionally it has been claimed that it is for this reason "unscientific" to explain the behavior of animals by theories that refer to the animal's conscious feelings, desires, and so on – the idea being that if the behavior in question can be explained without invoking consciousness or feelings, that will be the simpler theory. Yet we can now see that such explanations, when assessed with respect to the actual behavior of both human and nonhuman animals, are actually far more complex than rival explanations. For we know from our own experience that explanations of our own behavior that did not refer to consciousness and the feeling of pain would be incomplete; and it is simpler to assume that the similar behavior of animals with similar nervous systems is to be explained in the same way than to try to invent some other explanation for the behavior of nonhuman animals as well as an explanation for the divergence between humans and nonhumans in this respect.

The overwhelming majority of scientists who have addressed themselves to this question agree. Lord Brain, one of the most eminent neurologists of our time, has said:

I personally can see no reason for conceding mind to my fellow men and denying it to animals. . . . I at least cannot doubt that the interests and activities of animals are correlated with awareness and feeling in the same way as my own, and which may be, for aught I know, just as vivid.[5]

The author of a book on pain writes:

Every particle of factual evidence supports the contention that the higher mammalian vertebrates experience pain sensations at least as acute as our own. To say that they feel less because they are lower animals is an absurdity; it can easily be shown that many of their senses are far more acute than ours—visual acuity in certain birds, hearing in most wild animals, and touch in others; these animals depend more than we do today on the sharpest possible awareness of a hostile environment. Apart from the complexity of the cerebral cortex (which does not directly perceive pain) their nervous systems are almost identical to ours and their reactions to pain remarkably similar, though lacking (so far as we know) the philosophical and moral overtones. The emotional element is all too evident, mainly in the form of fear and anger.[6]

In Britain, three separate expert government committees on matters relating to animals have accepted the conclusion that animals feel pain. After noting the obvious behavioral evidence for this view, the members of the Committee on Cruelty to Wild Animals, set up in 1951, said:

we believe that the physiological, and more particularly the anatomical, evidence fully justifies and reinforces the commonsense belief that animals feel pain.

And after discussing the evolutionary value of pain the committee's report concluded that pain is "of clear-cut biological usefulness" and this is "a third type of evidence that animals feel pain." The committee members then went on to consider forms of suffering other than mere physical pain and added that they were "satisfied that animals do suffer from acute fear and terror." Subsequent reports by British government committees on experiments on animals and on the welfare of animals under intensive farming methods agreed with this view, concluding that animals are capable of suffering both from straightforward physical injuries and from fear, anxiety, stress, and so on. Finally, within the last decade, the publication of scientific studies with titles such as

Animal Thought, Animal Thinking, and *Animal Suffering: The Science of Animal Welfare* have made it plain that conscious awareness in non-human animals is now generally accepted as a serious subject for investigation.[7]

That might well be thought enough to settle the matter; but one more objection needs to be considered. Human beings in pain, after all, have one behavioral sign that nonhuman animals do not have: a developed language. Other animals may communicate with each other, but not, it seems, in the complicated way we do. Some philosophers, including Descartes, have thought it important that while humans can tell each other about their experience of pain in great detail, other animals cannot. (Interestingly, this once neat dividing line between humans and other species has now been threatened by the discovery that chimpanzees can be taught a language.) But as Bentham pointed out long ago, the ability to use language is not relevant to the question of how a being ought to be treated – unless that ability can be linked to the capacity to suffer, so that the absence of a language casts doubt on the existence of this capacity.

This link may be attempted in two ways. First, there is a hazy line of philosophical thought, deriving perhaps from some doctrines associated with the influential philosopher Ludwig Wittgenstein, which maintains that we cannot meaningfully attribute states of consciousness to beings without language. This position seems to me very implausible. Language may be necessary for abstract thought, at some level anyway; but states like pain are more primitive, and have nothing to do with language.

The second and more easily understood way of linking language and the existence of pain is to say that the best evidence we can have that other creatures are in pain is that they tell us that they are. This is a distinct line of argument, for it is denying not that non-language-users conceivably *could* suffer, but only that we could ever have sufficient reason to *believe* that they are suffering. Still, this line of argument fails too. As Jane Goodall has pointed out in her study of chimpanzees, *In the Shadow of Man,* when it comes to the expression of feelings and emotions language is less important

than nonlinguistic modes of communication such as a cheering pat on the back, an exuberant embrace, a clasp of the hands, and so on. The basic signals we use to convey pain, fear, anger, love, joy, surprise, sexual arousal, and many other emotional states are not specific to our own species.[8] The statement "I am in pain" may be one piece of evidence for the conclusion that the speaker is in pain, but it is not the only possible evidence, and since people sometimes tell lies, not even the best possible evidence.

Even if there were stronger grounds for refusing to attribute pain to those who do not have a language, the consequences of this refusal might lead us to reject the conclusion. Human infants and young children are unable to use language. Are we to deny that a year-old child can suffer? If not, language cannot be crucial. Of course, most parents understand the responses of their children better than they understand the responses of other animals; but this is just a fact about the relatively greater knowledge that we have of our own species and the greater contact we have with infants as compared to animals. Those who have studied the behavior of other animals and those who have animals as companions soon learn to understand their responses as well as we understand those of an infant, and sometimes better.

So to conclude: there are no good reasons, scientific or philosophical, for denying that animals feel pain. If we do not doubt that other humans feel pain we should not doubt that other animals do so too.

Animals can feel pain. As we saw earlier, there can be no moral justification for regarding the pain (or pleasure) that animals feel as less important than the same amount of pain (or pleasure) felt by humans. But what practical consequences follow from this conclusion? To prevent misunderstanding I shall spell out what I mean a little more fully.

If I give a horse a hard slap across its rump with my open hand, the horse may start, but it presumably feels little pain. Its skin is thick enough to protect it against a mere slap. If I slap a baby in the same way, however, the baby will cry and presumably feel pain, for its skin is more sensitive. So it is worse to slap a baby than a horse, if both slaps are administered with equal force. But there must be some kind of blow – I don't know exactly what it would be, but perhaps a blow with a heavy stick – that would cause the horse as much pain as we cause a baby by slapping it with our hand. That is what I mean by "the same amount of pain," and if we consider it wrong to inflict that much pain on a baby for no good reason then we must, unless we are speciesists, consider it equally wrong to inflict the same amount of pain on a horse for no good reason.

Other differences between humans and animals cause other complications. Normal adult human beings have mental capacities that will, in certain circumstances, lead them to suffer more than animals would in the same circumstances. If, for instance, we decided to perform extremely painful or lethal scientific experiments on normal adult humans, kidnapped at random from public parks for this purpose, adults who enjoy strolling in parks would become fearful that they would be kidnapped. The resultant terror would be a form of suffering additional to the pain of the experiment. The same experiments performed on nonhuman animals would cause less suffering since the animals would not have the anticipatory dread of being kidnapped and experimented upon. This does not mean, of course, that it would be *right* to perform the experiment on animals, but only that there is a reason, which is *not* speciesist, for preferring to use animals rather than normal adult human beings, if the experiment is to be done at all. It should be noted, however, that this same argument gives us a reason for preferring to use human infants – orphans perhaps – or severely retarded human beings for experiments, rather than adults, since infants and retarded humans would also have no idea of what was going to happen to them. So far as this argument is concerned nonhuman animals and infants and retarded humans are in the same category; and if we use this argument to justify experiments on nonhuman animals we have to ask ourselves whether we are also prepared to allow experiments on human infants and retarded adults; and if we make a distinction between animals and these humans, on what basis can we do it, other than a bare-faced – and morally indefensible – preference for members of our own species?

There are many matters in which the superior mental powers of normal adult humans make a difference: anticipation, more detailed memory, greater knowledge of what is happening, and so on. Yet these differences do not all point to greater suffering on the part of the normal human being. Sometimes animals may suffer more because of their more limited understanding. If, for instance, we are taking prisoners in wartime we can explain to them that although they must submit to capture, search, and confinement, they will not otherwise be harmed and will be set free at the conclusion of hostilities. If we capture wild animals, however, we cannot explain that we are not threatening their lives. A wild animal cannot distinguish an attempt to overpower and confine from an attempt to kill; the one causes as much terror as the other.

It may be objected that comparisons of the sufferings of different species are impossible to make and that for this reason when the interests of animals and humans clash the principle of equality gives no guidance. It is probably true that comparisons of suffering between members of different species cannot be made precisely, but precision is not essential. Even if we were to prevent the infliction of suffering on animals only when it is quite certain that the interests of humans will not be affected to anything like the extent that animals are affected, we would be forced to make radical changes in our treatment of animals that would involve our diet, the farming methods we use, experimental procedures in many fields of science, our approach to wildlife and to hunting, trapping and the wearing of furs, and areas of entertainment like circuses, rodeos, and zoos. As a result, a vast amount of suffering would be avoided.

So far I have said a lot about inflicting suffering on animals, but nothing about killing them. This omission has been deliberate. The application of the principle of equality to the infliction of suffering is, in theory at least, fairly straightforward. Pain and suffering are in themselves bad and should be prevented or minimized, irrespective of the race, sex, or species of the being that suffers. How bad a pain is depends on how intense it is and how long it lasts, but pains of the same intensity and duration are equally bad, whether felt by humans or animals.

The wrongness of killing a being is more complicated. I have kept, and shall continue to keep, the question of killing in the background because in the present state of human tyranny over other species the more simple, straightforward principle of equal consideration of pain or pleasure is a sufficient basis for identifying and protesting against all the major abuses of animals that human beings practice. Nevertheless, it is necessary to say something about killing.

Just as most human beings are speciesists in their readiness to cause pain to animals when they would not cause a similar pain to humans for the same reason, so most human beings are speciesists in their readiness to kill other animals when they would not kill human beings. We need to proceed more cautiously here, however, because people hold widely differing views about when it is legitimate to kill humans, as the continuing debates over abortion and euthanasia attest. Nor have moral philosophers been able to agree on exactly what it is that makes it wrong to kill human beings, and under what circumstances killing a human being may be justifiable.

Let us consider first the view that it is always wrong to take an innocent human life. We may call this the "sanctity of life" view. People who take this view oppose abortion and euthanasia. They do not usually, however, oppose the killing of nonhuman animals – so perhaps it would be more accurate to describe this view as the "sanctity of *human* life" view. The belief that human life, and only human life, is sacrosanct is a form of speciesism. To see this, consider the following example.

Assume that, as sometimes happens, an infant has been born with massive and irreparable brain damage. The damage is so severe that the infant can never be any more than a "human vegetable," unable to talk, recognize other people, act independently of others, or develop a sense of self-awareness. The parents of the infant, realizing that they cannot hope for any improvement in their child's condition and being in any case unwilling to spend, or ask the state to spend, the thousands of dollars that would be needed annually for proper care of the infant, ask the doctor to kill the infant painlessly.

Should the doctor do what the parents ask? Legally, the doctor should not, and in this respect the law reflects the sanctity of life view. The life of every human being is sacred. Yet people who would say this about the infant do not object to the killing of nonhuman animals. How can they justify their different judgments? Adult chimpanzees, dogs, pigs, and members of many other species far surpass the brain-damaged infant in their ability to relate to others, act independently, be self-aware, and any other capacity that could reasonably be said to give value to life. With the most intensive care possible, some severely retarded infants can never achieve the intelligence level of a dog. Nor can we appeal to the concern of the infant's parents, since they themselves, in this imaginary example (and in some actual cases) do not want the infant kept alive. The only thing that distinguishes the infant from the animal, in the eyes of those who claim it has a "right to life," is that it is, biologically, a member of the species Homo sapiens, whereas chimpanzees, dogs, and pigs are not. But to use *this* difference as the basis for granting a right to life to the infant and not to the other animals is, of course, pure speciesism.[9] It is exactly the kind of arbitrary difference that the most crude and overt kind of racist uses in attempting to justify racial discrimination.

This does not mean that to avoid speciesism we must hold that it is as wrong to kill a dog as it is to kill a human being in full possession of his or her faculties. The only position that is irredeemably speciesist is the one that tries to make the boundary of the right to life run exactly parallel to the boundary of our own species. Those who hold the sanctity of life view do this, because while distinguishing sharply between human beings and other animals they allow no distinctions to be made within our own species, objecting to the killing of the severely retarded and the hopelessly senile as strongly as they object to the killing of normal adults.

To avoid speciesism we must allow that beings who are similar in all relevant respects have a similar right to life – and mere membership in our own biological species cannot be a morally relevant criterion for this right. Within these limits we could still hold, for instance, that it is worse to kill a normal adult human, with a capacity for selfawareness and the ability to plan for the future and have meaningful relations with others, than it is to kill a mouse, which presumably does not share all of these characteristics; or we might appeal to the close family and other personal ties that humans have but mice do not have to the same degree; or we might think that it is the consequences for other humans, who will be put in fear for their own lives, that makes the crucial difference; or we might think it is some combination of these factors, or other factors altogether.

Whatever criteria we choose, however, we will have to admit that they do not follow precisely the boundary of our own species. We may legitimately hold that there are some features of certain beings that make their lives more valuable than those of other beings; but there will surely be some non-human animals whose lives, by any standards, are more valuable than the lives of some humans. A chimpanzee, dog, or pig, for instance, will have a higher degree of self-awareness and a greater capacity for meaningful relations with others than a severely retarded infant or someone in a state of advanced senility. So if we base the right to life on these characteristics we must grant these animals a right to life as good as, or better than, such retarded or senile humans.

This argument cuts both ways. It could be taken as showing that chimpanzees, dogs, and pigs, along with some other species, have a right to life and we commit a grave moral offense whenever we kill them, even when they are old and suffering and our intention is to put them out of their misery. Alternatively one could take the argument as showing that the severely retarded and hopelessly senile have no right to life and may be killed for quite trivial reasons, as we now kill animals.

Since the main concern of this book is with ethical questions having to do with animals and not with the morality of euthanasia I shall not attempt to settle this issue finally. I think it is reasonably clear, though, that while both of the positions just described avoid speciesism, neither is satisfactory. What we need is some middle position that would avoid speciesism but would not make the lives of the retarded and senile as cheap as the lives of pigs and dogs now are, or make the lives of pigs and dogs so sacrosanct that we think it wrong to put them out of hopeless misery. What we must do is bring non-human animals within our sphere of moral concern and cease to treat their lives as expendable for whatever trivial purposes we may have. At the same time, once we realize that the fact that a being is a member of our own species is not in itself enough to make it always wrong to kill that being, we may come to reconsider our policy of preserving human lives at all costs, even when there is no prospect of a meaningful life or of existence without terrible pain.

I conclude, then, that a rejection of speciesism does not imply that all lives are of equal worth. While self-awareness, the capacity to think ahead and have hopes and aspirations for the future, the capacity for meaningful relations with others and so on are not relevant to the question of inflicting pain – since pain is pain, whatever other capacities, beyond the capacity to feel pain, the being may have – these capacities are relevant to the question of taking life. It is not arbitrary to hold that the life of a self-aware being, capable of abstract thought, of planning for the future, of complex acts of communication, and so on, is more valuable than the life of a being without these capacities. To see the difference between the issues of inflicting pain and taking life, consider how we would choose within our own species. If we had to choose to save the life of a normal human being or an intellectually disabled human being, we would probably choose to save the life of a normal human being; but if we had to choose between preventing pain in the normal human being or the intellectually disabled one – imagine that both have received painful but superficial injuries, and we only have enough painkiller for one of them – it is not nearly so clear how we ought to choose. The same is true when we consider other species. The evil of pain is, in itself, unaffected by the other characteristics of the being who feels the pain; the value of life is affected by these other characteristics. To give just one reason for this difference, to take the life of a being who has been hoping, planning, and working for some future goal is to deprive that being of the fulfillment of all those efforts; to take the life of a being with a mental capacity below the level needed to grasp that one is a being with a future – much less make plans for the future – cannot involve this particular kind of loss.

Normally this will mean that if we have to choose between the life of a human being and the life of another animal we should choose to save the life of the human; but there may be special cases in which the reverse holds true, because the human being in question does not have the capacities of a normal human being. So this view is not speciesist, although it may appear to be at first glance. The preference, in normal cases, for saving a human life over the life of an animal when a choice *has* to be made is a preference based on the characteristics that normal humans have, and not on the mere fact that they are members of our own species. This is why when we consider members of our own species who lack the characteristics of normal humans we can no longer say that their lives are always to be preferred to those of other animals. [. . .] In general, though, the question of when it is wrong to kill (painlessly) an animal is one to which we need give no precise answer. As long as we remember that we should give the same respect to the lives of animals as we give to the lives of those humans at a similar mental level, we shall not go far wrong.

In any case, the conclusions that are argued for in this book flow from the principle of minimizing suffering alone. The idea that it is also wrong to kill animals painlessly gives some of these conclusions additional support that is welcome but strictly unnecessary. Interestingly enough, this is true even of the conclusion that we ought to become vegetarians, a conclusion that in the popular mind is generally based on some kind of absolute prohibition on killing.

Notes

1. Letter to Henry Gregoire, February 25, 1809.
2. Reminiscences by Francis D. Gage, from Susan B. Anthony, *The History of Woman Suffrage*, vol. 1; the passage is to be found in the extract in Leslie Tanner, ed., *Voices From Women's Liberation* (New York: Signet, 1970).
3. *Introduction to the Principles of Morals and Legislation*, chapter 17.
4. Lord Brain, "Presidential Address," in C. A. Keele and R. Smith, eds., *The Assessment of Pain in Men and Animals* (London: Universities Federation for Animal Welfare, 1962).
5. Lord Brain, "Presidential Address," p. 11.
6. Richard Serjeant, *The Spectrum of Pain* (London: Hart Davis, 1969), p. 72.
7. See Stephen Walker, *Animal Thoughts* (London: Routledge and Kegan Paul, 1983); Donald-Griffin, *Animal Thinking* (Cambridge: Harvard University Press, 1984); and Marian Stamp Dawkins, *Animal Suffering: The Science of Animal Welfare* (London: Chapman and Hall, 1980).
8. *In the Shadow of Man* (Boston: Houghton Mifflin, 1971), p. 225.
9. I am here putting aside religious views, for example the doctrine that all and only human beings have immortal souls, or are made in the image of God. Historically these have been very important, and no doubt are partly responsible for the idea that human life has a special sanctity. [. . .] Logically, however, these religious views are unsatisfactory, since they do not offer a reasoned explanation of why it should be that all humans and no nonhumans have immortal souls. This belief too, therefore, comes under suspicion as a form of speciesism. In any case, defenders of the "sanctity of life" view are generally reluctant to base their position on purely religious doctrines, since these doctrines are no longer as widely accepted as they once were.

CHAPTER 44

The Rights of Animals
and Unborn Generations

JOEL FEINBERG

Every philosophical paper must begin with an unproved assumption. Mine is the assumption that there will still be a world five hundred years from now, and that it will contain human beings who are very much like us. We have it within our power now, clearly, to affect the lives of these creatures for better or worse by contributing to the conservation or corruption of the environment in which they must live. I shall assume furthermore that it is psychologically possible for us to care about our remote descendants, that many of us in fact do care, and indeed that we ought to care. My main concern then will be to show that it makes sense to speak of the rights of unborn generations against us, and that given the moral judgment that we ought to conserve our environmental inheritance for them, and its grounds, we might well say that future generations *do* have rights correlative to our present duties toward them. Protecting our environment now is also a matter of elementary prudence, and insofar as we do it for the next generation already here in the persons of our children, it is a matter of love. But from the perspective of our remote descendants it is

Joel Feinberg, "The Rights of Animals and Unborn Generations," pp. 43–6, 49–50, 55, 57–63 from William Blackstone (ed.), *Philosophy and Environmental Crisis*. Athens: University of Georgia Press, 1974. Reprinted by permission of Jean T. Blackstone.

basically a matter of justice, of respect for their rights. My main concern here will be to examine the concept of a right to better understand how that can be.

The Problem

To have a right is to have a claim *to* something and *against* someone, the recognition of which is called for by legal rules or, in the case of moral rights, by the principles of an enlightened conscience. In the familiar cases of rights, the claimant is a competent adult human being, and the claimee is an officeholder in an institution or else a private individual, in either case, another competent adult human being. Normal adult human beings, then, are obviously the sorts of beings of whom rights can meaningfully be predicated. Everyone would agree to that, even extreme misanthropes who deny that anyone in fact has rights. On the other hand, it is absurd to say that rocks can have rights, not because rocks are morally inferior things unworthy of rights (that statement makes no sense either), but because rocks belong to a category of entities of whom rights cannot be meaningfully predicated. That is not to say that there are no circumstances in which we ought to treat rocks carefully, but only that the rocks themselves cannot validly claim good treatment from us. In between the clear cases of rocks and normal human beings, however, is a spectrum of less obvious cases, including some bewildering borderline ones. Is it meaningful or conceptually possible to ascribe rights to our dead ancestors? to individual animals? to whole species of animals? to plants? to idiots and madmen? to fetuses? to generations yet unborn? Until we know how to settle these puzzling cases, we cannot claim fully to grasp the concept of a right, or to know the shape of its logical boundaries.

One way to approach these riddles is to turn one's attention first to the most familiar and unproblematic instances of rights, note their most salient characteristics, and then compare the borderline cases with them, measuring as closely as possible the points of similarity and difference. In the end, the way we classify the borderline cases may depend on whether we are more impressed with the similarities or the differences between them and the cases in which we have the most confidence.

It will be useful to consider the problem of individual animals first because their case is the one that has already been debated with the most thoroughness by philosophers so that the dialectic of claim and rejoinder has now unfolded to the point where disputants can get to the end game quickly and isolate the crucial point at issue. When we understand precisely what *is* at issue in the debate over animal rights, I think we will have the key to the solution of all the other riddles about rights.

Individual Animals

Almost all modern writers agree that we ought to be kind to animals, but that is quite another thing from holding that animals can claim kind treatment from us as their due. Statutes making cruelty to animals a crime are now very common, and these, of course, impose legal duties on people not to mistreat animals; but that still leaves open the question whether the animals, as beneficiaries of those duties, possess rights correlative to them. We may very well have duties *regarding* animals that are not at the same time duties *to* animals, just as we may have duties regarding rocks, or buildings, or lawns, that are not duties *to* the rocks,

buildings, or lawns. Some legal writers have taken the still more extreme position that animals themselves are not even the directly intended beneficiaries of statutes prohibiting cruelty to animals. During the nineteenth century, for example, it was commonly said that such statutes were designed to protect human beings by preventing the growth of cruel habits that could later threaten human beings with harm too. [. . .]

The very people whose sensibilities are invoked in the alternative explanation, a group that no doubt now includes most of us, are precisely those who would insist that the protection belongs primarily to the animals themselves, not merely to their own tender feelings. Indeed, it would be difficult even to account for the existence of such feelings in the absence of a belief that the animals deserve the protection in their own right and for their own sakes.

Even if we allow, as I think we must, that animals are the intended direct beneficiaries of legislation forbidding cruelty to animals, it does not follow directly that animals have legal rights, [. . .] Now, it is relatively easy to see why animals cannot have duties, and this matter is largely beyond controversy. Animals cannot be "reasoned with" or instructed in their responsibilities; they are inflexible and unadaptable to future contingencies; they are subject to fits of instinctive passion which they are incapable of repressing or controlling, postponing or sublimating. Hence, they cannot enter into contractual agreements, or make promises; they cannot be trusted; and they cannot (except within very narrow limits and for purposes of conditioning) be blamed for what would be called "moral failures" in a human being. They are therefore incapable of being moral subjects, of acting rightly or wrongly in the moral sense, of having, discharging, or breeching duties and obligations.

But what is there about the intellectual incompetence of animals (which admittedly disqualifies them for duties) that makes them logically unsuitable for rights? The most common reply to this question is that animals are incapable of *claiming* rights on their own. They cannot make motion, on their own, to courts to have their claims recognized or enforced; they cannot initiate, on their own, any kind of legal proceedings; nor are they capable of even understanding when their rights are being violated, of distinguishing harm from wrongful injury, and responding with indignation and an outraged sense of justice instead of mere anger or fear.

No one can deny any of these allegations, but to the claim that they are the grounds for disqualification of rights of animals, philosophers on the other side of this controversy have made convincing rejoinders. It is simply not true, says W. D. Lamont,[1] that the ability to understand what a right is and the ability to set legal machinery in motion by one's own initiative are necessary for the possession of rights. If that were the case, then neither human idiots nor wee babies would have any legal rights at all. Yet it is manifest that both of these classes of intellectual incompetents have legal rights recognized and easily enforced by the courts. Children and idiots start legal proceedings, not on their own direct initiative, but rather through the actions of proxies or attorneys who are empowered to speak in their names. If there is no conceptual absurdity in this situation, why should there be in the case where a proxy makes a claim on behalf of an animal? People commonly enough make wills leaving money to trustees for the care of animals. Is it not natural to speak of the animal's right to his inheritance in cases of this kind? If a trustee embezzles money from the animal's account, and a proxy speaking in the dumb brute's behalf presses the animal's claim, can he not be described as asserting the animal's *rights*? More exactly, the animal itself claims its rights through the vicarious actions of a human proxy speaking in its name and in its behalf. There appears to be no reason why we should require the animal to understand what is going on (so the argument concludes) as a condition for regarding it as a possessor of rights.
[...]

Now, there is a very important insight expressed in the requirement that a being have interests if he is to be a logically proper subject of rights. This can be appreciated if we consider just why it is that mere things cannot have rights. Consider a very precious "mere thing" – a beautiful natural wilderness, or a complex and ornamental artifact, like the Taj Mahal.

Such things ought to be cared for, because they would sink into decay if neglected, depriving some human beings, or perhaps even all human beings, of something of great value. Certain persons may even have as their own special job the care and protection of these valuable objects. But we are not tempted in these cases to speak of "thing-rights" correlative to custodial duties, because, try as we might, we cannot think of mere things as possessing interests of their own. Some people may have a duty to preserve, maintain, or improve the Taj Mahal, but they can hardly have a duty to help or hurt it, benefit or aid it, succor or relieve it. Custodians may protect it for the sake of a nation's pride and art lovers' fancy; but they don't keep it in good repair for "its own sake," or for "its own true welfare," or "well-being." A mere thing, however valuable to others, has no good of its own. The explanation of that fact, I suspect, consists in the fact that mere things have no conative life: no conscious wishes, desires, and hopes; or urges and impulses; or unconscious drives, aims, and goals; or latent tendencies, direction of growth, and natural fulfillments. Interests must be compounded somehow out of conations; hence mere things have no interests. *A fortiori*, they have no interests to be protected by legal or moral rules. Without interests a creature can have no "good" of its own, the achievement of which can be its due. Mere things are not loci of value in their own right, but rather their value consists entirely in their being objects of other beings' interests.

[...] I should think that the trustee of funds willed to a dog or cat is more than a mere custodian of the animal he protects. Rather his job is to look out for the interests of the animal and make sure no one denies it its due. The animal itself is the beneficiary of his dutiful services. Many of the higher animals at least have appetites, conative urges, and rudimentary purposes, the integrated satisfaction of which constitutes their welfare or good. We can, of course, with consistency treat animals as mere pests and deny that they have any rights; for most animals, especially those of the lower orders, we have no choice but to do so. But it seems to me, nevertheless, that in general, animals *are* among the sorts of beings of whom rights can meaningfully be predicated and denied.

Now, if a person agrees with the conclusion of the argument thus far, that animals are the sorts of beings that *can* have rights, and further, if he accepts the moral judgment that we ought to be kind to animals, only one further premise is needed to yield the conclusion that some animals do in fact have rights. We must now ask ourselves for whose sake ought we to treat (some) animals with consideration and humaneness? If we conceive our duty to be one of obedience to authority, or to one's own conscience merely, or one of consideration for tender human sensibilities only, then we might still deny that animals have rights, even though we admit that they are the kinds of beings that *can* have rights. But if we hold not only that we ought to treat animals humanely but also that we should do so for the animals' own sake, that such treatment is something we owe animals as their due, something that can be claimed for them, something the withholding of which would be an injustice and a wrong, and not merely a harm, then it follows that we do ascribe rights to animals. I suspect that the moral judgments most of us make about animals do pass these phenomenological tests, so that most of us do believe that animals have rights, but are reluctant to say so because of the conceptual confusions about the notion of a right that I have attempted to dispel above.

Now we can extract from our discussion of animal rights a crucial principle for tentative use in the resolution of the other riddles about the applicability of the concept of a right, namely, that the sorts of beings who *can* have rights are precisely those who have (or can have) interests. I have come to this tentative conclusion for two reasons: (1) because a right holder must be capable of being represented and it is impossible to represent a being that has no interests, and (2) because a right holder must be capable of being a beneficiary in his own person, and a being without interests is a being that is incapable of being harmed or benefitted, having no good or "sake" of its own. Thus, a being without interests has no "behalf" to act in, and no "sake" to act for. My strategy now will be to apply the "interest principle," as we can call it, to the other puzzles

about rights, while being prepared to modify it where necessary (but as little as possible), in the hope of separating in a consistent and intuitively satisfactory fashion the beings who can have rights from those which cannot.

Vegetables

It is clear that we ought not to mistreat certain plants, and indeed there are rules and regulations imposing duties on persons not to misbehave in respect to certain members of the vegetable kingdom. It is forbidden, for example, to pick wildflowers in the mountainous tundra areas of national parks, or to endanger trees by starting fires in dry forest areas. Members of Congress introduce bills designed, as they say, to "protect" rare redwood trees from commercial pillage. Given this background, it is surprising that no one speaks of plants as having rights. Plants, after all, are not "mere things"; they are vital objects with inherited biological propensities determining their natural growth. Moreover, we do say that certain conditions are "good" or "bad" for plants, thereby suggesting that plants, unlike rocks, are capable of having a "good." (This is a case, however, where "what we say" should not be taken seriously: we also say that certain kinds of paint are good or bad for the internal walls of a house, and this does not commit us to a conception of walls as beings possessed of a good or welfare of their own.) Finally, we are capable of feeling a kind of affection for particular plants, though we rarely personalize them, as we do in the case of animals, by giving them proper names.

Still, all are agreed that plants are not the kinds of beings that can have rights. Plants are never plausibly understood to be the direct intended beneficiaries of rules designed to "protect" them. We wish to keep redwood groves in existence for the sake of human beings who can enjoy their serene beauty, and for the sake of generations of human beings yet unborn. Trees are not the sorts of beings who have their "own sakes," despite the fact that they have biological propensities. Having no conscious wants or goals of their own, trees cannot know satisfaction or frustration, pleasure or pain. Hence, there is no possibility of kind or cruel treatment of trees. In these morally crucial respects, trees differ from the higher species of animals.

[...]

Whole Species

The topic of whole species, whether of plants or animals, can be treated in much the same way as that of individual plants. A whole collection, as such, cannot have beliefs, expectations, wants, or desires, and can flourish or languish only in the human interest-related sense in which individual plants thrive and decay. Individual elephants can have interests, but the species elephant cannot. Even where individual elephants are not granted rights, human beings may have an interest – economic, scientific, or sentimental – in keeping the species from dying out, and *that* interest may be protected in various ways by law. But that is quite another matter from recognizing a right to survival belonging to the species itself. Still, the preservation of a whole species may quite properly seem to be a morally more important matter than the preservation of an individual animal. Individual animals can have rights but it is implausible to ascribe to them a right to life on the human model. Nor do we normally have duties to keep individual animals alive or even to abstain from killing them provided we do it humanely and nonwantonly in the promotion of legitimate human interests. On the other hand, we do have duties to protect threatened species, not duties to the species themselves as such, but rather duties to future human beings, duties derived from our housekeeping role as temporary inhabitants of this planet.

[...]

Dead Persons

So far we have refined the interest principle but we have not had occasion to modify it. Applied to dead persons, however, it will have to be stretched to near the breaking point if it is to explain how our duty to honor commitments to the dead can be thought to be linked to the rights of the dead against us. The case against ascribing rights to dead men can be made very simply: a dead man is a mere corpse, a piece of decaying organic matter. Mere inanimate things can have no interests, and what is incapable of having interests is incapable of having rights. If, nevertheless, we grant dead men rights against us, we would seem to be treating the interests they had while alive as somehow surviving their deaths. There is the sound of paradox in this way of talking, but it may be the least paradoxical way of describing our moral relations to our predecessors. And if the idea of an interest's surviving its possessor's death is a kind of fiction, it is a fiction that most living men have a real interest in preserving.

Most persons while still alive have certain desires about what is to happen to their bodies, their property, or their reputations after they are dead. For that reason, our legal system has developed procedures to enable persons while still alive to determine whether their bodies will be used for purposes of medical research or organic transplantation, and to whom their wealth (after taxes) is to be transferred. Living men also take out life insurance policies guaranteeing that the accumulated benefits be conferred upon beneficiaries of their own choice. They also make private agreements, both contractual and informal, in which they receive promises that certain things will be done after their deaths in exchange for some present service or consideration. In all these cases promises are made to living persons that their wishes will be honored after they are dead. Like all other valid promises, they impose duties on the promisor and confer correlative rights on the promisee.

How does the situation change after the promisee has died? Surely the duties of the promisor do not suddenly become null and void. If that were the case, and known to be the case, there could be no confidence in promises regarding posthumous arrangements; no one would bother with wills or life insurance policies. Indeed the duties of courts and trustees to honor testamentary directions, and the duties of life insurance companies to pay benefits to survivors, are, in a sense, only conditional duties before a man dies. They come into existence as categorical demands for immediate action only upon the promisee's death. So the view that death renders them null and void has the truth exactly upside down.

The survival of the promisor's duty after the promisee's death does not prove that the promisee retains a right even after death, for we might prefer to conclude that there is one class of cases where duties to keep promises are not logically correlated with a promisee's right, namely, cases where the promisee has died. Still, a morally sensitive promisor is likely to think of his promised performance not only as a duty (i.e., a morally required action) but also as something owed to the deceased promisee as his due. Honoring such promises is a way of keeping faith with the dead. To be sure, the promisor will not think of his duty as something to be done for the promisee's "good," since the promisee, being dead, has no "good" of his own. We can think of certain of the deceased's interests, however, (including especially those enshrined in wills and protected by contracts and promises) as surviving their owner's death, and constituting claims against us that persist beyond the life of the claimant. Such claims can be represented by proxies just like the claims of animals. This way of speaking, I believe, reflects more accurately than any other an important fact about the human condition: we have an interest while alive that other interests of ours will continue to be recognized and served after we are dead. The whole practice of honoring wills and testaments, and the like, is thus for the sake of the living, just as a particular instance of it may be thought to be for the sake of one who is dead.

Conceptual sense, then, can be made of talk about dead men's rights; but it is still a wide open moral question whether dead men in fact have rights, and if so, what those rights are. In particular, commentators have disagreed over whether a man's interest in his reputation deserves to be protected from defamation even after his death. [...] A widow or a son may be wounded, or embarrassed, or even injured economically, by a defamatory attack on the memory of their dead husband or father. In Utah defamation of the dead is a misdemeanor, and in Sweden a cause of action in tort. The law rarely presumes, however, that a dead man himself has any interests, rep-

resentable by proxy, that can be injured by defamation, apparently because of the maxim that what a dead man doesn't know can't hurt him.

This presupposes, however, that the whole point of guarding the reputations even of living men, is to protect them from hurt feelings, or to protect some other interests, for example, economic ones, that do not survive death. A moment's thought, I think, will show that our interests are more complicated than that. If someone spreads a libelous description of me, without my knowledge, among hundreds of persons in a remote part of the country, so that I am, still without my knowledge, an object of general scorn and mockery in that group, I have been injured, even though I never learn what has happened. That is because I have an interest, so I believe, in having a good reputation *simpliciter*, in addition to my interest in avoiding hurt feelings, embarrassment, and economic injury. In the example, I do not know what is being said and believed about me, so my feelings are not hurt; but clearly if I did know, I would be enormously distressed. The distress would be the natural consequence of my belief that an interest other than my interest in avoiding distress had been damaged. How else can I account for the distress? If I had no interest in a good reputation as such, I would respond to news of harm to my reputation with indifference.

While it is true that a dead man cannot have his feelings hurt, it does not follow, therefore, that his claim to be thought of no worse than he deserves cannot survive his death. [...]

Human Vegetables

Mentally deficient and deranged human beings are hardly ever so handicapped intellectually that they do not compare favorably with even the highest of the lower animals, though they are commonly so incompetent that they cannot be assigned duties or be held responsible for what they do. Since animals can have rights, then, it follows that human idiots and madmen can too. It would make good sense, for example, to ascribe to them a right to be cured whenever effective therapy is available at reasonable cost, and even those incurables who have been consigned to a sanatorium for permanent "warehousing" can claim (through a proxy) their right to decent treatment.

Human beings suffering extreme cases of mental illness, however, may be so utterly disoriented or insensitive as to compare quite unfavorably with the brightest cats and dogs. Those suffering from catatonic schizophrenia may be barely distinguishable in respect to those traits presupposed by the possession of interests from the lowliest vegetables. So long as we regard these patients as potentially curable, we may think of them as human beings with interests in their own restoration and treat them as possessors of rights. We may think of the patient as a genuine human person inside the vegetable casing struggling to get out, just as in the old fairy tales a pumpkin could be thought of as a beautiful maiden under a magic spell waiting only the proper words to be restored to her true self. Perhaps it is reasonable never to lose hope that a patient can be cured, and therefore to regard him always as a person "under a spell" with a permanent interest in his own recovery that is entitled to recognition and protection.

What if, nevertheless, we think of the catatonic schizophrenic and the vegetating patient with irreversible brain damage as absolutely incurable? Can we think of them at the same time as possessed of interests and rights too, or is this combination of traits a conceptual impossibility? Shocking as it may at first seem, I am driven unavoidably to the latter view. If redwood trees and rose-bushes cannot have rights, neither can incorrigible human vegetables. The trustees who are designated to administer funds for the care of these unfortunates are better understood as mere custodians than as representatives of their interests since these patients no longer have interests. It does not follow that they should not be kept alive as long as possible: that is an open moral question not foreclosed by conceptual analysis. Even if we have duties to keep human vegetables alive, however, they cannot be duties *to* them. We may be obliged to keep them alive to protect the sensibilities of others, or to foster humanitarian tendencies in ourselves, but we cannot keep them alive for their own good, for they are no longer capable of having a "good" of their own. Without awareness, expectation, belief, desire, aim, and purpose, a being can have no interests; without

interests, he cannot be benefited; without the capacity to be a beneficiary, he can have no rights. But there may nevertheless be a dozen other reasons to treat him as if he did.

Fetuses

If the interest principle is to permit us to ascribe rights to infants, fetuses, and generations yet unborn, it can only be on the grounds that interests can exert a claim upon us even before their possessors actually come into being, just the reverse of the situation respecting dead men where interests are respected even after their possessors have ceased to be. Newly born infants are surely noisier than mere vegetables, but they are just barely brighter. They come into existence, as Aristotle said, with the capacity to acquire concepts and dispositions, but in the beginning we suppose that their consciousness of the world is a "blooming, buzzing confusion." They do have a capacity, no doubt from the very beginning, to feel pain, and this alone may be sufficient ground for ascribing both an interest and a right to them. Apart from that, however, during the first few hours of their lives, at least, they may well lack even the rudimentary intellectual equipment necessary to the possession of interests. Of course, this induces no moral reservations whatever in adults. Children grow and mature almost visibly in the first few months so that those future interests that are so rapidly emerging from the unformed chaos of their earliest days seem unquestionably to be the basis of their present rights. Thus, we say of a newborn infant that he has a right now to live and grow into his adulthood, even though he lacks the conceptual equipment at this very moment to have this or any other desire. A new infant, in short, lacks the traits necessary for the possession of interests, but he has the capacity to acquire those traits, and his inherited potentialities are moving quickly toward actualization even as we watch him. Those proxies who make claims in behalf of infants, then, are more than mere custodians: they are (or can be) genuine representatives of the child's emerging interests, which may need protection even now if they are to be allowed to come into existence at all.

The same principle may be extended to "unborn persons." After all, the situation of fetuses one day before birth is not strikingly different from that a few hours after birth. The rights our law confers on the unborn child, both proprietary and personal, are for the most part, placeholders or reservations for the rights he shall inherit when he becomes a full-fledged interested being. The law protects a potential interest in these cases before it has even grown into actuality, as a garden fence protects newly seeded flower beds long before blooming flowers have emerged from them. The unborn child's present right to property, for example, is a legal protection offered now to his future interest, contingent upon his birth, and instantly voidable if he dies before birth. As Coke put it: "The law in many cases hath consideration of him in respect of the apparent expectation of his birth"; but this is quite another thing than recognizing a right actually to be born. Assuming that the child will be born, the law seems to say, various interests that he will come to have after birth must be protected from damage that they can incur even before birth. Thus prenatal injuries of a negligently inflicted kind can give the newly born child a right to sue for damages which he can exercise through a proxy-attorney and in his own name any time *after* he is born.

[. . .]

It is important to reemphasize here that the questions of whether fetuses do or ought to have rights are substantive questions of law and morals open to argument and decision. The prior question of whether fetuses are the kind of beings that can have rights, however, is a conceptual, not a moral, question, amenable only to what is called "logical analysis," and irrelevant to moral judgment. The correct answer to the conceptual question, I believe, is that unborn children are among the sorts of beings of whom possession of rights can meaningfully be predicated, even though they are (temporarily) incapable of having interests, because their future interests can be protected now, and it does make sense to protect a potential interest even before it has grown into actuality. The interest principle, however, makes perplexing, at best, talk of a noncontingent fetal right to be born; for fetuses, lacking actual wants and beliefs, have no actual interest in being born, and it is difficult to think of any other reason for ascribing any rights to them other than on the assumption that they will in fact be born.

Future Generations

We have it in our power now to make the world a much less pleasant place for our descendants than the world we inherited from our ancestors. We can continue to proliferate in ever greater numbers, using up fertile soil at an even greater rate, dumping our wastes into rivers, lakes, and oceans, cutting down our forests, and polluting the atmosphere with noxious gases. All thoughtful people agree that we ought not to do these things. Most would say that we have a duty not to do these things, meaning not merely that conservation is morally required (as opposed to merely desirable) but also that it is something due our descendants, something to be done for their sakes. Surely we owe it to future generations to pass on a world that is not a used up garbage heap. Our remote descendants are not yet present to claim a livable world as their right, but there are plenty of proxies to speak now in their behalf. These spokesmen, far from being mere custodians, are genuine representatives of future interests.

Why then deny that the human beings of the future have rights which can be claimed against us now in their behalf? Some are inclined to deny them present rights out of a fear of falling into obscure metaphysics, by granting rights to remote and unidentifiable beings who are not yet even in existence. Our unborn great-great-grandchildren are in some sense "potential" persons, but they are far more remotely potential, it may seem, than fetuses. This, however, is not the real difficulty. Unborn generations are more remotely potential than fetuses in one sense, but not in another. A much greater period of time with a far greater number of causally necessary and important events must pass before their potentiality can be actualized, it is true; but our collective posterity is just as certain to come into existence "in the normal course of events" as is any given fetus now in its mother's womb. In that sense the existence of the distant human future is no more remotely potential than that of a particular child already on its way.

The real difficulty is not that we doubt whether our descendants will ever be actual, but rather that we don't know who they will be. It is not their temporal remoteness that troubles us so much as their indeterminacy – their present facelessness and namelessness. Five centuries from now men and women will be living where we live now. Any given one of them will have an interest in living space, fertile soil, fresh air, and the like, but that arbitrarily selected one has no other qualities we can presently envision very clearly. We don't even know who his parents, grandparents, or great-grandparents are, or even whether he is related to us. Still, whoever these human beings may turn out to be, and whatever they might reasonably be expected to be like, they will have interests that we can affect, for better or worse, right now. That much we can and do know about them. The identity of the owners of these interests is now necessarily obscure, but the fact of their interest-ownership is crystal clear, and that is all that is necessary to certify the coherence of present talk about their rights. We can tell, sometimes, that shadowy forms in the spatial distance belong to human beings, though we know not who or how many they are; and this imposes a duty on us not to throw bombs, for example, in their direction. In like manner, the vagueness of the human future does not weaken its claim on us in light of the nearly certain knowledge that it will, after all, be human.

Doubts about the existence of a right to be born transfer neatly to the question of a similar right to come into existence ascribed to future generations. The rights that future generations certainly have against us are contingent rights: the interests they are sure to have when they come into being (assuming of course that they will come into being) cry out for protection from invasions that can take place now. Yet there are no actual interests, presently existent, that future generations, presently nonexistent, have now. Hence, there is no actual interest that they have in simply coming into being, and I am at a loss to

think of any other reason for claiming that they have a right to come into existence (though there may well be such a reason). Suppose then that all human beings at a given time voluntarily form a compact never again to produce children, thus leading within a few decades to the end of our species. This of course is a wildly improbable hypothetical example but a rather crucial one for the position I have been tentatively considering. And we can imagine, say, that the whole world is converted to a strange ascetic religion which absolutely requires sexual abstinence for everyone. Would this arrangement violate the rights of anyone? No one can complain on behalf of presently nonexistent future generations that their future interests which give them a contingent right of protection have been violated since they will never come into existence to be wronged. My inclination then is to conclude that the suicide of our species would be deplorable, lamentable, and a deeply moving tragedy, but that it would violate no one's rights. Indeed if, contrary to fact, all human beings could ever agree to such a thing, that very agreement would be a symptom of our species' biological unsuitability for survival anyway.

Conclusion

For several centuries now human beings have run roughshod over the lands of our planet, just as if the animals who do live there and the generations of humans who will live there had no claims on them whatever. Philosophers have not helped matters by arguing that animals and future generations are not the kinds of beings who can have rights now, that they don't presently qualify for membership, even "auxiliary membership," in our moral community. I have tried in this essay to dispel the conceptual confusions that make such conclusions possible. To acknowledge their rights is the very least we can do for members of endangered species (including our own). But that is something.

Note

1. W. D. Lamont, *Principles of Moral Judgment* (Oxford: Clarendon Press, 1946), pp. 83–5.

CHAPTER 45

On Being Morally Considerable

KENNETH GOODPASTER

A thing is right when it tends to preserve the integrity, stability, and beauty of the biotic community. It is wrong when it tends otherwise.

(*Aldo Leopold*)

What follows is a preliminary inquiry into a question which needs more elaborate treatment than an essay can provide. The question can be and has been addressed in different rhetorical formats, but perhaps G. J. Warnock's formulation of it[1] is the best to start with:

> Let us consider the question to whom principles of morality apply from, so to speak, the other end—from the standpoint not of the agent, but of the "patient." What, we may ask here, is the condition of moral *relevance*? What is the condition of having a claim to be *considered*, by rational agents to whom moral principles apply? (148)

[...]

Kenneth Goodpaster, "On Being Morally Considerable," pp. 308, 310–25 from *Journal of Philosophy*, 75, 1978. Reprinted by permission of *The Journal of Philosophy*.

I

[...] Neither rationality nor the capacity to experience pleasure and pain seem to me necessary (even though they may be sufficient) conditions on moral considerability. And only our hedonistic and concentric forms of ethical reflection keep us from acknowledging this fact. Nothing short of the condition of *being alive* seems to me to be a plausible and non-arbitrary criterion. What is more, this criterion, if taken seriously, could admit of application to entities and systems of entities heretofore unimagined as claimants on our moral attention (such as the biosystem itself). Some may be inclined to take such implications as a *reductio* of the move "beyond humanism." I am beginning to be persuaded, however, that such implications may provide both a meaningful ethical vision and the hope of a more adequate action guide for the long-term future. Paradigms are crucial components in knowledge – but they can conceal as much as they reveal. Our paradigms of moral considerability are individual persons and their joys and sorrows. I want to venture the belief that the universe of moral consideration is more complex than these paradigms allow.

II

My strategy, now that my cards are on the table, will be to spell out a few rules of the game (in this section) and then to examine the "hands" of several respected philosophers whose arguments seem to count against casting the moral net as widely as I am inclined to (sections III, IV, and V). In the concluding section (VI), I will discuss several objections and touch on further questions needing attention.

The first (of four) distinctions that must be kept clear in addressing our question has already been alluded to. It is that between moral *rights* and moral *considerability*. My inclination is to construe the notion of rights as more specific than that of considerability, largely to avoid what seem to be unnecessary complications over the requirements for something's being an appropriate "bearer of rights." The concept of rights is used in wider and narrower senses, of course. Some authors (indeed, one whom we shall consider later in this paper) use it as roughly synonymous with Warnock's notion of "moral relevance." Others believe that being a bearer of rights involves the satisfaction of much more demanding requirements. The sentiments of John Passmore[2] are probably typical of this narrower view:

> The idea of "rights" is simply not applicable to what is non-human . . . It is one thing to say that it is wrong to treat animals cruelly, quite another to say that animals have rights (116/7).

I doubt whether it is so clear that the class of rights-bearers is or ought to be restricted to human beings, but I propose to suspend this question entirely by framing the discussion in terms of the notion of moral considerability (following Warnock), except in contexts where there is reason to think the widest sense of "rights" is at work. Whether beings who deserve moral consideration in themselves, not simply by reason of their utility to human beings, also possess moral *rights* in some narrow sense is a question which will, therefore, remain open here – and it is a question the answer to which need not be determined in advance.

A second distinction is that between what might be called a *criterion of moral considerability* and a *criterion of moral significance*. The former represents the central quarry here, while the latter, which might easily get confused with the former, aims at governing *comparative* judgments of moral "weight" in cases of conflict. Whether a tree, say, deserves any moral consideration is a question that must be kept separate from the question of whether trees deserve more or less consideration than dogs, or dogs than human persons. We should not expect that the criterion for having "moral standing" at all will be the same as the criterion for adjudicating competing claims to priority among beings that merit that standing. In fact, it may well be an insufficient appreciation of this distinction which leads some to a preoccupation with rights in dealing with morality. I suspect that the real force of attributions of "rights" derives from comparative contexts, contexts in which moral considerability is presupposed and the issue of strength is crucial. Eventually, of course, the priority issues have to be dealt with for an operational ethical account – this much I have already acknowledged – but in the interests of clarity, I set them aside for now.

Another important distinction, the third, turns on the difference between questions of intelligibility and questions of normative substance. An adequate treatment of this difficult and complicated division would take us far afield, but a few remarks are in order. It is tempting to assume, with Joel Feinberg,[3] that we can neatly separate such questions as

(2)   What sorts of beings can (logically) be *said* to deserve moral consideration?

from questions like

(3)   What sorts of beings do, as a matter of "ethical fact" deserve moral consideration?

But our confidence in the separation here wanes (perhaps more quickly than in other philosophical contexts where the conceptual/substantive distinction arises) when we reflect upon the apparent *flexibility* of our metamoral beliefs. One might argue plausibly, for example, that there were times and societies in which the moral standing of blacks was, as a matter of *conceptual analysis*, deniable. Examples could be multiplied to include women, children, fetuses, and various other instances of what might be called "metamoral disenfranchisement." I suspect that the lesson to be learned here is that,[. . .]metaethics is, and has always been, a partially normative discipline. Whether we are to take this to mean that it is really impossible ever to engage in morally neutral conceptual analysis in ethics is, of course, another question. In any case, it appears that, with respect to the issue at hand, keeping (2) and (3) apart will be difficult. At the very least, I think, we must be wary of arguments that purport to answer (3) *solely* on the basis of "ordinary language"–style answers to (2).

Though the focus of the present inquiry is more normative than conceptual [hence aimed more at (3) than at (2)], it remains what I called a "framework" inquiry nonetheless, since it prescinds from the question of relative weights (moral significance) of moral considerability claims.

Moreover – and this brings us to the fourth and last distinction – there is another respect in which the present inquiry involves framework questions rather than questions of application. There is clearly a sense in which we are subject to *thresholds* of moral sensitivity just as we are subject to thresholds of cognitive or perceptual sensitivity. Beyond such thresholds we are "morally blind" or suffer disintegrative consequences analogous to "information overload" in a computer. In the face of our conative limitations, we often will distinguish between moral demands that are relative to those limitations and moral demands that are not. The latter demands represent claims on our consideration or respect which we acknowledge as in some sense ideally determinative if not practically determinative. We might mark this distinction by borrowing Ross's categories of "prima facie vs. actual duty" except that (A) these

categories tend to map more naturally onto the distinction mentioned earlier between considerability and significance, and (B) these categories tend to evoke conditionality and lack thereof of a sort which is rooted more in a plurality of "external" moral pressures than in an agent's "internal" capacities for practical response. Let us, then, say that the moral considerability of X is *operative* for an agent A if and only if the thorough acknowledgment of X by A is psychologically (and in general, causally) possible for A. If the moral considerability of X is defensible on all grounds independent of operativity, we shall say that it is *regulative*. An agent may, for example, have an obligation to grant regulative considerability to all living things, but be able psychologically and in terms of his own nutrition to grant operative consideration to a much smaller class of things (though note that capacities in this regard differ among persons and change over time).

Using all these distinctions, and the rough and ready terminology that they yield, we can now state the issue in (1) as a concern for a relatively substantive (vs. purely logical) criterion of moral considerability (vs. moral significance) of a regulative (vs. operative) sort. As far as I can see, X's being a living thing is both necessary and sufficient for moral considerability so understood, whatever may be the case for the moral *rights* that rational agents should acknowledge.

III

Let us begin with Warnock's own answer to the question, now that the question has been clarified somewhat. In setting out his answer, Warnock argues (in my view, persuasively) against two more restrictive candidates. The first, what might be called the *Kantian principle*, amounts to little more than a reflection of the requirements of moral *agency* onto those of moral considerability:

(4)   For X to deserve moral consideration from A, X must be a rational human person.

Observing that such a criterion of considerability eliminates children and mentally handicapped adults, among others, Warnock dismisses it as intolerably narrow.

The second candidate, actually a more generous variant of the first, sets the limits of moral considerability by disjoining "potentiality":

(5) For all A, X deserves moral consideration from A if and only if X is a rational human person or is a potential rational human person.

Warnock's reply to this suggestion is also persuasive. Infants and imbeciles are no doubt potentially rational, but this does not appear to be the reason why we should not maltreat them. And we would not say that an imbecile reasonably judged to be incurable would thereby reasonably be taken to have no moral claims (151). In short, it seems arbitrary to draw the boundary of moral *considerability* around rational human beings (actual or potential), however plausible it might be to draw the boundary of moral *responsibility* there!

Warnock then settles upon his own solution. The basis of moral claims, he says, may be put as follows:

> . . . just as liability to be judged as a moral agent follows from one's general capability of alleviating, by moral action, the ills of the predicament, and is for that reason confined to rational beings, so the condition of being a proper "beneficiary" of moral action is the capability of *suffering* the ills of the predicament – and for that reason is not confined to rational beings, nor even to potential members of that class (151).

The criterion of moral considerability then, is located in the *capacity to suffer*:

(6) For all A, X deserves moral consideration from A if and only if X is capable of suffering pain (or experiencing enjoyment).

And the defense involves appeal to what Warnock considers to be (analytically) the *object* of the moral enterprise: amelioration of "the predicament."

Now two issues arise immediately in the wake of this sort of appeal. The first has to do with Warnock's own over-all strategy in the context of the quoted passage. Earlier on in his book, he insists that the appropriate analysis of the concept of morality will lead us to an "object" whose pursuit provides the framework for ethics. But the "object" seems to be more restrictive:

> . . . the general object of moral evaluation must be to contribute in some respects, by way of the actions of rational beings, to the amelioration of the human predicament – that is, of the conditions in which *these* rational beings, humans, actually find themselves (16; emphasis in the original).

It appears that, by the time moral considerability comes up later in the book, Warnock has changed his mind about the object of morality by enlarging the "predicament" to include nonhumans.

The second issue turns on the question of analysis itself. As I suggested earlier, it is difficult to keep conceptual and substantive questions apart in the present context. We can, of course, stipulatively *define* "morality" as both having an object and having the object of mitigating suffering. But, in the absence of more argument, such definition is itself in need of a warrant. Twentieth-century preoccupation with the naturalistic or definist fallacy should have taught us at least this much.

Neither of these two observations shows that Warnock's suggested criterion is wrong, of course. But they do, I think, put us in a rather more demanding mood. And the mood is aggravated when we look to two other writers on the subject who appear to hold similar views.

W. K. Frankena, in a recent paper,[4] joins forces:

> Like Warnock, I believe that there are right and wrong ways to treat infants, animals, imbeciles, and idiots even if or even though (as the case may be) they are not persons or human beings – just because they are capable of pleasure and suffering, and not just because their lives happen to have some value to or for those who clearly are persons or human beings.

And Peter Singer[5] Writes:

> If a being is not capable of suffering, or of experiencing enjoyment or happiness, there is

nothing to be taken into account. This is why the limit of sentience (using the term as a convenient, if not strictly accurate, shorthand for the capacity to suffer or experience enjoyment or experience enjoyment or happiness) is the only defensible boundary of concern for the interests of others (154).

I say that the mood is aggravated because, although I acknowledge and even applaud the conviction expressed by these philosophers that the capacity to suffer (or perhaps better, *sentience*) is sufficient for moral considerability, I fail to understand their reasons for thinking such a criterion necessary. To be sure, there are hints at reasons in each case. Warnock implies that nonsentient beings could not be proper "beneficiaries" of moral action. Singer seems to think that beyond sentience "there is nothing to take into account." And Frankena suggests that nonsentient beings simply do not provide us with moral reasons for respecting them unless it be potentiality for sentience. Yet it is so clear that there *is* something to take into account, something that is not merely "potential sentience" and which surely does qualify beings as beneficiaries and capable of harm – namely, *life* – that the hints provided seem to me to fall short of good reasons.

Biologically, it appears that sentience is an adaptive characteristic of living organisms that provides them with a better capacity to anticipate, and so avoid, threats to life. This at least suggests, though of course it does not prove, that the capacities to suffer and to enjoy are ancillary to something more important rather than tickets to considerability in their own right. In the words of one perceptive scientific observer:

If we view pleasure as rooted in our sensory physiology, it is not difficult to see that our neurophysiological equipment must have evolved via variation and selective retention in such a way as to record a positive signal to adaptationally satisfactory conditions and a negative signal to adaptationally unsatisfactory conditions . . . The pleasure signal is only an evolutionarily derived indicator, not the goal itself. It is the applause which signals a job well done, but not the actual completion of the job.[6]

Nor is it absurd to imagine that evolution might have resulted (indeed might still result?) in beings whose capacities to maintain, protect, and advance their lives did not depend upon mechanisms of pain and pleasure at all.

So far, then, we can see that the search for a criterion of moral considerability takes one quickly and plausibly beyond humanism. But there is a tendency, exhibited in the remarks of Warnock, Frankena, and Singer, to draw up the wagons around the notion of sentience. I have suggested that there is reason to go further and not very much in the way of argument not to. But perhaps there is a stronger and more explicit case that can be made for sentience. I think there is, in a way, and I propose to discuss it in detail in the section that follows.

IV

Joel Feinberg offers (51) what may be the clearest and most explicit case for a restrictive criterion on moral considerability (restrictive with respect to life). I should mention at the outset, however, that the context for his remarks is

(I)   the concept of "rights," which, we have seen, is sometimes taken to be narrower than the concept of "considerability" and

(II) the *intelligibility* of rights-attributions, which, we have seen, is problematically related to the more substantive issue of what beings deserve moral consideration.

These two features of Feinberg's discussion might be thought sufficient to invalidate my use of that discussion here. But the context of his remarks is clearly such that "rights" is taken very broadly, much closer to what I am calling moral considerability than to what Passmore calls "rights." And the thrust of the arguments, since they are directed against the *intelligibility* of certain rights attributions, is *a fortiori* relevant to the more substantive issue set out in (1). So I propose to treat Feinberg's arguments as if they were addressed to the considerability issue in its more substantive form, whether or not they were or would be intended to have such general application. I do so with due notice to the possible need for scare-quotes around Feinberg's name, but with the conviction that it is really in Feinberg's discussion that we discover the clearest line of argument in favor of something like sentience, an argument which was only hinted at in the remarks of Warnock, Frankena, and Singer.

The central thesis defended by Feinberg is that a being cannot intelligibly be said to possess moral rights (read: deserve moral consideration) unless that being satisfies the "interest principle," and that only the subclass of humans and higher animals among living beings satisfies this principle:

> . . . the sorts of beings who can have rights are precisely those who have (or can have) interests. I have come to this tentative conclusion for two reasons: (1) because a right holder must be capable of being represented and it is impossible to represent a being that has no interests, and (2) because a right holder must be capable of being a beneficiary in his own person, and a being without interests is a being that is incapable of being harmed or benefited, having no good or "sake" of its own (51).

Implicit in this passage are the following two arguments, interpreted in terms of moral considerability:

(A1)   Only beings who can be represented can deserve moral consideration.

Only beings who have (or can have) interests can be represented.

Therefore, only beings who have (or can have) interests can deserve moral consideration.

(A2)   Only beings capable of being beneficiaries can deserve moral consideration.

Only beings who have (or can have) interests are capable of being beneficiaries.

Therefore, only beings who have (or can have) interests can deserve moral consideration.

I suspect that these two arguments are at work between the lines in Warnock, Frankena, and

Singer, though of course one can never be sure. In any case, I propose to consider them as the best defense of the sentience criterion in recent literature.

I am prepared to grant, with some reservations, the first premises in each of these obviously valid arguments. The second premises, though, are *both* importantly equivocal. To claim that only beings who have (or can have) interests can be represented might mean that "mere things" cannot be represented because they have nothing to represent, no "interests" as opposed to "usefulness" to defend or protect. Similarly, to claim that only beings who have (or can have) interests are capable of being beneficiaries might mean that "mere things" are incapable of being benefited or harmed – they have no "well-being" to be sought or acknowledged by rational moral agents. So construed, Feinberg seems to be right; but he also seems to be committed to allowing any *living* thing the status of moral considerability. For as he himself admits, even plants

> . . . are not "mere things"; they are vital objects with inherited biological propensities determining their natural growth. Moreover we do say that certain conditions are "good" or "bad" for plants, thereby suggesting that plants, unlike rocks, are capable of having a "good" (51).

But Feinberg pretty clearly wants to draw the nets tighter than this – and he does so by interpreting the notion of "interests" in the two second premises more narrowly. The contrast term he favors is not "mere things" but "mindless creatures". And he makes this move by insisting that "interests" logically presuppose *desires* or *wants* or *aims*, the equipment for which is not possessed by plants (nor, we might add, by many animals or even some humans?).

But why should we accept this shift in strength of the criterion? In doing so, we clearly abandon one sense in which living organisms like plants do have interests that can be represented. There is no absurdity in imagining the representation of the needs of a tree for sun and water in the face of a proposal to cut it down or pave its immediate radius for a parking lot. We might of course, on reflection, decide to go ahead and cut it down or do the paving, but there is hardly an intelligibility problem about representing the tree's interest in our deciding not to. In the face of their obvious tendencies to maintain and heal themselves, it is very difficult to reject the idea of interests on the part of trees (and plants generally) in remaining alive.

Nor will it do to suggest, as Feinberg does, that the needs (interests) of living things like trees are not really their own but implicitly *ours*: "Plants may need things in order to discharge their functions, but their functions are assigned by human interests, not their own" (54). As if it were human interests that assigned to trees the tasks of growth or maintenance! The interests at stake are clearly those of the living things themselves, not simply those of the owners or users or other human persons involved. Indeed, there is a suggestion in this passage that, to be capable of being represented, an organism must *matter* to human beings somehow – a suggestion whose implications for human rights (disenfranchisement) let alone the rights of animals (inconsistently for Feinberg, I think – are grim.

The truth seems to be that the "interests" that nonsentient beings share with sentient beings (over and against "mere things") are far more plausible as criteria of *considerability* than the "interests" that sentient beings share (over and against "mindless creatures"). This is not to say that interests construed in the latter way are morally irrelevant – for they may play a role as criteria of moral *significance* – but it is to say that psychological or hedonic capacities seem unnecessarily sophisticated when it comes to locating the minimal conditions for something's deserving to be valued for its own sake. Surprisingly, Feinberg's own reflections on "mere things" appear to support this very point:

> . . . mere things have no conative life: no conscious wishes, desires, and hopes; or urges and impulses; or unconscious drives, aims, and goals; or latent tendencies, direction of growth, and natural fulfillments. Interests must be compounded somehow out of conations; hence mere things have no interests (49).

Together with the acknowledgment, quoted earlier, that plants, for example, are not "mere things," such observations seem to undermine the interest principle in its more restrictive form. I conclude, with appropriate caution, that the interest principle either grows to fit what we might call a "life principle" or requires an arbitrary stipulation of psychological capacities (for desires, wants, etc.) which are neither warranted by (A1) and (A2) nor independently plausible.

V

Thus far, I have examined the views of four philosophers on the necessity of sentience or interests (narrowly conceived) as a condition on moral considerability. I have maintained that these views are not plausibly supported, when they are supported at all, because of a reluctance to acknowledge in nonsentient living beings the presence of independent needs, capacities for benefit and harm, etc. I should like, briefly, to reflect on a more general level about the roots of this reluctance before proceeding to a consideration of objections against the "life" criterion which I have been defending. In the course of this reflection, we might gain some insight into the sources of our collective hesitation in viewing environmental ethics in a "nonchauvinistic" way.

When we consider the reluctance to go beyond sentience in the context of moral consideration – and look for both explanations and justifications – two thoughts come to mind. The first is that, given the connection between beneficence (or nonmaleficence) and morality, it is natural that limits on moral considerability will come directly from limits on the range of beneficiaries (or "maleficiaries"). This is implicit in Warnock and explicit in Feinberg. The second thought is that, if one's conception of the good is *hedonistic* in character, one's conception of a beneficiary will quite naturally be restricted to beings who are capable of pleasure and pain. If pleasure or satisfaction is the only ultimate gift we have to give, morally, then it is to be expected that only those equipped to receive such a gift will enter into our moral deliberation. And if pain or dissatisfaction is the only ultimate harm we can cause, then it is to be expected that only those equipped for it will deserve our consideration. There seems, therefore, to be a noncontingent connection between a hedonistic or quasi-hedonistic[7] theory of value and a response to the moral-considerability question which favors sentience or interest possession (narrowly conceived).

One must, of course, avoid drawing too strong a conclusion about this connection. It does not follow from the fact that hedonism leads naturally to the sentience criterion either that it entails that criterion or that one who holds that criterion must be a hedonist in his theory of value. For one might be a hedonist with respect to the good and yet think that moral consideration was, on other grounds, restricted to a subclass of the beings capable of enjoyment or pain. And one might hold to the sentience criterion for considerability while denying that pleasure, for example, was the only intrinsically good thing in the life of a human (or nonhuman) being. So hedonism about value and the sentience criterion of moral considerability are not logically equivalent. Nor does either entail the other. But there is some sense, I think, in which they mutually support each other – both in terms of "rendering plausible" and in terms of "helping to explain." [. . .]

Let me hazard the hypothesis, then, that there is a nonaccidental affinity between a person's or a society's conception of value and its conception of moral considerability. More specifically, there is an affinity between hedonism or some variation on hedonism and a predilection for the sentience criterion of considerability or some variation on it. The implications one might draw from this are many. In the context of a quest for a richer moral framework to deal with a new awareness of the environment, one might be led to expect significant resistance from a hedonistic society unless one forced one's imperatives into an instrumental form. One might also be led to an appreciation of how technology aimed at largely hedonistic goals could gradually "harden the hearts" of a civilization to the biotic community in which it lives — at least until crisis or upheaval raised some questions.

VI

Let us now turn to several objections that might be thought to render a "life principle" of moral considerability untenable quite independently of the adequacy or inadequacy of the sentience or interest principle.

(O1) A principle of moral respect or consideration for life in all its forms is mere Schweitzerian romanticism, even if it does not involve, as it probably does, the projection of mental or psychological categories beyond their responsible boundaries into the realms of plants, insects, and microbes.

(R1) This objection misses the central thrust of my discussion, which is *not* that the sentience criterion is necessary, but applicable to all life forms – rather the point is that the possession of sentience is not necessary for moral considerability. Schweitzer himself may have held the former view – and so have been "romantic" – but this is beside the point.

(O2) To suggest seriously that moral considerability is coextensive with life is to suggest that conscious, feeling beings have no more central role in the moral life than vegetables, which is downright absurd – if not perverse.

(R2) This objection misses the central thrust of my discussion as well, for a different reason. It is consistent with acknowledging the moral considerability of all life forms to go on to point out differences of moral significance among these life forms. And as far as perversion is concerned, history will perhaps be a better judge of our civilization's treatment of animals and the living environment on that score.

(O3) Consideration of life can serve as a criterion only to the degree that life itself can be given a precise definition; and it can't.

(R3) I fail to see why a criterion of moral considerability must be strictly decidable in order to be tenable. Surely rationality, potential rationality, sentience, and the capacity for or possession of interests fare no better here. Moreover, there do seem to be empirically respectable accounts of the nature of living beings available which are not intolerably vague or open-textured:

The typifying mark of a living system . . . appears to be its persistent state of low entropy, sustained by metabolic processes for accumulating energy, and maintained in equilibrium with its environment by homeostatic feedback processes.[8]

Granting the need for certain further qualifications, a definition such as this strikes me as not only plausible in its own right, but ethically illuminating, since it suggests that the core of moral concern lies in respect for self-sustaining organization and integration in the face of pressures toward high entropy.

(O4) If life, as understood in the previous response, is really taken as the key to moral considerability, then it is possible that larger systems besides our ordinarily understood "linear" extrapolations from human beings (e.g., animals, plants, etc.) might satisfy the conditions, such as the biosystem as a whole. This surely would be a *reductio* of the life principle.

(R4) At best, it would be a *reductio* of the life principle in this form or without qualification. But it seems to me that such (perhaps surprising) implications, if true, should be taken seriously. There is some evidence that the biosystem as a whole exhibits behavior approximating to the definition sketched above, and I see no reason to deny it moral considerability on that account. Why should the universe of moral considerability map neatly onto our medium-sized framework of organisms?

(O5) There are severe epistemological problems about imputing interests, benefits, harms, etc. to nonsentient beings. What is it for a tree to have needs?

(R5) I am not convinced that the epistemological problems are more severe in this context than they would be in numerous others which the objector would probably not find problematic. Christopher Stone has put this point nicely:

I am sure I can judge with more certainty and meaningfulness whether and when my lawn wants (needs) water than the Attorney General can judge whether and when the United States wants (needs) to take an appeal from an adverse judgment by a lower court. The lawn tells me that it wants water by a certain dryness of the blades and soil – immediately obvious to the touch – the appearance of bald spots, yellowing, and a lack of springiness after being walked on; how does "the United States" communicate to the Attorney General? (24).[9]

We make decisions in the interests of others or on behalf of others every day – "others" whose wants are far less verifiable than those of most living creatures.

(O6) Whatever the force of the previous objections, the clearest and most decisive refutation of the principle of respect for life is that one cannot *live* according to it, nor is there any indication in nature that we were intended to. We must eat, experiment to gain knowledge, protect ourselves from predation (macroscopic and microscopic), and in general deal with the overwhelming complexities of the moral life while remaining psychologically intact. To take seriously the criterion of considerability being defended, all these things must be seen as somehow morally wrong.

(R6) This objection, if it is not met by implication in (R2), can be met, I think, by recalling the distinction made earlier between regulative and operative moral consideration. It seems to me that there clearly are limits to the operational character of respect for living things. We must eat, and usually this involves killing (though not always). We must have knowledge, and sometimes this involves experimentation with living things and killing (though not always). We must protect ourselves from predation and disease, and sometimes this involves killing (though not always). The regulative character of the moral consideration due to all living things asks, as far as I can see, for sensitivity and awareness, not for suicide (psychic or otherwise). But it is not vacuous, in that it does provide a *ceteris paribus* encouragement in the direction of nutritional, scientific, and medical practices of a genuinely life-respecting sort.

As for the implicit claim, in the objection, that since nature doesn't respect life, we needn't, there are two rejoinders. The first is that the premise is not so clearly true. Gratuitous killing in nature is rare indeed. The second, and more important, response is that the issue at hand has to do with the appropriate moral demands to be made on rational moral agents, not on beings who are not rational moral agents. Besides, this objection would tell equally against *any* criterion of moral considerability so far as I can see, if the suggestion is that nature is amoral.

I have been discussing the necessary and sufficient conditions that should regulate moral consideration. As indicated earlier, however, numerous other questions are waiting in the wings. Central among them are questions dealing with how to balance competing claims to consideration in a world in which such competing claims seem pervasive. Related to these questions would be problems about the relevance of developing or declining status in life (the very young and the very old) and the relevance of the part-whole relation (leaves to a tree; species to an ecosystem). And there are many others.

Perhaps enough has been said, however, to clarify an important project for contemporary ethics, if not to defend a full-blown account of moral considerability and moral significance. Leopold's ethical vision and its implications for modern society in the form of an environmental ethic are important – so we should proceed with care in assessing it.

Notes

1. *The Object of Morality* (New York: Methuen, 1971).

2. *Man's Responsibility for Nature* (New York: Scribner's, 1974).

3. "The Rights of Animals and Unborn Generations," in Blackstone, *Philosophy and Environmental Crisis* (University of Georgia, 1974), p. 43; parenthetical page references to Feinberg will be to this paper.

4. "Ethics and the Environment," in K. Goodpaster and K. M. Sayre, eds., *Ethics and Problems of the 21st Century* (Notre Dame, IN: University Press, 1978).

5. "All Animals Are Equal," in Tom Regan and Peter Singer, *Animal Rights and Human Obliga-*
tions (Englewood Cliffs, N.J.: Prentice-Hall, 1976). See p. 316.

6. Mark W. Lipsey, "Value Science and Developing Society," paper delivered to the Society for Religion in Higher Education, Institute on Society, Technology and Values (July 15–Aug. 4, 1973), p. 11.

7. Frankena uses the phrase "quasi-hedonist" in *Ethics* (Prentice-Hall, 1973), p. 90.

8. K. M. Sayre, *Cybernetics and the Philosophy of Mind* (New York: Humanities, 1976), p. 91.

9. *Should Trees Move Standing?* (Los Altos, CA.: William Kaufmann, 1974).

CHAPTER 46
Abortion and Infanticide

MICHAEL TOOLEY

The Basic Issue: When is a Member of the Species Homo Sapiens a Person?

Settling the issue of the morality of abortion and infanticide will involve answering the following questions: What properties must something have to be a person, i.e., to have a serious right to life? At what point in the development of a member of the species Homo sapiens does the organism possess the properties that make it a person? The first question raises a moral issue. To answer it is to decide what basic moral principles involving the ascription of a right to life one ought to accept. The second question raises a purely factual issue, since the properties in question are properties of a purely descriptive sort.

[. . .]

Let us now turn to the first and most fundamental question: What properties must something have in order to be a person, i.e., to have a serious right to life? The claim I wish to defend is this: An organism possesses a serious right to life only if it possesses the concept of a self as a continuing subject of experiences and other mental states, and believes that it is itself a continuing entity.

Michael Tooley, "Abortion and Infanticide," pp. 44–55, 58–64 from *Philosophy of Public Affairs*, 1, 1972. Reprinted by permission of the publishers, Blackwell Publishing.

My basic argument in support of this claim, which I will call the self-consciousness requirement, will be clearest, I think, if I first offer a simplified version of the argument, and then consider a modification that seems desirable. The simplified version of my argument is this. To ascribe a right to an individual is to assert something about the prima facie obligations of other individuals to act, or to refrain from acting, in certain ways. However, the obligations in question are conditional ones, being dependent upon the existence of certain desires of the individual to whom the right is ascribed. Thus if an individual asks one to destroy something to which he has a right, one does not violate his right to that thing if one proceeds to destroy it. This suggests the following analysis: "A has a right to X" is roughly synonymous with "If A desires X, then others are under a prima facie obligation to refrain from actions that would deprive him of it."

Although this analysis is initially plausible, there are reasons for thinking it not entirely correct. I will consider these later. Even here, however, some expansion is necessary, since there are features of the concept of a right that are important in the present context, and that ought to be dealt with more explicitly. In particular, it seems to be a conceptual truth that things that lack consciousness, such as ordinary machines, cannot have rights. Does this conceptual truth follow from the above analysis of the concept of a right? The answer depends on how the term "desire" is interpreted. If one adopts a completely behavioristic interpretation of "desire," so that a machine that searches for an electrical outlet in order to get its batteries recharged is described as having a desire to be recharged, then it will not follow from this analysis that objects that lack consciousness cannot have rights. On the other hand, if "desire" is interpreted in such a way that desires are states necessarily standing in some sort of relationship to states of consciousness, it will follow from the analysis that a machine that is not capable of being conscious, and consequently of having desires, cannot have rights. I think those who defend analyses of the concept of a right along the lines of this one do have in mind an interpretation of the term "desire" that involves reference to something more than behavioral dispositions. However, rather than relying on this, it seems preferable to make such an interpretation explicit. The following analysis is a natural way of doing that: "A has a right to X" is roughly synonymous with "A is the sort of thing that is a subject of experiences and other mental states, A is capable of desiring X, and if A does desire X, then others are under a prima facie obligation to refrain from actions that would deprive him of it."

The next step in the argument is basically a matter of applying this analysis to the concept of a right to life. Unfortunately the expression "right to life" is not an entirely happy one, since it suggests that the right in question concerns the continued existence of a biological organism. That this is incorrect can be brought out by considering possible ways of violating an individual's right to life. Suppose, for example, that by some technology of the future the brain of an adult human were to be completely reprogrammed, so that the organism wound up with memories (or rather, apparent memories), beliefs, attitudes, and personality traits completely different from those associated with it before it was subjected to reprogramming. In such a case one would surely say that an individual has been destroyed, that an adult human's right to life had been violated, even though no biological organism had been killed. This example shows that the expression

"right to life" is misleading, since what one is really concerned about is not just the continued existence of a biological organism, but the right of a subject of experiences and other mental states to continue to exist.

Given this more precise description of the right with which we are here concerned, we are now in a position to apply the analysis of the concept of a right stated above. When we do so we find that the statement "A has a right to continue as a subject of experiences and other mental states" is roughly synonymous with the statement "A is a subject of experiences and other mental states, A is capable of desiring to continue to exist as a subject of experiences and other mental states, and if A does desire to continue to exist as such an entity, then others are under a prima facie obligation not to prevent him from doing so."

The final stage in the argument is simply a matter of asking what must be the case if something is to be capable of having a desire to continue existing as a subject of experiences and other mental states. The basic point here is that the desires a thing can have are limited by the concepts it possesses. For the fundamental way of describing a given desire is as a desire that a certain proposition be true.[1] Then, since one cannot desire that a certain proposition be true unless one understands it, and since one cannot understand it without possessing the concepts involved in it, it follows that the desires one can have are limited by the concepts one possesses. Applying this to the present case results in the conclusion that an entity cannot be the sort of thing that can desire that a subject of experiences and other mental states exist unless it possesses the concept of such a subject. Moreover, an entity cannot desire that it itself *continue* existing as a subject of experiences and other mental states unless it believes that it is now such a subject. This completes the justification of the claim that it is a necessary condition of something's having a serious right to life that it possess the concept of a self as a continuing subject of experiences, and that it believe that it is itself such an entity.

Let us now consider a modification in the above argument that seems desirable. This modification concerns the crucial conceptual claim advanced about the relationship between ascription of rights and ascription of the corresponding desires. Certain situations suggest that there may be exceptions to the claim that if a person doesn't desire something, one cannot violate his right to it. There are three types of situations that call this claim into question: (i) situations in which an individual's desires reflect a state of emotional disturbance; (ii) situations in which a previously conscious individual is temporarily unconscious; (iii) situations in which an individual's desires have been distorted by conditioning or by indoctrination.

As an example of the first, consider a case in which an adult human falls into a state of depression which his psychiatrist recognizes as temporary. While in the state he tells people he wishes he were dead. His psychiatrist, accepting the view that there can be no violation of an individual's right to life unless the individual has a desire to live, decides to let his patient have his way and kills him. Or consider a related case in which one person gives another a drug that produces a state of temporary depression; the recipient expresses a wish that he were dead. The person who administered the drug then kills him. Doesn't one want to say in both these cases that the agent did something seriously wrong in killing the other person? And isn't the reason the action was seriously wrong in each case the fact that it violated the individual's right to life? If so, the right to life cannot be linked with a desire to live in the way claimed above.

The second set of situations are ones in which an individual is unconscious for some reason – that is, he is sleeping, or drugged, or in a temporary coma. Does an individual in such a state have any desires? People do sometimes say that an unconscious individual wants something, but it might be argued that if such talk is not to be simply false it must be interpreted as actually referring to the desires the individual *would* have if he were now conscious. Consequently, if the analysis of the concept of a right proposed above were correct, it would follow that one does not violate an individual's right if one takes his car, or kills him, while he is asleep.

Finally, consider situations in which an individual's desires have been distorted, either by inculcation of irrational beliefs or by direct conditioning. Thus an individual may permit someone to kill him because he has been convinced that if he allows himself to be sacrificed to the gods he will be gloriously rewarded in a life to come. Or an individual may be enslaved after first having been conditioned to desire a life of slavery. Doesn't one want to say that in the former case an individual's right to life has been violated, and in the latter his right to freedom?

Situations such as these strongly suggest that even if an individual doesn't want something, it is still possible to violate his right to it. Some modification of the earlier account of the concept of a right thus seems in order. The analysis given covers, I believe, the paradigmatic cases of violation of an individual's rights, but there are other, secondary cases where one also wants to say that someone's right has been violated which are not included.

Precisely how the revised analysis should be formulated is unclear. Here it will be sufficient merely to say that, in view of the above, an individual's right to X can be violated not only when he desires X, but also when he *would* now desire X were it not for one of the following: (i) he is in an emotionally unbalanced state; (ii) he is temporarily unconscious; (iii) he has been conditioned to desire the absence of X.

The critical point now is that, even given this extension of the conditions under which an individual's right to something can be violated, it is still true that one's right to something can be violated only when one has the conceptual capability of desiring the thing in question. For example, an individual who would now desire not to be a slave if he weren't emotionally unbalanced, or if he weren't temporarily unconscious, or if he hadn't previously been conditioned to want to be a slave, must possess the concepts involved in the desire not to be a slave. Since it is really only the conceptual capability presupposed by the desire to continue existing as a subject of experiences and other mental states, and not the desire itself, that enters into the above argument, the modification required in the account of the conditions under which an individual's rights can be violated does not undercut my defense of the self-consciousness requirement.[2]

To sum up, my argument has been that having a right to life presupposes that one is capable of desiring to continue existing as a subject of experiences and other mental states. This in turn presupposes both that one has the concept of such a continuing entity and that one believes that one is oneself such an entity. So an entity that lacks such a consciousness of itself as a continuing subject of mental states does not have a right to life.

It would be natural to ask at this point whether satisfaction of this requirement is not only necessary but also sufficient to ensure that a thing has a right to life. I am inclined to an affirmative answer. However, the issue is not urgent in the present context, since as long as the requirement is in fact a necessary one we have the basis of an adequate defense of abortion and infanticide. If an organism must satisfy some other condition before it has a serious right to life, the result will merely be that the interval during which infanticide is morally permissible may be somewhat longer. Although the point at which an organism first achieves self-consciousness and hence the capacity of desiring to continue existing as a subject of experiences and other mental states may be a theoretically incorrect cutoff point, it is at least a morally safe one: any error it involves is on the side of caution.

Some Critical Comments on Alternative Proposals

I now want to compare the line of demarcation I am proposing with the cutoff points traditionally advanced in discussions of abortion. My fundamental claim will be that none of these cutoff points can be defended by appeal to plausible, basic moral principles. The main suggestions as to the point past which it is seriously wrong to destroy something that will develop into an adult member of the species Homo sapiens are these: (a) conception; (b) the attainment of human form; (c) the achievement of the ability to move about spontaneously; (d) viability; (e) birth.[3] The corresponding moral principles suggested by these cutoff points are as follows: (1) It is seriously wrong to kill an organism, from a zygote on, that belongs to the species Homo sapiens. (2) It is seriously wrong to kill an organism that belongs to Homo sapiens and that has achieved human form. (3) It is seriously wrong to kill an organism that is a member of Homo sapiens and that is capable of spontaneous movement. (4) It is seriously wrong to kill an organism that belongs to Homo sapiens and that is capable of existing outside the womb. (5) It is seriously wrong to kill an organism that is a member of Homo sapiens that is no longer in the womb.

My first comment is that it would not do *simply* to omit the reference to membership in the species Homo sapiens from the above principles, with the exception of principle (2). For then the principles would be applicable to animals in general, and one would be forced to conclude that it was seriously wrong to abort a cat fetus, or that it was seriously wrong to abort a motile cat fetus, and so on.

The second and crucial comment is that none of the five principles given above can plausibly be viewed as a *basic* moral principle. To accept any of them as such would be akin to accepting as a basic moral principle the proposition that it is morally permissible to enslave black members of the species Homo sapiens but not white members. Why should it be seriously wrong to kill an unborn member of the species Homo sapiens but not seriously wrong to kill an unborn kitten? Difference in species is not per se a morally relevant difference. If one holds that it is seriously wrong to kill an unborn member of the species Homo sapiens but not an unborn kitten, one should be prepared to point to some property that is morally significant and that is possessed by unborn members of Homo sapiens but not by unborn kittens. Similarly, such a property must be identified if one believes it seriously wrong to kill unborn members of Homo sapiens that have achieved viability but not seriously wrong to kill unborn kittens that have achieved that state.

What property might account for such a difference? That is to say, what *basic* moral principles might a person who accepts one of these five principles appeal to in support of his secondary moral judgment? Why should events such as the achievement of human form, or the

achievement of the ability to move about, or
the achievement of viability, or birth serve to
endow something with a right to life? What the
liberal must do is to show that these events
involve changes, or are associated with changes,
that are morally relevant.

Let us now consider reasons why the events
involved in cutoff points (b) through (e) are
not morally relevant, beginning with the last
two: viability and birth. The fact that an organism is not physiologically dependent upon another organism, or is capable of such
physiological independence, is surely irrelevant
to whether the organism has a right to life. In
defense of this contention, consider a speculative case where a fetus is able to learn a language while in the womb. One would surely
not say that the fetus had no right to life until it
emerged from the womb, or until it was capable of existing outside the womb. A less speculative example is the case of Siamese twins who
have learned to speak. One doesn't want to say
that since one of the twins would die were the
two to be separated, it therefore has no right to
life. Consequently it seems difficult to disagree
with the conservative's claim that an organism
which lacks a right to life before birth or before
becoming viable cannot acquire this right immediately upon birth or upon becoming viable.

This does not, however, completely rule out
viability as a line of demarcation. For instead of
defending viability as a cutoff point on the
ground that only then does a fetus acquire a
right to life, it is possible to argue rather that
when one organism is physiologically dependent upon another, the former's right to life
may conflict with the latter's right to use its
body as it will, and moreover, that the latter's
right to do what it wants with its body may
often take precedence over the other organism's
right to life. Thomson has defended this view:
"I am arguing only that having a right to life
does not guarantee having either a right to the
use of or a right to be allowed continued use of
another person's body – even if one needs it for
life itself. So the right to life will not serve the
opponents of abortion in the very simple and
clear way in which they seem to have thought
it would."[4] I believe that Thomson is right
in contending that philosophers have been
altogether too casual in assuming that if one

grants the fetus a serious right to life, one must
accept a conservative position on abortion. I
also think the only defense of viability as a
cutoff point which has any hope of success at
all is one based on the considerations she advances. I doubt very much, however, that this
defense of abortion is ultimately tenable. I
think that one can grant even stronger assumptions than those made by Thomson and still
argue persuasively for a semiconservative view.
What I have in mind is this. Let it be granted,
for the sake of argument, that a woman's right
to free her body of parasites which will inhibit
her freedom of action and possibly impair her
health is stronger than the parasite's right to
life, and is so even if the parasite has as much
right to life as an adult human. One can still
argue that abortion ought not to be permitted.
For if A's right is stronger than B's, and it is
impossible to satisfy both, it does not follow
that A's should be satisfied rather than B's. It
may be possible to compensate A if his right
isn't satisfied, but impossible to compensate B
if his right isn't satisfied. In such a case the best
thing to do may be to satisfy B's claim and to
compensate A. Abortion may be a case in
point. If the fetus has a right to life and the
right is not satisfied, there is certainly no way
the fetus can be compensated. On the other
hand, if the woman's right to rid her body of
harmful and annoying parasites is not satisfied,
she can be compensated. Thus it would seem
that the just thing to do would be to prohibit
abortion but to compensate women for the
burden of carrying a parasite to term. Then,
however, we are back at a (modified) conservative position. Our conclusion must be that it
appears unlikely there is any satisfactory defense either of viability or of birth as cutoff
points.

Let us now consider the third suggested line
of demarcation, the achievement of the power
to move about spontaneously. It might be argued that acquiring this power is a morally
relevant event on the grounds that there is a
connection between the concept of an agent
and the concept of a person, and being motile
is an indication that a thing is an agent.

It is difficult to respond to this suggestion
unless it is made more specific. Given that one's
interest here is in defending a certain cutoff

point, it is natural to interpret the proposal as suggesting that motility is a necessary condition of an organism's having a right to life. But this won't do, because one certainly wants to ascribe a right to life to adult humans who are completely paralyzed. Maybe the suggestion is rather that motility is a sufficient condition of something's having a right to life. However, it is clear that motility alone is not sufficient, since this would imply that all animals, and also certain machines, have a right to life. Perhaps, then, the most reasonable interpretation of the claim is that motility together with some other property is a sufficient condition of somethings having a right to life, where the other property will have to be a property possessed by unborn members of the species Homo sapiens but not by unborn members of other familiar species.

The central question, then, is what this other property is. Until one is told, it is very difficult to evaluate either the moral claim that motility together with that property is a sufficient basis for ascribing to an organism a right to life or the factual claim that a motile human fetus possesses that property while a motile fetus belonging to some other species does not. A conservative would presumably reject motility as a cutoff point by arguing that whether an organism has a right to life depends only upon its potentialities, which are of course not changed by its becoming motile. If, on the other hand, one favors a liberal view of abortion, I think that one can attack this third suggested cutoff point, in its unspecified form, only by determining what properties are necessary, or what properties sufficient, for an individual to have a right to life. Thus I would base my rejection of motility as a cutoff point on my claim, defended above, that a necessary condition of an organism's possessing a right to life is that it conceive of itself as a continuing subject of experiences and other mental states.

The second suggested cutoff point – the development of a recognizably human form – can be dismissed fairly quickly. I have already remarked that membership in a particular species is not itself a morally relevant property. For it is obvious that if we encountered other "rational animals," such as Martians, the fact that their physiological makeup was very different from our own would not be grounds for

denying them a right to life.[5] Similarly, it is clear that the development of human form is not in itself a morally relevant event. Nor do there seem to be any grounds for holding that there is some other change, associated with this event, that is morally relevant. The appeal of this second cutoff point is, I think, purely emotional.

The overall conclusion seems to be that it is very difficult to defend the cutoff points traditionally advanced by those who advocate either a moderate or a liberal position on abortion. The reason is that there do not seem to be any basic moral principles one can appeal to in support of the cutoff points in question. We must now consider whether the conservative is any better off.

Refutation of the Conservative Position

Many have felt that the conservative's position is more defensible than the liberal's because the conservative can point to the gradual and continuous development of an organism as it changes from a zygote to an adult human being. He is then in a position to argue that it is morally arbitrary for the liberal to draw a line at some point in this continuous process and to say that abortion is permissible before, but not after, that particular point. The liberal's reply would presumably be that the emphasis upon the continuity of the process is misleading. What the conservative is really doing is simply challenging the liberal to specify the properties a thing must have in order to be a person, and to show that the developing organism does acquire the properties at the point selected by the liberal. The liberal may then reply that the difficulty he has meeting this challenge should not be taken as grounds for rejecting his position. For the conservative cannot meet this challenge either; the conservative is equally unable to say what properties something must have if it is to have a right to life.

Although this rejoinder does not dispose of the conservative's argument, it is not without bite. For defenders of the view that abortion is always wrong have failed to face up to the question of the basic moral principles on which their position rests. They have been content to assert the wrongness of killing any organism, from a zygote on, if that organism is a member of the species Homo sapiens. But they have overlooked the point that this cannot be an acceptable *basic* moral principle, since difference in species is not in itself a morally relevant difference. The conservative can reply, however, that it is possible to defend his position – but not the liberal's – *without* getting clear about the properties a thing must possess if it is to have a right to life. The conservative's defense will rest upon the following two claims: first, that there is a property, even if one is unable to specify what it is, that (i) is possessed by adult humans, and (ii) endows any organism possessing it with a serious right to life. Second, that if there are properties which satisfy (i) and (ii) above, at least one of those properties will be such that any organism potentially possessing that property has a serious right to life even now, simply by virtue of that potentiality, where an organism possesses a property potentially if it will come to have that property in the normal course of its development. The second claim – which I shall refer to as the potentiality principle – is critical to the conservative's defense. Because of it he is able to defend his position without deciding what properties a thing must possess in order to have a right to life. It is enough to know that adult members of Homo sapiens do have such a right. For then one can conclude that any organism which belongs to the species Homo sapiens, from a zygote on, must also have a right to life by virtue of the potentiality principle.

The liberal, by contrast, cannot mount a comparable argument. He cannot defend his position without offering at least a partial answer to the question of what properties a thing must possess in order to have a right to life.

The importance of the potentiality principle, however, goes beyond the fact that it provides support for the conservative's position. If the principle is unacceptable, then so is his position.

[. . .]

Let us now turn to the task of finding a direct refutation of the potentiality principle. The basic issue is this. Is there any property J which satisfies the following conditions: (1) There is a property K such that any individual possessing property K has a right to life, and there is a scientific law L to the effect that any organism possessing property J will in the normal course of events come to possess property K at some later time. (2) Given the relationship between property J and property K just described, anything possessing property J has a right to life. (3) If property J were not related to property K in the way indicated, it would not be the case that anything possessing property J thereby had a right to life. In short, the question is whether there is a property J that bestows a right to life on an organism *only because* J stands in a certain causal relationship to a second property K, which is such that anything possessing that property ipso facto has a right to life.

My argument turns upon the following critical principle: Let C be a causal process that normally leads to outcome E. Let A be an action that initiates process C, and B be an action involving a minimal expenditure of energy that stops process C before outcome E occurs. Assume further that actions A and B do not have any other consequences, and that E is the only morally significant outcome of process C. Then there is no moral difference between intentionally performing action B and intentionally refraining from performing action A, assuming identical motivation in both cases. This principle, which I shall refer to as the moral symmetry principle with respect to action and inaction, would be rejected by some philosophers. They would argue that there is an important distinction to be drawn between "what we owe people in the form of aid and what we owe them in the way of non-interference,"[6] and that the latter, "negative duties," are duties that it is more serious to neglect than the former, "positive" ones. This view arises from an intuitive response to examples such as the following. Even if it is wrong not to send food to starving people in other parts of the world, it is more wrong still to kill someone. And isn't the conclusion, then, that one's obligation to refrain from killing someone is a more serious obligation than one's obligation to save lives?

I want to argue that this is not the correct conclusion. I think it is tempting to draw this conclusion if one fails to consider the motivation that is likely to be associated with the respective actions. If someone performs an action he knows will kill someone else, this will usually be grounds for concluding that he wanted to kill the person in question. In contrast, failing to help someone may indicate only apathy, laziness, selfishness, or an amoral outlook: the fact that a person knowingly allows another to die will not normally be grounds for concluding that he desired that person's death. Someone who knowingly kills another is more likely to be seriously defective from a moral point of view than someone who fails to save another's life.

If we are not to be led to false conclusions by our intuitions about certain cases, we must explicitly assume identical motivations in the two situations. Compare, for example, the following: (1) Jones sees that Smith will be killed by a bomb unless he warns him. Jones's reaction is: "How lucky, it will save me the trouble of killing Smith myself." So Jones allows Smith to be killed by the bomb, even though he could easily have warned him. (2) Jones wants Smith dead, and therefore shoots him. Is one to say there is a significant difference between the wrongness of Jones's behavior in these two cases? Surely not. This shows the mistake of drawing a distinction between positive duties and negative duties and holding that the latter impose stricter obligations than the former. The difference in our intuitions about situations that involve giving aid to others and corresponding situations that involve not interfering with others is to be explained by reference to probable differences in the motivations operating in the two situations, and not by reference to a distinction between positive and negative duties. For once it is specified that the motivation is the same in the two situations, we realize that inaction is as wrong in the one case as action is in the other.

There is another point that may be relevant. Action involves effort, while inaction usually does not. It usually does not require any effort on my part to refrain from killing someone, but saving someone's life will require an expenditure of energy. One must then ask how large a sacrifice a person is morally required to make to save the life of another. If the sacrifice of time and energy is quite large it may be that one is not morally obliged to save the life of

another in that situation. Superficial reflection upon such cases might easily lead us to introduce the distinction between positive and negative duties, but again it is clear that this would be a mistake. The point is not that one has a greater duty to refrain from killing others than to perform positive actions that will save them. It is rather that positive actions require effort, and this means that in deciding what to do a person has to take into account his own right to do what he wants with his life, and not only the other person's right to life. To avoid this confusion, we should confine ourselves to comparisons between situations in which the positive action involves minimal effort.

The moral symmetry principle, as formulated above, explicitly takes these two factors into account. It applies only to pairs of situations in which the motivations are identical and the positive action involves minimal effort. Without these restrictions, the principle would be open to serious objection; with them, it seems perfectly acceptable. For the central objection to it rests on the claim that we must distinguish positive from negative duties and recognize that negative duties impose stronger obligations than positive ones. I have tried to show how this claim derives from an unsound account of our moral intuitions about certain situations.

My argument against the potentiality principle can now be stated. Suppose at some future time a chemical were to be discovered which when injected into the brain of a kitten would cause the kitten to develop into a cat possessing a brain of the sort possessed by humans, and consequently into a cat having all the psychological capabilities characteristic of adult humans. Such cats would be able to think, to use language, and so on. Now it would surely be morally indefensible in such a situation to ascribe a serious right to life to members of the species Homo sapiens without also ascribing it to cats that have undergone such a process of development: there would be no morally significant differences.

Secondly, it would not be seriously wrong to refrain from injecting a newborn kitten with the special chemical, and to kill it instead. The fact that one could initiate a causal process that would transform a kitten into an entity that would eventually possess properties such that anything possessing them ipso facto has a serious right to life does not mean that the kitten has a serious right to life even before it has been subjected to the process of injection and transformation. The possibility of transforming kittens into persons will not make it any more wrong to kill newborn kittens than it is now.

Thirdly, in view of the symmetry principle, if it is not seriously wrong to refrain from initiating such a causal process, neither is it seriously wrong to interfere with such a process. Suppose a kitten is accidentally injected with the chemical. As long as it has not yet developed those properties that in themselves endow something with a right to life, there cannot be anything wrong with interfering with the causal process and preventing the development of the properties in question. Such interference might be accomplished either by injecting the kitten with some "neutralizing" chemical or simply by killing it.

But if it is not seriously wrong to destroy an injected kitten which will naturally develop the properties that bestow a right to life, neither can it be seriously wrong to destroy a member of Homo sapiens which lacks such properties, but will naturally come to have them. The potentialities are the same in both cases. The only difference is that in the case of a human fetus the potentialities have been present from the beginning of the organism's development, while in the case of the kitten they have been present only from the time it was injected with the special chemical. This difference in the time at which the potentialities were acquired is a morally irrelevant difference.

It should be emphasized that I am not here assuming that a human fetus does not possess properties which in themselves, and irrespective of their causal relationships to other properties, provide grounds for ascribing a right to life to whatever possesses them. The point is merely that if it is seriously wrong to kill something, the reason cannot be that the thing will later acquire properties that in themselves provide something with a right to life.

Finally, it is reasonable to believe that there are properties possessed by adult members of Homo sapiens which establish their right to life, and also that any normal human fetus will come to possess those properties shared by adult humans. But it has just been shown that if it is wrong to kill a human fetus, it cannot be because of its potentialities. One is therefore forced to conclude that the conservative's potentiality principle is false.

In short, anyone who wants to defend the potentiality principle must either argue against the moral symmetry principle or hold that in a world in which kittens could be transformed into "rational animals" it would be seriously wrong to kill newborn kittens. It is hard to believe there is much to be said for the latter moral claim. Consequently one expects the conservative's rejoinder to be directed against the symmetry principle. While I have not attempted to provide a thorough defense of that principle, I have tried to show that what seems to be the most important objection to it – the one that appeals to a distinction between positive and negative duties – is based on a superficial analysis of our moral intuitions. I believe that a more thorough examination of the symmetry principle would show it to be sound. If so, we should reject the potentiality principle, and the conservative position on abortion as well.

Summary and Conclusions

Let us return now to my basic claim, the self-consciousness requirement: An organism possesses a serious right to life only if it possesses the concept of a self as a continuing subject of experiences and other mental states, and believes that it is itself such a continuing entity. My defense of this claim has been twofold. I have offered a direct argument in support of it, and I have tried to show that traditional conservative and liberal views on abortion and infanticide, which involve a rejection of it, are unsound. I now want to mention one final reason why my claim should be accepted. Consider the example mentioned in the second section – that of killing, as opposed to torturing, newborn kittens. I suggested there that while in the case of adult humans most people would consider it worse to kill an individual than to torture him for an hour, we do not usually view the killing of a newborn kitten as morally outrageous, although we would regard someone who tortured a newborn kitten for an hour as heinously evil. I pointed out that a possible conclusion that might be drawn from this is that newborn kittens have a right not to be tortured, but do not have a serious right to life. If this is the correct conclusion, how is one to explain it? One merit of the self-consciousness requirement is that it provides an explanation of this situation. The reason a newborn kitten does not have a right to life is explained by the fact that it does not possess the concept of a self. But how is one to explain the kitten's having a right not to be tortured? The answer is that a desire not to suffer pain can be ascribed to something without assuming that it has any concept of a continuing self. For while something that lacks the concept of a self cannot desire that a self not suffer, it can desire that a given sensation not exist. The state desired – the absence of a particular sensation, or of sensations of a certain sort – can be described in a purely phenomenalistic language, and hence without the concept of a continuing self. So long as the newborn kitten possesses the relevant phenomenal concepts, it can truly be said to desire that a certain sensation not exist. So we can ascribe to it a right not to be tortured even though, since it lacks the concept of a continuing self, we cannot ascribe to it a right to life.

This completes my discussion of the basic moral principles involved in the issue of abortion and infanticide. But I want to comment upon an important factual question, namely, at what point an organism comes to possess the concept of a self as a continuing subject of experiences and other mental states, together with the belief that it is itself such a continuing entity. This is obviously a matter for detailed psychological investigation, but everyday observation makes it perfectly clear, I believe, that a newborn baby does not possess the concept of a continuing self, any more than a newborn kitten possesses such a concept. If so, infanticide during a time interval shortly after birth must be morally acceptable.

But where is the line to be drawn? What is the cutoff point? If one maintained, as some philosophers have, that an individual possesses concepts only if he can express these concepts in language, it would be a matter of everyday observation whether or not a given organism possessed the concept of a continuing self. Infanticide would then be permissible up to the time an organism learned how to use certain expressions. However, I think the claim that acquisition of concepts is dependent on acquisition of language is mistaken. For example, one wants to ascribe mental states of a conceptual sort – such as beliefs and desires – to organisms that are incapable of learning a language. This issue of prelinguistic understanding is clearly outside the scope of this discussion. My point is simply that *if* an organism can acquire concepts without thereby acquiring a way of expressing those concepts linguistically, the question of whether a given organism possesses the concept of a self as a continuing subject of experiences and other mental states, together with the belief that it is itself such a continuing entity, may be a question that requires fairly subtle experimental techniques to answer.

If this view of the matter is roughly correct, there are two worries one is left with at the level of practical moral decisions, one of which may turn out to be deeply disturbing. The lesser worry is where the line is to be drawn in the case of infanticide. It is not troubling because there is no serious need to know the exact point at which a human infant acquires a right to life. For in the vast majority of cases in which infanticide is desirable, its desirability will be apparent within a short time after birth. Since it is virtually certain that an infant at such a stage of its development does not possess the concept of a continuing self, and thus does not possess a serious right to life, there is excellent reason to believe that infanticide is morally permissible in most cases where it is otherwise desirable. The practical moral problem can thus be satisfactorily handled by choosing some period of time, such as a week after birth, as the interval during which infanticide will be permitted. This interval could then be modified once psychologists have established the point at which a human organism comes to believe that it is a continuing subject of experiences and other mental states.

The troubling worry is whether adult animals belonging to species other than Homo sapiens may not also possess a serious right to life. For once one says that an organism can possess the concept of a continuing self, together with the belief that it is itself such an entity, without having any way of expressing that concept and that belief linguistically, one has to face up to the question of whether animals may not possess properties that bestow a serious right to life upon them. The suggestion itself is a familiar one, and one that most of us are accustomed to dismiss very casually. The line of thought advanced here suggests that this attitude may turn out to be tragically mistaken. Once one reflects upon the question of the *basic* moral principles involved in the ascription of a right to life to organisms, one may find himself driven to conclude that our everyday treatment of animals is morally indefensible, and that we are in fact murdering innocent persons.

Notes

1. In everyday life one often speaks of desiring things, such as an apple or a newspaper. Such talk is elliptical, the context together with one's ordinary beliefs serving to make it clear that one wants to eat the apple and read the newspaper. To say that what one desires is that a certain proposition be true should not be construed as involving any particular ontological commitment. The point is merely that it is sentences such as "John wants it to be the case that he is eating an apple in the next few minutes" that provide a completely explicit description of a person's desires. If one fails to use such sentences one can be badly misled about what concepts are presupposed by a particular desire.

2. There are, however, situations other than those discussed here which might seem to count against the claim that a person cannot have a right unless he is conceptually capable of having the corresponding desire. Can't a young child, for example, have a right to an estate, even though he may not be conceptually capable of wanting the estate? It is clear that such situations have to be carefully considered if one is to arrive at a satisfactory account of the concept of a right. My inclination is to say that the correct description is not that the child now has a right to the estate, but that he will come to have such a right when he is mature, and that in the meantime no one else has a right to the estate. My reason for saying that the child does not now have a right to the estate is that he cannot now do things with the estate, such as selling it or giving it away, that he will be able to do later on.

3. Another frequent suggestion as to the cutoff point not listed here is quickening. I omit it because it seems clear that if abortion after quickening is wrong, its wrongness must be tied up with the motility of the fetus, not with the mother's awareness of the fetus' ability to move about.

4. Judith Jarvis Thomson, "A Defense of Abortion," *Philosophy and Public Affairs* 1(1) (1971): 56.

5. This requires qualification. If their central nervous systems were radically different from ours, it might be thought that one would not be justified in ascribing to them mental states of an experiential sort. And then, since it seems to be a conceptual truth that only things having experiential states can have rights, one would be forced to conclude that one was not justified in ascribing any rights to them.

6. Phillipa Foot, "The Problem of Abortion and the Doctrine of the Double Effect," *The Oxford Review* 5 (1967): 5–15. See the discussion on pp. 11ff.

CHAPTER 47

An Argument that Abortion is Wrong

DON MARQUIS

The purpose of this essay is to set out an argument for the claim that abortion, except perhaps in rare instances, is seriously wrong.[1] One reason for these exceptions is to eliminate from consideration cases whose ethical analysis should be controversial and detailed for clear-headed opponents of abortion. Such cases include abortion after rape and abortion during the first fourteen days after conception when there is an argument that the fetus is not definitely an individual. Another reason for making these exceptions is to allow for those cases in which the permissibility of abortion is compatible with the argument of this essay. Such cases include abortion when continuation of a pregnancy endangers a woman's life and abortion when the fetus is anencephalic. When I speak of the wrongness of abortion in this essay, a reader should presume the above qualifications. I mean by an abortion an action intended to bring about the death of a fetus for the sake of the woman who carries it. (Thus, as is standard on the literature on this subject, I eliminate spontaneous abortions from consideration.) I mean by a fetus a developing human being from the time of conception to the time of birth. (Thus, as is standard, I call embryos and zygotes, fetuses.)

The argument of this essay will establish that abortion is wrong for the same reason as killing a reader of this essay is wrong. I shall just assume, rather than establish, that killing you is seriously wrong. I shall make no attempt to offer a complete ethics of killing. Finally, I shall make no attempt to resolve some very fundamental and difficult general philosophical issues into which this analysis of the ethics of abortion might lead.

Why the Debate Over Abortion Seems Intractable

Symmetries that emerge from the analysis of the major arguments on either side of the abortion debate may explain why the abortion debate seems intractable. Consider the following standard antiabortion argument: Fetuses are both human and alive. Humans have the right to life. Therefore, fetuses have the right to life. Of course, women have the right to control their own bodies, but the right to life overrides the right of a woman to control her own body. Therefore, abortion is wrong.

Thomson's view

Judith Thomson (1971) has argued that even if one grants (for the sake of argument only) that fetuses have the right to life, this argument

Don Marquis, "An Argument that Abortion is Wrong," pp. 91–102 from Hugh LaFollette (ed.), *Ethics in Practice*. Oxford: Blackwell, 1997. Reprinted by permission of the publishers, Blackwell Publishing.

fails. Thomson invites you to imagine that you have been connected while sleeping, bloodstream to bloodstream, to a famous violinist. The violinist, who suffers from a rare blood disease, will die if disconnected. Thomson argues that you surely have the right to disconnect yourself. She appeals to our intuition that having to lie in bed with a violinist for an indefinite period is too much for morality to demand. She supports this claim by noting that the body being used is *your* body, not the violinist's body. She distinguishes the right to life, which the violinist clearly has, from the right to use someone else's body when necessary to preserve one's life, which it is not at all obvious the violinist has. Because the case of pregnancy is like the case of the violinist, one is no more morally obligated to remain attached to a fetus than to remain attached to the violinist.

It is widely conceded that one can generate from Thomson's vivid case the conclusion that abortion is morally permissible when a pregnancy is due to rape [. . .]. But this is hardly a general right to abortion. Do Thomson's more general theses generate a more general right to an abortion? Thomson draws our attention to the fact that in a pregnancy, although a fetus uses a woman's body as a life-support system, a pregnant woman does not use a fetus's body as a lifesupport system. However, an opponent of abortion might draw our attention to the fact that in an abortion the life that is lost is the fetus's, not the woman's. This symmetry seems to leave us with a stand-off.

Thomson points out that a fetus's right to life does not entail its right to use someone else's body to preserve its life. However, an opponent of abortion might point out that a woman's right to use her own body does not entail her right to end someone else's life in order to do what she wants with her body. In reply, one might argue that a pregnant woman's right to control her own body doesn't come to much if it is wrong for her to take any action that ends the life of the fetus within her. However, an opponent of abortion can argue that the fetus's right to life doesn't come to much if a pregnant woman can end it when she chooses. The consequence of all of these symmetries seems to be a stand-off. But if we

have the stand-off, then one might argue that we are left with a conflict of rights: a fetal right to life versus the right of a woman to control her own body. One might then argue that the right to life seems to be a stronger right than the right to control one's own body in the case of abortion because the loss of one's life is a greater loss than the loss of the right to control one's own body in one respect for nine months. Therefore, the right to life overrides the right to control one's own body and abortion is wrong. Considerations like these have suggested to both opponents of abortion and supporters of choice that a Thomsonian strategy for defending a general right to abortion will not succeed [. . .] In fairness, one must note that Thomson did not intend her strategy to generate a general moral permissibility of abortion.

Do fetuses have the right to life?

The above considerations suggest that whether abortion is morally permissible boils down to the question of whether fetuses have the right to life. An argument that fetuses either have or lack the right to life must be based upon some general criterion for having or lacking the right to life. Opponents of abortion, on the one hand, look around for the broadest possible plausible criterion, so that fetuses will fall under it. This explains why classic arguments against abortion appeal to the criterion of being human [. . .]. This criterion appears plausible: The claim that all humans, whatever their race, gender, religion or *age*, have the right to life seems evident enough. In addition, because the fetuses we are concerned with do not, after all, belong to another species, they are clearly human. Thus, the syllogism that generates the conclusion that fetuses have the right to life is apparently sound.

On the other hand, those who believe abortion is morally permissible wish to find a narrow, but plausible, criterion for possession of the right to life so that fetuses will fall outside of it. This explains, in part, why the standard pro-choice arguments in the philosophical literature appeal to the criterion of being a person [. . .]. This criterion appears plausible: The claim that only persons have the right to life seems evident enough.

Furthermore, because fetuses neither are rational nor possess the capacity to communicate in complex ways nor possess a concept of self that continues through time, no fetus is a person. Thus, the syllogism needed to generate the conclusion that no fetus possesses the right to life is apparently sound. Given that no fetus possesses the right to life, a woman's right to control her own body easily generates the general right to abortion. The existence of two apparently defensible syllogisms which support contrary conclusions helps to explain why partisans on both sides of the abortion dispute often regard their opponents as either morally depraved or mentally deficient.

Which syllogism should we reject? The anti-abortion syllogism is usually attacked by attacking its major premise: the claim that whatever is biologically human has the right to life. This premise is subject to scope problems because the class of the biologically human includes too much: human cancer-cell cultures are biologically human, but they do not have the right to life. Moreover, this premise also is subject to moral-relevance problems: the connection between the biological and the moral is merely assumed. It is hard to think of a good *argument* for such a connection. If one wishes to consider the category of "human" a moral category, as some people find it plausible to do in other contexts, then one is left with no way of showing that the fetus is fully human without begging the question. Thus, the classic anti-abortion argument appears subject to fatal difficulties.

These difficulties with the classic anti-abortion argument are well known and thought by many to be conclusive. The symmetrical difficulties with the classic pro-choice syllogism are not as well recognized. The pro-choice syllogism can be attacked by attacking its major premise: Only persons have the right to life. This premise is subject to scope problems because the class of persons includes too little: infants, the severely retarded, and some of the mentally ill seem to fall outside the class of persons as the supporter of choice understands the concept. The premise is also subject to moralrelevance problems: Being a person is understood by the pro-choicer as having certain psychological attributes. If the pro-choicer

questions the connection between the biological and the moral, the opponent of abortion can question the connection between the psychological and the moral. If one wishes to consider "person" a moral category, as is often done, then one is left with no way of showing that the fetus is not a person without begging the question.

Pro-choicers appear to have resources for dealing with their difficulties that opponents of abortion lack. Consider their moral-relevance problem. A pro-choicer might argue that morality rests on contractual foundations and that only those who have the psychological attributes of persons are capable of entering into the moral contract and, as a consequence, being a member of the moral community. [. . .] The great advantage of this contractarian approach to morality is that it seems far more plausible than any approach the anti-abortionist can provide. The great disadvantage of this contractarian approach to morality is that it adds to our earlier scope problems by leaving it unclear how we can have the duty not to inflict pain and suffering on animals.

Contractarians have tried to deal with their scope problems by arguing that duties to some individuals who are not persons can be justified even though those individuals are not contracting members of the moral community. For example, Kant argued that, although we do not have direct duties to animals, we "must practice kindness towards animals, for he who is cruel to animals becomes hard also in his dealings with men" (Kant, 1963, p. 240). Feinberg argues that infanticide is wrong, not because infants have the right to life, but because our society's protection of infants has social utility. If we do not treat infants with tenderness and consideration, then when they are persons they will be worse off and we will be worse off also (Feinberg, 1986, p. 271).

These moves only stave off the difficulties with the pro-choice view; they do not resolve them. Consider Kant's account of our obligations to animals. Kantians certainly know the difference between persons and animals. Therefore, no true Kantian would treat persons as she would treat animals. Thus, Kant's defense of our duties to animals fails to show that Kantians have a duty not to be cruel to animals.

Consider Feinberg's attempt to show that infanticide is wrong even though no infant is a person. All Feinberg really shows is that it is a good idea to treat with care and consideration the infants we intend to keep. That is quite compatible with killing the infants we intend to discard. This point can be supported by an analogy with which any pro-choicer will agree. There are plainly good reasons to treat with care and consideration the fetuses we intend to keep. This is quite compatible with aborting those fetuses we intend to discard. Thus, Feinberg's account of the wrongness of infanticide is inadequate.

Accordingly, we can see that a contractarian defense of the pro-choice personhood syllogism fails. The problem arises because the contractarian cannot account for our duties to individuals who are not persons, whether these individuals are animals or infants. Because the pro-choicer wishes to adopt a narrow criterion for the right to life so that fetuses will not be included, the scope of her major premise is too narrow. Her problem is the opposite of the problem the classic opponent of abortion faces.

The argument of this section has attempted to establish, albeit briefly, that the classic anti-abortion argument and the pro-choice argument favored by most philosophers both face problems that are mirror images of one another. A stand-off results. The abortion debate requires a different strategy.

The "Future Like Ours" Account of the Wrongness of Killing

Why do the standard arguments in the abortion debate fail to resolve the issue? The general principles to which partisans in the debate appeal are either truisms most persons would affirm in the absence of much reflection, or very general moral theories. All are subject to major problems. A different approach is needed.

Opponents of abortion claim that abortion is wrong because abortion involves killing someone like us, a human being who just happens to be very young. Supporters of choice claim that ending the life of a fetus is not in the same moral cateory as ending the life of an adult human being. Surely this controversy cannot be resolved in the absence of an account of what it is about killing us that makes killing us wrong. On the one hand, if we know what property we possess that makes killing us wrong, then we can ask whether fetuses have the same property. On the other hand, suppose that we do not know what it is about us that makes killing us wrong. If this is so, we do not understand even easy cases in which killing is wrong. Surely, we will not understand the ethics of killing fetuses, for if we do not understand easy cases, then we will not understand hard cases. Both pro-choicer and anti-abortionist agree that it is obvious that it is wrong to kill us. Thus, a discussion of what it is about us that makes killing us not only wrong, but seriously wrong, seems to be the right place to begin a discussion of the abortion issue.

Who is primarily wronged by a killing? The wrong of killing is not primarily explained in terms of the loss to the family and friends of the victim. Perhaps the victim is a hermit. Perhaps one's friends find it easy to make new friends. The wrong of killing is not primarily explained in terms of the brutalization of the killer. The great wrong to the victim explains the brutalization, not the other way around. The wrongness of killing us is understood in terms of what killing does to us. Killing us imposes on us the misfortune of premature death. That misfortune underlies the wrongness.

Premature death is a misfortune because when one is dead, one has been deprived of life. This misfortune can be more precisely specified. Premature death cannot deprive me of my past life. That part of my life is already gone. If I die tomorrow or if I live thirty more years my past life will be no different. It has occurred on either alternative. Rather than my past, my death deprives me of my future, of the life that I would have lived if I had lived out my natural life span.

The loss of a future biological life does not explain the misfortune of death. Compare two scenarios: In the former I now fall into a coma from which I do not recover until my death in thirty years. In the latter I die now. The latter scenario does not seem to describe a greater misfortune than the former.

The loss of our future conscious life is what underlies the misfortune of premature death. Not any future conscious life qualifies, however. Suppose that I am terminally ill with cancer. Suppose also that pain and suffering would dominate my future conscious life. If so, then death would not be a misfortune for me.

Thus, the misfortune of premature death consists of the loss to us of the future goods of consciousness. What are these goods? Much can be said about this issue, but a simple answer will do for the purposes of this essay. The goods of life are whatever we get out of life. The goods of life are those items toward which we take a "pro" attitude. They are completed projects of which we are proud, the pursuit of our goals, aesthetic enjoyments, friendships, intellectual pursuits, and physical pleasures of various sorts. The goods of life are what makes life worth living. In general, what makes life worth living for one person will not be the same as what makes life worth living for another. Nevertheless, the list of goods in each of our lives will overlap. The lists are usually different in different stages of our lives.

What makes the goods of my future good for me? One possible, but wrong, answer is my desire for those goods now. This answer does not account for those aspects of my future life that I now believe I will later value, but about which I am wrong. Neither does it account for those aspects of my future that I will come to value, but which I don't value now. What is valuable to the young may not be valuable to the middle-aged. What is valuable to the middle-aged may not be valuable to the old. Some of life's values for the elderly are best appreciated by the elderly. Thus it is wrong to say that the value of my future to me is just what I value now. What makes my future valuable to me are those aspects of my future that I will (or would) value when I will (or would) experience them, whether I value them now or not.

It follows that a person can believe that she will have a valuable future and be wrong. Furthermore, a person can believe that he will not have a valuable future and also be wrong. This is confirmed by our attitude toward many of the suicidal. We attempt to save the lives of the suicidal and to convince them that they have made an error in judgment. This does not mean that the future of an individual obtains value from the value that others confer on it. It means that, in some cases, others can make a clearer judgment of the value of a person's future *to that person* than the person herself. This often happens when one's judgment concerning the value of one's own future is clouded by personal tragedy. [. . .]

Thus, what is sufficient to make killing us wrong, in general, is that it causes premature death. Premature death is a misfortune. Premature death is a misfortune, in general, because it deprives an individual of a future of value. An individual's future will be valuable to that individual if that individual will come, or would come, to value it. We know that killing us is wrong. What makes killing us wrong, in general, is that it deprives us of a future of value. Thus, killing someone is wrong, in general, when it deprives her of a future like ours. I shall call this "an FLO."

Arguments in Favor of the FLO Theory

At least four arguments support this FLO account of the wrongness of killing.

The considered judgment argument

The FLO account of the wrongness of killing is correct because it fits with our considered judgment concerning the nature of the misfortune of death. The analysis of the previous section is an exposition of the nature of this considered judgment. This judgment can be confirmed. If one were to ask individuals with AIDS or with incurable cancer about the nature of their misfortune, I believe that they would say or imply that their impending loss of an FLO makes their premature death a misfortune. If they would not, then the FLO account would plainly be wrong.

The worst of crimes argument

The FLO account of the wrongness of killing is correct because it explains why we believe that killing is one of the worst of crimes. My being killed deprives me of more than does my being robbed or beaten or harmed in some other way because my being killed deprives me of all of the value of my future, not merely part of it. This explains why we make the penalty for murder greater than the penalty for other crimes.

As a corollary the FLO account of the wrongness of killing also explains why killing an adult human being is justified only in the most extreme circumstances, only in circumstances in which the loss of life to an individual is outweighed by a worse outcome if that life is not taken. Thus, we are willing to justify killing in self-defense, killing in order to save one's own life, because one's loss if one does not kill in that situation is so very great. We justify killing in a just war for similar reasons. We believe that capital punishment would be justified if, by having such an institution, fewer premature deaths would occur. The FLO account of the wrongness of killing does not entail that killing is always wrong. Nevertheless, the FLO account explains both why killing is one of the worst of crimes and, as a corollary, why the exceptions to the wrongness of killing are so very rare. A correct theory of the wrongness of killing should have these features.

The appeal to cases argument

The FLO account of the wrongness of killing is correct because it yields the correct answers in many life-and-death cases that arise in medicine and have interested philosophers.

Consider medicine first. Most people believe that it is not wrong deliberately to end the life of a person who is permanently unconscious. Thus we believe that it is not wrong to remove a feeding tube or a ventilator from a permanently comatose patient, knowing that such a removal will cause death. The FLO account of the wrongness of killing explains why this is so. A patient who is permanently unconscious cannot have a future that she would come to value, whatever her values. Therefore, according to the FLO theory of the wrongness of killing, death could not, *ceteris paribus*, be a misfortune to her. Therefore, removing the feeding tube or ventilator does not wrong her.

By contrast, almost all people believe that it is wrong, *ceteris paribus*, to withdraw medical treatment from patients who are temporarily unconscious. The FLO account of the wrongness of killing also explains why this is so. Furthermore, these two unconsciousness cases explain why the FLO account of the wrongness of killing does not include present consciousness as a necessary condition for the wrongness of killing.

Consider now the issue of the morality of legalizing active euthanasia. Proponents of active euthanasia argue that if a patient faces a future of intractable pain and wants to die, then, *ceteris paribus*, it would not be wrong for a physician to give him medicine that she knows would result in his death. This view is so universally accepted that even the strongest *opponents* of active euthanasia hold it. The official Vatican view (Sacred Congregation, 1980) is that it is permissible for a physician to administer to a patient morphine sufficient (although no more than sufficient) to control his pain even if she foresees that the morphine will result in his death. Notice how nicely the FLO account of the wrongness of killing explains this unanimity of opinion. A patient known to be in severe intractable pain is presumed to have a future without positive value. Accordingly, death would not be a misfortune for him and an action that would (foreseeably) end his life would not be wrong.

Contrast this with the standard emergency medical treatment of the suicidal. Even though the suicidal have indicated that they want to die, medical personnel will act to save their lives. This supports the view that it is not the mere *desire* to enjoy an FLO which is crucial to our understanding of the wrongness of killing. *Having* an FLO is what is crucial to the account, although one would, of course, want to make an exception in the case of fully autonomous people who refuse life-saving medical treatment. Opponents of abortion can, of course, be willing to make an exception for fully autonomous fetuses who refuse life support.

The FLO theory of the wrongness of killing also deals correctly with issues that have concerned philosophers. It implies that it would be wrong to kill (peaceful) persons from outer space who come to visit our planet even though they are biologically utterly unlike us.

Presumably, if they are persons, then they will have futures that are sufficiently like ours so that it would be wrong to kill them. The FLO account of the wrongness of killing shares this feature with the personhood views of the supporters of choice. Classical opponents of abortion who locate the wrongness of abortion somehow in the biological humanity of a fetus cannot explain this.

The FLO account does not entail that there is another species of animals whose members ought not to be killed. Neither does it entail that it is permissible to kill any non-human animal. On the one hand, a supporter of animals' rights might argue that since some non-human animals have a future of value, it is wrong to kill them also, or at least it is wrong to kill them without a far better reason than we usually have for killing non-human animals. On the other hand, one might argue that the futures of non-human animals are not sufficiently like ours for the FLO account to entail that it is wrong to kill them. Since the FLO account does not specify which properties a future of another individual must possess so that killing that individual is wrong, the FLO account is indeterminate with respect to this issue. The fact that the FLO account of the wrongness of killing does not give a determinate answer to this question is not a flaw in the theory. A sound ethical account should yield the right answers in the obvious cases; it should not be required to resolve every disputed question.

A major respect in which the FLO account is superior to accounts that appeal to the concept of person is the explanation the FLO account provides of the wrongness of killing infants. There was a class of infants who had futures that included a class of events that were identical to the futures of the readers of this essay. Thus, reader, the FLO account explains why it was as wrong to kill you when you were an infant as it is to kill you now. This account can be generalized to almost all infants. Notice that the wrongness of killing infants can be explained in the absence of an account of what makes the future of an individual sufficiently valuable so that it is wrong to kill that individual. The absence of such an account explains why the FLO account is indeterminate

with respect to the wrongness of killing non-human animals.

If the FLO account is the correct theory of the wrongness of killing, then because abortion involves killing fetuses and fetuses have FLOs for exactly the same reasons that infants have FLOs, abortion is presumptively seriously immoral. This inference lays the necessary groundwork for a fourth argument in favor of the FLO account that shows that abortion is wrong.

The analogy with animals argument

Why do we believe it is wrong to cause animals suffering? We believe that, in our own case and in the case of other adults and children, suffering is a misfortune. It would be as morally arbitrary to refuse to acknowledge that animal suffering is wrong as it would be to refuse to acknowledge that the suffering of persons of another race is wrong. It is, on reflection, suffering that is a misfortune, not the suffering of white males or the suffering of humans. Therefore, infliction of suffering is presumptively wrong no matter on whom it is inflicted and whether it is inflicted on persons or nonpersons. Arbitrary restrictions on the wrongness of suffering count as racism or speciesism. Not only is this argument convincing on its own, but it is the only way of justifying the wrongness of animal cruelty. Cruelty toward animals is clearly wrong. (This famous argument is due to Singer, 1979.)

The FLO account of the wrongness of abortion is analogous. We believe that, in our own case and the cases of other adults and children, the loss of a future of value is a misfortune. It would be as morally arbitrary to refuse to acknowledge that the loss of a future of value to a fetus is wrong as to refuse to acknowledge that the loss of a future of value to Jews (to take a relevant twentieth-century example) is wrong. It is, on reflection, the loss of a future of value that is a misfortune; not the loss of a future of value to adults or loss of a future of value to non-Jews. To deprive someone of a future of value is wrong no matter on whom the deprivation is inflicted and no matter whether the deprivation is inflicted on persons or nonpersons. Arbitrary restrictions on the wrongness of this deprivation count as racism, genocide or ageism. Therefore, abortion is wrong. This argument that abortion is wrong should be convincing because it has the same form as the argument for the claim that causing pain and suffering to non-human animals is wrong. Since the latter argument is convincing, the former argument should be also. Thus, an analogy with animals supports the thesis that abortion is wrong.

Replies to Objections

The four arguments in the previous section establish that abortion is, except in rare cases, seriously immoral. Not surprisingly, there are objections to this view. There are replies to the four most important objections to the FLO argument for the immorality of abortion.

The potentiality objection

The FLO account of the wrongness of abortion is a potentiality argument. To claim that a fetus *has* an FLO is to claim that a fetus now has the potential to be in a state of a certain kind in the future. It is not to claim that all ordinary fetuses *will* have FLOs. Fetuses who are aborted, of course, will not. To say that a standard fetus has an FLO is to say that a standard fetus either will have or would have a life it will or would value. To say that a standard fetus would have a life it would value is to say that it will have a life it will value if it does not die prematurely. The truth of this conditional is based upon the nature of fetuses (including the fact that they naturally age) and this nature concerns their potential.

Some appeals to potentiality in the abortion debate rest on unsound inferences. For example, one may try to generate an argument against abortion by arguing that because persons have the right to life, potential persons also have the right to life. Such an argument is plainly invalid as it stands. The premise one needs to add to make it valid would have to be something like: "If Xs have the right to Y, then potential Xs have the right to Y." This premise is plainly false. Potential presidents don't have the rights of the presidency; potential voters don't have the right to vote.

In the FLO argument potentiality is not used in order to bridge the gap between adults and fetuses as is done in the argument in the above paragraph. The FLO theory of the wrongness of killing adults is based upon the adult's potentiality to have a future of value. Potentiality is in the argument from the very beginning. Thus, the plainly false premise is not required. Accordingly, the use of potentiality in the FLO theory is not a sign of an illegitimate inference.

The argument from interests

A second objection to the FLO account of the immorality of abortion involves arguing that even though fetuses have FLOs, nonsentient fetuses do not meet the minimum conditions for having any moral standing at all because they lack interests. Steinbock (1992, p. 5) has presented this argument clearly:

> Beings that have moral status must be capable of caring about what is done to them. They must be capable of being made, if only in a rudimentary sense, happy or miserable, comfortable or distressed. Whatever reasons we may have for preserving or protecting nonsentient beings, these reasons do not refer to their own interests. For without conscious awareness, beings cannot have interests. Without interests, they cannot have a welfare of their own. Without a welfare of their own, nothing can be done for their sake. Hence, they lack moral standing or status.

Medical researchers have argued that fetuses do not become sentient until after 22 weeks of gestation (Steinbock, 1992, p. 50). If they are correct, and if Steinbock's argument is sound, then we have both an objection to the FLO account of the wrongness of abortion and a basis for a view on abortion minimally acceptable to most supporters of choice.

Steinbock's conclusion conflicts with our settled moral beliefs. Temporarily unconscious human beings are nonsentient, yet no one believes that they lack either interests or moral standing. Accordingly, neither conscious awareness nor the capacity for conscious awareness is a necessary condition for having interests.

The counter-example of the temporarily unconscious human being shows that there is something internally wrong with Steinbock's argument. The difficulty stems from an ambiguity. One cannot *take* an interest in something without being capable of caring about what is done to it. However, something can be *in* someone's interest without that individual being capable of caring about it, or about anything. Thus, life support can be *in* the interests of a temporarily unconscious patient even though the temporarily unconscious patient is incapable of *taking* an interest in that life support. If this can be so for the temporarily unconscious patient, then it is hard to see why it cannot be so for the temporarily unconscious (that is, nonsentient) fetus who requires placental life support. Thus the objection based on interests fails.

The problem of equality

The FLO account of the wrongness of killing seems to imply that the degree of wrongness associated with each killing varies inversely with the victim's age. Thus, the FLO account of the wrongness of killing seems to suggest that it is far worse to kill a five-year-old than an 89-year-old because the former is deprived of far more than the latter. However, we believe that all persons have an equal right to life. Thus, it appears that the FLO account of the wrongness of killing entails an obviously false view (Paske, 1994).

However, the FLO account of the wrongness of killing does not, strictly speaking, imply that it is worse to kill younger people than older people. The FLO account provides an explanation of the wrongness of killing that is sufficient to account for the serious presumptive wrongness of killing. It does not follow that killings cannot be wrong in other ways. For example, one might hold, as does Feldman (1992, p. 184), that in addition to the wrongness of killing that has its basis in the future life of which the victim is deprived, killing an individual is also made wrong by the admirability of an individual's past behavior. Now the amount of admirability will presumably vary directly with age, whereas the amount of deprivation will vary inversely with age. This tends to equalize the wrongness of murder.

However, even if, *ceteris paribus*, it is worse to kill younger persons than older persons, there are good reasons for adopting a doctrine of the legal equality of murder. Suppose that we tried to estimate the seriousness of a crime of murder by appraising the value of the FLO of which the victim had been deprived. How would one go about doing this? In the first place, one would be confronted by the old problem of interpersonal comparisons of utility. In the second place, estimation of the value of a future would involve putting oneself, not into the shoes of the victim at the time she was killed, but rather into the shoes the victim would have worn had the victim survived, and then estimating from that perspective the worth of that person's future. This task seems difficult, if not impossible. Accordingly, there are reasons to adopt a convention that murders are equally wrong.

Furthermore, the FLO theory, in a way, explains why we do adopt the doctrine of the legal equality of murder. The FLO theory explains why we regard murder as one of the worst of crimes, since depriving someone of a future like ours deprives her of more than depriving her of anything else. This gives us a reason for making the punishment for murder very harsh, as harsh as is compatible with civilized society. One should not make the punishment for younger victims harsher than that. Thus, the doctrine of the equal legal right to life does not seem to be incompatible with the FLO theory.

The contraception objection

The strongest objection to the FLO argument for the immorality of abortion is based on the claim that, because contraception results in one less FLO, the FLO argument entails that contraception, indeed, abstention from sex when conception is possible, is immoral. Because neither contraception nor abstention from sex when conception is possible is immoral, the FLO account is flawed.

There is a cogent reply to this objection. If the argument of the early part of this essay is correct, then the central issue concerning the morality of abortion is the problem of whether fetuses are individuals who are members of the class of individuals whom it is seriously presumptively wrong to kill. The properties of being human and alive, of being a person, and of having an FLO are criteria that participants in the abortion debate have offered to mark off the relevant class of individuals. The central claim of this essay is that having an FLO marks off the relevant class of individuals. A defender of the FLO view could, therefore, reply that since, at the time of contraception, there is no individual to have an FLO, the FLO account does not entail that contraception is wrong. The wrong of killing is primarily a wrong to the individual who is killed; at the time of contraception there is no individual to be wronged.

However, someone who presses the contraception objection might have an answer to this reply. She might say that the sperm and egg are the individuals deprived of an FLO at the time of contraception. Thus, there are individuals whom contraception deprives of an FLO and if depriving an individual of an FLO is what makes killing wrong, then the FLO theory entails that contraception is wrong.

There is also a reply to this move. In the case of abortion, an objectively determinate individual is the subject of harm caused by the loss of an FLO. This individual is a fetus. In the case of contraception, there are far more candidates (see Norcross, 1990). Let us consider some possible candidates in order of the increasing number of individuals harmed: (1) The single harmed individual might be the combination of the particular sperm and the particular egg that would have united to form a zygote if contraception had not been used. (2) The two harmed individuals might be the particular sperm itself, and, in addition, the ovum itself that would have physically combined to form the zygote. (This is modeled on the double homicide of two persons who would otherwise in a short time fuse. (1) is modeled on harm to a single entity some of whose parts are not physically contiguous, such as a university.) (3) The many harmed individuals might be the millions of *combinations* of sperm and the released ovum whose (small) chances of having an FLO were reduced by the successful contraception. (4) The even larger class of harmed individuals (larger by one) might be the class consisting of all of the individual sperm in an ejaculate and, in addition, the individual ovum released at the time of the successful contraception. (1) through (4) are all candidates for being the subject(s) of harm in the case of successful contraception or abstinence from sex. Which should be chosen? Should we hold a lottery? There seems to be no non-arbitrarily determinate subject of harm in the case of successful contraception. But if there is no such subject of harm, then no determinate thing was harmed. If no determinate thing was harmed, then (in the case of contraception) no wrong has been done. Thus, the FLO account of the wrongness of abortion does not entail that contraception is wrong.

Conclusion

This essay contains an argument for the view that, except in unusual circumstances, abortion is seriously wrong. Deprivation of an FLO explains why killing adults and children is wrong. Abortion deprives fetuses of FLOs. Therefore, abortion is wrong. This argument is based on an account of the wrongness of killing that is a result of our considered judgment of the nature of the misfortune of premature death. It accounts for why we regard killing as one of the worst of crimes. It is superior to alternative accounts of the wrongness of killing that are intended to provide insight into the ethics of abortion. This account of the wrongness of killing is supported by the way it handles cases in which our moral judgments are settled. This account has an analogue in the most plausible account of the wrongness of causing animals to suffer. This account makes no appeal to religion. Therefore, the FLO account shows that abortion, except in rare instances, is seriously wrong.

Note

1. This essay is an updated version of a view that first appeared in the *Journal of Philosophy* (1989).

References

Feinberg, J., "Abortion," *Matters of Life and Death: New Introductory Essays in Moral Philosophy*, ed. T. Regan (New York: Random House, 1986).

Feldman, F., *Confrontations with the Reaper: A Philosophical Study of the Nature and Value of Death* (New York: Oxford University Press, 1992).

Kant, I., *Lectures on Ethics*, tr. L. Infeld (New York: Harper, 1963).

Norcross, A., "Killing, abortion and contraception: a reply to Marquis," Journal of Philosophy, 87 (1990): 268–77.

Paske, G., "Abortion and the neo-natal right to life: a critique of Marquis's futurist argument," *The Abortion Controversy: A Reader*, ed. L. P. Pojman and F. J. Beckwith (Boston: Jones and Bartlett, 1994), pp. 343–53.

Sacred Congregation for the Propagation of the Faith, *Declaration on Euthanasia* (Vatican City, 1980).

Shirley, E. S., "Marquis' argument against abortion: a critique," *Southwest Philosophy Review*, 11 (1995): 79–89.

Singer, P., "Not for humans only: the place of non-humans in environmental issues," *Ethics and Problems of the 21st Century*, ed. K. E. Goodpaster and K. M. Sayre (South Bend: Notre Dame University Press, 1979).

Steinbock, B., *Life Before Birth: The Moral and Legal Status of Embryos and Fetuses* (New York: Oxford University Press, 1992).

Thomson, J. J., "A defense of abortion," *Philosophy and Public Affairs*, 1 (1971): 47–66.

PART VIII

Consequentialism

Introduction to Part VIII

Here is a very popular thought: an action cannot really be immoral if it generates only happiness for many, and no unhappiness for anyone. Here is another: sometimes life confronts us with only awful choices, and morality requires us to face this, and elect the option that will minimize harm. And here is another: the ends, if truly valuable and important, justify the sometimes hard-to-stomach means.

These are all consequentialist thoughts. Consequentialism is a family of theories that are united by one central idea – that the moral assessment of actions, motives or rules is, at bottom, a matter of how much good such things produce, or how much bad they allow us to avoid. There is a standard division within consequentialist views between *act* and *rule* consequentialism, and we will respect this division in what follows. According to act consequentialism, morally right actions are those that do, or are expected to, generate either the very best results, or sufficiently good results, as compared to all of the other actions available to a person at a given time. According to rule consequentialism, morally right actions are those that conform to optimal social rules, where such rules are those that would generate best results were they very widely endorsed or adhered to.

Consequentialist theories must all take a stand on what is intrinsically valuable. That is because the general mission of moral action, according to consequentialism, is to enhance the amount of intrinsic goodness in the world, and to diminish the amount of what is intrinsically bad. A distinct kind of consequentialism can be generated for each candidate intrinsic value. Some versions will direct us to maximize the amount of beauty in the world; others, the amount of love, or friendship, or peace. Still others are built upon a pluralistic value theory, and so reject the idea that there is any single value whose promotion is required for morally right action. *Utilitarianism*, historically the most prominent and well-developed form of consequentialism, combines a claim that happiness is the sole intrinsic value, with the consequentialist view that morally right action either actually maximizes happiness, is reasonably expected to maximize it, or tends to promote the greatest happiness. The great classical consequentialists – Jeremy Bentham, John Stuart Mill, and Henry Sidgwick – were each utilitarians who endorsed one of these variants.

For reasons that are conveyed in each of our first three readings – an excerpt from Mill's *Utilitarianism*, a contemporary exposition and defense of consequentialism from philosopher William Shaw, and a robust defense of act utilitarianism by Australian philosopher J.J.C. Smart – act consequentialism has for a long while proven more popular than rule consequentialism. The basis for this has been an argument, formulated crisply by Smart, to the effect that rule consequentialism is a form of irrational rule worship. Smart confines his attention to rule utilitarianism – the view that acts are right if and only if they are permitted by certain rules, namely, those that would maximize the overall amount of happiness were they generally adhered to. Yet Smart's criticism, if successful, applies to all forms of rule consequentialism. The argument is straightforward. Act utilitarianism requires the performance of actions that (are reasonably expected to) maximize happiness or minimize unhappiness, and forbids all other actions. If rule utilitarianism is really a distinct theory, generating different verdicts and recommendations from act utilitarianism, then rule utilitarianism must sometimes require the performance of suboptimal actions (i.e., actions that fail to maximize (expected) happiness), and forbid actions that (are reasonably expected to) maximize happiness. And yet, from a utilitarian perspective, this is completely irrational. It is irrational in that such recommendations defeat the ultimate goal of utilitarianism, which is to create a world of greatest possible happiness and the least possible misery.

Rule utilitarianism was developed to handle a variety of problems that beset act utilitarianism. Perhaps the three most important of these are (i) that act utilitarianism is a wholly impartialist doctrine; (ii) that act utilitarianism does not recognize the intrinsic moral importance of certain kinds of actions; and (iii) the so-called problem of justice. Let us consider these in turn.

It may sound quite strange to identify the act utilitarian's insistence on impartiality as any kind of problem for the doctrine. Certainly, its emphasis on impartiality is thought by many to be one of its great strengths, and provides support for the utilitarian's calls for important reforms of deeply inegalitarian social policies. Still, morality sometimes seems to require us to behave partially, rather than impartially. When faced with a choice between spending my money to feed and educate my children, or strangers, it seems morally permitted – perhaps even required – to give priority to my children. Yet this is to display partiality towards those I love, rather than to display an impartial concern for all whose needs and interests are similar. Act utilitarianism requires that we do the latter, and so forbids the kind of partiality that most of us take for granted as an acceptable element of morality.

Rule utilitarianism can handle this, provided that optimal social rules will allow us to allocate greater concern for our loved ones than for strangers. And most rule utilitarians have thought that this is the case – that society as a whole will be better off if we were to allow, or require, that people give some kinds of priority to the interests of loved ones over those of strangers.

Act utilitarianism does not endorse the idea that there is anything, in and of itself, either morally good or morally bad about any kind of action. On this view, an action's moral status depends entirely on its (likely) consequences. So there is nothing intrinsically right, for instance, about keeping one's promise, or displaying gratitude to a beneficiary; nothing intrinsically wrong about killing, or rape. Whether these actions are right or wrong depends not on their own nature, but rather on the results that they generate in any given instance. Rule utilitarianism, by contrast, does not make the moral status of actions such a contingent matter. Whether a grateful appreciation of gift in fact yields good results, or backfires of its intention, such behavior is still morally right, according to the rule utilitarian. And that is because a social rule that requires gratitude is very likely optimal, even if in specific cases the expression of gratitude fails to have the good effects it usually does.

Finally, we confront the problem of justice. The problem is that maximizing happiness (or minimizing unhappiness) can sometimes require a sacrifice of justice. If a murderer is well-connected, and can credibly threaten to wreak havoc if brought to trial and convicted, then act utilitarianism can require that legal officials let him go his way. Doing so will doubtless allow a number of bad things to happen. But if apprehending him will cause even greater harm, then letting him continue on his harmful path is what is morally required. And yet this is surely not what justice demands. The act utilitarian will say that this is a case where life presents us with only bad choices. When it does, we must choose the least worst option. That it has us allowing injustice is simply a hard fact that we must live with.

Act utilitarians (and act consequentialists generally) will deny that there are any absolute moral rules. Absolute rules are those that are never permissibly broken. According to act utilitarianism, whether we should abide by a moral rule depends entirely on the actual or expected results of doing so. No matter how firmly established a rule may be, we can always imagine a scenario in which the violation of the rule will reduce misery or maximize happiness. Consider such moral rules as those prohibiting the killing and torture of innocents, the deception of friends and family, or the enslavement of minorities. It is possible that the violation of each of these rules will, in highly unusual circumstances, indeed minimize misery or maximize happiness. And in those cases, act utilitarianism requires the violation of the relevant rules.

This may sometimes seem the path of wisdom. But we can envision situations in which, say, the torture of a wrongly despised person gives a great number of people some small pleasure. If the number is large enough, then their combined happiness will outweigh the happiness that the victim would have enjoyed were he spared his torture. In such a case, act utilitarianism requires that we go ahead and torture the innocent. Or imagine a case in which the enslavement of a very small minority population will make the much larger majority population very happy. Overall, happiness will be maximized by retaining, rather than abolishing, the system. In his carefully argued defense of act utilitarianism, R.M. Hare here argues that the preservation of slavery under such circumstances is indeed a moral requirement. Hare argues that our convictions about the importance of justice can be both explained and justified on act utilitarian grounds. When it comes to assessing the actual morality of our practices, we must sometimes set aside these strongly held conventional beliefs, and appeal directly to the act utilitarian principle that tells us that we are, after all, sometimes morally required to perpetrate injustice.

Rule utilitarians (and rule consequentialists generally) balk at this aspect of act utilitarianism.

They are concerned to preserve our convictions about the great moral importance of protecting justice, and so develop a view according to which justice is to be done even in those cases in which fulfilling its demands leads to suboptimal results. When we compare the overall utility of a social rule that prohibits enslavement, or torture, or the freeing of known murderers, with social rules that prohibit such conduct, we can see that these latter rules are ones that, if generally endorsed or obeyed, would lead to a far happier society. In that case, the moral rules are (as we believe) those that prohibit enslavement, torture, etc. If rule consequentialism is correct, that means that morally right action is determined by reference to these rules. And therefore, in the above examples, it would be wrong to torture the innocent, enslave the minority population, or fail to apprehend and try the well-connected murderer.

Brad Hooker, in his article here, develops a sophisticated version of rule consequentialism that both vindicates common sense, and seeks to avoid what most philosophers have thought to be its Achilles' heel – namely, its vulnerability to the charge of irrational rule worship. Hooker argues that the moral rules need not be ultimately justified by reference to the goal of making the world the happiest place it can be. If we abandon this goal, the basis for leveling a charge of irrationality disappears. Along the way, Hooker does a fine job of explaining the difficulties that beset act utilitarianism, and developing a version of consequentialism that rejects the utilitarian value theory. He believes that fairness is as important an intrinsic value as happiness, and so the moral rules, for him, are those that strike a balance between the two.

A powerful objection to standard versions of act consequentialism is that they demand too much of us. Their insistence that we maximize good results means that the realm of the supererogatory disappears. Supererogatory action is action that is "above and beyond the call of duty." It is good, praiseworthy behavior that falls short of being morally required, like that of a bystander who rushes into a burning building to save those trapped within. If act consequentialism is correct, nothing is beyond the call of duty, because our duty requires us always to maximize (likely) good results.

Peter Singer's contribution applies this doctrine to the subject of famine relief. We in the more prosperous countries can save a great many others from premature death were we to give up a good deal of what we have. We think that we have moral discretion over our possessions and our paychecks, but if Singer is correct, that thought is mistaken. Much of what we possess does not, he thinks, morally belong to us, even if the law protects us in our claims. If we can prevent suffering without thereby making ourselves as badly off as our intended beneficiaries, then we are morally required to do so. Those who balk at such a suggestion are well advised to read Singer's provocative piece, and use it as a kind of test case to determine the plausibility of the act utilitarianism that his advice embodies.

Another classic worry about act utilitarianism is that, despite its insistence that the like interests of everyone deserve equal respect, it nonetheless allows us to treat people without the respect they so deserve. If sacrificing a person's life or happiness is necessary to maximize good results, then that is what morality requires. This strikes many as a view that transforms those with moral standing into expendable instruments in the service of maximizing happiness.

As an illustration of this point, consider a thought experiment offered by our last author, John Harris. Imagine that a society instituted a lottery whose loser was required to submit to a vivisection, in order that his vital organs be redistributed to others whose lives would thereby be saved. The lottery is fairly run, and everyone knows that this is so. As a result, each citizen stands a better chance of living a healthy and longer life than she would were the lottery abolished. For each citizen required to give up his life, there would be at least two others whose lives would be saved. With a survival lottery, more lives would be saved than without it. And so, provided that saving life is the most significant thing we could do in such a situation, we morally must institute the lottery.

Harris considers a number of objections to such a view, and finds them all wanting. Like any good act utilitarian, he is not overly impressed by the fact that such a policy violates our deeply held beliefs about right and wrong. What counts is that we minimize misery in the world; a survival lottery will do that; therefore we are morally required to institute such a lottery. That it offends our sensibilities, and forces innocent people to sacrifice themselves for the sake of others whom they may not even care about, is not a potent objection to the enterprise. This is Hare's view, Singer's view, and Harris's, as well. For them, the requirement to maximize happiness or minimize misery takes priority over our particular moral convictions.

It is a highly controversial question within philosophy about the extent to which our theorizing should be constrained by what most of us regard as common sense. The question is no closer to resolution when it comes to ethics. Those who set greater store by our widely shared moral convictions will be to that extent suspicious of act consequentialism, despite the fact that it also preserves many of the moral beliefs we hold dear – witness the examples offered at the very beginning of this Introduction. For those less inclined to demand that moral theory preserve such widely held beliefs, consequentialism may well be the way to go.

CHAPTER 48
Utilitarianism

JOHN STUART MILL

[. . .] According to the Greatest Happiness Principle [. . .] the ultimate end, with reference to and for the sake of which all other things are desirable (whether we are considering our own good or that of other people), is an existence exempt as far as possible from pain, and as rich as possible in enjoyments, both in point of quantity and quality; the test of quality, and the rule for measuring it against quantity, being the preference felt by those who, in their opportunities of experience, to which must be added their habits of self-consciousness and self-observation, are best furnished with the means of comparison. This, being, according to the utilitarian opinion, the end of human action, is necessarily also the standard of morality; which may accordingly be defined, the rules and precepts for human conduct, by the observance of which an existence such as has been described might be, to the greatest extent possible, secured to all mankind; and not to them only, but, so far as the nature of things admits, to the whole sentient creation.

[. . .]

I must again repeat, what the assailants of utilitarianism seldom have the justice to acknowledge, that the happiness which forms the utilitarian standard of what is right in conduct, is not the agent's own happiness, but that of all concerned. As between his own happiness and that of others, utilitarianism requires him to be as strictly impartial as a disinterested and benevolent spectator. In the golden rule of Jesus of Nazareth, we read the complete spirit of the ethics of utility. To do as one would be done by, and to love one's neighbour as oneself, constitute the ideal perfection of utilitarian morality. As the means of making the nearest approach to this ideal, utility would enjoin, first, that laws and social arrangements should place the happiness, or (as speaking practically it may be called) the interest, of every individual, as nearly as possible in harmony with the interest of the whole; and secondly, that education and opinion, which have so vast a power over human character, should so use that power as to establish in the mind of every individual an indissoluble association between his own happiness and the good of the whole; especially between his own happiness and the practice of such modes of conduct, negative and positive, as regard for the universal happiness prescribes: so that not only he may be unable to conceive the possibility of happiness to himself, consistently with conduct opposed to the general good, but also that a direct impulse to promote the general good may be in every individual one of the habitual motives of action, and the sentiments connected therewith may fill a large and

John Stuart Mill, "Utilitarianism," from *Utilitarianism*, 1859.

prominent place in every human being's sentient existence. If the impugners of the utilitarian morality represented it to their own minds in this its true character, I know not what recommendation possessed by any other morality they could possibly affirm to be wanting to it: what more beautiful or more exalted developments of human nature any other ethical system can be supposed to foster, or what springs of action, not accessible to the utilitarian, such systems rely on for giving effect to their mandates.

The objectors to utilitarianism cannot always be charged with representing it in a discreditable light. On the contrary, those among them who entertain anything like a just idea of its disinterested character, sometimes find fault with its standard as being too high for humanity. They say it is exacting too much to require that people shall always act from the inducement of promoting the general interests of society. But this is to mistake the very meaning of a standard of morals, and to confound the rule of action with the motive of it. It is the business of ethics to tell us what are our duties, or by what test we may know them; but no system of ethics requires that the sole motive of all we do shall be a feeling of duty; on the contrary, ninety-nine hundredths of all our actions are done from other motives, and rightly so done, if the rule of duty does not condemn them. It is the more unjust to utilitarianism that this particular misapprehension should be made a ground of objection to it, inasmuch as utilitarian moralists have gone beyond almost all others in affirming that the motive has nothing to do with the morality of the action, though much with the worth of the agent. He who saves a fellow creature from drowning does what is morally right, whether his motive be duty, or the hope of being paid for his trouble: he who betrays the friend that trusts him, is guilty of a crime, even if his object be to serve another friend to whom he is under greater obligations.[1] But to speak only of actions done from the motive of duty, and in direct obedience to principle: it is a misapprehension of the utilitarian mode of thought, to conceive it as implying that people should fix their minds upon so wide a generality as the world, or society at large. The great majority of good actions are intended, not for the benefit of the world, but for that of individuals, of which the good of the world is made up; and the thoughts of the most virtuous man need not on these occasions travel beyond the particular persons concerned, except so far as is necessary to assure himself that in benefiting them he is not violating the rights – that is, the legitimate and authorized expectations – of any one else. The multiplication of happiness is, according to the utilitarian ethics, the object of virtue: the occasions on which any person (except one in a thousand) has it in his power to do this on an extended scale, in other words, to be a public benefactor, are but exceptional; and on these occasions alone is he called on to consider public utility; in every other case, private utility, the interest or happiness of some few persons, is all he has to attend to. Those alone the influence of whose actions extends to society in general, need concern themselves habitually about so large an object. In the case of abstinences indeed – of things which people forbear to do, from moral considerations, though the consequences in the particular case might be beneficial – it would be unworthy of an intelligent agent not to be consciously aware that the action is of a class which, if practised generally, would be generally injurious, and that this is the ground of the obligation to abstain from it. The amount of regard for the public interest implied in this recognition, is no greater than is demanded by every system of morals; for they all enjoin to abstain from whatever is manifestly pernicious to society.

The same considerations dispose of another reproach against the doctrine of utility, founded on a still grosser misconception of the purpose of a standard of morality, and of the very meaning of the words right and wrong. It is often affirmed that utilitarianism renders men cold and unsympathizing; that it chills their moral feelings towards individuals; that it makes them regard only the dry and hard consideration of the consequences of actions, not taking into their moral estimate the qualities from which those actions emanate. If the assertion means that they do not allow their judgment respecting the rightness or wrongness of an action to be influenced by their opinion of the qualities of the person who does it, this is a complaint not against utilitarianism, but against having any standard of morality at all; for certainly no known ethical standard decides an action to be good or bad because it is done by a good or a bad man, still less because done by an amiable, a brave, or a benevolent man, or the contrary. These considerations are relevant, not to the estimation of actions, but of persons; and there is nothing in the utilitarian theory inconsistent with the fact that there are other things which interest us in persons besides the rightness and wrongness of their actions. The Stoics, indeed, with the paradoxical misuse of language which was part of their system, and by which they strove to raise themselves above all concern about anything but virtue, were fond of saying that he who has that has everything; that he, and only he, is rich, is beautiful, is a king. But no claim of this description is made for the virtuous man by the utilitarian doctrine. Utilitarians are quite aware that there are other desirable possessions and qualities besides virtue, and are perfectly willing to allow to all of them their full worth. They are also aware that a right action does not necessarily indicate a virtuous character, and that actions which are blameable often proceed from qualities entitled to praise. When this is apparent in any particular case, it modifies their estimation, not certainly of the act, but of the agent. I grant that they are, notwithstanding, of opinion, that in the long run the best proof of a good character is good actions; and resolutely refuse to consider any mental disposition as good, of which the predominant tendency is to produce bad conduct. This makes them unpopular with many people; but it is an unpopularity which they must share with every one who regards the distinction between right and wrong in a serious light; and the reproach is not one which a conscientious utilitarian need be anxious to repel.

If no more be meant by the objection than that many utilitarians look on the morality of actions, as measured by the utilitarian standard, with too exclusive a regard, and do not lay sufficient stress upon the other beauties of character which go towards making a human being lovable or admirable, this may be admitted. Utilitarians who have cultivated their moral feelings, but not their sympathies nor their artistic perceptions, do fall into this mistake; and so do all other moralists under the same conditions. What can be said in excuse for other moralists is equally available for them, namely, that if there is to be any error, it is better that it should be on that side. As a matter of fact, we may affirm that among utilitarians as among adherents of other systems, there is every imaginable degree of rigidity and of laxity in the application of their standard: some are even puritanically rigorous, while others are as indulgent as can possibly be desired by sinner or by sentimentalist. But on the whole, a doctrine which brings prominently forward the interest that mankind have in the repression and prevention of conduct which violates the moral law, is likely to be inferior to no other in turning the sanctions of opinion against such violations. It is true, the question, What does violate the moral law? is one on which those who recognise different standards of morality are likely now and then to differ. But difference of opinion on moral questions was not first introduced into the world by utilitarianism, while that doctrine does supply, if not always an easy, at all events a tangible and intelligible mode of deciding such differences.

It may not be superfluous to notice a few more of the common misapprehensions of utilitarian ethics, even those which are so obvious and gross that it might appear impossible for any person of candour and intelligence to fall into them: since persons, even of considerable mental endowments, often give themselves so little trouble to understand the bearings of any opinion against which they entertain a prejudice, and men are in general so little conscious of this voluntary ignorance as a defect, that the vulgarest misunderstandings of ethical doctrines are continually met with in the deliberate writings of persons of the greatest pretensions both to high principle and to philosophy. We not uncommonly hear the doctrine of utility inveighed against as a *godless* doctrine. If it be necessary to say anything at all against so mere an assumption, we may say that the question depends upon what idea we have formed of the moral character of the Deity. If it be a true belief that God desires, above all things, the happiness of his creatures, and that this was his purpose in their creation, utility is not only not a godless doctrine, but more profoundly religious than any other. If it be meant that utilitarianism does not recognise the revealed will of God as the supreme law of morals, I answer, that an utilitarian who believes in the perfect goodness and wisdom of God, necessarily believes that whatever God has thought fit to reveal on the subject of morals, must fulfil the requirements of utility in a supreme degree. But others besides utilitarians have been of opinion that the Christian revelation was intended, and is fitted, to inform the hearts and minds of mankind with a spirit which should enable them to find for themselves what is right, and incline them to do it when found, rather than to tell them, except in a very general way, what it is: and that we need a doctrine of ethics, carefully followed out, to *interpret* to us the will of God. Whether this opinion is correct or not, it is superfluous here to discuss; since whatever aid religion, either natural or revealed, can afford to ethical investigation, is as open to the utilitarian moralist as to any other. He can use it as the testimony of God to the usefulness or hurtfulness of any given course of action, by as good a right as others can use it for the indication of a transcendental law, having no connexion with usefulness or with happiness.

Again, Utility is often summarily stigmatized as an immoral doctrine by giving it the name of Expediency, and taking advantage of the popular use of that term to contrast it with Principle. But the Expedient, in the sense in which it is opposed to the Right, generally means that which is expedient for the particular interest of the agent himself; as when a minister sacrifices the interest of his country to keep himself in place. When it means anything better than this, it means that which is expedient for some immediate object, some temporary purpose, but which violates a rule whose observance is expedient in a much higher degree. The Expedient, in this sense, instead of being the same thing with the useful, is a branch of the hurtful. Thus, it would often be expedient, for the purpose of getting over some momentary embarrassment, or attaining some object immediately useful to ourselves or others, to tell a lie. But inasmuch as the cultivation in ourselves of a sensitive feeling on the subject of veracity, is one of the most useful, and the enfeeblement of that feeling one of the most hurtful, things to which our conduct can be instrumental; and inasmuch as any, even unintentional, deviation from truth does that much towards weakening the trustworthiness of human assertion, which is not only the principal support of all present social well-being, but the insufficiency of which does more than any one thing that can be named to keep back civilization, virtue, everything on which human happiness on the largest scale depends; we feel that the violation, for a present advantage, of a rule of such transcendant expediency, is not expedient, and that he who, for the sake of a convenience to himself or to some other individual, does what depends on him to deprive mankind of the good, and inflict upon them the evil, involved in the greater or less reliance which they can place in each other's word, acts the part of one of their worst enemies. Yet that even this rule, sacred as it is, admits of possible exceptions, is acknowledged by all moralists; the chief of which is when the withholding of some fact (as of information from a malefactor, or of bad news from a person dangerously ill) would preserve some one (especially a person other than oneself) from great and unmerited evil, and when the withholding can only be effected by denial. But in order that the exception may not extend itself beyond the need, and may have the least possible effect in weakening reliance on veracity, it ought to be recognised, and, if possible, its limits defined; and if the principle of utility is good for anything, it must be good for weighing these conflicting utilities against one another, and marking out the region within which one or the other preponderates.

Again, defenders of utility often find themselves called upon to reply to such objections as this – that there is not time, previous to action, for calculating and weighing the effects of any line of conduct on the general happiness. This is exactly as if any one were to say that it is impossible to guide our conduct by Christianity, because there is not time, on every occasion on which anything has to be done, to read through the Old and New Testaments. The answer to the objection is, that there has been ample time, namely, the whole past duration of the human species. During all that time mankind have been learning by experience the tendencies of actions; on which experience all the prudence, as well as all the morality of life, is dependent. People talk as if the commencement of this course of experience had hitherto been put off, and as if, at the moment when some man feels tempted to meddle with the property or life of another, he had to begin considering for the first time whether murder and theft are injurious to human happiness. Even then I do not think that he would find the question very puzzling; but, at all events, the matter is now done to his hand. It is truly a whimsical supposition that if mankind were agreed in considering utility to be the test of morality, they would remain without any agreement as to what *is* useful, and would take no measures for having their notions on the subject taught to the young, and enforced by law and opinion. There is no difficulty in proving any ethical standard whatever to work ill, if we suppose universal idiocy to be conjoined with it; but on any hypothesis short of that, mankind must by this time have acquired positive beliefs as to the effects of some actions on their happiness; and the beliefs which have thus come down are the rules of morality for the multitude, and for the philosopher until he has succeeded in finding better. That philosophers might easily do this, even now, on many subjects; that the received code of ethics is by no means of divine right; and that mankind have still much to learn as to the effects of actions on the general happiness, I admit, or rather, earnestly maintain. The corollaries from the principle of utility, like the precepts of every practical art, admit of indefinite improvement, and, in a progressive state of human mind, their improvement is perpetually going on. But to consider the rules of morality as improvable, is one thing; to pass over the intermediate generalizations entirely, and endeavour to test each individual action directly by the first principle, is another. It is a strange notion that the acknowledgment of a first principle is inconsistent with the admission of secondary ones. To inform a traveller respecting the place of his ultimate destination, is not to forbid the use of landmarks and direction-posts on the way. The proposition

that happiness is the end and aim of morality, does not mean that no road ought to be laid down to that goal, or that persons going thither should not be advised to take one direction rather than another. Men really ought to leave off talking a kind of nonsense on this subject, which they would neither talk nor listen to on other matters of practical concernment. Nobody argues that the art of navigation is not founded on astronomy, because sailors cannot wait to calculate the Nautical Almanack. Being rational creatures, they go to sea with it ready calculated; and all rational creatures go out upon the sea of life with their minds made up on the common questions of right and wrong, as well as on many of the far more difficult questions of wise and foolish. And this, as long as foresight is a human quality, it is to be presumed they will continue to do. Whatever we adopt as the fundamental principle of morality, we require subordinate principles to apply it by: the impossibility of doing without them, being common to all systems, can afford no argument against any one in particular: but gravely to argue as if no such secondary principles could be had, and as if mankind had remained till now, and always must remain, without drawing any general conclusions from the experience of human life, is as high a pitch, I think, as absurdity has ever reached in philosophical controversy.

The remainder of the stock arguments against utilitarianism mostly consist in laying to its charge the common infirmities of human nature, and the general difficulties which embarrass conscientious persons in shaping their course through life. We are told that an utilitarian will be apt to make his own particular case an exception to moral rules, and, when under temptation, will see an utility in the breach of a rule, greater than he will see in its observance. But is utility the only creed which is able to furnish us with excuses for evil doing, and means of cheating our own conscience? They are afforded in abundance by all doctrines which recognise as a fact in morals the existence of conflicting considerations; which all doctrines do, that have been believed by sane persons. It is not the fault of any creed, but of the complicated nature of human affairs, that rules of conduct cannot be so framed as to require no exceptions, and that hardly any kind of action can safely be laid down as either always obligatory or always condemnable. There is no ethical creed which does not temper the rigidity of its laws, by giving a certain latitude, under the moral responsibility of the agent, for accommodation to peculiarities of circumstances; and under every creed, at the opening thus made, self-deception and dishonest casuistry get in. There exists no moral system under which there do not arise unequivocal cases of conflicting obligation. These are the real difficulties, the knotty points both in the theory of ethics, and in the conscientious guidance of personal conduct. They are overcome practically with greater or with less success according to the intellect and virtue of the individual; but it can hardly be pretended that anyone will be the less qualified for dealing with them, from possessing an ultimate standard to which conflicting rights and duties can be referred. If utility is the ultimate source of moral obligations, utility may be invoked to decide between them when their demands are incompatible. Though the application of the standard may be difficult, it is better than none at all: while in other systems, the moral laws all claiming independent authority, there is no common umpire entitled to interfere between them; their claims to precedence one over another rest on little better than sophistry, and unless determined, as they generally are, by the unacknowledged influence of considerations of utility, afford a free scope for the actions of personal desires and partialities. We must remember that only in these cases of conflict between secondary principles is it requisite that first principles should be appealed to. There is no case of moral obligation in which some secondary principle is not involved; and if only one, there can seldom be any real doubt which one it is in the mind of any person by whom the principle itself is recognised.

Note

1. An opponent, whose intellectual and moral fairness it is a pleasure to acknowledge (the Rev. J. Llewellyn Davies), has objected to this passage, saying, "Surely the rightness or wrongness of saving a man from drowning does depend very much upon the motive with which it is done. Suppose that a tyrant, when his enemy jumped into the sea to escape from him, saved him from drowning simply in order that he might inflict upon him more exquisite tortures, would it tend to clearness to speak of that rescue as 'a morally right action?' Or suppose again, according to one of the stock illustrations of ethical inquiries, that a man betrayed a trust received from a friend, because the discharge of it would fatally injure that friend himself or some one belonging to him, would utilitarianism compel one to call the betrayal 'a crime' as much as if it had been done from the meanest motive?"

I submit, that he who saves another from drowning in order to kill him by torture afterwards, does not differ only in motive from him who does the same thing from duty or benevolence; the act itself is different. The rescue of the man is, in the case supposed, only the necessary first step of an act far more atrocious than leaving him to drown would have been. Had Mr Davies said, "The rightness or wrongness of saving a man from drowning does depend very much" – not upon the motive, but – "upon the *intention*," no utilitarian would have differed from him. Mr Davies, by an oversight too common not to be quite venial, has in this case confounded the very different ideas of Motive and Intention. There is no point which utilitarian thinkers (and Bentham pre-eminently) have taken more pains to illustrate than this. The morality of the action depends entirely upon the intention – that is, upon what the agent *wills to do*. But the motive, that is, the feeling which makes him will so to do, when it makes no difference in the act, makes none in the morality: though it makes a great difference in our moral estimation of the agent, especially if it indicates a good or a bad habitual *disposition* – a bent of character from which useful, or from which hurtful actions are likely to arise.

CHAPTER 49

The Consequentialist Perspective

WILLIAM SHAW

Philosophers use the term *consequentialism* to identify a general way of thinking about right and wrong and thereby provide a convenient label for a whole family of theories or possible theories in normative ethics. *Consequentialist* ethical theories maintain that right and wrong are a function of the consequences of our actions – more precisely, that our actions are right or wrong because, and only because, of their consequences. The *only because* is important because almost all ethical theories take consequences into account when assessing actions, and almost all philosophers believe that the consequences of our actions at least sometimes affect their rightness or wrongness. What distinguishes consequentialist from non-consequentialist ethical theories is the insistence that when it comes to rightness or wrongness, nothing matters but the results of our actions.

When consequentialists affirm that the results or consequences of an action determine whether it is right or wrong, they have in mind, more specifically, the value of those results. That is, it is the goodness or badness of an action's consequences that determines its rightness or wrongness. Different consequentialist theories spell out this relationship in different ways. In other words, if right and wrong are a function of the goodness and badness of the results of our actions, then different functions are possible, different ways of connecting consequences to rightness and wrongness. What I shall call *standard consequentialism* advances some further theses that distinguish it from other possible types of consequentialism.

Standard consequentialism asserts that the morally right action for an agent to perform is the action, of those actions that the agent could perform at the time, that has the best consequences or results in the most good. Standard consequentialism is a maximizing doctrine. By instructing us to bring about as much good as we can, standard consequentialism distinguishes itself from the thesis that an action is right if and only if it has good consequences (or consequences that are sufficiently good or that are good enough). Standard consequentialism holds, furthermore, that we are not merely permitted or encouraged to act so as to maximize good; we are required to do so. Accordingly, standard consequentialism rejects the idea that there can be degrees of rightness so that an agent might have several options open to him, all of which are right but some of which are more right than others. On the other hand, of the actions open to the agent, several might have equally optimal results. Thus, there may be no single best action and,

William Shaw, "The Consequentialist Perspective," pp. 5–20 from James Dreier, *Contemporary Debates in Moral Theory.* Oxford: Blackwell, 2005. Reprinted by permission of the publishers, Blackwell Publishing.

hence, no uniquely right action. Put more precisely, then, standard consequentialism holds that an action is morally right if and only if there is no other action, among those available to the agent, that has better consequences; otherwise, the action is wrong. Thus, several actions might be equally right, and what morality requires is that the agent do one of them. Finally, an action might have bad consequences and yet be right. This will be the case if all alternative actions have worse results.

Further Features of Standard Consequentialism

In this section, I describe some further features of standard consequentialism. I call it standard consequentialism because it is the most familiar and widely discussed form of consequentialism; it is what I usually have in mind when discussing the subject. I am also inclined to think it is the most plausible form of consequentialism. But even if I am wrong on both counts, for purposes of discussion it will be helpful to focus on one reasonably specific version of consequentialism.

Outcome includes the value of the action itself

When consequentialists refer to the results or consequences of an action, they have in mind the entire upshot of the action, that is, its overall outcome. They are concerned with whether, and to what extent, the world is better or worse because the agent has elected a given course of conduct. Thus, consequentialists take into account whatever value, if any, the action has in itself, not merely the value of its subsequent effects.

This might sound odd, because when speaking of the "results" or "consequences" of an action, we frequently have in mind effects that are distinct from, subsequent to, and caused by the action. Consequentialists, however, don't limit results to effects in a narrow or causal sense, because they are interested in the consequences not only of one's acting in various positive ways, but also of one's refraining from acting. For example, it would seem odd to say that, by ignoring a panhandler's request

for rent money, I "caused" his family to sleep outside tonight. Still, this may be one result of my not stopping to help him; if so, then consequentialists will take it into account in assessing my conduct.

Consequentialists, moreover, needn't assume that the line between an action and the effects that flow from it, between what we do and what results from what we do, is set in nature. Rather, this line is a function of how the situation is described. For example, what I did at the faculty seminar at 4.36 p.m. might be described as "opening my mouth wide and covering my ears with my hands," "feigning shock and horror," "expressing my disdain for the ontological argument," or "insulting my colleague." "Feigning shock and horror" is a subsequent effect of my action when it is described as "opening my mouth wide and covering my ears," but not when it is described as "insulting my colleague." This fact buttresses the point that consequentialism is properly concerned with the entire upshot of our actions, with whether they make the world as a whole better or worse. We are to assess and compare the overall outcomes of the various actions we could perform, and these outcomes include the positive or negative value, if any, of each action viewed by itself as well as the positive or negative value of its subsequent effects.

The good is agent-neutral and independent of the right

Standard consequentialism assumes that we can sometimes makes objective, impartial, and agent-neutral judgments about the comparative goodness or badness of different states of affairs. At least sometimes it will be the case that one outcome is better than another outcome – not better merely from some particular perspective, but simply better, better *tout court*. Thus, for example, it is a better outcome (all other things being equal) when eight people have headaches and two people die than when two people have headaches and eight people die. Most people believe this, as do most philosophers, including many non-consequentialists. However, some non-consequentialists contend that this idea makes no sense (e.g., Thomson 2001: 12–19, 41). One state of affairs can be better for Fred or worse for Sarah than another state of affairs, they say, but it can't be said to be just plain better. There is no such thing as being just plain better, only better along some particular dimension or better for someone or better from some perspective. In line with this, some philosophers have proposed variants of consequentialism in which all or some judgments regarding the comparative value of states of affairs are agent-relative as opposed to agent-neutral. I shan't discuss these non-standard variants of consequentialism.

Standard consequentialism takes it for granted not only that the goodness or badness of an action's outcome is an agent-neutral matter, but also that this is something that can be identified prior to, and independently of, the normative assessment of the action. The point, after all, of consequentialism is to use the goodness or badness of an action to determine its rightness or wrongness. And circularity would threaten the theory if our notions of right and wrong were to infect our assessment of consequences as good or bad. Standard consequentialism thus assumes that we can identify states of affairs as good or bad, better or worse, without reference to normative principles of right and wrong. If we cannot do this, then the distinction between consequentialism and non-consequentialism begins to dissolve – leaving us, for example, unable to avoid labeling as consequentialist the deontological theorist who says that the right thing for an agent to do is to bring about the best state of affairs that he can, where the best state of affairs always consists in the agent's doing his duty, which in turn consists in his performing tokens of act types that are intrinsically right and refraining from performing tokens of act types that are intrinsically wrong.

Most non-consequentialists would agree with what I have just written. They grant that the good can be identified prior to, and independently of, the right, but they distinguish themselves from consequentialists by holding that the good doesn't, or doesn't always, determine the right. However, some self-described consequentialists would challenge the previous paragraph. They believe that it is theoretically acceptable for some normative notions to enter into our assessments of goodness and badness

and that their doing so neither is viciously circular nor undermines the spirit of consequentialism. They might hold, for example, that one state of affairs may be better than another because it is just and the other unjust and that this fact may make bringing about the first state of affairs the right thing to do. Again, however, I'll be ignoring non-standard forms of consequentialism like this.

Expected consequences, not actual consequences, are what count

According to standard consequentialism, an action is right if and only if nothing the agent could do would have better results. However, we rarely know ahead of time and for certain what the consequences will be of each of the possible actions we could perform. Standard consequentialism therefore says that we should choose the action, the expected value of the outcome of which is at least as great as that of any other action open to us. The notion of expected value is mathematical in origin and conceptualized as follows. Every action that we might perform has a number of possible outcomes. The likelihood of those outcomes varies, but each can be assumed to have a certain probability of happening. In addition, each possible outcome of a given action has a certain value; that is, it is good or bad to some specified degree. Assume for the sake of discussion that we can assign numbers both to probabilities and to values. One would then calculate the expected value of hypothetical action A, with (let us suppose) three possible outcomes, by multiplying the probability of each outcome times its value and summing the three figures. Suppose that the first outcome has a probability of 0.7 and a value of 3, the second outcome has a probability of 0.2 and a value of -1, and the third outcome a probability of 0.1 and value of 2. The expected value of A is thus 2.1, which equals $(3 \times 0.7) + (-1 \times 0.2) + (2 - 0.1)$. A is the right action to perform if and only if no alternative has greater expected value.

In reality, of course, we never have more than rough, qualitative estimates of probabilities and values. Indeed, we are likely to be ignorant of some possible outcomes or misjudge their goodness or badness, and we may overlook altogether some possible courses of action. Nevertheless, the point being made is important. Standard consequentialism instructs the agent to do what has the highest expectation of good as judged by what a reasonable and conscientious person in the agent's circumstances could be expected to know. It might turn out, however, that because of untoward circumstances, the action with the greatest expected value ends up producing poor results – worse results, in fact, than several other things the agent could have done instead. Assuming that the agent's original estimate of expected value was correct (or, at least, the most accurate estimate one could have arrived at in the circumstances), then this action remains the right thing to have done. Indeed, it is what the agent should do if he or she were faced with the same situation again. On the other hand, an agent might perform an action that has less expected value than several other actions the agent could have performed, and yet, through a fortuitous chain of circumstances, it turns out that the action has better results, brings more good into the world, than anything else the agent could have done. Nevertheless, standard consequentialism asserts that the agent acted wrongly.

Some consequentialists adopt the rival view that the right action is the one that actually brings about the best results (or would in fact have brought about the best results, had it been performed), regardless of its expected value. How can it be right, they ask, to do what in fact had suboptimal results? Or wrong to do the thing that had the best results? Because these consequentialists still want the agent to act in whatever way is likely to maximize value, they draw a distinction between objective rightness and the action it would have been reasonable (or subjectively right) for the agent to perform. Comparing the actual results of what we did with what the actual results would have been, had we done an alternative action, raises philosophical puzzles. But the main reason for orienting consequentialism toward probable results rather than actual results is that the theory, like other ethical theories, is supposed to be prospective and action-guiding. In acting so as to maximize expected value, the agent is doing what the theory wants him to do, and he is not to be blamed, nor is he necessarily to modify his future conduct, if this action does not, in fact, maximize value. Accordingly, standard consequentialism holds that this is not merely the reasonably, but also the morally right, way for the agent to act.

Further comments on the uncertainty of consequences

Critics of consequentialism perennially point to the inevitable uncertainty of our knowledge of future events, arguing that this uncertainty undermines the viability of consequentialism. Although, as was just discussed, we don't have to know what the outcome of an action will be in order to estimate its expected value, in fact we are unlikely to know all the possible outcomes an action might have, or to do more than guess at their comparative probabilities. And, depending on the particular theory of value the consequentialist adopts, he or she will have greater or lesser difficulty assigning values to those outcomes. These problems are compounded by the fact that the consequences of our actions continue indefinitely into the future, often in ways that are far from trivial even if they are unknowable.

Consequentialists can concede these points, yet affirm the viability of their theory. First, they can stress that, despite our ignorance, we already know quite a lot about the likely results of different actions. The human race wasn't born yesterday, and in reflecting on the possible consequences of an action, we do so with a wealth of experience behind us. Although by definition the specific situation in which one finds oneself is always unique, it is unlikely to be the first time human beings have pondered the results of performing actions of type A, B, or C in similar sorts of circumstances. Second, consequentialists can stress that the difficulties we face in identifying the best course of action do not undermine the goal of endeavoring to bring about as much good as we can. Whether we are consequentialists or not, we must act. And even though ignorance and uncertainty plague human action, they don't prevent us from striving to do as much good as we can. Third, and finally, consequentialists can point out that uncertainty about the future is a problem for other normative theories as well. Almost all normative theories take into account the likely consequences of the actions open to the agent and are thus to some extent infected by uncertainty about the future.

Utilitarianism

Consequentialism is not a complete ethical theory. (From now on by "consequentialism" I mean "standard consequentialism", unless otherwise indicated.) It tells us to act so as to bring about as much expected good as we can, but it doesn't say what the good is. Thus, depending on one's theory of value, there are different ways of filling out consequentialism and turning it into a complete ethical theory. Utilitarianism represents one way, and it is worth saying a little about it because utilitarianism is the most influential as well as the most widely discussed consequentialist ethical theory. In fact, only a couple of decades ago did philosophers begin to appreciate fully that an ethical theory could retain the consequentialist normative structure of utilitarianism while relinquishing its specific value commitments – that is, that an ethical theory could agree with utilitarianism that our actions should bring about as much good as possible and yet disagree with it about what the good is.

Utilitarianism takes happiness or, more broadly, well-being to be the only thing that is good in itself or valuable for its own sake. We don't need to explore what well-being involves to point out some important features of utilitarianism's value theory. First, the good, as utilitarians understand it, attaches only to particular individuals (that is, to human beings or other sentient creatures). Thus, a state of affairs is good or bad to some degree (and better or worse than some other state of affairs) only in virtue of the goodness or badness of the lives of particular individuals. There is no good or bad above and beyond that, no good or bad above and beyond the happiness or unhappiness of individuals. Second, utilitarians believe that the good is additive, that total or net happiness is just the sum of the happiness or unhappiness of each individual. More

happiness here counterbalances less happiness there. Underlying this, of course, is the assumption that in principle we can compare people's levels of happiness or well-being. But one shouldn't interpret this assumption too rigorously. Utilitarians have always granted that interpersonal comparisons of happiness or well-being are difficult, and they can even concede that some issues of comparison and addition may be irresolvable in principle. Utilitarians need believe only that we can rank many states of affairs as better or worse. Finally, utilitarians believe that each person's well-being is equally valuable, and his happiness or unhappiness, her pleasure or pain, carries the same weight as that of any other person. As Bentham wrote, each person counts as one, and no one as more than one.

In sum, utilitarianism has a welfarist value theory, which holds that the happiness or well-being of persons is the only thing that is valuable for its own sake and that the well-being of any person is neither more nor less valuable than the well-being of any other. It holds that the good is additive and that we can – sometimes and to some extent – compare the relative gains and losses in the well-being of different persons. As a consequentialist theory, utilitarianism thus asserts that the standard of moral assessment is well-being and that the right course of action is the one that brings about the greatest expected net well-being.

Non-utilitarian variants of consequentialism drop this exclusive commitment to well-being, seeing things other than or in addition to it as having intrinsic non-moral value. A utilitarian believes that the things we normally take to be valuable – say, close personal bonds, knowledge, autonomy, or beauty – are valuable only because they typically lead, directly or indirectly, to enhanced well-being. Friendship, for instance, usually makes people happier, and human lives almost always go better with it than without it. By contrast, the non-utilitarian consequentialist holds that some things are valuable independently of their impact on well-being. Some of these things, like autonomy, say, may be things that are believed to be an intrinsically valuable component of any human life. They are thought to be good for an individual, regardless of whether they promote the individual's well-being. Some non-utilitarian consequentialists go further, however and cut the link between being good and being good for someone that is characteristic of utilitarianism. They hold that some states of affairs are intrinsically better than others even if they are not better for anyone. For example, a world with more equality or beauty or biological diversity might be thought intrinsically better than a world with less even if no one is aware of the increased equality, beauty, or diversity and it makes no individual's life more valuable.

In addition to, or instead of, challenging the unique value placed on well-being, a non-utilitarian consequentialist might deviate from utilitarianism by declining to count equally the well-being of each. For example, the non-utilitarian might believe that enhancing the well-being of those whose current level of well-being is below average is more valuable than enhancing by an equal amount the well-being of those whose current level of well-being is above average. Or the non-utilitarian consequentialist might give up the belief that the good is additive and that the net value of an outcome is a straightforward function of various individual goods and bads. G. E. Moore (1903), for example, famously urged that the value of a state of affairs bears no regular relation to the values of its constituent parts. Although the non-utilitarian consequentialist would, in these ways, be challenging the value theory of utilitarianism, he or she would remain committed to the proposition that one is always required to act so as to bring about as much good as possible.

Two common objections to utilitarianism

Many critics of utilitarianism object to its maximizing approach to right and wrong on the grounds that the theory sometimes condones immoral conduct and that it is indifferent to the distribution of well-being. Because utilitarianism entails that an action's rightness or wrongness depends on its expected consequences in the particular circumstances facing the agent, it follows that the theory might require an action that commonsense morality repudiates as evil because, in the given circumstances, the action would produce more

well-being than any alternative would produce. Furthermore, utilitarianism places no intrinsic value on how well-being is distributed among individuals. It cares only about total well-being. As a result, critics charge that utilitarianism too easily permits one person's happiness to be sacrificed for the benefit of others and, more generally, that it subordinates considerations of justice, equality, and fairness to the principle of utility. Utilitarianism's critics have illustrated these two points with various imaginary but vivid examples, intended to embarrass the theory by showing that its implications are out of step with ordinary moral thinking.

Utilitarians, for their part, have a lot to say in their defense, and it is far from obvious that the above criticisms carry the day (see Shaw 1999: chs 4 and 5). Here, however, I wish only to note that these criticisms have less force against consequentialist theories that identify as intrinsically valuable various goods other than, or in addition to, well-being or that put greater priority on the well-being of those who are less well-off.

Consequentialism in Practice

According to consequentialism, an action is morally right if and only if, among the actions that the agent could perform, there is no other action, the outcome of which has greater expected value. To act in any other way is wrong. The consequentialist criterion of rightness is straightforward, but the theory's practical implications can be surprisingly subtle.

Praise and blame

For consequentialists, whether an agent acted wrongly is distinct from the question whether he or she should be blamed or criticized for so acting (and, if so, how severely). Consequentialists apply their normative standard to questions of blame or praise just as they do to other questions. In particular, they will ask whether it will maximize expected good to criticize someone for failing to maximize expected good. Blame, criticism, and rebuke, although hurtful, can have good results by encouraging both the agent and other people to do better in the future, whereas neglecting to reproach misconduct increases the likelihood that the agent (or others) will act in the same unsatisfactory way in the future. However, in some circumstances, to blame or criticize someone for acting wrongly would be pointless or even counterproductive – for example, if the person did so accidentally, was innocently misinformed, or was suffering from emotional distress. In such circumstances, chastising the person for not living up to the consequentialist standard might do more harm than good.

Suppose that a well intentioned agent acted in a beneficial way, but that she could have produced even more (expected) good had she acted in some other way. Should consequentialists criticize her? Depending on the circumstances, the answer may well be "no". Suppose she acted spontaneously but in a way that was unselfish or showed regard for others, or suppose that she could have produced more good only by violating a generally accepted rule, the following of which usually produces good results. Or imagine that pursuing the second course of conduct would have required a disregard for self-interest or for the interests of those who are near and dear to her that is more than we normally (or, perhaps, can reasonably) expect from human beings. In these cases, blame would seem to have little or no point. Indeed, if the agent behaved in a way that usually produces good, we may want to encourage others to follow her example (that is, to adhere to the same rule or act from the same motive) when they encounter similar situations. Praising an agent for an action that fails to live up to the consequentialist standard can sometimes be right. Consequentialists applaud instances of act-types they want to encourage, and they commend motivations, dispositions, and character traits they want to reinforce.

Motives, dispositions, and character traits

Consequentialists generally take an instrumental approach to motives. Good motives are those that tend to produce right conduct, whereas bad motives are those that tend to produce wrongful conduct. Consequentialists generally assess dispositions, behavioral patterns, and character traits in the same instrumental way: one determines which ones are good, and how good they are, by looking at the actions they lead to. According to some value theories, however, certain motives are intrinsically, not just instrumentally, good or bad; likewise, the exercise of certain dispositions or character traits might be judged intrinsically good or bad. If so, then the presence or absence of these factors will make a difference to the overall value of a state of affairs. This fact, in turn, will make more complex the consequentialist's analysis of how one ought to act.

Even if a consequentialist adopts an entirely instrumental approach to the assessment of motives, dispositions, and traits, it doesn't follow that the agent's only concern ought to be the impartial maximization of good. On the contrary, the consequentialist tradition has long urged that more good may come from people acting from other, more particular motivations, commitments, and dispositions than from their acting only and always from a desire to promote the general good. For one thing, a consequentialist should not try to compute the probabilities of all possible outcomes before each and every action. Even if this were humanly possible, it would be absurd and counterproductive. At least in trivial matters and routine situations, stopping and calculating will generally lead to poor results. One does better to act from habit or do what has proved right in similar situations or what seems intuitively or at a glance to be the best course of conduct. Thus, consequentialism implies that one should not always reason as a consequentialist or, at least, that one should not always reason in a fully and directly consequentialist way. Better results may come from people acting in accord with principles, procedures, or motives other than the basic consequentialist one.

This last statement may sound paradoxical, but the consequentialist standard itself determines in what circumstances we should employ that standard as our direct guide to acting. The proper criterion for assessing actions is one matter; in what ways we should deliberate, reason, or otherwise decide what to do (so as to meet that criterion as best we can) is another issue altogether. Consequentialists will naturally want to guide their lives, make decisions, and base their actions on principles, procedures, and motives, the following of which will produce the best results over the long run. Which principles, procedures, and motives produce the best results is a contingent matter, which depends in part on one's value theory. But a consequentialist will approve of people's acting out of a concern for things other than the general good or on the basis of values that his theory does not believe to be basic if the consequentialist believes that people's so acting is likely to bring about more good in the long run.

Following moral rules

Although consequentialism bases morality on one fundamental principle, it also stresses the importance in ordinary circumstances of following certain well-established rules or guidelines that can generally be relied upon to produce good results. Utilitarians, for example, believe that we should make it a practice to tell the truth and keep our promises, rather than try to calculate possible pleasures and pains in every routine case, because we know that in general telling the truth and keeping our promises result in more good than lying and breaking promises. Relying on secondary rules helps consequentialists deal with the no-time-to-calculate problem and the future-consequences-are-hard-to-foresee problem. It can also counteract the fact that even conscientious agents can err in estimating the likelihood of a particular result and thus the expected value of a given action. In particular, when our interests are engaged or when something we care about is at stake, bias can unconsciously skew our deliberations. For this reason, we are generally less likely to go wrong and more likely to promote good by cleaving to well-established secondary rules. Finally, when secondary rules are well known and generally followed, then people know what others are going to do in certain routine and easily recognizable situations, and they can rely on this knowledge. This improves social coordination and makes society more stable and secure.

An analogy with traffic laws and regulations illuminates these points. Society's goal, let's assume, is that the overall flow of automobile traffic maximize benefit by getting everyone to his or her destination as safely and promptly as possible. Now imagine a traffic system with just one law or rule: drive your car so as to maximize benefit. It's easy to see that such a one-rule traffic system would be far from ideal and that we do much better with a variety of more specific traffic regulations. Without secondary rules telling them, for example, to drive on the right side of the road and obey traffic signals, drivers would be left to do whatever they thought best at any given moment depending on their interpretation of the traffic situation and their calculation of the probable results of alternative actions. Some philosophers seem to think that if people were smart enough and well informed enough, and if time and effort were no consideration, then secondary rules would be unnecessary. But this is a delusion, as Brian Barry explains:

> The optimal course of action for me depends upon what I expect others to do, while the optimal course of action for others depends upon what they expect me to do. . . . Expectations can be coordinated only by a system of rules (such as that enjoining promise-keeping) which are adhered to without regard to consequences. Only within a matrix of stable expectations created in this way does it make sense for people to make judgments about the likely consequences of acting in one way or another. (1995: 220)

For the reasons just canvassed, consequentialists of all stripes agree that to promote the good effectively, we should, at least sometimes, rely and encourage others to rely on secondary rules, precepts, and guidelines. Moreover, it is widely agreed among consequentialists that the full benefit of secondary rules can only be reaped when they are treated as moral rules and not merely as rules of thumb or practical aids to decision-making. Having people strongly inclined to act in certain rule-designated ways, to feel guilty about failing to do so, and to use those rules to assess the conduct of others can have enormous utility. This is because it produces good results to have people strongly disposed to act in certain predictable ways, ways that generally (but perhaps not always) maximize expected benefit.

In practice, then, consequentialists approach issues of character and conduct from several distinct angles. First, about any action they can ask whether it was right in the sense of maximizing expected value. Second, they can ask whether it was an action the agent should have performed, knowing what she knew (or should have known) and feeling the obligation she should have felt to adhere to the rules that consequentialists would want people in her society to stick to. Third, if the action fell short in this respect, consequentialists can ask whether the agent should be criticized and, if so, how much. This will involve taking into account, among other things, how far the agent fell short, whether there were extenuating factors, what the alternatives were, and what could reasonably have been expected of someone in the agent's shoes, as well as the likely effects of criticizing the agent (and others like her) for the conduct in question. Finally, consequentialists can ask whether the agent's motivations are ones that should be reinforced and strengthened, or weakened and discouraged, and they can ask the same question about the broader character traits of which these motivations are an aspect. Looking at the matter from these various angles produces a nuanced, multidimensional assessment, but one that reflects the complicated reality of our moral lives.

The Appeal of Consequentialism

Although this essay abstains from metaethical questions, I incline toward the view that moral theories are "necessarily grounded in intuitions of truth or value that cannot be objectively demonstrated or disproved" (Hardin 1988: 179). At any rate, I know of no proof of consequentialism. G. E. Moore once thought otherwise. In his famous work *Principia Ethica* (1903), he argued that consequentialism is true by definition because "morally right" simply means "maximizes the good." "The assertion 'I am morally bound to perform this action,'" he wrote, "is identical with the assertion 'This action will produce the greatest amount of good in the Universe'" (p. 82). A few years

later, however, Moore admitted that he was mistaken, as indeed he was, to assert that these statements are identical in meaning. Nevertheless, Moore continued to maintain that the two propositions "morally right" and "produces the most good" are logically equivalent – that there is a "necessary and reciprocal connection" between them – even though they are not identical in meaning. Why? Moore's answer was simply that it is self-evident "that it must always be our duty to do what will produce the best effects *upon the whole*" (1912: 100; 1952: 562–3).

Too many reflective thinkers have rejected consequentialism for a Moore-like assertion of self-evidence to carry the day. But if this is so and if, as I suspect, ethical theories cannot be proved, then the question is whether one finds the ethical ideas, values, or assumptions that inspire consequentialism more attractive and convincing than those that guide non-consequentialist approaches to ethics and whether one believes that consequentialism provides the most coherent, systematic, and plausible orientation to ethics that one is likely to find.

As we have seen, consequentialists share the intuition that the morality of our actions must be a function of the goodness or badness of their outcomes and, more specifically, that an action is right if and only if it brings about the best outcome the agent could have brought about. Consequentialists find it difficult to see what the point of morality could be if it is not about acting in ways that directly or indirectly bring about as much good as possible. True, consequentialism may tell us not to guide ourselves directly by the consequential standard of right in our day-to-day actions, but the correctness of that basic standard has struck most thinkers in the consequentialist tradition as obvious. How, they ask, could the foundational principle of morality deem actions as morally right that fail to maximize expected benefit? Acting so as to maximize benefit strikes consequentialists as the essence of rationality. As John Stuart Mill writes:

Whether happiness be or be not the end to which morality should be referred – that it be referred to an *end* of some sort, and not left in the dominion of vague feeling or inexplicable internal conviction, that it be made a matter of reason and calculation, and not merely of sentiment, is essential to the very idea of moral philosophy; is, in fact, what renders argument or discussion on moral questions possible. That the morality of actions depends on the consequences which they tend to produce, is the doctrine of rational persons of all schools; that the good or evil of those consequences is measured solely by pleasure and pain, is all of the doctrine of the school of utility, which is peculiar to it (1838: 83)

Consequentialism's goal-oriented, maximizing approach to ethics coheres with what we implicitly believe to be rational conduct in other contexts, in particular, when it comes to assessing prudential behavior. When seeking to advance our personal interests, we take for granted that practical rationality requires us to weigh, balance, and make tradeoffs among the things we seek in order to maximize the net amount of good we obtain. Only a consequentialist approach tallies with that.

The conviction that moral assessment turns on consequences and that the promotion of what ultimately matters ought to be the guiding principle of ethics lies at the heart of consequentialism. Rival normative theories, of course, rely on other moral assumptions and appeal to different considered moral judgments. Compared to most non-consequentialist approaches, however, consequentialism requires a very small number of ethical assumptions, and these yield, or so consequentialists believe, a powerful but structurally simple normative theory, capable of unifying our understanding of a diverse range of ethical phenomena. By contrast, non-consequentialist approaches to ethics (such as the popular reflective equilibrium method of Rawls [1971] or the common-sense pluralism of Ross [1930]) typically have recourse to intuition at an array of different points. In practice, the result can be a hodgepodge of rules, principles, and injunctions of varying degrees of generality. Moreover, the ethical assumptions on which consequentialists rely are not only few in number, but also very general in character, whereas non-consequentialist theorists typically have recourse to various more specific lower-level intuitions, concerning the legitimacy

of particular rules or the moral necessity of particular deontological permissions and restrictions. Intuitions about the rightness or wrongness of specific types of conduct seem more likely to be distorted by the authority of cultural tradition and the influence of customary practice than are the more abstract, high-level intuitions upon which consequentialism relies.

Objections to Consequentialism

Non-consequentialists believe either that it is sometimes wrong to act so as to maximize expected benefit, or that failing to so act is sometimes permissible, or both. That is, they distinguish themselves from consequentialists by affirming certain deontological restrictions or embracing certain deontological permissions.

Deontological restrictions

As mentioned earlier, the likelihood that a consequentialist theory will require conduct that conflicts with the injunctions of ordinary commonsense morality will depend on the particular value theory one adopts. However, even if consequentialists concede that unusual circumstances could, in theory, make it right to perform an action that people normally consider immoral, our earlier discussion should have made it clear that in practice the priority consequentialists give to promoting rules, motives, and dispositions that typically produce good results implies that they will endorse most of the deontological restrictions of everyday morality because doing so maximizes expected benefit.

Even if a consequentialist theory entailed that in the abstract it could be right, if the circumstances were bizarre enough, to do something that would normally be judged morally despicable, like, say, torturing an innocent child, in practice it will make for a much better world if people's characters are such that they would never even entertain the idea of torturing a child, regardless of the circumstances. True, if placed in the imaginary world where torturing the child maximizes good, such people will do the wrong thing (as judged by the consequentialist standard) by refraining from torturing the child. But the real world in which we live is certainly better the more widespread the inhibition on harming children is and the more deeply entrenched it is in people's psychology. Consequentialists prefer people to have the moral motivations that bring the best results in the everyday world, even if these motivations might lead them to behave suboptimally in fanciful situations. To this, non-consequentialists often reply that the consequentialist gets the right answer but for the wrong reason. Consequentialists, it is alleged, overlook the intrinsic wrongness of torturing. But consequentialists can explain perfectly well why torture is evil. And unless the non-consequentialist is an absolutist, he cannot say that torturing an innocent child is always wrong. What if doing so was the only way to stop a war of aggression? So, the non-consequentialist is reduced to saying that the consequentialist takes the possibility of torturing the child too lightly or is too ready to do it. But these allegations seem specious.

In fact, non-consequentialism's commitment to deontological restrictions is vulnerable to consequentialist counterattack. The non-consequentialist sees it as an important fact about our moral lives that an action can sometimes be wrong even though its outcome would be better than that of all alternative actions. Now suppose that somehow your violating a certain deontological restriction (call it R) would result in there being fewer violations of R overall. According to the deontologist, it would still be wrong for you to violate R. This is puzzling, and it is natural to ask: "If non-violation of R is so important, shouldn't that be the goal? How can a concern for the non-violation of R lead to the refusal to violate R when this would prevent more extensive violations of R?" (Nozick 1974: 30 [slightly modified]). Admittedly, these are abstract questions, but one can imagine circumstances in which only by telling a lie (breaking a promise, killing an innocent person) can one prevent several other people from telling lies (breaking promises, killing innocent people). Faced with such situations, deontological theories will, at least sometimes, forbid an action of a certain type even when performing it would

result in fewer actions of the forbidden type. This point does not presuppose that the deontologist is an absolutist. Even a moderate non-consequentialist endorses restrictions that it would be wrong for one to violate, at least in some circumstances, even though one's doing so would minimize violations of the very same restriction. This fact leads consequentialists to argue that deontological restrictions are paradoxical or even irrational. For how can a normative theory plausibly say that it is wrong to act so as to decrease immoral conduct (that is, conduct that the theory itself identifies as immoral)? It seems illogical for a theory to forbid the performance of a morally objectionable act when doing so would reduce the total number of such actions and would have no other relevant consequences.

In practice consequentialists are likely to endorse many of the restrictions that deontologists insist upon. But these restrictions will be part of the moral code that consequentialists uphold in order to promote the good in the most effective way they can. However strongly agents are encouraged to adhere to these rules and to internalize a commitment to them, these restrictions are not, for the consequentialist, foundational, but derive from a more basic principle of morality.

Deontological permissions

Critics of consequentialism claim that it sets too high a standard and demands too much of us. Their argument goes like this. At many points in our day, when we are innocently relaxing, talking with friends, or simply at work doing our jobs, we could probably be doing something else instead that would create more good. Instead of watching television tonight, we could visit a nursing home to chat and play cards with its elderly residents. Instead of going to the beach with friends, we could work with the homeless. Instead of buying a new car, we could make do with our old one and give the rest of the money to charity. And so on: our lives are rarely so productive of good that it would be impossible for us to do more. In principle, or so the critics contend, consequentialism could require us to sacrifice our most basic interests in the name of the general good.

Because I have discussed this matter elsewhere (Shaw 1999: 129–32, 261–87) [. . .] I will be brief. How much sacrifice consequentialism demands of us will, again, depend on the values the consequentialist wants to see maximized. We must bear in mind the good that (on almost any plausible value theory) is likely to come from permitting people to pursue, as much as possible, their own goals and plans, as well as the possibility that it may bring better results "for a man to aim rather at goods affecting himself and those in whom he has a strong personal interest, than to attempt a more extended beneficence" (Moore 1903: 166–7). Suppose, however, that when conjoined with our most plausible theory of good, consequentialism entails that morality demands much, much more of us than people ordinarily think. It doesn't follow from this that consequentialism is mistaken. Intuitions about these matters, in particular, intuitions about how much effort, time, or money morality obliges us to give to assist those who need our assistance, are an unreliable foundation for normative theorizing because those intuitions reflect social expectations and customary practice in a socioeconomic system, the norms of which are themselves open to assessment.

There are, however, compelling reasons for believing that consequentialists will not advocate a norm requiring (for example) that people give away most of what they have to help those in other parts of the world who need it more. Instead, they will uphold the less demanding norm that we should aid strangers when the benefit to them is great and the cost to ourselves comparatively minor. Trying to instill the more demanding norm would be difficult, and the psychological and other costs of doing so (that is, of getting people to feel guilty about not giving away most of what they have) would be high. It is doubtful whether we could ever succeed in motivating people to comply with such a norm – at least not over the long run. In addressing problems like hunger and disease in the Third World, consequentialists will arguably do more good by upholding a less demanding norm and by supporting the institutions necessary to take over the task and reduce the burden on individual beneficence.

Conclusion

This essay has explained the consequentialist approach to ethics, sketched the rich normative resources at its disposal, given reasons for finding the theory appealing, and defended it against some common criticisms. In this way, I hope to have shown that consequentialism provides an account of right and wrong that is morally attractive, philosophically respectable, and viable in practice. However, a full explication and defense of consequentialism would require further discussion of many matters. Among other things, it would require us to say more about the good and to assess in more detail rival normative approaches.

References

Barry, B. (1995). *Justice as Impartiality.* Oxford: Oxford University Press.

Hardin, R. (1988). *Morality Within the Limits of Reason.* Chicago: University of Chicago Press.

Mill, J. S. (1838 [2003]). "Bentham." In J. S. Mill, *Utilitarianism* and *On liberty,* ed M. Warnock. 2nd edn. Oxford: Blackwell.

Moore, G. E. (1903 [1968]). *Principia Ethica.* Cambridge: Cambridge University Press.

Moore, G. E. (1912 [1965]). *Ethics.* New York: Oxford University Press.

Moore, G. E. (1952). "A reply to my critics." In P. A. Schilpp (ed.), *The Philosophy of G. E. Moore.* 2nd edn. New York: Tudor.

Nozick, R. (1974). *Anarchy, State, and Utopia.* New York: Basic Books.

Rawls, J. (1971). *A Theory of Justice.* Cambridge, Mass.: Harvard University Press.

Ross, W. E. (1930). *The Right and the Good.* Oxford: Oxford University Press.

Shaw, W. H. (1999). *Contemporary Ethics: Taking Account of Utilitarianism.* Oxford: Blackwell.

Thomson, J. J. (2001). *Goodness and Advice.* Princeton, NJ: Princeton University Press.

CHAPTER 50

Extreme and Restricted Utilitarianism

J. J. C. SMART

1

Utilitarianism is the doctrine that the rightness of actions is to be judged by their consequences. What do we mean by "actions" here? Do we mean particular actions or do we mean classes of actions? According to which way we interpret the word "actions" we get two different theories, both of which merit the appellation "utilitarian."

(1) If by "actions" we mean particular individual actions we get the sort of doctrine held by Bentham, Sidgwick, and Moore. According to this doctrine we test individual actions by their consequences, and general rules, like "keep promises," are mere rules of thumb which we use only to avoid the necessity of estimating the probable consequences of our actions at every step. The rightness or wrongness of keeping a promise on a particular occasion depends only on the goodness or badness of the consequences of keeping or of breaking the promise on that particular occasion. Of course part of the consequences of breaking the promise, and a part to which we will normally ascribe decisive importance, will be the weakening of faith in the institution of promising. However, if the goodness of the

consequences of breaking the rule is *in toto* greater than the goodness of the consequences of keeping it, then we must break the rule, irrespective of whether the goodness of the consequences of *everybody's* obeying the rule is or is not greater than the consequences of *everybody's* breaking it. To put it shortly, rules do not matter, save *per accidens* as rules of thumb and as *de facto* social institutions with which the utilitarian has to reckon when estimating consequences. I shall call this doctrine "extreme utilitarianism."

(2) A more modest form of utilitarianism has recently become fashionable. The doctrine is to be found in Toulmin's book *The Place of Reason in Ethics*, in Nowell-Smith's *Ethics* (though I think Nowell-Smith has qualms), in John Austin's *Lectures on Jurisprudence* (Lecture II), and even in J. S. Mill, if Urmson's interpretation of him is correct (*Philosophical Quarterly*, vol. 3, pp. 33–9, 1953). Part of its charm is that it appears to resolve the dispute in moral philosophy between intuitionists and utilitarians in a way which is very neat. The above philosophers hold, or seem to hold, that moral rules are more than rules of thumb. In general the rightness of an action is *not* to be tested by evaluating its consequences but only by considering whether or not it falls under a certain rule. Whether the rule is to be considered an acceptable moral rule, is, however, to be decided by considering the consequences of

J. J. C. Smart, "Extreme and Restricted Utilitarianism," pp. 344–54 from *Philosophical Quarterly*, 6, 1956. Reprinted by permission of the publishers, Blackwell Publishing.

adopting the rule. Broadly, then, actions are to be tested by rules and rules by consequences. The only cases in which we must test an individual action directly by its consequences are *(a)* when the action comes under two different rules, one of which enjoins it and one of which forbids it, and *(b)* when there is no rule whatever that governs the given case. I shall call this doctrine "restricted utilitarianism."

[. . .]

2

For an extreme utilitarian moral rules are rules of thumb. In practice the extreme utilitarian will mostly guide his conduct by appealing to the rules ("do not lie," "do not break promises," etc.) of common sense morality. This is not because there is anything sacrosanct in the rules themselves but because he can argue that probably he will most often act in an extreme utilitarian way if he does not think as a utilitarian. For one thing, actions have frequently to be done in a hurry. Imagine a man seeing a person drowning. He jumps in and rescues him. There is no time to reason the matter out, but usually this will be the course of action which an extreme utilitarian would recommend if he did reason the matter out. If, however, the man drowning had been drowning in a river near Berchtesgaden in 1938, and if he had had the well known black forelock and moustache of Adolf Hitler, an extreme utilitarian would, if he had time, work out the probability of the man's being the villainous dictator, and if the probability were high enough he would, on extreme utilitarian grounds, leave him to drown. The rescuer, however, has not time. He trusts to his instincts and dives in and rescues the man. And this trusting to instincts and to moral rules can be justified on extreme utilitarian grounds. Furthermore, an extreme utilitarian who knew that the drowning man was Hitler would nevertheless praise the rescuer, not condemn him. For by praising the man he is strengthening a courageous and benevolent disposition of mind, and in general this disposition has great positive utility. (Next time, perhaps, it will be Winston Churchill that the man saves!) We must never forget that an extreme utilitarian may praise actions which he knows to be wrong. Saving Hitler was wrong, but it was a member of a class of actions which are generally right, and the motive to do actions of this class is in general an optimific one. In considering questions of praise and blame it is not the expediency of the praised or blamed action that is at issue, but the expediency of the praise. It can be expedient to praise an inexpedient action and inexpedient to praise an expedient one.

Lack of time is not the only reason why an extreme utilitarian may, on extreme utilitarian principles, trust to rules of common sense morality. He knows that in particular cases where his own interests are involved his calculations are likely to be biased in his own favor. Suppose that he is unhappily married and is deciding whether to get divorced. He will in all probability greatly exaggerate his own unhappiness (and possibly his wife's) and greatly underestimate the harm done to his children by the break up of the family. He will probably also underestimate the likely harm done by the weakening of the general faith in marriage vows. So probably he will come to the correct extreme utilitarian conclusion if he does not in this instance think as an extreme utilitarian but trusts to common sense morality.

There are many more and subtle points that could be made in connection with the relation between extreme utilitarianism and the morality of common sense. All those that I have just made and many more will be found in Book IV Chapters 3–5 of Sidgwick's *Methods of Ethics*. I think that this book is the best book ever written on ethics, and that these chapters are the best chapters of the book. As they occur so near the end of a very long book they are unduly neglected. I refer the reader, then, to Sidgwick for the classical exposition of the relation between (extreme) utilitarianism and the morality of common sense. One further point raised by Sidgwick in this connection is whether an (extreme) utilitarian ought on (extreme) utilitarian principles to propagate (extreme) utilitarianism among the public. As most people are not very philosophical and not good at empirical calculations, it is probable that they will most often act in an extreme utilitarian way if they do not try to think as extreme utilitarians. We have seen how easy it would be to misapply the extreme utilitarian criterion in the case of divorce. Sidgwick seems to think it quite probable that an extreme utilitarian should not propagate his doctrine too widely. However, the great danger to humanity comes nowadays on the plane of public morality – not private morality. There is a greater danger to humanity from the hydrogen bomb than from an increase of the divorce rate, regrettable though that might be, and there seems no doubt that extreme utilitarianism makes for good sense in international relations. When France walked out of the United Nations because she did not wish Morocco discussed, she said that she was within her rights because Morocco and Algiers are part of her metropolitan territory and nothing to do with UN. This was clearly a legalistic if not superstitious argument. We should not be concerned with the so-called "rights" of France or any other country but with whether the cause of humanity would best be served by discussing Morocco in UN. (I am not saying that the answer to this is "Yes." There are good grounds for supposing that more harm than good would come by such a discussion.) I myself have no hesitation in saying that on extreme utilitarian principles we ought to propagate extreme utilitarianism as widely as possible. But Sidgwick had respectable reasons for suspecting the opposite.

The extreme utilitarian, then, regards moral rules as rules of thumb and as sociological facts that have to be taken into account when deciding what to do, just as facts of any other sort have to be taken into account. But in themselves they do not justify any action.

3

The restricted utilitarian regards moral rules as more than rules of thumb for short-circuiting calculations of consequences. Generally, he argues, consequences are not relevant at all when we are deciding what to do in a particular case. In general, they are relevant only to deciding what rules are good reasons for acting in a certain way in particular cases. This doctrine

is possibly a good account of how the modern unreflective twentieth century Englishman often thinks about morality, but surely it is monstrous as an account of how it is most rational to think about morality. Suppose that there is a rule R and that in 99% of cases the best possible results are obtained by acting in accordance with R. Then clearly R is a useful rule of thumb; if we have not time or are not impartial enough to assess the consequences of an action it is an extremely good bet that the thing to do is to act in accordance with R. But is it not monstrous to suppose that if we *have* worked out the consequences and if we have perfect faith in the impartiality of our calculations, and if we *know* that in this instance to break R will have better results than to keep it, we should nevertheless obey the rule? Is it not to erect R into a sort of idol if we keep it when breaking it will prevent, say, some avoidable misery? Is not this a form of superstitious rule-worship (easily explicable psychologically) and not the rational thought of a philosopher?

The point may be made more clearly if we consider Mill's comparison of moral rules to the tables in the nautical almanac (*Utilitarianism*, Everyman Edition, pp. 22–3). This comparison of Mill's is adduced by Urmson as evidence that Mill was a restricted utilitarian, but I do not think that it will bear this interpretation at all. (Though I quite agree with Urmson that many other things said by Mill are in harmony with restricted rather than extreme utilitarianism. Probably Mill had never thought very much about the distinction and was arguing for utilitarianism, restricted or extreme, against other and quite non-utilitarian forms of moral argument.) Mill says: "Nobody argues that the art of navigation is not founded on astronomy, because sailors cannot wait to calculate the Nautical Almanac. Being rational creatures, they go out upon the sea of life with their minds made up on the common questions of right and wrong, as well as on many of the far more difficult questions of wise and foolish. . . . Whatever we adopt as the fundamental principle of morality, we require subordinate principles to apply it by." Notice that this is, as it stands, only an argument for subordinate principles as rules of thumb. The example of the nautical almanac is misleading because the information given in the almanac is in all cases the same as the information one would get if one made a long and laborious calculation from the original astronomical data on which the almanac is founded. Suppose, however, that astronomy were different. Suppose that the behavior of the sun, moon and planets was very nearly as it is now, but that on rare occasions there were peculiar irregularities and discontinuities, so that the almanac gave us rules of the form "in 99% of cases where the observations are such and such you can deduce that your position is so and so." Furthermore, let us suppose that there were methods which enabled us, by direct and laborious calculation from the original astronomical data, not using the rough and ready tables of the almanac, to get our correct position in 100% of cases. Seafarers might use the almanac because they never had time for the long calculations and they were content with a 99% chance of success in calculating their positions. Would it not be absurd, however, if they *did* make the direct calculation, and finding that it disagreed with the almanac calculation, nevertheless they ignored it and stuck to the almanac conclusion? Of course the case would be altered if there were a high enough probability of making slips in the direct calculation: then we might stick to the almanac result, liable to error though we knew it to be, simply because the direct calculation would be open to error for a different reason, the fallibility of the computer. This would be analogous to the case of the extreme utilitarian who abides by the conventional rule against the dictates of his utilitarian calculations simply because he thinks that his calculations are probably affected by personal bias. But if the navigator were sure of his direct calculations would he not be foolish to abide by his almanac? I conclude, then, that if we change our suppositions about astronomy and the almanac (to which there are no exceptions) to bring the case into line with that of morality (to whose rules there are exceptions), Mill's example loses its appearance of supporting the restricted form of utilitarianism. Let me say once more that I am not here concerned with how ordinary men think about morality but with how they ought to think. We could

quite well imagine a race of sailors who acquired a superstitious reverence for their almanac, even though it was only right in 99% of cases, and who indignantly threw overboard any man who mentioned the possibility of a direct calculation. But would this behavior of the sailors be rational?

Let us consider a much discussed sort of case in which the extreme utilitarian might go against the conventional moral rule. I have promised to a friend, dying on a desert island from which I am subsequently rescued, that I will see that his fortune (over which I have control) is given to a jockey club. However, when I am rescued I decide that it would be better to give the money to a hospital, which can do more good with it. It may be argued that I am wrong to give the money to the hospital. But why? (a) The hospital can do more good with the money than the jockey club can. (b) The present case is unlike most cases of promising in that no one except me knows about the promise. In breaking the promise I am doing so with complete secrecy and am doing nothing to weaken the general faith in promises. That is, a factor, which would normally keep the extreme utilitarian from promise breaking even in otherwise unoptimific cases, does not at present operate. (c) There is no doubt a slight weakening in my own character as an habitual promise keeper, and moreover psychological tensions will be set up in me every time I am asked what the man made me promise him to do. For clearly I shall have to say that he made me promise to give the money to the hospital, and, since I am an habitual truth teller, this will go very much against the grain with me. Indeed I am pretty sure that in practice I myself would keep the promise. But we are not discussing what my moral habits would probably make me do; we are discussing what I ought to do. Moreover, we must not forget that even if it would be most rational of me to give the money to the hospital it would also be most rational of you to punish or condemn me if you did, most improbably, find out the truth (e.g. by finding a note washed ashore in a bottle). Furthermore, I would agree that though it was most rational of me to give the money to the hospital it would be most rational of you to condemn me for it. We revert again to Sidgwick's distinction between the utility of the action and the utility of the praise of it.

Many such issues are discussed by A. K. Stout[1] [. . .] It will be useful [. . .] to consider one [. . .] example that he gives. Suppose that during hot weather there is an edict that no water must be used for watering gardens. I have a garden and I reason that most people are sure to obey the edict, and that as the amount of water that I use will be by itself negligible no harm will be done if I use the water secretly. So I do use the water, thus producing some lovely flowers which give happiness to various people. Still, you may say, though the action was perhaps optimific, it was unfair and wrong.

There are several matters to consider. Certainly my action should be condemned. We revert once more to Sidgwick's distinction. A right action may be rationally condemned. Furthermore, this sort of offense is normally found out. If I have a wonderful garden when everybody else's is dry and brown there is only one explanation. So if I water my garden I am weakening my respect for law and order, and as this leads to bad results an extreme utilitarian would agree that I was wrong to water the garden. Suppose now that the case is altered and that I can keep the thing secret: there is a secluded part of the garden where I grow flowers which I give away anonymously to a home for old ladies. Are you still so sure that I did the wrong thing by watering my garden? However, this is still a weaker case than that of the hospital and the jockey club. There will be tensions set up within myself: my secret knowledge that I have broken the rule will make it hard for me to exhort others to keep the rule. These psychological ill effects in myself may be not inconsiderable: directly and indirectly they may lead to harm which is at least of the same order as the happiness that the old ladies get from the flowers. You can see that on an extreme utilitarian view there are two sides to the question.

So far I have been considering the duty of an extreme utilitarian in a predominantly non-utilitarian society. The case is altered if we consider the extreme utilitarian who lives in a society every member, or most members, of which can be expected to reason as he does. Should he water his flowers now? (Granting, what is doubtful, that in the case already considered he would have been right to water his flowers.) As a first approximation, the answer is that he should not do so. For since the situation is a completely symmetrical one, what is rational for him is rational for others. Hence, by a *reductio ad absurdum* argument, it would seem that watering his garden would be rational for none. Nevertheless, a more refined analysis shows that the above argument is not quite correct, though it is correct enough for practical purposes. The argument considers each person as confronted with the choice either of watering his garden or of not watering it. However there is a third possibility, which is that each person should, with the aid of a suitable randomizing device, such as throwing dice, give himself a certain probability of watering his garden. This would be to adopt what in the theory of games is called "a mixed strategy." If we could give numerical values to the private benefit of garden watering and to the public harm done by 1, 2, 3, etc., persons using the water in this way, we could work out a value of the probability of watering his garden that each extreme utilitarian should give himself. Let a be the value which each extreme utilitarian gets from watering his garden, and let $f(1), f(2), f(3)$, etc., be the public harm done by exactly 1, 2, 3, etc., persons respectively watering their gardens. Suppose that p is the probability that each person gives himself of watering his garden. Then we can easily calculate, as functions of p, the probabilities that exactly 1, 2, 3, etc., persons will water their gardens. Let these probabilities be $p_1, p_2, \cdots p_n$. Then the total net probable benefit can be expressed as

$$V = p_1(a - f(1)) + p_2(2a - f(2)) + \ldots p_n(na - f(n))$$

Then if we know the function $f(x)$ we can calculate the value of p for which $(dV/dp) = 0$. This gives the value of p which it would be rational for each extreme utilitarian to adopt. The present argument does not of course depend on a perhaps unjustified assumption that the values in question are measurable, and in a practical case such as that of the garden watering we can doubtless assume that

p will be so small that we can take it near enough as equal to zero. However the argument is of interest for the theoretical underpinning of extreme utilitarianism, since the possibility of a mixed strategy is usually neglected by critics of utilitarianism, who wrongly assume that the only relevant and symmetrical alternatives are of the form "everybody does X" and "nobody does X."

I now pass on to a type of case which may be thought to be the trump card of restricted utilitarianism. Consider the rule of the road. It may be said that since all that matters is that everyone should do the same it is indifferent which rule we have, "go on the left hand side" or "go on the right hand side." Hence the only *reason* for going on the left hand side in British countries is that this is the rule. Here the rule does seem to be a reason, in itself, for acting in a certain way. I wish to argue against this. The rule in itself is not a reason for our actions. We would be perfectly justified in going on the right hand side if *(a)* we knew that the rule was to go on the left hand side, and *(b)* we were in a country peopled by super-anarchists who always on principle did the opposite of what they were told. This shows that the rule does not give us a reason for acting so much as an indication of the probable actions of others, which helps us to find out what would be our own most rational course of action. If we are in a country not peopled by anarchists, but by non-anarchist extreme Utilitarians, we expect, other things being equal, that they will keep rules laid down for them. Knowledge of the rule enables us to predict their behavior and to harmonize our own actions with theirs. The rule "keep to the left hand side," then, is not a logical *reason* for action but an anthropological *datum* for planning actions.

I conclude that in every case if there is a rule R the keeping of which is in general optimific, but such that in a special sort of circumstances the optimific behavior is to break R, then in these circumstances we should break R. Of course we must consider all the less obvious effects of breaking R, such as reducing people's faith in the moral order, before coming to the conclusion that to break R is right: in fact we shall rarely come to such a conclusion. Moral rules, on the extreme utilitarian view, are rules

of thumb only, but they are not bad rules of thumb. But if we *do* come to the conclusion that we should break the rule and if we have weighed in the balance our own fallibility and liability to personal bias, what good reason remains for keeping the rule? I can understand "it is optimific" as a reason for action, but why should "it is a member of a class of actions which are usually optimific" or "it is a member of a class of actions which as a class are more optimific than any alternative general class" be a good reason? You might as well say that a person ought to be picked to play for Australia just because all his brothers have been, or that the Australian team should be composed entirely of the Harvey family because this would be better than composing it entirely of any other family. The extreme utilitarian does not appeal to artificial feelings, but only to our feelings of benevolence, and what better feelings can there be to appeal to? Admittedly we can have a pro-attitude to anything, even to rules, but such artificially begotten pro-attitudes smack of superstition. Let us get down to realities, human happiness and misery, and make these the objects of our pro-attitudes and anti-attitudes.

The restricted utilitarian might say that he is talking only of *morality*, not of such things as rules of the road. I am not sure how far this objection, if valid, would affect my argument, but in any case I would reply that as a philosopher I conceive of ethics as the study of how it would be *most rational* to act. If my opponent wishes to restrict the word "morality" to a narrower use he can have the word. The fundamental question is the question of rationality of action *in general*. Similarly if the restricted utilitarian were to appeal to ordinary usage and say "it might be most rational to leave Hitler to drown but it would surely not be *wrong* to rescue him," I should again let him have the words "right" and "wrong" and should stick to "rational" and "irrational." We already saw that it would be rational to praise Hitler's rescuer, even though it would have been most rational not to have rescued Hitler. In ordinary language, no doubt, "right" and "wrong" have not only the meaning "most rational to do" and "not most rational to do" but also have the meaning "praiseworthy" and "not praiseworthy." Usually to the utility of an action corresponds utility of praise of it, but as we saw, this is not always so. Moral language could thus do with tidying up, for example by reserving "right" for "most rational" and "good" as an epithet of praise for the motive from which the action sprang. It would be more becoming in a philosopher to try to iron out illogicalities in moral language and to make suggestions for its reform than to use it as a court of appeal whereby to perpetuate confusions.

Note

1. "But Suppose Everybody Did the Same?", *Australasian Journal of Philosophy* vol. 32, pp. 1–29.

CHAPTER 51

Rule-Consequentialism

BRAD HOOKER

1 Introduction

Just what is the connection between moral rightness and consequences? For nearly half a century now, consequentialists have divided themselves into different camps with respect to this question. Act-consequentialists believe that the moral rightness of an act depends entirely on whether the act's consequences are at least as good as that of any alternative act. Rule-consequentialists believe that the rightness of an act depends not on its own consequences, but rather on the consequences of a code of rules. [. . .] This essay explores the prospects for rule-consequentialism.

2 What Constitutes Benefit?

Rule-consequentialism holds that any code of rules is to be evaluated in terms of how much *good* could reasonably be expected to result from the code. By 'good' here I mean whatever has non-instrumental value. What has non-instrumental value?

Utilitarians, who have been the most prominent kind of consequentialists, believe that the

Brad Hooker, "Rule-Consequentialism," pp. 183–204 from Hugh LaFollette (ed.), *The Blackwell Guide to Ethical Theory*. Oxford: Blackwell, 1999. Reprinted by permission of the publishers, Blackwell Publishing.

only thing with non-instrumental value is utility. All utilitarians have held that pleasure and the absence of pain are at least a large part of utility. Indeed, utilitarianism is often said to maintain that pleasure and the absence of pain are the *only* things that matter non-instrumentally. Certainly, this was the official view of the classic utilitarians Jeremy Bentham, J. S. Mill, and Henry Sidgwick – though in Sidgwick's case, equality seems to have independent weight as a tie breaker [. . .]

Perhaps more common over the last thirty years has been the view that utility is constituted by the fulfillment of people's desires, even if these desires are for things other than pleasure. Many people, even when fully informed and thinking carefully, persistently want things in addition to pleasure. They care, for example, about knowing important truths, about achieving valuable goals, about having deep personal relationships, about living their lives in broad accordance with their own choices rather than always in accordance with someone else's [. . .]. The pleasure these things can bring is of course important. Still, human beings can care about these things in themselves, i.e., in addition to whatever pleasure they bring.

This view, however, can be challenged. Some desires seem to be about things too unconnected with you for them to play a direct role in determining your good. Would your desiring that a stranger recovers fully from her illness make her recovery good for you, even if you never see or hear from her again? [. . .] Naturally, the fulfillment of such a desire would *indirectly* benefit you *if* it brought you pleasure or peace of mind. But this is not to say that the fulfillment of your desire that the stranger recovers herself constitutes a benefit to you. Rather if you get pleasure or peace of mind from the fulfillment of this desire, this pleasure or peace of mind constitutes a benefit to you (since you doubtless also desire pleasure and peace of mind for yourself).

The view that the fulfillment of your desires itself *constitutes* a benefit to you – if this view is to be at all plausible – will have to limit the desires in question. The only desires the fulfillment of which constitutes a benefit to you are your desires for states of affairs in which you are an essential constituent [. . .], You are not an essential constituent of the state of affairs in which this stranger recovers. So her recovery doesn't itself constitute a benefit to you.

There seem to be reasons for further restrictions on the desires directly relevant to personal good. Think how bizarre desires can be. When we encounter particularly bizarre ones, we might begin to wonder whether the things are good simply because they are desired. Would my desiring to count all the blades of grass in the lawns on the street make this good for me? [. . .] Whatever *pleasure* I get from the activity would be good for me. But it seems that the *desire-fulfillment as such* is worthless in this case. Intuitively, the fulfillment of my desires constitutes a benefit to me only if these desires are for the right things [. . .] Indeed, some things seem to be desired because they are perceived as valuable, not valuable merely because desired or pleasant. [. . .]

Views holding that something benefits a person if and only if it increases the person's pleasure or desire-fulfillment are in a sense "subjectivist" theories of personal good. For these theories make something's status as a benefit depend always on the person's subjective mental states. "Objectivist" theories claim that the contribution to personal good made by such things as important knowledge, important achievement, friendship, and autonomy is not exhausted by the extent to which these things bring people pleasure or fulfil their desires. These things can constitute benefits even when they don't increase pleasure. Likewise, they can constitute benefits even when they are not the objects of desire. Objectivist theories will typically add that pleasure is of course an objective good. These theories will also hold that ignorance, failure, friendlessness, servitude, and pain constitute harms.

For the most part, I will be neutral in this essay about which theory of personal good is best. *Usually* what gives people pleasure or enjoyment is also what satisfies their desires and involves the objective goods that could plausibly be listed. So usually we don't need to decide as among these theories of personal good.

But not always. Suppose the ruling elite believed that quantity of pleasure were all that matters. Then (to take a familiar leaf from *Nineteen Eighty-Four*) they might feel justified in manipulating the people and even giving them drugs that induce contentment but drain ambition and curiosity, if they thought such practices would maximize aggregate pleasure. Or suppose the ruling elite believed that the fulfillment of desire were all that matters. Again, the ruling elite might feel justified in manipulating the formation of preferences and development of desires such that these are easily satisfied. Now we can accept that – to some extent – our desires should be modified so that there is some reasonable hope of fulfilling them. But this could be pushed too far either in the name of maximizing pleasure or in the name of maximizing desire-fulfillment. A life could be maximally pleasurable, have maximum desire-fulfillment, and still be empty – if it lacked desires for friendship, achievement, knowledge, and autonomy.

3   Distribution

The term "rule-utilitarianism" is usually used to refer to theories that evaluate acts in terms of rules selected for their utility – i.e., for their effects on social well-being. The term "rule-consequentialism" is usually used to refer to a broader class of theories of which rule-utilitarian theories are a subclass. Rule-consequentialist theories evaluate acts in terms of rules selected for their good consequences. Non-utilitarian versions of rule-consequentialism say the consequences that matter are not limited to net effects on overall well-being. Most prominently, some versions of rule-consequentialism say that what matters are not only how much well-being results but also how it is distributed, in particular the fairness of alternative distributions. Table 51.1 might prove helpful.

Which version of rule-consequentialism is best? The problem with rule-utilitarianism is that it has the potential to be unfairly inegalitarian. [. . .] Consider a set of rules which leaves each member of a smaller group very badly off, and each member of a much larger group very well off (table 51.2).

Now if no alternative rule would provide greater net aggregate benefit, then utilitarians would endorse this code. Yet suppose the next best rule *from the point of view of utility* would be one with the results set out in table 51.3.

Let us assume that the first code leaves the people in group A less well off for some reason other than that these people opted to work less hard or imprudently took bad risks. In that case, the second code seems morally superior to, because fairer than, the first code. This is why we should reject rule-utilitarianism in favor of a distribution-sensitive rule-consequentialism that considers fairness as well as well-being.

What are the relative weights given to well-being and fairness by this distribution-sensitive rule-consequentialism? Clearly, well-being does not have overriding weight. For there can be cases in which the amount of aggregate net benefit produced would not justify rules that were unfair to some group. That was what my schematic example above was meant to show.

Does fairness have overriding weight? This is particularly unsettled territory, since even what constitutes fairness is unclear. Nevertheless, we cannot rule out the possibility that some unfair practice so greatly increases overall

Table 51.1

Consequentialist Theories   vs.   Non-consequentialist Theories

| Act-consequentialist Theories | Rule-consequentialist Theories | Other-consequentialist Theories |

| Rule-utilitarianism | The version of rule-consequentialism which selects rules on basis of welfare and fairness only | Other versions of rule-consequentialism |

Table 51.2   Well-being

First Code:	per person	per group	for both groups
10,000 people in group A	1	10,000	
100,000 people in group B	10	1,000,000	
			1,010,000

Table 51.3 Well-being

Second Code:	per person	per group	for both groups
10,000 people in group A	8	80,000	
100,000 people in group B	9	900,000	
			980,000

well-being that the practice is justified. But it is certainly unclear where the threshold is for fairness to trump well-being. Perhaps the best we can say is that, in the choice between codes, judgment will be needed in balancing fairness against well-being. By evaluating rules in terms of two values (well-being and fairness) instead of one (well-being), distribution-sensitive rule-consequentialism is messier than rule-utilitarianism. Still, this seems to be a case where the more plausible theory is the messier one.

4   Criteria of Rightness versus Decision Procedures

Rule-consequentialism is often portrayed as merely part of a broader consequentialist theory. This broader theory evaluates *all things* by their consequences. So it evaluates the desirability of acts by their consequences, the desirability of rules by their consequences, etc. The standard point to make along these lines is that, even if the rightness of an act depends on its consequences, better consequences will result if people do *not* try always to decide what to do by calculating consequences than if they try always to decide in this way. In other words, consequentialists can and should deny that

> On every occasion, an agent should decide which act to do by ascertaining which act has the greatest expected good.

Consequentialists agree that our *decision procedure* for day-to-day moral thinking should instead be as follows:

At least normally, an agent should decide how to act by referring to tried and true rules, such as "Don't harm others", "Don't steal", "Keep your promises", "Tell the truth", etc.

Why? First, we frequently lack information about the probable consequences of various acts we might do. Where we cannot even estimate the consequences, we can hardly choose on the basis of maximizing the good. Second, we often do not have the time to collect this information. Third, human limitations and biases are such that we are not accurate calculators of the expected overall consequences of our alternatives. For example, most of us are biased in such a way that we tend to underestimate the harm to others of acts that would benefit us.

Now if there will be greater overall good where people are largely disposed to focus and act on non-consequentialist considerations, then consequentialism itself endorses such dispositions. So consequentialists advocate firm dispositions to follow certain rules, including firm dispositions not to harm others, not to steal, not to break promises, etc. Different consequentialists thus by and large agree about how people should do their day-to-day moral thinking.

What different kinds of consequentialists disagree about is what makes an act morally permissible, i.e., about the criterion for moral rightness.

> *Act-consequentialism* claims that an act is morally right (both permissible and required) if and only if the actual (or expected) good produced by *that particular act* would be at least as great as that of any other act open to the agent.

In contrast,

> *Rule-consequentialism* claims that an act is permissible if and only if it is allowed by a code that could reasonably be expected to result in as much good as could reasonably be expected to result from any other identifiable code.

The distinction between act-consequentialism's criterion of rightness and the dispositions it favors is important in many ways. It is important if we want to know what act-consequentialism wants from us. It is also important if act-consequentialism had better not conflict too sharply with our intuitive moral reactions. For if act-consequentialism claimed that we should always be focused on and motivated by calculations of what would maximize the good impartially conceived, many philosophers have thought it would be ridiculous. But the idea that act-consequentialism must make this ridiculous prescription is undermined by the distinction between act-consequentialism's criterion of rightness and the decision procedures it favors.

Nevertheless, the distinction is powerless to protect act-consequentialism from other objections. True, act-consequentialism's implications *about focus and motivation* are not as counter-intuitive as might initially be thought. But this is irrelevant to objections about act-consequentialism's criterion of rightness.

5   Formulations of Rule-Consequentialism

We need to augment our formulation of rule-consequentialism. All recognizable forms of rule-consequentialism make moral rightness depend on rules which are evaluated in terms of their consequences. But different forms of rule-consequentialism disagree about the conditions under which rules are to be evaluated. For instance, one version of rule-consequentialism is formulated in terms of the rules the *compliance with which* would be optimific. Another version is formulated in terms of rules the *acceptance of which* would produce the

most good. Should rule-consequentialism be formulated in terms of compliance or in terms of acceptance?

Although compliance with the right rules is the first priority, it isn't the only thing of importance. We also care about people's having *moral concerns.* So we had better consider the costs of securing not only compliance but also adequate moral motivation. From a rule-consequentialist point of view, "moral motivation" means acceptance of moral rules. By "acceptance of moral rules", I mean a disposition to comply with them, dispositions to feel guilt when one breaks them and to resent others' breaking them, and a belief that the rules and these dispositions are justified. [. . .]

The focus on *acceptance of rules,* i.e., *dispositions,* is crucial because the acceptance of a rule – or perhaps at this point it would be better to say the *internalization* of a rule – can have consequences over and above compliance with the rule. [. . .]

The most obvious example of this involves rules that deter perfectly. Suppose you accept a rule prescribing that you retaliate against attackers. Suppose also that you are totally transparent, in the sense that people can see exactly what your dispositions are. So everyone knows about your disposition to retaliate, and therefore *never* attacks you. Thus, your accepting the rule is so successful at deterring attack that you *never* have an opportunity to comply with the rule. Your accepting the rule thus obviously has important consequences that simply *cannot* come from your acting on the rule, since you in fact never do. [. . .]

Now suppose everyone internalized rules such as "Don't kill except when killing will maximize the aggregate good," "Don't steal except when stealing will maximize the aggregate good," "Don't break your promises except when breaking them will maximize the good," etc. Presumably, if everyone had internalized these rules, sooner or later awareness of this would become widespread. And people's becoming aware of this would undermine their ability to rely confidently on others to behave in agreed-upon ways. Trust would break down. The consequences would be terrible. And these terrible consequences would result, not from individual acts of complying with these rules, but from public awareness that the rules's exception clauses – the ones prescribing killing, stealing, and so on when such acts would maximize the good – were too available. [. . .]

I am aware that there has been some controversy over the argument just outlined. But there is another way in which a cost-benefit analysis of *internalization* is richer than a cost-benefit analysis of compliance. Getting one code of rules internalized might involve greater costs than getting another code internalized. These costs are immensely important. For example, one possible objection to a code might be that it is so complicated or calls for so much self-sacrifice that too much of humanity's resources would have to be devoted to getting it widely internalized. The internalization costs would be so high that internalizing this code would not, on balance, be optimal. When this is the case, rule-consequentialists hold that the code isn't justified, and complying with it isn't required.

These points about internalization costs beg to be deployed at a number of places in the discussion of rule-consequentialism. One such place I explore in the next section.

6   Collapse

If we formulate rule-consequentialism in terms of *compliance*, we risk having rule-consequentialism collapse into act-consequentialism. The objection that rule-consequentialism collapses into extensional equivalence with act-consequentialism assumes rules are to be evaluated in terms of only the effects of compliance. While compliance can be one effect of internalizing rules, we have seen that there are also other effects. We must consider not only the benefits of compliance but also the other effects of rule internalization. With these effects factored into the evaluation of rules, the cost-benefit analysis will not favor rules extensionally equivalent to act-consequentialism.

One version of the objection that rule-consequentialism collapses into act-consequentialism claims that rule-consequentialism must favor just the one simple rule that one must always do what will maximize the good. [. . .] The objection assumes that, if each person

successfully complies with a rule requiring the maximization of the good, then the good would be maximized. That the good would be maximized under these conditions has been challenged (see Hodgson 1967, ch. 2; Regan 1980, ch. 5). But whether or not everyone's *complying* with the act-consequentialist principle would maximize the good, we should again consider the wider costs and benefits of rule *internalization*. The impartial good would not in fact be maximized by the internalization of just this one act-consequentialist rule. To internalize just the one act-consequentialist rule is to have just one moral disposition, the disposition to try to comply with act-consequentialism. To have just this one moral disposition is to have act-consequentialism as one's moral decision procedure. But we've already seen why act-consequentialism is not a good decision procedure.

In addition, the costs of getting a disposition to try to comply with act-consequentialism internalized would be extremely high. For getting that one rule internalized amounts to getting people to be disposed always to do what would be impartially best. Such a disposition would have to overcome people's immensely powerful natural biases towards themselves and their loved ones. To be sure, there are great benefits to be gained from getting people to care about others, and to be willing to make sacrifices for strangers. But think how much time, energy, attention, and psychological conflict that would be required to get people to internalize an overriding completely impartial altruism (if this is even possible at all). The costs of trying to make humans into saints would be too great.

That may seem like a paradoxical thing to assert. Wouldn't a world full of people each with an overriding disposition to maximize the impartial good be so ideal as to be worth any costs of getting from here to there? I think not. Bear in mind that the costs would hardly be a once-and-for-all-time sacrifice. Rather, getting this overriding impartiality internalized would have to be done for every new generation. We are contemplating here a radical reshaping of something deep in human nature. It is not as if the impartiality internalized by one generation will be reflected in the genes of their children. Rather, there will be the high cost of getting the overriding impartiality internalized in their children, just as there was when the parents were children themselves. (I am ignoring here the possibility of genetic engineering to create more altruistic humans.) The internalization costs will be incurred for each new generation of humans.

I have been arguing as if getting overriding impartiality internalized by the vast majority is a serious possibility, though one with prohibitive transition costs. It may not, however, be a serious possibility. In any case, the only *realistic* way to make humans totally and always impartial would be to reduce their special concern for themselves and those with whom they have special attachments. What would be left might be merely a life of insipid impartiality, devoid of deep personal attachments and inimical to great enthusiasm and joy. Strong concern and commitment focused on particular projects and individuals play an ineliminable role in a rewarding human life. But these features would have to be eliminated if human beings are to internalize an overriding motivation to maximize the impartial good. [. . .]

So in the light of the transition and permanent costs of getting internalized an overriding impartiality, I hold that there must be some point short of this where the costs of going further outweigh the benefits. Remember why this matters here. Getting internalized an overriding impartiality would be part of getting internalized an overriding disposition to do what will maximize the impartial good. So if there is a compelling rule-consequentialist reason against getting internalized an overriding impartiality, there is a compelling rule-consequentialist reason against getting internalized an overriding disposition to do what will maximize the impartial good. I have just argued that there is a compelling rule-consequentialist reason against getting internalized an overriding impartiality. Such a disposition would *not* find favor with rule-consequentialism. So there is a compelling rule-consequentialist reason against getting internalized an overriding disposition to do what will maximize the impartial good. This kills the first way of developing the collapse objection.

The other way of developing the collapse objection starts by admitting that internalization of just the one act-consequentialist rule would lead to bad consequences. But this way of developing the collapse objection maintains that utility could be gained from the provision of specific exception clauses to moral rules against harming others, breaking promises, etc. If this is right, then rule-consequentialists are forced by their own criterion for rule selection to embrace rules with these exception clauses. The same sort of reasoning will militate in favor of adding specific exceptions aimed at each situation in which following some rule would not bring about the best consequences. Once all the exception clauses are added, rule-consequentialism will have the same implications for action that act-consequentialism has. This would be a fatal collapse.

To this way of developing the collapse objection, rule-consequentialists will reply by returning to the points about trust and expectations that I alluded to earlier. How much confidence would you have in others if you knew they accepted such highly qualified rules? How much mutual trust would there be in a society of agents who accepted endless exceptions to rules against harming others, breaking promises, lying, etc.?

Furthermore, the point about internalization costs is again relevant. The more plentiful and more complicated the rules to be learned, the higher the costs of learning them would be. At some point the costs of having to learn more rules, or more complications, would outweigh the benefits. Hence, the rules whose teaching and internalization would have the best results are limited in number and complexity. These limitations will keep the code from being extensionally equivalent with act-consequentialism. So this kind of rule-consequentialism does *not* collapse into act-consequentialism.

7   Rule-Consequentialism and the Distribution of Acceptance

A relatively simple form of rule-consequentialism selects rules by their consequences given internalization of them by 100 percent of the population. But I think the theory should be formulated in terms of internalization by less than 100 percent of the population. Rule-consequentialism needs to be formulated this way in order to make room for rules about what to do when others have no moral conscience at all. Let us refer to such people as unmitigated amoralists.

Suppose we assume internalization of the rules by 100 percent of the population. We might still need rules for dealing with non-compliance, since *internalization* by 100 percent of the people does not guarantee 100 percent *compliance*. Some people might fully accept the best rules and yet sometimes, seduced by temptation, act wrongly. Thus there is need for rules dealing with non-compliance. These rules might specify, for example, what penalties apply for what crimes. They might also specify what to do when those around you accept that they should be helping to save others but aren't.

Contrast what is needed to deter or rehabilitate someone with a moral conscience too weak to ensure good behavior in some circumstances, with what is needed to deal with unmitigated amoralists (people who have no moral conscience at all). If we imagine a world with acceptance of the best code by 100 percent of the population, we have simply imagined unmitigated amoralists out of existence. Hence, we have imagined out of existence any rule-consequentialist rationale for having rules for deterring and dealing with unmitigated amoralists.

Here is why. On the rule-consequentialist view, there is always at least some cost associated with every additional rule added to the code. Every additional rule takes at least a little time to learn and at least a little memory to store. Then the question is whether there is some benefit from internalization of the rule that outweighs the cost. We can of course frame rules applying to non-existent situations. For example, "be kind to any rational non-humans living on the moon." But, if the situation envisaged really is non-existent, where is the benefit of including such a rule in the code to be internalized? Presumably there are no benefits from such never-to-be-applied rules. These rules, which have *some* costs and *no* benefits, fail a cost-benefit analysis.

The reasoning seems to me to generate the following important conclusion. Rule-consequentialism cannot generate or justify rules about how to deter murder, rape, robbery, fraud, etc. *by unmitigated amoralists*, unless rule-consequentialism picks its rules with reference to an imagined world where there is internalization of the envisaged rules by less than 100 percent of the population. So rule-consequentialism should evaluate rules in terms of internalization by less than 100 percent of the population.

But should we assume internalization by 99, or 90, or 80 percent, or even less? Any precise number will of course be somewhat arbitrary, but we do have some relevant factors to consider. On one hand, we want a percentage close enough to 100 percent to hold on to the idea that moral rules are for acceptance *by the whole society of human beings*. On the other hand, we want a percentage far enough short of 100 percent to *make salient the problems about non-compliance* – such problems should not be thought of as incidental. Acknowledging that any one percentage will nevertheless be somewhat arbitrary, I propose we take internalization by 90 percent of people in each future generation as the condition under which rules have to be optimal. Let me just add that this distinction between the 90 percent who are moral and the 10 percent who are amoral is supposed to cut across all other distinctions, such as distinctions in nationality and financial status.

8 Arguments for Rule-Consequentialism

One argument for rule-consequentialism is that general internalization of rule-consequentialism would actually maximize the impartial good. The idea is that *from a purely consequentialist point of view* rule-consequentialism seems better than act-consequentialism and all other theories.

Many act-consequentialists reply by invoking their distinction between their criterion of rightness and the decision procedure for day-to-day moral decisions. They admit act-consequentialism is not a good procedure for agents to use when deciding what to do.

But they think this does not invalidate act-consequentialism's criterion of rightness. They would add that, even if rule-consequentialism is an optimal decision procedure, this would not entail that rule-consequentialism correctly identifies what makes right acts right and wrong acts wrong.

Let us turn, then, to arguments for rule-consequentialism other than the one that internalizing rule-consequentialism would maximize the good. Consider the moral code whose acceptance by society would be best, i.e., would maximize net good, impartially calculated. Shouldn't we try to follow that code? Isn't the code best for general adoption by the group of which we are members the one we should try to follow? These general thoughts about morality seem intuitively attractive and broadly rule-consequentialist.

And consider the related question "What if everyone felt free to do what you're doing?" This question may in the end prove to be an inadequate test of moral rightness. But there is no denying its initial appeal. And there is no denying that rule-consequentialism is an (at least initially) appealing interpretation of the test.

Rule-consequentialism thus taps into and develops familiar and intuitively plausible ideas about morality. Morality is to be understood as a social code, a collective enterprise, something people are to pursue together. And the elements of this code are to be evaluated in terms of both fairness and the overall effects on the well-being of individuals, impartially considered.

But rule-consequentialism's leading rivals all likewise emerge from attractive general ideas about morality. For example, act-utilitarianism can be seen as emerging from the idea that all that ultimately matters from the moral point of view is whether individuals are benefitted or harmed, that everything else is only instrumentally important. [. . .] And act-consequentialism, the broader theory than act-utilitarianism, can be seen as emerging from the intuition that it can't be wrong to do what produces the most good. [. . .]

Now consider moral contractualism, the theory that an act is right if and only if allowed by rules which could not be reasonably rejected by anyone motivated to find rules that no one with this same motivation could reject. Contractualism develops from the idea that morality consists of rules to which everyone would consent under appropriate conditions. This seems a very appealing general idea – moral rules grounded in reasonable agreement.

Consider yet another theory. The moral particularism of Jonathan Dancy (1993) builds on the idea that moral truth is found not in cold inflexible principles but rather through a finely tuned sensitivity to particular cases in all their rich complexity. Actually, to be distinct, moral particularism must go beyond the claim that there are some conflicts between competing moral considerations which are so difficult that agents would have to have fine moral sensitivity and judgement to resolve them correctly. To be distinct, moral particularism must be the view that what counts as a consideration at all can be decided only on a case by case basis. This is just how Dancy frames his theory: the very same consideration can count morally in favor of doing an action in one case, and against in another, and there are few if any considerations that must always count on the same side morally. (Dancy points out that such properties as moral rightness itself do *always* count morally in favor of an act.)

Finally, as I understand what has come to be called virtue ethics, this approach grows from the thought that right and wrong actions can be understood only in terms of choices that a fully virtuous person would make. This thought then suggests that we take the nature of and rationale for the virtues as the primary focal points for our moral philosophy.

Thus all these moral theories – rule-consequentialism, act-utilitarianism, act-consequentialism, contractualism, particularism, virtue ethics – tap into familiar and intuitively attractive general ideas about morality, though different ones. So no one could claim that any one theory is the only one with this feature. The conclusion to draw from this is simple. The fact that a theory arises from and develops attractive general ideas about morality is hardly enough to show that it is superior to all its rivals.

Now among the questions we can go on to ask about competing moral theories are (1) whether they are coherent and develop from initially attractive ideas about morality, and (2) whether the claims they end up making about right and wrong in various circumstances are intuitively plausible. I have already argued that rule-consequentialism develops from attractive ideas about morality. But I shall not fully discuss here the objection that rule-consequentialism *incoherently* claims that maximizing the good is the overarching goal and then that following certain rules can be right even when breaking them would produce more good. I admit that if we start from an overarching commitment to maximize overall good, then our rule-consequentialism might be an incoherent account of moral rightness. But I propose our route to rule-consequentialism starts elsewhere: we don't start from, and indeed don't have, an overarching commitment to maximize overall good. If I am right about that, then this objection falls apart. [. . .]

What other route to rule-consequentialism might there be? In the next few sections, I will show that rule-consequentialism's implications about what is right or wrong in particular circumstances match our confident moral convictions quite well. But let me immediately address the familiar challenge to the idea that moral theories are to be tested by their match with intuitions. The familiar challenge is that moral convictions are merely inherited prejudices and as such cannot provide good reason for anything.

In reply to this challenge, let me say I of course recognize that people from different cultures have different moral intuitions, as do people even from the same culture. We must always be willing to reconsider our moral intuitions. They are scarcely infallible.

But, while they are not infallible, they can be crucial. Suppose we have two moral theories which are each coherent developments of appealing general ideas about morality. Suppose one of these theories has implications that match our convictions quite closely, and the other has implications that conflict with many of our most confidently held moral convictions. In this case, I cannot see what could reasonably keep us from thinking better of the theory with the more intuitively plausible implications. Indeed, it seems to me that we are at least as confident about what is right in *some* specific kinds of situation as we are about any of the general ideas about morality that get developed into different moral theories such as Aristotelianism, Kantianism, contractualism, and act-consequentialism. This is why almost all moral philosophers are unable to resist "testing" these theories by comparing the judgments that follow from them with our confident convictions about right and wrong in various kinds of situations.

Let me take stock. I've suggested three different ways of arguing for rule-consequentialism.

One is that rule-consequentialism is, from a purely consequentialist point of view, best. I myself am not relying on this argument.

The second is that rule-consequentialism develops from some very attractive general ideas about morality. Though this is an important feature of rule-consequentialism, I acknowledge rule-consequentialism is hardly the only theory that plugs into or develops from attractive general ideas about morality. So the fact that a theory is a coherent development of some initially very attractive ideas is not enough to make it superior to all its rivals.

The third argument for rule-consequentialism is that we can reach a reflective equilibrium between rule-consequentialism and our confident moral convictions. At least *some* moral convictions seem more secure than any theory that could oppose them. If this is right, then appeal to reflective equilibrium between abstract theory and moral conviction must be part of the defense of rule-consequentialism.

9   Rule-Consequentialism on Prohibitions

Whatever act-consequentialism says about day-to-day moral thinking, act-consequentialism's criterion of moral rightness entails that *whenever* killing an innocent person, or stealing, or breaking a promise, etc., would maximize the good, such acts would be morally right. W. D. Ross put forward the following example (table 51.4) to illustrate that keeping one's promises can be right even when this would produce *slightly* less good (Ross 1930: 34–5):

Table 51.4 Numbers below represent units of good

	Effect on person A	*Effect on person B*	*Total good*
Keeping promise to A	1000	0	1000
Keeping promise to A	0	1001	1001

Most of us would agree with Ross that keeping the promise would be morally right in this case. Act-consequentialism, of course, favors breaking the promise in this case, since that is the alternative with the most good. So, if we agree with Ross about this case, we must reject act-consequentialism.

Most of us also believe (as Ross went on to observe) that, if breaking the promise would produce *much greater* good than keeping it, breaking the promise could be right. We believe parallel things about inflicting harm on innocent people, stealing, lying, etc. Thus most of us reject what is sometimes called "absolutism" in ethics. Absolutists hold that certain acts (e.g., physical attack on the innocent, promise-breaking, stealing, lying) are *always* wrong, even when they would prevent the most extreme *disasters*.

Absolutism and act-consequentialism are, we might say, two ends of a spectrum. Whereas absolutism never permits certain kinds of act, even when necessary to prevent extreme disaster, act-consequentialism insists such act are right not only when a great disaster is at stake but also when a *marginal* gain in net good is in the offing. Act-consequentialists seem mistaken about these cases of marginal gain, just as absolutists seem mistaken about the disaster cases. Thus, absolutism seems to go too far in one direction, act-consequentialism in the other.

Rule-consequentialism, on the other hand, concurs with our beliefs both about when we can, and when we cannot, do normally forbidden acts for the sake of the overall good. It claims that individual acts of murder, torture, promise-breaking, and so on, can be wrong even when they result in somewhat more good than not doing them would. The rule-consequentialist reason for this is that the general internalization of a code prohibiting murder, torture, promise-breaking, and so on would clearly result in more good than general internalization of a code with no prohibitions on such acts.

Another rule whose general internalization would be optimal is a rule telling us to do what is necessary to prevent disasters. This rule is relevant when the only way to prevent a disaster is to break a promise or do some other normally prohibited act. In such cases, rule-consequentialism holds that the normally prohibited act should be done. I mention this rule about preventing disaster because its existence undermines the objection that rule-consequentialism would, in a counterintuitive way, prescribe sticking to rules even when this would result in disaster.

10 Doing Good for Others

Morality paradigmatically requires us to be willing to make sacrifices for others. Yet act-consequentialism is widely accused of going too far here too. Utility, impartially calculated, would be maximized if I gave away most of my material goods to the appropriate charities. Giving away most of my material goods is therefore required of me by (most versions of) act-consequentialism. I should probably even change to some more lucrative employment so that I would then have more money to give to charity. [. . .] I could make much more money as a corporate lawyer, banker, stockbroker, accountant, gossip-columnist, or bounty-hunter than as an employee of a philosophy department. If people should be willing to make any sacrifices that are smaller than the benefits thereby secured for others, then I should move to the better paying job so that I will have a bigger salary to contribute to the needy. With a bigger salary, I would then have to give an even larger percentage of my earnings to aid agencies. The result would be a life of devoted money-making – only then to deny myself virtually all the rewards I could buy for myself with the money. After all, from an act-consequentialist perspective, my own enjoyment is insignificant compared to the very lives of those who would be saved by my additional contributions. Such reflections give special poignancy to Shelly Kagan's remark: "Given the parameters of the actual world, there is no question that [maximally] promoting the good would require a life of hardship, self-denial, and austerity" (1989: 360).

But many of us may on reflection think that it would be *morally unreasonable* to demand this level of self-sacrifice for the sake of others[1] However praiseworthy such self-sacrifice may be, most of us are quite confident that perpetual self-impoverishment for the sake of strangers is above and beyond what morality *requires* of us.

I have been discussing the objection that act-consequentialism requires us to make *huge* sacrifices in order to maximize our contribution to famine relief. Act-consequentialism also requires self-sacrifice even when the benefit to the other person is only *slightly* larger than the cost to the agent. Consider, for example, the corner office in our building. Offices are allotted on the basis of seniority. Suppose you are the most senior person who might want this corner office. But if you do not take it, it will go to an acquaintance who spends ten percent more time in her office than you do in yours. Suppose we therefore reasonably guess that she would benefit a bit more from moving into this office than you would. This is not a life and death matter. Nor will she be so depressed by not getting the corner office that her work or domestic life will be seriously compromised. Nevertheless, she would get a bit more enjoyment out of the better office than you would. But you still take it for yourself. No one would think you unreasonable or immoral for doing so. Except in special circumstances, morality does not, we think, really *require* you to sacrifice your own good for the sake of slightly larger gains to others.

I have offered two objections about the demands of act-consequentialism. (1) Act-consequentialism requires *huge* sacrifices from you. (2) Act-consequentialism requires you to sacrifice your own good even when the aggregate

good will be only *slightly* increased by the your sacrifice. In both ways, act-consequentialism is *unreasonably demanding*.

In contrast, rule-consequentialism would *not* require you to pass up the corner office and let your colleague have it. You are certainly permitted to do that if you want, but rule-consequentialism would not *require* such impartiality in your decisions about what to do with your own time, energy, money, or place in line. The rules the internalization of which could reasonably be thought to produce the most good would *allow* each person considerable partiality towards self (and even *require* partiality towards friends and family. [. . .] For, as I noted earlier, the costs of getting a complete impartiality internalized by each new generation would be prohibitive.

Likewise, whereas act-consequentialism requires huge sacrifices for the sake of maximizing the good, rule-consequentialism seems not to require more than a reasonable amount of sacrifice for this purpose. Why? A rule-consequentialist might point out that, if everyone relatively well off in the world were to contribute quite modest amounts to the best aid agencies, the worst elements of poverty could be overcome.

The World Bank has been calling for contributions from the rich countries of 0.7 percent of GDP, the current average being less than half that. Much of this aid does not go to the most needy, but instead to countries that offer business for, or military alliances with, the donor country. The UN estimates that if merely 60 percent of the aid that the rich countries now give (i.e., 60 percent of about $57 billion) were intelligently spent on providing basic health services and clean water and on eliminating illiteracy, these problems could be fixed (*The Economist*, June 22, 1996: 64).

A rule-consequentialist will be interested in redistribution beyond what is required to secure the very basic necessities. But even after including these other potential benefits in the cost-benefit analysis, we might well conclude that the amount the world's relatively well off would each be required to give would not be unreasonably severe. [. . .]

Consider the following example. Walking along a deserted road on your way to the airport for a flight to the other side of the world, you see a child drowning in a shallow pool beside the road. You could easily save the child, at no risk to yourself. But if you do save the child, you will miss your flight and lose the cost of the nonrefundable ticket.[2]

Everyone agrees you are obligated to save the child. This is true even if you are not terribly rich. Suppose the ticket costs as much as a tenth of your annual income. You would still be morally wrong not to make the sacrifice and save the child. And even if the probability of the child's drowning without your rescue is less than 100 percent – suppose, for example, it is 80 percent – you are obligated to sacrifice your ticket to save the child.

Now consider a variant of the example. [. . .] You and I are walking to the airport when we see two small children drowning in a lake. You and I could each easily save the children, at no risk to ourselves. The two children are positioned in the lake in such a way that you and I could each save one and still get to our flights. But if one of us saves both children, he will miss his flight. Suppose you save one child, but I do nothing. Surely, you should now save the other.

Yet, were rule-consequentialism framed in terms of 100 percent compliance, how could it tell you to save the other? With 100 percent compliance, there would be no need for you to save the second child. With 100 percent compliance, once you'd done your share, you'd have done all that was needed. The rule that would be best given 100 percent compliance would presumably not require you to sacrifice more than you would have to sacrifice if everyone did their part. But if this rule is applied to our case, where I am in fact not coming to the rescue, you are *not* obligated to save this child. This is clearly an implausible implication.

But I argued that rule-consequentialism should be framed in terms of less that 100 percent compliance. If rule-consequentialism is framed in terms of 90 percent compliance, we can envisage that there is a need for rules about how to act when others around you aren't doing their part. The rule might be, "When you happen to be surrounded by others who are not helping, then prevent disaster even if this involves doing more than you would

have to do if the others helped." This rule *would* require you to save the second child from the shallow pond.

But if the world we live in – the real world – is one where partial compliance is ubiquitous, then a rule requiring you to make up for the non-compliance of others could become unreasonably demanding. Just how much would rule-consequentialism require you to make up for non-compliance by other people in a position to help? In earlier work, I assumed that rule-consequentialism would formulate a rule about aiding the needy in terms of a *fairly precise* level of contribution or sacrifice to the reduction of world poverty.

I now think this approach is hopeless. Consider a concrete moral code that could reasonably be expected to produce at least as much good as any other we can identify. It would contain rules requiring us not to injure others physically, not to steal, not to break promises, not to lie, etc. These rules might have *some* exceptions built into them (though not a general break-the-rule-whenever-you-could-thereby-produce-more-good exception, nor an unlimited set of much more specific exceptions). Nonetheless, there is pressure to have *fairly general* rules that can be applied to a wide array of situations. Oxfam's petitioning the rich to help the very poor is hardly the only situation where some people have an opportunity to help others at relatively little cost to themselves. There will be situations where the rich can help other rich, situations where poor can help other poor, even situations where the poor can help the rich. And there will be situations where the help needs to be in the form of physical effort, other situations where the help needs to be in the form of money or time.

Given all this, perhaps the optimific rule for such a world would not be "the rich should give the very needy at least precisely n percent of their annual income", but rather "people should help others in great need when they can do so at modest to themselves, cost being assessed aggregatively, not iteratively" (Cullity 1995: 293–5). Such a rule would apply in a wide array of situations – indeed, whenever some person can help another in great need. It is not limited to what the rich should do nor to what should be done concerning world poverty.

But because cost to the agent is to be assessed aggregatively rather than iteratively, the rule does not require one to help another in great need whenever the cost of helping *on that particular occasion* is modest. Having to help others whenever doing so *on that occasion* involves modest cost could easily be very costly. For each of us faces an indefinitely long string of such occasions, because any day on which we could give money to UNICEF or Oxfam counts as such an occasion. But many small sacrifices added together can amount to a huge sacrifice. The end of that road is self-impoverishment. If I am right, rule-consequentialism instead endorses a rule requiring sacrifices over the course of your life that add up to something significant. It allows but does not require personal sacrifice beyond this point.

I propose that this rule *would* have good consequences even in possible worlds that are either much poorer or much richer than ours. I don't have space here to argue either that rule-consequentialism would indeed end up with this rule in *all* possible worlds, or that this rule *always* has intuitively acceptable consequences. I mention this rule only in order to sketch one way in which a defense of rule-consequentialism might go. [...]

11   Conclusion

Rule-consequentialism has an uncertain future. It needs to be carefully formulated if it is to avoid being a sitting target. In this essay, I have tried to improve its defenses by fine-tuning its formulation. I have also argued here that the theory develops from appealing general beliefs about morality, that it does not collapse into act-consequentialism, and that it coheres well with our intuitions about moral prohibitions and permissible partiality. As I see things, the theory is healthy now. But it is hardly invulnerable. Like someone walking through a dangerous city who has so far managed to fight off muggers emerging from behind every corner, the theory might meet an attack it cannot survive. I am curious to see whether that happens.

Notes

1. See Quinn 1993: 171: "We think there is something morally amiss when people are forced to be farmers or flute players just because the balance of social needs tips in that direction. Barring great emergencies, we think people's lives must be theirs to lead."

2. This example has been central to the contemporary philosophical debate about beneficence. The example and the debate owe their prominence to Singer 1972.

References

Cullity, Garrett: "Moral Character and the Iteration Problem," *Utilitas*, 7 (1995): 289–99.

Dancy, Jonathan: *Moral Reasons* (Oxford: Blackwell, 1993).

Hodgson, D. H.: *Consequences of Utilitarianism* (Oxford: Clarendon Press, 1967).

Kagan, Shelly: *The Limits of Morality* (Oxford: Clarendon Press, 1989).

Quinn, Warren: *Morality and Action* (New York: Cambridge University Press, 1993).

Regan, D.: *Utilitarianism and Co-operation* (Oxford: Clarendon Press, 1980).

Ross, W. D.: *The Right and the Good* (Oxford: Clarendon Press, 1930).

Singer, Peter: "Famine, Affluence, and Morality," *Philosophy and Public Affairs*, 1 (1972): 229–43.

CHAPTER 52

What is Wrong with Slavery

R. M. HARE

Nearly everybody would agree that slavery is wrong; and I can say this perhaps with greater feeling than most, having in a manner of speaking *been* a slave. However, there are dangers in just taking for granted that something is wrong; for we may then assume that it is obvious that it is wrong and indeed obvious why it is wrong; and this leads to a prevalence of very bad arguments with quite silly conclusions, all based on the so-called absolute value of human freedom. If we could see more clearly what *is* valuable about freedom, and why it is valuable, then we might be protected against the rhetoric of those who, the moment anything happens that is disadvantageous or distasteful to them, start complaining loudly about some supposed infringement of their liberty, without telling us why it is wrong that they should be prevented from doing what they would like to do. It may well *be* wrong in many such cases; but until we have some way of judging when it is and when it is not, we shall be at the mercy of every kind of demagogy.

This is but one example of the widespread abuse of the appeal to human rights. We may even be tempted to think that our politics would be more healthy if rights had never been heard of; but that would be going too

R. M. Hare, "What is Wrong with Slavery," pp. 103–21 from *Philosophy and Public Affairs*, 8(2), 1979. Reprinted by permission of the publishers, Blackwell Publishing.

far. It is the unthinking appeal to ill-defined rights, unsupported by argument, that does the harm. There is no doubt that arguments justifying some of these appeals are possible; but since the forms of such arguments are seldom understood even by philosophers, it is not surprising that many quite unjustified claims of this sort go unquestioned, and thus in the end bring any sort of appeal to human rights into disrepute. It is a tragedy that this happens, because there really are rights that ought to be defended with all the devotion we can command. Things are being done the world over which can properly be condemned as infringements of human rights; but so long as rights are used so loosely as an all-purpose political weapon, often in support of very questionable causes, our protests against such infringements will be deprived of most of their force.

Another hazard of the appeal to rights is that it is seldom that such an appeal by one side cannot be countered with an appeal to some conflicting right by the opposite side. The controversies which led finally to the abolition of slavery provide an excellent example of this, with one side appealing to rights of liberty and the other to rights of property. But we do not have to go so far back in history to find examples of this sort of thing. We have only to think of the disputes about distributive justice between the defenders of equality and of individual liberty; or of similar arguments about education. I have written about both these disputes elsewhere, in the attempt to substitute for intuitions some more solid basis for argument.[1] I have the same general motive in raising the topic of slavery, and also a more particular motive. Being a utilitarian, I need to be able to answer the following attack frequently advanced by opponents of utilitarianism. It is often said that utilitarianism must be an objectionable creed because it could in certain circumstances condone or even commend slavery, given that circumstances can be envisaged in which utility would be maximized by preserving a slave-owning society and not abolishing slavery. The objectors thus seek to smear utilitarians with the taint of all the atrocious things that were done by slave-traders and slave-owners. The objection, as I hope to show, does not stand up; but in order to see through this rhetoric we shall have to achieve a quite deep understanding of some rather difficult issues in moral philosophy; and this, too, adds to the importance and interest of the topic.

First, we have to ask what this thing, slavery, is, about whose wrongness we are arguing. As soon as we ask this question we see at once, if we have any knowledge of history, that it is, in common use, an extremely ill-defined concept. Even if we leave out of account such admittedly extended uses as 'wage-slave' in the writings of Marxists, it is clear that the word 'slave' and its near-equivalents such as 'servus' and 'doulos' have meant slightly different things in different cultures; for slavery is, primarily, a *legal* status, defined by the disabilities or the liabilities which are imposed by the law on those called slaves; and obviously these may vary from one jurisdiction to another. Familiar logical difficulties arise about how we are to decide, of a word in a foreign language, that it means the same as the English word 'slave'. Do the relevant laws in the country where the language is spoken have to be identical with those which held in English-speaking countries before slavery was abolished? Obviously not; because it would be impossible for them to be identical with the laws of all such countries at all periods, since these did not remain the same. Probably we have a rough idea of the kind of laws which have to hold in a country before we can say that that country has an institution properly called 'slavery'; but it is pretty rough.

It would be possible to pursue at some length, with the aid of legal, historical and anthropological books on slavery in different cultures and jurisdictions, the different shades of meaning of the word 'slave'. But since my purpose is philosophical, I shall limit myself to asking what is essential to the notion of slavery in common use. The essential features are, I think, to be divided under two heads: slavery is, first, a *status* in society, and secondly, a *relation* to a master. The slave is so called first of all because he occupies a certain place in society, lacking certain rights and privileges secured by the law to others, and subject to certain liabilities from which others are free. And secondly, he is the slave *of* another person or body (which might be the state itself). The first head is not enough to distinguish slavery from other legal disabilities; for example the lowest castes in some societies are as lacking in legal rights as slaves in some others, or more so, but are not called slaves because they are not the slaves *of* anybody.

The *status* of a slave was defined quite early by the Greeks in terms of four freedoms which the slave lacks. These are: a legally recognized position in the community, conferring a right of access to the courts; protection from illegal seizure and detention and other personal violence; the privilege of going where he wants to go; and that of working as he pleases. The first three of these features are present in a manumission document from Macedonia dated about 235 BC; the last is added in the series of manumission documents from Delphi which begins about thirty years later.[2] The state could to some extent regulate by law the treatment of slaves without making us want to stop calling them slaves, so that the last three features are a bit wobbly at the edges. But we are seeking only a rough characterization of slavery, and shall have to put up with this indefiniteness of the concept.

[. . .]

I shall put my philosophical argument, to which we have now come, in terms of an imaginary example, to which I shall give as much verisimilitude as I can. It will be seen, however, that quite unreal assumptions have to be made in order to get the example going – and this is very important for the argument between the utilitarians and their opponents. It must also be noted that to play its role in the argument the example will have to meet certain requirements. It is intended as a fleshed-out substitute for the rather jejune examples often to be found in anti-utilitarian writers. To serve its purpose it will have to be a case in which to abolish slavery really and clearly would diminish utility. This means, first, that the slavery to be abolished must really be slavery, and, secondly, that it must have a total utility clearly, but not enormously, greater than the total utility of the kind of regime which would be, in that situation, a practical alternative to slavery.

If it were not *clearly* greater, utilitarians could argue that, since all judgements of this sort are only probable, caution would require them to stick to a well-tried principle favouring liberty, the principle itself being justified on utilitarian grounds (see below); and thus the example would cease to divide them from their opponents, and would become inapposite.

If, on the other hand, the utility of slavery were *enormously* greater, anti-utilitarians might complain that their own view was being made too strong; for many anti-utilitarians are pluralists and hold that among the principles of morality a principle requiring beneficence is to be included. Therefore, if the advantages of retaining slavery are made sufficiently great, a non-utilitarian with a principle of beneficence in his repertory could agree that it ought to be retained – that is, that *in this case* the principle of beneficence has greater weight than that favouring liberty. Thus there would again be no difference, in this case, between the verdicts of the utilitarians and their opponents, and the example would be inapposite.

There is also another dimension in which the example has to be carefully placed. An anti-utilitarian might claim that the example I shall give makes the difference between the conditions of the slaves and those of the free in the supposed society too small, and the number of slaves too great. If, he might claim, I had made the number of slaves small and the difference between the miseries of the slaves and the pleasures of the slave-owners much

greater, then the society might have the same total utility as mine (that is, greater than that of the free society with which I compare it), but it would be less plausible for me to maintain that if such a comparison had to be made in real life, we ought to follow the utilitarians and prefer the slave society.

I cannot yet answer this objection without anticipating my argument; I shall merely indicate briefly how I would answer it. The answer is that the objection rests on an appeal to our ordinary intuitions; but that these are designed to deal with ordinary cases. They give no reliable guide to what we ought to say in highly unusual cases. But, further, the case desiderated is never likely to occur. How could it come about that the existence of a small number of slaves was necessary in order to preserve the happiness of the rest? I find it impossible to think of any technological factors (say, in agriculture or in transport by land or sea) which would make the preservation of slavery for a small class necessary to satisfy the interests of the majority. It is quite true that in the past there have been *large* slave populations supporting the higher standard of living of *small* minorities. But in that case it is hard to argue that slavery has more utility than its abolition, if the difference in happiness between slaves and slave-owners is great. Yet if, in order to produce a case in which the retention of slavery really would be optimal, we reduce the number of slaves relative to slave-owners, it becomes hard to say how the existence of this relatively small number of slaves is necessary for the happiness of the large number of free men. What on earth are the slaves doing that could not be more efficiently done by paid labour? And is not the abolition (perhaps not too abrupt) of slavery likely to promote those very technical changes which are necessary to enable the society to do without it?

The crux of the matter, as we shall see, is that in order to use an appeal to our ordinary intuitions as an argument, the opponents of utilitarianism have to produce cases which are not too far removed from the sort of cases with which our intuitions are designed to deal, namely the ordinary run of cases. If the cases they use fall outside this class, then the fact that our common intuitions give a different verdict from utilitarianism has no bearing on the argument; our intuitions could well be wrong about such cases, and be none the worse for that, because they will never have to deal with them in practise.

We may also notice, while we are sifting possible examples, that cases of *individual* slave-owners who are kind to their slaves will not do. The issue is one of whether slavery as an institution protected by law should be preserved; and if it is preserved, though there may be individuals who do not take advantage of it to maltreat their slaves, there will no doubt be many others who do.

Let us imagine, then, that the battle of Waterloo, that 'damned nice thing, the nearest run thing you ever saw in your life',[3] as Wellington called it, went differently from the way it actually did go, in two respects. The first was that the British and Prussians lost the battle; the last attack of the French Guard proved too much for them, the Guard's morale having been restored by Napoleon who in person led the advance instead of handing it over to Ney. But secondly, having exposed himself to fire as Wellington habitually did, but lacking Wellington's amazing good fortune, Napoleon was struck by a cannon ball and killed instantly. This so disorganized the French, who had no other commanders of such ability, that Wellington was able to rally his forces and conduct one of those holding operations at which he was so adept, basing himself on the Channel ports and their intricate surrounding waterways; the result was a cross between the Lines of Torres Vedras and the trench warfare of the first World War. After a year or two of this, with Napoleon out of the way and the war party discredited in England, liberal (that is, neither revolutionary nor reactionary) regimes came into power in both countries, and the Congress of Vienna reconvened in a very different spirit, with the French represented on equal terms.

We have to consider these events only as they affected two adjacent islands in the Caribbean which I am going to call Juba and Camaica. I need not relate what happened in the rest of the world, because the combined European powers could at that time command absolute supremacy at sea, and the Caribbean could therefore be effectively isolated from world politics by the agreement which they reached to take that area out of the imperial war game. All naval and other forces were withdrawn from it except for a couple of bases on small islands for the suppression of the slave trade, which, in keeping with their liberal principles, the parties agreed to prohibit (those that had not already done so). The islands were declared independent and their white inhabitants, very naturally, all departed in a hurry, leaving the government in the hands of local black leaders, some of whom were of the calibre of Toussaint l'Ouverture and others of whom were very much the reverse.

On Juba, a former Spanish colony, at the end of the colonial period there had been formed, under pressure of military need, a militia composed of slaves under white officers, with conditions of service much preferable to those of the plantation slaves, and forming a kind of elite. The senior serjeant-major of this force found himself, after the white officers fled, in a position of unassailable power, and, being a man of great political intelligence and ability, shaped the new regime in a way that made Juba the envy of its neighbours.

What he did was to retain the institution of slavery but to remedy its evils. The plantations were split up into smaller units, still under overseers, responsible to the state instead of to the former owners. The slaves were given rights to improved conditions of work; the wage they had already received as a concession in colonial times was secured to them and increased; all cruel punishments were prohibited. However, it is still right to call them slaves, because the state retained the power to direct their labour and their place of residence and to enforce these directions by sanctions no more severe than are customary in countries without slavery, such as fines and imprisonment. The Juban government, influenced by early communist ideas (though Marx had not yet come on the scene) kept the plantations in its own hands; but private persons were also allowed to own a limited number of slaves under conditions at least as protective to the slaves as on the state-owned plantations.

The island became very prosperous, and the slaves in it enjoyed a life far preferable in every way to that of the free inhabitants of the neighbouring island of Camaica. In Camaica there had been no such focus of power in the early days. The slaves threw off their bonds and each seized what land he could get hold of. Though law and order were restored after a fashion, and democracy of a sort prevailed, the economy was chaotic, and this, coupled with a population explosion, led to widespread starvation and misery. Camaica lacked what Juba had: a government with the will *and the instrument, in the shape of the institution of slavery,* to control the economy and the population, and so make its slave-citizens, as I said, the envy of their neighbours. The flood of people in fishing boats seeking to emigrate from free Camaica and insinuate themselves as slaves into the plantations of Juba became so great that the Juban government had to employ large numbers of coastguards (slaves of course) to stop it.

That, perhaps, will do for our imaginary example. Now for the philosophical argument. It is commonly alleged that utilitarianism could condone or commend slavery. In the situation described, utility would have been lessened and not increased if the Juban government had abolished slavery and if as a result the economy of Juba had deteriorated to the level of that of Camaica. So, it might be argued, a utilitarian would have had to oppose the abolition. But everyone agrees, it might be held, that slavery is wrong; so the utilitarians are convicted of maintaining a thesis which has consequences repugnant to universally accepted moral convictions.

What could they reply to this attack? There are, basically, two lines they could take. These lines are not incompatible but complementary; indeed, the defence of utilitarianism could be put in the form of a dilemma. Either the defender of utilitarianism is allowed to question the imagined facts of the example, or he is not. First let us suppose that he is not. He might then try, as a first move, saying that in the situation *as portrayed* it would indeed be wrong to abolish slavery. If the argument descends to details, the anti-utilitarians may be

permitted to insert any amount of extra details (barring the actual abolition of slavery itself) in order to make sure that its retention really does maximize utility. But then the utilitarian sticks to his guns and maintains that in that case it *would* be wrong to abolish slavery, and that, further, most ordinary people, if they could be got to consider the case on its merits and not allow their judgement to be confused by association with more detestable forms of slavery, would agree with this verdict. The principle of liberty which forbids slavery is a prima facie principle admitting of exceptions, and this imaginary case is one of the exceptions. If the utilitarians could sustain this line of defence, they would win the case; but perhaps not everyone would agree that it is sustainable.

So let us allow the utilitarian another slightly more sophisticated move, still staying, however, perched on the first horn of the dilemma. He might admit that not everyone would agree on the merits of this case, but explain this by pointing to the fantastic and unusual nature of the case, which, he might claim, would be unlikely to occur in real life. *If* he is not allowed to question the facts of the case, he has to admit that abolition would be wrong; but ordinary people, he might say, cannot see this because the principles of political and social morality which we have all of us *now* absorbed (as contrasted with our eighteenth-century ancestors), and with which we are deeply imbued, prevent us from considering the case on its merits. The principles are framed to cope with the cases of slavery which actually occur (all of which are to a greater or less degree harmful). Though they are the best principles for us to have when confronting the actual world, they give the wrong answer when presented with this fantastic case. But all the same, the world being as it is, we should be morally worse people if we did not have these principles; for then we might be tempted, whether through ignorance or by self-interest, to condone slavery in cases in which, though actually harmful, it could be colourably represented as being beneficial. Suppose, it might be argued, that an example of this sort had been used in anti-abolitionist writings in, say, 1830 or thereabouts. Might it not have persuaded many people that slavery *could* be an admirable thing, and thus have secured their votes against abolition; and would this not have been very harmful? For the miseries caused by the *actual* institution of slavery in the Caribbean and elsewhere were so great that it was desirable from a utilitarian point of view that people should hold and act on moral convictions which condemned slavery as such and without qualification, because this would lead them to vote for its abolition.

If utilitarians take this slightly more sophisticated line, they are left saying at one and the same time that it would have been wrong to abolish slavery in the imagined circumstances, *and* that it is a good thing that nearly everyone, if asked about it, would say that it was right. Is this paradoxical? Not, I think, to anybody who understands the realities of the human situation. What resolves the paradox is that the example *is* imaginary and that therefore people are not going to have to pronounce, as a practical issue, on what the laws of Juba are to be. In deciding what principles it is good that people have, it is not necessary or even desirable to take into account such imaginary cases. It does not really matter, from a practical point of view, what judgements people reach about imaginary cases, provided that this does not have an adverse effect upon their judgements about real cases. From a practical point of view, the principles which it is best for them to have are those which will lead them to make the highest proportion of right decisions in actual cases where their decisions make a difference to what happens – weighted, of course, for the importance of the cases, that is, the amount of difference the decisions make to the resulting good or harm.

It is therefore perfectly acceptable that we should at one and the same time feel a strong moral conviction that even the Juban slave system, however beneficial, is wrong, *and* confess, when we reflect on the features of this imagined system, that we cannot see anything specifically wrong about it, but rather a great deal to commend. This is bound to be the experience of anybody who has acquired the sort of moral convictions that one ought to acquire, and at the same time is able to reflect rationally on the features of some unusual imagined situation. I have myself constantly

had this experience when confronted with the sort of anti-utilitarian examples which are the stock-in-trade of philosophers like Bernard Williams. One is led to think, on reflection, that *if* such cases were to occur, one ought to do what is for the best in the circumstances (as even Williams himself appears to contemplate in one of his cases)[4] but one is bound also to find this conclusion repugnant to one's deepest convictions; if it is not, one's convictions are not the best convictions one could have.

Against this, it might be objected that if one's deep moral convictions yield the wrong answer even in imaginary or unusual cases, they are *not* the best one could have. Could we not succeed, it might be asked, in inculcating into ourselves convictions of a more accommodating sort? Could we not, that is to say, absorb principles which had written into them either exceptions to deal with awkward cases like that in my example, or even provision for writing in exceptions ad hoc when the awkward cases arose? Up to a point this is a sensible suggestion; but beyond that point (a point which will vary with the temperament of the person whose principles they are to be) it becomes psychologically unsound. There are some simple souls, no doubt, who really cannot keep themselves in the straight and narrow way unless they cling fanatically and in the face of what most of us would call reason to extremely simple and narrow principles. And there are others who manage to have very complicated principles with many exceptions written into them (only 'written' is the wrong word, because the principles of such people defy formulation). Most of us come somewhere in between. It is also possible to have fairly simple principles but to attach to them a rubric which allows us to depart from them, either when one conflicts with another in a particular case, or where the case is such an unusual one that we find ourselves doubting whether the principles were designed to deal with it. In these cases we may apply utilitarian reasoning directly; but it is most unwise to do this in more normal cases, for those are precisely the cases (the great majority) which our principles *are* designed to deal with, since they were chosen to give the best results in the general run of cases. In normal cases, therefore, we are more likely to achieve the right decision (even from the utilitarian point of view) by sticking to these principles than by engaging in utilitarian reasoning about the particular case, with all its temptations to special pleading.

I have dealt with these issues at length elsewhere.[5] Here all I need to say is that there is a psychological limit to the complexity and to the flexibility of the moral principles that we can wisely seek to build deeply, as moral convictions, into our character; and the person who tries to go beyond this limit will end up as (what he will be called) an unprincipled person, and will not in fact do the best he could with his life, even by the test of utility. This may explain why I would always vote for the abolition of slavery, even though I can admit that cases could be *imagined* in which slavery would do more good than harm, and even though I am a utilitarian.

So much, then, for the first horn of the dilemma. Before we come to the second horn, on which the utilitarian is allowed to object to his opponents' argument on the ground that their example would not in the actual world be realized, I wish to make a methodological remark which may help us to find our bearings in this rather complex dispute. Utilitarianism, like any other theory of moral reasoning that gets anywhere near adequacy, consists of two parts, one formal and one substantial. The formal part is no more than a rephrasing of the requirement that moral prescriptions be universalizable; this has the consequence that equal interests of all are to be given equal weight in our reasoning: everybody to count for one and nobody for more than one. One should not expect such a formal requirement to generate, by itself, any substantial conclusions even about the actual world, let alone about all logically possible worlds. But there is also a substantial element in the theory. This is contributed by factual beliefs about what interests people in the real world actually have (which depends on what they actually want or like or dislike, and on what they would want or like or dislike under given conditions); and also about the actual effects on these interests of different actions in the real world. Given the truth of these beliefs, we can reason morally and shall come to certain morally and shall

come to certain moral conclusions. But the conclusions are not generated by the formal part of the theory alone.

Utilitarianism therefore, unlike some other theories, is *exposed* to the facts. The utilitarian cannot reason a priori that *whatever* the facts about the world and human nature, slavery is wrong. He has to show that it is wrong by showing, through a study of history and other factual observation, that slavery does have the effects (namely the production of misery) which make it wrong. This, though it may at first sight appear a weakness in the doctrine, is in fact its strength. A doctrine, like some kinds of intuitionism, according to which we can think up examples as fantastic as we please and the doctrine will still come up with the same old answers, is really showing that it has lost contact with the actual world with which the intuitions it relies on were designed to cope. Intuitionists think they can face the world armed with nothing but their inbred intuitions; utilitarians know that they have to look at what actually goes on in the world and see if the intuitions are really the best ones to have in that sort of world.

I come now to the second horn of the dilemma, on which the utilitarian is allowed to say, "Your example won't do: it would never happen that way". He may admit that Waterloo and the Congress of Vienna could have turned out differently – after all it was a damned nice thing, and high commanders were in those days often killed on the battlefield (it was really a miracle that Wellington was not), and there were liberal movements in both countries. But when we come to the Caribbean, things begin to look shakier. Is it really likely that there would have been such a contrast between the economies of Juba and Camaica? I do not believe that the influence of particular national leaders is ever so powerful, or that such perfectly wise leaders are ever forthcoming. And I do not believe that in the Caribbean or anywhere else a system of nationalized slavery could be made to run so smoothly. I should, rather, expect the system to deteriorate very rapidly. I base these expectations on general beliefs about human nature, and in particular upon the belief that people in the power of other people will be exploited, whatever the good intentions of those who founded the system.

Alternatively, if there really had been leaders of such amazing statesmanship, could they not have done better by abolishing slavery and substituting a free but disciplined society? In the example, they gave the slaves some legal rights; what was to prevent them giving others, such as the right to change residences and jobs, subject of course to an overall system of land-use and economic planning such as exists in many free countries? Did the retention of *slavery* in particular contribute very much to the prosperity of Juba that could not have been achieved by other means? And likewise, need the government of Camaica have been so incompetent? Could it not, without reintroducing slavery, have kept the economy on the rails by such controls as are compatible with a free society? In short, did not the optimum solution lie somewhere *between* the systems adopted in Juba and Camaica, but on the free side of the boundary between slavery and liberty?

These factual speculations, however, are rather more superficial than I can be content with. The facts that it is really important to draw attention to are rather deep facts about human nature which must always, or nearly always, make slavery an intolerable condition. I have mentioned already a fact about slave ownership: that ordinary, even good, human beings will nearly always exploit those over whom they have absolute power. We have only to read the actual history of slavery in all centuries and cultures to see that. There is also the effect on the characters of the exploiters themselves. I had this brought home to me recently when, staying in Jamaica, I happened to pick up a history book[6] written there at the very beginning of the nineteenth century, before abolition, whose writer had added at the end an appendix giving his views on the abolition controversy, which was then at its height. Although obviously a kindly man with liberal leanings, he argues against abolition; and one of his arguments struck me very forcibly. He argues that although slavery can be a cruel fate, things are much better in Jamaica now: there is actually a law that a slave on a plantation may not be given more than thirty-six lashes by the foreman without running him up in front of the overseer. The contrast between the niceness of the man and what he says here does perhaps more than any philosophical argument to make the point that our moral principles have to be designed for human nature as it is.

The most fundamental point is one about the human nature of the slave which makes ownership by another more intolerable for him than for, say, a horse (not that we should condone cruelty to horses). Men are different from other animals in that they can look a long way ahead, and therefore can become an object of deterrent punishment. Other animals, we may suppose, can only be the object of Skinnerian reinforcement and Pavlovian conditioning. These methods carry with them, no doubt, their own possibilities of cruelty; but they fall short of the peculiar cruelty of human slavery. One can utter to a man threats of punishment in the quite distant future which he can understand. A piece of human property, therefore, unlike a piece of inanimate property or even a brute animal in a man's possession, can be subjected to a sort of terror from which other kinds of property are immune; and, human owners being what they are, many will inevitably take advantage of this fact. That is the reason for the atrocious punishments that have usually been inflicted on slaves; there would have been no point in inflicting them on animals. A slave is the only being that is *both* able to be held responsible in this way, *and* has no escape from, or even redress against, the power that this ability to threaten confers upon his oppressor. If he were a free citizen, he would have rights which would restrain the exercise of the threat; if he were a horse or a piece of furniture, the threat would be valueless to his owner because it would not be understood. By being subjected to the threat of legal and other punishment, but at the same time deprived of legal defences against its abuse (since he has no say in what the laws are to be, nor much ability to avail himself of such laws as there are) the slave becomes, or is likely to become if his master is an ordinary human, the most miserable of all creatures.

No doubt there are other facts I could have adduced. But I will end by reiterating the general point I have been trying to illustrate. The wrongness of slavery, like the wrongness of anything else, has to be shown in the world as it actually is. We can do this by first reaching an understanding of the meaning of this and the other moral words, which brings with it certain rules of moral reasoning, as I have tried to show in other places.[7] One of the most important of these rules is a formal requirement reflected in the Golden Rule: the requirement that what we say we ought to do to others we have to be able to say ought to be done to ourselves were we in precisely their situation with their interests. And this leads to a way of moral reasoning (utilitarianism) which treats the equal interests of all as having equal weight. Then we have to apply this reasoning to the world as it actually is, which will mean ascertaining what will actually be the result of adopting certain principles and policies, and how this will actually impinge upon the interests of ourselves and others. Only so can we achieve a morality suited for use in real life; and nobody who goes through this reasoning in real life will adopt principles which permit slavery, because of the miseries which in real life it causes. Utilitarianism can thus show what is wrong with slavery; and so far as I can see it is the kind of moral reasoning best able to show this, as opposed to merely *protesting* that slavery is wrong.

Notes

1. 'Justice and Equality', in J. Arthur and W. H. Shaw, eds., *Justice and Economic Distribution* (Englewood Cliffs: Prentice-Hall, 1978); 'Opportunity for What?: Some Remarks on Current Disputes about Equality in Education', *Oxford Review of Education* 3 (1977).

2. See W. L. Westermann, *The Slave Systems of Greek and Roman Antiquity* (Philadelphia: American Philosophical Society, 1995), p. 35.

3. For references, see E. Longford, *Wellington: The Years of the Sword* (London: Weidenfeld and Nicholson, 1969), p. 489.

4. See Williams, 'A Critique of Utilitarianism,' in J. J. C. Smart and B. Williams, *Utilitarianism: For and Against* (Cambridge: Cambridge University Press, 1973), p. 99.

5. See my 'Ethical Theory and Utilitarianism', in H. D. Lewis, ed., *Contemporary British Philosophy 4* (London: Allen and Unwin, 1976), and the references given there.

6. R. C. Dallas, *The History of the Maroons* (London: Longman and Rees, 1803; reprinted by Frank Cass, 1968). I have not been able to obtain the book again to verify this reference.

7. See n. 5 above, and my *Freedom and Reason* (Oxford: Oxford University Press, 1963), especially chap. 6.

CHAPTER 53

Famine, Affluence and Morality

PETER SINGER

As I write this, in November 1971, people are dying in East Bengal from lack of food, shelter, and medical care. The suffering and death that are occurring there now are not inevitable, not unavoidable in any fatalistic sense of the term. Constant poverty, a cyclone, and a civil war have turned at least nine million people into destitute refugees; nevertheless, it is not beyond the capacity of the richer nations to give enough assistance to reduce any further suffering to very small proportions. The decisions and actions of human beings can prevent this kind of suffering. Unfortunately, human beings have not made the necessary decisions. At the individual level, people have, with very few exceptions, not responded to the situation in any significant way. Generally speaking, people have not given large sums to relief funds; they have not written to their parliamentary representatives demanding increased government assistance; they have not demonstrated in the streets, held symbolic fasts, or done anything else directed toward providing the refugees with the means to satisfy their essential needs. At the government level, no government has given the sort of massive aid that would enable the refugees to survive for more than a few days. Britain, for instance, has given

rather more than most countries. It has, to date, given £14,750,000. For comparative purposes, Britain's share of the nonrecoverable development costs of the Anglo-French Concorde project is already in excess of £275,000,000, and on present estimates will reach £440,000,000. The implication is that the British government values a supersonic transport more than thirty times as highly as it values the lives of the nine million refugees. Australia is another country which, on a per capita basis, is well up in the "aid to Bengal" table. Australia's aid, however, amounts to less than one-twelfth of the cost of Sydney's new opera house. The total amount given, from all sources, now stands at about £65,000,000. The estimated cost of keeping the refugees alive for one year is £464,000,000. Most of the refugees have now been in the camps for more than six months. The World Bank has said that India needs a minimum of £300,000,000 in assistance from other countries before the end of the year. It seems obvious that assistance on this scale will not be forthcoming. India will be forced to choose between letting the refugees starve or diverting funds from her own development program, which will mean that more of her own people will starve in the future.[1]

These are the essential facts about the present situation in Bengal. So far as it concerns us here, there is nothing unique about this situation except its magnitude. The Bengal

Peter Singer, "Famine, Affluence and Morality," pp. 229–43 from *Philosophy and Public Affairs*, 1(3), 1972. Reprinted by permission of the publishers, Blackwell Publishing.

emergency is just the latest and most acute of a series of major emergencies in various parts of the world, arising both from natural and from man-made causes. There are also many parts of the world in which people die from malnutrition and lack of food independent of any special emergency. I take Bengal as my example only because it is the present concern, and because the size of the problem has ensured that it has been given adequate publicity. Neither individuals nor governments can claim to be unaware of what is happening there.

What are the moral implications of a situation like this? In what follows, I shall argue that the way people in relatively affluent countries react to a situation like that in Bengal cannot be justified; indeed, the whole way we look at moral issues – our moral conceptual scheme – needs to be altered, and with it, the way of life that has come to be taken for granted in our society.

In arguing for this conclusion I will not, of course, claim to be morally neutral. I shall, however, try to argue for the moral position that I take, so that anyone who accepts certain assumptions, to be made explicit, will, I hope, accept my conclusion.

I begin with the assumption that suffering and death from lack of food, shelter, and medical care are bad. I think most people will agree about this, although one may reach the same view by different routes. I shall not argue for this view. People can hold all sorts of eccentric positions, and perhaps from some of them it would not follow that death by starvation is in itself bad. It is difficult, perhaps impossible, to refute such positions, and so for brevity I will henceforth take this assumption as accepted. Those who disagree need read no further.

My next point is this: if it is in our power to prevent something bad from happening, without thereby sacrificing anything of comparable moral importance, we ought, morally, to do it. By "without sacrificing anything of comparable moral importance" I mean without causing anything else comparably bad to happen, or doing something that is wrong in itself, or failing to promote some moral good, comparable in significance to the bad thing that we can prevent. This principle seems almost as uncon-

troversial as the last one. It requires us only to prevent what is bad, and not to promote what is good, and it requires this of us only when we can do it without sacrificing anything that is, from the moral point of view, comparably important. I could even, as far as the application of my argument to the Bengal emergency is concerned, qualify the point so as to make it: if it is in our power to prevent something very bad from happening, without thereby sacrificing anything morally significant, we ought, morally, to do it. An application of this principle would be as follows: if I am walking past a shallow pond and see a child drowning in it, I ought to wade in and pull the child out. This will mean getting my clothes muddy, but this is insignificant, while the death of the child would presumably be a very bad thing.

The uncontroversial appearance of the principle just stated is deceptive. If it were acted upon, even in its qualified form, our lives, our society, and our world would be fundamentally changed. For the principle takes, firstly, no account of proximity or distance. It makes no moral difference whether the person I can help is a neighbor's child ten yards from me or a Bengali whose name I shall never know, ten thousand miles away. Secondly, the principle makes no distinction between cases in which I am the only person who could possibly do anything and cases in which I am just one among millions in the same position.

I do not think I need to say much in defense of the refusal to take proximity and distance into account. The fact that a person is physically near to us, so that we have personal contact with him, may make it more likely that we *shall* assist him, but this does not show that we *ought* to help him rather than another who happens to be further away. If we accept any principle of impartiality, universalizability, equality, or whatever, we cannot discriminate against someone merely because he is far away from us (or we are far away from him). Admittedly, it is possible that we are in a better position to judge what needs to be done to help a person near to us than one far away, and perhaps also to provide the assistance we judge to be necessary. If this were the case, it would be a reason for helping those near to us first. This may once have been a justification for being more concerned with the poor in one's own town than with the famine victims in India. Unfortunately for those who like to keep their moral responsibilities limited, instant communication and swift transportation have changed the situation. From the moral point of view, the development of the world into a "global village" has made an important, though still unrecognized, difference to our moral situation. Expert observers and supervisors, sent out by famine relief organizations or permanently stationed in famine-prone areas, can direct our aid to a refugee in Bengal almost as effectively as we could get it to someone in our own block. There would seem, therefore, to be no possible justification for discriminating on geographical grounds.

There may be a greater need to defend the second implication of my principle – that the fact that there are millions of other people in the same position, in respect to the Bengali refugees, as I am, does not make the situation significantly different from a situation in which I am the only person who can prevent something very bad from occurring. Again, of course, I admit that there is a psychological difference between the cases; one feels less guilty about doing nothing if one can point to others, similarly placed, who have also done nothing. Yet this can make no real difference to our moral obligations.[2] Should I consider that I am less obliged to pull the drowning child out of the pond if on looking around I see other people, no further away than I am, who have also noticed the child but are doing nothing? One has only to ask this question to see the absurdity of the view that numbers lessen obligation. It is a view that is an ideal excuse for inactivity; unfortunately most of the major evils – poverty, overpopulation, pollution – are problems in which everyone is almost equally involved.

The view that numbers do make a difference can be made plausible if stated in this way: if everyone in circumstances like mine gave £5 to the Bengal Relief Fund, there would be enough to provide food, shelter, and medical care for the refugees; there is no reason why I should give more than anyone else in the same circumstances as I am; therefore I have no obligation to give more than £5. Each premise in this

argument is true, and the argument looks sound. It may convince us, unless we notice that it is based on a hypothetical premise, although the conclusion is not stated hypothetically. The argument would be sound if the conclusion were: if everyone in circumstances like mine were to give £5, I would have no obligation to give more than £5. If the conclusion were so stated, however, it would be obvious that the argument has no bearing on a situation in which it is not the case that everyone else gives £5. This, of course, is the actual situation. It is more or less certain that not everyone in circumstances like mine will give £5. So there will not be enough to provide the needed food, shelter, and medical care. Therefore by giving more than £5 I will prevent more suffering than I would if I gave just £5.

It might be thought that this argument has an absurd consequence. Since the situation appears to be that very few people are likely to give substantial amounts, it follows that I and everyone else in similar circumstances ought to give as much as possible, that is, at least up to the point at which by giving more one would begin to cause serious suffering for oneself and one's dependents – perhaps even beyond this point to the point of marginal utility, at which by giving more one would cause oneself and one's dependents as much suffering as one would prevent in Bengal. If everyone does this, however, there will be more than can be used for the benefit of the refugees, and some of the sacrifice will have been unnecessary. Thus, if everyone does what he ought to do, the result will not be as good as it would be if everyone did a little less than he ought to do, or if only some do all that they ought to do.

The paradox here arises only if we assume that the actions in question – sending money to the relief funds – are performed more or less simultaneously, and are also unexpected. For if it is to be expected that everyone is going to contribute something, then clearly each is not obliged to give as much as he would have been obliged to had others not been giving too. And if everyone is not acting more or less simultaneously, then those giving later will know how much more is needed, and will have no obligation to give more than is necessary to reach this amount. To say this is not to deny the principle that people in the same circumstances have the same obligations, but to point out that the fact that others have given, or may be expected to give, is a relevant circumstance: those giving after it has become known that many others are giving and those giving before are not in the same circumstances. So the seemingly absurd consequence of the principle I have put forward can occur only if people are in error about the actual circumstances – that is, if they think they are giving when others are not, but in fact they are giving when others are. The result of everyone doing what he really ought to do cannot be worse than the result of everyone doing less than he ought to do, although the result of everyone doing what he reasonably believes he ought to do could be.

If my argument so far has been sound, neither our distance from a preventable evil nor the number of other people who, in respect to that evil, are in the same situation as we are, lessens our obligation to mitigate or prevent that evil. I shall therefore take as established the principle I asserted earlier. As I have already said, I need to assert it only in its qualified form: if it is in our power to prevent something very bad from happening, without thereby sacrificing anything else morally significant, we ought, morally, to do it.

The outcome of this argument is that our traditional moral categories are upset. The traditional distinction between duty and charity cannot be drawn, or at least, not in the place we normally draw it. Giving money to the Bengal Relief Fund is regarded as an act of charity in our society. The bodies which collect money are known as "charities." These organizations see themselves in this way – if you send them a check, you will be thanked for your "generosity." Because giving money is regarded as an act of charity, it is not thought that there is anything wrong with not giving. The charitable man may be praised, but the man who is not charitable is not condemned. People do not feel in any way ashamed or guilty about spending money on new clothes or a new car instead of giving it to famine relief. (Indeed, the alternative does not occur to them.) This way of looking at the matter cannot be justified. When we buy new clothes not to keep ourselves warm but to look "well-dressed" we are not providing for any important need. We would not be sacrificing anything significant if we were to continue to wear our old clothes, and give the money to famine relief. By doing so, we would be preventing another person from starving. It follows from what I have said earlier that we ought to give money away, rather than spend it on clothes which we do not need to keep us warm. To do so is not charitable, or generous. Nor is it the kind of act which philosophers and theologians have called "supererogatory" – an act which it would be good to do, but not wrong not to do. On the contrary, we ought to give the money away, and it is wrong not to do so.

I am not maintaining that there are no acts which are charitable, or that there are no acts which it would be good to do but not wrong not to do. It may be possible to redraw the distinction between duty and charity in some other place. All I am arguing here is that the present way of drawing the distinction, which makes it an act of charity for a man living at the level of affluence which most people in the "developed nations" enjoy to give money to save someone else from starvation, cannot be supported. It is beyond the scope of my argument to consider whether the distinction should be redrawn or abolished altogether. There would be many other possible ways of drawing the distinction – for instance, one might decide that it is good to make other people as happy as possible, but not wrong not to do so.

Despite the limited nature of the revision in our moral conceptual scheme which I am proposing, the revision would, given the extent of both affluence and famine in the world today, have radical implications. These implications may lead to further objections, distinct from those I have already considered. I shall discuss two of these.

One objection to the position I have taken might be simply that it is too drastic a revision of our moral scheme. People do not ordinarily judge in the way I have suggested they should. Most people reserve their moral condemnation for those who violate some moral norm, such as the norm against taking another person's property. They do not condemn those who indulge in luxury instead of giving to famine relief. But given that I did not set out to present a morally neutral description of the way people make moral judgments, the way people do in fact judge has nothing to do with the validity of my conclusion. My conclusion follows from the principle which I advanced earlier, and unless that principle is rejected, or the arguments shown to be unsound, I think the conclusion must stand, however strange it appears.

It might, nevertheless, be interesting to consider why our society, and most other societies, do judge differently from the way I have suggested they should. In a well-known article, J. O. Urmson suggests that the imperatives of duty, which tell us what we must do, as distinct from what it would be good to do but not wrong not to do, function so as to prohibit behavior that is intolerable if men are to live together in society.[3] This may explain the origin and continued existence of the present division between acts of duty and acts of charity. Moral attitudes are shaped by the needs of society, and no doubt society needs people who will observe the rules that make social existence tolerable. From the point of view of a particular society, it is essential to prevent violations of norms against killing, stealing, and so on. It is quite inessential, however, to help people outside one's own society.

If this is an explanation of our common distinction between duty and supererogation, however, it is not a justification of it. The moral point of view requires us to look beyond the interests of our own society. Previously, as I have already mentioned, this may hardly have been feasible, but it is quite feasible now. From the moral point of view, the prevention of the starvation of millions of people outside our society must be considered at least as pressing as the upholding of property norms within our society.

It has been argued by some writers, among them Sidgwick and Urmson, that we need to have a basic moral code which is not too far beyond the capacities of the ordinary man, for otherwise there will be a general breakdown of compliance with the moral code. Crudely stated, this argument suggests that if we tell people that they ought to refrain from murder and give everything they do not really need to famine relief, they will do neither, whereas if we tell them that they ought to refrain from murder and that it is good to give to famine relief but not wrong not to do so, they will at least refrain from murder. The issue here is: Where should we draw the line between conduct that is required and conduct that is good although not required, so as to get the best possible result? This would seem to be an empirical question, although a very difficult one. One objection to the Sidgwick-Urmson line of argument is that it takes insufficient account of the effect that moral standards can have on the decisions we make. Given a society in which a wealthy man who gives five percent of his income to famine relief is regarded as most generous, it is not surprising that a proposal that we all ought to give away half our incomes will be thought to be absurdly unrealistic. In a society which held that no man should have more than enough while others have less than they need, such a proposal might seem narrow-minded. What it is possible for a man to do and what he is likely to do are both, I think, very greatly influenced by what people around him are doing and expecting him to do. In any case, the possibility that by spreading the idea that we ought to be doing very much more than we are to relieve famine we shall bring about a general breakdown of moral behavior seems remote. If the stakes are an end to widespread starvation, it is worth the risk. Finally, it should be emphasized that these considerations are relevant only to the issue of what we should require from others, and not to what we ourselves ought to do.

The second objection to my attack on the present distinction between duty and charity is one which has from time to time been made against utilitarianism. It follows from some forms of utilitarian theory that we all ought, morally, to be working full time to increase the balance of happiness over misery. The position I have taken here would not lead to this conclusion in all circumstances, for if there were no bad occurrences that we could prevent without sacrificing something of comparable moral importance, my argument would have no application. Given the present conditions in many parts of the world, however, it does follow from my argument that we ought, morally, to be working full time to relieve great suffering of the sort that occurs as a result of famine or other disasters. Of course, mitigating circumstances can be adduced – for instance, that if we wear ourselves out through overwork, we shall be less effective than we would otherwise have been. Nevertheless, when all considerations of this sort have been taken into account, the conclusion remains: we ought to be preventing as much suffering as we can without sacrificing something else of comparable moral importance. This conclusion is one which we may be reluctant to face. I cannot see, though, why it should be regarded as a criticism of the position for which I have argued, rather than a criticism of our ordinary standards of behavior. Since most people are self-interested to some degree, very few of us are likely to do everything that we ought to do. It would, however, hardly be honest to take this as evidence that it is not the case that we ought to do it.

It may still be thought that my conclusions are so wildly out of line with what everyone else thinks and has always thought that there must be something wrong with the argument somewhere. In order to show that my conclusions, while certainly contrary to contemporary Western moral standards, would not have seemed so extraordinary at other times and in other places, I would like to quote a passage from a writer not normally thought of as a way-out radical, Thomas Aquinas.

> Now, according to the natural order instituted by divine providence, material goods are provided for the satisfaction of human needs. Therefore the division and appropriation of property, which proceeds from human law, must not hinder the satisfaction of man's necessity from such goods. Equally, whatever a man has in super-abundance is owed, of natural right, to the poor for their sustenance. So Ambrosius says, and it is also to be found in the *Decretum Gratiani*: "The bread which you withhold belongs to the hungry; the clothing you shut away, to the naked; and the money you bury in the earth is the redemption and freedom of the penniless."[4]

I now want to consider a number of points, more practical than philosophical, which are relevant to the application of the moral conclusion we have reached. These points challenge not the idea that we ought to be doing all we can to prevent starvation, but the idea that giving away a great deal of money is the best means to this end.

It is sometimes said that overseas aid should be a government responsibility, and that therefore one ought not to give to privately run charities. Giving privately, it is said, allows the government and the noncontributing members of society to escape their responsibilities.

This argument seems to assume that the more people there are who give to privately organized famine relief funds, the less likely it is that the government will take over full responsibility for such aid. This assumption is unsupported, and does not strike me as at all plausible. The opposite view – that if no one gives voluntarily, a government will assume that its citizens are uninterested in famine relief and would not wish to be forced into giving aid – seems more plausible. In any case, unless there were a definite probability that by refusing to give one would be helping to bring about massive government assistance, people who do refuse to make voluntary contributions are refusing to prevent a certain amount of suffering without being able to point to any tangible beneficial consequence of their refusal. So the onus of showing how their refusal will bring about government action is on those who refuse to give.

I do not, of course, want to dispute the contention that governments of affluent nations should be giving many times the amount of genuine, nostrings-attached aid that they are giving now. I agree, too, that giving privately is not enough, and that we ought to be campaigning actively for entirely new standards for both public and private contributions to famine relief. Indeed, I would sympathize with someone who thought that campaigning was more important than giving oneself, although I doubt whether preaching what one does not practice would be very effective. Unfortunately, for many people the idea that "it's the government's responsibility" is a reason for not giving which does not appear to entail any political action either.

Another, more serious reason for not giving to famine relief funds is that until there is effective population control, relieving famine merely postpones starvation. If we save the Bengal refugees now, others, perhaps the children of these refugees, will face starvation in a few years' time. In support of this, one may cite the now well-known facts about the population explosion and the relatively limited scope for expanded production.

This point, like the previous one, is an argument against relieving suffering that is happening now, because of a belief about what might happen in the future; it is unlike the previous point in that very good evidence can be adduced in support of this belief about the future. I will not go into the evidence here. I accept that the earth cannot support indefinitely a population rising at the present rate. This certainly poses a problem for anyone who thinks it important to prevent famine. Again, however, one could accept the argument without drawing the conclusion that it absolves one from any obligation to do anything to prevent famine. The conclusion that should be drawn is that the best means of preventing famine, in the long run, is population control. It would then follow from the position reached earlier that one ought to be doing all one can to promote population control (unless one held that all forms of population control were wrong in themselves, or would have significantly bad consequences). Since there are organizations working specifically for population control, one would then support them rather than more orthodox methods of preventing famine.

A third point raised by the conclusion reached earlier relates to the question of just how much we all ought to be giving away. One possibility, which has already been mentioned, is that we ought to give until we reach the level of marginal utility – that is, the level at which, by giving more, I would cause as much suffering to myself or my dependents as I would relieve by my gift. This would mean, of course, that one would reduce oneself to very nearly the material circumstances of a Bengali refugee. It will be recalled that earlier I put forward both a strong and a moderate version of the principle of preventing bad occurrences. The strong version, which required us to prevent bad things from happening unless in doing so we would be sacrificing something of comparable moral significance, does seem to require reducing

ourselves to the level of marginal utility. I should also say that the strong version seems to me to be the correct one. I proposed the more moderate version – that we should prevent bad occurrences unless, to do so, we had to sacrifice something morally significant – only in order to show that even on this surely undeniable principle a great change in our way of life is required. On the more moderate principle, it may not follow that we ought to reduce ourselves to the level of marginal utility, for one might hold that to reduce oneself and one's family to this level is to cause something significantly bad to happen. Whether this is so I shall not discuss, since, as I have said, I can see no good reason for holding the moderate version of the principle rather than the strong version. Even if we accepted the principle only in its moderate form, however, it should be clear that we would have to give away enough to ensure that the consumer society, dependent as it is on people spending on trivia rather than giving to famine relief, would slow down and perhaps disappear entirely. There are several reasons why this would be desirable in itself. The value and necessity of economic growth are now being questioned not only by conservationists, but by economists as well.[5] There is no doubt, too, that the consumer society has had a distorting effect on the goals and purposes of its members. Yet looking at the matter purely from the point of view of overseas aid, there must be a limit to the extent to which we should deliberately slow down our economy; for it might be the case that if we gave away, say, forty percent of our Gross National Product, we would slow down the economy so much that in absolute terms we would be giving less than if we gave twenty-five percent of the much larger GNP that we would have if we limited our contribution to this smaller percentage.

I mention this only as an indication of the sort of factor that one would have to take into account in working out an ideal. Since Western societies generally consider one percent of the GNP an acceptable level for overseas aid, the matter is entirely academic. Nor does it affect the question of how much an individual should give in a society in which very few are giving substantial amounts.

It is sometimes said, though less often now than it used to be, that philosophers have no special role to play in public affairs, since most public issues depend primarily on an assessment of facts. On questions of fact, it is said, philosophers as such have no special expertise, and so it has been possible to engage in philosophy without committing oneself to any position on major public issues. No doubt there are some issues of social policy and foreign policy about which it can truly be said that a really expert assessment of the facts is required before taking sides or acting, but the issue of famine is surely not one of these. The facts about the existence of suffering are beyond dispute. Nor, I think, is it disputed that we can do something about it, either through orthodox methods of famine relief or through population control or both. This is therefore an issue on which philosophers are competent to take a position. The issue is one which faces everyone who has more money than he needs to support himself and his dependents, or who is in a position to take some sort of political action. These categories must include practically every teacher and student of philosophy in the universities of the Western world. If philosophy is to deal with matters that are relevant to both teachers and students, this is an issue that philosophers should discuss.

Discussion, though, is not enough. What is the point of relating philosophy to public (and personal) affairs if we do not take our conclusions seriously? In this instance, taking our conclusion seriously means acting upon it. The philosopher will not find it any easier than anyone else to alter his attitudes and way of life to the extent that, if I am right, is involved in doing everything that we ought to be doing. At the very least, though, one can make a start. The philosopher who does so will have to sacrifice some of the benefits of the consumer society, but he can find compensation in the satisfaction of a way of life in which theory and practice, if not yet in harmony, are at least coming together.

Notes

1. There was also a third possibility: that India would go to war to enable the refugees to return to their lands. Since I wrote this paper, India has taken this way out. The situation is no longer that described above, but this does not affect my argument, as the next paragraph indicates.

2. In view of the special sense philosophers often give to the term, I should say that I use "obligation" simply as the abstract noun derived from "ought," so that "I have an obligation to" means no more, and no less, than "I ought to." This usage is in accordance with the definition of "ought" given by the *Shorter Oxford English Dictionary*: "the general verb to express duty or obligation." I do not think any issue of substance hangs on the way the term is used; sentences in which I use "obligation" could all be rewritten, although somewhat clumsily, as sentences in which a clause containing "ought" replaces the term "obligation."

3. J. O. Urmson, "Saints and Heroes," in *Essays in Moral Philosophy*, ed. Abraham I. Melden (Seattle and London, 1958), p. 214. For a related but significantly different view see also Henry Sidgwick, *The Methods of Ethics*, 7th edn. (London, 1907), pp. 220–1, 492–3.

4. *Summa Theologica*, II-II, Question 66, Article 7, in *Aquinas, Selected Political Writings*, ed. A. P. d'Entreves, trans. J. G. Dawson (Oxford, 1948), p. 171.

5. See, for instance, John Kenneth Galbraith, *The New Industrial State* (Boston, 1967); and E. J. Mishan, *The Costs of Economic Growth* (London, 1967).

CHAPTER 54
The Survival Lottery

JOHN HARRIS

Let us suppose that organ transplant procedures have been perfected; in such circumstances if two dying patients could be saved by organ transplants then, if surgeons have the requisite organs in stock and no other needy patients, but nevertheless allow their patients to die, we would be inclined to say, and be justified in saying, that the patients died because the doctors refused to save them. But if there are no spare organs in stock and none otherwise available, the doctors have no choice, they cannot save their patients and so must let them die. In this case we would be disinclined to say that the doctors are in any sense the cause of their patients' deaths. But let us further suppose that the two dying patients, Y and Z, are not happy about being left to die. They might argue that it is not strictly true that there are no organs which could be used to save them. Y needs a new heart and Z new lungs. They point out that if just one healthy person were to be killed his organs could be removed and both of them be saved. We and the doctors would probably be alike in thinking that such a step, while technically possible, would be out of the question. We would not say that the doctors were killing

John Harris, "The Survival Lottery," pp. 81–7 from *Philosophy*, 50, 1975. © by The Royal Institute of Philosophy, published by Cambridge University Press, reproduced with permission. Reprinted with permission of Professor John Harris.

their patients if they refused to prey upon the healthy to save the sick. And because this sort of surgical Robin Hoodery is out of the question we can tell Y and Z that they cannot be saved, and that when they die they will have died of natural causes and not of the neglect of their doctors. Y and Z do not however agree, they insist that if the doctors fail to kill a healthy man and use his organs to save them, then the doctors will be responsible for their deaths.

Many philosophers have for various reasons believed that we must not kill even if by doing so we could save life. They believe that there is a moral difference between killing and letting die. On this view, to kill A so that Y and Z might live is ruled out because we have a strict obligation not to kill but a duty of some lesser kind to save life. A. H. Clough's dictum "Thou shalt not kill but need'st not strive officiously to keep alive" expresses bluntly this point of view. The dying Y and Z may be excused for not being much impressed by Clough's dictum. They agree that it is wrong to kill the innocent and are prepared to agree to an absolute prohibition against so doing. They do not agree, however, that A is more innocent than they are. Y and Z might go on to point out that the currently acknowledged right of the innocent not to be killed, even where their deaths might give life to others, is just a decision to prefer the lives of the fortunate to those of the unfortunate. A is innocent in the sense that he has done nothing to deserve death, but Y and Z are also innocent in this sense. Why should they be the ones to die simply because they are so unlucky as to have diseased organs? Why, they might argue, should their living or dying be left to chance when in so many other areas of human life we believe that we have an obligation to ensure the survival of the maximum number of lives possible?

Y and Z argue that if a doctor refuses to treat a patient, with the result that the patient dies, he has killed that patient as sure as shooting, and that, in exactly the same way, if the doctors refuse Y and Z the transplants that they need, then their refusal will kill Y and Z, again as sure as shooting. The doctors, and indeed the society which supports their inaction, cannot defend themselves by arguing that they are neither expected, nor required by law or convention, to kill so that lives may be saved (indeed, quite the reverse) since this is just an appeal to custom or authority. A man who does his own moral thinking must decide whether, in these circumstances, he ought to save two lives at the cost of one, or one life at the cost of two. The fact that so called "third parties" have never before been brought into such calculations, have never before been thought of as being involved, is not an argument against their now becoming so. There are of course, good arguments against allowing doctors simply to haul passers-by off the streets whenever they have a couple of patients in need of new organs. And the harmful side-effects of such a practice in terms of terror and distress to the victims, the witnesses and society generally, would give us further reasons for dismissing the idea. Y and Z realize this and have a proposal, which they will shortly produce, which would largely meet objections to placing such power in the hands of doctors and eliminate at least some of the harmful side-effects.

In the unlikely event of their feeling obliged to reply to the reproaches of Y and Z, the doctors might offer the following argument: they might maintain that a man is only responsible for the death of someone whose life he might have saved, if, in all the circumstances of the case, he ought to have saved the man by the means available. This is why a doctor might be a murderer if he simply refused or neglected to treat a patient who would die without treatment, but not if he could only save the patient by doing something he ought in no circumstances to do – kill the innocent. Y and Z readily agree that a man ought not to do what he ought not to do, but they point out that if the doctors, and for that matter society at large, ought on balance to kill one man if two can thereby be saved, then failure to do so will involve responsibility for the consequent deaths. The fact that Y's and Z's proposal involves killing the innocent cannot be a reason for refusing to consider their proposal, for this would just be a refusal to face the question at issue and so avoid having to make a decision as to what ought to be done in circumstances like these. It is Y's and Z's claim that failure to adopt their plan will also involve killing the innocent, rather more of the innocent than the proposed alternative.

To back up this last point, to remove the arbitrariness of permitting doctors to select their donors from among the chance passers-by outside hospitals, and the tremendous power this would place in doctors' hands, to mitigate worries about side-effects and lastly to appease those who wonder why poor old A should be singled out for sacrifice, Y and Z put forward the following scheme: they propose that everyone be given a sort of lottery number. Whenever doctors have two or more dying patients who could be saved by transplants, and no suitable organs have come to hand through "natural" deaths, they can ask a central computer to supply a suitable donor. The computer will then pick the number of a suitable donor at random and he will be killed so that the lives of two or more others may be saved. No doubt if the scheme were ever to be implemented a suitable euphemism for "killed" would be employed. Perhaps we would begin to talk about citizens being called upon to "give life" to others. With the refinement of transplant procedures such a scheme could offer the chance of saving large numbers of lives that are now lost. Indeed, even taking into account the loss of the lives of donors, the numbers of untimely deaths each year might be dramatically reduced, so much so that everyone's chance of living to a ripe old age might be increased. If this were to be the consequence of the adoption of such a scheme, and it might well be, it could not be dismissed lightly. It might of course be objected that it is likely that more old people will need transplants to prolong their lives than will the young, and so the scheme would inevitably lead to a society dominated by the old. But if such a society is thought objectionable, there is no reason to suppose that a program could not be designed for the computer that would ensure the maintenance of whatever is considered to be an optimum age distribution throughout the population.

Suppose that inter-planetary travel revealed a world of people like ourselves, but who organized their society according to this scheme. No one was considered to have an absolute right to life or freedom from interference, but everything was always done to ensure that as many people as possible would enjoy long and happy lives. In such a world a man who attempted to escape when his number was up or who resisted on the grounds that no one had a right to take his life, might well be regarded as a murderer. We might or might not prefer to live in such a world, but the morality of its inhabitants would surely be one that we could respect. It would not be obviously more barbaric or cruel or immoral than our own.

Y and Z are willing to concede one exception to the universal application of their scheme. They realize that it would be unfair to allow people who have brought their misfortune on themselves to benefit from the lottery. There would clearly be something unjust about killing the abstemious B so that W (whose heavy smoking has given him lung cancer) and X (whose drinking has destroyed his liver) should be preserved to over-indulge again.

What objections could be made to the lottery scheme? A first straw to clutch at would be the desire for security. Under such a scheme we would never know when we would hear *them* knocking at the door. Every post might bring a sentence of death, every sound in the night might be the sound of boots on the stairs. But, as we have seen, the chances of actually being called upon to make the ultimate sacrifice might be slimmer than is the present risk of being killed on the roads, and most of us do not lie trembling a-bed, appalled at the prospect of being dispatched on the morrow. The truth is that lives might well be more secure under such a scheme.

If we respect individuality and see every human being as unique in his own way, we might want to reject a society in which it appeared that individuals were seen merely as interchangeable units in a structure, the value of which lies in its having as many healthy units as possible. But of course Y and Z would want to know why A's individuality was more worthy of respect than theirs.

Another plausible objection is the natural reluctance to play God with men's lives, the feeling that it is wrong to make any attempt to re-allot the life opportunities that fate has determined, that the deaths of Y and Z would be "natural," whereas the death of anyone killed to save them would have been perpetrated by men. But if we are able to change things, then to elect not to do so is also to determine what will happen in the world.

Neither does the alleged moral differences between killing and letting die afford a respectable way of rejecting the claims of Y and Z. For if we really want to counter proponents of the lottery, if we really want to answer Y and Z and not just put them off, we cannot do so by saying that the lottery involves killing and object to it for that reason, because to do so would, as we have seen, just beg the question as to whether the failure to save as many people as possible might not also amount to killing.

To opt for the society which Y and Z propose would be then to adopt a society in which saintliness would be mandatory. Each of us would have to recognize a binding obligation to give up his own life for others when called upon to do so. In such a society anyone who reneged upon this duty would be a murderer. The most promising objection to such a society, and indeed to any principle which required us to kill A in order to save Y and Z, is, I suspect, that we are committed to the right of self-defence. If I can kill A to save Y and Z then he can kill me to save P and Q, and it is only if I am prepared to agree to this that I will opt for the lottery or be prepared to agree to a man's being killed if doing so would save the lives of more than one other man. Of course there is something paradoxical about basing objections to the lottery scheme on the right of self-defence since, *ex hyposthesi*, each person would have a better chance of living to a ripe old age if the lottery scheme were to be implemented. None the less, the feeling that no man should be required to lay down his life for others makes many people shy away from such a scheme, even though it might be rational to accept it on prudential grounds, and perhaps even mandatory on utilitarian grounds. Again, Y and Z would reply that the right of self-defence must extend to them as much as to anyone else; and while it is true that they can only live if another man is killed, they would claim that it is also true that if they are left to die, then someone who lives on does so over their dead bodies.

It might be argued that the institution of the survival lottery has not gone far to mitigate the harmful side-effects in terms of terror and distress to victims, witnesses and society generally, that would be occasioned by doctors simply snatching passers-by off the streets and disorganizing them for the benefit of the unfortunate. Donors would after all still have to be procured, and this process, however it was carried out, would still be likely to prove distressing to all concerned. The lottery scheme would eliminate the arbitrariness of leaving the life and death decisions to the doctors, and remove the possibility of such terrible power falling into the hands of any individuals, but the terror and distress would remain. The effect of having to apprehend presumably unwilling victims would give us pause. Perhaps only a long period of education or propaganda could remove our abhorrence. What this abhorrence reveals about the rights and wrongs of the situation is however more difficult to assess. We might be inclined to say that only monsters could ignore the promptings of conscience so far as to operate the lottery scheme. But the promptings of conscience are not necessarily the most reliable guide. In the present case Y and Z would argue that such promptings are mere squeamishness, an over-nice self-indulgence that costs lives. Death, Y and Z would remind us, is a distressing experience whenever and to whomever it occurs, so the less it occurs the better. Fewer victims and witnesses will be distressed as part of the side-effects of the

lottery scheme than would suffer as part of the side-effects of not instituting it.

Lastly, a more limited objection might be made, not to the idea of killing to save lives, but to the involvement of "third parties." Why, so the objection goes, should we not give X's heart to Y or Y's lungs to X, the same number of lives being thereby preserved and no one else's life set at risk? Y's and Z's reply to this objection differs from their previous line of argument. To amend their plan so that the involvement of so called "third parties" is ruled out would, Y and Z claim, violate their right to equal concern and respect with the rest of society. They argue that such a proposal would amount to treating the unfortunate who need new organs as a class within society whose lives are considered to be of less value than those of its more fortunate members. What possible justification could there be for singling out one group of people whom we would be justified in using as donors but not another? The idea in the mind of those who would propose such a step must be something like the following: since Y and Z cannot survive, since they are going to die in any event, there is no harm in putting their names into the lottery, for the chances of their dying cannot thereby be increased and will in fact almost certainly be reduced. But this is just to ignore everything that Y and Z have been saying. For if their lottery scheme is adopted they are not going to die anyway – their chances of dying are no greater and no less than those of any other participant in the lottery whose number may come up. This ground for confining selection of donors to the unfortunate therefore disappears. Any other ground must discriminate against Y and Z as members of a class whose lives are less worthy of respect than those of the rest of society.

It might more plausibly be argued that the dying who cannot themselves be saved by transplants, or by any other means at all, should be the priority selection group for the computer programme. But how far off must death be for a man to be classified as "dying"? Those so classified might argue that their last few days or weeks of life are as valuable to them (if not more valuable) than the possibly longer span remaining to others. The problem of narrowing down the class of possible donors without discriminating unfairly against some sub-class of society is, I suspect, insoluble.

Such is the case for the survival lottery. Utilitarians ought to be in favour of it, and absolutists cannot object to it on the ground that it involves killing the innocent, for it is Y's and Z's case that any alternative must also involve killing the innocent. If the absolutist wishes to maintain his objection he must point to some morally relevant difference between positive and negative killing. This challenge opens the door to a large topic with a whole library of literature, but Y and Z are dying and do not have time to explore it exhaustively. In their own case the most likely candidate for some feature which might make this moral difference is the malevolent intent of Y and Z themselves. An absolutist might well argue that while no one intends the deaths of Y and Z, no one necessarily wishes them dead, or aims at their demise for any reason, they do mean to kill A (or have him killed). But Y and Z can reply that the death of A is no part of their plan, they merely wish to use a couple of his organs, and if he cannot live without them . . . *tant pis*! None would be more delighted than Y and Z if artificial organs would do as well, and so render the lottery scheme otiose.

One form of absolutist argument perhaps remains. This involves taking an Orwellian stand on some principle of common decency. The argument would then be that even to enter into the sort of "macabre" calculations that Y and Z propose displays a blunted sensibility, a corrupted and vitiated mind. Forms of this argument have recently been advanced by Noam Chomsky (*American Power and the New Mandarins*) and Stuart Hampshire (*Morality and Pessimism*). The indefatigable Y and Z would of course deny that their calculations are in any sense "macabre," and would present them as the most humane course available in the circumstances. Moreover they would claim that the Orwellian stand on decency is the product of a closed mind, and not susceptible to rational argument. Any reasoned defence of such a principle must appeal to notions like

respect for human life, as Hampshire's argument in fact does, and these Y and Z could make conformable to their own position.

Can Y and Z be answered? Perhaps only by relying on moral intuition, on the insistence that we do feel there is something wrong with the survival lottery and our confidence that this feeling is prompted by some morally relevant difference between our bringing about the death of A and our bringing about the deaths of Y and Z. Whether we could retain this confidence in our intuitions if we were to be confronted by a society in which the survival lottery operated, was accepted by all, and was seen to save many lives that would otherwise have been lost, it would be interesting to know.

There would of course be great practical difficulties in the way of implementing the lottery. In so many cases it would be agonizingly difficult to decide whether or not a person had brought his misfortune on himself. There are numerous ways in which a person may contribute to his predicament, and the task of deciding how far, or how decisively, a person is himself responsible for his fate would be formidable. And in those cases where we can be confident that a person is innocent of responsibility for his predicament, can we acquire this confidence in time to save him? The lottery scheme would be a powerful weapon in the hands of someone willing and able to misuse it. Could we ever feel certain the lottery was safe from unscrupulous computer programmers? Perhaps we should be thankful that such practical difficulties make the survival lottery an unlikely consequence of the perfection of transplants. Or perhaps we should be appalled.

It may be that we would want to tell Y and Z that the difficulties and dangers of their scheme would be too great a price to pay for its benefits. It is as well to be clear, however, that there is also a high, perhaps an even higher, price to be paid for the rejection of the scheme. That price is the lives of Y and Z and many like them, and we delude ourselves if we suppose that the reason why we reject their plan is that we accept the sixth commandment.

PART IX
Deontology

Introduction to Part IX

Here is a familiar thought: there are some things one just shouldn't do, no matter what. A common list of such things includes intentionally killing innocents, raping them, and torturing them. Even if a very unusual circumstance arose in which more happiness was created by doing any of these things, one simply ought not to do them.

The view that there are moral constraints on the pursuit of recognized goods such as love, happiness, and peace is a classic deontological theme. Deontologists believe that certain actions are intrinsically morally right or wrong. That is, many actions have the moral character they do by virtue of their own nature, considered entirely apart from any good or bad consequences they generate. There is something about murder, or intentional deception, or humiliation, that makes such actions wrong in and of themselves.

The most famous defender of a deontological ethic is Immanuel Kant, whose *Groundwork of the Metaphysics of Morals* (excerpted here) contains the underpinnings of his developed ethical view. Kant thought that reason alone was capable of discovering correct moral principles. He regarded such principles as absolute, that is, as never permissibly broken. He considered consequences to be irrelevant in determining the moral worth of actions and persons. He thought that there was only one thing that was unconditionally

good, i.e., good in any and every circumstance whatever – namely, a good will. A good will is the steady motivation to do one's duty for its own sake.

Kant thought that moral principles had a special status among the dictates of reason. Moral principles are, in his terms, *categorical imperatives*. These are requirements of reason that apply to all individuals, regardless of their contingent commitments. They also, for Kant, are rationally compelling, in the sense that those who violate them do so at the cost of their own irrationality. Moral demands apply to us even if they fail to get us what we want, or fail to promote our self-interest. We flout such demands at the cost of our own irrationality.

Kant offered different accounts of the content of the ultimate moral standard, what he called The Categorical Imperative (as opposed to the many more specific such imperatives that constituted the variety of moral rules). The two versions of the Categorical Imperative that have attracted by far the most attention are the Principle of Universalizability, and the Principle of Humanity.

The Principle of Universalizability, here discussed in an article by Christine Korsgaard, tells us to act only on those maxims that one can will to be a universal law. A maxim is a principle of action that one gives oneself, stating what one is going to do, and why one is going to do it. The very difficult exegetical and philosophical issue is how to understand the relevant sense of "universal law." Kant tells us that we are to imagine a world in which everyone acts in accordance with our maxim, and then consider whether such a world is strictly impossible, or whether it somehow involves the defeat of an essential commitment that any rational agent must have. If either of these so-called "contradictions" ensues, then one is morally and rationally required to refrain from performing the action called for by the maxim. If no such contradiction ensues, then one's action is morally permitted.

Kant's thinking here is hardly transparent, but it certainly repays the effort at understanding. At its core, what Kant is doing is insisting on the crucial importance of justice in morality. Utilitarians see benevolence as the central moral virtue; Kant sees justice playing this role. The Principle of Universalizability is essentially a requirement not to make an exception of oneself, a demand that one live according to principles that one can coherently see others living by. And this often conforms quite well to our considered moral judgments. It is immoral for a senior banker to embezzle funds, even if his theft is never detected, no one is harmed, and he, his friends and his family are greatly benefited. When confronting such a perpetrator, we are inclined to ask a very basic moral question: what if everyone did that? Kant's Principle of Universalizability is meant to provide us with a formula for interpreting and applying this central moral question.

Kant sometimes favors his Principle of Humanity as the best expression of the ultimate moral standard. This principle counsels us always to treat humanity as an end, and never as a mere means. What it is to be an end, or a mere means, is not immediately clear, and the Kant scholar Onora O'Neill gives us an excellent exposition of these ideas in the context of applying them to some of the moral problems raised by famine relief. To treat someone as an end is to treat her with the respect she deserves, by virtue of her rationality and autonomy. To treat someone as a mere means is to treat her as a tool, as nothing more than an instrument that can usefully serve one's own purposes. Inanimate objects are rightly treated as mere means; human beings are not. Human beings, says Kant, are alone in being literally priceless. We can fix an appropriate price on all other things in the world, a price that can identify the exchange value of an item. Our value is based on our dignity, which in turn is founded on the special capacities of rationality and autonomy. These are the capacities that, according to Kant, generate the moral demand of respectful treatment. What it is to treat others with respect is, of course, itself a contested notion. O'Neill helps us to understand what Kant had in mind here. It is instructive to compare the Kantian perspective on famine relief with the utilitarian view, offered by Peter Singer in the previous Part. Reading both pieces in tandem will help to make the sometimes highly abstract and theoretical discussions surrounding these ethical views more comprehensible and easier to assess.

One problem that has received much discussion over the past few decades is the so-called *paradox of deontology*. A short piece here by Robert Nozick provides the basis for thinking critically about this paradox. A deontological requirement – what Nozick calls a *side constraint* – forbids us from doing a certain kind of action. But what if doing that action reduced the number of violations of that very requirement? What if one had to kill someone in order to prevent even more killings, or lie to someone in order to prevent many more deceptions? A valid deontological requirement will protect something of great value (e.g., an innocent life, or a person's integrity). If the value is so important as to generate a deontological requirement, then why isn't the value so important as to license a violation of that requirement if such violation would better protect the relevant value? If we are forbidden from killing, then we must not kill, even if refraining will lead to many more killings. But if it is the value of protecting life that generates the moral rule in the first place, then it seems that we should do what we can to protect that value as much as possible. And that would mean that we should be allowed to break the moral rules, if doing so would better protect the values they serve. But then there would be no deontological requirements, no side constraints on the pursuit of what is valuable.

This of course is precisely what act consequentialists believe. And though talk of a paradox is relatively new, the challenge is ages old. What could substantiate the existence of an absolute prohibition on various actions? A divine command, perhaps. But short of that, aren't all moral rules made to be broken, should the circumstances be extreme enough? And if the answer to that question is "yes," isn't the rationale the one offered by act consequentialism – namely, that there are intrinsic values, and that we are morally obligated to maximize their presence in the world?

One classic way of responding to the act consequentialist challenge is to cite a fundamental moral principle that can give rise to absolute moral rules, and so offer a principled way to resist the challenge of act consequentialism. The Golden Rule has often played this role. Like Kant's theory, the Golden Rule is an effort to capture the central importance of fairness in the moral life. In its basic formula – do unto others as you would have them do unto you – the rule is problematic. Kant himself made note of this. If we take this formula literally, says Kant, then a judge would be prevented from sentencing a criminal, since the judge, were he in the criminal's shoes, would not want to be punished. Moreover, the Golden Rule would permit us to commit actions that we all believe to be immoral. A masochist would be entitled to impose a great amount of pain on others, just because he'd be delighted were such pain imposed on him. But his unusual inclinations don't, of course, give him moral license to go around spanking others.

Alan Gewirth here offers a sophisticated discussion of the Golden Rule, and describes a way in which its guiding spirit can be adapted to provide a basis for deontological requirements. The amended rule reads as follows: do unto others as you would *rationally* want them to do unto you. Naturally, everything hinges on understanding what it is to rationally want something. A standard way to interpret such desires is to see them as desires for things that would help a person achieve her goals. For instance, a budding journalist rationally wants to play an active role on the student newspaper, since that is what is going to help her achieve

what she ultimately wants. Gewirth, like Kant before him, must say that this instrumental conception of rationality is unduly limited. Gewirth believes that reason dictates certain requirements that may only frustrate the fulfillment of one's actual aims.

The basic Kantian picture, which Gewirth endorses, claims that there is something distinctive about being an agent – someone capable of reflecting on the merit of various purposes, deciding among them, and conforming one's behavior to one's decisions – that generates rational requirements to respect oneself *and others*. Here, the relevant opponent is not the consequentialist, but the egoist – one who sees the only moral and rational requirements as those that protect self-interest. It is easy to see that reason requires me to look after myself. But why does it require me to respect others, especially if I don't care about them, and if their welfare just stands in the way of my getting what I want? Gewirth claims that simply being an agent commits one to thinking that one has certain basic rights. These rights are grounded in one's agency – in one's capacity to deliberate and act on those deliberations. But consistency requires that one recognize the like capacities in others. Since these capacities serve as the basis of one's own rights, they serve as the basis of the rights of others. Therefore, if one is rational, one will recognize that others have basic rights that are as valid as one's own. Failure to see this is evidence of an internal contradiction, and hence an irrationality.

For the last two entries in this section, we return to the consequentialist challenge, and the deontologist's effort to reply to it. The first of these articles is by Philippa Foot, who introduces an example that has become quite famous in the philosophical literature, and is taken up in the last of our articles here, by Judith Thomson. This is the example of the runaway trolley, in which a conductor is faced with a choice of allowing the trolley (whose brakes have failed) to remain on its present course, or steering it onto a side track. The problem is that there are five innocent people on the main track, and they will undoubtedly be killed if the trolley does not shift to the side track. But (you guessed it) there is a lone innocent person on that side track, and he, too, will surely be killed if the trolley is diverted his way. What should the conductor do?

Consequentialist reasoning tells us that when faced with such a choice, we are to minimize harm. So there is no real moral conundrum – the conductor morally must steer away from the five, and into the one. But many feel that things are not so simple. Some think that the conductor must not divert the trolley. Others think that he may do so, but is not required to do so. But if protecting human life is so valuable, then why not do whatever is necessary to maximize the protection of this value? We are back to the paradox of deontology again.

One reply is to invoke the doctrine of double effect. The double effect refers to two kinds of outcome – those that one directly intends to produce, and those that one merely foresees but does not aim at. The doctrine states that it is sometimes permissible to bring about an outcome if one does not directly aim at doing so, even though it would be immoral to bring it about as a result of directly intending to produce it. A common example is from wartime strategy. Many think it permissible, for instance, to set out to destroy an enemy weapons depot, even if such an attack is foreseeably going to produce heavy civilian casualties in the surrounding neighborhood. Yet many would also think it immoral to undermine the enemy by directly targeting these civilian populations, even if the number of civilian deaths that would result from such an attack is the same as the "collateral damage" that results from the depot's destruction.

One explanation of the difference in moral verdicts between these two wartime cases is the doctrine of double effect. According to this doctrine, our intentions matter crucially to the moral character of our actions, such that directly intending harm may render them morally forbidden, whereas a more benign intention may render them permissible. This is so even if the (likely) outcomes of these two acts are the same.

Now consider this case, discussed by both Foot and Thomson: a healthy patient pays a visit to the surgeon. The surgeon proceeds to trick him into being anesthetized, and then removes his vital organs, so that they may be distributed to five people who need them to survive. If the surgeon does this, he kills one to save five. If the conductor is morally permitted to divert the trolley, he too kills one in order to save five. Yet even for those who balk at the conductor's actions, they are likely to provoke nothing like the outrage that would greet those of the surgeon. Here, too, we register a moral difference despite the fact that the (expected) outcomes are identical. This puts great pressure on act consequentialism, which lacks the resources to morally distinguish such cases from one another. But it also puts pressure on the deontologist to account for the moral difference between the trolley and the surgeon cases.

Both Foot and Thomson consider a variety of deontological strategies for handling this problem. They both agree that the doctrine of double effect won't survive scrutiny, but are divided on the appropriate non-consequentialist rationale for solving these extremely difficult questions. Indeed, accounting for our intuitions in such cases as those above is a continuing source of fruitful philosophical research, both on the part of contemporary consequentialists and deontologists.

CHAPTER 55

Groundwork of the Metaphysics of Morals

IMMANUEL KANT

The Good Will

It is impossible to think of anything at all in the world, or indeed even beyond it, that could be considered good without limitation except a *good will*. Understanding, wit, judgment and the like, whatever such *talents* of mind may be called, or courage, resolution, and perseverance in one's plans, as qualities of *temperament*, are undoubtedly good and desirable for many purposes, but they can also be extremely evil and harmful if the will which is to make use of these gifts of nature, and whose distinctive constitution is therefore called *character*, is not good. It is the same with *gifts of fortune*. Power, riches, honor, even health and that complete well-being and satisfaction with one's condition called *happiness*, produce boldness and thereby often arrogance as well unless a good will is present which corrects the influence of these on the mind and, in so doing, also corrects the whole principle of action and brings it into conformity with universal ends – not to mention that an impartial rational spectator can take no delight in seeing the uninterrupted

Immanuel Kant, pp. 7–16, 25–39 from *Groundwork of the Metaphysics of Morals*, trans. Mary J. Gregor. Cambridge: Cambridge University Press, 1998. © by Cambridge University Press, reprinted with permission. Reprinted by permission of Betty Kiehl, The Estate of Professor M. J. Gregor.

prosperity of a being graced with no feature of a pure and good will, so that a good will seems to constitute the indispensable condition even of worthiness to be happy.

Some qualities are even conducive to this good will itself and can make its work much easier; despite this, however, they have no inner unconditional worth but always presuppose a good will, which limits the esteem one otherwise rightly has for them and does not permit their being taken as absolutely good. Moderation in affects and passions, self-control, and calm reflection are not only good for all sorts of purposes but even seem to constitute a part of the *inner* worth of a person; but they lack much that would be required to declare them good without limitation (however unconditionally they were praised by the ancients); for, without the basic principles of a good will they can become extremely evil, and the coolness of a scoundrel makes him not only far more dangerous but also immediately more abominable in our eyes than we would have taken him to be without it.

A good will is not good because of what it effects or accomplishes, because of its fitness to attain some proposed end, but only because of its volition, that is, it is good in itself and, regarded for itself, is to be valued incomparably higher than all that could merely be brought about by it in favor of some inclination and indeed, if you will, of the sum of all inclinations. Even if, by a special disfavor of fortune or by the niggardly provision of a stepmotherly nature, this will should wholly lack the capacity to carry out its purpose – if with its greatest efforts it should yet achieve nothing and only the good will were left (not, of course, as a mere wish but as the summoning of all means insofar as they are in our control) – then, like a jewel, it would still shine by itself, as something that has its full worth in itself. Usefulness or fruitlessness can neither add anything to this worth nor take anything away from it. Its usefulness would be, as it were, only the setting to enable us to handle it more conveniently in ordinary commerce or to attract to it the attention of those who are not yet expert enough, but not to recommend it to experts or to determine its worth.

There is, however, something so strange in this idea of the absolute worth of a mere will, in the estimation of which no allowance is made for any usefulness, that, despite all the agreement even of common understanding with this idea, a suspicion must yet arise that its covert basis is perhaps mere high-flown fantasy and that we may have misunderstood the purpose of nature in assigning reason to our will as its governor. Hence we shall put this idea to the test from this point of view.

In the natural constitution of an organized being, that is, one constituted purposively for life, we assume as a principle that there will be found in it no instrument for some end other than what is also most appropriate to that end and best adapted to it. Now in a being that has reason and a will, if the proper end of nature were its *preservation*, its *welfare*, in a word its *happiness*, then nature would have hit upon a very bad arrangement in selecting the reason of the creature to carry out this purpose. For all the actions that the creature has to perform for this purpose, and the whole rule of its conduct, would be marked out for it far more accurately by instinct, and that end would have thereby been attained much more surely than it ever can be by reason; and if reason should have been given, over and above, to this favored creature, it must have served it only to contemplate the fortunate constitution of its nature, to admire this, to delight in it, and to be grateful for it to the beneficent cause, but not to submit its faculty of desire to that weak and deceptive guidance and meddle with nature's purpose. In a word, nature would have taken care that reason should not break forth into *practical use* and have the presumption, with its weak insight, to think out for itself a plan for happiness and for the means of attaining it. Nature would have taken upon itself the choice not only of ends but also of means and, with wise foresight, would have entrusted them both simply to instinct.

And, in fact, we find that the more a cultivated reason purposely occupies itself with the enjoyment of life and with happiness, so much the further does one get away from true satisfaction; and from this there arises in many, and indeed in those who have experimented most with this use of reason, if only they are candid enough to admit it, a certain degree of *misology*, that is, hatred of reason; for, after calculating all the advantages they draw – I do not say from the invention of all the arts of common luxury, but even from the sciences (which seem to them to be, at bottom, only a luxury of the understanding) – they find that they have in fact only brought more trouble upon themselves instead of gaining in happiness; and because of this they finally envy rather than despise the more common run of people, who are closer to the guidance of mere natural instinct and do not allow their reason much influence on their behavior. And to this extent we must admit that the judgment of those who greatly moderate, and even reduce below zero, eulogies extolling the advantages that reason is supposed to procure for us with regard to the happiness and satisfaction of life is by no means surly or ungrateful to the goodness of the government of the world; we must admit, instead, that these judgments have as their covert basis the idea of another and far worthier purpose of one's existence, to which therefore, and not to happiness, reason is properly destined, and to which, as supreme condition, the private purpose of the human being must for the most part defer.

Since reason is not sufficiently competent to guide the will surely with regard to its objects and the satisfaction of all our needs (which it to some extent even multiplies) – an end to which an implanted natural instinct would have led much more certainly; and since reason is nevertheless given to us as a practical faculty, that is, as one that is to influence the *will*; then, where nature has everywhere else gone to work purposively in distributing its capacities, the true vocation of reason must be to produce a will that is good, not perhaps *as a means* to other purposes, but *good in itself*, for which reason was absolutely necessary. This will need not, because of this, be the sole and complete good, but it must still be the highest good and the condition of every other, even of all demands for happiness. In this case it is entirely consistent with the wisdom of nature if we perceive that the cultivation of reason, which is requisite to the first and unconditional purpose, limits in many ways – at least in this life – the attainment of the second, namely happiness, which is always conditional; indeed it may reduce it below zero without nature proceeding unpurposively in the matter, because reason, which cognizes its highest practical vocation in the establishment of a good will, in attaining this purpose is capable only of its own kind of satisfaction, namely from fulfilling an end which in turn only reason determines, even if this should be combined with many infringements upon the ends of inclination.

We have, then, to explicate the concept of a will that is to be esteemed in itself and that is good apart from any further purpose, as it already dwells in natural sound understanding and needs not so much to be taught as only to be clarified – this concept that always takes first place in estimating the total worth of our actions and constitutes the condition of all the rest. In order to do so, we shall set before ourselves the concept of *duty*, which contains that of a good will though under certain subjective limitations and hindrances, which, however, far from concealing it and making it unrecognizable, rather bring it out by contrast and make it shine forth all the more brightly.

I here pass over all actions that are already recognized as contrary to duty, even though they may be useful for this or that purpose; for in their case the question whether they might have been done *from duty* never arises, since they even conflict with it. I also set aside actions that are really in conformity with duty

but to which human beings have *no inclination* immediately and which they still perform because they are impelled to do so through another inclination. For in this case it is easy to distinguish whether an action in conformity with duty is done *from duty* or from a self-seeking purpose. It is much more difficult to note this distinction when an action conforms with duty and the subject has, besides, an *immediate* inclination to it. For example, it certainly conforms with duty that a shopkeeper not overcharge an inexperienced customer, and where there is a good deal of trade a prudent merchant does not overcharge but keeps a fixed general price for everyone, so that a child can buy from him as well as everyone else. People are thus served *honestly*; but this is not nearly enough for us to believe that the merchant acted in this way from duty and basic principles of honesty; his advantage required it; it cannot be assumed here that he had, besides, an immediate inclination toward his customers, so as from love, as it were, to give no one preference over another in the matter of price. Thus the action was done neither from duty nor from immediate inclination but merely for purposes of self-interest.

On the other hand, to preserve one's life is a duty, and besides everyone has an immediate inclination to do so. But on this account the often anxious care that most people take of it still has no inner worth and their maxim has no moral content. They look after their lives *in conformity with duty* but not *from duty*. On the other hand, if adversity and hopeless grief have quite taken away the taste for life; if an unfortunate man, strong of soul and more indignant about his fate than despondent or dejected, wishes for death and yet preserves his life without loving it, not from inclination or fear but from duty, then his maxim has moral content.

To be beneficent where one can is a duty, and besides there are many souls so sympathetically attuned that, without any other motive of vanity or self-interest they find an inner satisfaction in spreading joy around them and can take delight in the satisfaction of others so far as it is their own work. But I assert that in such a case an action of this kind, however it may conform with duty and however amiable it may be, has nevertheless no true moral worth but is on the same footing with other inclinations, for example, the inclination to honor, which, if it fortunately lights upon what is in fact in the common interest and in conformity with duty and hence honorable, deserves praise and encouragement but not esteem; for the maxim lacks moral content, namely that of doing such actions not from inclination but *from duty*. Suppose, then, that the mind of this philanthropist were over-clouded by his own grief, which extinguished all sympathy with the fate of others, and that while he still had the means to benefit others in distress their troubles did not move him because he had enough to do with his own; and suppose that now, when no longer incited to it by any inclination, he nevertheless tears himself out of this deadly insensibility and does the action without any inclination, simply from duty; then the action first has its genuine moral worth. Still further: if nature had put little sympathy in the heart of this or that man; if (in other respects an honest man) he is by temperament cold and indifferent to the sufferings of others, perhaps because he himself is provided with the special gift of patience and endurance toward his own sufferings and presupposes the same in every other or even requires it; if nature had not properly fashioned such a man (who would in truth not be its worst product) for a philanthropist, would he not still find within himself a source from which to give himself a far higher worth than what a mere good-natured temperament might have? By all means! It is just then that the worth of character comes out, which is moral and incomparably the highest, namely that he is beneficent not from inclination but from duty.

To assure one's own happiness is a duty (at least indirectly); for, want of satisfaction with one's condition, under pressure from many anxieties and amid unsatisfied needs, could easily become a great *temptation to transgression of duty*. But in addition, without looking to duty here, all people have already, of themselves, the strongest and deepest inclination to happiness because it is just in this idea that all inclinations unite in one sum. However, the precept of happiness is often so constituted that it greatly infringes upon some inclinations,

and yet one can form no determinate and sure concept of the sum of satisfaction of all inclinations under the name of happiness. Hence it is not to be wondered at that a single inclination, determinate both as to what it promises and as to the time within which it can be satisfied, can often outweigh a fluctuating idea, and that a man – for example, one suffering from gout – can choose to enjoy what he likes and put up with what he can since, according to his calculations, on this occasion at least he has not sacrificed the enjoyment of the present moment to the perhaps groundless expectation of a happiness that is supposed to lie in health. But even in this case, when the general inclination to happiness did not determine his will; when health, at least for him, did not enter as so necessary into this calculation, there is still left over here, as in all other cases, a law, namely to promote his happiness not from inclination but from duty; and it is then that his conduct first has properly moral worth.

It is undoubtedly in this way, again, that we are to understand the passages from scripture in which we are commanded to love our neighbor, even our enemy. For, love as an inclination cannot be commanded, but beneficence from duty – even though no inclination impels us to it and, indeed, natural and unconquerable aversion opposes it – is *practical* and not *pathological* love, which lies in the will and not in the propensity of feeling, in principles of action and not in melting sympathy; and it alone can be commanded.

Thus the moral worth of an action does not lie in the effect expected from it and so too does not lie in any principle of action that needs to borrow its motive from this expected effect. For, all these effects (agreeableness of one's condition, indeed even promotion of others' happiness) could have been also brought about by other causes, so that there would have been no need, for this, of the will of a rational being, in which, however, the highest and unconditional good alone can be found. Hence nothing other than the *representation of the law* in itself, *which can of course occur only in a rational being*, insofar as it and not the hoped-for effect is the determining ground of the will, can constitute the preeminent good we call moral, which is already present in the person himself who acts in accordance with this representation and need not wait upon the effect of his action.[1]

But what kind of law can that be, the representation of which must determine the will, even without regard for the effect expected from it, in order for the will to be called good absolutely and without limitation? Since I have deprived the will of every impulse that could arise for it from obeying some law, nothing is left but the conformity of actions as such with universal law, which alone is to serve the will as its principle, that is, *I ought never to act except in such a way that I could also will that my maxim should become a universal law.* Here mere conformity to law as such, without having as its basis some law determined for certain actions, is what serves the will as its principle, and must so serve it, if duty is not to be everywhere an empty delusion and a chimerical concept. Common human reason also agrees completely with this in its practical appraisals and always has this principle before its eyes. Let the question be, for example: may I, when hard pressed, make a promise with the intention not to keep it? Here I easily distinguish two significations the question can have: whether it is prudent or whether it is in conformity with duty to make a false promise. The first can undoubtedly often be the case. I see very well that it is not enough to get out of a present difficulty by means of this subterfuge but that I must reflect carefully whether this lie may later give rise to much greater inconvenience for me than that from which I now extricate myself; and since, with all my supposed *cunning*, the results cannot be so easily foreseen but that once confidence in me is lost this could be far more prejudicial to me than all the troubles I now think to avoid, I must reflect whether the matter might be handled *more prudently* by proceeding on a general maxim and making it a habit to promise nothing except with the intention of keeping it. But it is soon clear to me that such a maxim will still be based only on results feared. To be truthful from duty, however, is something entirely different from being truthful from anxiety about detrimental results, since in the first case the concept of the action in itself already contains a law for me while in the second I must first look about

elsewhere to see what effects on me might be combined with it. For, if I deviate from the principle of duty this is quite certainly evil; but if I am unfaithful to my maxim of prudence this can sometimes be very advantageous to me, although it is certainly safer to abide by it. However, to inform myself in the shortest and yet infallible way about the answer to this problem, whether a lying promise is in conformity with duty, I ask myself: would I indeed be content that my maxim (to get myself out of difficulties by a false promise) should hold as a universal law (for myself as well as for others)? and could I indeed say to myself that every one may make a false promise when he finds himself in a difficulty he can get out of in no other way? Then I soon become aware that I could indeed will the lie, but by no means a universal law to lie; for in accordance with such a law there would properly be no promises at all, since it would be futile to avow my will with regard to my future actions to others who would not believe this avowal or, if they rashly did so, would pay me back in like coin; and thus my maxim, as soon as it were made a universal law, would have to destroy itself.

I do not, therefore, need any penetrating acuteness to see what I have to do in order that my volition be morally good. Inexperienced in the course of the world, incapable of being prepared for whatever might come to pass in it, I ask myself only: can you also will that your maxim become a universal law? If not, then it is to be repudiated, and that not because of a disadvantage to you or even to others forthcoming from it but because it cannot fit as a principle into a possible giving of universal law, for which lawgiving reason, however, forces from me immediate respect. Although I do not yet *see* what this respect is based upon (this the philosopher may investigate), I at least understand this much: that it is an estimation of a worth that far outweighs any worth of what is recommended by inclination, and that the necessity of my action from *pure* respect for the practical law is what constitutes duty, to which every other motive must give way because it is the condition of a will good *in itself*, the worth of which surpasses all else.

Thus, then, we have arrived, within the moral cognition of common human reason, at its principle, which it admittedly does not think so abstractly in a universal form but which it actually has always before its eyes and uses as the norm for its appraisals. Here it would be easy to show how common human reason, with this compass in hand, knows very well how to distinguish in every case that comes up what is good and what is evil, what is in conformity with duty or contrary to duty, if, without in the least teaching it anything new, we only, as did Socrates, make it attentive to its own principle; and that there is, accordingly, no need of science and philosophy to know what one has to do in order to be honest and good, and even wise and virtuous. We might even have assumed in advance that cognizance of what it is incumbent upon everyone to do, and so also to know, would be the affair of every human being, even the most common. Yet we cannot consider without admiration how great an advantage the practical faculty of appraising has over the theoretical in common human understanding. In the latter, if common reason ventures to depart from laws of experience and perceptions of the senses it falls into sheer incomprehensibilities and self-contradictions, at least into a chaos of uncertainty, obscurity, and instability. But in practical matters, it is just when common understanding excludes all sensible incentives from practical laws that its faculty of appraising first begins to show itself to advantage. It then becomes even subtle, whether in quibbling tricks with its own conscience or with other claims regarding what is to be called right, or in sincerely wanting to determine the worth of actions for its own instruction; and, what is most admirable, in the latter case it can even have as good a hope of hitting the mark as any philosopher can promise himself; indeed, it is almost more sure in this matter, because a philosopher, though he cannot have any other principle than that of common understanding, can easily confuse his judgment by a mass of considerations foreign and irrelevant to the matter and deflect it from the straight course. Would it not therefore be more advisable in moral matters to leave the judgment of common reason as it is and, at most, call in philosophy only to present the system of morals all the more completely and apprehensibly and to

present its rules in a form more convenient for use (still more for disputation), but not to lead common human understanding, even in practical matters, away from its fortunate simplicity and to put it, by means of philosophy, on a new path of investigation and instruction?

There is something splendid about innocence; but what is bad about it, in turn, is that it cannot protect itself very well and is easily seduced. Because of this, even wisdom – which otherwise consists more in conduct than in knowledge – still needs science, not in order to learn from it but in order to provide access and durability for its precepts. The human being feels within himself a powerful counterweight to all the commands of duty, which reason represents to him as so deserving of the highest respect – the counterweight of his needs and inclinations, the entire satisfaction of which he sums up under the name happiness. Now reason issues its precepts unremittingly, without thereby promising anything to the inclinations, and so, as it were, with disregard and contempt for those claims, which are so impetuous and besides so apparently equitable (and refuse to be neutralized by any command). But from this there arises a *natural dialectic*, that is, a propensity to rationalize against those strict laws. . . .

The Categorical Imperative

Now, all imperatives command either *hypothetically* or *categorically*. The former represent the practical necessity of a possible action as a means to achieving something else that one wills (or that it is at least possible for one to will). The categorical imperative would be that which represented an action as objectively necessary of itself, without reference to another end.

Since every practical law represents a possible action as good and thus as necessary for a subject practically determinable by reason, all imperatives are formulae for the determination of action that is necessary in accordance with the principle of a will which is good in some way. Now, if the action would be good merely as a means *to something else* the imperative is *hypothetical*; if the action is represented as *in itself* good, hence as necessary in a will in itself conforming to reason, as its principle, *then it is categorical.*

The imperative thus says which action possible by me would be good, and represents a practical rule in relation to a will that does not straightaway do an action just because it is good, partly because the subject does not always know that it is good, partly because, even if he knows this, his maxims could still be opposed to the objective principles of a practical reason.

Hence the hypothetical imperative says only that the action is good for some *possible* or *actual* purpose. In the first case it is a *problematically* practical principle, in the second an *assertorically* practical principle. The categorical imperative, which declares the action to be of itself objectively necessary without reference to some purpose, that is, even apart from any other end, holds as an *apodictically* practical principle.

One can think of what is possible only through the powers of some rational being as also a possible purpose of some will; accordingly, principles of action, insofar as this is represented as necessary for attaining some possible purpose to be brought about by it, are in fact innumerable. All sciences have some practical part, consisting of problems [which suppose] that some end is possible for us and of imperatives as to how it can be attained. These can therefore be called, in general, imperatives of *skill*. Whether the end is rational and good is not at all the question here, but only what one must do in order to attain it. The precepts for a physician to make his man healthy in a well-grounded way, and for a poisoner to be sure of killing his, are of equal worth insofar as each serves perfectly to bring about his purpose. Since in early youth it is not known what ends might occur to us in the course of life, parents seek above all to have their children learn *a great many things* and to provide for *skill* in the use of means to all sorts of *discretionary* ends, about none of which can they determine whether it might in the future actually become their pupil's purpose, though it is always *possible* that he might at some time have it; and this concern is so great that they commonly neglect to form and correct their children's judgment about the worth of the things that they might make their ends.

There is, however, *one* end that can be presupposed as actual in the case of all rational beings (insofar as imperatives apply to them, namely as dependent beings), and therefore one purpose that they not merely *could* have but that we can safely presuppose they all actually *do have* by a natural necessity, and that purpose is *happiness*. The hypothetical imperative that represents the practical necessity of an action as a means to the promotion of happiness is assertoric. It may be set forth not merely as necessary to some uncertain, merely possible purpose but to a purpose that can be presupposed surely and a priori in the case of every human being, because it belongs to his essence. Now, skill in the choice of means to one's own greatest well-being can be called *prudence*[2] in the narrowest sense. Hence the imperative that refers to the choice of means to one's own happiness, that is, the precept of prudence, is still always *hypothetical*; the action is not commanded absolutely but only as a means to another purpose.

Finally there is one imperative that, without being based upon and having as its condition any other purpose to be attained by certain conduct, commands this conduct immediately. This imperative is *categorical.* It has to do not with the matter of the action and what is to result from it, but with the form and the principle from which the action itself follows; and the essentially good in the action consists in the disposition, let the result be what it may. This imperative may be called the imperative *of morality.*

Volition in accordance with these three kinds of principles is also clearly distinguished by *dissimilarity* in the necessitation of the will. In order to make this dissimilarity evident, I think they would be most suitably named in their order by being said to be either *rules* of skill, or *counsels* of prudence, or *commands* (*laws*) of morality. For, only law brings with it the concept of an *unconditional* and objective and hence universally valid *necessity*, and commands are laws that must be obeyed, that is, must be followed even against inclination. *Giving counsel* does involve necessity, which, however, can hold only under a subjective and contingent condition, whether this or that man counts this or that in his happiness; the categorical imperative, on the contrary, is limited by no condition and, as absolutely although practically necessary, can be called quite strictly a command. The first imperative could also be called *technical* (belonging to art), the second pragmatic[3] (belonging to welfare), the third moral (belonging to free conduct as such, that is, to morals).

Now the question arises: how are all these imperatives possible? This question does not inquire how the performance of the action that the imperative commands can be thought, but only how the necessitation of the will, which the imperative expresses in the problem, can be thought. How an imperative of skill is possible requires no special discussion. Whoever wills the end also wills (insofar as reason has decisive influence on his actions) the indispensably necessary means to it that are within his power. This proposition is, as regards the volition, analytic; for in the volition of an object as my effect, my causality as acting cause, that is, the use of means, is already thought, and the imperative extracts the concept of actions necessary to this end merely from the concept of a volition of this end (synthetic propositions no doubt belong to determining the means themselves to a purpose intended, but they do not have to do with the ground for actualizing the act of will but for actualizing the object). That in order to divide a line into two equal parts on a sure principle I must make two intersecting arcs from its ends, mathematics admittedly teaches only by synthetic propositions; but when I know that only by such an action can the proposed effect take place, then it is an analytic proposition that if I fully will the effect I also will the action requisite to it; for, it is one and the same thing to represent something as an effect possible by me in a certain way and to represent myself as acting in this way with respect to it.

If only it were as easy to give a determinate concept of happiness, imperatives of prudence would agree entirely with those of skill and would be just as analytic. For it could be said, here just as there: who wills the end also wills (necessarily in conformity with reason) the sole means to it that are within his control. But it is

a misfortune that the concept of happiness is such an indeterminate concept that, although every human being wishes to attain this, he can still never say determinately and consistently with himself what he really wishes and wills. The cause of this is that all the elements that belong to the concept of happiness are without exception empirical, that is, they must be borrowed from experience, and that nevertheless for the idea of happiness there is required an absolute whole, a maximum of well-being in my present condition and in every future condition. Now, it is impossible for the most insightful and at the same time most powerful but still finite being to frame for himself a determinate concept of what he really wills here. If he wills riches, how much anxiety, envy and intrigue might he not bring upon himself in this way! If he wills a great deal of cognition and insight, that might become only an eye all the more acute to show him, as all the more dreadful, ills that are now concealed from him and that cannot be avoided, or to burden his desires, which already give him enough to do, with still more needs. If he wills a long life, who will guarantee him that it would not be a long misery? If he at least wills health, how often has not bodily discomfort kept someone from excesses into which unlimited health would have let him fall, and so forth. In short, he is not capable of any principle by which to determine with complete certainty what would make him truly happy, because for this omniscience would be required. One cannot therefore act on determinate principles for the sake of being happy, but only on empirical counsels, for example, of a regimen, frugality, courtesy, reserve and so forth, which experience teaches are most conducive to well-being on the average. From this it follows that imperatives of prudence cannot, to speak precisely, command at all, that is, present actions objectively as practically *necessary*; that they are to be taken as counsels (*consilia*) rather than as commands (*praecepta*) of reason; that the problem of determining surely and universally which action would promote the happiness of a rational being is completely insoluble, so that there can be no imperative with respect to it that would, in the strict sense, command him to do what would make him happy; for happiness is not an ideal of reason but of imagination, resting merely upon empirical grounds, which it is futile to expect should determine an action by which the totality of a series of results in fact infinite would be attained. This imperative of prudence would, nevertheless, be an analytic practical proposition if it is supposed that the means to happiness can be assigned with certainty; for it is distinguished from the imperative of skill only in this: that in the case of the latter the end is merely possible, whereas in the former it is given; but since both merely command the means to what it is presupposed one wills as an end, the imperative that commands volition of the means for him who wills the end is in both cases analytic. Hence there is also no difficulty with respect to the possibility of such an imperative.

On the other hand, the question of how the imperative of *morality* is possible is undoubtedly the only one needing a solution, since it is in no way hypothetical and the objectively represented necessity can therefore not be based on any presupposition, as in the case of hypothetical imperatives. Only we must never leave out of account, here, that it cannot be made out *by means of any example*, and so empirically, whether there is any such imperative at all, but it is rather to be feared that all imperatives which seem to be categorical may yet in some hidden way be hypothetical. For example, when it is said "you ought not to promise anything deceitfully," and one assumes that the necessity of this omission is not giving counsel for avoiding some other ill – in which case what is said would be "you ought not to make a lying promise lest if it comes to light you destroy your credit" – but that an action of this kind must be regarded as in itself evil and that the imperative of prohibition is therefore categorical: one still cannot show with certainty in any example that the will is here determined merely through the law, without another incentive, although it seems to be so; for it is always possible that covert fear of disgrace, perhaps also obscure apprehension of other dangers, may have had an influence on the will. Who can prove by experience the nonexistence of a cause when all that experience teaches is that we do not perceive it? In such

a case, however, the so-called moral imperative, which as such appears to be categorical and unconditional, would in fact be only a pragmatic precept that makes us attentive to our advantage and merely teaches us to take this into consideration.

We shall thus have to investigate entirely a priori the possibility of a *categorical* imperative, since we do not here have the advantage of its reality being given in experience, so that the possibility would be necessary not to establish it but merely to explain it. In the meantime, however, we can see this much: that the categorical imperative alone has the tenor of a practical **law**; all the others can indeed be called *principles* of the will but not laws, since what it is necessary to do merely for achieving a discretionary purpose can be regarded as in itself contingent and we can always be released from the precept if we give up the purpose; on the contrary, the unconditional command leaves the will no discretion with respect to the opposite, so that it alone brings with it that necessity which we require of a law.

Second, in the case of this categorical imperative or law of morality the ground of the difficulty (of insight into its possibility) is also very great. It is an a priori synthetic practical proposition; and since it is so difficult to see the possibility of this kind of proposition in theoretical cognition, it can be readily gathered that the difficulty will be no less in practical cognition.

In this task we want first to inquire whether the mere concept of a categorical imperative may not also provide its formula containing the proposition which alone can be a categorical imperative. For, how such an absolute command is possible, even if we know its tenor, will still require special and difficult toil, which, however, we postpone to the last section.

When I think of a *hypothetical* imperative in general I do not know beforehand what it will contain; I do not know this until I am given the condition. But when I think of a *categorical* imperative I know at once what it contains. For, since the imperative contains, beyond the law, only the necessity that the maxim[4] be in conformity with this law, while the law contains no condition to which it would be limited, nothing is left with which the maxim of action is to conform but the universality of a law as such; and this conformity alone is what the imperative properly represents as necessary.

There is, therefore, only a single categorical imperative and it is this: *act only in accordance with that maxim through which you can at the same time will that it become a universal law.*

Now, if all imperatives of duty can be derived from this single imperative as from their principle, then, even though we leave it undecided whether what is called duty is not as such an empty concept, we shall at least be able to show what we think by it and what the concept wants to say.

Since the universality of law in accordance with which effects take place constitutes what is properly called *nature* in the most general sense (as regards its form) – that is, the existence of things insofar as it is determined in accordance with universal laws – the universal imperative of duty can also go as follows: *act as if the maxim of your action were to become by your will a universal law of nature.*

We shall now enumerate a few duties in accordance with the usual division of them into duties to ourselves and to other human beings and into perfect and imperfect duties.[5]

1) Someone feels sick of life because of a series of troubles that has grown to the point of despair, but is still so far in possession of his reason that he can ask himself whether it would not be contrary to his duty to himself to take his own life. Now he inquires whether the maxim of his action could indeed become a universal law of nature. His maxim, however, is: from self-love I make it my principle to shorten my life when its longer duration threatens more troubles than it promises agreeableness. The only further question is whether this principle of self-love could become a universal law of nature. It is then seen at once that a nature whose law it would be to destroy life itself by means of the same feeling whose destination is to impel toward the furtherance of life would contradict itself and would therefore not subsist as nature; thus that maxim could not possibly be a law of nature and, accordingly, altogether opposes the supreme principle of all duty.

2) Another finds himself urged by need to borrow money. He well knows that he will not be able to repay it but sees also that nothing will be lent him unless he promises firmly to repay it within a determinate time. He would like to make such a promise, but he still has enough conscience to ask himself: is it not forbidden and contrary to duty to help oneself out of need in such a way? Supposing that he still decided to do so, his maxim of action would go as follows: when I believe myself to be in need of money I shall borrow money and promise to repay it, even though I know that this will never happen. Now this principle of self-love or personal advantage is perhaps quite consistent with my whole future welfare, but the question now is whether it is right. I therefore turn the demand of self-love into a universal law and put the question as follows: how would it be if my maxim became a universal law? I then see at once that it could never hold as a universal law of nature and be consistent with itself, but must necessarily contradict itself. For, the universality of a law that everyone, when he believes himself to be in need, could promise whatever he pleases with the intention of not keeping it would make the promise and the end one might have in it itself impossible, since no one would believe what was promised him but would laugh at all such expressions as vain pretenses.

3) A third finds in himself a talent that by means of some cultivation could make him a human being useful for all sorts of purposes. However, he finds himself in comfortable circumstances and prefers to give himself up to pleasure than to trouble himself with enlarging and improving his fortunate natural predispositions. But he still asks himself whether his maxim of neglecting his natural gifts, besides being consistent with his propensity to amusement, is also consistent with what one calls duty. He now sees that a nature could indeed always subsist with such a universal law, although (as with the South Sea Islanders) the human being should let his talents rust and be concerned with devoting his life merely to idleness, amusement, procreation – in a word, to enjoyment; only he cannot possibly *will* that this become a universal law or be put in us as such by means of natural instinct. For, as a

rational being he necessarily wills that all the capacities in him be developed, since they serve him and are given to him for all sorts of possible purposes.

Yet a *fourth*, for whom things are going well while he sees that others (whom he could very well help) have to contend with great hardships, thinks: what is it to me? let each be as happy as heaven wills or as he can make himself; I shall take nothing from him nor even envy him; only I do not care to contribute anything to his welfare or to his assistance in need! Now, if such a way of thinking were to become a universal law the human race could admittedly very well subsist, no doubt even better than when everyone prates about sympathy and benevolence and even exerts himself to practice them occasionally, but on the other hand also cheats where he can, sells the right of human beings or otherwise infringes upon it. But although it is possible that a universal law of nature could very well subsist in accordance with such a maxim, it is still impossible to will that such a principle hold everywhere as a law of nature. For, a will that decided this would conflict with itself, since many cases could occur in which one would need the love and sympathy of others and in which, by such a law of nature arisen from his own will, he would rob himself of all hope of the assistance he wishes for himself.

These are a few of the many actual duties, or at least of what we take to be such, whose derivation from the one principle cited above is clear. We must *be able to will* that a maxim of our action become a universal law: this is the canon of moral appraisal of action in general. Some actions are so constituted that their maxim cannot even be *thought* without contradiction as a universal law of nature, far less could one *will* that it *should* become such. In the case of others that inner impossibility is indeed not to be found, but it is still impossible to *will* that their maxim be raised to the universality of a law of nature because such a will would contradict itself. It is easy to see that the first is opposed to strict or narrower (unremitting) duty, the second only to wide (meritorious) duty; and so all duties, as far as the kind of obligation (not the object of their action) is concerned, have by these examples been set

out completely in their dependence upon the one principle.

If we now attend to ourselves in any transgression of a duty, we find that we do not really will that our maxim should become a universal law, since that is impossible for us, but that the opposite of our maxim should instead remain a universal law, only we take the liberty of making an *exception* to it for ourselves (or just for this once) to the advantage of our inclination. Consequently, if we weighed all cases from one and the same point of view, namely that of reason, we would find a contradiction in our own will, namely that a certain principle be objectively necessary as a universal law and yet subjectively not hold universally but allow exceptions. Since, however, we at one time regard our action from the point of view of a will wholly conformed with reason but then regard the very same action from the point of view of a will affected by inclination, there is really no contradiction here but instead a resistance of inclination to the precept of reason (*antagonismus*), through which the universality of the principle (*universalitas*) is changed into mere generality (*generalitas*) and the practical rational principle is to meet the maxim half way. Now, even though this cannot be justified in our own impartially rendered judgment, it still shows that we really acknowledge the validity of the categorical imperative and permit ourselves (with all respect for it) only a few exceptions that, as it seems to us, are inconsiderable and wrung from us.

We have therefore shown at least this much: that if duty is a concept that is to contain significance and real lawgiving for our actions it can be expressed only in categorical imperatives and by no means in hypothetical ones; we have also – and this is already a great deal – set forth distinctly and as determined for every use the content of the categorical imperative, which must contain the principle of all duty (if there is such a thing at all). But we have not yet advanced so far as to prove a priori that there really is such an imperative, that there is a practical law, which commands absolutely of itself and without any incentives, and that the observance of this law is duty.

For the purpose of achieving this it is of the utmost importance to take warning that we must not let ourselves think of wanting to derive the reality of this principle from the *special property of human nature*. For, duty is to be practical unconditional necessity of action and it must therefore hold for all rational beings (to which alone an imperative can apply at all) and *only because of this* be also a law for all human wills. On the other hand, what is derived from the special natural constitution of humanity – what is derived from certain feelings and propensities and even, if possible, from a special tendency that would be peculiar to human reason and would not have to hold necessarily for the will of every rational being – that can indeed yield a maxim for us but not a law; it can yield a subjective principle on which we might act if we have the propensity and inclination, but not an objective principle on which we would be *directed* to act even though every propensity, inclination, and natural tendency of ours were against it – so much so that the sublimity and inner dignity of the command in a duty is all the more manifest the fewer are the subjective causes in favor of it and the more there are against it, without thereby weakening in the least the necessitation by the law or taking anything away from its validity.

Here, then, we see philosophy put in fact in a precarious position, which is to be firm even though there is nothing in heaven or on earth from which it depends or on which it is based. Here philosophy is to manifest its purity as sustainer of its own laws, not as herald of laws that an implanted sense or who knows what tutelary nature whispers to it, all of which – though they may always be better than nothing at all – can still never yield basic principles that reason dictates and that must have their source entirely and completely a priori and, at the same time, must have their commanding authority from this: that they expect nothing from the inclination of human beings but everything from the supremacy of the law and the respect owed it or, failing this, condemn the human being to contempt for himself and inner abhorrence.

Hence everything empirical, as an addition to the principle of morality, is not only quite inept for this; it is also highly prejudicial to the purity of morals, where the proper worth of an absolutely good will – a worth raised above all price – consists just in the principle of action being free from all influences of contingent grounds, which only experience can furnish. One cannot give too many or too frequent warnings against this laxity, or even mean cast of mind, which seeks its principle among empirical motives and laws; for, human reason in its weariness gladly rests on this pillow and in a dream of sweet illusions (which allow it to embrace a cloud instead of Juno) it substitutes for morality a bastard patched up from limbs of quite diverse ancestry, which looks like whatever one wants to see in it but not like virtue for him who has once seen virtue in her true form.[6]

The question is therefore this: is it a necessary law *for all rational beings* always to appraise their actions in accordance with such maxims as they themselves could will to serve as universal laws? If there is such a law, then it must already be connected (completely a priori) with the concept of the will of a rational being as such. But in order to discover this connection we must, however reluctantly, step forth, namely into metaphysics, although into a domain of it that is distinct from speculative philosophy, namely into metaphysics of morals. In a practical philosophy, where we have to do not with assuming grounds for what *happens* but rather laws for what *ought to happen* even if it never does, that is, objective practical laws, we do not need to undertake an investigation into the grounds on account of which something pleases or displeases; how the satisfaction of mere sensation differs from taste, and whether the latter differs from a general satisfaction of reason; upon what the feeling of pleasure or displeasure rests, and how from it desires and inclinations arise, and from them, with the cooperation of reason, maxims; for all that belongs to an empirical doctrine of the soul, which would constitute the second part of the doctrine of nature when this is regarded as *philosophy of nature* insofar as it is based *on empirical laws*. Here, however, it is a question of objective practical laws and hence of the relation of a will to itself insofar as it determines itself only by reason; for then everything that has reference to the empirical falls away of itself, since if reason entirely by itself determines conduct (and the possibility of this is just what we want now to investigate), it must necessarily do so a priori.

The will is thought as a capacity to determine itself to acting in conformity with the *representation of certain laws*. And such a capacity can be found only in rational beings. Now, what serves the will as the objective ground of its self-determination is an end, and this, if it is given by reason alone, must hold equally for all rational beings. What, on the other hand, contains merely the ground of the possibility of an action the effect of which is an end is called a *means*. The subjective ground of desire is an *incentive*; the objective ground of volition is a *motive*; hence the distinction between subjective ends, which rest on incentives, and objective ends, which depend on motives, which hold for every rational being. Practical principles are *formal* if they abstract from all subjective ends, whereas they are *material* if they have put these, and consequently certain incentives, at their basis. The ends that a rational being proposes at his discretion as *effects* of his actions (material ends) are all only relative; for only their mere relation to a specially constituted faculty of desire on the part of the subject gives them their worth, which can therefore furnish no universal principles, no principles valid and necessary for all rational beings and also for every volition, that is, no practical laws. Hence all these relative ends are only the ground of hypothetical imperatives.

But suppose there were something the *existence of which in itself* has an absolute worth, something which as *an end in itself* could be a ground of determinate laws; then in it, and in it alone, would lie the ground of a possible categorical imperative, that is, of a practical law.

Now I say that the human being and in general every rational being *exists* as an end in itself, *not merely as a means* to be used by this or that will at its discretion; instead he must in all his actions, whether directed to himself or also to other rational beings, always be regarded *at the same time as an end*. All objects of the inclinations have only a conditional worth; for, if there were not inclinations and the needs based on them, their object would be without worth. But the inclinations themselves, as sources of needs, are so far from having an absolute worth, so as to make one wish to have

them, that it must instead be the universal wish of every rational being to be altogether free from them. Thus the worth of any object *to be acquired* by our action is always conditional. Beings the existence of which rests not on our will but on nature, if they are beings without reason, still have only a relative worth, as means, and are therefore called *things*, whereas rational beings are called *persons* because their nature already marks them out as an end in itself, that is, as something that may not be used merely as a means, and hence so far limits all choice (and is an object of respect). These, therefore, are not merely subjective ends, the existence of which as an effect of our action has a worth *for us*, but rather *objective ends*, that is, beings the existence of which is in itself an end, and indeed one such that no other end, to which they would serve *merely* as means, can be put in its place, since without it nothing of *absolute worth* would be found anywhere; but if all worth were conditional and therefore contingent, then no supreme practical principle for reason could be found anywhere.

If, then, there is to be a supreme practical principle and, with respect to the human will, a categorical imperative, it must be one such that, from the representation of what is necessarily an end for everyone because it is an *end in itself*, it constitutes an *objective* principle of the will and thus can serve as a universal practical law. The ground of this principle is: *rational nature exists as an end in itself*. The human being necessarily represents his own existence in this way; so far it is thus a *subjective* principle of human actions. But every other rational being also represents his existence in this way consequent on just the same rational ground that also holds for me; thus it is at the same time an *objective* principle from which, as a supreme practical ground, it must be possible to derive all laws of the will. The practical imperative will therefore be the following: *So act that you use humanity, whether in your own person or in the person of any other, always at the same time as an end, never merely as a means.* We shall see whether this can be carried out.

To keep to the preceding examples:

First, as regards the concept of necessary duty to oneself, someone who has suicide in mind will ask himself whether his action can be consistent with the idea of humanity *as an end in itself*. If he destroys himself in order to escape from a trying condition he makes use of a person *merely as a means* to maintain a tolerable condition up to the end of life. A human being, however, is not a thing and hence not something that can be used *merely* as a means, but must in all his actions always be regarded as an end in itself. I cannot, therefore, dispose of a human being in my own person by maiming, damaging or killing him. (I must here pass over a closer determination of this principle that would prevent any misinterpretation, e.g., as to having limbs amputated in order to preserve myself, or putting my life in danger in order to preserve my life, and so forth; that belongs to morals proper.)

Second, as regards necessary duty to others or duty owed them, he who has it in mind to make a false promise to others sees at once that he wants to make use of another human being *merely as a means*, without the other at the same time containing in himself the end. For, he whom I want to use for my purposes by such a promise cannot possibly agree to my way of behaving toward him, and so himself contain the end of this action. This conflict with the principle of other human beings is seen more distinctly if examples of assaults on the freedom and property of others are brought forward. For then it is obvious that he who transgresses the rights of human beings intends to make use of the person of others merely as means, without taking into consideration that, as rational beings, they are always to be valued at the same time as ends, that is, only as beings who must also be able to contain in themselves the end of the very same action.

Third, with respect to contingent (meritorious) duty to oneself, it is not enough that the action does not conflict with humanity in our person as an end in itself; it must also *harmonize with it*. Now there are in humanity predispositions to greater perfection, which belong to the end of nature with respect to humanity in our subject; to neglect these might admittedly be consistent with the *preservation* of humanity as an end in itself but not with the *furtherance* of this end.

Fourth, concerning meritorious duty to others, the natural end that all human beings have is their own happiness. Now, humanity might indeed subsist if no one contributed to the happiness of others but yet did not intentionally withdraw anything from it; but there is still only a negative and not a positive agreement with *humanity as an end in itself* unless everyone also tries, as far as he can, to further the ends of others. For, the ends of a subject who is an end in itself must as far as possible be also *my* ends, if that representation is to have its *full* effect in me.

This principle of humanity, and in general of every rational nature, *as an end in itself* (which is the supreme limiting condition of the freedom of action of every human being) is not borrowed from experience; first because of its universality, since it applies to all rational beings as such and no experience is sufficient to determine anything about them; second because in it humanity is represented not as an end of human beings (subjectively), that is, not as an object that we of ourselves actually make our end, but as an objective end that, whatever ends we may have, ought as law to constitute the supreme limiting condition of all subjective ends, so that the principle must arise from pure reason. That is to say, the ground of all practical lawgiving lies (in accordance with the first principle) *objectively in the rule* and the form of universality which makes it fit to be a law (possibly a law of nature); *subjectively*, however, it lies in the *end*; but the subject of all ends is every rational being as an end in itself (in accordance with the second principle); from this there follows now the third practical principle of the will, as supreme condition of its harmony with universal practical reason, the idea *of the will of every rational being as a will giving universal law*.

In accordance with this principle all maxims are repudiated that are inconsistent with the will's own giving of universal law. Hence the will is not merely subject to the law but subject to it in such a way that it must be viewed as also giving the law to itself and just because of this as first subject to the law (of which it can regard itself as the author).

Notes

1. It could be objected that I only seek refuge, behind the word *respect*, in an obscure feeling, instead of distinctly resolving the question by means of a concept of reason. But though respect is a feeling, it is not one *received* by means of influence; it is, instead, a feeling *self-wrought* by means of a rational concept and therefore specifically different from all feelings of the first kind, which can be reduced to inclination or fear. What I cognize immediately as a law for me I cognize with respect, which signifies merely consciousness of the *subordination* of my will to a law without the mediation of other influences on my sense. Immediate determination of the will by means of the law and consciousness of this is called *respect*, so that this is regarded as the *effect* of the law on the subject, and not as the *cause* of the law. Respect is properly the representation of a worth that infringes upon my self-love. Hence there is something that is regarded as an object neither of inclination nor of fear, though it has something analogous to both. The *object* of respect is therefore simply the *law*, and indeed the law that we impose upon *ourselves* and yet as necessary in itself. As a law we are subject to it without consulting self-love; as imposed upon us by ourselves it is nevertheless a result of our will; and in the first respect it has an analogy with fear, in the second with inclination. Any respect for a person is properly only respect for the law (of integrity and so forth) of which he gives us an example. Because we also regard enlarging our talents as a duty, we represent a person of talents also as, so to speak, an *example of the law* (to become like him in this by practice), and this is what constitutes our respect. All so-called moral *interest* consists simply in *respect* for the law.

2. The word "prudence" is taken in two senses: in the one it may bear the name of "knowledge of the world," in the other that of "private prudence." The first is a human being's skill in influencing others so as to use them for his own purposes. The second is the insight to unite all these purposes to his own enduring advantage. The latter is properly that to which the worth even of the former is reduced, and if

someone is prudent in the first sense but not in the second, we might better say of him that he is clever and cunning but, on the whole, nevertheless imprudent.

3. It seems to me that the proper meaning of the word *pragmatic* can be most accurately determined in this way. For *sanctions* are called "pragmatic" that do not flow strictly from the right of *states* as necessary laws but from *provision* for the general welfare. A *history* is composed pragmatically when it makes us *prudent*, that is, instructs the world how it can look after its advantage better than, or at least as well as, the world of earlier times.

4. A *maxim* is the subjective principle of acting, and must be distinguished from the *objective* principle, namely the practical law. The former contains the practical rule determined by reason conformably with the conditions of the subject (often his ignorance or also his inclinations), and is therefore the principle in accordance with which the subject *acts*; but the law is the objective principle valid for every rational being, and the principle in accordance with which he *ought to act*, i.e., an imperative.

5. It must be noted here that I reserve the division of duties entirely for a future *Metaphysics of Morals*, so that the division here stands only as one adopted at my discretion (for the sake of arranging my examples). For the rest, I understand here by a perfect duty one that admits no exception in favor of inclination, and then I have not merely external but also internal *perfect duties*; although this is contrary to the use of the word adopted in the schools, I do not intend to justify it here, since for my purpose it makes no difference whether or not it is granted me.

6. To behold virtue in her proper form is nothing other than to present morality stripped of any admixture of the sensible and of any spurious adornments of reward or self-love. By means of the least effort of his reason everyone can easily become aware of how much virtue then eclipses everything else that appears charming to the inclinations, provided his reason is not altogether spoiled for abstraction.

CHAPTER 56
Kant's Formula of Universal Law

CHRISTINE KORSGAARD

Kant's first formulation of the categorical imperative, the Formula of Universal Law, runs:

> Act only according to that maxim by which you can at the same time will that it should become a universal law. (G 421)

A few lines later, Kant says that this is equivalent to acting as though your maxim were by your will to become a law of nature, and he uses this latter formulation in his examples of how the imperative is to be applied. Elsewhere, Kant specifies that the test is whether you could will the universalization for a system of nature "of which you yourself were a part" (C2 69); and in one place he characterizes the moral agent as asking "what sort of world he would create under the guidance of practical reason, . . . a world into which, moreover, he would place himself as a member" (R 5). But how do you determine whether or not you can will a given maxim as a law of nature? Since the will is practical reason, and since everyone must arrive at the same conclusions in matters of duty, it cannot be the case that what you are able to will is a matter of personal taste, or relative to your individual desires. Rather, the

question of what you can will is a question of what you can will *without contradiction.*

According to Kant, willing universalized maxims may give rise to contradictions in two ways:

> Some actions are of such a nature that their maxim cannot even be *thought* as a universal law of nature without contradiction, far from it being possible that one could will that it should be such. In others this internal impossibility is not found, though it is still impossible to *will* that their maxim should be raised to the universality of a law of nature, because such a will would contradict itself. We easily see that the former maxim conflicts with the stricter or narrower (imprescriptible) duty, the latter with broader (meritorious) duty. (G 424)

The first sort of contradiction is usually called a contradiction in conception, and the second a contradiction in the will.

In this paper I am concerned with identifying the sense in which there is a "contradiction" in willing the universalization of an immoral maxim, and especially with the sense in which the universalization of such a maxim can be said to have a contradiction *in* it – that is, with the idea of a contradiction in conception. There are three different interpretations of the kind of contradiction Kant

Christine Korsgaard, "Kant's Formula of Universal Law," pp. 24–47 from *Pacific Philosophical Quarterly*, 66, 1985. Reprinted by permission of the publishers, Blackwell Publishing.

has (or ought to have) in mind found in the literature. They are:

i) The Logical Contradiction Interpretation. On this interpretation, there is something like a logical impossibility in the universalization of the maxim, or in the system of nature in which the maxim is a natural law: if the maxim were universalized, the action or policy that it proposes would be inconceivable.

ii) The Teleological Contradiction Interpretation. On this interpretation, it would be contradictory to will your maxim as a law for a system of nature teleologically conceived: either you are acting against some natural purpose, or your maxim could not be a teleological law. The maxim is inconsistent with a systematic harmony of purposes, or with the principle that any organ, instinct, or action-type has a natural purpose for which it must be the one best suited.

iii) The Practical Contradiction Interpretation. On this interpretation, the contradiction is that your maxim would be self-defeating if universalized: your action would become ineffectual for the achievement of your purpose if everyone (tried to) use it for that purpose. Since you propose to use that action for that purpose at the same time as you propose to universalize the maxim, you in effect will the thwarting of your own purpose.

In trying to determine which of these views is correct, it is important to remember that it is not just because of the contradiction in the universalized maxim that immoral action is irrational. Kant is not claiming that immoral conduct is contradictory – if he were, the moral law would be analytic rather than synthetic. In any event, a contradiction in the universalization of your maxim would not prove that there is a contradiction in your maxim, for these are different. The Formula of Universal Law is a test of the sufficiency of the reasons for action and choice which are embodied in our maxims. The idea that universalizability is a test for sufficiency ("what if everybody did that?") is a familiar one, and shows in an intuitive way

why it is rational to attend to a universalizability requirement. But the claim that universalizability is a test for a reason sufficient to motivate a rational being cannot be fully defended at this stage of the argument, for the full defense requires the connection to autonomy. Kant's critical ethical project is to prove that perfect rationality includes conformity to the categorical imperative: but in the *Groundwork* this project is not directly taken up until the Third Section. The Second Section, where the Formula of Universal Law appears, is devoted to showing us what the content of the categorical imperative will be *if there is one*. The question of contradictions arises not in the context of determining *why* you must conform your conduct to the categorical imperative, but of *how* you do so.

Yet in trying to come to an understanding of how the Formula of Universal Law is to be applied, we must not lose sight of this further goal. Any view of how the Formula of Universal Law is applied must presuppose some view of what rational willing is. The problem is most obviously pressing for the case of contradictions in the will, for it seems impossible to say what contradicts a rational will until we know what a rational will is, or what it necessarily contains. There is a contradiction in one's beliefs if one believes both x and not-x, or things that imply both x and not-x. There is a contradiction in one's will if one wills both x and not-x, or things that imply both x and not-x. But until one knows what things are involved in or implied by "willing x," one will not know how to discover these contradictions. So in determining which maxims can be willed as universal law without contradiction, we will have to employ some notion of what rational willing is. Some of the interpretations of the contradiction in conception test also rely on particular views of what rational willing is. This is why we must keep in view Kant's eventual aim of showing that moral conduct is rational conduct. Whatever view of the nature of rational willing is used in determining how the formula is to be applied must also be used in determining why it is rational to act as the formula prescribes.

One constraint this places on interpretations of the test is this: it must not employ a notion of rational willing that already has moral content. An example will show what I mean. John Stuart Mill says of Kant:

> But when he begins to deduce from this precept any of the actual duties of morality, he fails, almost grotesquely, to show that there would be any contradiction, any logical (not to say physical) impossibility, in the adoption by all rational beings of the most outrageously immoral rules of conduct. All he shows is that the consequences of their universal adoption would be such as no one would choose to incur.[1]

Mill thinks that Kant's view really amounts to an appeal to utility, to what we would now call rule-utilitarianism. A rule-utilitarian interpretation of the Formula of Universal Law gives, as Mill points out, no sense to Kant's use of the word "contradiction" in this context. Yet, we could give it sense by claiming that a rational being is *by definition* opposed to undesirable consequences, and therefore cannot, without contradiction, will the universalization of any maxim if that universalization would have undesirable consequences. But roughly this kind of connection between a rational will and a moral will is what Kant is trying to *establish*, and therefore to use such a definition in explaining the contradiction test would make the Kantian argument circular. For if we use this definition we are already presupposing a morality-laden conception of what it is to be rational: we are assuming the sort of connection between moral goodness and rationality that Kant is preparing to demonstrate. So although the contradiction tests by themselves do not show us why immoral action is irrational, the notion of rational willing which they presuppose must be one that can be used at the later stage of the argument.

My question is which of the three "kinds" of contradiction we should expect to find in the universalized version of an immoral maxim, and my aim is to defend the third answer, that it is a practical contradiction. I should say from the outset that although there is one important piece of textual evidence for this answer, it is my view that no interpretation can be based on textual considerations alone.

Language supporting all of them can be found in Kant's texts, and it seems possible that he was not aware of the differences among them. My defense of the practical contradiction interpretation will therefore be based primarily on philosophical considerations. For each interpretation I will ask (i) what kinds of cases it can handle, (ii) whether it can meet some standard objections, (iii) what sort of distinction between the contradiction in conception test and the contradiction in the will test is implied by it, and, most importantly, (iv) what presuppositions about rationality it makes and so what kind of case it will allow Kant to make when he turns to the critical project of showing that morality *is* pure rationality.

I   The Logical Contradiction Interpretation

Some of Kant's defenders have tried to identify a contradiction of just the sort Mill denies can be found. [. . .] I suppose hardly any of this interpretation's proponents have held it in the pure form that Mill describes: what they have looked for is something very like a logical or physical impossibility. Part of the reason for this is that it is clear that nothing like a logical contradiction can be found for the contradiction in the will test, since we are explicitly told that maxims that fail that test are conceivable. But there is no question that much of Kant's language favors a Logical Contradiction Interpretation for the contradiction in conception test. He says that universalizations of immoral maxims destroy themselves (G 403), annihilate themselves (C2 27), are inconceivable or cannot be thought, and so on. The example that fits this view best is the false promising example. A man in financial difficulties considers "borrowing" money which he knows he can never repay. Kant explains how this fails the contradiction in conception test this way:

> . . . the universality of a law which says that anyone who believes himself to be in need could promise what he pleased with the intention of not fulfilling it would make the promise itself and the end to be accomplished by it

impossible; no one would believe what was promised to him but would only laugh at any such assertion as vain pretense. (G 422)

Proponents of the Logical Contradiction Interpretation tend to focus on the remark that the promise itself would be impossible, as this seems to be where a logical inconceivability would lie. Kant tells us that promises would be impossible if this maxim were universalized because no one would believe them. There are various ways to find a contradiction here. One could say that the contradiction is that we are trying to conceive a world in which the agent (and everyone with his purpose) is making a certain sort of false promise, but at the same time we are necessarily conceiving a world in which no one can be making this sort of promise, since you cannot make a promise (of this sort) to someone who will not accept it. Perhaps the clearest way to bring out a logical contradiction is to say that there would be no such thing as a promise (or anyway a repayment-promise) in the world of the universalized maxim. The practice of offering and accepting promises would have died out under stress of too many violations. Thus we are imagining a world in which the agent and everyone with his purpose is making a certain sort of promise, but also a world in which there is no such thing. And this is logically inconceivable. If universalizing a maxim makes the action proposed inconceivable, then, we can get a logical contradiction.

A problem about violence

The difficulty in taking this line shows up in a problem that Dietrichson describes in "Kant's Criteria of Universalizability." He considers the case of a woman who has decided to consider the maxim "if I give birth to a baby weighing less than six pounds, I shall do everything in my power to kill it."[2] Dietrichson points out that it is certainly possible to conceive the idea of every mother behaving according to this rule. In my view, Dietrichson's example is not a properly formulated maxim, since it does not mention the mother's reason for killing the child. The child's weighing less than six pounds is not by itself recognizable as a *prima facie*

reason for killing it. Since the Formula of Universal Law is a test of the sufficiency of reasons, the maxim must include them. But this is not the problem brought out by Dietrichson's example. We can make the maxim one of killing children that tend to cry at night more than average, in order to get enough sleep. Either Dietrichson's maxim or mine could clearly be a universal law without a logical contradiction. There could in fact be worlds where these things happen. They could happen in our world.

Dietrichson's solution is to appeal to the second contradiction test, and to place this among the maxims whose universalizations cannot be willed although they can be conceived. But this will not work. Different ways of deriving duties lead to different kinds of duty, with different moral and legal consequences. In the *Groundwork*, Kant associates the contradiction in the will test with wide, meritorious duties (G 424), and the duty not to kill a child is obviously not of that kind.
[. . .]

Natural and conventional actions

The problem that is demonstrated by Dietrichson's example springs from the fact that the action contemplated is one of natural violence. In the promising case we were able to generate a logical contradiction because the practice of promising was, under stress of universal violation, ushered off the scene. There would no longer be such a thing as promising. No such analysis is available here, because killing cannot be ushered off the scene by the way it is employed. The reason is obvious. Promising is, in the sense developed by Rawls in "Two Concepts of Rules,"[3] a practice. Both the possibility and the efficacy of actions performed within a convention such as promising – such as making, accepting, and keeping promises – depend on the existence, by conventional establishment, of the practice. The practice is comprised of certain rules, and its existence (where it is not embodied in an institution with sanctions) consists in the general acknowledgement and following of those rules. Now it is perhaps difficult to say exactly under what conditions a practice exists. We know that practices can exist if their rules are violated sometimes, for they do. But they cannot exist if their rules are universally violated. One may generate the contradiction by saying that when this happens the practice has new rules and becomes a different practice, but this is somewhat obscure. The clearer thing to say is this: a practice has a standard purpose, and if its rules are universally violated it ceases to be efficacious for this purpose, and so ceases to exist. People find some other way to achieve it, and the practice simply goes out of business. This is what happens in Kant's false promising example. Repayment promises, because they are never accepted, become nonexistent. People either make no loans or find another way to ensure repayment. For this reason, all actions which could not intelligibly exist or would not be efficacious without the existence of practices, and yet violate the rules of those practices, are easily handled by both the Logical and the Practical Interpretations of the contradiction test. Willing universal violation creates an inconsistency by making the action-type that it universalizes a non-existent one, and *ipso facto*, ineffectual.

But in Dietrichson's case there is no practice. The action is killing, and no amount or kind of use of the action of killing is going to make it impossible. And this is because the existence of this kind of action and its efficacy depend only on the laws of nature, not on any conventional practice. For shorthand, I am going to call actions like promising "conventional actions" and actions like killing "natural actions." The Logical Contradiction interpretation works well for immoral conventional actions, but it is not very clear how it can handle immoral natural actions. When an action's possibility depends only on the laws of nature it cannot become inconceivable through universal practice.

[. . .]

II The Teleological Contradiction Interpretation

According to the Teleological Contradiction interpretation, when we test our maxim by the two contradiction tests under the Formula of the Law of Nature, we are to consider whether we could will the universalized maxim as a possible law in a teleologically organized system of nature. There are two versions of this view. The first, which I will call the simple view, is usually understood this way: the contradiction emerges when an action or instinct is used in a way that is inconsistent with its natural purpose, or is not used in a way that its natural purpose calls for. A problem with this view as I have just stated it is that it makes no real use of universalization. Yet, there is some textual support for this interpretation: Kant does not scruple to use teleological language, and there are five arguments in the published ethical writings in which Kant's reasoning is explicitly teleological. One is the argument about the function of practical reasoning in the first section of the *Groundwork* (G 395–6). That argument is certainly teleological – Kant indeed carefully sets forth its teleological basis – but it is not a derivation of duty. Of the other four, two appear in the *Groundwork*, in connection with the first set of examples: in deriving the duty not to commit suicide (G 421–2) and in deriving the duty of self-cultivation (G 423). The other two are in the *Metaphysics of Morals*, where lying is said to violate the natural purpose of the power of communication (MPV 429) and carnal self-defilement is denounced by appeal to the natural purpose of the sexual instincts (MPV 424–5).

The second version of this view is that of H. J. Paton, spelled out in Chapter XV of *The Categorical Imperative*. [. . .] Paton thinks that it is clear that the laws of nature Kant had in mind were teleological rather than causal, and that the test is whether "a will which aimed at a systematic harmony of purposes in human nature could consistently will this particular maxim as a law of human nature."[5] Paton's view differs from the simple view in that he thinks that a teleological system serves as the *type* of the moral law, rather than thinking that our actions must not contradict actual natural purposes. However, in his account of the examples he takes Kant's explicitly teleological language as evidence for his interpretation, although that language suits the simple view. The difference matters more than

Paton seems to realize, for the presuppositions about rationality are different. On his own view the claim must be that a rational being as such values a systematic harmony of human purposes, whereas on the simple view we must claim that a rational being as such values natural purposes. In what follows I will consider both versions.

As I mentioned, the usual understanding of the teleological view is that we find some way to assign natural purposes to various instincts and types of actions and then find the contradiction when universalized maxims involve uses of those instincts and actions that defeat the natural purpose or perhaps are merely deviant. The best evidence that Kant understood the contradiction test this way is the suicide example, and it can be made to fit this pattern.

In the first teleological argument in the *Groundwork*, Kant offers this as a general principle of teleological judgment: "we assume as an axiom that no organ will be found for any purpose which is not the fittest and best adapted to that purpose" (G 395). We can use this regulative principle to assign natural purposes to action-types as well as to organs, instincts, and other organic arrangements. Kant uses it to establish that the attainment of happiness is not the natural purpose of practical reason – the argument being that since instinct would be a better guide to happiness than reason is, reason is not the fittest and best adapted thing for that purpose. So let us say that there is a teleological contradiction if we propose as a universal law that a certain organ, instinct, or action-type be used in a way that makes it less than the fittest and best device for achieving its natural purpose. For example, we will say that the "natural purpose" of promising is to establish trust and confidence and the cooperation which they make possible. False promising on a universal scale makes promising less than the best device for this natural purpose. The suicide case will work this way: self-love is for the natural purpose of self-preservation; in the system of nature that results from universalizing the maxim of committing suicide out of self-love, self-love would not be the instinct fittest and best adapted to the purpose of self-preservation. As Kant says, "One sees immediately a contradiction in a system of nature whose law would be to destroy life by the feeling whose special office is to impel the improvement of life" (G 422). So the standard set by the regulative principle of teleological judgment is not met.

An attraction of the Teleological Contradiction Interpretation is that it looks at first as if it is going to resolve the most difficult problem faced by the Logical Contradiction Interpretation, that of natural actions. Suicide, after all, is such an action. The reason that it is not hard to find a contradiction in willing the universal violation of a practice is that the practice has a standard purpose: universal violation causes people to find some other way to carry out this purpose, and that is why the practice is abandoned. The Teleological view promises to allow us to treat natural actions in a similar way, for it assigns these actions or the instincts that prompt them standard purposes like the ones practices have – namely natural purposes. Of course it is true that a natural action or instinct, unlike a practice, will survive its universal abuse. But this is not a problem for the Teleological Contradiction Interpretation, for the defender of this view can say that the action or instinct will not, if universally misused, be best fitted for its purpose. That, not the existence of the action-type or instinct, is his criterion for establishing the contradiction.

But there is a difficulty with this solution to the problem of natural actions and with the proposed reading of the suicide case generally. It is that the suicide *himself* is not supposed to be able to will the teleological system based on the universalization of his maxim. Now it may be said that the suicide certainly cannot will the teleological system resulting from the universalization of his maxim, since, *qua* teleological system, it has a contradiction in it (an instinct not best adapted to its purpose). But this is a curiously abstract way to make a case against suicide. The contradiction in the teleological system is, after all, that a mechanism designed for the protection of life is malfunctioning. But the suicide doesn't want the mechanism to function well in his own case, and he may be indifferent about other cases. So neither his own purpose nor anything else commits him to the purpose. So if Kant's point were that the suicide cannot will the teleological system in question because *qua* teleological system it has a contradiction in it, Kant would simply be committed to the view that a rational being as such wills a well-functioning teleological system, regardless of whether he wills the purposes that it serves. But then it is hard to see how the argument can go through. This instinct would be malfunctioning with regard to *this* purpose, but nothing prevents the suicide from willing that both the instinct and its purpose be scrapped.

[. . .]

[A] problem shows up in Paton's analysis of the false promising case. He reads the Teleological Contradiction Interpretation into the promising case by suggesting that the purpose of promises is to produce trust and mutual confidence; false promises destroy trust and therefore universalization makes the purpose of promising impossible. Paton comments:

> What Kant says is true enough so far as it goes, but it does not offer a satisfactory basis for moral judgment unless we make the further assumption that the keeping of such promises and the mutual confidence thereby aroused are essential factors in the systematic harmony of human purposes[6]

[. . .] On either Paton's or the simple view, the teleological analysis requires a commitment to specific purposes: either purposes of nature (like the preservation of life in the suicide example) or purposes required for the systematic harmony of human purposes. The trouble with bringing in teleological considerations in order to assign these purposes to natural as well as conventional actions is that such purposes may have nothing to do with what the agent wants or ought rationally to want, or even with what any human being wants. Unless we can show that the agent is committed to the purpose, it is possible to say that the system can do without the teleological arrangement because it can do without the purpose.

The Practical Contradiction Interpretation, which appeals to thwarting of the agent's *own* purpose in formulating the maxim in the first place, will solve this problem.

III   The Practical Contradiction Interpretation

According to the Practical Contradiction Interpretation of the contradiction in conception test, the contradiction that is involved in the universalization of an immoral maxim is that the agent would be unable to act on the maxim in a world in which it were universalized so as to achieve his own purpose – that is, the purpose that is specified in the maxim. Since he wills to act on his maxim, this means that his purpose will be frustrated. If this interpretation is correct, then it is essential that in testing maxims of actions the purpose always be included in the formulation of the maxim. It is what happens to the purpose that is the key to the contradiction.

The test is carried out by imagining, in effect, that the action you propose to perform in order to carry out your purpose is the standard procedure for carrying out that purpose. What the test shows to be forbidden are just those actions whose efficacy in achieving their purposes depends upon their being exceptional. If the action no longer works as a way of achieving the purpose in question when it is universalized, then it is an action of this kind. Intuitively speaking, the test reveals unfairness, deception, and cheating. For instance, in the false promising case, the difficulty is that the man's end – getting the money – cannot be achieved by his means – making a false promise – in the world of the universalized maxim. The efficacy of the false promise as a means of securing the money depends on the fact that not everyone uses promises this way. Promises are efficacious in securing loans only because they are believed, and they are believed only if they are normally true. Since promising is the means he proposes to use, his end would not be achieved at all, but frustrated. In willing the world of the universalized maxim and – as Kant says – *at the same time* – willing the maxim itself, the man wills the frustration of his own end. As Kant says, the man "would make the promise itself and the end to be accomplished by it impossible" (G 422). This way of looking at the test also shows us one sense in which violations of the universal law test imply that you are using others as mere means. If you do something that only works because most people do not do it, their actions are making your action work. In the false promising case, other people's honesty makes your deceit effective.

Practical contradictions

Even proponents of this view, or versions of it, sometimes describe a practical contradiction as being a contradiction in a weaker sense than a theoretical one. This is not correct. Kant's ethics is based on the idea that there is a specifically practical employment of reason, which is not the same as an application of theoretical reason. It includes a specifically practical sense of "contradiction." The argument that shows this seems to me to be an almost decisive one in favor of this interpretation.

After laying out the three kinds of imperatives, Kant tells us that hypothetical imperatives are analytic. This means, ordinarily, two things: the relation expressed is one of conceptual containment, and the opposite or denial is a flat contradiction. Intuitively, we can see why failing to conform your conduct to relevant hypothetical imperatives, and thus frustrating your own purposes, is contradictory. Someone who wills an end, knows that it will be brought about by a certain necessary and available means, has no extraneous reason not to use that means, and yet is utterly unmoved to take it, is irrational in a way that does seem to amount to contradiction. We might capture the sense that there is a contradiction here by saying that such a person is acting as if she both did and didn't will the end. But Kant can do better than that, for he also explains the containment relation that makes the hypothetical imperative analytic:

> Whoever wills the end, so far as reason has decisive influence on his action, wills also the indispensably necessary means to it that lie in his power. This proposition, in what concerns the will, is analytical; for, in willing the object as my effect, my causality as an acting cause, i.e., the use of means, is already thought, and the imperative derives the concept of necessary actions to this end from the concept of willing this end. (G 417)

[. . .] In the argument above, Kant's point is this: willing is regarding yourself as the cause of the end in question – as the one who will bring it about. This distinguishes willing from mere wanting or wishing or desiring. Conceiving yourself as a cause of the end is conceiving yourself as setting off a causal chain that will result in the production of the end. It is conceiving yourself as using the available causal connections. But the available causal connections are, by definition, "means." So, willing the end contains, or insofar as you are rational is already, willing the means. It is because this is a "containment" relation – in the logic of practical reason – that acting against the hypothetical imperative is contradictory. This gives us a sense of practical contradiction – of contradiction in the will – which is different from but not weaker than "theoretical" contradiction.

Since this is the sort of contradiction implied by the analyticity of hypothetical imperatives, it is reasonable to think that this will be the sort of contradiction employed in the categorical imperative tests. On the Practical Contradiction Interpretation, such a contradiction in the universalization of an immoral maxim is exactly what the test shows. In the world of the universalized maxim, the *hypothetical* imperative from which the false promiser constructs his maxim is no longer true. It was "if you want some ready cash, you ought to make a false promise." But at the same time that he employs this hypothetical imperative in constructing his maxim, he wills its falsification, by willing a state of affairs (the world of the universalized maxim) in which it will be false. In that world, false promising is not a means to getting ready cash. Kant, therefore, not only has a specifically practical sense of "contradiction," but should be seen as employing it in his contradiction tests.

[. . .]

Contradictions in conception and in the will

Another advantage of this view is that it should enable us to employ the same sense of contradiction in interpreting the two contradiction tests, and yet still to distinguish between them. Consider what the other two interpretations say about this question. The Logical

Contradiction Interpretation forces us to look for a different sort of contradiction altogether for the contradiction in the will test, since Kant is explicit about the fact that no logical inconceivability is involved there. The Logical Contradiction Interpretation seems initially to have the virtue that it involves no presuppositions about rationality that are not completely uncontroversial. The contradiction it identifies in universalizing immoral maxims is of a familiar kind. But this advantage is lost if we must use different presuppositions in order to understand the contradiction in the will test. Often, proponents of the Logical Contradiction Interpretation for the contradictions in conception end up with something like a utilitarian or a teleological view about contradictions in the will. But the utilitarian reading has the same problem for the second test as it does for the first: it presupposes a morality-laden conception of rationality. The Teleological Contradiction Interpretation, on the other hand, does not seem to allow for a very well-defined distinction between the two tests. I suppose one may say that in the case of a contradiction in conception, some specific instinct or action is found not to be best adapted to its particular purpose; and in the case of a contradiction in the will, we lose some positive good needed for a teleological system, or for the systematic harmony of human purposes. But it is not really obvious that these are distinct. Recall that Paton could not find a contradiction in the false promising case without assuming that promises are needed for the harmony of human purposes. This problem tends to collapse the two tests.

Now consider the Practical Contradiction Interpretation. If a thwarted purpose is a practical contradiction, we must understand the contradiction in the will test this way: we must find some purpose or purposes which belong essentially to the will, and in the world where maxims that fail these tests are universal law, these essential purposes will be thwarted, because the means of achieving them will be unavailable. Examples of purposes that might be thought to be essential to the will are its general effectiveness in the pursuit of its ends, and its freedom to adopt and pursue new ends. The arguments for self-development

and mutual aid will then be that without the development of human talents and powers and the resources of mutual cooperation, the will's effectiveness and freedom would be thwarted. This is of course just a sketch. Exactly which purposes are essential to the will and how they can be shown to be so is a topic in its own right, which I will not pursue further here. The point is that the Practical Contradiction Interpretation gives a better account of the relation between the two tests than either of the others. The difference between the two tests will not lie in the use of a different kind of contradiction, as it does in the Logical Contradiction Interpretation. And yet there will be a difference. The purpose thwarted in the case of a maxim that fails the contradiction in the conception test is *the one in the maxim itself,* and so the contradiction can be said to be *in* the universalized maxim. The purpose thwarted in the case of the contradiction in the will test is not one that is in the maxim,[7] but one that is essential to the will.

The problem of natural actions

The Practical Contradiction Interpretation, like the Logical, works especially well with respect to wrong actions which are conventional. But the reason why it works is slightly different. On the Logical Contradiction Interpretation, the contradiction arises because the agent wills to engage in a conventional action, but he also wills a state of affairs in which that kind of action will no longer *exist.* On the Practical Contradiction Interpretation, the contradiction arises because the agent wills to engage in a conventional action, but he also wills a state of affairs in which the action will no longer *work.* When we are dealing with an action that falls under a practice, the two views are readily confused, because the reason the action no longer works is *because* it no longer exists. But on the Practical Contradiction Interpretation it is the failure of efficacy, not the non-existence, that really matters.

This gives rise to the possibility that with the Practical Contradiction Interpretation we will be able to derive at least some of our duties of omission with respect to natural actions. Natural actions are not going to cease to exist if used wrongly, but their efficacy for some purposes may depend on their exceptional use. A great deal depends here on what the purpose is taken to be and how it is described. One case that is borderline between natural and conventional is stealing. That might seem wholly conventional, since property is a practice, but it is difficult to imagine an economic system in which the means of production and action were not guaranteed to the use of particular persons at particular times. And any violation of these guaranteed assignments would be "stealing." Now if the purpose of stealing is to acquire something for your personal use or possession – to get something you want when you want it – and you imagine that anyone in your situation – anyone who wants something not assigned to him – steals it, as a standard procedure – then you see that under these conditions it is quite impossible to acquire something for your use or possession, to have it when you want it. The idea here is that what the thief really wants is to make something his property, to have some *guarantee* that he will have it when he wants it. His purpose is therefore thwarted if his maxim is universalized.

That case is borderline, but a similar analysis might apply to wholly natural acts. Here is a silly example. Suppose you are second in line for a job, and are considering murder as a way of dealing with your more successful rival. Can this be universalized? Killing is a natural act, not a conventional one. We cannot say that if this sort of action is abused the practice will die out, for that makes no sense whatever. Nor can we say that any amount or kind of use of killing will destroy its efficacy in achieving its purpose *if* we specify that purpose simply as that of getting someone dead. So here the test will only work if the purpose is specified differently. We must say that the purpose is that of securing a job, and we must emphasize the fact that if anyone else wants this job, or any job you hold, universalization makes you the victim. Now, it may seem that the purpose that is thwarted by universalization – that of staying alive – is not the same as the purpose in your maxim – that of securing the job. This would be bad. It is the fact that it is the purpose in the maxim that gets thwarted in the world of the

universalized maxim that enables us to carry out the test without any extraneous information about the agent's desires and purposes. If it is some other, contingent, purpose that gets thwarted, then it looks as if the test (i) requires empirical information about what other purposes people have and (ii) functions idiosyncratically, giving different results to people with different desires. These are both conclusions the Kantian wants to avoid. We shall avoid them here by pointing out that this is not a case of an extraneous end being thwarted. Staying alive matters in this example because it is a necessary condition of having the job.

That might seem like a silly thing to say in this case, but it is an application of a point which is not in general silly at all. In *Utilitarianism*, Mill argues that justice is specifically concerned with a special object of human interest – that of security. Security is not merely one good thing among others, but to put it in Kantian language, a condition of the goodness of anything else:

> . . . but security no human being can possibly do without; on it we depend for all our immunity from evil, and for the whole value of all and every good, beyond the passing moment, since nothing but the gratification of the instant could be of any worth to us, if we could be deprived of anything the next instant by whoever was momentarily stronger than ourselves.[8]

The Kantian may avail himself of this insight. To want something is to want to be secure in the possession of it. The use of violent natural means for achieving ends cannot be universalized because that would leave us insecure in the possession of these goods, and without that security these goods are no good to us at all. So, if we include as part of the purpose that the agent wants to be secure in the possession of the end, we can get a practical contradiction in the universalization of violent methods. And in fact, Kant's argument in the *Metaphysical Principles of Justice* about why there must be proprietary rights is not very different from Mill's: it is that we need to be secure in the possession of certain sorts of goods in order to successfully make use of them (MPJ 246ff.).

The method of dealing with natural acts which I have just suggested focuses on the question whether you could really achieve your purpose – with everything that purpose involves (i.e., security in its possession) in a world where your action was the universal method of achieving that purpose. Another way to approach this problem is to consider whether the social conditions that allow violence to work as a method of achieving this purpose would exist if it were the universal method. It is true that natural laws are all that is needed to make violent methods yield their natural effects, but more is needed to make them yield their social effects. For example, the simplest way of making the argument against cheating on an entrance examination is to point out that if everyone did this the entrance examination would cease to be used as a criterion for selection. Since a lot of incompetent people would get in, it would be found impracticable and some other method would be chosen. ("Everyone would laugh at entrance examinations as vain pretenses.") Placing people in jobs is like this: it is something for which there must be a method, and if one method were universally abused, another, not liable to that abuse, would be found. Now if murder to get a job were universally practiced, the best candidates would not get the jobs. So whatever it is about the old selection process that makes this possible would be changed. Perhaps no one would be told who the candidates were, or people would even keep it a secret what jobs they held. Again, the argument sounds silly in this case but is meant to bring out something that is not silly. Cheating could not be the first or standard procedure for getting into an educational program. It is essentially parasitic on the existence of another method. Violence, in many cases, also has this parasitic nature when it is a way of achieving a purpose in society.

The Practical Contradiction Interpretation can therefore handle some cases of natural actions. A harder kind of case would be something like killing for revenge, or out of hatred. In these cases it is not some enduring condition that the agent wants to achieved – he wants the immediate result – so the security consideration will not help us here. These grim kinds

of cases are managed without difficulty when using the Formula of Humanity, but it will be difficult to find any contradiction of the sort needed here. And this problem applies to the suicide case as well. On the Practical Contradiction Interpretation we cannot get an analysis of that case, for the suicide's purpose, if it is release from his own misery, will not be thwarted by universal practice. There is an important parallel to this problem. Kant's theory is least helpful and least plausible when one is dealing with a case where other people around the agent have already introduced evil into the situation. His debate with Benjamin Constant about whether you may lie to the murderer whose victim is hidden in your house, and his insistence that there is never a right to revolution, are infamous examples of cases in which his view seems to forbid us to try to prevent or to set right the wrongs committed by others. I believe that there is a similar sort of difficulty in making out what Kant is to say about cases where something has gone wrong inside, where the problem is not the selfish pursuit of an ordinary purpose, but a diseased purpose. I do not say that Kant is unable to give us an account of these cases. But the kind of case around which the view is framed, and which it handles best, is the temptation to make oneself an exception: selfishness, meanness, advantage-taking, and disregard for the rights of others. It is this sort of thing, not violent crimes born of despair or illness, that serves as Kant's model of immoral conduct. I do not think we can fault him on this, for this and not the other is the sort of evil that most people are tempted by in their everyday lives.

Conclusion

It is conceivable that Kant did not perceive the differences among these three readings, and that this is why language supporting all of them can be found in his texts. In a certain kind of case, the three readings are very close. Where the immoral action involves the abuse of a practice, the Logical Contradiction Interpretation says you cannot universalize because the practice will not exist and the action will be inconceivable; the Teleological Contradiction

Interpretation says you cannot universalize because the practice will then not be best suited for what in a teleological system would be its natural purpose; and the Practical Contradiction Interpretation says you cannot universalize because if the practice disappears it will of course no longer be efficacious in producing your purpose. These three analyses are very close, and for this kind of case the differences are insignificant. It is only when we begin to consider the problems created by natural actions [. . .] and the need to extend our analysis in the right way to the contradiction in the will test that differences emerge. In my view, the Practical Contradiction Interpretation deals with these problems better than the other two, although not always with complete success.

The best argument for it, however, is that it employs the sense of contradiction which Kant identifies in his analysis of the hypothetical imperative. Each interpretation must presuppose some notion of rationality in determining whether a rational being can will the universalization of a maxim at the same time as that maxim without contradiction. The Logical Contradiction view works with a notion of contradiction indistinguishable from that of theoretical rationality and this is a great advantage. But this advantage is lost when we turn to contradictions in the will, which then require another interpretation. The Teleological Contradiction view works with a rather rich notion of rationality as aiming at a harmony of purposes. I think on Kant's view pure reason does aim at a harmony of purposes, but that only morality tells us how that is to be achieved. We cannot reason morally from that idea. The Practical Contradiction view uses a specifically practical notion of rationality and of contradiction which springs from the notion of the will as a causality. This is not a morality-laden notion of rationality, for on Kant's view this notion is needed to explain *instrumental* rationality.

Yet the same notion will also be employed in explaining why the moral law applies to us. The Practical Contradiction Interpretation allows us to sketch an explanation, in terms of autonomy, of why conformity to the Formula of Universal Law is a requirement of reason. Start with a parallel to theoretical reasoning: as a rational being, you may take the connection between two events to be a causal one. But this connection must always hold – must hold universally – if the cause you have identified is indeed *sufficient* to produce that effect. Only in this case is what you have identified a law. The rational will, regarding itself as a causality, models its conception of a law on a causal law. As a rational being you may take the connection between a purpose you hold and an action that would promote it to be a reason for you to perform the action. But this connection must be universalizable *if the reason is sufficient*. Only in this case have you identified a law. If universalization would destroy the connection between action and purpose, the purpose is not a sufficient reason for the action. This is how, on the Practical Contradiction Interpretation, the contradiction in conception test shows an immoral maxim to be unfit to be an objective practical law. As an autonomous rational being, you must act on your conception of a law. This is why autonomy requires comformity to the Formula of Universal Law.

Notes

1. John Stuart Mill, *Utilitarianism*, p. 4.
2. Dietrichson, "Kant's Criteria of Universalizability," p. 188.
3. John Rawls, "Two Concepts of Rules."
4. H. J. Paton, *The Categorical Imperative*, pp. 146–57.
5. Paton, *The Categorical Imperative*, p. 151.
6. Paton, *The Categorical Imperative*, p. 153.
7. In Kant's first set of examples of the contradiction in the will test in the *Groundwork*, there is no purpose given in the maxim. But even if we assigned purposes to the agents who adopt these maxims the point will hold. The man who does not develop his talents and powers presumably has the purpose of taking his ease. But the purpose that is thwarted is the development of his rational nature.
8. Mill, *Utilitarianism*, p. 53.

Abbreviations for Kant's Works

C2 *Critique of Practical Reason* (1788), trans. Lewis White Beck. The Library of Liberal Arts, 1956. Formerly published in Indianapolis by Bobbs-Merrill, now published in New York by Macmillan. Hereinafter referred to simply as Library of Liberal Arts. (V)

G *Groundwork of the Metaphysics of Morals* (1785), trans. Lewis White Beck as *Foundations of the Metaphysics of Morals*. Library of Liberal Arts, 1959. (VI)

MPJ *The Metaphysical Principles of Justice* (1797), trans. John Ladd. Library of Liberal Arts, 1965. (VI)

MPV *The Metaphysical Principles of Virtue* (1797), trans. James Ellington in *Immanuel Kant: Ethical Philosophy*, cited above. (VI)

R *Religion within the Limits of Reason Alone* (1793), trans. Theodore M. Greene and Hoyt H. Hudson. La Salle, Illinois: Open Court, 1934. Rpt. New York: Harper Torchbooks, 1960. (VI)

CHAPTER 57

Kantian Approaches to Some Famine Problems

ONORA O'NEILL

The second moral theory whose scope and determinacy in dealing with famine problems I shall consider was developed by the German philosopher Immanuel Kant (1724–1804). First I shall offer a simplified version of Kantian ethics [...] I shall set out some of its implications for action toward those who are hungry and at risk of famine, and then I shall summarize some differences between utilitarian and Kantian ethics.

A Simplified Account of Kant's Ethics

Kant's theory is frequently and misleadingly assimilated to theories of human rights. It is, in fact, a theory of human obligations; therefore it is wider in scope than a theory of human rights. (Not all obligations have corresponding rights.) Kant does not, however, try to generate a set of precise rules defining human obligations in all possible circumstances; instead, he attempts to provide a set of *principles of obligation* that can be used as the starting points for moral reasoning in actual contexts of action. The primary focus of Kantian ethics is, then, on *action* rather than either *results*, as

Onora O'Neill, "Kantian Approaches to Some Famine Problems," pp. 258–70 from Tom Regan (ed.), *Matters of Life and Death: New Introductory Essays in Moral Philosophy*, Third Edition. New York: McGraw-Hill, 1980.

in utilitarian thinking, or *entitlements*, as in theories that make human rights their fundamental category. Morality requires action of certain sorts. But to know *what* sort of action is required (or forbidden) in which circumstances, we should not look just at the expected results of action or at others' supposed entitlements but, in the first instance, at the nature of the proposed actions themselves.

When we engage in moral reasoning, we often need go no further than to refer to some quite specific principle or tradition. We may say to one another, or to ourselves, things like "It would be hypocritical to pretend that our good fortune is achieved without harm to the Third World" or "Redistributive taxation shouldn't cross national boundaries." But when these specific claims are challenged, we may find ourselves pushed to justify or reject or modify them. Such moral debate, on Kant's account, rests on appeals to what he calls the *Supreme Principle of Morality*, which can (he thinks) be used to work out more specific principles of obligation. This principle, the famous Categorical Imperative, plays the same role in Kantian thinking that the Greatest Happiness Principle plays in utilitarian thought.

A second reason why Kant's moral thought often appears difficult is that he offers a number of different versions of this principle, which he claims are equivalent but which look very different. A straightforward way in which to simplify Kantian moral thought is to concentrate on just one of these formulations of the Categorical Imperative. For present purposes I shall choose the version to which he gives the sonorous name, *The Formula of the End in Itself.*

The Formula of the End in Itself

The Formula of the End in Itself runs as follows:

> Act in such a way that you always treat humanity, whether in your own person or in the person of any other, never simply as a means but always at the same time as an end.

To understand this principle we need in the first place to understand what Kant means by the term 'maxim'. The maxim of an act or policy or activity is the *underlying principle* of the act, policy, or activity, by which other, more superficial aspects of action are guided. Very often interpretations of Kant have supposed that maxims can only be the (underlying) intentions of individual human agents. If that were the case it would limit the usefulness of Kantian modes of moral thought in dealing with world hunger and famine problems. For it is clear enough that individual action (while often important) cannot deal with all the problems of Third World poverty. A moral theory that addresses *only* individual actors does not have adequate scope for discussing famine problems. As we have seen, one of the main attractions of utilitarianism as an approach to Third World poverty is that its scope is so broad: it can be applied with equal appropriateness to the practical deliberations of individuals, of institutions and groups, and even of nation states and international agencies. Kantian ethical thinking can be interpreted (though it usually isn't) to have equally broad scope.

Since maxims are *underlying* principles of action, they may not always be obvious either to the individuals or institutions whose maxims they are, or to others. We can determine what the underlying principles of some activity or institution are only by seeing the patterns made by various more superficial

aspects of acts, policies, and activities. Only those principles that would generate that pattern of activity are maxims of action. Sometimes more than one principle might lie behind a given pattern of activity, and we may be unsure what the maxim of the act was. For example, we might wonder (as Kant does) how to tell whether somebody gives change accurately only out of concern to have an honest reputation or whether he or she would do so anyhow. In such cases we can sometimes set up an "isolation test" – for example, a situation in which it would be open to somebody to be dishonest without any chance of a damaged reputation. But quite often we can't set up any such situation and may be to some extent unsure which maxim lies behind a given act. Usually we have to rely on whatever individual actors tell us about their maxims of action and on what policymakers or social scientists may tell us about the underlying principles of institutional or group action. What they tell us may well be mistaken. While mistakes can be reduced by care and thoughtfulness, there is no guarantee that we can always work out which maxim of action should be scrutinized for purposes of judging what others do. On the other hand, there is no problem when we are trying to guide our own action: if we can find out what duty demands, we can try to meet those demands.

It is helpful to think of some examples of maxims that might be used to guide action in contexts where poverty and the risk of famine are issues. Somebody who contributes to famine-relief work or advocates development might have an underlying principle such as, "Try to help reduce the risk or severity of world hunger." This commitment might be reflected in varied surface action in varied situations. In one context a gift of money might be relevant; in another some political activity such as lobbying for or against certain types of aid and trade might express the same underlying commitment. Sometimes superficial aspects of action may seem at variance with the underlying maxim they in fact express. For example, if there is reason to think that indiscriminate food aid damages the agricultural economy of the area to which food is given, then the maxim of seeking to relieve hunger might be expressed in action aimed at *limiting* the extent of food aid. More lavish use of food aid might *seem* to treat the needy more generously, but if in fact it will damage their medium- or long-term economic prospects, then it is not (contrary to superficial appearances) aimed at improving and securing their access to subsistence. On a Kantian theory, the basis for judging action should be its *fundamental* principle or policy, and superficially similar acts may be judged morally very different. Regulating food aid in order to drive up prices and profit from them is one matter; regulating food aid in order to enable local farmers to sell their crops and to stay in the business of growing food is quite another.

When we want to work out whether a proposed act or policy is morally required we should not, on Kant's view, try to find out whether it would produce more happiness than other available acts. Rather we should see whether the act or policy is required if we are to avoid acting on maxims that use others as mere means and act on maxims that treat others as ends in themselves. These two aspects of Kantian duty can each be spelled out and shown to have determinate implications for acts and policies that may affect the persistence of hunger and the risk and course of famines.

Using Others as Mere Means

We use others as *mere means* if what we do reflects some maxim *to which they could not in principle consent*. Kant does not suggest that there is anything wrong about using someone as a means. Evidently every cooperative scheme of action does this. A government that agrees to provide free or subsidized food to famine-relief agencies both uses and is used by the agencies; a peasant who sells food in a local market both uses and is used by those who buy the food. In such examples each party to the transaction can and does consent to take part in that transaction. Kant would say that the parties to such transactions use one another but do not use one another as *mere means*. Each party assumes that the other has its own maxims of action and is not just a thing or prop to be used or manipulated.

But there are other cases where one party to an arrangement or transaction not only uses the other but does so in ways that could only be done on the basis of a fundamental principle or maxim to which the other could not in principle consent. If, for example, a false promise is given, the party that accepts the promise is not just used but used as a mere means, because it is *impossible* for consent to be given to the fundamental principle or project of deception that must guide every false promise, whatever its surface character. Those who accept false promises *must* be kept ignorant of the underlying principle or maxim on which the "undertaking" is based. If this isn't kept concealed, the attempted promise will either be rejected or will not be a *false* promise at all. In false promising, the deceived party becomes, as it were, a prop or tool – a *mere means* – in the false promisor's scheme. Action based on any such maxim of deception would be wrong in Kantian terms, whether it is a matter of a breach of treaty obligations, of contractual undertakings, or of accepted and relied upon modes of interaction. Maxims of deception *standardly* use others as mere means, and acts that could only be based on such maxims are unjust.

Other standard ways of using others as mere means is by violence or coercion. Here too victims have no possibility of refusing what is done to them. If a rich or powerful landowner or nation destroys a poorer or more vulnerable person, group, or nation or threatens some intolerable difficulty unless a concession is made, the more vulnerable party is denied a genuine choice between consent and dissent. While the boundary that divides violence and coercion from mere bargaining and negotiation varies and is therefore often hard to discern, we have no doubt about the clearer cases. Maxims of violence destroy or damage agents or their capabilities. Maxims of coercion may threaten physical force, seizure of possessions, destruction of opportunities, or any other harm that the coerced party is thought to be unable to absorb without grave injury or danger. For example, a grain dealer in a Third World village who threatens not to make or renew an indispensable loan without which survival until the next harvest would be impossible, unless he is sold the current crop at pitifully low prices, uses the peasant as mere means. The peasant does not have the possibility of genuinely consenting to the "offer he can't refuse." In this way the outward form of some coercive transactions may *look* like ordinary commercial dealings: but we know very well that some action that is superficially of this sort is based on maxims of coercion. To avoid coercion, action must be governed by maxims that the other party can choose to refuse and is not forced to accept. The more vulnerable the other party in any transaction or negotiation, the less that party's scope for refusal, and the more demanding it is likely to be to ensure that action is noncoercive.

In Kant's view, acts done on maxims that endanger, coerce, or deceive others, and thus cannot in principle have the consent of those others, are wrong. When individuals, institutions, or nation states act in ways that can only be based on such maxims, they fail in their duty. They treat the parties who are either deceived or coerced unjustly. To avoid unjust action it is not enough to observe the outward forms of free agreement, cooperation, and market disciplines; it is also essential to see that the weaker party to any arrangement has a genuine option to refuse the fundamental character of the proposal.

Treating Others as Ends in Themselves

For Kant, as for utilitarians, justice is only one part of duty. We may fail in our duty, even when we don't use anyone as mere means, if we fail to treat others as "ends in themselves." To treat others as ends in themselves we must not only avoid using them as mere means but also treat them as rational and autonomous beings with their own maxims. In doing so we must also remember that (as Kant repeatedly stressed, but later Kantians have often forgotten) human beings are *finite* rational beings in several ways. First, human beings are not ideal rational calculators. We *standardly* have neither a complete list of the actions possible in a given situation nor more than a partial view of their likely consequences. In addition, abilities to assess and to use available information are usually quite limited. Second, these cognitive

limitations are *standardly* complemented by limited autonomy. Human action is limited not only by various sorts of physical barrier and inability but by further sorts of (mutual or asymmetrical) *dependence*. To treat one another as ends in themselves such beings have to base their action on principles that do not undermine but rather sustain and extend one another's capacities for autonomous action. A central requirement for doing so is to share and support one another's ends and activities to some extent. Since finite rational beings cannot generally achieve their aims without some help and support from others, a general refusal of help and support amounts to failure to treat others as rational and autonomous beings, that is, as ends in themselves. Hence Kantian principles require us not only to act justly, that is, in accordance with maxims that don't injure, coerce, or deceive others, but also to avoid manipulation and to lend some support to others' plans and activities. Since hunger, great poverty, and powerlessness all undercut the possibility of autonomous action, and the requirement of treating others as ends in themselves demands that Kantians standardly act to support the possibility of autonomous action where it is most vulnerable, Kantians are required to do what they can to avert, reduce, and remedy hunger. They cannot of course do everything to avert hunger: but they may not do nothing.

Justice and Beneficence in Kant's Thought

Kant is often thought to hold that justice is morally required, but beneficence is morally less important. He does indeed, like Mill, speak of justice as a *perfect duty* and of beneficence as an *imperfect duty*. But he does not mean by this that beneficence is any less a duty; rather, he holds that it has (unlike justice) to be selective. We cannot share or even support *all* others' maxims *all* of the time. Hence support for others' autonomy is always selective. By contrast we can make all action and institutions conform fundamentally to standards of nondeception and noncoercion. Kant's understanding of the distinction between perfect and imperfect duties differs from Mill's. In a Kantian perspective justice is more than the core of beneficence, as in Mill's theory, and beneficence isn't just an attractive but optional moral embellishment of just arrangements (as tends to be assumed in most theories that take human rights as fundamental).

Justice to the Vulnerable in Kantian Thinking

For Kantians, justice requires action that conforms (at least outwardly) to what could be done in a given situation while acting on maxims that use nobody. Since anyone hungry or destitute is more than usually vulnerable to deception, violence, and coercion, the possibilities and temptations to injustice are then especially strong. They are often strongest for those who are nearest to acute poverty and hunger, so could (if they chose) exploit others' need.

Examples are easily suggested. I shall begin with some situations that might arise for somebody who happened to be part of a famine-stricken population. Where shortage of food is being dealt with by a reasonably fair rationing scheme, any mode of cheating to get more than one's allocated share involves using some others and is unjust. Equally, taking advantage of others' desperation to profiteer – for example, selling food at colossal prices or making loans on the security of others' future livelihood, when these are "offers they can't refuse" – constitutes coercion, uses others as mere means, and so is unjust. Transactions that have the outward form of normal commercial dealings may be coercive when one party is desperate. Equally, forms of corruption that work by deception – such as bribing officials to gain special benefits from development schemes, or deceiving others about these entitlements – use others unjustly. Such requirements are far from trivial and are frequently violated in hard times; acting justly in such conditions may involve risking one's own life and livelihood and may require the greatest courage.

It is not so immediately obvious what justice, Kantianly conceived, requires of agents and agencies who are remote from destitution.

Might it not be sufficient to argue that those of us fortunate enough to live in the developed world are far from famine and destitution, so if we do nothing but go about our usual business will successfully avoid injustice to the destitute? This conclusion has often been reached by those who take an abstract view of rationality and forget the limits of human rationality and autonomy. To such people it seems that there is nothing more to just action than noninterference with others. But once we remember the limitations of human rationality and autonomy, and the particular ways in which they are limited for those living close to the margins of subsistence, we can see that mere "noninterfering" conformity to ordinary standards of commercial honesty and political bargaining is not enough for justice toward the destitute. If the demands of the powerful constitute "offers that cannot be refused" by the government or by the citizens of a poor country, or if the concessions required for investment by a transnational corporation or a development project reflect the desperation of recipients rather than an appropriate contribution to the project, then (however benevolent the motives of some parties) the weaker party to such agreements is used by the stronger.

In the earlier days of European colonial penetration of the now underdeveloped world it was evident enough that some of the ways in which "agreements" were made with native peoples were in fact violent, deceptive, or coercive – or all three. "Sales" of land by those who had no grasp of market practices and "cession of sovereignty" by those whose forms of life were prepolitical constitute only spurious consent to the agreements struck. But it is not only in these original forms of bargaining between powerful and powerless that injustice is frequent. There are many contemporary examples. For example, if capital investment in a poorer country requires the receiving country or some of its institutions or citizens to contribute disproportionately to the maintenance of a developed, urban "enclave" economy that offers little local employment but lavish standards of life for a small number of (possibly expatriate) "experts," while guaranteeing long-term exemption from local taxation for the investors, then we may doubt that the agreement could have been struck without the element of coercion provided by the desperation of the weaker party. Often enough the coercers in such cases are members of the local as well as the international elite. Or if a trade agreement extracts political advantages (such as military bases) that are incompatible with the fundamental political interests of the country concerned, we may judge that at least some leaders of that country have been "bought" in a sense that is not consonant with ordinary commercial practice.

Even when the actions of those who are party to an agreement don't reflect a fundamental principle of violence, coercion, or deception, the agreement may alter the life circumstances and prospects of third parties in ways to which they patently could not have not consented. For example, a system of food aid and imports agreed upon by the government of a Third World country and certain developed states or international agencies may give the elite of that Third World country access to subsidized grain. If that grain is then used to control the urban population and also produces destitution among peasants (who used to grow food for that urban population), then those who are newly destitute probably have not been offered any opening or possibility of refusing their new and worsened conditions of life. If a policy is imposed, those affected *cannot* have been given a chance to refuse it: had the chance been there, they would either have assented (and so the policy would not have been *imposed*) or refused (and so proceeding with the policy would have been evidently coercive), or they would have been able to renegotiate the terms of trade.

Beneficence to the Vulnerable in Kantian Thinking

In Kantian moral reasoning, the basis for beneficent action is that without it we fail to treat others of limited rationality and autonomy as ends in themselves. This is not to say that Kantian beneficence won't make others happier, for it will do so whenever they would be happier if (more) capable of autonomous action, but that happiness secured by purely

paternalistic means, or at the cost (for example) of manipulating others' desires, will not count as beneficent in the Kantian picture. Clearly the vulnerable position of those who lack the very means of life, and their severely curtailed possibilities for autonomous action, offer many different ways in which it might be possible for others to act beneficently. Where the means of life are meager, almost any material or organizational advance may help extend possibilities for autonomy. Individual or institutional action that aims to advance economic or social development can proceed on many routes. The provision of clean water, of improved agricultural techniques, of better grain storage systems, or of adequate means of local transport may all help transform material prospects. Equally, help in the development of new forms of social organization – whether peasant self-help groups, urban cooperatives, medical and contraceptive services, or improvements in education or in the position of women – may help to extend possibilities for autonomous action. While the central core of such development projects will be requirements of justice, their full development will also demand concern to treat others as ends in themselves, by paying attention to their particular needs and desires. Kantian thinking does not provide a means by which all possible ways of treating others as ends in themselves could be listed and ranked. But where some activity helps secure possibilities for autonomous action for more people, or is likely to achieve a permanent improvement in the position of the most vulnerable, or is one that can be done with more reliable success, this provides reason for furthering that way of treating others as ends.

Clearly the alleviation of need must rank far ahead of the furthering of happiness in other ways in the Kantian picture. I might make my friends very happy by throwing extravagant parties: but this would probably not increase anybody's possibility for autonomous action to any great extent. But the sorts of development-oriented changes that have just been mentioned may *transform* the possibilities for action of some. Since hunger and the risk of famine are always and evidently highly damaging to human autonomy, any action that helps avoid or reduce famine must have a strong claim on any Kantian who is thinking through what beneficence requires. Depending on circumstances, such action may have to take the form of individual contribution to famine relief and development organizations, of individual or collective effort to influence the trade and aid policies of developed countries, or of attempts to influence the activities of those Third World elites for whom development does not seem to be an urgent priority. Some approaches can best be undertaken by private citizens of developed countries by way of lobbying, publicity, and education; others are best approached by those who work for governments, international agencies, or transnational corporations, who can "work from within" to influence the decisions and policies of these institutions. Perhaps the most dramatic possibilities to act for a just or an unjust, a beneficent or selfish future belongs to those who hold positions of power or influence within the Third World. But wherever we find ourselves, our duties are not, on the Kantian picture, limited to those close at hand. Duties of justice arise whenever there is some involvement between parties – and in the modern world this is never wholly lacking. Duties of beneficence arise whenever destitution puts the possibility of autonomous action in question for the more vulnerable. When famines were not only far away, but nothing could be done to relieve them, beneficence or charity legitimately began – and stayed – near home. In an interconnected world, the moral significance of distance has shrunk, and we may be able to affect the capacities for autonomous action of those who are far away.

The Scope of Kantian Deliberations about Hunger and Famine

In many ways Kantian moral reasoning is less ambitious than utilitarian moral reasoning. It does not propose a process of moral reasoning that can (in principle) rank *all* possible actions or all possible institutional arrangements from the happiness-maximizing "right" action or institution downward. It aims rather to offer a pattern of reasoning by which we can identify

whether *proposed action or institutional arrangements* would be just or unjust, beneficent or lacking in beneficence. While *some* knowledge of causal connections is needed for Kantian reasoning, it is far less sensitive than is utilitarian reasoning to gaps in our causal knowledge. It may therefore help us reach conclusions that are broadly accurate even if they are imprecise. The conclusions reached about particular proposals for action or about institutional arrangements will not hold for all time, but be relevant for the contexts for which action is proposed. For example, if it is judged that some institution – say, the World Bank – provides, under present circumstances, a just approach to certain development problems, it will not follow that under all other circumstances such an institution would be part of a just approach. There may be other institutional arrangements that are also just; and there may be other circumstances under which the institutional structure of the World Bank would be shown to be in some ways unjust.

These points show us that Kantian deliberations about hunger can lead only to conclusions that are useful in determinate contexts. This, however, is standardly what we need to know for action, whether individual or institutional. We do not need to be able to generate a complete list of available actions in order to determine whether proposed lines of action are not unjust and whether any are beneficent. Kantian patterns of moral reasoning cannot be guaranteed to identify the optimal course of action in a situation. They provide methods neither for listing nor for ranking all possible proposals for action. But any line of action that is considered can be checked to see whether it is part of what justice and beneficence require – or of what they forbid.

The reason this pattern of reasoning will not show any action or arrangement of the most beneficent one available is that the Kantian picture of beneficence is less mathematically structured than the utilitarian one. It judges beneficence by its overall contribution to the prospects for human autonomy and not by the quantity of happiness expected to result. To the extent that the autonomous pursuit of goals is what Mill called "one of the principal ingredients of human happiness" (but only to that extent), the requirements of Kantian and of utilitarian beneficence will coincide. But whenever expected happiness is not a function of the scope for autonomous action, the two accounts of beneficent action diverge. For utilitarians, paternalistic imposition of, for example, certain forms of aid and development assistance need not be wrong and may even be required. But for Kantians, who think that beneficence should secure others' possibilities for autonomous action, the case for paternalistic imposition of aid or development projects without the recipients' involvement must always be questionable.

In terms of some categories in which development projects are discussed, utilitarian reasoning may well endorse "top-down" aid and development projects that override whatever capacities for autonomous choice and action the poor of a certain area now have in the hopes of securing a happier future. If the calculations work out in a certain way, utilitarians may even think a "generation of sacrifice" – or of forced labor or of imposed population-control policies – not only permissible but mandated. In their darkest Malthusian moments some utilitarians have thought that average happiness might best be maximized not by improving the lot of the poor but by minimizing their numbers, and so have advocated policies of harsh neglect of the poorest and most desperate. Kantian patterns of reasoning are likely to endorse less global and less autonomy-overriding aid and development projects; they are not likely to endorse neglect or abandoning of those who are most vulnerable and lacking in autonomy. If the aim of beneficence is to keep or put others in a position to act for themselves, then emphasis must be placed on "bottom-up" projects, which from the start draw on, foster, and establish indigenous capacities and practices for self-help and local action.

Utilitarians, Kantians, and Respect for Life: Respect for Life in Utilitarian Reasoning

In the contrasting utilitarian and Kantian pictures of moral reasoning and of their implications for hunger, we can also discern two sharply contrasting pictures of the value of human life.

Utilitarians, since they value happiness above all, aim to achieve the happiest possible world. If their life plans remain unclear, this is because the means to this end are often unclear. But one implication of this position is entirely clear. It is that if happiness is the supreme value, then anything may and ought to be sacrificed for the sake of a greater happiness. Lesser possibilities of happiness and even life itself ought to be sacrificed to achieve maximal happiness. Such sacrifices may be required even when those whose happiness or lives are sacrificed are not willing. Rearing the fabric of felicity may be a bloody business. It all depends on the causal connections.

As our control over the means of ending and preserving lives has increased, utilitarians have confronted many uncomfortable questions. Should life be preserved at the cost of pain when modern medicine makes this possible? Or will happiness be greater if euthanasia is permitted under certain circumstances? Should the most afflicted be left to starve in famine situations if the happiness of all, and perhaps the average happiness, will be greater if those whose recovery is not likely to be complete are absent? Should population growth be fostered so long as total (or again perhaps average) happiness is increased, even if other sorts of difficulties arise? Should forced labor and enforced redistribution of income across national boundaries be imposed for the sake of a probably happier world? How far ought utilitarians to insist on the sacrifice of comforts, liberties, and even lives in order to "rear the fabric of felicity"?

Utilitarians do not deny that their moral reasoning raises many questions of these sorts. But the imprecision of our knowledge of consequences often blurs the answers to these questions. As we peer through the blur, we can see that on a utilitarian view lives must be sacrificed to build a happier world if this is the most efficient way to do so, whether or not those who lose their lives are willing. There is nothing wrong with using another as mere means, provided that the end in view is a happier result than could have been achieved any other way, taking account of the misery the means may have caused. In utilitarian thinking, persons are not ends in themselves. Their special moral status, such as it is, derives from their being means to the production of happiness. But they are not even necessary means for this end, since happiness can be located in nonhuman lives. It may even turn out that maximal happiness requires the sacrifice of human for the sake of animal lives.

In utilitarian thinking life has a high but derivative value, and some lives may have to be sacrificed for the sake of greater happiness or reduced misery in other lives. Nor is there a deep difference between ending others' lives by not helping (as some Malthusians suggest) and doing so as a matter of deliberate intervention or policy.

Respect for Life in Kantian Reasoning

Kantians reach different conclusions about human life. They see it as valuable because humans have considerable (but still quite incomplete) capacities for autonomous action. There may be other beings with more complete capacities, but we are not acquainted with them. Christian tradition speaks of angels; Kant referred to hypothetical beings he called Holy Wills; writers of science fiction have multiplied the varieties. There are certainly other beings with fewer capacities for autonomous action than humans standardly have. Whether we think that (some) animals should not be used as mere means, or should be treated as ends in themselves, is going to depend on the particular picture we have of partial autonomy and on the capacities we find that certain sorts of animals have or are capable of acquiring. This is a large question, around which I shall put some hasty brackets. It is quite an important issue in working out the famine and development implications of Kantian thinking, since development strategies have different implications for various animal species. For the moment, however, I shall consider only some implications of human capacities for (partially) autonomous action in Kantian thinking on respect for human life in contexts of acute vulnerability, such as destitution and (threatened) hunger.

The fundamental idea behind the Categorical Imperative is that the actions of a plurality of rational beings can be mutually consistent. A minimal condition for their mutual consistency is that each, in acting autonomously, not preclude others' autonomous action. This requirement can be spelled out, as in the formula of the end in itself, by insisting that each avoid action that the other could not freely join in (hence avoid violence, deception, and coercion) and that each seek to foster and secure others' capacities for autonomous action. What this actually takes will, as we have seen, vary with circumstances. But it is clear enough that the partial autonomy of human beings is undermined by life-threatening and destroying circumstances, such as hunger and destitution. Hence a fundamental Kantian commitment must be to preserve life in two senses. First, others must not be deprived of life. The dead (as well as the moribund, the gravely ill, and the famine-stricken) cannot act. Second, others' lives must be preserved in forms that offer them sufficient physical energy, psychological space, and social security for action. Partial autonomy is vulnerable autonomy, and in human life psychological and social as well as material needs must be met if any but the most meager possibility of autonomous action is to be preserved. Kantians are therefore committed to the preservation not only of biological but of biographical life. To act in the typical ways humans are capable of we must not only be alive, but have a life to lead.

On a Kantian view, we may justifiably – even nobly – risk or sacrifice our lives for others. When we do so, we act autonomously, and nobody uses us as a mere means. But we cannot justly use others (nor they us) as mere means in a scheme that could only be based on violence, deception, or coercion. Nor may we always refuse others the help they need to sustain the very possibility of autonomous action. Of course, no amount of beneficence could put anyone in the position to do all possible actions: that is not what we need to be concerned about. What we do need to be concerned about is failure to secure for others a possibility of some range of autonomous action.

Where others' possibilities for autonomous action are eroded by poverty and malnutrition, the necessary action must clearly include moves to change the picture. But these moves will not meet Kantian requirements if they provide merely calories and basic medicine; they must also seek to enable those who began to be adequately fed to act autonomously. They must foster the capabilities that human beings need to function effectively. They must therefore aim at least at minimal security and subsistence. Hence the changes that Kantians argue or work for must always be oriented to development plans that create enough economic self-sufficiency and social security for independence in action to be feasible and sustainable. There is no royal road to this result and no set of actions that is likely to be either universally or totally effective. Too many changes are needed, and we have too little understanding of the precise causal connections that limit some possibilities and guarantee others. But some broadly accurate, if imprecise indication of ranges of required action, or ranges of action from which at least some are required, is possible.

Nearby Hunger and Poverty: Hunger and Welfare in Rich Countries

So far we have been considering how we might think about and respond to the poverty, hunger, and famine that are characteristic of parts of the developing world. However, both poverty and hunger can be found nearer home. Poverty in the developed world is nowhere so widespread or acute as to risk famine; but it is well documented. Hunger in the developed world is doubly hidden. As always, it shows more in the blighting of lives and health than in literal deaths. However, in contrast to Third World poverty, poverty in rich countries is a minority problem that affects parts of the population whom not everybody meets. Perhaps the most visible aspect of this poverty-amid-wealth in the 1990s is the number of homeless people now to be found on the streets of great and once-great cities in some of the richest societies of the world. In the warmer climates of the Third World, the need for warm and decent housing is also often unmet – but homelessness is nowhere a worse experience

than in the colder parts of the developed world. Although the homeless of the rich world may be able to command money that would constitute wealth in a very poor country, its purchasing power where they are is not enough for minimal housing, decent hygiene, and clothing and may not be enough for adequate food. Apart from the highly visible homeless there are many others in the richer countries who for one reason or another go hungry.

The utilitarian and Kantian ways of thinking considered in this chapter have clear implications for responses to nearby hunger. For utilitarians there will be no doubt that this hunger too produces misery, and should be ended by whatever means will add to the total of human happiness. Many of the strategies that have been used successfully to eradicate hunger in some developed countries have been strongly influenced by this utilitarian thinking. For example, in many western European states social welfare systems guarantee basic welfare, including health care for all, and minimal income. The public policies of these welfare states are funded by taxation, and there would be wide public agreement that these policies produce a greater total happiness than would *laissez-faire* policies, which would leave the poor without a publicly funded "safety net." Opposition to welfare state policies, which can reliably reduce poverty and end hunger, is not likely to come from utilitarians. On the contrary, utilitarian activism has been one of the major forces behind the emergence of welfare states.

Opposition to a welfare state has, however, been vocal among some sorts of human rights thinkers. They articulate the worry that a welfare state, like foreign aid or food aid, is unjust to those who are taxed to provide the funds, and damaging to those who become dependent on what they often disparagingly call welfare handouts.

The objection to redistributive taxation has been part of a long-standing polemic between advocates of "equality" and of "liberty" during the period of the Cold War. Some of the advocates of liberty (often called libertarians) have adopted an extreme view of the demands of liberty, and argue that unrestricted rights to property-without-taxation are a human right.

They conclude that the welfare state is an attack on human liberty. Equally, some advocates of equality have argued for a very strong imposition of material equality, which would indeed make heavy inroads into individual liberty. The underlying arguments for both extreme positions, and for their favored interpretations of human rights, are quite unconvincing. In practice, societies have to strike some balance between liberty and equality. Good social welfare policies are an attractive way of accommodating liberty and equality because they ensure that nobody is so vulnerable that their liberty is wholly eroded, but they do so without a heavy reduction of liberty of those who pay the necessary taxes. The even-handed collection of just taxes leaves richer citizens very great liberty to lead their lives as they will, and enables poorer citizens to reach a minimally decent standard of living that secures their capabilities for leading their lives with dignity. The real issues for social policymakers in the area of taxation have to do with questions about the containment of costs, the fairness of taxation, and the efficiency of its collection rather than with illusory attempts to create societies that embody liberty without equality, or equality without liberty.

The second of these worries, that welfare creates dependence, is a rather implausible objection to policies that end hunger: nothing damages autonomy and creates vulnerability and dependence as much as debilitating hunger and demeaning homelessness. A lack of welfare systems perhaps guarantees that the poor do not depend on the state, but it increases rather than ends their dependence. Worries about dependence have a limited appropriate role in considering *what sort* of welfare policies to pursue. Should welfare payments be in cash or in kind? How far is means testing needed? Should support go to families or to individuals? Do some welfare systems damage the incentive to work? These detailed questions, rather than ideological defense either of unrestricted liberty or of unrestricted equality, are the real issues for social policymakers today.

The Kantian position presented here stresses the importance of not using others as mere means and of treating them as ends in themselves. This position demands commitment to institutions that enable people to become and remain autonomous agents. Hence Kantians would be particularly concerned to prevent the extremes of poverty that lead to hunger and homelessness. The hungry and homeless are particularly vulnerable to every sort of injustice, and above all to violence, coercion, and deception, all of which use people as mere means. On the other hand, this same commitment to autonomy would lead Kantians to demand that welfare policies leave welfare recipients as much in charge of their lives as possible. They would argue that welfare policies (e.g., minimum wage, health care, unemployment pay, child benefit, and many others) can all be structured to enhance rather than restrict the autonomy of those who receive benefits or payments. Good welfare policies manifest rather than damage respect for persons. Kantians do not, of course, advocate justice alone, but also insist that beneficence is important and should be manifested in support and concern for particular others and for their projects. This commitment would also be relevant to actions to relieve poverty, hunger, and homelessness. A society that manages not to use any of its members as mere means, and funds adequate levels of welfare payment, can either succeed in treating its more vulnerable members as ends in themselves, whose particular lives and plans must be respected, or fail to do so by leaving them to the undermining and humiliating procedures of an ill-trained welfare bureaucracy. Because Kantians are concerned for justice and beneficence, they would never see beneficence alone as an adequate response to poverty, homelessness, and hunger at home or abroad. Mere charity is too capricious to secure for the poor capabilities to lead their own lives. Equally, unlike persons with rights-based sorts of ethical thinking, they would never see justice alone as a morally adequate response to human vulnerability.

Whether poverty and hunger are in the next street or far away, whether we articulate the task in utilitarian, in Kantian, or in other terms, the claims of justice and of beneficence for the two cases are similar. What may differ in the two cases are our opportunities for action. Sometimes we have far greater possibilities to affect what goes on in the next street than we do to affect what goes on on distant continents. Since nobody can do everything, we not only *may* but *must* put our efforts where they will bear fruit. This, however, provides no license for injustice to distant others. Nearby neighbors need justice, but they are not entitled to justice at the expense of those who are far away. Hence legitimate concern for justice and welfare for those who are nearby fellow-citizens has always to work with and not against the vast efforts of countless agents and institutions across the world and across the generations of mankind to put an end to world hunger. In a world in which action affects distant others, justice cannot be stopped at local or national boundaries: there is no such thing as social justice in one country. It is only our activism, and not our thinking or concern, that can legitimately be local. If we act by the ecologist's slogan "Think globally, act locally" not only in protecting vulnerable environments but in protecting vulnerable humans, we may, however, become part of the solution rather than part of the problem of world hunger.

CHAPTER 58

The Rationality of Side Constraints

ROBERT NOZICK

A proponent of the ultraminimal state may seem to occupy an inconsistent position. Greatly concerned to protect rights against violation, he makes this the sole legitimate function of the state; and he protests that all other functions are illegitimate because they themselves involve the violation of rights. Since he accords paramount place to the protection and nonviolation of rights, how can he support the ultraminimal state, which would seem to leave some persons' rights unprotected or illprotected? How can he support this *in the name of* the nonviolation of rights?

Moral Constraints and Moral Goals

This question assumes that a moral concern can function only as a moral *goal*, as an end state for some activities to achieve as their result. It may, indeed, seem to be a necessary truth that 'right,' 'ought,' 'should,' and so on, are to be explained in terms of what is, or is intended to be, productive of the greatest good, with all goals built into the good. Thus it is often thought that what is wrong with

Robert Nozick, "The Rationality of Side Constraints," pp. 27–33 from *Anarchy, State and Utopia*. New York: Basic Books. © 1974 by Basic Books. Reprinted by permission of Basic Books, a member of Perseus Books, LLC.

utilitarianism (which *is* of this form) is its too narrow conception of good. Utilitarianism doesn't, it is said, properly take rights and their nonviolation into account; it instead leaves them a derivative status. Many of the counterexample cases to utilitarianism fit under this objection, for example, punishing an innocent man to save a neighborhood from a vengeful rampage. But a theory may include in a primary way the nonviolation of rights, yet include it in the wrong place and the wrong manner. For suppose some condition about minimizing the total (weighted) amount of violations of rights is built into the desirable end state to be achieved. We then would have something like a 'utilitarianism of rights'; violations of rights (to be *minimized*) merely would replace the total happiness as the relevant end state in the utilitarian structure. (Note that we do not hold the nonviolation of our rights as our sole greatest good or even rank it first lexicographically to exclude trade-offs, if there is some desirable society we would choose to inhabit even though in it some rights of ours sometimes are violated, rather than move to a desert island where we could survive alone.) This still would require us to violate someone's rights when doing so minimizes the total (weighted) amount of the violation of rights in the society. For example, violating someone's rights might deflect others from *their* intended action of gravely violating rights, or might remove their motive for doing so, or might divert their attention, and so on. A mob rampaging through a part of town killing and burning *will* violate the rights of those living there. Therefore, someone might try to justify his punishing another *he* knows to be innocent of a crime that enraged a mob, on the grounds that punishing this innocent person would help to avoid even greater violations of rights by others, and so would lead to a minimum weighted score for rights violations in the society.

In contrast to incorporating rights into the end state to be achieved, one might place them as side constraints upon the actions to be done: don't violate constraints C. The rights of others determine the constraints upon your actions. (A *goal-directed* view with constraints added would be: among those acts available to you that don't violate constraints C, act so as to maximize goal G. Here, the rights of others would constrain your goal-directed behavior. I do not mean to imply that the correct moral view includes mandatory goals that must be pursued, even within the constraints.) This view differs from one that tries to build the side constraints C *into* the goal G. The side-constraint view forbids you to violate these moral constraints in the pursuit of your goals; whereas the view whose objective is to minimize the violation of these rights allows you to violate the rights (the constraints) in order to lessen their total violation in the society.[1]

The claim that the proponent of the ultra-minimal state is inconsistent, we now can see, assumes that he is a 'utilitarian of rights.' It assumes that his goal is, for example, to minimize the weighted amount of the violation of rights in the society, and that he should pursue this goal even through means that themselves violate people's rights. Instead, he may place the nonviolation of rights as a constraint upon action, rather than (or in addition to) building it into the end state to be realized. The position held by this proponent of the ultraminimal state will be consistent one if his conception of rights holds that your being *forced* to contribute to another's welfare violates your rights, whereas someone else's not providing you with things

you need greatly, including things essential to the protection of your rights, does not *itself* violate your rights, even though it avoids making it more difficult for someone else to violate them. (That conception will be consistent provided it does not construe the monopoly element of the ultraminimal state as itself a violation of rights.) That it is a consistent position does not, of course, show that it is an acceptable one.

Why Side Constraints?

Isn't it *irrational* to accept a side constraint C, rather than a view that directs minimizing the violations of C? (The latter view treats C as a condition rather than a constraint.) If nonviolation of C is so important, shouldn't that be the goal? How can a concern for the non-violation of C lead to the refusal to violate C even when this would prevent other more extensive violations of C? What is the rationale for placing the nonviolation of rights as a side constraint upon action instead of including it solely as a goal of one's actions?

Side constraints upon action reflect the underlying Kantian principle that individuals are ends and not merely means; they may not be sacrificed or used for the achieving of other ends without their consent. Individuals are inviolable. More should be said to illuminate this talk of ends and means. Consider a prime example of a means, a tool. There is no side constraint on how we may use a tool, other than the moral constraints on how we may use it upon others. There are procedures to be followed to preserve it for future use ("don't leave it out in the rain"), and there are more and less efficient ways of using it. But there is no limit on what we may do to it to best achieve our goals. Now imagine that there was an overrideable constraint C on some tool's use. For example, the tool might have been lent to you only on the condition that C not be violated unless the gain from doing so was above a certain specified amount, or unless it was necessary to achieve a certain specified goal. Here the object is not *completely* your tool, for use according to your wish or whim.

But it is a tool nevertheless, even with regard to the overrideable constraint. If we add constraints on its use that may not be overridden, then the object may not be used as a tool *in those ways*. *In those respects*, it is not a tool at all. Can one add enough constraints so that an object cannot be used as a tool at all, in *any* respect?

Can behavior toward a person be constrained so that he is not to be used for any end except as he chooses? This is an impossibly stringent condition if it requires everyone who provides us with a good to approve positively of every use to which we wish to put it. Even the requirement that he merely should not object to any use we plan would seriously curtail bilateral exchange, not to mention sequences of such exchanges. It is sufficient that the other party stands to gain enough from the exchange so that he is willing to go through with it, even though he objects to one or more of the uses to which you shall put the good. Under such conditions, the other party is not being used solely as a means, in that respect. Another party, however, who would not choose to interact with you if he knew of the uses to which you *intend* to put his actions or good, *is* being used as a means, even if he receives enough to choose (in his ignorance) to interact with you. ('All along, you were just *using* me' can be said by someone who chose to interact only because he was ignorant of another's goals and of the uses to which he himself would be put.) Is it morally incumbent upon someone to reveal his intended uses of an interaction if he has good reason to believe the other would refuse to interact if he knew? Is he *using* the other person, if he does not reveal this? And what of the cases where the other does not choose to be of use at all? In getting pleasure from seeing an attractive person go by, does one use the other solely as a means? Does someone so use an object of sexual fantasies? These and related questions raise very interesting issues for moral philosophy; but not, I think, for political philosophy.

Political philosophy is concerned only with *certain* ways that persons may not use others; primarily, physically aggressing against them. A specific side constraint upon action toward others expresses the fact that others may not be used in the specific ways the side constraint excludes. Side constraints express the inviolability of others, in the ways they specify. These modes of inviolability are expressed by the following injunction: 'Don't use people in specified ways.' An end-state view, on the other hand, would express the view that people are ends and not merely means (if it chooses to express this view at all), by a different injunction: 'Minimize the use in specified ways of persons as means.' Following this precept itself may involve using someone as a means in one of the ways specified. Had Kant held this view, he would have given the second formula of the categorical imperative as, 'So act as to minimize the use of humanity simply as a means,' rather than the one he actually used: 'Act in such a way that you always treat humanity, whether in your own person or in the person of any other, never simply as a means, but always at the same time as an end.'

Side constraints express the inviolability of other persons. But why may not one violate persons for the greater social good? Individually, we each sometimes choose to undergo some pain or sacrifice for a greater benefit or to avoid a greater harm: we go to the dentist to avoid worse suffering later; we do some unpleasant work for its results; some persons diet to improve their health or looks; some save money to support themselves when they are older. In each case, some cost is borne for the sake of the greater overall good. Why not, *similarly*, hold that some persons have to bear some costs that benefit other persons more, for the sake of the overall social good? But there is no *social entity* with a good that undergoes some sacrifice for its own good. There are only individual people, different individual people, with their own individual lives. Using one of these people for the benefit of others, uses him and benefits the others. Nothing more. What happens is that something is done to him for the sake of others. Talk of an overall social good covers this up. (Intentionally?) To use a person in this way does not sufficiently respect and take account of the fact that he is a separate person, that his is the only life he has. *He* does not get some overbalancing good from his sacrifice, and no one is entitled to force this upon him – least of all a state or government that claims his allegiance (as other individuals do not) and that therefore scrupulously must be *neutral* between its citizens.

Note

1. The question of whether these side constraints are absolute, or whether they may be violated in order to avoid catastrophic moral horror, and if the latter, what the resulting structure might look like, is one I hope largely to avoid.

CHAPTER 59
The Golden Rule Rationalized

ALAN GEWIRTH

The Golden Rule is the common moral denominator of all the world's major religions.[1] In one of its most famous formulations it says, "Do unto others as you would have them do unto you." The Rule's imperative ("Do . . .") may be interpreted as an "ought," as prescribing how persons morally ought to act toward others or at least how it is morally right for them to act toward others. Thus the Golden Rule sets forth a criterion of the moral rightness of interpersonal actions, or transactions. This criterion consists in the agent's desires or wishes for himself *qua* recipient: what determines the moral rightness of a transaction initiated or controlled by some person is whether he would himself want to undergo such a transaction at the hands of other persons.

I

There are at least two traditional criticisms of the Golden Rule as a moral criterion or principle. First, the agent's wishes for himself *qua* recipient may not be in accord with his recipient's own wishes as to how he is to be treated. As Bernard Shaw put it in a famous quip, "Do not do unto others as you would that they

Alan Gewirth, "The Golden Rule Rationalized," pp. 133–47 from *Midwest Studies in Philosophy*, 3, 1978. Reprinted by permission of the publishers, Blackwell Publishing.

should do unto you. Their tastes may not be the same."[2] Thus, if the agent A treats his recipient B as A himself would want to be treated, this may inflict gratuitous suffering on B, for B may not want to be treated in this way. For example, a person who likes others to quarrel or intrigue with him would be authorized by the Golden Rule to quarrel with others or involve them in networks of intrigue regardless of their own wishes in the matter; a *roué* who would want some young woman to climb into his bed at night would be justified in climbing into her bed at night; a fanatical believer in the sanctity of contracts who would want others to imprison him for defaulting on his debts would be allowed to imprison persons who default on their debts to him, and so forth.

A second criticism of the Golden Rule is that the agent's wishes for himself *qua* recipient may go counter to many justified social rules, legal, economic, and other. Even if the agent's wishes for himself are not opposed to those of his recipient, both sets of wishes may be immoral. As Sidgwick put it, "one might wish for another's cooperation in sin, and be willing to reciprocate it."[3] For example, a law-violator A who bribes a corrupt policeman B may be treating B as A would himself want to be treated.

The point of this criticism can be brought out further if the Golden Rule is given its negative formulation: "Do not do unto others as you would not have them do unto you." On this formulation together with the preceding positive one, accord with the agent's wishes for himself *qua* recipient is both the necessary and the sufficient condition of the moral rightness of transactions. The difficulty of its being a necessary condition is frequently illustrated by the case of a criminal before a judge; as Kant put it, "on the basis (of the Golden Rule), the criminal would be able to dispute with the judges who punish him."[4] For on this interpretation of the Golden Rule the judges would be justified in meting out punishment to the criminal only if they would be willing to receive such treatment themselves, so that the criminal could appeal to their own dislike for being punished as a basis for arguing that their sentencing of him is morally wrong. Not only criminal punishment but the collection of money owed by recalcitrant borrowers, the payment of lesser wages for inferior work, the giving of lower grades to poorer students, and the infliction of many similar sorts of hardships would be prohibited by the Golden Rule whenever it could be shown that the respective agents would not themselves want to undergo such adverse treatment. The Rule does not recognize the existence of justified disparities of merit and reward among agents and their recipients, including those which arise in competitive relations. More generally, in making the agent's wishes for himself *qua* recipient the criterion of right actions, the Rule ignores that various institutions may set requirements which are justified without regard to those wishes.

It is sometimes held that these difficulties of the Golden Rule can be avoided if it is given a "general interpretation" rather than a "particular interpretation."[5] These interpretations differ with regard to just which desires or wishes of the agent *qua* recipient should determine how he ought to act. The particular interpretation makes decisive the agent's particular wishes or preferences as to the particular actions which he would want to receive from others. The general interpretation, on the other hand, makes decisive the more general principles or standards on which the agent would want others to act toward him. As Marcus Singer puts it, according to the particular interpret-

ation, "whatever in particular I would have others do to or for me, I should do to or for them," but according to the general interpretation "I am to treat others . . . on the same principles or standards as I would have them apply in their treatment of me."[6]

This distinction is a plausible one, and it might be thought that the general interpretation is able to surmount at least the first difficulty stemming from the difference between an agent's particular desires for himself *qua* recipient and the particular desires of his recipients. Closer scrutiny, however, shows that this is not the case. For the "general interpretation" turns out to embody two different conceptions, neither of which is able to resolve the difficulties of the Golden Rule.

One conception is that which Singer calls the "Inversion" of the Golden Rule. This says, "Do unto others as *they* would have you do unto them." As Singer correctly notes, this conception is quite unacceptable, for it "is tantamount to: 'Always do what anyone else wants you to do,' which in turn is equivalent to a universal requirement of perfect or absolute altruism, the absurdity of which is so manifest as not to require detailing."[7] Nevertheless, some of Singer's own formulations of the general interpretation of the Golden Rule embody precisely this Inversion conception. For example, he writes:

> What I have to consider is the general ways in which I would have others behave in their treatment of me. And what I would have them do, in abstraction from any of my particular desires, and all that I am entitled to expect them to do, is to take account of my interests, desires, needs, and wishes – which may be different from theirs – and either satisfy them or at least not willfully frustrate them. If I would have others take account of my interests and wishes in their treatment of me, even though my interests and wishes may differ considerably from their own, then what the Golden Rule in this interpretation requires of me is that I should take account of the interests and wishes of others in my treatment of them.[8]

The phrase "take account of" is vague; a sadist, for example, takes account of his victim's wishes, since such taking account is necessary to his aim of violating those wishes. What Singer means, of course, as the second sentence of the quoted passage shows, is that the agent should either "satisfy" his recipient's wishes or else "not willfully frustrate them." But this then is largely identical with the Inversion conception of the Golden Rule: it requires that the agent always treat his recipient as the latter wishes to be treated, or at least that he not intentionally contravene those wishes. And, as has been emphasized, this is unacceptable as a general principle. It is too permissive for the recipient and too restrictive for the agent.[9]

The other conception of the general interpretation which Singer offers, without explicitly differentiating it from the Inversion conception, is one which I shall call that of Rule-Reciprocity. He presents this in such passages as the following: "I am to treat others *as* I would have them treat me, that is, on the same principle or standard as I would have them apply in their treatment of me." "One should act in relation to others *on the same principles or standards* that one would have them apply in their treatment of oneself."[10] According to this conception, the independent variable determining what the agent ought to do consists in the general principle or standard which the agent would want to have applied to him by others. The result, however, is that the Golden Rule is now too restrictive for the recipient and too permissive for the agent. For on this conception the Rule authorizes an agent to do whatever he wishes to his recipients so long as the general standard or principle on which he acts is one that he would also want or be willing to have applied to himself. But this view incurs the first difficulty of the Golden Rule sketched above. It would allow recipients to be oppressed by the principles or standards upheld by the quarreler, the *roué*, the fanatical believer in the sanctity of contracts, and so forth. The principles of action which such agents would be willing to undergo as recipients may be excessively onerous to other recipients because the latter do not share the agents' preferences or ideals or for other reasons.[11]

We may summarize these difficulties of the "general interpretation" of the Golden Rule as follows. This interpretation seems to admit of two distinct emphases: one which looks at proposed actions from the standpoint of the recipient and one which looks at them from the standpoint of the agent. In the former case the agent is to act toward others as he would want them to act toward him if he had their desires; he must hence treat them as they want to be treated. In the latter case the agent is to act toward others according to the principles on which he would want them to act toward him. Which of these emphases is adopted seems to depend on how the agent's wants for himself *qua* recipient are described. "Do unto others as you would have them do unto you." But I would have others treat me as I wish; therefore, I ought to treat them as they wish. Or, I would have others act toward me according to certain principles which I accept; therefore, I ought to act according to those principles in relation to them. (If I act toward them according to principles which *they* accept, this is equivalent to the former case, where I treat them as they want to be treated.) Thus, the description of the agent's wants for himself *qua* recipient may say either that he wants others to accede to his own wishes or that he wants others to act toward him according to certain principles. Each description yields different and unacceptable results. The former description supports the Inversion conception, to the possible detriment of the agent's wishes; the latter description supports the Rule-Reciprocity conception, to the possible detriment of the recipient's wishes.

Is there any way, then, of "saving" the Golden Rule and thereby avoiding the contrast between its universal (and universalist) appeal and its crippling difficulties? A frequent reaction to the presentation of these difficulties is that one must look to the "spirit" rather than to the "letter" of the Rule. This is fair enough; but it leaves untouched the question of how, specifically, the Rule is to be interpreted so as to conform to its spirit while avoiding literal difficulties like those just presented.

Let us, however, try to follow up this suggestion. It seems safe to say that the spirit or intention of the Golden Rule, violated by all the interpretations so far considered, is mutualist or egalitarian: the actions it requires must be such as fulfill neither the agent's desires alone at the potential expense of his recipients' desires, nor the recipients' desires alone at the potential expense of the agent's desires. Instead, the actions must be such as make proper provision for fulfilling the desires both of the agent and of the recipient. It might be thought that the formulation which most directly satisfies this requirement is: Act in accord with your recipient's desires as well as your own, including the principles upheld by your recipient as well as by yourself. I shall call this the *Generic* interpretation of the Golden Rule, since it refers to desires as such without restriction to specific descriptions of desires either of the agent or of the recipient. Since this interpretation provides that the agent act in accord with his own desires, it avoids the difficulty of the Inversion conception; and since it provides that the agent act also in accord with his recipient's desires, it avoids the difficulty of the Rule-Reciprocity conception. Its difference from the latter needs some further comment. It is one thing to say that an action or a principle of action is justified if its agent is willing to be the recipient of such an action. It is quite a different thing to say that an action or a principle of action is justified if both its recipient and its agent are willing to accept it. In the former case the *justificans* of the principle consists in the desires of only the agent, although in two different capacities, while in the latter case it consists in the desires of both the agent and the recipient, that is, of all the persons who are involved in transactions according to the principle. This makes a considerable difference. Thus while the Rule-Reciprocity interpretation of the Golden Rule may provide for satisfying the agent's desires at the expense of his recipient's desires, this is prohibited by the Generic interpretation.

This interpretation, however, does not solve all the difficulties of the Golden Rule. For it does not tell the agent what to do when his desires conflict with those of his actual or potential recipients. If the *roué* acts in accord with his own desires, including the principles he upholds, he will climb into the girl's bed; if he acts in accord with her desires, he will not. If the hard-working citizen acts in accord with his own desires, he will refuse to give money to the drunken beggar, but if he acts in accord with

the latter's desires, he will give him money to spend on further liquor. The Generic interpretation does indeed pose a challenge to the agent to act so as to accommodate his own wants or desires, including the general principles he upholds, to those of his recipient while not frustrating either set of wants or desires. But the interpretation provides no guidance concerning how this accommodation or compromise is to proceed in cases of conflict.

In addition, the second difficulty mentioned earlier must still be met: even if, following the Generic interpretation, the agent acts in accord with his recipient's desires as well as his own, his action may go counter to justified social rules. Thus the previous example of the law-violator who bribes the corrupt policeman applies also against the Generic interpretation. It may be held that in such a case the law-violator is offending against the desires of the many law-abiding citizens who would be affronted or wronged by his bribery, so that he is not acting in accord with their desires as well as his own. This, however, raises the question of just which persons are to count as the "others" toward whom one acts. If the wishes or desires of even those persons who are affected only remotely or by way of principled disapproval are to be included among such "others," then the possibility of conflicting desires becomes even more acute.

The trouble with all the interpretations so far considered is that, amid the mutualist form of the Golden Rule, they take as their contents contingent wants or desires, whether of the agent or of his recipients or both, and whether particular or general. The interpretations make such wants or desires the independent bases for determining the rightness of actions. Now wants may be of various kinds: There are differences between what one actively wants, what one idly wishes for, and what one would merely be willing to accept, perhaps with various degrees of enthusiasm or reluctance; there are also differences between self-interested wants, including hedonic inclinations, and disinterested wants, including those which seek to achieve some general principle or ideal; in addition, there are differences between long-range wants and immediate wants, between wants based on adequate information and wants based on ignorance, between conscious and unconscious wants, and so forth. The Golden Rule would have to be interpreted differently insofar as "want" is interpreted in these different ways. In its standard formulations, however, the Golden Rule does not explicitly provide any clue for differentiating among these sorts of wants or desires. Thus in the New Testament the Greek word translated as "would have" or "would want" is $\Theta \acute{\epsilon} \lambda \eta \tau \epsilon$ (*thelēte*, Latin *vultis*),[12] which has a quite general desiderative sense.

When wants or desires are taken indiscriminately as the independent bases for determining the rightness of actions, including the desires of the agent *qua* recipient or of the recipient himself, the result is either the potential oppressiveness and one-sidedness of the Rule-Reciprocity and Inversion conceptions or the potential unresolved conflicts of the Generic interpretation. The reason why the basis in wants or desires may have these results is that the wants in question include contingent predilections which may vary from one person to another, so that the desires of the agent and of his recipient may conflict both with one another and with justified social rules. The Golden Rule is most plausible when it focuses on certain standard desires which all persons are normally thought to have for themselves, such as protection against physical violence and other harms. But the Rule is not, of course, limited to such desires, nor are they held so universally that some persons may not be willing to surrender them for the sake of various ideals or interests. If the Golden Rule is to be saved, then, its criterion of rightness must be separated from the contingency and potential arbitrariness which attach to desires taken without qualification.

II

I now want to suggest that these difficulties of the Golden Rule are to be resolved not by completely surrendering the Rule's substantive basis in the desires of the agent for himself *qua* recipient, but rather by adding the requirement that the desires in question must be *rational*. Thus the Golden Rule should be amended to read: Do unto others as you would rationally want them to do unto you. I shall call this the *Rational Golden Rule*, and I shall say that the Golden Rule is "rationalized" when its form and content are made to include this reference to rationality. Similarly, the Generic interpretation of the Rule should be amended to read: Act in accord with your recipient's rational desires as well as your own. The difficulties of the Golden Rule noted above have been elicited by noting that its applications may conflict with intuitions most of us have about the morally right ways to act toward other persons. To rationalize the Rule by grounding it in rational desires serves not only to save these intuitions but also to show how they and all other correct moral judgments have a rational basis.

It is obviously of crucial importance how "rational" is interpreted in this context. Although the word has been used with many different meanings which have given rise to a sizeable literature, for present purposes we may distinguish just two possibilities. Either "rational" is used in a normatively moral sense or in a morally neutral sense. By a normatively moral sense I mean one where its user takes sides on normative moral issues by directly identifying "rational" with one or another preferred way of treating other persons. Such identification sometimes occurs by giving a certain egalitarian moral content to the concept of a "moral reason," as when it is said that a moral reason for rules of action requires that the rules must be for the good of everyone alike or that they must serve to harmonize the interests of all the persons affected.[13]

This normative moral interpretation of "rational" incurs serious problems. It does not, of itself, show why the opposed contents or ways of treating other persons may not be rational; it seems to settle substantive moral issues by linguistic fiat; it does not indicate how this use of "rational" is related to other standard uses of the word and to more general criteria of rationality. In the present context, moreover, such an interpretation of "rational" would make the Golden Rule superfluous. For the Rule purports to set forth the criterion of moral rightness. But if the word "rational" already comprises such a criterion, then there is no need to tell the agent that he should act toward others as he would rationally desire *that they act toward him.* It would be sufficient to tell the agent to act rationally, for "rational" would already mean or include the criterion of moral rightness. Hence, the Golden Rule's emphasis on mutuality or reciprocity of desires would be redundant.

A parallel difficulty is incurred by Samuel Clarke's principle of "equity," which Sidgwick said is "the 'Golden Rule' precisely stated." According to Clarke's principle, "Whatever I judge reasonable or unreasonable for another to do for me, that, by the same judgment, I declare reasonable or unreasonable that I in the like case should do for him."[14] If criteria of reasonableness vary from one person to another, then the problem of divergent "tastes" is not resolved; while if "reasonable" is interpreted as having some definite normative moral sense, then the mutuality of the Golden Rule becomes superfluous since one must already know what is morally right. In any case, we are still left with the problem of determining what it is reasonable for other persons to do to oneself.

A similar point applies to the move made by St. Augustine and Thomas Aquinas when, having distinguished between "rational will" (*voluntas*) and "appetite" (*cupiditas*), they insisted that only the former figures in the Golden Rule,[15] which is thus to be interpreted as saying: Do unto others as you would rationally will that they do unto you. The distinction between *voluntas* and *cupiditas* is said to be that the objects of the former are goods (*bona*) while the objects of the latter are evils (*mala*). The question now turns on the nature of the "goods" which are held to be uniquely the objects of *voluntas* as against *cupiditas*. They cannot include non-moral goods like sexual pleasure or wealth, since these are also the objects of *cupiditas*. If, on the other hand, the goods in question are intended to be moral ones, as seems likely, then the Golden Rule would now say that an agent ought to do others only those morally good things which he would want others to do to him. This would mean, however, that the Rule would no longer be a first moral principle determining what are moral goods and evils. For on this interpretation, in order to apply the Rule one would already have to know, independently of the Rule, what are the moral goods and evils. Moreover, on this interpretation there would again be little or no point in the Rule's referring to the agent's rational wants for himself *qua* recipient as determining what he ought to do. For insofar as what one ought to do is what is morally good, the latter, if we know what it consists in, provides of itself a sufficient criterion of right action; there is no need to add that the agent must want that other persons do these morally good things to him.

If, however, a normative moral interpretation of "rational" incurs these failings, is anything better forthcoming from a morally neutral interpretation, which directly takes no sides on the moral issue of how persons ought to treat one another? From a morally neutral meaning of "rational" whereby the agent is to act toward his recipients as he would rationally want them to act toward him, how can an acceptable normatively moral content be derived for the Golden Rule? The answer is given by the consideration that when certain morally neutral rational requirements are imposed on the agent's desires, there logically emerges a normative moral content which resolves the traditional difficulties of the Rule.

The morally neutral rational requirements in question are the canons of deductive and inductive logic, including among the latter its beginning-points in sense-experience. Deductive logic is here viewed as including the conceptual analysis by which the components of a complex concept are found to pertain to the concept with logical necessity, so that it is contradictory to affirm that the complex concept applies and to deny that its component concepts apply. When conceptual analysis is brought to bear on the concepts of action and wanting, a principle is derived which replaces the contingent desires of the traditional interpretations of the Golden Rule by a certain necessary content. This content is one of *rights* to the generic features of action. In this new formulation, the Golden Rule will read as follows: Do unto others as you have a right that they do unto you. Or, to put it in its Generic formulation: Act in accord with the generic rights of your recipients as well as of yourself.

Since I have presented the argument for this in various other places,[16] I shall merely summarize the main points here. We begin from the agent who wants to attain various of his purposes. Such wants are necessarily attributable to every agent, for what it means to be an agent is that one controls one's behavior with a view to achieving ends which constitute one's reasons for acting, and which one hence intends to achieve. Since the agents regards his purposes as good according to whatever criteria (not necessarily moral ones) are involved in his reasons for acting, he must hold *a fortiori* that the generic features which characterize all his actions, and which are the proximate necessary conditions of his acting for purposes, are necessary goods. These generic features consist in the freedom or voluntariness whereby he controls or initiates his behavior by his unforced choice, and in the purposiveness or well-being whereby he sets goals for himself and has the abilities required for achieving them. Because freedom and well-being are necessary goods to the agent, he must hold at least implicitly that he has rights to them, in that all other persons ought to refrain from interfering with his having freedom and well-being. I shall call these *generic rights*, since they are rights to the generic features of action. If some agent were to deny that he has these rights, he would contradict himself. For he would then judge both that freedom and well-being are necessary goods which he upholds for himself as the conditions of his acting for any other goods, and also that it is permissible for other persons to interfere with his having these necessary goods.

Every agent must hold that he has the generic rights on the ground or for the sufficient reason that he is a prospective agent who has purposes he wants to fulfill. Suppose some agent were to maintain that he has these rights only for some more restrictive reason R. Since this would entail that in lacking R he would lack the generic rights, A would thereby contradict himself. For since, as we have seen, it is necessarily true of every agent that he holds implicitly that he has the generic rights, A would be in the position of holding both that he has the generic rights and that, as lacking R, he does not have these rights. Thus, on pain of

self-contradiction, every agent must accept the generalization that all prospective purposive agents have the generic rights because, as we have seen, he must hold that being a prospective purposive agent is a sufficient condition or reason for having the generic rights. This generalization entails that the agent ought to refrain from interfering with the freedom and well-being of all other persons insofar as they are prospective purposive agents; this is the same as to say that he must refrain from coercing and harming them. Since to refrain from such interferences is to act in such a way that one's actions are in accord with the generic rights of all other persons, every agent is logically committed, on pain of inconsistency, to accept the following precept: *Act in accord with the generic rights of your recipients as well as yourself.* I call this the *Principle of Generic Consistency (PGC)*, since it combines the formal consideration of consistency with the material consideration of the generic features and rights of action.

It will be noted that the *PGC* is the same as the Generic interpretation of the Golden Rule, except that the "desires" of the latter are replaced by "generic rights." The *PGC* also retains the mutualist, egalitarian form of the spirit of the Golden Rule, but again with the substantive difference that the agent is to act toward others not according to his wishes or desires for himself *qua* recipient but rather according to his generic rights as well as those of his recipients. By the above analysis, however, the agent rationally desires to act in this way. He rationally desires to act in accord with his own generic rights because, if his freedom and well-being are interfered with by other persons, he will not be able to act, either at all or at least successfully. The force of "rational" is here in part a matter of means-end calculation and hence of inductive inference, but it is mainly a matter of conceptual analysis whereby the agent becomes aware of the necessary conditions of his action and applies this awareness to his conative concern with achievement of his purposes. Since it is necessarily true of the agent that he wants to achieve his purposes and since his having the generic rights is logically necessary to such achievement, the rational agent, being aware of this logical necessity, wants to have and act in accord with his generic rights.

The agent also rationally desires to act in accord with the generic rights of his recipients. As we have seen, if he violates or denies the *PGC* he contradicts himself. To incur or accept self-contradiction is to violate the most basic logical canon of rationality. Thus when the requirement of rationality is imposed on the wants or desires of an agent who intends to achieve his purposes, there logically emerges a certain normative moral principle consisting in equality or mutuality of rights to freedom and well-being. Every rational agent, in the sense of "rational" just indicated, necessarily accepts this principle.

When it is said that every agent rationally desires to act in accord with the generic rights of his recipients as well as of himself, the force of "rationally" is not that every agent always has or acts from rational desires. It is rather that, insofar as his desires are rational, they have such action as their object. If the agent heeds the canons of deductive logic as these are applied to the analysis of what it is to be an agent who wants to achieve his purposes, he will recognize that in order to avoid self-contradiction he must act in accord with the generic rights of his recipients as well as of himself, and he will also recognize that he must control his effective desires accordingly. Thus the canons of deductive rationality when applied to the concept of agency entail a normative moral conclusion. Since these canons, consisting ultimately in the principle of contradiction, are the most basic conditions of any justificatory argument, the agent logically must accept the *PGC* on pain of losing all justification for his actions. But since the desires from which the agent acts may not in fact be rational ones, the *PGC*'s prescriptive force is not redundant: What the *PGC* tells the agent to do is not something which he inevitably does.

We must now consider how the *PGC* is logically equivalent to the Rational Golden Rule which tells the agent that he should do unto others as he would rationally want them to do unto him. There seems to be a difference here. For in the Rational Golden Rule the object of the agent's rational desires is the

actions of *other persons* toward himself – do unto others as you rationally want *them* to do unto you. But in the *PGC* as just explicated, the object of the agent's rational desires is rather *his own* actions toward other persons – do unto others as *you* rationally want to do unto them – since the agent rationally wants that *he* act in accord with his recipients' generic rights as well as his own. In view of this difference, the following question arises. The agent's rightful actions are to be determined by his rational desires; but are these to be his rational desires as to how *others* are to act toward himself, or are they to be his rational desires as to how *he* is to act toward others, that is, in accord with their generic rights as well as his own? It might seem that these two alternatives would yield different results.

The most direct answer to this question is that, according to both the Rational Golden Rule and the *PGC*, all persons should act toward one another according to their rational desires for such interpersonal action. The objects of these rational desires, as shown by the argument given above, are the generic rights of the respective recipients as well as of the respective agents. Since there are these same objects in each case, there is no difference between what one rationally wants others to do to oneself and what one rationally wants oneself to do to others. Thus the Rational Golden Rule's precept – Do unto others as you rationally want them to do unto you – is logically equivalent to the *PGC*, which may now be put as follows: Do unto others as you rationally want to do unto them, namely, to act in accord with their generic rights as well as your own.

Let us examine somewhat more fully how it is that the agent's rational desires for the actions of other persons toward himself have the same general contents or objects as are had by his rational desires for his own actions toward other persons. He rationally wants other persons to act toward himself in accord with his own generic rights, since the objects of these rights are the necessary conditions of his own actions. Hence, by the Rational Golden Rule, he also ought to act toward other persons in accord with their generic rights. Since this logical consequence of the Rational Golden

Rule is rationally derived from the Rule, the agent whose desires are governed by it has rational desires as determined by the Rule. But these desires of his, by this logical consequence of the Rational Golden Rule, now have as their objects his own actions toward other persons: he ought to act in accord with his recipients' generic rights. Thus the Rational Golden Rule, like the *PGC*, sets for the agent's conduct requirements based on his rational desires as to how he is to act toward other persons, namely, in accord with their generic rights.

This result can also be established in another way. The requirement that one act in accord with the generic rights of one's recipients is not only a logical consequence of the Rational Golden Rule; it also logically follows, independently of this Rule, from the agent's rational desire for himself *qua* recipient. For in rationally wanting that other persons act toward himself in accord with his generic rights, he holds (because of the correlativity of rights and "oughts") that other persons ought to refrain from interfering with his freedom and well-being, and he holds this for the sufficient reason that he is a prospective purposive agent. Hence, he must also hold, on pain of self-contradiction, that there ought to be such refraining from interference in the case of all prospective purposive agents: their freedom and well-being too ought to be respected and not interfered with. From this it follows that the agent himself ought to refrain from interfering with the freedom and well-being of other persons insofar as they are prospective purposive agents, so that he ought to act toward them in accord with their generic rights. Moreover, he rationally desires to act in this way, since it logically follows from his rational desire for himself *qua* recipient. But this rational desire of his now has as its object his own actions toward other persons: he rationally wants that he act toward other persons in accord with their generic rights. Since this rational desire is identical in its object with what is required by the Rational Golden Rule, it follows that this Rule, like the *PGC*, requires that the agent act toward others as he rationally wants himself to act toward them, namely, in accord with their generic rights.

In the above arguments I have assumed what may be called rational-desire-transfers: if A rationally desires that *p*, and *p* entails *q*, then A rationally desires that *q*. Now desire-transfers do not obtain universally, any more than do belief-transfers. But rational-desire-transfers do obtain. For insofar as one's desires are rational in the sense of conforming to the canons of deductive logic, one must rationally desire, or at least be predisposed to desire, whatever is entailed by what one rationally desires in the first place. If one rejects the logical consequent, then, so far as one becomes aware of this, one will also reject, and in this sense not rationally desire, the antecedent.

There still remains a question about the limits of the agent's rational desires for himself *qua* recipient. Why should he confine his demands on other persons, his rational desires concerning how they should treat him, to the generic rights? Since the basis of his right-claim is prudential, why shouldn't he rationally want that they fulfill *all* his desires? If this were indeed what he rationally wanted, then the Rational Golden Rule would unacceptably entail the Inversion of the Golden Rule: Do unto others whatever they desire that you do unto them.

The main answer to this question is that the Rational Golden Rule, including its criterion of rationality, must be interpreted in the light of the *PGC* with its own fuller development of rationality. This development proceeds in terms of the agent's right-claim to the necessary conditions of action. For the *PGC* is derived from the conceptual analysis of action, including what every agent must claim on the basis of the necessary conditions of his agency, which conditions are themselves ascertained by conceptual analysis. Thus the argument to the *PGC* abstracts from the divergent and possibly idiosyncratic desires which may characterize different agents. The argument for every agent's having to make an implicit right-claim holds only insofar as the object of the right-claim is the necessary goods of action, namely, freedom and well-being. The agent is in the position of saying that because these goods are necessary for his action, it is necessary that other persons not interfere with his having them; and this latter necessity, viewed in terms of the agent's conative pursuit of his purposes, is equivalent to his "ought"-judgment that other persons ought to refrain from interfering with his freedom and well-being. Since the agent regards this as a duty owed to himself which he is entitled to have fulfilled, his "ought"-judgement is logically equivalent to a right-claim. Thus it is only to the necessary goods of action that the agent is logically justified in making a right-claim. As we have seen, if he were to deny that he has rights to these goods, he would contradict himself. But he would not contradict himself if he were to deny that he does not have rights to other goods.

If the agent were to claim rights to whatever he might want, including all the objects of his particular contingent desires, then not only would there be a tremendous proliferation of right-claims, but the agent would also be aware that he would be subject to an unmanageable barrage of right-claims from other persons. For the agent, as rational, knows that if he makes a claim on other persons for a certain sufficient reason, then he logically must accept that other persons too have such claims on him insofar as they too fulfill that sufficient reason. Since, as we have seen, the only sufficient reason on which the agent is logically entitled to base his right-claim is that he is a prospective purposive agent, he must accept that all other prospective purposive agents also have the rights he claims for himself. Hence, to avoid burdening himself with such an unfulfillable plethora of claims from other persons, the agent must limit his claims to the necessary conditions of action, the generic rights.

It has now been shown how the Rational Golden Rule is logically equivalent to the PGC. For the sake of convenience the following respective parallel formulations of them may be given: (1) Do unto others as you rationally want them to do unto you. (2) Do unto others in accord with their generic rights as well as your own. Still another formulation was also given above: (3) Do unto others as you have a right that they do unto you. The equivalence of (3) to (2) obtains once it is recognized that (3), like (1), must be interpreted in the light of (2). For what the agent has a right that other persons do to him is that they act in accord

with his generic rights, that is, that they respect his freedom and well-being. Thus, he ought to respect the freedom and well-being of his recipients. Such respect is also what the agent rationally wants that other persons exhibit toward himself, as the PGC requires.

III

As we have seen, the generic rights are rights to freedom and well-being. The PGC and the Rational Golden Rule tell every agent that he should preserve a rationally grounded mutuality or equality between his generic rights and those of his recipients. The specific applications of the PGC are of two kinds, direct and indirect. In the direct applications, the PGC's requirements are imposed on particular transactions, while in the indirect applications the requirements are imposed in the first instance on social rules and institutions, so that particular transactions are right or justified when they conform to social rules which are themselves justified through the PGC. Since the nature of man is associative and interactive, wherever there is a conflict between the direct and the indirect applications, the latter have priority.

The PGC's direct applications require that the agent act in accord with his recipients' rights to freedom as well as his own. Since it is necessarily true of the agent that he participates freely or voluntarily in transactions he initiates or controls, he must also allow his recipients to participate freely or voluntarily. This means that he must refrain from coercing his recipients, so that their participation in transactions must be subject to their own unforced choice or consent.

Similarly, the agent must act in accord with his recipients' rights to well-being as well as his own. Most generally, well-being consists in having the various abilities and conditions which every agent must regard as goods because they are needed for successful action. These fall into a hierarchy determined by the degree of their necessity for action. Basic goods, such as life and physical integrity, are the necessary preconditions of action. Non-subtractive goods are the abilities and conditions needed for maintaining undiminished one's level of purpose-fulfillment, and additive goods are the abilities and conditions needed for raising that level. Thus the *PGC*, in its well- being component, prohibits interferences with basic goods through killing and physical assault (except in self-defense); it also prohibits lying, stealing, and promise-breaking, which interfere with non-subtractive goods; and it requires the parental care and the social arrangements which contribute to additive goods. The *PGC* also requires positive actions in circumstances where voluntary inaction would cause or permit the occurrence of basic harms.

The *PGC* and the Rational Golden Rule overcome the difficulties of the Golden Rule indicated above. The general reason for this is that whereas the traditional Golden Rule allows the rightness of actions to be determined by the agent's even arbitrary or contingent desires for himself *qua* recipient, the *PGC* and the Rational Golden Rule require that the agent's desires for himself *qua* recipient be subjected to rational requirements. As we have seen, these requirements serve both to limit the scope of the agent's determining desires for himself *qua* recipient and to assure that his own recipients are entitled to the same generic emoluments of action as he claims for himself. Thus the mutualist and beneficent intentions of the traditional Golden Rule are fulfilled and its crippling difficulties avoided.

Where the traditional Golden Rule allows the agent to oppress his recipients when his own desires for himself *qua* recipient go counter to his recipient's desires, the *PGC* prohibits such oppression. For the rightness of a transaction is now determined by the agent's rational desires for himself *qua* recipient, and such rational desires require that he act in accord with his recipients' generic rights as well as his own. Thus the actions of the quarreler, of the *roué*, and of the imprisoner of debtors are prohibited by the Rational Golden Rule, since such actions violate their recipients' rights to freedom or well-being or both. The requirement that the agent's desires for himself *qua* recipient be rational also obviates the difficulty of the Inversion conception

of the traditional Golden Rule, whereby the agent must fulfill his recipients' arbitrary desires regardless of the cost to himself. For the Rational Golden Rule and the *PGC* require that the agent act in accord with his own generic rights as well as those of his recipient.

We saw above that in the Generic interpretation of the traditional Golden Rule, which tells the agent to act in accord with his recipients' desires as well as his own, no provision was made for situations where the agent's desires conflict with the desires of his recipients. The case is otherwise, however, when the desires in question must be rational. For this involves that desires are ruled out from consideration when they require actions which violate the generic rights of their recipients; similarly, the recipients' desires must not intend violation of other persons' generic rights.

There may still be conflicts between the generic rights of the agent and of his recipients. For example, the agent's right to freedom may conflict with his recipients' right to well-being, and indeed the agent's right to freedom may also conflict with his own right to well-being. But in the first place, such conflicts are far fewer than the conflicts among desires taken indiscriminately. And in the second place, the fact that the generic rights are derived from the necessary conditions of agency provides a rational basis for resolving conflicts among specific rights. For, other things being equal, one right takes precedence over another to the degree to which the former is more necessary for action than is the latter. For example, A's right not to be killed takes precedence over B's right to be told the truth when the two are in conflict, and C's right to be saved from drowning takes precedence over D's right to be free from any encumbrances on his leisure.

Where the traditional Golden Rule permits actions which go counter to justified social rules, this is not the case with the Rational Golden Rule or the *PGC*. For the *PGC* provides the ultimate basis for the justification of social rules. All such rules, to be justified, must be derivable from the *PGC* either procedurally or instrumentally, that is, either as deriving from voluntary agreement and hence from the right to freedom, or as deriving from the requirements of well-being. The rules of voluntary associations such as baseball teams are justified in the former way; the rules of the minimum state with its criminal law are justified in the latter way. It is hence not open to any person who participates in such justified groupings to try to evade the requirements of their rules on the ground that he would not want to be treated as the rules require. The arbitrary or contingent desires of the participants, including the law-violator and the corrupt policeman, must here give way to the rational desires which are in conformity with the respective social rules.

Although the *PGC* as the basis of the Rational Golden Rule deals primarily with the generic rights and hence prescribes strict "oughts" to agents, it can also deal with the myriad moral situations which involve other rights, as well as those which bear on supererogatory rather than strict duties, whether they concern simple amenities or heroic and saintly actions. On the one hand, all other rights, in order to be justified, must derive directly or indirectly from the generic rights. On the other hand, so far as concerns supererogatory actions, their recipients, by definition, do not have rights to them, such that severe censure or even coercion is justified if the conduct in question is not forthcoming. Nevertheless, every person insofar as he is rational must desire that he be the recipient of such supererogatory actions in relevant circumstances; hence, according to the Rational Golden Rule, it is right or fitting that he perform such actions toward others. For although the actions in question are not matters of rights or strict duties, they go in the same direction as do the generic rights, serving to advance the freedom or well-being of their recipients either directly or by promoting a social context in which these necessary goods are furthered. Because of these connections with the generic rights, every rational person must want that he be the recipient of such supererogatory actions in relevant circumstances. Hence, the Rational Golden Rule provides for the rightness of such actions. The Rational Golden Rule and the *PGC*, like the traditional Golden Rule, require that an agent treat his recipients according to the same rules or principles as the agent wants for his

own treatment. But whereas the traditional Golden Rule leaves completely open and indeterminate the contents of the agent's wants for himself and hence of the rules or principles, the *PGC* focuses on what the agent necessarily wants or values insofar as he is rational, namely that he be acted on in accord with his generic rights. Applications of the *PGC* and the Rational Golden Rule, unlike those of the traditional Golden Rule, cannot be immoral because they cannot be tailored, in their antecedents, to the agent's variable inclinations or ideals without regard to the generic rights of their recipients. The Rational Golden Rule and the *PGC* hence provide in their applications an indefeasible guarantee of reciprocal fairness to both agents and recipients.

This normative moral point also has a deeper logical corollary. The traditional Golden Rule leaves open the question of why any person ought to act in accordance with it. Even if the Rule is assimilated to or derived from a principle of universalizability, that what is right for one person must be right for any relevantly similar person in similar circumstances, the criterion of relevant similarity is still left subject to all the variabilities which we saw to attach to the contingent desires or predilections of agents. The Rational Golden Rule, on the other hand, contains within itself both a formal and a material necessity which determines quite conclusively why every person ought to obey it. Formally, the Rational Golden Rule, like the *PGC*, is necessary in that to deny or violate it is to contradict oneself. Materially, this self-contradiction is inescapable because, unlike the traditional Golden Rule, the Rational Golden Rule and the *PGC* are derived from the necessities of purposive agency. It is not the contingent desires of agents but rather aspects of agency which cannot rationally be varied or evaded by any agent that determine the content of the Rational Golden Rule and the *PGC*. Thus, when the Golden Rule is rationalized it has a conclusive rational justification which the traditional Golden Rule lacks. Nevertheless, such rationality may be said to be implicit in the traditional Golden Rule because it serves to preserve and elucidate the Rule's mutualist intentions in a logically necessary way.

Notes

1. See. *The Eleven Religions and Their Proverbial Love*, ed. S. G. Champion (London, 1944), pp. xvi–xviii, 18, 44, 84, 90, 104, 129, 153, 160, 161, 194, 215, 218, 265, 302; R. E. Hume, *The World's Living Religions* (New York, 1949), pp. 265–6.

2. George Bernard Shaw, *Man and Superman*, app., "Maxims for Revolutionists" in *Collected Works of Bernard Shaw* X (New York, 1930): 217.

3. Henry Sidgwick, *The Methods of Ethics*, 7th ed. (London, 1907), p. 380.

4. *Foundations of the Metaphysics of Morals* VI (Akademie ed.): 430 n.; trans., H. J. Paton, *The Moral Law* (London, 1947), p. 97 n. See John Selden, "Equity" in *Table Talk*, xxxvii, s.v., ed. S. H. Reynolds (Oxford, 1892), pp. 61–2.

5. See Marcus G. Singer, "The Golden Rule," *Philosophy* 38 (1963): 293–314; W. T. Blackstone, "The Golden Rule: A Defense," *Southern Journal of Philosophy* 3 (1965): 172–7. Despite the criticisms of Singer's interpretation which I present below, his article helped to clarify the Golden Rule's import. For another statement of the "general interpretation," see R. M. Hare, *Freedom and Reason* (Oxford, 1963), p. 113.

6. Singer, "The Golden Rule," pp. 299–300.

7. *Ibid.*, pp. 294–6.

8. *Ibid.*, p. 300.

9. The Inversion conception is also upheld by G. H. von Wright, *The Varieties of Goodness* (London, 1963), p. 201: "If the Golden Rule is formulated in a way which is independent of the presupposition of similar wants, it would run as follows: Do to others what they want you to do to them, and don't do to others what they do not want you to do to them." Subsequently (p. 202), von Wright recognizes that the "positive part" of this rule requires "some 'check' on the demands which men have on their neighbour's good services."

10. Singer, "The Golden Rule," pp. 300, 301; emphases in original.

11. This criticism also applies to what Kurt Baier calls "the condition of 'reversibility,' that is, that the behavior in question must be acceptable to a person whether he is at the 'giving' or 'receiving' end of it" (*The Moral Point of View* (Ithaca, N.Y., 1958), p. 202). Such behavior, while acceptable to its agent in his capacity both as agent and as recipient, may still not be acceptable to its recipient.

12. Matthew 7:12; Luke 6:31.

13. See Baier, *The Moral Point of View*, pp. 200–1; Stephen E. Toulmin, *An Examination of the Place of Reason in Ethics* (Cambridge, 1950), p. 145.

14. Samuel Clarke, *Discourse upon Natural Religion*, in *British Moralists*, ed. L. A. Selby-Bigge II (Oxford, 1897): 24; or in *British Moralists, 1650–1800*, ed. D. D. Raphael I (Oxford, 1969): 208. See also Sidgwick, *The Methods of Ethics*, p. 385.

15. St. Augustine, *De Sermone Domini in Monte*, II. 74, in *Augustini Opera Omnia*, vol. III, Pars Altera, col. 1587 (Paris, 1837). Thomas Aquinas, *Catena Aurea Super Matthaei Evangelium*, cap. vii, 6, in *Sancti Thomae Aquinatis Opera Omnia* XI (New York, 1949):99.

16. See my "Categorial Consistency in Ethics," *Philosophical Quarterly* 17 (1967): 289–99; "Obligation: Political, Legal, Moral," *Nomos XII: Political and Legal Obligation* (1970), pp. 55–88; "The Normative Structure of Action," *Review of Metaphysics* 25 (1971): 38–61; "The Justification of Egalitarian Justice," *American Philosophical Quarterly* 8 (1971): 331–41; "Moral Rationality," Lindley Lecture, University of Kansas (1972), "The 'Is-Ought' Problem Resolved," *Proceedings and Addresses of the American Philosophical Association* 47 (1974): 34–61. In my book, *Reason and Morality* (Chicago, 1981), I present the whole argument more extensively.

CHAPTER 60

The Problem of Abortion and the Doctrine of the Double Effect

PHILIPPA FOOT

One of the reasons why most of us feel puzzled about the problem of abortion is that we want, and do not want, to allow to the unborn child the rights that belong to adults and children. When we think of a baby about to be born it seems absurd to think that the next few minutes or even hours could make so radical a difference to its status; yet as we go back in the life of the foetus we are more and more reluctant to say that this is a human being and must be treated as such. No doubt this is the deepest source of our dilemma, but it is not the only one. For we are also confused about the general question of what we may and may not do where the interests of human beings conflict. We have strong intuitions about certain cases; saying, for instance, that it is all right to raise the level of education in our country, though statistics allow us to predict that a rise in the suicide rate will follow, while it is not all right to kill the feeble-minded to aid cancer research. It is not easy, however, to see the principles involved, and one way of throwing light on the abortion issue will be by setting up parallels involving adults or children once born. So we will be able to isolate the "equal rights" issue, and should be able to make some advance.

I shall not, of course, discuss all the principles that may be used in deciding what to do where the interest or rights of human beings conflict. What I want to do is to look at one particular theory, known as the "doctrine of the double effect," which is invoked by Catholics in support of their views on abortion but supposed by them to apply elsewhere. As used in the abortion argument this doctrine has often seemed to non-Catholics to be a piece of complete sophistry. In the last number of the *Oxford Review* it was given short shrift by Professor Hart.[1] And yet this principle has seemed to some non-Catholics as well as to Catholics to stand as the only defence against decisions on other issues that are quite unacceptable. It will help us in our difficulty about abortion if this conflict can be resolved.

The doctrine of the double effect is based on a distinction between what a man foresees as a result of his voluntary action and what, in the strict sense, he intends. He intends in the strictest sense both those things that he aims at as ends and those that he aims at as means to his ends. The latter may be regretted in themselves but nevertheless desired for the sake of the end, as we may intend to keep dangerous lunatics confined for the sake of our safety. By contrast a man is said not strictly, or directly, to intend the foreseen consequences of his voluntary actions where these are neither the end at which he is aiming nor the means to this end. Whether the word "intention" should

Philippa Foot, "The Problem of Abortion and the Doctrine of the Double Effect," pp. 5–15 from *Oxford Review*, 5, 1967.

be applied in both cases is not of course what matters: Bentham spoke of "oblique intention," contrasting it with the "direct intention" of ends and means, and we may as well follow his terminology. Everyone must recognize that some such distinction can be made, though it may be made in a number of different ways, and it is the distinction that is crucial to the doctrine of the double effect. The words "double effect" refer to the two effects that an action may produce: the one aimed at, and the one foreseen but in no way desired. By "the doctrine of the double effect" I mean the thesis that it is sometimes permissible to bring about by oblique intention what one may not directly intend. Thus the distinction is held to be relevant to moral decision in certain difficult cases. It is said for instance that the operation of hysterectomy involves the death of the foetus as the foreseen but not strictly or directly intended consequence of the surgeon's act, while other operations kill the child and count as the direct intention of taking an innocent life, a distinction that has evoked particularly bitter reactions on the part of non-Catholics. If you are permitted to bring about the death of the child, what does it matter how it is done? The doctrine of the double effect is also used to show why in another case, where a woman in labour will die unless a craniotomy operation is performed, the intervention is not to be condoned. There, it is said, we may not operate but must not operate but must let the mother die. We foresee her death but do not directly intend it, whereas to crush the skull of the child would count as direct intention of its death.[2]

This last application of the doctrine has been queried by Professor Hart on the ground that the child's death is not strictly a means to saving the mother's life and should logically be treated as an unwanted but foreseen consequence by those who make use of the distinction between direct and oblique intention. To interpret the doctrine in this way is perfectly reasonable given the language that has been used; it would, however, make nonsense of it from the beginning. A certain event may be desired under one of its descriptions, unwanted under another, but we cannot treat these as two different events, one of which is aimed at and the other not. And even if it be argued that

there are here two different events – the crushing of the child's skull and its death – the two are obviously much too close for an application of the doctrine of the double effect. To see how odd it would be to apply the principle like this we may consider the story, well known to philosophers, of the fat man stuck in the mouth of the cave. A party of potholers have imprudently allowed the fat man to lead them as they make their way out of the cave, and he gets stuck, trapping the others behind him. Obviously the right thing to do is to sit down and wait until the fat man grows thin; but philosophers have arranged that flood waters should be rising within the cave. Luckily (luckily?) the trapped party have with them a stick of dynamite with which they can blast the fat man out of the mouth of the cave. Either they use the dynamite or they drown. In one version the fat man, whose head is *in* the cave, will drown with them; in the other he will be rescued in due course.[3] Problem: may they use the dynamite or not? Later we will find parallels to this example. Here it is introduced for light relief and because it will serve to show how ridiculous one version of the doctrine of the double effect would be. For suppose that the trapped explorers were to argue that the death of the fat man might be taken as a merely foreseen consequence of the act of blowing him up. ("We didn't want to kill him . . . only to blow him into small pieces" or even " . . . only to blast him out of the mouth of the cave.") I believe that those who use the doctrine of the double effect would rightly reject such a suggestion, though they will, of course, have considerable difficulty in explaining where the line is to be drawn. What is to be the criterion of "closeness" if we say that anything very close to what we are literally aiming at counts as if part of our aim?

Let us leave this difficulty aside and return to the arguments for and against the doctrine, supposing it to be formulated in the way considered most effective by its supporters, and ourselves bypassing the trouble by taking what must on any reasonable definition be clear cases of "direct" or "oblique" intention.

The first point that should be made clear, in fairness to the theory, is that no one is suggesting that it does not matter what you bring about as long as you merely foresee and do not strictly intend the evil that follows. We might think, for instance, of the (actual) case of wicked merchants selling, for cooking, oil they knew to be poisonous and thereby killing a number of innocent people, comparing and contrasting it with that of some unemployed gravediggers, desperate for custom, who got hold of this same oil and sold it (or perhaps *they* secretly gave it away) in order to create orders for graves. They strictly (directly) intend the deaths they cause, while the merchants could say that it was not part of their *plan* that anyone should die. In morality, as in law, the merchants, like the gravediggers, would be considered as murderers; nor are the supporters of the doctrine of the double effect bound to say that there is the least difference between them in respect of moral turpitude. What they are committed to is the thesis that *sometimes* it makes a difference to the permissibility of an action involving harm to others that this harm, although foreseen, is not part of the agent's direct intention. An end such as earning one's living is clearly not such as to justify *either* the direct or oblique intention of the death of innocent people, but in certain cases one is justified in bringing about knowingly what one could not directly intend.

It is now time to say why this doctrine should be taken seriously in spite of the fact that it sounds rather odd, that there are difficulties about the distinction on which it depends, and that it seemed to yield one sophistical conclusion when applied to the problem of abortion. The reason for its appeal is that its opponents have often *seemed* to be committed to quite indefensible views. Thus the controversy has raged around examples such as the following. Suppose that a judge or magistrate is faced with rioters demanding that a culprit be found for a certain crime and threatening otherwise to take their own bloody revenge on a particular section of the community. The real culprit being unknown, the judge sees himself as able to prevent the bloodshed only by framing some innocent person and having him executed. Beside this example is placed another in which a pilot whose aeroplane is about to crash is deciding whether to steer from a more to a less inhabited area. To make the parallel as close as possible it may rather be supposed that he is the driver of a runaway tram which he can only steer from one narrow track on to another; five men are working on one track and one man on the other; anyone on the track he enters is bound to be killed. In the case of the riots the mob have five hostages, so that in both the exchange is supposed to be one man's life for the lives of five. The question is why we should say, without hesitation, that the driver should steer for the less occupied track, while most of us would be appalled at the idea that the innocent man could be framed. It may be suggested that the special feature of the latter case is that it involves the corruption of justice, and this is, of course, very important indeed. But if we remove that special feature, supposing that some private individual is to kill an innocent person and pass him off as the criminal we still find ourselves horrified by the idea. The doctrine of the double effect offers us a way out of the difficulty, insisting that it is one thing to steer towards someone foreseeing that you will kill him and another to aim at his death as part of your plan. Moreover there is one very important element of good in what is here insisted. In real life it would hardly ever be certain that the man on the narrow track would be killed. Perhaps he might find a foothold on the side of the tunnel and cling on as the vehicle hurtled by. The driver of the tram does not then leap off and brain him with a crowbar. The judge, however, needs the death of the innocent man for his (good) purposes. If the victim proves hard to hang he must see to it that he dies another way. To choose to execute him is to choose that this evil *shall come about*, and this must therefore count as a *certainty* in weighing up the good and evil involved. The distinction between direct and oblique intention is crucial here, and is of great importance in an uncertain world. Nevertheless this is no way to defend the doctrine of the double effect. For the question is whether the difference between aiming at something and obliquely intending it is *in itself* relevant to moral decisions; not whether it is important when correlated with a difference of certainty in the balance of good and evil. Moreover we are particularly interested in the application of the doctrine of the double effect to the question of abortion, and no one can deny that in medicine there are sometimes certainties so complete that it would be a mere quibble to speak of the "probable outcome" of this course of action or that. It is not, therefore, with a merely philosophical interest that we should put aside the uncertainty and scrutinize the examples to test the doctrine of the double effect. Why can we not argue from the case of the steering driver to that of the judge?

Another pair of examples poses a similar problem. We are about to give to a patient who needs it to save his life a massive dose of a certain drug in short supply. There arrive, however, five other patients each of whom could be saved by one-fifth of that dose. We say with regret that we cannot spare our whole supply of the drug for a single patient, just as we should say that we could not spare the whole resources of a ward for one dangerously ill individual when ambulances arrive bringing in the victims of a multiple crash. We feel bound to let one man die rather than many if that is our only choice. Why then do we not feel justified in killing people in the interests of cancer research or to obtain, let us say, spare parts for grafting on to those who need them? We can suppose, similarly, that several dangerously ill people can be saved only if we kill a certain individual and make a serum from his dead body. (These examples are not over fanciful considering present controversies about prolonging the life of mortally ill patients whose eyes or kidneys are to be used for others.) Why cannot we argue from the case of the scarce drug to that of the body needed for medical purposes? Once again the doctrine of the double effect comes up with an explanation. In one kind of case but not the other we aim at the death of the innocent man.

A further argument suggests that if the doctrine of the double effect is rejected this has the consequence of putting us hopelessly in the power of bad men. Suppose for example that some tyrant should threaten to torture five men if we ourselves would not torture one. Would it be our duty to do so, supposing we believed him, because this would be no different from choosing to rescue five men from his tortures rather than one? If so anyone who wants us to do something we think wrong has only to threaten that otherwise he himself will do something we think worse. A mad murderer, known to keep his promises, could thus make it our duty to kill some innocent citizen to prevent him from killing two. From this conclusion we are again rescued by the doctrine of the double effect. If we refuse, we foresee that the greater number will be killed but we do not intend it: it is he who intends (that is strictly or directly intends) the death of innocent persons; we do not.

At one time I thought that these arguments in favour of the doctrine of the double effect were conclusive, but I now believe that the conflict should be solved in another way. The clue that we should follow is that the strength of the doctrine seems to lie in the distinction it makes between what we do (equated with direct intention) and what we allow (thought of as obliquely intended). Indeed it is interesting that the disputants tend to argue about whether we are to be held responsible for what we allow as we are for what we do.[4] Yet it is not obvious that this is what they should be discussing, since the distinction between what one does and what one allows to happen is not the same as that between direct and oblique intention. To see this one has only to consider that it is possible *deliberately* to allow something to happen, aiming at it either for its own sake or as part of one's plan for obtaining something else. So one person might want another person dead, and deliberately allow him to die. And again one may be said to do things that one does not aim at, as the steering driver would kill the man on the track. Moreover there is a large class of things said to be brought about rather than either done or allowed, and either kind of intention is possible. So it is possible to *bring about* a man's death by getting him to go to sea in a leaky boat, and the intention of his death may be either direct or oblique.

Whatever it may, or may not, have to do with the doctrine of the double effect, the idea of *allowing* is worth looking into in this context. I shall leave aside the special case of giving permission, which involves the idea of authority, and consider the two main divisions into which cases of allowing seem to fall. There is firstly the allowing which is forbearing to prevent. For this we need a sequence thought of as somehow already in train, and something that the agent could do to intervene. (The agent must be able to intervene, but does not do so.) So, for instance, he could warn someone, but *allows* him to walk into a trap. He could feed an animal but *allows* it to die for lack of food. He could stop a leaking tap but *allows* the water to go on flowing. This is the case of allowing with which we shall be concerned, but the other should be mentioned. It is the kind of allowing which is roughly equivalent to *enabling*, the root idea being the removal of some obstacle which is, as it were, holding back a train of events. So someone may remove a plug and *allow* water to flow; open a door and *allow* an animal to get out; or give someone money and *allow* him to get back on his feet.

The first kind of allowing requires an omission, but there is no other general correlation between omission and allowing, commission and bringing about or doing. An actor who fails to turn up for a performance will generally spoil it rather than allow it to be spoiled. I mentioned the distinction between omission and commission only to not set it aside.

Thinking of the first kind of allowing (forebearing to prevent), we should ask whether there is any difference, from the moral point of view, between what one does or causes and what one merely allows. It seems clear that on occasions one is just as bad as the other, as is recognized in both morality and law. A man may murder his child or his aged relatives, by allowing them to die of starvation as well as by giving poison; he may also be convicted of murder on either account. In another case we would, however, make a distinction. Most of us allow people to die of starvation in India and Africa, and there is surely something wrong with us that we do; it would be nonsense, however, to pretend that it is only in law that we make a distinction between allowing people in the underdeveloped countries to die of starvation and sending them poisoned food. There is worked into our moral system a distinction between what we owe people in the form of aid and what we owe them in the way of non-interference. Salmond, in his *Jurisprudence*, expressed as follows the distinction between the two.

A positive right corresponds to a positive duty, and is a right that he on whom the duty lies shall do some positive act on behalf of the person entitled. A negative right corresponds to a negative duty, and is a right that the person bound shall refrain from some act which would operate to the prejudice of the person entitled. The former is a right to be positively benefited; the latter is merely a right not to be harmed.[5]

As a general account of rights and duties this is defective, since not all are so closely connected with benefit and harm. Nevertheless for our purposes it will do well. Let us speak of negative duties when thinking of the obligation to refrain from such things as killing or robbing, and of the positive duty, e.g., to look after children or aged parents. It will be useful, however, to extend the notion of positive duty beyond the range of things that are strictly called duties, bringing acts of charity under this heading. These are owed only in a rather loose sense, and some acts of charity could hardly be said to be owed at all, so I am not following ordinary usage at this point.

Let us now see whether the distinction of negative and positive duties explains why we see differently the action of the steering driver and that of the judge, of the doctors who withhold the scarce drug and those who obtain a body for medical purposes, of those who choose to rescue the five men rather than one man from torture and those who are ready to torture the one man themselves in order to save five. In each case we have a conflict of duties, but what kind of duties are they? Are we, in each case, weighing positive duties against positive, negative against negative, or one against the other? Is the duty to refrain from injury, or rather to bring aid?

The steering driver faces a conflict of negative duties, since it is his duty to avoid injuring five men and also his duty to avoid injuring one. In the circumstances he is not able to avoid both, and it seems clear that he should do the least injury he can. The judge, however, is weighing the duty of not inflicting injury against the duty of bringing aid. He wants to rescue the innocent people threatened with death but can do so only by inflicting injury himself. Since one does not *in general* have the same duty to help people as to refrain from injuring them, it is not possible to argue to a conclusion about what he should do from the steering driver case. It is interesting that, even where the strictest duty of positive aid exists, this still does not weigh as if a negative duty were involved. It is not, for instance, permissible to commit a murder to bring one's starving children food. If the choice is between inflicting injury on one or many there seems only one rational course of action; if the choice is between aid to some at the cost of injury to others, and refusing to inflict the injury to bring the aid, the whole matter is open to dispute. So it is not inconsistent of us to think that the driver must steer for the road on which only one man stands while the judge (or his equivalent) may not kill the innocent person in order to stop the riots. Let us now consider the second pair of examples, which concern the scarce drug on the one hand and on the other the body needed to save lives. Once again we find a difference based on the distinction between the duty to avoid injury and the duty to provide aid. Where one man needs a massive dose of the drug and we withhold it from him in order to save five men, we are weighing aid against aid. But if we consider killing a man in order to use his body to save others, we are thinking of doing him injury to bring others aid. In an interesting variant of the model, we may suppose that instead of killing someone we deliberately let him die. (Perhaps he is a beggar to whom we are thinking of giving food, but then we say "No, they need bodies for medical research.") Here it does seem relevant that in allowing him to die we are aiming at his death, but presumably we are inclined to see this as a violation of negative rather than positive duty. If this is right, we see why we are unable in either case to argue to a conclusion from the case of the scarce drug.

In the examples involving the torturing of one man or five men, the principle seems to be the same as for the last pair. If we are bringing aid (rescuing people about to be tortured by the tyrant), we must obviously rescue the larger rather than the smaller group. It does not follow, however, that we would be justified in inflicting the injury, or getting a third person to

do so, in order to save the five. We may therefore refuse to be forced into acting by the threats of bad men. To refrain from inflicting injury ourselves is a stricter duty than to prevent other people from inflicting injury, which is not to say that the other is not a very strict duty indeed.

So far the conclusions are the same as those at which we might arrive following the doctrine of the double effect, but in others they will be different, and the advantage seems to be on the side of the alternative. Suppose, for instance, that there are five patients in a hospital whose lives could be saved by the manufacture of a certain gas, but that this inevitably releases lethal fumes into the room of another patient whom for some reason we are unable to move. His death, being of no use to us, is clearly a side effect, and not directly intended. Why then is the case different from that of the scarce drug, if the point about that is that we foresaw but did not strictly intend the death of the single patient? Yet it surely is different. The relatives of the gassed patient would presumably be successful if they sued the hospital and the whole story came out. We may find it particularly revolting that someone should be *used* as in the case where he is killed or allowed to die in the interest of medical research, and the fact of *using* may even determine what we would decide to do in some cases, but the principle seems unimportant compared with our reluctance to bring such injury for the sake of giving aid.

My conclusion is that the distinction between direct and oblique intention plays only a quite subsidiary role in determining what we say in these cases, while the distinction between avoiding injury and bringing aid is very important indeed. I have not, of course, argued that there are no other principles. For instance it clearly makes a difference whether our positive duty is a strict duty or rather an act of charity: feeding our own children or feeding those in far away countries. It may also make a difference whether the person about to suffer is one thought of as uninvolved in the threatened disaster, and whether it is his presence that constitutes the threat to the others. In many cases we find it very hard to know what to say, and I have not been arguing for any general conclusion such as that we may never, whatever the balance of good and evil, bring injury to one for the sake of aid to others, even when this injury amounts to death. I have only tried to show that even if we reject the doctrine of the double effect we are not forced to the conclusion that the size of the evil must always be our guide.

Let us now return to the problem of abortion, carrying out our plan of finding parallels involving adults or children rather than the unborn. We must say something about the different cases in which abortion might be considered on medical grounds.

First of all there is the situation in which nothing that can be done will save the life of child and mother, but where the life of the mother can be saved by killing the child. This is parallel to the case of the fat man in the mouth of the cave who is bound to be drowned with the others if nothing is done. Given the certainty of the outcome, as it was postulated, there is no serious conflict of interests here, since the fat man will perish in either case, and it is reasonable that the action that will save someone should be done. It is a great objection to those who argue that the direct intention of the death of an innocent person is never justifiable that the edict will apply even in this case. The Catholic doctrine on abortion must here conflict with that of most reasonable men. Moreover we would be justified in performing the operation whatever the method used, and it is neither a necessary nor a good justification of the special case of hysterectomy that the child's death is not directly intended, being rather a foreseen consequence of what is done. What difference could it make as to how the death is brought about?

Secondly we have the case in which it is possible to perform an operation which will save the mother and kill the child or kill the mother and save the child. This is parallel to the famous case of the shipwrecked mariners who believed that they must throw someone overboard if their boat was not to founder in a storm, and to the other famous case of the two sailors, Dudley and Stephens, who killed and ate the cabin boy when adrift on the sea without food. Here again there is no conflict

of interests so far as the decision to act is concerned; only in deciding whom to save. Once again it would be reasonable to act, though one would respect someone who held back from the appalling action either because he preferred to perish rather than do such a thing or because he held on past the limits of reasonable hope. In real life the certainties postulated by philosophers hardly ever exist, and Dudley and Stephens were rescued not long after their ghastly meal. Nevertheless if the certainty were absolute, as it might be in the abortion case, it would seem better to save one than none. Probably we should decide in favour of the mother when weighing her life against that of the unborn child, but it is interesting that, a few years later, we might easily decide it the other way.

The worst dilemma comes in the third kind of example where to save the mother we must kill the child, say by crushing its skull, while if nothing is done the mother will perish but the child can be safely delivered after her death. Here the doctrine of the double effect has been invoked to show that we may not intervene, since the child's death would be directly intended while the mother's would not. On a strict parallel with cases not involving the unborn we might find the conclusion correct though the reason given was wrong. Suppose, for instance, that in later life the presence of a child was certain to bring death to the mother. We would surely not think ourselves justified in ridding her of it by a process that involved its death. For in general we do not think that we can kill one innocent person to rescue another, quite apart from the special care that we feel is due to children once they have prudently got themselves born. What we would be prepared to do when a great many people were involved is another matter, and this is probably the key to one quite common view of abortion on the part of those who take quite seriously the rights of the unborn child. They probably feel that if *enough* people are involved one must be sacrificed, and they think of the mother's life against the unborn child's life as if it were many against one. But of course many people do not view it like this at all, having no inclination to accord to the foetus or unborn child anything like ordinary human status in the matter of rights. I have not been arguing for or against these points of view but only trying to discern some of the currents that are pulling us back and forth. The levity of the examples is not meant to offend.

Notes

1. H. L. A. Hart, "Intention and Punishment," *Oxford Review*, no. 4, Hilary 1967. Reprinted in H. L. A. Hart, *Punishment and Responsibility* (Oxford, England: Oxford University Press 1968). I owe much to this article and to a conversation with Professor Hart though I do not know whether he will approve of what follows.

2. For discussions of the Catholic doctrine on abortion see Glanville Williams, *The Sanctity of Life and the Criminal Law* (New York, 1957); also N. St. John-Stevas, *The Right to Life* (London, 1963).

3. It was Professor Hart who drew my attention to this distinction.

4. See, e.g., J. Bennett, "Whatever the Consequences," *Analysis*, January 1966, and G. E. M. Anscombe's reply in *Analysis*, June 1966. See also Miss Anscombe's "Modern Moral Philosophy" in *Philosophy*, 33 (January 1958).

5. J. Salmond, *Jurisprudence*, 11th edition, p. 283.

CHAPTER 61

Killing, Letting Die, and the Trolley Problem

JUDITH JARVIS THOMSON

1

Morally speaking it may matter a great deal how a death comes about, whether from natural causes, or at the hands of another, for example. Does it matter whether a man was killed or only let die? A great many people think it does: they think that killing is worse than letting die. And they draw conclusions from this for abortion, euthanasia, and the distribution of scarce medical resources. Others think it doesn't, and they think this shown by what we see when we construct a pair of cases which are so far as possible in all other respects alike, except that in the one case the agent kills, in the other he only lets die. So, for example, imagine that

1. Alfred hates his wife and wants her dead. He puts cleaning fluid in her coffee, thereby killing her,

and that

2. Bert hates his wife and wants her dead. She puts cleaning fluid in her coffee (being

Judith Jarvis Thomson, "Killing, Letting Die, and the Trolley Problem," *The Monist*, 59(2), April 1976. © 1976, *The Monist: An International Quarterly Journal of General Philosophical Inquiry*, Peru, IL, USA 61354. Reprinted by permission.

muddled, thinking it's cream). Bert happens to have the antidote to cleaning fluid, but he does not give it to her; he lets her die.[1]

Alfred kills his wife out of a desire for her death; Bert lets his wife die out of a desire for her death. But what Bert does is surely every bit as bad as what Alfred does. So killing isn't worse than letting die.

But I am now inclined to think that this argument is a bad one. Compare the following argument for the thesis that cutting off a man's head is no worse than punching a man in the nose. "Alfrieda knows that if she cuts off Alfred's head he will die, and, wanting him to die, cuts it off; Bertha knows that if she punches Bert in the nose he will die – Bert is in peculiar physical condition – and, wanting him to die, punches him in the nose. But what Bertha does is surely every bit as bad as what Alfrieda does. So cutting off a man's head isn't worse than punching a man in the nose." It's not easy to say just exactly what goes wrong in this argument, because it's not clear what we mean when we say, as we do, such things as that cutting off a man's head is worse than punching a man in the nose. The argument brings out that we don't mean by it anything which entails that for every pair of acts, actual or possible, one of which is a nose-punching, the other of which is a head-cutting-off, but which are so far as possible in all other respects alike, the second is worse than the first. Or at least the argument brings out that we can't mean anything which entails this by "Cutting off a man's head is worse than punching a man in the nose" if we want to go on taking it for true. Choice is presumably in question, and the language which comes most readily is perhaps this: if you can cut off a man's head or punch him in the nose, then if he is in "normal" condition – and if other things are equal – you had better not choose cutting off his head. But there is no need to go into any of this for present purposes. Whatever precisely we do mean by "Cutting off a man's head is worse than punching a man in the nose," it surely (a) is not disconfirmed by the cases of Alfrieda and Bertha, and (b) is confirmed by the fact that if you can now either cut off my head, or punch me in the nose, you had better not choose cutting off my head. This latter is a fact. I don't say that you had better choose punching me in the nose: best would be to do neither. Nor do I say it couldn't have been the case that it would be permissible to choose cutting off my head. But things being as they are, you had better not choose it.

I'm not going to hazard a guess as to what precisely people mean by saying "Killing is worse than letting die." I think the argument of the first paragraph brings out that they can't mean by it anything which entails that for every pair of acts, actual or possible, one of which is a letting die, the other of which is a killing, but which are so far as possible in all other respects alike, the second is worse than the first – they can't, that is, if they want to go on taking it for true. I think here too that choice is in question, and that what they mean by it is something which is not disconfirmed by the cases of Alfred and Bert. And isn't what they mean by it confirmed by the fact – isn't it a fact? – that in the following case, Charles must not kill, that he must instead let die:

3. Charles is a great transplant surgeon. One of his patients needs a new heart, but is of a relatively rare blood-type. By chance, Charles learns of a healthy specimen with that very blood-type. Charles can take the healthy specimen's heart, killing him, and

install it in his patient, saving him. Or he can refrain from taking the healthy specimen's heart, letting his patient die.

I should imagine that most people would agree that Charles must not choose to take out the one man's heart to save the other: he must let his patient die.

And isn't what they mean by it further confirmed by the fact – isn't it a fact? – that in the following case, David must not kill, that he must instead let die:

4. David is a great transplant surgeon. Five of his patients need new parts – one needs a heart, the others need, respectively, liver, stomach, spleen, and spinal cord – but all are of the same, relatively rare, blood-type. By chance, David learns of a healthy specimen with that very blood-type. David can take the healthy specimen's parts, killing him, and install them in his patients, saving them. Or he can refrain from taking the healthy specimen's parts, letting his patients die.

If David may not even choose to cut up one where *five* will thereby be saved, surely what people who say "Killing is worse than letting die" mean by it must be right!

On the other hand, there is a lovely, nasty difficulty which confronts us at this point. Philippa Foot says[2] – and seems right to say – that it is permissible for Edward, in the following case, to kill:

5. Edward is the driver of a trolley, whose brakes have just failed. On the track ahead of him are five people; the banks are so steep that they will not be able to get off the track in time. The track has a spur leading off to the right, and Edward can turn the trolley onto it. Unfortunately there is one person on the right-hand track. Edward can turn the trolley, killing the one; or he can refrain from turning the trolley, killing the five.

If what people who say "Killing is worse than letting die" mean by it is true, how is it that Edward may choose to turn that trolley?

Killing and letting die apart, in fact, it's a lovely, nasty difficulty: why is it that Edward may turn that trolley to save his five, but David may not cut up his healthy specimen to save his five? I like to call this the trolley problem, in honor of Mrs. Foot's example.

Mrs. Foot's own solution to the trolley problem is this. We must accept that our "negative duties," such as the duty to refrain from killing, are more stringent than our "positive duties," such as the duty to save lives. If David does nothing, he violates a positive duty to save five lives; if he cuts up the healthy specimen, he violates a negative duty to refrain from killing one. Now the negative duty to refrain from killing one is not merely more stringent than the positive duty to save one, it is more stringent even than the positive duty to save five. So of course Charles may not cut up his one to save one; and David may not cut up his one even to save five. But Edward's case is different. For if Edward "does nothing," he doesn't just do nothing; he kills the five on the track ahead, for he drives right into them with his trolley. Whichever Edward does, turn or not turn, he kills. There is, for Edward, then, not a conflict between a positive duty to save five and a negative duty to refrain from killing one; there is, for Edward, a conflict between a negative duty to refrain from killing five and a negative duty to refrain from killing one. But this is no real conflict: a negative duty to refrain from killing five is surely more stringent than a negative duty to refrain from killing one. So Edward may, indeed must, turn that trolley.

Now I am inclined to think that Mrs. Foot is mistaken about why Edward may turn his trolley, but David may not cut up his healthy specimen. I say only that Edward "may" turn his trolley, and not that he must: my intuition tells me that it is not required that he turn it, but only that it is permissible for him to do so. But this isn't important now: it is, at any rate, permissible for him to do so. Why? Compare (5) with

6. Frank is a passenger on a trolley whose driver has just shouted that the trolley's brakes have failed, and who then died of the shock. On the track ahead are five people; the banks are so steep that they will not be able to get off the track in time. The track has a spur leading off to the right, and Frank can turn the trolley onto it. Unfortunately there is one person on the right-hand track. Frank can turn the trolley, killing the one; or he can refrain from turning the trolley, letting the five die.

If Frank turns his trolley, he plainly kills his one, just as if Edward turns his trolley, he kills his one: anyone who turns a trolley onto a man presumably kills him. Mrs. Foot thinks that if Edward does nothing, he kills his five, and I agree with this: if a driver of a trolley drives it full speed into five people, he kills them, even if he only drives it into them because his brakes have failed. But it seems to me that if Frank does nothing, he kills no one. He at worst lets the trolley kill the five; he does not himself kill them, but only lets them die.

But then by Mrs. Foot's principles, the conflict for Frank is between the negative duty to refrain from killing one, and the positive duty to save five, just as it was for David. On her view, the former duty is the more stringent: its being more stringent was supposed to explain why David could not cut up his healthy specimen. So by her principles, Frank may no more turn that trolley than David may cut up his healthy specimen. Yet I take it that anyone who thinks Edward may turn his trolley will also think that Frank may turn his. Certainly the fact that Edward is driver, and Frank only passenger could not explain so large a difference.

So we stand in need, still, of a solution: why can Edward and Frank turn their trolleys, whereas David cannot cut up his healthy specimen? One's intuitions are, I think, fairly sharp on these matters. Suppose, for a further example, that

7. George is on a footbridge over the trolley tracks. He knows trolleys, and can see that the one approaching the bridge is out of control. On the track back of the bridge there are five people; the banks are so steep that they will not be able to get off the track in time. George knows that the only way to stop an out-of-control trolley is to

drop a very heavy weight into its path. But the only available, sufficiently heavy weight is a fat man, also watching the trolley from the footbridge. George can shove the fat man onto the track in the path of the trolley, killing the fat man; or he can refrain from doing this, letting the five die.

Presumably George may not shove the fat man into the path of the trolley; he must let the five die. Why may Edward and Frank turn their trolleys to save their fives, whereas George must let his five die? George's shoving the fat man into the path of the trolley seems to be very like David's cutting up his healthy specimen. But what is the relevant likeness?

Further examples come from all sides. Compare, for example, the following two cases:

8. Harry is President, and has just been told that the Russians have launched an atom bomb towards New York. The only way in which the bomb can be prevented from reaching New York is by deflecting it; but the only deflection-path available will take the bomb onto Worcester. Harry can do nothing, letting all of New York die; or he can press a button, deflecting the bomb, killing all of Worcester.
9. Irving is President, and has just been told that the Russians have launched an atom bomb towards New York. The only way in which the bomb can be prevented from reaching New York is by dropping one of our own atom bombs on Worcester: the blast of the American bomb will pulverize the Russian bomb. Irving can do nothing, letting all of New York die; or he can press a button, which launches an American bomb onto Worcester, killing all of Worcester.

Most people, I think, would feel that Harry may act in (8): he may deflect the Russian bomb from its New York path onto Worcester, in order to minimize the damage it does. (Notice that if Harry doesn't deflect that bomb, he kills no one – just as Frank kills no one if he doesn't turn his trolley.) But I think most people would feel that Irving may not drop an American bomb onto Worcester: a President

simply may not launch an atomic attack on one of his own cities, even to save a larger one from a similar attack.

Why? I think it is the same problem.

2

Perhaps the most striking difference between the cases I mentioned in which the agent may act, and the cases I mentioned in which he may not, is this: in the former what is in question is deflecting a threat from a larger group onto a smaller group, in the latter what is in question is bringing a different threat to bear on the smaller group. But it is not easy to see why this should matter so crucially. I think it does, and have a suggestion as to why, but it is no more than a suggestion.

I think we may be helped if we turn from evils to goods. Suppose there are six men who are dying. Five are standing in one clump on the beach, one is standing further along. Floating in on the tide is a marvelous pebble, the Health-Pebble, I'll call it: it cures what ails you. The one needs for cure the whole Health-Pebble; each of the five needs only a fifth of it. Now in fact that Health-Pebble is drifting towards the one, so that if nothing is done to alter its course, the one will get it. We happen to be swimming nearby, and are in a position to deflect it towards the five. Is it permissible for us to do this? It seems to me that it is permissible for us to deflect the Health-Pebble if and only if the one who has no more claim on it than any of the five does.

What could make it be the case that the one has more claim on it than any of the five does? One thing that I think *doesn't* is the fact that the pebble is headed for the one, and that he will get it if we do nothing. There is no Principle of Moral Inertia: there is no prima facie duty to refrain from interfering with existing states of affairs just because they are existing states of affairs. A burglar whose burgling we interfere with cannot say that since, but for our interference, he would have got the goods, he had a claim on them; it is not as if we weigh the burglar's claim on the goods against the owner's claim on them, and find the owner's claim weightier, and therefore interfere – the burglar has no claim on the goods to be weighed.

Well, the Health-Pebble might actually belong to the one. (It fell off his boat.) Or it might belong to us, and we had promised it to the one. If either of these is the case, the one has a claim on it in the sense of a right to it. If the one alone owns it, or if we have promised it only to the one, then he plainly has more claim on it than any of the five do; and we may not deflect it away from him.

But I mean to be using the word "claim" more loosely. So, for example, suppose that the five are villains who had intentionally caused the one's fatal illness, hoping he would die. (Then they became ill themselves.) It doesn't seem to me obvious that a history like this gives the one a *right* to that pebble; yet it does seem obvious that in some sense it gives the one a claim on it – anyway, more of a claim on it than any of the five has. Certainly anyway one feels that if it comes to a choice between them and him, he ought to get it. Again, suppose the six had played pebble-roulette: they had seen the pebble floating in, and agreed to flip a coin for positions on the beach and take their chances. And now the pebble is floating in towards the one. It doesn't seem to me that a history like this gives the one a *right* to that pebble; yet it does seem obvious that in some sense it gives him a claim on it, anyway, more claim on it than any of the five has. (While the fact that a pebble is floating towards one does not give him more claim on it, the compound fact that a pebble is floating towards him and that there was a background of pebble-roulette does, I think, give him more claim. If two groups have agreed to take what comes, and have acted in good faith in accordance with that agreement, I think we cannot intervene.)

I leave it open just precisely what sorts of things might give the one more claim on that Health-Pebble than any of the five has. What seems clear enough, however, is this: if the one has no more claim on it than any of the five has, we may deflect it away from him and towards the five. If the one has no more claim on it than any of the five has, it is permissible for us to deflect it in order to bring about that it saves more lives than it would do if we did not act.

Now that Health-Pebble is good to those dying men on the beach: if they get to eat it, they live. The trolley is an evil to the living men on the tracks: if they get run down by it, they die. And deflecting the Health-Pebble away from one and towards five is like deflecting the trolley away from five and towards one. For if the pebble is deflected, one life is lost and five are saved; and if the trolley is deflected, so also is one life lost and five saved. The analogy suggests a thesis: that Edward (or Frank) may deflect his trolley if and only if the one has no more claim against the trolley than any of the five has – that is, that under these circumstances he may deflect it in order to bring about that it takes fewer lives than it would do if he did not.

But while it was at least relatively clear what sorts of things might give the one more of a claim *on* the Health-Pebble, it is less clear what could give the one more of a claim *against* a trolley. Nevertheless there are examples in which it is clear enough that the one has more of a claim against the trolley than any of the five does. Suppose that

i. The five on the track ahead are regular track workmen, repairing the track – they have been warned of the dangers of their job, and are paid specially high salaries to compensate. The righthand track is a dead end, unused in ten years. The Mayor, representing the City, has set out picnic tables on it, and invited the convalescents at the nearby City Hospital to have lunch there, guaranteeing them safety from trolleys. The one on the right-hand track is a convalescent having his lunch there; it would never have occurred to him to have his lunch there but for the Mayor's invitation and guarantee of safety. And Edward (Frank) is the Mayor.

The situation if (i) is true is very like the situation if we own the Health-Pebble which is floating in on the tide, and have promised it to the one. If we have promised the Health-Pebble to the one and not to the five, the one has more claim on it than any of the five does, and we therefore may not deflect it away from him; if Edward (Frank) has promised that no trolley shall run down the one, and has not made this promise to the five, the one has more claim against it – more claim to not be run down by it – than any of the five does, and Edward therefore may not deflect it onto him.

So in fact I cheated: it isn't permissible for Edward and Frank to turn their trolleys in *every* possible instance of (5) and (6). Why did it seem as if it would be? The cases were under-described, and what you supplied as filler was that the six on the tracks are on a par: that there was nothing further true of any of them which had a bearing on the question whether or not it was permissible to turn the trolleys. In particular, then, you were assuming that it was not the case that the one had more claim against the trolleys than any of the five did.

Compare, by contrast, the situation if

ii. All six on the tracks are regular track work-men, repairing the tracks. As they do every day, they drew straws for their assignments for the day. The one who is on the right-hand track just happened to draw the straw tagged "Right-hand track."

Or if

iii. All six are innocent people whom villains have tied to the trolley tracks, five on one track, one on the other.

If (ii) or (iii) is true, all six are on a par in the relevant respect: the one has no more claim against the trolley than any of the five has and so the trolley may be turned.

Again, consider the situation if

iv. The five on the track ahead are regular track workmen, repairing the track. The one on the right-hand track is a school-boy, collecting pebbles on the track. He knows he doesn't belong there: he climbed the fence to get onto the track, ignoring all warning signs, thinking "Who could find it in his heart to turn a trolley onto a schoolboy?"

At the risk of seeming hardhearted about schoolboys, I have to say I think that if (iv) is true, the trolley not only may be, but must be turned. So it seems to me arguable that if – as I take to be the case if (iv) is true – the five have more claim against the trolley than the one does, the trolley not only may be, but must be turned. But for present purposes what counts is only what makes it permissible to turn it where it is permissible to turn it.

President Harry's case, (8), is of course like the cases of Edward and Frank. Harry also deflects something which will harm away from a larger group onto a smaller group. And my proposal is that he may do this because (as we may presume) the Worcesters have no more claim against a Russian bomb than the New Yorkers do.

The situation could have been different. Suppose an avalanche is descending towards a large city. It is possible to deflect it onto a small one. May we? Not if the following is the case. Large City is in avalanche country – the risk of an avalanche is very high there. The founders of Large City were warned of this risk when they built there, and all settlers in it were warned of it before settling there. But lots and lots of people did accept the risk and settle there, because of the beauty of the countryside and the money to be made there. Small City, however, is not in avalanche country – it's flat for miles around; and settlers in Small City settled for a less lovely city, and less money, precisely because they did not wish to run the risk of being overrun by an avalanche. Here it seems plain we may not deflect that avalanche onto Small City to save Large City: the Small Cityers have more claim against it than the Large Cityers do. And it could have been the case that New York was settled in the teeth of Russian-bomb-risk.

The fact that is permissible for President Harry in (8) to deflect that atom bomb onto Worcester brings out something of interest. Mrs. Foot had asked us to suppose "that some tyrant should threaten to torture five men if we ourselves would not torture one." She then asked: "Would it be our duty to do so, supposing we believed him . . . ?" Surely not, she implies: for "if so anyone who wants us to do something we think wrong has only to threaten that otherwise he himself will do something we think worse. A mad murderer, known to keep his promises, could thus make it our duty to kill some innocent citizen to prevent him from killing two."[3] Mrs. Foot is surely right. But it would be unfair to Mrs. Foot to summarize her point in this way: we must not do a villain's dirty work for him. And wrong, in any case, for suppose the Russians don't really care about New York. The city they really want to destroy is Worcester. But for some reason they can only aim their bomb at New York, which they do in the hope that President Harry will himself deflect it onto Worcester. It seems to me it makes no difference what their aim is: whether they want Worcester or not, Harry can still deflect their bomb onto Worcester But in doing so, he does the villains' dirty work for them: for if he deflects their bomb, he kills Worcester for them.

Similarly, it doesn't matter whether or not the villains in (iii) want the one on the right-hand track dead: Edward and Frank can all the same turn their trolleys onto him. That a villain wants a group dead gives them no more claim against a bomb or a trolley than these in the other group have.

Mrs. Foot's examples in the passages I quoted are of villains who have not yet launched their threat against anyone, but only threaten to: they have not yet set in train any sequence of events – e.g., by launching a bomb, or by starting a trolley down a track – such that if we don't act, a group will be harmed. The villains have as yet only *said* they would set such a sequence of events in train. I don't object to our acting on the ground of uncertainties: one may, as Mrs. Foot supposes, be perfectly certain that a villain will do exactly what he says he will do. There are two things that make it impermissible to act in this kind of case. In the first place, there are straightforward utilitarian objections to doing so: the last thing we need is to give further villains reason to think they'll succeed if they too say such things.[4] But this doesn't take us very far, for as I said, we may deflect an already launched threat away from one group and onto another, and we don't want further villains thinking they'll succeed if they only manage to get such a sequence of events set in train. So the second point is more important: in such cases, to act is *not* to deflect a threat away from one group and onto another, but instead to bring a different

threat to bear on the other group. It is to these cases we should now turn.

3

Edward and Frank may turn their trolleys if and only if the one has no more claim against the trolleys than any of the five do. Why is it impermissible for David to cut up his healthy specimen?

I think the Health-Pebble helps here. I said earlier that we might suppose that the one actually owns the Health-Pebble which is floating in on the tide. (It fell off his boat.) And I said that in that case, he has more claim on it than any of the five has, so that we may not deflect it away from him and towards the five. Let's suppose that deflecting isn't in question any more: the pebble has already floated in, and the one has it. Let's suppose he's already put it in his mouth. Or that he's already swallowed it. We certainly may not cut him open to get it out – even if it's not yet digested, and can still be used to save five. Analogously, David may not cut up his healthy specimen to give his parts to five. One doesn't come to own one's parts in the way in which one comes to own a pebble, or a car, or one's grandfather's desk, but a man's parts are his all the same. And therefore that healthy specimen has more claim on those parts than any of the five has – just as if the one owns the Health-Pebble, he has more claim on it than any of the five do.

I do not, and did not, mean to say that we may *never* take from one what belongs to him to give to five. Perhaps there are situations in which we may even take from one something that he needs for life itself in order to give to five. Suppose, for example, that the healthy specimen had caused the five to catch the ailments because of which they need new parts – he deliberately did this in hope the five would die. No doubt a legal code which permitted a surgeon to transplant in situations such as this would be open to abuses, and bad for that reason; but it seems to me it would not be unjust.

So perhaps we can bring David's case in line with Edward's and Frank's, and put the matter like this: David may cut up his healthy specimen and give his parts to the five if and only if the healthy specimen has no more claim on his parts than any of the five do. This leaves it open that in some instances of (4), David may act.

But I am inclined to think there is more to be said of David's case than this. I suggested earlier that if George, in (7), shoves the fat man into the path of the trolley, he does something very like what David does if David cuts up his healthy specimen. Yet George wouldn't be taking anything away from the one in order to give it to the five. George would be "taking" the fat man's life, of course; but what this means is only that George would be killing the fat man, and Edward and Frank kill someone too. And similarly for Irving, in (9): if he bombs Worcester, he doesn't take anything away from the Worcesters in order to give it to the New Yorkers.

Moreover, consider the following variant on David's case:

4'. Donald is a great diagnostician. Five of his patients are dying. By chance Donald learns of a healthy specimen such that if Donald cuts him up into bits, a peculiar physiological process will be initiated in the five, curing them. Donald can cut his healthy specimen up into bits, killing him, thereby saving his patients. Or he can refrain from doing this, letting his patients die.

In (4'), Donald does not need to give anything which belongs to his healthy specimen to his five; unlike David, he need only cut his healthy specimen up into bits, which can then be thrown out. Yet presumably in whatever circumstances David may not act, Donald may not act either.

So something else is involved in George's, Irving's, and Donald's cases than I drew attention to in David's; and perhaps this other thing is present in David's too.

Suppose that in the original story, where the pebble is floating in on the tide, we are for some reason unable to deflect the pebble away from the one and towards the five. All we can do, if we want the five to get it instead of the one, is to shove the one away, off the beach, out

of reach of where the pebble will land; or all we can do is to drop a bomb on the one; or all we can do is to cut this one up into bits.

I suppose that there might be circumstances in which it would be permissible for us to do one or another of these things to the one – even circumstances which include that the one owns the pebble. Perhaps it would be permissible to do them if the one had caused the five to catch the ailments because of which they need the pebble, and did this deliberately, in hope the five would die. The important point, however, is this. The fact that the one has no more claim on the pebble than any of the five do does make it permissible for us to deflect the pebble away from the one and towards the five; it does not make it permissible for us to shove the one away, bomb him, or cut him to bits in order to bring about that the five get it.

Why? Here is a good, up for distribution, a Health-Pebble. If we do nothing, one will get it, and five will not; so one will live and five will die. It strikes us that it would be better for five to live and one die than for one to live and five die, and therefore that a better distribution of the good would be for the five to get it, and the one not to. If the one has no more claim on the good than any of the five has, he cannot complain if we do something to *it* in order to bring about that it is better distributed; but he can complain if we do something to *him* in order to bring about that it is better distributed.

If there is a pretty shell on the beach and it is unowned, I cannot complain if you pocket it to give to another person who would get more pleasure from it than I would. But I can complain if you shove me aside so as to be able to pocket it to give to another person who would get more pleasure from it than I would. It's unowned; so you can do to it whatever would be necessary to bring about a better distribution of it. But a *person* is not something unowned, to be knocked about in order to bring about a better distribution of something else.

Here is something bad, up for distribution, a speeding trolley. If nothing is done, five will get it, and one will not; so five will die and one will live. It strikes us that it would be better for five to live and one to die than for one to live and five to die, and therefore that a better distribution of the bad thing would be for the one to get it, and the five not to. If the one has no more claim against the bad thing than any of the five has, he cannot complain if we do something to *it* in order to bring about that it is better distributed: that is, it is permissible for Edward and Frank to turn their trolleys. But even if the one has no more claim against the bad thing than any of the five has, he can complain if we do something to *him* in order to bring about that the bad thing is better distributed: that is, it is not permissible for George to shove his fat man off the bridge into the path of the trolley.

It is true that if Edward and Frank turn their trolleys, they don't merely turn their trolleys: they turn their trolleys onto the one, they run down and thereby kill him. And if you turn a trolley onto a man, if you run him down and thereby kill him, you certainly do something to *him*. (I don't know whether or not it should be said that if you deflect a Health-Pebble away from one who needs it for life, and would get it if you didn't act, you have killed him; perhaps it would be said that you killed him, perhaps it would be said that you didn't kill him, but only caused his death. It doesn't matter: even if you only caused his death, you certainly did something to him.) So haven't their ones as much ground for complaint as George's fat man? No, for Edward's (Frank's) turning his trolley onto the one, his running the one down and thereby killing him, isn't something he does to the one to bring about that the trolley is better distributed. The trolley's being better distributed *is* its getting onto the one, it *is* running the one down and thereby killing him; and Edward doesn't turn his trolley onto the one, he doesn't run the one down and thereby kill him, in order to bring this about – what he does to bring it about is to turn his trolley. You don't bring about that a thing melts or breaks by melting or breaking it; you bring about that it melts or breaks by (as it might be) putting it on the stove or hitting it with a brick. Similarly, you don't bring about that a thing gets to a man by getting it to him; you bring about that it gets to him by (as it might be) deflecting it, turning it, throwing it – whatever it is you do, by the doing of which you will have got it to the man.

By contrast, George, if he acts, does something to the fat man (shoves him off the bridge

into the path of the trolley) to bring about the better distribution of the trolley, namely, that the one (the fat man) gets it instead of the five.

A good bit more would have to be said about the distinction I appeal to here if my suggestion is to go through. In part we are hampered by the lack of a theory of action, which should explain, in particular, what it is to bring something about by doing something. But perhaps the intuition is something to take off from: that what matters in these cases in which a threat is to be distributed is whether the agent distributes it by doing something to it, or whether he distributes it by doing something to a person.

The difference between Harry's case and Irving's is, I think, the same. Harry, if he acts, does something to the Russian bomb (deflect it), in order to bring about that it is better distributed: the few Worcesters get it instead of the many New Yorkers. Irving, however, does something to the Worcesters (drops one of our own bombs on them) in order to bring about that the Russian bomb is better distributed: instead of the many New Yorker's getting it, nobody does. Hence the fact that the Worcesters have no more claim against the Russian bomb than the New Yorkers do makes it permissible for Harry to act; but not for Irving to.

If we can speak of making a better distribution of an ailment, we can say of Donald too that if he acts, he does something to his healthy specimen (cut him up into bits) in order to bring about a better distribution of the ailments threatening his five patients: instead of the five patients getting killed by them, nobody is.

And then the special nastiness in David, if he acts, lies in this: in the first place, he gives to five what belongs to the one (bodily parts), *and* in the second place, in order to bring about a better distribution of the ailments threatening his five – that is, in order to bring about that instead of the five patients getting killed by them, nobody is – he does something to the one (cuts him up).

4

Is killing worse than letting die? I suppose that what those who say it is have in mind may well be true. But this is because I suspect that they do not have in mind anything which is discon-firmed by the fact that there are pairs of acts containing a killing and letting die in which the first is no worse than the second (for example, the pair containing Alfred's and Bert's) *and* also do not have in mind anything which is discon-firmed by the fact that there are cases in which an agent may kill instead of letting die (for example, Frank's and Harry's). What I suspect they have in mind is something which is con-firmed by certain cases in which an agent may not kill instead of letting die (for example, David's and Donald's). So as I say, I think they may be right. More generally, I suspect that Mrs. Foot and others may be right to say that negative duties are more stringent than positive duties. But we shan't be able to decide until we get clearer what these things

come to. I think it's no special worry for them, however. For example, I take it most people think that cutting a man's head off is worse than punching a man in the nose, and I think we aren't any clearer about what this means than they are about their theses. The larger question is a question for all of us.

Meanwhile, however, the thesis that killing is worse than letting die cannot be used in any simple, mechanical way in order to yield con-clusions about abortion, euthanasia, and the distribution of scarce medical resources. The cases have to be looked at individually. If noth-ing else comes out of the preceding discussion, it may anyway serve as a reminder of this: that there are circumstances in which – even if it is true that killing is worse than letting die – one may choose to kill instead of letting die.

Notes

1. See J.J. Thomson, "Rights and Deaths," *Philoso-phy and Public Affairs* 2 (1973), sec. 3 See also Michael Tooley, "Abortion and Infanticide," *Philosophy and Public Affairs* 2 (Fall 1972), sec. 5, and James Rachels, "Active and Passive Eutha-nasia," *New England Journal of Medicine* 292 (January 9, 1975).

2. In her very rich article, "Abortion and the Doc-trine of the Double Effect," *Oxford Review* 5

(1967). Most of my examples are more or less long-winded expansions of hers. See also G. E. M. Anscome's brief reply, "Who is Wronged?" in the same issue of the *Oxford Review.*

3. Foot, ibid., p. 10.

4. See D. H. Hodgson, *Consequences of Utilit-arianism: A Study in Normative Ethics & Legal Theory* (Oxford: Oxford University Press, 1967), pp. 77–87.

PART X
Contractarianism

Introduction to Part X

The social contract tradition finds its natural home within political philosophy. In this context, those writing within this tradition (so-called *contractarians*) have offered nuanced and powerful accounts of the origins and justification of state authority, and the moral basis of a citizen's duty to obey the law. The state earns its right to govern by virtue of an agreement among the governed to give it this authority, and the fact that citizens have promised one another to obey the law is what generates their duty to do so.

The social contract theory has received less attention in the moral realm, though its historical antecedents reach all the way back to Book II of Plato's *Republic*. There, Plato describes (but ultimately rejects) an account of the origins of morality very like Thomas Hobbes' account of the origins of the state. According to such an account, each of us has a natural desire to become the richest and most powerful person around. However, each of us also knows that only a very few can make it to the top of the economic and political heap, and none of us wants to be the loser in such a highly competitive game. So we compromise. Rather than a competitive free-for-all, in which misery is par for the course, we settle for a system that protects us from the worst, at the cost of our renouncing our chances to get all that we want. Morality is a system of rules based on two things: a desire to get as much

as you can for yourself, and a fear that others, pursuing the same agenda, will act on this very desire and victimize you in the process.

Hobbes begins his account by having us envision a state of nature (a situation in which there are no enforceable laws). Hobbes conceives of such a state as one in which "the life of man is solitary, poore, nasty, brutish, and short." Not a very pleasant prospect. Any rational person will want to escape such a situation, and the way to do this is to agree amongst ourselves to limit our liberty. We forgo the freedom to pursue self-interest at the expense of others, provided that they do so as well. What results is a system of mutually beneficial cooperation that leaves each of us much better off than we would be in a state of nature. On this view, morality is a system of rules that restrains people from unlimited pursuit of personal gain, and in so doing, guarantees its participants a certain minimum of peace and security.

This account does a good job of explaining the origin of many familiar moral rules. Those that prohibit killing, cheating, stealing and lying are ones that all rational people would endorse as the basis of mutual cooperation. No one wants to be the victim of such practices, and forgoing the liberty to engage in them is a reasonable price to pay for some protection that one won't be victimized in these ways.

Suppose that one has signed on to a set of these mutually beneficial rules, but then sees a chance to break one of them, and in so doing, to reap a windfall. If the society is a well-structured one, then penalties for rule violations will be stiff enough to discourage people from taking the risk. But suppose that one has done all of the calculations, and has decided that the chances of getting away with such a violation are pretty good, that the potential gain is very substantial, and the price to be paid if caught is worth the risk. Then isn't it rational to go ahead and break the rules?

Hobbes puts just this challenge into the mouth of his Foole, and offers an answer that is open to a variety of interpretations. The deep problem here stems from an assumption that Hobbes endorses, and that the contemporary Hobbesian, David Gauthier, also accepts. Whereas Hobbes offers just a couple of paragraphs by way of response to the Foole's challenge, Gauthier devotes much of his article here to addressing it. The difficulty for the contractarian stems from the assumption of *rational egoism*. This is the view that one has good reason to do something only if doing it will serve one's self-interest. The reason one should enter a social contract, and abide by its terms, is that in doing so, one will escape from the state of nature, and thereby enhance self-interest. If there really were a chance of doing very well without agreeing to the many restrictions imposed by the moral rules, then there would be no reason to adhere to them.

But aren't there such chances? Gauthier counsels a move that is quite similar to that endorsed by Gregory Kavka, in his article in Part III. In that piece, Kavka argues that cultivating a moral character is usually in one's long-term self-interest, even if, once one has such a character, one will forgo opportunities to enhance self-interest by breaking the moral rules. Being a moral person means being indifferent, or positively hostile, to opportunities to reap rewards through immorality. It also means being inattentive to various opportunities for such self-enrichment, for the moral person won't be on the lookout for chances to break the moral rules. Gauthier thinks that our disposition to violate moral rules is more or less transparent, and if this is so, then our unreliability is pretty well advertised to others, who will be reluctant to share the benefits of

cooperation that come from allegiance to the moral rules. So if one really wants to promote one's self-interest, as we all want to do, and as we all have excellent reason to do, then one will try to maintain a highly moral character, which will prevent one from succumbing to any temptation to immorality.

If this picture is largely on target, then we have here an account that can both explain much of the paradigmatic content of morality, while at the same time providing a justification for our being moral. Yet this Hobbesian picture has always had its critics. Its account of the scope of the moral community, and in particular the moral standing of animals and vulnerable human beings, has long been contested. (For a brief discussion of this, see the Introduction to Part VII.) Its allegiance to rational egoism has also been subject to criticism (this matter is pursued at greater length in a number of the readings in Part III). Relatedly, many have argued that the link between moral action and the likely enhancement of self-interest is contingent, at best. If the link is severed, there is no basis, according to Hobbes and Gauthier, for our continued adherence to our moral agreements.

Enter a different form of contractarianism, this one descended from Kant and Rousseau, rather than from Hobbes. This sort of theory, represented here by the work of John Rawls and Thomas Scanlon, does not locate the origin of morality, or the justification of moral conduct, in the rational pursuit of self-interest.

Each contractarian theory can be distinguished by its views on three subjects. The first is the characterization of the contracting parties – what they know, what their interests are, how rational they are, etc. The second is what the conditions of choice look like – is everyone equally situated, or are there discrepancies of power? Are deliberations time-sensitive, made under external pressure, meant to bind only temporarily, or in perpetuity? The third is the subject matter of negotiations – are parties intending to fix rules to govern all aspects of their lives together, or just some portion thereof? And if the latter, which portion?

The selection we have here, from John Rawls's *A Theory of Justice*, provides the basics of his contractarian view. Though his account is explicitly restricted to providing a justification only of the basic social institutions, rather than the whole of morality, we can fairly easily extrapolate in order to get a well-developed ethic. Rawls claims that the basic principles of justice are those that would be agreed to by mutually disinterested, rational people who have been placed under a "veil of ignorance." The social contract, for Rawls, is entirely a theoretical device, and not meant to reflect any actual agreement among those who are bound by the decisions that would be made by the highly idealized contractors. The veil strips away all knowledge from the contractors that would introduce partiality into their deliberations. None of the contractors knows any distinguishing features about himself or herself – all knowledge of one's sex, race, religion, wealth, and social status are withheld, so as to ensure that the outcome of the joint deliberations are fair.

Rawls coined the phrase "justice as fairness" to describe the essence of his view. The idea is that the rules of justice are those that would be agreed to by people who were fairly situated to make choices about the rules that are to govern their interactions. The main difference between the Rawlsian conception and the one favored by Gauthier and Hobbes is in the depiction of the contractors. Rawls does not envision any one of us as the relevant contractor; Hobbes and Gauthier do precisely that. For them, it would be, in a way, deeply unfair to imagine away all of the specifics of a person's situation in trying to determine the content of the rules that would be rational for him to agree upon. Indeed, one of Gauthier's central criticisms of Rawls's account is that its central principles of justice can leave a rational person completely indifferent. In that case, there is no compelling reason to adhere to them, and they are, in Gauthier's eyes, thereby both useless and unjustified.

Thomas Scanlon is the last of our representatives of the social contract tradition. For Scanlon, an action is wrong if it would be forbidden by a system of rules governing social interaction that no one could reasonably reject. The essence of the Scanlonian view is this notion of reasonable rejection. That a person actually does reject a rule, or a set of rules, does not automatically immunize him from a duty of obedience, since his rejection may be unreasonable. Part of what it is to be reasonable in this context is to have a care for one's own well-being. Another part is to have a care for what others, given their outlooks, could consider to be acceptable terms of interaction. The guiding thought is that one is looking explicitly for terms of cooperation that no one will reject, were they each seeking to identify terms of cooperation that avoid imposing undue sacrifices on any party to the agreement.

Scanlon frames his discussion against the background of what he calls *philosophical utilitarianism* – the idea that the only fundamental moral facts are those about individual well-being. This view, he thinks, accounts for the great popularity and influence of act and rule utilitarianism. Scanlon rejects these forms of utilitarianism, and uses them as a foil to develop his contractarianism. One problem he finds for utilitarianism is that of moral motivation. Though there is a natural connection between one's own well-being and one's motivation, the utilitarian emphasis on impartiality, and its insistence that actions maximize overall happiness, can leave the rational agent cold. Scanlon thinks he can do better, by citing as the central moral motivation the desire to act on a basis that others could not reasonably reject. If we consider paradigmatically moral people, we see that each of them has this desire. They are directly concerned to be able to justify their actions to others, at least so long as these others are willing to listen to reason. As Scanlon sees it, this motivation, rather than a concern that happiness be maximized, is the distinctively moral one.

CHAPTER 62
Leviathan

THOMAS HOBBES

Of the Natural Condition of Mankind as Concerning their Felicity and Misery

Nature has made men so equal in the faculties of the body and mind as that, though there be found one man sometimes manifestly stronger in body or of quicker mind than another, yet, when all is reckoned together, the difference between man and man is not so considerable as that one man can thereupon claim to himself any benefit to which another may not pretend as well as he. For as to the strength of body, the weakest has strength enough to kill the strongest, either by secret machination or by confederacy with others that are in the same danger with himself.

And as to the faculties of the mind, setting aside the arts grounded upon words, and especially that skill of proceeding upon general and infallible rules called science – which very few have and but in few things, as being not a native faculty born with us, nor attained, as prudence, while we look after somewhat else – I find yet a greater equality among men than that of strength. For prudence is but experience, which equal time equally bestows on all men in those things they equally apply themselves unto. That which may perhaps make such equality incredible is but a vain conceit of

one's own wisdom, which almost all men think they have in a greater degree than the vulgar – that is, than all men but themselves and a few others whom, by fame or for concurring with themselves, they approve. For such is the nature of men that howsoever they may acknowledge many others to be more witty or more eloquent or more learned, yet they will hardly believe there be many so wise as themselves; for they see their own wit at hand and other men's at a distance. But this proves rather that men are in that point equal than unequal. For there is not ordinarily a greater sign of the equal distribution of anything than that every man is contented with his share.

From this equality of ability arises equality of hope in the attaining of our ends. And therefore if any two men desire the same thing, which nevertheless they cannot both enjoy, they become enemies; and in the way to their end, which is principally their own conservation, and sometimes their delectation only, endeavor to destroy or subdue one another. And from hence it comes to pass that where an invader has no more to fear than another man's single power, if one plant, sow, build, or possess a convenient seat, others may probably be expected to come prepared with forces united to dispossess and deprive him, not only of the fruit of his labor, but also of his life or liberty. And the invader again is in the like danger of another.

Thomas Hobbes, from *Leviathan*, 1651.

And from this diffidence of one another there is no way for any man to secure himself so reasonable as anticipation – that is, by force or wiles to master the persons of all men he can, so long till he see no other power great enough to endanger him; and this is no more than his own conservation requires, and is generally allowed. Also, because there be some that take pleasure in contemplating their own power in the acts of conquest, which they pursue farther than their security requires, if others that otherwise would be glad to be at ease within modest bounds should not by invasion increase their power, they would not be able, long time, by standing only on their defense, to subsist. And by consequence, such augmentation of dominion over men being necessary to a man's conservation, it ought to be allowed him.

Again, men have no pleasure, but on the contrary a great deal of grief, in keeping company where there is no power able to overawe them all. For every man looks that his companion should value him at the same rate he sets upon himself; and upon all signs of contempt or undervaluing naturally endeavors, as far as he dares (which among them that have no common power to keep them in quiet is far enough to make them destroy each other), to extort a greater value from his contemners by damage and from others by the example.

So that in the nature of man we find three principal causes of quarrel: first, competition; secondly, diffidence; thirdly, glory.

The first makes men invade for gain, the second for safety, and the third for reputation. The first use violence to make themselves masters of other men's persons, wives, children, and cattle; the second, to defend them; the third, for trifles, as a word, a smile, a different opinion, and any other sign of undervalue, either direct in their persons or by reflection in their kindred, their friends, their nation, their profession, or their name.

Hereby it is manifest that, during the time men live without a common power to keep them all in awe, they are in that condition which is called war, and such a war as is of every man against every man. For WAR consists not in battle only, or the act of fighting, but in a tract of time wherein the will to contend by battle is sufficiently known; and therefore the notion of *time* is to be considered in the nature of war as it is in the nature of weather. For as the nature of foul weather lies not in a shower or two of rain but in an inclination thereto of many days together, so the nature of war consists not in actual fighting but in the known disposition thereto during all the time there is no assurance to the contrary. All other time is PEACE.

Whatsoever, therefore, is consequent to a time of war where every man is enemy to every man, the same is consequent to the time wherein men live without other security than what their own strength and their own invention shall furnish them withal. In such condition there is no place for industry, because the fruit thereof is uncertain: and consequently no culture of the earth; no navigation nor use of the commodities that may be imported by sea; no commodious building; no instruments of moving and removing such things as require much force; no knowledge of the face of the earth; no account of time; no arts; no letters; no society; and, which is worst of all, continual fear and danger of violent death; and the life of man solitary, poor, nasty, brutish, and short.

It may seem strange to some man that has not well weighed these things that nature should thus dissociate and render men apt to invade and destroy one another; and he may therefore, not trusting to this inference made from the passions, desire perhaps to have the same confirmed by experience. Let him therefore consider with himself – when taking a journey he arms himself and seeks to go well accompanied, when going to sleep he locks his doors, when even in his house he locks his chests, and this when he knows there be laws and public officers, armed, to revenge all injuries shall be done him – what opinion he has of his fellow subjects when he rides armed, of his fellow citizens when he locks his doors, and of his children and servants when he locks his chests. Does he not there as much accuse mankind by his actions as I do by my words? But neither of us accuse man's nature in it. The desires and other passions of man are in themselves no sin. No more are the actions that proceed from those passions till they know a law that forbids them, which, till laws be made, they cannot know, nor can any law be made till they have agreed upon the person that shall make it.

It may peradventure be thought there was never such a time nor condition of war as this, and I believe it was never generally so over all the world; but there are many places where they live so now. For the savage people in many places of America, except the government of small families, the concord whereof depends on natural lust, have no government at all and live at this day in that brutish manner as I said before. Howsoever, it may be perceived what manner of life there would be where there were no common power to fear by the manner of life which men that have formerly lived under a peaceful government use to degenerate into in a civil war.

But though there had never been any time wherein particular men were in a condition of war one against another, yet in all times kings and persons of sovereign authority, because of their independency, are in continual jealousies and in the state and posture of gladiators, having their weapons pointing and their eyes fixed on one another – that is, their forts, garrisons, and guns upon the frontiers of their kingdoms, and continual spies upon their neighbors – which is a posture of war. But because they uphold thereby the industry of their subjects, there does not follow from it that misery which accompanies the liberty of particular men.

To this war of every man against every man, this also is consequent: that nothing can be unjust. The notions of right and wrong, justice and injustice, have there no place. Where there is no common power, there is no law; where no law, no injustice. Force and fraud are in war the two cardinal virtues. Justice and injustice are none of the faculties neither of the body nor mind. If they were, they might be in a man that were alone in the world, as well as his senses and passions. They are qualities that relate to men in society, not in solitude. It is consequent also to the same condition that there be no propriety, no dominion, no *mine* and *thine* distinct; but only that to be every man's that he can get, and for so long as he can keep it. And thus much for the ill condition which man by mere nature is actually placed

in, though with a possibility to come out of it consisting partly in the passions, partly in his reason.

The passions that incline men to peace are fear of death, desire of such things as are necessary to commodious living, and a hope by their industry to obtain them. And reason suggests convenient articles of peace, upon which men may be drawn to agreement. These articles are they which otherwise are called the Laws of Nature, whereof I shall speak more particularly in the two following chapters.

Of the First and Second Natural Laws, and of Contracts

The RIGHT OF NATURE, which writers commonly call *jus naturale*, is the liberty each man has to use his own power, as he will himself, for the preservation of his own nature – that is to say, of his own life – and consequently of doing anything which, in his own judgment and reason, he shall conceive to be the aptest means thereunto.

By LIBERTY is understood, according to the proper signification of the word, the absence of external impediments; which impediments may oft take away part of a man's power to do what he would, but cannot hinder him from using the power left him according as his judgment and reason shall dictate to him.

A LAW OF NATURE, *lex naturalis*, is a precept or general rule, found out by reason, by which a man is forbidden to do that which is destructive of his life or takes away the means of preserving the same and to omit that by which he thinks it may be best preserved. For though they that speak of this subject use to confound *jus* and *lex*, right and law, yet they ought to be distinguished; because RIGHT consists in liberty to do or to forbear, whereas LAW determines and binds to one of them; so that law and right differ as much as obligation and liberty, which in one and the same matter are inconsistent.

And because the condition of man [. . .], is a condition of war of every one against every one – in which case everyone is governed by his own reason and there is nothing he can make use of that may not be a help unto him in preserving his life against his enemies – it follows that in such a condition every man has a right to everything, even to one another's body. And therefore, as long as this natural right of every man to everything endures, there can be no security to any man, how strong or wise soever he be, of living out the time which nature ordinarily allows men to live. And consequently it is a precept or general rule of reason *that every man ought to endeavor peace, as far as he has hope of obtaining it; and when he cannot obtain it, that he may seek and use all helps and advantages of war.* The first branch of which rule contains the first and fundamental law of nature, which is *to seek peace and follow it.* The second, the sum of the right of nature, which is, *by all means we can to defend ourselves.*

From this fundamental law of nature, by which men are commanded to endeavor peace, is derived this second law: *that a man be willing, when others are so too, as far forth as for peace and defense of himself he shall think it necessary, to lay down this right to all things, and be contented with so much liberty against other men as he would allow other men against himself.* For as long as every man holds this right of doing anything he likes, so long are all men in the condition of war. But if other men will not lay down their right as well as he, then there is no reason for anyone to divest himself of his, for that were to expose himself to prey, which no man is bound to, rather than to dispose himself to peace. This is that law of the gospel: *whatsoever you require that others should do to you, that do ye to them.* And that law of all men, *quod tibi fieri non vis, alteri ne feceris.*[1]

To lay down a man's *right* to anything is to *divest* himself of the *liberty* of hindering another of the benefit of his own right to the same. For he that renounces or passes away his right gives not to any other man a right which he had not before – because there is nothing to which every man had not right by nature – but only stands out of his way, that he may enjoy his own original right without hindrance from him, not without hindrance from another. So that the effect which redounds to one man by another man's defect of right is but so much diminution of impediments to the use of his own right original. Right is laid aside either by simply renouncing it or by transferring it to another. By *simply* RENOUNCING, when he cares not to whom the benefit thereof redounds. By TRANSFERRING, when he intends the benefit thereof to some certain person or persons. And when a man has in either manner abandoned or granted away his right, then he is said to be OBLIGED or BOUND not to hinder those to whom such right is granted or abandoned from the benefit of it; and that he *ought,* and it is his DUTY, not to make void that voluntary act of his own; and that such hindrance is INJUSTICE and INJURY as being *sine jure,*[2] the right being before renounced or transferred. So that *injury* or *injustice* in the controversies of the world is somewhat like to that which in the disputations of scholars is called *absurdity.* For as it is there called an absurdity to contradict what one maintained in the beginning, so in the world it is called injustice and injury voluntarily to undo that which from the beginning he had voluntarily done. The way by which a man either simply renounces or transfers his right is a declaration or signification by some voluntary and sufficient sign or signs that he does so renounce or transfer, or has so renounced or transferred, the same to him that accepts it. And these signs are either words only or actions only; or as it happens most often, both words and actions. And the same are the BONDS by which men are bound and obliged – bonds that have their strength, not from their own nature, for nothing is more easily broken than a man's word, but from fear of some evil consequence upon the rupture.

Whensoever a man transfers his right or renounces it, it is either in consideration of some right reciprocally transferred to himself or for some other good he hopes for thereby. For it is a voluntary act; and of the voluntary acts of every man, the object is some *good to himself.* And therefore there be some rights which no man can be understood by any words or other signs to have abandoned or transferred. As, first, a man cannot lay down the right of resisting them that assault him by force to take away his life, because he cannot be understood to aim thereby at any good to himself. The same may be said of wounds and chains and imprisonment, both because there is no benefit consequent to such patience as there is to the patience of suffering another to be wounded or imprisoned, as also because a man cannot tell, when he sees men proceed against him by violence, whether they intend his death or not. And, lastly, the motive and end for which this renouncing and transferring of right is introduced is nothing else but the security of a man's person in his life and in the means of so preserving life as not to be weary of it. And therefore if a man by words or other signs seem to despoil himself of the end for which those signs were intended, he is not to be understood as if he meant it or that it was his will, but that he was ignorant of how such words and actions were to be interpreted.

The mutual transferring of right is that which men call CONTRACT.

There is difference between transferring of right to the thing and transferring, or tradition – that is, delivery – of the thing itself. For the thing may be delivered together with the translation of the right, as in buying and selling with ready money or exchange of goods or lands, and it may be delivered some time after.

Again, one of the contractors may deliver the thing contracted for on his part and leave the other to perform his part at some determinate time after and in the meantime be trusted, and then the contract on his part is called PACT or COVENANT; or both parts may contract now to perform hereafter, in which cases he that is to perform in time to come, being trusted, his performance is called *keeping of promise* or faith, and the failing of performance, if it be voluntary, *violation of faith.*

When the transferring of right is not mutual, but one of the parties transfers in hope to gain thereby friendship or service from another or from his friends, or in hope to gain the reputation of charity or magnanimity, or to deliver his mind from the pain of compassion, or in hope of reward in heaven – this is not contract but GIFT, FREE GIFT, GRACE, which words signify one and the same thing.

Signs of contract are either *express* or *by inference.* Express are words spoken with understanding of what they signify, and such words are either of the time *present* or *past* – as *I give, I grant, I have given, I have granted, I will that this be yours* – or of the future – as *I will give, I will grant* – which words of the future are called PROMISE.

Signs by inference are sometimes the consequence of words, sometimes the consequence of silence, sometimes the consequence of actions, sometimes the consequence of forbearing an action; and generally a sign by inference of any contract is whatsoever sufficiently argues the will of the contractor.

Words alone, if they be of the time to come and contain a bare promise, are an insufficient sign of a free gift and therefore not obligatory. For if they be of the time to come, as *tomorrow I will give,* they are a sign I have not given yet and consequently that my right is not transferred but remains till I transfer it by some other act. But if the words be of the time present or past, as *I have given* or *do give to be delivered tomorrow,* then is my tomorrow's right given away today, and that by the virtue of the words though there were no other argument of my will. And there is a great difference in the signification of these words: *volo hoc tuum esse cras* and *cras dabo* – that is, between *I will that this be yours tomorrow* and *I will give it you tomorrow* – for the word *I will,* in the former manner of speech, signifies an act of the will present, but in the latter it signifies a promise of an act of the will to come; and therefore the former words, being of the present, transfer a future right; the latter, that be of the future, transfer nothing. But if there be other signs of the will to transfer a right besides words, then, though the gift be free, yet may the right be understood to pass by words of the future: as if a man propound a prize to him that comes first to the end of a race, the gift is free; and though the words be of the future, yet the right passes; for if he would not have his words so be understood, he should not have let them run.

In contracts, the right passes not only where the words are of the time present or past but also where they are of the future, because all contract is mutual translation or change of right, and therefore he that promises only because he has already received the benefit for which he promises is to be understood as if he intended the right should pass; for unless he had been content to have his words so understood, the other would not have performed his part first. And for that cause, in buying and selling and other acts of contract a promise is equivalent to a covenant and therefore obligatory.

He that performs first in the case of a contract is said to MERIT that which he is to receive by the performance of the other; and he has it as *due*. Also when a prize is propounded to many which is to be given to him only that wins, or money is thrown among many to be enjoyed by them that catch it, though this be a free gift, yet so to win or so to catch is to *merit* and to have it as DUE. For the right is transferred in the propounding of the prize and in throwing down the money, though it be not determined to whom but by the event of the contention. But there is between these two sorts of merit this difference: that in contract I merit by virtue of my own power and the contractor's need, but in this case of free gift I am enabled to merit only by the benignity of the giver; in contract I merit at the contractor's hand that he should depart with his right, in this case of gift I merit not that the giver should part with his right but that when he has parted with it, it should be mine rather than another's. And this I think to be the meaning of that distinction of the Schools between *meritum congrui* and *meritum condigni*.[3] For God Almighty having promised Paradise to those men, hoodwinked with carnal desires, that can walk through this world according to the precepts and limits prescribed by him, they say he that shall so walk shall merit Paradise *ex congruo*. But because no man can demand a right to it, by his own righteousness or any other power in himself, but by the free grace of God only, they say no man can merit Paradise *ex condigno*. This, I say, I think is the meaning of that distinction; but because disputers do not agree upon the signification of their own terms of art longer than it serves their turn, I will not affirm anything of their meaning; only this I say: when a gift is given indefinitely, as a prize to be contended for, he that wins merits and may claim the prize as due.

If a covenant be made wherein neither of the parties perform presently but trust one another, in the condition of mere nature, which is a condition of war of every man against every man, upon any reasonable suspicion, it is void; but if there be a common power set over them both, with right and force sufficient to compel performance, it is not void. For he that performs first has no assurance the other will perform after, because the bonds of words are too weak to bridle men's ambition, avarice, anger, and other passions without the fear of some coercive power which in the condition of mere nature, where all men are equal and judges of the justness of their own fears, cannot possibly be supposed. And therefore he which performs first does but betray himself to his enemy, contrary to the right he can never abandon of defending his life and means of living.

But in a civil estate, where there is a power set up to constrain those that would otherwise violate their faith, that fear is no more reasonable; and for that cause, he which by the covenant is to perform first is obliged so to do.

The cause of fear which makes such a covenant invalid must be always something arising after the covenant made, as some new fact or other sign of the will not to perform; else it cannot make the covenant void. For that which could not hinder a man from promising ought not to be admitted as a hindrance of performing.

He that transfers any right transfers the means of enjoying it, as far as lies in his power. As he that sells land is understood to transfer the herbage and whatsoever grows upon it; nor can he that sells a mill turn away the stream that drives it. And they that give to a man the right of government in sovereignty are understood to give him the right of levying money to maintain soldiers and of appointing magistrates for the administration of justice.

To make covenants with brute beasts is impossible because, not understanding our speech, they understand not nor accept of any translation of right, nor can translate any right to another; and without mutual acceptation there is no covenant.

To make covenant with God is impossible but by mediation of such as God speaks to, either by revelation supernatural or by his lieutenants that govern under him and in his name; for otherwise we know not whether our covenants be accepted or not. And therefore they that vow anything contrary to any law of nature vow in vain, as being a thing unjust to pay such vow. And if it be a thing commanded by the law of nature, it is not the vow but the law that binds them.

The matter or subject of a covenant is always something that falls under deliberation, for to covenant is an act of the will – that is to say, an act, and the last act, of deliberation – and is therefore always understood to be something to come, and which is judged possible for him that covenants to perform.

And therefore to promise that which is known to be impossible is no covenant. But if that prove impossible afterwards which before was thought possible, the covenant is valid, and binds, though not to the thing itself, yet to the value, or, if that also be impossible, to the unfeigned endeavor of performing as much as is possible, for to more no man can be obliged.

Men are freed of their covenants two ways: by performing or by being forgiven. For performance is the natural end of obligation, and forgiveness the restitution of liberty, as being a retransferring of that right in which the obligation consisted.

Covenants entered into by fear, in the condition of mere nature, are obligatory. For example, if I covenant to pay a ransom or service for my life to an enemy, I am bound by it; for it is a contract, wherein one receives the benefit of life, the other is to receive money or service for it; and consequently, where no other law, as in the condition of mere nature, forbids the performance, the covenant is valid. Therefore prisoners of war, if trusted with the payment of their ransom, are obliged to pay it; and if a weaker prince make a disadvantageous peace with a stronger, for fear, he is bound to keep it; unless, as has been said before, there arises some new and just cause of fear to renew the war. And even in commonwealths, if I be forced to redeem myself from a thief by promising him money, I am bound to pay it till the civil law discharge me. For whatsoever I may lawfully do without obligation, the same I may lawfully covenant to do through fear; and what I lawfully covenant, I cannot lawfully break. A former covenant makes void a later. For a man that has passed away his right to one man today has it not to pass tomorrow to another; and therefore the later promise passes no right, but is null.

A covenant not to defend myself from force by force is always void. For, as I have showed before, no man can transfer or lay down his right to save himself from death, wounds, and imprisonment, the avoiding whereof is the only end of laying down any right; and therefore the promise of not resisting force in no covenant transfers any right, nor is obliging. For though a man may covenant thus: *unless I do so or so, kill me*, he cannot covenant thus: *unless I do so or so, I will not resist you when you come to kill me*. For man by nature chooses the lesser evil, which is danger of death in resisting, rather than the greater, which is certain and present death in not resisting. And this is granted to be true by all men, in that they lead criminals to execution and prison with armed men, notwithstanding that such criminals have consented to the law by which they are condemned.

A covenant to accuse oneself, without assurance of pardon, is likewise invalid. For in the condition of nature, where every man is judge, there is no place for accusation; and in the civil state, the accusation is followed with punishment, which, being force, a man is not obliged not to resist. The same is also true of the accusation of those by whose condemnation a man falls into misery, as of a father, wife, or benefactor. For the testimony of such an accuser, if it be not willingly given, is presumed to be corrupted by nature, and therefore not to be received; and where a man's testimony is not to be credited, he is not bound to give it. Also accusations upon torture are not to be reputed as testimonies. For torture is to be used but as means of conjecture and light in the further examination and search of truth; and what is in that case confessed tends to the ease of him that is tortured, not to the informing of the torturers, and therefore ought not to have the credit of a sufficient testimony; for whether he deliver himself by true or false accusation, he does it by the right of preserving his own life.

The force of words being, as I have formerly noted, too weak to hold men to the performance of their covenants, there are in man's nature but two imaginable helps to strengthen it. And those are either a fear of the consequence of breaking their word, or a glory or pride in appearing not to need to break it. This latter is a generosity too rarely found to be presumed on, especially in the pursuers of wealth, command, or sensual pleasure – which are the greatest part of mankind. The passion to be reckoned upon is fear, whereof there be two very general objects: one, the power of spirits invisible; the other, the power of those men they shall therein offend. Of these two, though the former be the greater power, yet the fear of the latter is commonly the greater fear. The fear of the former is in every man his own religion, which has place in the nature of man before civil society. The latter has not so, at least not place enough to keep men to their promises, because in the condition of mere nature the inequality of power is not discerned but by the event of battle. So that before the time of civil society, or in the interruption thereof by war, there is nothing can strengthen a covenant of peace agreed on against the temptations of avarice, ambition, lust, or other strong desire but the fear of that invisible power, which they everyone worship as God and fear as a revenger of their perfidy. All therefore that can be done between two men not subject to civil power is to put one another to swear by the God he fears, which *swearing* or OATH is a *form of speech, added to a promise, by which he that promises signifies that, unless he perform, he renounces the mercy of his God, or calls to him for vengeance on himself.* Such was the heathen form, *Let Jupiter kill me else, as I kill this beast.* So is our form, *I shall do thus and thus, so help me God.* And this, with the rites and ceremonies which everyone uses in his own religion, that the fear of breaking faith might be the greater.

By this it appears that an oath taken according to any other form or rite than his that swears is in vain and no oath, and that there is no swearing by anything which the swearer thinks not God. For though men have sometimes used to swear by their kings, for fear or flattery, yet they would have it thereby understood they attributed to them divine honor. And that swearing unnecessarily by God is but profaning of his name; and swearing by other things, as men do in common discourse, is not swearing but an impious custom gotten by too much vehemence of talking.

It appears also that the oath adds nothing to the obligation. For a covenant, if lawful, binds in the sight of God without the oath as much as with it; if unlawful, binds not at all, though it be confirmed with an oath.

Of Other Laws of Nature

From that law of nature by which we are obliged to transfer to another such rights as, being retained, hinder the peace of mankind, there follows a third, which is this: *that men perform their covenants made*; without which covenants are in vain and but empty words, and, the right of all men to all things remaining, we are still in the condition of war.

And in this law of nature consists the fountain and original of JUSTICE. For where no covenant has preceded there has no right been transferred, and every man has right to every thing; and consequently no action can be unjust. But when a covenant is made, then to break it is *unjust*; and the definition of INJUSTICE is no other than *the not performance of covenant.* And whatsoever is not unjust is *just.*

But because covenants of mutual trust, where there is a fear of not performance on either part, as has been said in the former chapter, are invalid, though the original of justice be the making of covenants, yet injustice actually there can be none till the cause of such fear be taken away, which, while men are in the natural condition of war, cannot be done. Therefore, before the names of just and unjust can have place, there must be some coercive power to compel men equally to the performance of their covenants by the terror of some punishment greater than the benefit they expect by the breach of their covenant, and to make good that propriety which by mutual contract men acquire in recompense of the universal right they abandon; and such power there is none before the erection of a commonwealth. And this is also to be gathered out of the ordinary definition of justice in the Schools, for they say that *justice is the constant will of giving to every man his own.* And therefore where there is no *own* – that is, no propriety – there is no injustice; and where there is no coercive power erected – that is, where there is no commonwealth – there is no propriety, all men having right to all things; therefore, where there is no commonwealth, there nothing is unjust. So that the nature of justice consists in keeping of valid covenants; but the validity of covenants begins not but with the constitution of a civil power sufficient to compel men to keep them; and then it is also that propriety begins.

The fool hath said in his heart, there is no such thing as justice,[4] and sometimes also with his tongue, seriously alleging that, every man's conservation and contentment being committed to his own care, there could be no reason why every man might not do what he thought conduced thereunto; and therefore also to make or not make, keep or not keep covenants was not against reason when it conduced to one's benefit. He does not therein deny that there be covenants and that they are sometimes broken, sometimes kept, and that such breach of them may be called injustice and the observance of them justice; but he questions whether injustice, taking away the fear of God – for the same fool hath said in his heart there is no God – may not sometimes stand with that reason which dictates to every man his own good, and particularly then when it conduces to such a benefit as shall put a man in a condition to neglect not only the dispraise and revilings, but also the power of other men. The kingdom of God is gotten by violence; but what if it could be gotten by unjust violence? Were it against reason so to get it, when it is impossible to receive hurt by it? And if it be not against reason, it is not against justice, or else justice is not to be approved for good. From such reasoning as this, successful wickedness has obtained the name of virtue; and some that in all other things have disallowed the violation of faith yet have allowed it when it is for the getting of a kingdom. And the heathen that believed that Saturn was deposed by his son Jupiter believed nevertheless the same Jupiter to be the avenger of injustice – somewhat like to a piece of law in Coke's *Commentaries on Littleton*[5] where he says: if the right heir of the crown be attainted of treason, yet the crown shall descend to him and *eo instante* the attainder be void; from which instances a man will be very prone to infer that when the heir apparent of a kingdom shall kill him that is in possession, though his father, you may call it injustice or

by what other name you will, yet it can never be against reason, seeing all the voluntary actions of men tend to the benefit of themselves, and those actions are most reasonable that conduce most to their ends. This specious reasoning is nevertheless false.

For the question is not of promises mutual where there is no security of performance on either side – as when there is no civil power erected over the parties promising – for such promises are no covenants; but either where one of the parties has performed already or where there is a power to make him perform there is the question whether it be against reason – that is, against the benefit of the other – to perform or not. And I say it is not against reason. For the manifestation whereof we are to consider, first, that when a man does a thing which, notwithstanding anything can be foreseen and reckoned on, tends to his own destruction, howsoever some accident which he could not expect, arriving, may turn it to his benefit, yet such events do not make it reasonably or wisely done. Secondly, that in a condition of war, wherein every man to every man, for want of a common power to keep them all in awe, is an enemy, there is no man who can hope by his own strength or wit to defend himself from destruction without the help of confederates, where everyone expects the same defense by the confederation that anyone else does; and therefore he which declares he thinks it reason to deceive those that help him can in reason expect no other means of safety than what can be had from his own single power. He, therefore, that breaks his covenant, and consequently declares that he thinks he may with reason do so, cannot be received into any society that unite themselves for peace and defense, but by the error of them that receive him; nor, when he is received, be retained in it without seeing the danger of their error, which errors a man cannot reasonably reckon upon as the means of his security; and therefore if he be left or cast out of society he perishes, and if he live in society, it is by the errors of other men, which he could not foresee nor reckon upon, and consequently against the reason of his preservation; and so, as all men that contribute not to his destruction, forbear him only out of ignorance of what is good for themselves.

As for the instance of gaining the secure and perpetual felicity of heaven by any way, it is frivolous, there being but one way imaginable, and that is not breaking but keeping of covenant.

And for the other instance of attaining sovereignty by rebellion, it is manifest that, though the event follow, yet because it cannot reasonably be expected, but rather the contrary, and because by gaining it so others are taught to gain the same in like manner, the attempt thereof is against reason. Justice, therefore – that is to say, keeping of covenant – is a rule of reason by which we are forbidden to do anything destructive to our life, and consequently a law of nature.

There be some that proceed further and will not have the law of nature to be those rules which conduce to the preservation of man's life on earth but to the attaining of an eternal felicity after death, to which they think the breach of covenant may conduce and consequently be just and reasonable; such are they that think it a work of merit to kill or depose or rebel against the sovereign power constituted over them by their own consent. But because there is no natural knowledge of man's estate after death – much less of the reward that is then to be given to breach of faith – but only a belief grounded upon other men's saying that they know it supernaturally, or that they know those that knew them that knew others that knew it supernaturally, breach of faith cannot be called a precept of reason or nature.

Others that allow for a law of nature the keeping of faith do nevertheless make exception of certain persons, as heretics and such as use not to perform their covenant to others; and this also is against reason. For if any fault of a man be sufficient to discharge our covenant made, the same ought in reason to have been sufficient to have hindered the making of it.

The names of just and unjust, when they are attributed to men, signify one thing, and when they are attributed to actions, another. When they are attributed to men, they signify conformity or inconformity of manners to reason. But when they are attributed to actions, they signify the conformity or inconformity to reason, not of manners

or manner of life, but of particular actions. A just man, therefore, is he that takes all the care he can that his actions may be all just; and an unjust man is he that neglects it. And such men are more often in our language styled by the names of righteous and unrighteous than just and unjust, though the meaning be the same. Therefore a righteous man does not lose that title by one or a few unjust actions that proceed from sudden passion or mistake of things or persons; nor does an unrighteous man lose his character for such actions as he does or forbears to do for fear, because his will is not framed by the justice but by the apparent benefit of what he is to do. That which gives to human actions the relish of justice is a certain nobleness or gallantness of courage, rarely found, by which a man scorns to be beholden for the contentment of his life to fraud or breach of promise. This justice of the manners is that which is meant where justice is called a virtue and injustice a vice.

But the justice of actions denominates men, not just, but *guiltless;* and the injustice of the same, which is also called injury, gives them but the name of *guilty.*

Again, the injustice of manners is the disposition or aptitude to do injury, and is injury, and is injustice before it proceed to act and without supposing any individual person injured. But the injustice of an action – that is to say, injury – supposes an individual person injured – namely, him to whom the covenant was made – and therefore many times the injury is received by one man when the damage redounds to another. As when the master commands his servant to give money to a stranger: if it be not done, the injury is done to the master, whom he had before covenanted to obey; but the damage redounds to the stranger, to whom he had no obligation and therefore could not injure him. And so also in common-wealths private men may remit to one another their debts but not robberies or other violences whereby they are endamaged; because the detaining of debt is an injury to themselves, but robbery and violence are injuries to the person of the commonwealth.

Whatsoever is done to a man, conformable to his own will signified to the doer, is no injury to him. For if he that does it has not passed away his original right to do what he please by some antecedent covenant, there is no breach of covenant and therefore no injury done him. And if he have, then his will to have it done, being signified, is a release of that covenant, and so again there is no injury done him.

Justice of actions is by writers divided into *commutative* and *distributive;* and the former they say consists in proportion arithmetical, the latter in proportion geometrical. Commutative, therefore, they place in the equality of value of the things contracted for, and distributive in the distribution of equal benefit to men of equal merit. As if it were injustice to sell dearer than we buy, or to give more to a man than he merits. The value of all things contracted for is measured by the appetite of the contractors, and therefore the just value is that which they be contented to give. And merit (besides that which is by covenant, where the performance on one part merits the performance of the other part, and falls under justice commutative, not distributive) is not due by justice, but is rewarded of grace only. And therefore this distinction, in the sense wherein it uses to be expounded, is not right. To speak properly, commutative justice is the justice of a contractor – that is, a performance of covenant in buying and selling, hiring and letting to hire, lending and borrowing, exchanging, bartering, and other acts of contract.

And distributive justice, the justice of an arbitrator – that is to say, the act of defining what is just. Wherein, being trusted by them that make him arbitrator, if he perform his trust, he is said to distribute to every man his own; and this is indeed just distribution, and may be called, though improperly, distributive justice, but more properly equity, which also is a law of nature, as shall be shown in due place.

As justice depends on antecedent covenant, so does GRATITUDE depend on antecedent grace – that is to say, antecedent free gift – and is the fourth law of nature, which may be conceived in this form: *that a man which receives benefit from another of mere grace endeavor that he which gives it have no reasonable cause to repent him of his good will.* For no man gives but with intention of good to himself, because gift is voluntary, and of all voluntary acts the object is to every man his own good; of which if men see they shall be frustrated, there will be no beginning of benevolence or trust nor consequently of mutual help nor of reconciliation of one man to another; and therefore they are to remain still in the condition of *war,* which is contrary to the first and fundamental law of nature, which commands men to *seek peace.* The breach of this law is called *ingratitude,* and has the same relation to grace that injustice has to obligation by covenant.

A fifth law of nature is COMPLAISANCE – that is to say, *that every man strive to accommodate himself to the rest.* For the understanding whereof we may consider that there is in men's aptness to society a diversity of nature rising from their diversity of affections not unlike to that we see in stones brought together for building of an edifice. For as that stone which by the asperity and irregularity of figure takes more room from others than itself fills, and for the hardness cannot be easily made plain and thereby hinders the building, is by the builders cast away as unprofitable and troublesome, so also a man that by asperity of nature will strive to retain those things which to himself are superfluous and to others necessary, and for the stubbornness of his passions cannot be corrected, is to be left or cast out of society as cumbersome thereunto. For seeing every man, not only by right but also by necessity of nature, is supposed to endeavor all he can to obtain that which is necessary for his conservation, he that shall oppose himself against it for things superfluous is guilty of the war that thereupon is to follow, and therefore does that which is contrary to the fundamental law of nature, which commands *to seek peace.* The observers of this law may be called SOCIABLE (the Latins call them *commodi*), the contrary *stubborn, insociable, forward, intractable.*

A sixth law of nature is this: *that upon caution of the future time, a man ought to pardon the offenses past of them that, repenting, desire it.* For PARDON is nothing but granting of peace, which, though granted to them that persevere in their hostility, be not peace but fear, yet, not granted to them that give caution of the future time, is sign of an aversion to peace, and therefore contrary to the law of nature.

A seventh is *that in revenges* – that is, retribution of evil for evil – *men look not at the greatness of the evil past, but the greatness of the good to follow.* Whereby we are forbidden to inflict punishment with any other design than for correction of the offender or direction of others. For this law is consequent to the next before it that commands pardon upon security of the future time. Besides, revenge without respect to the example and profit to come is a triumph or glorying in the hurt of another, tending to no end; for the end is always somewhat to come, and glorying to no end is vainglory and contrary to reason; and to hurt without reason tends to the introduction of war, which is against the law of nature and is commonly styled by the name of *cruelty*.

And because all signs of hatred or contempt provoke to fight, insomuch as most men choose rather to hazard their life than not to be revenged, we may in the eighth place for a law of nature set down this precept: *that no man by deed, word, countenance, or gesture declare hatred or contempt of another.* The breach of which law is commonly called *contumely*.

The question who is the better man has no place in the condition of mere nature, where, as has been shown before, all men are equal. The inequality that now is has been introduced by the laws civil. I know that Aristotle in the first book of his *Politics*, for a foundation of his doctrine, makes men by nature some more worthy to command, meaning the wiser sort such as he thought himself to be for his philosophy, others to serve, meaning those that had strong bodies but were not philosophers as he; as if master and servant were not introduced by consent of men but by difference of wit, which is not only against reason but also against experience. For there are very few so foolish that had not rather govern themselves than be governed by others; nor when the wise in their own conceit contend by force with them who distrust their own wisdom, do they always, or often, or almost at any time, get the victory. If nature therefore have made men equal, that equality is to be acknowledged; or if nature have made men unequal, yet because men that think themselves equal will not enter into conditions of peace but upon equal terms, such equality must be admitted. And therefore for

the ninth law of nature, I put this: *that every man acknowledge another for his equal by nature.* The breach of this precept is *pride*.

On this law depends another: *that at the entrance into conditions of peace, no man require to reserve to himself any right which he is not content should be reserved to every one of the rest.* As it is necessary for all men that seek peace to lay down certain rights of nature – that is to say, not to have liberty to do all they list – so is it necessary for man's life to retain some, as right to govern their own bodies, enjoy air, water, motion, ways to go from place to place, and all things else without which a man cannot live or not live well. If in this case, at the making of peace, men require for themselves that which they would not have to be granted to others, they do contrary to the precedent law that commands the acknowledgment of natural equality and therefore also against the law of nature. The observers of this law are those we call *modest*, and the breakers *arrogant* men. The Greeks call the violation of this law πλεονεξία – that is, a desire of more than their share.

Also if *a man be trusted to judge between man and man*, it is a precept of the law of nature *that he deal equally between them.* For without that, the controversies of men cannot be determined but by war. He, therefore, that is partial in judgment does what in him lies to deter men from the use of judge and arbitrators, and consequently, against the fundamental law of nature, is the cause of war.

The observance of this law, from the equal distribution to each man of that which in reason belongs to him, is called EQUITY and, as I have said before, distributive justice; the violation, *acception of persons*, προσωποληψία.

And from this follows another law: *that such things as cannot be divided be enjoyed in common, if it can be; and if the quantity of the thing permit, without stint; otherwise proportionably to the number of them that have right.* For otherwise the distribution is unequal and contrary to equity.

But some things there be that can neither be divided nor enjoyed in common. Then the law of nature, which prescribes equity, requires *that the entire right, or else – making the use alternate – the first possession, be determined by lot.* For equal distribution is of the law of nature; and other means of equal distribution cannot be imagined.

Of *lots* there be two sorts: *arbitrary* and *natural.* Arbitrary is that which is agreed on by the competitors; natural is either *primogeniture* (which the Greek calls κληρονομία, which signifies *given by lot*) or *first seizure.*

And therefore those things which cannot be enjoyed in common, nor divided, ought to be adjudged to the first possessor; and in some cases to the first-born, as acquired by lot.

It is also a law of nature *that all men that mediate peace be allowed safe conduct.* For the law that commands peace, as the *end,* commands intercession, as the *means;* and to intercession the means is safe conduct.

And because, though men be never so willing to observe these laws, there may nevertheless arise questions concerning a man's action – first, whether it were done or not done; secondly, if done, whether against the law or not against the law; the former whereof is called a question *of fact,* the latter a question *of right* – therefore, unless the parties to the question covenant mutually to stand to the sentence of another, they are as far from peace as ever. This other to whose sentence they submit is called an ARBITRATOR. And therefore it is of the law of nature *that they that are at controversy submit their right to the judgment of an arbitrator.*

And seeing every man is presumed to do all things in order to his own benefit, no man is a fit arbitrator in his own cause; and if he were never so fit, yet, equity allowing to each party equal benefit, if one be admitted to be judge the other is to be admitted also; and so the controversy – that is, the cause of war – remains against the law of nature.

For the same reason no man in any cause ought to be received for arbitrator to whom greater profit or honor or pleasure apparently arises out of the victory of one party than of the other; for he has taken, though an unavoidable bribe, yet a bribe, and no man can be obliged to trust him. And thus also the controversy and the condition of war remains, contrary to the law of nature.

And in a controversy of *fact,* the judge being to give no more credit to one than to the other, if there be no other arguments, must give credit to a third, or to a third and fourth, no more; for else the question is undecided and left to force, contrary to the law of nature.

These are the laws of nature dictating peace for a means of the conservation of men in multitudes, and which only concern the doctrine of civil society. There be other things tending to the destruction of particular men – as drunkenness and all other parts of intemperance – which may therefore also be reckoned among those things which the law of nature has forbidden, but are not necessary to be mentioned nor are pertinent enough to this place.

And though this may seem too subtle a deduction of the laws of nature to be taken notice of by all men – whereof the most part are too busy in getting food and the rest too negligent to understand – yet to leave all men inexcusable they have been contracted into one easy sum, intelligible even to the meanest capacity, and that is *Do not that to another which you would not have done to yourself;* which shows him that he has no more to do in learning the laws of nature but, when weighing the actions of other men with his own they seem too heavy, to put them into the other part of the balance and his own into their place, that his own passions and self-love may add nothing to the weight, and then there is none of these laws of nature that will not appear unto him very reasonable.

The laws of nature oblige *in foro interno*[6] – that is to say, they bind to a desire they should take place – but *in foro externo*[7] – that is, to the putting them in act – not always. For he that should be modest and tractable and perform all he promises in such time and place where no man else should do so should but make himself a prey to others and procure his own certain ruin, contrary to the ground of all laws of nature, which tend to nature's preservation. And again, he that, having sufficient security that others shall observe the same laws toward him, observes them not himself, seeks not peace but war and consequently the destruction of his nature by violence.

And whatsoever laws bind *in foro interno* may be broken, not only by a fact contrary to the law, but also by a fact according to it, in case a man think it contrary. For though his action in this case be according to the law, yet is purpose was against the law, which, where he obligation is *in foro interno,* is a breach.

The laws of nature are immutable and ternal, for injustice, ingratitude, arrogance, ride, iniquity, acception of persons, and the est can never be made lawful. For it can ever be that war shall preserve life and peace estroy it.

The same laws, because they oblige only to a esire and endeavor – I mean an unfeigned and onstant endeavor – are easy to be observed. or in that they require nothing but endeavor, e that endeavors their performance fulfills hem; and he that fulfills the law is just.

And the science of them is the true and only noral philosophy. For moral philosophy is othing else but the science of what is *good* nd *evil* in the conversation and society of nankind. *Good* and *evil* are names that signify ur appetites and aversions, which in different empers, customs, and doctrines of men are ifferent; and divers men differ not only in heir judgment on the senses of what is pleasnt and unpleasant to the taste, smell, hearing, ouch, and sight but also of what is conformble or disagreeable to reason in the actions of ommon life. Nay, the same man in divers imes differs from himself, and one time raises – that is, calls good – what another ime he dispraises and calls evil; from whence rise disputes, controversies, and at last war.

And therefore so long as a man is in the condition of mere nature, which is a condition of war, private appetite is the measure of good and evil; and consequently all men agree on this: that peace is good, and therefore also the way or means of peace, which, as I have showed before, are *justice, gratitude, modesty, equity, mercy,* and the rest of the laws of nature, are good – that is to say, *moral virtues* – and their contrary *vices* evil. Now the science of virtue and vice is moral philosophy; and therefore the true doctrine of the laws of nature is the true moral philosophy. But the writers of moral philosophy, though they acknowledge the same virtues and vices, yet, not seeing wherein consisted their goodness nor that they come to be praised as the means of peaceable, sociable, and comfortable living, place them in a mediocrity of passions; as if not the cause but the degree of daring made fortitude, or not the cause but the quantity of a gift made liberality.

These dictates of reason men used to call by the name of laws, but improperly, for they are but conclusions or theorems concerning what conduces to the conservation and defense of themselves, whereas law, properly, is the word of him that by right has command over others. But yet if we consider the same theorems as delivered in the word of God, that by right commands all things, then are they properly called laws.

Notes

. [Matt. 7:12; Luke 6:31. The Latin expresses the same rule negatively: "What you would not have done to you, do not do to others."]

. [Without legal basis.]

. [Merit based on conformity and merit based on worthiness.]

. [Pss. 14, 53.]

. [Sir Edward Coke (1552–1634), English jurist, the first Lord Chief Justice of England. The first

volume of his *Institutes* was a translation of, and commentary on, the *Treatise on Tenures* of Sir Thomas de Littleton (*c.* 1407–1481). It is commonly called *Coke on Littleton.*]

6. [In conscience.]

7. [In civil law.]

CHAPTER 63
Why Contractarianism?

DAVID GAUTHIER

I

As the will to truth thus gains self-consciousness – there can be no doubt of that – morality will gradually perish *now: this is the great spectacle in a hundred acts reserved for the next two centuries in Europe – the most terrible, most questionable, and perhaps also the most hopeful of all spectacles.*

Nietzsche[1]

Morality faces a foundational crisis. Contractarianism offers the only plausible resolution of this crisis. These two propositions state my theme. What follows is elaboration.

Nietzsche may have been the first, but he has not been alone, in recognizing the crisis to which I refer. Consider these recent statements. "The hypothesis which I wish to advance is that in the actual world which we inhabit the language of morality is in . . . [a] state of grave disorder . . . we have – very largely, if not entirely – lost our comprehension, both theoretical and practical, of morality" (Alasdair MacIntyre).[2] "The resources of most modern moral philosophy are not well adjusted to the modern world" (Bernard Williams).[3] "There are no objective values . . . [But] the main tradition of European moral philosophy includes the contrary claim" (J. L. Mackie).[4] "Moral hypotheses do not help explain why people observe what they observe. So ethics is problematic and nihilism must be taken seriously. . . . An extreme version of nihilism holds that morality is simply an illusion. . . . In this version, we should abandon morality, just as an atheist abandons religion after he has decided that religious facts cannot help explain observations" (Gilbert Harman).[5]

I choose these statements to point to features of the crisis that morality faces. They suggest that moral language fits a world view that we have abandoned – a view of the world as purposively ordered. Without this view we no longer truly understand the moral claims we continue to make. They suggest that there is a lack of fit between what morality

David Gauthier, "Why Contractarianism?," pp. 15–30 from Peter Vallentyne (ed.), *Contractarianism and Rational Choice*. New York: Cambridge University Press, 1991. Reprinted by permission of Cambridge University Press.

presupposes – objective values that help explain our behavior, and the psychological states – desires and beliefs – that, given our present world view, actually provide the best explanation. This lack of fit threatens to undermine the very idea of a morality as more than an anthropological curiosity. But how could this be? How could morality *perish*?

I

To proceed, I must offer a minimal characterization of the morality that faces a foundational crisis. And this is the morality of justified constraint. From the standpoint of the agent, moral considerations present themselves as constraining his choices and actions, in ways independent of his desires, aims, and interests. Later, I shall add to this characterization, but for the moment it will suffice. For it reveals clearly what is in question – the ground of constraint. This ground seems absent from our present world view. And so we ask, what reason can a person have for recognizing and accepting a constraint that is independent of his desires and interests? He may agree that such a constraint would be *morally* justified; he would have a reason for accepting it *if* he had a reason for accepting morality. But what justifies paying attention to morality, rather than dismissing it as an appendage of outworn beliefs? We ask, and seem to find no answer. But before proceeding, we should consider three objections.

The first is to query the idea of constraint. Why should morality be seen as constraining our choices and actions? Why should we not rather say that the moral person chooses most freely, because she chooses in the light of a true conception of herself, rather than in the light of the false conceptions that so often predominate? Why should we not link morality with self-understanding? Plato and Hume might be enlisted to support this view, but Hume would be at best a partial ally, for his representation of "virtue in all her genuine and most engaging charms, . . . talk[ing] not of useless austerities and rigors, suffering and self-denial," but rather making "her votaries . . . , during every instant of their existence,

if possible, cheerful and happy," is rather overcast by his admission that "in the case of justice, . . . a man, taking things in a certain light, may often seem to be a loser by his integrity."[6] Plato, to be sure, goes further, insisting that only the just man has a healthy soul, but heroic as Socrates' defense of justice may be, we are all too apt to judge that Glaucon and Adeimantus have been charmed rather than reasoned into agreement, and that the unjust man has not been shown necessarily to be the loser.[7] I do not, in any event, intend to pursue this direction of thought. Morality, as we, heirs to the Christian and Kantian traditions, conceive it, constrains the pursuits to which even our reflective desires would lead us. And this is not simply or entirely a constraint on self-interest; the affections that morality curbs include the social ones of favoritism and partiality, to say nothing of cruelty.

The second objection to the view that moral constraint is insufficiently grounded is to query the claim that it operates independently of, rather than through, our desires, interests, and affections. Morality, some may say, concerns the well-being of all persons, or perhaps of all sentient creatures.[8] And one may then argue, either with Hume, that morality arises in and from our sympathetic identification with our fellows, or that it lies directly in well-being, and that our affections tend to be disposed favorably toward it. But, of course, not all of our affections. And so our sympathetic feelings come into characteristic opposition to other feelings, in relation to which they function as a constraint.

This is a very crude characterization, but it will suffice for the present argument. This view grants that morality, as we understand it, is without purely *rational* foundations, but reminds us that we are not therefore unconcerned about the well-being of our fellows. Morality is founded on the widespread, sympathetic, other-directed concerns that most of us have, and these concerns do curb self-interest, and also the favoritism and partiality with which we often treat others. Nevertheless, if morality depends for its practical relevance and motivational efficacy entirely on our sympathetic feelings, it has no title to the prescriptive grip with which it has been invested in the Christian and Kantian views to which I have referred, and which indeed Glaucon and Adeimantus demanded that Socrates defend to them in the case of justice. For to be reminded that some of the time we do care about our fellows and are willing to curb other desires in order to exhibit that care tells us nothing that can guide us in those cases in which, on the face of it, we do not care, or do not care enough – nothing that will defend the demands that morality makes on us in the hard cases. That not all situations in which concern for others combats self-concern are hard cases is true, but morality, as we ordinarily understand it, speaks to the hard cases, whereas its Humean or naturalistic replacement does not.

These remarks apply to the most sustained recent positive attempt to create a moral theory – that of John Rawls. For the attempt to describe our moral capacity, or more particularly, for Rawls, our sense of justice, in terms of principles, plausible in the light of our more general psychological theory, and coherent with "our considered judgments in reflective equilibrium,"[9] will not yield any answer to why, in those cases in which we have no, or insufficient, interest in being just, we should nevertheless follow the principles. John Harsanyi, whose moral theory is in some respects a utilitarian variant of Rawls' contractarian construction, recognizes this explicitly: "All we can prove by rational arguments is that anybody who wants to serve our common human interests in a rational manner must obey these commands."[10] But although morality may offer itself in the service of our common human interests, it does not offer itself only to those who want to serve them.

Morality is a constraint that, as Kant recognized, must not be supposed to depend solely on our feelings. And so we may not appeal to feelings to answer the question of its foundation. But the third objection is to dismiss this question directly, rejecting the very idea of a foundational crisis. Nothing justifies morality, for morality needs no justification. We find ourselves, in morality as elsewhere, in mediis rebus. We make, accept and reject, justify and criticize moral judgments. The concern of moral theory is to systematize that practice, and so to give us a deeper understanding of what moral justification is. But there are no extramoral foundations for moral justification, any more than there are extraepistemic foundations for epistemic judgments. In morals as in science, foundationalism is a bankrupt project.

Fortunately, I do not have to defend *normative* foundationalism. One problem with accepting moral justification as part of our ongoing practice is that, as I have suggested, we no longer accept the world view on which it depends. But perhaps a more immediately pressing problem is that we have, ready to hand, an alternative mode for justifying our choices and actions. In its more austere and, in my view, more defensible form, this is to show that choices and actions maximize the agent's expected utility, where utility is a measure of considered preference. In its less austere version, this is to show that choices and actions satisfy, not a subjectively defined requirement such as utility, but meet the agent's objective interests. Since I do not believe that we have objective interests, I shall ignore this latter. But it will not matter. For the idea is clear; we have a mode of justification that does not require the introduction of moral considerations.[11]

Let me call this alternative nonmoral mode of justification, neutrally, deliberative justification. Now moral and deliberative justification are directed at the same objects – our choices and actions. What if they conflict? And what do we say to the person who offers a deliberative justification of his choices and actions and refuses to offer any other? We can say, of course, that his behavior lacks *moral* justification, but this seems to lack any hold, unless he chooses to enter the moral framework. And such entry, he may insist, lacks any deliberative justification, at least for him.

If morality perishes, the justificatory enterprise, in relation to choice and action, does not perish with it. Rather, one mode of justification perishes, a mode that, it may seem, now hangs unsupported. But not only unsupported, for it is difficult to deny that deliberative justification is more clearly basic, that it cannot be avoided insofar as we are rational agents, so that if moral justification conflicts with it, morality seems not only unsupported but opposed by what is rationally more fundamental.

Deliberative justification relates to our deep sense of self. What distinguishes human beings from other animals, and provides the basis for rationality, is the capacity for semantic representation. You can, as your dog on the whole cannot, represent a state of affairs to yourself, and consider in particular whether or not it is the case, and whether or not you would want it to be the case. You can represent to yourself the contents of your beliefs, and your desires or preferences. But in representing them, you bring them into relation with one another. You represent to yourself that the Blue Jays will win the World Series, and that a National League team will win the World Series, and that the Blue Jays are not a National League team. And in recognizing a conflict among those beliefs, you find rationality thrust upon you. Note that the first two beliefs could be replaced by preferences, with the same effect.

Since in representing our preferences we become aware of conflict among them, the step from representation to choice becomes complicated. We must, somehow, bring our conflicting desires and preferences into some sort of coherence. And there is only one plausible candidate for a principle of coherence – a maximizing principle. We order our preferences, in relation to decision and action, so that we may choose in a way that maximizes our expectation of preference fulfillment. And in so doing, we show ourselves to be rational agents, engaged in deliberation and deliberative justification. There is simply nothing else for practical rationality to be.

The foundational crisis of morality thus cannot be avoided by pointing to the existence of a practice of justification within the moral framework, and denying that any extramoral foundation is relevant. For an extramoral mode of justification is already present, existing not side by side with moral justification, but in a manner tied to the way in which we unify our beliefs and preferences and so acquire our deep sense of self. We need not suppose that this deliberative justification is itself to be understood foundationally. All that we need suppose is that moral justification does not plausibly survive conflict with it.

III

In explaining why we may not dismiss the idea of a foundational crisis in morality as resulting from a misplaced appeal to a philosophically discredited or suspect idea of foundationalism, I have begun to expose the character and dimensions of the crisis. I have claimed that morality faces an alternative, conflicting, deeper mode of justification, related to our deep sense of self, that applies to the entire realm of choice and action, and that evaluates each *action* in terms of the reflectively held concerns of its *agent*. The relevance of the agent's concerns to practical justification does not seem to me in doubt. The relevance of anything else, except insofar as it bears on the agent's concerns, does seem to me very much in doubt. If the agent's reflectively endorsed concerns, his preferences, desires, and aims, are, with his considered beliefs, constitutive of his self-conception, then I can see no remotely plausible way of arguing from their relevance to that of anything else that is not similarly related to his sense of self. And, indeed, I can see no way of introducing anything as relevant to practical justification except through the agent's self-conception. My assertion of this practical individualism is not a conclusive argument, but the burden of proof is surely on those who would maintain a contrary position. Let them provide the arguments – if they can.

Deliberative justification does not refute morality. Indeed, it does not offer morality the courtesy of a refutation. It ignores morality, and seemingly replaces it. It preempts the arena of justification, apparently leaving morality no room to gain purchase. Let me offer a controversial comparison. Religion faces – indeed, has faced – a comparable foundational crisis. Religion demands the worship of a divine being who purposively orders the universe. But it has confronted an alternative mode of explanation. Although the emergence of a cosmological theory based on efficient, rather than teleological, causation provided warning of what was to come, the supplanting of teleology in biology by the success of evolutionary theory in providing a mode of explanation that accounted in efficient-causal terms for the *appearance* of a purposive order among living beings, may seem to toll the death knell for religion as an intellectually respectable enterprise. But evolutionary biology and, more generally, modern science do not refute religion. Rather they ignore it, replacing its explanations by ontologically simpler ones. Religion, understood as affirming the justifiable worship of a divine being, may be unable to survive its foundational crisis. Can morality, understood as affirming justifiable constraints on choice independent of the agent's concerns, survive?

There would seem to be three ways for morality to escape religion's apparent fate. One would be to find, for moral facts or moral properties, an explanatory role that would entrench them prior to any consideration of justification.[12] One could then argue that any mode of justification that ignored moral considerations would be ontologically defective. I mention this possibility only to put it to one side. No doubt there are persons who accept moral constraints on their choices and actions, and it would not be possible to explain those choices and actions were we to ignore this. But our explanation of their behavior need not commit us to their view. Here the comparison with religion should be straightforward and uncontroversial. We could not explain many of the practices of the religious without reference to their beliefs. But to characterize what a religious person is doing as, say, an act of worship, does not commit us to supposing that an object of worship actually exists, though it does commit us to supposing that she believes such an object to exist. Similarly, to characterize what a moral agent is doing as, say, fulfilling a duty does not commit us to supposing that there are any duties, though it does commit us to supposing that he believes that there are duties. The skeptic who accepts neither can treat the apparent role of morality in explanation as similar to that of religion. Of course, I do not consider that the parallel can be ultimately sustained, since I agree with the religious skeptic but not with the moral skeptic. But to establish an explanatory role for morality, one must first demonstrate its justificatory credentials. One may not assume that it has a prior explanatory role.

The second way would be to reinterpret the idea of justification, showing that, more fully understood, deliberative justification is incomplete, and must be supplemented in a way that makes room for morality. There is a long tradition in moral philosophy, deriving primarily from Kant, that is committed to this enterprise. This is not the occasion to embark on a critique of what, in the hope again of achieving a neutral characterization, I shall call universalistic justification. But critique may be out of place. The success of deliberative justification may suffice. For theoretical claims about its incompleteness seem to fail before the simple practical recognition that it works. Of course, on the face of it, deliberative justification does not work to provide a place for morality. But to suppose that it must, if it is to be fully adequate or complete as a mode of justification, would be to assume what is in question, whether moral justification is defensible.

If, independent of one's actual desires, and aims, there were objective values, and if, independent of one's actual purposes, one were part of an objectively purposive order, then we might have reason to insist on the inadequacy of the deliberative framework. An objectively purposive order would introduce considerations relevant to practical justification that did not depend on the agent's self-conception. But the supplanting of teleology in our physical and biological explanations closes this possibility, as it closes the possibility of religious explanation.

I turn then to the third way of resolving morality's foundational crisis. The first step is to embrace deliberative justification, and recognize that morality's place must be found within, and not outside, its framework. Now this will immediately raise two problems. First of all, it will seem that the attempt to establish any constraint on choice and action, within the framework of a deliberation that aims at the maximal fulfillment of the agent's considered preferences, must prove impossible. But even if this be doubted, it will seem that the attempt to establish a constraint *independent of the agent's preferences*, within such a framework, verges on lunacy. Nevertheless, this is precisely the task accepted by my third way. And, unlike its predecessors, I believe that it can be successful, indeed, I believe that my recent book, *Morals by Agreement*, shows how it can succeed.[13]

I shall not rehearse at length an argument that is now familiar to at least some readers, and, in any event, can be found in that book. But let me sketch briefly those features of deliberative rationality that enable it to constrain maximizing choice. The key idea is that in many situations, if each person chooses what, given the choices of the others, would maximize her expected utility, then the outcome will be mutually disadvantageous in comparison with some alternative – everyone could do better.[14] Equilibrium, which obtains when each person's action is a best response to the others' actions, is incompatible with (Pareto-) optimality, which obtains when no one could do better without someone else doing worse. Given the ubiquity of such situations, each person can see the benefit, to herself, of participating with her fellows in practices requiring each to refrain from the direct endeavor to maximize her own utility, when such mutual restraint is mutually advantageous. No one, of course, can have reason to accept any unilateral constraint on her maximizing behavior; each benefits from, and only from, the constraint accepted by her fellows. But if one benefits more from a constraint on others than one loses by being constrained oneself, one may have reason to accept a practice requiring everyone, including oneself, to exhibit such a constraint. We may represent such a practice as capable of gaining unanimous agreement among rational persons who were choosing the terms on which they would interact with each other. And this agreement is the basis of morality.

Consider a simple example of a moral practice that would command rational agreement. Suppose each of us were to assist her fellows only when either she could expect to benefit herself from giving assistance, or she took a direct interest in their well-being. Then, in many situations, persons would not give assistance to others, even though the benefit to the recipient would greatly exceed the cost to the giver, because there would be no provision for the giver to share in the benefit. Everyone would then expect to do better were each to give assistance to her fellows, regardless of her own benefit or interest, whenever the cost of assisting was low and the benefit of receiving assistance was

considerable. Each would thereby accept a constraint on the direct pursuit of her own concerns, not unilaterally, but given a like acceptance by others. Reflection leads us to recognize that those who belong to groups whose members adhere to such a practice of mutual assistance enjoy benefits in interaction that are denied to others. We may then represent such a practice as rationally acceptable to everyone.

This rationale for agreed constraint makes no reference to the content of anyone's preferences. The argument depends simply on the *structure* of interaction, on the way in which each person's endeavor to fulfill her own preferences affects the fulfillment of everyone else. Thus, each person's reason to accept a mutually constraining practice is independent of her particular desires, aims and interests, although not, of course, of the fact that she has such concerns. The idea of a purely rational agent, moved to act by reason alone, is not, I think, an intelligible one. Morality is not to be understood as a constraint arising from reason alone on the fulfillment of nonrational preferences. Rather, a rational agent is one who acts to achieve the maximal fulfillment of her preferences, and morality is a constraint on the manner in which she acts, arising from the effects of interaction with other agents.

Hobbes's Foole now makes his familiar entry onto the scene, to insist that however rational it may be for a person to agree with her fellows to practices that hold out the promise of mutual advantage, yet it is rational to follow such practices only when so doing directly conduces to her maximal preference fulfillment.[15] But then such practices impose no real constraint. The effect of agreeing to or accepting them can only be to change the expected payoffs of her possible choices, making it rational for her to choose what in the absence of the practice would not be utility maximizing. The practices would offer only true prudence, not true morality.

The Foole is guilty of a twofold error. First, he fails to understand that real acceptance of such moral practices as assisting one's fellows, or keeping one's promises, or telling the truth is possible only among those who are disposed to comply with them. If my disposition to comply extends only so far as my interests or concerns at the time of performance, then you will be the real fool if you interact with me in ways that demand a more rigorous compliance. If, for example, it is rational to keep promises only when so doing is directly utility maximizing, then among persons whose rationality is common knowledge, only promises that require such limited compliance will be made. And opportunities for mutual advantage will be thereby forgone.

Consider this example of the way in which promises facilitate mutual benefit. Jones and Smith have adjacent farms. Although neighbors, and not hostile, they are also not friends, so that neither gets satisfaction from assisting the other. Nevertheless, they recognize that, if they harvest their crops together, each does better than if each harvests alone. Next week, Jones's crop will be ready for harvesting; a fortnight hence, Smith's crop will be ready. The harvest in, Jones is retiring, selling his farm, and moving to Florida, where he is unlikely to encounter Smith or other members of their community. Jones would like to promise Smith that, if Smith helps him harvest next week, he will help Smith harvest in a fortnight. But Jones and Smith both know that in a fortnight, helping Smith would be a pure cost to Jones. Even if Smith helps him, he has nothing to gain by returning the assistance, since neither care for Smith nor, in the circumstances, concern for his own reputation, moves him. Hence, if Jones and Smith know that Jones acts straightforwardly to maximize the fulfillment of his preferences, they know that he will not help Smith. Smith, therefore, will not help Jones even if Jones pretends to promise assistance in return. Nevertheless, Jones would do better could he make and keep such a promise – and so would Smith.

The Foole's second error, following on his first, should be clear; he fails to recognize that in plausible circumstances, persons who are genuinely disposed to a more rigorous compliance with moral practices than would follow from their interests at the time of performance can expect to do better than those who are not so disposed. For the former, constrained maximizers as I call them, will be welcome partners in mutually advantageous cooperation, in which each relies on the voluntary adherence of the others, from which the latter,

straightforward maximizers, will be excluded. Constrained maximizers may thus expect more favorable opportunities than their fellows. Although in assisting their fellows, keeping their promises, and complying with other moral practices, they forgo preference fulfillment that they might obtain, yet they do better overall than those who always maximize expected utility, because of their superior opportunities.

In identifying morality with those constraints that would obtain agreement among rational persons who were choosing their terms of interaction, I am engaged in rational reconstruction. I do not suppose that we have actually agreed to existent moral practices and principles. Nor do I suppose that all existent moral practices would secure our agreement, were the question to be raised. Not all existent moral practices need be justifiable – need be ones with which we ought willingly to comply. Indeed, I do not even suppose that the practices with which we ought willingly to comply need be those that would secure our present agreement. I suppose that justifiable moral practices are those that would secure our agreement ex ante, in an appropriate premoral situation. They are those to which we should have agreed as constituting the terms of our future interaction, had we been, per impossible, in a position to decide those terms. Hypothetical agreement thus provides a test of the justifiability of our existent moral practices.

IV

Many questions could be raised about this account, but here I want to consider only one. I have claimed that moral practices are rational, even though they constrain each person's attempt to maximize her own utility, insofar as they would be the objects of unanimous ex ante agreement. But to refute the Foole, I must defend not only the rationality of agreement, but also that of compliance, and the defense of compliance threatens to preempt the case for agreement, so that my title should be "Why Constraint?" and not "Why Contractarianism?" It is rational to dispose oneself to accept certain constraints on direct maximization in choosing and acting, if and only if so disposing oneself maximizes one's expected utility. What then is the relevance of agreement, and especially of hypothetical agreement? Why should it be rational to dispose oneself to accept only those constraints that would be the object of mutual agreement in an appropriate premoral situation, rather than those constraints that are found in our existent moral practices? Surely it is acceptance of the latter that makes a person welcome in interaction with his fellows. For compliance with existing morality will be what they expect, and take into account in choosing partners with whom to cooperate.

I began with a challenge to morality – how can it be rational for us to accept its constraints? It may now seem that what I have shown is that it is indeed rational for us to accept constraints, but to accept them whether or not they might be plausibly considered moral. Morality, it may seem, has nothing to do with my argument; what I have shown is that it is rational to be disposed to comply with whatever constraints are generally accepted and expected, regardless of their nature. But this is not my view.

To show the relevance of agreement to the justification of constraints, let us assume an ongoing society in which individuals more or less acknowledge and comply with a given set of practices that constrain their choices in relation to what they would be did they take only their desires, aims, and interests directly into account. Suppose that a disposition to conform to these existing practices is prima facie advantageous, since persons who are not so disposed may expect to be excluded from desirable opportunities by their fellows. However, the practices themselves have, or at least need have, no basis in agreement. And they need satisfy no intuitive standard of fairness or impartiality, characteristics that we may suppose relevant to the identification of the practices with those of a genuine morality. Although we may speak of the practices as constituting the morality of the society in question, we need not consider them morally justified or acceptable. They are simply practices constraining individual behavior in a way that each finds rational to accept.

Suppose now that our persons, as rational maximizers of individual utility, come to reflect on the practices constituting their morality. They will, of course, assess the practices in relation to their own utility, but with the awareness that their fellows will be doing the same. And one question that must arise is: Why these practices? For they will recognize that the set of actual moral practices is not the only possible set of constraining practices that would yield mutually advantageous, optimal outcomes. They will recognize the possibility of alternative moral orders. At this point it will not be enough to say that, as a matter of fact, each person can expect to benefit from a disposition to comply with existing practices. For persons will also ask themselves: Can I benefit more, not from simply abandoning any morality, and recognizing no constraint, but from a partial rejection of existing constraints in favor of an alternative set? Once this question is asked, the situation is transformed; the existing moral order must be assessed, not only against simple noncompliance, but also against what we may call alternative compliance.

To make this assessment, each will compare her prospects under the existing practices with those she would anticipate from a set that, in the existing circumstances, she would expect to result from bargaining with her fellows. If her prospects would be improved by such negotiation, then she will have a real, although not necessarily sufficient, incentive to demand a change in the established moral order. More generally, if there are persons whose prospects would be improved by renegotiation, then the existing order will be recognizably unstable. No doubt those whose prospects would be worsened by renegotiation will have a clear incentive to resist, to appeal to the status quo. But their appeal will be a weak one, especially among persons who are not taken in by spurious ideological considerations, but focus on individual utility maximization. Thus, although in the real world, we begin with an existing set of moral practices as constraints on our maximizing behavior, yet we are led by reflection to the idea of an amended set that would obtain the agreement of everyone, and this amended set has, and will be recognized to have, a stability lacking in existing morality.

The reflective capacity of rational agents leads them from the given to the agreed, from existing practices and principles requiring constraint to those that would receive each person's assent. The same reflective capacity, I claim, leads from those practices that would be agreed to, in existing social circumstances, to those that would receive ex ante agreement, premoral and presocial. As the status quo proves unstable when it comes into conflict with what would be agreed to, so what would be agreed to proves unstable when it comes into conflict with what would have been agreed to in an appropriate presocial context. For as existing practices must seem arbitrary insofar as they do not correspond to what a rational person would agree to, so what such a person would agree to in existing circumstances must seem arbitrary in relation to what she would accept in a presocial condition.

What a rational person would agree to in existing circumstances depends in large part on her negotiating position vis-à-vis her fellows. But her negotiating position is significantly affected by the existing social institutions, and so by the currently accepted moral practices embodied in those institutions. Thus, although agreement may well yield practices differing from those embodied in existing social institutions, yet it will be influenced by those practices, which are not themselves the product of rational agreement. And this must call the rationality of the agreed practices into question. The arbitrariness of existing practices must infect any agreement whose terms are significantly affected by them. Although rational agreement is in itself a source of stability, yet this stability is undermined by the arbitrariness of the circumstances in which it takes place. To escape this arbitrariness, rational persons will revert from actual to hypothetical agreement, considering what practices they would have agreed to from an initial position not structured by existing institutions and the practices they embody.

The content of a hypothetical agreement is determined by an appeal to the equal rationality of persons. Rational persons will voluntarily accept an agreement only insofar as they perceive it to be equally advantageous to each.

To be sure, each would be happy to accept an agreement more advantageous to herself than to her fellows, but since no one will accept an agreement perceived to be less advantageous, agents whose rationality is a matter of common knowledge will recognize the futility of aiming at or holding out for more, and minimize their bargaining costs by coordinating at the point of equal advantage. Now the extent of advantage is determined in a twofold way. First, there is advantage internal to an agreement. In this respect, the expectation of equal advantage is assured by procedural fairness. The step from existing moral practices to those resulting from actual agreement takes rational persons to a procedurally fair situation, in which each perceives the agreed practices to be ones that it is equally rational for all to accept, given the circumstances in which agreement is reached. But those circumstances themselves may be called into question insofar as they are perceived to be arbitrary – the result, in part, of compliance with constraining practices that do not themselves ensure the expectation of equal advantage, and so do not reflect the equal rationality of the complying parties. To neutralize this arbitrary element, moral practices to be fully acceptable must be conceived as constituting a possible outcome of a hypothetical agreement under circumstances that are unaffected by social institutions that themselves lack full acceptability. Equal rationality demands consideration of external circumstances as well as internal procedures.

But what is the practical import of this argument? It would be absurd to claim that mere acquaintance with it, or even acceptance of it, will lead to the replacement of existing moral practices by those that would secure presocial agreement. It would be irrational for anyone to give up the benefits of the existing moral order simply because he comes to realize that it affords him more than he could expect from pure rational agreement with his fellows. And it would be irrational for anyone to accept a long-term utility loss by refusing to comply with the existing moral order, simply because she comes to realize that such compliance affords her less than she could expect from pure rational agreement. Nevertheless, these realizations do transform, or perhaps bring to the surface, the character of the relationships between persons that are maintained by the existing constraints, so that some of these relationships come to be recognized as coercive. These realizations constitute the elimination of false consciousness, and they result from a process of rational reflection that brings persons into what, in my theory, is the parallel of Jürgen Habermas's ideal speech situation.[16] Without an argument to defend themselves in open dialogue with their fellows, those who are more than equally advantaged can hope to maintain their privileged position only if they can coerce their fellows into accepting it. And this, of course, may be possible. But coercion is not agreement, and it lacks any inherent stability.

Stability plays a key role in linking compliance to agreement. Aware of the benefits to be gained from constraining practices, rational persons will seek those that invite stable compliance. Now compliance is stable if it arises from agreement among persons each of whom considers both that the terms of agreement are sufficiently favorable to herself that it is rational for her to accept them, and that they are not so favorable to others that it would be rational for them to accept terms less favorable to them and more favorable to herself. An agreement affording equally favorable terms to all thus invites, as no other can, stable compliance.

V

In defending the claim that moral practices, to obtain the stable voluntary compliance of rational individuals, must be the objects of an appropriate hypothetical agreement, I have added to the initial minimal characterization of morality. Not only does morality constrain our choices and actions, but it does so in an impartial way, reflecting the equal rationality of the persons subject to constraint. Although it is no part of my argument to show that the requirements of contractarian morality will satisfy the Rawlsian test of cohering with our considered judgments in reflective equilibrium, yet it would be misleading to treat

rationally agreed constraints on direct utility maximization as constituting a morality at all, rather than as replacing morality, were there no fit between their content and our pretheoretical moral views. The fit lies, I suggest, in the impartiality required for hypothetical agreement.

The foundational crisis of morality is thus resolved by exhibiting the rationality of our compliance with mutual, rationally agreed constraints on the pursuit of our desires, aims, and interests. Although bereft of a basis in objective values or an objectively purposive order, and confronted by a more fundamental mode of justification, morality survives by incorporating itself into that mode. Moral considerations have the same status, and the same role in explaining behavior, as the other reasons acknowledged by a rational deliberator. We are left with a unified account of justification, in which an agent's choices and actions are evaluated in relation to his preferences – to the concerns that are constitutive of his sense of self. But since morality binds the agent independently of the particular content of his preferences, it has the prescriptive grip with which the Christian and Kantian views have invested it.

In incorporating morality into deliberative justification, we recognize a new dimension to the agent's self-conception. For morality requires that a person have the capacity to commit himself, to enter into agreement with his fellows secure in the awareness that he can and will carry out his part of the agreement without regard to many of those considerations that normally and justifiably would enter into his future deliberations. And this is more than the capacity to bring one's desires and interests together with one's beliefs into a single coherent whole. Although this latter unifying capacity must extend its attention to past and future, the unification it achieves may itself be restricted to that extended present within which a person judges and decides. But in committing oneself to future action in accordance with one's agreement, one must fix at least a subset of one's desires and beliefs to hold in that future. The self that agrees and the self that complies must be one. "Man himself must first of all have become *calculable, regular, necessary,* even in his own image of himself, if he is to be able to stand security for *his own future*, which is what one who promises does!"[17]

In developing *"the right to make promises,"*[18] we human beings have found a contractarian bulwark against the perishing of morality.

Notes

1. *On the Genealogy of Morals,* trans. by Walter Kaufmann and R. J. Hollingdale (New York: Random House, 1967), third essay, sec. 27, p. 161.
2. *After Virtue* (Notre Dame, IN: University of Notre Dame Press, 1981), p. 2.
3. *Ethics and the Limits of Philosophy* (Cambridge, MA: Harvard University Press, 1985), p. 197.
4. *Ethics: Inventing Right and Wrong* (Harmondsworth: Penguin, 1977), pp. 15, 30.
5. *The Nature of Morality* (New York: Oxford University Press, 1977), p. II.
6. David Hume, *An Equiry Concerning the Principles of Morals,* 1751, sec. IX, pt. II.
7. See Plato, *Republic,* esp. books II and IV.
8. Some would extend morality to the nonsentient, but sympathetic as I am to the rights of trolley cars and steam locomotives, I propose to leave this view quite out of consideration.
9. John Rawls, *A Theory of Justice* (Cambridge, MA: Harvard University Press, 1971), p. 51.
10. John C. Harsanyi, "Morality and the Theory of Rational Behavior," in *Utilitarianism and Beyond,* edited by Amartya Sen and Bernard Williams (Cambridge: Cambridge University Press, 1982), p. 62.
11. To be sure, if we think of morality as expressed in certain of our affections and/or interests, it will incorporate moral considerations to the extent that they actually are present in our

preferences. But this would be to embrace the naturalism that I have put to one side as inadequate.
12. This would meet the challenge to morality found in my previous quotation from Gilbert Harman.
13. See David Gauthier, *Morals by Agreement* (Oxford: Oxford University Press, 1986), especially chaps. V and VI.
14. The now-classic example of this type of situation is the Prisoner's Dilemma; see *Morals by Agreement,* pp. 79–80. More generally, such situations may be said, in economists' parlance, to exhibit market failure. See, for example, "Market Contractarianism" in Jules Coleman, *Markets, Morals, and the Law* (Cambridge: Cambridge University Press, 1988), chap. 10.
15. See Hobbes, *Leviathan,* London, 1651, chap. 15.
16. See Raymond Geuss, *The Idea of a Critical Theory: Habermas and the Frankfurt School* (Cambridge: Cambridge University Press, 1981), p. 65 ff.
17. Nietzsche, *On the Genealogy of Morals,* trans. by Walter Kaufmann and R. J. Hollingdale (New York: Random House, 1967), second essay, sec. 1, p. 58.
18. Ibid., p. 57.

CHAPTER 64
A Theory of Justice

JOHN RAWLS

The Main Idea of the Theory of Justice

My aim is to present a conception of justice which generalizes and carries to a higher level of abstraction the familiar theory of the social contract as found, say, in Locke, Rousseau, and Kant.[1] In order to do this we are not to think of the original contract as one to enter a particular society or to set up a particular form of government. Rather, the guiding idea is that the principles of justice for the basic structure of society are the object of the original agreement. They are the principles that free and rational persons concerned to further their own interests would accept in an initial position of equality as defining the fundamental terms of their association. These principles are to regulate all further agreements; they specify the kinds of social cooperation that can be entered into and the forms of government that can be established. This way of regarding the principles of justice I shall call justice as fairness.

Thus we are to imagine that those who engage in social cooperation choose together, in one joint act, the principles which are to assign basic rights and duties and to determine the division of social benefits. Men are to decide in advance how they are to regulate their claims against one another and what is to be the foundation charter of their society. Just as each person must decide by rational reflection what constitutes his good, that is, the system of ends which it is rational for him to pursue, so a group of persons must decide once and for all what is to count among them as just and unjust. The choice which rational men would make in this hypothetical situation of equal liberty, assuming for the present that this choice problem has a solution, determines the principles of justice.

In justice as fairness the original position of equality corresponds to the state of nature in the traditional theory of the social contract. This original position is not, of course, thought of as an actual historical state of affairs, much less as a primitive condition of culture. It is understood as a purely hypothetical situation characterized so as to lead to a certain conception of justice.[2] Among the essential features of this situation is that no one knows his place in society, his class position or social status, nor does any one know his fortune in the distribution of natural assets and abilities, his intelligence, strength, and the like. I shall even assume that the parties do not know their conceptions of the good or their special psychological propensities. The principles of justice are chosen behind a veil of ignorance.

John Rawls, "A Theory of Justice," pp. 11–21, 60–3, 136–40, 153–6 from *A Theory of Justice*. Cambridge, MA: Harvard University Press, 1971. Reprinted by permission of the publisher, Harvard University Press.

This ensures that no one is advantaged or disadvantaged in the choice of principles by the outcome of natural chance or the contingency of social circumstances. Since all are similarly situated and no one is able to design principles to favor his particular condition, the principles of justice are the result of a fair agreement or bargain. For given the circumstances of the original position, the symmetry of everyone's relations to each other, this initial situation is fair between individuals as moral persons, that is, as rational beings with their own ends and capable, I shall assume, of a sense of justice. The original position is, one might say, the appropriate initial status quo, and thus the fundamental agreements reached in it are fair. This explains the propriety of the name "justice as fairness": it conveys the idea that the principles of justice are agreed to in an initial situation that is fair. The name does not mean that the concepts of justice and fairness are the same, any more than the phrase "poetry as metaphor" means that the concepts of poetry and metaphor are the same.

Justice as fairness begins, as I have said, with one of the most general of all choices which persons might make together, namely, with the choice of the first principles of a conception of justice which is to regulate all subsequent criticism and reform of institutions. Then, having chosen a conception of justice, we can suppose that they are to choose a constitution and a legislature to enact laws, and so on, all in accordance with the principles of justice initially agreed upon. Our social situation is just if it is such that by this sequence of hypothetical agreements we would have contracted into the general system of rules which defines it. Moreover, assuming that the original position does determine a set of principles (that is, that a particular conception of justice would be chosen), it will then be true that whenever social institutions satisfy these principles those engaged in them can say to one another that they are cooperating on terms to which they would agree if they were free and equal persons whose relations with respect to one another were fair. They could all view their arrangements as meeting the stipulations which they would acknowledge in an initial situation that embodies widely accepted and reasonable constraints on the choice of principles. The general recognition of this fact would provide the basis for a public acceptance of the corresponding principles of justice. No society can, of course, be a scheme of cooperation which men enter voluntarily in a literal sense; each person finds himself placed at birth in some particular position in some particular society, and the nature of this position materially affects his life prospects. Yet a society satisfying the principles of justice as fairness comes as close as a society can to being a voluntary scheme, for it meets the principles which free and equal persons would assent to under circumstances that are fair. In this sense its members are autonomous and the obligations they recognize self-imposed.

One feature of justice as fairness is to think of the parties in the initial situation as rational and mutually disinterested. This does not mean that the parties are egoists, that is, individuals with only certain kinds of interests, say in wealth, prestige, and domination. But they are conceived as not taking an interest in one another's interests. They are to presume that even their spiritual aims may be opposed, in the way that the aims of those of different religions may be opposed. Moreover, the concept of rationality must be interpreted as far as possible in the narrow sense, standard in economic theory, of taking the most effective means to given ends. I shall modify this concept to some extent, but one must try to avoid introducing into it any controversial ethical elements. The initial situation must be characterized by stipulations that are widely accepted.

In working out the conception of justice as fairness one main task clearly is to determine which principles of justice would be chosen in the original position. To do this we must describe this situation in some detail and formulate with care the problem of choice which it presents. These matters I shall take up in the immediately succeeding chapters. It may be observed, however, that once the principles of justice are thought of as arising from an original agreement in a situation of equality, it is an open question whether the principle of utility would be acknowledged. Offhand it hardly seems likely that persons who view themselves as equals, entitled to press their claims upon one another, would agree to a principle which may require lesser life prospects for some simply for the sake of a greater sum of advantages enjoyed by others. Since each desires to protect his interests, his capacity to advance his conception of the good, no one has a reason to acquiesce in an enduring loss for himself in order to bring about a greater net balance of satisfaction. In the absence of strong and lasting benevolent impulses, a rational man would not accept a basic structure merely because it maximized the algebraic sum of advantages irrespective of its permanent effects on his own basic rights and interests. Thus it seems that the principle of utility is incompatible with the conception of social cooperation among equals for mutual advantage. It appears to be inconsistent with the idea of reciprocity implicit in the notion of a well-ordered society. Or, at any rate, so I shall argue.

I shall maintain instead that the persons in the initial situation would choose two rather different principles: the first requires equality in the assignment of basic rights and duties, while the second holds that social and economic inequalities, for example inequalities of wealth and authority, are just only if they result in compensating benefits for everyone, and in particular for the least advantaged members of society. These principles rule out justifying institutions on the grounds that the hardships of some are offset by a greater good in the aggregate. It may be expedient but it is not just that some should have less in order that others may prosper. But there is no injustice in the greater benefits earned by a few provided that the situation of persons not so fortunate is thereby improved. The intuitive idea is that since everyone's well-being depends upon a scheme of cooperation without which no one could have a satisfactory life, the division of advantages should be such as to draw forth the willing cooperation of everyone taking part in it, including those less well situated. Yet this can be expected only if reasonable terms are proposed. The two principles mentioned seem to be a fair agreement on the basis of which those better endowed, or more fortunate in their social position, neither of which we can be said to deserve, could expect the willing cooperation of others when some workable scheme is a necessary condition of the welfare of all. Once we decide to look for a conception of justice that nullifies the accidents of natural endowment and the contingencies of social circumstance as counters in quest for political and economic advantage, we are led to these principles. They express the result of leaving aside those aspects of the social world that seem arbitrary from a moral point of view.

The problem of the choice of principles, however, is extremely difficult. I do not expect the answer I shall suggest to be convincing to everyone. It is, therefore, worth nothing from the outset that justice as fairness, like other contract views, consists of two parts: (1) an interpretation of the initial situation and of the problem of choice posed there, and (2) a set of principles which, it is argued, would be agreed to. One may accept the first part of the theory (or some variant thereof), but not the other, and conversely. The concept of the initial contractual situation may seem reasonable although the particular principles proposed are rejected. To be sure, I want to maintain that the most appropriate conception of this situation does lead to principles of justice contrary to utilitarianism and perfectionism, and therefore that the contract doctrine provides an alternative to these views. Still, one may dispute this contention even though one grants that the contractarian method is a useful way of studying ethical theories and of setting forth their underlying assumptions.

Justice as fairness is an example of what I have called a contract theory. Now there may be an objection to the term "contract" and related expressions, but I think it will serve reasonably well. Many words have misleading connotations which at first are likely to confuse. The terms "utility" and "utilitarianism" are surely no exception. They too have unfortunate suggestions which hostile critics have been willing to exploit; yet they are clear enough for those prepared to study utilitarian doctrine. The same should be true of the term "contract" applied to moral theories. As I have mentioned, to understand it one has to keep in mind that it implies a certain level of abstraction. In particular, the content of the relevant agreement is not to enter a given society or to adopt a given form of government, but to accept certain moral principles. Moreover, the undertakings referred to are purely hypothetical: a contract view holds that certain prnciples would be accepted in a well-defined initial situation.

The merit of the contract terminology is that it conveys the idea that principles of justice may be conceived as principles that would be chosen by rational persons, and that in this way conceptions of justice may be explained and justified. The theory of justice is a part, perhaps the most significant part, of the theory of rational choice. Furthermore, principles of justice deal with conflicting claims upon the advantages won by social cooperation; they apply to the relations among several persons or groups. The word "contract" suggests this plurality as well as the condition that the appropriate division of advantages must be in accordance with principles acceptable to all parties. The condition of publicity for principles of justice is also connoted by the contract phraseology. Thus, if these principles are the outcome of an agreement, citizens have a knowledge of the principles that others follow. It is characteristic of contract theories to stress the public nature of political principles. Finally there is the long tradition of the contract doctrine. Expressing the tie with this line of thought helps to define ideas and accords with natural piety. There are then several advantages in the use of the term "contract." With due precautions taken, it should not be misleading.

A final remark. Justice as fairness is not a complete contract theory. For it is clear that the contractarian idea can be extended to the choice of more or less an entire ethical system, that is, to a system including principles for all the virtues and not only for justice. Now for the most part I shall consider only principles of justice and others closely related to them; I make no attempt to discuss the virtues in a systematic way. Obviously if justice as fairness succeeds reasonably well, a next step would be to study the more general view suggested by the name "rightness as fairness." But even this wider theory fails to embrace all moral relationships, since it would seem to include only our relations with other persons and to leave out of account how we are to conduct ourselves toward animals and the rest of nature. I do not contend that the contract notion offers a way to approach these questions which are certainly of the first importance; and I shall have to put them aside. We must recognize the limited scope of justice as fairness and of the general type of view that it exemplifies. How far its conclusions must be revised once these other matters are understood cannot be decided in advance.

The Original Position and Justification

I have said that the original position is the appropriate initial status quo which insures that the fundamental agreements reached in it are fair. This fact yields the name "justice as fairness." It is clear, then, that I want to say that one conception of justice is more reasonable than another, or justifiable with respect to it, if rational persons in the initial situation would choose its principles over those of the other for the role of justice. Conceptions of justice are to be ranked by their acceptability to persons so circumstanced. Understood in this way the question of justification is settled by working out a problem of deliberation: we have to ascertain which principles it would be rational to adopt given the contractual situation. This connects the theory of justice with the theory of rational choice.

If this view of the problem of justification is to succeed, we must, of course, describe in some detail the nature of this choice problem. A problem of rational decision has a definite answer only if we know the beliefs and interests of the parties, their relations with respect to one another, the alternatives between which they are to choose, the procedure whereby they make up their minds, and so on. As the circumstances are presented in different ways, correspondingly different principles are accepted. The concept of the original position, as I shall refer to it, is that of the most philosophically favored interpretation of this initial choice situation for the purposes of a theory of justice.

But how are we to decide what is the most favored interpretation? I assume, for one thing, that there is a broad measure of agreement that principles of justice should be chosen under certain conditions. To justify a particular description of the initial situation one shows that it incorporates these commonly shared presumptions. One argues from widely accepted but weak premises to more specific conclusions. Each of the presumptions should by itself be natural and plausible; some of them may seem innocuous or even trivial. The aim of the contract approach is to establish that taken together they impose significant bounds on acceptable principles of justice. The ideal outcome would be that these conditions determine a unique set of principles; but I shall be satisfied if they suffice to rank the main traditional conceptions of social justice.

One should not be misled, then, by the some-what unusual conditions which characterize the original position. The idea here is simply to make vivid to ourselves the restrictions that it seems reasonable to impose on arguments for principles of justice, and therefore on these principles themselves. Thus it seems reasonable and generally acceptable that no one should be advantaged or disadvantaged by natural fortune or social circumstances in the choice of principles. It also seems widely agreed that it should be impossible to tailor principles to the circumstances of one's own case. We should insure further that particular inclinations and aspirations, and persons' conceptions of their good do not affect the principles adopted. The aim is to rule out those principles that it would be rational to propose for acceptance, however little the chance of success, only if one knew certain things that are irrelevant from the standpoint of justice. For example, if a man knew that he was wealthy, he might find it rational to advance the principle that various taxes for welfare measures be counted unjust; if he knew that he was poor, he would most likely propose the contrary principle. To represent the desired restrictions one imagines a situation in which everyone is deprived of this sort of information. One excludes the knowledge of those contingencies which sets men at odds and allows them to be guided by their prejudices. In this manner the veil of ignorance is arrived at in a natural way. This concept should cause no difficulty if we keep in mind the constraints

on arguments that it is meant to express. At any time we can enter the original position, so to speak, simply by following a certain procedure, namely, by arguing for principles of justice in accordance with these restrictions.

It seems reasonable to suppose that the parties in the original position are equal. That is, all have the same rights in the procedure for choosing principles; each can make proposals, submit reasons for their acceptance, and so on. Obviously the purpose of these conditions is to represent equality between human beings as moral persons, as creatures having a conception of their good and capable of a sense of justice. The basis of equality is taken to be similarity in these two respects. Systems of ends are not ranked in value; and each man is presumed to have the requisite ability to understand and to act upon whatever principles are adopted. Together with the veil of ignorance, these conditions define the principles of justice as those which rational persons concerned to advance their interests would consent to as equals when none are known to be advantaged or disadvantaged by social and natural contingencies.

There is, however, another side to justifying a particular description of the original position. This is to see if the principles which would be chosen match our considered convictions of justice or extend them in an acceptable way. We can note whether applying these principles would lead us to make the same judgments about the basic structure of society which we now make intuitively and in which we have the greatest confidence; or whether, in cases where our present judgments are in doubt and given with hesitation, these principles offer a resolution which we can affirm on reflection. There are questions which we feel sure must be answered in a certain way. For example, we are confident that religious intolerance and racial discrimination are unjust. We think that we have examined these things with care and have reached what we believe is an impartial judgment not likely to be distorted by an excessive attention to our own interests. These convictions are provisional fixed points which we presume any conception of justice must fit. But we have much less assurance as to what is the correct distribution of wealth and authority. Here we may be looking for a way to remove our doubts. We can check an interpretation of the initial situation, then, by the capacity of its principles to accommodate our firmest convictions and to provide guidance where guidance is needed.

In searching for the most favored description of this situation we work from both ends. We begin by describing it so that it represents generally shared and preferably weak conditions. We then see if these conditions are strong enough to yield a significant set of principles. If not, we look for further premises equally reasonable. But if so, and these principles match our considered convictions of justice, then so far well and good. But presumably there will be discrepancies. In this case we have a choice. We can either modify the account of the initial situation or we can revise our existing judgments, for even the judgments we take provisionally as fixed points are liable to revision. By going back and forth, sometimes altering the conditions of the contractual circumstances, at others withdrawing our judgments and conforming them to principle, I assume that eventually we shall find a description of the initial situation that both expresses reasonable conditions and yields principles which match our considered judgments duly pruned and adjusted. This state of affairs I refer to as reflective equilibrium.[3] It is an equilibrium because at last our principles and judgments coincide; and it is reflective since we know to what principles our judgments conform and the premises of their derivation. At the moment everything is in order. But this equilibrium is not necessarily stable. It is liable to be upset by further examination of the conditions which should be imposed on the contractual situation and by particular cases which may lead us to revise our judgments. Yet for the time being we have done what we can to render coherent and to justify our convictions of social justice. We have reached a conception of the original position.

I shall not, of course, actually work through this process. Still, we may think of the interpretation of the original position that I shall present as the result of such a hypothetical course of reflection. It represents the attempt to accommodate within one scheme both reasonable philosophical conditions on principles as well as our considered judgments of justice. In arriving at the favored interpretation of the initial situation there is no point at which an appeal is made to self-evidence in the traditional sense either of general conceptions or particular convictions. I do not claim for the principles of justice proposed that they are necessary truths or derivable from such truths. A conception of justice cannot be deduced from self-evident premises or conditions on principles; instead, its justification is a matter of the mutual support of many considerations, of everything fitting together into one coherent view.

A final comment. We shall want to say that certain principles of justice are justified because they would be agreed to in an initial situation of equality. I have emphasized that this original position is purely hypothetical. It is natural to ask why, if this agreement is never actually entered into, we should take any interest in these principles, moral or otherwise The answer is that the conditions embodied in the description of the original position are ones that we do in fact accept. Or if we do not, then perhaps we can be persuaded to do so by philosophical reflection. Each aspect of the contractual situation can be given supporting grounds. Thus what we shall do is to collect together into one conception a number of conditions on principles that we are ready upon due consideration to recognize as reasonable. These constraints express what we are prepared to regard as limits on fair terms of social cooperation. One way to look at the idea of the original position, therefore, is to see it as an expository device which sums up the meaning of these conditions and helps us to extract their consequences. On the other hand, this conception is also an intuitive notion that suggests its own elaboration, so that led on by it we are drawn to define more clearly the standpoint from which we can best interpret moral relationships. We need a conception that enables us to envision our objective from afar: the intuitive notion of the original position is to do this for us. . . .

Two Principles of Justice

I shall now state in a provisional form the two principles of justice that I believe would be chosen in the original position. In this section I wish to make only the most general comments, and therefore the first formulation of these principles is tentative. As we go on I shall run through several formulations and approximate step by step the final statement to be given much later. I believe that doing this allows the exposition to proceed in a natural way.

The first statement of the two principles reads as follows.

First: each person is to have an equal right to the most extensive basic liberty compatible with a similar liberty for others.

Second: social and economic inequalities are to be arranged so that they are both (a) reasonably expected to be to everyone's advantage, and (b) attached to positions and offices open to all. . . .

By way of general comment, these principles primarily apply, as I have said, to the basic structure of society. They are to govern the assignment of rights and duties and to regulate the distribution of social and economic advantages. As their formulation suggests, these principles presuppose that the social structure can be divided into two more or less distinct parts, the first principle applying to the one, the second to the other. They distinguish between those aspects of the social system that define and secure the equal liberties of citizenship and those that specify and establish social and economic inequalities. The basic liberties of citizens are, roughly speaking, political liberty (the right to vote and to be eligible for public office) together with freedom of speech and assembly; liberty of conscience and freedom of thought; freedom of the person along with the right to hold (personal) property; and freedom from arbitrary arrest and seizure as defined by the concept of the rule of law. These liberties are all required to be equal by the first principle, since citizens of a just society are to have the same basic rights.

The second principle applies, in the first approximation, to the distribution of income and wealth and to the design of organizations that make use of differences in authority and responsibility, or chains of command. While the distribution of wealth and income need not be equal, it must be to everyone's advantage, and at the same time, positions of author-

ity and offices of command must be accessible to all. One applies the second principle by holding positions open, and then, subject to this constraint, arranges social and economic inequalities so that everyone benefits.

These principles are to be arranged in a serial order with the first principle prior to the second. This ordering means that a departure from the institutions of equal liberty required by the first principle cannot be justified by, or compensated for, by greater social and economic advantages. The distribution of wealth and income, and the hierarchies of authority, must be consistent with both the liberties of equal citizenship and equality of opportunity.

It is clear that these principles are rather specific in their content, and their acceptance rests on certain assumptions that I must eventually try to explain and justify. A theory of justice depends upon a theory of society in ways that will become evident as we proceed. For the present, it should be observed that the two principles (and this holds for all formulations) are a special case of a more general conception of justice that can be expressed as follows.

> [All social values – liberty and opportunity, income and wealth, and the bases of self-respect – are to be distributed equally unless an unequal distribution of any, or all, of these values is to everyone's advantage.]

Injustice, then, is simply inequalities that are not to the benefit of all. Of course, this conception is extremely vague and requires interpretation.

As a first step, suppose that the basic structure of society distributes certain primary goods, that is, things that every rational man is presumed to want. These goods normally have a use whatever a person's rational plan of life. For simplicity, assume that the chief primary goods at the disposition of society are rights and liberties, powers and opportunities, income and wealth. . . . [the primary good of self-respect has a central place.] These are the social primary goods. Other primary goods such as health and vigor, intelligence and imagination, are natural goods; although their possession is influenced by the basic structure, they are not so directly under its control. Imagine, then, a hypothetical initial arrangement in which all the social primary goods are equally distributed: everyone has similar rights and duties, and income and wealth are evenly shared. This state of affairs provides a benchmark for judging improvements. If certain inequalities of wealth and organizational powers would make everyone better off than in this hypothetical starting situation, then they accord with the general conception.

Now it is possible, at least theoretically, that by giving up some of their fundamental liberties men are sufficiently compensated by the resulting social and economic gains. [The general conception of justice imposes no restrictions on what sort of inequalities are permissible; it only requires that everyone's position be improved.] We need not suppose anything so drastic as consenting to a condition of slavery. Imagine instead that men forego certain political rights when the economic returns are significant and their capacity to influence the course of policy by the exercise of these rights would be marginal in any case. It is this kind of exchange which the two principles as stated rule out; being arranged in serial order they do not permit exchanges between basic liberties and economic and social gains. The serial ordering of principles expresses an underlying preference among primary social goods. When this preference is rational so likewise is the choice of these principles in this order. . . .

The Veil of Ignorance

The idea of the original position is to set up a fair procedure so that any principles agreed to will be just. The aim is to use the notion of pure procedural justice as a basis of theory. Somehow we must nullify the effects of specific contingencies which put men at odds and tempt them to exploit social and natural circumstances to their own advantage. Now in order to do this I assume that the parties are situated behind a veil of ignorance. They do not know how the various alternatives will affect their own particular case and they are obliged to evaluate principles solely on the basis of general considerations.

It is assumed, then, that the parties do not know certain kinds of particular facts. First of all, no one knows his place in society, his class position or social status; nor does he know his fortune in the distribution of natural assets and abilities, his intelligence and strength, and the like. Nor, again, does anyone know his conception of the good, the particulars of his rational plan of life, or even the special features of his psychology such as his aversion to risk or liability to optimism or pessimism. More than this, I assume that the parties do not know the particular circumstances of their own society. That is, they do not know its economic or political situation, or the level of civilization and culture it has been able to achieve. The persons in the original position have no information as to which generation they belong. These broader restrictions on knowledge are appropriate in part because questions of social justice arise between generations as well as within them, for example, the question of the appropriate rate of capital saving and of the conservation of natural resources and the environment of nature. There is also, theoretically anyway, the question of a reasonable genetic policy. In these cases too, in order to carry through the idea of the original position, the parties must not know the contingencies that set them in opposition. They must choose principles the consequences of which they are prepared to live with whatever generation they turn out to belong to.

As far as possible, then, the only particular facts which the parties know is that their society is subject to the circumstances of justice and whatever this implies. It is taken for granted, however, that they know the general facts about human society. They understand political affairs and the principles of economic theory; they know the basis of social organization and the laws of human psychology. Indeed, the parties are presumed to know whatever general facts affect the choice of the principles of justice. There are no limitations on general information, that is, on general laws and theories, since conceptions of justice must be adjusted to the characteristics of the systems of social cooperation which they are to regulate, and there is no reason to rule out these facts. It is, for example, a consideration against a conception of justice that in view of the laws of moral psychology, men would not acquire a desire to act upon it even when the institutions of their society satisfied it. For in this case there would be difficulty in securing the stability of social cooperation. It is an important feature of a conception of justice that it should generate its own support. That is, its principles should be such that when they are embodied in the basic structure of society men tend to acquire the corresponding sense of justice. Given the principles of moral learning, men develop a desire to act in accordance with its principles. In this case a conception of justice is stable. This kind of general information is admissible in the original position.

The notion of the veil of ignorance raises several difficulties. Some may object that the exclusion of nearly all particular information makes it difficult to grasp what is meant by the original position. Thus it may be helpful to observe that one or more persons can at any time enter this position, or perhaps, better, simulate the deliberations of this hypothetical situation, simply by reasoning in accordance with the appropriate restrictions. In arguing for a conception of justice we must be sure that it is among the permitted alternatives and satisfies the stipulated formal constraints. No considerations can be advanced in its favor unless they would be rational ones for us to urge were we to lack the kind of knowledge that is excluded. The evaluation of principles must proceed in terms of the general consequences of their public recognition and universal application, it being assumed that they will be complied with by everyone. To say that a certain conception of justice would be chosen in the original position is equivalent to saying that rational deliberation satisfying certain conditions and restrictions would reach a certain conclusion. If necessary, the argument to this result could be set out more formally. I shall, however, speak throughout in terms of the notion of the original position. It is more economical and suggestive, and brings out certain essential features that otherwise one might easily overlook.

These remarks show that the original position is not to be thought of as a general assembly which includes at one moment everyone who will live at some time; or, much less, as an assembly of everyone who could live at some time. It is not a gathering of all actual or possible persons. To conceive of the original position in either of these ways is to stretch fantasy too far; the conception would cease to be a natural guide to intuition. In any case, it is important that the original position be interpreted so that one can at any time adopt its perspective. It must make no difference when one takes up this viewpoint, or who does so: the restrictions must be such that the same principles are always chosen. The veil of ignorance is a key condition in meeting this requirement. It insures not only that the information available is relevant, but that it is at all times the same.

It may be protested that the condition of the veil of ignorance is irrational. Surely, some may object, principles should be chosen in the light of all the knowledge available. There are various replies to this contention. Here I shall sketch those which emphasize the simplifications that need to be made if one is to have any theory at all. . . . To begin with, it is clear that since the differences among the parties are unknown to them, and everyone is equally rational and similarly situated, each is convinced by the same arguments. Therefore, we can view the choice in the original position from the standpoint of one person selected at random. If anyone after due reflection prefers a conception of justice to another, then they all do, and a unanimous agreement can be reached. We can, to make the circumstances more vivid, imagine that the parties are required to communicate with each other through a referee as intermediary, and that he is to announce which alternatives have been suggested and the reasons offered in their support. He forbids the attempt to form coalitions, and he informs the parties when they have come to an understanding. But such a referee is actually super-fluous, assuming that the deliberations of the parties must be similar.

Thus there follows the very important consequence that the parties have no basis for bargaining in the usual sense. No one knows his situation in society nor his natural assets, and therefore no one is in a position to tailor principles to his advantage. We might imagine that one of the contractees threatens to hold out unless the others agree to principles favorable to him. But how does he know which principles are especially in his interests? The same holds for the formation of coalitions: if a group were to decide to band together to the disadvantage of the others, they would not know how to favor themselves in the choice of principles. Even if they could get everyone to agree to their proposal, they would have no assurance that it was to their advantage, since they cannot identify themselves either by name or description. The one case where this conclusion fails is that of saving. Since the persons in the original position know that they are contemporaries (taking the present time of entry interpretation), they can favor their generation by refusing to make any sacrifices at all for their successors; they simply acknowledge the principle that no one has a duty to save for posterity. Previous generations have saved or they have not; there is nothing the parties can now do to affect that. So in this instance the veil of ignorance fails to secure the desired result. Therefore I resolve the question of justice between generations in a different way by altering the motivation assumption. But with this adjustment no one is able to formulate principles especially designed to advance his own cause. Whatever his temporal position, each is forced to choose for everyone.

The restrictions on particular information in the original position are, then, of fundamental importance. Without them we would not be able to work out any definite theory of justice at all. We would have to be content with a vague formula stating that justice is what would be agreed to without being able to say much, if anything, about the substance of the agreement itself. The formal constraints of the concept of right, those applying to principles directly, are not sufficient for our purpose. The veil of ignorance makes possible a unanimous choice of a particular conception of justice.

Without these limitations on knowledge the bargaining problem of the original position would be hopelessly complicated. Even if theoretically a solution were to exist, we would not, at present anyway, be able to determine it. . . .

A final comment. For the most part I shall suppose that the parties possess all general information. No general facts are closed to them. I do this mainly to avoid complications. Nevertheless a conception of justice is to be the public basis of the terms of social cooperation. Since common understanding necessitates certain bounds on the complexity of principles, there may likewise be limits on the use of theoretical knowledge in the original position. Now clearly it would be very difficult to classify and to grade for complexity the various sorts of general facts. I shall make no attempt to do this. We do however recognize an intricate theoretical construction when we meet one. Thus it seems reasonable to say that other things equal one conception of justice is to be preferred to another when it is founded upon markedly simpler general facts, and its choice does not depend upon elaborate calculations in the light of a vast array of theoretically defined possibilities. It is desirable that the grounds for a public conception of justice should be evident to everyone when circumstances permit. This consideration favors, I believe, the two principles of justice over the criterion of utility.
[. . .]

The Reasoning Leading to the Two Principles of Justice

It seems clear from these remarks that the two principles are at least a plausible conception of justice. The question, though, is how one is to argue for them more systematically. Now there are several things to do. One can work out their consequences for institutions and note their implications for fundamental social policy. In this way they are tested by a comparison with our considered judgments of justice. . . . But one can also try to find arguments in their favor that are decisive from the standpoint of the original position. In order to see how this might be done, it is useful as a heuristic device to think of the two principles as the maximin solution to the problem of social justice. There is an analogy between the two principles and the maximin rule for choice under uncertainty. This is evident from the fact that the two principles are those a person would choose for the design of a society in which his enemy is to assign him is place. The maximin rule tells us to rank alternatives by their worst possible outcomes: we are to adopt the alternative the worst outcome of which is superior to the worst outcomes of the others. The persons in the original position do not, of course, assume that their initial place in society is decided by a malevolent opponent. As I note below, they should not reason from false premises. The veil of ignorance does not violate this idea, since an absence of information is not misinformation. But that the two principles of justice would be chosen if the parties were forced to protect themselves against such a contingency explains the sense in which this conception is the maximin solution. And this analogy suggests that if the original position has been described so that it is rational for the parties to adopt the conservative attitude expressed by this rule, a conclusive argument can indeed be constructed for these principles. Clearly the maximin rule is not, in general, a suitable guide for choices under uncertainty. But it is attractive in situations marked by certain special features. My aim, then, is to show that a good case can be made for the two principles based on the fact that the original position manifests these features to the fullest possible degree, carrying them to the limit, so to speak.

Consider the gain-and-loss table below [Table 64.1]. It represents the gains and losses for a situation which is not a game of strategy. There is no one playing against the person making the decision; instead he is faced with several possible circumstances which may or may not obtain. Which circumstances happen to exist does not depend upon what the person choosing decides or whether he announces his moves in advance. The numbers in the table are monetary values (in hundreds of dollars) in comparison with some initial situation. The gain (g) depends upon the individual's decision

(d) and the circumstances (c). Thus $g = f(d,c)$. Assuming that there are three possible decisions and three possible circumstances, we might have this gain-and-loss table.

The maximin rule requires that we make the third decision. For in this case the worst that can happen is that one gains five hundred dollars, which is better than the worst for the other actions. If we adopt one of these we may lose either eight or seven hundred dollars. [. . .] "maximin" means the *maximum minimorum;* and the rule directs our attention to the worst that can happen under any proposed course of action, and to decide in the light of that.

Now there appear to be three chief features of situations that give plausibility to this unusual rule. First, since the rule takes no account of the likelihoods of the possible circumstances, there must be some reason for sharply discounting estimates of these probabilities. Offhand, the most natural rule of choice would seem to be to compute the expectation of monetary gain for each decision and then to adopt the course of action with the highest prospect. [. . .] Thus it must be, for example, that the situation is one in which a knowledge of likelihoods is impossible, or at best extremely insecure. In this case it is unreasonable not to be skeptical of probabilistic calculations unless there is no other way out, particularly if the decision is a fundamental one that needs to be justified to others.

The second feature that suggests the maximin rule is the following: the person choosing has a conception of the good such that he cares very little, if anything, for what he might gain above the minimum stipend that he can, in fact, be sure of by following the maximin rule. It is not worthwhile for him to take a chance for the sake of a further advantage, especially when it may turn out that he loses much that is important to him. This last provision brings in the third feature; namely, that the rejected alternatives have outcomes that one can hardly accept. The situation involves grave risks. Of course these features work most effectively in combination. The paradigm situation for following the maximin rule is when all three features are realized to the highest degree. This rule does not, then, generally apply, nor

Table 64.1

	Circumstances		
Decisions	C1	C2	C3
d1	−7	8	12
d2	−8	7	14
d3	5	6	8

of course is it self-evident. Rather, it is a maxim, a rule of thumb, that comes into its own in special circumstances. Its application depends upon the qualitative structure of the possible gains and losses in relation to one's conception of the good, all this against a background in which it is reasonable to discount conjectural estimates of likelihoods.

It should be noted, as the comments on the gain-and-loss table say, that the entries in the table represent monetary values and not utilities. This difference is significant since for one thing computing expectations on the basis of such objective values is not the same thing as computing expected utility and may lead to different results. The essential point, though, is that in justice as fairness the parties do not know their conception of the good and cannot estimate their utility in the ordinary sense. In any case, we want to go behind de facto preferences generated by given conditions. Therefore, expectations are based upon an index or primary goods and the parties make their choice accordingly. The entries in the example are in terms of money and not utility to indicate this aspect of the contract doctrine.

Now, as I have suggested, the original position has been defined so that it is a situation in which the maximin rule applies. In order to see this, let us review briefly the nature of this situation with these three special features in mind. To begin with, the veil of ignorance excludes all but the vaguest knowledge of likelihoods. The parties have no basis for determining the probable nature of their society, or their place in it. Thus they have strong reasons for being wary of probability calculations if any other course is open to them. They must also take into account the fact that their choice of principles should seem reasonable to others, in particular their descendants, whose rights will be deeply affected by it. There are further grounds for discounting that I shall mention as we go along. For the present it suffices to note that these considerations are strengthened by the fact that the parties know very little about the gain-and-loss table. Not only are they unable to conjecture the likelihoods of the various possible circumstances, they cannot say much about what the possible circumstances are, much less enumerate them and foresee the outcome of each alternative available. Those deciding are much more in the dark than the illustration by a numerical table suggests. It is for this reason that I have spoken of an analogy with the maximin rule.

Several kinds of arguments for the two principles of justice illustrate the second feature. Thus, if we can maintain that these principles provide a workable theory of social justice and that they are compatible with reasonable demands of efficiency, then this conception guarantees a satisfactory minimum. There may be, on reflection, little reason for trying to do better. Thus much of the argument . . . is to show, by their application to the main questions of social justice, that the two principles are a satisfactory conception. These details have a philosophical purpose. Moreover, this line of thought is practically decisive if we can establish the priority of liberty, the lexical ordering of the two principles. For this priority implies that the persons in the original position have no desire to try for greater gains at the expense of the equal liberties. The minimum assured by the two principles in lexical order is not one that the parties wish to jeopardize for the sake of greater economic and social advantages. . . .

Finally, the third feature holds if we can assume that other conceptions of justice may lead to institutions that the parties would find intolerable. For example, it has sometimes been held that under some conditions the utility principle (in either form) justifies, if not slavery or serfdom, at any rate serious infractions of liberty for the sake of greater social benefits. We need not consider here the truth of this claim, or the likelihood that the requisite conditions obtain. For the moment, this contention is only to illustrate the way in which conceptions of justice may allow for outcomes which the parties may not be able to accept. And having the ready alternative of the two principles of justice which secure a satisfactory minimum, it seems unwise, if not irrational, for them to take a chance that these outcomes are not realized.

So much, then, for a brief sketch of the features of situations in which the maximin rule comes into its own and of the way in which the arguments for the two principles of justice can be subsumed under them. . . .

Notes

1. As the text suggests, I shall regard Locke's *Second Treatise of Government*, Rousseau's The *Social Contract*, and Kant's ethical works beginning with *The Foundations of the Metaphysics of Morals* as definitive of the contract tradition. For all of its greatness, Hobbes's *Leviathan* raises special problems. A general historical survey is provided by J. W. Gough, The *Social Contract*, 2nd ed. (Oxford, The Clarendon Press, 1957), and Otto Gierke, *Natural Law and the Theory of Society*, trans. with an introduction by Ernest Barker (Cambridge, The University Press, 1934). A presentation of the contract view as primarily an ethical theory is to be found in G. R. Grice, *The Grounds of Moral Judgment* (Cambridge, The University Press, 1967). See also §19, note 30.

2. Kant is clear that the original agreement is hypothetical. See *The Metaphysics of Morals*, pt. I (*Rechtslehre*), especially §§47, 52; and pt. II of the essay "Concerning the Common Saying: This May Be True in Theory but It Does Not Apply in Practice," in *Kant's Political Writings*, ed. Hans Reiss and trans. by H. B. Nisbet (Cambridge, The University Press, 1970), pp. 73–87. See Georges Vlachos, *La Pensée politique de Kant* (Paris, Presses Universitaires de France, 1962), pp. 326–35; and J. G. Murphy, *Kant: The Philosophy of Right* (London, Macmillan, 1970), pp. 109–12, 133–6, for a further discussion.

3. The process of mutual adjustment of principles and considered judgments is not peculiar to moral philosophy. See Nelson Goodman, *Fact, Fiction, and Forecast* (Cambridge, Mass., Harvard University Press, 1955), pp. 65–8, for parallel remarks concerning the justification of the principles of deductive and inductive inference.

CHAPTER 65
Contractualism and Utilitarianism

T. M. SCANLON

Utilitarianism occupies a central place in the moral philosophy of our time. It is not the view which most people hold; certainly there are very few who would claim to be act utilitarians. But for a much wider range of people it is the view towards which they find themselves pressed when they try to give a theoretical account of their moral beliefs. Within moral philosophy it represents a position one must struggle against if one wishes to avoid it. This is so in spite of the fact that the implications of act utilitarianism are wildly at variance with firmly held moral convictions, while rule utilitarianism, the most common alternative formulation, strikes most people as an unstable compromise.

The wide appeal of utilitarianism is due, I think, to philosophical considerations of a more or less sophisticated kind which pull us in a quite different direction than our first order moral beliefs. In particular, utilitarianism derives much of its appeal from alleged difficulties about the foundations of rival views.

T. M. Scanlon, "Contractualism and Utilitarianism," pp. 103–29 from Amartya Sen and Bernard Williams (eds.), *Utilitarianism and Beyond*. Cambridge: Cambridge University Press, 1982. © 1982 by Maison des Sciences de l'Homme and Cambridge University Press, reproduced with permission. Reprinted by permission of Professor T. Scanlon.

What a successful alternative to utilitarianism must do, first and foremost, is to sap this source of strength by providing a clear account of the foundations of non-utilitarian moral reasoning. In what follows I will first describe the problem in more detail by setting out the questions which a philosophical account of the foundations of morality must answer. I will then put forward a version of contractualism which, I will argue, offers a better set of responses to these questions than that supplied by straightforward versions of utilitarianism. Finally I will explain why contractualism, as I understand it, does not lead back to some utilitarian formula as its normative outcome.

Contractualism has been proposed as the alternative to utilitarianism before, notably by John Rawls in *A Theory of Justice* (Rawls 1971). Despite the wide discussion which this book has received, however, I think that the appeal of contractualism as a foundational view has been underrated. In particular, it has not been sufficiently appreciated that contractualism offers a particularly plausible account of moral motivation. The version of contractualism that I shall present differs from Rawls' in a number of respects. In particular, it makes no use, or only a different and more limited kind of use, of his notion of choice from behind a veil of ignorance. One result of this difference is to make the contrast between contractualism and utilitarianism stand out more clearly.

I

There is such a subject as moral philosophy for much the same reason that there is such a subject as the philosophy of mathematics. In moral judgments, as in mathematical ones, we have a set of putatively objective beliefs in which we are inclined to invest a certain degree of confidence and importance. Yet on reflection it is not at all obvious what, if anything, these judgments can be about, in virtue of which some can be said to be correct or defensible and others not. This question of subject matter, or the grounds of truth, is the first philosophical question about both morality and mathematics. Second, in both morality and mathematics it seems to be possible to discover the truth simply by thinking or reasoning about it. Experience and observation may be helpful, but observation in the normal sense is not the standard means of discovery in either subject. So, given any positive answer to the first question – any specification of the subject matter or ground of truth in mathematics or morality – we need some compatible epistemology explaining how it is possible to discover the facts about this subject matter through something like the means we seem to use.

Given this similarity in the questions giving rise to moral philosophy and to the philosophy of mathematics, it is not surprising that the answers commonly given fall into similar general types. If we were to interview students in a freshman mathematics course many of them would, I think, declare themselves for some kind of conventionalism. They would hold that mathematics proceeds from definitions and principles that are either arbitrary or instrumentally justified, and that mathematical reasoning consists in perceiving what follows from these definitions and principles. A few others, perhaps, would be realists or platonists according to whom mathematical truths are a special kind of non-empirical fact that we can perceive through some form of intuition. Others might be naturalists who hold that mathematics, properly understood, is just the most abstract empirial science. Finally there are, though perhaps not in an average freshman course, those who hold that there are no mathematical facts in the world "outside of us," but that the truths of mathematics are objective truths about the mental constructions of which we are capable. Kant held that pure mathematics was a realm of objective mind-dependent truths, and Brouwer's mathematical Intuitionism is another theory of this type (with the important difference that it offers grounds for the warranted assertability of mathematical judgments rather than for their truth in the classical sense). All of these positions have natural correlates in moral philosophy. Intuitionism of the sort espoused by W. D. Ross is perhaps the closest analogue to mathematical platonism, and Kant's theory is the most familiar version of the thesis that morality is a sphere of objective, mind-dependent truths.

All of the views I have mentioned (with some qualification in the case of conventionalism) give positive (i.e. non-sceptical) answers to the first philosophical question about mathematics. Each identifies some objective, or at least intersubjective, ground of truth for mathematical judgments. Outright scepticism and subjective versions of mind-dependence (analogues of emotivism or prescriptivism) are less appealing as philosophies of mathematics than as moral philosophies. This is so in part simply because of the greater degree of intersubjective agreement in mathematical judgment. But it is also due to the difference in the further questions that philosophical accounts of the two fields must answer.

Neither mathematics nor morality can be taken to describe a realm of facts existing in isolation from the rest of reality. Each is supposed to be connected with other things. Mathematical judgments give rise to predictions about those realms to which mathematics is applied. This connection is something that a philosophical account of mathematical truth must explain, but the fact that we can observe and learn from the correctness of such predictions also gives support to our belief in objective mathematical truth. In the case of morality the main connection is, or is generally supposed to be, with the will. Given any candidate for the role of subject matter of morality we must explain why anyone should care about it, and the need to answer this question of motivation has given strong support to subjectivist views.

But what must an adequate philosophical theory of morality say about moral motivation? It need not, I think, show that the moral truth gives anyone who knows it a reason to act which appeals to that person's present desires or to the advancement of his or her interests. I find it entirely intelligible that moral requirement might correctly apply to a person even though that person had no reason of either of these kinds for complying with it. Whether moral requirements give those to whom they apply reasons for compliance of some third kind is a disputed question which I shall set aside. But what an adequate moral philosophy must do, I think, is to make clearer to us the nature of the reasons that morality does provide, at least to those who are concerned with it. A philosophical theory of morality must offer an account of these reasons that is, on the one hand, compatible with its account of moral truth and moral reasoning and, on the other, supported by a plausible analysis of moral experience. A satisfactory moral philosophy will not leave concern with morality as a simple special preference, like a fetish or a special taste, which some people just happen to have. It must make it understandable why moral reasons are ones that people can take seriously, and why they strike those who are moved by them as reasons of a special stringency and inescapability.

There is also a further question whether susceptibility to such reasons is compatible with a person's good or whether it is, as Nietzsche argued, a psychological disaster for the person who has it. If one is to defend morality one must show that it is not disastrous in this way, but I will not pursue this second motivational question here. I mention it only to distinguish it from the first question, which is my present concern.

The task of giving a philosophical explanation of the subject matter of morality differs both from the task of analysing the meaning of moral terms and from that of finding the most coherent formulation of our first order moral beliefs. A maximally coherent ordering of our first order moral beliefs could provide us with a valuable kind of explanation: it would make clear how various, apparently disparate moral notions, precepts and judgments are related to one another, thus indicating to what degree conflicts between them are fundamental and to what degree, on the other hand, they can be resolved or explained away. But philosophical inquiry into the subject matter of morality takes a more external view. It seeks to explain what kind of truths moral truths are by describing them in relation to other things in the world and in relation to our particular concerns. An explanation of how we can come to know the truth about morality must be based on such an external explanation of the kind of things moral truths are rather than on a list of particular moral truths, even a maximally coherent list. This seems to be true as well about explanations of how moral beliefs can give one a reason to act.

Coherence among our first-order moral beliefs – what Rawls has called narrow reflective equilibrium – seems unsatisfying as an account of moral truth or as an account of the basis of justification in ethics just because, taken by itself, a maximally coherent account of our moral beliefs need not provide us with what I have called a philosophical explanation of the subject matter of morality. However internally coherent our moral beliefs may be rendered, the nagging doubt may remain that there is nothing to them at all. They may be merely a set of socially inculcated reactions, mutually consistent perhaps but not judgments of a kind which can properly be said to be correct or incorrect. A philosophical theory of the nature of morality can contribute to our confidence in our first order moral beliefs chiefly by allaying these natural doubts about the subject. Insofar as it includes an account of moral epistemology, such a theory may guide us towards new forms of moral argument, but it need not do this. Moral argument of more or less the kind we have been familiar with may remain as the only form of justification in ethics. But whether or not it leads to revision in our modes of justification, what a good philosophical theory should do is to give us a clearer understanding of what the best forms of moral argument amount to and what kind of truth it is that they can be a way of arriving at. (Much the same can be said, I believe, about the contribution which philosophy of mathematics makes to our confidence in particular mathematical judgments and particular forms of mathematical reasoning.)

Like any thesis about morality, a philosophical account of the subject matter of morality must have some connection with the meaning of moral terms: it must be plausible to claim that the subject matter described is in fact what these terms refer to at least in much of their normal use. But the current meaning of moral terms is the product of many different moral beliefs held by past and present speakers of the language, and this meaning is surely compatible with a variety of moral views and with a variety of views about the nature of morality. After all, moral terms are used to express many different views of these kinds, and people who express these views are not using moral terms incorrectly, even though what some of them say must be mistaken. Like a first-order moral judgment, a philosophical characterization of the subject matter of morality is a substantive claim about morality, albeit a claim of a different kind.

While a philosophical characterization of morality makes a kind of claim that differs from a first-order moral judgment, this does not mean that a philosophical theory of morality will be neutral between competing normative doctrines. The adoption of a philosophical thesis about the nature of morality will almost always have some effect on the plausibility of particular moral claims, but philosophical theories of morality vary widely in the extent and directness of their normative implications. At one extreme is intuitionism, understood as the philosophical thesis that morality is concerned with certain non-natural properties. Rightness, for example, is held by Ross to be the property of "fittingness" or "moral suitability." Intuitionism holds that we can identify occurrences of these properties, and that we can recognize as self-evident certain general truths about them, but that they cannot be further analyzed or explained in terms of other notions. So understood, intuitionism is in principle compatible with a wide variety of normative positions. One could, for example, be an intuitionistic utilitarian or an intuitionistic believer in moral rights, depending on the general truths about the property of moral rightness which one took to be self-evident.

The other extreme is represented by philosophical utilitarianism. The term "utilitarianism" is generally used to refer to a family of specific normative doctrines – doctrines which might be held on the basis of a number of different philosophical theses about the nature of morality. In this sense of the term one might, for example, be a utilitarian on intuitionist or on contractualist grounds. But what I will call "philosophical utilitarianism" is a particular philosophical thesis about the subject matter of morality, namely the thesis that the only fundamental moral facts are facts about individual well-being. I believe that this thesis has a great deal of plausibility for many people, and that, while some people are utilitarians for other reasons, it is the attractiveness of philosophical utilitarianism which accounts for the widespread influence of utilitarian principles.

It seems evident to people that there is such a thing as individuals' being made better or worse off. Such facts have an obvious motivational force; it is quite understandable that people should be moved by them in much the way that they are supposed to be moved by moral considerations. Further, these facts are clearly relevant to morality as we now understand it. Claims about individual well-being are one class of valid starting points for moral argument. But many people find it much harder to see how there could be any other, independent starting points. Substantive moral requirements independent of individual well-being strike people as intuitionist in an objectionable sense. They would represent "moral facts" of a kind it would be difficult to explain. There is no problem about recognizing it as a fact that a certain act is, say, an instance of lying or of promise breaking. And a utilitarian can acknowledge that such facts as these often have (derivative) moral significance: they are morally significant because of their consequences for individual well-being. The problems, and the charge of "intuitionism," arise when it is claimed that such acts are wrong in a sense that is not reducible to the fact that they decrease individual well-being. How could this independent property of moral wrongness be understood in a way that would give it the kind of importance and motivational force which moral considerations have been taken to have? If one accepts the idea that there are no moral properties having this kind of intrinsic significance, then philosophical utilitarianism may seem to be the only tenable account of morality. And once philosophical utilitarianism is accepted, some form of normative utilitarianism seems to be forced on us as the correct first-order moral theory. Utilitarianism thus has, for many people, something like the status which Hilbert's Formalism and Brouwer's Intuitionism have for their believers. It is a view which seems to be forced on us by the need to give a philosophically defensible account of the subject. But it leaves us with a hard choice: we can either abandon many of our previous first-order beliefs or try to salvage them by showing that they can be obtained as derived truths or explained away as useful and harmless fictions.

It may seem that the appeal of philosophical utilitarianism as I have described it is spurious, since this theory must amount either to a form of intuitionism (differing from others only in that it involves just one appeal to intuition) or else to definitional naturalism of a kind refuted by Moore and others long ago. But I do not think that the doctrine can be disposed of so easily. Philosophical utilitarianism is a philosophical thesis about the nature of morality. As such, it is on a par with intuitionism or with the form of contractualism which I will defend later in this paper. None of these theses need claim to be true as a matter of definition; if one of them is true it does not follow that a person who denies it is misusing the words "right," "wrong" and "ought." Nor are all these theses forms of intuitionism, if intuitionism is understood as the view that moral facts concern special non-natural properties, which we can apprehend by intuitive insight but which do not need or admit of any further analysis. Both contractualism and philosophical utilitarianism are specifically incompatible with this claim. Like other philosophical theses about the nature of morality (including, I would say, intuitionism itself), contractualism and philosophical utilitarianism are to be appraised on the basis of their success in giving an account of

moral belief, moral argument and moral motivation that is compatible with our general beliefs about the world: our beliefs about what kinds of things there are in the world, what kinds of observation and reasoning we are capable of, and what kinds of reasons we have for action. A judgment as to which account of the nature of morality (or of mathematics) is most plausible in this general sense is just that: a judgment of overall plausibility. It is not usefully described as an insight into concepts or as a special intuitive insight of some other kind.

If philosophical utilitarianism is accepted then some form of utilitarianism appears to be forced upon us as a normative doctrine, but further argument is required to determine which form we should accept. If all that counts morally is the well-being of individuals, no one of whom is singled out as counting for more than the others, and if all that matters in the case of each individual is the degree to which his or her well-being is affected, then it would seem to follow that the basis of moral appraisal is the goal of maximising the *sum* of individual well-being. Whether this standard is to be applied to the criticism of individual actions, or to the selection of rules or policies, or to the inculcation of habits and dispositions to act is a further question, as is the question of how "well-being" itself is to be understood. Thus the hypothesis that much of the appeal of utilitarianism as a normative doctrine derives from the attractiveness of philosophical utilitarianism explains how people can be convinced that some form of utilitarianism must be correct while yet being quite uncertain as to which form it is, whether it is "direct" or "act" utilitarianism or some form of indirect "rule" or "motive" utilitarianism. What these views have in common, despite their differing normative consequences, is the identification of the same class of fundamental moral facts.

II

If what I have said about the appeal of utilitarianism is correct, then what a rival theory must do is to provide an alternative to philosophical utilitarianism as a conception of the subject matter of morality. This is what the theory which I shall call contractualism seeks to do. Even if it succeeds in this, however, and is judged superior to philosophical utilitarianism as an account of the nature of morality, normative utilitarianism will not have been refuted. The possibility will remain that normative utilitarianism can be established on other grounds, for example as the normative outcome of contractualism itself. But one direct and, I think, influential argument for normative utilitarianism will have been set aside.

To give an example of what I mean by contractualism, a contractualist account of the nature of moral wrongness might be stated as follows.

An act is wrong if its performance under the circumstances would be disallowed by any system of rules for the general regulation of behavior which no one could reasonably reject as a basis for informed, unforced general agreement.

This is intended as a characterization of the kind of property which moral wrongness is. Like philosophical utilitarianism, it will have normative consequences, but it is not my present purpose to explore these in detail. As a contractualist account of one moral notion, what I have set out here is only an approximation, which may need to be modified considerably. Here I can offer a few remarks by way of clarification.

The idea of "informed agreement" is meant to exclude agreement based on superstition or false belief about the consequences of actions, even if these beliefs are ones which it would be reasonable for the person in question to have. The intended force of the qualification "reasonably," on the other hand, is to exclude rejections that would be unreasonable *given* the aim of finding principles which could be the basis of informed, unforced general agreement. Given this aim, it would be unreasonable, for example, to reject a principle because it imposed a burden on you when every alternative principle would impose much greater burdens on others. I will have more to say about grounds for rejection later in the paper.

The requirement that the hypothetical agreement which is the subject of moral argument be unforced is meant not only to rule out coercion, but also to exclude being forced to accept an agreement by being in a weak bargaining position, for example because others are able to hold out longer and hence to insist on better terms. Moral argument abstracts from such considerations. The only relevant pressure for agreement comes from the desire to find and agree on principles which no one who had this desire could reasonably reject. According to contractualism, moral argument concerns the possibility of agreement among persons who are all moved by this desire, and moved by it to the same degree. But this counterfactual assumption characterizes only the agreement with which morality is concerned, not the world to which moral principles are to apply. Those who are concerned with morality look for principles for application to their imperfect world which they could not reasonably reject, and which others in this world, who are not now moved by the desire for agreement, could not reasonably reject should they come to be so moved.

The contractualist account of moral wrongness refers to principles "which no one could reasonably reject" rather than to principles "which everyone could reasonably accept" for the following reason. Consider a principle under which some people will suffer severe hardships, and suppose that these hardships are avoidable. That is, there are alternative principles under which no one would have to bear comparable burdens. It might happen, however, that the people on whom these hardships fall are particularly self-sacrificing, and are willing to accept these burdens for the sake of what they see as the greater good of all. We would not say, I think, that it would be unreasonable of them to do this. On the other hand, it might not be unreasonable for them to refuse these burdens, and, hence, not unreasonable for someone to reject a principle requiring him to bear them. If this rejection would be reasonable, then the principle imposing these burdens is put in doubt, despite the fact that some particularly self-sacrificing people could (reasonably) accept it. Thus it is the reasonableness of rejecting a principle, rather than the reasonableness of accepting it, on which moral argument turns.

It seems likely that many non-equivalent sets of principles will pass the test of non-rejectability. This is suggested, for example, by the fact that there are many different ways of defining important duties, no one of which is more or less "rejectable" than the others. There are, for example, many different systems of agreement-making and many different ways of assigning responsibility to care for others. It does not follow, however, that any action allowed by at least one of these sets of principles cannot be morally wrong according to contractualism. If it is important for us to have *some* duty of a given kind (some duty of fidelity to agreements, or some duty of mutual aid) of which there are many morally acceptable forms, then one of these forms needs to be established by convention. In a setting in which one of these forms *is* conventionally established, acts disallowed by it will be wrong in the sense of the definition given. For, given the need for such conventions, one thing that could not be generally agreed to would be a set of principles allowing one to disregard conventionally established (and morally acceptable) definitions of important duties. This dependence on convention introduces a degree of cultural relativity into contractualist morality. In addition, what a person can reasonably reject will depend on the aims and conditions that are important in his life, and these will also depend on the society in which he lives. The definition given above allows for variation of both of these kinds by making the wrongness of an action depend on the circumstances in which it is performed.

The partial statement of contractualism which I have given has the abstract character appropriate in an account of the subject matter of morality. On its face, it involves no specific claim as to which principles could be agreed to or even whether there is a unique set of principles which could be the basis of agreement. One way, though not the only way, for a contractualist to arrive at substantive moral claims would be to give a technical definition of the relevant notion of agreement, e.g. by specifying the conditions under which agreement is to be reached, the parties to this agreement and the

criteria of reasonableness to be employed. Different contractualists have done this in different ways. What must be claimed for such a definition is that (under the circumstances in which it is to apply) what it describes is indeed the kind of unforced, reasonable agreement at which moral argument aims. But contractualism can also be understood as an informal description of the subject matter of morality, on the basis of which ordinary forms of moral reasoning can be understood and appraised without proceeding via a technical notion of agreement.

Who is to be included in the general agreement to which contractualism refers? The scope of morality is a difficult question of substantive morality, but a philosophical theory of the nature of morality should provide some basis for answering it. What an adequate theory should do is to provide a framework within which what seem to be relevant arguments for and against particular interpretations of the moral boundary can be carried out. It is often thought that contractualism can provide no plausible basis for an answer to this question. Critics charge either that contractualism provides no answer at all, because it must begin with some set of contracting parties taken as given, or that contractualism suggests an answer which is obviously too restrictive, since a contract requires parties who are able to make and keep agreements and who are each able to offer the others some benefit in return for their cooperation. Neither of these objections applies to the version of contractualism that I am defending. The general specification of the scope of morality which it implies seems to me to be this: morality applies to a being if the notion of justification to a being of that kind makes sense. What is required in order for this to be the case? Here I can only suggest some necessary conditions. The first is that the being have a good, that is, that there be a clear sense in which things can be said to go better or worse for that being. This gives partial sense to the idea of what it would be reasonable for a trustee to accept on the being's behalf. It would be reasonable for a trustee to accept at least those things that are good, or not bad, for the being in question. Using this idea of trusteeship we can extend the notion of acceptance to apply to beings that are incapable of literally agreeing to anything. But this minimal notion of trusteeship is too weak to provide a basis for morality, according to contractualism. Contractualist morality relies on notions of what it would be reasonable to accept, or reasonable to reject, which are essentially comparative. Whether it would be unreasonable for me to reject a certain principle, given the aim of finding principles which no one with this aim could reasonably reject, depends not only on how much actions allowed by that principle might hurt me in absolute terms but also on how that potential loss compares with other potential losses to others under this principle and alternatives to it. Thus, in order for a being to stand in moral relations with us it is not enough that it have a good, it is also necessary that its good be sufficiently similar to our own to provide a basis for some system of comparability. Only on the basis of such a system can we give the proper kind of sense to the notion of what a trustee could reasonably reject on a being's behalf.

But the range of possible trusteeship is broader than that of morality. One could act as a trustee for a tomato plant, a forest or an ant colony, and such entities are not included in morality. Perhaps this can be explained by appeal to the requirement of comparability: while these entities have a good, it is not comparable to our own in a way that provides a basis for moral argument. Beyond this, however, there is in these cases insufficient foothold for the notion of justification *to* a being. One further minimum requirement for this notion is that the being constitute a point of view; that is, that there be such a thing as what it is like to be that being, such a thing as what the world seems like to it. Without this, we do not stand in a relation to the being that makes even hypothetical justification to *it* appropriate.

On the basis of what I have said so far contractualism can explain why the capacity to feel pain should have seemed to many to count in favor of moral status: a being which has this capacity seems also to satisfy the three conditions I have just mentioned as necessary for the idea of justification to it to

make sense. If a being can feel pain, then it constitutes a center of consciousness to which justification can be addressed. Feeling pain is a clear way in which the being can be worse off; having its pain alleviated a way in which it can be benefited; and these are forms of weal and woe which seem directly comparable to our own.

It is not clear that the three conditions I have listed as necessary are also sufficient for the idea of justification to a being to make sense. Whether they are, and, if they are not, what more may be required, are difficult and disputed questions. Some would restrict the moral sphere to those to whom justifications could in principle be communicated, or to those who can actually agree to something, or to those who have the capacity to understand moral argument. Contractualism as I have stated it does not settle these issues at once. All I claim is that it provides a basis for argument about them which is at least as plausible as that offered by rival accounts of the nature of morality. These proposed restrictions on the scope of morality are naturally understood as debatable claims about the conditions under which the relevant notion of justification makes sense, and the arguments commonly offered for and against them can also be plausibly understood on this basis.

Some other possible restrictions on the scope of morality are more evidently rejectable. Morality might be restricted to those who have the capacity to observe its constraints, or to those who are able to confer some reciprocal benefit on other participants. But it is extremely implausible to suppose that the beings excluded by these requirements fall entirely outside the protection of morality. Contractualism as I have formulated it can explain why this is so: the absence of these capacities alone does nothing to undermine the possibility of justification to a being. What it may do in some cases, however, is to alter the justifications which are relevant. I suggest that whatever importance the capacities for deliberative control and reciprocal benefit may have is as factors altering the duties which beings have and the duties others have towards them, not as conditions whose absence suspends the moral framework altogether.

III

I have so far said little about the normative content of contractualism. For all I have said, the act utilitarian formula might turn out to be a theorem of contractualism. I do not think that this is the case, but my main thesis is that whatever the normative implications of contractualism may be it still has distinctive content as a philosophical thesis about the nature of morality. This content – the difference, for example, between being a utilitarian because the utilitarian formula is the basis of general agreement and being a utilitarian on other grounds – is shown most clearly in the answer that a contractualist gives to the first motivational question.

Philosophical utilitarianism is a plausible view partly because the facts which it identifies as fundamental to morality – facts about individual well-being – have obvious motivational force. Moral facts can motivate us, on this view, because of our sympathetic identification with the good of others. But as we move from philosophical utilitarianism to a specific utilitarian formula as the standard of right action, the form of motivation that utilitarianism appeals to becomes more abstract. If classical utilitarianism is the correct normative doctrine then the natural source of moral motivation will be a tendency to be moved by changes in aggregate well-being, however these may be composed. We must be moved in the same way by an aggregate gain of the same magnitude whether it is obtained by relieving the acute suffering of a few people or by bringing tiny benefits to a vast number, perhaps at the expense of moderate discomfort for a few. This is very different from sympathy of the familiar kind toward particular individuals, but a utilitarian may argue that this more abstract desire is what natural sympathy becomes when it is corrected by rational reflection. This desire has the same content as sympathy – it is a concern for the good of others – but it is not partial or selective in its choice of objects.

Leaving aside the psychological plausibility of this even-handed sympathy, how good a candidate is it for the role of moral motivation? Certainly sympathy of the usual kind is one of the many motives that can sometimes impel one to do the right thing. It may be the dominant motive, for example, when I run to the aid of a suffering child. But when I feel convinced by Peter Singer's article[1] on famine, and find myself crushed by the recognition of what seems a clear moral requirement, there is something else at work. In addition to the thought of how much good I could do for people in drought-stricken lands, I am overwhelmed by the further, seemingly distinct thought that it would be wrong for me to fail to aid them when I could do so at so little cost to myself. A utilitarian may respond that his account of moral motivation cannot be faulted for not capturing this aspect of moral experience, since it is just a reflection of our non-utilitarian moral upbringing. Moreover, it must be groundless. For what kind of fact could this supposed further fact of moral wrongness be, and how could it give us a further, special reason for acting? The question for contractualism, then, is whether it can provide a satisfactory answer to this challenge.

According to contractualism, the source of motivation that is directly triggered by the belief that an action is wrong is the desire to be able to justify one's actions to others on grounds they could not reasonably reject. I find this an extremely plausible account of moral motivation – a better account of at least my moral experience than the natural utilitarian alternative – and it seems to me to constitute a strong point for the contractualist view. We all might like to be in actual agreement with the people around us, but the desire which contractualism identifies as basic to morality does not lead us simply to conform to the standards accepted by others whatever these may be. The desire to be able to justify one's actions to others on grounds they could not reasonably reject will be satisfied when we know that there is adequate justification for our action even though others in fact refuse to accept it (perhaps because they have no interest in finding principles which we and others could not reasonably reject). Similarly, a person moved by this desire will not be satisfied by the fact that others accept a justification for his action if he regards this justification as spurious.

One rough test of whether you regard a justification as sufficient is whether you would accept that justification if you were in another person's position. This connection between the idea of "changing places" and the motivation which underlies morality explains the frequent occurrence of "Golden Rule" arguments within different systems of morality and in the teachings of various religions. But the thought experiment of changing places is only a rough guide; the fundamental question is what would it be unreasonable to reject as a basis for informed, unforced, general agreement. As Kant observed,[3] our different individual points of view, taken as they are, may in general by simply irreconcilable. "Judgmental harmony" requires the construction of a genuinely interpersonal form of justification which nonetheless something that each individual could agree to. From this interpersonal standpoint, a certain amount of how things look from another person's point of view, like a certain amount of how they look from my own, will be counted as bias.

I am not claiming that the desire to be able to justify one's actions to others on grounds they could not reasonably reject is universal or "natural." "Moral education" seems to me plausibly understood as a process of cultivating this desire and shaping it, largely by learning what justifications others are in fact willing to accept, by finding which ones you yourself find acceptable as you confront them from a variety of perspectives, and by appraising your own and others' acceptance or rejection of these justifications in the light of greater experience.

In fact it seems to me that the desire to be able to justify one's actions (and institutions) on grounds one takes to be acceptable is quite strong in most people. People are willing to go to considerable lengths, involving quite heavy sacrifices, in order to avoid admitting the unjustifiability of their actions and institutions. The notorious insufficiency of moral motivation as a way of getting people to do the right thing is not due to simple weakness of the underlying motive, but rather to the fact that it is easily deflected by self-interest and self-deception.

It could reasonably be objected here that the source of motivation I have described is not tied exclusively to the contractualist notion of moral truth. The account of moral motivation which I have offered refers to the idea of a justification which it would be unreasonable to reject, and this idea is potentially broader than the contractualist notion of agreement. For let M be some non-contractualist account of moral truth. According to M, we may suppose, the wrongness of an action is simply a moral characteristic of that action in virtue of which it ought not to be done. An act which has this characteristic, according to M, has it quite independently of any tendency of informed persons to come to agreement about it. However, since informed persons are presumably in a position to recognize the wrongness of a type of action, it would seem to follow that if an action is wrong then such persons would agree that it is not to be performed. Similarly, if an act is not morally wrong, and there is adequate moral justification to perform it, then there will presumably be a moral justification for it which an informed person would be unreasonable to reject. Thus, even if M, and not contractualism, is the correct account of moral truth, the desire to be able to justify my actions to others on grounds they could not reasonably reject could still serve as a basis for moral motivation.

What this shows is that the appeal of contractualism, like that of utilitarianism, rests in part on a qualified scepticism. A non-contractualist theory of morality can make use of the source of motivation to which contractualism appeals. But a moral argument will trigger this source of motivation only in virtue of being a good justification for acting in a certain way, a justification which others would be unreasonable not to accept. So a non-contractualist theory must claim that there are moral properties which have justificatory force quite independent of their recognition in any ideal agreement. These would represent what John Mackie has called instances of intrinsic "to-be-doneness" and "not-to-be-doneness." Part of contractualism's appeal rests on the view that, as Mackie puts it, it is puzzling how there could be such properties "in the world." By contrast, contractualism seeks to explain the justificatory status of moral properties, as well as their motivational force, in terms of the notion of reasonable agreement. In some cases the moral properties are themselves to be understood in terms of this notion. This is so, for example, in the case of the property of moral wrongness, considered above. But there are also right- and wrong-making properties which are themselves independent of the contractualist notion of agreement. I take the property of being an act of killing for the pleasure of doing so to be a wrong-making property of this kind. Such properties are wrong-making because it would be reasonable to reject any set of principles which permitted the acts they characterize. Thus, while there are morally relevant properties "in the world" which are independent of the contractualist notion of agreement, these do not constitute instances of intrinsic "to-be-doneness" and "not-to-be-doneness": their moral relevance – their force in justifications as well as their link with motivation – is to be explained on contractualist grounds.

In particular, contractualism can account for the apparent moral significance of facts about individual well-being, which utilitarianism takes to be fundamental. Individual well-being will be morally significant, according to contractualism, not because it is intrinsically valuable or because promoting it is self-evidently a right-making characteristic, but simply because an individual could reasonably reject a form of argument that gave his well-being no weight. This claim of moral significance is, however, only approximate, since it is a further difficult question exactly how "well-being" is to be understood and in what ways we are required to take account of the well-being of others in deciding what to do. It does not follow from this claim, for example, that a given desire will always and everywhere have the same weight in determining the rightness of an action that would promote its satisfaction, a weight proportional to its strength or "intensity." The right-making force of a person's desires is specified by what might be called a conception of morally legitimate interests. Such a conception is a product of moral argument; it is not given, as the notion of individual well-being may be, simply by the idea of what it is rational for an individual to desire. Not everything for which I have a rational desire will be something

in which others need concede me to have a legitimate interest which they undertake to weigh in deciding what to do. The range of things which may be objects of my rational desires is very wide indeed, and the range of claims which others could not reasonably refuse to recognize will almost certainly be narrower than this. There will be a tendency for interests to conform to rational desire – for those conditions making it rational to desire something also to establish a legitimate interest in it – but the two will not always coincide.

One effect of contractualism, then, is to break down the sharp distinction, which arguments for utilitarianism appeal to, between the status of individual well-being and that of other moral notions. A framework of moral argument is required to define our legitimate interests and to account for their moral force. This same contractualist framework can also account for the force of other moral notions such as rights, individual responsibility and procedural fairness.

IV

It seems unlikely that act utilitarianism will be a theorem of the version of contractualism which I have described. The positive moral significance of individual interests is a direct reflection of the contractualist requirement that actions be defensible to each person on grounds he could not reasonably reject. But it is a long step from here to the conclusion that each individual must agree to deliberate always from the point of view of maximum aggregate benefit and to accept justifications appealing to this consideration alone. It is quite possible that, according to contractualism, *some* moral questions may be properly settled by appeal to maximum aggregate well-being, even though this is not the sole or ultimate standard of justification.

What seems less improbable is that contractualism should turn out to coincide with some form of "two-level" utilitarianism. I cannot fully assess this possibility here. Contractualism does share with these theories the important features that the defense of individual actions must proceed via a defense of principles that would allow those acts. But contractualism differs from *some* forms of two level utilitarianism in an important way. The role of principles in contractualism is fundamental; they do not enter merely as devices for the promotion of acts that are right according to some other standard. Since it does not establish two potentially conflicting forms of moral reasoning, contractualism avoids the instability which often plagues rule utilitarianism.

The fundamental question here, however, is whether the principles to which contractualism leads must be ones whose general adoption (either ideally or under some more realistic conditions) would promote maximum aggregate well-being. It has seemed to many that this must be the case. To indicate why I do not agree I will consider one of the best known arguments for this conclusion and explain why I do not think it is successful. This will also provide an opportunity to examine the relation between the version of contractualism I have advocated here and the version set forth by Rawls.

The argument I will consider, which is familiar from the writings of Harsanyi[4] and others, proceeds via an interpretation of the contractualist notion of acceptance and leads to the principle of maximum average utility. To think of a principle as a candidate for unanimous agreement I must think of it not merely as acceptable to *me* (perhaps in virtue of my particular position, my tastes, etc.) but as acceptable to others as well. To be relevant, my judgment that the principle is acceptable must be impartial. What does this mean? To judge impartially that a principle is acceptable is, one might say, to judge that it is one which you would have reason to accept no matter who you were. That is, and here is the interpretation, to judge that it is a principle which it would be rational to accept if you did not know which person's position you occupied and believed that you had an equal chance of being in any of these positions. ("Being in a person's position" is here understood to mean being in his objective circumstances and evaluating these from the perspective of his tastes and preferences.) But, it is claimed, the principle which it would be rational to prefer under these circumstances – the one which would offer the chooser greatest expected utility – would be that principle under which the average utility of the affected parties would be highest.

This argument might be questioned at a number of points, but what concerns me at present is the interpretation of impartiality. The argument can be broken down into three stages. The first of these is the idea that moral principles must be impartially acceptable. The second is the idea of choosing principles in ignorance of one's position (including one's tastes, preferences, etc.). The third is the idea of rational choice under the assumption that one has an equal chance of occupying anyone's position. Let me leave aside for the moment the move from stage two to stage three, and concentrate on the first step, from stage one to stage two. There is a way of making something like this step which is, I think, quite valid, but it does not yield the conclusion needed by the argument. If I believe that a certain principle, *P,* could not reasonably be rejected as a basis for informed, unforced general agreement, then I must believe not only that it is something which it would be reasonable for me to accept but something which it would be reasonable for others to accept as well, insofar as we are all seeking a ground for general agreement. Accordingly, I must believe that I would have reason to accept *P* no matter which social position I were to occupy (though, for reasons mentioned above, I may not believe that I *would* agree to *P* if I were in some of these positions). Now it may be thought that no sense can be attached to the notion of choosing or agreeing to a principle in ignorance of one's social position, especially when this includes ignorance of one's tastes, preferences, etc. But there is at least a minimal sense that might be attached to this notion. If it would be reasonable for everyone to choose or agree to *P,* then my knowledge that I have reason to do so need not depend on my knowledge of my particular position, tastes, preferences, etc. So, insofar as it makes any sense at all to speak of choosing or agreeing to something in the absence of this knowledge, it could be said that I have reason to choose or agree to those things which everyone has reason to choose or agree to (assuming, again, the aim of finding principles on which all could agree). And indeed, this same reasoning can carry us through to a version of stage three. For if I judge P to be a principle which everyone has reason to agree to, then it could be said that I would have reason to agree to it if I thought that I had an equal chance of being anybody, or indeed, if I assign any other set of probabilities to being one or another of the people in question.

But it is clear that this is not the conclusion at which the original argument aimed. That conclusion concerned what it would be rational for a self-interested person to choose or agree to under the assumption of ignorance or equal probability of being anyone. The conclusion we have reached appeals to a different notion: the idea of what it would be unreasonable for people to reject given that they are seeking a basis for general agreement. The direction of explanation in the two arguments is quite different. The original argument sought to explain the notion of impartial acceptability of an ethical principle by appealing to the notion of rational self-interested choice under special conditions, a notion which appears to be a clearer one. My revised argument explains how *a* sense might be attached to the idea of choice or agreement in ignorance of one's position given some idea of what it would be unreasonable for someone to reject as a basis for general agreement. This indicates a problem for my version of contractualism: it may be charged with failure to explain the central notion on which it relies. Here I would reply that my version of contractualism does not seek to explain this notion. It only tries to describe it clearly and to show how other features of morality can be understood in terms of it. In particular, it does not try to explain this notion by reducing it to the idea of what would maximize a person's self-interested expectations if he were choosing from a position of ignorance or under the assumption of equal probability of being anyone.

The initial plausibility of the move from stage one to stage two of the original argument rests on a subtle transition from one of these notions to the other. To believe that a principle is morally correct one must believe that it is one which all could reasonably agree to and none could reasonably reject. But my belief

that this is the case may often be distorted by a tendency to take its advantage to me more seriously than its possible costs to others. For this reason, the idea of "putting myself in another's place" is a useful corrective device. The same can be said for the thought experiment of asking what I could agree to in ignorance of my true position. But both of these thought experiments are devices for considering more accurately the question of what *everyone* could reasonably agree to or what no one could reasonably reject. That is, they involve the pattern of reasoning exhibited in my revised form of the three-stage argument, not that of the argument as originally given. The question, what would maximize the expectations of a single self-interested person choosing in ignorance of his true position, is a quite different question. This can be seen by considering the possibility that the distribution with the highest average utility, call it A, might involve extremely low utility levels for some people, levels much lower than the minimum anyone would enjoy under a more equal distribution.

Suppose that A is a principle which it would be rational for a self-interested chooser with an equal chance of being in anyone's position to select. Does it follow that no one could reasonably reject A? It seems evident that this does not follow. Suppose that the situation of those who would fare worst under A, call them the Losers, is extremely bad, and that there is an alternative to A, call it E, under which no one's situation would be nearly as bad as this. Prima facie, the losers would seem to have a reasonable ground for complaint against A. Their objection may be rebutted, by appeal to the sacrifices that would be imposed on some other individual by the selection of E rather than A. But the mere fact that A yields higher average utility, which might be due to the fact that many people do very slightly better under A than under E while a very few do much worse, does not settle the matter.

Under contractualism, when we consider a principle our attention is naturally directed first to those who would do worst under it. This is because if anyone has reasonable grounds for objecting to the principle it is *likely* to be them. It does not follow, however, that contractualism always requires us to select the principle under which the expectations of the worse off are highest. The reasonableness of the Losers' objection to A is not established simply by the fact that they are worse off under A and no-one would be this badly off under E. The force of their complaint depends also on the fact that their position under A is, in absolute terms, very bad, and would be significantly better under E. This complaint must be weighed against those of individuals who would do worse under E. The question to be asked is, is it unreasonable for someone to refuse to put up with the Losers' situation under A in order that someone else should be able to enjoy the benefits which he would have to give up under E? As the supposed situation of the Loser under A becomes better, or his gain under E smaller in relation to the sacrifices required to produce it, his case is weakened.

One noteworthy feature of contractualist argument as I have presented it so far is that it is non-aggregative: what are compared are individual gains, losses and levels of welfare. How aggregative considerations can enter into contractualist argument is a further question too large to be entered into here.

I have been criticizing an argument for Average Utilitarianism that is generally associated with Harsanyi, and my objections to this argument (leaving aside the last remarks about maximin) have an obvious similarity to objections raised by Rawls. But the objections I have raised apply as well against some features of Rawls' own argument. Rawls accepts the first step of the argument I have described. That is, he believes that the correct principles of justice are those which "rational persons concerned to advance their interests" would accept under the conditions defined by his Original Position, where they would be ignorant of their own particular talents, their conception of the good, and the social position (or generation) into which they were born. It is the second step of the argument which Rawls rejects, i.e. the claim that it would be rational for persons so situated to choose those principles which would offer them greatest expected utility under the assumption that they have an equal chance of being anyone in the society in

question. I believe, however, that a mistake has already been made once the first step is taken.

This can be brought out by considering an ambiguity in the idea of acceptance by persons "concerned to advance their interests." On one reading, this is an essential ingredient in contractual argument; on another it is avoidable and, I think, mistaken. On the first reading, the interests in question are simply those of the members of society to whom the principles of justice are to apply (and by whom those principles must ultimately be accepted). The fact that they have interests which may conflict; and which they are concerned to advance, is what gives substance to questions of justice. On the second reading, the concern "to advance their interests" that is in question is a concern of the parties to Rawls' Original Position, and it is this concern which determines, in the first instance, what principles of justice they will adopt. Unanimous agreement among these parties, each motivated to do as well for himself as he can, is to be achieved by depriving them of any information that could give them reason to choose differently from one another. From behind the veil of ignorance, what offers the best prospects for one will offer the best prospects for all, since no-one can tell what would benefit him in particular. Thus the choice of principles can be made, Rawls says, from the point of view of a single rational individual behind the veil of ignorance.

Whatever rules of rational choice this single individual, concerned to advance his own interests as best he can, is said to employ, this reduction of the problem to the case of a single person's self-interested choice should arouse our suspicion. As I indicated in criticizing Harsanyi, it is important to ask whether this single individual is held to accept a principle because he judges that it is one he could not reasonably reject whatever position he turns out to occupy, or whether, on the contrary, it is supposed to be acceptable to a person in any social position because it would be the rational choice for a single self-interested person behind the veil of ignorance. I have argued above that the argument for average utilitarianism involves a covert transition from the first pattern of reasoning to the second. Rawls' argument also appears to be of this second form; his defence of his two principles of justice relies, at least initially, on claims about what it would be rational for a person, concerned to advance his own interests, to choose behind a veil of ignorance. I would claim, however, that the plausibility of Rawls' arguments favoring his two principles over the principle of average utility is preserved, and in some cases enhanced, when they are interpreted as instances of the first form of contractualist argument.

Some of these arguments are of an informal moral character. I have already mentioned his remark about the unacceptability of imposing lower expectations on some for the sake of the higher expectations of others. More specifically, he says of the parties to the Original Position that they are concerned "to choose principles the consequences of which they are prepared to live with whatever generation they turn out to belong to"[5] or, presumably, whatever their social position turns out to be. This is a clear statement of the first form of contractualist argument. Somewhat later he remarks, in favor of the two principles, that they "are those a person would choose for the design of a society in which his enemy is to assign him a place."[6] Rawls goes on to dismiss this remark, saying that the parties "should not reason from false premises,"[7] but it is worth asking why it seemed a plausible thing to say in the first place. The reason, I take it, is this. In a contractualist argument of the first form, the object of which is to find principles acceptable to each person, assignment by a malevolent opponent is a thought experiment which has a heuristic role like that of a veil of ignorance: it is a way of testing whether one really does judge a principle to be acceptable from all points of view or whether, on the contrary, one is failing to take seriously its effect on people in social positions other than one's own.

But these are all informal remarks, and it is fair to suppose that Rawls' argument, like the argument for average utility, is intended to move from the informal contractualist idea of principles "acceptable to all" to the idea of rational choice behind a veil of ignorance, an idea which is, he hopes, more precise and more capable of yielding definite results. Let me turn then to his more formal arguments for the choice of the Difference Principle by the parties to the Original Position. Rawls cites three features of the decision faced by parties to the Original Position which, he claims, make it rational for them to use the maximum rule and, therefore, to select his Difference Principle as a principle of justice. These are (1) the absence of any objective basis for estimating probabilities, (2) the fact that some principles could have consequences for them which "they could hardly accept" while (3) it is possible for them (by following maximin) to ensure themselves of a minimum prospect, advances above which, in comparison, matter very little.[8] The first of these features is slightly puzzling, and I leave it aside. It seems clear, however, that the other considerations mentioned have at least as much force in an informal contractualist argument about what all could reasonably agree to as they do in determining the rational choice of a single person concerned to advance his interests. They express the strength of the objection that the "losers" might have to a scheme that maximized average utility at their expense, as compared with the counter-objections that others might have to a more egalitarian arrangement.

In addition to this argument about rational choice, Rawls invokes among "the main grounds for the two principles" other considerations which, as he says, use the concept of contract to a greater extent.[9] The parties to the Original Position, Rawls says, can agree to principles of justice only if they think that this agreement is one that they will actually be able to live up to. It is, he claims, more plausible to believe this of his two principles than of the principle of average utility, under which the sacrifices demanded ("the strains of commitment") could be much higher. A second, related claim is that the two principles of justice have greater psychological stability than the principle of average utility. It is more plausible to believe, Rawls claims, that in a society in which they were fulfilled people would continue to accept them and to be motivated to act in accordance with them. Continuing acceptance of the principle of average utility, on the other hand, would require an exceptional degree of identification with the good of the whole on the part of those from who sacrifices were demanded.

These remarks can be understood as claims about the "stability" (in a quite practical sense) of a society founded on Rawls' two principles of justice. But they can also be seen as an attempt to show that a principle arrived at via the second form of contractualist reasoning will also satisfy the requirements of the first form, i.e. that it is something no one could reasonably reject. The question "Is the acceptance of this principle an agreement you could actually live up to?" is, like the idea of assignment by one's worst enemy, a thought experiment through which we can use our own reactions to test our judgment that certain principles are ones that no one could reasonably reject. General principles of human psychology can also be invoked to this same end.

Rawls' final argument is that the adoption of his two principles gives public support to the self-respect of individual members of society, and "give a stronger and more characteristic interpretation of Kant's idea"[10] that people must be treated as ends, not merely as means to the greater collective good. But, whatever difference there may be here between Rawls' two principles of justice and the principle of average utility, there is at least as sharp a contrast between the two patterns of contractualist reasoning distinguished above. The connection with self-respect, and with the Kantian formula, is preserved by the requirement that principles of justice be ones which no member of the society could reasonably reject. This connection is weakened when we shift to the idea of a choice which advances the interests of a single rational individual for whom the various individual lives in a society are just so many different possibilities. This is so whatever decision rule this rational chooser is said to employ. The argument from maximin seems to preserve this connection because it reproduces as a claim about rational choice what is, in slightly different terms, an appealing moral argument.

The "choice situation" that is fundamental to contractualism as I have described it is obtained by beginning with "mutually disinterested" individuals with full knowledge of their situations and adding to this (not, as is sometimes suggested, benevolence but) a desire on each of their parts to find principles which none could reasonably reject insofar as they

too have this desire. Rawls several times considers such an idea in passing.[11] He rejects it in favor of his own idea of mutually disinterested choice from behind a veil of ignorance on the ground that only the latter enables us to reach definite results: "if in choosing principles we required unanimity even where there is full information, only a few rather obvious cases could be decided."[12] I believe that this supposed advantage is questionable. Perhaps this is because my expectations for moral argument are more modest than Rawls'. However, as I have argued, almost all of Rawls' own arguments have at least as much force when they are interpreted as arguments within the form of contractualism which I have been proposing. One possible exception is the argument from maximin. If the Difference Principle were taken to be generally applicable to decisions of public policy, then the second form of contractualist reasoning through which it is derived would have more far reaching implications than the looser form of argument by comparison of losses, which I have employed. But these wider applications of the principle are not always plausible, and I do not think that Rawls intends it to be applied so widely. His intention is that the Difference Principle should be applied only to major inequalities generated by the basic institutions of a society, and this limitation is a reflection of the special conditions under which he holds maximin to be the appropriate basis for rational choice: some choices have outcomes one could hardly accept, while gains above the minimum one can assure one's self matter very little, and so on. It follows, then, that in applying the Difference Principle – in identifying the limits of its applicability – we must fall back on the informal comparison of losses which is central to the form of contractualism I have described.

V

I have described this version of contractualism only in outline. Much more needs to be said to clarify its central notions and to work out its normative implications. I hope that I have said enough to indicate its appeal as a philosophical theory of morality and as an account of moral motivation. I have put forward contractualism as an alternative to utilitarianism, but the characteristic feature of the doctrine can be brought out by contrasting it with a somewhat different view.

It is sometimes said that morality is a device for our mutual protection. According to contractualism, this view is partly true but in an important way incomplete. Our concern to protect our central interests will have an important effect on what we could reasonably agree to. It will thus have an important effect on the content of morality if contractualism is correct. To the degree that this morality is observed, these interests will gain from it. If we had no desire to be able to justify our actions to others on grounds they could reasonably accept, the hope of gaining this protection would give us reason to try to instil this desir in others, perhaps through mass hypnosis o conditioning, even if this also meant acquirin it ourselves. But given that we have thi desire already, our concern with morality i less instrumental.

The contrast might be put as follows. On on view, concern with protection is fundamenta and general agreement becomes relevant as means or a necessary condition for securin this protection. On the other, contractualis view, the desire for protection is an importar factor determining the content of moralit ecause it determines what can reasonably b agreed to. But the idea of general agreemer does not arise as a means of securing protec tion. It is, in a more fundamental sense, wha morality is about.

Notes

1. Singer, "Faminè, Affluence and Morality."
2. Reasonably, that is, given the desire to find principles which others similarly motivated could not reasonably reject.
3. Kant, *Groundwork of the Metaphysics of Morals*, Section 2, footnote 14.
4. See John Harsanyi, "Cardinal Utility in Welfare Economics and in the Theory of Risk-Taking," *Jounal of Political Economy* 61 (1953).
5. Rawls, *A Theory of Justice* (Harvard University Press) 1971, p. 137.
6. Rawls 1971, p. 152.
7. Rawls 1971, p. 153.
8. Rawls 1971, p. 154.
9. Rawls 1971, sec. 29, pp. 175ff.
10. Rawls 1971, p. 183.
11. E.g. Rawls 1971, pp. 141, 148, although thes passages may not clearly distinguish betwee this alternative and an assumption of benev lence.
12. Rawls 1971, p. 141.

PART XI
Virtue Ethics

Introduction to Part XI

There has been a resurgence of interest in virtue ethics over the past three decades, most of it inspired by reconsiderations of Aristotle's ethical thought. Despite a large body of recent work, the realm of virtue ethics isn't yet as well-defined in its central tenets and methodology as are, say, consequentialist and deontological views.

That said, we can identify some general trends within virtue ethics, and some points of disagreement, or at least differences in emphasis, with its competitors in normative ethics. In the first place, virtue ethicists will typically place a kind of explanatory priority on the virtues of character, rather than on moral rules of conduct. Whereas other kinds of ethical theory will ordinarily seek to identify a fundamental moral rule (say, the principle of utility), and then define a virtue as a steady disposition to conform to such a rule, the virtue ethicist will seek to explain appropriate conduct by reference to action that exemplifies virtue. Actions are morally good, for instance, because they exemplify virtuous character traits, and not because they conform to some already-specified moral rule.

Aristotle cautions us not to expect more precision than an inquiry allows. When it comes to ethics, we must accept that no set of rules will give us sufficient guidance to ascertain what is right and wrong. We instead look to moral exemplars, and determine proper conduct by reference to the choices that they would make in the situation. No set of precise rules can be given for identifying, in advance of the many situations we can find ourselves in, which such choices the exemplars would make.

Aristotle thinks that *eudaimonia* (happiness, or flourishing) is the proper end of human beings. We all seek it, and are right to do so. Happiness is, for him, activity of the soul in accordance with virtue. Virtue will not guarantee the best life – some things essential for such a life are beyond our control (e.g., having decent health, avoiding crushing debt). But virtue is essential for the best life, and, together with a modest amount of good fortune, is enough to make a life an excellent one for the person living it.

The ancients constantly returned to the puzzle of the virtuous parent whose son or daughter strayed from the path of virtue. If virtue is, as so many believed, the greatest good for human beings, why did those who possess it so often fail to pass it on to their beloved children? Aristotle's answer is that moral virtue is a quite different thing from intellectual virtue, which can be directly taught and learnt. The virtues of character, by contrast, require experience and habituation, and a modicum of external resources and good fortune. The virtue of courage, for instance, cannot be learned from a book, but is a trait that is developed through practice and experience. What unifies the moral virtues, according to Aristotle, is the famous golden mean – they are means that are located between extremes of vice. Courage, for instance, is a trait of character that is midway between the vice of rashness, and the vice of cowardice.

The philosopher and social critic Martha Nussbaum here offers an interpretation of Aristotle's ethics in light of recent work that is sympathetic to ethical relativism. Some virtue ethicists, impressed by the diversity of cultural norms and practices, have thought that the nature of a flourishing life will importantly differ depending on one's cultural milieu. Given this assumption, the virtue ethicist should resist any effort to identify just a single model of the good and virtuous life. This resistance can be bolstered by a central tenet of virtue ethics, namely, its rejection of the idea that there is just a single ultimate ethical principle that is applicable to all people, in all situations. This combination of views entails that there is no single picture of a virtuous life, but rather a variety of equally tenable pictures. This appears to lend support to the idea that a virtue ethicist should embrace some sort of ethical relativism.

Nussbaum thinks that this is the wrong lesson to take from the facts of cultural pluralism. She is intent on showing how Aristotle's conception of the virtuous life is rooted in an appreciation of various universal features of the human experience. Further, an embrace of ethical relativism would mean an uncritical kind of tolerance for the status quo, even where the ongoing situation is one in which women are treated as inferiors, caste members oppressed, and religious minorities routinely subjugated. A plausible virtue ethic will not license these sorts of practices, but will rather reveal the preconditions that everyone must exemplify, no matter his or her social situation, in order to live a truly flourishing life. Nussbaum reconstructs the essence of Aristotle's detailed picture of the moral virtues, and argues that they are each founded on an aspect of human life that is shared by all human beings, no matter the time or the culture in which they have lived. If she is right, then the Aristotelian virtue ethicist would do well to reject any allegiance to relativism.

One of the attractions of virtue ethics stems from the felt dissatisfaction with its main competitors. There does seem something morally important about an impartial concern for happiness, as stressed by utilitarians; something morally important about fairness, as emphasized by Kantians; and something quite important about fidelity to one's agreements as stressed by contractarians. But many have thought that these theories fall short by emphasizing just one of these important elements, at the expense of the others. Virtue ethics has seemed to many to represent a kind of ethical outlook that can explain the importance of impartiality, fairness, and fidelity, without giving any one of these the sole ultimate role in ethics. And yet many, too, have thought that this rejection of ethical monism brings with it a serious problem: namely, that virtue ethics fails to give sufficiently concrete guidance to how one ought to behave. The rule that requires us to maximize happiness, for instance, though not unproblematic, at least offers us a way, in principle, to determine where our duty on a given occasion really lies. But the counsel to do as the wise person would do is intolerably vague, and of next to no help in guiding our ethical deliberations.

Rosalind Hursthouse takes up this challenge directly. She argues in two ways. First, virtue ethics does have the resources to helpfully guide us in deciding what we ought to do. And second, despite initial appearances, its competitors fare no better in providing moral rules that can set out just what ought to be done in particular situations. Admittedly, virtue ethics will not yield a set of precise recommendations that can be applied without any judgment at all. But then neither will utilitarianism or deontology. Moreover, the aspiration to do so is completely misguided – just think of how incredible it would be were a moral theorist to present a slim volume containing a mathematical algorithm for moral decision-making. If there were a simple recipe for invariably getting it right in ethics, we would have seen it a long time ago. But if we really reflect on the difficulties of moral deliberation, we will come to reject the picture of it according to which we can more or less mechanically read off our moral duty from a fixed set of rules.

That said, virtue ethics can indeed formulate moral rules, such as those requiring us to act charitably, kindly and honestly. True, it will require some sensitivity to determine whether an act qualifies as kind, or generous, or honest. But this is no different from determining the moral implications of a Kantian rule, such as one requiring that we keep our promises. Whether something counts as a promise, and whether we must always be faithful to our promises, is something that no rule is going to tell us. The consequentialist requirement to maximize the good is not self-interpreting, either. We must discern what is intrinsically valuable. We must know how to balance options that generate some amount of happiness, as against those that lessen the amount of misery, in the world. We must know how to balance options that generate different goods, on the assumption that there is more than just one kind of intrinsic value. Again, there are no precise rules that offer guidance in resolving these sorts of puzzles.

A common worry about virtue ethics is that its emphasis on the primacy of character generates mistaken moral assessments. Suppose, as virtue ethicists such as Michael Slote contend, that an act is morally right if and only if it is undertaken by a person who is exemplifying virtue in its performance. If that were so, then it would be strictly impossible for a virtuous person, acting virtuously, to behave immorally. If her motivations were virtuous, then no matter her action, it would be morally right. And yet most of us believe that a person can end up doing the wrong action for the right (i.e., the virtuous) reasons. Further, such view seems to imply that a virtuous person can do anything she pleases, and still be doing what is right, since right action is defined as action that such a person would perform.

Michael Slote carefully considers both objections, which have received wide airing in the philosophical literature. He is prepared to bite the bullet with regard to the first objection. Actions done by virtuous people from virtuous motives are indeed morally right, even if they have disastrous consequences. And the second objection, he contends, is based on a mistaken assumption. His view is not that any action undertaken by a virtuous person is morally right. Rather, any action taken by such a person *insofar as she exemplifies virtue* is morally right. Virtuous people can act out of character – when they do, their actions are not morally right.

Christine Swanton's article on virtue ethics begins with a critical assessment of both Hursthouse's and Slote's views. Readers are encouraged to consider the merits of her critical discussion, and usefully compare and contrast her own views with those of our two other authors. Swanton herself develops a view that has two central theses. They are: (i) an action is virtuous in respect V (e.g., benevolent or generous) if and only if it realizes the end of virtue V; and (ii) an action is right if and only if it is overall virtuous.

A virtue's ends are given by the targets it aims at. Swanton spends a fair bit of time elucidating the notion of a virtue's target. Rather than recapitulate her discussion, we can illustrate the idea with a few examples: the target of connoisseurship is the nuanced appreciation of valuable items; the target of politeness is the exhibition of appropriate deference; the target of courage is to appropriately cope with fear, or to successfully handle dangerous situations (or both). One can act so as to hit these targets even if, in so doing, one's motives are less than virtuous. (One can act tactfully, for instance, even if one lacks the virtue of tact.) Right actions are those that are not only virtuous, but overall virtuous. This last notion is another tricky one, and Swanton devotes a good deal of attention to uncovering its complexities. Once she does, she proceeds to answer objections, and to argue that her view is more plausible than those of her fellow virtue ethicists.

Julia Annas next addresses a number of pressing concerns about virtue ethics. Annas initiates an interesting discussion about the nature of moral learning, why experience is required in its acquisition, and why a technical manual for moral education would be wholly implausible. Imagine, she says, that someone always did what his mother told him to do. This strikes us as immature, an abdication of responsibility. And why should things look any better when Mom is replaced by a moral decision procedure? The thought that moral theory is supposed to give us a complete set of rules for moral decision-making is itself a mistake. Therefore virtue ethics cannot be faulted for failing to provide such a thing.

Before setting out her own view, Annas criticizes a standard account of virtue ethics (endorsed by some of our authors, above), according to which an action is right just in case it is what a virtuous person would characteristically do in the circumstances. In addition to three standard criticisms of such a view – (i) it is difficult to know how to identify a virtuous person, (ii) there may be no truly virtuous people, and (iii) some actions are clearly right even though a virtuous person wouldn't (be in a position to) do them – Annas identifies what she considers to be the deepest problem for it. The fundamental problem is that such theorists are simply replacing the technical manual of ethical decision-making with a reliance on the decisions of a virtuous person. Rather than a technical manual telling us what to do, we are relying on the virtuous person to do that.

But what is the alternative to that? Annas takes us back to our beginnings, in Aristotle, to resuscitate his view that learning to be virtuous is not book learning. Nor is it rote emulation of virtuous people. Rather, it is a developmental process that includes a steep learning curve that is mastered (if at all) only with very extensive practice and experience. Becoming virtuous is very like acquiring a skill, and as with all such acquisition – becoming a master builder, or a concert pianist – it cannot be done overnight, and is not a matter solely (or even primarily) of intellectual competence. What is right for us to do is not necessarily just what the virtuous person would do, because we may still be at a relatively early stage of progress in attaining her level of practical wisdom. What is appropriate for a master may be ill-advised for the novice.

It follows, then, that right action is not the same for everyone, at all times. Even in the same context of decision, what is right for the moral learner may be one thing; right for the truly virtuous person, quite another. If Annas is correct, this picture will replace the standard model of ethical theorizing, according to which a theory is successful only if it can supply us with a principle that, in advance of a situation, and without regard to the character of the agent in that situation, will tell us what such an agent ought to do.

CHAPTER 66

The Nature of Virtue

ARISTOTLE

Book I: Happiness

Ends and goods

§1 Every craft and every line of inquiry, and likewise every action and decision, seems to seek some good; that is why some people were right to describe the good as what everything seeks. §2 But the ends [that are sought] appear to differ; some are activities, and others are products apart from the activities. Wherever there are ends apart from the actions, the products are by nature better than the activities.

§3 Since there are many actions, crafts, and sciences, the ends turn out to be many as well; for health is the end of medicine, a boat of boat building, victory of generalship, and wealth of house-hold management. §4 But some of these pursuits are subordinate to some one capacity; for instance, bridle making and every other science producing equipment for horses are subordinate to horsemanship, while this and every action in warfare are, in turn, subordinate to generalship, and in the same way other pursuits are subordinate to

Aristotle, "The Nature of Virtue," pp. 1–5, 7–12, 15–29, 163–9 from *Nichomachean Ethics*, Second Edition, trans. Terence Irwin. Indianapolis: Hackett, 1999. Reprinted by permission of Hackett Publishing Company, Inc. All rights reserved.

further ones. In all such cases, then, the ends of the ruling sciences are more choiceworthy than all the ends subordinate to them, since the lower ends are also pursued for the sake of the higher. §5 Here it does not matter whether the ends of the actions are the activities themselves, or something apart from them, as in the sciences we have mentioned.

The highest good and political science

§1 Suppose, then, that the things achievable by action have some end that we wish for because of itself, and because of which we wish for the other things, and that we do not choose everything because of something else – for if we do, it will go on without limit, so that desire will prove to be empty and futile. Clearly, this end will be the good, that is to say, the best good.

§2 Then surely knowledge of this good also carries great weight for [determining the best] way of life; if we know it, we are more likely, like archers who have a target to aim at, to hit the right mark. §3 If so, we should try to grasp, in outline at any rate, what the good is, and which is its proper science or capacity.

§4 It seems proper to the most controlling science – the highest ruling science. §5 And this appears characteristic of political science. §6 For it is the one that prescribes which of the sciences ought to be studied in cities, and which ones each class in the city should learn, and how far; indeed we see that even the most honored capacities – generalship, household management, and rhetoric, for instance – are subordinate to it. §7 And since it uses the other sciences concerned with action, and moreover legislates what must be done and what avoided, its end will include the ends of the other sciences, and so this will be the human good. §8 For even if the good is the same for a city as for an individual, still the good of the city is apparently a greater and more complete good to acquire and preserve. For while it is satisfactory to acquire and preserve the good even for an individual, it is finer and more divine to acquire and preserve it for a people and for cities. And so, since our line of inquiry seeks these [goods, for an individual and for a community], it is a sort of political science.

The method of political science

§1 Our discussion will be adequate if we make things perspicuous enough to accord with the subject matter; for we would not seek the same degree of exactness in all sorts of arguments alike, any more than in the products of different crafts. §2 Now, fine and just things, which political science examines, differ and vary so much as to seem to rest on convention only, not on nature. §3 But [this is not a good reason, since] goods also vary in the same way, because they result in harm to many people – for some have been destroyed because of their wealth, others because of their bravery. §4 And so, since this is our subject and these are our premises, we shall be satisfied to indicate the truth roughly and in outline; since our subject and our premises are things that hold good usually [but not universally], we shall be satisfied to draw conclusions of the same sort.

Each of our claims, then, ought to be accepted in the same way [as claiming to hold good usually]. For the educated person seeks exactness in each area to the extent that the nature of the subject allows; for apparently it is just as mistaken to demand demonstrations from a rhetorician as to accept [merely] persuasive arguments from a mathematician. §5 Further, each person judges rightly what he knows, and is a good judge about that; hence the good judge in a given area is the person

educated in that area, and the unqualifiedly good judge is the person educated in every area.

This is why a youth is not a suitable student of political science; for he lacks experience of the actions in life, which are the subject and premises of our arguments. §6 Moreover, since he tends to follow his feelings, his study will be futile and useless; for the end [of political science] is action, not knowledge. §7 It does not matter whether he is young in years or immature in character, since the deficiency does not depend on age, but results from following his feelings in his life and in a given pursuit; for an immature person, like an incontinent person, gets no benefit from his knowledge. But for those who accord with reason in forming their desires and in their actions, knowledge of political science will be of great benefit.

§8 These are the preliminary points about the student, about the way our claims are to be accepted, and about what we propose to do.

Common beliefs

§1 Let us, then, begin again. Since every sort of knowledge and decision pursues some good, what is the good that we say political science seeks? What, [in other words,] is the highest of all the goods achievable in action?

§2 As far as its name goes, most people virtually agree; for both the many and the cultivated call it happiness, and they suppose that living well and doing well are the same as being happy. But they disagree about what happiness is, and the many do not give the same answer as the wise.

§3 For the many think it is something obvious and evident – for instance, pleasure, wealth, or honor. Some take it to be one thing, others another. Indeed, the same person often changes his mind; for when he has fallen ill, he thinks happiness is health, and when he has fallen into poverty, he thinks it is wealth. And when they are conscious of their own ignorance, they admire anyone who speaks of something grand and above their heads. [Among the wise,] however, some used to think that besides these many goods there is some other good that exists in its own right and that causes all these goods to be goods.

§4 Presumably, then, it is rather futile to examine all these beliefs, and it is enough to examine those that are most current or seem to have some argument for them.

§5 We must notice, however, the difference between arguments from principles and arguments toward principles. For indeed Plato was right to be puzzled about this, when he used to ask if [the argument] set out from the principles or led toward them – just as on a race course the path may go from the starting line to the far end, or back again. For we should certainly begin from things known, but things are known in two ways; for some are known to us, some known without qualification. Presumably, then, *we* ought to begin from things known to *us*.

§6 That is why we need to have been brought up in fine habits if we are to be adequate students of fine and just things, and of political questions generally. §7 For we begin from the [belief] that [something is true]; if this is apparent enough to us, we can begin without also [knowing] why [it is true]. Someone who is well brought up has the beginnings, or can easily acquire them. Someone who neither has them nor can acquire them should listen to Hesiod: 'He who grasps everything himself is best of all; he is noble also who listens to one who has spoken well; but he who neither grasps it himself nor takes to heart what he hears from another is a useless man.'

The three lives

§1 But let us begin again from the point from which we digressed. For, it would seem, people quite reasonably reach their conception of the good, i.e., of happiness, from the lives [they lead]; §2 for there are roughly three most favored lives: the lives of gratification, of political activity, and, third, of study.

The many, the most vulgar, would seem to conceive the good and happiness as pleasure, and hence they also like the life of gratification. §3 In this they appear completely slavish, since the life they decide on is a life for grazing animals. Still, they have some argument in their defense, since many in positions of power feel as Sardanapallus felt, [and also choose this life].

§4 The cultivated people, those active [in politics], conceive the good as honor, since this is more or less the end [normally pursued] in the political life. This, however, appears to be too superficial to be what we are seeking; for it seems to depend more on those who honor than on the one honored, whereas we intuitively believe that the good is something of our own and hard to take from us. §5 Further, it would seem, they pursue honor to convince themselves that they are good; at any rate, they seek to be honored by prudent people, among people who know them, and for virtue. It is clear, then, that – in their view at any rate – virtue is superior [to honor].

§6 Perhaps, indeed, one might conceive virtue more than honor to be the end of the political life. However, this also is apparently too incomplete [to be the good]. For it seems possible for someone to possess virtue but be asleep or inactive throughout his life, and, moreover, to suffer the worst evils and misfortunes. If this is the sort of life he leads, no one would count him happy, except to defend a philosopher's paradox. Enough about this, since it has been adequately discussed in the popular works as well.

§7 The third life is the life of study, which we shall examine in what follows.

§8 The moneymaker's life is in a way forced on him [not chosen for itself]; and clearly wealth is not the good we are seeking, since it is [merely] useful, [choiceworthy only] for some other end. Hence one would be more inclined to suppose that [any of] the goods mentioned earlier is the end, since they are liked for themselves. But apparently they are not [the end] either; and many arguments have been presented against them. Let us, then, dismiss them.

An account of the human good

§1 But let us return once again to the good we are looking for, and consider just what it could be. For it is apparently one thing in one action or craft, and another thing in another; for it is one thing in medicine, another in generalship, and so on for the rest. What, then, is the good of each action or craft? Surely it is that for the sake of which the other things are done; in medicine this is health, in generalship victory, in house-building a house, in another case something else, but in every action and decision it is the end, since it is for the sake of the end that everyone does the other actions. And so, if there is some end of everything achievable in action, the good achievable in action will be this end; if there are more ends than one, [the good achievable in action] will be these ends.

§2 Our argument, then, has followed a different route to reach the same conclusion. But we must try to make this still more perspicuous. §3 Since there are apparently many ends, and we choose some of them (for instance, wealth, flutes, and, in general, instruments) because of something else, it is clear that not all ends are complete. But the best good is apparently something complete. And so, if only one end is complete, the good we are looking for will be this end; if more ends than one are complete, it will be the most complete end of these.

§4 We say that an end pursued in its own right is more complete than an end pursued because of something else, and that an end that is never choiceworthy because of something else is more complete than ends that are choiceworthy both in their own right and because of this end. Hence an end that is always choiceworthy in its own right, never because of something else, is complete without qualification.

§5 Now happiness, more than anything else, seems complete without qualification. For we always choose it because of itself, never because of something else. Honor, pleasure, understanding, and every virtue we certainly choose because of themselves, since we would choose each of them even if it had no further result; but we also choose them for the sake of happiness, supposing that through them we shall be happy. Happiness, by contrast, no one ever chooses for their sake, or for the sake of anything else at all.

§6 The same conclusion [that happiness is complete] also appears to follow from self-sufficiency. For the complete good seems to be self-sufficient. What we count as self-sufficient is not what suf-fices for a solitary person by himself, living an isolated life, but what suffices also for parents, children, wife, and, in general, for friends and fellow citizens, since a human

being is a naturally political [animal]. §7 Here, however, we must impose some limit; for if we extend the good to parents' parents and children's children and to friends of friends, we shall go on without limit; but we must examine this another time. Anyhow, we regard something as self-sufficient when all by itself it makes a life choiceworthy and lacking nothing; and that is what we think happiness does.

§8 Moreover, we think happiness is most choiceworthy of all goods, [since] it is not counted as one good among many. [If it were] counted as one among many, then, clearly, we think it would be more choiceworthy if the smallest of goods were added; for the good that is added becomes an extra quantity of goods, and the larger of two goods is always more choiceworthy. Happiness, then, is apparently something complete and selfsufficient, since it is the end of the things achievable in action.

§9 But presumably the remark that the best good is happiness is apparently something [generally] agreed, and we still need a clearer statement of what the best good is. §10 Perhaps, then, we shall find this if we first grasp the function of a human being. For just as the good, i.e., [doing] well, for a flautist, a sculptor, and every craftsman, and, in general, for whatever has a function and [characteristic] action, seems to depend on its function, the same seems to be true for a human being, if a human being has some function.

§11 Then do the carpenter and the leather worker have their functions and actions, but has a human being no function? Is he by nature idle, without any function? Or, just as eye, hand, foot, and, in general, every [bodily] part apparently has its function, may we likewise ascribe to a human being some function apart from all of these?

§12 What, then, could this be? For living is apparently shared with plants, but what we are looking for is the special function of a human being; hence we should set aside the life of nutrition and growth. The life next in order is some sort of life of sense perception; but this too is apparently shared with horse, ox, and every animal.

§13 The remaining possibility, then, is some sort of life of action of the [part of the soul] that has reason. One [part] of it has reason as obeying reason; the other has it as itself having reason and thinking. Moreover, life is also spoken of in two ways [as capacity and as activity], and we must take [a human being's special function to be] life as activity, since this seems to be called life more fully. We have found, then, that the human function is activity of the soul in accord with reason or requiring reason.

§14 Now we say that the function of a [kind of thing] – of a harpist, for instance – is the same in kind as the function of an excellent individual of the kind – of an excellent harpist, for instance. And the same is true without qualification in every case, if we add to the function the superior achievement in accord with the virtue; for the function of a harpist is to play the harp, and the function of a good harpist is to play it well. Moreover, we take the human function to be a certain kind of life, and take this life to be activity and actions of the soul that involve reason; hence the function of the excellent man is to do this well and finely.

§15 Now each function is completed well by being completed in accord with the virtue proper [to that kind of thing]. And so the human good proves to be activity of the soul in accord with virtue, and indeed with the best and most complete virtue, if there are more virtues than one. §16 Moreover, it must be in a complete life. For one swallow does not make a spring, nor does one day; nor, similarly, does one day or a short time make us blessed and happy.

§17 This, then, is a sketch of the good; for, presumably, we must draw the outline first, and fill it in later. If the sketch is good, anyone, it seems, can advance and articulate it, and in such cases time discovers more, or is a good partner in discovery. That is also how the crafts have improved, since anyone can add what is lacking [in the outline].

§18 We must also remember our previous remarks, so that we do not look for the same degree of exactness in all areas, but the degree that accords with a given subject matter and is proper to a given line of inquiry. §19 For the carpenter's and the geometer's inquiries about the right angle are different also; the carpenter restricts himself to what helps his work, but the geometer inquires into what, or what sort of thing, the right angle is, since he studies the truth. We must do the same, then, in other areas too, [seeking the proper degree of exactness], so that digressions do not overwhelm our main task.

§20 Nor should we make the same demand for an explanation in all cases. On the contrary, in some cases it is enough to prove rightly that [something is true, without also explaining why it is true]. This is so, for instance, with principles, where the fact that [something is true] is the first thing, that is to say, the principle.

§21 Some principles are studied by means of induction, some by means of perception, some by means of some sort of habituation, and others by other means. §22 In each case we should try to find them out by means suited to their nature, and work hard to define them rightly. §23 For they carry great weight for what follows; for the principle seems to be more than half the whole, and makes evident the answer to many of our questions.

Defense of the account of the good

§1 We should examine the principle, however, not only from the conclusion and premises [of a deduction], but also from what is said about it; for all the facts harmonize with a true account, whereas the truth soon clashes with a false one.

§2 Goods are divided, then, into three types, some called external, some goods of the soul, others goods of the body. We say that the goods of the soul are goods most fully, and more than the others, and we take actions and activities of the soul to be [goods] of the soul. And so our account [of the good] is right, to judge by this belief anyhow – and it is an ancient belief, and accepted by philosophers.

§3 Our account is also correct in saying that some sort of actions and activities are the end; for in that way the end turns out to be a good of the soul, not an external good.

§4 The belief that the happy person lives well and does well also agrees with our account, since we have virtually said that the end is a sort of living well and doing well.

§5 Further, all the features that people look for in happiness appear to be true of the end described in our account. §6 For to some people happiness seems to be virtue; to others prudence; to others some sort of wisdom; to others again it seems to be these, or one of these, involving pleasure or requiring it to be added; others add in external prosperity as well. §7 Some of these views are traditional, held by many, while others are held by a few men who are widely esteemed. It is reasonable for each group not to be completely wrong, but to be correct on one point at least, or even on most points.

§8 First, our account agrees with those who say happiness is virtue [in general] or some [particular] virtue; for activity in accord with virtue is proper to virtue. §9 Presumably, though, it matters quite a bit whether we suppose that the best good consists in possessing or in using – that is to say, in a state or in an activity [that actualizes the state]. For someone may be in a state that achieves no good – if, for instance, he is asleep or inactive in some other way – but this cannot be true of the activity; for it will necessarily act and act well. And just as Olympic prizes are not for the finest and strongest, but for the contestants – since it is only these who win – the same is true in life; among the fine and good people, only those who act correctly win the prize.

§10 Moreover, the life of these active people is also pleasant in itself. For being pleased is a condition of the soul, [and hence is included in the activity of the soul]. Further, each type of person finds pleasure in whatever he is called a lover of; a horse, for instance, pleases the horse-lover, a spectacle the lover of spectacles. Similarly, what is just pleases the lover of justice, and in general what accords with virtue pleases the lover of virtue.

§11 Now the things that please most people conflict, because they are not pleasant by nature, whereas the things that please lovers of the fine are things pleasant by nature. Actions in accord with virtue are pleasant by nature, so that they both please lovers of the fine and are pleasant in their own right.

§12 Hence these people's life does not need pleasure to be added [to virtuous activity] as some sort of extra decoration; rather, it has its pleasure within itself. For besides the reasons already given, someone who does not enjoy fine actions is not good; for no one would call a person just, for instance, if he did not enjoy doing just actions, or generous if he did not enjoy generous actions, and similarly for the other virtues.

§13 If this is so, actions in accord with the virtues are pleasant in their own right. Moreover, these actions are good and fine as well as pleasant; indeed, they are good, fine, and pleasant more than anything else is, since on this question the excellent person judges rightly, and his judgment agrees with what we have said.

§14 Happiness, then, is best, finest, and most pleasant, and the Delian inscription is wrong to distinguish these things: "What is most just is finest; being healthy is most beneficial; but it is most pleasant to win our heart's desire." For all three features are found in the best activities, and we say happiness is these activities, or [rather] one of them, the best one.

§15 Nonetheless, happiness evidently also needs external goods to be added, as we said, since we cannot, or cannot easily, do fine actions if we lack the resources. For, first of all, in many actions we use friends, wealth, and political power just as we use instruments. §16 Further, deprivation of certain [externals] – for instance, good birth, good children, beauty – mars our blessedness. For we do not altogether have the character of happiness if we look utterly repulsive or are ill-born, solitary, or childless; and we have it even less, presumably, if our children or friends are totally bad, or were good but have died.

§17 And so, as we have said, happiness would seem to need this sort of prosperity added also. That is why some people identify happiness with good fortune, and others identify it with virtue.

How is happiness achieved?

§1 This also leads to a puzzle: Is happiness acquired by learning, or habituation, or by some other form of cultivation? Or is it the result of some divine fate, or even of fortune?

§2 First, then, if the gods give any gift at all to human beings, it is reasonable for them to give us happiness more than any other human good, insofar as it is the best of human goods.

3 Presumably, however, this question is more suitable for a different inquiry.

But even if it is not sent by the gods, but instead results from virtue and some sort of learning or cultivation, happiness appears to be one of the most divine things, since the prize and goal of virtue appears to be the best good, something divine and blessed. §4 Moreover [if happiness comes in this way] it will be widely shared; for anyone who is not deformed in his capacity] for virtue will be able to achieve happiness through some sort of learning and attention.

§5 And since it is better to be happy in this way than because of fortune, it is reasonable for this to be the way [we become] happy. For whatever is natural is naturally in the finest state possible. §6 The same is true of the products of crafts and of every other cause, especially the best cause; and it would be seriously inappropriate to entrust what is greatest and finest to fortune.

§7 The answer to our question is also evident from our account. For we have said that happiness is a certain sort of activity of the soul in accord with virtue, [and hence not a result of fortune]. Of the other goods, some are necessary conditions of happiness, while others are naturally useful and cooperative as instruments [but are not parts of it].

§8 Further, this conclusion agrees with our opening remarks. For we took the goal of political science to be the best good; and most of its attention is devoted to the character of the citizens, to make them good people who do fine actions.

§9 It is not surprising, then, that we regard neither ox, nor horse, nor any other kind of animal as happy; for none of them can share in this sort of activity. §10 For the same reason a child is not happy either, since his age prevents him from doing these sorts of actions. If he is called happy, he is being congratulated [simply] because of anticipated blessedness; for, as we have said, happiness requires both complete virtue and a complete life.

§11 It needs a complete life because life includes many reversals of fortune, good and bad, and the most prosperous person may fall into a terrible disaster in old age, as the Trojan stories tell us about Priam. If someone has suffered these sorts of misfortunes and comes to a miserable end, no one counts him happy.

Praise and honor

§1 Now that we have determined these points, let us consider whether happiness is something praiseworthy, or instead something honorable; for clearly it is not a capacity [which is neither praiseworthy nor honorable].

§2 Whatever is praiseworthy appears to be praised for its character and its state in relation to something. We praise the just and the brave person, for instance, and in general the good person and virtue, because of their actions and achievements; and we praise the strong person, the good runner, and each of the others because he naturally has a certain character and is in a certain state in relation to something good and excellent. §3 This is clear also from praises of the gods; for these praises appear ridiculous because they are referred to us, but they are referred to us because, as we said, praise depends on such a reference.

§4 If praise is for these sorts of things, then clearly for the best things there is no praise, but something greater and better. And indeed this is how it appears. For the gods and the most godlike of men are [not praised, but] congratulated for their blessedness and happiness. The same is true of goods; for we never praise happiness, as we praise justice, but we count it blessed, as something better and more godlike [than anything that is praised].

§5 Indeed, Eudoxus seems to have used the right sort of argument in defending the supremacy of pleasure. By not praising pleasure, though it is a good, we indicate – so he thought – that it is superior to everything praiseworthy; [only] the god and the good have this superiority since the other goods are [praised] by reference to them.

§6 [Here he seems to have argued correctly.] For praise is given to virtue, since it makes us do fine actions; but celebrations are for achievements, either of body or of soul. §7 But an exact treatment of this is presumably more proper for specialists in celebrations. For us, anyhow, it is clear from what has been said that happiness is something honorable and complete.

§8 A further reason why this would seem to be correct is that happiness is a principle; for [the principle] is what we all aim at in all our other actions; and we take the principle and cause of goods to be something honorable and divine.

Introduction to the virtues

§1 Since happiness is a certain sort of activity of the soul in accord with complete virtue, we must examine virtue; for that will perhaps also be a way to study happiness better. §2 Moreover, the true politician seems to have put more effort into virtue than into anything else, since he wants to make the citizens good and law-abiding. §3 We find an example of this in the Spartan and Cretan legislators and in any others who share their concerns. §4 Since, then, the examination of virtue is proper for political science, the inquiry clearly suits our decision at the beginning.

§5 It is clear that the virtue we must examine is human virtue, since we are also seeking the human good and human happiness. §6 By human virtue we mean virtue of the soul, not of the body, since we also say that happiness is an activity of the soul. §7 If this is so, it is clear that the politician must in some way know about the soul, just as someone setting out to heal the eyes must know about the whole body as well. This is all the more true to the extent that political science is better and more honorable than medicine; even among doctors, the cultivated ones devote a lot of effort to finding out about the body. Hence the politician as well [as the student of nature] must study the soul. §8 But he must study it for his specific purpose, far enough for his inquiry [into virtue]; for a more exact treatment would presumably take more effort than his purpose requires.

§9 [We] have discussed the soul sufficiently [for our purposes] in [our] popular works as well [as our less popular], and we should use this discussion. We have said, for instance, that one [part] of the soul is nonrational, while one has reason. §10 Are these distinguished as parts of a body and everything divisible into parts are? Or are they two [only] in definition, and inseparable by nature, as the convex and the concave are in a surface? It does not matter for present purposes.

§11 Consider the nonrational [part]. One [part] of it, i.e., the cause of nutrition and growth, would seem to be plantlike and shared [with all living things]; for we can ascribe this capacity of the soul to everything that is nourished, including embryos, and the same capacity to full-grown living things, since this is more reasonable than to ascribe another capacity to them.

§12 Hence the virtue of this capacity is apparently shared, not [specifically] human. For this part and this capacity more than others seem to be active in sleep, and here the good and the bad person are least distinct; hence happy people are said to be no better off than miserable people for half their lives. §13 This lack of distinction is not surprising, since sleep is inactivity of the soul insofar as it is called excellent or base, unless to some small extent some movements penetrate [to our awareness], and in this way the decent person comes to have better images [in dreams] than just any random person has. §14 Enough about this, however, and let us leave aside the nutritive part, since by nature it has no share in human virtue.

§15 Another nature in the soul would also seem to be nonrational, though in a way it shares in reason. For in the continent and the incontinent person we praise their reason, that is to say, the [part] of the soul that has reason, because it exhorts them correctly and toward what is best; but they evidently also have in them some other [part] that is by nature something apart from reason, clashing and struggling with reason. For just as paralyzed parts of a body, when we decide to move them to the right, do the contrary and move off to the left, the same is true of the soul; for incontinent people have impulses in contrary directions. §16 In bodies, admittedly, we see the part go astray, whereas we do not see it in the soul; nonetheless, presumably, we should suppose that the soul also has something apart from reason, countering and opposing reason. The [precise] way it is different does not matter.

§17 However, this [part] as well [as the rational part] appears, as we said, to share in reason. At any rate, in the continent person it obeys reason; and in the temperate and the brave person it presumably listens still better to reason, since there it agrees with reason in everything.

§18 The nonrational [part], then, as well [as the whole soul] apparently has two parts. For while the plantlike [part] shares in reason not at all, the [part] with appetites and in general desires shares in reason in a way, insofar as it both listens to reason and obeys it. This is the way in which we are said to "listen to reason" from father or friends, as opposed to the way in which [we "give the reason"] in mathematics. The nonrational part also [obeys and] is persuaded in some way by reason, as is shown by correction, and by every sort of reproof and exhortation.

§19 If, then, we ought to say that this [part] also has reason, then the [part] that has reason, as well [as the nonrational part], will have two parts. One will have reason fully, by having it within itself; the other will have reason by listening to reason as to a father.

The division between virtues accords with this difference. For some virtues are called virtues of thought, others virtues of character; wisdom, comprehension, and prudence are called virtues of thought, generosity and temperance virtues of character. For when we speak of someone's character we do not say that he is wise or has good comprehension, but that he is gentle or temperate. And yet, we also praise the wise person for his state, and the states that are praiseworthy are the ones we call virtues.

Book II [Virtue of Character]

How a virtue of character is acquired

§1 Virtue, then, is of two sorts, virtue of thought and virtue of character. Virtue of thought arises and grows mostly from teaching; that is why it needs experience and time. Virtue of character [i.e., of *ēthos*] results from habit [*ethos*]; hence its name "ethical", slightly varied from "ethos".

§2 Hence it is also clear that none of the virtues of character arises in us naturally. For if something is by nature in one condition, habituation cannot bring it into another condition. A stone, for instance, by nature moves downwards, and habituation could not make it move upwards, not even if you threw it up ten thousand times to habituate it; nor could habituation make fire move downwards, or bring anything that is by nature in one condition into another condition. §3 And so the virtues arise in us neither by nature nor against nature. Rather, we are by nature able to acquire them, and we are completed through habit.

§4 Further, if something arises in us by nature, we first have the capacity for it, and later perform the activity. This is clear in the case of the senses; for we did not acquire them by frequent seeing or hearing, but we already had them when we exercised them, and did not get them by exercising them. Virtues, by contrast, we acquire, just as we acquire crafts, by having first activated them. For we learn a craft by producing the same product that we must produce when we have learned it; we become builders, for instance, by building, and we become harpists by playing the harp. Similarly, then, we become just by doing just actions, temperate by doing temperate actions, brave by doing brave actions. . . .

Habituation

§1 Our present discussion does not aim, as our others do, at study; for the purpose of our examination is not to know what virtue is, but to become good, since otherwise the inquiry would be of no benefit to us. And so we must examine the right ways of acting; for, as we have said, the actions also control the sorts of states we acquire.

§2 First, then, actions should accord with the correct reason. That is a common [belief], and let us assume it. We shall discuss it later, and say what the correct reason is and how it is related to the other virtues.

§3 But let us take it as agreed in advance that every account of the actions we must do has to be stated in outline, not exactly. As we also said at the beginning, the type of accounts we demand should accord with the subject matter; and questions about actions and expediency, like questions about health, have no fixed answers.

§4 While this is the character of our general account, the account of particular cases is still more inexact. For these fall under no craft or profession; the agents themselves must consider in each case what the opportune action is, as doctors and navigators do. §5 The account we offer, then, in our present inquiry is of this inexact sort; still, we must try to offer help.

§6 First, then, we should observe that these sorts of states naturally tend to be ruined by excess and deficiency. We see this happen with strength and health – for we must use evident cases [such as these] as witnesses to things that are not evident. For both excessive and deficient exercise ruin bodily strength, and, similarly, too much or too little eating or drinking ruins health, whereas the proportionate amount produces, increases, and preserves it.

§7 The same is true, then, of temperance, bravery, and the other virtues. For if, for instance, someone avoids and is afraid of everything, standing firm against nothing, he becomes cowardly; if he is afraid of nothing at all and goes to face everything, he becomes rash. Similarly, if he gratifies himself with every pleasure and abstains from none, he becomes intemperate; if he avoids them all, as boors do, he becomes some sort of insensible person. Temperance and bravery, then, are ruined by excess and deficiency, but preserved by the mean.

§8 But these actions are not only the sources and causes both of the emergence and growth of virtues and of their ruin; the activities of the virtues [once we have acquired them] also consist in these same actions. For this is also true of more evident cases; strength, for instance, arises from eating a lot and from withstanding much hard labor, and it is the strong person who is most capable of these very actions. §9 It is the same with the virtues. For abstaining from pleasures makes us become temperate, and once we have become temperate we are most capable of abstaining from pleasures. It is similar with bravery; habituation in disdain for frightening situations and in standing firm against them makes us become brave, and once we have become brave we shall be most capable of standing firm.

The importance of pleasure and pain

§1 But we must take someone's pleasure or pain following on his actions to be a sign of his state. For if someone who abstains from bodily pleasures enjoys the abstinence itself he is temperate; if he is grieved by it, he is intemperate. Again, if he stands firm against terrifying situations and enjoys it, or at least does not find it painful, he is brave; if he finds it painful, he is cowardly. For virtue of character is about pleasures and pains.

For pleasure causes us to do base actions and pain causes us to abstain from fine ones. §2 That is why we need to have had the appropriate upbringing – right from early youth, as Plato says – to make us find enjoyment or pain in the right things; for this is the correct education. . . .

§6 We assume, then, that virtue is the sort of state that does the best actions concerning pleasures and pains, and that vice is the contrary state. . . .

§11 To sum up: Virtue is about pleasures and pains; the actions that are its sources also increase it or, if they are done badly, ruin it; and its activity is about the same actions as those that are its sources.

Virtuous actions versus virtuous character

§1 Someone might be puzzled, however, about what we mean by saying that we become just by doing just actions and become temperate by doing temperate actions. For [one might suppose that] if we do grammatical or musical actions, we are grammarians or musicians, and, similarly, if we do just or temperate actions, we are thereby just or temperate.

§2 But surely actions are not enough, even in the case of crafts; for it is possible to produce a grammatical result by chance, or by following someone else's instructions. To be grammarians, then, we must both produce a grammatical result and produce it grammatically – that is to say, produce it in accord with the grammatical knowledge in us.

§3 Moreover, in any case, what is true of crafts is not true of virtues. For the products of a craft determine by their own qualities whether they have been produced well; and o it suffices that they have the right qualities when they have been produced. But for actions in accord with the virtues o be done temperately or justly it does not suffice that they themselves have the right qualities. Rather, the agent must also be in the right state when he does them. First, he must know [that he is doing virtuous actions]; second, he must decide on them, and decide on them for themselves; and, third, he must also do them from a firm and unchanging state. . . .

§4 Hence actions are called just or temperate when they are the sort that a just or temperate person would do. But the just and temperate person is not the one who [merely] does these actions, but the one who also does them in the way in which just or temperate people do them.

§5 It is right, then, to say that a person comes to be just from doing just actions and temperate from doing temperate actions; for no one has the least prospect of becoming good from failing to do them. . . .

Virtue of character: its genus

§1 Next we must examine what virtue is. Since there are three conditions arising in the soul – feelings, capacities, and states – virtue must be one of these. . . .

§3 First, then, neither virtues nor vices are feelings. For we are called excellent or base insofar as we have virtues or vices, not insofar as we have feelings. Further, we are neither praised nor blamed insofar as we have feelings; for we do not praise the angry or the frightened person, and do not blame the person who is simply angry, but only the person who is angry in a particular way. We are praised or blamed, however, insofar as we have virtues or vices. . . .

§5 For these reasons the virtues are not capacities either; for we are neither called good nor called bad, nor are we praised or blamed, insofar as we are simply capable of feelings. . . .

§6 If, then, the virtues are neither feelings nor capacities, the remaining possibility is that they are states. And so we have said what the genus of virtue is.

Virtue of character: its differentia

§1 But we must say not only, as we already have, that it is a state, but also what sort of state it is.

§2 It should be said, then, that every virtue causes its possessors to be in a good state and to perform their functions well. The virtue of eyes, for instance, makes the eyes and their functioning excellent, because it makes us see well; and similarly, the virtue of a horse makes the horse excellent, and thereby good at galloping, at carrying its rider, and at standing steady in the face of the enemy. §3 If this is true in every case, the virtue of a human being will likewise be the state that makes a human being good and makes him perform his function well.

§4 We have already said how this will be true, and it will also be evident from our next remarks, if we consider the sort of nature that virtue has.

In everything continuous and divisible we can take more, less, and equal, and each of them either in the object itself or relative to us; and the equal is some intermediate between excess and deficiency. §5 By the intermediate in the object I mean what is equidistant from each extremity; this is one and the same for all. But relative to us the intermediate is what is neither superfluous nor deficient; this is not one, and is not the same for all.

§6 If, for instance, ten are many and two are few, we take six as intermediate in the object, since it exceeds [two] and is exceeded [by ten] by an equal amount, [four]. §7 This is what is intermediate by numerical proportion. But that is not how we must take the intermediate that is relative to us. For if ten pounds [of food], for instance, are a lot for someone to eat, and two pounds a little, it does not follow that the trainer will prescribe six, since this might also be either a little or a lot for the person who is to take it – for Milo [the athlete] a little, but for the beginner in gymnastics a lot; and the same is true for running and wrestling. §8 In this way every scientific expert avoids excess and deficiency and seeks and chooses what is intermediate – but intermediate relative to us, not in the object. . . .

§10 By virtue I mean virtue of character; for this is about feelings and actions, and these admit of excess, deficiency, and an intermediate condition. We can be afraid, for instance, or be confident, or have appetites, or get angry, or feel pity, and in general have pleasure or pain, both too much and too little, and in both ways not well. §11 But having these feelings at the right times, about the right things, toward the right people, for the right end, and in the right way, is the intermediate and best condition, and this is proper to virtue. §12 Similarly, actions also admit of excess, deficiency, and an intermediate condition.

Now virtue is about feelings and actions, in which excess and deficiency are in error and incur blame, whereas the intermediate condition is correct and wins praise, which are both proper to virtue. §13 Virtue, then, is a mean, insofar as it aims at what is intermediate. . . .

§15 Virtue, then, is a state that decides, consisting in a mean, the mean relative to us, which is defined by reference to reason, that is to say, to the reason by reference to which the prudent person would define it. It is a mean between two vices, one of excess and one of deficiency.

§16 It is a mean for this reason also: Some vices miss what is right because they are deficient, others because they are excessive, in feelings or in actions, whereas virtue finds and chooses what is intermediate.

§17 That is why virtue, as far as its essence and the account stating what it is are concerned, is a mean, but, as far as the best [condition] and the good [result] are concerned, it is an extremity.

§18 Now not every action or feeling admits of the mean. For the names of some automatically include baseness – for instance, spite, shamelessness, envy [among feelings], and adultery, theft, murder, among actions. For all of these and similar things are called by these names because they themselves, not their excesses or deficiencies, are base. Hence in doing these things we can never be correct, but must invariably be in error. We cannot do them well or not well – by committing adultery, for instance, with the right woman at the right time in the right way. On the contrary, it is true without qualification that to do any of them is to be in error.

§19 [To think these admit of a mean], therefore, is like thinking that unjust or cowardly or intemperate action also admits of a mean, an excess and a deficiency. If it did, there would be a mean of excess, a mean of deficiency, an excess of excess and a deficiency of deficiency. §20 On the contrary, just as there is no excess or deficiency of temperance or of bravery (since the intermediate is a sort of extreme), so also there is no mean of these vicious actions either, but whatever way anyone does them, he is in error. For in general there is no mean of excess or of deficiency, and no excess or deficiency of a mean.

The particular virtues of character

§1 However, we must not only state this general account but also apply it to the particular cases. For among accounts concerning actions, though the general ones are common to more cases, the specific ones are truer, since actions are about particular cases, and our account must accord with these. Let us, then, find these from the chart.

§2 First, then, in feelings of fear and confidence the mean is bravery. The excessively fearless person is nameless (indeed many cases are nameless), and the one who is excessively confident is rash. The one who is excessive in fear and deficient in confidence is cowardly.

§3 In pleasures and pains – though not in all types, and in pains less than in pleasures – the mean is temperance and the excess intemperance. People deficient in pleasure are not often found, which is why they also lack even a name; let us call them insensible.

§4 In giving and taking money the mean is generosity, the excess wastefulness and the deficiency ungenerosity. Here the vicious people have contrary excesses and defects; for the wasteful person is excessive in spending and deficient in taking, whereas the ungenerous person is excessive in taking and deficient in spending. §5 At the moment we are speaking in outline and summary, and that is enough; later we shall define these things more exactly.

Relations between mean and extreme states

§1 Among these three conditions, then, two are vices – one of excess, one of deficiency – and one, the mean, is virtue. In a way, each of them s opposed to each of the others, since each extreme is contrary both to the intermediate condition and to the other extreme, while the intermediate is contrary to the extremes.

§2 For, just as the equal is greater in comparison to the smaller, and smaller in comparison to the greater, so also the intermediate states are excessive in comparison to the deficiencies and deficient in comparison to the excesses – both in feelings and in actions. For the brave person, for instance, appears rash in comparison to the coward, and cowardly in comparison to the rash person; the temperate person appears intemperate in comparison to the insensible person, and insensible in comparison with the intemperate person; and the generous person appears wasteful in comparison to the ungenerous, and ungenerous in comparison to the wasteful person. §3 That is why each of the extreme people tries to push the intermediate person to the other extreme, so that the coward, for instance, calls the brave person rash, and the rash person calls him a coward, and similarly in the other cases.

§4 Since these conditions of soul are opposed to each other in these ways, the extremes are more contrary to each other than to the intermediate. For they are further from each other than from the intermediate, just as the large is further from the small, and the small from the large, than either is from the equal.

§5 Further, sometimes one extreme – rashness or wastefulness, for instance – appears somewhat like the intermediate state, bravery or generosity. But the extremes are most unlike one another; and the things that are furthest apart from each other are defined as contraries. And so the things that are further apart are more contrary.

§6 In some cases the deficiency, in others the excess, is more opposed to the intermediate condition. For instance, cowardice, the deficiency, not rashness, the excess, is more opposed to bravery, whereas intemperance, the excess, not insensibility, the deficiency, is more opposed to temperance.

§7 This happens for two reasons: One reason is derived from the object itself. Since sometimes one extreme is closer and more similar to the intermediate condition, we oppose the contrary extreme, more than this closer one, to the intermediate condition. Since rashness, for instance, seems to be closer and more similar to bravery, and cowardice less similar, we oppose cowardice, more than rashness, to bravery; for what is further from the intermediate condition seems to be more contrary to it. This, then, is one reason, derived from the object itself.

§8 The other reason is derived from ourselves. For when we ourselves have some natural tendency to one extreme more than to the other, this extreme appears more opposed to the intermediate condition. Since, for instance, we have more of a natural tendency to pleasure, we drift more easily toward intemperance than toward orderliness. Hence we say that an extreme is more contrary if we naturally develop more in that direction; and this is why intemperance is more contrary to temperance, since it is the excess [of pleasure].

How can we reach the mean?

§1 We have said enough, then, to show that virtue of character is a mean and what sort of mean it is; that it is a mean between two vices, one of excess and one of deficiency; and that it is a mean because it aims at the intermediate condition in feelings and actions.

§2 That is why it is also hard work to be excellent. For in each case it is hard work to find the intermediate; for instance, not everyone, but only one who knows, finds the midpoint in a circle. So also getting angry, or giving and spending money, is easy and everyone can do it; but doing it to the right person, in the right amount, at the right time, for the right end, and in the right way is no longer easy, nor can everyone do it. Hence doing these things well is rare, praiseworthy, and fine.

§3 That is why anyone who aims at the intermediate condition must first of all steer clear of the more contrary extreme, following the advice that Calypso also gives: 'Hold the ship outside the spray and surge.' For one extreme is more in error, the other less. §4 Since, therefore, it is hard to hit the intermediate extremely accurately, the secondbest tack, as they say, is to take the lesser of the evils. We shall succeed best in this by the method we describe.

We must also examine what we ourselves drift into easily. For different people have different natural tendencies toward different goals, and we shall come to know our own tendencies from the pleasure or pain that arises in us. §5 We must drag ourselves off in the contrary direction; for if we pull far away from error, as they do in straightening bent wood, we shall reach the intermediate condition.

§6 And in everything we must beware above all of pleasure and its sources; for we are already biased in its favor when we come to judge it. Hence we must react to it as the elders reacted to Helen, and on each occasion repeat what they said; for if we do this, and send it off, we shall be less in error.

§7 In summary, then, if we do these things we shall best be able to reach the intermediate condition. But presumably this is difficult, especially in particular cases, since it is not easy to define the way we should be angry, with whom, about what, for how long. For sometimes, indeed, we ourselves praise deficient people and call them mild, and sometimes praise quarrelsome people and call them manly.

§8 Still, we are not blamed if we deviate a little in excess or deficiency from doing well, but only if we deviate a long way, since then we are easily noticed. But how great and how serious a deviation receives blame is not easy to define in an account; for nothing else perceptible is easily defined either. Such things are among particulars, and the judgment depends on perception.

§9 This is enough, then, to make it clear that in every case the intermediate state is praised, but we must sometimes incline toward the excess, sometimes toward the deficiency; for that is the easiest way to hit the intermediate and good condition.

Book X

Happiness and theoretical study

§1 If happiness is activity in accord with virtue, it is reasonable for it to accord with the supreme virtue, which will be the virtue of the best thing. The best is understanding, or whatever else seems to be the natural ruler and leader, and to understand what is fine and divine, by being itself either divine or the most divine element in us. Hence complete happiness will be its activity in accord with its proper virtue; and we have said that this activity is the activity of study.

§2 This seems to agree with what has been said before, and also with the truth. For this activity is supreme, since understanding is the supreme element in us, and the objects of understanding are the supreme objects of knowledge.

Further, it is the most continuous activity, since we are more capable of continuous study than any continuous action.

§3 Besides, we think pleasure must be mixed into happiness; and it is agreed that the activity in accord with wisdom is the most pleasant of the activities in accord with virtue. Certainly philosophy seems to have remarkably pure and firm pleasures, and it is reasonable for those who have knowledge to spend their lives more pleasantly than those who seek it.

§4 Moreover, the self-sufficiency we spoke of will be found in study more than in anything else. For admittedly the wise person, the just person, and the other virtuous people all need the good things necessary for life. Still, when these are adequately supplied, the just person needs other people as partners and recipients of his just actions; and the same is true of the temperate person, the brave person, and each of the others. But the wise person is able, and more able the wiser he is, to study even by himself; and though he presumably does it better with colleagues, even so he is more self-sufficient than any other [virtuous person].

§5 Besides, study seems to be liked because of itself alone, since it has no result beyond having studied. But from the virtues concerned with action we try to a greater or lesser extent to gain something beyond the action itself. . . .

But the activity of understanding, it seems, is superior in excellence because it is the activity of study, aims at no end apart from itself, and has its own proper pleasure, which increases the activity. Further, self-sufficiency, leisure, unwearied activity (as far as is possible for a human being), and any other features ascribed to the blessed person, are evidently features of his activity. Hence a human being's complete happiness will be this activity, if it receives a complete span of life, since nothing incomplete is proper to happiness.

§8 Such a life would be superior to the human level. For someone will live it not insofar as he is a human being, but insofar as he has some divine element in him. And the activity of this divine element is as much superior to the activity in accord with the rest of virtue as this element is superior to the compound. Hence if understanding is something divine in comparison with a human being, so also will the life in accord with understanding be divine in comparison with human life. We ought not to follow the makers of proverbs and 'Think human, since you are human', or 'Think mortal, since you are mortal'. Rather, as far as we can, we ought to be proimmortal, and go to all lengths to live a life in accord with our supreme element; for however much this element may lack in bulk, by much more it surpasses everything in power and value.

§9 Moreover, each person seems to be his understanding, if he is his controlling and better element. It would be absurd, then, if he were to choose not his own life, but something else's. And what we have said previously will also apply now. For what is proper to each thing's nature is supremely best and most pleasant for it; and hence for a human being the life in accord with understanding will be supremely best and most pleasant, if understanding, more than anything else, is the human being. This life, then, will also be happiest.

Theoretical study and the other virtues . . .

§4 Moreover, it seems to need external supplies very little, or [at any rate] less than virtue of character needs them. For let us grant that they both need necessary goods, and to the same extent; for there will be only a very small difference, even though the politician labors more about the body and such-like. Still, there will be a large difference in [what is needed] for the [proper] activities [of each type of virtue]. For the generous person will need money for generous actions; and the just person will need it for paying debts, since wishes are not clear, and

people who are not just pretend to wish to do justice. Similarly, the brave person will need enough power, and the temperate person will need freedom [to do intemperate actions], if they are to achieve anything that the virtue requires. For how else will they, or any other virtuous people, make their virtue clear?

§5 Moreover, it is disputed whether decision or action is more in control of virtue, on the assumption that virtue depends on both. Well, certainly it is clear that the complete [good] depends on both; but for actions many external goods are needed, and the greater and finer the actions the more numerous are the external goods needed.

§6 But someone who is studying needs none of these goods, for that activity at least; indeed, for study at least, we might say they are even hindrances. Insofar as he is a human being, however, and [hence] lives together with a number of other human beings, he chooses to do the actions that accord with virtue. Hence he will need the sorts of external goods [that are needed for the virtues], for living a human life.

§7 In another way also it appears that complete happiness is some activity of study. For we traditionally suppose that the gods more than anyone are blessed and happy; but what sorts of actions ought we to ascribe to them? Just actions? Surely they will appear ridiculous making contracts, returning deposits, and so on. Brave actions? Do they endure what [they find] frightening and endure dangers because it is fine? Generous actions? Whom will they give to? And surely it would be absurd for them to have currency or anything like that. What would their temperate actions be? Surely it is vulgar praise to say that they do not have base appetites. When we go through them all, anything that concerns actions appears trivial and unworthy of the gods. Nonetheless, we all traditionally suppose that they are alive and active, since surely they are not asleep like Endymion. Then if someone is alive, and action is excluded, and production even more, what is left but study? Hence the gods' activity that is superior in blessedness will be an activity of study. And so the human activity that is most akin to the gods' activity will, more than any others, have the character of happiness.

§8 A sign of this is the fact that other animals have no share in happiness, being completely deprived of this activity of study. For the whole life of the gods is blessed, and human life is blessed to the extent that it has something resembling this sort of activity; but none of the other animals is happy, because none of them shares in study at all. Hence happiness extends just as far as study extends, and the more someone studies, the happier he is, not coincidentally but insofar as he studies, since study is valuable in itself. And so [on this argument] happiness will be some kind of study.

§9 But happiness will need external prosperity also, since we are human beings; for our nature is not self-sufficient for study, but we need a healthy body, and need to have food and the other services provided. Still, even though no one can be blessedly happy without external goods, we must not think that to be happy we will need many large goods. For self-sufficiency and action do not depend on excess.

§10 Moreover, we can do fine actions even if we do not rule earth and sea; for even from moderate resources we can do the actions that accord with virtue. This is evident to see, since many private citizens seem to do decent actions no less than people in power do – even more, in fact. It is enough if moderate resources are provided; for the life of someone whose activity accords with virtue will be happy.

§11 Solon surely described happy people well, when he said they had been moderately supplied with external goods, had done what he regarded as the finest actions, and had lived their lives temperately. For it is possible to have moderate possessions and still to do the right actions. And Anaxagoras would seem to have supposed that the happy person was neither rich nor powerful, since he said he would not be surprised if the happy person appeared an absurd sort of person to the many. For the many judge by externals, since these are all they perceive. §12 Hence the beliefs of the wise would seem to accord with our arguments.

These considerations, then, produce some confidence. But the truth in questions about action is judged from what we do and how we live, since these are what control [the answers to such questions]. Hence we ough to examine what has been said by applying i to what we do and how we live; and i it harmonizes with what we do, we shoulc accept it, but if it conflicts we should coun it [mere] words.

§13 The person whose activity accords with understanding and who takes care of understanding would seem to be in the best condi tion, and most loved by the gods. For if the gods pay some attention to human beings, a they seem to, it would be reasonable for then to take pleasure in what is best and most akir to them, namely understanding; and reason able for them to benefit in return those whc most of all like and honor understanding, or the assumption that these people attend tc what is beloved by the gods, and act correctly and finely. Clearly, all this is true of the wise person more than anyone else; hence he is mos loved by the gods. And it is likely that this same person will be happiest; hence, by this argu ment also, the wise person, more than anyone else, will be happy.

From Ethics to Politics

Moral education

§1 We have now said enough in outlines about happiness and the virtues, and about friendship and pleasure also. Should we, then, think that our decision [to study these] has achievec its end? On the contrary, the aim of studies about action, as we say, is surely not to study and know about a given thing, but rather to act on our knowledge. §2 Hence knowing about virtue is not enough, but we must also try to possess and exercise virtue, or become good in any other way. . . .

It is difficult, however, for someone to be trained correctly for virtue from his youth if he has not been brought up under correct laws: for the many, especially the young, do not find it pleasant to live in a temperate and resistant way. That is why laws must prescribe their upbringing and practices; for they will not find these things painful when they get used to them.

§9 Presumably, however, it is not enough if they get the correct upbringing and attention when they are young; rather, they must continue the same practices and be habituated to them when they become men. Hence we need laws concerned with these things also, and in general with all of life. For the many yield to compulsion more than to argument, and to sanctions more than to the fine.

§10 That is why legislators must, in some people's view, urge people toward virtue and exhort them to aim at the fine – on the assumption that anyone whose good habits have prepared him decently will listen to them – but must impose corrective treatments and penalties on anyone who disobeys or lacks the right nature, and must completely expel an incurable. For the decent person, it is assumed, will attend to reason because his life aims at the fine, whereas the base person, since he desires pleasure, has to receive corrective treatment by pain, like a beast of burden. That is why it is said that the pains imposed must be those most contrary to the pleasures he likes.

CHAPTER 67

Non-Relative Virtues:
An Aristotelian Approach

MARTHA NUSSBAUM

All Greeks used to go around armed with swords.
Thucydides, *History of the Peloponnesian War*

The customs of former times might be said to be too simple and barbaric. For Greeks used to go around armed with swords; and they used to buy wives from one another, and there are surely other ancient customs that are extremely stupid. (For example, in Cyme there is a law about homicide, that if a man prosecuting a charge can produce a certain number of witnesses from among his own relations, the defendant will automatically be convicted of murder.) In general, all human beings seek not the way of their ancestors, but the good.
Aristotle, *Politics 1268a39 ff.*

One may also observe in one's travels to distant countries the feelings of recognition and affiliation that link every human being to every other Human Being.
Aristotle, *Nicomachean Ethics 1155a21–22*

I

The virtues are attracting increasing interest in contemporary philosophical debate. From many different sides one hears of a dissatisfaction with ethical theories that are remote from concrete human experience. Whether this remoteness results from the utilitarian's interest in arriving at a universal calculus of satisfactions or from a Kantian concern with universal principles of broad generality, in which the names of particular contexts, histories, and persons do not occur, remoteness is now being seen by an increasing number of moral philosophers as a defect in an approach to ethical questions. In the search for an alternative approach, the concept of virtue is playing a prominent role. So, too, is the work of Aristotle, the greatest defender of an ethical approach based on the concept of virtue. For Aristotle's work seems, appealingly, to combine rigor with concreteness, theoretical power with sensitivity to the actual circumstances of

Martha Nussbaum, "Non-Relative Virtues: An Aristotelian Approach," pp. 32–50 from Peter A. French, Theodore E. Uehling, Jr., and Howard K. Wettstein (eds.), *Ethical Theory: Character and Virtue*, Midwest Studies in Philosophy 13. Notre Dame, IN: University of Notre Dame Press, 1988.

ıman life and choice in all their multiplicity,
ıriety, and mutability.

But on one central point there is a striking
ıvergence between Aristotle and contempor-
y virtue theory. To many current defenders of
ı ethical approach based on the virtues, the
turn to the virtues is connected with a turn
ıward relativism – toward, that is, the view
ıat the only appropriate criteria of ethical
ıodness are local ones, internal to the tradi-
ıns and practices of each local society or
oup that asks itself questions about the
ıod. The rejection of general algorithms and
ıstract rules in favor of an account of the
ıod life based on specific modes of virtuous
ıtion is taken, by writers as otherwise diverse
ı Alasdair MacIntyre, Bernard Williams, and
ıilippa Foot,[1] to be connected with the aban-
ınment of the project of rationally justifying a
ıngle norm of flourishing life for and to all
ıman beings and with a reliance, instead, on
ırms that are local both in origin and in
ıplication.

The positions of all of these writers, where
ılativism is concerned, are complex; none un-
ıuivocally endorses a relativist view. But all
ınnect virtue ethics with a relativist denial
ıat ethics, correctly understood, offers any
ıans-cultural norms, justifiable with reference
ı reasons of universal human validity, with
ıference to which we may appropriately criti-
ıze different local conceptions of the good.
ınd all suggest that the insights we gain by
ıursuing ethical questions in the Aristotelian
ırtue-based way lend support to relativism.

For this reason it is easy for those who are
ıterested in supporting the rational criticism
ı local traditions and in articulating an idea of
ıhical progress to feel that the ethics of
ırtue can give them little help. If the position
ı women, as established by local traditions
ı many parts of the world, is to be improved,
ı traditions of slave holding and racial inequ-
ıity, if religious intolerance, if aggressive
ıd warlike conceptions of manliness, if une-
ıual norms of material distribution are to
ıe criticized in the name of practical reason,
ıis criticizing (one might easily suppose) will
ıave to be done from a Kantian or utilitarian
ıewpoint, not through the Aristotelian
ıpproach.

This is an odd result, where Aristotle is concerned. For it is obvious that he was not only
the defender of an ethical theory based on the
virtues, but also the defender of a single objective account of the human good, or human
flourishing. This account is supposed to be
objective in the sense that it is justifiable with
reference to reasons that do not derive merely
from local traditions and practices, but rather
from features of humanness that lie beneath
all local traditions and are there to be seen
whether or not they are in fact recognized in
local traditions. And one of Aristotle's most
obvious concerns is the criticism of existing
moral traditions, in his own city and in
others, as unjust or repressive, or in other
ways incompatible with human flourishing.
He uses his account of the virtues as a basis
for this criticism of local traditions: prominently, for example, in Book II of the *Politics*,
where he frequently argues against existing
social forms by pointing to ways in which
they neglect or hinder the development of
some important human virtue. Aristotle evidently believes that there is no incompatibility
between basing an ethical theory on the virtues
and defending the singleness and objectivity of
the human good. Indeed, he seems to believe
that these two aims are mutually supportive.

Now the fact that Aristotle believes something
does not make it true. (Though I have sometimes been accused of holding that position!)
But it does, on the whole, make that something a
plausible *candidate* for the truth, one deserving
our most serious scrutiny. In this case, it would
be odd indeed if he had connected two elements
in ethical thought that are self-evidently incompatible, or in favor of whose connectedness and
compatibility there is nothing interesting to be
said. The purpose of this paper is to establish
that Aristotle does indeed have an interesting
way of connecting the virtues with a search for
ethical objectivity and with the criticism of
existing local norms, a way that deserves our
serious consideration as we work on these questions. Having described the general shape of the
Aristotelian approach, we can then begin to
understand some of the objections that might
be brought against such a non-relative account
of the virtues, and to imagine how the Aristotelian could respond to those objections.

II

The relativist, looking at different societies, is impressed by the variety and the apparent non-comparability in the lists of virtues she encounters. Examining the different lists, and observing the complex connections between each list and a concrete form of life and a concrete history, she may well feel that any list of virtues must be simply a reflection of local traditions and values, and that, virtues being (unlike Kantian principles or utilitarian algorithms) concrete and closely tied to forms of life, there can in fact be no list of virtues that will serve as normative for all these varied societies. It is not only that the specific forms of behavior recommended in connection with the virtues differ greatly over time and place, it is also that the very areas that are singled out as spheres of virtue, and the manner in which they are individuated from other areas, vary so greatly. For someone who thinks this way, it is easy to feel that Aristotle's own list, despite its pretensions to universality and objectivity, must be similarly restricted, merely a reflection of one particular society's perceptions of salience and ways of distinguishing. At this point, relativist writers are likely to quote Aristotle's description of the "great-souled" person, the *megalopsuchos*, which certainly contains many concrete local features and sounds very much like the portrait of a certain sort of Greek gentleman, in order to show that Aristotle's list is just as culture-bound as any other.

But if we probe further into the way in which Aristotle in fact enumerates and individuates the virtues, we begin to notice things that cast doubt upon the suggestion that he has simply described what is admired in his own society. First of all, we notice that a rather large number of virtues and vices (vices especially) are nameless, and that, among the ones that are not nameless, a good many are given, by Aristotle's own account,

names that are somewhat arbitrarily chosen b Aristotle, and do not perfectly fit the behavic he is trying to describe.[2] Of such modes conduct he writes, "Most of these are nameles but we must try . . . to give them names in orde to make our account clear and easy to follow (*NE* 1108a16–19). This does not sound lik the procedure of someone who is simply study ing local traditions and singling out the virtu names that figure most prominently in thos traditions.

What *is* going on becomes clearer when w examine the way in which he does, in fac introduce his list. For he does so, in the *Nic machean Ethics*, by a device whose very straigh forwardness and simplicity has caused it escape the notice of most writers on this topi What he does, in each case, is to isolate a spher of human experience that figures in more or le any human life, and in which more or less an human being will have to make *some* choic rather than others, and act in *some* way rathe than some other. The introductory chapter enu merating the virtues and vices begins from a enumeration of these spheres (*NE* 2.7); and eac chapter on a virtue in the more detailed accoun that follows begins with "Concerning X . . ." words to this effect, where "X" names a spher of life with which all human beings regularl and more or less necessarily have dealing Aristotle then asks: What is it to choose an respond well within that sphere? What is it, o the other hand, to choose defectively? The "thi account" of each virtue is that it is whatever it to be stably disposed to act appropriately in th sphere. There may be, and usually are, variou competing specifications of what acting well, i each case, in fact comes to. Aristotle goes on t defend in each case some concrete specifica tions, producing, at the end, a full or "thick definition of the virtue.

Here are the most important spheres experience recognized by Aristotle, along wit the names of their corresponding virtues:

Sphere	Virtue
1. Fear of important damages, esp. death	courage
2. Bodily appetites and their pleasures	moderation
3. Distribution of limited resources	justice

4. Management of one's personal property, where others are concerned	generosity
5. Management of personal property, where hospitality is concerned	expansive hospitality
6. Attitudes and actions with respect to one's own worth	greatness of soul
7. Attitude to slights and damages	mildness of temper
8. "Association and living together and the fellowship of words and actions"	
a. truthfulness in speech	truthfulness
b. social association of a playful kind	easy grace (contrasted with coarseness, rudeness, insensitivity)
c. social association more generally	nameless, but a kind of friendliness (contrasted with irritability and grumpiness)
9. Attitude to the good and ill fortune of others	proper judgment (contrasted with enviousness, spitefulness, etc.)
10. Intellectual life	the various intellectual virtues (such as perceptiveness, knowledge, etc.)
11. The planning of one's life and conduct	practical wisdom

There is, of course, much more to be said about this list, its specific members, and the names Aristotle chooses for the virtue in each case, some of which are indeed culture bound. What I want, however, to insist is the care with which Aristotle articulates his general approach, beginning from a characterization of a sphere of universal experience and choice, and introducing the virtue name as the name (as yet undefined) of whatever it is to choose appropriately in that area of experience. On this approach, it does not seem possible to say, as the relativist wishes to, that a given society does not contain anything that corresponds to a given virtue. Nor does it seem to be an open question, in the case of a particular agent, whether a certain virtue should or should not be included in his or her life – except in the sense that she can always choose to pursue the corresponding deficiency instead. The points is that everyone makes some choices and acts somehow or other in these spheres: if not properly, then improperly. Everyone has *some* attitude and behavior toward her own death; toward her bodily appetites and their management; toward her property and its use; toward the distribution of social goods; toward telling the truth; toward being kindly or not kindly to others; toward cultivating or not cultivating a sense of play and delight; and so on. No matter where one

lives one cannot escape these questions, so long as one is living a human life. But then this means that one's behavior falls, willy nilly, within the sphere of the Aristotelian virtue, in each case. If it is not appropriate, it is inappropriate; it cannot be off the map altogether. People will of course disagree about what the appropriate ways of acting and reacting in fact *are*. But in that case, as Aristotle has set things up, they are arguing about the same thing, and advancing competing specifications of the same virtue. The reference of the virtue term in each case is fixed by the sphere of experience – by what we shall from now on call the "grounding experiences." The thin or "nominal definition" of the virtue will be, in each case, that it is whatever it is that being disposed to choose and respond well consists in, in that sphere. The job of ethical theory will be to search for the best further specification corresponding to this nominal definition, and to produce a full definition.

III

We have begun to introduce considerations from the philosophy of language. We can now make the direction of the Aristotelian account clearer by considering his own account of linguistic indicating (referring) and defining, which guides his treatment of both scientific and ethical terms, and of the idea of progress in both areas.

Aristotle's general picture is as follows. We begin with some experiences – not necessarily our own, but those of members of our linguistic community, broadly construed. On the basis of these experiences, a word enters the language of the group, indicating (referring to) whatever it is that is the content of those experiences. Aristotle gives the example of thunder.[3] People hear a noise in the clouds, and they then refer to it, using the word "thunder." At this point, it may be that nobody has any concrete account of the noise or any idea about what it really is. But the experience fixes a subject for further inquiry. From now on, we can refer to thunder, ask "What is thunder?" and advance and assess competing theories. The thin or, we might say, "nominal definition" of thunder is "That noise in the clouds, whatever it is." The competing explanatory theories are rival candidates for correct full or thick definition. So the explanation story citing Zeus' activities in the clouds is a false account of the very same thing of which the best scientific explanation is a true account. There is just one debate here, with a single subject.

So too, Aristotle suggests, with our ethical terms. Heraclitus, long before him, already had the essential idea, saying, "They would not have known the name of justice, if these things did not take place."[4] "These things," our source for the fragment informs us, are experiences of injustice – presumably of harm, deprivation, inequality. These experiences fix the reference of the corresponding virtue word. Aristotle proceeds along similar lines. In the *Politics* he insists that only human beings, and not either animals or gods, will have our basic ethical terms and concepts (such as just and unjust, noble and base, good and bad), because the beasts are unable to form the concepts, and gods lack the experiences of limit and finitude that give a concept such as justice its point.[5] In the *Nicomachean Ethics* enumeration of the virtues, he carries the line of thought further, suggesting that the reference of the virtue terms is fixed by spheres of choice, frequently connected with our finitude and limitation, that we encounter in virtue of shared

conditions of human existence. The question about virtue usually arises in areas in which human choice is both non-optional and somewhat problematic. (Thus, he stresses, there is no virtue involving the regulation of listening to attractive sounds or seeing pleasing sights.) Each family of virtue and vice or deficiency words attaches to some such sphere. And we can understand progress in ethics, like progress in scientific understanding, to be progress in finding the correct fuller specification of a virtue, isolated by its thin or "nominal" definition. This progress is aided by a perspicuous mapping of the sphere of the grounding experiences. When we understand more precisely what problems human beings encounter in their lives with one another, what circumstances they face in which choice of some sort is required, we will have a way of assessing competing responses to those problems, and we will begin to understand what it might be to act well in the face of them.

Aristotle's ethical and political writings provide many examples of how such progress (or more generally, such a rational debate) might go. We find argument against Platonic asceticism, as the proper specification of moderation (appropriate choice and response vis-à-vis the bodily appetites) and the consequent proneness to anger over slights, that was prevalent in Greek ideals of maleness and in Greek behavior, together with a defense of a more limited and controlled expression of anger, as the proper specification of the virtue that Aristotle calls "mildness of temper." (Here Aristotle evinces some discomfort with the virtue term he has chosen, and he is right to do so, since it certainly loads the dice heavily in favor of his concrete specification and against the traditional one.)[6] And so on for all the virtues.

In an important section of *Politics* II, part of which forms one of the epigraphs to this paper, Aristotle defends the proposition that law should be revisable and not fixed by pointing to evidence that there is progress toward greater correctness in our ethical conceptions as also in the arts and sciences. Greeks used to think that courage was a matter of waving swords around; now they have (the *Ethics* informs us) a more inward and a more civic and communally attuned understanding of proper behavior toward the possibility of death. Women used to be regarded as property, bought and sold; now this would be thought barbaric. And in the case of justice as well we have, the *Politics* passage claims, advanced toward a more adequate understanding of what is fair and appropriate. Aristotle gives the example of an existing homicide law that convicts the defendent automatically on the evidence of the prosecutor's relatives (whether they actually witnessed anything or not, apparently). This, Aristotle says, is clearly a stupid and unjust law; and yet it once seemed appropriate – and, to a tradition-bound community, must still be so. To hold tradition fixed is then to prevent ethical progress. What human beings want and seek is not conformity with the past, it is the good. So our systems of law should make it possible for them to progress beyond the past, when they have agreed that a change is good. (They should not, however, make change too easy, since it is no easy matter to see one's way to the good, and tradition is frequently a sounder guide than current fashion.)

In keeping with these ideas, the *Politics* as a whole presents the beliefs of the many different societies it investigates not as unrelated local norms, but as competing answers to questions of justice and courage (and so on) with which all the societies (being human) are concerned, and in response to which they are all trying to find what is good. Aristotle's analysis of the virtues gives him an appropriate framework for these comparisons, which seem perfectly appropriate inquiries into the ways in which different societies have solved common human problems.

In the Aristotelian approach it is obviously of the first importance to distinguish two stages of the inquiry: the initial demarcation of the sphere of choice, of the "grounding experiences" that fix the reference of the virtue term; and the ensuing more concrete inquiry into what appropriate choice, in that sphere, *is*. Aristotle does not always do this carefully, and the language he has to work with is often not helpful to him. We do not have much difficulty with terms like "moderation" and "justice" and even "courage," which seem vaguely normative but relatively empty, so far, of concrete moral content. As the approach requires, they can serve as extension-fixing labels under which many competing specifications may be investigated. But we have already noticed the problem with "mildness of temper," which seems to rule out by fiat a prominent contender for the appropriate disposition concerning anger. And much the same thing certainly seems to be true of the relativists' favorite target, *megalopsuchia*, which implies in its very name an attitude to one's own worth that is more Greek than universal. (For example, a Christian will feel that the proper attitude to one's own worth requires understanding one's lowness, frailty, and sinfulness. The virtue of humility requires considering oneself *small*, not great.) What we ought to get at this point in the inquiry is a word for the proper behavior toward anger and offense and a word for the proper behavior toward one's worth that are more truly neutral among the competing specifications, referring only to the sphere of experience within which we wish to determine what is appropriate. Then we could regard the competing conceptions as rival accounts of one and the same thing, so that, for example, Christian humility would be a rival specification of the same virtue whose Greek specification is given in Aristotle's account of *megalopsuchia*, namely, the proper way to behave toward the question of one's own worth.

And in fact, oddly enough, if one examines the evolution in the use of this word from Aristotle through the Stoics to the Christian fathers, one can see that this is more or less what happened, as "greatness of soul" became associated, first, with Stoic emphasis on the supremacy of virtue and the worthlessness of externals, including the body, and, through this, with the Christian denial of the body and of the worth of earthly life. So even in this apparently unpromising case, history shows that the Aristotelian approach not only provided the materials for a single debate but actually succeeded in organizing such a debate, across enormous differences of both place and time.

Here, then, is a sketch for an objective human morality based upon the idea of virtuous action – that is, of appropriate functioning in each human sphere. The Aristotelian claim is that, further developed, it will retain virtue morality's immersed attention to actual human experiences, while gaining the ability to criticize local and traditional moralities in the name of a more inclusive account of the circumstances of human life, and of the needs for human functioning that these circumstances call forth.

IV

The proposal will encounter many objections. The concluding sections of this paper will present three of the most serious and will sketch the lines along which the Aristotelian conception might proceed in formulating a reply. To a great extent these objections are not imagined or confronted by Aristotle himself, but his position seems capable of confronting them.

The first objection concerns the relationship between singleness of problem and singleness of solution. Let us grant for the moment that the Aristotelian approach has succeeded in coherently isolating and describing areas of human experience and choice that form, so to speak, the *terrain* of the virtues, and in giving thin definitions of each of the virtues as whatever it is that consists in choosing and responding well within that sphere. Let us suppose that the approach succeeds in doing this in a way that embraces many times and places, bringing disparate cultures together into a single debate about the good human being and the good human life. Different cultural accounts of good choice within the sphere in question in each case are now seen not as untranslatably different forms of life, but as competing answers to a single general question about a set of shared human experiences. Still, it might be argued, what has been achieved is, at best, a single discourse or debate about virtue. It has not been shown that this debate will have, as Aristotle believes, a single answer. Indeed, it has not even been shown that the discourse we have set up will have the form of a *debate* at all, rather than that of a plurality of culturally specific narratives, each giving the thick definition of a virtue that corresponds to the experience and traditions of a particular group. There is an important disanalogy with the case of thunder, on which the Aristotelian so much

relies in arguing that our questions will have a single answer. For in that case what is given in experience is the definiendum itself, so that experiences establish a rough extension, to which any good definition must respond. In the case of the virtues, things are more indirect. What is given in experience across groups is only the *ground* of virtuous action, the circumstances of life to which virtuous action is an appropriate response. Even if these grounding experiences are shared, that does not tell us that there will be a shared appropriate response.

In the case of thunder, furthermore, the conflicting theories are clearly put forward as competing candidates for the truth; the behavior of those involved in the discourse suggests that they are indeed, as Aristotle says, searching "not for the way of their ancestors, but for the good." And it seems reasonable in that case for them to do so. It is far less clear where the virtues are concerned (the objector continues) that a unified practical solution is either sought by the actual participants or a desideratum for them. The Aristotelian proposal makes it possible to conceive of a way in which the virtues might be non-relative. It does not, by itself, answer the question of relativism.

The second objection goes deeper. For it questions the notion of spheres of shared human experience that lies at the heart of the Aristotelian approach. The approach, says this objector, seems to treat the experiences that ground the virtues as in some way primitive given, and free from the cultural variation that we find in the plurality of normative conceptions of virtue. Ideas of proper courage may vary, but the fear of death is shared by all human beings. Ideas of moderation may vary, but the experiences of hunger, thirst, and sexual desire are (so the Aristotelian seems to claim) invariant. Normative conceptions introduce an element of cultural interpretation that is not present in the grounding experiences which are, for that very reason, the Aristotelian's starting point.

But, the objector continues, such assumptions are naive. They will not stand up either to our best account of experience or to a close examination of the ways in which these so-called grounding experiences have in fact

een differently constructed by different cultures. In general, first of all, our best accounts
f the nature of experience, even perceptual
xperience, inform us that there is no such
1ing as an "innocent eye" that receives an
ninterpreted "given." Even sense-perception is
nterpretive, heavily influenced by belief, teach-
1g, language, and in general by social and con-
xtual features. There is a very real sense in
hich members of different societies do not
e the same sun and stars, encounter the same
lants and animals, hear the same thunder.

But if this seems to be true of human experi-
nce of nature, which was the allegedly unprob-
ma
tic starting point for Aristotle's account of
aming, it is all the more plainly true, the
bjector claims, in the area of the human
ood. Here it is only a very naive and historic-
lly insensitive moral philosopher who would
y that the experience of the fear of death or
1e experience of bodily appetites is a human
onstant. Recent anthropological work on
1e social construction of the emotions,[7] for
xample, has shown to what extent the experi-
nce of fear has learned and culturally variant
lements. When we add that the object of the
ar in which the Aristotelian takes an interest
; death, which has been so variously inter-
reted and understood by human beings at
ifferent times and in different places, the con-
lusion that the "grounding experience" is
n irreducible plurality of experiences, highly
arious and in each case deeply infused with
ultural interpretation, becomes even more
1escapable.

Nor is the case different with the apparently
ess complicated experience of the bodily appe-
tes. Most philosophers who have written
bout the appetites have treated hunger, thirst,
nd sexual desire as human universals, stem-
1ing from our shared animal nature. Aristotle
imself was already more sophisticated, since
e insisted that the object of appetite is
the apparent good" and that appetite is there-
1re something interpretive and selective, a
ind of intentional awareness. But he does not
2em to have reflected much about the ways in
/hich historical and cultural differences
ould shape that awareness. The Hellenistic
hilosophers who immediately followed him
id so reflect, arguing that the experience of

sexual desire and of many forms of the desire
for food and drink are, at least in part, social
constructs, built up over time on the basis of a
social teaching about value that is external to
start with, but that enters so deeply into the
perceptions of the individual that it actually
forms and transforms the experience of desire.
Let us take two Epicurean examples. People are
taught that to be well fed they require luxuri-
ous fish and meat, that a simple vegetarian diet
is not enough. Over time, the combination of
teaching with habit produces an appetite for
meat, shaping the individual's perceptions of
the objects before him. Again, people are
taught that what sexual relations are all about
is a romantic union or fusion with an object
who is seen as exalted in value, or even as
perfect. Over time, this teaching shapes sexual
behavior and the experience of desire, so that
sexual arousal itself responds to this culturally
learned scenario.

This work of social criticism has recently
been carried further by Michel Foucault in his
History of Sexuality. This work has certain gaps
as a history of Greek thought on this topic, but
it does succeed in establishing that the Greeks
saw the problem of the appetites and their
management in an extremely different way
from the way of twentieth-century Westerners.
To summarize two salient conclusions of his
complex argument, the Greeks did not single
out the sexual appetite for special treatment;
they treated it alongside hunger and thirst, as
a drive that needed to be mastered and kept
within bounds. Their central concern was with
self-mastery, and they saw the appetites in the
light of this concern. Furthermore, where
the sexual appetite is concerned, they did not
regard the gender of the partner as particularly
important in assessing the moral value of the
act. Nor did they identify or treat as morally
salient a stable disposition to prefer partners
of one sex rather than the other. Instead, they
focused on the general issue of activity and
passivity, connecting it in complex ways with
the issue of self-mastery.

Work like Foucault's – and there is a lot of it
in various areas, some of it very good – shows
very convincingly that the experience of bodily
desire, and of the body itself, has elements
that vary with cultural and historical change.

The names that people call their desires and themselves as subjects of desire, the fabric of belief and discourse into which they integrate their ideas of desiring, all this influences, it is clear, not only their reflection about desire, but also their experience of desire itself. Thus, for example, it is naive to treat our modern debates about homosexuality as continuations of the very same debate about sexual activity that went on in the Greek world. In a very real sense there was no "homosexual experience" in a culture that did not contain our emphasis on the gender of the object, our emphasis on the subjectivity of inclination and the permanence of appetitive disposition, our particular ways of problematizing certain forms of behavior.

If we suppose that we can get underneath this variety and this constructive power of social discourse in at least one case – namely, with the universal experience of bodily pain as a bad thing – even here we find subtle arguments against us. For the experience of pain seems to be embedded in a cultural discourse as surely as the closely related experiences of the appetites; and significant variations can be alleged here as well. The Stoics already made this claim against the Aristotelian virtues. In order to establish that bodily pain is not bad by its very nature, but only by cultural tradition, the Stoics had to provide some explanation for the ubiquity of the belief that pain is bad and of the tendency to shun it. This explanation would have to show that the reaction was learned rather than natural, and to explain why, in the light of this fact, it is learned so widely. This they did by pointing to certain features in the very early treatment of infants. As soon as an infant is born, it cries. Adults, assuming that the crying is a response to its pain at the unaccustomed coldness and harshness of the place where it finds itself, hasten to comfort it. This behavior, often repeated, teaches the infant to regard its pain as a bad thing – or, better, teaches it the concept of pain, which includes the notion of badness, and teaches it the forms of life its society shares concerning pain. It is all social teaching, they claim, though this usually escapes our notice because of the early and non-linguistic nature of the teaching.

These and related arguments, the objecto concludes, show that the Aristotelian idea tha there is a single non-relative discourse abou human experiences such as mortality or desir is a naive idea. There is no such bedrock o shared experience, and thus no single spher of choice within which the virtue is the dispo ition to choose well. So the Aristotelian proje cannot even get off the ground.

Now the Aristotelian confronts a thir objector, who attacks from a rather differer direction. Like the second, she charges tha the Aristotelian has taken for a universal an necessary feature of human life an experienc that is contingent on certain non-necessar historical conditions. Like the second, sh argues that human experience is much mor profoundly shaped by non-necessary soci features than the Aristotelian has allowec But her purpose is not simply, like secon objector's, to point to the great variety c ways in which the "grounding experiences corresponding to the virtues are actuall understood and lived by human beings. It more radical still. It is to point out that w could imagine a form of human life that doc not contain these experiences – or some c them – at all, in any form. Thus the virtu that consists in acting well in that sphere nee not be included in an account of the huma good. In some cases, the experience may eve be a sign of *bad* human life, and the corre sponding virtue, therefore, no better than form of non-ideal adaptation to a bad state c affairs. The really good human life, in such case, would contain neither the groundin deficiency nor the remedial virtue.

This point is forcefully raised by some c Aristotle's own remarks about the virtu of generosity. One of his points against soci eties that eliminate private ownership is tha they have thereby done away with the oppor tunity for generous action, which requires hav ing possessions of one's own to give to others. This sort of remark is tailor-made for th objector, who will immediately say that gener osity, if it really rests upon the experienc of private possession, is a dubious candidat indeed for inclusion in a purportedly non relative account of the human virtues. If rests upon a "grounding experience" that on-necessary and is capable of being evaluated in different ways, and of being either included or eliminated in accordance with that valuation, then it is not the universal the Aristotelian said it was.

Some objectors of the third kind will stop at this point, or use such observations to support the second objector's relativism. But in another prominent form this argument takes a non-relativist direction. It asks us to assess the "grounding experiences" against an account of human flourishing, produced in some independent manner. If we do so, the objector urges, we will discover that some of the experiences are remediable deficiencies. The objection to Aristotelian virtue ethics will then be that it limits our social aspirations, getting us to regard as permanent and necessary what we might in fact improve to the benefit of all human life. This is the direction in which the third objection to the virtues was pressed by Karl Marx, its most famous proponent.[9] According to Marx's argument, a number of the leading bourgeois virtues are responses to defective relations of production. Bourgeois justice, generosity, etc. presuppose conditions and structures that are non-ideal and that will be eliminated when communism is achieved. And it is not only the current *specification* of these virtues that will be superceded with the removal of deficiency. It is the virtues themselves. It is in this sense that communism leads human beings beyond ethics.

Thus the Aristotelian is urged to inquire into the basic structures of human life with the daring of a radical political imagination. It is claimed that when she does so she will see that human life contains more possibilities than are dreamed of in her list of virtues.

V

Each of these objections is profound. To answer any one of them adequately would require a treatise. But we can still do something at this point to map out an Aristotelian response to each one, pointing the direction in which a fuller reply might go.

The first objector is right to insist on the distinction between singleness of framework and singleness of answer, and right, again, to

stress that in constructing a debate about the virtues based on the demarcation of certain spheres of experience we have not yet answered any of the "What is X?" questions that this debate will confront. We have not even said very much about the structure of the debate itself, beyond its beginnings – about how it will both use and criticize traditional beliefs, how it will deal with conflicting beliefs, how it will move critically from the "way of one's ancestors" to the "good" – in short, about whose judgments it will trust. [. . .]. At this point, [. . .] we can make four observations to indicate how the Aristotelian might deal with some of the objector's concerns here. First, the Aristotelian position that I wish to defend need not insist, in every case, on a single answer to the request for a specification of a virtue. The answer might well turn out to be a disjunction. The process of comparative and critical debate will, I imagine, eliminate numerous contenders – for example, the view of justice that prevailed in Cyme. But what remains might well be a (probably small) plurality of acceptable accounts. These accounts may or may not be capable of being subsumed under a single account of greater generality. Success in the eliminative task will still be no trivial accomplishment. For example, if we should succeed in ruling out conceptions of the proper attitude to one's own human worth that are based on a notion of original sin, this would be moral work of enormous significance, even if we got no further than that in specifying the positive account.

Second, the general answer to a "What is X?" question in any sphere may well be susceptible of several or even of many concrete specifications, in connection with other local practices and local conditions. For example, the normative account where friendship and hospitality are concerned is likely to be extremely general, admitting of many concrete "fillings." Friends in England will have different customs, where regular social visiting is concerned, from friends in ancient Athens. And yet both sets of customs can count as further specifications of a general account of friendship that mentions, for example, the Aristotelian criteria of mutual benefit and well-wishing, mutual enjoyment, mutual awareness, a shared conception of the good, and some form of "living together." Sometimes we may want to view such concrete accounts as optional alternative specifications, to be chosen by a society on the basis of reasons of ease and convenience. Sometimes, on the other hand, we may want to insist that this account gives the only legitimate specification of the virtue in question for that concrete context; in that case, the concrete account could be viewed as a part of a longer or fuller version of the single normative account. The decision between these two ways of regarding it will depend upon our assessment of its degree of non-arbitrariness for its context (both physical and historical), its relationship to other non-arbitrary features of the moral conception of that context, and so forth.

Third, whether we have one or several general accounts of a virtue, and whether this account or these accounts do or do not admit of more concrete specifications relative to ongoing cultural contexts, the particular choices that the virtuous person, under this conception, makes will always be a matter of being keenly responsive to the local features of his or her concrete context. So in this respect, again, the instructions the Aristotelian gives to the person of virtue do not differ from one part of what a relativist would recommend. The Aristotelian virtues involve a delicate balancing between general rules and the keen awareness of particulars, in which process, as Aristotle stresses, the perception of the particular takes priority. It takes priority in the sense that a good rule is a good summary of wise particular choices and not a court of last resort. Like rules in medicine and in navigation, ethical rules should be held open to modification in the light of new circumstances; and the good agent must therefore cultivate the ability to perceive and correctly describe his or her situation finely and truly, including in this perceptual grasp even those features of the situation that are not covered under the existing rule. [. . .]

What I want to stress here is that Aristotelian particularism is fully compatible with Aristotelian objectivity. The fact that a good and virtuous decision is context-sensitive does not imply that it is right only *relative to*, or *inside*, a limited context, any more than the fact that

a good navigational judgment is sensitive to particular weather conditions shows that it is correct only in a local or relational sense. It is right absolutely, objectively, from anywhere in the human world, to attend to the particular features of one's context; and the person who so attends and who chooses accordingly is making, according to Aristotle, the humanly correct decision, period. If another situation ever should arise with all the same morally relevant features, including contextual features, the same decision would again be absolutely right.

Thus the virtue-based morality can capture a great deal of what the relativist is after and still lay claim to objectivity. In fact, we might say that the Aristotelian virtues do better than the relativist virtues in explaining what people are actually doing when they scrutinize the features of their context carefully, looking at both the shared and the non-shared features with an eye to what is best. For as Aristotle says, people who do this are usually searching for the good, not just for the way of their ancestors. They are prepared to defend their decisions as good or right, and to think of those who advocate a different course as disagreeing about what is right, not just narrating a different tradition.

Finally, we should point out that the Aristotelian virtues, and the deliberations they guide, unlike some systems of moral rules, remain always open to revision in the light of new circumstances and new evidence. In this way, again, they contain the flexibility to local conditions that the relativist would desire but, again, without sacrificing objectivity. Sometimes the new circumstances may simply give rise to a new concrete specification of the virtue as previously defined; in some cases it may cause us to change our view about what the virtue itself is. All general accounts are held provisionally, as summaries of correct decisions and as guides to new ones. This flexibility, built into the Aristotelian procedure, will again help the Aristotelian account to answer the questions of the relativist, without relativism.

VI

We must now turn to the second objection. Here, I believe, is the really serious threat to he Aristotelian position. Past writers on virtue, including Aristotle himself, have lacked sensitivity to the ways in which different traditions of discourse, different conceptual schemes, articulate the world, and also to the profound connections between the structure of discourse and the structure of experience itself. Any contemporary defense of the Aristotelian position must display this sensitivity, responding somehow to the data that the relativist historian or anthropologist brings forward.

The Aristotelian should begin, it seems to me, by granting that with respect to any complex matter of deep human importance there is no "innocent eye" – no way of seeing the world that is entirely neutral and free of cultural shaping. The work of philosophers such as Putnam, Goodman, and Davidson[10] – following, one must point out, from the arguments of Kant and, I believe, from those Aristotle himself – have shown convincingly that even where sense-perception is concerned, the human mind is an active and interpretive instrument and that its interpretations are a function of its history and its concepts, as well as of its innate structure. The Aristotelian should also grant, it seems to me, that the nature of human world-interpretations is holistic and that the criticism of them must, equally well, be holistic. Conceptual schemes, like languages, hang together as whole structures, and we should realize, too, that a change in any single element is likely to have implications for the system as a whole.

But these two facts do not imply, as some relativists in literary theory and in anthropology tend to assume, that all world interpretations are equally valid and altogether non-comparable, that there are no good standards of assessment and "anything goes." The rejection of the idea of ethical truth as correspondence to an altogether uninterpreted reality does not imply that the whole idea of searching for the truth is an old-fashioned error. Certain ways in which people see the world can still be criticized exactly as Aristotle criticized them: as stupid, pernicious, and false. The standards used in such criticisms must come from inside human life. (Frequently they will come from the society in question itself, from its own rationalist and critical traditions.) And the inquirer must attempt, prior to criticism, to develop an inclusive understanding of the conceptual scheme being criticized, seeing what motivates each of its parts and how they hang together. But there is so far no reason to think that the critic will not be able to reject the institution of slavery or the homicide law of Cyme as out of line with the conception of virtue that emerges from reflection on the variety of different ways in which human cultures have had the experiences that ground the virtues.

The "grounding experiences" will not, the Aristotelian should concede, provide precisely a single language – neutral bedrock on which an account of virtue can be straightforwardly and unproblematically based. The description and assessment of the ways in which different cultures have constructed these experiences will become one of the central tasks of Aristotelian philosophical criticism. But the relativist has, so far, shown no reasons why we could not, at the end of the day, say that certain ways of conceptualizing death are more in keeping with the totality of our evidence and with the totality of our wishes for flourishing life than others; that certain ways of experiencing appetitive desire are for similar reasons more promising than others.

Relativists tend, furthermore, to understate the amount of attunement, recognition, and overlap that actually obtains across cultures, particularly in the areas of the grounding experiences. The Aristotelian in developing her conception in a culturally sensitive way, should insist, as Aristotle himself does, upon the evidence of such attunement and recognition. Despite the evident differences in the specific cultural shaping of the grounding experiences, we do recognize the experiences of people in other cultures as similar to our own. We do converse with them about matters of deep importance, understand them, allow ourselves to be moved by them. When we read Sophocles' *Antigone*, we see a good deal that seems strange to us; and we have not read the play well if we do not notice how far its conceptions of death, womanhood, and so on differ from our own. But it is still possible for us to be moved by the drama, to care about its people, to regard their debates as reflections upon virtue that speak to our own experience, and their choices as choices in spheres of conduct in which we too must choose. Again, when one sits down at a table with people from other parts of the world and debates with them concerning hunger or just distribution or in general the quality of human life, one does find, in spite of evident conceptual differences, that it is possible to proceed as if we are all talking about the same human problem; and it is usually only in a context in which one or more of the parties is intellectually committed to a theoretical relativist position that this discourse proves impossible to sustain. This sense of community and overlap seems to be especially strong in the areas that we have called the areas of the grounding experiences. And this, it seems, supports the Aristotelian claim that those experiences can be a good starting point for ethical debate.

Furthermore, it is necessary to stress that hardly any cultural group today is as focused upon its own internal traditions and as isolated from other cultures as the relativist argument presupposes. Cross-cultural communication and debate are ubiquitous facts of contemporary life. Our experience of cultural interaction indicates that in general the inhabitants of different conceptual schemes do tend to view their interaction in the Aristotelian and not the relativist way. A traditional society, confronted with new technologies and sciences, and the conceptions that go with them, does not, in fact, simply fail to understand them or regard them as totally alien incursions upon a hermetically sealed way of life. Instead, it assesses the new item as a possible contributor to flourishing life, making it comprehensible to itself and incorporating elements that promise to solve problems of flourishing. Examples of such assimilation, and the debate that surrounds it, suggest that the parties do, in fact, recognize common problems and that the traditional society is perfectly capable of viewing an external innovation as a device to solve a problem that it shares with the innovating society. The parties do, in fact, search for the good, not the way of their ancestors; only traditionalist anthropologists insist, nostalgically, on the absolute preservation of the ancestral.

And this is so even when cross-cultural discourse reveals a difference at the level of the conceptualization of the grounding experiences. Frequently the effect of work like Foucault's, which reminds us of the non-necessary and non-universal character of one's own ways of seeing in some such area, is precisely to prompt a critical debate in search of the human good. It is difficult, for example, to read Foucault's observations about the history of our sexual ideas without coming to feel that certain ways in which the Western contemporary debate on these matters has been organized, as a result of some combination of Christian morality with nineteenth-century pseudo-science, are especially silly, arbitrary, and limiting, inimical to a human search for flourishing. Foucault's moving account of Greek culture, as he himself insists in a preface,[11] provides not only a sign that someone once thought differently, but also evidence that it is possible for *us* to think differently. Foucault announced that the purpose of his book was to "free thought" so that it could think differently, imagining new and more fruitful possibilities. And close analysis of spheres of cultural discourse, which stresses cultural differences in the spheres of the grounding experiences, is being combined, increasingly, in current debates about sexuality and related matters, with the critique of existing social arrangements and attitudes, and with the elaboration of a new norm of human flourishing. There is no reason to think this combination incoherent.

As we pursue these possibilities, the basic spheres of experience identified in the Aristotelian approach will no longer, we have said, be seen as spheres of *uninterpreted* experience. But we have also insisted that there is much family relatedness and much overlap among societies. And certain areas of relatively greater universality can be specified here, on which we should insist as we proceed to areas that are more varied in their cultural expression. Not without a sensitive awareness that we are speaking of something that is experienced differently in different contexts, we can nonetheless identify certain features of our common humanity closely related to Aristotle's original list, from which our debate might proceed.

Mortality. No matter how death is understood, all human beings face it and (after a certain age) know that they face it. This fact shapes every aspect of more or less every human life.

The Body. Prior to any concrete cultural shaping, we are born with human bodies, whose possibilities and vulnerabilities do not as such belong to one culture rather than any other. Any given human being might have belonged to any culture. The experience of the body is culturally influenced; but the body itself, prior to such experience, provides limits and parameters that ensure a great deal of overlap in what is going to be experienced, where hunger, thirst, desire, the five senses are concerned. It is all very well to point to the cultural component in these experiences. But when one spends time considering issues of hunger and scarcity, and in general of human misery, such differences appear relatively small and refined, and one cannot fail to acknowledge that "there are no known ethnic differences in human physiology with respect to metabolism of nutrients. Africans and Asians do not burn their dietary calories or use their dietary protein any differently from Europeans and Americans. It follows then that dietary requirements cannot vary widely as between different races."[12] This and similar facts should surely be focal points for debate about appropriate human behavior in this sphere. And by beginning with the body, rather than with the subjective experience of desire, we get, furthermore, an opportunity to criticize the situation of people who are so persistently deprived that their *desire* for good things has actually decreased. This is a further advantage of the Aristotelian approach, when contrasted with approaches to choice that stop with subjective expressions of preference.

Pleasure and pain. In every culture, there is a conception of pain; and these conceptions, which overlap very largely with one another, can be plausibly seen as grounded in universal and pre-cultural experience. The Stoic story of infant development is highly implausible; the negative response to bodily pain is surely primitive and universal, rather than learned and optional, however much its specific "grammar" may be shaped by later learning.

4. *Cognitive capability.* Aristotle's famous claim that "all human beings by nature reach out for understanding"[13] seems to stand up to the most refined anthropological analysis. It points to an element in our common humanity that is plausibly seen, again, as grounded independently of particular acculturation, however much it is later shaped by acculturation.

5. *Practical reason.* All human beings, whatever their culture, participate (or try to) in the planning and managing of their lives, asking and answering questions about how one should live and act. This capability expresses itself differently in different societies, but a being who altogether lacked it would not be likely to be acknowledged as a human being, in any culture.

6. *Early infant development.* Prior to the greatest part of specific cultural shaping, though perhaps not free from all shaping, are certain areas of human experiences and development that are broadly shared and of great importance for the Aristotelian virtues: experiences of desire, pleasure, loss, one's own finitude, perhaps also of envy, grief, gratitude. One may argue about the merits of one or another psychoanalytical account of infancy. But it seems difficult to deny that the work of Freud on infant desire and of Klein on grief, loss, and other more complex emotional attitudes has identified spheres of human experience that are to a large extent common to all humans, regardless of their particular society. All humans begin as hungry babies, perceiving their own helplessness, their alternating closeness to and distance from those on whom they depend, and so forth. Melanie Klein records a conversation with an anthropologist in which an event that at first looked (to Western eyes) bizarre was interpreted by Klein as the expression of a universal pattern of mourning. The anthropologist accepted her interpretation.[14]

7. *Affiliation.* Aristotle's claim that human beings as such feel a sense of fellowship with other human beings, and that we are by nature social animals, is an empirical claim, but it seems to be a sound one. However varied our specific conceptions of friendship and love are, there is a great point in seeing them as overlapping expressions of the same family of shared human needs and desires.

8. *Humor.* There is nothing more culturally varied than humor, and yet, as Aristotle insists, some space for humor and play seems to be a need of any human life. The human being was not called the "laughing animal" for nothing; it is certainly one of our salient differences from almost all animals, and (in some form or other) a shared feature, I somewhat boldly assert, of any life that is going to be counted as fully human.

This is just a list of suggestions, closely related to Aristotle's list of common experiences. One could subtract some of these items and/or add others. But it seems plausible to claim that in all these areas we have a basis for further work on the human good. We do not have a bedrock of completely uninterpreted "given" data, but we do have nuclei of experience around which the construction of different societies proceed. There is no Archimedean point here, and no pure access to unsullied "nature" – even, here, human nature – as it is in and of itself. There is just human life as it is lived. But in life as it is lived, we do find a family of experiences, clustering around certain foci, which can provide reasonable starting points for cross-cultural reflection.

VII

The third objection raises, at bottom, a profound conceptual question: What is it to inquire about the *human* good? What circumstances of existence go to define what it is to live the life of a *human being*, and not some other life? Aristotle likes to point out that an inquiry into the human good cannot, on pain of incoherence, end up describing the good of some other being, say a god, a good, that on account of our circumstances, it is impossible for us to attain (cf. *NE* 1159a10–12, 1166a18–23). Which circumstances then? The virtues are defined relatively to certain problems and limitations, and also to certain endowments. Which ones are sufficiently central that their removal would make us into different beings and open up a wholly new and different debate about the good? This question is itself part of the ethical debate we propose. For there is no way to answer it but ask ourselves which elements of our experience seem to us so important that they count, for us, as part of who we are. I discuss Aristotle's attitude to this question elsewhere, and I shall simply summarize here.[15] It seems clear, first of all, that our mortality is an essential feature of our circumstances as human beings. An immortal being would have such a different form of life, and such different values and virtues, that it does not seem to make sense to regard that being as part of the same search for good. Essential, too, will be our dependence upon the world outside of us: some sort of need for food, drink, the help of others. On the side of abilities, we would want to include cognitive functioning and the activity of practical reasoning as elements of any life that we would regard as human. Aristotle argues, plausibly, that we would want to include sociability as well, some sensitivity to the needs of and pleasure in the company of other beings similar to ourselves.

But it seems to me that the Marxian question remains, as a deep question about human forms of life and the search for the human good. For one certainly can imagine forms of human life that do not contain the holding of private property – and, therefore, not those virtues that have to do with its proper management. And this means that it remains an open question whether these virtues ought to be regarded as virtues, and kept upon our list. Marx wished to go much further, arguing that communism would remove the need for justice, courage, and most of the bourgeois virtues. I think we might be skeptical here. Aristotle's general attitude to such transformations of life is to suggest that they usually have a tragic dimension. If we remove one sort of problem – say, by removing private property we frequently do so by introducing another – say, the absence of a certain sort of freedom of choice, the freedom that makes it possible to do fine and generous actions for others. If things are complex even in the case of generosity, where we can rather easily imagine the transformation that removes the virtue, they are surely far more so in the cases of justice and courage. And we would need a far more detailed description than Marx ever gives us of the form of life under communism, before we would be able even to begin to see whether this form of life has in fact transformed things where these virtues are concerned, and whether it has or has not introduced new problems and limitations in their place.

In general it seems that all forms of life, including the imagined life of a god, contain boundaries and limits. All structures, even that of putative limitlessness, are closed to something, cut off from something – say, in that case, from the specific value and beauty inherent

in the struggle against limitation. Thus it does not appear that we will so easily get beyond the virtues. Nor does it seem to be so clearly a good thing for human life that we should.

VIII

The best conclusion to this sketch of an Aristotelian program for virtue ethics was written by Aristotle himself, at the end of his discussion of human nature in *Nicomachean Ethics* I:

> So much for our outline sketch for the good. For it looks as if we have to draw an outline first, and fill it in later. It would seem to be open to anyone to take things further and to articulate the good parts of the sketch. And time is a good discoverer or ally in such things. That's how the sciences have progressed as well: it is open to anyone to supply what is lacking. (*NE* 1098a20–26)

Notes

1. A. MacIntyre, *After Virtue* (Notre Dame, IN, 1981); P. Foot, *Virtues and Vices* (Los Angeles, 1978); B. Williams, *Ethics and the Limits of Philosophy* (Cambridge, MA, 1985) and Tanner Lectures, Harvard, 1983. See also M. Walzer, *Spheres of Justice* (New York, 1983) and Tanner Lectures, Harvard, 1985.

2. For "nameless" virtues and vices, see *NE* 1107b1–2, 1107b8, 1107b30–31, 1108a17, 1119a10–11, 1126b20, 1127a12, 1127a14; for recognition of the unsatisfactoriness of names given, see 1107b8, 1108a5–6, 1108a20 ff. The two categories are largely overlapping, on account of the general principles enunciated at 1108a16–19, that where there is no name a name should be given, unsatisfactory or not.

3. *Posterior Analytics*, 2.8, 93a21 ff.

4. Heraclitus, fragment DK B23; see Nussbaum, "*Psuche* in Heraclitus, II," *Phronesis* 17(1972): 153–70.

5. See *Politics* 1.2. 1253a1–18; that discussion does not deny the virtues to gods explicitly, but this denial is explicit at *NE* 1145a25–7 and 1178 b10 ff.

6. 1108a5, where Aristotle says that the virtues and the corresponding person are "pretty much nameless," and says "Let us call . . ." when he

introduces the names. See also 1125b29, 1126a3–4.

7. See, for example, *The Social Construction of the Emotions*, edited by Rom Harré (Oxford, 1986).

8. *Politics* 1263b11 ff.

9. For a discussion of the relevant passages, see S. Lukes, *Marxism and Morality* (Oxford, 1987). For an acute discussion of these issues I am indebted to an exchange between Alan Ryan and Stephen Lukes at the Oxford Philosophical Society, March 1987.

10. See H. Putnam, *Reason, Truth, and History* (Cambridge, 1981); *The Many Faces of Realism*, The Carus Lectures, forthcoming; and *Meaning and the Moral Sciences* (London, 1979); N. Goodman, *Languages of Art* (Indianapolis, 1968) and *Ways of World-Making* (Indianapolis, 1978); D. Davidson, *Inquiries into Truth and Interpretation* (Oxford, 1984).

11. Foucault, *Histoire de la Sexualité*, vol. 2, preface.

12. C. Gopalan, "Undernutrition: Measurement and Implications," paper prepared for the WIDER Conference on Poverty, Undernutrition, and Living Standards, Helsinki, 27–31 July 1987, in Osmani, S. R. *Nutrition and Poverty* (Oxford, 1992).

13. *Metaphysics* 1.1.
14. M. Klein, in Postscript to "Our Adult World and Its Roots in Infancy," in *Envy, Gratitude and Other Works 1946–1963* (London, 1984), 247–63.

15. "Aristotle on Human Nature and the Foundation of Ethics," in Altham, J. E. and Harrison, R. *World Mind and Ethics: Essays on the Ethical Philosophy of Bernard Williams* (Cambridge, 1995). This paper will be a WIDER Working Paper.

CHAPTER 68
Normative Virtue Ethics

ROSALIND HURSTHOUSE

A common belief concerning virtue ethics is that it does not tell us what we should do. This belief is sometimes manifested merely in the expressed assumption that virtue ethics, in being 'agent-centred' rather than 'act-centred', is concerned with Being rather than Doing, with good (and bad) character rather than right (and wrong) action, with the question 'What sort of person should I be?' rather than the question 'What should I do?' On this assumption, 'virtue ethics' so-called does not figure as a normative rival to utilitarian and deontological ethics; rather, its (fairly) recent revival is seen as having served the useful purpose of reminding moral philosophers that the elaboration of a normative theory may fall short of giving a full account of our moral life. Thus prompted, deontologists have turned to Kant's long neglected 'Doctrine of Virtue', and utilitarians, largely abandoning the old debate about rule- and act-utilitarianism, are showing interest in the general-happiness-maximizing consequences of inculcating such virtues as friendship, honesty, and loyalty.

On this assumption, it seems that philosophers who 'do virtue ethics', having served this purpose, must realize that they have been

doing no more than supplementing normative theory, and should now decide which of the two standard views they espouse. Or, if they find that too difficult, perhaps they should confine themselves to writing detailed studies of particular virtues and vices, indicating where appropriate that 'a deontologist would say that an agent with virtue X will characteristically . . . , whereas a utilitarian would say that she will characteristic-ally . . . ' But anyone who wants to espouse virtue ethics as a rival to deontological or utilitarian ethics (finding it distinctly bizarre to suppose that Aristotle espoused either of the latter) will find this common belief voiced against her as an objection: 'Virtue ethics does not, because it cannot, tell us what we should do. Hence it cannot be a normative rival to deontology and utilitarianism.'

This paper is devoted to defending virtue ethics against this objection.

1. Right Action

What grounds might someone have for believing that virtue ethics cannot tell us what we should do? It seems that sometimes the ground is no more than the claim that virtue ethics is concerned with good (and bad) character rather than right (and wrong) action. But that claim does no more than highlight an interesting contrast between virtue ethics on the one

Rosalind Hursthouse, "Normative Virtue Ethics," pp. 19–33 from Roger Crisp (ed.), *How Should One Live?*. Oxford: Oxford University Press, 1996.

hand, and deontology and utilitarianism on the other; the former is agent-centred, the latter (it is said) are act-centred. It does not entail that virtue ethics has nothing to say about the concept of right action, nor about which actions are right and which wrong. Wishing to highlight a different contrast, the one between utilitarianism and deontology, we might equally well say, 'Utilitarianism is concerned with good (and bad) states of affairs rather than right (and wrong) action', and no one would take that to mean that utilitarianism, unlike deontology, had nothing to say about right action, for what utilitarianism does say is so familiar.

Suppose an act-utilitarian laid out her account of right action as follows:

U1. An action is right iff it promotes the best consequences.

This premiss provides a specification of right action, forging the familiar utilitarian link between the concepts of *right action* and *best consequences*, but gives one no guidance about how to act until one knows what to count as the best consequences. So these must be specified in a second premiss, for example:

U2. The best consequences are those in which happiness is maximized,

which forges the familiar utilitarian link between the concepts of *best consequences* and *happiness*.

Many different versions of deontology can be laid out in a way that displays the same basic structure. They begin with a premiss providing a specification of right action:

D1. An action is right iff it is in accordance with a correct moral rule or principle.

Like the first premiss of act-utilitarianism, this gives one no guidance about how to act until, in this case, one knows what to count as a correct moral rule (or principle). So this must be specified in a second premiss which begins

D2. A correct moral rule (principle) is one that . . . ,

and this may be completed in a variety of ways for example:

(i) is on the following list (and then a list does follow)

or

(ii) is laid on us by God

or

(iii) is universalizable

or

(iv) would be the object of choice of all rational beings and so on.

Although this way of laying out fairly familiar versions of utilitarianism and deontology is hardly controversial, it is worth noting that it suggests some infelicity in the slogan 'Utilitarianism begins with (or takes as its fundamental concept etc.) the Good, whereas deontology begins with the Right.' If the concept a normative ethics 'begins with' is the one it uses to specify right action, then utilitarianism might be said to begin with the Good (if we take this to be the 'same' concept as that of the *best*), but we should surely hasten to add 'but only in relation to consequences; not, for instance, in relation to *good* agents, or to living *well*'. And even then, we shall not be able to go on to say that most versions of deontology 'begin with' the Right, for they use the concept of moral rule or principle to specify right action. [. . .]

And if the dictum is supposed to single out, rather vaguely, the concept which is 'most important', then the concepts of *consequences* or *happiness* seem as deserving of mention as the concept of the Good for utilitarianism, and what counts as most important (if any one concept does) for deontologists would surely vary from case to case. For some it would be God, for others universalizability, for others the Categorical Imperative, for others rational acceptance, and so on.

It is possible that too slavish an acceptance of this slogan, and the inevitable difficulty of finding a completion of 'and virtue ethics begins with . . . ' which does not reveal its inadequacy, has contributed to the belief that virtue ethics cannot provide a specification of right action. I have heard people say, 'Utilitarianism defines the Right in terms of the Good, and deontology defines the Good in terms of the Right; but how can virtue ethics possibly define both in terms of the (virtuous) Agent?', and indeed, with no answer forthcoming to the questions Good *what*? Right *what*?', I have no idea. But if the question is 'How can virtue ethics specify right action?', the answer is easy:

V1. An action is right iff it is what a virtuous agent would characteristically (i.e. acting in character) do in the circumstances.

This specification rarely, if ever, silences those who maintain that virtue ethics cannot tell us what we should do. On the contrary, it tends to provoke irritable laughter and scorn. '*That's* no use', the objectors say. 'It gives us no guidance whatsoever. Who are the virtuous agents?' But if the failure of the first premiss of a normative ethics which forges a link between the concept of right action and a concept distinctive of that ethics may provoke scorn because it provides no practical guidance, why not direct a similar scorn at the first premisses of act-utilitarianism and deontology in the form in which I have given them? Of each of them I remarked, apparently *en passant* but with intent, that they gave us no guidance. Utilitarianism must specify what are to count as the best consequences, and deontology what is to count as a correct moral rule, producing a second premiss, before any guidance is given. And similarly, virtue ethics must specify who is to count as a virtuous agent. So far, the three are all in the same position.

Of course, if the virtuous agent can only be specified as an agent disposed to act in accordance with moral rules, as some have assumed, then virtue ethics collapses back into deontology and is no rival to it. So let us add a subsidiary premiss to this skeletal outline, with the intention of making it clear that virtue ethics aims to provide a non-deontological specification of the virtuous agent via a specification of the virtues, which will be given in its second premiss:

V1a. A virtuous agent is one who acts virtuously, that is, one who has and exercises the virtues.

V2. A virtue is a character trait that . . .

This second premiss of virtue ethics might, like the second premiss of some versions of deontology, be completed simply by enumeration ('a virtue is one of the following', and then the list is given). Or we might, not implausibly, interpret the Hume of the second *Enquiry* as espousing virtue ethics. According to him, a virtue is a character trait (of human beings) that is useful or agreeable to its possessor or to others (inclusive 'or' both times). The standard neo-Aristotelian completion claims that a virtue is a character trait a human being needs for *eudaimonia*, to flourish or live well.

Here, then, we have a specification of right action, whose structure closely resembles those of act-utilitarianism and many forms of deontology. Given that virtue ethics can come up with such a specification, can it still be maintained that it, unlike utilitarianism and deontology, cannot tell us what we should do? Does the specification somehow fail to provide guidance in a way that the other two do not?

At this point, the difficulty of identifying the virtuous agent in a way that makes V1 action-guiding tends to be brought forward again. Suppose it is granted that deontology has just as much difficulty in identifying the correct moral rules as virtue ethics has in identifying the virtues and hence the virtuous agent. Then the following objection may be made.

'All the same,' it may be said, 'if we imagine that that has been achieved – perhaps simply by enumeration – deontology yields a set of clear prescriptions which are readily applicable ("Do not lie", "Do not steal", "Do not inflict evil or harm on others", "Do help others", "Do keep promises", etc.). But virtue ethics yields only the prescription "Do what the virtuous agent (the one who is honest, charitable, just, etc.) would do in these circumstances." And this gives me no guidance unless I am (and know I am) a virtuous agent myself (in which case I am hardly in need of it). If I am less than fully virtuous, I shall have no idea what a virtuous agent would do, and hence cannot apply the only prescription that virtue ethics has given me. (Of course, act-utilitarianism also yields a single prescription, "Do what maximises happiness", but there are no *parallel* difficulties in applying that.) So there is the way in which V1 fails to be action-guiding where deontology and utilitarianism succeed.'

It is worth pointing out that, if I acknowledge that I am far from perfect, and am quite unclear what a virtuous agent would do in the circumstances in which I find myself, the obvious thing to do is to go and ask one, should this be possible. This is far from being a trivial point, for it gives a straightforward explanation of an aspect of our moral life which should not be ignored, namely the fact that we do seek moral guidance from people who we think are morally better than ourselves. When I am looking for an excuse to do something I have a horrid suspicion is wrong, I ask my moral inferiors (or peers if I am bad enough), 'Wouldn't you do such and such if you were in my shoes?' But when I am anxious to do what is right, and do not see my way clear, I go to people I respect and admire – people who I think are kinder, more honest, more just, wiser, than I am myself – and ask them what they would do in my circumstances. How utilitarianism and deontology would explain this fact, I do not know; but, as I said, the explanation within the terms of virtue ethics is straightforward. If you want to do what is right, and doing what is right is doing what a virtuous agent would do in the circumstances, then you should find out what she would do if you do not already know.

Moreover, seeking advice from virtuous people is not the only thing an imperfect agent trying to apply the single prescription of virtue ethics can do. For it is simply false that, in general, 'if I am less than fully virtuous, then I shall have no idea what a virtuous agent would do', as the objection claims. Recall that we are assuming that the virtues have been enumerated, as the deontologist's rules have been. The latter have been enumerated as, say, 'Do not lie', 'Do not inflict evil or harm', etc.; the former as, say, honesty, charity, justice, etc. So, *ex hypothesi*, a virtuous agent is one who is honest, charitable, just, etc. So what she characteristically does is act honestly, charitably, justly, etc., and not dishonestly, uncharitably, unjustly. So given an enumeration of the virtues, I may well have a perfectly good idea of what the virtuous person would do in my circumstances despite my own imperfection.

Would she lie in her teeth to acquire an unmerited advantage? No, for that would be to act both dishonestly and unjustly. Would she help the naked man by the roadside or pass by on the other side? The former, for she acts charitably. Might she keep a deathbed promise even though living people would benefit from its being broken? Yes, for she acts justly. And so on.

2. Moral Rules

The above response to the objection that V fails to be action-guiding clearly amounts to a denial of the oft-repeated claim that virtue ethics does not come up with any rules (another version of the thought that it is concerned with Being rather than Doing and needs to be supplemented with rules). We can now see that it comes up with a large number; not only does each virtue generate a prescription – act honestly, charitably, justly – but each vice a prohibition – do not act dishonestly, uncharitably, unjustly. Once this point about virtue ethics is grasped (and it is remarkable how often it is overlooked), can there remain any reason for thinking that virtue ethics cannot tell us what we should do? Yes. The reason given is, roughly, that rules such as 'Act honestly', 'Do not act uncharitably', etc. are, like the rule 'Do what the virtuous agent would do', still the wrong sort of rule, still somehow doomed to fail to provide the action guidance supplied by the rules (or rule) of deontology and utilitarianism.

But how so? It is true that these rules of virtue ethics (henceforth 'v-rules') are couched in terms, or concepts, which are certainly 'evaluative' in *some* sense, or senses, of that difficult word. Is it this which dooms them to failure? Surely not, unless many forms of deontology fail too. If we concentrate on the single example of lying, defining lying to be 'asserting what you believe to be untrue, with the intention of deceiving your hearer(s)', then we might, for a moment, preserve the illusion that a deontologist's rules do not contain 'evaluative' terms. But as soon as we remember that few deontologists will want to forgo principles of non-maleficence or beneficence, the lusion vanishes. For those principles, and their corresponding rules ('Do no evil or harm to others', 'Help others', 'Promote their well-being'), rely on terms or concepts which are at least as 'evaluative' as those employed in the v-rules. Few deontologists rest content with the simple quasi-biological 'Do not kill', but more refined versions of that rule such as 'Do not murder', or 'Do not kill the innocent', once again employ 'evaluative' terms, and 'Do not kill unjustly' is itself a particular instantiation of a v-rule.

Supposing this point were granted, a deontologist might still claim that the v-rules are markedly inferior to deontological rules as far as providing guidance for children is concerned. Granted, adult deontologists must think hard about what really constitutes harming someone, or promoting their well-being, or respecting their autonomy, or murder, but surely the simple rules we learnt at our mother's knee are indispensable? How could virtue ethics plausibly seek to dispense with these and expect toddlers to grasp 'Act charitably, honestly, and kindly', 'Don't act unjustly', and so on? Rightly are these concepts described as 'thick'! Far too thick for a child to grasp.

Strictly speaking, this claim about learning does not really support the *general* claim that v-rules fail to provide action-guidance, but the claim about learning, arising naturally as it does in the context of the general claim, is one I am more than happy to address. For it pinpoints a condition of adequacy that any normative ethics must meet, namely that such an ethics must not only come up with action-guidance for a clever rational adult but also generate some account of moral education, of how one generation teaches the next what they should do. But an ethics inspired by Aristotle is unlikely to have forgotten the question of moral education, and the objection fails to hit home. First, the implicit empirical claim that toddlers are taught *only* the deontologist's rules, not the 'thick' concepts, is false. Sentences such as 'Don't do that, it hurts, you mustn't be *cruel*', 'Be *kind* to your brother, he's only little', 'Don't be so *mean*, so *greedy*' are commonly addressed to toddlers. Secondly, why should a proponent of virtue ethics deny the significance of such mother's-knee rules as

'Don't lie', 'Keep promises', 'Don't take more than your fair share', 'Help others'? Although it is a mistake, I have claimed, to define a virtuous agent simply as one disposed to act in accordance with moral rules, it is a very understandable mistake, given the obvious connection between, for example, the exercise of the virtue of honesty and refraining from lying. Virtue ethicists want to emphasize the fact that, if children are to be taught to be honest, they must be taught to prize the truth, and that *merely* teaching them not to lie will not achieve this end. But they need not deny that to achieve this end teaching them not to lie is useful, even indispensable.

So we can see that virtue ethics not only comes up with rules (the v-rules, couched in terms derived from the virtues and vices), but further, does not exclude the more familiar deontologists' rules. The theoretical distinction between the two is that the familiar rules, and their applications in particular cases, are given entirely different backings. According to virtue ethics, I must not tell this lie, since it would be dishonest, and dishonesty is a vice; must not break this promise, since it would be unjust, or a betrayal of friendship, or, perhaps (for the available virtue and vice terms do not neatly cover every contingency), simply because no virtuous person would.

However, the distinction is not merely theoretical. It is, indeed, the case that, with respect to a number of familiar examples, virtue ethicists and deontologists tend to stand shoulder to shoulder against utilitarians, denying that, for example, this lie can be told, this promise broken, this human being killed because the consequences of so doing will be generally happiness-maximizing. But, despite a fair amount of coincidence in action-guidance between deontology and virtue ethics, the latter has its own distinctive approach to the practical problems involved in dilemmas.

3.   The Conflict Problem

It is a noteworthy fact that, in support of the general claim that virtue ethics cannot tell us what we should do, what is often cited is the 'conflict problem'. The requirements of different virtues, it is said, can point us in opposed directions. Charity prompts me to kill the person who would (truly) be better off dead, but justice forbids it. Honesty points to telling the hurtful truth, kindness and compassion to remaining silent or even lying. And so on. So virtue ethics lets us down just at the point where we need it, where we are faced with the really difficult dilemmas and do not know what to do.

In the mouth of a utilitarian, this may be a comprehensible criticism, for, as is well known, the only conflict that classical utilitarianism's one rule can generate is the tiresome logical one between the two occurrences of 'greatest' in its classical statement. But it is strange to find the very same criticism coming from deontologists, who are notoriously faced with the same problem. 'Don't kill', 'Respect autonomy', 'Tell the truth', 'Keep promises' may all conflict with 'Prevent suffering' or 'Do no harm', which is precisely why deontologists so often reject utilitarianism's deliverances on various dilemmas. Presumably, they must think that deontology can solve the 'conflict problem' and, further, that virtue ethics cannot. Are they right?

With respect to a number of cases, the deontologist's strategy is to argue that the 'conflict' is merely apparent, or *prima facie*. The proponent of virtue ethics employs the same strategy: according to her, many of the putative conflicts are merely apparent, resulting from a misapplication of the virtue or vice terms. Does kindness require not telling hurtful truths? Sometimes, but in *this* case, what has to be understood is that one does people no kindness by concealing this sort of truth from them, hurtful as it may be. Or, in a different case, the importance of the truth in question puts the consideration of hurt feelings out of court, and the agent does not show herself to be unkind, or callous, by speaking out. Does charity require that I kill the person who would be better off dead but who wants to stay alive, thereby conflicting with justice? [. . .]

One does not have to agree with the three judgements expressed here to recognize this as a *strategy* available to virtue ethics, any more than one has to agree with the particular judgements of deontologists who, for example, may

claim that one rule outranks another, or that a certain rule has a certain exception clause built in, when they argue that a putative case of conflict is resolvable. Whether an individual has resolved a putative moral conflict or dilemma rightly is one question; whether a normative ethics has the wherewithal to resolve it is an entirely different question, and it is the latter with which we are concerned here.

The form the strategy takes within virtue ethics provides what may plausibly be claimed to be the deep explanation of why, in some cases agents do not know the answer to 'What should I do in these circumstances?' despite the fact that there *is* an answer. Trivially, the explanation is that they lack moral knowledge of what to do in this situation; but why? In what way? The lack, according to virtue ethics strategy, arises from lack of moral wisdom, from an inadequate grasp of what is involved in acting *kindly* (unkindly) or *charitably* (uncharitably), in being *honest*, or *just*, or *lacking in charity*, or, in general, of how the virtue (and vice) terms are to be correctly applied.

Here we come to an interesting defence of the v-rules, often criticized as being too difficult to apply for the agent who lacks moral wisdom. The defence relies on an (insufficiently acknowledged) insight of Aristotle's – namely that moral knowledge, unlike mathematical knowledge, cannot be acquired merely by attending lectures and is not characteristically to be found in people too young to have much experience of life. Now *if* right action were determined by rules that any clever adolescent could apply correctly, how could this be so? Why are there not moral whiz-kids, the way there are mathematical (or quasi-mathematical) whiz-kids? But if the rules that determine right action are, like the v-rules, very difficult to apply correctly, involving, for instance, a grasp of the *sort* of truth that one does people no kindness by concealing, the explanation is readily to hand. Clever adolescents do not, in general, have a good grasp of that sort of thing. And *of course* I have to say 'the sort of truth that . . . ' and 'that sort of thing', relying on my readers' knowledgeable uptake. For if I could define either sort, then, once again, clever adolescents could acquire moral wisdom from textbooks.

So far, I have described one strategy available to virtue ethics for coping with the 'conflict problem', a strategy that consists in arguing that the conflict is merely apparent, and can be resolved. According to one – only one of many – versions of 'the doctrine of the unity of the virtues', this is the only possible strategy (and ultimately successful), but this is not a claim I want to defend. One general reason is that I still do not know what I think about 'the unity of the virtues' (all those different versions!); a more particular, albeit related, reason is that, even if I were (somehow) sure that the requirements of the particular virtues could never conflict, I suspect that I would still believe in the possibility of moral dilemmas. I have been talking so far as though examples of putative dilemmas and examples of putative conflict between the requirements of different virtues (or deontologists' rules) coincided. But it may seem to many, as it does to me, that there are certain (putative) dilemmas which can only be described in terms of (putative) conflict with much artifice and loss of relevant detail.

Let us, therefore, consider the problem of moral dilemmas without bothering about whether they can be described in the simple terms of a conflict between the requirements of two virtues (or two deontologists' rules). Most of us, it may be supposed, have our own favoured example(s), either real or imaginary, of the case (or cases) where we see the decision about whether to do A or B as a very grave matter, have thought a great deal about what can be said for and against doing A, and doing B, and have still not managed to reach a conclusion which we think is the right one. How, if at all, does virtue ethics direct us to think about such cases?

4. Dilemmas and Normative Theory

As a preliminary to answering that question, we should consider a much more general one, namely 'How should any normative ethics direct us to think about such cases?' This brings us to the topic of normative theory.

It is possible to detect a new movement in moral philosophy, a movement which has already attracted the name 'anti-theory in ethics'. Its various representatives have as a common theme the rejection of normative ethical theory; but amongst them are numbered several philosophers usually associated with virtue ethics, [. . .]. This does not mean that they maintain what I have been denying, namely that virtue ethics is not normative; rather, they assume that it does not constitute a normative *theory* (and, mindful of this fact, I have been careful to avoid describing virtue ethics as one). What is meant by a 'normative theory' in this context is not easy to pin down, but, roughly, a normative theory is taken to be a set (possibly one-membered in the case of utilitarianism) of general principles which provide a *decision procedure* for all questions about how to act morally.

Part of the point of distinguishing a normative ethics by calling it a normative 'theory' is that a decent theory, as we know from science, enables us to answer questions that we could not answer before we had it. It is supposed to resolve those difficult dilemmas in which, it is said, our moral intuitions clash, and, prior to our grasp of the theory, we do not know what we should do. And a large part of the motivation for subscribing to 'anti-theory in ethics' is the belief that we should not be looking to science to provide us with our model of moral knowledge. Our 'intuitions' in ethics do not play the same role *vis-à-vis* the systematic articulation of moral knowledge as our 'observations' play *vis-à-vis* the systematic articulation of scientific knowledge; many of the goals appropriate to scientific knowledge – universality, consistency, completeness, simplicity – are not appropriate to moral knowledge; the acquisition of moral knowledge involves the training of the emotions in a way that the acquisition of scientific knowledge does not; and so on.

Clearly, many different issues are involved in the question of the extent to which moral knowledge should be modelled on scientific knowledge. The one I want to focus on here is the issue of whether a normative ethics should provide a decision procedure which enables us to resolve all moral dilemmas. Should it, to rephrase the question I asked above, (1) direct us to think about moral dilemmas in the belief that they *must* have a resolution, and that it is the business of the normative ethics in question to provide one? Or should it (2) have built into it the possibility of there being, as David Wiggins puts it, some 'absolutely undecidable questions – e.g. cases where . . . nothing could count as *the* reasonable practical answer',[1] counting questions about dilemmas of the sort described as amongst them? Or should it (3) be sufficiently flexible to allow for a comprehensible disagreement on this issue between two proponents of the normative ethics in question?

If we are to avoid modelling normative ethics mindlessly on scientific theory, we should not simply assume that the first position is the correct one. But rejection of such a model is not enough to justify the second position either. Someone might believe that for *any* dilemma there must be something that counts as the right way out of it, without believing that normative ethics remotely resembles scientific theory, perhaps because they subscribe to a version of realism. [. . .] More particularly, someone might believe on religious grounds that if I find myself, through no fault of my own, confronted with a dilemma (of the sort described), there must be something that counts as the right way out of it. [. . .] It seems to me that a normative ethics should be able to accommodate such differences, and so I subscribe to the third position outlined above.

Which position utilitarians and deontologists might espouse is not my concern here; I want to make clear how it is that virtue ethics is able to accommodate the third.

Let us return to V1 – 'An action is right iff it is what a virtuous agent would characteristically do in the circumstances.' This makes it clear that if two people disagree about the possibility of irresolvable moral dilemmas, their disagreement will manifest itself in what they say about the virtue of agents. So let us suppose that two candidates for being virtuous agents are each faced with their own case of the same dilemma. (I do not want to defend the view that each situation is unique in such a way that nothing would count as two agents being in the same circumstances and faced with the same dilemma.) And, after much thought, one does A and the other does B.

Now, those who believe that there cannot be irresolvable dilemmas (of the sort described) can say that, in the particular case, at least one agent, say the one who did A, thereby showed themselves to be lacking in virtue, perhaps in that practical wisdom which is an essential aspect of each of the 'non-intellectual' virtues. [. . .] Or they can say that at least one agent must have been lacking in virtue, without claiming to know which.

But those who believe that there are, or may be, irresolvable dilemmas can suppose that both agents are not merely candidates for being, but actually are, virtuous agents. For to believe in such dilemmas is to believe in cases in which even the perfect practical wisdom that the most idealized virtuous agent has does not direct her to do, say, A rather than B. And then the fact that these virtuous agents acted differently, despite being in the same circumstances, *determines* the fact that there is no answer to the question 'What is *the* right thing to do in these circumstances?' For if it is true both that *a* virtuous agent would do A, and that *a* virtuous agent would do B (as it is, since, *ex hypothesi*, one did do A and the other B), then both A and B are, in the circumstances, right, according to V1.

The acceptance of this should not be taken as a counsel of despair, nor as an excuse for moral irresponsibility. It does not license coin-tossing when one is faced with a putative dilemma, for the moral choices we find most difficult do not come to us conveniently labelled as 'resolvable' or 'irresolvable'. I was careful to specify that the two candidates for being virtuous agents acted only 'after much thought'. It will always be necessary to think very hard before accepting the idea that a particular moral decision does not have one right issue, and, even on the rare occasions on which she eventually reached the conclusion that this is such a case, would the virtuous agent toss a coin? Of course not.

No doubt someone will say, 'Well, if she really thinks the dilemma is irresolvable, why not, according to virtue ethics?', and the answer must, I think, be *ad hominem*. *If* their conception of the virtuous agent – of someone with the character traits of justice, honesty, compassion, kindness, loyalty, wisdom, etc. – really is of someone who would resort to coin-tossing when confronted with what she believed to be an irresolvable dilemma, then that is the bizarre conception they bring to virtue ethics, and they must, presumably, think that there is nothing morally irresponsible or light-minded about coin-tossing in such cases. So they should not want virtue ethics to explain 'why not'. But if their conception of the virtuous agent does not admit of her acting thus – if they think such coin-tossing would be irresponsible, or light-minded, or indeed simply insane – then they have no need to ask the question. *My* question was, 'Would the virtuous agent toss a coin?'; they agree that of course she would not. Why not? Because it would be irresponsible, or light-minded, or the height of folly.

The acceptance of the possibility of irresolvable dilemmas within virtue ethics (by those of us who do accept it) should not be seen in itself as conceding much to 'pluralism'. If I say that I can imagine a case in which two virtuous agents are faced with a dilemma, and one does A while the other does B, I am not saying that I am imagining a case in which the two virtuous agents each think that what the other does is wrong (vicious, contrary to virtue) because they have radically different views about what is required by a certain virtue, or about whether a certain character trait is a vice, or about whether something is to be greatly valued or of little importance. I am imagining a case in which my two virtuous agents have the same 'moral views' about everything, up to and including the view that, in this particular case, neither decision is *the* right one, and hence neither is wrong. Each recognizes the propriety of the other's reason for doing what she did – say, 'To avoid *that* evil', 'To secure *this* good' – for her recognition of the fact that this is as good a moral reason as her own (say, 'To avoid *this* evil', 'To secure *that*

good') is what forced each to accept the idea that the dilemma was irresolvable in the first place. Though each can give such a reason for what they did (A in one case, B in the other), neither attempts to give 'the moral reason' why they did one *rather than* the other. The 'reason' for or explanation of *that* would be, if available at all, in terms of psychological autobiography ('I decided to sleep on it, and when I woke up I just found myself thinking in terms of doing A', or 'I just felt terrified at the thought of doing A: I'm sure this was totally irrational, but I did, so I did B').

The topic of this chapter has been the view that virtue ethics cannot be a normative rival to utilitarianism and deontology because 'it cannot tell us what we should do'. In defending the existence of normative virtue ethics I have not attempted to argue that it can 'tell us what we should do' in such a way that the difficult business of acting well is made easy for us. I have not only admitted but welcomed the fact that, in some cases, moral wisdom is required if the v-rules are to be applied correctly and apparent dilemmas thereby resolved (or indeed identified, since a choice that may seem quite straightforward to the foolish or wicked may rightly appear difficult, calling for much thought, to the wise). Nor have I attempted to show that virtue ethics is guaranteed to be able to resolve every dilemma. It seems bizarre to insist that a normative ethics must be able to do this prior to forming a reasonable belief that there cannot be irresolvable dilemmas, but those who have formed such a belief may share a normative ethics with those who have different views concerning realism, or the existence of God. A normative ethics, I suggested, should be able to accommodate both views on this question, as virtue ethics does, not model itself mindlessly on scientific theory.

Note

1. D. Wiggins, 'Truth, Invention and the Meaning of Life', *Proceedings of the British Academy* 62 (1976), 371, my italics.

CHAPTER 69
Agent-Based Virtue Ethics

MICHAEL SLOTE

A tremendous revival of interest in virtue ethics has recently been taking place, but in this paper I would like to discuss some important virtue-ethical possibilities that have yet to be substantially explored. Till now Aristotle has been the principal focus of new interest in virtue ethics, but it is possible to pursue virtue ethics in a more *agent-based* fashion than what we (or some of us) find in Aristotle. I am going to explore that possibility here and attempt to explain why such a more radical approach is not as outré, misconceived, inappropriate, or obviously unpromising as it is sometimes held to be.

1. Agent-Based versus Agent-Focused Virtue Ethics

An agent-based approach to virtue ethics treats the moral or ethical status of acts as entirely derivative from independent and fundamental aretaic (as opposed to deontic) ethical characterizations of motives, character traits, or individuals, and such agent-basing is arguably not to be found in Aristotle, at least on one kind of standard interpretation. To be sure, Aristotle

seems to put a greater emphasis on the evaluation of agents and character traits than he does on the evaluation of actions. Moreover, for Aristotle an act is noble or fine if it is one that a noble or virtuous individual would perform, and he does say that the virtuous individual is the measure of virtue in action. But Aristotle also allows that properly guided or momentarily inspired individuals can perform fine or good or virtuous acts even if the individuals are not themselves good or virtuous, and, in addition, he characterizes the virtuous individual as someone who *sees* or *perceives* what is good or fine or right to do in any given situation.

Such language clearly implies that the virtuous individual does what is noble or virtuous because it is the noble – e.g., courageous – thing to do, rather than its being the case that what is noble – or courageous – to do has this status simply because the virtuous individual will choose or has chosen it. Even if right or fine actions cannot be defined in terms of rules, what makes them right or fine, for Aristotle, is not that they have been chosen in a certain way by a certain sort of individual. So their status as right or fine or noble is treated as in some measure independent of agent-evaluations, and that is incompatible with agent-basing as we defined it just above. (If the virtuous individual is the measure of what is fine or right, that may simply mean that she is in the *best possible*

Michael Slote, "Agent-Based Virtue Ethics," pp. 83–101 from *Midwest Studies in Philosophy*, 20, 1995. Reprinted by permission of the publishers, Blackwell Publishing.

osition *to know or perceive* what is fine or ight.)

Thus we must distinguish a virtue-ethical theory like Aristotle's (as commonly inter-preted), which focuses more on virtuous indi-iduals and individual traits than on actions nd is thus in some sense *agent-focused*, from gent-based views which, unlike Aristotle, treat he moral or ethical status of actions as entirely derivative from independent and fundamental thical aretaic facts (or claims) about the notives, dispositions, or inner life of the indi-viduals who perform them. Views of the latter ind clearly represent an extreme or radical orm of virtue ethics, and indeed it is some-what difficult to find clear-cut historical examples of such agent-basing. I have found s that of the nineteenth-century British ethicist James Martineau. Other potential historical examples of agent-basing – notably, Hume, Leslie Stephen, Nietzsche, Abelard, Augustine, and Kant – offer different forms of resistance to such interpretation, and even Plato, who insists that we evaluate actions by reference to the health and virtue of the individual soul, seems to think that appreciation of the Form of the Good represents a level of evaluation prior to the evaluation of souls, with souls counting as virtuous when properly appreciating and being guided by the value inherent in the Form of the Good. To that extent, Plato's view is not agent-based, but I believe there is a way of freeing the Platonic approach from dependence on the Forms, and the first form of agent-basing I shall be describing has its ultimate inspiration in Plato. The other ways of agent-basing I shall go on to describe can be seen as more plausible simplifying variants on Martineau's moral the-ory. But before I say more about particular ways of developing agent-based virtue theories, there are some very worrying objections to the whole idea of agent-basing that must first be addressed.

2. Two Objections to Agent-Basing

One thing that seems wrong in principle with any agent-based approach to moral evaluation is that it appears to obliterate the common distinction between doing the right thing and doing the right thing for the right reasons. Sidgwick's well-known example of the prosecu-tor who does his duty by trying to convict a defendant, but who is motivated by malice rather than by a sense of duty, seems to illus-trate the distinction in question, and it may well seem that agent-based virtue ethics would have difficulty here because of the way it understands rightness in terms of having good motivations and wrongness in terms of having bad motives. If actions are wrong when they result from morally bad motives, does that not mean that the prosecutor does the wrong thing in prosecuting someone out of malice (assuming that malice is morally criticizable in general or in this particular case)? And isn't that a rather unfortunate consequence of the agent-based approach?

I am not sure. Sidgwick himself seems to grant a certain plausibility to the idea that the prosecutor acts wrongly if he prosecutes from malice. What *is* implausible is merely the claim that the prosecutor has no obligation to pros-ecute, which doesn't follow from the agent-based assumption that he acts wrongly if he prosecutes from malice. Sidgwick of course points out that if he is sufficiently motivated by malice, the prosecutor may be unable to do his duty entirely or even substantially for the right kind of reason. But this merely entails that there is no way the prosecutor who is motivated thus can avoid acting wrongly if he prosecutes. It does not mean it is morally all right for him *not* to prosecute, or thus that he has no duty or obligation to prosecute.

But how can such a duty be understood in agent-based terms? Consider the possibility that *if he does not prosecute*, the prosecutor's motivation will *also* be bad. Those who talk about the malicious prosecutor case often fail to mention the motives that might lead him *not* to prosecute. With malice present or even in the absence of malice, if the prosecutor doesn't prosecute, one very likely explanation will be that he lacks real or strong concern for doing his job and playing the contributing social role which that involves. Imagine, for example, that horrified by his own malice he decides not to prosecute. This too will be motivated by a bad motive, insufficient con-cern for the public (or general human) good or for making his contribution to society – motives I shall have a good deal more to say about in discussing positive versions of agent-based views.

So the idea that motives are the basis for evaluating actions that they cause or that express them doesn't have particularly untoward results. And it allows us something like the distinction between doing the right thing and doing the right thing for the right reason. In particular, it allows us to say that the prosecutor has a duty to prosecute, because if he does not we shall in the normal course (barring a heart attack, nervous breakdown, religious conversion, and such like) be able to attribute to him motivation, or deficient or defective motivation, of a kind that makes his act wrong. Yet we can also say that if he prosecutes, he acts wrongly, even if another person, with different motivation, would have acted rightly in doing so. This allows us then to distinguish between doing one's duty for the right reasons and thus acting rightly, on the one hand, and doing one's duty for the wrong reasons and thus acting wrongly. This is very close to the distinction between right action and acting rightly for the right reasons, except for the fact it supposes that when the reasons aren't right, the action itself is actually *wrong*. But we have already seen that this idea is not in itself particularly implausible. And what we now see is that the above-mentioned complaint against agent-basing boils down to a faulty assumption about the inability of such views to make fine-grained distinctions of the sort we have just succeeded in making.

However, there is another objection to the whole idea of agent-basing that may more fundamentally represent what seems objectionable and even bizarre about any such approach to morality or ethics. If the evaluation of actions ultimately derives from that of (the inner states of) agents, then it would appear to follow that if one is the right sort of person or possesses the right sort of inner states, it doesn't morally matter what one actually *does*, so that the person, or at least her actions, are subject to no genuine moral requirements or constraints. In this light, agent-basing seems a highly autistic and antinomian approach to ethics, an approach that seems to undermine the familiar,

intuitive notion that the moral or ethical life involves, among other things, *living up to* certain *standards* of behavior or action. Such an implication would seem to be totally unacceptable from the standpoint of anyone who takes ethics and the moral life seriously. Indeed, this train of reasoning once caused me to abandon the whole idea of agent-based morality, before I saw that the implications drawn just now do not in fact follow in any way from agent-basing. A view can be agent-based and still not treat actions as right or admirable simply because they are done by a virtuous individual or by someone with an admirable or good inner state. Nor does an agent-based theory have to say, with respect to each and every action a virtuous agent is capable of performing, that if she were to perform that action, it would automatically count as a good or admirable thing for her to have done.

Thus consider a very simple view according to which (roughly) benevolence is the only good motive and acts are right, admirable, or good to the extent they exhibit or express benevolent motivation. (We can also assume actions are wrong or bad if they exhibit the opposite of benevolence or are somehow deficient in benevolence.) To the extent this view treats benevolence as fundamentally and inherently admirable or morally good, it is agent-based; but such a view doesn't entail that the virtuous individual with admirable inner states can simply choose any actions she pleases (among those lying within her power) without the admirability or goodness of her behavior or actions being in any way compromised or diminished. For, assuming only some reasonable form of free-will compatibilism, a benevolent agent is typically *capable* of choosing many actions that *fail to express or exhibit* her benevolence. And if one is not *entirely* or *perfectly* benevolent, then one may well be capable of choosing actions that exhibit the opposite of, or a deficiency in, this motive. Thus if one is benevolent and sees an individual who needs one's help, one may help and, in doing so, exhibit one's benevolence. But it is also presumably within one's power to refuse to help, and if one does, then one's actions won't exhibit benevolence and will presumably be less admirable than they could or would have een otherwise. Of course, the really or perfectly benevolent person will not refuse to help, out the point is that she could, and such refusal and the actions it would give rise to don't count as admirable according to the simplified agent-based view that makes benevolence the touchstone of all moral evaluation.

So it is not true to say that agent-basing entails that what one does doesn't matter morally or that it doesn't matter given that one has a good enough inner character or motivation. The person who expresses and exhibits benevolence in her actions performs actions that, in agent – based terms, can count as ethically superior to other actions she might or could have performed, namely, actions (perhaps including refrainings) that would *not* have expressed or exhibited benevolence. Acts therefore do not count as admirable or virtuous for an agent-based theory of the sort just roughly introduced merely because they are or would be done by someone who in fact is admirable or possessed of admirable motivation; acts have to exhibit, express, or further such motivation, or be such that they *would* exhibit, express, or further such motivation if they occurred, in order to qualify as admirable or virtuous. We may conclude, then, that it is simply not true that agent-based theories inevitably treat human actions as subject to no moral standards or requirements.

In order to avoid wrongdoing, one must (on agent-based theories of the sort just mentioned) avoid actions that exhibit bad or deficient inner motives (one way to do this of course would be to have perfect or univocally good inner motivation). Likewise, in order to be highly admirable, actions must express or further the realization of highly admirable inner motives. So agent-based views clearly allow for agents to be subject to moral requirements or constraints or standards governing their actions. But those requirements, standards, and constraints operate and bind, as it were, *from within*.

But even this metaphor must be taken with caution because it seems to imply that for agent-based views the direction of fit between world and moral agent is all one-way: from agent to world, and this too suggests a kind of autism or isolation from the world that makes

one wonder how any such form of ethics can possibly be plausible or adequate. However, agent-basing does not entail isolation from or the irrelevance of facts about the world; in fact, the kinds of motivation such theories specify as fundamentally admirable invariably wish and need to take the world into account. If one is really benevolent, for example, one doesn't just throw good things around or give them to the first person one sees. Benevolence isn't really benevolence in the fullest sense unless one cares about who exactly is needy and to what extent they are needy, and such care, in turn, essentially involves wanting and making efforts to know relevant facts, so that one's benevolence can be really useful. Thus even if universal benevolence is a ground floor moral value, someone who acts from such a motive must be open to, seek contact with, and be influenced by the world round her – her decisions will not be made in splendid causal and epistemic isolation from what most of us would take to be the morally relevant realities, so the worries mentioned just above really have no foundation.

3. Morality as Inner Strength

Having quelled the charges of autism and antinomianism that it is initially so tempting to launch against agent-basing, I would like now to consider – too briefly, I'm afraid – how agent-based approaches might best be developed in the current climate of ethics. Looking back at the somewhat sparse history of agent-based approaches, it strikes me that there are basically two possible ways in which one may naturally develop the idea of agent-basing: one of them I call "cool," the other "warm." I mentioned earlier that Plato relates the morality of individual actions to the health and virtue of the soul, but in the *Republic* (Book IV) Plato also uses the images of a strong soul and a beautiful soul to convey what he takes to be the inner touchstone of all good human action. And I believe that ideas about health and, especially, strength can serve as the aretaic foundations for one kind of agent-based virtue ethics. Since, in addition, it is natural to wonder how any sort of *humane concern for other people* can be derived from notions like health and strength, agent-based approaches of this first kind can be conveniently classified as "cool."

By contrast, James Martineau's agent-based conception of morality treats compassion as the highest of secular motives, and some of the philosophers who have come closest to presenting agent-based views (Hume, Hutcheson, and now Jorge Garcia) have placed a special emphasis on compassion or, to use a somewhat more general term, *benevolence* as a motive. I believe the latter notion can provide the focus for a second kind of agent-based view (actually, as it turns out, a pair of views) that deserves our attention, and since this second kind of view builds humane concern explicitly into its aretaic foundations, it is natural to think of it as "warm."

Since Plato's discussion of health and strength is older than any discussion of benevolence I know, I would like first to consider agent-basing as anchored in the cool idea of strength. Metaphors of health and strength also play an important role in Stoicism, in Spinoza, and in Nietzsche, though none of these offers a perfectly clear-cut example of an agent-based account of ethics. Still, these views cluster around the same notions that fascinate and influence Plato, and I believe they can naturally be extrapolated to a modern version of Plato's virtue-ethical approach: a genuinely agent-based theory that regards inner strength, in various forms, as the sole foundation for an understanding of the morality of human action.

For Plato, good action is to be understood in terms of the seemingly consequentialistic idea of creating and/or sustaining the strength (or health, etc.) of the soul. But it seems more promising to explore the idea of actions that *express* or *exhibit* inner strength, and so *morality as inner strength*, as it seems natural to call it, will proceed on that basis (without making any appeal to the supposed value of the Forms).

Now the idea that there is something intuitively admirable about being strong inside, something requiring no appeal to or defense from *other ideas*, can perhaps be made more plausible by being more specific about the kinds of inner disposition and motivation I have in mind in speaking of inner strength. What *does not* seem plausible, however, is the idea that any contemporaneously relevant and inclusive morality of human action could be based *solely* in ideas about inner strength. What does inner strength have to do with being kind to people, with not deceiving them, with not harming them? If it does not relate to these sorts of things, it clearly cannot function as a general groundwork for morality.

The same problem comes up in connection with Plato's defense of morality in the *Republic*. The *Republic* begins with the problem of explaining why anyone should be moral or just in the conventional sense of not deceiving, stealing, and the like, but Plato ends up defining justice in terms of the health or strength of the soul and never adequately explains why such a soul would refrain from what are ordinarily regarded as unjust or immoral actions. Even the appeal to the Form of the Good seems just a form of handwaving in connection with these difficulties because even though Plato holds that the healthy soul must be guided by the Good, we are not told enough about the Good to know why it would direct us away from lying and stealing. Doesn't a similar problem arise for any cool agent-based theory appealing fundamentally to the notion of inner strength? It certainly appears to, but perhaps the appearance can be dispelled by pointing out connections between certain kinds of strength and other-regarding morality that have largely gone unnoticed. Let us begin by considering how strength in the form of *self-reliance* gives rise to a concern for the well-being of others.

Most children envy the self-reliance of their parents and want to be like them, rather than continuing to depend on them or others to do things for them. Moreover, the effort to learn to do things for oneself and eventually make one's own way in the world expresses a kind of inner self-sufficiency that we think well of. The contrary desire, which we would call parasitism, is, most of us think, inherently deplorable; someone who willingly remains dependent on others rather than in any substantial degree striking out on her own seems to us pathetic and *weak*. Notice here too that the accusation weak dependency depends more on the motivation than on the abilities of the accused. A person who is *capable* of leaving the family nest but *unwilling* to do so is considered dependent and weak and a parasite *because of his motivation*. The accusation of parasitism doesn't apply to a handicapped person who strives but fails to be entirely self-supporting or to a welfare mother in a similar position. So a morality that bases everything on *inner strength* can say that motivational (as opposed to achieved) self-reliance demonstrates inner strength and self-sufficiency and is thus inherently admirable, whereas motivational parasitism is a form of dependency and inherently weak and deplorable. It can then go on to say that acts that exhibit the one motive are right and even good, whereas those exhibiting the latter are wrong. And having appealed to our aretaic intuitions about strength and self-sufficiency in this way and without recourse to any further arguments, morality as inner strength is thus far at least an example of agent-basing. The admirability of wanting to be independent and not a parasite is not a function of its consequences for anyone's happiness, but, according to the present view, is and can be recognized to be admirable apart from any consequences. To be sure, we think it will have good results if people want to be and succeed in being self-reliant in their lives – they will help themselves and, as we shall shortly see, they will tend to help others too. (I am not assuming that attempts at *total, godlike* self-reliance make any sense for beings with our social and personal needs.) Yet our low opinion of dependent weakness is not based, or solely based, on assumptions about results.

Consider, for example, the courage it takes to face unpleasant facts about oneself or the universe. Self-deception about whether one has cancer may make the end of one's life less miserable and even make things easier for those taking care of one; but still it seems far more admirable to face such facts. Intuitively such courage is not admired for the good it does people, but rather because we find courage, and the inner or personal strength it demonstrates, inherently admirable and in need of no further defense or justification. All arguments, all theories need to start

somewhere in intuitive or convincing assumptions, and in this case it would appear that the admirability of inner strength is a fundamental aretaic assumption of the sort appropriate to agent-basing.

By the same token motivational (as opposed to *achieved*) self-reliance and self-sufficiency seems admirable to us independently of any (further) argument or justification. We admire, for example, a handicapped person who makes persistent but largely unsuccessful efforts to do things for himself and earn his own money, but in such a case those efforts may frustrate and annoy the handicapped individual, and he may be less happy and contented than if he had simply allowed things to be done for him. For all we know, his motivational self-reliance might also do nothing to lift the burden of caring for him from others, and our admiration for such a person as compared with someone with no qualms about taking everything from others is thus not reasonably thought to be based on consequentialistic considerations. Rather, we seem to think of this form of strength and self-sufficiency in the same way we regard the strength to face facts, as something inherently and fundamentally admirable; and so the question now before us is: Just *how much* of our ordinary other-regarding morality can be based in considerations of inner strength?

Our admiration for self-reliance as opposed to parasitism can be used, in the first instance, to undergird and justify a good deal of activity devoted to the well-being of other people. To depend passively on society or others in the way a child depends on his parents counts as an instance of parasitism and is wrong and deplorable as such, whether we are talking about welfare chiseling, on the one hand, or, on the other, the leisured existence of the wealthy; and a person who is opposed to parasitism will presumably want to *be* useful and *make* a contribution to society, so as to counterbalance all that has been done for him by others.

Notice, furthermore, that this desire is not egoistic or self-interested, even if it presupposes one's self-interest has been served by others. For one's motive here is not the instrumental one of making a contribution in order that others may be more likely to help one in the future, but looks back to help one has already received and seeks *with no ulterior motive to counterbalance or repay that help.*

The appeal to a desire to repay and make a positive contribution to society and to particular individuals allows us to criticize both the harming of others and failures to contribute to others' well-being. But the imperative of self-reliance or non-parasitism also connects with the "deontological" side of our ordinary moral thinking – with our obligations to keep promises, not to be deceptive, to tell the truth, etc. For those who rely on others to believe their promises and who have benefitted from others' keeping promises to *them* would count as parasites upon the social practice of promising if they refused to keep their promises. More needs to be said here, but given space constraints, we ought to move on to consider some forms of inner strength we have not mentioned yet.

I have spoken of self-sufficiency understood in the sense of self-reliance, but such self-sufficiency and strength *vis-à-vis* other *people* is different from a kind of self-sufficiency in regard to *things* that we also think well of, namely, the self-sufficiency shown by those who are moderate in their needs or desires. Those who do not desire (or so strongly desire) many things that most of us desire, those who are contented with what would not be enough to satisfy most people, seem less needy, less greedy, less dependent on things than those others. Since neediness and dependency seem to be ways of being weak (inside), a certain independence from and self-sufficiency in regard to things that people can crave represents another form of inner strength that is admirable in itself.

Interestingly, this new form of self-sufficient strength can help us to justify some further kinds of altruistic behavior, and, ironically enough, it is Nietzsche, the self-avowed egoist, who shows us how to do this. The kind of moderation of desire that can be justified in terms of an ideal of self-sufficiency is not particularly directed to the good of others, but as Nietzsche points out in *Beyond Good and Evil* (section 260), *Joyful Wisdom* (section 55), and many other places, one can also be moved to

give things to other people out of a self-sufficient sense of having more than enough, superabundance, of things. Nietzsche think this kind of "noble" giving is ethically superic to giving based in pity or a sense of obligatio but quite apart from this further judgment, seems clear that Nietzsche has pointed out further way in which benefiting others can b justified in terms of our ideal of inner strengtl The person who begrudges things to others n matter how much he has seems needy, patheti too dependent on the things he keeps fo himself, and can be criticized as lacking self sufficiency in regard to the good things c this world.

Notice that although generosity based o this kind of self-sufficiency presupposes tha the giver is genuinely satisfied with the good things she has, it is not egoistic. One generousl gives to others out of a sense of one's own wellbeing but not in order to *promote* one' well-being or (necessarily) in order to *repay* people for previous help, and this therefore counts as a form of altruism in addition to the kind that develops out of self-reliance. Such self-sufficient generosity can serve rathe widely as a touchstone for social and individua moral criticism but, once again, there is no space here to go into the details. What is important at this point is that the cool notion of inner strength has sides to it that allow for a defense of various forms of altruism and of the honoring of commitments.

In fact, I believe there are four basic facets to the idea of inner strength, all with a role to play in morality as inner strength. We have mentioned three: courage to face facts and, let me add, to face danger; self-sufficient self-reliance; and self-sufficient moderation and generosity. The fourth kind of inner strength is *strength of purpose* as involving both keeping to purposes and intentions over time and following one's better judgment (not being weak-willed) at the time one is supposed to act on some intention. I don't propose at this point to go any further, though, into the details of morality as strength. Clearly, if we have four different kinds of inner strength, we need to say something about their relative importance and about how they interact to yield an intuitive and thoroughgoing account of ethical phenomena. But I want at

is point to indicate a general problem with
is whole approach that has led me to think
ere are probably more promising ways to
evelop an agent-based virtue ethics.

The problem, in a nutshell, is that morality
s strength treats benevolence, compassion,
indness, and the like as only *derivatively*
dmirable and morally good; and this seems
ighly implausible to the modern moral con-
ciousness. To be sure, compassion cannot
lways have its way; it sometimes must yield
o considerations of justice, and a compassion
r generosity that never pays any heed to the
gent's own needs seems self-depreciating,
nasochistic, and ethically unattractive. But
till, even if compassion has to be limited or
ualified by other values, it counts with us as a
ery important basic moral value. And it seems
o distort the aretaic value we place on warm
:ompassion, benevolence, and kindness to
egard them as needing justification in terms
of the cool ideal of inner strength or any other
different value. (Such a criticism clearly also
touches the Kantian account of benevolence.)
So I would propose at this point to introduce
and discuss certain warm forms of agent-based
virtue ethics that are immune to this problem
precisely because they base all morality on the
aretaic value, the moral admirability, of one or
another kind of benevolence. Moreover, as I
mentioned earlier, Martineau's *Types of Ethical
Theory* is the clearest example of agent-basing
one can find in the entire history of ethics, and
I believe that the advantages of virtue ethics
based on compassion or benevolence can best
be brought to light by first considering the
structure of Martineau's theory and the criticisms that Henry Sidgwick made of that theory.

4. Morality as Universal Benevolence

Martineau gives a ranking of human motives
from lowest to highest and, assuming that all
moral decisions involve a conflict between two
such motives, holds that right action is action
from the higher of the two motives, and wrong
action action from the lower of the two.
Martineau's hierarchy of motives ascends
(roughly) as follows: vindictiveness; love of
sensual pleasure; love of gain; resentment

– fear – antipathy; ambition – love of power;
compassion; and, at the apex, reverence for the
Deity.

Sidgwick objects to the rigidity of this
hierarchy, pointing out that circumstances and
consequences may affect the preferability of
acting from one or another of the motives
Martineau has ranked. Thus contrary to
Martineau, there are times when it is better
for reasons of justice to act from resentment
rather than compassion, and the love of sensual
pleasure might sometimes prevail over a love
of power or gain (especially if the latter were
already being given ample play). Sidgwick concludes that conflicts between lower motives can
only be resolved by appeal to the highest ranked
motive or, alternatively, to some supremely
regulative general motive like justice, prudence,
or universal benevolence – none of which is
contained among the more particular motives
of Martineau's hierarchy. That is, all conflicts of
Martineau's lower motives should be settled by
reference to reverence for the Deity or by reference to some regulative or "master" motive like
benevolence. (This would not be necessary if we
could devise a more plausible and less priggish
hierarchy than Martineau's, but no one has yet
suggested a way of doing that.)

Sidgwick then goes on to make one further
mistake, assumption. He assumes that for a
motive to be regulative, it must be regulative
in relation to the ultimate *ends* or *goals* of that
motive. This entails that if we confine ourselves
to secular motives, take seriously the fact that
compassion is the highest secular motive in
Martineau's ranking, and as a result choose
universal benevolence as supremely regulative,
then actions and motives will be judged in
terms of the goal of universal benevolence,
namely, human or sentient happiness. Somehow, we have ended up not with a more orderly
or unified form of agent-based view, but with
act-utilitarianism. And this has happened
because Sidgwick ignores the possibility of an
agent-based view that judges actions from
either of two conflicting motives in terms
of how well the two motives exemplify or
approximate to the motive of universal benevolence, *rather than* in terms of whether those
actions achieve (or are likely to achieve) certain
goals that universal benevolence aims at.

Thus suppose someone knows that he can help a friend in need, but that he could instead have fun swimming. The good he can do for himself by swimming is a great deal less than what he can do for his friend, but he also knows that if he swims, certain strangers will somehow indirectly benefit and the benefit will be greater than anything he can provide for his needy friend. However the man doesn't at all care about the strangers, and though he does care about his friend, he ends up taking a swim. In that case, both actualist and expectabilist versions of act-utilitarianism will regard his action as the morally best available to him in the circumstances. It has better consequences for human happiness than any alternative, and its expectable utility is greater than the alternative of helping his friend, since the man *knows* he will do more good, directly and indirectly, by swimming. But there is a difference between *expecting* or *knowing* that an act will have good consequences and *being motivated* to produce those consequences, and if we judge actions in agent-based fashion by how closely their motives exemplify or approximate to universal benevolence, then it is morally *less* good for him to go swimming for his selfish reason than to try to help his needy friend, and this is precisely the opposite of what standard forms of act-utilitarianism would conclude.

Thus in order to rule out agent-based views making use of the notion of compassion or benevolence, it is not enough to undermine complicated views like Martineau's, for we have seen that there can be an agent-based *analogue* (or "*interiorization*") of utilitarianism that morally judges everything, in unified or monistic fashion, by reference to universal benevolence as a *motive that seeks* certain ends rather than, in the utilitarian manner, by reference to the actual or probable *occurrence* of those ends. In addition, this distinctive *morality as universal benevolence* contrasts with utilitarianism in some striking further ways we have not yet mentioned.

Utilitarians and other consequentialists evaluate motives and intentions in the same way as actions, namely, in terms of their consequences. (I shall here ignore rule-utilitarianism because of what I take to be its inherent difficulties.) Thus consider someone whose motives would ordinarily be thought not to be morally good, a person who gives money for the building of a hospital, but who is motivated only by desire to see her name on a building or a desire to get a reputation for generosity as a means to launching a political career. Utilitarians and consequentialists will typically say that her particular motivation, her motivation in those circumstances, is morally good, whereas morality as universal benevolence, because it evaluates motives in terms of how well they approximate to universal benevolence, will be able, more intuitively, to treat such motivation as less than morally good (even if not very *bad* either). Of course, when we learn of what such a person is doing and of her selfish motivation, we may well be happy and think it a good thing that she has the egotistical motives she has on the occasion in question, given their good consequences (and our own benevolence). But we ordinarily distinguish between motives that, relative to circumstances we are glad to see and it is good to have occur and those motives we genuinely admire as morally good. Consequentialism, however, standardly leads to a denial and collapse of this plausible distinction by morally evaluating motives solely in terms of their consequences. By contrast, morality as universal benevolence, precisely because it insists that the *moral* evaluation of motives depends on their inherent character as motives rather than on their consequences, allows for the distinction and comes much closer to an intuitive conception of what makes motives morally better or worse.

As an agent-based analogue of utilitarianism, morality as universal benevolence is, however, open to many of the criticisms that have recently been directed at utilitarianism, including the claim that such views demand too much self-sacrifice. But this last problem can perhaps be dealt with on analogy with the way utilitarianism and consequentialism have attempted to deal with the criticism of over-demandingness: namely, either by arguing against it outright, or by accommodating it through an adjustment of their principle(s) of right action. A satisficing version of (utilitarian) consequentialism can say that right action requires only that one do *enough* good, and it can then offer some agent-neutral conception f what it is, in various situations, to do nough good for humankind considered as a whole. And a satisficing version of morality as universal benevolence can say (in a manner indicated above) that acts are right if they come from a motive (together with underlying moral dispositions) that is *close enough* to universal benevolence – rather than insisting that only acts exemplifying the highest motive, universal benevolence, can count as morally acceptable. Someone who devoted most of her time, say, to the rights of consumers or to peace in Northern Ireland might then count as acting and living rightly, even if she were not concerned with universal human welfare and sometimes preferred simply to enjoy herself. So there are versions of morality as universal benevolence that allow us to meet the criticism of overdemandingness, even if we think that this criticism does have force against versions of the view that require us always to have the morally best motives or moral dispositions when we act.

Some forms of utilitarianism are also, however, criticized for having an overly narrow conception of human well-being and in particular for treating all well-being as a matter of the balance of pleasure over pain. This criticism doesn't hold for certain pluralistic forms of consequentialism, nor does it apply to morality as universal benevolence, interestingly enough. The latter is not committed to any particular conception of human well-being, and happily allows us to admire a person's concern and compassion for human beings without attributing to that person or ourselves having a settled view of what human well-being consists in.

Finally, utilitarianism has been criticized for its inability to account for certain aspects of deontology, and these criticisms would undoubtedly also extend to morality as universal benevolence. Strict deontology tells us we would be wrong to kill one person in a group in order to prevent everyone in the group, including the person in question, from being killed by some menacing third party. But although Kantian ethics indeed seems to demand that we refrain from killing the one person, it is not clear that our ordinary thinking actually insists on such a requirement. Bernard Williams, for example, says that the question

whether to kill one to save the rest is more difficult than utilitarianism can allow, but he also grants that utilitarianism probably gives the right answer about what to do in such a case. Moreover, since benevolence involves not only the desire to do what is good or best overall for the people one is concerned about, *but also the desire that no one of those people should suffer*, morality as universal benevolence can explain why we might be horrified at killing one to save many, even if in the end it holds that that is what we morally ought to do.

I conclude, then, that although both consequentialism and morality as universal benevolence are open to a good many familiar criticisms, they have ways of responding to the criticisms. Moreover, they have systematic advantages over many other approaches to morality because of their relative systematicity or unified structure. But, as I suggested earlier, morality as universal benevolence seems to have intuitive advantages over its more familiar utilitarian/consequentialist analogues. Though it is a view that to the best of my knowledge has not previously been explicitly stated or defended, it is in many ways more commonsensical and plausible than utilitarianism and consequentialism. At the same time its reliance on the ideas of benevolence and universality should render it attractive to defenders of the latter views and make them ask themselves whether it wouldn't be better to accept an agent-based "interiorized" version of their own doctrines. If consequentialism and utilitarianism have present-day viability and appeal, agent-based morality as universal benevolence does too.

[. . .]

5.   Can Agent-Based Theories be Applied?

[. . .]

Some defenders of virtue ethics are willing to grant that virtue ethics – whether agent-based or otherwise – cannot be applied to practical moral issues, but would claim nonetheless that virtue ethics can give us the correct theory or view of morality. However, it would be better for virtue ethics if we could show that (agent-based) virtue ethics *can* be applied, and I believe we can accomplish this by making further use of the way that an internal state like benevolence focuses on and concerns itself with gathering facts about the world. If one morally judges a certain course of action or decision by reference to, say, the benevolence of the motives of its agent, one is judging in relation to an inner factor that itself takes into account facts about people in the world. One's inward gaze effectively "doubles back" on the world and allows one, as we shall see in more detail in a moment, to take facts about the world into account in one's attempt to determine what is morally acceptable or best to do. On the other hand this doubling back is not unnecessarily duplicative or wasteful of moral effort, if we assume that motive is fundamentally at least relevant to the *moral* character of any action. For if we judge the actions of ourselves or others simply by their effects in the world, we end up unable to distinguish accidentally or ironically useful actions (or slips on banana peels) from actions that we actually morally admire and that are morally good and praiseworthy.

Consider, then, someone who hears that her aged mother has suddenly been taken to the hospital and who flies from a distant city to be with her. Given morality as benevolence in some form or other and assuming she is her mother's sole living relative, how should she resolve the issue of what morally she ought to do with or for her parent when she gets to the hospital: Should she or should she not, for example, advocate heroic measures to save her mother? Surely morality as some form of benevolence doesn't given her an answer to this question, but what is worth noting is that given the woman's assumed ignorance of her mother's particular condition and prospects, there is no reason for most moral theories to offer an answer to that question at this point. But morality as benevolence *does* offer her an answer to the question what morally she should do when she gets to the hospital. It tells her she morally ought (would be wrong not) to find out more about her mother's condition and prospects, as regards quality and duration of life and certainly as regards future suffering and incapacity. And it can tell her this by reference to her actual motives, because if

she does not find out more and decides what to do or to advocate about her mother solely on the basis of present relative ignorance, she will demonstrate a callousness (toward her mother) that is very far from benevolent. To decide to pull the plug or not allow heroic measures without finding out more about her mother would demonstrate indifference or callousness toward her and on that basis morality as benevolence can make the moral judgment that she ought to find out more before making any decision. (Morality as inner strength could be shown to yield a similar conclusion.)

Then, once the facts have emerged, and assuming they are fairly clear-cut and point to horrendously painful and debilitating prospects for her mother, the woman's decision is once again plausibly derivable from morality as benevolence. At that point, it would be callous of her to insist on heroic measures and benevolent not to do so, and the proper moral decision can thus be reached by agent-based considerations.

But surely, someone might say, the woman herself does not think in such terms. She is worried about whether her mother would have a painful or pleasant future existence, for example, not about whether she herself would be acting callously if she sought to prolong the mother's existence. I would think that she could morally justify her decision not to allow heroic measures *either* by reference simply to likely future suffering if the mother were kept alive, or by saying, more complexly and richly: it would be (would have been) callous of me to try to keep her alive, given her prospects. Surely, there is nothing unusual or untoward about the latter as an expression of moral problem-solving.

Think, for example, about the arguments that were made in advocacy of the North American Free Trade Agreement (NAFTA). Both Vice President Gore and House Minority Leader Robert Michel defended the agreement on the grounds that to reject it would be to adopt a cringing, fearful, or despairing attitude to the world and America's future. They could have spoken more directly about consequences, but there is nothing unreasonable about the way they addressed the issue. So I want to conclude that, given the outward-looking character of inner motives, agent-based views have resources for the resolution of moral issues that parallel those available to such practically applicable moral theories as utilitarianism and consequentialism more generally.

Our ordinary thinking in response to difficult or not-so-difficult practical moral issues can invoke either motives or consequences or both. Consequentialism, however, solves such issues by appealing ultimately to consequences and only indirectly and as a method of useful approximation to considerations of motives like impartial benevolence. Agent-based morality as benevolence solves the problem in the opposite fashion by appealing ultimately to motives, but taking in consequences indirectly, to the extent they are considered by people with such motives and investigated in response to such motives. Each approach allows for the case-by-case solution of many moral difficulties or problems, and so with regard to the whole question of applied ethics, neither approach seems to have the advantage, and there is no reason to criticize agent-basing for being irrelevant to practical moral problems or making their solutions impossible.

To be sure, there will be times when morality as benevolence won't be able to solve our moral difficulties. For example, if the facts about her mother's prospects cannot be learned or turn out to be highly complicated, morality as benevolence will be stymied. But any consequentialism worthy of the name will also come up empty in such a case. It is a strength of such views, but no less of agent-based morality as benevolence, whether in partialistic or universalistic form, that such views do not presume to know the answers to difficult moral questions in cases that *outrun our human knowledge or reasoning powers*. Any ethical theory that makes it too easy always to know what to do or to feel will seem to that extent flawed or even useless because untrue to our soberer sense of the wrenching complexity of moral phenomena.

Since the revival of virtue ethics, those interested in the subject have focused mainly on Aristotle and on neo-Aristotelian ideas. I have myself defended neo-Aristotelian agent-focused ideas *From Morality to Virtue*, but we have seen here that certain forms of agent-based virtue ethics also have real promise and possibilities. In a period when virtue ethics is flexing its muscles, it needs a more varied diet than Aristotle or Aristotelianism alone can provide.

CHAPTER 70

A Virtue Ethical Account
of Right Action

CHRISTINE SWANTON

I. Introduction

It is a common view of virtue ethics that it emphasizes the evaluation of agents and downplays or ignores the evaluation of acts, especially their evaluation as right or wrong. Despite this view, some contemporary proponents of virtue ethics have explicitly offered a virtue ethical criterion of the right, contrasting that criterion with Kantian and consequentialist criteria. I too believe that though the virtues themselves require excellence in affective and motivational states, they can also provide the basis of accounts of rightness of actions, where the criteria for rightness can deploy notions of success extending beyond such agent-centered excellences. They can do this, I shall claim, through the notion of the target or aim of a virtue. This notion can provide a distinctively virtue ethical notion of rightness of actions. In this article I make two basic assumptions: first, that a virtue ethical search for a virtue ethical criterion of rightness is an appropriate search, and second, since virtue ethics in modern guise is still in its infancy, relatively speaking, more work needs to be done in the exploration of virtue ethical criteria of the right.

I wish to show in particular that a virtu[e] ethics can offer a criterion of rightness th[at] has certain structural similarities with act co[n]seqentialism. These are (i) a criterion of righ[t]ness offers an account of success in action n[ot] entirely reducible to inner properties of a vi[r]tuous agent; (ii) such a criterion allows a virtu[e] ethics to distinguish between rightness of ac[ts] and praiseworthiness of acts, wrongness of ac[ts] and blame-worthiness of acts; and (iii) such [a] criterion is not tantamount to a decision pr[o]cedure or a method of guiding actions.

My aim is not to defend the need for [a] criterion of rightness of this kind in virtu[e] ethics. Rather, I appeal to those who share (a[s] I do) commonly held intuitions of both con[-] sequentialists and W. D. Ross that moral goo[d]ness and rightness are not the same thing. I ai[m] to show how a virtue ethicist, too often accuse[d] of being too "agent-centered," can accommo[-] date such intuitions.

This article offers a virtue ethical criterion [of] rightness of acts as an alternative to certa[in] other virtue ethical criteria, which are di[s]cussed in Section II. Indeed, there are tw[o] types of explicit, developed, virtue ethic[al] accounts of right action in modern virtu[e] ethics. One I call a "qualified agent" accou[nt] of rightness; the other is motive-centered. I[n] "Virtue Theory and Abortion," Rosalin[d] Hursthouse proposed the following "qualifie[d] agent" account, which has received widesprea[d]

Christine Swanton, "A Virtue Ethical Account of Right Action," pp. 32–52 from *Ethics*, 112, 2001. Reprinted by permission of the publisher, The University of Chicago Press.

tention and which has often been thought
anonical for a virtue ethical account of right-
ess: "An act is right if and only if it is what a
irtuous agent would do in the circumstan-
s."[1] In a later article, Hursthouse modified
he above as follows: "An act is right if and only
if it is what a virtuous agent would character-
tically (i.e., acting in character) do in the
rcumstances."[2]

A second kind of virtue ethical account
f rightness is proposed in Michael Slote's
agent-based virtue ethics," according to
hich an action is right if and only if it exhibits
r expresses a virtuous (admirable) motive, or
least does not exhibit or express a vicious
leplorable) motive.[3]

In this article I propose a third account,
hose central theses are (1) an action is virtuous
respect V (e.g., benevolent, generous) if and
nly if it hits the target of (realizes the end of)
rtue V (e.g., benevolence, generosity); (2) an
tion is right if and only if it is overall virtuous.

In Section II, I consider difficulties in Hurst-
ouse's and Slote's accounts. In Section III, I
xplain what it is for an act to be virtuous, by
xplaining what it is to hit the target of (realize
e end of) the relevant virtue. In Section IV, I
ffer an account of what it is for an action to be
verall virtuous, and thereby right.

. Rival Accounts

he following problem arises in Hursthouse's
otion of rightness. The rightness of an act is
iterially determined by a qualified agent, but
ow qualified is a virtuous agent? If "virtue" is
threshold concept, then it is possible that you,
and our friends are virtuous, but it is also
ossible (indeed likely) that others are yet more
rtuous. The problem has both a vertical and a
orizontal dimension. On the latter dimension,
standardly temperate, courageous, just, gen-
ous individual does not have expertise in all
eas of endeavor. She may be inexperienced in
edicine, or law, or in child rearing. She may
erefore lack practical wisdom in those areas.
ven though we may call her virtuous *tout
ourt*, she is not a qualified agent in the areas
here she lacks practical wisdom. On the ver-
cal dimension, our virtuous agents (you, I,

and our friends) are surpassed in temperance,
courage, generosity, and justice by greater
moral paragons. So even though on a threshold
concept of "virtue", you, I, and our friends are
virtuous, we are not as virtuous as we might be,
let alone ideally so, and maybe we should defer
to our betters in moral decision making.

Hursthouse could resolve the above problem
in the following ways. She may assume that
"virtue" is a threshold notion, but where
the threshold is set depends on context. For
example, in the field of medical ethics not
any virtuous agent will be a qualified agent. A
medical ethicist, for example, needs to be not
merely benevolent, kind, and a respecter of
autonomy, but also knowledgeable about
medicine or, at the very least, in excellent communication with those who are. She needs
to possess the full array of dialogical virtues.
Another resolution is to drop the threshold
concept of virtue in the definition of rightness.
Perhaps "virtue" is an idealized notion. However, it seems clear that Hursthouse wants
actual human agents to be qualified agents.
In her later account of rightness, Hursthouse
realizes the danger that actual virtuous agents
may at times judge and act out of character, so
she inserts into the definition a qualification
to rule out this possibility.

However, the above resolutions do not completely resolve the problem of whether a virtuous agent is a qualified agent. Actual human
agents, no matter how virtuous and wise, are
not omniscient. As a result, an important end
of a virtue may be something about which
there is large scale ignorance and for which
no blame can be attached to individuals or
even cultures. To illustrate the point I am making, consider the relatively newly discovered
virtue, that of environmental friendliness. As
the debates in journals like *Scientific American*
show, controversy rages about whether or not
environmental friendliness requires various
drastic measures to reduce a perceived threat –
for example, global warming. The Aristotelian
virtuous agent possesses phronesis, but phronesis, with its connotations of fine sensibilities
and discriminatory powers, is impotent in the
face of massive ignorance of the entire human
species. No matter how well motivated and
practically wise the virtuous policy maker, if

her policies prove environmentally disastrous, one would think, they cannot be regarded as right. Here is another example. Wise, suitably cautious, and benevolent policy makers may decide to severely restrict genetically modified food on the grounds that large-scale ignorance about genetic modification still persists. But it may be that though the caution expresses practical wisdom, it does not exhibit knowledge. For though the possible dangers of genetically modified products of various kinds may not, in fact, be realized, reasonable people in the face of ignorance should guard against such possible dangers. The caution, even if wise, may have the result that important ends of the virtue of benevolence, such as the production of cheaper and more plentiful food, may be missed.

The above problem has a more general manifestation. Any virtuous agent is necessarily limited, and in a variety of ways. Janna Thompson puts the problem this way: "The belief that the right answer to an ethical problem is what the virtuous person judges is right is not compatible with the recognition that ethical judgments of individuals are limited and personal. It would be irrational for us to place our trust in what a single individual, however virtuous, thinks is right."[4]

The problems facing Slote's account are quite different from those facing Hursthouse's. Slote does not aspire to a "qualified agent" account of rightness, and so avoids the above difficulties. Rightness is tied firmly to quality of motive, but this arguably leads to counterintuitive results. A foolish but well-motivated agent may not be blameworthy in her misguided actions, but should we call such actions morally right? Slote deals with this problem in the following way. The well-motivated agent is concerned to determine facts: an agent genuinely desirous of being helpful is concerned that her help reaches its target, in a suitable way.[5] To a reply that such an agent may not be aware of her ignorance, Slote would claim that a motive to help contaminated with intellectual arrogance is not an admirable motive. However, not all ignorance about one's expertise need be so contaminated.[6]

In general, it could be argued that Slote has failed to take account of a distinction between rightness and goodness of action. For W.] Ross, quality of motive has nothing to with rightness (although, as will be seen, n own view will not be so stark). Ross claims:

> Suppose, for instance, that a man pays a pa ticular debt simply from fear of the legal co sequences of not doing so, some people wou say he had done what was right, and othe would deny this: they would say that no mor value attaches to such an act, and that sin "right" is meant to imply moral value, the a cannot be right. They might generalize and s that no act is right unless it is done from sense of duty, or if they shrank from so rigo ous a doctrine, they might at least say th no act is right unless done from *some* go motive, such as either sense of duty or benev lence.[7]

Ross distinguishes between a right act and morally good act understood as one which well motivated. Virtue ethicists are inclined sidestep or belittle this distinction by speakin of acting well, but this idea does not obliterat or even downgrade the importance of, the di tinction Ross is trying to draw. Unsurprising however, on my view, a virtue ethical emplo ment of the distinction between right act ar good act is not going to be quite the sam as Ross's. First, on my view, quality of moti can sometimes make a difference to rightne and second, as Aristotle believes, goodness motive is not the only inner state of the age relevant to acting well. Since this article about rightness and not about acting well ge erally, I shall not elaborate further on the latt point.

III.   A Target-Centered Virtue Ethical Conception of Rightness

The first stage in the presentation of my virt ethical account of rightness is the provision an account of a virtuous act (or more precise an act which is virtuous in respect V). The bas of my account of such an act is Aristotl distinction between virtuous act and actic from (a state of) virtue. On my account, righ ness (as opposed to full excellence) of action

ed not to action from virtue but to virtuous
ct.

Let me first present Aristotle's distinction,
efore elaborating further on the notion of
irtuous act. Aristotle introduces the distinc-
on thus:

> A difficulty, however, may be raised as to how
> we can say that people must perform just
> actions if they are to become just, and temper-
> ate ones if they are to become temperate;
> because if they do what is just and temperate,
> they are just and temperate already, in the same
> way that if they use words or play music cor-
> rectly they are already literate or musical. But
> surely this is not true even of the arts. It is
> possible to put a few words together correctly
> by accident, or at the prompting of another
> person; so the agent will only be literate if he
> does a literate act in a literate way, viz. in virtue
> of his own literacy. Nor, again, is there an
> analogy between the arts and the virtues.
> Works of art have their merit in themselves;
> so it is enough for them to be turned out with
> a certain quality of their own. But virtuous acts
> are not done in a just or temperate way merely
> because *they* have a certain quality, but only if
> the agent also acts in a certain state, viz. (1) if he
> knows what he is doing, (2) if he chooses it, and
> chooses it for its own sake, and (3) if he does it
> from a fixed and permanent disposition.[8]

[ow can an action be just or temperate if it
oes not exhibit a just or temperate state? The
nswer I shall propose is this: an action can be
ıst or temperate if it hits the target of the
ırtues of justice or temperance, and an action
ıay hit those targets without exhibiting a just
r temperate state. According to Robert Audi,
ne "dimension" of virtue is "the characteristic
ırgets it aims at."[9] This idea requires explica-
on if it is to be employed in the service of an
ccount of rightness. The task of the remainder
f this article is precisely to offer what may
e termed a "target-centered" virtue ethical
ccount of rightness.

It will first be noticed that a target-centered
iew will tolerate moral luck in the attainment
f rightness, for rightness may depend in part
n results not entirely within the control of
ıe agent. This understanding sits well with
ristotle, one of whose strengths on my view

is his distinction between character (virtue)
which is concerned with choice (rather than
the results of choice) and the target of a virtue
which may be missed. He allows for the possibility that the target of choice (virtue) may
be missed through no fault of the agent. For
example, the aim of magnificence is a result:
"The result must be worthy of the expense, and
the expense worthy of the result, or even in
excess of it."[10] Though of course the magnificent person has wisdom, are all results of
largesse predictable by the wise? Aristotle seems
to allow for the possibility that a choice from
the virtue of magnificence may not be a magnificent act. And, indeed, that will be my position. To revert to an earlier example, choice
from the virtue of environmental friendliness
may not be an environmentally friendly act.

Let me now explicate the idea of hitting the
target of a virtue. To understand the idea of
hitting the target of a virtue it is necessary to
propose a schematic definition of a virtue:

(V_1): A virtue is a good quality or excellence
of character. It is a disposition of acknowledging or responding to items in the field of a
virtue in an excellent (or good enough) way.

Three points need to be made about this
definition. The qualification "good enough" is
intended to accommodate the possibility that
"virtue", especially in worlds full of evil, catas-
trophe, neediness, and conflict, is a threshold
concept. Second, the definition is intended to
be neutral with respect to a variety of virtue
theories and virtue ethics. In particular, it entails neither eudaemonistic nor noneudaemo-
nistic virtue ethics. Third, the definition is
neutral about the issue of how broadly or
how narrowly we should understand the notion of (moral) virtue.

I can now present schematic definitions of an
act from virtue and a virtuous act in the light
of (V_1). First, a definition of action from virtue:

(V_2): An action from virtue is an action
which displays, expresses, or exhibits all (or a
sufficient number of) the excellences comprising virtue in sense (V_1), to a sufficient degree.

In the light of (V_1) also, we can understand
what it is to hit the target of a virtue:

(V_3): Hitting the target of a virtue is a
form (or forms) of success in the moral
acknowledgment of or responsiveness to items

in its field or fields, appropriate to the aim of the virtue in a given context.

A virtuous act can now be defined:

(V_4): An act is virtuous (in respect V) if and only if it hits the target of V.

In the remainder of this section, I first elucidate the idea of hitting the target of a virtue, before showing how a virtuous act differs from an action from virtue.

Recall that to hit the target of a virtue is to respond successfully to items in its field according to the aim of a virtue. I need now to discuss this idea further in order to clarify the distinction between virtuous act and action from virtue. What counts as hitting the target of a virtue is relatively easy to grasp when the aim of a virtue is simply to promote the good of individuals and hitting that target is successfully promoting that good. However, this relatively simple paradigm is complicated by several features. I shall discuss five. These are: (1) there are several modes of moral response or acknowledgment appropriate to one kind of item in a virtue's field, so hitting the target of a virtue may involve several modes of moral response; (2) the target of a virtue may be internal to the agent; (3) the target of a virtue may be plural; (4) what counts as the target of a virtue may depend on context; (5) the target of a virtue may be to avoid things. Features 1–5 are discussed in turn.

1. *Hitting the targets of virtue may involve several modes of moral response.* – Given that hitting the target of a virtue is constituted by successful response to items in its field, according to the virtue's aim, I need briefly to explain the ideas of a virtue's field and the types of response to items in it.

The field of a virtue consists of the items which are the sphere of concern of the virtue. These items may be within the agent, for example, the bodily pleasures which are the focus of temperance, or outside the agent, for example, human beings, property, money, honors. They may be situations, for example, the dangerous situations which are the focus of courage; abstract items such as knowledge or beauty; physical objects, such as one's children, friends, sentient beings in general; art works or cultural icons; or the natural objects which are the focus of the environmental virtues.

What are the types of response to items in a virtue's field? That responsiveness to, or acknowledgment of, items in the field of a virtue required by a virtue may take several forms is at least suggested by an investigation of individual virtues. These forms I shall call modes of moral responsiveness or acknowledgment. They include not only promoting or bringing about (benefit or value) but also honoring value (roughly, not dirtying one's hands with respect to a value, e.g., by not being unjust in promoting justice); honoring things such as rules; producing; appreciating; loving; respecting; creating; being receptive or open to; using or handling. One may respect an individual in virtue of her status as an elder or one's boss; promote or enhance value; promote the good of a stranger or friend; appreciate the value of an artwork, nature, or the efforts of a colleague; create a valuable work of art; creatively solve a moral problem; love an individual in ways appropriate to various types of bonds; be open or receptive to situations and individuals; use money, or natural objects.

The modes of moral acknowledgment of items are richly displayed in the virtues. The virtue of justice is primarily concerned with the honoring of rules of justice by adhering to those rules oneself and with respect for the status of individuals. The virtues of connoisseurship are concerned not with the promoting of, for example, art (by giving money to art foundations, say) but with the appreciation of valuable items such as art. Virtues of creativity require more than appreciation. Thrift is a virtue concerned with use of money; temperance, a virtue concerned with handling of and pursuit of pleasure; consideration, politeness, appropriate deference, virtues concerned with respect for others and their status. Many virtues, for example, that of friendship, exhibit many modes of moral acknowledgment. A good friend does not merely promote the good of her friend: she appreciates her friend, respects, and even loves her friend. Caring as a virtue involves receptivity, perhaps love in some sense, and to a large extent promotion of good.

What I shall call the profile of a virtue is that constellation of modes of moral responsiveness which comprise the virtuous disposition. On ny view, not only do the virtues exhibit many modes of moral acknowledgment, but a single virtue, such as benevolence, friendship, or justice, may require that we acknowledge items in its field through several different modes. The plurality of modes of moral acknowledgment comprising the profiles of the virtues reflects the complexity of human responsiveness to the world. The virtues, with their complex profiles, recognize that we are beings who are not only agents of change in the attempt to promote good but also agents of change in the attempt to produce and to create. They also recognize that we are not only agents who are active in changing the world by promoting good (often at the expense of causing harm) but also agents who love and respect (often at the expense of maximizing good). And they recognize that we are not only active beings hell-bent on change but also are passive in a sense: in our openness, receptivity to, and appreciation of value and things. Not all ethics is "task-oriented." In short, attention to the profiles of the virtues reminds us of the complexity of our human nature and our modes of moral response. This complexity will feed into the account of rightness.

What counts as success in exhibiting modes of moral responsiveness appropriate to the aim of a virtue is a complex matter, requiring discussion of each mode. Of course, to give a full account of each mode of moral acknowledgment as it is manifested in the profiles of the virtues is a very large undertaking. I cannot, therefore, within the confines of this article provide such an account but shall instead be briefly illustrative in the service of my discussion of rightness.

2. *The targets of some virtues are internal.* – It is granted that the target of many virtues is external, for example, the target of beneficence, efficiency, justice. A just act is one that, for example, conforms to legitimate rules of procedure; an efficient act is timely and poses little cost for a worthwhile gain; a beneficent act successfully promotes human welfare. We sometimes speak too of a generous act of giving without any knowledge of, or even interest in, the motivation of the donor. The same point applies to wrongness. Consider the action of former Prime Minister Keating of Australia,

who ushered the Queen to her place by putting his arm round her waist. Many considered this action wrong – even egregious, even outrageous – because it was disrespectful or impolite. He did not suitably keep his distance (as Kant puts it), and his action was therefore deemed wrong because disrespectful by many, regardless of his motivations. He may have been innocently operating within Australian mores of informality and egalitarianism, or he may have been striking another blow for turning Australia into a republic by subtly undermining the Queen's prestige or mystique.

However, the supposition that the target of all virtue is external to the agent or is only external to the agent is false. Though the target of some virtues is external or is external in many contexts, the target of others seems to be entirely internal, for example, determination or (mental) strength. The target of the former virtue is trying hard in a sustained way, and that target may be reached even if the agent fails rather consistently in her endeavors. More commonly, the targets of virtues such as caring are a mixture of features within the agent's mind, features of an agent's behavior (her manner) and features external to the agent. Similarly, the target of the virtue of (racial) toleration is not merely external: the pro forma respecting of the rights of people in certain racial groups. We may call an act wrong because racist if the agent, in respecting a right, possessed racist motivation, even if that motivation was not displayed. Notice, however, that the application of terms such as "racist" to acts is controversial, and what is required for an act not to be racist may be more or less demanding, depending on context. Though the full virtue of racial toleration may demand that we morally acknowledge those of other races through a variety of different modes (e.g., respect, promotion of good, appreciation, even a form of love), the conditions under which we call an act racist and thereby wrong may be more or less stringent.

3. *Some targets of virtue are plural.* – According to Robert Audi, the target of courage is the control of fear. However, one may have thought that hitting the target of courage is to successfully handle dangerous or threatening situations. Perhaps then, the target of courage

is plural, embracing both regulating certain inner states and handling certain sorts of external situations. On my view, regardless of what one wants to say about courage, there is no requirement for a virtue to have only one target, for a virtue may have more than one field. Even with respect to inner states, Aristotle thought that courage involved the regulation of both fear and confidence.

4. *Contextual variability of targets.* – One might wonder how the target of a virtue is to be determined if the profile of a virtue is complex. Part of the answer to this question lies in the contextual variability of the target of a virtue. What counts as a virtuous act is more heavily contextual than what counts as an action from virtue. In some contexts, for example, where there is considerable need, one may be said to have performed a generous act if one donates a large amount of money, say, even if that donation is made with bad grace. However, in other contexts, we may deny that an act of giving is generous on the grounds that it was not made in a generous spirit. Here the target of generosity is to alleviate need, in the right way, where "in the right way" makes reference to manner of giving and even motivation. Perhaps the context is a more personal one, and the hostility or ill grace noticed by the recipients. We may at other times mark the fact that the target of a virtue is reached, but only in a minimalist sense, by claiming of an action that it is all right but not right *tout court*. At yet other times we may mark the fact that the target of a virtue has been reached in its richest sense, by claiming of an action not merely that it was right but that it was splendid or admirable because lavish, nobly performed, or performed in the face of great difficulty or cost.

Here is another example illustrating the contextual nature of the target of a virtue and thereby of a virtuous act. I am an aid worker, working ceaselessly saving lives. Are my actions benevolent because successful in saving lives or not benevolent since they do not manifest caring or loving attitudes? People at this point may not worry about whether my actions manifest love for others. The target of benevolence here is simply to alleviate need. My actions are deemed benevolent and right –

indeed admirable. However, after several years of tireless activity in famine stricken areas I come home in a state of deep depression. I feel burdened by an inability to love or be creative. I am filled with resentment and rush to an analyst. She is worried about my tendencies to promote good. She tries to teach me that truly benevolent actions flow from love of humanity (in a particularized form) and inner strength. My continued knee-jerk "beneficent" actions are wrong. In this context the aim or target of benevolence is richer. It is no longer mere promotion of others' good.

Contextual variation and disagreement about salience occurs also with the attribution of vice terms to acts. A term such as "cruel" may, when applied to acts, sometimes make reference to inner states of agents and sometimes not. Sometimes one will say of an act of poisoning opossums of Australian origin with cyanide bait in New Zealand forests over-run with these pests, "That's cruel." The action is said to be cruel simply because of its effects on the opossums. Another person, knowing the mental anguish suffered by the poisoner (who is nonetheless determined to save coastline pohutukawa trees) says, "Sure, the act hurt the opossums, but it's not a cruel act."

5. *Some targets of virtue are to avoid things.* Talk of "hitting the target" of a virtue suggests that the aim of a virtue is always positive, as opposed to the avoiding of certain things. However, some virtues seem to be targeted at the avoidance of certain states, and to illustrate this, let me briefly discuss the controversial virtue of modesty. There is disagreement about the targets aimed at by the virtue of modesty, and such disagreement may be explained by differing views about what makes a trait a virtue. On a consequentialist view, such as Julia Driver's, a trait is a virtue if and only if its exercise tends to bring about valuable states of affairs.[11] According to Driver, what makes modesty a virtue is that "stops problems from arising in social situations," such problems as jealousy.[12] It does not follow that this is the aim of the virtue but a consequentialist view of what makes a trait of virtue may drive the account of its aim, and this is the case with Driver's account of modesty.

On Driver's view, the modest agent avoids spending time ranking herself and avoids seeking information to enable her to have a correct estimation of her worth. But so far, modesty as a virtue has not been distinguished from laziness as a vice. Driver goes further. The target of modesty is not just to avoid these things, it is to attain something positive: the ignorance of underestimation. The agent need not directly aim at this but must achieve it if the target of the virtue of modesty is to be reached. And it is the hitting of this target which leads to the valuable social consequences of absence of jealousy.

On my view, by contrast, the target of modesty is simply to avoid certain things. The modest agent avoids certain behaviors, including those mentioned by Driver, but it is also the case (if modesty is to be distinguished from laziness) that the modest agent avoids drawing attention to herself, talking about herself excessively, boasting, and so forth. One might accept all this without buying into the consequentialist justification of modesty as a virtue and without buying into an account of its target as something positive: the ignorance of underestimation. One may reject that account because one may believe (as I do) that what makes modesty a virtue is not its tendency to promote valuable states of affairs (absence of jealousy, etc.) but its being the expression of a valuable or flourishing state of the agent – namely, an agent who has self-love and who does not need therefore to get a sense of self-worth from comparisons with others. Though this is what makes modesty a virtue on my view, that is not its target, however. Its target is simply to avoid certain things – the kinds of behavior mentioned above.

I am now in a position to give an account of the distinction between an action from (a state of) virtue and a virtuous act. The requirements for hitting the target of a virtue and for action from virtue are demanding in different kinds of ways. We have seen already that an act from virtue may fail to hit the target of a virtue if the virtuous agent's practical wisdom does not amount to complete knowledge. So an agent with virtues of benevolence or environmental friendliness may act out of those virtues and miss the targets of those virtues.

Second, for an action to be from a state of virtue, in an ideal case, all modes of acknowledgment of items in a virtue's field, constituting the profile of the relevant virtue, must be displayed. However, this is not always, or even standardly, a requirement for virtuous action, even in an ideal case. Furthermore, for an act to be from a state of virtue (in an ideal case), not only must all modes of moral acknowledgment comprising the virtuous disposition be displayed, they must be displayed in an excellent way, in a way which expresses fine inner states. For Aristotle, this involves fine motivation (including having fine ends), fine emotions, practical wisdom, and the possession of a stable disposition of fine emotions, feelings, and other affective states. But even though the targets of some virtues are internal (at least in part), it is not generally the case that they involve the expression of all those fine inner states required for action from virtue. For example, we might say that obedience (to legitimate authority) as a virtue requires the existence of fine depth states: not only the practical wisdom which distinguishes obedience as a virtue from related vices such as blind obedience but also the absence of deep-seated hostile resentment of all authority figures, whether legitimate or not. However, the end or target of that virtue is compliance with legitimate rules and instructions, not the elimination of such deep-seated feelings.

I now summarize the key differences between action from virtue and virtuous act.

1. An action from a state of virtue may not be a virtuous act because it misses the target of (the relevant) virtue.
2. A virtuous act may fail to be an action from virtue because it fails to manifest aspects of the profile of the relevant virtue at all.
3. A virtuous act may fail to be an action from virtue because it fails to manifest the profile of a virtue in a good enough way, namely, it fails to express sufficiently fine inner states (such as practical wisdom, fine motivation, or dispositions of fine emotion).
4. What counts as a virtuous act is more heavily contextual than what counts as an act from virtue.

We have seen how it is possible to draw a distinction between virtuous act and action from virtue. We have also seen that the drawing of this distinction in particular cases is by no means easy, for there is a constellation of modes of moral acknowledgment constituting the profiles of the virtues, and it is often a matter of context which aspects of the profile of a virtue are salient in determining the target of a virtue. It is time now to discuss rightness as the overall virtuousness of an act.

IV.   Overall Virtuousness

According to my account, an act is right if and only if it is overall virtuous. There is much ambiguity about the idea of rightness. In particular, a target-centered virtue ethical view is compatible with three possible accounts which are now discussed. I illustrate with the virtue of generosity.

1. An act is right if and only if it is overall virtuous, and that entails that it is the (or a) best action possible in the circumstances. Assuming that no other virtues or vices are involved, we could say that a given act is right insofar as it was the most generous possible. The target of generosity on this view is very stringent: there is no large penumbra such that any act which falls within it is deemed right.

2. An act is right if and only if it is overall virtuous, and that entails that it is good enough even if not the (or a) best action. Here it is assumed that there is much latitude in hitting the target of virtues such as generosity. Right acts range from the truly splendid and admirable to acts which are "all right."

3. An act is right if and only if it is not overall vicious. Here it is assumed that not being overall vicious does not entail being overall virtuous. An act may avoid the vices of meanness or stinginess, for example, without hitting the target of generosity, which demands more than mere avoidance of stingy, mean acts. This may be true even if the target of generosity is interpreted as in 2, rather than 1.

My own target-centered view rules out 3, since rightness is understood in terms of overall virtuousness rather than the avoidance of overall viciousness. This leaves open a choice between 1 and 2. I prefer 1. Provided distinction is made between rightness and praiseworthiness, and wrongness and blameworthiness, it seems natural to think of the targets of a virtue as best acts (relative to the virtue) though it does not follow that a rational agent should always aim at such a target directly or should necessarily deliberate about reaching that target.

It should also be noted that a belief in 1 is compatible with considerable indeterminacy about what is best. "What is best" may not be a single action but any of a number of actions none of which are ruled out by reasons that could be defeated.

Finally, the distinction between 1, 2, and raises the issue of what should be called wrong. Should wrong actions include or exclude actions which fall short of rightness in sense 1 but are "all right" in the sense of "good enough"? My own preference is to employ three categories: right actions (conforming to 1), "all right" actions (which exclude actions which are overall vicious), and wrong actions (actions which are overall vicious).

We turn now to the account of rightness as overall virtuousness. Assume that it is determined whether an act is properly describable as hitting the target of an individual virtue, such as justice, generosity, friendship, and so forth. Disagreement about overall virtuousness centers on the resolution of conflict when an action is said to be virtuous in respect V and nonvirtuous or even vicious in respect W. Given that an act can be virtuous in respect V if merely certain aspects of the profile of V are displayed, it is not necessary that such an act is in all ways excellent. It is possible for vice terms to also apply. Actions, for example, can be both just and weak, or just and malicious, or friendly and unjust, or self-protective and nonbeneficent, or independent and unkind, or cruel and environmentally sound, or assertive and hurtful, or efficient and uncaring. Of course, it is possible for an action to be right (overall) simply because it is friendly or generous.

How is overall virtuousness determined? Like Jonathan Dancy, I wish to highlight the holism of right-making features of action.[1] Dancy subscribes to a form of particularism

ccording to which "the behaviour of a reason
or of a consideration which serves as a reason)
1 a new case cannot be predicted from its
ehaviour elsewhere."[14] The point is this. We
annot claim that certain features always con-
ribute positively (or negatively) to the overall
irtuousness of an act, even if those kinds of
eature characteristically contribute positively
or negatively).

A strong version of particularism should be
istinguished from a weaker version. Accord-
1g to the strong version, there are no moral
rinciples at all. According to the weaker ver-
ion, though there may be a very few moral
rinciples, characteristically reasons relevant to
ightness or wrongness function holistically. I
o not want to commit myself to the strong
ersion but merely wish to emphasize that even
irtue-based reasons can function holistically.

Though it is beyond the scope of this article
o write at length about the moral view labeled
particularism", it is important to clear away
ne misunderstanding. Particularism, even in
s strong version, does not deny the existence
f moral "principles" in a weak sense described
hus by Tom Sorrell: "By a 'principle' I mean a
eason for doing or committing something, a
eason that is, in the first place, general. It must
pply in a wide range of situations."[15]

Indeed, what Hursthouse calls virtue rules
re principles in exactly this sense. What is
enied in the strong version of particularism
s the existence of any universal moral prin-
iples in the sense that reasons (which may
onstitute principles in the above sense) always
ave negative or positive valence (as opposed
o operating holistically). Dancy makes it clear
hat principles of the form "characteristically
hus and so" or "normally thus and so" are
erfectly acceptable to the particularist.[16] This
act undermines the objection that moral life
nder particularism would be unpredictable.

Let us now see how virtue-based reasons
unction holistically in the assessment of ac-
ions as overall virtuous. Say that we have a
unch of virtues, such as kindness, generosity,
rankness, tactfulness, assertiveness, justice.
emember that for an action to be described
s virtuous (insofar as it is frank, tactful,
ind, generous, just, etc.), it has to hit the
arget of the relevant virtue, but it does not

characteristically have to display all the excellences which would make it an act from the
relevant virtuous state. Indeed, the agent who
performs a tactful action on an occasion may
not possess the virtue of tact at all. It is possible
even for such terms as "tactful" and "kind",
which normally contribute positively to the
rightness of actions, to contribute neutrally or
even negatively on occasion. I want now to show
how this can be possible, using two illustrations.

Consider an act which hits the target of the
virtue of kindness. We are at a conference
where a stranger looks lonely. It turns out he
is a person from overseas with a poor command of English and cannot participate in the
scintillating and sophisticated discussion on
moral theory. Our agent Tim performs a kind
act, namely, going to talk to the stranger. However, let us look at further features of this
situation. Tim is exceptionally keen to participate in the discussion but leaves in order to talk
to the stranger who could have made more
effort to amuse himself in other ways and
whose hangdog expression is expressive of a
rather weak, spoiled approach to life. The conversation with the stranger is difficult, and Tim
does not enjoy it. Furthermore, Tim is always
doing this kind of thing, sacrificing his interests
in the performance of such kind acts. He has
resolved to be more self-protective and strong,
and encourage others to do their share of burdensome tasks. But he consistently fails to
abide by the resolution. In this context, the
kindness of the act contributes negatively to
the overall virtuousness of the act.

The second example concerns intrafamilial
justice. I have been training my children not to
be obsessive about justice or fairness, particularly in an intrafamily context and where the
stakes are not high. I want them to be more
caring, magnanimous, generous. Despite my
personal tendencies to be overly concerned
with justice, I resolve to drive the lesson home
at the next opportunity. An opportunity soon
arises. A family tradition of "fair shares"
requires that the person making the division
has last choice. There is a cake to be cut. I allow
my older son to cut the cake. I notice that he
has cut carelessly, but in a state of unawareness
takes the biggest piece. The target of (procedural) justice has not been reached. My younger

son, apparently unnoticing and uncaring, looks delightedly at the smaller piece that he has been left with. Instead of praising my younger son, I make my older son swap pieces telling him that the division, and his action in going first, having cut, is unjust. My intervention is just, but in the circumstances that is a wrong-making feature of the situation. The justice of the intervention is in this context expressive of the obsessive, weak quality of my behavior.

My point in the above examples is that the virtuousness of an act in a given respect (e.g., its friendliness, justice, kindness) can be wrong making (i.e., can contribute negatively to the rightness of an act). My point is not that the virtuousness of an act is not characteristically right making. Indeed, if the virtuousness of acts were not characteristically right making, we could not subsume features under virtue concepts.

V.   Objections

A number of objections to my target-centered virtue ethical notion of rightness might be raised. The first objection is that virtuousness (or viciousness) may not feature at all in the list of right-making properties. In the claim "it's wrong because it is distasteful," it may be thought that "distasteful" is not a vice term. In reply one should note the following. It should first be determined how properties such as being distasteful are to be understood as relevant to rightness. The notion of distasteful-ness, for example, needs to be unpacked. One would need to say, for example, "it is distasteful because indecent." Ideally, the vice term "indecent" needs itself to be further unpacked into such notions as "manipulative", "dishonest", "disrespectful", "lacking integrity".

Another example is "it's right to stop considering this problem because there isn't enough time." It may be supposed that "because there is not enough time" is a right-making property not involving virtue. However, to know the impact of "lack of time" on rightness, we need to see how it affects virtues and vices. The sense that there is no time may reflect laziness. Or it may involve self-indulgence or lack of temperance. Perhaps we are wanting to rush off

to a party. On the other hand, the reason may implicate the virtues of courage, self-protection or parental virtue. Virtues such as these need to operate in the face of a pressuring adminis-tration which thinks that we have limitless cap-acities to cope with stress or no families to go back to.

Second, it may be objected that my account of rightness is too agent centered. Rightness, it may be claimed, has nothing to do with an agent's motives or reasons but has entirely to do with success in the external realm. However my target-centered virtue ethical view (by com-parison with some virtue ethical and Kantian views) does accommodate this consequentialist intuition about rightness. My problem with consequentialism is that it has too narrow a conception of modes of moral acknowledg-ment or response that are relevant to rightness. Once the plurality of modes of moral response is accepted, it can be appreciated that the target of some virtues, such as caring, can include the internal.

Indeed, the fact that my account allows for some agent centeredness overcomes an objec-tion that can be leveled at some versions of qualified agent accounts. The objection is this: an action which is one that a virtuous agent would perform could be one that merely mim-ics an action of a virtuous agent. It seems possible therefore that a nonvirtuous agent could perform an act describable as, for example, uncaring, even though it is an act which a virtuous agent would perform and which would therefore be right on a qualified agent account of rightness. The act is uncaring because, though mimicking a virtuous agent's act, it nonetheless fails to exhibit the internal qualities that would be exhibited by a virtuous agent's caring act. We may wish to say therefore that such an act was unvirtuous, even though mimicking the act of a virtuous agent. Indeed, on my view, an act which mimics the action of a virtuous agent may be wrong, because in the hands of the actor it is unvirtuous. It is uncar-ing, for example, or racist because it is expres-sive of racist attitudes.

The following reply could be made to this possible difficulty in a qualified agent formula of rightness. As Justin Oakley points out in "Varieties of Virtue Ethics," the formula that

n action is right if and only if it is what an
gent with a virtuous character would do in the
circumstances is ambiguous between two interpretations.[17] The formula could furnish what
Oakley calls an "external criterion" of right
action, or the idea of "doing what the virtuous
person would do" is to be understood as
requiring more than "merely the performance
of certain acts." Acting rightly also "requires
our acting out of the appropriate dispositions
and motives."[18] However, the strong interpretation would tie rightness not to the virtuousness of action but to action out of virtue, and
that is implausibly strong as a criterion of
rightness. The point of connecting rightness
to the former idea is to recognize a virtue
ethical variant of a distinction between good
and right act and to recognize that the latter
notion is less agent-centered than the former.

Another objection to my account of rightness is this: if the claim that an act is virtuous
in respect V is the claim that the act falls under
a virtue term "V", then, it may be argued, the
idea of rightness does not track the truth but
merely culturally dependent beliefs. For virtue
terms reflect our culturally determined and
possibly false beliefs about virtue.

Notice, however, that to say that an act is
virtuous in respect V if and only if it hits the
target of V is not quite the same as saying that
an act is virtuous in respect V if and only if it
falls under a virtue-term "V". This is so for two
reasons. First, some virtue terms refer to states
which only approximate to virtue. Take for
example "honest". We are happy to say that
"honest" is a virtue term, but "honesty" is
arguably not an accurate description of a vir-
ue. Honesty is a disposition to tell the truth, or
at least a disposition to not lie. We do not
describe an act of evasiveness or an act of
telling a lie as honest acts. Yet such acts may
hit the target of a virtue – namely, a virtue of a
correct disposition with respect to the field of
divulging information. Certainly, this dispos-
tion involves being a respecter of truth and is
normally manifested in honest acts, but arguably practical wisdom in this area does not
always mandate honest acts. Furthermore,
some of our virtue terms may not refer even
to states which approximate virtues, and a correct theory of virtue may demonstrate this.

Nietzsche's "revaluation of values," for example, called into question pity as a virtue
and (egalitarian conceptions of) justice as a
virtue, on the assumption that "justice" refers
to egalitarian propensities expressive of resentment. Second, as Aristotle remarks, not all virtues have names. The fact that our language is
insufficiently rich to capture all forms of virtue
does not tell against (V_4).

A slightly different accusation of relativism is
this. According to Soran Reader, "we are told
[by the particularist] that rationality is a matter
of judgement anchored in a way of life (anthropology), and that we are all competent to
recognize it even if we can never make it explicit (intuition)."[19] A particularism embedded
within a virtue ethics need not be wedded to
an intuitionistic epistemology. An epistemology
suitable for a virtue ethical particularism is
a completely open question. Particularism is a
theory emphasizing the holism of reasons, it
is not a theory about the basis of those reasons
nor is it an epistemological theory.

Finally, it is sometimes claimed that since
virtue ethical accounts of rightness are not
rule-based, they lack resources for resolving
moral dilemmas. In fact virtue ethics has
more resources for determining overall rightness of acts in dilemmatic situations than may
be appreciated.

The question is whether it is possible that an
agent cannot do something which is virtuous
overall and therefore right, when faced with
alternatives, all of which are extremely repugnant. The richness of virtue and vice vocabulary
allows us to admit the possibility of right action,
even in such cases. For virtue-based act evaluations allow us to think of "actions" as embracing demeanor, motivation, processes of
deliberation and thought, reactions and attitudes. We can describe demeanor, motivation,
thought processes, and reactions as callous,
arrogant, or light-minded, or as anguished.
We can describe them as strong, or decisive, or
courageous; or as cowardly, feeble, pathetic,
vacillating. We can describe them as dignified
or weak.[20] In short, the choice of a repugnant
option can be understood as right (virtuous
overall) when we take account of the full nature
of the action, including the way it was done. In
Sophie's Choice, for example, it is possible that

Sophie acted virtuously overall.[21] One might argue that she acted virtuously because she acted as a good mother in that situation. Or (someone may argue) in such a tragic situation, Sophie had to rise above the normal traits of goodness in mothers, and virtuous action required a certain coolness and deliberateness. One might in that case say her choice was not overall virtuous because it failed to display virtuous calmness and strength in the process of choice. This kind of question (of how a good mother would react) cannot be answered from within the resources of the philosopher. For a start, research on the behavior of mothers required to make life and death decisions for their children, in different kinds of contexts of scarcity and evil, would be required.

Finally, the idea that virtue ethics is not rule-based should not be misunderstood. On my account, the determination of rightness is partly a matter of publicly accessible rules, rather than the essentially private deliberations and intuitions of a virtuous agent. For rightness depends on the applicability of terms like "caring", "efficient", "kind", "friendly", and their applicability is rule-governed. But I do want to express an important caveat here. The correct applicability of virtue concepts in any sophisticated context is not a matter of the application of relatively perspicuous rules. When, for example, I praise an act as right because strong, or right because caring, or wrong because weak or uncaring, ensuing controversy may precipitate entire accounts of the concepts of strength, weakness, and caring. And good accounts will extend into terrain well beyond the expertise of the analytic philosopher.

Notes

1. Rosalind Hursthouse, "Virtue Theory and Abortion," *Philosophy & Public Affairs* 20 (1991): 223–46.
2. Rosalind Hursthouse, "Normative Virtue Ethics," in *How Should One Live? Essays in the Philosophy of Virtue*, ed. Roger Crisp (Oxford: Clarendon Press, 1996).
3. Michael Slote, "Agent-Based Virtue Ethics," in *Midwest Studies in Philosophy*, vol. 20, *Moral Concepts*, ed. Peter A. French, Theodore E. Uehling, Jr., and Howard K. Wettstein (Notre Dame, Ind.: University of Notre Dame Press, 1996), pp. 83–101.
4. Janna Thompson, *Discourse and Knowledge: A Defence of Collectivist Ethics* (London: Routledge, 1988), p. 73.
5. Slote, "Agent-Based Virtue Ethics," and "The Justice of Caring," *Social Philosophy and Policy* 15 (1998): 171–95.
6. For further criticism of Slote's failure to incorporate notions of successful relation to the external world in his criterion of rightness, see Julia Driver, "Monkeying with Motives: Agent-Basing Virtue Ethics," *Utilitas* 7 (1995): 281–8.
7. W. D. Ross, *The Right and the Good* (Oxford: Oxford University Press, 1930), p. 2.
8. Aristotle, *Nicomachean Ethics*, trans. J. A. K. Thomson (New York: Penguin Classics, 1976), p. 97, sec. 2 iv.
9. Robert Audi, *Moral Knowledge and Ethical Character* (New York: Oxford University Press, 1997), p. 180.
10. Aristotle, *Nicomachean Ethics* 1122b1–21.
11. Julia Driver, "The Virtues and Human Nature," in *How Should One Live? Essays in the Philosophy of Virtue*, ed. Roger Crisp (Oxford: Clarendon Press, 1996), pp. 111–29.
12. Julia Driver, "Modesty and Ignorance," *Ethics* 109 (1999): 827–34, p. 828.
13. Jonathan Dancy, *Moral Reasons* (Oxford: Blackwell, 1993).
14. Ibid., p. 60.
15. Tom Sorrell, *Moral Theory and Capital Punishment* (Oxford: Blackwell, 1987), p. 3.
16. Dancy, *Moral Reasons*, p. 60.
17. Justin Oakley, "Varieties of Virtue Ethics," *Ratio* 9 (1996): 128–52.
18. Ibid., p. 136.
19. Soran Reader, "Principle Ethics, Particularism and Another Possibility," *Philosophy* 72 (1997): 269–96, p. 275.
20. For more on a virtue ethical understanding of "irresolvable dilemmas," see Hursthouse, *On Virtue Ethics*.
21. William Styron, *Sophie's Choice* (New York: Random House, 1979).

CHAPTER 71

Being Virtuous and Doing the Right Thing

JULIA ANNAS

One common objection to virtue ethics is that it is 'not applicable'; it is, allegedly, a theory which is too vague for us to apply it to the actual world. There is a quick response to this: we do apply it all the time, for we take people to be brave or cowardly, generous or mean. This is, of course, not what the objectors have in mind: they mean that it is not applicable in the special sense, familiar to moral philosophers, of being too vague to be capable of *telling us what to do*. But here again there is a quick response: someone whose ethical thinking is in terms of the virtues can tell people (perhaps his children) what to do: they should do what's kind, avoid mean actions and not be dishonest.[1]

This is unlikely to satisfy the objectors. Among the objections brought at this point two have been prominent: Since we pick up our understanding of virtue terms from our family and social contexts, and our culture in general, virtue ethics will tend to be parochial in a way unsuitable for ethical thinking. Further, the recommendations of virtue ethics will be too vague to resolve ethical disagreement, which, again, ethical thinking ought to be able to do.

Before meeting these points on the level of theory, I think it is interesting to point out that if you get on the Web you will find the Virtues Project, an organization which specializes in moral education and conflict resolution, which has been particularly successful in the First Nations areas of western Canada and in Maori areas of New Zealand. It does this by using the language of the virtues, which they have found to be the most effective inter-cultural ethical language. The website features a list of 52 virtues which the project has found to be character traits respected in seven world spiritual traditions. The Virtues Project is unaffected by ethical philosophy; it uses the language of educational psychology. It is also not hard to find many respects in which it is strikingly under-theorized; it treats the virtues on a very elementary level. Despite all this, it strikes me as worthy of reflection that the Virtues Project has for some years and in many countries actually been successfully using the virtues to resolve conflicts in schools and inter-cultural situations, while some philosophers have been deeming from their armchairs that thinking in terms of the virtues is ethnocentric and can't resolve disagreements. It also strikes me as worthy of reflection that, for all that on the theoretical level consequentialism is often praised as a practical, problem-solving theory, it has, as far as I know, no similar facts on the ground; no teachers (again, as far as I know)

Julia Annas, "Being Virtuous and Doing the Right Thing," p. 61–74 from *Proceedings and Addresses of the American Philosophical Association*, 78, 2004. Reprinted by permission of the American Philosophical Association.

are successfully teaching children and actually resolving conflicts in intercultural situations using the language of consequences.

Still, at the level of theory doubt remains. We do learn to apply virtue terms in our own social and cultural contexts. And recommendations to be honest, or brave, are on the face of them somewhat unspecific. Ethical theories, in the tradition in which they have developed in the twentieth century, have raised a certain expectation about ethical theory: that it will apply to everyone in the same way, and that it will do so by telling people what to do in a fairly specific manner. This expectation cannot, I think, just be rejected; it has to be met on its own terms before we are entitled to proceed without it.

When we ask, before getting to theory, what we or other people should do, it is unlikely that we will appeal to principles or methods of deciding which are pulled out of thin air. We are most likely to appeal to the rules, conventions and ideals of our social and cultural context. For what other source has given us directives as to what to do, and how to live, which are likely to have any authority with us? One way of putting this point is that by the time we get to reflecting about ethical matters at all, we are not blank slates; we already have firm views about right and wrong ways to act, worthy and unworthy ways to be.

As we get to reflecting about the principles and ideals we have acquired, we come to see that there is much in them that is due merely to convention. Worse, some aspects of our moral outlook, when we think about them, appear to be due merely to prejudice. Few of us grow up thinking that our moral education has been entirely adequate; we need to think how to do better.[2] How do we do this?

Ethical theories that have been orthodox among philosophers in the twentieth century have typically thought that what we do is to take the directives that we find in our unreflective ethical thought, and refine them so that they do one thing clearly and specifically, namely direct us. We look at the rules in everyday ethical discourse, notice that they are vague and may conflict, and try to refine them so that conflict is ruled out. Or we follow Sidgwick in looking for principles behind everyday ethical rules – principles which do not suffer from the flexibility of those everyday rules. This general direction of thought can be reasonably summed up in the claim that as we move to the level of explicit ethical theory we search for a *decision procedure* which will tell us what to do.

The term 'decision procedure' has had a bad press in some quarters, so it is worth stressing that it does not itself import the idea of a mechanical, algorithmic procedure. The idea is simply that as we get to the level of moral theory, we discover a better moral methodology than the one we have been using, a methodology which will deliver an organized and systematic way of telling us what is the right thing to do.

(It is sometimes suggested that there is a parallel here to the development of a more sophisticated scientific methodology from everyday naïve views of the world. But this is surely a mistake, on two grounds. Firstly, the idea of 'scientific method' is scarcely a help here. There are far more divergences between the ways different sciences develop than between different moral theories. And secondly, the purpose of science, insofar as it can be said to have a purpose, is theoretical understanding, which is precisely the wrong analogue for ethical theory insofar as that is taken to be practical, and hence focussed on particular people and actions.)

If we need a decision procedure, a systematic and theorizable way of telling us what to do, then it will seem reasonable to think of the major aim of moral theory as being that of producing a *theory of right action*. This will be a theory which will produce, and defend theoretically, some decision procedure for telling us what to do, where 'telling us what to do' means: giving specific instructions for how to act which are applicable to everyone in the same way. Consequentialism is standardly the clearest example of this kind of theory. It isolates one simple principle behind the directives of our everyday ethical discourse, and then tells us how to formulate this principle and apply it to tell us, systematically and specifically, what to do. This task is simple in principle, although difficult and technical in practice.[3]

This is very like the kind of help we seek in [ar]eas of our lives where we have theoretically [si]mple but practically complex decisions to [m]ake. This model of a theory of right action, [i]n this way of looking at ethics, is rather like [th]e model often provided in these technical [ar]eas, for example by a computer manual. [T]he computer manual does the technical [w]ork for us and makes clear to us the theoret[ic]ally simple grounds of the decisions we need [to] make when we use the computer. The com[m]on model of a theory of right action, as [w]e meet it explicitly in many introductions to [m]oral theory, and implicitly in the work of [m]any moral theorists, can be called the *com[pu]ter manual model*.

I have found that some people think that [co]mparison to a computer manual is in some [w]ay a dismissive or reductive way of thinking [of] a theory of right action. I am not sure why [th]is should be so, especially since the model [em]bodies an important, and in many ways [at]tractive, feature of this way of thinking of a [th]eory of right action. It is *egalitarian* – it is, in [pr]inciple, equally available to anyone. It is not, [of] course, available to everyone equally just as [th]ey are, any more than a computer manual is. [H]owever, this difference is standardly taken, [su]rely correctly, as a difference merely in edu[ca]tion, where this is training in technical mat[te]rs which are, we suppose, equally accessible [to] all who have the opportunity. Similarly, [ap]plying the theory will on this account be [av]ailable equally to all who take the trouble to [m]aster the decision procedure. Thus, what a [th]eory of this type offers is something which is [in] principle available to anyone; inequities in [it]s possession will be due to social contingen[ci]es rather than to the characters of the people [co]ncerned. It is this egalitarianism, I think, [wh]ich helps to give this model continued [ap]peal in the face of difficulties.

There are some obvious problems with this [m]odel. Two of them have been stressed by [Ro]salind Hursthouse.[4] Firstly, given the point [th]at the understanding required is technical, [an]d that mastering this kind of information is [n]otoriously something which some people can [do] at a very young age, it would follow that [th]ere could (and predictably would) be clever [te]enagers who had mastered the relevant

theory of right action, and thus would be, since the computer manual model is a model of moral theory, reliable and sound sources of moral advice and direction. But of course as soon as we pose this suggestion we can see how absurd it is. We do not go to clever teenagers for advice on what to do or how to live, because we realize that the technical cleverness they often do have may, because of their comparative lack of experience, be accompanied by naïvete and credulity, rendering their advice shaky at best. We could call this the objection from the idiot savant: the young person with technically brilliant understanding may be a moral idiot.[5]

Secondly, if the theory of right action is to have this kind of form, then it would be possible in principle for someone to be brilliant at it, and to offer outstanding moral advice, while having a character and values that were morally detestable. After all, it is a supposed advantage of this model that the moral understanding it offers is available to all regardless of their moral character. So, I could in principle go to someone for moral advice, and take it, regardless of the fact that her character was marked by, for example, great cruelty and sadism. As long as this was unconnected to her theory of right action, there would be no reason for this to bother me. Indeed, I might be intrigued by the interesting complexity of her character. 'I hate the way you torture kittens,' I might say, 'but I appreciate the excellence of your theory of right action. What a good job it is unconnected to your character and values – for I will do what your theory of right action tells me to do, though of course I would be horrified at the thought of my being in the least like you.' I take it that this is deeply absurd, and indicates that divorcing right action from character is problematic. We could call this the objection from the loathsome advisor.

Some may object that this example is a travesty, but if so the reasons are going to be interesting. The objection has to be some variant on the thought that people with horrible characters are just not going to come up with excellent theories of right action; so we will not be faced by the loathsome advisor. But is this just a massive and fortunate accident? That is not very plausible. And if not, it will suggest the idea that such a theory is not in fact accessible to anyone with the required technical ability, but might involve character and its development. But one of the advantages of this kind of theory of right action was that it was supposed to be available to anyone, regardless of character, who could be taught the necessary technical skills.

However, strong as these two objections are, I think that there is a more important one. It emerges from the discomfort that I, at any rate, feel when faced by the common idea that what we need from a moral theory is to be 'told what to do'. Do I really want to be told what to do? I have a moral problem: should I do this action? I get the answer, Yes (or alternatively the answer, No). Or I recount my problem and get told to do, or not do, action A. I have been told what to do, but is this what I want from a moral theory? It is certainly the kind of answer I want from a computer manual. I have a computer problem; I consult the manual, and get a specific and decisive answer, Yes, do that, or No, don't do it; or I recount my problem and get told the steps to follow to put it right. But in the moral case this gives us what the theory was supposed to be so good at, and yet clearly something is missing.

Perhaps this is so far an insufficiently charitable interpretation of what a theory of right action is supposed to do. Perhaps so far I am leaving out something else the theory gives us, namely the justification for doing (or not doing) the action it tells us to do. So a theory of right action won't just tell us what to do; it will tell us what to do and give reasons why this is the right answer. After all, it's a *theory*: it will show us why the answer is correct, in terms of the way that the considerations relevant in this situation are processed by the theory (which will differ, of course, as the theories differ).

This does not remove the discomfort, however. Theories of right action are supposed to be practical, to give us specific directions. Since it is taken to be a fault in such a theory to be vague or unspecific, the desired result has to be, precisely, my being told what to do here and now, Yes or No. Reasons to back this up and enlarge my understanding of why the answer is Yes, on this occasion, rather than No, do not remove this feature. So the original discomfort

remains: do we really want a moral theory t tell us what to do? Aren't we losing an impor ant sense in which we should be making ou *own* decisions? Suppose I later come to thin that what I did was actually the wrong thing t do. In the computer case I think that either got the manual wrong, or the manual wa wrong. And this is unproblematic; there is n soul-searching to be done as to why I made th wrong decision. But in the moral case there surely something problematic in the thoug that either I got the theory wrong or the theor was wrong, but there is no worry as to m making the wrong decision.

The idea that we want a theory of righ action which tells anybody (with the right tech nical skills) what to do seems so far to leave ou something important about the making c moral decisions. My moral decisions are mir in that I am responsible for them, but in further way as well. They reveal somethin about me such that I can be praised or blame for them in a way that cannot be shifted to th theory I was following. This is so even when is true that the theory was correct, I was fo lowing the theory correctly, and the point c my following the theory was to be told wha to do.

This point can be put vividly. Suppose (un realistically!) someone always does what h mother tells him to do. He always follows he orders; if he fails to do so he feels guilt, regre and so on. We take this to be immature, a cas of arrested development; at his age, we sa he should be making his own decisions. Nov why should this picture become all right whe we replace Mom by a decision procedure? Pre sumably a decision procedure, supported by theory of right action, can be expected to t correct more often, and more reliably, tha Mom can; but how could this remove th worry?

Once again we may be told that this is a uncharitable way to be interpreting a theory c right action and people who think we nee one. The idea, it will be claimed, is not that ask the theory to tell me what to do in the wa I consult the computer manual. Rather, th theory is supposed to be something I interna ize, a way of thinking which, when I adopt i enables me to have the correct criteria fc oral decisions. So the theory does not strictly tell me what to do; it gives me the criteria for doing it myself. The theory of right action is supposed to be like a computer manual in specificity, and in being accessible to all with the technical skills, but unlike it in that I am supposed to internalize it to come to my own decisions.

But again this does not meet the fundamental point. Granted that the theory does not literally tell me what to do, it still gives me the criteria for coming to the right decision. But if the theory is practical and specific, in the way stressed so far, what it is doing, in doing this, is enabling me to tell myself what to do. And furthermore, my acceptance that this is, in fact, the right thing to do comes entirely from my acceptance of, and internalization of, the theory of right action. So whether the theory is pictured as outside me, like a manual, or inside me, like a set of directions as to how to think, it is still telling me what to do. The point remains: what I should be doing is interpreting the theory correctly. If we bothered to internalize computer manuals it would be somewhat similar.

So we can see that the idea of a decision procedure backed by a theory of right action, that has been assumed in much moral philosophy, runs into serious problems. And apart from these we can feel the force of a more general dissatisfaction. Informally this can be put as the query whether we do in fact think of the moral life this way, as our going round all the time telling one another what to do. Is the moral life really this endless busybodying? Further, what on this model do we make of our concern for our own moral lives? It looks as though it has to come from the thought that amidst all this telling other people what to do, we from time to time, if only out of fairness, tell ourselves what to do too. And this definitely gets the concern wrong.

Virtue ethics has, for much of the period of its recent revival, been taken to offer an appealing alternative to this anxious and obsessive picture of the moral life. It is an alternative in which issues of the best life to live, a good person to be and a good character to have are important along with doing the right thing. It is by now clear that the nature of this shift from focus on right action to concern with being a good person is complex, and diverse accounts of it have been given. I will first give a common account of what virtue ethics is alleged to hold about right action and the virtuous person. Bringing out what is wrong with this account will point us in the direction of a better alternative.

A common view is that, by way of an alternative to the egalitarian, computer manual model of a theory of right action, virtue ethics offers a theory of right action that starts from some version of the following:

An action is right if and only if it is what a virtuous person would do, adding 'reliably (or characteristically)' or the like, since virtue is a matter of character. There are many ways of interpreting this schema.[6] What I take to be the common view holds that the virtuous person must be identified independently of their performance of right actions. Otherwise, we would not have an account of right action which was explanatory. If we define right action as what the virtuous person would do, but it turns out that the virtuous person is even in part defined in turn by the doing of right action, the claim goes, we have a circle, and so no explanation.

So construed, the account has been attacked by well-known objections. Firstly, how are we to identify the virtuous person? We can, of course, point to actual examples of alleged virtuous people. 'Fred and Jane are the virtuous people around here,' we are supposed to say, 'so do what they do.' But there is an obvious response to this: our account will be parochial, for people in other places or cultures might not think Fred and Jane virtuous.

Secondly, we can avoid this objection by saying that unfortunately there are no virtuous people, at least not around here; virtue is an ideal, so that we cannot point to any actual virtuous people (though figures like Socrates and Gandhi may give us some inkling). This might be all right from some points of view, but is unfortunate if we want to give an account of right action in terms of the virtuous person, since the account will now be vague, and it will not be obvious how it is supposed to apply to particular circumstances.

Thirdly, we are taken to recognize clear cases where there would be agreement on what was the right thing to do, but this is patently not what the virtuous person would (reliably or characteristically) do. A familiar example is this: I have behaved badly: what would be the right thing to do in the circumstances? It is no good appealing to what the virtuous person would do, since the virtuous person wouldn't have behaved badly in the first place.[7] Recently Robert Johnson has added to the list.[8] The right thing to do, he claims, might be for me to improve my character (by controlling myself more); or to organize my life so that I am forced to do the right thing when my own motivation is insufficient; or to ask for guidance in an area where I know I am faulty. But none of these actions can be plausibly taken to be what the virtuous person does, reliably or as a matter of character. For the virtuous person does not need to improve; does not need to strategize to make up for absent motivation; does not need to ask for guidance where she is faulty.

We can't, I think, see how these objections can be met until we look at a more adequate alternative account of virtue and right action. And before doing this I shall raise what I take to be a further, more fundamental objection to this standard view. Suppose that we *can* define the virtuous person in a way satisfactorily independent from performance of right action. We then define right action in terms of what the virtuous person, so understood, would (reliably, or whatever) do. Whatever we have or haven't done, we haven't produced an *alternative* to the kind of theory of right action that has been so problematic all along. At most we have put a loop in it. Instead of trying to produce a theory of right action with the form of a computer manual, we have called up the figure of the computer expert. The expert might use a manual herself, in which case we have merely postponed the application of the manual to tell us what to do. But even if the expert is supposed not to use a manual herself, but to have an understanding of right and wrong action which cannot be codified in a manual, we are still, on this model, *using* the expert to tell us what to do, in exactly the way we used the manual: namely, to tell us what to do.

We find, then, that bringing in the virtuous person in this way does not help with the deepest problem we found with theories of right action. Appeal to the virtuous person certainly helps with some of the problems, for at least we will not be getting our theory of right action from a precocious teenager, or somebody with loathsome values. But the deepest problem remains intact, indeed is worse than anything. We still have a theory of right action which tells us what to do. All that has changed is the criterion for locating the right thing to do. It is still the case that what we have to do is to get the theory right; our decisions are the decisions that come from applying the theory correctly, as anybody could in principle do. Hence, this kind of appeal to the virtuous person still doesn't let the character of the person deciding make any difference; for, whether we appeal to Fred and Jane or to the ideal virtuous person, we are still applying the theory in a way that anybody might have done regardless of character.

So far, then, we have not found a real alternative to the problematic role of a theory of right action, understood as importing a decision procedure. If we assume that the virtuous person must be defined independently of right action, then importing the virtuous person into our theory of right action does no good at all.

A lot of people see this as an impasse. What, after all, is the alternative supposed to be? If we bring right action into our definition of the virtuous person, haven't we just given up on the prospect of a non-circular account of right action?

Obviously we do not want an account in which being virtuous and doing the right thing are trivially defined in terms of each other. But we might, I suggest, try an alternative: producing a developmental account, in which we give an account of being virtuous and doing the right thing in a way which involves a developmental process. If so, we would have a theory involving not two items but three: the virtuous person, right action and the relevant developmental process.

This prospect becomes more attractive if we can find an analogous example which is convincing in its own right and also indicates that we can think of virtue in this way. And this is what we find if we look at the classical tradition

f virtue ethics, which points us to a model
which was fundamental in thinking of virtue
for many centuries. It emerges most dramatic-
lly when we notice that Aristotle urges us to
think of becoming virtuous on the lines of
learning to be a builder.[9] This passage is well-
known and we have to remind ourselves that,
in terms of what modern theories require, it is
outrageous in its mundanity. Learning to be
moral is like acquiring a *practical skill*? But
es, this is the point of the analogy. A practical
kill is a useful model for the intellectual struc-
ure of a virtue in several ways: it is, of course,
practical, it is undergirded by general under-
tanding of the relevant field and, most im-
ortant, it is an area where there is a process
f *learning*, of passage from the state of being a
earner to the state of being an expert.

This is a large topic, on which a lot has been
written, and here I am just bringing out points
elevant to our understanding of virtue and
ction. The beginning builder has to learn by
icking a role model and copying what she
oes, repeating her actions. Gradually he learns
o build better, that is, to engage in the prac-
ical activity in a way which is less dependent
n the examples of others and expresses more
nderstanding of his own. He progresses from
iecemeal and derivative understanding of
uilding to a more unified and explanatory
nderstanding of his own. His actions may at
his point differ from those of his role model
recisely because he is a better builder. This is
ecause he is learning, and learning contains
he notion of aspiration to improve.

We can see how this leads to an improvement in both activity and understanding if we
ake an example from the performance arts.
uppose I aim to be an expert piano player,
nd take Alfred Brendel as my role model.
Clearly I am making a mistake if I think that I
will learn to 'play like Alfred Brendel' if I listen
obsessively to his recordings, copy his manner-
sms, play only pieces he performs. The development from learner to expert essentially
nvolves acquiring *your own* understanding of
he field you are learning. The learner depends
n the expert to learn in the first place, but the
oal of learning is to have your own under-
tanding of what you have learned from the
xpert. The expert in a practical field aims not

to produce clone-like disciples who will mimic
what she does, but pupils who will go on to
become experts themselves, which they can do
only if they acquire their own understanding
of the subject. The person who succeeds in
playing like Alfred Brendel ends up performing
in a way which sounds rather different.

It is these points about practical skill which
make it a good model for thinking of virtue.
This in no way implies, it should be stressed,
that virtue is going to be in all ways like a skill –
clearly in some ways it is quite different. Nor
does it imply that this story is all there is to an
account of the development of virtue. I have
just emphasized the initial point, that we start
as learners dependent on models and progress
to acquire our own understanding. There
remains much further story to tell.[10] However,
the importance of the movement from learner
to expert in a practical skill is important for
understanding the initial development of virtue. Let us recall the story at the start of this
paper: we grow up in a particular social and
cultural context and acquire corresponding
beliefs, principles and ideals, along with conceptions of the virtues as those are practised
and thought of in our society. We then reach a
point where we realize that our moral upbringing has left us with much that is merely conventional, or wrong. Many moral theories react
at this point, as was noted, by trying to systematize the rules and principles of everyday
thought, with the aim of producing a decision
procedure to be used by anyone.

Here is the point of decisive difference with
virtue ethics – at least virtue ethics as I take it
to be defensible. For instead of trying to force
our everyday moral thoughts into a system of a
one-size-fits-all kind, virtue ethics tells us to
look elsewhere – at what happens when we try
to become a builder or a pianist. The moral
beliefs we have taken over from others are just
the beginning stage. It is up to us to put in the
work needed to develop into someone who has
more understanding. Virtue ethics assumes
that this is something that we will all tend to
do. Other factors may prevent this becoming
effective, but it is a rare person who if
unaffected by other factors grows up morally
in a purely passive and dependent way, never
reflecting on the moral beliefs they have

grown up with or wondering whether what they were told to do was a complete guide to right action.

What we should do, then, at the stage when we realize the merely conventional status of many of our moral beliefs? In the spirit of other theories, but in a different way, virtue ethics tries to improve our understanding in a way which will lead to our acting in better ways. But virtue ethics regards it as misguided to try to produce a theory-based decision procedure for anyone at any stage to use. This would be like trying to improve building by insisting that all builders learn from the same books. These might be helpful, but they don't produce expert builders; it is people who have to make themselves into expert builders. Similarly, each of us has to do the work in our own case, aiming to become a virtuous person with understanding and not just derivative copying of others. No manual will do it for us.

If we take this developmental model seriously, we can see that it is important to differentiate the initial, uncritical grasp of virtue from the kind of understanding that the developed virtuous person has. We all start with some conventional grasp of virtue that we pick up as we grow up from parents, teachers and so on. It is up to us to recognize at this point that we are *learners*, and so to aspire to improve. To the extent that we do, we are on the way to becoming more fully virtuous. What form will this improvement take? A number of accounts have been defended here. The fully virtuous person, analogous to the practical expert, may have developed an uncodifiable ability to discern morally relevant features of situations. Or he may have developed practical wisdom which develops from, but goes beyond, that of his role models.[11] Or he may have developed a grasp of rules and principles such that he can apply them intelligently and with insight.[12] I take it that the term 'virtue ethics' picks out a cluster of theories,[13] so that these and others are options within virtue ethics, and decision between them is not needed here. One thing, however, is true of all of them: becoming more fully virtuous requires each of us to think for ourselves, hard and critically, about the moral concepts, especially those of the virtues, that we have picked up from our surroundings.

How does this help us with the issue of being virtuous and doing the right thing? The learner starts by doing what he is taught is the right thing to do, copying the actions which in his society are conventionally marked off as the kinds of thing that, for example, a brave person does. As he progresses in virtue, he does these things as a virtuous person does them, with understanding, and also gets better at doing the right thing. He acts bravely with greater understanding of what bravery requires, for example, and does the right thing as the truly brave person would do it – from the right reasons, as a result of having the right disposition, and so on.

It is generally true that brave people in our society, for example, do certain actions, which can be independently specified. But most people in our society are only at the beginning, learner stage of virtue. They do the right thing for people at that stage. It is what bravery requires of them, demanded by society's rules, exemplified in people who are role models of bravery. When the completely virtuous brave person does the right thing it is not because is required of him by the conventional account of bravery, but as a result of his own reflective understanding of bravery and its requirements and his development of the appropriate disposition.

So if we return to the schema:

An action is right if and only if it is what virtuous person would (reliably, characteristically) do

we can see that it can be applied in two quite different kinds of way. The beginner does the right thing in the following way: it is what bravery requires, it is the right, not the wrong thing to do; it is praised, emulated and so on. The fully virtuous person also does the right thing; in this case it is the right thing done for the all the right reasons and from a disposition that has developed virtuously in both its intellectual and affective aspects, based on fully developed understanding of all relevant ethical factors.[14] These are obviously very different ways of being the right thing to do. We cannot, of course, give an account of doing the right thing as the virtuous person would do it ithout reference to the virtuous person. So we nnot come up with independent character-ations of the virtuous person and the right ing to do if we take into account not merely e beginner in virtue but also the fully virtu-us person. And if we omit the latter from our count of virtue, we are failing to notice a ucial point: the fully virtuous person is the eal that the beginner in virtue is aspiring be.

We can now see why we cannot give a satis-ctory virtue ethical account of right action if e insist on independent characterizations of e virtuous person and the right thing to do; ch an account (whatever else can be said for d against it) will capture only the learner, the rson whose virtue is limited to doing the nventionally right thing. But the learner es not exhaust our conception of virtue; we so need to take account of the expert. And we ill not get the point even of what the learner is ing if we take him to be merely doing the nventional thing, failing to notice that he is so aspiring to do better, and thus to get closer an ideal. So we can also now see why reject-g independent characterization of the virtu-s person and right action is far from landing with a trivially circular account.

meone might say that if we are going to dis-guish the way the beginner does the right ing from the way the fully virtuous person es the right thing, then what the theory ould say is that the right thing to do just is hat the fully virtuous person would do, and e beginning virtuous person is not doing the ght thing. This would be a rigorist approach, e that of consequentialists who hold that the ght thing to do is what the ideal calculator of nsequences would do, so that we ordinary ople, however admirable our intentions, aracter and so on, almost never do the right ing. This way of looking at things, however, s to hold that some of us are worthy of praise, nulation and so on, even though we are not ing the right thing; and this is at least awk-ard. It is also difficult to make sense of moral lucation and improvement on this view; meone becoming brave, for example, would ill never be doing the right thing until ey became completely virtuous. It is worth

noticing here that the Stoics were rigorists about virtue, holding that only the completely virtuous have virtue, while we are all vicious and base – but even they held that the non-virtuous, as well as the virtuous, can do the right thing, though only the virtuous do the right thing in the fully virtuous way.[15]

Another response might be to suggest that we have two senses of 'right' here. But this is surely implausible, for the same kind of reason that it is implausible that we would have dif-ferent senses of 'right' when the apprentice carpenter and the skilled carpenter both fix the shelves in the right way.

We can see, then, why the familiar schema cannot produce a decision procedure for virtue ethics if we take into account the point that virtue involves aspiring to an ideal; any account that could produce a decision procedure would be stuck at the level of the learner, helpless to deal with our ethical aspirations.

So, if I am wondering what the right thing is to do, and approach the virtuous person's char-acteristic actions for guidance as to what that is, there are two important factors. Firstly, to what extent is the person I look to an expert or a mere learner? How virtuous are they, really? If they are a mere learner then their actions may be right, but only through doing what they were told without deep understanding. Only if they have developed the right kind of understanding will their examples be good ones from which I can learn. And secondly, to what extent am I an expert or a mere learner? How virtuous am I, really? If I am a mere learner then I may not have chosen the right model, and even if I have, I may not be emulating the right aspect of it.

If we bear these two factors in mind we see that and why the virtuous person cannot pro-vide an all-purpose decision procedure that I can apply regardless of my character to find out what the right thing is for me to do. Even if I try to go through the virtuous person to find the right thing to do, the merits of my decision will depend not just on the goodness of my model but the degree of my own virtu-ous development in discerning what in it to emulate.

Some people regard this result as a disaster, for it loses the one attractive aspect of the com-puter manual model, namely its egalitarianism.

We no longer have a decision procedure for working out the right thing to do in a way which is available to everyone. However, I have worked to undermine the thought that a decision procedure is what we want. And the result here is, I claim, supported by our everyday ethical discourse. We do recognize that the worth of the advice and direction we get from other people depends on their degree of moral development. We don't emulate, or get advice from, airheads, or untrustworthy people. When we take moral advice we assess its source; we know that the character of the person we go to will be shown in the advice we get. It would be bizarre for me to say that I will do what John tells me to do, though I thoroughly despise John. And we do take my actions to show something about me as a person, not just my ability to understand a theory; they show what sort of character I have.

What of the three common objections to virtue ethics I mentioned earlier? We can see, briefly, that and why they lose their force once we recognize that virtue involves a progress from the beginner to the fully virtuous.

How do we identify the virtuous people? We do so in the way that we identify good builders and pianists – that is, in a way which is initially hostage to our own lack of expertise. At first we just have to accept their credentials; as we improve in the relevant area we might end up by challenging them.

What of the unhelpful vagueness of the ideally virtuous person? This need not matter if it is not the ideally virtuous person we are appealing to for guidance in how we are to act. We start with teachers and role models who are braver, more generous and so on than we are, but we do not need, or expect, them to be already completely virtuous for the process to get going.

What of the clear cases of right action which are not actions which a virtuous person would

characteristically do? Again, we need to distinguish between what the ordinarily virtuous person, the learner, would do, and what the fully virtuous person would do. The person who is at the stage of learning to be virtuous and still aspiring to do better might quite well do the wrong thing and have to apologize. He might well try to improve his character, organize his life to help his improvement along, and need guidance from a person who is in the relevant respect better. These are all normal actions characteristic of someone who is developing a virtuous disposition, given ordinary facts about human weaknesses. Fully virtuous person would never need to do such things; but we are not fully virtuous people, though hopefully we are trying to improve.

We have seen, then, how virtue ethics applicable. It is not a theory which tells us what to do; we have seen that we neither have nor should want any such thing. Rather, guides us by improving the practical reasoning with which we act. It directs us, as we are wondering what to do, towards emulating people who are braver, more generous and generally better than we are, and does so in way which recognizes the constraints put on this by the level of our development as well as that of the people we emulate. This result will be disappointing only to those who think that acting well can be reduced to the results of formula applied across the board with no further moral effort. Virtue ethics does better, have suggested, because it has a built-in recognition of the point that the moral life is not static; it is always developing. When it comes to working out the right thing to do, we cannot shift the work to a theory, however excellent because we, unlike the theories, are always learning, and so we are always aspiring to do better.

Notes

1. This is what Rosalind Hursthouse calls thinking in terms of the 'v-rules'; see her *On Virtue Ethics*, Oxford University Press 1999.
2. It is sometimes suggested that this happens only in relatively open societies, whose members are

exposed to different ways of life and encouraged to think for themselves about them; in relatively closed and traditional societies this is unlikely to happen. I think that this makes an unwarranted inference from the fact that in traditional societies ethically more reflective thought may be repressed (sometimes harshly) to the claim that in such societies people are satisfied with unreflective thought. History strongly suggests otherwise.

There are theories which do not make this kind of demand, or which make it in their simpler versions but reject it in their more sophisticated versions. While I do not have the scope to develop the point here, I think that virtue ethics will converge with these theories, rather than providing an alternative to them. However, in my experience the need for a decision procedure is often assumed to be a requirement on a respectable moral theory. Cf Mark Timmons, *Moral Theory*, Rowman and Littlefield 2002, p. 3: 'The main practical aim of a moral theory is to discover a decision procedure that can be used to guide correct moral reasoning about matters of moral concern'. Successfully meeting this demand is thus necessary for virtue ethics to be recognized as even a contender for being a type of moral theory.

In much of her work, but particularly in *On Virtue Ethics* (Oxford University Press, 1999).

Followers of the *Fox Trot* daily cartoon can think of this point as the Jason Fox point.

Hursthouse has made extensive use of this schema, but not to produce a decision procedure, something she rightly takes virtue ethics not to do.

This common example is found in Gilbert Harman, 'Moral Philosophy Meets Social Psychology,' *Proceedings of the Aristotelian Society* New Series 2000, 223–36, and John Doris, "Persons, Situations and Virtue Ethics," *Nous* 32.4, 1998, 504–30.

Robert N. Johnson, 'Virtue and Right,' *Ethics* 113.4, July 2003, 810–34.

Nicomachean Ethics II 1.

10. The analogy with building is relevant to the initial stage of moving from acquiring a conventional understanding of virtue to coming to have your own understanding of that virtue. Most versions of virtue ethics will also move on to further stages. The practice of the several virtues is not compartmentalized; reflection on the ways in which they interrelate generally leads to some form of unification of the virtues via the exercise of the practical reasoning displayed in them. Further, people both within a culture and between cultures will learn to respect one another's reasoning insofar as they recognize the practice of the virtues in different contexts and across cultural boundaries.

11. This, the Aristotelian model, is the most familiar, which is why I have used it as illustration in the present paper.

12. This would be required by religious versions of virtue ethics, in which the content of the virtuous person's reasonings would be initially given by religiously sanctioned rules (such as Mosaic law) which are not open to rejection or revision, but do demand intelligent interpretation to be correctly applied.

13. In a way precisely paralled by consequentialism and deontology.

14. This is a gesture at what full virtue might require; different theories have different accounts here.

15. The distinction drawn here, between doing the right thing as the beginner (the learner) does it and doing the right thing as the fully virtuous person (the expert) does it, maps well onto the Stoic distinction between a *kathekon*, a right action which anyone can perform, and a *katorthoma*, a right action performed by a virtuous person. (For the Stoics, however, this would be limited to the sage or ideally virtuous person, nobody else being virtuous.)

PART XII

Prima Facie Duties
and Particularism

Introduction to Part XII

moral rule is absolute just in case it may ever be permissibly broken. Are there any such rules?

Here is a reason for thinking that there are no absolute moral rules. The reason is that morality cannot require us to perpetrate disastrous results. But for every moral rule, we can imagine a case in which abiding by it yields disastrous results. So every moral rule, no matter how initially plausible, may be permissibly broken in at least some circumstances. Therefore, there are no absolute moral rules.

One way to reply to this argument is to say that we need only to craft the moral rules in a finer-grained way, so that permissible exceptions turn out to be impossible. The relevant moral rule will not, for instance, prohibit killing humans, but rather will prohibit killing humans in all circumstances except (say) in cases of self-defense, or in the prosecution of just war. Once we have refined the principle against homicide, we will have a truly exceptionless rule.

There are many, however, who are skeptical that such a filling-in can ever be done. No matter the exceptions, we might always encounter or imagine another circumstance in which adherence to even the amended rule would engender a horrific result, while its violation would spare us this disaster.

The natural home for such a skeptical thought is act consequentialism. Indeed, one of the main arguments for act consequentialism is that it can account for our suspicions about the existence of absolute moral rules. W. D. Ross, in an excerpt from his classic work, *The Right and the Good*, sees the temptation to endorse act consequentialism on this basis, and encourages us strongly to resist it. Indeed, if Ross is right, then we should steer a middle path between both act consequentialism, and its traditional sparring partner, Kantian deontology.

Ross identifies two basic problems with act consequentialism. The first is its mistaken insistence that the distribution of goodness is morally irrelevant. If I can generate an equal amount of goodness by either keeping my promise, or by violating it, then act consequentialism regards these actions as morally equivalent. But that, says Ross, is just false, as every mature person would recognize. Its second error is that it ignores the highly personal character of duty. Moral duty is much more than a requirement to impartially generate as much happiness (or love, or beauty, etc.) as possible. We are friends, parents, debtors, and wrongdoers, relations we bear only to specific people, rather than to everyone, and each of these relations generates duties of its own. Ross agrees that there is a duty to prevent misery for others, and to cultivate their happiness, but these are not the only duties that we have. Nor are they always the most important.

Kant's views do not escape Ross's scrutiny, either. Ross thought that Kant's fundamental error lay in conceiving of moral rules as absolute. Kant's unqualified opposition to any instance of lying and suicide (among other things) struck Ross, as so many others, as deeply mistaken. Ross suggested instead that we see all moral rules as generating *prima facie duties*, i.e., duties that can be permissibly broken when competing considerations are weighty enough. In any specific case, such duties represent decisive, all-things-considered moral requirements if no other prima facie duties are as significant in the given context. There are prima facie duties of beneficence and non-maleficence, but also of fidelity (to past agreements), reparations (for past wrongdoing), justice (to align reward with merit), etc. There is no fixed ranking of these duties – sometimes it is morally more important to prevent harm than to keep a promise, for instance, but at other times, the reverse is true.

The basic idea here is that there is a plurality of basic, non-derivative sources of moral duty. The core ideas of utilitarianism, Kantianism, and contractarianism are each represented by a distinct prima facie duty, no one of which invariably takes moral priority over the others. Many people have found this a deeply satisfying account of morality, since it allows us to preserve something of the basic intuitions that underlie each of the major normative ethical theories, while avoiding the problems that arise due to their exclusivity of moral focus.

That said, there are three major difficulties for the view. The first is that of arbitrariness. It seems that Ross has offered us an unconnected heap of duties, with no systematic rationale available to justify his favored candidate duties. The second is that of balancing. In the absence of any permanent ranking of the prima facie duties, or any more basic rule that could adjudicate conflicts between them, it simply isn't clear why one such duty takes priority in some cases, while the priority is reversed in others. The third, related, difficulty is understanding how we might know both the prima facie duties, and the final, conclusive duty in particular cases. Ross tells us that the prima facie duties are self-evident, and we have seen, in Part II, the many challenges to claims of

self-evidence. Further, Ross offers no procedure, and almost no advice, about how to discern one's actual, all-things-considered moral duty in any case in which prima facie duties conflict. Addressing these long-standing worries is the main focus of David McNaughton's sympathetic reconstruction and defense of Ross's views, given here in our second reading.

Though McNaughton comes to Ross's defense, he was earlier known for his allegiance to a different sort of view: ethical particularism. Particularism is the most extreme rejection of the idea that morality must be structured by reference to a set of moral rules. Particularists deny that there are any useful moral rules. Not only are there no absolute moral rules; there are no prima facie ones, either.

The particularist rejection of moral rules is founded on a central claim: that there are no uniformly morally relevant features of the world. Despite their disagreements on other fronts, those who endorse absolute moral rules, and those in favor of prima facie ones, both agree that certain kinds of action (e.g., harming others, or keeping one's word) always, and of necessity, incline in favor of an action, or against it. If there is a moral rule against lying, for instance, then there is always something wrong about lying – no exceptions. If absolutists are right, then there is always decisive reason not to lie. If Ross is right, then there is always some defeasible (i.e., defeatable) reason not to lie, even if lying is, in a particular case, morally acceptable, all things considered.

Particularists will reject both pictures of the moral rules. And their rejection does not depend on the specific example of lying. For them, whether a feature is morally relevant cannot be discerned in advance, but only after a sensitive appreciation of the entire context in which the feature is located. Just as a certain brushstroke of a particular color may be a positive contribution to one painting, but a terrible addition to another, so too any feature may sometimes contribute favorably to the morality of an action, and yet at other times detract from it. According to Jonathan Dancy, the most renowned contemporary ethical particularist, even those features enshrined in Ross's prima facie duties are only variably morally relevant. That an action makes others appy, for instance, is often, but not always, a reason to do it. Sometimes an action's contribution to happiness is either no reason at all to undertake it, or a positive reason not to do so. That the action of torturing someone makes the sadist happy, for example, is a reason against such torture, not a reason for it. Dancy thinks that we will be able to offer a similar diagnosis for any feature of the world. There are some contexts in which, when combined with other facts of the case, a feature will favor an action. Other contexts, where the accompanying facts are different, will render the feature a strike against the action. And in other cases still, the feature may be wholly neutral, making the action neither more nor less justified than it would otherwise be.

Philosophers are usually quite sympathetic to system building, to seeking an explanation that will unify a diverse set of phenomena. In this they are no different from thinkers in most other disciplines. Particularism denies that ethics is a systematic area of inquiry. Moral phenomena cannot be ordered and classified by reference to moral rules, whether absolute or prima facie. Ethical particularism stands at the far end of the spectrum of theoretical order and simplicity. At the opposite terminus is ethical egoism and act utilitarianism, which insist on just a single moral rule, requiring the maximization of just a single intrinsic value. On such views, the moral realm is ultimately explicable by reference to the basic consideration. Particularism denies that the moral realm is explicable by reference to any rules at all.

It may seem difficult to envision a middle path between particularism and Ross's view, but Margaret Little seeks its course. What needs clarification is the notion of what she calls a *defeasible generalization*. This is an "other things equal," or a "for the most part" moral rule, as in "other things being equal, one ought to keep one's promises," or "killing people is, for the most part, immoral." What do we mean when we use such phrases? One thing we might mean is what Ross himself meant – namely, that there is (at the least) always a reason to keep one's word, and always a reason against killing. Or we might mean that fidelity is usually right, and killing ordinarily wrong, though in some cases there isn't anything morally right about fidelity, and nothing morally amiss about killing. Or we might consider such generalizations handy rules of thumb. In this last case, we might imagine that, with sufficient time and attention, we could specify exactly what the appropriate exceptions are to the rule, but, for ease of use, we simply employ the rule as shorthand to give us reliable practical guidance.

Little offers us a different alternative. Moral rules specify conditions under which kinds of actions are (for example) morally right or wrong, virtuous or vicious, praiseworthy or blameworthy. For Little, the connections linking kinds of actions and specific moral features need not hold always, or even usually. In this, she agrees with particularists. Still, there are many plausible moral rules, so long as we understand them as claiming to identify something especially revealing about the nature of the actions they describe. A correct moral rule entitles us to take as privileged those cases in which an action has the moral feature attributed to it by the rule. For instance, moral rules can identify paradigm cases of (im)morality. The moral rule against killing human beings does this. If there are cases in which such killing is permissible, the rule's function is to show where the burden of argument and explanation lies.

To illustrate this point, consider a nonmoral rule: Chairs are, for the most part, to be sat on. This identifies a paradigmatic feature of chairs. Yet some chairs, such as those high-end art objects intended for museum display cases, aren't to be sat on. This exceptional example doesn't undermine the rule. Rather, the rule serves as a way of establishing a privileged kind of case, one that, when it fails to hold, calls out for some explanation.

Certainly one of the most difficult problems faced by all of the authors in this Part is the epistemological problem of justifying our beliefs about our all-things-considered duties. Some help can be gained from the readings in Part II, but our present authors seem to be in more difficult straits. If there are no moral rules at all (Dancy), or only prima facie rules or defeasible generalizations (Ross, McNaughton, Little), then how can we know our actual duty in particular cases?

This challenge is set against a very common assumption, namely, that a person has justified belief that something is her conclusive duty only if her belief can be supported by a general moral principle. The thought is that without the ability to invoke a general principle, a person has nothing to substantiate the claim that a certain action is her all-things-considered moral duty. And if she has nothing to substantiate such a claim, then she can't be justified in believing it.

Gerald Dworkin challenges this common assumption by showing that the particularist's approach to gaining moral knowledge is in reality just standard practice. If we consider how we actually go about rendering moral verdicts, we see that we do not, in fact, ordin-arily invoke general rules in order to identi[f]y our all-in moral duty. Rather, we attend [to] specific details, do not feel constrained b[y] general rules, and rely on sound practical judg-ment to arrive at the right answer to mor[al] questions. This is a highly unsystematic unde[r]taking, and confounds what Dworkin regar[ds] as a philosopher's fantasy (*viz.*, that we ordi[n]arily justify our claims about specific duties b[y] introducing general moral rules). He offers [a] detailed account of our actual practices [of] moral deliberation and interpersonal justifica-tion, and claims that if we attend to the[m] carefully, and regard them as largely reliabl[e,] then we will no longer see moral rules [as] an indispensable element in acquiring mor[al] knowledge.

CHAPTER 72

What Makes Right Acts Right?

W. D. ROSS

. .]

hen a plain man fulfils a promise because he
inks he ought to do so, it seems clear that he
es so with no thought of its total conse-
ences, still less with any opinion that these
e likely to be the best possible. He thinks in
ct much more of the past than of the future.
hat makes him think it right to act in a
rtain way is the fact that he has promised
do so – that and, usually, nothing more.
at his act will produce the best possible
nsequences is not his reason for calling it
ght. What lends colour to the theory we are
amining, then, is not the actions (which
rm probably a great majority of our actions)
which some such reflection as "I have prom-
d" is the only reason we give ourselves for
inking a certain action right, but the excep-
nal cases in which the consequences of ful-
ing a promise (for instance) would be so
sastrous to others that we judge it right not
do so. It must of course be admitted that
ch cases exist. If I have promised to meet a
end at a particular time for some trivial
rpose, I should certainly think myself justi-
d in breaking my engagement if by doing so I
uld prevent a serious accident or bring relief
the victims of one. And the supporters of the

view we are examining hold that my thinking
so is due to my thinking that I shall bring more
good into existence by the one action than by
the other. A different account may, however, be
given of the mater, an account which will, I
believe, show itself to be the true one. It may
be said that besides the duty of fulfilling promises I have and recognize a duty of relieving
distress, and that when I think it right to do the
latter at the cost of not doing the former, it is
not because I think I shall produce more good
thereby but because I think it the duty which
is in the circumstances more of a duty. This
account surely corresponds much more closely
with what we really think in such a situation. If,
so far as I can see, I could bring equal amounts
of good into being by fulfilling my promise and
by helping some one to whom I had made no
promise, I should not hesitate to regard the
former as my duty. Yet on the view that what
is right is right because it is productive of the
most good I should not so regard it.

There are two theories, each in its way
simple, that offer a solution of such cases of
conscience. One is the view of Kant, that there
are certain duties of perfect obligation, such as
those of fulfilling promises, of paying debts, of
telling the truth, which admit of no exception
whatever in favour of duties of imperfect obligation, such as that of relieving distress. The
other is the view of, for instance, Professor
Moore and Dr. Rashdall, that there is only the

D. Ross, "What Makes Right Acts Right?," pp. 18–22,
-32, 39–41 from *The Right and the Good*. Oxford: Oxford
iversity Press, 1930.

duty of producing good, and that all "conflicts of duties" should be resolved by asking "by which action will most good be produced?" But it is more important that our theory fit the facts than that it be simple, and the account we have given above corresponds (it seems to me) better than either of the simpler theories with what we really think, viz. That normally promise-keeping, for example, should come before benevolence, but that when and only when the good to be produced by the benevolent act is very great and the promise comparatively trivial, the act of benevolence becomes our duty.

In fact the theory of "ideal utilitarianism," if I may for brevity refer so to the theory of Professor Moore, seems to simplify unduly our relations to our fellows. It says, in effect, that the only morally significant relation in which my neighbours stand to me is that of being possible beneficiaries by my action. They do stand in this relation to me, and this relation is morally significant. But they may also stand to me in the relation of promisee to promiser, of creditor to debtor, of wife to husband, of child to parent, of friend to friend, of fellow countryman to fellow countryman, and the like; and each of these relations is the foundation of a *prima facie* duty, which is more or less incumbent on me according to the circumstances of the case. When I am in a situation, as perhaps I always am, in which more than one of these *prima facie* duties is incumbent on me, what I have to do is to study the situation as fully as I can until I form the considered opinion (it is never more) that in the circumstances one of them is more incumbent than any other; then I am bound to think that to do this *prima facie* duty is my duty *sans phrase* in the situation.

I suggest "*prima facie* duty" or "conditional duty" as a brief way of referring to the characteristic (quite distinct from that of being a duty proper) which an act has, in virtue of being of a certain kind (e.g. the keeping of a promise), of being an act which would be a duty proper if it were not at the same time of another kind which is morally significant. Whether an act is a duty proper or actual duty depends on *all* the morally significant kinds it is an instance of. . . .

There is nothing arbitrary about these *prima facie* duties. Each rests on a definite circumstance which cannot seriously be held to be without moral significance. Of *prima facie* duties I suggest, without claiming completeness or finality for it, the following division.[1]

(1) Some duties rest on previous acts of my own. These duties seem to include two kinds. (a) those resting on a promise or what may fairly be called an implicit promise, such as the implicit undertaking not to tell lies which seems to be implicit in the act of entering into conversation (at any rate by civilized men), or of writing books that purport to be history and not fiction. These may be called the duties of fidelity. (b) Those resting on a previous wrongful act. These may be called the duties of reparation. (2) Some rest on previous acts of other men, i.e. services done by them to me. These may be loosely described as the duties of gratitude. (3) Some rest on the fact or possibility of a distribution of pleasure or happiness (or of the means thereto) which is not in accordance with the merit of the persons concerned; in such cases there arises a duty to upset or prevent such a distribution. These are the duties of justice. (4) Some rest on the mere fact that there are other beings in the world whose condition we can make better in respect of virtue, or of intelligence, or of pleasure. These are the duties of beneficence. (5) Some rest on the fact that we can improve our own condition in respect of virtue or of intelligence. These are the duties of self-improvement. (6) I think that we should distinguish from (4) the duties that may be summed up under the title of "not injuring others." No doubt to injure others is incidentally to fail to do them good; but it seems to me clear that non-maleficence is apprehended as a duty distinct from that of beneficence, and as a duty of a more stringent character. It will be noticed that this alone among the types of duty has been stated in a negative way. An attempt might no doubt be made to state this duty, like the others, in a positive way. It might be said that it is really the duty to prevent ourselves from acting either from an inclination to harm others or from an inclination to seek our own pleasure, in doing which we should incidentally harm them. But on reflection it seems clear that the

imary duty here is the duty not to harm others, this being a duty whether or not we have an inclination that if followed would lead to our harming them; and that when we have such an inclination the primary duty not to harm others gives rise to a consequential duty to resist the inclination. The recognition of this duty of non-maleficence is the first step in the way to the recognition of the duty of beneficence; and that accounts for the prominence of the commands "thou shalt not kill," "thou shalt not commit adultery," "thou shalt not steal," "thou shalt not bear false witness," in so early a code as the Decalogue. But even when we have come to recognize the duty of beneficence, it appears to me that the duty of non-maleficence is recognized as a distinct one, and as *prima facie* more binding. We should not in general consider it justifiable to kill one person in order to keep another alive, or to steal from one in order to give alms to another.

The essential defect of the "ideal utilitarian" theory is that it ignores, or at least does not do full justice to, the highly personal character of duty. If the only duty is to produce the maximum of good, the question who is to have the good – whether it is myself, or my benefactor, or a person to whom I have made a promise to confer that good on him, or a mere fellow man to whom I stand in no such special relation – should make no difference to my having a duty to produce that good. But we are all in fact sure that it makes a vast difference. . . .

If the objection be made, that this catalogue of the main types of duty is an unsystematic one resting on no logical principle, it may be replied, first, that it makes no claim to being ultimate. It is a *prima facie* classification of the duties which reflection on our moral convictions seems actually to reveal. And if these convictions are, as I would claim that they are, of the nature of knowledge, and if I have not misstated them, the list will be a list of authentic conditional duties, correct as far as it goes though not necessarily complete. The list of *goods* put forward by the rival theory is reached by exactly the same method – the only sound one in the circumstances – viz. that of direct reflection on what we really think. Loyalty to the facts is worth more than a

symmetrical architectonic or a hastily reached simplicity. If further reflection discovers a perfect logical basis for this or for a better classification, so much the better.

It may, again, be objected that our theory that there are these various and often conflicting types of *prima facie* duty leaves us with no principle upon which to discern what is our actual duty in particular circumstances. But this objection is not one of which the rival theory is in a position to bring forward. For when we have to choose between the production of two heterogeneous goods, say knowledge and pleasure, the "ideal utilitarian" theory can only fall back on an opinion, for which no logical basis can be offered, that one of the goods is the greater; and this is no better than a similar opinion that one of two duties is the more urgent. And again, when we consider the infinite variety of the effects of our actions in the way of pleasure, it must surely be admitted that the claim which *hedonism* sometimes makes, that it offers a readily applicable criterion of right conduct, is quite illusory.

I am unwilling, however, to content myself with an *argumentum ad hominem*, and I would contend that in principle there is no reason to anticipate that every act that is our duty is so for one and the same reason. Why should two sets of circumstances, or one set of circumstances, *not* possess different characteristics, any one of which makes a certain act our *prima facie* duty? When I ask what it is that makes me in certain cases sure that I have a *prima facie* duty to do so and so, I find that it lies in the fact that I have made a promise; when I ask the same question in another case, I find the answer lies in the fact that I have done a wrong. And if on reflection I find (as I think I do) that neither of these reasons is reducible to the other, I must not on any *a priori* ground assume that such a reduction is possible. . . .

It is necessary to say something by way of clearing up the relation between *prima facie* duties and the actual or absolute duty to do one particular act in particular circumstances. If, as almost all moralists except Kant are agreed, and as most plain men think, it is sometimes right to tell a lie or to break a promise, it must be maintained that there is a difference between *prima facie* duty and actual or absolute duty. When we think our-selves justified in breaking, and indeed morally obliged to break, a promise in order to relieve some one's distress, we do not for a moment cease to recognize a *prima facie* duty to keep our promise, and this leads us to feel, not indeed shame or repentance, but certainly compunction, for behaving as we do; we rec-ognize, further, that it is our duty to make up somehow to the promise for the breaking of the promise. We have to distinguish from the characteristic of being our duty that of tending to be our duty. Any act that we do contains various elements in virtue of which it falls under various categories. In virtue of being the breaking of a promise, for instance, it tends to be wrong; in virtue of being an instance of relieving distress it tends to be right. Tendency to be one's duty may be called a parti-resultant attribute, i.e. one which belongs to an act in virtue of some one com-ponent in its nature. *Being* one's duty is a toti-resultant attribute, one which belongs to an act in virtue of its whole nature and of nothing less than this. . . .

Another instance of the same distinction may be found in the operation of natural laws. *Qua* subject to the force of gravitation towards some other body, each body tends to move in a particular direction with a particular velocity; but its actual movement depends on *all* the forces to which it is subject. It is only by recognising this distinction that we can pre-serve the absoluteness of laws of nature, and only by recognising a corresponding distinc-tion that we can preserve the absoluteness of the general principles of morality. But an important difference between the two cases must be pointed out. When we say that in virtue of gravitation a body tends to move in a certain way, we are referring to a casual influence actually exercised on it by another body or other bodies. When we say that in virtue of being deliberately untrue a certain remark tends to be wrong, we are referring to no causal relation, to no relation that involves succession in time, but to such a relation as connects the various attributes of a mathemat-ical figure. And if the word "tendency" is thought to suggest too much a causal relation,

it is better to talk of certain types of act as bei**n** *prima facie* right or wrong (or of differe**nt** persons as having different and possibly co**n**flicting claims upon us), than of their tendi**ng** to be right or wrong.

Something should be said of the relati**on** between our apprehension of the *prima fa**cie*** rightness of certain types of act and our men**tal** attitude towards particular acts. It is proper **to** use the word "apprehension" in the form**er** case and not in the latter. That an act, q**ua** fulfilling a promise, or *qua* effecting a ju**st** distribution of good, or *qua* returning servic**e** rendered, or *qua* promoting the good of othe**rs** or *qua* promoting the virtue or insight of t**he** agent, is *prima facie* right, is self-evident; not **in** the sense that it is evident from the beginni**ng** of our lives, or as soon as we attend to t**he** proposition for the first time, but in the sen**se** that when we have reached sufficient men**tal** maturity and have given sufficient attenti**on** to the proposition it is evident without a**ny** need of proof, or of evidence beyond itself. **It** is self-evident just as a mathematical axio**m,** or the validity of a form of inference, is evide**nt.** The moral order expressed in these propo**si**tions is just as much part of the fundament**al** nature of the universe (and, we may add, of a**ny** possible universe in which there were mo**ral** agents at all) as is the spatial or numeric**al** structure expressed in the axioms of geomet**ry** or arithmetic. In our confidence that the**se** propositions are true there is involved t**he** same trust in our reason that is involved **in** our confidence in mathematics; and we shou**ld** have no justification for trusting it in the latt**er** sphere and distrusting it in the former. In bo**th** cases we are dealing with propositions th**at** cannot be proved, but that just as certai**nly** need no proof. . . .

Our judgements about our actual duty **in** concrete situations have none of the certai**nty** that attaches to our recognition of the gene**ral** principles of duty. A statement is certain, i.**e.** is an expression of knowledge, only in one **or** other of two cases: when it is either se**lf-**evident, or a valid conclusion from self-evide**nt** premisses. And our judgements about our pa**r**ticular duties have neither of these characte**r.** (1) They are not self-evident. Where a possi**ble**

ct is seen to have two characteristics, in virtue
f one of which it is *prima facie* right,
nd in virtue of the other *prima facie* wrong,
e are (I think) well aware that we are not
ertain whether we ought or ought not to do
; that whether we do it or not, we are taking a
noral risk. We come in the long run, after
onsideration, to think one duty more pressing
han the other, but we do not feel certain that it
 so. And though we do not always recognize
hat a possible act has two such characteristics,
nd though there *may* be cases in which it has
ot, we are never certain that any particular
ossible act has not, and therefore never certain
hat it is right, nor certain that it is wrong. For,
o go no further in the analysis, it is enough to
oint out that any particular act will in all
robability in the course of time contribute to
he bringing about of good or of evil for many
uman beings, and thus have a *prima facie*
ightness or wrongness of which we know
othing. (2) Again, our judgements about our
articular duties are not logical conclusions
rom self-evident premises. The only possible
remises would be the general principles stat-
ng their *prima facie* rightness or wrongness
ua having the different characteristics they
o have; and even if we could (as we cannot)
pprehend the extent to which an act will tend
n the one hand, for example, to bring about
dvantages for our benefactors, and on the
ther hand to bring about disadvantages for
ellow men who are not our benefactors, there
s no principle by which we can draw the con-
lusion that it is on the whole right or on the
vhole wrong. In this respect the judgement as
o the rightness of a particular act is just like
he judgement as to the beauty of a particular
natural object or work of art. A poem is, for
nstance, in respect of certain qualities beauti-
ul and in respect of certain others not beauti-
ul; and our judgement as to the degree of
beauty it possesses on the whole is never
eached by logical reasoning from the appre-
nension of its particular beauties or particular
defects. Both in this and in the moral case we
nave more or less probable opinions which are
not logically justified conclusions from the
general principles that are recognized as
elf-evident.

There is therefore much truth in the description of the right act as a fortunate act. If we
cannot be certain that it is right, it is our good
fortune if the act we do is the right act. This
consideration does not, however, make the
doing of our duty a mere matter of chance.
There is a parallel here between the doing of
duty and the doing of what will be to our
personal advantage. We never *know* what act
will in the long run be to our advantage. Yet it
is certain that we are more likely in general to
secure our advantage if we estimate to the best
of our ability the probable tendencies of our
actions in this respect, than if we act on caprice.
And similarly we are more likely to do our duty
if we reflect to the best of our ability on the
prima facie rightness or wrongness of various
possible acts in virtue of the characteristics
we perceive them to have, than if we act without reflection. With this greater likelihood we
must be content.

[. . .]

The general principles of duty are obviously
not self-evident from the beginning of our
lives. How do they come to be so? The answer
is, that they come to be self-evident to us just as
mathematical axioms do. We find by experience that this couple of matches and that
couple make four matches, that this couple of
balls on a wire and that couple make four balls;
and by reflection on these and similar discoveries we come to see that it is of the nature of
two and two to make four. In a precisely similar
way, we see the *prima facie* rightness of an act
which would be the fulfilment of a particular
promise, and of another which would be the
fulfilment of another promise, and when we
have reached sufficient maturity to think in
general terms, we apprehend *prima facie* rightness to belong to the nature of any fulfilment
of promise. What comes first in time is the
apprehension of the self-evident *prima facie*
rightness of an individual act of a particular
type. From this we come by reflection to
apprehend the self-evident general principle
of *prima facie* duty. From this, too, perhaps
along with the apprehension of the self-evident
prima facie rightness of the same act in virtue
of its having another characteristic as well, and
perhaps in spite of the apprehension of its

prima facie wrongness in virtue of its having some third characteristic, we come to believe something not self-evident at all, but an object of probable opinion, viz. that this particular act is (not *prima facie* but) actually right. . . .

Supposing it to be agreed, as I think on reflection it must, that no one *means* by "right" just "productive of the best possible consequences," or "optimific," the attributes "right" and "optimific" might stand in either of two kinds of relation to each other. (1) They might be so related that we could apprehend *a priori*, either immediately or deductively, that any act that is optimific is right and any act that is right is optimific, as we can apprehend that any triangle that is equilateral is equiangular and *vice versa*. Professor Moore's view is, I think, that the coextensiveness of "right" and "optimific" is apprehended immediately. He rejects the possibility of any proof of it. Or (2) the two attributes might be such that the question whether they are invariably connected had to be answered by means of an inductive inquiry. Now at first sight it might seem as if the constant connexion of the two attributes could be immediately apprehended. It might seem absurd to suggest that it could be right for any one to do an act which would produce consequences less good than those which would be produced by some other act in his power. Yet a little thought will convince us that this is not absurd. The type of case in which it is easiest to see that this is so is, perhaps, that in which one has made a promise. In such a case we all think that *prima facie* it is our duty to fulfil the promise irrespective of the precise goodness of the total consequences. And though we do not think it is necessarily our actual or absolute duty to do so, we are far from thinking that any, even the slightest, gain in the value of the total consequences will necessarily justify us in doing something else instead. Suppose, to simplify the case by abstraction, that the fulfilment of a promise to *A* would produce 1,000 units of good for him, but that by doing some other act I could produce 1,001 units of good for *B*, to whom I have made no promise, the other consequences of the two acts being of equal value; should we really think it self-evident that it was our duty

to do the second act and not the first? I think not. We should, I fancy, hold that only a much greater disparity of value between the total consequences would justify us in failing to discharge our *prima facie* duty to *A*. After all, a promise is a promise, and is not to be treated so lightly as the theory we are examining would imply. What, exactly, a promise is, is not so easy to determine, but we are surely agreed that it constitutes a serious moral limitation to our freedom of action. To produce the 1,001 units of good for *B* rather than fulfil our promise to *A* would be to take, not perhaps our duty as philanthropists too seriously, but certainly our duty as makers of promises too lightly. . . .

Such instances – and they might easily be added to – make it clear that there is no self-evident connexion between the attributes "right" and "optimific." The theory we are examining has a certain attractiveness when applied to our decision that a particular act is our duty (though I have tried to show that it does not agree with our actual moral judgements even here). But it is not even plausible when applied to our recognition of *prima facie* duty. For if it were self-evident that the right coincides with the optimific, it should be self-evident that what is *prima facie* right is *prima facie* optimific. But whereas we are certain that keeping a promise is *prima facie* right, we are not certain that it is *prima facie* optimific (though we are perhaps certain that it is *prima facie* bonific). Our certainty that it is *prima facie* right depends not on its consequences but on its being the fulfilment of a promise. The theory we are examining involves too much difference between the evident ground of our conviction about *prima facie* duty and the alleged ground of our conviction about actual duty. . . .

I conclude that the attributes "right" and "optimific" are not identical, and that we do not know either by intuition, by deduction, or by induction that they coincide in their application, still less that the latter is the foundation of the former. It must be added, however, that if we are ever under no special obligation such as that of fidelity to a promisee or of gratitude to a benefactor, we ought to do what will roduce most good; and that even when we re under a special obligation the tendency f acts to promote general good is one of ne main factors in determining whether they re right.

In what has preceded, a good deal of use has een made of "what we really think" about noral questions; a certain theory has been ejected because it does not agree with what 'e really think. It might be said that this is in rinciple wrong; that we should not be content) expound what our present moral conscious-ess tells us but should aim at a criticism of ur existing moral consciousness in the light f theory. Now I do not doubt that the moral onsciousness of men has in detail undergone good deal of modifications as regards the nings we think right, at the hands of moral neory. But if we are told, for instance, that we nould give up our view that there is a special bligatoriness attaching to the keeping of romises because it is self-evident that the nly duty is to produce as much good as ossible, we have to ask ourselves whether we eally, when we reflect, *are* convinced that this self-evident, and whether we really *can* get d of our view that promise-keeping has a indingness independent of productiveness of naximum good. In my own experience I find nat I cannot, in spite of a very genuine ttempt to do so; and I venture to think that nost people will find the same, and that just ecause they cannot lose the sense of special bligation, they cannot accept as self-evident, r even as true, the theory which would equire them to do so. In fact it seems, on eflection, self-evident that a promise, simply s such, is something that *prima facie* ought to e kept, and it does *not*, on reflection, seem elf-evident that production of maximum ood is the only thing that makes an act bligatory. And to ask us to give up at the idding of a theory our actual apprehension f what is right and what is wrong seems like sking people to repudiate their actual experi-nce of beauty, at the bidding of a theory hich says" only that which satisfies such nd such conditions can be beautiful." If hat I have called our actual apprehension is

(as I would maintain that it is) truly an appre-hension, i.e. an instance of knowledge, the request is nothing less than absurd.

I would maintain, in fact, that what we are apt to describe as "what we think" about moral questions contains a considerable amount that we do not think but know, and that this forms the standard by reference to which the truth of any moral theory has to be tested, instead of having itself to be tested by reference to any theory. I hope that I have in what precedes indicated what in my view these elements of knowledge are that are involved in our ordin-ary moral consciousness.

It would be a mistake to found a natural science on "what we really think," i.e. on what reasonably thoughtful and well-educated people think about the subjects of the science before they have studied them scientifically. For such opinions are interpretations, and often misinterpretations, of sense-experience; and the man of science must appeal from these to sense-experience itself, which furnishes his real data. In ethics no such appeal is possible. We have no more direct way of access to the facts about rightness and goodness and about what things are right or good, than by thinking about them; the moral convictions of thought-ful and well-educated people are the data of ethics just as sense-perceptions are the data of a natural science. Just as some of the latter have to be rejected as illusory, so have some of the former; but as the latter are rejected only when they are in conflict with other more accurate sense-perceptions, the former are rejected only when they are in conflict with other convic-tions which stand better the test of reflection. The existing body of moral convictions of the best people is the cumulative product of the moral reflection of many generations, which has developed an extremely delicate power of appreciation of moral distinctions; and this the theorist cannot afford to treat with anything other than the greatest respect. The verdicts of the moral consciousness of the best people are the foundation on which he must build; though he must first compare them with one another and eliminate any contradictions they may contain.

Note

1. I should make it plain at this state that I am *assuming* the correctness of some of our main convictions as to *prima facie* duties, or, more strictly, am claiming that we *know* them to be true. To me it seems as self-evident as anything could be, that to make a promise, for instance, is to create a moral claim on us in someone else. Many readers will perhaps say that they do *not* know this to be true. If so, I certainly cannot prove it to them; I can only ask them to reflect again, in the hope that they will ultimately agree that they also know it to be true. The mai[n] moral convictions of the plain man seem to m[e] to be, not opinions which it is for philosoph[y] to prove or disprove, but knowledge from th[e] start; and in my own case I seem to find litt[le] difficulty in distinguishing these essential co[n]victions from other moral convictions which [I] also have, which are merely fallible opinio[ns] based on an imperfect study of the working f[or] good or evil of certain institutions or types [of] action.

CHAPTER 73

An Unconnected Heap
of Duties?

DAVID McNAUGHTON

Despite its name, the school of ethical intu-itionism which flourished between the world wars, and whose greatest proponents were H. A. Prichard and W. D. Ross, was not distin-guished from its competitors by a distinctive epistemology. The dispute between intuition-ism and its main rival, the utilitarian tradition, revolved around the issue of whether there was more than one fundamental moral principle. The utilitarian tradition in ethical thought can be represented as holding that there is just one fundamental duty or moral principle: the duty of beneficence. In the hands of G. E. Moore, whom Ross and Prichard saw as their main opponent, the theory had developed into a sophisticated consequentialism which subscribed to a pluralist account of the good. Even so, in determining which action is right, only one consideration is relevant: which action will produce the most good? Ethical intuitionism rejected this monism about what makes right actions right as over-simple, and insisted that there are a number of distinct and irreducible basic duties or moral principles, all of which can be relevant in determining whether some action is right. Both parties to this debate were taken to agree that an ethical

theory rests on intuition, by which was meant no more than that the most basic ethical prin-ciples, since they could not be inferred from more basic ones, must be self-evident.

It has become commonplace to dismiss the deontic pluralism of an ethical intuitionist such as Ross fairly briskly, for a variety of reasons. In this paper I examine two main charges. First, intuitionism is held to be unsystematic, offer-ing us merely a 'heap of unconnected duties' with no unifying rationale. Thus D. D. Raphael complains that, while intuitionism 'gives a reasonably accurate picture of everyday moral judgement . . . it does not meet the needs of a philosophical theory, which should try to show connections and tie things up in a coherent system'[1] Second, intuitionism can give nothing in the way of general guidance to the agent who is faced with a conflict of duties, because it refuses to rank duties in order of importance or stringency.[2] In fact Ross, who offers the most fully worked-out version of intuitionism, does offer a systematic justification for the list of fundamental duties he puts forward, and does claim that some duties are more stringent than others. To the best of my knowledge, Ross's remarks on these topics have not been much discussed in the standard literature. This is due, in part, to the failure of many critics to read Ross with either the care or the sympathy with which they would approach other major writers in the subject. I shall argue, firstly, that

David McNaughton, "An Unconnected Heap of Duties?," pp. 433–47 from *Philosophical Quarterly*, 46, 1996. Reprinted by permission of the publishers, Blackwell Publishing.

Ross has an entire answer to those who maintain his theory is unsystematic; second, that Ross fails to sustain his claim that some duties are more stringent than others, but that this is not a defect in his theory.

1

We can expand the first complaint as follows. Common-sense morality appeals to a large variety of moral principles, which have no discernible structure. Intuitionism does not attempt to systematize ordinary morality, but simply mirrors it. An intuitionist, such as Ross, merely presents us with a more or less arbitrarily selected list of the more common (prima facie) duties, and announces them to be self-evident. Since there is no structure to this list, there seems to be no explanation of why some items are on the list and not others, and therefore no room for rational debate in the event of disagreement about what should be included. Given the unavailability of reasoned discussion we simply have one bare intuition pitted against another. Even a philosopher who admits that we may eventually have to appeal to intuition may rightly feel that this is too quick. Moral theory should facilitate reasoned debate, not forestall it. Indeed, in the absence of such structure it is doubtful whether intuitionism, unlike utilitarianism, can lay claim to be a moral *theory* at all.

Such a criticism fails to recognize that philosophical intuitionism does seek to systematize common-sense morality, and in much the same way as many utilitarians have tried to do. For it seeks to show that the plethora of precepts which constitutes common-sense morality can be derived from a very small number of self-evident basic duties. 'The general principles which [intuitionism] regards as intuitively seen to be true are very few in number and very general in character.'[3] Both utilitarianism and intuitionism can therefore be seen as sharing the theoretical goal of explaining and justifying our everyday moral judgements by appeal to the fewest number of most general principles. In this sense, intuitionism is as much engaged as is utilitarianism in constructing a moral theory; they only differ over how

many basic principles they need to accomplish the task.

In fairness to his critics it must be admitted that Ross does not explicitly state in his famous exposition of his theory in chapter 2 of *The Right and the Good* that his theory has this explanatory structure, but it is implicit throughout his long and detailed discussion. He begins by offering a categorization or division of prima facie duties for which he does not claim 'completeness or finality' but which he maintains is not 'arbitrary' because "Each rests on a definite circumstance which cannot seriously be held to be without moral significance."[4] Subsequent discussion makes it clear that this list of prima facie duties is a first shot at a complete list of basic and underivative duties. As Ross points out, it is slightly misleading to think of these as distinct or fundamental *duties*, since on Ross's account prima facie duties are not strictly duties at all, 'but something related in a special kind of way to duty'.[5] One's duty proper is what one ought actually to do, all things considered, in some particular situation. The list might more accurately be thought of as a list of fundamental morally relevant characteristics of actions; or features of actions which are right- or wrong-making characteristics which always carry weight when we are considering whether a particular action is right or wrong. With that proviso, here is my summary of the items on Ross's original list.

1. Duties resting on a previous act of my own. These in turn divide into two main categories:
    (*a*) duties of *fidelity*; these result from my having made a promise or something like a promise;
    (*b*) duties of *reparation*; these stem from my having done something wrong so that I am now required to make amends.
2. Duties resting on previous acts of others; these are duties of *gratitude*, which I owe to those who have helped me.
3. Duties to prevent (or overturn) a distribution of benefits and burdens which is not in accordance with the merit of the person concerned; these are duties of *justice*.

. Duties which rest on the fact that there are other people in the world whose condition we could make better; these are duties of *beneficence*.

. Duties which rest on the fact that I could better myself; these are duties of *self-improvement*.

. Duties of not injuring others; these are duties of *non-maleficence*.

This list is only provisional; Ross goes on to discuss whether it can be further reduced by showing that some of these duties are not really basic. Since the dialectic of the argument dictates that a duty cannot remain on the list if it can be shown to be derivative, we need to know what it is for one duty to be derived from another.

Unfortunately, Ross gives no systematic account of the relation of derivation, but one can be gleaned from scattered remarks throughout the text. After reviewing and revising his list of basic duties, he writes: 'These seem to be, in principle, all the ways in which *prima facie* duties arise. In actual experience they are compounded together in highly complex ways.'[6] He then gives as an example the citizen's duty to obey the laws of her country. That duty "arises from" (at least in the ideal case) three basic duties: gratitude, fidelity, and beneficence. We should be grateful for the benefits we have received from the state; we have made an implicit promise to obey by retaining permanent residence in a country whose laws we know we are expected to obey; beneficence also requires us to obey the laws because they are 'a potent instrument for the general good'. Ross later[7] gives a similar account of the duty not to lie. He claims that this duty, which he does not sharply distinguish from the duty of veracity, stems from two of the basic duties on his list: those of non-maleficence and fidelity. To lie to someone is (normally) to do an injury to that person (and perhaps to others). In addition, Ross holds that communication standardly presupposes an implicit mutual undertaking by all parties that they will use language to convey their real opinions. In such cases, to lie is to breach this implicit promise. We show what is wrong with lawbreaking and lying by showing that to act in

these ways is, normally, to be in breach of more than one of our fundamental duties.

In his discussion of both these cases, Ross makes it clear that there can be special circumstances in which some of the considerations which count against acting in these ways do not apply. In such cases, the force or bindingness of the duty in question may be weakened. For example, a very bad government will not be promoting the general good, and then there will be no duty arising from considerations of beneficence to support it. In the case of lying, the presupposition that there is a mutual agreement to make true assertions can lapse. If someone is a habitual liar, then she has announced, by her actions, her refusal to be bound by this implicit contract, thus releasing others from their obligation to honour it. Similarly, if I am in a strange society and know nothing of their social practices, not even whether they are friendly or hostile, then there is no such implicit understanding. In Ross's opinion, a large part of the stringency of the duty not to lie stems from the supposed implicit promise; where it is not present then the obligation not to lie is much weakened.[8]

Although Ross does not discuss this point, it seems perfectly possible that there might be cases where none of the considerations which normally make lawbreaking or lying wrong apply. For example, if I play a game of Cheat with my children, I must lie, because that is part of the game. On Ross's account of what makes lying wrong, it may be that there is absolutely nothing wrong with lying in such cases. The tacit agreement to tell the truth is explicitly cancelled in such games and it is at least arguable that I am, in this context, doing no harm whatever to my children in lying to them. Similarly, there can surely be governments so bad that there is nothing to be said in favour of obeying them, and everything to be said against.

If there are circumstances, such as playing Cheat, where the fact that saying something would be a lie does not furnish any reason whatever for not saying it, then in what sense can it be said, as Ross does, that there is a duty not to lie? On Ross's official account of prima facie duty, refraining from lying cannot be such a duty because, as we saw, that would imply that lying was universally a wrong-making characteristic; that it always counted against an action that it involved lying. But this claim is arguably false; it does not count at all against my playing Cheat with my children that we shall all lie as hard as we can. In the case of derivative duties, such as the duty not to lie or to obey the law, we must say rather that it is only normally or standardly that we have a prima facie duty to act in this way.

If the duty not to lie is understood in this way, can we still maintain *of a particular act* that it is prima facie wrong in virtue of being a lie? We might be tempted to interpret Ross's account of lying as holding that in a normal case, where it does count against an action that it would involve lying, the act is prima facie wrong, *not* in virtue of being a lie, but in virtue of its being a case of promise-breaking and causing harm. But this, I think, is a false contrast. Acts can get to be instances of promise-breaking or maleficence in a number of ways. It may be true of some particular act that it is in virtue of its being a lie (rather than, for example, the non-payment of a debt) that it is an instance of promise-breaking and malefi-cence. If this is right, then the fact that *this* act is a lie may make it prima facie wrong, even though there can be acts which, though they involve lying, are not made prima facie wrong by that fact. On this interpretation, lying is not a fundamental moral consideration (which is why it does not occur on the list of basic duties) but not all morally relevant con-siderations need be fundamental. The fact that some act is a lie can still be a reason why that act is prima facie wrong.

The examples of derivative duties we have so far considered are cases where our prima facie duties are, in Ross's words, 'compounded together in highly complex ways'. But deriva-tive duties need not be complex in this manner. For some kind of action may be a derivative duty in virtue of its falling, in standard cases, under just one basic duty. Take the duty a child has to honour its parents; it might plausibly be claimed that this duty rests on the single basic duty of gratitude. As in the previous examples, there could be exceptional cases where there was not even a prima facie duty to honour one's parents. Where the child had received

nothing from its parents there would be, on this view, no duty to honour them. Ross gives another example himself in his discussion of punishment. He dissents from the common intuitionist view that there is 'a fundamental and underivative duty' to reward the virtuous and punish the innocent. Rather, he claims, the state of affairs in which the good are happy and the bad unhappy is better than the reverse. Since we have a general duty of beneficence we have a duty to bring about the better state of affairs. 'The duty of reward and punishment seems to me to be . . . derivative. It can be subsumed under the duty of producing as much good as we can.'[9] There may be cases where no good would come of punishing (per-haps because the wrongdoer has suffered enough) and here punishing would not be even prima facie right.

In sum, derivative duties are not on the list of basic duties because the characteristic by which they are picked out is not itself morally fundamental, nor does it entail the presence of a morally fundamental characteristic. They still count as duties, however, because acts having that character normally or standardly have one or more of the morally fundamental character-istics that figure on Ross's basic list.

Being underivative is not, however, sufficient for inclusion in Ross's list of basic duties, for he is also striving for as high a level of generality as possible. Thus there may be duties which are not derivative in the sense just defined, but are not on the list because insufficiently gen-eral. Thus it is plausible to hold that the fact that an act would be the paying of a debt always counts in its favour. Here, the reason why we are unable to imagine a particular case where debt-paying is not prima facie right may be supposed to lie in the fact that one could not be in debt unless one had made an (implicit) promise to repay. That an act is paying of a debt thus entails that it is the keeping of a promise. The duty to pay debts will then not appear on the list of basic duties because it is only a specific instance of the more general duty of fidelity.

I am not here concerned to defend Ross's analysis of any of these duties; I cite them merely to illustrate his general approach. With the two distinctions between derivative and

nderivative duties and between more and less
general underivative duties now in place, we
can now see how one might make a case for
mending Ross's list. Challenges can come
from one of two directions. It may be claimed
either that the list needs shortening because it
contains some duty that is not really basic, or
that the list needs lengthening because it leaves
out a basic duty.

The list needs shortening if it can be shown
to contain duties that are either derivable from
other duties on the list, or are insufficiently
general in form. The latter challenge will have
been made out if it can be shown either that
the duty on the list is just a specific instance of
a more general basic duty, or that two of the
putative basic duties are just specific instances
of one wider inclusive basic duty. Immediately
after drawing up his initial list Ross embarks on
a discussion to see if it can be made more
'systematic'. His conclusion is that the list
does need shortening, and his discussion provides two examples of the latter kind of challenge at work.

First, he considers whether beneficence and
self-improvement are distinct duties.[10] The
main reason for thinking that they are lies in
the fact that, while we have a duty to give
others pleasure, as well as to make them
knowledgeable and virtuous, we normally
think we have no corresponding obligation to
give ourselves pleasure. Ross discusses whether
the belief that we have no duty to give ourselves pleasure arises merely from the fact that
it is redundant to require us to do something
which we are already (too) strongly motivated
to do. If we think, as Ross is inclined to, that
there is in fact a duty to give ourselves pleasure, a duty which is rarely if ever necessary
to invoke, then categories 4 and 5 can be
merged under the wider head of universal
beneficence.

Second, Ross argues that the duty of justice
is simply a specific instance of the general duty
to bring about the good since, as we saw when
discussing punishment, Ross's view is that the
distribution of goods in accord with merit is a
specific kind of good. So Ross's final list is
whittled down to five: the duty to bring about
as much good as possible, under which now fall
justice, beneficence, and self-improvement, and

the distinct duties of non-maleficence, fidelity,
gratitude, and reparation.[11]

The other way to criticize the list would be to
claim that it is too short, because there are
underivative moral considerations that have
not been included. We should note that, in
order to exclude some putative basic duty
from the list it would have to be shown that it
is *wholly* derivative. Thus lying should only be
excluded if our moral objection to lying rests
solely on the fact that lying would normally
involve us in breaching other duties, such as
fidelity and non-maleficence; the claim must be
that the mere fact that an act is a lie carries no
independent moral weight, however slight.

Critics of intuitionism are wont to point out
that different intuitionist philosophers cannot
agree about which are the basic duties, as if this
were itself a sufficient refutation of the theory.
But this would only be an objection to intuitionism if the theory held that the contents of
the list should be immediately obvious, which
it does not. What is important is that there
should be some rational and principled way
to settle such disputes, and this is what I have
tried to show. There is no need to resort to
a blank appeal to intuition. Nor should we
imagine that intuitionism of this stripe need
be conservative. Nothing in Ross's procedure
prevents moral criticism of the prevailing
mores of a society.

It may, of course, be that there is no one way
of structuring these duties that will be uncon-
troversially the right one. That is not, however,
a matter that can be determined in advance.
Moreover, the discovery that there were several
possible ways of carving up the territory
between which it was hard to decide would
itself constitute important philosophical
progress.

A critic of Rossian intuitionism might now
complain, rather more cautiously, that while
Ross's list is by no means an arbitrary heap,
the basic duties are still unconnected, and
that this is a weakness in his theory. But why
might one think it a weakness? One suggestion
might be that the simpler a theory is the better
and, all else equal, the fewer independent
axioms, postulates, or underived principles to
which it appeals the better. The intuitionist
need not deny this, but he will point out that

there are other desiderata for a theory, among which fitting the facts and explanatory adequacy rank highly. Ross's main complaint about consequentialist theories is that they oversimplify and thus fail to account convincingly for the nature of our moral thought. By this he means, not only that they deliver counter-intuitive verdicts in particular cases, but that they give a distorted account of the reasons we would offer for those verdicts.[12] Nor is it always the case that the theory with the fewest underived principles is the simplest; for simplicity at the level of principle may lead to complexity at a higher level.

The second suggestion might be that a theory which admits the existence of distinct and irreducible moral principles gains in systematic unity if those principles are generated by some unitary justificatory procedure, as is the case perhaps with Kantianism, or with rule-consequentialism. To this Ross might reply that he also offers a single test. The difference between his test and the Kantian one is that the latter is atomistic, generating each principle independently of the others, whereas his is holistic, testing each principle by seeing whether it can be derived from the others. But why should a holistic test be less systematic than an atomistic one? The real worry here, I suspect, may be about not the lack of systematic unity in Ross's theory, but the perceived need for a justificatory grounding for each duty. But that is, of course, just to beg the question against the intuitionist who maintains that these basic duties stand in no need of grounding.

A third worry might be that duties that are distinct and irreducible may also be disparate, having nothing significant in common, except that they are all duties. But of course they may have a great deal in common, and if they do, then the theory would have a further unity. Ross in fact seems to suggest at various points[13] that at least some, and perhaps all, of our duties, both basic and derivative, do have something in common; they rest on relationships between persons, each different relationship generating a different duty. Positional duties, contractual duties, and duties of special relationship are the model here. Of the seven basic duties which Ross has on his original list, three – fidelity, gratitude, and rep aration – seem to fit this description neatl The others, however, raise problems. In orde for me to have a duty of beneficence, nor maleficence, or justice towards some particula person or group, it does not have to be the cas that I previously stood in any particular rela tionship to them; it is enough that they are i need, or that they could be harmed, or tha goods are unjustly distributed among then Nor, in the case of duties of self-improvemen is it clear what it means to talk about m relationship with myself. These difficultie may or may not be soluble; my only purpos here was to illustrate how it might be tha distinct duties may yet have some commo structural element that gives them a unity.

My conclusion is that intuitionism, at lea in Ross's version, is not systematically less un fied than its major rivals. If there are objection to it, they lie elsewhere.

II

I turn now to my second topic, the issue c what Ross has to say about the respective rank ing of the basic moral duties in cases of mora conflict. Ross rejects what he calls 'out-and-ou intuitionism', which says that there are absolut duties that should be fulfilled irrespective c the consequences.[14] Duties are prima facie fc Ross; where they conflict we have to decide, i each particular case, which is here the weight est. Now Ross's view commits him to th wholly plausible claim that the stringency of duty can vary from one occasion to anothe Some promises, for example, are solemn an binding, and ought only to be broken, if at al in the most serious circumstances; others a less weighty and can more easily be overridde by other considerations. Ross is standardl interpreted as claiming that a conflict betwee duties in a particular case can only be resolve by determining what weight those duties carr in that case; nothing *in general* can be sai about the relative weight of different kinds c duty. Even as careful a commentator as Auc makes this claim. '[Ross] seems committed t the view that ethical generalizations do nc *independently* carry evidential weight in suc

onflicts. One should not, e.g., appeal to a
second-order generalization that duties of justice are stronger than duties of fidelity.'[15]

This interpretation runs counter to the text.
On several occasions Ross explicitly claims that
one duty is more binding or more stringent
than another, although no very clear overall
picture emerges of their precise relations.
Both fidelity[16] and non-maleficence[17] are held
to be more stringent than beneficence. Later on
he adds to the list of more stringent duties,
albeit in a cagey remark:

> For the estimation of the comparative strin-
> gency of these *prima facie* obligations no gen-
> eral rules can, so far as I can see, be laid down.
> We can only say that a great deal of stringency
> belongs to the duties of 'perfect obligation' –
> the duties of keeping our promises, of repair-
> ing wrongs we have done, and of returning the
> equivalent of services we have received. For
> the rest, 'the decision rests with perception.'[18]

Ross appears, therefore, to be trying to find
room for a position midway between the complete generalism of absolutism (or indeed of a
lexical ordering of duties) which gives no consideration to the circumstances of the particular
case, and a doctrine of prima facie duties that
makes the outcome of any conflict depend solely
upon the wholly individual circumstances of
the particular case. That midway position is
intended to allow us to say something about
the ranking of duties in general which falls
short of absolutism: namely, that some kinds
of basic duty might be thought to be, in their
intrinsic nature, more weighty than others. This
does not mean that the less weighty duty will
never win out, only that it starts with an initial
handicap which it will have to work hard to
overcome. In deciding what to do, it seems, we
must take into account not only how weighty an
instance of each particular duty we have in the
case before us, but also the *general* weight that is
to be given to each of these duties.

This doctrine of 'double weighing' is hard
to grasp in the abstract; it is not clear what it
means, still less whether we hold such a view.
Ross supplies a couple of examples which
are supposed to do the double duty both of
illustrating the claim and of showing that the

particular moral judgements we make commit
us to it. His first claim is that the duty of non-
maleficence is recognized both as distinct from
and as more binding than the duty of beneficence. 'We should not in general consider it
justifiable to kill one person in order to keep
another alive, or to steal from one in order to
give alms to another.'[19] But this example will
not help Ross to illustrate the claim that non-
maleficence is the more stringent duty because,
as I shall now go on to show, we only need
the claim that non-maleficence is *distinct*
from beneficence to explain our judgement in
this case.

In any choice I make, considerations of beneficence are always relevant, because what I
choose will have some influence on the well-
being of others. Where beneficence is the only
relevant duty, then the right action is completely determined by the amount of good I
can produce: the right action is the one that
brings about the best state of affairs. If two
courses of action produce the same amount of
value, then, from the point of view of beneficence, there is nothing to choose between
them.

Ross holds, of course, that there are other
duties, such as fidelity and non-maleficence,
distinct from beneficence, which have to be
taken into account where relevant. Since they
are distinct duties, they must carry independent weight in determining which action is my
duty proper, though what weight they will have
in the particular case will depend on the circumstances. Two consequences follow. First,
where the balance of good between the two
courses of action is (roughly) equal, the other
duty will be decisive, because beneficence will
not favour one course over the other. Second,
where the balance of good, and therefore
beneficence, counts morally in favour of one
course of action, but some other duty, say the
duty to keep promises, counts against doing it,
then beneficence will only win out if it has
sufficient weight to outweigh the other duty
in this case. But the weight that we should
give to the duty of beneficence in any particular
case depends solely on the surplus of good
produced by following one course of action
rather than another. So beneficence will only
win out over the other duty if the course of

action favoured by beneficence will produce a considerably better state of affairs than that which will result if we act in accordance with the other duty. In fact, it will have to produce a surplus of good sufficiently large for us to judge that, in this case, the good to be achieved outweighs all the weight against that course which stems from the fact that it would involve a breach of the other duty.

These consequences follow simply from the fact that, on Ross's view, the other duties are *distinct* from beneficence. In weighing up what to do, one must take account not only of how much good will be produced, as the duty of beneficence requires, but also of the independent weight of the other duties. There is thus no need to bring in any doctrine about one duty being weightier than another at the general level in order to explain, for example, why it is wrong 'to kill one person in order to keep another alive, or to steal from one in order to give alms to another'. We do think it wrong to kill one person to save another, but that may simply be because, given that the benefit to one is roughly counterbalanced by the loss to the other, the duty not to harm tells against killing the one, but not against failing to save the other. (If we think that the benefit and loss are not equal, this will be because we think being killed is a greater evil than not having one's life saved, and that will not help Ross's case.) Similar remarks will be true, not just of conflicts between fidelity or non-maleficence and beneficence, but of a conflict between beneficence and any other duty.

This diagnosis is confirmed when we see that Ross claims that the distinctness of fidelity and beneficence *alone* is sufficient to account for our judgement in a structurally similar case.

> . . . if . . . I could bring equal amounts of good into being by fulfilling my promise and by helping someone to whom I had made no promise, I should not hesitate to regard the former as my duty.[20]

Ross's other example seems to get us closer to what we need.

> We . . . think . . . that normally promise-keeping, for example, should come before

benevolence, but that when and only when the good to be produced by the benevolent act is very great and the promise comparatively trivial, the act of benevolence becomes our duty.[21]

One way of understanding this remark is as follows. We are to imagine separate rankings of instances of both duties in order, from the least to the most weighty instances. We then claim that a beneficent action can only make breach of fidelity right when it is located significantly higher on its scale than the breach of fidelity is on its scale. But it is not clear that we can make any sense of these cross-scale comparisons. To mention just one obvious difficulty: in order to know roughly how high up the scale one is, one must have a sense of where its top is as well as its base. Since, however, there seems to be no limit to the amount of benefit that might flow from a single action, there is no top to the scale of beneficence. If there is no measure of how high one is on that scale, then an act cannot be significantly higher on it than it is on the scale of fidelity. So we are still no nearer making sense of the idea that one duty is in itself more binding than another.

Ross's remarks could be taken to suggest a different interpretation that would, finally, give us a sense in which one duty might be more stringent than another. The claim that the promise must be 'comparatively trivial' might naturally be read as meaning, not that is trivial as compared with the substantial amount of good which might be achieved, but that it is trivial *compared with other promises*. So understood, this would impose an additional condition that must be met before it could be our duty to break a promise. Not only must the balance of good greatly favour the breaking of the promise, but the promise itself must not be of a particularly serious, solemn, or binding kind. On that interpretation, where a promise is particularly solemn and binding, no amount of good to be achieved, however great, could make it our duty to break it.

Since, on Ross's view, the weight to be accorded to a duty is not just a function of the good produced, there does not seem to be anything in Ross's system that prevents him laiming that serious cases of promise-breaking ould have a moral weight that could not be utweighed by any amount of good to be chieved on the other side. Nevertheless, it eems to me unlikely that Ross actually held his view; there is no other textual evidence for . Moreover, it is a position that does not seem o me very attractive with regard to promise-eeping. Most of us feel that there are situ-tions in which it would be right to break a romise, however solemn. In the case of non-aleficence, however, there does seem a case or claiming that it is intrinsically weightier han beneficence in the sense just defined. For hile it can be right to inflict some compara-vely slight harm in order to secure a great ood or avert a disaster, it may be that it can ever be right to inflict a very serious harm, uch as killing an innocent child, to achieve a ood end. Here the end really cannot justify the leans in any circumstances.

Such a position might make room, within system of prima facie duties, for something ke an absolute constraint against killing the nnocent. (The fact that Ross is opposed to ut-and-out intuitionism' is further reason to hink that he cannot be advocating this view.) or, while the duty not to harm in general is nly prima facie, the duty not to inflict certain erious kinds of harm, such as killing the inno-ent, would be one that cannot be overridden. Ioral considerations on the other side would ot be *silenced*, however. On this view, the fact hat killing an innocent person would do good ill always be a reason in its favour; it will just e that it will never be strong enough to over-de the duty of non-maleficence in this case.

We have had great difficulty in finding an nterpretation of Ross's claim that some duties re more stringent than others which made nse and which there was good reason to hink that Ross held. It seems best, therefore, o suppose that Ross was just confused when e thought that he needed, in order to explain ur moral judgements, to claim not only that here were duties distinct from beneficence, ut also that the former were more stringent an the latter. We are left, then, with the claim at all we can do, when faced with a moral onflict, is to look carefully at the particular se in all its complexity and form a reasonable

judgement as to which duty (or duties) carry the most weight.

Does his failure to come up with any general guidance as to how to resolve moral conflicts constitute a complaint, as his critics seem to suppose, against Ross's system, as distinct from a complaint against Ross's account of his own system? I think not. It is only a complaint against intuitionism that it does not offer any general guidance about what to do in a situation of moral conflict if one thinks that this is a reasonable job to expect a moral theory to do. Ross has a much less ambitious picture of the role of moral theory than that. The job of moral theory is simply to see which general account of the nature of our duties (and of goodness) gives the best overall picture of our moral thinking. There is no question of theory revealing answers to moral questions that can-not otherwise be answered, or justifying what would not otherwise be justified. In particular, where there are puzzling moral conflicts, moral theory will not help to resolve them. This does not mean that we must simply blankly 'intuit' what to do in such cases, or else make an arbi-trary decision. Deciding what to do in complex cases involves discernment, sensitivity, and judgement, but those skills have to be exercised at the level of the particular case. To look to abstract theory to help out is to look in the wrong place. If Ross is right in this, as I believe he is, then it is not a defect in his theory that it turns out after all to have nothing general to say about the relative stringency of our basic duties.

III

The heart of most objections to intuitionism lies in the belief that it is a profoundly anti-theoretical ethical view. This claim is partly true and partly false; intuitionism seeks to per-form some but by no means all of the tasks that are often demanded of moral theory. One such task is to reveal the structure of our moral thought, to impose order and systematic unity on what otherwise seems rather unstruc-tured and even inchoate. Here, as I have tried to show, Ross's theory does as well as its rivals. A second task is that of justification. Different theories construe this task differently. On

Ross's theory, it is not a matter of finding or constructing a justification for our moral beliefs, which might otherwise remain unsupported. It consists, Ross claims, in showing both that the general principles of duty (the items on the basic list) are self-evident and that we bring our knowledge of those general principles to bear on each particular case. Since almost all morally significant acts will fall under more than one of these principles, we cannot have more than probable opinion about what is the right thing to do in any particular case.[22] The third task some have hoped that moral theory might perform is to supply guidance in making difficult moral choices. I hope have shown that, on Ross's account of moral judgement, this is a task that moral *theory* cannot perform. To complain, therefore, that Ross's system fails to perform it is to miss the point of his theory.

Notes

1. Raphael, *Moral Philosophy* (Oxford: Oxford University Press, 1981), 55.
2. The classic contemporary version of this complaint is voiced by Rawls (*A Theory of Justice* (Cambridge, Mass.: Harvard University Press, 1971), 34).
3. Ross, *The Foundations of Ethics* (Oxford: Clarendon Press, 1939), 190. Sidgwick also saw this as the aim of philosophical intuitionism. See Sidgwick, *The Methods of Ethics*, 7th edn. (London: Macmillan, 1967), 102.
4. Ross, *The Right and the Good* (Oxford: Clarendon Press, 1930), 20.
5. Ibid., 20.
6. Ibid., 27.
7. Ibid., 54–5.
8. Ibid.
9. Ibid., 58.
10. Ibid., 24–6.
11. Ibid., 27.
12. Ibid., 19 and 37–9.
13. e.g. *The Right and the Good*, 19 and 22.
14. See Ross, *The Foundations of Ethics*, 79.
15. R. Audi, 'Ethical Reflectionism', *Monist*, 7 (1993), 297. I have been equally at fault in this regard: see my *Moral Vision* (Oxford: Blackwell, 1988), 198. B. Gaut ('Moral Pluralism', *Philosophical Papers*, 22 (1993), 17–40) an honourable exception to the general rule.
16. *The Right and the Good*, 19.
17. Ibid., 22.
18. Ibid. 41–2. The quotation (which appears in the original Greek in Ross) is from Aristotle *Nicomachean Ethics* 1109^{b}23 and 1126^{b}4.
19. *The Right and the Good*, 22. Nor did Ross change his view in his later work; see *The Foundations of Ethics*, 75.
20. *The Right and the Good*, 18.
21. Ibid., 19.
22. Ibid., 32 and 42.

CHAPTER 74
An Unprincipled Morality

JONATHAN DANCY

---

study reasons in the sort of way that one
ight study rats. One might ask whether the
udy of one rat in isolation is likely to tell us
ow it will behave in company or what is likely
 happen if one puts a large rat in against two
naller ones: and the same with reasons. One
n ask whether two rats on the same side
ways make a stronger team than either rat
 its own: and the same with reasons, again.
ne answer to this last question about reasons
 no. Suppose I said that there are two reasons
hy I don't eat veal: first, the appalling condi-
ons under which veal calves are kept, and
cond, one just can't get good veal any more.
hough these reasons are on the same side,
ey don't go well together.

One of the first things that one learns when
udying how reasons behave is that a certain
eory, atomism, is false. Atomism holds that
y feature that is a reason in favour of action
 one case will always be a reason in favour of
tion wherever it occurs. The same feature
ways makes the same reason; or, a reason is
 general reason. This theory is false; some-
ing that is a reason in favour of action in
e case may in another case be no reason at
, or even a reason against action. It all
pends on the circumstances; reasons are
nsitive to context.

nathan Dancy, "An Unprincipled Morality." Reprinted by
mission of Professor Jonathan Dancy.

This needs to be shown. Reasons come in
two sorts. There are reasons for belief and
reasons for action. First, reasons for belief do
not behave in the way that atomism claims.
Ordinarily, that something before me looks
red is some reason to believe that it is red. (It
may not be enough reason, of course, since
there may be reasons, better reasons, on the
other side.) But suppose that I know I have
just taken a drug that makes red things look
blue and blue things look red. In that case, that
the thing before me looks red is a reason to
believe that it is not red. Here, it is no reason at
all to believe the thing to be red; it is a reason
to believe it to be blue. Reasons for belief are
sensitive to context.

Actually nobody has ever thought to defend
atomism as a theory about reasons for belief,
because nobody has thought about the matter
at all, so far as I know. The opposite view,
which I call holism, is uncontentious in this
case.

But with reasons for action similar examples
are easy to find. That someone is very keen to
get the job is sometimes a reason to give it
to her, and sometimes not. That there will be
hardly anyone else there is sometimes a reason
to go there, and sometimes a reason to stay well
away. That an action is against the law is sometimes a reason for doing it, though normally
not. That there are two people claiming to have
witnessed the same event is sometimes a reason

to believe what they say, and sometimes a reason to disbelieve it; it might even be both at the same time.

This again is uncontentious, one would have thought. It is only when we turn to a special brand of reasons for action, moral reasons, that things become debatable. For most people think that moral reasons are based on principles. But, as I will argue, if atomism is false, there can be no moral principles. *Moral particularism* holds that, because of the falsehood of atomism, there are plenty of moral reasons but no moral principles. And it is very hard to persuade anybody of this. People are convinced that moral reasons are quite different in this respect from other reasons – that atomism is true of moral reasons even if not of other sorts of reason. For them, moral reasons must be general reasons even if others are not. I call this view 'moral generalism'.

Straight off, generalism seems implausible. There are all sorts of counter-examples to atomism in ethics. Ordinarily, that someone will enjoy it is some reason to let them do it: but not always. If people are going to enjoy watching public executions, that is probably some reason not to let them do so. That there is a law against a certain sort of action normally gives us some moral reason not to do actions of that sort; but sometimes it might do exactly the opposite. Many in the pioneering days of the New World thought that the laws curtailing hunting were ones that it was important to break. And so on. This makes it plausible to suppose that atomism is as false of moral reasons as of all others. A feature can be a moral reason for action in one case, and no reason at all in another.

If this is true, however, there can be no moral principles. For all moral principles specify features which they suppose to constitute the same reason wherever they occur, regardless of context. The principle that it is wrong to lie asserts that if an action requires you to lie, this is always some reason against it. And if atomism is false there are no such features.

Sadly, that is too quick. But something pretty close to it is true. It might be that there are some features that constitute the same moral reason wherever they occur. Call these 'invariant reasons'. I have done nothing to

show that there are no invariant reasons; best, I have shown that reasons do not *need* be invariant, and that many are not. So the could be a set of perfectly good reasons, eve moral reasons, none of which is invariant; a if things were like this there would be no mor principles at all. However, many people a convinced that there are at least *some* invaria moral reasons. It may be, for instance, that it always wrong, so far as that goes, to torture baby, even if in terrible circumstances th might be the thing we should do, all thin considered.

Still, I claim that few reasons are like th Most vary with the circumstances, being som times a reason in favour and sometimes a re son against. *How often* this happens is not t main point. That it *can* happen is enough show that we are not dealing with a general invariant reason. This means that not all mor reasons are based on principles. Should we s that at least the invariant ones are? This wou give us a hybrid picture of moral reasons, som being principle-based and others (probably t majority) not. I find it very implausible suggest that some features can only be t reasons they are because they are keyed into principle, while others need no such suppo Surely that I am torturing the baby is as mu of a reason against what I am doing as it nee to be, whether or not all such actions would b so far as that goes, wrong. How this featu behaves elsewhere just has nothing to do wi the way it is functioning as a reason here. the fact, if it is a fact, that it is invariant as reason has nothing to do with the way in whi it functions as a reason in any particular cas

Atomism, then, as a theory about how mor reasons work, is false; and since it is false the can be no moral principles. For many, t means that there is no such thing as morali so tight is the link between morality and pri ciples for them. But for me it means that unle we can make sense of an unprincipled morali there is no morality at all. We need to devel an understanding of moral judgement whi does not think of us as subsuming the ca before us under one or many principl Rather, we will have to work out a concepti of moral judgement as a sensitivity to t nature of the situation we find ourselves nd to the demands that it places on us. There will be a structure to that situation, a structure of reasons, features that combine with each other to make it the case that here we should to this rather than that. The competent moral udge is the person capable of recognising such a thing when it occurs. The question is always, what is the nature of the case before us?', not in what way is my decision here determined by previous decisions, or general principles?'. The development of this approach to ethics s the construction of a fully-fledged moral particularism.

When I try to persuade people of these things, I meet extraordinary resistance. People reject the persuasive charms of particularism for, broadly, two sorts of reasons: reasons to do with rationality, and reasons to do with motivation. I take rationality first. Three points are made. The first and most direct is that thinking rationally requires at least that one think consistently, and in ethics this just means taking the same feature to be the same reason wherever it occurs. Particularism, therefore, denies the rationality of moral thought. Second, what is the difference between moral choice and choosing chocolates? The difference is that when choosing morally we are required to make similar choices in similar circumstances; not so for the choice between rum truffles and peppermint creams. Third, what account can the particularist give of our ability to learn from our moral experience? Such moral self-education is certainly possible. An adolescent who has so far refused to accept that tact is a virtue can be brought to see the importance of being tactful in a particular case, and is then in a position to apply this knowledge more generally. The generalist can understand this as the extraction of a principle from an earlier case, which we then apply to later ones. What can the particularist offer as an alternative account?

Of these three points, the third is the hardest. The answer to the first is that, when we are thinking of reasons for belief, the sort of consistency required of us is merely that we do not adopt beliefs that cannot all be true together. Why should we understand the consistency requirement in a different way when we turn to moral reasons? Simply to insist that

this is so must be to beg the question against particularism.

The second question asks us to justify a distinction between matters of whim, such as the choosing of chocolates, and matters of weighty reasons, such as those involved in moral choice. But this need not be a problem. Moral reasons as my particularist understands them occur in the one case and not in the other. Nothing at all like them applies to the choosing of chocolates (normally). This does nothing to show that in morality, unlike in the area of whim, we are required to make similar choices in similar situations. There are quite enough other differences between morality and whim.

The third question asks us what relevance other cases do have to a new case, if not the sort of relevance that the generalist supposes. The answer to this is that experience of similar cases can tell us what sort of thing to look out for, and the sort of relevance that a certain feature can have; in this way our judgement in a new case can be informed, though it is not forced or constrained, by our experience of similar cases in the past. There is no need to suppose that the way in which this works is by the extraction of principles from the earlier cases, which we then impose on the new case.

So much for one sort of complaint. I now turn to questions which focus on motivation. The general idea here is that a particularist morality is a lax morality: without principles, anything goes. But there are various ways in which this thought can be built up. The first is just to say that morality is in the business of imposing constraints on our choices. For there to be constraints, there needs to be regulation, and regulation means rules, and rules mean principles. This, however, is just wrong. There can be fully particular constraints on action, and the judgement that this action would be wrong is surely just such a thing. Constraints do not need to be general constraints, any more than reasons need to be general reasons.

Another line is that the person of principle will be unbudgeable; having taken a stand on an issue, he will not be moved from it. A particularist will not be like this. But here I have two things to say. First, nothing prevents a particularist from being of firm conviction case by case; an unbudgeable conviction need not be founded on principle, but simply on the nature of the case. Unbudgeability and principle have nothing essentially in common. Second, even if it were true that a principled person will on some points be unbudgeable, the question is whether those points are the right points. What worries me is that they will not be – that in being driven by principle, our principled person will distort the relevance of relevant features by insisting on filtering them through principles, in a way that is at odds with the falsehood of atomism. One might think here of Christian Scientist parents denying their child a blood transfusion. In my view, unbudgeability and principles go very badly together. Unbudgeability may be a virtue in its place, but to be unbudgeably involved in a distortion is not a great triumph. If you are going to be incorrigible you had better always be right; incorrigible error is the worst of all worlds.

A different suggestion is that morality has the sort of authority over us that can only be provided by a rule. Here, however, I think that I should simply dig my heels in, and insist that moral reasons have all the authority they need already. She is needs medical help, and I am the only person around to summon it. This situation demands a certain response from me, in a way that has authority over me because there is nothing that I can do to get out of it.

Still, we might say, there is the ever-present danger of backsliding in ethics; we see the right, but somehow cannot bring ourselves to do it. With principles, we have something capable of stiffening our waning resolve. Without principles, we will fall short all too often. My view about this is that it is an empirical hypothesis for which I see little real evidence. What is more, the need for moral stiffening only arises once we have already decided what morality requires of us here, and the real question was whether that decision needed to be based on principle. As far as the point about backsliding goes, it does not; the need, if any, for principles comes later.

More to the point might be a worry about special pleading. This is different from backsliding, because the special pleader is the person who makes exceptions in their own favour.

It would not be right for most people to do what I propose to do, but I am special; so I am left off the moral hook that others are caught by. This sort of special pleading occurs in the process of making our moral decision; it is no to do with motivation thereafter, as backsliding is. With backsliding I say 'this is wrong but I am going to do it all the same'; with special pleading I say 'this would be wrong for others, but not for me'.

The reason why there is a genuine worry about special pleading is that one can always find some difference between this act and a plain duty, and there seems to be no way, within the resources available to particularism, to prevent such differences from being appealed to by those who, in bad faith, want to let themselves off the moral hook. A principle, we might say, would, or at least should, stop this sort of thing.

My general view about this is that we are appealing to principles to rectify a natural distortion in moral judgement. If such judgement focuses only on the reasons present in the case before us, it is all too easy to twist those reasons to suit oneself. So we use principles to stop ourselves from doing that. But really the remedy for poor moral judgement is not a different style of moral judgement, principle-based judgement, but just better moral judgement. There is only one real way to stop oneself distorting things in one's own favour, and that is to look again, as hard as one can, at the reasons present in the case, and see if really one is so different from others that what would be required of them is not required of oneself. This method is not infallible, I know; but then nor was the appeal to principle.

My conclusion, then, is that there are no successful objections to moral particularism, and that the development of this position is the best chance we have of freeing ourselves from the distortions caused by the long association of morality with the exercise of moral principles. Moral reasons are not this different from other reasons, they do not need this sort of support, and they are better off without it. But to accept particularism is to accept a change at the very centre of one's conception of the moral - a change in moral theory that will lead to a change in moral practice.

CHAPTER 75

On Knowing the "Why": Particularism and Moral Theory

MARGARET OLIVIA LITTLE

If particularism is right, the broad moral claims we make are usually riddled with exceptions. But such generalizations can still be a useful, even necessary part of moral life. They help us know what we should do, and they are essential for understanding why we should do it.

Moral particularism – or situationism, as it has sometimes been called – seems to present an especially radical objection to the enterprise of moral theory. While the project of many "antitheorists" has been to battle philosophers' tendency toward and or overly tidy pictures of morality, particularism seems to put pressure on the point or possibility of doing moral theory at all. It argues, (in)famously, that the moral import of any consideration is irreducibly context dependent, that exceptions can be found to any proffered principles, and that moral wisdom consists in the ability to discern and interpret the shape of situations one encounters, not the ability to subsume them under codified rules. The position thus seems, in the minds of many, to suggest not that moral theory needs to be richer than has been its make & wont, but that there

is no such thing, or at least no such thing we need.

Contemplation of such an idea often provokes feelings of vertigo – not to mention derision. But it also provokes confusion. Is the particularist really saying that theory has no place in the moral life? Such a view seems curious. After all, the philosopher most often claimed as an ally to particularism, Aristotle, didn't seem to eschew theory so entirely. He didn't confine himself to commenting on individual cases; and he insisted that the person of moral wisdom must know the "why," not just the "that"-something that sounds, one might have thought, like a call to theoretical abstraction. Add to this the fact that many particularists agree that principles have some role or other, and it's fair to wonder whether some notion of theory is compatible with particularism – and what that notion might be.

As a card-carrying moral particularist who makes a living doing something I'd be happy to call moral theory, I do think the two are compatible. But I think the insights underlying particularism offer profoundly important lessons on how moral theory should be conceived. For one thing, theory turns out to be less central to the moral life than certain traditions have thought. More importantly, particularism, properly understood, presents a different picture of the kinds of generalizations

Margaret Olivia Little, "On Knowing the 'Why': Particularism and Moral Theory," pp. 32–40 from *Hastings Center Report*, 31(4), 2001. Reprinted by permission of The Hastings Center.

that make up moral theory-that make up, in the end, our understanding of the "why."

Varieties of Antitheory

I want to start by isolating the distinctive challenge that particularism seems to pose for moral theory. As many have noted, the objections presented under the "antitheory" rubric form a diverse class. Sometimes, the point has been to object to ambitiously reductive theories, in which a very few concepts are said to be able to generate all of our moral considerations if only we spin them out properly – such as Kant's theory that all of morality (including the virtues, as it turns out) could be generated out of the notions of respect for self and others. Such views, it is argued, buy simplicity at the cost of accuracy: the moral landscape cannot be understood by reference to some one or two concepts.

Other objections target theories that bleed out any distinctive role for judgment. On some treatments of morality (hedonic utilitarianism comes to mind), the considerations said to have moral import are ones we could in principle design a sensor to detect for us, and their relative weights something a computer could render algorithmically (they are lexically ordered, say, or commensurable in the strong sense that renders all weightings quantitative). In contrast, it is argued, moral expertise just isn't the sort of thing a machine could have. It takes interpretation to determine when an action counts as merciful, and again when the demands of mercy trump those of justice instead of the other way around.

At other times, the objection is to theories preoccupied with an overarching ideal. Thus Stuart Hampshire objects to approaches that try to locate all of morality in what is common to rational beings or human creatures as such; some of the most important moral values and directives in life, he urges, are those that flow from social practices or ways of life that can permissibly vary from person to person or culture to culture.[1] Pursuing a related theme, Annette Baier criticizes the idea that we best gain direction on how to live by modeling a morally ideal world.[2] Given that our own struggles are animated most centrally by the

presence of moral imperfection, it is folly t think we can best understand morality by start ing with a removed ideal – say, the Kingdom c Ends – and then adding layers of failure, rathe than imagining incremental improvements t the imperfections we confront.

And of course, many have objected to pro posals eliminating elements that seem, o reflection, essential to the richness of mor life – to theories that deny the existence c genuine dilemmas or the moral importanc of emotion, or again, to theories that seem t think that merely possessing a moral theory i enough to make us moral.

I myself think all these objections are im portant (if sometimes levied a bit indiscrimin ately in discussions of historic figures). Bu whatever one thinks of them, they are clearl objections to impoverished moral theory, nc to moral theory per se. Someone persuaded c the above criticisms could nonetheless find moral theory to make her happy – one that pluralist about values and duties and nonre ductive about what carries theoretical weigh that admits of dilemmas and the importance c directives specific to idiosyncratic ways of lif that addresses imperfection directly rather tha by approximation to an ideal, and that require judgment in its application. In short, th "antitheory" objections just canvassed are pe fectly consistent with the idea that we can an should build a moral theory.

Somewhat more radical are objections to th idea that the moral terrain forms any "unifie system" at all. As classically used, the notion c a system is more than just an amalgam of a true propositions about some subject matte the idea of unity more robust than mere con pleteness and consistency. Rather, the phras imports the notion of a well-ordered set, i which a finite number of concepts suffice t capture the terrain, in which each concept related to the others in a codified, law-like wa in which axiom can be ordered to postulat and which admits of a neat taxonomy who crisp edges are marred only by whatever vagu ness is inherent in its member concepts.

In contrast, some have urged, the categorie that together make up the moral terrain are motley crew. The concepts needed to captu the terrain are open-ended, and are ofte

rthogonal to each other or assume overlap-
ing shapes that don't cleanly fit any genus-
pecies taxonomy. Thus Amelie Rorty argues
against attempts to recover some final unity
ut of the concepts – indispensable, every
ne – belonging variously to virtue theory,
eontology, and utilitarianism. To do so would
e to bleed out the substantive historical allegi-
nces that give each approach its greatest wis-
om.[3] And Iris Murdoch argues that the
ategories needed for accurate moral descrip-
ons of the situations one confronts (the central
ask, she thinks, in moral life) is a thoroughly
pen-ended affair. There is no notion of an
ndpoint to that discovery: moral description
unboundedly rich.[4] On these views, then, it's
ot that we need to acknowledge a richer system
a morality, it's that strictly speaking, morality
orms no system at all.

This sort of objection is obviously more
adical than the first. Nonetheless, its accept-
nce is still consistent with an important no-
on of theory. Even if morality doesn't admit
f "a" theory, understood as a well-ordered
nodel, we can still theorize about the moral
ealm. After all, for all that's been said, we
an give definitions of all those many useful
oncepts – outlining when cases fit under their
mbrellas – or sort them as values and disva-
ues, as things to pursue and things to avoid;
nd in doing so we would have constructed bits
f moral theory. "Interference without consent
a moral violation;" "generosity is the mean
ith respect to sharing scarce resources;" pain
a bad;" "kindness is solicitous concern for
nother's well-being," and so on. We may not
e able to corral these pieces of theory into one
nified model, but we can articulate the pieces
nemselves. What we can still have, in short, are
neoretical generalizations – broad claims that
o more than assess individual cases, and do
o, not just contingently (as when we point
ut that Dora is usually cruel to Jack), but as
xplanatory generalizations that seem to get at
ne nature of various moral considerations.
hese are the constitutive elements of theory.
Moreover, one might well think, they are the
nost important such elements, for they are
hat allow us to explain, to extend our know-
edge most ambitiously, to make explicit the
asis for criticizing others.

But it is here that the particularist's position
seems to present a distinctive challenge. For it
is this very notion – the building blocks of
theory, as it were – that particularism seems
to press on. The particularist argues that considerations carry their moral import only holistically. A consideration that in one context
counts for an action, can in another count
against it or be irrelevant, and all in a way
that cannot be cashed out in finite or helpful
terms. Pain is bad – well, except when it's
constitutive of athletic challenge; intentionally
telling a falsehood is prima facie wrong – well,
but not when done to Nazi guards, to whom
the truth is not owed, or when playing the
game Diplomacy. Pleasure always counts in
favor of a situation – well, except when it's
the sadist's delight in her victim's agony,
where her pleasure is precisely what is wrong
with the situation, not its "moral silver lining."[5]

The claim is not just that the moral contribution made by these considerations gets outweighed by others (as when the pain of a shot
is justified by the utility it brings); the claim is
that the moral "valence" of the consideration, as
it were, itself depends irreducibly on the context
in which it appears. The claim, in essence, is the
cousin to claims of holism in the theory of
knowledge. Having a perception of a red cup
can provide excellent evidence that there is
indeed such a cup; but there are contexts in
which having such an appearance counts precisely against drawing that conclusion – as when
you know the evil demon is playing with your
eyesight – and there's no cashing out in finite or
helpful terms the contexts in which the evidence
tips for rather than against the conclusion.

Moral particularists vary in how broadly
they cast their claim of context-dependency.
Some believe it is only so-called naturalistic
features (those describable without obvious
use of evaluative language) that carry moral
import holistically; moral considerations so
identified are granted invariant reason-giving
force – that an action is just always counts in
its favor, that it causes pleasure does not. For
others, it's in for a penny, in for a pound: even
"cruelty" is said to switch valence depending
on the context in which it appears, and the
aphorism that you sometimes have to be cruel
to be kind is to be taken at face value.

And whether the valence of such moral properties varies or not, some particularists will look skeptically at the idea that we can succeed in providing them with exhaustive, nontrivial definitions. Generosity is the mean with respect to sharing scarce resources – well, except when the generosity in question is the generosity of interpretation. Cruelty is wanton infliction of pain – well, except when the cruelty is constitutive of kindness. Again, the scope of skepticism here need not be universal: virtually all will agree we can recover exceptionless generalizations if we get sufficiently abstract. The question is whether those areas not admitting of such generalizations are now placed beyond the bounds of theory.

The particularist's position thus seems to cast into doubt, not just whether bits of theory can be well-ordered in the classical sense, but whether for large portions of morality, at least, we can isolate any bits of theory to lean on.

Questioning the Need for Theory

Now one of the points particularists rightly insist on when such claims raise a worried eyebrow is that the need for theoretical generalizations is badly overblown by theory – loving philosophers. On a view familiar from the Enlightenment, theoretical generalizations are at the very heart of all sorts of moves integral to the moral life. We're told that to persuade rationally (as opposed to converting by head blow), we must give arguments; to teach, we must give definitions; to be able to critically dislodge our own or others' faulty intuitions on more than a case by case basis, we must appeal to broad principles; to justify our intuitions about cases, we need to subsume those intuitions under, or secure their coherence with, articulated generalizations.

But it's just wrong to think we can accomplish these important aims only by appeal to explanatory generalizations. In real life, we teach in all sorts of ways – telling fables, pointing to exemplars, interpreting a case jointly witnessed. In real life, moral views are changed by experience and art as much as by argument: someone's sexist views about women change by fighting alongside them in battle, their views

of unfettered capitalism are undermined by working as a night janitor, and their views about eating animals shift by reading a poem. And while justification sometimes proceeds by subsumption under, or coherence with, explanatory generalizations, it doesn't always. Someone who sees that a rose is yellow, for instance, is hardly appealing (even tacitly) to a general principle to license some inference: she is instead justified in believing the rose yellow because her faculty of sight is in good working condition. So, too, we can be justified in our moral conclusions, not just by subsuming the situation under some general law, but by taking in the situation, exercising discernment and wisdom – Aristotle's phronesis – and seeing that it's cruel.

These are important points, and we can move from Aristotle to Wittgenstein to explain the general insight. To teach is to do something that enables another to catch on to the shape of a concept; to convert or dislodge a view is to get someone to apply a different concept from the one they were deploying; and these are changes we can effect in all sorts of extra-theoretic ways. Certainly, we don't need to provide some set of necessary and sufficient conditions: few concepts even admit of such definitions. A chair is functionally understood as something to sit on – well, except that many things that aren't chairs (including Uncle Fred) can be grand to sit on, and many things that are chairs, such as ornamental chairs made intentionally frail, are things we can't sit on at all. There is no saying once and for all what counts – when the object at the Museum of Modern Art is a chair, or a work of art, or both. If a concept as easily learned as "chair" resists such attempts, we shouldn't be surprised that concepts such as "kindness" similarly resist capture. It takes experience – sometimes a lifetime – to understand the nuance that separates tough love from abandonment.

We may not be able to spell out any but the most trivial definition, then, but this doesn't keep us from being able to catch on, or get others to catch on, to the shape and point of a concept. (To be rule-guided in Wittgenstein's sense one does not need access to codified principles, only a sense of how to go on. Once we do catch on, we can come to see that a situation is kind, or cruel – not because we have some spooky faculty of moral intuition, but because what it is to have mastery of a concept (whether "proton," "chair," or "cruelty") is to possess the ability to see directly rather than infer its instances in the world. And we can teach others, not just by defending arguments, but by introducing, endorsing, and highlighting some concept as more apt for interpreting a given situation than the one that might traditionally be used.

It is absolutely true that all of these moves – teaching, criticism, justification – involve the need for and invocation of generality. But a concept is, perforce, something of generality and abstraction. It applies to many individuals; it groups them together in virtue of what they share in common. Thus when Julia Annas argues that moral expertise requires a "principled" understanding of morality, everything depends on what is meant by "principled."[6] If it's read as a requirement that one possess exceptionless definitions or codified generalizations, it simply isn't true. For "principled" can mean mastery of the set of relevant concepts – having a deep understanding of the concepts, not just surface competence, and the skill to navigate them when they tangle together in concrete situations. Nor is it true, as it's often claimed, that we are limited to dislodging opinion case by case if we don't have theory. Where we succeed in introducing "subordination" as a telling concept, or in shunning the appropriateness of "chastity," we have succeeded in one fell swoop in changing others' opinions on an enormous number of cases. Generality, in short, is not just found in theoretical generalization.

Recovering a Role for Theory

All of this strikes me as clearly correct, so far as it goes. But how far is that? Are we really to think from all of this that we never make use of theoretical generalizations in morality? Aristotle – the great advocate of phronesis – didn't think so. His treatise on the virtues is suffused with theoretic moves. He didn't just point to exemplars or tell stories; and while he insisted that moral wisdom requires life

experience, he saw fit to articulate all manner of theoretical generalizations intended to guide and illuminate what that experience will reveal.

And so do we. If we reflect on our shared moral life, it certainly looks as though an important part of how we justify, convince, teach, and clarify is by pointing to explanatory generalizations whose truth we seem to endorse. Sometimes we convert by showing a film; then again, sometimes we do it by giving an argument (say, that one shouldn't discriminate on the basis of sex). Sometimes we teach by modeling behavior; but sometimes we do it by articulating a generalization (say, that wrongful interference is measured by lack of consent). And when we want to understand what someone means when she invokes a contested concept (say, "equality"), sometimes we ask for her verdict on a test case, but sometimes (if only to control for differing factual interpretations) we ask her to give us her definition. In short, we seem to theorize – to appeal to explanatory generalizations – about morality all over the place.

Particularists often respond to this point by re-interpreting the service to which these generalizations are put. Such principles, it is said, are useful pedagogic devices-helpful crutches for novices in moral judgment who, like beginning cooks, often need intentionally simplified rules or recipes to guide them as they gather needed experience. Or again, they are valuable heuristics: they aid our ability to interpret a case by serving to remind us of what can be salient. Or again, they are summaries of past cases, useful not just as records of history, but as shorthand memos of what tends to be relevant. Or again, they are rules of thumb, giving us a set of presumptions ("don't stab!") to take with us when we head out into the world.

These are surely some of the uses to which moral principles are put. But to think these functions exhaust their use seems profoundly at odds with moral practice. When we teach our children that it is morally problematic to inflict pain on their toddler siblings (to give an example dear to my heart just now), we're surely not just saying that infliction of pain can have moral import. That's something we can say of anything, including shoelace color. But the morally wise person, one would have thought, is someone who understands that there is a deep difference in moral status between infliction of pain and shoelace color, even if both can, against the right narrative, be bad-making.

Nor is it enough to say that moral generalizations just assert what usually carries moral import. To be sure, many of the moral presumptions we arm ourselves with are inductively based, as it were: part of why I presume not to lie to those I meet is because, fortunately, my misanthropic enemies are few and far between. This, though, is a thoroughly contingent fact. There are possible worlds (life in your favorite post-apocalyptic movie) in which enemies outnumber friends by a wide margin, and most of the lies in fact told are honorable rather than shameful. Are we really to think that the generalizations we work so hard to isolate are just meant to be statements of local frequencies – as though the only thing we mean when we make generalizations about the morally problematic nature of lying is that, in our neck of the woods, the situations in which lying is wrong-making outnumber those in which it is not?

So, too, with principles' claimed pedagogic function. Sometimes the directives we issue are very crude ones (the sweeping "never lie!" uttered to a five-year-old), meant to be left behind once one moves from novice to expert. But it is difficult to imagine that the hard-won insights of philosophy discussions are all just temporary crutches toward enlightenment; they sometimes seem, not what the person of practical wisdom leaves behind, but precisely what she understands.

But if particularists are often deflationary in their views of moral generalities, it's because it can seem unclear how they can say anything more robust. Exceptions, after all, are everywhere: anything could have, and nothing must have, moral import. Such puzzlement can lead to skepticism about the very possibility of doing theory beyond endorsing or objecting to the use of various concepts: one may conclude that there is no room left for theoretical moral generalizations.

I think particularism carries a different lesson. What it really invites us to consider are statements that are law-like despite admitting irreducibly of exceptions. What it really invites us to think about is what Aristotle might have meant by the claims he called "for the most part" generalizations.

Defeasible Generalizations and Moral Theory

The qualifier "for the most part" gets bandied about rather casually, as do its sometimes substitutes "ceteris paribus" and "all things equal." These phrases are often used interchangeably as all-purpose qualifiers whose meaning is left opaque. But what do we mean when we advance a generalization thusly qualified? If we say "ceteris paribus, lying is wrong-making," or "for the most part, pain has a negative valence," or "the prospect of pleasure counts, all things equal, in favor of an action," just what is it that we are saying?

Some read these claims as purely statistical ones (understandably, really, given the quantitative ring of Aristotle's phrase). On this interpretation, use of "for the most part" means, quite literally, that the asserted connection between, say, lying and wrong-making, or pleasure and good-making, holds with high frequency. To read such generalizations in this way, however, is to give up any pretense that they are robustly explanatory. Except in areas like quantum mechanics, which are ruled by genuinely statistical laws, statistical generalizations are contingent ones. (If catfish "usually" weigh about four pounds, this means not just that people occasionally catch six-pounders, but that there are some rivers – and possible worlds – in which most of them tip the scales at six.) On this interpretation, then, the connection asserted doesn't get at the nature of the subject it concerns, but at the features the subject usually displays as a matter of fact.

Those explicit in maintaining the explanatory nature of "for the most part" generalizations, on the other hand, usually do so by interpreting that qualification as a signal that we're talking shorthand. The assertion, it turns out, is an enthymeme" – a claim containing suppressed premises we could fill in if we just had the time. (There is a concrete exceptionless generalization in the offing, we just don't quite now yet what fills in the gaps – or it's so obvious we needn't bother to state it.) On this reading, "for the most part" generalizations are indeed explanatory, but they are thought capable of serving that function only because the exceptions are in principle eliminable. Here, explanation is a species of deduction.

On the first, statistical, interpretation, qualified generalizations are not robustly explanatory – they are, at best, locally useful as inductive guides to one's neighborhood. On the second interpretation, qualified generalizations are explanatory, but only because the qualification is capable of being expunged.

These interpretations seem to me to get exactly wrong the sort of generalization Aristotle was actually hinting at. While one could think these options exhaust the possibilities, it is also possible – and truer to Aristotle's own views – that the lesson here is a quite different one: namely, there are generalizations that are porous and genuinely explanatory.

When we issue a generalization to the effect that something has a certain feature, sometimes what we really want to say is not that such a connection always, or even usually, holds, but that the conditions in which it does hold are particularly revealing of that items nature. We might put it by saying that we're asserting what happens in "normal" conditions, except that the notion of "normalcy" is so freighted with misleading connotations. Better put, then, we are taking as privileged, in one way or another, cases in which the item has the feature specified. There are various ways in which that privileging move can take place; I'll mention two prominent ones. In one, the conditions are elevated in an evaluative sense: where the connection fails to hold, it means that something has gone awry. In another, we are saying that cases instantiating the feature in question count as a paradigm against which departures are understood.

For an example of the first, return to the case we used in illustration of holism in the theory of knowledge. While having a perception of a red cup often counts as an excellent reason to think such a cup sits before you, we noted, there are all sorts of cases in which it counts in just the opposite way, as when you remember you've taken an hallucinogenic drug. Nonethe-

less, it seems natural to think there is some sort of intimate connection between appearances and justification. Appearances can mislead, to be sure; but when they do, it's a sign that something is epistemically amiss. Someone who has entered the circus's Hall of Holograms has entered a situation that, however fun, is defective. If the "evidential valence," of appearances turns negative, it's a signal that one has entered a deviant context. Appearances, we might put it, have a default evidential valence of being trustworthy; put in another way, they are defeasibly trustworthy.

When we say "all things equal, appearances are the sorts of things we can take at their word," then, we are not claiming that appearances are usually trustworthy. Someone who gets stuck in the Hall of Holograms may never again be able to trust her eyes; the unfortunate brain in a vat is misled most of the time. What we are saying, rather, is that such a situation is thereby marked as defective by knowledge's own lights. The situation is deviant, not in a statistical, but in an evaluative sense.

In the second sort of case, we mark exceptions as deviant in a different way. To illustrate, return to our example of the concept "chair." Ornamental chairs, we noted, are still chairs even though we can't sit on them. Nonetheless, it seems natural to think there is some sort of intimate connection between "chair" and the function of holding people in repose; and we might intuitively think to put the point by saying something like "ceteris paribus, chairs are things we can sit on." Once again, such a claim is not a statistical one. We're not committed to saying we can usually sit on chairs: a very opulent society might in fact have more ornamental than functional chairs lying about. But we need not be finding fault here with ornamental chairs. It's not as though there is something deficient or defective about them (they're no good to sit on, to be sure, but that doesn't keep them from being fabulous – and fabulously sought-after – chairs). What we mean, instead, is that there is something like theme and variation involved. The ornamental chair is, if you like, a riff on the theme of chair; and one can't understand a riff without understanding the theme to which it stands as variation. The privileging move here, then, is not about what is better, but about what has, as it were, conceptual priority: to understand something as an ornamental chair one must understand the notion of chairs that are for sitting on, but not vice versa.

In neither of these cases, then, are we saying that the items in question usually have the features we highlight. Nor, though, must we think we can exhaustively specify the conditions under which they in fact would – filling in just when a chair can and cannot be sat upon, or specifying once and for all the conditions in which appearances are and are not trustworthy. For one needn't think we can specify the conditions in which a connection does obtain in order to say that where it does counts as a privileged case. Such generalizations tell us about the nature of something, in essence, not by getting rid of exceptions to the isolated connection, but by maintaining and demarcating their status as exceptions. ("Exceptions," again, that can outnumber the rule in all sorts of contexts, for the measure of exception here is not a statistical one.)

In short, "ceteris paribus," or "for the most part" generalizations need be neither statistical nor enthymematic. When we use them, we may instead be asserting what we might call defeasible generalizations: generalizations that privilege the conditions or cases in which a certain connection holds. This is also, I believe, just what Aristotle was doing (or often doing) when he offered his theoretical generalizations. When he talks about the "usual" nature of repaying one's debts, say, he is making explicit its default status, and, in doing so, he is implicitly calling our attention to what is theme and variation, deviance and normality, paradigm and emendation.

On this theory, when we say "ceteris paribus, lying has a negative valence," we are not saying that it always, must, or even usually has that status; we are saying that this is the valence it has in conditions that are privileged in various ways. When we say "all things equal, pain is bad-making," we are not saying that pain always carries this valence, nor merely asserting that it usually does in our neck of the woods. We are saying, instead, that pain is defeasibly bad-making; it has a default negative valence.

Where lying and pain lack this valence, as they sometimes or even often do, it is because they occupy a context defective by morality's own lights, or again because the cases in question are operating as variations that cannot be understood except by reference to a paradigm that carries the privileged valence.

Thus telling a falsehood to the Nazi guard, for instance, may indeed be honorable rather than shameful, but it's because something has gone awry: there is something badly amiss (namely, the Nazi's evil) from the moral point of view. (It is, if you will, a bad-making feature of the situation that lying is now a moral plus; would that it weren't honorable here to lie!) Telling a lie while playing Diplomacy, in turn, involves nothing morally amiss, but understanding its moral status relies on invoking a notion, consent, that itself cannot be understood without invoking a framework in which the normal case is not to lie. And while pain can be an integral and even cherished part of the athletic challenge, we understand it as pain only if we understand that this situation is the riff, not the theme. And if generosity cannot be defined as the mean with respect to sharing scarce resources, we may still think its nature is best illuminated by regarding that notion – or even the metaphors it evokes – as paradigmatic.

Thus it is not true that particularism allows no theoretical generalizations. It can acknowledge defeasible generalizations. These are completely consistent with even a radically holistic doctrine of morality, according to which we cannot identify once and for all, in any concrete terms, the contexts in which a given consideration counts for or against an action. For once again, one needn't be able to delineate the conditions under which a consideration has a given import in order to elevate as privileged those cases in which it does.

This means, to be sure, that using such generalizations won't give us a moral analysis of lying, or interference, or inflicting pain. We won't get from them some set of conditions laying out when lying is justified and unjustified, or even when it counts as a moral plus instead of minus. The particularist still insists that navigating the moral world is at bottom a matter of skill, including now a skill

nderstanding and recognizing what is deviant
nd normal, what paradigmatic and emend-
tion, what conceptually prior or central.
Defeasible generalizations, that is, will not
oncretely specify what the moral nature of
omething is.

What defensible generalizations do allow the
articularist to do, though, is to preserve a
istinction between actions or dispositions
aat can, and those that cannot, properly be
aid to have a moral nature. Shoelace color and
afliction of pain can both be bad-making. In
cknowledging this, though, we needn't be
ommitted to the radical particularist thesis
aat they are therefore on a par (as though,
' we single out the latter rather than the
ormer in our teaching and reflection, it
, only because doing so is locally useful).
hoelace color doesn't have a moral nature;
ing does. The former doesn't have a moral
ature because, while it can have various moral
mports (good-making, bad-making, indiffer-
nt) in various contexts, it has none of them
efensibly It has, we might put it, no privileged
mport.

The availability of defensible generalizations
lso means that particularists can do more than
ndorse or descry the use of various concepts
hen trying to make progress in illuminating
ae moral landscape. Without trying to ex-
austively define the paradigmatic case, or spe-
ify the conditions in which a privileged
onnection holds, she can make explicit which
efensible generalizations she advances as true.
Vhich types of actions does she believe have a
aoral nature, in the sense used above? What
alence forms their default? And, crucially,
hich sort of privileging – conceptual priority,
entrality, evaluative privilege – is she here
efending? This, in turn, is all fodder for
ebate. Does lying have a moral nature in the
ense used above? Do we illuminate respect for
ersons' best by centering the self-sufficient,
r the vulnerable agent, in our reflections?
low we resolve all of this is, of course, a
aessy matter, and not one we can codify (the
articularist gives a model of resolving dis-
greement no more than she gives one of
ring). But the point is that the particularist
not, as the usual image has it, confined to
ae sidelines of theoretical moral debate – as

though all she can do is watch the play from
the bench, at most throwing in the occasional
story or concept while others trade theoretical
claims. For better or worse, particularists can –
and do – join the fray.

If particularism is right, most of the moral
generalizations we deploy in everyday life turn
out to be irreducibly porous. They are shot
through with expectations we cannot eliminate. By the particularist's own lights, though,
these generalizations can nonetheless count as
robustly explanatory and insightful. Adducing
them has a power a list of instances does not,
for it situates instances within a framework
that maintains some as exceptions to others'
rule.

Once we recover this sort of generalization,
it turns out that theory is in fact essential to
moral life. Defeasible generalizations will, as we
noted, be useful when it comes time to teach,
convert, and justify; but these tasks, as we also
noted, are ones that can in principle be effected
through moral discernment. What theory turns
out to be necessary for is understanding – for
knowing what Aristotle called the "why" rather
than the "that." For mastery of moral concepts
is mastery of defeasible generalizations. To be
sure, one can understand the concepts without
ever stating these generalizations explicitly
(and one certainly need have no thought,
as such, of the terms in which they have here
been put). But one cannot be said to understanding moral concepts without appreciation
the privileging moves that lie at their heart.
Indeed, I doubt there are any concepts whose
mastery doesn't involve appreciation of defensible generalizations. An integral aspect of
knowing "how to go on" is knowing what
counts as, and having the skill to navigate,
what is deviant and normal, paradigm and
emendation, theme and variation. If it is
wrong to interpret Annas's notion of principled
understanding as possession of codifiable generalizations, it's equally wrong to think it
empty of generalization altogether.

Even the particularist thus must acknowledge an indispensable role for the explanatory
generalizations that make up the theoretical. To
agree to this, though, is a far cry from agreeing
to the goal of theory as traditionally construed.
The particularist's lesson about the nature of

explanatory generalization counsels against the usual quest for theory, which is to spend all of our time filling in the holes of our generaliza-tions. We get moral wisdom, in the end, not b filling in the exceptions, but by knowing wh counts as one in the first place.

Notes

1. S. Hampshire, "Morality and Conflict," in *Morality and Conflict* (Oxford: Blackwell Publishers, 1983).
2. A. Baier, "Theory and Reflective Practices," in *Postures of the Mind. Essays in Mind and Morals* (Minneapolis: University of Minnesota Press, 1985).
3. A. Rorty, "The Advantages of Moral Diversity," *Social Philosophy and Policy* 9, no. 2 (1992): 38–62.
4. I. Murdoch, *The Sovereignty of Good* (Londo Routledge Kegan Paul, 1970)
5. The pain example is from Elijah Milgram, t Diplomacy example from Mark Lance, and t pleasure example from Dancy, who further a tributes it to Roy Hattersley.
6. J. Annas, "Virtue as a Skill," *Internation Journal of Philosophical Studies* 3, no. 2 (199⁵ 227–43.

CHAPTER 76
Unprincipled Ethics

GERALD DWORKIN

. . . if the particular case can be satisfactorily settled by conscience without reference to general rules, "Casuistry" which consists in the application of general rules to particular cases, is at best superfluous. But then, on this view, we shall have no practical need of any such general rules, or of scientific Ethics at all.
—Sidgwick *Methods of Ethics*

General propositions do not decide concrete cases.
—O. W. Holmes *Lochner v. New York*

1

My topic is the nature of moral judgment. In particular how we make particular moral judgments about what to do. My task is three-fold. First, to show that contrary to much moral philosophy there is no necessity that we use moral principles or rules in deductive reasoning to arrive at particular judgments. Second, to suggest that there are reasons to suppose that we do not in fact reason this way. Third, to suggest some alternative models about how we do make moral judgments.

2

Let me begin by defining some central terms. By a *moral judgment* I shall mean an answer to

a question of the form: What is the right thing to do in this particular situation? It is obvious that this is only one of many different kinds of moral judgment that we make. We evaluate not only in the first-person but in the third-person. We evaluate not only what we should do now but what we have done in the past. We judge not only actions but persons, policies, character traits, desires, thoughts, institutions. We judge not only whether actions are right but whether they are courageous, virtuous, cruel, excusable, sentimental, above and beyond the call of duty, sincere, just, and so forth. I see no reason, in advance, to suppose that all of these judgments work in the same logical fashion. I shall concentrate on what many have supposed to be the central moral judgment, the one about what I ought to do in this particular case – first-person practical action judgments.

I want to emphasize that I concentrate on this issue not because I think it is the only, or the most important, or the central issue in

Gerald Dworkin, "Unprincipled Ethics," pp. 224–38 from *Midwest Studies in Philosophy*, 20, 1995. Reprinted by permission of the publishers, Blackwell Publishing.

ethics. It is just as plausible to suppose that discovering what are the major conceptions of the good life for persons is the central problem of ethics. Nor do I wish to put the emphasis on action and choice that Murdoch criticizes so effectively.[1] But in accordance with the methodological principle that one should make life as hard as possible for one's views, I take the area in which it is most reasonable that principles or rules play a major role in moral judgment. If the picture of moral thought and decision making is quite different from the received view here, it must be even further from the truth on these alternative conceptions.

By a *moral principle* I shall mean a general statement, containing moral terms, which in conjunction with other principles and statements describing the relevant, particular features of a case is supposed to provide deductive support for a judgment about what one ought to do in the particular situation. By a *general statement* I do not limit myself to universal generalizations, e.g., 'all killing of innocent persons is wrong'. It can include ceteris paribus generalizations such as, 'leaving people to themselves is always better, ceteris paribus, than interfering with them'. It can include what I have called quasi-generalizations such as Mill's 'All restraint, *qua* restraint, is an evil.' I wish to include comparative principles such as 'It is worse to harm somebody deliberately than to do so accidentally'. And, finally, I wish to include what might be called "criterial generalizations:" that an act is a lie is a reason for thinking it wrong to do.

There is a use of principles which I shall only indirectly be concerned with. This is their theoretical use in moral theories which purport to tell us in virtue of what characteristics certain acts are right or wrong. Regarded in this fashion the traditional utilitarian principle of acting so as to produce the best consequences provides us with a standard in terms of which to assess actions. As consequentialists in recent years have emphasized, there is no guarantee that such theoretical propositions, even if correct, are the ones that agents use or ought to use in making their moral decisions; it is this latter function in which I am interested.

3

My first claim is that there is no philosophic reason to suppose that the actual structure of most people's moral reasoning about what t do in particular situations is a deductive conclusion from some set of facts and principle Any claim about the actual structure of our reasoning is a descriptive, psychological claim Unfortunately there is very little empirica work on exactly how people do reason abou moral matters, and I am not in a position t produce new evidence. So instead I shall argu that there is no a priori or philosophical reaso to suppose that we do, or must, reason in th fashion.

Why have so many philosophers though that we must reason deductively, using prin ciples, in the absence of any empirical eviden to support that view? I believe it is because the assumed that there was no alternative accoun that was possible.

If there were a number of possible structure for moral reasoning it would have seeme obvious that the question of which one w actually used would have to be settled b observation and evidence. Now by possib structures I do not mean particular normativ theories such as utilitarianism or Kantianisn For it is obvious to all that there are man such systems and that the question of whicl if any, of these are used by people to make thei moral decisions must be settled by empirica observations.

This is the level at which investigations pic neered by Kohlberg, and continued by other have been conducted. But it is assumed b most philosophical theorists that the structur of moral reasoning is the same: a set of prin ciples or morally relevant considerations fron which, together with a description of the fact in the particular case, one deductively reasor to the appropriate conclusion about what to dc

Philosophers have thought that there ar a number of different considerations whic converge on the idea that there is one basi structure to moral reasoning. It is though that in the absence of this model it would b impossible to learn how to act rightly, to justir our actions to others, to teach our childre

ow to act well. In addition it is thought that
ne very idea of there being a *structure* or logic
o moral reasoning requires there be some gen-
ral principles or rules which explain the
gent's judgment that one particular act, rather
han another, is the right one to perform. It
s these ideas which I propose to examine
ritically.

4

n his attack on what Sidgwick labeled *unphilo-
sophical Intuitionism* (by which is meant the
doctrine' that we 'pronounce on the morality
of particular courses of conduct at the moment
of action'), Hastings Rashdall presents a number of reasons why rules or principles must be
involved in moral decisions. The first is that
without such rules moral decision making is
arbitrary.

> If it is supposed that the injunctions of the
> moral faculty are so wholly arbitrary that they
> proceed upon no general or rational principle
> whatever, if it is supposed that I may to-day in
> one set of circumstances feel bound by an
> inexplicable impulse within me to act in one
> way, while tomorrow I may be directed or
> direct myself to act differently under circum-
> stances in no way distinguishable from the
> former, then moral judgments are reduced to
> an arbitrary caprice which is scarcely compat-
> ible with the belief in any objective standard of
> duty.[2]

None of this is sound. Why should the process
be one of 'impulse'? Why should it be 'inexplicable'? Why should the intuitionist be committed to the view that he would judge
differently in circumstances indistinguishable
from those in which he judged before? The
argument about this last is that

> . . . there must be some rule or principle by
> which it must be possible to distinguish be-
> tween circumstances which do and circum-
> stances which do not alter our duty, however
> little this rule or principle may be present in an
> abstract form to the moral consciousness of
> the individual. Granted, therefore, that the
> moral judgments may as a matter of psycho-

logical fact reveal themselves first and most
clearly in particular cases . . . it must still, it
would seem, be possible by analysis of our
particular moral judgments to discover the
general principles upon which they *proceed*.[3]

But this is to confuse what is possible ex post
judgment with what is possible ex ante. From
the assertion that there must be some set of
properties which *make* one act right and the
other wrong it cannot be inferred that there is
some non-trivial rule or principle which is *used*
by us to make the discrimination. Given that
we have made differing judgments in two cases,
given some view about moral properties as
supervenient on non-moral ones, there must
be some difference between the two cases
which accounts for our different judgments.
But all the following are consistent with this:
We are not able to formulate even ex post *what*
those differences consist in. If we are able to do
so for the two cases at hand, we are not able to
formulate a principle which is *generally* applicable. If we are able to formulate such a principle, it is not one that is capable of being
actually used (whether explicitly or implicitly)
to make our judgment. If there is such a principle which is theoretically capable of being
used, we do not actually use the principle to
make our judgment.

The next argument Rashdall gives is connected with the possibility of teaching morality
to others.

> If this [the existence of "some rough rules or
> principles"] be denied, moral instruction must
> be treated as absolutely impossible. . . . We
> do not say to a child who asks whether he
> may pick a flower in somebody else's garden,
> "My good child, that depends entirely upon
> the circumstances of the particular case: to lay
> down any general rule on the subject would be
> a piece of unwarranted dogmatism on my
> part: consult your own Conscience, as each
> case arises, and all will be well." On the con-
> trary, we say at once: "You must not pick the
> flower: because that would be stealing, and
> stealing is wrong."[4]

Again we see an a priori thesis asserted about
matters that are contingent and upon which
there is evidence that the thesis is mistaken.

In the first place much of morality is picked up, like language, and not taught at all. We see how others act, how they talk about what they do, how they react to others, how they criticize their own behavior. We read stories about good and bad people. Much of this takes place at a very early age and without conscious intent or effort.

There is undoubtedly a certain amount of explicit instruction on the matter. But again much of the instruction does not take the form of laying out even rough rules or principles.

Consider all the different ways in which more or less explicit moral instruction takes place:

- the use of parables (the Good Samaritan) or fables (the ant and the grasshopper);
- golden rule considerations (How would you like it if Johnny wouldn't let you play with his toy?);
- appeals to consistency (You remember not wanting to play with Harry because you thought he was selfish? Aren't you behaving the same way?);
- appeals to procedure (What would be a fair way of choosing up the teams?);
- appeals to some indeterminate process of weighing competing considerations (What do you think is more important, Susan feeling bad because she is not invited to your party or your other friends feeling that she is icky to be around?);
- appeals to characteristics of the decision making process (Perhaps you ought to wait before deciding so that you aren't so angry when making the decision.);
- appeals to the virtues (If you lie it's because you are afraid to be unpopular.); and
- appeals to moral authority (If you are having trouble deciding what to do maybe you should talk it over with the rabbi. Or: What do you think Jesus would have done in this situation?).

In light of all these different ways of imparting moral advice and instruction, how could it be thought 'absolutely impossible' to transmit morality in the absence of general rules and principles? Of course, one might claim that all of these modes of transmission assume, perhaps implicitly, that we use such rules and principles. But this reductionist move requires a good deal of argument which is so far absent.

Much has been made of the idea that there must be some generality involved in the learning and teaching of moral conduct if only because of the universality requirement. This, as stated by Sidgwick, is the view that 'if a kind of conduct that is right (or wrong) for me is not right (or wrong) for someone else, it must be on the ground of some difference between the two cases, other than the fact that I and he are different persons.'[5] But this formal truth (as opposed to some substantive interpretations of impartiality) yields only the trivial generalization, "If one comes across another situation which is exactly like this one then, unless one has changed one's mind about the former judgment, one must (on pain of inconsistency) decide the new case in the same manner". Not only does this not commit one to some view that the agent must be using some general principle in deciding the initial case, it does not even provide one with reasons for supposing there is some interesting generalization which could be used in future cases. It is as uninformative to be told that this generalization must hold as it would be to be told in the case of chicken-sexing that the sexer must be using (unconsciously) some algorithm over (unknown) features of the chicken to arrive at his judgments because, after all, any other chicken which was exactly like this one (a male) must be judged to be a male also.[6]

5

Undoubtedly the strongest reason for supposing that moral agents must be using some general principles in a deductive fashion to make moral judgments has to do with the practice of *justification*. It is thought essential to moral judgment – indeed what distinguishes it from, say, judgments of taste – that one be prepared to give reasons for one's views. One must be prepared to make assertions of the form: 'X is the right thing to do *because* of p,q,r'. And this is thought to require the istence of rules or principles. Here are some xamples of this kind of support for the exist- nce of rules or principles.

To justify requires one to put one's claim, defence or decisions on the footing that *because* the facts are F1, F2, . . . Fn, the judgment *j* ought to be pronounced. But such a 'because . . .' requires a commitment to the universal, 'whenever f1, f2, . . . fn, then *j*', coupled with: 'and in this case, F1, F2, . . . Fn, which are instances of f1, f2, . . . fn'. . . . That justification requires universalization or universalizability in this sense follows from the idea that justifying involves propounding good rational grounds for what one does.[7]

ow, strictly speaking, it would be a non sequi- r to conclude, even if one accepted the above, at we must be using such univeralizations in riving at our judgments. For it is compatible ith our giving such a rationale that we arrive them by some completely different method. ompare, for example, how I answer the ques- on, 'How many days are there in July?' by e mnemonic '30 days hath September', etc. ther people may in fact have that answer directly stored in memory. But if asked to stify that number I would show somebody calendar. So the process of justification is uite different from the process of forming e judgment.

But though logically correct, this is not a reply should feel comfortable with since I would like weaken the distinction between practical rea- ning on the one hand and, on the other, a urely theoretical account of what makes moral dgments correct. If I am disposed to give counts of why I reach a judgment in terms ich as 'it would be wrong, because it would be quivalent to stealing', then I am committed to ving an account of that '*because*' as entering to my process of moral decision making. The uestion then becomes how to explain the force f the 'because' without assuming the correct- ess of the deductive model. That is, without suming the reasoning as being of the form, stealing is wrong. This would be stealing. herefore, this is wrong'.

Suppose I make a great sacrifice to help mebody out. Suppose I also believe that this

is what was required of me in the situation, not just that it was permissible. I am asked why and reply "because he is a good friend." This is both an explanatory and justificatory claim. I have made the action both intelligible and reason- able. The 'because' functions as an indication of the salient, goodmaking feature which both led me to act as I did, and which provided me with a good reason for the action. My claim is that all this is consistent with the idea that there is no deductive argument of the above form available to me. For what would the major premise be – 'Always make large sacri- fices for one's friends'? That is just not a rea- sonable principle. 'It is required, other things being equal, to make large sacrifices for one's friends'. This does not seem correct either, and even if it were, are other things equal? This just means that one of the indefinite number of defeating conditions for the principle is not present. Even if the list were definite, it might be very large and is it the case that I ran through the list to see if any of the conditions were present? All that I am committed to is the view that in this particular case, given these particular facts, the decision to make the sacri- fice cannot be criticized, and the alternative decision can be.

The same issue of deductivism, it should be noted, arises in purely explanatory contexts as well. Consider the following: 'Why did he close the window? Because he was cold'. The deduc- tivist claims that this is an explanation only if there is a valid argument of the form: 'He wanted to achieve x; x would be achieved only if he did y; therefore he did y'. But note that although closing the window, in the con- text, was sufficient for his avoiding cold it was not necessary. He could have put on a sweater, turned up the heat, exercised vigorously, gone to his neighbor's apartment, got into a hot bath, and so forth. And this 'so forth' is indef- inite. So it doesn't even make sense to suppose he went through the list of alternatives and ruled out each one for particular reasons. Again, as in the moral case it seems to me a perfectly good explanation to suppose that closing the window simply struck him as the way to solve his problem. And since it *is* a perfectly reasonable way of solving his problem it not only explains but rationalizes his action, makes it intelligible. Now there may be an additional story to be told about why one thing strikes a person rather than another (although that could be simply a matter of chance) but that is *another* story – not part of this one.

6

So far I have given reasons why there is no argument to the effect that we must reach moral judgments deductively by the use of rules and principles. This, of course, does not show that we do not in fact do so, but merely that there is no necessity to do so. I now want to consider why there is reason to suppose that in fact we do not do so.

One line of argument has been produced recently by Holly Smith.[8] She objects against both consequentialist and deontological principles that we may simply not have enough knowledge to use these principles. If for example the principle we are using is 'maximize good consequences' or 'give victims adequate compensation' we may have no way of knowing what the consequences of our actions are, or what adequate compensation consists in. She calls this the problem of doubt.

I think even if the problem of doubt were not a serious one, we would still be faced with a problem that those working in artificial intelligence refer to as the 'frame problem.' For descriptive problem-solving, e.g., how to solve the puzzle of the cannibals and the missionaries, the problem is that, as Dennett puts it:

> What is needed is a system that genuinely ignores most of what it knows, and operates with a well-chosen portion of its knowledge at any moment. Well-chosen, but not chosen by exhaustive considerations. How, though, can you give a system rules for ignoring – or better, since explicit rule-following is not the problem, how can you design a system that reliably ignores what it ought to ignore under a wider variety of different circumstances in a complex action environment.[9]

A similar problem emerges when we consider normative problem-solving. The most plausible form of principles is that of ceteris paribus

statements. Other things being equal, loss should rest where they fall. Leaving people alone is better, ceteris paribus, than interfering with them. But to draw deductive conclusion from such principles it is necessary to determine that other things are equal. The strategies for doing so, given the very large number of considerations which might make things unequal and the sensitivity of moral judgment to small changes in these factors, are very unlikely to be rule-governed or reducible to articulated propositions. The most likely strategies involve sensitivity to patterns of salience, and tendencies to pay attention to certain sorts of features and to ignore others. The agent would be 'primed' for certain kinds of paradigm cases and, as in the factual problem-solving cases, "differentially alert to relevant divergences from the stereotypes it would always begin by 'expecting.' "[10]

7

Undoubtedly part of the attraction of the deductive model, here as elsewhere, lies in what Hilary Putnam calls the 'What else' argument. If we do not reason deductively from general rules or principles how else could we arrive at our particular moral judgments? I want in this section to give a number of alternative models for how we make particular moral judgments. Which of them, if any, closest to how we actually think about these matters is a psychological question. But each of them has some plausibility as a correct account. The first model is based in part on recent work by cognitive psychologists as to how we use concepts and categories. The story that developed is plausible for various moral conceptions as well, and ties in with alternative speculations as to how we make moral judgments that range from Aristotle on practical wisdom to Edward Levi on judicial decision making.

Consider a word such as 'bird' and the associated concept. Philosophers when asked the basis on which people are able to classify accurately instances of birds have typically supposed that there is a 'definition' of the concept, consisting of necessary and sufficient nditions, and that people are employing this ·finition, perhaps unconsciously, to deter-·ine whether any particular object is a bird is not. According to what the linguist ·harles Fillmore calls the 'checklist' theory, ·e definition of a term consists of a set of ·atures such that any given object falls into ·e extension of the term just when it possess ·e property named by each feature in the ·finition.

Philosophers and others have failed to actu-·y come up with such a checklist for any ·oderately complex concept. Various experi-·ental studies in human categorization in the ·main of color terms and natural kinds, and ·rious linguistic and philosophical arguments ·ve led recent theorists to propose an alterna-·e model. According to prototype semantics ·r what cognitive psychologists call 'prototy-·cality effects') the meaning of a concept is ·termined by a cognitive schema or image, ·d speakers determine whether some new in-·ance falls under the concept by judging the ·gree to which the new instance matches the ·ototypical schema or image.

Thus, when experimental subjects are asked ·list features that characterize birds they list ·ies' although this is not a necessary feature, ·d the subjects themselves recognize penguins ·birds. It is true, however, that subjects take ·uch less time to categorize flying animals as ·rds than those who do not fly. Thus a robin is ·garded as more 'typical' of a bird than a ·icken. In addition, concepts almost always ·ve fuzzy boundaries and allow for degrees ·membership. So for most people a sparrow ·some sense is more clearly a bird than an ·gle. It is also true that various properties do ·t contribute equally to the degree of mem-·rship of an individual in a category.

Most of the evidence of prototypicality effects ·s been with artifacts, natural kinds, and per-·ptual terms. But there is at least one study ·ich deals with a moral concept, that of a lie. The prototypical lie, according to Coleman ·d Kay, is characterized by a falsehood which ·deliberate and intended to deceive.[11] Notice ·at while this might be taken as a 'classical' ·finition, in this study an instance which ·ars all three of these features is considered a ·llfledged lie, but instances which lack one or

more of the elements might still be thought of as lies, but as less of a lie. A questionnaire was constructed which had eight stories (represent-ing all the combinations of the three features) and the subjects were asked whether a particu-lar utterance was a lie, not a lie, or they couldn't say. They were also asked whether they were very sure, fairly sure, or not too sure that others would agree with their choice.

Here, for example, is a story with only the intent to deceive present:

John and Mary have recently started going together. Valentino is Mary's ex-boyfriend. One evening John asks Mary, 'Have you seen Valentino this week?' Mary answers, 'Valenti-no's been sick with mononucleosis for the past two weeks.' Valentino has in fact been sick with mononucleosis for the past two weeks, but it is also the case that Mary had a date with Valentino the night before. Did Mary lie?[12]

The results of the experiment support the prototype hypothesis. The more prototype elements a story contains, the higher it scores on the lie scale. In addition the prototypical elements could be ranked in terms of their contribution to the classification as a lie. The agent believing his assertion to be false is the most important element; the intent to deceive is next most important; and the assertion in fact being false is least important.

This result about the concept of a lie does not have immediate implications for the issue of whether we use moral principles deductively in decision making. It does create problems for a deductivist who supposes that the minor premise in such an argument is always a matter of determining what the *facts* of the situation are. For someone who supposes that we use a moral principle of the form 'lying is wrong' in conjunction with the factual determination that 'this speech act is a lie' to deduce that we should not perform this speech act, and that the only difficult question is what the facts are (since whether these facts amount to a lie is determined by a classical definition of a lie), the evidence supports the view that matters are more complicated. But this does not directly affect the deductivist claim since the model can concede that it is often difficult to tell whether the minor premises are true. Compare the utilitarian who believes that we use rules about producing good and avoiding harm but who concedes that it is often difficult to tell whether a given act does produce good or harm.[13]

I am arguing that this is an alternative model for understanding the production of particular moral judgments. They are reached, not by the use of general principles or rules but by the comparison of new instances with prototypes or exemplars. The process of judgment involves making comparisons of the new instance with an exemplar which has been classified as right or wrong and making a determination that the new case is similar or close enough to the exemplar to warrant the same classification. Now it is still a matter of controversy as to how these similarity determinations are made. It is possible that we work by forming some abstract description of the two patterns and checking for identical features. In this case the reasoning would seem similar to rule-governed procedures. But it is also possible that we simply compare different patterns and see the pattern before us as more like one of these than the others.

8

Let me now present a slightly different model of how we might actually make moral judgments. This is also based on the idea of pattern recognition but differs from the previous model in not relying on a reference to a prototypical pattern. This model which has been studied by cognitive psychologists in various perceptual areas such as face recognition would lend empirical support to the philosophical views of Ross and Prichard. According to them there is no process of moral reasoning; rather, having assembled all the facts, we simply 'see' that the act is to be done or not.

This again is a model that involves 'seeing-that' rather than 'reasoning-that' but it is important to note that the 'seeing' is a kind of recognizing that is not necessarily perceptual in nature. Although many of the best-known studies have been in the area of perception (facial recognition, identification of phonemes, etc.) the same model is postulated for non-perceptual cognition.

The basic idea here is that we make various judgments by recognizing patterns on the basis of various cues or features. We do not infer the conclusion on the basis of the presence of features. We simply perceive that a certain pattern is present.

Consider for example how radiologists make diagnoses from x-rays. The computational (deductive) model supposes that the radiologist notices, perhaps unconsciously, various features of the x-ray (dark and light regions etc.) and then, using some implicit rule connecting certain features with certain diseases makes a diagnosis. The alternative model is that having stored various previous patterns in memory, the current film simply 'looks like' one of the previous patterns.

Studies of chess masters have shown that they have stored a very large number of positions in memory – probably on the order of 50,000. Upon being faced with a certain position in a current game, the master simply calls up one of the previous positions and the associated knowledge of how the prior game was played. Just as you can recognize hundreds of faces you have previously encountered, a chess master can recognize hundreds of positions.

The corresponding model for moral judging is that we have stored in our memory lots of moral situations with which we have had experience. We also have a knowledge base concerning how the various decisions we made in those situations "worked out." Faced with a new situation we see that it "looks like" one of the stored patterns and make a judgment based on the similarity of patterns.

An alternative model is that what is stored is not specific situations but rather a conception of an idealized moral agent. When faced with a new situation we try to match our beliefs about how such an agent would judge the situation. This corresponds to the Aristotelian notion of the right actions as that which the man of practical wisdom would choose.

9

The next model I want to present which has certain similarities to the prototypical model is suggested by various discussions of legal

asoning.[14] At least with respect to common-
w decision making the claim is made that
dges do not reason deductively from rules
ut reason by analogy from prior cases. A typi-
al example is *Adams v. New Jersey Steamboat
o*. The case was brought by a steamboat pas-
nger who had money stolen from his state-
oom. There was no negligence either on his
art or on the part of the steamboat company.
dge O'Brien argued by analogy from the
rior cases involving innkeepers.

> The principle upon which innkeepers are
> charged by the common law as insurer of the
> money or personal effects of their guests ori-
> ginated in public policy. It was deemed to be a
> sound and necessary rule that this class of
> persons should be subjected to a high degree
> of responsibility in cases where an extraordin-
> ary confidence is necessarily reposed in them,
> and where great temptation to fraud and dan-
> ger of plunder exists by reasons of the peculiar
> relations of the parties. . . . The relations that
> exist between a steamboat company and its
> passengers, who have procured staterooms
> for their comfort during the journey, differ
> in no essential respect from those that exist
> between the innkeeper and his guests.
>
> The passenger procures and pays for his
> room for the same reasons that a guest at an
> inn does. There are the same opportunities for
> fraud and plunder on the part of the carrier that
> was originally supposed to furnish a temptation
> to the landlord to violate his duty to the guest.
> A steamer carrying passengers upon the water,
> and furnishing them with rooms and entertain-
> ment is, for all practical purposes, a floating inn,
> and hence the duties which the proprietors owe
> to their charge ought to be the same. No good
> reason is apparent for relaxing the rigid rule of
> the common law which applies as between inn-
> keeper and guest since the same considerations
> of public policy apply to both relations. . . .
>
> The two relations, if not identical, bear such
> close analogy to each other that the same rule
> of responsibility should govern. We are of the
> opinion, therefore, that the defendant was
> properly held liable in this case for the
> money stolen from the plaintiff, without any
> proof of negligence.[15]

ote that although there is a rule which
lays an important role in the reasoning, the
decision does not follow from the rule. It cannot, since the rule is about innkeepers and the
case is about a steamboat company. Rather, the
claim is made that the case is sufficiently similar so that it is appropriate to render the same
judgment, namely liability without proof of
negligence.

I suggest then the following model for how
we make particular moral judgments. Prior to
being confronted with a particular case we have
built up a series of judgments in paradigm
cases. For the most part, at least when we are
young, these paradigm cases are not a product
of reasoning. They are inculcated by the emotional reactions of our parents and peers, they
are conveyed by storybooks, perhaps some of
them are even innate (some primitive sense of
fairness). When faced with a new case we
search for some appropriate paradigm case
and judge whether the new case is sufficiently
similar or 'close' to the paradigm case to warrant the same judgment. Having found such a
paradigm, we may also search for other paradigms which seem to give a contrary judgment.
We then try to preserve consistency of judgment by distinguishing the present case from
the paradigm with the contrary judgment.
Notice that this process of reasoning is 'creative' in the sense that nothing guarantees that
we will be able to find appropriate paradigms,
nor that we will be able to find relevant distinctions when faced with contrary judgments.

Notice also that having found a satisfactory
analogy justifying our judgment does not
involve appeal to some general principle. It is
always possible, of course, to find features a, b,
c, . . . and formulate a universal principle of
the form 'Whenever a, b, c . . . then x ought
to be done'. But in most cases such a principle
will either be false or empty (because one of the
features will be something like 'in circumstances sufficiently similar to these').

While this process of argument from analogy
bears certain resemblances to the prototype
model discussed earlier it is not the same
model. This process is more 'reasoned' in the
sense that we articulate features of the paradigm situations which are claimed to be the
relevant features for deciding the new case,
and make a judgment that those features, or
ones sufficiently similar, warrant making the

same judgment in the new case. It is not simply a matter of 'seeing' that two cases are sufficiently 'close.' It is also important that this process involves the search for paradigms that give differing results and the necessity of 'distinguishing' cases. There is nothing that approximates this in the prototype model.

10

The general lesson is that we know from psychological research that there is evidence that the way we reach judgments and solve problems in a host of different areas is not via deductive reasoning from general rules. Indeed we even know that we do not reason about syllogisms according to the deductive model. Why should moral reasoning be any different? In conclusion let me consider one possible line of argument to support the view that moral judgment *is* different.

There is a commonsense datum which seems to support the deductive model and to count against the alternative models I have been suggesting, namely, that when asked why they have arrived at a certain conclusion people most frequently reconstruct their reasoning according to the deductive model. They present their judgment as a conclusion from some general rules or principles. The simplest explanation is that this is in fact how they reach their judgments.

In further support of this line of reasoning is the asymmetry with other kinds of judgments, e.g., facial recognition. Here people do not claim to recognize a face on the basis of certain features. They have no idea how they reached their judgment. They just do it (usually) successfully.

While it is true that the simplest explanation is that our subjective reports accurately reflect the real causes of our judgments there is impressive evidence from other areas in cognitive psychology that in fact we have no reliable access to the actual causes of our judgments in many areas. The best summary of this literature is an article by Nisbett and Wilson called 'Telling More Than We Can Know: Verbal Reports on Mental Processes.'[16] Their general conclusion is that:

People often cannot report accurately on the effects of particular stimuli on higher order inference-based responses. Indeed, sometimes they cannot report on the existence of critical stimuli, sometimes cannot report on the existence of their responses, and sometimes cannot even report that an inferential process of any kind has occurred. The accuracy of subjective reports is so poor as to suggest that any introspective access that may exist is not sufficient to produce generally correct or reliable reports.[17]

To give you some of the flavor of the evidence for these conclusions, consider the following experiment. Subjects were faced with the classic Maier experiment in which two cords were hung from the ceiling in such a fashion that the subject could not, while holding onto one cord, reach the other. Various objects were strewn about the laboratory such as clamps, pliers, and extension cords. The subjects were told to tie the two ends of the cord together. Some possible solutions, such as tying the extension cord to one of the ceiling cords, came fairly easily to the subjects. But one of the solutions was often not hit upon by the subjects. Maier would then casually put one of the cords in motion. Often, shortly thereafter, the subject would pick up the pliers, tie to the end of one of the cords, set it swinging like a pendulum, and succeed in the task. Now the interesting phenomenon is that when subjects were asked how they got the idea for the pendulum solution they would either have no idea what the stimulus was and say things like "It just came to me" or, more frequently, they would confabulate answers. They would make up a story. Here, for example, is the tale of a psychology professor who was a subject.

Having exhausted everything else, the next thing was to swing it. I thought of the situation of swinging across a river. I had images of monkeys swinging from trees. The imagery appeared simultaneously with the solution. The idea appeared complete.[18]

Further, when Maier gave a useless hint, twirling a weight on a cord, and presented this before the helpful cue, many of the subjects when probed persistently about what cue

em reported that the useless cue had been
pful but not the helpful cue.

After summing up a large body of literature,
sbett and Wilson conclude that

> the evidence suggests that people's erroneous
> reports about their cognitive processes are not
> capricious or haphazard, but instead are regu-
> lar and systematic. . . . It seems equally clear
> that the subjects . . . are drawing on a similar
> source for their verbal reports about stimulus
> effects. . . . We propose that when people are
> asked to report how a particular stimulus
> influenced a particular response, they do not
> do so by consulting a memory of the mediat-
> ing process, but by applying or generating
> causal theories about the effects of that type
> of stimulus on that type of response.[19]

sbett and Wilson believe that the causal the-
ies are generated by the culture of the sub-
ts either explicitly or implicitly and are held
an a priori basis.

While much of the evidence comes from
idies of perceptual cues, Wason and Evans
ve found much the same evidence for what
ppens when people make logical inferences
ch as those involving modus tollens. It is a
ll-known result that faced with four cards,
ch of which has an 'A' or a 'B' on one side,
d a '3' or a '4' on the other, and asked
iich cards must be turned over to verify
iether the following statement is true 'If a
rd has a "A" on one side it has a "3" on the

other,' most subjects get it wrong. But the
interesting study, for our purposes, is that
when asked about their reasoning processes
(whether they get the solution or not) again
we find confabulation. Wason and Evans
believe the following two assumptions explain
best the data in various experiments they performed:

(1) The processes underlying the reasoning
performance . . . are not generally available for introspective report.
(2) Introspective accounts of performance
reflect a tendency for the subject to *construct* a justification for his own behavior
consistent with his knowledge of the
situation.[20]

My suggestion, then, is that the fact that people
may *say* that they reached a particular moral
judgment on the basis of a deduction from
general rules or principles may represent the
same kind of confabulation that we observe in
other areas of judgment and reasoning. Just as
subjects construct explanations based on the
causal theories of their culture, moral agents
who live in a culture which stresses the importance of rules and principles may borrow this
a priori structure to fashion their explanation
of how they reached their conclusions. Only
experimental evidence can settle this question
one way or the other. But it is not an objection
against my account that people's introspective
accounts contradict it.

otes

I. Murdoch, "Vision and Choice in Morality,"
Proceedings of the Aristotelian Society supple-
mentary volume no. 30 (1956): 191–218.
Hastings Rashdall, *The Theory of Good and Evil*
(Oxford, 1907), 81.
Ibid., 82, italics mine.
Ibid., 83.
Sigdwick, *The Methods of Ethics*, (London,
1962), 379.
John H. Lunn, "Chick Sexing," *American Scien-
tist* 36 (1948): 280–81.
Neil McCormick, "Why Cases Have Rationes
and What These Are," in *Precedent*, edited by
Goldstein (Oxford, 1987), 162. This is presented

as a claim about legal argument but similar
claims are made for moral argument.
8. H. Smith, "Making Moral Decisions," *Nous* 22
(1988): 89–108.
9. D. Dennett, "Cognitive Wheels: The Frame
Problem of Artificial Intelligence," in *Minds,
Machines and Evolution*, edited by C. Hookway
(Cambridge, England, 1984), 143.
10. Ibid., 141. De Sousa suggests in *The Rationality
of Emotions* (Cambridge, Mass., 1987) that
emotions play precisely this role: "emotions
are determinate patterns of salience among
objects of attention, lines of inquiry and inferential strategies" (p. 246).

11. L. Coleman and P. Kay, "Prototype Semantics: The English Verb *Lie*," *Language* 57, no. 1 (1981): 26–44.

12. Ibid., 31.

13. Cf. Smith's "Making Moral Decisions" on the difficulty in applying principles.

14. For typical examples see Martin Golding, *Legal Reasoning* (New York, 1984); Edward Levi, *An Introduction to Legal Reasoning* (Chicago, 1949).

15. As quoted in Golding, *Legal Reasoning*, 46–47.

16. Nisbett and Wilson, "Telling More Than Can Know: Verbal Reports on Mental P' cesses," *Psychological Review* 84, no. 3 (N 1977): 231–54.

17. Ibid., 253.

18. Ibid., 241.

19. Ibid., 248.

20. P.C. Wason and J. St. B. T. Evans, "Dual P cesses in Reasoning," *Cognition* 3 (1974– 141–54.